HOLLYWOOD CREATIVE DIRECTORY

FROM THE PUBLISHERS OF

58TH EDITION • FALL 2006

CONTENTS

Resource Guide	**iv**
The Concierge: Los Angeles	**1**
The Concierge: New York	**15**
Section A. Deals by Company	**25**
Section B. New Listings at a Glance	**33**
Section C. Companies and Staff	**37**
Section D. TV Shows and Staff	**351**
Section E. Index by Type	**381**
Section F. Index by Name	**407**

WELCOME
TO Fabulous
LAS VEGAS
NEVADA

STATE FILM COMMISSIONS

ALABAMA

Alabama Film Office
www.alabamafilm.org
401 Adams Ave., Ste. 630
Montgomery, AL 36104
Phone 334-242-4195
Fax 334-242-2077
Email film@ado.state.al.us
Brenda Hobbie, Film Office Coordinator
Courtney Murphy, Film Liaison Specialist
Tommy Fell, Location Coordinator

ALASKA

Alaska Film Program
www.alaskafilm.org
c/o Office of Economic Development
550 W. Seventh Ave., Ste. 1770
Anchorage, AK 99501
Phone 907-269-8190
Fax 907-269-8125
Email alaskafilm@commerce.state.ak.us
Shelley James, Director

ARIZONA

Arizona Film Commission
www.azcommerce.com
1700 W. Washington, Ste. 220
Phoenix, AZ 85007
Phone 602-771-1193
800-523-6695
Fax 602-771-1211
Harry Tate, Director
Ken Chapa, Film Resource Coordinator

ARKANSAS

Arkansas Film Office
www.1-800-arkansas.com/film
One Capitol Mall, Ste. 4B-505
Little Rock, AR 72201
Phone 501-682-7676
800-ARKANSAS
Fax 501-682-FILM
Email jglass@1800arkansas.com
Joe Glass, Film Commissioner

CALIFORNIA

California Film Commission
www.film.ca.gov
7080 Hollywood Blvd., Ste. 900
Hollywood, CA 90028
Phone 323-860-2960
800-858-4749
Fax 323-860-2972
Email filmca@film.ca.gov
Amy Lemish, Director

COLORADO

Colorado Film Commission
www.coloradofilm.org
1625 Broadway, Ste. 950
Denver, CO 80202
Phone 303-620-4500
800-SCOUT-US
Fax 303-620-4545
Email coloradofilm@state.co.us
Sara Bell, Interim Film Commissioner

CONNECTICUT

Connecticut Commission on Culture and Tourism Film Division
www.ctfilm.com
805 Brook St., Bldg. 4
Rocky Hill, CT 06067
Phone 860-571-7130
Fax 860-721-7088
Email info@ctfilm.com
Ellen Woolf, Project Manager

DELAWARE

Delaware Film Office
www.state.de.us/dedo
99 Kings Hwy.
Dover, DE 19901
Phone 302-739-4271
302-672-6857
Fax 302-739-5749
Christine Serio, Public Relations Specialist

DISTRICT OF COLUMBIA

District of Columbia - Office of Motion Picture & TV Development
www.film.dc.gov
441 Fourth St. NW, Ste. 760N
Washington, DC 20001
Phone 202-727-6608
Fax 202-727-3246

FLORIDA

Governor's Office of Film & Entertainment
www.filminflorida.com
c/o Executive Office of the Governor
The Capital
400 S. Monroe St., Ste. 2002
Tallahassee, FL 32399-0001
Phone 877-352-3456
Fax 850-410-4770
Email film1@myflorida.com
Paul Sirmons, Film Commissioner
Niki Welge, Production Coordinator
Susan Simms, Los Angeles Liaison
Raquel Cisneros, Communications Coordinator

Jacksonville Film & Television Office
www.coj.net
220 E. Bay St., 14th Fl.
Jacksonville, FL 32202
Phone 904-630-2522
Fax 904-630-2919
Email troobin@coj.net
Todd Roobin, Chief

GEORGIA

Georgia Film, Video & Music Office
www.georgia.org
75 Fifth St. NW, Ste. 1200
Atlanta, GA 30308
Phone 404-962-4052
Fax 404-962-4053
Email film@georgia.org
Greg Torre, Director

HAWAII

Hawaii Film Office
www.hawaiifilmoffice.com
PO Box 2359
Honolulu, HI 96804
Phone 808-586-2570
Fax 808-586-2572
Email info@hawaiifilmoffice.com
ddawson@dbedt.hawaii.gov
Donne Dawson, Film Commissioner

Big Island Film Office (Island of Hawaii)
www.filmbigisland.com
25 Aupuni St., Rm. 109
Hilo, HI 96720
Phone 808-326-2663
808-961-8366
Fax 808-935-1205
Email film@bigisland.com
Marilyn Killeri, Film Commissioner

Honolulu Film Office (Island of Oahu)
www.filmhonolulu.com
530 S. King St., Ste. 306
Honolulu, HI 96813
Phone 808-527-6108
Fax 808-527-6102
Email info@filmhonolulu.com
Walea Constantinau, Film Commissioner

Kauai Film Commission
www.filmkauai.com
4444 Rice St., Ste. 200
Lihue, HI 96766
Phone 808-241-6386
Fax 808-241-6399
Email info@filmkauai.com
Tiffani Lizama, Film Commissioner
Art Umezu, Film Commissioner

Maui County Film Office (Islands of Maui, Molokai, Lanai)
www.filmmaui.com
200 S. High St., 6th Fl.
Wailuku, HI 96793
Phone 808-270-7415
Fax 808-270-7995
Email info@filmmaui.com
Benita Brazier, Film Commissioner

IDAHO

Idaho Film Bureau
www.filmidaho.com
700 W. State St.
Boise, ID 83720
Phone 208-334-2470
800-942-8338
Fax 208-334-2631
Email peg.owens@tourism.idaho.gov
Peg Owens, Director

ILLINOIS

Illinois Film Office
www.filmillinois.state.il.us
100 W. Randolph St., Ste. 3-400
Chicago, IL 60601
Phone 312-814-3600
Fax 312-814-8874
Email bsexton@ildceo.net
Brenda Sexton, Film Commissioner

IOWA

Iowa Film Office
www.filmiowa.com
200 E. Grand Ave.
Des Moines, IA 50309
Phone 515-242-4726
Fax 515-242-4718
Email filmiowa@iowalifechanging.com
Tom Wheeler, Contact

KANSAS

Kansas Film Commission
www.filmkansas.com
1000 S.W. Jackson St., Ste. 100
Topeka, KS 66612
Phone 785-296-4927
888-701-3456
Fax 785-296-3490
Email kdfilm@kansascommerce.com
Peter Jasso, Director
Erin Schroeder, Scouting & Production Manager

KENTUCKY

Kentucky Film Commission
www.kyfilmoffice.com
c/o Capital Plaza Tower
500 Mero St.,
2200 Capital Plaza Tower
Frankfort, KY 40601
Phone 502-564-3456
800-345-6591
Fax 502-564-7588
Email todd.cassidy@ky.gov
Todd Cassidy, Director

LOUISIANA

Louisiana Governor's Office of Film & TV Development
www.lafilm.org
800 Distributors Row, Ste. 101
Harahan, LA 70123
Phone 504-736-7280
Fax 504-736-7287
Email schott@la.gov
Alex J. Schott, Film Commissioner

MAINE

Maine Film Office
www.filminmaine.com
59 State House Station
111 Sewall St., 3rd Fl.
Augusta, ME 04333
Phone 207-624-7631
207-624-7851
(Production Hotline)
Fax 207-287-8070
Email filmme@earthlink.net
Lea Girardin, Director

MARYLAND

Maryland Film Office
www.marylandfilm.org
217 E. Redwood St.
Baltimore, MD 21202
Phone 410-767-6340
800-333-6632
410-767-0067 (Hotline)
Fax 410-333-0044
Email filminfo@marylandfilm.org
Jack Gerbes, Director
Catherine Batavick, Deputy Director
Ken Haber, Manager, Los Angeles Office
Kathi Ash, Project Manager, Film/TV
Jason Thomas, Marketing Coordinator
Katie Pelura, Visual Communications Assistant
Brenda Lee, Administrative Assistant

MASSACHUSETTS

Massachusetts Sports & Entertainment Commission
www.masportsandfilm.org
31 St. James Ave., Ste. 260
Boston, MA 02116
Phone 617-423-1155
Fax 617-423-1158
Email info@masportsandfilm.org
Mark R. Drago, VP/Executive Director, Film & Entertainment

MICHIGAN

Michigan Film Office
www.michigan.gov/filmoffice
702 W. Kalamazoo St.
Lansing, MI 48909
Phone 517-373-0638
800-477-3456
Fax 517-241-2930
Email jlockwood@michigan.gov
filmassistant@michigan.gov
Mailing Address
PO Box 30739
Lansing, MI 48909
Janet Lockwood, Director

MINNESOTA

Minnesota Film & TV Board
www.mnfilmandtv.org
2446 University Ave. West, #100
St. Paul, MN 55104
Phone 651-645-3600
Fax 651-645-7373
Email info@mnfilmandtv.org
Riki McManus, Interim Manager

MISSISSIPPI

Mississippi Film Office
www.visitmississippi.org/film
Woolfolk State Office Bldg.
501 N. West St., 5th Fl.
Jackson, MS 39201
Phone 601-359-3297
Fax 601-359-5048
Email wemling@mississippi.org
Mailing Address
PO Box 849
Jackson, MS 39205
Ward Emling, Manager (601-359-3422)
Nina Parikh, Associate Manager (601-359-3034)
Betty Black, Office Coordinator (601-259-6564)

MISSOURI

Missouri Film Commission
www.mofilm.org
301 W. High St., Rm. 720,
PO Box 118
Jefferson City, MO 65102
Phone 573-751-9050
Fax 573-522-1719
Email mofilm@ded.mo.gov
Jerry Jones, Director
Traci Albertson, Assistant Director

MONTANA

Montana Film Office
www.montanafilm.com
301 S. Park Ave.
Helena, MT 59620
Phone 406-841-2876
800-553-4563
Fax 406-841-2877
Email montanafilm@visitmt.com
siversen@mt.gov
Sten Iversen, Manager
Bill Kuney, Sr. Location Coordinator
Maribeth Goodrich, Office Coordinator/Crew Liaison
John Ansotegui, Digital Media Projects Coordinator

NEBRASKA

Nebraska Film Office
www.filmnebraska.org
301 Centenial Mall South
PO Box 94666
Lincoln, NE 68509
Phone 402-471-3746
800-228-4307
Fax 402-471-3365
Email info@filmnebraska.org
Laurie J. Richards, Nebraska Film Officer

NEVADA

Nevada Film Office, Reno/Tahoe
www.nevadafilm.com
108 E. Proctor St.
Carson City, NV 89701
Phonc 775-687-1814
Fax 775-687-4450
Email ccnfo@bizopp.state.nv.us
Robin Holabird, Deputy Director
Kristen Anderson, Operations Coordinator

Nevada Film Office, Las Vegas
www.nevadafilm.com
555 E. Washington Ave., Ste. 5400
Las Vegas, NV 89101
Phone 702-486-2711
877-638-3456
Fax 702-486-2712
Email lvnfo@bizopp.state.nv.us
Charles Geocaris, Director

NEW HAMPSHIRE

New Hampshire Film & TV Office
www.filmnh.org
20 Park St.
Concord, NH 03301
Phone 603-271-2220
Fax 603-271-6826
Email film@nh.gov
Matthew W. Newton, Director

NEW JERSEY

New Jersey Motion Picture & Television Commission
www.njfilm.org
153 Halsey St., 5th Fl.
PO Box 47023
Newark, NJ 07101
Phone 973-648-6279
Fax 973-648-7350
Email njfilm@njfilm.org
Joseph Friedman, Executive Director
Steven Gorelick, Associate Director

NEW MEXICO

New Mexico Film Office
www.nmfilm.com
1100 St. Francis Dr., Ste. 1200
Santa Fe, NM 87505-4147
Phone 505-827-9810
800- 545-9871
Fax 505-827-9799
Email film@nmfilm.com
Lisa Strout, Director

NEW YORK

New York State Governor's Office for Motion Picture & Television Development
www.nylovesfilm.com/index.asp
633 Third Ave., 33rd Fl.
New York, NY 10017
Phone 212-803-2330
Fax 212-803-2339
Pat Swinney Kaufman, Deputy Commissioner & Director

The City of New York Mayor's Office of Film, Theatre & Broadcasting
www.nyc.gov/film
1697 Broadway, 6th Fl.
New York, NY 10019
Phone 212-489-6710
Fax 212-307-6237
Email info@film.nyc.gov
Katherine Oliver, Commissioner

NORTH CAROLINA

North Carolina Film Office
www.ncfilm.com
4324 Mail Service Center
Raleigh, NC 27699-4324
Phone 919-733-9900
800-232-9227
Fax 919-715-0151
Email barnold@nccommerce.com
Bill Arnold, Film Commissioner

NORTH DAKOTA

North Dakota Film Commission
www.ndtourism.com
c/o Century Center
North Dakota Tourism Division
1600 E. Century Ave., Ste. 2
Bismarck, ND 58503-2057
Phone 800-435-5663
701-328-2525
Fax 701-328-4878
Email tourism@state.nd.us
Sara Otte Coleman, Film Commissioner

OKLAHOMA

Oklahoma Film & Music Commission
www.oklahomafilm.org
120 N. Robinson, Ste. 600
Oklahoma City, OK 73102
Phone 800-766-3456
405-230-8440
Fax 405-230-8640
Email filminfo@oklahomafilm.org
Jill Simpson, Director
Dino Lalli, Field Representative
Julie Porte, Film Development Coordinator

OREGON

Oregon Film & Video Office
www.oregonfilm.org
c/o One World Trade Center
121 SW Salmon, Ste. 1205
Portland, OR 97204
Phone 503-229-5832
Fax 503-229-6869
Email shoot@oregonfilm.org
Susan Haley, Marketing & Administrative Manager
Bob Schmaling, Project Manager
Kayla Thames Berge, Contact, Los Angeles Office (323-656-0889, kayla@oregonfilm.org)

PENNSYLVANIA

Pennsylvania Film Office
www.filminpa.com
Commonwealth Keystone Bldg.
400 North St., 4th Fl.
Harrisburg, PA 17120-0225
Phone 717-783-3456
Fax 717-787-0687
Jane Saul, Contact

RHODE ISLAND

Rhode Island Film & Television Office
www.film.ri.gov
One Capitol Hill, 3rd Fl.
Providence, RI 02908
Phone 401-222-3456 (FILM)
401-222-6666 (Hotline)
Fax 401-222-3018
Email steven@arts.ri.gov
Steven Feinberg, Director

SOUTH CAROLINA

South Carolina Film Commission
www.filmsc.com
1201 Main St., Ste. 1600
Columbia, SC 29201
Phone 803-737-0490
Fax 803-737-3104
Email scfilmoffice@sccommerce.com
Jeff Monks, Film Commssioner
Dan Rogers, Sr. Manager
Melinda Peterson, Business Development

SOUTH DAKOTA

South Dakota Film Office
www.filmsd.com
711 E. Wells Ave.
Pierre, SD 57501
Phone 605-773-3301
Fax 605-773-3256
Email ann.garry@state.sd.us
Ann Garry, Contact

TENNESSEE

Tennessee Film, Entertainment & Music Commission
www.state.tn.us/film
312 Eighth Ave. North
Tennessee Tower, 9th Fl.
Nashville, TN 37243
Phone 615-741-3456
877-818-3456
Fax 615-741-5554
Email tn.film@state.tn.us
David Bennett, Executive Director

TEXAS

Texas Film Commission
www.texasfilmcommission.com
PO Box 13246
Austin, TX 78711
Phone 512-463-9200
Fax 512-463-4114
Email film@governor.state.tx.us

UTAH

Utah Film Commission
www.film.utah.gov
Council Hall/Capitol Hill
300 N. State St.
Salt Lake City, UT 84114
Phone 801-538-8740
Fax 801-538-1397
Email asyrett@uthan.gov
Aaron Syrett, Film Commissioner

VERMONT

Vermont Film Commission
www.vermontfilm.com
10 Baldwin St., Drawer 33
Montpelier, VT 05633
Phone 802-828-3618
Fax 802-828-0607
Email vermontfilm@vermontfilm.com
Danis Regal, Executive Director

VIRGINIA

Virginia Film Office
www.filmvirginia.org
901 E. Byrd St., 19th Fl.
Richmond, VA 23219-4048
Phone 804-545-5530
800-854-6233
Fax 804-545-5531
Email vafilm@virginia.org
Rita McClenny, VP, Industry Relations & Film (rmcclenny@virginia.org)
Rebecca Albert Beckstoffer, Marketing Manager (balbert@virginia.org)

WASHINGTON

Washington State Film Office
www.filmwashington.com
2001 Sixth Ave., Ste. 2600
Seattle, WA 98121
Phone 206-256-6151
Fax 206-256-6154
Email wafilm@cted.wa.gov
Suzy Kellett, Director

WEST VIRGINIA

West Virginia Film Office
www.wvfilm.com
90 MacCorkle Ave. SW
South Charleston, WV 25303
Phone 304-558-2200, x382
800-225-5982, x382
Fax 304-558-1662
Email phaynes@wvfilm.com
Pamela Haynes, Director

WYOMING

Wyoming Film Office
www.filmwyoming.com
I-25 @ College Dr.
Cheyenne, WY 82002
Phone 307-777-3400
800-458-6657
Fax 307-777-2877
Email info@filmwyoming.com

INTERNATIONAL FILM COMMISSIONS

AUSTRALIA

Ausfilm
www.ausfilm.com.au
2049 Century Park East, 19th Fl.
Los Angeles, CA 90067
Phone 310-229-4833
Fax 310-277-2258
Email tracey.montgomery@ausfilm.com.au
info@ausfilm.com.au
Tracey Montgomery, Film Commissioner (Australia)

Film Victoria
Melbourne Film Office
www.film.vic.gov.au
189 Flinders Ln., Level 7
Melbourne, Victoria 3000
Australia
Phone 61-3-9660-3200
Fax 61-3-9660-3201
Email mfo@film.vic.gov.au
contact@film.vic.gov.au
Caroline Pitcher, General Manager
Neil McCart, Production & Policy Manager

New South Wales Film & Television Office
www.fto.nsw.gov.au
Level 7, 157 Liverpool St.
Sydney, NSW 2000 Australia
Phone 61-2-9264-6400
Fax 61-2-9264-4388
Email fto@fto.nsw.gov.au
Gary Brennan, Film Commissioner

Pacific Film & Television Commission
www.pftc.com.au
Level 15, 111 George St.
Brisbane, QLD 4000 Australia
Phone 61-7-3224-4114
Fax 61-7-3224-6717
Email mwalmsley@pftc.com.au
Michelle Walmsley, Mktg./Locations Advisor

South Australian Film Corporation
www.safilm.com.au
c/o Hendon Common
3 Butler Dr.
Hendon Adelaide, South Australia
5014 Australia
Phone 61-8-8348-9300
61-8-8348-9336
Fax 61-8-8347-0385
Email safilm@safilm.com.au
gelliel@safilm.com.au
Lisa Gellie, Head, Marketing & Locations Services

CHINA

Hong Kong Film Services Office
www.fso-tela.gov.hk
40/F Revenue Tower
5 Gloucester Rd.
Wanchai, Hong Kong China
Phone 852-2594-5757
Fax 852-2824-0595
Email info@fso-tela-gov.hk
Camy Mak, Contact

FRANCE

Film France
www.filmfrance.net
c/o National Film Commission France
33 rue des Jeûneurs
Paris, 75002 France
Phone 33-1-5383-9898
Fax 33-1-5383-9899
Email film@filmfrance.net
Patrick Lamassoure, Contact

GERMANY

Berlin Brandenburg Film Commission
www.bbfc.de
August-Bebel-Str. 26-53
Potsdam, Babelsberg D-14482
Germany
Phone 49-331-743-87-30
Fax 49-331-743-87-99
Email location@medienboard.de
c.raab@medienboard.de
Christiane Raab, Film Commissioner

IRELAND

Irish Film Board
www.filmboard.ie
Rockford House
St. Augustine St.
Galway, Ireland
Phone 353-91-561-398
Fax 353-91-561-405
Email info@filmboard.ie

ITALY

Italian Film Commission
www.filminginitaly.com
1801 Avenue of the Stars, Ste. 700
Los Angeles, CA 90067
Phone 323-879-0950
Fax 310-203-8335
Email losangeles@losangeles.ice.it
Fortunato Celi Zullo, Film Commissioner

MEXICO

National Film Commission - Mexico
www.conafilm.org.mx
Ave. Division Del Norte,
2462 5th Fl.
Colonia, Portales, 03300
Mexico
Phone 52-55-5688-7813
Fax 52-55-5688-7027
Email conafilm@conafilm.org.mx
US Office
233 Wilshire Blvd., Ste. 400
Santa Monica, CA 90401
Phone 310-270-6600
Fax 310-836-7159
Sergio Molina, Film Commissioner
Ted Perkins, Chief US Liaison (Santa Monica)

NEW ZEALAND

Film New Zealand
www.filmnz.com
23 Frederick St., PO Box 24142
Wellington, New Zealand
Phone 64-4-385-0766
Fax 64-4-384-5840
Email info@filmnz.org.nz
Judith McCann, CEO

New Zealand Film Commission
www.nzfilm.co.nz
The Film Centre, PO Box 11-546
Wellington, 6001 New Zealand
Phone 64-4-382-7680
Fax 64-4-384-9719
Email marketing@nzfilm.co.nz
Barrie Everard, Chairman
Ruth Harley, CEO
Kathleen Drumm, Sales & Marketing

PUERTO RICO

Puerto Rico Film Commission
www.puertoricofilm.com
355 F.D. Roosevelt Ave., Fomento Bldg., Ste. 106, PO Box 362350
San Juan, Puerto Rico 00936
Phone 787-758-4747, x2251
Fax 787-756-5706
Luis A. Riefkohl, Executive Director (lriefkohl@pridco.com)
Marvin Crespo, Project Coordinator (crespo@pridco.com)
Louis De-Moura, Project Coordinator (demoura@pridco.com)

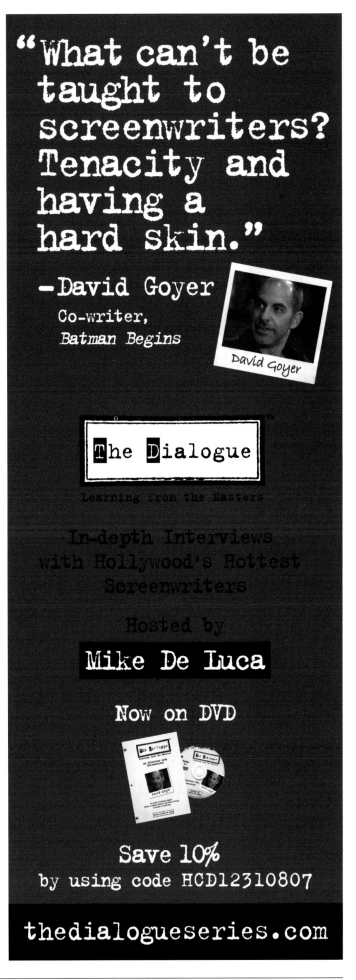

UNITED KINGDOM

Film London
www.filmlondon.org.uk
20 Euston Centre
Regent's Pl.
London, NW1 3JH UK
Phone 44-207-387-8787
Fax 44-207-387-8788
Email info@filmlondon.org.uk
Sue Hayes, Film Commissioner

UK Film Council International
www.ukfilmcouncil.org.uk
10 Little Portland St.
London, W1W 7JG England
Phone 44-207-861-7861
Fax 44-207-861-7864
Email international@ukfilmcouncil.org.uk
Steve Norris, British Film Commissioner

UK Film Council US
www.ukfilmcouncil-us.org
8533 Melrose Ave., Ste. C
West Hollywood, CA 90069
Phone 310-652-6169
Fax 310-652-6232
Email info@ukfilmcouncil-us.org
Claire Chapman, Executive Director

GUILDS, UNIONS AND ASSOCIATIONS

Academy of Motion Picture Arts and Sciences (AMPAS)
www.oscars.org
Honorary organization of motion picture professionals founded to advance the arts and sciences of motion pictures.
8949 Wilshire Blvd.
Beverly Hills, CA 90211-1972
Phone 310-247-3000
Fax 310-859-9619
Sid Ganis, President
Bruce Davis, Executive Director

Academy of Television Arts & Sciences (ATAS)
www.emmys.tv
Nonprofit corporation for the advancement of telecommunications arts and sciences.
5220 Lankershim Blvd.
North Hollywood, CA 91601
Phone 818-754-2800
Fax 818-761-2827
Alan Perris, President

Actors' Equity Association (AEA)
www.actorsequity.org
Labor union representing US actors and stage managers working in the professional theatre.

New York
165 W. 46th St., 15th Fl.
New York, NY 10036
Phone 212-869-8530
Fax 212-719-9815

Chicago
125 S. Clark St., Ste. 1500
Chicago, IL 60603
Phone 312-641-0393
Fax 312-641-6365

Orlando
10319 Orangewood Blvd.
Orlando, FL 32821
Phone 407-345-8600
Fax 407-345-1522

Los Angeles
5757 Wilshire Blvd., Ste. 1
Los Angeles, CA 90036
Phone 323-634-1750
Fax 323-634-1777

San Francisco
350 Sansome St., Ste. 900
San Francisco, CA 94104
Phone 415-391-3838
Fax 415-391-0102

Actors' Fund of America
www.actorsfund.org
Nonprofit organization providing for the social welfare of entertainment professionals.

New York
729 Seventh Ave., 10th Fl.
New York, NY 10019
Phone 212-221-7300
Fax 212-764-0238

Los Angeles
5757 Wilshire Blvd., Ste. 400
Los Angeles, CA 90036
Phone 323-933-9244
Fax 323-933-7615

Chicago
203 N. Wabash, Ste. 2104
Chicago, IL 60601
Phone 312-372-0989
Fax 312-372-0272

Actors' Work Program
www.actorsfund.org
Career counseling for members of the Actors' Fund of America.

Los Angeles
5757 Wilshire Blvd., Ste. 400
Los Angeles, CA 90036
Phone 323-933-9244
Fax 323-933-7615

New York
729 Seventh Ave., 11th Fl.
New York, NY 10019
Phone 212-354-5480
Fax 212-921-4295

Alliance of Canadian Cinema, Television & Radio Artists (ACTRA)
www.actra.ca
Labor union founded to negotiate, safeguard, and promote the professional rights of Canadian performers working in film, television, video, and all recorded media.
625 Church St., 3rd Fl.
Toronto, ON M4Y 2G1 Canada
Phone 800-387-3516
416-489-1311
Fax 416-489-8076
Email national@actra.ca
info@actratoronto.com

Alliance of Motion Pictures & Television Producers (AMPTP)
www.amptp.org
Trade association involved with labor issues within the motion picture and television industries.
15503 Ventura Blvd.
Encino, CA 91436
Phone 818-995-3600
Fax 818-382-1793

American Academy of Dramatic Arts (AADA)
www.aada.org
Offers a two-year professional actor's training program, a third year advanced performance program and a six-week summer program. Nonprofit and accredited.

Los Angeles
1336 N. La Brea Ave.
Los Angeles, CA 90028
Phone 323-464-2777
800-463-8990
Fax 323-464-1250

New York
120 Madison Ave.
New York, NY 10016
Roger Croucher, President
Marguerite Artura, President, Los Angeles Division

American Booksellers Association (ABA)
www.bookweb.org
Nonprofit organization of independently owned bookstores with retail storefront locations.
200 White Plains Rd.
Tarrytown, NY 10591
Phone 800-637-0037
914-591-2665
Fax 914-591-2720
Email info@bookweb.org

American Cinema Editors, Inc. (ACE)
www.ace-filmeditors.org
Honorary society made up of editors deemed to be outstanding in their field.
100 Universal City Plaza,
Verna Fields Bldg. 2282, Rm. 190
Universal City, CA 91608
Phone 818-777-2900
Fax 818-733-5023

American Cinematheque at the Egyptian & Aero Theatres
www.egyptiantheatre.com
www.americancinematheque.com
Nonprofit cultural arts organization programming specialty film series at the Egyptian and Aero Theatres.
6712 Hollywood Blvd.
Los Angeles, CA 90028
Phone 323-461-2020
323-466-FILM
Fax 323-461-9737
Margot Gerber, Marketing & Publicity Manager
Barbara Smith, Director

American Federation of Film Producers (AFFP)
www.filmfederation.net
Trade organization of creative professionals committed to excellence in filmmaking.
3000 W. Alameda Ave., Ste. 1585
Burbank, CA 91523
Phone 818-840-4924
Brent Roske, President

American Federation of Television & Radio Artists (AFTRA)
www.aftra.org
Labor organization representing broadcast performers.

Los Angeles
5757 Wilshire Blvd., Ste. 900
Los Angeles, CA 90036
Phone 323-634-8100
Fax 323-634-8246
Email losangeles@aftra.com
aftrany@aftra.com

New York
260 Madison Ave., 7th Fl.
New York, NY 10016
Phone 212-532-0800
Fax 212-545-1238
Stephen Burrow, Executive Director, New York Chapter
Mathis L. Dunn Jr., Interim Executive Director, Los Angeles Chapter

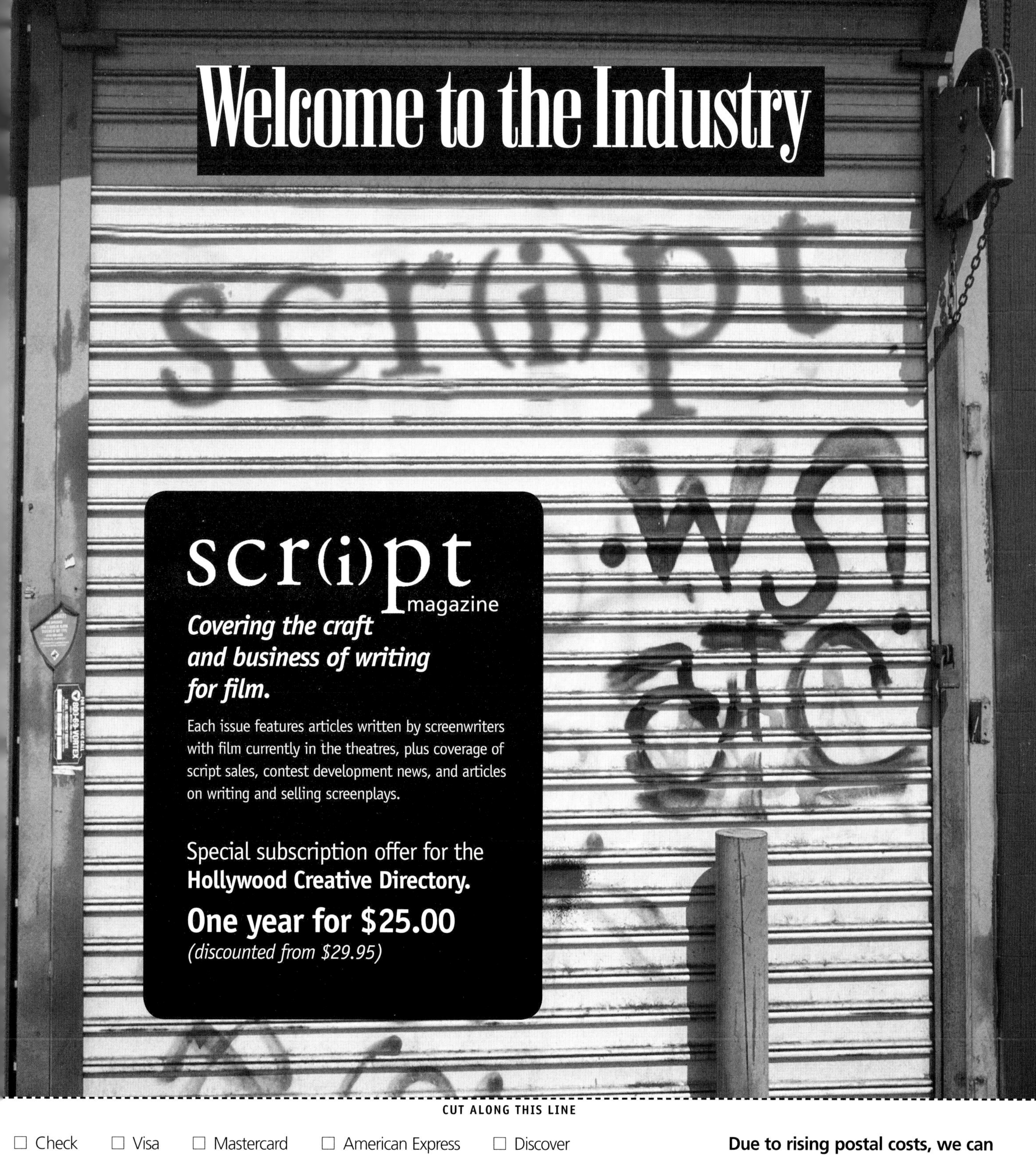

Welcome to the Industry
scr(i)pt
scr(i)pt magazine
Covering the craft and business of writing for film.
Each issue features articles written by screenwriters with film currently in the theatres, plus coverage of script sales, contest development news, and articles on writing and selling screenplays.
Special subscription offer for the Hollywood Creative Directory.
One year for $25.00
(discounted from $29.95)

CUT ALONG THIS LINE

☐ Check ☐ Visa ☐ Mastercard ☐ American Express ☐ Discover

Credit Card # ______ Expiration Date ______

Phone ______ E-mail ______

Name ______

Address ______ Apartment # ______

City ______ State ______ Zip ______

Due to rising postal costs, we can only accept prepaid subscriptions.

5638 Sweet Air Rd, Baldwin, MD, 21013
tf. 888-245-2228 f. 410-592-8062

MD residents add 5% sales tax. Canada and Mexico add $8/yr all other non-American add $20/yr funds must be drawn from a U.S. bank.

American Film Institute (AFI)
www.afi.com
Organization dedicated to preserving and advancing the art of the moving image through events, exhibitions and education.
2021 N. Western Ave.
Los Angeles, CA 90027
Phone 323-856-7600
Fax 323-467-4578
Jean Picker Firstenberg, Director/CEO
Jonathan Estrin, Executive VP

American Guild of Variety Artists (AGVA)
Labor union representing performers in Broadway, off-Broadway, and cabaret productions, as well as theme park and nightclub performers.
Los Angeles
4741 Laurel Canyon Blvd., Ste. 208
Valley Village, CA 91607
Phone 818-508-9984
Fax 818-508-3029
Email agvawest@earthlink.net
New York
363 Seventh Ave., 17th Fl.
New York, NY 10001
Phone 212-675-1003
Fax 212-633-0097

American Humane Association (AHA) Film & TV Unit
www.americanhumane.org/film
Watchdog organization dedicated to preventing cruelty to animal actors performing in films and television.
15366 Dickens St.
Sherman Oaks, CA 91403
Phone 818-501-0123
800-677-3420 (Hotline)
Fax 818-501-8725
Marie Belew Wheatley, President/CEO, AHA

American Screenwriters Association (ASA)
www.goasa.com
Nonprofit organization dedicated to the promotion and encouragement of the art and craft of screenwriting.
269 S. Beverly Dr., Ste. 2600
Beverly Hills, CA 90212-3807
Phone 866-265-9091
Email asa@goasa.com
John E. Johnson, Executive Director

American Society of Cinematographers (ASC)
www.theasc.com
Society representing professional cinematographers, dedicated to improving the quality of motion picture presentation.
1782 N. Orange Dr.
Hollywood, CA 90028
Phone 323-969-4333
800-448-0145
Fax 323-882-6391
Email office@theasc.com
Daryn Okada, President
Delphine Figueras, Administrative Assistant

American Society of Composers, Authors & Publishers (ASCAP)
www.ascap.com
Performing rights organization representing composers, lyricists, songwriters, and music publishers; Additional offices in New York, Nashville, Chicago, Miami, Atlanta, Puerto Rico, and London.
7920 W. Sunset Blvd., 3rd Fl.
Los Angeles, CA 90046
Phone 323-883-1000
212-621-6000
615-742-5000
Fax 323-883-1049
212-724-9064
615-742-5020
Email info@ascap.com

American Society of Young Musicians (ASYM)
www.asymusicians.org
National nonprofit organization committed to the enrichment of young musicians; Sponsor of the annual ASYM Spring Benefit Concert and Awards.
6100 Wilshire Blvd., Ste. 230
Los Angeles, CA 90048
Phone 310-358-8300
Fax 310-358-8304
Email info@asymusicians.org

American Women in Radio & Television (AWRT)
www.awrt.org
National organization supporting the advancement of women in the communications industry.
8405 Greensboro Dr., Ste. 800
McLean, VA 22102
Phone 703-506-3290
Fax 703-506-3266
Email info@awrt.org
Maria Brennan, Executive Director

Art Directors Guild & Scenic, Title and Graphic Artists
www.artdirectors.org
Organization representing production designers, art directors, assistant art directors and scenic, title and graphic designers.
c/o Local 800 I.A.T.S.E.
11969 Ventura Blvd., Ste. 200
Studio City, CA 91604
Phone 818-762-9995
Fax 818-762-9997
Lydia Zimmer, Office Manager

Association of Film Commissioners International (AFCI)
www.afci.org
Organization providing representation and support to member film commissions.
314 N. Main, Ste. 308
Helena, MT 59601
Phone 406-495-8040
323-462-6092
Fax 406-495-8039
323-462-6091
Email info@afci.org
Bill Lindstrom, CEO

Association of Independent Commercial Producers (AICP)
www.aicp.com
Organization representing interests of US companies that specialize in producing commericals in various media (film, video, Internet, etc.) for advertisers and agencies.
Los Angeles
650 N. Bronson Ave., Ste. 223-B
Los Angeles, CA 90004
Phone 323-960-4763
Fax 323-960-4766
New York
3 W. 18th St., 5th Fl.
New York, NY 10011
Phone 212-929-3000
Fax 212-929-3359
Steve Caplan, Executive VP
Farah Fima, Events Coordinator

Association of Independent Video and Filmmakers (AIVF)
www.aivf.org
Nonprofit membership organization serving local, national and international filmmakers, including documentarians and experimental artists.
304 Hudson St., 6th Fl.
New York, NY 10013
Phone 212-807-1400
Fax 212-463-8519
Email info@aivf.org
Priscilla Grim, Membership/ Advocacy Director

Association of Moving Image Archivists
www.amianet.org
Non-profit professional association established to advance the field of moving image archiving by fostering cooperation among individuals and organizations concerned with the acquisition, preservation, exhibition and use of moving image materials
1313 N. Vine St.
Los Angeles, CA 90028
Phone 323-463-1500
Fax 323-463-1506
Email amia@amianet.org
Janice Simpson, President
Keith LaQua, Executive Director

Association of Talent Agents (ATA)
www.agentassociation.com
www.actorsagentsearch.com
Nonprofit trade association for talent agencies representing clients in the motion picture and television industries, as well as literary, theatre, radio, and commercial clients.
9255 Sunset Blvd., Ste. 930
Los Angeles, CA 90069
Phone 310-274-0628
Fax 310-274-5063
Shellie Jetton, Administrative Director

The Black Filmmaker Foundation (BFF)
www.dvrepublic.org
Nonprofit organization which administers an online community and a filmmaker lab.
11 W. 42nd St., 9th Fl.
New York, NY 10036
Phone 212-253-1690
Fax 718-407-0608
Email hudlin@dvrepublic.org
Warrington Hudlin, Founder/Chief

Breakdown Services
www.breakdownservices.com
Communications network and casting system providing integrated tools for casting directors and talent representatives, as well as casting information for actors.
2140 Cotner Ave.
Los Angeles, CA 90025
Phone 310-276-9166
212-869-2003
604-943-7100

Broadcast Music, Inc. (BMI)
www.bmi.com
Nonprofit performing rights organization of songwriters, composers and music publishers. Additional offices in Nashville, New York, Atlanta, Miami, Puerto Rico, and London.
8730 Sunset Blvd., 3rd Fl. West
West Hollywood, CA 90069-2211
Phone 310-659-9109
615-401-2000
212-586-2000

California Arts Council (CAC)
www.cac.ca.gov
State organization encouraging artistic awareness, expression, and participation reflecting California's diverse cultures.
1300 I St., Ste. 930
Sacramento, CA 95814
Phone 916-322-6555
800-201-6201
Fax 916-322-6575
Mary Beth Barber, Communications Director

Casting Society of America
www.castingsociety.com
Trade organization of professional film and television casting directors.
Los Angeles
606 N. Larchmont Blvd., Ste. 4B
Los Angeles, CA 90004
Phone 323-463-1925
Fax 323-463-5753
New York
C/O Bernard Telsey
145 W. 28th St., Ste. 12F
New York NY 10001
Phone 212-868-1260
Fax 212-868-1261
Larry Raab
Alice S. Cassidy

CFI Film Preservation
Offers film preservation and restoration services for motion pictures.
4050 Lankershim Blvd.
North Hollywood, CA 91604
Phone 818-260-3844
Fax 818-260-3851

Cinewomen
www.cinewomen.org
Nonprofit organization dedicated to supporting the advancement of women within the motion picture industry.
Los Angeles
PO Box 691637
Los Angeles, CA 90069
Phone 310-288-1160
Email info@cinewomen.com (LA)
info@cinewomenny.org (NY)
New York
PO Box 1477
Cooper Station
New York, NY 10276
Phone 212-604-4264

Clear, Inc.
www.clearinc.org
Organization of clearance and research professionals working in the film, television, and multimedia industries.
PO Box 628
Burbank, CA 91503-0628
Fax 413-647-3380
Email info@clearinc.org
Rob Meyers, Executive Director

Commercial Casting Directors Association (CCDA)
Organization dedicated to providing a level of professionalism for casting directors within the commercial industry.
c/o Jeff Gerard/Chelsea Studios
11340 Moorpark St.
Studio City, CA 91604
Phone 818-782-9900

Costume Designers Guild (CDG)
www.costumedesignersguild.com
Union representing motion picture, television, and commercial costume designers. Promotes research, artistry and technical expertise in the field of film and television costume design.
4730 Woodman Ave., Ste. 430
Sherman Oaks, CA 91423
Phone 818-905-1557
Fax 818-905-1560
Email cdgia@earthlink.net
Cheryl Downey, Executive Director
Rachael Stanley, Assistant Executive Director

The Digital Entertainment Group (DEG)
www.dvdinformation.com
Nonprofit trade consortium dedicated to promoting DVD and video; Partnership between hardware and software manufacturers to ensure all aspects of the home enterainment industry are accurately represented
9229 Sunset Blvd., Ste. 425
Los Angeles, CA 90069
Phone 310-888-2201
Fax 310-888-2205
Email getinfo@digitalentertainmentinfo.com

Directors Guild of America (DGA)
www.dga.org
Labor union representing film and television directors, unit production managers, first assistant directors, second assistant directors, technical coordinators, tape associate directors, stage managers and production associates.
Los Angeles
7920 Sunset Blvd.
Los Angeles, CA 90046
Phone 800-421-4173
310-289-2000
Fax 310-289-2029
New York
110 W. 57th St.
New York, NY 10019
Phone 212-581-0370
Fax 212-581-1441
Chicago
400 N. Michigan Ave., Ste. 307
Chicago, IL 60611
Phone 312-644-5050
Fax 312-644-5776
Michael Apted, President

Doculink
www.doculink.org
An online community for documentary filmmakers who share information, leads, ideas, and a commitment to support each other's growth as nonfiction filmmakers.
Robert Bahar, Founder
Antonia Kao, Founder

The Dramatists Guild of America, Inc.
www.dramaguild.com
Professional association of playwrights, composers and lyricists.
1501 Broadway, Ste. 701
New York, NY 10036
Phone 212-398-9366
Fax 212-944-0420
Email director@dramatistsguild.com
Ralph Sevush, Associate Director

Entertainment Industries Council, Inc.
www.eiconline.org
Nonprofit organization founded in 1983 by leaders in the entertainment industry to provide information, awareness and understanding of major health and social issues among the entertainment industries and to audiences at large.
2600 W. Olive St., Ste. 574
Burbank, CA 91505
Phone 818-333-5001
Fax 818-333-5005
Email eicwest@eiconline.org

Festival Consulting Group
www.festivalconsultinggroup.com
Consulting service to film festivals around the world, specializing in start-up strategies, administration, sponsorship, marketing, special events and technical production.
4712 Admiralty Way, Ste. 244
Los Angeles, CA 90292
Phone 310-827-9100
Fax 310-827-9101
Email
info@festivalconsulting.com

Film Independent (FIND)
www.filmindependent.org
Nonprofit service organization providing resources and information for independent filmmakers and industry professionals.
8750 Wilshire Blvd., 2nd Fl.
Beverly Hills, CA 90211
Phone 310-432-1200
Fax 310-432-1203
Dawn Hudson, Executive Director

Film Music Network
www.filmmusicworld.com
Organization for film and television music professionals, including supervisors, composers, editors and contractors.
13101 Washington Blvd., Ste. 466
Los Angeles, CA 90066
Phone 310-909-8418
800-774-3700
Fax 310-496-0917
Email info@filmmusicworld.com

Filmmakers Alliance (FA)
www.filmmakersalliance.com
Community of film artists bound by a commitment to realize the full creative potential of independent film; Hosts monthly meetings, screenings, seminars, discussion forums, writers groups and staged readings.
10920 Ventura Blvd.
Studio City, CA 91604
Phone 818-980-8161
Fax 213-228-1156
Email info@filmmakersalliance.com

Hollywood Radio & Television Society (HRTS)
www.hrts.org
Recognized as the entertainment industry's premiere networking and information forum. Through the signature Newsmaker Luncheon Series and other HRTS events, provides industry executives the opportunity to stay abreast of current trends while also staying connected to other key entertainment industry leaders.
13701 Riverside Dr., Ste. 205
Sherman Oaks, CA 91423
Phone 818-789-1182
Fax 818-789-1210
Email info@hrts.org
Andy Friendly, President, Board of Directors
Dave Ferrara, Executive Director

Horror Writers Association
www.horror.org
Worldwide organization of horror and dark fantasy writers and publishing professionals.
PO Box 50577
Palo Alto, CA 94303
Email hwa@horror.org

The Humanitas Prize
www.humanitasprize.org
Prestigious prizes awarded to film and television writers whose produced scripts communicate values which most enrich the human person.
17575 Pacific Coast Highway
PO Box 861
Pacific Palisades, CA 90272
Phone 310-454-8769
Fax 310-459-6549
Email humanitasmail@aol.com
Frank Desiderio C.S.P., President
Chris Donahue, Executive Director
Cara D'Antoni, Assistant to Executive Director

IFP - Independent Feature Project
www.ifp.org
Notprofit organization designed to foster a more sustainable infrastructure that supports independent filmmaking, and ensures opportunities for the public to see films more accurately reflecting the full diversity of American culture; Presents the IFP Market, Gotham Awards and Filmmaker Magazine.
104 W. 29th St., 12th Fl.
New York, NY 10001
Phone 212-465-8200
Fax 212-465-8525
Email newyorkmembership@ifp.org
Michelle Byrd, Executive Director

Independent Film & Television Alliance (IFTA)
www.ifta-online.org
Trade association for the independent film and television industries.
10850 Wilshire Blvd., 9th Fl.
Los Angeles, CA 90024-4321
Phone 310-446-1000
Fax 310-446-1600
Email info@ifta-online.org
Jean Prewitt, President/CEO

International Alliance of Theatrical Stage Employees (IATSE)
www.iatse-intl.org
Union representing technicians, artisans and craftpersons in the entertainment industry including live theatre, film and television production and trade shows.

Los Angeles
10045 Riverside Dr.
Toluca Lake, CA 91602
Phone 818-980-3499
Fax 818-980-3496

New York
1430 Broadway, 20th Fl.
New York, NY 10018
Phone 212-730-1770
Fax 212-730-7809

International Documentary Association
www.documentary.org
Dedicated to supporting the efforts of nonfiction film and video makers throughout the United States and the world; Promotes the documentary form, expands opportunities for the production, distribution, and exhibition of documentary
1201 W. Fifth St., Ste. M320
Los Angeles, CA 90017
Phone 213-534-3600
Fax 213-534-3610
Sandra J. Ruch, Executive Director (sandra@documentary.org)
Diane Estelle Vicari, President

International Press Academy
www.pressacademy.com
Association of professional entertainment journalists.
9601 Wilshire Blvd., Ste. 755
Beverly Hills, CA 90210
Phone 310-271-7041
818-989-1589
Fax 818-787-3627
Email info@pressacademy.com

The Norman Lear Center
www.learcenter.org
A multidisciplinary research and public policy center exploring implications of the convergence of entertainment, commerce, and society.
USC Annenberg School of Communication
Los Angeles, CA 90089
Phone 213-821-1343
Fax 213-821-1580
Email enter@usc.edu

Location Managers Guild of America
www.locationmanagers.org
Professional association of Location Managers and Scouts in film, TV, commercials, music videos and print advertising
10940 Wilshire Blvd., Ste. 1400
Los Angeles, CA 90024
Phone 310-967-2007
Kayla Thames-Berge, President

Motion Picture Association of America (MPAA)
www.mpaa.org
Trade association for the US motion picture, home video and television industries.
15503 Ventura Blvd.
Encino, CA 91436
Phone 818-995-6600
Fax 818-382-1799
Dan Glickman, Chairman/CEO

Motion Picture Editors Guild
www.editorsguild.com
Union representing motion pictures, television, and commercial editors, sound technicians and story analysts.

Los Angeles
7715 Sunset Blvd., Ste. 200
Hollywood, CA 90046
Phone 323-876-4770
Fax 323-876-0861
Email mail@editorsguild.com

New York
145 Hudson St., Ste. 201
New York, NY 10013
Phone 212-302-0700
Fax 212-302-1091

Chicago
6317 N. Northwest Hwy.
Chicago, IL 60631
Phone 773-594-6598
Fax 773-594-6599
Serena Kung, Director, Membership Services

Multicultural Motion Picture Association (MMPA)
www.thediversityawards.org
Association promoting and encouraging diversity of ideas, cultures and perspectives in film. Sponsor of the annual Diversity Awards.
6100 Wilshire Blvd., Ste. 230
Los Angeles, CA 90048
Phone 310-358-8300
Fax 310-358-8304
Email info@diversityawards.org

Music Video Production Association (MVPA)
www.mvpa.com
Nonprofit trade organization made up of music video production and post production companies, as well as editors, directors, producers, cinematographers, choreographers, script supervisors, computer animators and make-up artists involved in the production of music videos.
201 N. Occidental Blvd., Bldg. 7, Unit B
Los Angeles, CA 90026
Phone 213-387-1590
Fax 213-385-9507
Email info@mvpa.com
Andrea Clark, Executive Director
Amy E, Executive

Mystery Writers of America (MWA)
www.mysterywriters.org
Organization of published mystery authors, editors, screenwriters, and other professionals in the field. Sponsors symposia, conferences and The Edgar Awards.
17 E. 47th St., 6th Fl.
New York, NY 10017
Phone 212-888-8171
Fax 212-888-8107
Email mwa@mysterywriters.org

Nashville Association of Talent Directors (NATD)
www.n-a-t-d.com
Professional entertainment organization comprised of industry professionals involved in all aspects of the music and entertainment industries.
PO Box 23903
Nashville, TN 37202-3903
Phone 615-297-0100
Email info@n-a-t-d.com

National Academy of Recording Arts & Sciences (NARAS)
www.grammy.com
Organization dedicated to improving the quality of life and cultural condition for musicians, producers, and other recording professionals. Provides outreach, professional development, cultural enrichment, education and human services programs. Sponsors The Grammy Awards.
The Recording Academy
3402 Pico Blvd.
Santa Monica, CA 90405
Phone 310-392-3777
Fax 310-399-3090
Email losangeles@grammy.com

National Association of Latino Independent Producers (NALIP)
www.nalip.org
Organization of Latino/Latina film, television and documentary makers.

Los Angeles
1323 Lincoln Blvd., Ste. 220
Santa Monica, CA 90401
Phone 310-395-8880
Fax 310-395-8811
Email membership@nalip.info
naliped@msn.com

New York
32 Broadway, 14th Fl.
New York, NY 10004
Phone 646-336-6333
Fax 212-727-0549
Kathryn Galán, Executive Director
Octavio Marin, Signature Programs Director
Jose Murillo, Membership Coordinator

National Association of Television Program Executives (NATPE)
www.natpe.org
Global, nonprofit organization dedicated to the creation, development and distribution of televised programming in all forms, across all platforms. Develops and nurtures opportunities for the buying, selling and sharing of content and ideas.
5757 Wilshire Blvd., Penthouse 10
Los Angeles, CA 90036-3681
Phone 310-453-4440
Fax 310-453-5258
Email info@natpe.org
Rick Feldman, President/CEO

National Conference of Personal Managers (NCOPM)
www.ncopm.com
Association for the advancement of personal managers and their clients.

Los Angeles
1440 Beaumont Ave., Ste. A2-360
Beaumont, CA 92223
Phone 310-492-5983

New York
330 W. 38th St., Ste. 904
New York, NY 10018
Phone 212-245-2063
Fax 212-245-2367
Daniel Abrahamsen, Executive Director, Eastern Division
Candee Barshop, Executive Director, Western Division

National Council of La Raza (NCLR)
www.nclr.org
Private, nonprofit, nonpartisan, tax-exempt organization dedicated, in part, to promoting fair, accurate, and balanced portrayals of Latinos in film, television and music. Sponsor of the ALMA Awards.
c/o Raul Yzaguirre Bldg.
1126 16th Street NW
Washington, DC 20036
Phone 202-785-1670
Fax 202-785-7620

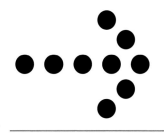

Nosotros/Ricardo Montalban Foundation
www.nosotros.org
Organization established to improve the image of Latinos/Hispanics as they are portrayed in the entertainment industry, both in front of and behind the camera, as well as to expand employment opportunities within the entertainment industry. Producers of The Golden Eagle Awards.
650 N. Bronson Ave., Ste. 102
Hollywood, CA 90004
Phone 323-466-8566 (President's Office)
323-465-4167 (Nosotros/Theatre Office)
Fax 323-466-8540

Organization of Black Screenwriters (OBS)
www.obswriter.com
Nonprofit organization developing and supporting Black screenwriters.
4648 Mioland Dr.
Los Angeles, CA 90048
Phone 323-735-2050
Email sfranklin@obswriter.com
Sylvia Franklin, President

PEN
www.pen.org
Nonprofit organization made up of poets, playwrights, essayists, novelists, television writers, screenwriters, critics, historians, editors, journalists, and translators. Dedicated to protecting the rights of writers around the world, to stimulate interest in the written word and to foster a vital literary community.
Pen American Center
568 Broadway, Ste. 303
New York, NY 10012-3225
Phone 212-334-1660
Fax 212-334-2181

Players Directory
www.playersdirectory.com
Casting directory published every six months as a cooperative service to the players and production studios of Hollywood.
1313 N. Vine St.
Hollywood, CA 90028
Phone 310-247-3058
Fax 310-550-5034
Email players@oscars.org
Su Hyatt, Associate Editor

Producers Guild of America (PGA)
www.producersguild.org
Organization representing the interests of all members of the producing team.
8530 Wilshire Blvd., Ste. 450
Beverly Hills, CA 90211
Phone 310-358-9020
Fax 310-358-9520
Marshall Herskovitz, President

Professional Electronic Entertainment Recruiters (PEER)
www.peer-org.com
Professional Electronic Entertainment Recruiters (PEER) is an interactive entertainment software industry trade association comprised of recruiters committed to better serving the gaming industry.
Email join@peer-org.com
David Musgrove, President

Rock the Vote
www.rockthevote.org
Dedicated to protecting freedom of expression and mobilizing young people to get out and vote.
Los Angeles
409 N. Pacific Coast Hwy., #589
Redondo Beach, CA 90277
Phone 310-234-0665
Email info@rockthevote.org
Washington, DC
1313 L St., NW, 1st Fl.
Washington, DC 20005
Phone 202-962-9710
Fax 202-962-9715

Screen Actors Guild (SAG)
www.sag.org
Union representing actors in feature films, short films and digital projects.
Los Angeles
5757 Wilshire Blvd.
Los Angeles, CA 90036
Phone 323-954-1600
New York
360 Madison Ave., 12th Fl.
New York, NY 10017
Phone 212-944-1030
Fax 212-944-6774

Scriptwriters Network
www.scriptwritersnetwork.org
Organization providing information and career counseling for film and television writers.
11684 Ventura Blvd., Ste. 508
Studio City, CA 91604
Phone 323-848-9477
Email info@scriptwritersnetwork.org

Society of Operating Cameramen (SOC)
www.soc.org
Organization promoting excellence in the fields of camera operation and the allied camera crafts.
PO Box 2006
Toluca Lake, CA 91610
Phone 818-382-7070
Email info@soc.org

Society of Stage Directors & Choreographers (SSDC)
www.ssdc.org
Union representing directors and choreographers of Broadway national tours, regional theatre, dinner theatre and summer stock, as well as choreographers for motion pictures, television and music videos.
1501 Broadway, Ste. 1701
New York, NY 10036-5653
Phone 212-391-1070
800-541-5204
Fax 212-302-6195

Stunts-Ability, Inc.
www.stuntsability.com
Nonprofit organization training amputees and other disabled persons for stunts, acting and effects for the entertainment industry.
PO Box 600711
San Diego, CA 92160-0711
Phone 619-542-7730
Fax 619-542-7731
Email info@stuntsability.com

Talent Managers Association (TMA)
www.talentmanagers.org
Nonprofit organization promoting and encouraging the highest standards of professionalism in the practice of talent management.
4804 Laurel Canyon Blvd., Ste. 611
Valley Village, CA 91607
Phone 310-205-8495
Fax 818-765-2903
Steven Nash, President
Betty McCormick Aggas, Marketing & Benefits Director

U.S. Copyright Office
www.copyright.gov
Promotes progress of the arts and protection for the works of authors; Web site serves the copyright community of creators and users, as well as the general public.
Library of Congress
101 Independence Avenue S.E.
Washington, D.C. 20559
Phone 202-707-3000
202-707-9100 (Hotline)

Women In Film (WIF)
www.wif.org
Organization dedicated to empowering, promoting and nurturing women in the film and television industries.
8857 W. Olympic Blvd., Ste. 201
Beverly Hills, CA 90211-3605
Phone 310-657-5144
Fax 310-657-5154
Email info@wif.org
CiCi Holloway, President
Gayle Nachlis, Executive Director

Women's Image Network (WIN)
www.winfemme.com
www.thewinawards.com
Nonprofit corporation encouraging positive portrayals of women in theatre, television and film.
2118 Wilshire Blvd., Ste. 144
Santa Monica, CA 90403
Phone 310-229-5365
Email info@winfemme.com
Phyllis Stuart, President

Writers Guild of America (WGA)
www.wga.org
www.wgaeast.org
Union representing writers in the motion pictures, broadcast cable and new technologies industries.
Los Angeles
7000 W. Third St.
Los Angeles, CA 90048-4329
Phone 323-951-4000
Fax 323-782-4800
New York
555 W. 57th St., Ste. 1230
New York, NY 10019
Phone 212-767-7800
Fax 212-582-1909

LIBRARIES AND MUSEUMS

Academy of Motion Picture Arts & Sciences - Margaret Herrick Library
www.oscars.org
Extensive and comprehensive research and reference collections documenting film as an art form and an industry.
333 S. La Cienega Blvd.
Beverly Hills, CA 90211
Phone 310-247-3020
Fax 310-657-5193
Linda Harris Mehr, Director

Library of Congress
www.loc.gov/rr/mopic
Acquisition, cataloging and preservation of the motion picture and television collections. Operates the Motion Picture and Television Reading Room to provide access and information services to an international community of film and television professionals, archivists, scholars and researchers.
c/o Motion Pictures & Television Reading Room
101 Independence Ave., SE
James Madison Bldg., Ste. 336
Washington, DC 20540
Phone 202-707-8572
202-707-5000
Fax 202-707-2371

The Library of Moving Images, Inc.
www.libraryofmovingimages.com
Independent film archives including 19th Century experimental film footage, silent film footage, 20th Century newsreel footage, short subjects, education and industrial films, classic documentaries, vintage cartoons, home movies and world news feeds.
6671 Sunset Blvd., Bungalow 1581
Hollywood, CA 90028
Phone 323-469-7499
Fax 323-469-7559

Lillian Michelson Research Library
c/o DreamWorks SKG
1000 Flower St.
Glendale, CA 91201
Phone 818-695-6445
Fax 818-695-6450

Los Angeles County Museum of Art (LACMA)
collectionsonline.lacma.org
www.lacma.org
Holdings include entertainment-related photographs, prints, costumes and costume sketches. Museum also has film department and film series.
5905 Wilshire Blvd.
Los Angeles, CA 90036
Phone 323-857-6118
323-857-6000
(General Information)
Email library@lacma.org

Louis B. Mayer Library
www.afi.com
Books, periodicals and other special collections covering various aspects of motion pictures and television. Serves the research needs of the American Film Institute's staff, faculty and students. Library is available on a non-circulating basis to visiting scholars, researchers, and advanced graduate students, as well as members of the entertainment industry.
c/o American Film Institute
2021 N. Western Ave.
Los Angeles, CA 90027
Phone 323-856-7654
323-856-7600

Museum of the Moving Image
www.movingimage.us
Dedicated to educating the public about the art, history, technique, and technology of film, television, and digital media and to examining their impact on culture and society. Nation's largest permanent collection of moving image artifacts.
35th Avenue at 36th St.
Astoria, NY 11106
Phone 718-784-4520
718-784-0077
Fax 718-784-4681
Rochelle Slovin, Director

New York Public Library for the Performing Arts
www.nypl.org
Extensive combination of circulating, reference and rare archival collections in the performing arts.
40 Lincoln Center Plaza
New York, NY 10023-7498
Phone 212-870-1630
Email performingarts@nypl.org

Warner Bros. Studio Research Library
2777 N. Ontario St.
Burbank, CA 91504
Phone 818-977-5050
Fax 818-567-4366
Steve Bingen, Research Librarian
Linda Cummings, Research Librarian

Writers Guild Foundation Shavelson-Webb Library
www.wga.org
www.wgfoundation.org
Collection dedicated to the art, craft, and history of writing for motion pictures, radio, television and new media. Open to the public and Guild members.
7000 W. Third St.
Los Angeles, CA 90048-4329
Phone 323-782-4544
Fax 323-782-4695
Karen Pedersen, Library Director

WORKSHEET

FREQUENTLY CALLED PHONE NUMBERS

NAME	COMPANY	PHONE #	FAX #

WORKSHEET

DATE	PROJECT	CONTACT	NOTES

WORKSHEET

FREQUENTLY CALLED PHONE NUMBERS

NAME	COMPANY	PHONE #	FAX #

WORKSHEET

DATE	PROJECT	CONTACT	NOTES

THE CONCIERGE™

LOS ANGELES ✦ NEW YORK

CONTENTS

FOOD & DRINK

- Commissaries & Executive Dining Rooms 2
- Restaurants 2
- Dinner Delivery 5
- Catering 5
- Event Planning 5

ACCOMMODATIONS

- Hotels 6
- Corporate Retreats 7
- Corporate Housing 7
- Real Estate 8

TRAVEL & TRANSPORTATION

- Travel Agencies 8
- Airlines - Domestic 8
- Airlines - International 8
- Charter Planes 9
- Car Rentals 9
- Limos 9
- Executive Car Leasing 9

GIFTS & SHOPPING

- Florists 10
- Gift Baskets 10
- Personal Shoppers 10

SCREENING ROOMS 10

VIP TICKETS 12

MAIL & DELIVERY

- Messengers 12
- FedEx Kinko's Stores 12
- UPS Stores & Drop Boxes 13
- Post Offices 13

OFFICE SERVICES & SUPPLIES 14

FOOD & DRINK

Commissaries & Executive Dining Rooms

PARAMOUNT PICTURES
The Cafe 323-956-5101
Contact – Mari Gutierrez

Executive Dining Room 323-956-8399
Contact – Mari Gutierrez

Special Functions 323-956-8599
Contact – Uschi Wilson

SONY PICTURES ENTERTAINMENT
The Grill 310-244-5134
Contact – Allen Artcliff

Rita Hayworth Dining Room....310-244-5521
Contact – Allen Artcliff

TWENTIETH CENTURY FOX
Cafeteria....310-369-2621
Executive Dining Room 310-369-2759
Contact – Cathy

UNIVERSAL CITY STUDIOS
Commissary....818-777-2414
Executive Dining Room 818-777-5405
Catering 818-777-5402
Contact – Scott Ackerman

THE WALT DISNEY COMPANY
Buena Vista Commissary 818-560-5546
Contact – Lucy Barraza

Riverside Commissary 818-460-5777
Contact – Tracey Riddle

The Rotunda 818-560-1051
Contact – Nora Titner

WARNER BROS.
Commissary....818-954-4203
Contact – Maurizio Binotto

Executive Dining Room 818-954-4220
Contact – Julene Rury

Restaurants

BEVERLY HILLS

BARNEY GREENGRASS 310-777-5877
Barney's, 9570 Wilshire Blvd. (Camden Dr.), Beverly Hills
General Manager – Sharon Kerbyn

THE BLVD 310-275-5200
The Regent Beverly Wilshire Hotel, 9500 Wilshire Blvd. (Rodeo Dr.), Beverly Hills
Restaurant Managers – Felipe Gomez & Ara Aederi

CRUSTACEAN 310-205-8990
9646 Little Santa Monica Blvd. (Bedford Dr.), Beverly Hills
Operation Manager – Christopher Kulow

CUT 310-275-5200
The Regent Beverly Wilshire Hotel, 9500 Wilshire Blvd. (Rodeo Dr.), Beverly Hills
General Manager – Mateo Ferdinandi

DA PASQUALE 310-859-3884
9749 Little Santa Monica Blvd. (Wilshire Blvd.), Beverly Hills
General Manager – Bruno Morra

FOOD & DRINK

Restaurants

BEVERLY HILLS

THE FRIARS OF BEVERLY HILLS 310-553-0850
9900 Santa Monica Blvd. (Charleville Blvd.), Beverly Hills
General Manager – Colin Trauberman

GRILL ON THE ALLEY....310-276-0615
9560 Dayton Way (Wilshire Blvd.), Beverly Hills
General Manager – Arthur Meola

IL CIELO 310-276-9990
9018 Burton Way (Doheny Dr.), Beverly Hills
www.ilcielo.com
General Manager – Massimo Mazzarini

THE IVY 310-274-8303
113 N. Robertson Blvd. (Beverly Blvd.), Beverly Hills
General Manager – Ann Parker

KATE MANTILINI 310-278-3699
9101 Wilshire Blvd. (Doheny Dr.), Beverly Hills
General Manager – Mark Richards

MAPLE DRIVE....310-274-9800
345 N. Maple Dr. (Alden Rd.), Beverly Hills
General Manager – Michael Morrisette

MASTRO'S STEAKHOUSE 310-888-8782
246 N. Canon Dr. (Wilshire Blvd.), Beverly Hills
General Manager – Jason Talsky

MATSUHISA 310-659-9639
129 N. La Cienega Blvd. (Wilshire Blvd.), Beverly Hills
General Manager – Mark Varo

NATE 'N AL'S 310-274-0101
414 N. Beverly Dr. (Little Santa Monica Blvd.), Beverly Hills
Owner – Mark Mendelson

NIC'S 310-550-5707
453 N. Canon Dr. (Little Santa Monica Blvd.), Beverly Hills
Owner – Larry Nicola

POLO LOUNGE 310-887-2777
Beverly Hills Hotel, 9641 Sunset Blvd. (Rodeo Dr.), Beverly Hills
Manager – Pepe De Anda

PREGO 310-277-7346
362 N. Camden Dr. (Wilshire Blvd.), Beverly Hills
General Manager – Dusko Radonic

SPAGO 310-385-0880
176 N. Canon Dr. (Wilshire Blvd.), Beverly Hills
General Manager – Tracey Spillane

TRADER VIC'S....310-276-6345
9876 Wilshire Blvd. (Santa Monica Blvd.), Beverly Hills
General Manager – Chai Rojana

WINDOWS LOUNGE 310-273-2222
Four Seasons Hotel, 300 S. Doheny Dr. (Burton Way), Beverly Hills
General Manager – Mehdi Eftekari

DOWNTOWN

CAFÉ PINOT 213-239-6500
700 W. Fifth St. (Flower St.), Los Angeles
General Manager – Adam Rosenbaum

CICADA....213-488-9488
617 S. Olive St. (6th St.), Los Angeles
www.cicadarestaurant.com
Owner – Adelmo Zarif

FOOD & DRINK

Restaurants

DOWNTOWN

CIUDAD 213-486-5171
445 S. Figueroa St. (4th St.), Los Angeles
www.ciudad-la.com
General Manager – Iona Muir

FLIX CAFÉ 213-534-2337
451 S. Beaudry Ave. (W. 4th St.), Los Angeles
Food Service Manager – Art Haga

NICK & STEF'S STEAKHOUSE 213-680-0330
330 S. Hope St. (W. 3rd St.), Los Angeles
www.patinagroup.com
General Manager – Steve Meyer

NOE 213-356-4100
Omni Hotel, 251 S. Olive St. (3rd St.), Los Angeles
General Manager – Abraham Rubio

THE PALM (DOWNTOWN) 213-763-4600
1100 S. Flower St. (11th St.), Los Angeles
General Manager – Johnathan Scott

PATINA 213-972-3331
Walt Disney Concert Hall, 141 S. Grand (W. 3rd St.), Los Angeles
General Manager – Christian Philippo

SAI SAI, MILLENNIUM BILTMORE HOTEL....................213-624-1100
501 S. Olive St., Los Angeles
www.millenniumhotels.com
General Manager – Keiko Terry

WATER GRILL 213-891-0900
544 S. Grand Ave. (5th St.), Los Angeles
General Manager – Fred Buhler

ZUCCA 213-614-7800
801 S. Figueroa St. (8th St.), Los Angeles
General Manager – Erwan Channo

HOLLYWOOD/WEST HOLLYWOOD

AGO RESTAURANT 323-655-6333
8478 Melrose Ave. (La Cienega Blvd.), West Hollywood
General Manager – Stefano Carella

A.O.C. 323-653-6359
8022 W. 3rd St. (Crescent Heights Blvd.), Los Angeles
General Manager – Cynthia Mendoza

AMMO 323-467-3293
1155 N. Highland Ave. (Santa Monica Blvd.), Hollywood
General Manager – Benny Bohm

ASIA DE CUBA 323-848-6000
Mondrian Hotel, 8440 Sunset Blvd. (La Cienega Blvd.), West Hollywood
Food & Beverage Director – Jan Henningsen

BALBOA 323-650-8383
8462 Sunset Blvd. (La Cienega Blvd.), West Hollywood
General Manager – Jacques Perwin

BASTIDE 323-651-0426
8475 Melrose Ave. (La Cienega Blvd.), West Hollywood
General Manager – Gregory Castells

BLOWFISH SUSHI LA, LLC 310-887-3848
9929 Sunset Blvd. (Doheny Rd.), West Hollywood
General Manager – Amy Pierson

FOOD & DRINK

Restaurants

HOLLYWOOD/WEST HOLLYWOOD

CA'BREA 323-938-2863
346 S. La Brea Ave. (3rd St.), Los Angeles
Owner - Antonio Tommasi
General Manager – Aurora Simeone

CAFÉ STELLA 323-666-0265
3932 Sunset Blvd. (Sanborn Ave.), Silverlake
General Manager – Alain Jue

CAMPANILE 323-938-1447
624 S. La Brea Ave. (Wilshire Blvd.), Los Angeles
General Manager – Jay Perrin

CHAYA BRASSERIE 310-859-8833
8741 Alden Dr. (Robertson Blvd.), Los Angeles
General Manager – Francis Liong

CINESPACE 323-817-3456
6356 Hollywood Blvd. (Ivar Ave.), Los Angeles
General Manager – Ginger Reyes

CRAVINGS 310-652-6103
8653 W. Sunset Blvd. (Sunset Plaza), Hollywood
Owner – Abraham Oztok

DAN TANA'S 310-275-9444
9071 Santa Monica Blvd. (Doheny Dr.), West Hollywood

DOLCE 323-852-7174
8284 Melrose Ave. (Sweetzer Ave.), Los Angeles
General Manager – Maurizio La Rosa

EAT ON SUNSET 323-461-8800
1448 N. Gower St. (Sunset Blvd.)
General Manager – Johnathan Rollo

FORMOSA CAFÉ 323-850-9050
7156 Santa Monica Blvd. (La Brea Ave.), West Hollywood
General Manager – Spike Spengel

GEISHA HOUSE 323-460-6300
6633 Hollywood Blvd. (Cherokee Ave.)
www.geishahousehollywood.com
General Manager – Steven Herbert

GRACE 323-934-4400
7360 Beverly Blvd. (N. Fuller Ave.), Los Angeles
General Manager – Amy Knoll-Frasier

HOLLYWOOD CANTEEN 323-465-0961
1006 N. Seward St. (Santa Monica Blvd.), Los Angeles
General Manager – Minsoo

HOUSE OF BLUES 323-848-5100
8430 W. Sunset Blvd. (La Cienega Blvd.), West Hollywood
General Manager – Steve Simon

HUGO'S 323-654-3993
8401 Santa Monica Blvd. (La Cienega Blvd.), West Hollywood
General Manager – Keith Woiswillow

JONES CAFE 323-850-1727
7205 Santa Monica Blvd. (Formosa Ave.), West Hollywood
General Manager – Jared Meisler

KATANA 323-650-8585
8439 W. Sunset Blvd. (La Cienega Blvd.), West Hollywood
General Manager – Christian Corben

FOOD & DRINK

Restaurants

HOLLYWOOD/WEST HOLLYWOOD

LOCANDA VENETA 310-274-1893
8638 W. Third St. (Robertson Blvd.), Los Angeles
General Manager – Denis Boaro

M CAFÉ' DE CHAYA 323-525-0588
7119 Melrose Ave. (La Brea Ave.)
General Manager – Yuta Tsunoda

MINIBAR...323-882-6965
3413 Cahuenga Blvd. West (Barham Blvd.), Los Angeles
www.minibarlounge.com
Contact – Rebekah Barrow

MORTON'S 310-276-5205
8764 Melrose Ave. (Robertson Blvd.), Los Angeles
General Manager – Pamela Morton

MUSSO & FRANK GRILL 323-467-7788
6667 Hollywood Blvd. (Las Palmas Ave.), Hollywood
General Manager – John Garcia

OFF VINE 323-962-1900
6263 Leland Way (Vine St.), Hollywood
General Manager – Richard Falzone

THE PALM 310-550-8811
9001 Santa Monica Blvd. (Robertson Blvd.), West Hollywood
General Manager – Tommy Saboni

PANE E VINO 323-651-4600
8265 Beverly Blvd. (Sweetzer Ave.), Los Angeles
General Manager – Tom Space

PROVIDENCE 323-460-4170
5955 Melrose Ave. (Cole Ave.), Los Angeles
General Manager – Donato Poto

THE RESTAURANT AT THE HYATT ON SUNSET 323-848-3884
8401 Sunset Blvd. (Kings Rd.), West Hollywood
Food & Beverage Manager – Heather Holbrook

THE STANDARD CAFÉ..323-650-9090
The Standard Hotel, 8300 W. Sunset Blvd. (Sweetzer Ave.), West Hollywood
General Manager – Domenic Chiodi

TABLE 8 323-782-8258
7661 Melrose Ave. (N. Stanley Ave.), Los Angeles
www.table8la.com
General Manger – Mike Ilic

THE TOWER BAR...323-848-6677
The Sunset Tower Hotel, 8358 Sunset Blvd. (Sweetzer Ave.), West Hollywood
www.sunsettowerhotel.com
General Manager – Shaw McPherson

VERT 323-491-1300
Hollywood & Highland Center, 801 Hollywood Blvd. (Highland Ave.), Hollywood
www.wolfgangpuck.com
General Manager – Shannon Buckley

WHITE LOTUS...323-463-0060
1743 N. Cahuenga Blvd. (Hollywood Blvd.), Hollywood
General Manager – Natalie Beydoun

FOOD & DRINK

Restaurants

SANTA MONICA/WESTSIDE

BALLONA FISH MARKET 310-822-8979
13455 Maxella Ave. (Lincoln Blvd.), Marina del Rey
Manager – Jason Lohs

BORDER GRILL..310-451-1655
1445 4th St. (Broadway St.), Santa Monica
General Manager – Brian Strassburger

BROADWAY DELI..310-451-0616
1457 3rd Street Promenade (Broadway St.), Santa Monica
General Manager – Camille Marinelli

BUFFALO CLUB..310-450-8600
1520 Olympic Blvd. (15th St.), Santa Monica
General Manager – Patrick Doherty

CAFÉ BIZOU...310-582-8203
2450 Colorado Ave. (Cloverfield Blvd.), Santa Monica
General Manager – Wilfred Leon

DRAGO 310-828-1585
2628 Wilshire Blvd. (26th St.), Santa Monica
Owner – Celestino Drago

EUROCHOW 310-209-0066
1099 Westwood Blvd. (Kinross St.), Westwood
General Manager – Sandro Oliviero

GARDENS ON GLENDON 310-824-1818
1139 Glendon Ave. (Lindbrook), Westwood
General Manager – John Patterson

IVY AT THE SHORE 310-393-3113
1541 Ocean Ave. (Broadway St.), Santa Monica
General Manager – Ann Parker

JIRAFFE 310-917-6671
502 Santa Monica Blvd. (5th St.), Santa Monica
General Manager – Heather Posner

JUNIOR'S DELI..310-475-5771
2379 Westwood Blvd. (Pico Blvd.), Los Angeles
Owner/General Manager – David Saul

LA CACHETTE 310-470-4992
10506 Santa Monica Blvd. (Thayer Ave.), Los Angeles
Owner – Jean Francois Meteigener

LA FARM 310-449-4000
3000 W. Olympic Blvd. (Centinela Ave.), Santa Monica
General Manager – Dawn Acrey

MÉLISSE 310-395-0881
1104 Wilshire Blvd. (11th St.), Santa Monica
Maitre d' – Matthew Nathanson

NOBU MALIBU 310-317-9140
383 Cross Creek Rd. (Pacific Coast Highway), Malibu
Catering Manager - Krissy Forzano
General Manager – Erica Matsunaga

RöCKENWAGNER 310-399-6504
2435 Main St. (Ocean Park Blvd.), Santa Monica
General Manager – Marsha Henrickson

SUSHI ROKU 310-458-4771
1401 Ocean Ave. (Santa Monica Blvd.), Santa Monica
General Manager – Eddie Sevilla

FOOD & DRINK

Restaurants

SANTA MONICA/WESTSIDE

TENGU 310-209-0071
10853 Lindbrook Dr. (Glendon Ave.), Westwood
General Manager – Charles Hueston

VALENTINO 310-829-4313
3115 W. Pico Blvd. (31st St.), Santa Monica
General Manager – Rachel Thomas Turner

WHIST 310-260-7500
Viceroy Santa Monica, 1819 Ocean Ave. (Pico Blvd.), Santa Monica
Restaurant Manager – Sandro Coppola

WILSHIRE RESTAURANT 310-586-1707
2454 Wilshire Blvd. (25th St.), Santa Monica
www.wilshirerestaurant.com
General Manager – Harvey Friend

VALLEY

ART'S DELI 818-762-1221
12224 Ventura Blvd. (Laurel Canyon Blvd.), Studio City
Owner & General Manager – Harold Ginsburg

BISTRO GARDEN AT COLDWATER 818-501-0202
12950 Ventura Blvd. (Coldwater Canyon Ave.), Studio City
General Manager – Greg Pappas

CA'DEL SOLE 818-985-4669
4100 Cahuenga Blvd. (Lankershim Blvd.), North Hollywood
General Manager – Angelo Calderan

CAFÉ BIZOU...818-788-3536
14016 Ventura Blvd. (Costello Ave.), Sherman Oaks
General Manager – Ryan Herrera

FIREFLY 818-762-1833
11720 Ventura Blvd. (Laurel Canyon Blvd.), Studio City
General Manager – Tiffany Russo

JERRY'S FAMOUS DELI 818-980-4245
12655 Ventura Blvd. (Coldwater Canyon Ave.), Studio City
General Manager – Robin Stubbs

MEXICALI 818-985-1744
12161 Ventura Blvd. (Laurel Canyon Blvd.), Studio City
Owner/General Manager – Glen Dobbs

PINOT BISTRO 818-990-0500
12969 Ventura Blvd. (Coldwater Canyon Ave.), Studio City
General Manager – Alyssa McDiarmid

SMOKEHOUSE..818-845-3731
4420 Lakeside Dr. (Barham Blvd.), Studio City
General Manager – Israel Aviles

Dinner Delivery

GOURMET COURIER 323-655-8666
Beverly Hills, West Hollywood, Hollywood

WHY COOK LA 310-278-3955
www.whycookla.com

Catering

CATERED OCCASIONS 310-568-1004
www.cateredoccasionsevents.com

CHEERS CATERING, INC. 818-772-0233
www.cheerscateringinc.com

FOOD & DRINK

Catering

CHEF J'S KITCHEN 818-901-8671
www.chefj.com

CHRISTOPHE BERNARD CATERING 310-441-7623

DEBBIE'S DINNERS 323-936-4545
www.debbiesdinners.com

FOODWORKS 310-280-6050
www.foodworksla.com
Contact – Celia Hollander

JOAN'S ON THIRD 323-655-2285
www.joansonthird.com

KAI'S EUROPEAN CATERING 310-204-4450
www.eurocaters.com

MICHAEL'S EPICUREAN, INC. 818-509-0558
www.michaelsepicurean.com

THE PIG CATERING (Memphis-Style BBQ) 323-935-1116
www.thepigcatering.com
Contact – Daly Thompson

RICK ROYCE PREMIER BBQ CATERING 310-441-RIBS
www.rickroycebbqcatering.com
Contact – Rick Royce

WOLFGANG PUCK'S CATERING & EVENTS.................. 323-491-1250
www.wolfgangpuck.com/catering
Contact – Barbara Brass

Event Planning

ALONG CAME MARY! PRODUCTIONS, INC. 323-931-9082
www.alongcamemary.com

BEAUTIFUL BARTENDERS, LLC.......................310-600-1077
www.beautifulbartenders.com
Contact – Ana Gallegos

JEFFREY BEST/BEST EVENTS LA......................323-857-5577

BRENT BOLTHOUSE PRODUCTIONS 323-848-9300
www.BolthouseProductions.com
Contact – Brent Bolthouse

CARAVENTS, INC. 323-933-9993
www.caravents.com

COLIN COWIE LIFESTYLE 310-286-9600
www.colincowie.com

DINE WITH 9 CATERING...............................818-769-1883
www.dinewith9.com

LEVY, PAZANTI & ASSOCIATES.......................310-201-5033

MINDY WEISS PARTY CONSULTANTS 310-205-6000
www.mindyweiss.com

MOONDANCE EVENTS & ENTERTAINMENT...........310-287-2329
www.moondanceevents.com
Contact – Benita Karroll

NJK Productions...818-789-3688
www.njkproductions.com
Contact – Nancy Kim

SILVER BIRCHES...626-796-1431
www.silverbirches.net
Contact – David van der Velde

ACCOMMODATIONS

Hotels

BEVERLY HILLS

AVALON 310-277-5221/800-535-4715
9400 W. Olympic Blvd. (Beverly Dr.), Beverly Hills
www.avalonbeverlyhills.com
General Manager – Janne Clare

THE BEVERLY HILLS HOTEL 310-276-2251/800-283-8885
9641 Sunset Blvd. (Beverly Dr.), Beverly Hills
www.thebeverlyhillshotel.com
General Manager – Alberto Del Hoyo

THE BEVERLY HILTON 310-274-7777/800-HILTONS
9876 Wilshire Blvd., (Santa Monica Blvd.), Beverly Hills
www.hilton.com
General Manager – Denny Fitzpatrick

FOUR SEASONS HOTEL LA
AT BEVERLY HILLS 310-273-2222/800-819-5053
300 S. Doheny Dr. (Burton Way.), Beverly Hills
www.fourseasons.com/losangeles
General Manager – Mehdi Eftekari

LE MERIDIEN 310-247-0400/800-543-4300
465 S. La Cienega Blvd. (San Vicente Blvd.), Beverly Hills
www.beverlyhills.lemeridien.com
Acting Manager – Robert Leak

MAISON 140 ....310-281-4000/800-670-6182
140 Lasky Dr. (Little Santa Monica Blvd.), Beverly Hills
www.maison140.com
General Manager – Joachim Reitmen

THE PENINSULA 310-551-2888/800-462-7899
9882 S. Santa Monica Blvd. (Wilshire Blvd.), Beverly Hills
www.beverlyhills.peninsula.com
General Manager – Ali Kasicki

RAFFLES L'ERMITAGE.........................310-278-3344/800-800-2113
9291 Burton Way (Maple Dr.), Beverly Hills
www.lermitagehotel.com
General Manager – Jack Naderkhani

THE REGENT BEVERLY WILSHIRE 310-275-5200/800-545-4000
9500 Wilshire Blvd. (Rodeo Dr.), Beverly Hills
www.regenthotels.com
General Manager – Radha Arora

DOWNTOWN

FIGUEROA HOTEL 213-627-8971/800-421-9092
939 S. Figueroa St. (8th St.), Los Angeles
www.figueroahotel.com
General Manager – Uno Thimansson

MILLENNIUM BILTMORE 213-624-1011/800-245-8673
506 S. Grand Ave. (5th St.), Los Angeles
www.thebiltmore.com
General Manager – Iva Lee

THE STANDARD (DOWNTOWN LA).............................213-892-8080
550 S. Flower St. (6th St.), Los Angeles
www.standardhotel.com
General Manager – Karim ElRaheb

WILSHIRE GRAND LA 213-688-7777/888-773-2888
930 Wilshire Blvd. (Figueroa St.), Los Angeles
www.wilshiregrand.com
General Manager – John Stoddard

ACCOMMODATIONS

Hotels

HOLLYWOOD/WEST HOLLYWOOD

BAMBOO 323-962-0270
Beachwood Canyon, Los Angeles
General Manager – Pete Henry, info@HotelBamboo.com

CHAMBERLAIN WEST HOLLYWOOD 310-657-7400
1000 Westmount Dr. (Holloway Dr.), West Hollywood
www.chamberlainwesthollywood.com
General Manager – David Lemmond

CHATEAU MARMONT 323-656-1010/800-CHATEAU
8221 Sunset Blvd. (Crescent Heights Blvd.), West Hollywood
www.chateaumarmont.com
General Manager – Phil Pavel

LE MONTROSE SUITE HOTEL 800-776-0666/310-855-1115
900 Hammond St. (Cynthia St.), West Hollywood
www.LeMontrose.com
General Manager – Claudia Jackson

LE PARC SUITE HOTEL........................310-855-8888/800-578-4837
733 N. West Knoll Dr. (Melrose Ave.), West Hollywood
www.leparcsuites.com
General Manager – Ira Kleinrock

MONDRIAN 323-650-8999/800-606-6090
8440 Sunset Blvd. (La Cienega Blvd.), West Hollywood
www.mondrianhotel.com
Acting Manager – Joseph Kirkley

THE ROOSEVELT HOTEL 323-466-7000/800-950-7667
7000 Hollywood Blvd. (N. Orange Dr.), Hollywood
www.hollywoodroosevelt.com
General Manager – Brett Blass

THE STANDARD (HOLLYWOOD).................................323-650-9090
8300 Sunset Blvd. (Sweetzer Ave.), West Hollywood
www.standardhotel.com
General Manager – Domenic Chiodi

SUNSET MARQUIS HOTEL & VILLAS 310-657-1333/800-858-9758
1200 N. Alta Loma Rd. (Sunset Blvd.), West Hollywood
www.sunsetmarquishotel.com
General Manager – Rod Gruendyke

THE SUNSET TOWER HOTEL 323-654-7100/800-225-2637
8358 Sunset Blvd. (Sweetzer Ave.), West Hollywood
www.sunsettowerhotel.com
General Manager – Rick Friaglia

WYNDHAM BEL AGE HOTEL 310-854-1111/800-WYNDHAM
1020 N. San Vicente Blvd. (Sunset Blvd.), West Hollywood
www.wyndham.com/belage
General Manager – Armel Santens

SANTA MONICA/WESTSIDE

HOTEL BEL-AIR 310-472-1211/800-648-4097
701 Stone Canyon Rd. (Sunset Blvd.), Bel-Air
www.hotelbelair.com
General Manager – Carlos Lopes

CASA DEL MAR 310-581-5533/800-898-6999
1910 Ocean Way, Santa Monica
General Manager – James Barela

THE HYATT REGENCY CENTURY PLAZA.......................310-277-2000
2025 Avenue of the Stars (Olympic Blvd.), Century City
www.westincenturyplaza.com
General Manager – David Horwitz

ACCOMMODATIONS

Hotels

SANTA MONICA/WESTSIDE

LOEWS SANTA MONICA BEACH HOTEL.. 310-458-6700/800-23-LOWES
1700 Ocean Ave. (Colorado Ave.), Santa Monica
www.loewshotels.com/santamonica
General Manager – John Thacker

PARK HYATT LOS ANGELES.................310-277-1234/800-233-1234
2151 Avenue of the Stars (Olympic Blvd.), Century City
www.parklosangeles.hyatt.com
General Manager – Malcolm Thompson

RITZ-CARLTON, MARINA DEL REY........ 310-823-1700/800-241-3333
4375 Admiralty Way (Bali Way), Marina del Rey
www.ritzcarlton.com
General Manager – Andrew Zephirin

SHUTTERS ON THE BEACH 310-458-0030/800-334-9000
1 Pico Blvd. (Ocean Front Walk), Santa Monica
www.shuttersonthebeach.com
General Manager – Henri Birmele

VICEROY HOTEL 310-451-8711/800-622-8711
1819 Ocean Ave. (Pico Blvd.), Santa Monica
www.viceroysantamonica.com
General Manager – Vincent Piro

W LOS ANGELES-WESTWOOD 310-208-8765/877-WHOTELS
930 Hilgard Ave. (Le Conte Ave.), Westwood
www.whotels.com/losangeles
General Manager – Valeriano Antonioli

VALLEY

HILTON UNIVERSAL CITY......................818-506-2500/800-HILTONS
555 Universal Hollywood Dr. (Lankershim Blvd.), Universal City
www.universalcity.hilton.com
General Manager – Juan Aquinde

SHERATON UNIVERSAL HOTEL.............818-980-1212/888-625-5144
333 Universal Hollywood Dr. (Lankershim Blvd.), Universal City
www.sheraton.com/universal
General Manager – Wolf Walther

Corporate Retreats

DESERT TOWNS

LA QUINTA RESORT AND CLUB 760-564-4111/800-598-3828
49-499 Eisenhower Dr., La Quinta
www.laquintaresort.com
General Manager – Paul McCormick

THE LODGE AT RANCHO MIRAGE 760-321-8282/888-FOR-ROCK
68-900 Frank Sinatra Dr., Rancho Mirage
www.ranchomirage.rockresorts.com
Managing Director – Regula Wipf

MARRIOTT RANCHO LAS PALMAS 760-568-2727/800-228-9290
41000 Bob Hope Dr., Rancho Mirage
www.rancholaspalmas.com
General Manager – Scott Blalock

VICEROY PALM SPRINGS 760-320-4117/800-237-3687
415 S. Belardo Rd., Palm Springs
www.viceroypalmsprings.com
General Manager – Mark VanCooney

ACCOMMODATIONS

Corporate Retreats

NORTH OF LA

BACARA RESORT & SPA......................805-968-0100/877-422-4245
8301 Hollister Ave., Santa Barbara
www.bacararesort.com
Managing Director – Jacque Villeneuve

FOUR SEASONS BILTMORE 805-969-2261/800-819-5053
1260 Channel Dr., Santa Barbara
www.fourseasons.com/santabarbara
General Manager – Karen Earp

OJAI VALLEY INN & SPA 805-646-5511/888-697-8780
905 Country Club Rd., Ojai
www.ojairesort.com
General Manager – Anna Olson

SADDLE PEAK LODGE..818-222-3888
419 Cold Canyon, Calabasas
www.saddlepeaklodge.com
General Manager – Gerhard Tratter

SAN YSIDRO RANCH 805-969-5046/800-368-6788
900 San Ysidro Lane, Santa Barbara
www.sanysidroranch.com
General Manager – Duncan Graham

SOUTH OF LA

LA COSTA RESORT & SPA....................760-438-9111/800-854-5000
Costa Del Mar Rd., Carlsbad
www.lacosta.com
General Manager – April Shute

MONTAGE RESORT & SPA 949-715-6000/866-271-6953
30801 S. Coast Hwy., Laguna Beach
www.montagelagunabeach.com
General Manager – James Bermingham

RITZ-CARLTON, LAGUNA NIGEL............949-240-2000/800-241-3333
1 Ritz-Carlton Dr., Dana Point
www.ritzcarlton.com
General Manager – John Dravinski

SURF & SAND HOTEL 949-497-4477/888-869-7569
1555 S. Coast Hwy., Laguna Beach
www.surfandsand.com
General Manager – Blaise Bartell

Corporate Housing

CITRUS SUITES-SANTA MONICA 800-410-0409
www.citrussuites.com
Leasing Director – Ryan Powers

OAKWOOD CORPORATE HOUSING 866-327-3077
www.oakwood.com
National Account Manager – Joni Rodenbusch

PARK LA BREA APARTMENTS..................................323-549-5450
www.parklabrea.com
Corporate Housing Director – Lisa Holbrook

THE SEACASTLE IN SANTA MONICA 310-917-1998/800-295-0022
www.theseacastle.com
General Manager – Richard Paschke

ACCOMMODATIONS

Real Estate

COLDWELL BANKER
23661 Pacific Coast Highway, Malibu
Irene Dazzan-Palmer 310-456-1747

HILTON & HYLAND
250 N. Canon Drive, Beverly Hills
Ann Eysenring 310-278-3311
Sandy Feldman 310-278-3311
Steve Levine 310-278-3311

KMD REALTY GROUP
8560 W. Sunset Blvd., Los Angeles
Brad Djukich 310-623-1441

MICHELLE BLACKMON ESTATES
310 Washington Blvd, Plaza 5, Marina Del Rey
Michelle Blackmon 310-301-0701

MOSSLER, DEASY & DOE
345 N. Maple Drive, Ste. 105, Beverly Hills
Rachel Busch 310-995-1969
Barry Gray 310-666-1107
Aaron Kirman 310-994-9515

PRUDENTIAL CALIFORNIA REALTY
9696 Wilshire Blvd., 3rd Fl., Beverly Hills
Joe Babajian 310-248-6400
Nanette Marchand 310-777-2810

8687 Melrose Ave., Ste. B110, Los Angeles
Scott Howard 323-660-6072

SOTHEBY'S INTERNATIONAL REALTY
451 N. Rodeo Dr., Beverly Hills
Jory Burton 310-275-8686

3900 Cross Creek Rd., #5, Malibu
Amy Alcini 310-456-1511

11911 San Vicente Blvd., Ste. 200, Los Angeles
Rodrigo Iglesias 310-699-3435

9200 Sunset Blvd., Ste. 200, West Hollywood
Sharona Alperin 310-888-3708
Dorothy Carter 310-205-0305
Brett Lawyer 310-888-3808
Jonah Wilson 310-888-3870

WESTSIDE ESTATE AGENCY
210 N. Canon Dr., Beverly Hills
Aileen Comora 310-300-1082

TRAVEL & TRANSPORTATION

Travel Agencies

MANSOUR TRAVEL 310-276-2768
www.mansourtravel.com

PRODUCTION TRAVEL & TOURS 818-760-0327
clubtrvl@aol.com
Contact – Sylvia Frommer-Mracky

WORLD TRAVEL BTI 404-841-6600/800-342-3234
www.worldtravel.com

TRAVEL & TRANSPORTATION

Airlines - Domestic

AIRTRAN 800-247-8726
www.airtran.com

ALASKA AIRLINES 800-252-7522
www.alaskaairlines.com

ALOHA AIRLINES 800-367-5250
www.alohaairlines.com

AMERICA WEST 800-235-9292
www.americawest.com

AMERICAN AIRLINES 800-433-7300
www.aa.com

AMERICAN TRANS AIR 800-435-9282
www.ata.com

CONTINENTAL 800-525-0280
www.continental.com

DELTA 800-221-1212
www.delta.com

FRONTIER 800-432-1359
www.frontierairlines.com

HAWAIIAN 800-367-5320
www.hawaiianair.com

HORIZON AIR 800-547-9308
www.horizonair.com

JETBLUE 800-538-2583
www.jetblue.com

MIDWEST AIRLINES 800-452-2022
www.midwestairlines.com

NORTHWEST 800-225-2525
www.nwa.com

SONG AIRLINES 800-FLY-SONG
www.flysong.com

SOUTHWEST 800-435-9792
www.southwest.com

SPIRIT AIRLINES 800-772-7117
www.spiritairlines.com

SUN COUNTRY AIRLINES 800-359-6786
www.suncountry.com

UNITED 800-241-6522
www.united.com

US AIRWAYS 800-428-4322
www.usairways.com

Airlines - International

AER LINGUS 800-474-7424
www.aerlingus.com

AIR CANADA 888-247-2262
www.aircanada.com

AIR FRANCE 800-237-2747
www.airfrance.net

AIR NEW ZEALAND 800-262-1234
www.airnewzealand.com

ALITALIA 800-223-5730
www.alitaliausa.com

TRAVEL & TRANSPORTATION

Airlines - International

AUSTRIAN AIRLINES 800-843-0002
www.aua.com

AVIANCA...800-284-2622
www.avianca.com

BRITISH AIRWAYS..800-247-9297
www.ba.com

CATHAY PACIFIC 800-233-2742
www.cathaypacific.com

EL AL 800-223-6700
www.elal.com

FINNAIR 800-950-5000
www.finnair.com

IBERIA AIRLINES 800-772-4642
www.iberia.com

ICELANDAIR 800-223-5500
www.icelandair.com

KLM ROYAL DUTCH 800-225-2525
www.klm.com

KOREAN AIR 800-438-5000
www.koreanair.com

LUFTHANSA...800-645-3880
www.lufthansa.com

QANTAS 800-227-4500
www.qantas.com

SWISS 877-359-7947
www.swiss.com

VIRGIN ATLANTIC..800-862-8621
www.virgin-atlantic.com

Charter Planes

AVJET CORPORATION 818-841-6190/800-342-8538
www.avjet.com
Contact – Mark Lefever, Executive Vice President

CLAY LACY AVIATION 818-989-2900/800-423-2904
www.claylacy.com

ELITE AVIATION 818-988-5387
www.eliteaviation.com

FOUR DIRECTIONS AIR, INC.....................................866-359-9355
www.fourdirectionsair.com
Contact – Maggie Begley, mbegley@aol.com

JET NETWORK 888-255-5387
www.jetnetwork.com

KOMAR AVIATION GROUP 949-250-1359/800-555-0996
www.komaraviation.com

METRO JET, LTD...888-682-6227
www.metrojet.com

PRESIDENTIAL AVIATION 310-279-6387
www.presidential-aviation.com
Contact – Leslie Guthrie, leslie@presidential-aviation.com

RAYTHEON AIRCRAFT CHARTER
AND MANAGEMENT...........................800-519-6283/316-676-0778
www.raytheonaircraft.com
Contact – Ron Gottschalk

TRAVEL & TRANSPORTATION

Charter Planes

SENTIENT PRIVATE JET MEMBERSHIP 800-641-6917
www.sentient.com

TELLURIDE FLIGHTS 970-728-1011
www.tellurideflights.com
Contact – Don

Car Rentals

ALAMO 800-462-5266
www.alamo.com

AVIS...800-230-4898
www.avis.com

BUDGET 800-527-0700
www.budget.com

DOLLAR 800-800-4000
www.dollar.com

ENTERPRISE..800-261-7331
www.enterprise.com

HERTZ 800-654-3131
www.hertz.com

NATIONAL 800-227-7368
www.nationalcar.com

THRIFTY 800-847-4389
www.thrifty.com

Limos

AFFORDABLE CLASS LIMOUSINE
& SEDAN SERVICE 818-881-6116/310-470-6111

BLS LIMOUSINE SERVICE 800-843-5752
www.blslimo.com

DIVA LIMOUSINE 310-278-3482/800-427-DIVA
www.divalimo.com

EXOTIC LIMO 310-414-0550
www.exoticlimo.com

FONTANA'S 310-877-7181/800-FON-TANAS
www.1800fontanas.com

MUSIC EXPRESS 800-421-9494
www.musiclimo.com

Executive Car Leasing

CENTURY WEST BMW 800-447-8871
4245 Lankershim Blvd. (Valley Spring Ln.), Universal City
www.centurywestbmw.com

ED CAR GUY 818-563-4499
www.edcarguy.com
Contact – Ed Levitt, ed@edcarguy.com

LAND ROVER ENCINO...818-990-9870
15800 Ventura Blvd. (Haskell Ave.), Encino
www.landroverencino.com

MERCEDES BENZ BEVERLY HILLS, LTD. ..310-659-2980/800-749-2758
9250 Beverly Blvd. (Santa Monica Blvd.), Beverly Hills
www.bhbenz.com

O'GARA COACH COMPANY 310-659-4050
8833 W. Olympic Blvd. (Robertson Blvd.), Beverly Hills
www.ogaracoachcompany.com

GIFTS & SHOPPING

Florists

BRYAN WARK DESIGNS..310-858-8640
8670 Washington Blvd. (Caroline Ave.), Culiver City
www.bryanwarkdesigns.com

DAVID JONES...310-659-6347
450 N. Robertson Blvd. (Melrose Ave.), West Hollywood

FLORALART 310-392-1633
1338 Abbot Kinney Blvd. (Andalusia Ave.), Venice
www.floralartla.com

JACOB MAARSE FLORIST 213-629-6949/626-449-0246
545 S. Figueroa St. (5th St.), Los Angeles

L.A. PREMIER 310-276-4665
8928 W. Olympic Blvd. (S. Robertson Blvd.), Beverly Hills

MARK'S GARDEN...818-906-1718
13838 Ventura Blvd. (Woodman Ave.), Sherman Oaks
www.marksgarden.net

RITA FLORA 323-938-3900/800-748-2356
468 S. La Brea Ave. (6th St.), Los Angeles
www.ritaflora.com

SANDY ROSE FLORAL DESIGNS 818-980-4371
www.sandyrose.com

TFS (THE FLOWER SHOP) 310-274-8491
616 N. Almont Dr., Ste. C (Melrose Ave.), West Hollywood

TIC TOCK 323-874-3034/800-893-6688
1603 N. La Brea Ave. (Hawthorne Ave.), Los Angeles
www.tictock.com

VELVET GARDEN 323-852-1766
8327 W. 3rd Street (San Vicente Blvd.), Los Angeles

THE WOODS EXQUISITE FLOWERS 310-826-0711
11711 San Vicente Blvd., Los Angeles

Z'S GARDEN 310-860-7557
468 Camden Dr., Ste. 200 (W. Olympic Blvd), Beverly Hills
www.zsgarden.com

Gift Baskets

DEB'S DELIGHTS..323-936-4545
www.debsdelights.com

DELIGHTFUL DELIVERIES 877-442-6333
www.delightfuldeliveries.com

DeLUSCIOUS COOKIES & MILK.................................323-460-2370
www.delusciouscookies.com

FAVOR FORTE..310-998-3464
www.favorforte.com
Contacts – Susan Leslie & Renee Lee

FIRENZE...818-832-4740/800-964-8259
www.firenzegifts.com
Contact – Steve Gagliano

FRAICHE 323-655-2880/888-654-7002
www.fraichegifts.com

GARRETT POPCORN SHOPS 800-476-7267
www.garrettpopcorn.com

GOURMET BY DESIGN 310-605-4955/888-982-2275
www.gourmetbydesign.com

JJ SUMMERLAND 800-610-6650
www.jjsummerlandgifts.com

GIFTS & SHOPPING

Gift Baskets

K CHOCOLATIER 310-248-2626
www.dkron.com

MAISON CONNOISSEUR 818-346-1520/866-590-0977
www.maisonconnoisseur.com

MANHATTAN FRUITIER 323-254-1127/800-841-5718
www.manhattanfruitier.com

SCHMERTY'S GOURMET COOKIES 877-422-5336
www.schmertys.com
Contacts – Syrna & Jeffrey

WALLY'S...310-475-0606/888-9WALLYS
www.wallywine.com

WHO'S BROWNIES, INC. 818-343-1685/866-946-7276
www.whosbrownies.com
Contacts – Mark Sferas & Kelly Hartleip

Personal Shoppers

DONUM CELEBRITY &
CORPORATE GIFTS 310-317-4577/508-358-7447
www.donumgifts.com
Contacts – Kristy Barrett Wylie & Amy Frankel Nau

STAR TREATMENT GIFT SERVICES 818-781-9016/800-444-9059
www.startreatment.com
Contact – Diane

SCREENING ROOMS

BEVERLY HILLS

ACADEMY OF MOTION PICTURES ARTS & SCIENCES 310-247-3000
Samuel Goldwyn Theater/Little Theater
8949 Wilshire Blvd. (La Peer Dr.), Beverly Hills
www.oscars.org/facilities/theaterops
Contact – Moray Greenfield

CHARLES AIDIKOFF SCREENING ROOM 310-274-0866
150 S. Rodeo Dr., Ste. 140 (Wilshire Blvd.), Beverly Hills
www.aidikoff.tv

CLARITY THEATRE 310-385-4092
100 N. Crescent Dr. (Wilshire Blvd.), Beverly Hills

FOX STUDIOS SCREENING ROOMS............................310-369-2405
10201 W. Pico Blvd. (Motor Ave.), Los Angeles
www.foxstudios.com/los_angeles/postproduction/screeningrooms.htm

WILSHIRE SCREENING ROOM 310-659-3875
8670 Wilshire Blvd. (Willaman Dr.), Los Angeles
www.studioscreenings.com

WRITERS GUILD THEATRE.......................................323-782-4525
135 S. Doheny Dr. (Wilshire Blvd.), Beverly Hills
www.wga.org/theater/theaterrental.html
Theatre Administrator – Caren Mandoyan

HOLLYWOOD/WEST HOLLYWOOD

ACADEMY OF MOTION PICTURES ARTS & SCIENCES 310-247-3000
Pickford Center for Motion Picture Study - Linwood Dunn Theater
1313 N. Vine St. (Fountain), Hollywood
www.oscars.org/facilities/theaterops
Contact – Moray Greenfield

SCREENING ROOMS

HOLLYWOOD/WEST HOLLYWOOD

AMERICAN FILM INSTITUTE 323-856-7828
2021 N. Western Ave. (Franklin Ave.), Los Angeles
www.afi.com

DIRECTORS GUILD OF AMERICA 310-289-2021/310-289-2023
7920 Sunset Blvd. (Fairfax Ave.), Los Angeles
www.dga.org
Contact – Tim Webber

HARMONY GOLD PREVIEW HOUSE 323-436-7204
7655 Sunset Blvd. (Fairfax Ave.), Los Angeles
www.harmonygold.com/theatre
Contact – Kathryn Davolio

LOS ANGELES CENTER STUDIOS 213-534-2311
1201 W. 5th St. (S. Beaudry Ave.), Los Angeles
www.lacenterstudios.com
Contact – Erica Chambers

PACIFIC DESIGN CENTER 310-360-6415
8687 Melrose Ave., 2nd Fl. (San Vicente Blvd.), Los Angeles
www.pacificdesigncenter.com

PARAMOUNT PICTURES 323-956-1652
5555 Melrose Ave. (Vine St.), Los Angeles
www.paramountstudiogroup.com
Contact – Frank Estrada

SCREENING ROOMS

HOLLYWOOD/WEST HOLLYWOOD

RALEIGH STUDIOS 323-466-3111
5300 Melrose Ave. (Western Ave.), Los Angeles
1600 Rosecrans Ave. (Sepulveda Blvd.), Manhattan Beach
www.raleighstudios.com

SUNSET SCREENING ROOM 310-652-1933
8730 Sunset Blvd. (La Cienega Blvd.), Los Angeles

THE LOT/WARNER BROS. 323-850-2581
1041 N. Formosa Ave. (Santa Monica Blvd.), Los Angeles
www.wbpostproduction.com
VP of Operations – Robert Winder

SANTA MONICA/WESTSIDE

ARTISAN THEATRE/LIONS GATE 310-255-4000
2700 Colorado Ave. (26th St.), Santa Monica

BENDETTI MOBILE, INC. 310-587-3377/888-834-8439
1549 11th St. (Broadway St.), Santa Monica
www.bendettimobile.com

BIG TIME PICTURE COMPANY 310-207-0921
12210-1/2 Nebraska Ave. (Bundy Dr.), Los Angeles
www.bigtimepic.com

CULVER STUDIOS 310-202-3253/310-202-1234
9336 W. Washington Blvd. (Culver Blvd.), Culver City
www.theculverstudios.com

SCREENING ROOMS

SANTA MONICA/WESTSIDE

METRO-GOLDWYN-MAYER 310-449-3456
10250 Constellation Blvd. (Avenue of the Stars), Santa Monica
www.mgm.com
Contact – Bill Cook

NEW DEAL STUDIOS 310-578-9929
4121 Redwood Ave. (Washington Blvd.), Los Angeles
www.newdealstudios.com

OCEAN SCREENING ROOM 310-576-1831
1401 Ocean Ave. (Santa Monica Blvd.), Santa Monica
www.oceanscreening.com

SONY PICTURES STUDIOS 310-244-5721
10202 W. Washington Blvd., Thalberg Bldg. (Overland Ave.), Culver City
Contact – Michael McLaren

TWENTIETH CENTURY FOX 310-369-2406
10201 W. Pico Blvd. (Avenue of the Stars), Los Angeles
www.fox.com
Contact – Valerie Zelinka

VALLEY

ACADEMY OF TELEVISION ARTS & SCIENCES 818-754-2800
5220 Lankershim Blvd. (Magnolia Blvd.), North Hollywood
www.emmys.org
Contact – Bob Gould

LEONARD H. GOLDENSON THEATRE. 818-242-3839
5230 Lankershim Blvd. (Magnolia Blvd.), North Hollywood
www.emmys.org
Contact – Vicky Compobasso

ICS SERVICES, INC. 818-242-3839
920 Allen Ave. (San Fernando Rd.), Glendale
www.icsfilm.com

SUNSET SCREENING ROOM 818-556-5190
2212 W. Magnolia Blvd. (Buena Vista St.), Burbank

UNIVERSAL STUDIOS...818-777-131
100 Universal City Plaza (Cahuenga Blvd.), Universal City
www.universalstudios.com
Contact – Kei Gilson

THE WALT DISNEY STUDIOS 818-560-5506
500 S. Buena Vista St. (Riverside Dr.), Burbank
www.buenavistapost.com
Contact – Sal Valletta

WARNER BROS. STUDIO FACILITIES......818-954-2144/818-954-2515
4000 Warner Blvd. (Hollywood Way), Burbank
www.wbpostproduction.warnerbros.com
Contact – Chelsea Simons

VIP TICKETS

ANAHEIM MIGHTY DUCKS.......................................714-940-2911
www.mightyducks.com
Director, Public Relations – Alex Gilchrist

LOS ANGELES ANGELS OF ANAHEIM 714-940-2014
www.angelsbaseball.com
VP, Communications – Tim Mead

LOS ANGELES CLIPPERS 213-742-7500
www.nba.com/clippers
Director, Communications – Rob Raichlen

VIP TICKETS

LOS ANGELES DODGERS 323-224-1301
www.dodgers.com
VP, Public Relations – John Olguin

LOS ANGELES KINGS 310-535-4545
www.lakings.com
VP, Communications – Mike Altieri

LOS ANGELES LAKERS 310-426-6004
www.nba.com/lakers
Director, Public Relations – John Black

LOS ANGELES SPARKS 310-341-1000
www.wnba.com/sparks
Director, Public Relations – Ashley King

MAIL & DELIVERY

Messengers

A1 EXPRESS...877-219-7737
www.a1express.com

ACCURATE EXPRESS MESSENGER SERVICE 323-906-1000
www.accurateexpress.net

EXACTA MESSENGER SERVICE 310-855-8800
www.exactamessenger.com

THE EXPRESS GROUP 310-478-8000/800-539-7737
www.expressgroup.net

THE GO-BETWEEN, INC. 310-276-6266
www.gobetween.com

LE COURIER, INC. 818-848-8089
www.lecourier.com

SECURITY COURIERS.........................818-789-3999/323-464-2673
www.securitycouriers.com

UNIVERSAL COURIER...310-410-4500
www.universalcourier.com

FedEx Kinko's Stores

Information...800-254-6567
www.fedexkinkos.com

BEVERLY HILLS

9334 Wilshire Blvd. (S. Elm Dr.), Beverly Hills
8471 Beverly Blvd., Ste. 103/104 (N. La Cienega), Los Angeles

HOLLYWOOD/WEST HOLLYWOOD

1440 Vine St. (Leland Way), Los Angeles
5500 Wilshire Blvd. (Miracle Mile), Los Angeles
7630 Sunset Blvd. (N. Stanley Ave.), Los Angeles

DOWNTOWN

835 Wilshire Blvd. (S. Flower St.), Los Angeles
2723 S. Figueroa St. (W. 27th St.), Los Angeles

SANTA MONICA/WESTSIDE

1520 Westwood Blvd. (Ohio Ave.), Los Angeles
5855 W. Century Blvd. (LA Airport Marriott), Los Angeles
10924 Weyburn Ave. (Westwood Blvd.), Los Angeles
2139 S. Bundy Dr. (W. Olympic Blvd.), Los Angeles
11819 Wilshire Blvd. (Granville Ave.), Los Angeles
601 Wilshire Blvd. (6th St.), Santa Monica

MAIL & DELIVERY

FedEx Kinko's Stores

VALLEY

12101 Ventura Blvd. (Laurel Canyon Blvd.), Studio City
4100 W. Riverside Dr. (N. Pass Ave.), Burbank
250 E. Olive Ave. (N. San Fernando Blvd.), Burbank

UPS Stores & Drop Boxes

Information 1-800-PICK-UPS
www.ups.com

BEVERLY HILLS

9777 Wilshire Blvd. (Little Santa Monica Blvd.), Beverly Hills
433 N. Camden Dr. (Little Santa Monica Blvd.), Beverly Hills
1171 S. Robertson Blvd. (W. Pico Blvd.), Beverly Hills
10573 W. Pico Blvd. (Prosser Ave.), Beverly Hills

DOWNTOWN

316 W. 2nd St. (N. Broadway), Los Angeles
717 W. Temple St. (N. Hope St.), Los Angeles
2202 S. Figueroa St. (W. 23rd St.), Los Angeles

HOLLYWOOD/WEST HOLLYWOOD

5419 Hollywood Blvd. (N. Western Ave.), Hollywood
1304 N. Highland Ave. (Fountain Ave.), Hollywood
7060 Hollywood Blvd. (N. Sycamore Ave.), Hollywood
8033 W. Sunset Blvd. (Laurel Canyon Blvd.), Hollywood

SANTA MONICA/WESTSIDE

1223 Wilshire Blvd. (12th St.), Santa Monica
926 Colorado Ave. (9th St.), Santa Monica
2633 Lincoln Blvd. (Ocean Park Blvd.), Santa Monica
100 Wilshire Blvd. (Ocean Ave.), Santa Monica
12405 Venice Blvd. (S. Centinela Ave.), Los Angeles

VALLEY

14622 Ventura Blvd. (Van Nuys Blvd.), Sherman Oaks
4024 Radford Ave. (Ventura Blvd.), Studio City
121 S. Glenoaks Blvd. (E. Olive Ave.), Burbank

Post Offices

Information..800-275-8777
www.usps.com

BEVERLY HILLS

BEVERLY HILLS POST OFFICE
325 N. Maple Dr. (3rd St.), Beverly Hills

BEVERLY POST OFFICE
312 S. Beverly Dr. (Olympic Blvd.), Beverly Hills

CRESCENT POSTAL STORE
323 N. Crescent Dr. (Burton Way), Beverly Hills

EASTGATE POST OFFICE
8383 Wilshire Blvd. (S. San Vicente Blvd.), Beverly Hills

DOWNTOWN

ALAMEDA POST OFFICE
1055 N. Vignes St. (Rosabell St.), Los Angeles

ARCADE POST OFFICE
508 S. Spring St. (6th St.), Los Angeles

MAIL & DELIVERY

Post Offices

DOWNTOWN

ARCO POST OFFICE
505 S. Flower St. (6th St.), Los Angeles

BUNKER HILL POST OFFICE
350 S. Grand Ave. (4th St.), Los Angeles

FEDERAL POST OFFICE
300 N. Los Angeles St. (Temple St.), Los Angeles

HOLLYWOOD/WEST HOLLYWOOD

BICENTENNIAL POST OFFICE
7610 Beverly Blvd. (Fairfax Ave.), Los Angeles

COLE BRANCH POST OFFICE
1125 N. Fairfax Ave. (Santa Monica Blvd.), West Hollywood

HOLLYWOOD POST OFFICE
1615 N. Wilcox St. (Cahuenga Blvd.), Hollywood

LOS FELIZ POST OFFICE
1825 N. Vermont Ave. (Franklin Ave.), Los Angeles

MIRACLE MILE STATION
5350 Wilshire Blvd. (S. La Brea Ave.), Los Angeles

SANTA WESTERN POST OFFICE
1385 N. Western Ave. (Sunset Blvd.), Los Angeles

SUNSET POST OFFICE
1425 N. Cherokee Ave. (Sunset Blvd.), Hollywood

WEST BRANCH POST OFFICE
820 N. San Vicente Blvd. (Santa Monica Blvd.), West Hollywood

WILCOX STATION
6457 Santa Monica Blvd. (Cahuenga Blvd.), Hollywood

SANTA MONICA/WESTSIDE

CENTURY CITY POST OFFICE
9911 W. Pico Blvd., Ste. 100 (Century Park East), Century City

OCEAN PARK POST OFFICE
2720 Neilson Way (Ocean Park Blvd.), Santa Monica

SANTA MONICA POST OFFICE
1248 Fifth St. (Arizona Ave.), Santa Monica

VENICE MAIN POST OFFICE
1601 Main St. (Venice Way), Venice

WEST LOS ANGELES POST OFFICE
11420 Santa Monica Blvd. (Sawtelle Blvd.), Los Angeles

WILL ROGERS POST OFFICE
1217 Wilshire Blvd. (12th St.), Santa Monica

VALLEY

BURBANK DOWNTOWN POST OFFICE
135 E. Olive Ave. (San Fernando Blvd.), Burbank

BURBANK MAIN POST OFFICE
2140 N. Hollywood Way (Pacific Ave.), Burbank

CHANDLER POST OFFICE
11304 Chandler Blvd. (Tujunga Ave.), North Hollywood

GLENOAKS POST OFFICE
1634 N. San Fernando Blvd. (Scott Rd.), Burbank

MAGNOLIA PARK POST OFFICE
3810 W. Magnolia Blvd. (Hollywood Way), Burbank

MAIL & DELIVERY

Post Offices

VALLEY

STUDIO CITY POST OFFICE
3950 Laurel Canyon Blvd. (Ventura Blvd.), Studio City

TOLUCA LAKE POST OFFICE
10063 Riverside Dr. (N. Pass Ave.), Toluca Lake

VALLEY PLAZA POST OFFICE
6242 Vantage Ave. (Laurel Canyon Blvd.), North Hollywood

VALLEY VILLAGE POST OFFICE
12450 Magnolia Blvd. (Whitsett Ave.), Valley Village

OFFICE SERVICES & SUPPLIES

DOWNTOWN

OFFICE DEPOT
401 E. Second St. (Central Ave.), Los Angeles 213-628-5000
2020 S. Figueroa St. (20th St.), Los Angeles 213-741-0576

STAPLES
1701 S. Figueroa St. (Venice Blvd.), Los Angeles 213-746-6330

HOLLYWOOD/WEST HOLLYWOOD

OFFICE DEPOT
1240 Vine St. (Fountain Ave.), Los Angeles 323-957-1274
5665 Wilshire Blvd. (Masselin Ave.), Los Angeles 323-965-0637

STAPLES
6450 Sunset Blvd. (Cahuenga Blvd.), Los Angeles......323-467-2155
5407 Wilshire Blvd. (La Brea Ave.), Los Angeles 323-965-5240
1833 La Cienega Blvd. (Venice Blvd.), Los Angeles 310-202-5343

OFFICE SERVICES & SUPPLIES

SANTA MONICA/WESTSIDE

OFFICE DEPOT
5640 Sepulveda Blvd. (Slauson Ave.), Culver City 310-390-4023
2231 S. Barrington Ave. (Olympic Blvd.), Los Angeles 310-478-7103

STAPLES
2052 Bundy Dr. (Olympic Blvd.), Los Angeles 310-826-0442
1501 Lincoln Blvd. (California Ave.), Venice.............310-577-6740

VALLEY

OFFICE DEPOT
11211 Ventura Blvd. (Fulton Ave.), Studio City..........818-760-4414
228 E. Burbank Blvd. (San Fernando Blvd.), Burbank..818-848-2591
6440 Sepulveda Blvd. (Victory Blvd.), Van Nuys 818-780-9916
16571 Ventura Blvd. (Rubio Ave.), Encino 818-907-1741

STAPLES
12605 Ventura Blvd. (Whitsett Ave.), Studio City 818-753-6390
1060 W. Alameda St. (Main St.), Burbank 818-558-3350
12807 Sherman Way (Coldwater Canyon Ave.),
North Hollywood...818-503-7960

CONTENTS

FOOD & DRINK
- Restaurants 16
- Catering 18
- Event Planning 18

ACCOMMODATIONS
- Hotels 19
- Corporate Retreats 20
- Corporate Housing 20
- Real Estate 20

TRAVEL & TRANSPORTATION
- Travel Agencies 20
- Airlines – Domestic 21
- Airlines – International 21
- Charter Planes 21
- Car Rentals 22
- Car Services/Limos 22

GIFTS & SHOPPING
- Florists 22
- Gift Baskets 22
- Personal Assistants 22
- Personal Shoppers 22

SCREENING ROOMS 22

VIP TICKETS 23

MAIL & DELIVERY
- Messengers 23
- FedEx Kinko's Stores 23
- UPS Stores & Drop Boxes 24
- Post Offices 24

OFFICE SERVICES & SUPPLIES 24

FOOD & DRINK

Restaurants

DOWNTOWN

5 Ninth 212-929-9460
5 Ninth Ave. (12th St.)
General Manager – Vincent Seufert

66 212-925-0202
241 Church St. (Leonard St.)
Owner – Jean-Georges Vongerichten

71 CLINTON FRESH FOOD 212-614-6960
71 Clinton (Rivington St.)
Owner – Janet Nelson

AQUAGRILL 212-274-0505
210 Spring St. (Avenue of the Americas)
Owners & General Managers – Jennifer Marshall & Jeremy Marshall

BABBO 212-777-0303
110 Waverly Pl. (Washington Square West)
www.babbonyc.com
General Manager – David Lynch
Maitre d' – John Mainieri

BALTHAZAR 212-965-1414
80 Spring St. (Crosby St.)
www.balthazarny.com
General Manager – Michael Lahara

BLUE RIBBON BAKERY 212-337-0404
33 Downing St. (Bedford St.)
General Manager – Sean Santamour

BLUE RIBBON SUSHI 212-343-0404
119 Sullivan St. (Prince St.)
Night Manager – Tom Wong

BLUE WATER GRILL 212-675-9500
31 Union Square West (16th St.)
www.brguestrestaurants.com
General Manager – Douglas Crowell

BOND STREET 212-777-2500
6 Bond St. (Broadway & Lafayette)
General Manager – Steven Durbahn

BOULEY BAKERY 212-964-2525
120 W. Broadway (Duane St.)
www.bouley.net
Maitre d' – Didier Palange

CRAFT 212-780-0880
43 E. 19th St. (Broadway)
www.craftrestaurant.com
General Manager – Katie Grieco

DANAL 212-982-6930
90 E. 10th St. (Third Ave.)
Owner – Danny Saltiel
General Manager – Bobby Allen

DA SILVANO 212-982-2343
260 Sixth Ave. (Houston)
www.dasilvano.com
General Manager – Alesandro Bandini

DOMINIC 212-343-0700
349 Greenwich St. (Jay St.)
www.dominicrestaurant.com
General Manager – John Villa

FOOD & DRINK

Restaurants

DOWNTOWN

GOTHAM BAR & GRILL 212-620-4020
12 E. 12th St. (Fifth Ave.)
www.gothambarandgrill.com
General Manager – Dana Madigan

GRADISCA 212-691-4886
126 W. 13th St. (Avenue of the Americas)
www.gradiscanyc.com
General Manager – Massiamo

THE HARRISON 212-274-9310
355 Greenwich St. (Harrison St.)
www.theharrison.com
Director of Operations – Alicia Nosenzo

IL BUCO 212-533-1932
47 Bond St. (LaFayette St.)
www.ilbuco.com
General Manager – Roberto Paris

JEWEL BAKO 212-979-1012
239 E. 5th St. (Second Ave.)
Owner – Jack Lamb

LA LUNCHEONETTE 212-675-0342
130 Tenth Ave. (18th St.)
General Manager – Melva Max

MATSURI 212-243-6400
The Maritime Hotel, 369 W. 16th St. (Ninth Ave.)
General Managers – Liz Teo & Buanao Konyak

MEET 212-242-0990
71-73 Gansevoort St. (Washington St.)
www.the-meet.com
General Manager – Milana Teodorovich

MERCER KITCHEN 212-966-5454
The Mercer, 99 Prince St. (Mercer St.)
www.jean-georges.com
General Manager – James Liakokos

NEXT DOOR NOBU 212-334-4445
105 Hudson St. (Franklin St.)
www.myriadrestaurantgroup.com
General Manager – Richard Notar

NOBU 212-219-0500
105 Hudson St. (Franklin St.)
www.myriadrestaurantgroup.com
General Manager – Richard Notar

ONE IF BY LAND, TWO IF BY SEA 212-228-0822
17 Barrow St. (Seventh Ave. South)
www.oneifbyland.com
General Manager – Rosanne Manetta

THE PARK 212-352-3313
118 Tenth Ave. (18th St.)
www.theparknyc.com
General Manager – Cassandra Davidson

PARIS COMMUNE 212-929-0509
99 Bank St. (Greenwich St.)
www.pariscommune.net
General Manager – Arvin Bonet

FOOD & DRINK

Restaurants

DOWNTOWN

PASTIS 212-929-4844
9 Ninth Ave. (Little W. 12th St.)
www.pastisny.com
General Manager – Eddie Pinto

PRAVDA 212-226-4944
281 Lafayette St. (Houston St.)
www.pravadany.com
General Manager – Ana Opitz

PROVENCE 212-475-7500
38 MacDougal St. (Prince St.)
www.provence-soho.com
Owner – Michel Jean

RAOUL'S 212-966-3518
180 Prince St. (Sullivan St.)
www.raouls.com
General Manager – Cindy Smith

SAVOY 212-219-8570
70 Prince St. (Crosby St.)
www.savoynyc.com
General Manager – Gil Abital

SPICE MARKET 212-675-2322
403 W. 13th St. (Ninth Ave.)
www.jean-georges.com
Owner – Jean-Georges Vongerichten

TRIBECA GRILL 212-941-3900
375 Greenwich St. (Franklin St.)
www.tribecagrill.com
General Manager – Martin Shapiro

VERITAS 212-353-3700
43 E. 20th St. (Park Avenue South)
www.veritas-nyc.com
General Manager – Tim Bellardo

WOO LAE OAK 212-925-8200
148 Mercer St. (Prince St.)
www.woolaeoaksoho.com
General Manager – Dan Reiser

MIDTOWN

21 CLUB 212-582-7200
21 W. 52nd St. (Fifth Ave.)
www.21club.com
General Manager – Bryan McGuire

ALAIN DUCASSE 212-265-7300
Essex House, 155 W. 58th St. (Avenue of the Americas)
www.alain-ducasse.com
General Manager – Yannis Stanisiere

ASIATE 212-805-8881
Mandarin Oriental Hotel, 80 Columbus Circle
www.mandarineoriental.com
General Manager – Rudy Tausher

AQUAVIT 212-307-7311
65 E. 55th St. (Park Ave.)
www.aquavit.org
General Manager – Olivier Zardoni

FOOD & DRINK

Restaurants

MIDTOWN

ASIA DE CUBA 212-726-7755
Morgans Hotel, 237 Madison Ave. (37th St.)
www.chinagrillmanagement.com
General Manager – Kelly Cresham

ATELIER 212-521-6125
50 Central Park South (Sixth Ave.)
www.atelierrestaurant.com
General Manager – Jean-Jacques Termolle

BARBETTA 212-246-9171
321 W. 46th St. (Eighth Ave.)
www.barbettarestaurant.com
Owner – Laura Maioglio

CELLAR BAR 212-642-2255
The Bryant Park Hotel, 40 W. 40th St. (Avenue of the Americas)
General Manager – Meghan Howard

DB BISTRO MODERNE 212-391-2400
City Club Hotel, 55 W. 44th St. (Avenue of the Americas)
www.danielnyc.com
General Manager – Dominique Paulin

ESTIATORIOS MILOS 212-245-7400
125 W. 55th St. (Avenue of the Americas)
www.milos.ca
General Manager – Mario Zeniou

FOUR SEASONS RESTAURANT 212-754-9494
99 E. 52nd St. (Park Ave.)
www.fourseasonsrestaurant.com
Owners – Julian Niccolini/Alex von Bidder

HUDSON CAFETERIA 212-554-6000
Hudson Hotel, 356 W. 58th St. (Eighth Ave.)
www.hudsoncafeteriany.com
General Manager – Anthony Stephenson

INAGIKU 212-355-0440
Waldorf Astoria Hotel, 111 E. 49th St. (Lexington Ave.)
www.inagiku.com
General Manager – Shimura Masayuki

JOSEPH'S CITARELLA 212-332-1515
1240 Avenue of the Americas (49th St.)
www.josephscitarella.com
General Managers – Helen Guerrera/Ron Levine

LA GRENOUILLE 212-752-1495
3 E. 52nd St. (Fifth Ave.)
www.la-grenoulle.com
Owner – Charles Masson

LCB BRASSERIE 212-688-6525
60 W. 55th St. (Avenue of the Americas)
General Manager – Gabriella Ene-Neagv

LE CHARLOT 212-794-1628
19 E. 69th St. (Madison Ave.)
Owner – Bruno Gelormini

LE PÉRIGORD 212-755-6244
405 E. 52nd St. (First Ave.)
www.leperigord.com
Owner – Georges Briguet

FOOD & DRINK

Restaurants

MIDTOWN

MICHAEL'S 212-767-0555
24 W. 55th St. (Fifth Ave.)
www.michaelsnewyork.com
General Manager – Steve Millington

NICOLE'S 212-223-2288
10 E. 60th St. (Madison Ave.)
www.nicolefarhi.com
General Manager – Oscar Henquet

OPIA 212-688-3939
130 E. 57th St. (Lexington Ave.)
www.opiarestaurant.com
General Manager – Azdine Sallem

REMI 212-581-4242
145 W. 53rd St. (Avenue of the Americas)
General Manager – Franchesco Pistorio

RUBY FOO'S 212-489-5600
1626 Broadway (49th St.)
www.brguestrestaurants.com
General Manager – Phillip Lee

SARDI'S 212-221-8440
234 W. 44th St. (Broadway)
www.sardis.com
General Manager – Sean Rickettes

TAO 212-888-2288
42 E. 58th St. (Madison Ave.)
www.taorestaurant.com
General Manager – Paul Goldstein

TOWN 212-582-4445
Chambers Hotel, 15 W. 56th St. (Fifth Ave.)
www.townnyc.com
Contact – Paul Guzzardo

VONG 212-486-9592
200 E. 54th St. (Third Ave.)
www.jean-georges.com
General Manager – Christian Amestoy

EASTSIDE

540 PARK 212-339-4050
Regency Hotel, 540 Park Ave. (61st St.)
General Manager – Stuart Schwartz

AUREOLE 212-319-1660
34 E. 61st St. (Madison Ave.)
www.aureolerestaurant.com
General Manager – Richard Lepoozo

DANIEL 212-288-0033
60 E. 65th St. (Park Ave.)
www.danielnyc.com
General Manager – Ignace Leclair

KING'S CARRIAGE HOUSE 212-734-5490
251 E. 82nd St. (Second Ave.)
Owners – Paul King & Elizabeth King

FOOD & DRINK

Restaurants

WESTSIDE

CAFÉ DES ARTISTES 212-877-3500
1 W. 67th St. (Central Park West)
www.cafedes.com
General Manager – Orlando Santana

CALLE OCHO 212-873-5025
446 Columbus Ave. (81st St.)
General Manager – Chris Cammer

ISABELLA'S 212-724-2100
359 Columbus Ave. (77th St.)
General Manager – Chris Dorsey

JEAN GEORGES 212-299-3900/888-44-TRUMP
1 Central Park West (60th St.)
www.trumpintl.com/jeangeorges.asp
General Manager – Phillipe Vongerichten

JEAN-LUC 212-712-1700
507 Columbus Ave. (17th St.)
www.jeanlucrestaurant.com
General Manager/Managing Partner – Doug Alexander

RUBY FOO'S 212-724-6700
2182 Broadway (77th St.)
www.brguestrestaurants.com
General Manager – Nestor Gonzales

TERRACE IN THE SKY 212-666-9490
400 W. 119th St. (Amsterdam Ave.)
www.terraceinthesky.com
General Manager – Richard Fuhrmann

Catering

GREAT PERFORMANCES 212-727-2424
287 Spring St. (Hudson St.)
www.greatperformances.com

NEW YORK CATERERS & PARTY PLANNERS 212-396-9351
421 E. 65th St. (First Ave.)
www.ny-caterers.com

THOMAS PRETI CATERERS 212-764-3188/914-667-2331
38-03 24th St., Long Island City
www.thomaspreti.com

YURA & COMPANY 212-860-8060
1645 Third Ave. (92nd St.)

Event Planning

B. RODWIN & COMPANY, LLC. 212-255-0355
www.brodwinco.com
Partner – Brian Rodwin

BEAUTIFUL BARTENDERS, LLC 310-600-1077
www.beautifulbartenders.com
Contact – Ana Gallegos

COLIN COWIE LIFESTYLE 212-396-9007
www.colincowie.com

DAVID LEES PRODUCTIONS 212-629-4321
www.davidleesproductions.com

IN ANY EVENT 212-472-7751
www.inanyevent.biz

FOOD & DRINK

Event Planning

LAWRENCE SCOTT EVENTS LTD. 516-933-7535

TRAVESTIES ENTERTAINMENT 800-938-6464
www.travestiesent.com

ACCOMMODATIONS

Hotels

DOWNTOWN

60 THOMPSON.................................212-431-0400/877-431-0400
60 Thompson St. (Broome St.)
www.60thompson.com
General Manager – Stephen Brandman

HOTEL GANSEVOORT..........................212-206-6700/877-426-7386
18 Ninth Ave. (13th St.)
www.hotelgansevoort.com
General Manager – Joel Freyberg

THE MARCEL 212-696-3800
201 E. 24th St. (Third Ave.)
www.nychotels.com
General Manager – Najib Ayed

THE MARITIME HOTEL 212-242-4300
363 W. 16th St. (Ninth Ave.)
www.themaritimehotel.com
General Manager – Mark O'Brian

MERCER HOTEL 212-966-6060/888-918-6060
147 Mercer St. (Prince St.)
www.mercerhotel.com
General Manager – Philip Truelove

RITZ CARLTON BATTERY PARK 212-344-0800
2 West St. (1st Pl.)
General Manager – Jacqueline Volkart

SOHO GRAND HOTEL..........................212-965-3000/800-965-3000
310 W. Broadway (Canal St.)
www.sohogrand.com
General Manager – Ian Nicholson

TRIBECA GRAND HOTEL......................212-519-6600/877-519-6600
2 Avenue of the Americas (Walker St.)
www.tribecagrand.com
General Manager – Ian Nicholson

MIDTOWN

THE BENJAMIN 212-715-2500/888-423-6526
125 E. 50th St. (Lexington Ave.)
www.thebenjamin.com
General Manager – Tom Chamberlain

THE BLAKELY NEW YORK 212-245-1800
136 W. 55th St. (Avenue of the Americas)
www.blakelynewyork.com
General Manager – Frederick Hartman

THE BRYANT PARK 212-869-0100/877-640-9300
40 W. 40th St. (Avenue of the Americas)
www.bryantparkhotel.com
Genereal Manarger – Phil Columbo

ACCOMMODATIONS

Hotels

MIDTOWN

CHAMBERS 212-974-5656/866-204-5656
15 W. 56th St. (Fifth Ave.)
www.chambersnyc.com
General Manager – Ansell Hawkins

CITY CLUB HOTEL 212-921-5500
55 W. 44th St. (Avenue of the Americas)
www.cityclubhotel.com
General Manager – Jeffrey Felshaw

FLATOTEL 212-887-9400/800-352-8683
135 West 52nd St. (Avenue of the Americas)
www.flatotel.com
General Manager – Else Nissen

FOUR SEASONS HOTEL 212-758-5700
57 E. 57th St. (Madison Ave.)
www.fourseasons.com
General Manager – Christoph Schmidinger

HUDSON..212-554-6000/800-606-6090
356 W. 58th St. (Eighth Ave.)
www.hudsonhotel.com
General Manager – John Beier

MILLENNIUM HOTEL 212-768-4400/866-866-6455
145 W. 44th St. (Avenue of the Americas)
www.millennium-hotels.com
General Manager – Per Hellman

THE MUSE 212-485-2400/877-692-6873
130 W. 46th St. (Avenue of the Americas)
www.themusehotel.com
General Manager – Dan Bergmann

PARAMOUNT 212-764-5500/800-225-7474
235 W. 46th St. (Broadway)
www.nycparamounthotel.com
General Manager – Andrew Tilley

THE PENINSULA 212-956-2888/800-262-9467
700 Fifth Ave. (55th St.)
www.peninsula.com
General Manager – Nikalus Leuenberger

RIHGA ROYAL 212-307-5000/800-937-5454
151 W. 54th St. (Seventh Ave.)
www.rihgaroyalny.com
General Manager – Alex Alexander

ROYALTON......................................212-869-4400/800-606-6090
44 W. 44th St. (Fifth Ave.)
www.royalton.com
General Manager – Ed Maynard

THE ST. REGIS 212-753-4500/877-STREGIS
2 E. 55th St. (Fifth Ave.)
www.stregis.com
General Manager – Scott Geraghty

THE SHOREHAM...............................212-247-6700/800-553-3347
33 W. 55th St. (Fifth Ave.)
www.shorehamhotel.com
General Manager – Joe Reyes

ACCOMMODATIONS

Hotels

MIDTOWN

THE WALDORF ASTORIA......................212-355-3000/800-925-3673
301 Park Ave. (49th St.)
www.waldorf.com
General Manager – Eric Long

W NEW YORK 212-755-1200
541 Lexington Ave. (49th St.)
www.whotels.com/newyork
General Manager – Ed Baten

W NEW YORK - THE TUSCANY 212-686-1600
120 E. 39th St. (Lexington Ave.)
www.whotels.com/thetuscany
General Manager – Deborah McCluskey

EASTSIDE

THE CARLYLE 212-744-1600
35 E. 76th St. (Madison Ave.)
www.thecarlyle.com
General Manager – James McBride

THE LOWELL HOTEL 212-838-1400/800-221-4444
28 E. 63rd St. (Madison Ave.)
www.lowellhotel.com
General Manager – Ralph Renz

THE MARK 212-744-4300/800-843-6275
25 E. 77th St. (Madison Ave.)
www.themarkhotel.com
General Manager – Alain Negueloua

PIERRE HOTEL.................................212-838-8000/800-743-7734
2 E. 61st St. (Fifth Ave.)
www.tajhotel.com
General Manager – Heiko Kunstle

WESTSIDE

MANDARIN ORIENTAL HOTEL 212-805-8800
80 Columbus Circle (60th St.)
www.mandarinoriental.com
General Manager – Rudy Tauscher

THE PHILLIPS CLUB 212-835-8800/877-854-8800
155 W. 66th St. (Broadway)
www.phillipsclub.com
General Manager – Alan Tennant

TRUMP INTERNATIONAL
HOTEL & TOWER 212-299-1000/888-448-7867
1 Central Park West (60th St.)
www.trumpintl.com
General Manager – Tom Downing

Corporate Retreats

NEW YORK

GENEVA ON THE LAKE 315-789-7190/800-3GENEVA
1001 Lochland Rd., Route 14, Geneva
www.genevaonthelake.com
General Manager – William Schickel

SOUTHAMPTON INN 631-283-6500/800-832-6500
91 Hill St., Southampton
www.southamptoninn.com
General Manager – Paula Lewis

ACCOMMODATIONS

Corporate Retreats

NEW YORK

VILLA ROMA RESORT HOTEL 845-887-4880/800-533-6767
356 Village Roma Rd., Callicoon
www.villaroma.com
General Manager – Terry Moses

CONNECTICUT

THE INN AT NATIONAL HALL............. 203-221-1351/800-628-4255
Two Post Road West, Westport
www.innatnationalhall.com
General Manager – Marco Deglinnocenti

THE MAYFLOWER INN 860-868-9466
118 Woodbury Rd., Washington
www.mayflowerinn.com
General Manager – John Trevenen

WATER'S EDGE RESORT 860-399-5901/800-222-5901
1525 Boston Post Rd., Westbrook
www.watersedgeresortandspa.com
General Manager – Tina Dattilo

Corporate Housing

AVALON COMMUNITIES 212-370-9269
www.avaloncommunities.com

CHURCHILL CORPORATE SERVICES 800-658-7366
www.churchillcorp.com

ENVOY CLUB 212-481-4600
www.envoyclub.com

FURNISHED QUARTERS 212-367-9400/800-255-8117
www.furnishedquarters.com

THE MARMARA MANHATTAN 212-427-3100
www.marmara-manhattan.com

OAKWOOD CORPORATE HOUSING 800-259-6914
www.oakwood.com

Real Estate

BROWN HARRIS STEVENS 212-906-9200
www.brownharrisstevens.com

THE COCORAN GROUP 800-544-4055
www.corcoran.com

SOTHEBY'S INTERNATIONAL REALTY 212-431-2440
www.sothebysrealty.com

STRIBLING & ASSOCIATES 212-570-2440
www.striblingny.com

TRAVEL & TRANSPORTATION

Travel Agencies

FRENCHWAY 212-243-3500/800-243-3575
www.frenchwaytravel.com

MARGO TRAVEL, INC. 212-944-1333

TRAVELCRAFT...800-777-2723
www.travelcraftusa.com

TRAVEL & TRANSPORTATION

Airlines - Domestic

AIRTRAN 800-247-8726
www.airtran.com

ALASKA AIRLINES 800-252-7522
www.alaskaairlines.com

ALOHA AIRLINES 800-367-5250
www.alohaairlines.com

AMERICA WEST 800-235-9292
www.americawest.com

AMERICAN AIRLINES 800-433-7300
www.aa.com

AMERICAN TRANS AIR 800-435-9282
www.ata.com

CONTINENTAL 800-525-0280
www.continental.com

DELTA 800-221-1212
www.delta.com

FRONTIER 800-432-1359
www.frontierairlines.com

HAWAIIAN 800-367-5320
www.hawaiianair.com

HORIZON AIR 800-547-9308
www.horizonair.com

JETBLUE 800-538-2583
www.jetblue.com

MIDWEST AIRLINES 800-452-2022
www.midwestairlines.com

NORTHWEST 800-225-2525
www.nwa.com

SONG AIRLINES 800-FLY-SONG
www.flysong.com

SOUTHWEST 800-435-9792
www.southwest.com

SPIRIT AIRLINES 800-772-7117
www.spiritairlines.com

SUN COUNTRY AIRLINES 800-359-6786
www.suncountry.com

UNITED 800-241-6522
www.united.com

US AIRWAYS 800-428-4322
www.usairways.com

Airlines - International

AER LINGUS 800-474-7424
www.aerlingus.com

AIR CANADA 888-247-2262
www.aircanada.com

AIR FRANCE 800-237-2747
www.airfrance.net

AIR NEW ZEALAND 800-262-1234
www.airnewzealand.com

ALITALIA 800-223-5730
www.alitaliausa.com

TRAVEL & TRANSPORTATION

Airlines - International

AUSTRIAN AIRLINES 800-843-0002
www.aua.com

AVIANCA 800-284-2622
www.avianca.com

BRITISH AIRWAYS 800-247-9297
www.ba.com

CATHAY PACIFIC 800-233-2742
www.cathaypacific.com

EL AL 800-223-6700
www.elal.com

FINNAIR 800-950-5000
www.finnair.com

IBERIA AIRLINES 800-772-4642
www.iberia.com

ICELANDAIR 800-223-5500
www.icelandair.com

KLM ROYAL DUTCH 800-225-2525
www.klm.com

KOREAN AIR 800-438-5000
www.koreanair.com

LUFTHANSA 800-645-3880
www.lufthansa.com

QANTAS 800-227-4500
www.qantas.com

SWISS 877-359-7947
www.swiss.com

VIRGIN ATLANTIC 800-862-8621
www.virgin-atlantic.com

Charter Planes

AVJET CORPORATION 818-841-6190/800-342-8538
www.avjet.com
Contact – Mark Lefever, Executive Vice President

CLAY LACY AVIATION 818-989-2900/800-423-2904
www.claylacy.com

ELITE AVIATION 818-988-5387
www.eliteaviation.com

FOUR DIRECTIONS AIR, INC. 866-359-9355
www.fourdirectionsair.com
Contact – Maggie Begley, mbegley@aol.com

JET NETWORK 888-255-5387
www.jetnetwork.com

KOMAR AVIATION GROUP 949-250-1359/800-555-0996
www.komaraviation.com

METRO JET, LTD. 888-682-6227
www.metrojet.com

PRESIDENTIAL AVIATION 310-279-6387
www.presidential-aviation.com
Contact – Leslie Guthrie, leslie@presidential-aviation.com

RAYTHEON AIRCRAFT CHARTER
AND MANAGEMENT 800-519-6283/316-676-0778
www.raytheonaircraft.com
Contact – Ron Gottschalk

TRAVEL & TRANSPORTATION

Charter Planes

SENTIENT PRIVATE JET MEMBERSHIP 800-641-6917
www.sentient.com

TELLURIDE FLIGHTS 970-728-1011
www.tellurideflights.com
Contact – Don

Car Rentals

ALAMO 800-462-5266
www.alamo.com

AVIS..800-230-4898
www.avis.com

BUDGET 800-527-0700
www.budget.com

DOLLAR 800-800-4000
www.dollar.com

ENTERPRISE...800-261-7331
www.enterprise.com

HERTZ 800-654-3131
www.hertz.com

NATIONAL 800-227-7368
www.nationalcar.com

THRIFTY 800-847-4389
www.thrifty.com

Car Services/Limos

ALLSTATE PRIVATE CAR & LIMOUSINE.......................212-333-3333

ATTITUDE NEW YORK...212-397-0004

BERMUDA LIMOUSINE INTERNATIONAL.....................800-223-1383
www.bermudalimo.com

BLS LIMOUSINE INTERNATIONAL.............................800-843-5752
www.blslimo.com

CARMEL CAR & LIMOUSINE SERVICE 212-666-6666/800-9-CARMEL
www.carmellimo.com

DIVA..800-427-DIVA
www.divalimo.com

MUSIC EXPRESS 800-421-9494
www.musiclimo.com

SURREY CADILLAC LIMOUSINE SERVICE 718-937-5700

TEL AVIV 212-777-7777/800-222-9888
www.telavivlimo.com

GIFTS & SHOPPING

Florists

COUNTRY GARDENS...212-966-2015

ELIZABETH RYAN FLORAL DESIGNS 212-995-1111

LOTUS 212-463-0555
www.lotus212.com

RENNY AND REED 212-288-7000
www.rennyandreed.com

SURROUNDING FLOWERS 800-567-7007
www.surroundingflowers.com

WILD POPPY 212-717-5757

GIFTS & SHOPPING

Gift Baskets

DELIGHTFUL DELIVERIES 877-442-6333
www.delightfuldeliveries.com

MANHATTAN FRUITIER 212-686-0404/800-841-5718
www.manhattanfruitier.com

THE ORCHARD.................................718-377-1799/800-222-0240
www.orchardfruit.com

Personal Assistants

IZZY BUSY..212-475-7289
Contact – Isabel Novoa, eneryisa@yahoo.com

Personal Shoppers

CONCIERGE CONNECTION OF NEW YORK 917-763-7878
cnyinc@yahoo.com
Contact – Barbara

CROSS IT OFF YOUR LIST 212-725-0122/888-XOFFLIST
www.crossitoffyourlist.com
Contact – Linda Rothschild

DONUM CELEBRITY &
CORPORATE GIFTS 310-317-4577/508-358-7447
www.donumgifts.com
Contacts – Kristy Barrett Wylie & Amy Frankel Nau

VISUAL THERAPY 212-315-2233
www.visual-therapy.com

SCREENING ROOMS

DOWNTOWN

ANTHOLOGY FILM ARCHIVES...................................212-505-5181
32 Second Ave. (E. 2nd St.)
www.anthologyfilmarchives.org

GRAND SCREEN 212-519-6600
Tribeca Grand Hotel, 2 Avenue of the Americas (Walker St.)
www.tribecagrand.com

IFC CENTER 212-924-7771
323 Avenue of the Americas (W. 3rd St.)
www.ifccenter.com

QUAD CINEMAS 212-255-8800
34 W. 13th St. (Fifth Ave.)
www.quadcinema.com

TRIBECA SCREENING ROOM 212-941-2000
Tribeca Film Center, 375 Greenwich St. (N. Moore St.)
www.tribecafilm.com

MIDTOWN

BROADWAY SCREENING ROOM 212-307-0990
1619 Broadway, 5th Fl. (49th St.)
www.mybsr.com

THE BRYANT PARK SCREENING ROOM 212-869-0100
The Bryant Park Hotel, 40 W. 40th St. (Avenue of the Americas)
www.bryantparkhotel.com

DISNEY SCREENING ROOM 212-735-5348
500 Park Ave. (59th St.)
www.buenavistapost.com
Contact – Bob Dickey

SCREENING ROOMS

MIDTOWN

FOX SCREENING ROOM 212-556-2406
1211 Avenue of the Americas, 3rd fl. (47th St.)
Contact – Michael Goucher

MAGNO SOUND & VIDEO 212-302-2505
729 Seventh Ave. (48th St.)
www.magnosoundandvideo.com

MGM SCREENING ROOM 212-708-0300
1350 Avenue of the Americas, 1st fl. (55th St.)
Contact – Bill Lopatto

SONY PICTURES 212-833-7652
550 Madison Ave. (55th St.)
Contact – Graham Smith

WARNER BROS. 212-636-5087
1325 Avenue of the Americas (53rd St.)
Contact – Vivan Tibbtts

EASTSIDE

FRENCH INSTITUTE ALLIANCE FRANÇAIS 212-355-6100
55 E. 59th St. (Madison Ave.)
www.fiaf.org/rental

MUSEUM OF THE MOVING IMAGE 718-784-4520
35th Ave. (36th St.), Astoria
www.movingimage.us

WESTSIDE

JAZZ AT LINCOLN CENTER, FREDERICK P. ROSE HALL.... 212-258-9803
33 W. 60th St., 11th fl. (Broadway)
www.jalc.org
Contact – Bret Silver, booking@jalc.org

WALTER READE THEATER 212-875-5608
165 W. 65th St. (Amsterdam Ave.)
www.filmlinc.com/wrt/theaterrental.htm
Contact – Sharon Bauhs

VIP TICKETS

NEW JERSEY NETS 201-635-3155
www.njnets.com
VP, Entertainment Development
& Talent Relations – Petra Pope

NEW YORK GIANTS 201-935-8111
www.giants.com
VP of Marketing – Rusty Hawley

NEW YORK ISLANDERS 516-501-6725
www.newyorkislanders.com
VP, Marketing & Sales – Paul Lancey

NEW YORK JETS 516-560-8107
www.newyorkjets.com
Director, Public Relations – Ron Colangelo

NEW YORK KNICKS 212-465-6102
www.nba.com/knicks
Director, VIP Services – Anne Marie Dunleavy

NEW YORK LIBERTY 212-465-6695
www.wnba.com/liberty
VP, Marketing & Communications – Amy Scheer

NEW YORK METS 718-507-6387
www.mets.mlb.com
Public Relations – Jay Horwitz

VIP TICKETS

NEW YORK RANGERS 212-465-6405
www.newyorkrangers.com
VP, Marketing – Jeanie Baumgartner

NEW YORK YANKEES 718-293-4300
www.yankees.mlb.com
Director, Community Relations – Brian Smith

MAIL & DELIVERY

Messengers

CITY EXPEDITOR, INC. 212-353-2042
www.cityexpeditor.com

MOBILE MESSENGER SERVICE 212-247-7400

PERSONAL MESSENGER SERVICES 212-505-7930

QUICK TRAK MESSENGER SERVICE 212-463-7070
www.quik-trak.com

SUPERSONIC MESSENGER SERVICE 212-446-2100
www.slsonline.com

FedEx Kinko's Stores

Information 800-254-6567
www.fedexkinkos.com

DOWNTOWN

245 7th Ave. (24th St.) 212-929-0623
650 Ave. of the Americas (20th St.) 646-638-9238
257 Park Ave. South (Grammercy Park) 646-602-0074
21 Astor Pl. (Lafayette) 212-228-9511
250 E. Houston St. (East Village) 212-253-9020
105 Duane St. (City Hall) 212-406-1220
110 William St. (John St.) 212-766-4646
100 Wall St. (Water St.) 212-269-0024

MIDTOWN

60 W. 40th St. (Bryant Park) 212-921-1060
500 Seventh Ave. (37th St.) 646-366-9166
350 Fifth Ave. (Empire State Bldg.) 212-629-5534
191 Madison Ave. (34th St.) 212-685-3449
16 E. 52nd St. (Madison Ave.) 212-308-2679
233 W. 54th St. (Broadway) 212-977-2679
1211 Ave. of the Americas (47th St.) 212-391-2679
230 Park Ave. (Vanderbilt) 212-949-2534
600 Third Ave. (39th St.) 212-370-0754
747 Third Ave. (47th St.) 212-753-7778
153 E. 53rd St. (Citicorp Ctr.) 212-753-7580
240 Central Park South (Columbus Cir.) 212-258-3750

EASTSIDE

641 Lexington Ave. (54th St.) 212-572-9995
1122 Lexington Ave. (78th St.) 212-628-5500

WESTSIDE

221 W. 72nd St. (Broadway) 212-362-5288
600 W. 116th St. (Broadway) 212-749-3515
2211 Broadway (79th St.) 212-787-6799

MAIL & DELIVERY

UPS Stores & Drop Boxes

Information 1-800-PICK-UPS
www.ups.com

DOWNTOWN

64 Beaver St. (Hanover Sqare)
305 W. Broadway (Canal St.)
118-A Fulton St. (Dutch St.)
342 W. Broadway (Catherine Ln.)

MIDTOWN

1514 Broadway (44th St.)
1357 Broadway (36th St.)
132 E. 43rd St. (Lexington Ave.)

EASTSIDE

527 Third Ave. (35th St.)
1173 Second Ave. (62nd St.)
1562 First Ave. (81st St.)
217 E. 86th St. (Third Ave.)

WESTSIDE

888-C Eighth Ave. (53rd St.)
119 W. 72nd St. (Columbus Ave.)
366 W. Amsterdam Ave. (89th St.)
2753 Broadway (105th St.)

Post Offices

Information...800-275-8777
www.usps.com

DOWNTOWN

CANAL STATION
350 Canal St. (Wooster St.)

PECK SLIP STATION
1 Peck Slip (Water St.)

VILLAGE STATION
201 Varick St. (W. Houston St.)

PRINCE STATION
124 Greene St. (Prince St.)

CANAL STREET RETAIL
6 Doyers St. (Confucius Plaza)

MIDTOWN

BRYANT STATION
23 W. 43rd St. (Fifth Ave.)

MURRAY HILL STATION
115 E. 34th St. (Lexington Ave.)

EMPIRE STATE STATION
19 W. 33rd St. (Fifth Ave.)

GREELEY SQUARE STATION
39 W. 31st St. (Seventh Ave.)

MIDTOWN STATION
223-241 W. 38th St. (Seventh Ave.)

TIMES SQUARE STATION
340 W. 42nd St. (Eighth Ave.)

ROCKEFELLER CENTER STATION
610 Fifth Ave. (48th St.)

RADIO CITY STATION
322 W. 52nd St. (Eighth Ave.)

MAIL & DELIVERY

Post Offices

EASTSIDE

CHEROKEE STATION
1483 York Ave. (79th St.)

GRACIE STATION
229 E. 85th St. (Third Ave.)

YORKVILLE STATION
1617 Third Ave. (94th St.)

LENOX HILL STATION
217 E. 70th St. (Third Ave.)

WESTSIDE

ANSONIA STATION
178 Columbus Ave. (68th St.)

PLANETARIUM STATION
127 W. 83rd St. (Columbus Ave.)

COLUMBUS CIRCLE STATION
27 W. 60th St. (Broadway)

PARK WEST STATION
693 Columbus Ave. (94th St.)

COLUMBIA UNIVERSITY STATION
534 W. 112 St. (Amsterdam Ave.)

OFFICE SERVICES & SUPPLIES

DOWNTOWN

STAPLES
488 Broadway (Broome St.)..................................212-219-1299
345 Park Avenue South (26th St.) 212-683-3267
200 Water St. (Fulton St.)....................................212-785-9521

THE NEW YORK COPY CENTER
204 E. 11th St. (Third Ave.) 212-673-5628

MIDTOWN

OFFICE DEPOT
1441 Broadway (41st St.) 212-764-2465

STAPLES
16 E. 34th St. (Fifth Ave.)....................................212-683-8009
730 Third Ave. (45th St.) 212-867-9486
205 E. 42nd St. (Third Ave.) 212-697-1591
1065 Avenue of the Americas (40th St.) 212-997-4446
57 W. 57th St. (Avenue of the Americas).................212-308-0335
575 Lexington Ave. (51st St.) 212-644-2118
425 Park Ave. (56th St.) 212-753-9640

EASTSIDE

STAPLES 212-426-6190
1280 Lexington Ave. (86th St.)

WESTSIDE

STAPLES 212-712-9617
2248 Broadway (81st St.)

SECTION A

DEALS BY COMPANY

ABC Entertainment Television Group
Bad Hat Harry Productions .818-954-4043
The Bedford Falls Company .310-394-5022
Big Light Productions .818-560-4782
Bungalow 78 Productions .818-560-4878
Embassy Row LLC .212-627-3439
Four Boys Films .818-560-1230
Harpo Films, Inc. .310-278-5559
Launa Newman Productions (LNP) .310-288-8383
Bill Melendez Productions .818-382-7382
Misher Films .323-956-8333
Next Entertainment .818-972-0077
Olmos Productions, Inc. .818-560-8651
Marc Platt Productions .818-777-8811

ABC Sports
MRB Productions, Inc. .323-465-7676

Alcon Entertainment, LLC
Rocklin Entertainment .310-789-3066

Craig Anderson Productions
Beth Grossbard Productions .310-841-2555

Baldwin Entertainment Group, Ltd.
Nick Grillo Productions .310-453-1351

Bauer Martinez Entertainment
Forest Park Pictures .323-848-2942

Blumhouse Productions
ROOM 101, Inc. .323-956-3038

Brookwell McNamara Entertainment, Inc.
MarVista Entertainment .310-737-0950

Buena Vista Motion Pictures Group
Scott Rudin Productions .323-956-4600

Mark Burnett Productions
AOL Media Networks .212-652-6400

John Calley Productions
Avenue Pictures .310-244-6868

Castle Rock Entertainment
Reiner/Greisman .310-285-2300

CBS Entertainment
Braga Productions .323-956-5799
Gran Via Productions .310-859-3060
High Horse Films .323-939-8802
Parkchester Pictures .310-289-5988
Scott Free Productions .310-360-2250

CBS Paramount Network Television
The Axelrod/Edwards Company .323-956-3705
Belisarius Productions .323-468-4500
Rick Berman Productions .323-956-5037
Braga Productions .323-956-5799
Charles Bros. .323-956-5962
Charles Floyd Johnson Productions .323-468-4520
Circle of Confusion Productions .310-253-7777
Grammnet Productions .323-956-5455
Gran Via Productions .310-859-3060
Hazy Mills Productions .818-655-5000
Humble Journey Films .323-882-6376
Nuance Productions .818-754-5484
Joe Roth Television .818-655-7266
Scott Free Productions .310-360-2250
Solaris .323-956-8899
Tooley Productions .310-777-8733
Simon West Productions .323-956-8994

Columbia Pictures
Michael De Luca Productions .310-244-4916
Gittes, Inc. .310-244-4333
The Mark Gordon Company .310-943-6401
The Hal Lieberman Company .310-244-4744
Out of the Blue . . . Entertainment .310-244-7811
Outlaw Productions .310-244-3445
Phoenix Pictures .310-244-6100
Spyglass Entertainment Group .310-443-5800
Wonderland Sound and Vision .310-659-4451
Laura Ziskin Productions .310-244-7373

Comedy Central
Busboy Productions .212-262-6165
Parallel Entertainment, Inc. .310-279-1123

Constantin Film Development, Inc./Constantin Television
Impact Pictures .310-247-1803

Court TV Networks
KLS Communications, Inc. .818-887-0308

Creative Differences
Rive Gauche Entertainment .818-784-9912

Dimension Films
Cube Vision .310-255-7100
Platinum Dunes .310-394-9200
Trancas International Films .310-553-5599

Discovery Health Channel
Weller/Grossman Productions .818-755-4800

Disney ABC Cable Networks Group
M3 Television .818-558-3633

The Walt Disney Company
Farrell Paura Productions, LLC .818-560-3000
Harpo Films, Inc. .310-278-5559
The Jim Henson Company .323-802-1500
Hyde Park Entertainment .818-783-6060
Janicek-Marino Creative .303-860-0070
Junction Entertainment .818-560-2800
LivePlanet .310-664-2400
Mandeville Films .818-560-4077

Walt Disney Pictures/Touchstone Pictures
Beacon .310-260-7000
Jerry Bruckheimer Films & Television .310-664-6246
Cider Mill Productions .818-560-8016
Gunn Films .818-560-6156
Martin Chase Productions .818-560-3952
Mayhem Pictures .310-393-5005
Pandemonium .310-385-4088
Pfeffer Film .818-560-3177
Rocket Pictures Limited .44-207-603-9530
Tollin/Robbins Productions .818-755-3000

Double Nickel Entertainment
Foremost Films .646-662-0829

DreamWorks SKG
Aardman Animations .44-117-984-8485
Ember Entertainment Group .310-230-9759
Jason Hoffs Productions .818-733-9926
Kurtzman/Orci .818-733-9645
The Montecito Picture Company .805-565-8590
Neal Street Productions Ltd. .44-207-240-8890
Red Hour Films .323-602-5000
The Zanuck Company .310-274-0261

E! Networks
Ryan Seacrest Productions 323-954-2400

ESPN Original Entertainment (EOE)
Embassy Row LLC 212-627-3439
Mango Tree Pictures 203-259-7771
MRB Productions, Inc. 323-465-7676

Focus Features/Rogue Pictures
Completion Films 718-693-2057
Deacon Entertainment 818-733-0814
Flavor Unit Entertainment 201-333-4883
Intrepid Pictures 310-264-3995
Primary Productions 212-620-4582
Random House Films 212-782-9000
Vertigo Entertainment 310-288-5160

Food Network
Weller/Grossman Productions 818-755-4800

Fortress Entertainment
Bonnie Forbes Productions 323-606-4403

fox 21
Benderspink 323-904-1800

Fox Atomic
OZLA Pictures, Inc. 323-876-0180

Fox Broadcasting Company
Heel & Toe Films 310-264-1866

Fox Television Studios
Avenue Pictures 310-244-6868
Fuse Entertainment 323-850-3873
Grand Productions, Inc. 310-369-5027
Key Creatives, LLC 310-273-3004
KLS Communications, Inc. 818-887-0308
Landscape Entertainment 310-248-6200
MobiTV 510-450-5000
The Shuman Company 310-841-4344

FremantleMedia North America
Krasnow Productions 310-255-4824
Nasser Entertainment Group 818-505-8030

Fried Films
Daniel Fried Productions 310-689-2460

Gold Circle Films
Lloyd Entertainment 310-278-4800
Safran Company 310-278-1450

The Hatchery
Janicek-Marino Creative 303-860-0070

HBO Entertainment
Comedy Arts Studios 310-382-3677
Face Productions/Jennilind Productions 310-205-2746
Pretty Matches Productions 212-512-5755
Q Media Partners 415-252-2868
Red Board Productions 310-264-4285
Simmons/Lathan 323-634-6400
Studios International 310-300-9130
SUperFInger Entertainment 818-295-8013

HBO Films
Cine Mosaic 212-625-3797
Duly Noted 323-525-1855

The History Channel
Weller/Grossman Productions 818-755-4800

HIT Entertainment
The Jim Henson Company 323-802-1500

Home & Garden Television (HGTV)
Weller/Grossman Productions 818-755-4800

Icon Productions, LLC
Rive Gauche Entertainment 818-784-9912

Initial Entertainment Group
Blueprint Films 212-625-0530
Infinitum Nihil 310-273-6700

Jaffe/Braunstein Films, LLC
Chotzen/Jenner Productions 323-465-9877

Lionsgate
Alchemy Entertainment 310-278-8889
Bayonne Entertainment 310-889-9222
City Entertainment 310-273-3101
Element Films 323-330-8000
Ithaka 310-314-9585
Panamax Films 305-421-6336
Sobini Films 310-255-5111

LMNO Productions
Rive Gauche Entertainment 818-784-9912

Madison Road Entertainment
Once A Frog Productions 310-432-6630

Mandate Pictures
Three Strange Angels, Inc. 310-601-2291

Metro-Goldwyn-Mayer Studios, Inc. (MGM)
Danjaq, LLC 310-449-3185
Irish DreamTime 310-449-3411
The Robert Simonds Company 310-789-2200
Winkler Films 310-858-5780

Millennium Films
Emmett/Furla Films 310-659-9411
Two Sticks Productions 323-822-2300

Morningstar Entertainment
Rive Gauche Entertainment 818-784-9912

MPH Entertainment, Inc.
Rive Gauche Entertainment 818-784-9912

MTV Films
Bona Fide Productions 310-273-6782
MM Productions 310-434-1477

MTV Networks
Amp'd Mobile 310-575-2500
Bad Boy Films 212-381-2057
Carson Daly Productions 818-827-7123
Generate 310-255-0460
Liquid Theory 310-276-1094
Terence Michael Productions, Inc. .310-823-3432

National Lampoon
Half Shell Entertainment 310-314-7672
Hand Picked Films 310-456-3444

NBC Entertainment
Darkwoods Productions 323-454-4580

NBC Universal Television Studio
40 Acres & A Mule Filmworks, Inc. 718-624-3703
Ars Nova 212-489-9800
Baby Cow Productions Ltd. 44-20-7399-1267
Big Cattle Productions 818-506-7200
Broadway Video 212-265-7600
Broadway Video Entertainment 323-956-5655
Carson Daly Productions 818-827-7123
Doozer 818-623-1880, x104
DreamWorks SKG 818-733-7000
Galán Entertainment 310-823-2822
Hypnotic 310-806-6930
Is Or Isn't Entertainment 310-248-2000
MobiTV 510-450-5000
Principato-Young Entertainment 310-274-4474
Raines 323-960-4725
Reveille, LLC 818-733-1218
Superb Entertainment 212-664-3493
Tapestry Films, Inc. 310-275-1191
Tollin/Robbins Productions 818-755-3000
Upright Citizens Brigade 323-908-8702
Wolf Films, Inc. 818-777-6969

New Line Cinema
Benderspink 323-904-1800
Stokely Chaffin Productions 323-802-1790
Chick Flicks 310-967-6541
Contrafilm 323-467-8787
j.k. livin productions 310-556-0079
Rat Entertainment/Rat TV 310-228-5000
Storyline Entertainment 818-560-2928
Temple Hill Productions 310-270-4383

Nickelodeon Movies
Lawrence Bender Productions 323-951-4600

Nickelodeon/MTVN Kids & Family Group
Frederator Studios 818-736-3606
Worldwide Biggies 212-846-7521

Paramount Pictures
Bad Robot Productions 818-560-7064
Blumhouse Productions 323-956-8855
Bona Fide Productions 310-273-6782
Broadway Video Entertainment 323-956-5655
CFP Productions 323-956-8866
C/W Productions 323-956-8199
The Sean Daniel Company 323-956-4855
Darkwoods Productions 323-454-4580
Deep River Productions 310-432-1800
di Bonaventura Pictures, Inc. 323-956-5454
Double Feature Films 310-887-1100
DreamWorks SKG 818 733 7000
The Robert Evans Company 323-956-8800
John Goldwyn Productions 323-956-5054
Guy Walks Into a Bar 323-930-9935
Interscope/Shady/Aftermath Films 323-956-5989
Tom Jacobson Productions 323-956-5040
The Jinks/Cohen Company 323-956-8411
Lakeshore Entertainment Group LLC 310-867-8000
Misher Films 323-956-8333
MM Productions 310-434-1477
MTV Films 323-956-8023
Nickelodeon Movies 323-956-8650
Lynda Obst Productions 323-956-8744
Paramount Vantage/Paramount Classics 323-956-5000
Plan B Entertainment 310-275-6135
Revelations Entertainment 310-394-3131
Southern Cross the Dog 323-956-2080
Trunity, a Mediar Company, a Division of
True Mediar, a Unity Corpbopoly 310-306-8110
Watermark 323-956-5000

Paramount Vantage/Paramount Classics
Interscope/Shady/Aftermath Films 323-956-5989

Participant Productions
Edward Saxon Productions (ESP) .310-246-7700

Radar Pictures
American Work 212-905-2325
Frederic Golchan Productions 310-208-8525

Regency Television
Avalon Television, Inc. 323-930-6010
OZLA Pictures, Inc. 323-876-0180

Revolution Studios
Broken Road Productions 310-255-7210
Team Todd 310-255-7265

Shoreline Entertainment, Inc.
Chic Productions 310-391-2152

Showtime Networks Inc.
Elkins Entertainment 323-932-0400
Peace Arch Entertainment Group Inc. 416-487-0377
Sacred Dogs Entertainment, LLC .323-656-6900

Sony Pictures Entertainment
360 Pictures/FGM Entertainment .310-205-9900
Apostle 212-541-4323
Avenue Pictures 310-244-6868
John Baldecchi Productions 310-244-8232
Blue Star Pictures 310-255-7018
Buckaroo Entertainment 310-244-4646
John Calley Productions 310-244-7777
Escape Artists II 310-244-8833
Wendy Finerman Productions 310-244-8800
Fresh Paint 310-656-4300
Gracie Films 310-244-4222
The Jim Henson Company 323-802-1500
Laurence Mark Productions 310-244-5239
O.N.C. Entertainment Inc. 310-244-4555
Original Film 310-575-6950
Overbrook Entertainment 310-432-2400
Pariah 310-276-3500
Red Wagon Entertainment 310-244-4466
Revolution Studios 310-255-7000
Paul Schiff Productions 310-244-5454
Trilogy Entertainment Group 310-656-9733
Winkler Films 310-858-5780

Sony Pictures Television
25C Productions 310-244-2980
BBC Worldwide Americas 818-299-9715
Bull's Eye Entertainment 310-979-7117
Embassy Row LLC 212-627-3439
Giraffe Productions 310-244-2230
Dean Hargrove Productions 310-244-8383
Diana Kerew Productions 310-838-3931
Krasnoff Foster Productions 310-244-3282
Original Film 310-575-6950
P.A.T. Productions 310-244-8881
Darren Star Productions 310-244-4000
Storyline Entertainment 818-560-2928
von Zerneck-Sertner Films 818-789-2766
Warrior Poets 212-219-7617

Spike TV
Liquid Theory 310-276-1094

Touchstone Television

Battle Plan Productions 818-560-2616
Berlanti Productions 818-560-4846
Big Light Productions 818-560-4782
Steven Bochco Productions 310-566-6900
Brancato/Salke Productions 818-560-1520
Brillstein-Grey Entertainment 310-275-6135
Bungalow 78 Productions 818-560-4878
Bushwacker Productions 213-534-3145
Coquette Productions 323-801-1000
The Edelstein Company 818-560-3884
The Mark Gordon Company 310-943-6401
Gross Entertainment 818-560-8117
Infront Productions 310-288-8000
The Littlefield Company 818-560-2280
LivePlanet 310-664-2400
Love Spell Entertainment 818-560-5376
Mandeville Films 818-560-4077
Mojo Films 818-560-8370
New Amsterdam Entertainment, Inc. 212-922-1930
Q Media Partners 415-252-2868
Sachs Judah Productions 818-560-5435
Sander/Moses Productions, Inc. 818-560-4500
Shady Acres Entertainment 818-777-4446
Silly Robin Productions 818-560-8585
SMG Productions 310-777-8200
Spyglass Entertainment Group 310-443-5800
Storyline Entertainment 818-560-2928
Wass-Stein 818-560-1950

TV Guide Channel

Keep Clear 310-854-2300

Twentieth Century Fox

21 Laps Entertainment 310-369-4466
Bazmark, Inq. 61-2-9361-6668
Blossom Films 310-369-5359
Conundrum Entertainment 310-319-2800
Davis Entertainment Company 310-556-3550
Dominant Pictures 310-369-0707
Firm Films 310-860-8000
Hyde Park Entertainment 818-783-6060
Josephson Entertainment 310-369-7501
Lightstorm Entertainment 310-656-6100
Penn Station Entertainment 310-207-2501
Zak Penn's Company 323-939-1700
Point Road, Inc. 323-850-2670
Principato-Young Entertainment 310-274-4474
Regency Enterprises 310-369-8300
Scott Free Productions 310-360-2250
Seed Productions 310-369-1900
Tapestry Films, Inc. 310-275-1191
Ralph Winter Productions, Inc. 310-369-4723

Twentieth Century Fox - Fox 2000

Blossom Films 310-369-5359
State Street Pictures 310-369-5099
Sunswept Entertainment 310-859-1060
Zucker/Netter Productions 310-394-1644

Twentieth Century Fox - Searchlight Pictures

Ad Hominem Enterprises 310-394-1444
DNA Films 44-207-292-8700

Twentieth Century Fox Animation

Blue Sky Studios 914-259-6500

Twentieth Century Fox Television

Adelstein Productions 310-362-2200
Callahan Filmworks 323-878-0645
Imagine Television 310-858-2000
Josephson Entertainment 310-369-7501
David E. Kelley Productions 310-727-2200
Phase Two Productions 310-369-8555
Roundtable Entertainment 323-769-2567
Watson Pond Productions 310-369-5701

Universal Pictures

Black & White Productions 818-777-0999
Bobker/Kruger Films 323-802-1567
Class 5 Films 917-414-9404
Everyman Pictures 310-264-4211
Film 44 310-689-2929
Gold Circle Films 310-278-4800
Greasy Entertainment 310-586-2300
Identity Films 818-733-3378
Imagine Entertainment 310-858-2000
The Kennedy/Marshall Company 310-656-8400
Larger Than Life Productions 818-777-4004
Mandalay Pictures 323-549-4300
Barry Mendel Productions 818-733-3076
Morgan Creek Productions 310-432-4848
New Deal Productions 323-299-2183
Marc Platt Productions 818-777-8811
Protozoa Pictures 212-244-3369
Shady Acres Entertainment 818-777-4446
The Sommers Company 310-917-9200
Strike Entertainment 310-315-0550
Terra Firma Films 818-777-4457
Tribeca Productions 212-941-4040
Type A Films 818-777-6222
Vertigo Entertainment 310-288-5160
Working Title Films 310-777-3100
Yari Film Group (YFG) 310-234-8970

VH1

51 Minds Entertainment 323-463-6100

Village Roadshow Pictures

This is that corporation 212-994-8455

Walden Media

Bristol Bay Productions 310-887-1000
Gran Via Productions 310-859-3060

Warner Bros. Pictures

1492 Pictures 818-954-4939
Alcon Entertainment, LLC 310-789-3040
Appian Way 310-300-1390
Bad Hat Harry Productions 818-954-4043
The Bedford Falls Company 310-394-5022
Broken Lizard Industries 818-954-5600
Castle Rock Entertainment 310-285-2300
De Line Pictures 818-954-5200
Di Novi Pictures 310-581-1355
Double Nickel Entertainment 212-636-5488
Esperanto Films 212-219-7610
The Film Department 818-954-4015
Flower Films, Inc. 818-954-5840
Fortis Films 310-659-4533
Gambit Pictures 818-954-3100
Gerber Pictures 310-385-5880
Heyday Films 818-954-3004
Initial Entertainment Group 310-315-1722
Legendary Pictures 818-954-1940
Malpaso Productions 818-954-3367
Management 360 310-272-7000
Maple Shade Films 818-954-3137
The Todd Phillips Company 818-954-6000
Radiant Productions 310-656-1400
Dylan Sellers Productions 818-954-4929
Jon Shestack Productions 323-468-1113

Warner Bros. Pictures (Continued)

Silver Pictures .818-954-4490
Smoke House .818-954-4840
Spring Creek Productions, Inc. .310-270-9000
Thunder Road Pictures .818-954-3130
Village Roadshow Pictures .818-260-6000
Weed Road Pictures .818-954-3771
Jerry Weintraub Productions .818-954-2500
Wigram Productions .818-954-2412
The Wolper Organization .818-954-1421

Warner Bros. Television Production

Acme Productions .818-954-7779
Bad Robot Productions .818-560-7064
Jerry Bruckheimer Films & Television .310-664-6246
Class IV Productions .818-954-7206
Double Nickel Entertainment .212-636-5488
Fort Hill Productions .818-954-7575
Genrebend Productions, Inc. .310-917-1064
Good Game .818-954-3414
The Jinks/Cohen Company .323-956-8411
Johnenelly Productions .818-954-6445
KoMut Entertainment .818-655-5563
Last Straw Productions .818-954-1064
Miller/Boyett Productions .212-702-9779
Mohawk Productions .818-954-7442
The Shephard/Robin Company .323-871-4412
Shoe Money Productions .818-954-2682
Silver Pictures .818-954-4490
Smoke House .818-954-4840
Tannenbaum Company .818-954-1113
John Wells Productions .818-954-1687
Wonderland Sound and Vision .310-659-4451

Warner Horizon Television

Next Entertainment .818-972-0077

Warner Independent Pictures

Bonne Pioche .33-1-4929-4600
Cherry Road Films, LLC .310-458-6550

The Weinstein Company

Cube Vision .310-255-7100
Mirage Enterprises .310-888-2830
Outerbanks Entertainment .310-858-8711
Trancas International Films .310-553-5599
View Askew Productions, Inc. .323-969-9423

John Wells Productions

Harms Way Productions .818-954-2160
Killer Films, Inc. .212-473-3950

Yari Film Group (YFG)

Brooklyn Media .323-851-5585

WORKSHEET

DATE	PROJECT	CONTACT	NOTES

SECTION **B**

NEW LISTINGS AT A GLANCE

COMPANIES

Adelstein Productions 47
Adult Swim 47
Ahimsa Films 48
And Then Productions 51
Anonymous Creators Productions 52
Arramis Films 55
Article 19 Films 56
Baby Cow Productions Ltd. 59
Big Cattle Productions 67
Blossom Films 68
The Bremer Goff Company 75
Bridge Films, LLC 75
CBS Corporation 86
Creative Coalition 103
Cyan Pictures 105
Disney Online 112
Elevation Filmworks 121
Endemol USA Latino 123
Eye in the Sky Entertainment 129
The Film Department 132
Foremost Films 137
Fox Cable Networks 139
Gordonstreet Pictures 150
Gorilla Pictures 150
Graymark Productions Inc. 153
The Group Entertainment 156
G-Unit Television & Films 157
House of Rock Productions, Inc. 169
Infinitum Nihil 174
Infinity Features Entertainment 174
ISBE Productions 177
Liddell Entertainment 197
Live Animals 201
LJ Film 201
L'Orange 203
Macgowan Films 206
Madhouse Entertainment 206
Mango Tree Pictures 210
The Mayhem Project 213
mistRE films 218
My Network TV 228
National Geographic Giant Screen Films & Special Projects 229
OZLA Pictures, Inc. 246
Partizan 250
Perry Films 253
Picturehouse 254
Playtone Productions 258
Potboiler Productions 260
Rocklin Entertainment 274
ROOM 101, Inc. 274
Safran Company 278
SenArt Films 284
Senator Entertainment, Inc. 284
Sinovoi Entertainment 290
Sirocco Media 290
Sleuth 291
Smoke House 292
SOAPnet 293
Station 3 300
Story and Film, Inc. 302
Superb Entertainment 305
Veoh Networks, Inc. 329
Warner Horizon Television 335
Water Channel 336
Yellow Cab Pictures 347

Asterisks (*) next to companies denote new listings

TV SHOWS

20 Good Years (NBC/30 mins.)........................353
3 lbs. (CBS/60 mins.) 353
30 Rock (NBC/30 mins.)..................................353
Big Day (ABC/30 mins.) 355
The Class (CBS/30 mins.) 357
Day Break (ABC/60 mins.) 359
Dirt (FX/60 mins.) 360
Friday Night Lights (NBC/60 mins.) 361
The Game (The CW/30 mins.)..........................361
Happy Hour (Fox/30 mins.)..............................362
Help Me Help You (ABC/30 mins.)....................363
Heroes (NBC/60 mins.)....................................363
Hidden Palms (The CW/60 mins.) 363
Jericho (CBS/60 mins.) 364
Justice (Fox/60 mins.) 364
The Knights of Prosperity (ABC/30 mins.) 365
My Boys (TBS/30 mins.) 369
The Nine (ABC/60 mins.) 370
Notes From the Underbelly (ABC/30 mins.) 370
Raines (NBC/60 mins.) 372
Rules of Engagement (CBS/30 mins.) 373
Runaway (The CW/60 mins.)............................373
Saved (TNT/60 mins.) 374
Shark (CBS/60 mins.) 374
The Singles Table (NBC/30 mins.) 375
Six Degrees (ABC/60 mins.) 375
Standoff (Fox/60 mins.) 376
'Til Death (Fox/30 mins.) 377
Traveler (ABC/60 mins.) 377
Ugly Betty (ABC/60 mins.)................................378
Vanished (Fox/60 mins.) 378
Waterfront (CBS/60 mins.)................................379

Asterisks (*) next to companies denote new listings

SECTION C

COMPANIES AND STAFF

@RADICAL.MEDIA

435 Hudson St.
New York, NY 10014

PHONE . . . 212-462-1500/310-664-4500
FAX . . . 212-462-1600/310-664-4600
EMAIL . . . info@radicalmedia.com
WEB SITE . . . www.radicalmedia.com

TYPES	Commercials - Documentaries - Features - Mobile Content - Music Videos - Theatre - TV Series
CREDITS	Iconoclasts (Sundance Channel) - The Gamekillers (MTV) - Nike Battlegrounds (MTV) - Metallica: Some Kind of Monster - The Fog of War - Concert for George - Jay Z in Fade to Black - The Exonerated - Left of the Dial - Gray Matter - Road to Paris - Erskineville Kings - The Cell - The Life - Report from Ground Zero - A Day in the Life of Africa - Shots in the Dark - Victoria Secret Fashion Show - Poem - Brotherhood - Meet the Lucky Ones - Lovely by Surprise - The Adventures of Seinfeld & Superman
SUBMISSION POLICY	No unsolicited submissions

Jon Kamen . . . Chairman
Frank Scherma . . . President
Cathy Shannon . . . VP, Worldwide Business Affairs
Aric Ackerman . . . COO
Sabrina Padwa . . . Head, Business Affairs/General Counsel
Chris Kim . . . Director, Marketing
Justin Wilkes . . . Executive Producer/Head, Content Group (NY)
Michael Hilliard . . . Head, Production, Content Group (NY)
Mike Bonfiglio . . . Producer (NY)
Andrew Fried . . . Producer (NY)
Rachel Dawson . . . Associate Producer (NY)
Nicole Pusateri . . . Coordinator, Content Group (NY)
Katy Leibold . . . Executive Assistant to Jon Kamen (NY)

100% ENTERTAINMENT

c/o Stanley Isaacs
322 S. Lucerne Blvd.
Los Angeles, CA 90020

PHONE . . . 323-461-6360
FAX . . . 323-934-0440
EMAIL . . . sisaacs100@mac.com
SECOND EMAIL . . . 100percent@iname.com
WEB SITE . . . www.100percentent.com

TYPES	Direct-to-Video/DVD - Features - Made-for-TV/Cable Movies - Mobile Content
DEVELOPMENT	Crush Depth - Everything Dies - Every Neighborhood Has One - Bite Me...A Love Story - Five Came Back
PRE-PRODUCTION	Marauders - Carnotaur
CREDITS	Megalodon - Last Gasp - Within the Rock - Ravager - Raptor Island (Sci Fi)
COMMENTS	Deal with Unreal Productions, Film and Music Entertainment, Inc.

Stanley Isaacs . . . President
Cooper Boone . . . Creative Executive

1492 PICTURES

4000 Warner Blvd., Producers Bldg. 3, Ste. 201
Burbank, CA 91522

PHONE . . . 818-954-4939
FAX . . . 818-954-7933

TYPES	Features
HAS DEAL WITH	Warner Bros. Pictures
UPCOMING RELEASES	Night at the Museum
CREDITS	Rent - Christmas with the Kranks - Harry Potter 1-3 - Bicentennial Man - Monkeybone - Stepmom - Jingle All the Way - Nine Months
SUBMISSION POLICY	No unsolicited material or query letters

Chris Columbus . . . Writer/Director/Producer/Partner
Michael Barnathan . . . President/Producer/Partner
Mark Radcliffe . . . Producer/Partner
Paula DuPré Pesmen . . . Associate Producer
Jennifer Blum . . . Sr. VP, Production
Karen Swallow . . . VP
Michelle Miller . . . Director, Development
Elizabeth Devereux . . . Assistant to Mr. Columbus
Jeanne Austin . . . Assistant to Mr. Radcliffe

19 ENTERTAINMENT, INC.

8560 West Sunset Blvd., 9th Fl.
West Hollywood, CA 90069

PHONE . . . 310-777-1940
FAX . . . 310-777-1949
WEB SITE . . . www.19.co.uk

TYPES	Animation - Direct-to-Video/DVD - Features - Music Videos - Reality TV - TV Series
CREDITS	American Idol - So You Think You Can Dance - From Justin to Kelly
SUBMISSION POLICY	No unsolicited submissions

Simon Fuller . . . CEO
Tom Ennis . . . President, 19 Recordings Ltd.
Iain Pirie . . . President, 19 Entertainment USA
Mal Young . . . President, Drama Development & Production, 19 TV
Staci Weiss . . . Sr. VP, 19 TV

21 LAPS ENTERTAINMENT

c/o Twentieth Century Fox
10201 W. Pico Blvd., Bldg. 49, Rm. 1
Los Angeles, CA 90035

PHONE . . . 310-369-4466
FAX . . . 310-969-0443

TYPES	Features - TV Series
HAS DEAL WITH	Twentieth Century Fox
DEVELOPMENT	Back Magick - Me, Me, Me
UPCOMING RELEASES	Night at the Museum
CREDITS	Cheaper by the Dozen 2 - Pepper Dennis
SUBMISSION POLICY	Through representaion only; No unsolicited material

Shawn Levy . . . Principal
Tom McNulty . . . President, Production
JJ Klein . . . VP, Television Production
Gene Roepke . . . VP, Production
Judd Cherry . . . Assistant to Shawn Levy
Regina Taufen . . . Assistant to Shawn Levy
Missy Foster . . . Assistant to Tom McNulty
Mazen Hassan . . . Assistant to JJ Klein

25C PRODUCTIONS
10202 W. Washington Blvd., Gable Bldg., Stes. 209-212
Culver City, CA 90232
PHONE 310-244-2980
TYPES TV Series
HAS DEAL WITH Sony Pictures Television
DEVELOPMENT Untitled Jeff Rake Project

Sarah Timberman . . . . . President/CEO (310-244-2980)
Carl Beverly . . . . . Partner (310-244-2975)
Chris Leanza . . . . . Executive Director, Development (310-244-2986)
Shana C. Waterman . . . . . Manager, Development (310-244-2978)

2929 PRODUCTIONS
9100 Wilshire Blvd., Ste. 500 West
Beverly Hills, CA 90212
PHONE 310-309-5200
FAX 310-309-5716
WEB SITE www.2929entertainment.com
TYPES Features
DEVELOPMENT Gambit - 342 - Infidelity for First-Time Fathers - Picaresque Revenge - Untitled Korean War Project - Belle Glade
PRODUCTION In Bloom
POST PRODUCTION Turistas (Fox Atomic) - Fast Track (Weinstein Co.)
UPCOMING RELEASES Black Christmas (Dimension)
CREDITS Akeelah and the Bee (Lionsgate) - Good Night and Good Luck - Godsend - Criminal - The Jacket - Herbie Hancock: Possibilities

Todd Wagner . . . . . Principal
Mark Cuban . . . . . Principal
Marc Butan . . . . . President (310-309-5704)
Mike Upton . . . . . Sr. VP, Physical Production Executive (310-309-5702)
Shebnem Askin . . . . . President, International (310-309-5706)
Jessica Roddy . . . . . Sr. VP, Business & Legal Affairs (310-309-5707)
Kent Kubena . . . . . Development & Production Executive (310-309-5705, kkubena@2929ent.com)
Couper Samuelson . . Development & Production Executive (310-309-5701, csamuelson@2929ent.com)
Robyn Heath . . . . . Development Assistant/Assistant to Marc Butan (310-309-5710, rheath@2929ent.com)
Dorka Hegedus-Lum . . . Physical Production Assistant/Assistant to Mike Upton (310-309-5799, dhegedus@2929ent.com)
Deanna Sanchez . . . . . Business Affairs Executive
Ellen Nicholson . . . . . Business & Legal Affairs Assistant/Assistant to Jessica Roddy (310-309-5780, dhorwich@2929.com)
Stephanie Rich . . . . . International Assistant/Assistant to Shebnem Askin (310-309-5703, srich@2929international.com)

3 ARTS ENTERTAINMENT, INC.
9460 Wilshire Blvd., 7th Fl.
Beverly Hills, CA 90212
PHONE 310-888-3200
FAX 310-888-3210
TYPES Features - TV Series
CREDITS The Office - It's Always Sunny in Philadelphia - Everybody Hates Chris - The Chris Rock Show - King of the Hill - The Hughleys - Carnivàle
COMMENTS Also a management company

Dave Becky . . . . . Talent Manager
Stephanie Davis . . . . . Talent Manager
Nick Frenkel . . . . . Talent Manager
Howard Klein . . . . . Partner/Talent Manager/Producer
Pam Kohl . . . . . Talent Manager
Tom Lassally . . . . . Talent Manager/Producer
Molly Madden . . . . . Talent Manager
David Miner . . . . . Talent Manager
Michael Rotenberg . . . . . Partner/Talent Manager/Producer
Mark Schulman . . . . . Talent Manager
Erwin Stoff . . . . . Partner/Talent Manager/Producer
Tucker Voorhees . . . . . Talent Manager
Greg Walter . . . . . Talent Manager
Scott Wexler . . . . . Talent Manager
Brad Bertner . . . . . Executive Director, Development

3 BALL PRODUCTIONS
1600 Rosecrans Ave., Bldg. 7
Manhattan Beach, CA 90266
PHONE 310-727-3337
FAX 310-727-3339
TYPES Reality TV
CREDITS Supergroup - Beauty and the Geek - The Biggest Loser - For Love or Money - Endurance - Moolah Beach - Breaking Bonaduce - Going Hollywood - Unan1mous

Todd Nelson . . . . . Executive Producer
JD Roth . . . . . Executive Producer
Adam Greener . . . . . VP, Development
Angela Malloy . . . . . Director, Development

3 RING CIRCUS FILMS
3699 Wilshire Blvd., Ste.1250
Los Angeles, CA 90010
PHONE 213-251-3300
FAX 213-251-3350
EMAIL . . . . . johnsid@3ringcircus.tv
WEB SITE www.3ringcircus.tv
TYPES Commercials - Features - Made-for-TV/Cable Movies - Reality TV
DEVELOPMENT Traces - Christmas City - Second Wind
CREDITS The Darwin Awards - Dream with the Fishes - Tear It Down - One - Cherish - Confessions
COMMENTS Independent film production

John Sideropoulos . . . . . CEO

360 PICTURES/FGM ENTERTAINMENT

301 N. Canon Dr., Ste. 207
Beverly Hills, CA 90210
PHONE 310-205-9900

TYPES	Features
HAS DEAL WITH	Sony Pictures Entertainment
POST PRODUCTION	Crossover
CREDITS	Stigmata - Species - Internal Affairs - Ronin
SUBMISSION POLICY	No unsolicited submissions; No faxed resumés or queries

Frank Mancuso Jr. . . . . Producer/President
Ittay Arad . . . . VP
Jennifer Nieves . . . . VP

3N1 ENTERTAINMENT

11726 San Vicente Blvd., Ste. 360
Los Angeles, CA 90049
PHONE 310-773-1147
EMAIL . . . . info@3n1ent.com
WEB SITE www.3n1ent.com

TYPES	Features - TV Series
DEVELOPMENT	3:52 (Sci Fi Channel)
PRODUCTION	Mercy
CREDITS	Club Meds
SUBMISSION POLICY	No unsolicited submissions

John Tinker . . . . Writer/Producer/Partner
Laura Hudson . . . . Writer/Producer/Partner
Celeste Wade . . . . Writer/Producer/Partner

3WOLVES PRODUCTIONS

8491 Sunset Blvd., Ste. 553
West Hollywood, CA 90069
PHONE 310-592-7613
FAX 310-260-8996
EMAIL . . . . roger@3wolvesproductions.com
SECOND EMAIL . . . . rita@3wolvesproductions.com
WEB SITE www.3wolvesproductions.com

TYPES	Direct-to-Video/DVD - Features
DEVELOPMENT	Nomads - A World Away
PRE-PRODUCTION	Curlow Creek
POST PRODUCTION	Chasing Dinner
UPCOMING RELEASES	Even Money
CREDITS	Find Me Guilty
SUBMISSION POLICY	No unsolicited phone calls or materials
COMMENTS	East Coast office: 125 W. 55th St., New York, NY 10019

Roger Zamudio . . . . CEO
Rita Branch . . . . COO
Mikuil Elias . . . . CFO (NY) (212-424-8133)
Judah Levi . . . . President/Producer
Joseph Gad . . . . Development/Production

40 ACRES & A MULE FILMWORKS, INC.

124 DeKalb Ave.
Brooklyn, NY 11217
PHONE 718-624-3703

TYPES	Animation - Features - Reality TV - TV Series
HAS DEAL WITH	NBC Universal Television Studio
CREDITS	When the Levee Broke (HBO) - Inside Man - She Hate Me - 25th Hour - 3 A.M. - Bamboozled - The Original Kings of Comedy - Love and Basketball - The Best Man - Summer of Sam - He Got Game - 4 Little Girls - Get on the Bus - Girl 6 - Clockers - Crooklyn - Malcolm X - Do the Right Thing

Spike Lee . . . . Chairman

44 BLUE PRODUCTIONS, INC.

4040 Vineland Ave., Ste. 105
Studio City, CA 91604
PHONE 818-760-4442
FAX 818-760-1509
EMAIL . . . . reception@44blue.com
WEB SITE www.44blue.com

TYPES	Documentaries - Features - Reality TV - TV Series
DEVELOPMENT	Home Sweet Home - Operation: Bootstrap - Stringers
PRE-PRODUCTION	Salvage Sqaud (Pilot) - Rocco (Pilot)
PRODUCTION	Survive This (Discovery) - Designing Blind (A&E) - City in Fear (MSNBC) - Find & Design (A&E) - Mega Movers (The History Channel) - Lockup (MSNBC) - Inside (Court TV)
CREDITS	Caesars 24/7 (A&E) - MSNBC Investigates - Investigative Reports (A&E) - Lock Up (MSNBC) - Headliners & Legends (MSNBC) - Small Shots (TNN) - The True Story of Black Hawk Down (History Channel) - Wide Open (A&E) - Cell Dogs (Animal Planet) - What Should You Do? (Lifetime) - Collector Inspector (HGTV)

Rasha Drachkovitch . . . . President/Executive Producer
Stephanie Drachkovitch . . . . Sr. VP/Executive Producer
Glenn Meehan . . . . VP, Development
Stuart Zwagil . . . . VP, Production
Sarah Poage . . . . Executive in Charge of Production

4TH ROW FILMS
27 W. 20th St., Ste. 1006
New York, NY 10011
PHONE .212-974-0082
FAX .212-627-3090
TYPES: Documentaries - Features - Internet Content - Made-for-TV/Cable Movies - Reality TV - TV Series
DEVELOPMENT: Do I Look Fat in This? - Crazy White Mother - Wilton Dedge - Sudden Rain
PRE-PRODUCTION: Victor in December
PRODUCTION: The Meaning of Life - All In: America's New Obsession with Poker - The Story of My Parents
CREDITS: Anytown, USA - A Reason to Believe - Killing Time - Twelve - The Lucky Ones
COMMENTS: Produces branding and marketing films for Fortune 500 companies

Douglas Tirola .President/Producer
Susan Bedusa .Director, Development
Robert Greene .Post Production Supervisor

51 MINDS ENTERTAINMENT
6565 Sunset Blvd., Ste. 301
Los Angeles, CA 90028
PHONE .323-463-6100/323-466-9200
FAX .323-466-9202
TYPES: Miniseries - Reality TV - Specials - TV Series
HAS DEAL WITH: VH1
PRODUCTION: Celebrity Paranormal Project
POST PRODUCTION: Surreal Life Fame Games
CREDITS: My Fair Brady - The Surreal Life - Flavor of Love

Cris Abrego .Executive Producer
Mark Cronin .Executive Producer

57-T PRODUCTIONS, INC.
2800 Neilson Way, Ste. 911
Santa Monica, CA 90405
PHONE .310-281-8688
FAX .310-392-8669
EMAIL .todoroff@ix.netcom.com
WEB SITE .www.tomtodoroff.com
TYPES: Features - Direct-to-Video/DVD - Made-for-TV/Cable Movies - TV Series
CREDITS: Borrowed Hearts - Monday After the Miracle - A Test of Love - Second Honeymoon - The Sons of Mistletoe - The Survivors Club (CBS) - No Vacancy - RSC Meets USA: Working Shakespeare

Tom Todoroff .Producer
Stephanie Carrie .Executive Assistant to Mr. Todoroff

6 PICTURES
14358 Magnolia Blvd., Ste. 135
Sherman Oaks, CA 91423
PHONE .818-789-7666
EMAIL .6pictures@earthlink.net
TYPES: Direct-to-Video/DVD - Features - Made-for-TV/Cable Movies
CREDITS: Tail Sting - Wes Craven Presents Carnival of Souls - Fat Man and Mr. Taco - Being Ron Jeremy - Three Shots - Captain Apache: Laugh Track Edition

Peter Soby Jr. .Producer
Kit Klehm .Partner
Scott Kimball .Director, Finance
Brad Parnell .Production Coordinator

777 ENTERTAINMENT GROUP, LTD.
1015 Gayley Ave., Ste. 1128
Los Angeles, CA 90024
PHONE .310-824-0664
EMAIL .admin@777entgroup.com
WEB SITE .www.777entgroup.com
TYPES: Animation - Direct-to-Video/DVD - Documentaries - Features - Music Videos - Reality TV - TV Series
DEVELOPMENT: Wraith - Where There's a Will - Springer & Co. - Hip Hop Superstar - Lotto People - Clinch - Nine Lives - Mercy's Mission - Double Doors - Soul Feud - Most Hated Man
PRE-PRODUCTION: The Roaches - Am I My Brother's Keeper? - Untitled Jazz Project
POST PRODUCTION: Richard III
CREDITS: The Beat - Red Is the Color of...

Marcello Robinson .President

7PONIES PRODUCTIONS
6230 Wilshire Blvd., Ste. 2060
Los Angeles, CA 90048
PHONE .323-634-9091
FAX .323-634-9091
EMAIL .7ponies@7ponies.com
WEB SITE .www.7ponies.com
TYPES: Direct-to-Video/DVD - Documentaries - Features - Reality TV - TV Series
DEVELOPMENT: Untitled College Feature - Bring It to the Table - Untitled Sports Docudrama - Debutantes: The Road to the Ball - Heaven's Gate Cult
CREDITS: Tripped Out - 10 Things Every Guy Should Experience - Crash Test - Sorority Life 1-3 - Fraternity Life 1&2 - E! True Hollywood Story: Redd Foxx, Linda Blair, Bo Derek - Heaven's Gate: The Untold Story

Sergio Myers .Executive Producer

THE 7TH FLOOR
19 W. 21st St., Ste. 706
New York, NY 10010
PHONE .212-244-2317
FAX .212-244-1218
EMAIL .general@the7thfloor.com
WEB SITE .www.the7thfloor.com
TYPES Commercials - Features - Music Videos - TV Series
PRODUCTION The Cake Eaters (57th & Irving Productions)
POST PRODUCTION Gardener of Eden (Appian Way)
CREDITS Manito - Twentynine Palms - Room - Blackballed: The Bobby Dukes Story - Cry Funny Happy
SUBMISSION POLICY No unsolicited material; Logline and synopsis only

Allen Bain .Producer
Jesse Scolaro .Producer
Darren Goldberg .Producer

8790 PICTURES, INC.
c/o Perry & Neidorf, LLC
9720 Wilshire Blvd., 3rd Fl.
Beverly Hills, CA 90212
PHONE .310-471-9983/310-550-1254
FAX .310-471-6366/310-550-2039
EMAIL .8790pictures@gmail.com
TYPES Direct-to-Video/DVD - Features
DEVELOPMENT Teen Idol - Every Boy's Got One - Staying Fat for Sarah Byrnes - No Flying in the House
CREDITS Because of Winn-Dixie
SUBMISSION POLICY No unsolicited material; Email query letters only

Joan Singleton .Writer/Producer
Ralph Singleton .Producer

9 SQUARED
1999 Broadway, Ste. 1250
Denver, CO 80202
PHONE .720-889-0014
FAX .720-889-0016
EMAIL .info@9squared.com
SECOND EMAIL .bizdev@9squared.com
WEB SITE .www.9squared.com
TYPES Mobile Content

Brian Casazza .CEO
Ted Suh .Chief Marketing Officer

9.14 PICTURES
1124 Walnut St., Ste. 4
Philadelphia, PA 19107
PHONE .215-238-0707
FAX .215-238-0663
EMAIL .info@914pictures.com
WEB SITE .www.914pictures.com
TYPES Commercials - Documentaries - Features - Miniseries - Music Videos - Reality TV - Specials - TV Series
COMPLETED UNRELEASED Two Days in April
CREDITS Rock School

Don Argott .Owner
Sheena M. Joyce .Owner
Gary E. Irwin .UPM/Producer

900 FILMS
1611-A S. Melrose Dr., #362
Vista, CA 92081
PHONE .760-477-2470
FAX .760-477-2478
EMAIL .irene@900films.com
WEB SITE .www.900films.com
TYPES Commercials - Direct-to-Video/DVD - Documentaries - Features - Reality TV - TV Series
CREDITS Grind (Warner Bros.) - King of Skate (Pay-per-view) - Tony Hawk: Gigantic Skatepark Tour (ESPN) - Tony Hawk's Trick Tips (DVD) - Hawk's HuckJam Diaries (Fuel)

Tony Hawk .Principal/Professional Skateboarder
Irene Navarro .COO/Producer
Jared Prindle .Producer
Matt Haring .Editor

A BAND APART
8530 Wilshire Blvd., Ste. 500
Beverly Hills, CA 90211
PHONE .323-951-4600
FAX .323-951-4601
WEB SITE .www.abandapart.com
TYPES Commercials - Direct-to-Video/DVD - Documentaries - Features - Internet Content - Miniseries - Music Videos - Reality TV - TV Series
CREDITS An Inconvenient Truth - Pulp Fiction - Reservoir Dogs - Good Will Hunting - Jackie Brown - The Mexican - Kill Bill - Havana Nights - Goal - Sherman Halsey - Dodge/HHR (Commercial) - Build or Bust (TV) - Earthsea

Lawrence Bender .Producer/Partner
Quentin Tarantino .Writer/Director/Partner
Karen Barber .Producer
Janet Jeffries .Creative Executive
Jason Olin .Creative Executive
Zac Minor .Executive Assistant

A WINK AND A NOD PRODUCTIONS
843 12th St., Ste. 4
Santa Monica, CA 90403
PHONE .310-394-5752
EMAIL .queries@awinkandanod.com
WEB SITE .www.awinkandanod.com
TYPES Features - Made-for-TV/Cable Movies - Specials
DEVELOPMENT Unsportsmanlike Conduct (Shutt/Jones Productions) - The Clio Awards (Actuality Productions) - City of 9 Dragons (Blue Star Movies/Lion Rock Productions)
PRE-PRODUCTION Miss Cupid's Beau (Hallmark Channel) - Stand by Love (Blue Star Movies) - Take a Number (Reunion Pictures)
POST PRODUCTION Hunter's Moon (Stouffer Entertainment)
CREDITS Santa Junior (Hallmark Channel)
SUBMISSION POLICY Not currently accepting queries; Referrals only
COMMENTS No reality programming

Wendy Winks .President
C. J. Helm .Assistant

A&E NETWORK

235 E. 45th St.
New York, NY 10017
PHONE 212-210-1400
FAX 212-983-4370
WEB SITE . . . . . www.aetv.com
SECOND WEB SITE . . . . . www.biography.com

TYPES	Direct-to-Video/DVD - Documentaries - Made-for-TV/Cable Movies - TV Series
DEVELOPMENT	American Teen Movie - Jesus Camp - Gene Simmons' Family Jewels - Wedding March - Sons of Hollywood - Big Spender - Move This House - Sell This House - Designing Blind - Wildfires - Kings of South Beach - Last Requests - Six Months
CREDITS	Intervention - Knievel's Wild Ride - Caesars 24/7 - Family Plots - Growing Up Gotti - Dog the Bounty Hunter - The First 48 - Biography - Airline - American Justice - Cold Case Files - City Confidential - King of Cars - Investigative Reports - MI-5 - Inked - Criss Angel: Mindfreak - Driving Force - Dallas SWAT
COMMENTS	Includes The Biography Channel

Nickolas Davatzes . . . . . CEO Emeritus, AETN
Abbe Raven . . . . . President/CEO, AETN
Daniel Davids . . . . . President, The History Channel, USA
Whitney Goit . . . . . Sr. Executive VP, AETN
Gerard Gruosso . . . . . CFO/Executive VP, AETN
Melvin Berning . . . . . Executive VP, Ad Sales, AETN
Robert DeBitetto . . . . . Executive VP/General Manager, A&E Network
Jim Greiner . . . . Executive VP, New Enterprises, Production & Internet Services
David Zagin . . . . . Executive VP, Distribution, A&E Television Networks
Nancy Dubuc . . . . . Sr. VP, Nonfiction Programming & New Media Content, A&E/A&E IndieFilms
Nick Febrizio . . . . . Sr. VP, Research & Strategy
Michael Feeney . . . . . Sr. VP, Corporate Communications
Joan Gundlach . . . . . Sr. VP, Affiliate Sales & Marketing
Bill Harris . . . . . Sr. VP, Production & Network Operations, AETN
Tom Heymann . . . . . Sr. VP/General Manager, The Biography Channel
Macie Huwiler . . . . . Sr. VP, National Ad Sales
Tana Nugent Jamieson . . . . . Sr. VP, Drama, A&E Network
Maria Komodikis . . . . . Sr. VP/General Manager, A&E International
Melinda McLaughlin . . . . . Sr. VP, Integrated Sales & Marketing
Dr. Libby O'Connell . . . . . Sr. VP, Corporate Outreach, Chief Historian
Peter Olsen . . . . . Sr. VP, Ad Sales
Joy Phoenix . . . . . Sr. VP, National Accounts
Steve Ronson . . . . . Sr. VP, Enterprises
Jennifer Ball . . . . . VP, Affiliate Marketing
Neil A. Cohen . . . . . VP, Non-Fiction & Alternative Programming
Delia Fine . . . . . VP, Film & Drama Programming
Mary Heed . . . . . VP, Sales Research
Risa Rosenthal . . . . . VP, Direct Response Advertising
Robert Sharenow . . . . . VP, Nonfiction & Alternative Programming
Nani Shin-Wannemacher . . VP, Affiliate Sales & Marketing, Northeast Region
Scott Vila . . . . . VP, Original Programming
Kate Winn . . . . . VP, Video Sales & Marketing, Consumer Marketing
Dan Silberman . . . . . Sr. Director, Publicity
Laura Fleury . . . . . Director, Documentary Programming, A&E
Lynn Gardner . . . . . Director, Public Relations, The History Channel
Kerri Tarmey . . . . . Director, Corporate Communications, AETN
Carrie Trimmer . . . . . Director, Licensing, Consumer Products
Marlea Willis . . . . . Director, Program Publicity, A&E
Gina Nocero . . . . . Manager, Program Publicity, A&E
Carlos Baez . . . . . Account Director, Southeast Region
Eileen Fitzpatrick . . . . . Listings Editor
Mark Silverman . . . . . Coordinator, Corporate Communications

AARDMAN ANIMATIONS

Gasferry Rd.
Bristol BS1 6UN, United Kingdom
PHONE 44-117-984-8485
FAX 44-117-984-8486
WEB SITE . . . . . www.aardman.com

TYPES	Animation - Commercials - Features - TV Series
HAS DEAL WITH	DreamWorks SKG
DEVELOPMENT	Creature Comforts (TV Series) - Chop Socky Chooks (CG Animation)
CREDITS	Wallace and Gromit: The Curse of the Were-Rabbit - Chicken Run

Nick Park . . . . . Managing Director
Peter Lord . . . . . Managing Director
David Sproxton . . . . . Managing Director
Miles Bullough . . . . . Head, Broadcast & Development
Stephen Moore . . . . . Head, Features/CEO
Heather Wright . . . . . Head, Commercials

ABANDON PICTURES, INC.

810 Seventh Ave., 11th Fl.
New York, NY 10019
PHONE 212-246-4445
FAX 212-397-8361
WEB SITE . . . . . www.abandonent.com

TYPES	Features - Mobile Content
DEVELOPMENT	And Soon the Darkness - Otherwise Engaged
PRE-PRODUCTION	Picasso at the Lapin Agile
CREDITS	Oxygen - Pros and Cons - Time Shifters - Off the Lip - Mexico City - Scotland, PA - Glory Days
SUBMISSION POLICY	No unsolicited material
COMMENTS	Partner in Mythic Entertainment; Online games

Karen Lauder . . . . . President/CEO
Deborah Marinoff . . . . . Producer

ABC DAYTIME

77 W. 66th St.
New York, NY 10023
PHONE 212-456-7777/818-560-1000
WEB SITE . . . . . www.abc.com

TYPES	TV Series - Reality TV
COMMENTS	West Coast office: 500 S. Buena Vista St., Burbank, CA 91521

Brian Frons . . . . . President, Daytime, Disney-ABC Television Group
Dominick Nuzzi . . . . . Sr. VP, Production & Administration
Harriet Abraham . . . . . VP, Programming Operations
Sue Johnson . . . . . VP, Talent Development & East Coast Programming
Abbie Schiller . . . . . VP, Media & Talent Relations
Julie Carruthers . . . . . Executive Producer, *All My Children*
Bill Geddie . . . . . Executive Producer, *The View*
Jill Farren Phelps . . . . . Executive Producer, *General Hospital*
Frank Valentini . . . . . Executive Producer, *One Life to Live*
Randall Barone . . . . . Director, Reality Programming

ABC ENTERTAINMENT TELEVISION GROUP

500 S. Buena Vista St.
Burbank, CA 91521

PHONE	818-460-7777
WEB SITE	www.abc.com
TYPES	Made-for-TV/Cable Movies - Reality TV - TV Series
PROVIDES DEAL TO	The Bedford Falls Company - Big Light Productions - Bungalow 78 Productions - Embassy Row LLC - Four Boys Films - Harpo Films, Inc. - Launa Newman Productions (LNP) - Bill Melendez Productions - Misher Films - Next Entertainment - Olmos Productions, Inc. - Marc Platt Productions

Anne Sweeney	Co-Chair, Disney Media Networks/President, Disney-ABC Television Group
Stephen McPherson	President, ABC Entertainment
Alex Wallau	President, ABC Network Operations & Administration
Eleo Hensleigh	Chief Marketing Officer/Executive VP, Marketing & Brand Strategy, Disney-ABC Television Group
Alan N. Braverman	Sr. Executive VP/General Counsel/Secretary, ABC Inc. & Walt Disney Company
Jeffrey Bader	Executive VP, ABC Entertainment
Francie Calfo	Executive VP, Development & Current Programming, ABC Entertainment
James Hedges	Executive VP/CFO, ABC Television Network
Keli Lee	Executive VP, Casting
Jana Winograde	Executive VP, Business Affairs, ABC Entertainment
Andrea Wong	Executive VP, Alternative Programming, Specials & Latenight
Kevin Brockman	Sr. VP, Communications, Disney-ABC Television Group
Olivia Cohen-Cutler	Sr. VP, Broadcast Standards & Practices
Samie Kim Falvey	Sr. VP, Comedy Development
Bruce Gersh	Sr. VP, Business Development, ABC Entertainment Group
Jennifer Mayo	Sr. VP, Business Affairs
Jim McClintock	Sr. VP, ABC Television Network, Network Media
Milinda McNeely	Sr. VP, Legal Affairs
Suzanne Patmore-Gibbs	Sr. VP, Drama Development
Kim Rozenfeld	Sr. VP, Current Drama
Quinn Taylor	Sr. VP, Movies/Minis, *Wonderful World of Disney*
Sharon Williams	Sr. VP, Communications Resources, Disney-ABC Television Group
Josh Barry	VP, Drama Development
David Cohen	VP, Legal Affairs, ABC
Vicki Dummer	VP, Alternative Series Programming
Channing Dungey	VP, Drama Development
Danielle Greene	VP, ABC Latenight
Amy Hartwick	VP, Comedy Development
Rosalie Joseph	VP, Casting
Brian Morewitz	VP, Drama Development
Deborah O'Brien	VP, Contracts Administration
Kevin Plunkett	VP, Current Comedy
Alison Rou	VP, Media Relations
John Saade	VP, Alternative Series & Specials
Cheryl Stanley	VP, Current Drama
Kenneth Warun	VP, Comedy Promotion
Hope Hartman	Head, Publicity, ABC Entertainment
Jocelyn Diaz	Executive Director, Drama Development
Brian Harvey	Executive Director, Drama Development
Michael McDonald	Executive Director, Drama Series
Marci Phillips	Executive Director, Casting
Michael Erlinger	Director, Business Affairs
Esrin Gozukizil	Director, Current Drama
Cathy Korda	Director, Program Planning & Scheduling
Kelly Luegenbiehl	Director, Comedy Development
Patrick Maguire	Director, Comedy Development
Adam Myman	Director, Current Programming
Zack Olin	Director, Current Comedy Programming

(Continued)

ABC ENTERTAINMENT TELEVISION GROUP (Continued)

Nicholas Pepper	Director, Drama Development
Brandon Reigg	Director, Alternative Series & Specials
Raymond Ricord	Director, Movies/Minis, *Wonderful World of Disney*
Heather Roth	Director, Comedy Development
Anne Delavigne	Manager, Movies/Minis, *Wonderful World of Disney*
Erin Horowitz	Manager, Current Programming
Sarah Hughes	Manager, Comedy Development
Rob Mills	Manager, Alternative Series & Specials

ABC FAMILY

3800 W. Alameda Ave.
Burbank, CA 91505

PHONE	818-560-1000
FAX	818-840-1973
WEB SITE	www.abcfamily.com
TYPES	Internet Content - Made-for-TV/Cable Movies - Miniseries - Reality TV - Specials - TV Series
DEVELOPMENT	The Other Mall - The Initiation of Sarah
PRE-PRODUCTION	Three Moons Over Milford - Lincoln Heights
PRODUCTION	Mary Christmas
UPCOMING RELEASES	Back on Campus
CREDITS	Kyle XY - Wildfire - Beautiful People - Falcon Beach - Fallen

Paul Lee	President
Laura Nathanson	Executive VP, Sales & Marketing, ABC Family & Kids
Kate Juergens	Sr. VP, Original Programming & Development
Ben Pyne	Sr. VP, Affiliate Sales & Marketing
John Rood	Sr. VP, Brand Marketing
Tricia Wilber	Sr. VP, Sales & Promotions
Tom Zappala	Sr. VP, Program Acquisitions & Scheduling
Brooke Bowman	VP, Programming & Development
Annie Fort	VP, Media Relations
Mina Lefevre	VP, Programming & Development

ABC SPORTS

A Division of ESPN
47 W. 66th St., 13th Fl.
New York, NY 10023

PHONE	212-456-7777
FAX	212-456-4317
WEB SITE	www.abcsports.com
TYPES	TV Series
PROVIDES DEAL TO	MRB Productions, Inc.
COMMENTS	Sports programming

George Bodenheimer	President, ESPN, Inc. & ABC Sports/Co-Chairman, Disney Media Networks
Ed Erhardt	President, ESPN/ABC Sports Customer Marketing & Sales
Ben Pyne	President, Disney & ESPN Networks Affiliate Sales & Marketing
Steve Anderson	Executive VP, Production & Technical Operations
Sean Bratches	Executive VP, Affiliate Sales & Marketing
Christine Driessen	Executive VP/CFO
Ed Durso	Executive VP, Administration
Chuck Gerber	Executive VP, Collegiate Sports
Salil Mehta	Executive VP, ESPN Enterprises
Chuck Pagano	Executive VP, Technology
John Skipper	Executive VP, Content
Norby Williamson	Executive VP, Studio & Remote Productions
Russell Wolff	Executive VP/Managing Director, ESPN International
Michael Pearl	Sr. VP, Production
Bob Toms	VP, Production
Mark Mandel	Sr. Director, Media Relations

ABERRATION FILMS
311 N. Robertson Blvd., Ste. 737
Beverly Hills, CA 90211
PHONE . . . 310-385-0585
EMAIL . . . aberrationfilms@yahoo.com
WEB SITE . . . www.aberrationfilms.com
TYPES: Documentaries - Features - TV Series
DEVELOPMENT: Film: Lost Not Found - Coyote Highway; TV Series: The Jury - Tribute - The Skeptics
POST PRODUCTION: Punk's Not Dead
CREDITS: Brick (Focus Features)

Susan Dynner . . . Director/Producer

ACAPPELLA PICTURES
8271 Melrose Ave., Ste. 101
Los Angeles, CA 90046
PHONE . . . 323-782-8200
FAX . . . 323-782-8210
TYPES: Documentaries - Features - TV Series
DEVELOPMENT: Addiction, Inc. - Good Country - Question of Sex
CREDITS: The Aviator - The Brave - The House of Mirth

Charles Evans Jr. . . . President
Charmaine Parcero . . . Development/Production

ACME PRODUCTIONS
4000 Warner Blvd., Bldg. 19, Rm. 221B
Burbank, CA 91522
PHONE . . . See Below
TYPES: TV Series
HAS DEAL WITH: Warner Bros. Television Production
DEVELOPMENT: Untitled Adam Ferrara Project - Untitled Chris Case Project - Unititled Kevin Abbott Project
CREDITS: The War at Home - Reba - Titus

Mindy Schultheis . . . Executive Producer (818-954-7779)
Michael Hanel . . . Executive Producer (818-954-7771)
Adam Blutt . . . No Title (818-954-7440)

ACT III PRODUCTIONS
100 N. Crescent Dr., Ste. 250
Beverly Hills, CA 90210
PHONE . . . 310-385-4111
FAX . . . 310-385-4080
TYPES: Features - TV Series
CREDITS: Fried Green Tomatoes - 704 Hauser - The Powers That Be
COMMENTS: Also Act III Licensing

Norman Lear . . . Chairman/CEO, Act III Communications
Julia Dyer . . . CFO
Marilyn Pessin . . . Executive Assistant to Norman Lear

ACTUAL REALITY PICTURES
6725 Sunset Blvd., Ste. 350
Los Angeles, CA 90028
PHONE . . . 310-202-1272
FAX . . . 310-202-1502
EMAIL . . . info@actualreality.tv
WEB SITE . . . www.actualreality.tv
TYPES: Documentaries - Features - Reality TV - TV Series
DEVELOPMENT: Untitled Nonscripted TV Project (Tribeca Productions/NBC)
PRODUCTION: Coach K (Discovery) - Ten Days That Changed America (History Channel)
COMPLETED UNRELEASED: Thin (HBO)
CREDITS: Black.White. (FX) - 30 Days (FX) - American High (FOX/PBS) - Military Diaries (VH1) - Freshman Diaries (Showtime) - American Candidate (Showtime) - Residents (TLC/Discovery Health) - Flip that House (Discovery) - Bound for Glory (ESPN) - Making Dazed (AMC)

R.J. Cutler . . . President
Michael Bernstein . . . Executive in Charge of Production
Mary Lisio . . . Director, Development

ACTUALITY PRODUCTIONS
20335 Ventura Blvd., Ste. 300
Woodland Hills, CA 91364
PHONE . . . 818-444-5000
FAX . . . 818-444-5001
WEB SITE . . . www.actualityproductions.com
TYPES: Documentaries - Internet Content - Mobile Content - Reality TV - Specials - TV Series

Bruce L. Paisner . . . President
Jerry Shevick . . . Executive VP, Documentary & Reality Programming
Bari Carrelli . . . VP, Documentary & Reality Programming
Jim Deutch . . . VP, Intergrated Marketing
Aurelia White . . . Manager, Development

AD HOMINEM ENTERPRISES
506 Santa Monica Blvd., Ste. 400
Santa Monica, CA 90401
PHONE . . . 310-394-1444
FAX . . . 310-394-5401
TYPES: Features
HAS DEAL WITH: Twentieth Century Fox - Searchlight Pictures
DEVELOPMENT: The King of California

Alexander Payne . . . Director/Producer
Jim Taylor . . . Writer/Director
Jim Burke . . . Producer
Evan Endicott . . . Director, Development
Anna Musso . . . Assistant to Alexander Payne

ORLY ADELSON PRODUCTIONS
12304 Santa Monica Blvd., Ste. 115
Los Angeles, CA 90025
PHONE . . . 310-442-2012
FAX . . . 310-442-2013
TYPES: Features - Made-for-TV/Cable Movies - Reality TV - TV Series
CREDITS: Code Breakers - The Junction Boys - The Man Who Saved Christmas - D.C. Sniper - Playmakers - Hustle - 3: The Dale Earnhardt Story - Mrs. Ashboro's Cat - Mystery Woman - Twelve Days of Terror - The Madam's Family: The Truth About the Canal Street Brothel - Plainsong - Cavedweller - Odd Girl Out - Tilt
SUBMISSION POLICY: No unsolicited submissions

Orly Adelson . . . President
Troy Westergaard . . . Executive Producer
Jon Eskenas . . . Sr. VP, Development
Kevin Meisler . . . Development Assistant

*ADELSTEIN PRODUCTIONS

9606 Santa Monica Blvd., 2nd Fl.
Beverly Hills, CA 90210
PHONE .310-362-2200
FAX .310-248-4969
TYPES Features - TV Series
HAS DEAL WITH Twentieth Century Fox Television
CREDITS Black Christmas - Prison Break - Tru Calling - Point Pleasant

Marty Adelstein .Executive Producer/Principal (2222)
Michael Thorn .President, TV Development (2207)
Scott Nemes .Sr. VP, Feature Production (2206)
Heather Fox .Manager, TV Development (2203)
Nick Valenta .Assistant to Michael Thorn (2209)
Jarrod Murray .Assistant to Scott Nemes (2214)

ADIRONDACK PICTURES

451 Greenwich St., 7th Fl.
New York, NY 10013
PHONE .212-343-2405
EMAIL .info@adirondackpics.com
WEB SITE .www.adirondackpics.com
TYPES Documentaries - Features
POST PRODUCTION The Night of the White Pants
SUBMISSION POLICY Accepted through an agent or lawyer only
COMMENTS Also finances

Paul Hardart .Partner
Tom Hardart .Partner
Pauline Piechota .No Title

[adult swim]

*ADULT SWIM

1050 Techwood Dr. NW
Atlanta, GA 30318
PHONE .404-885-2263
FAX .404-885-4312
WEB SITE .www.adultswim.com
TYPES Animation - TV Series
CREDITS Morel Orel - Minoriteam - Metalocalypse - Frisky Dingo - Assy McGee - Saul of the Mole Man - Lucy, The Daughter of the Devil - Robot Chicken - Family Guy - Tom Goes to the Mayor - Harvey Birdman, Attorney at Law - The Venture Bros. - Aqua Teen Hunger Force - 12 oz. Mouse - Squidbillies - The Boondocks - Futurama; Animé: InuYasha - The Big O - Cowboy Bebop - Witch Hunter Robin - Trigun - The Super Milk Chan Show - Fullmetal Alchemist - Ghost in the Shell: Stand Alone Complex

Jim Samples .Executive VP/General Manager, Cartoon Network
Mike Lazzo .Sr. VP, Programming & Production
Keith Crofford .VP, Production
Nick Weidenfeld .Manager, Development

AEI-ATCHITY ENTERTAINMENT INTERNATIONAL, INC.

9601 Wilshire Blvd., Box 1202
Beverly Hills, CA 90210
PHONE .323-932-0407/212-421-0256
FAX .323-932-0321
EMAIL .submissions@aeionline.com
WEB SITE .www.aeionline.com
SECOND WEB SITE .www.thewriterslifeline.com
TYPES Direct-to-Video/DVD - Documentaries - Features - Made-for-TV/Cable Movies - Miniseries - Reality TV - TV Series
DEVELOPMENT Henry's List of Wrongs (New Line) - Ripley's Believe It or Not (Paramount) - Demon Keeper (Fox 2000) - Prince of Pools - Nano - End of the Line - Abduction - Haunt - Stepshow - The Un-Dead - The Secret Castle - Hang Time - Code Gray - Cool Kids - The Last Valentine
PRE-PRODUCTION Meg (New Line)
CREDITS Features: Falling Over Backwards (Astral) - Joe Somebody (Fox 2000) - Life or Something Like It (New Regency); TV: Shades of Love (Cinemax) - Amityville: The Evil Escapes - Shadow of Obsession (NBC) - The Madam's Family: The Truth About the Canal Street Brothel (CBS)
COMMENTS Literary management (writers and writer-directors); Book publishing; Affiliated with Writers' Lifeline (phone: 323-932-0905), Warp & Weft Inc., The Studio Matrix LLC and with Daystar Entertainment, a division of AEI

Ken Atchity .Chairman/Partner
Chi-Li Wong .President/Partner
Greg F. Dix .VP/CEO, Daystar Entertainment
Brenna Lui .VP, Development
Michael Kuciak .Associate Manager/VP, Acquisitions & Marketing, Film & TV
Jennifer Pope .Development

AGAMEMNON FILMS, INC.

650 N. Bronson Ave., Ste. B-225
Los Angeles, CA 90004
PHONE .323-960-4066
FAX .323-960-4067
WEB SITE .www.agamemnon.com
TYPES Animation - Documentaries - Features - Made-for-TV/Cable Movies
DEVELOPMENT Tundra - The Search for Michael Rockefeller - DeMille Directs - Freya of the Seven Isles
CREDITS Treasure Island - The Crucifer of Blood - A Man for All Seasons - Mother Lode - Antony and Cleopatra - Alaska - Needful Things - The Bible - Ben Hur (Animated Feature)

Fraser C. Heston .President/Director
Alex Butler .Producer
Heather Thomas .Development

AGUA FILMS

5482 Wilshire Blvd., #193
Los Angeles, CA 90036
PHONE 323-571-2723
FAX 323-571-0210
EMAIL . . . . . . info@aguafilms.com
WEB SITE . . . . . . www.aguafilms.com

TYPES	Direct-to-Video/DVD - Features - Made-for-TV/Cable Movies - Reality TV - TV Series
DEVELOPMENT	San Antonio - Killing Pablo
CREDITS	Suzanne's Diary for Nicholas - And Starring Pancho Villa as Himself - Imagining Argentina
COMMENTS	Latino-themed projects

Lourdes Diaz . . . . . . Producer
Leyani Diaz . . . . . . Story Editor

*AHIMSA FILMS

6671 Sunset Blvd., Ste. 1593
Los Angeles, CA 90028
PHONE 323-464-8500
FAX 323-464-8535

TYPES	Documentaries - Features
DEVELOPMENT	On the Road - Right as Rain
PRE-PRODUCTION	The Kite Runner
PRODUCTION	Searching for On the Road (Documentary) - Anvil (Documentary)

Rebecca Yeldham . . . . . . President
Lauren McClard . . . . . . No Title

AIR2WEB, INC.

1230 Peachtree St. NE, 12th Fl.
Atlanta, GA 30309
PHONE 404-942-5300
FAX 404-815-7708
EMAIL . . . . . . info@air2web.com
WEB SITE www.air2web.com

TYPES	Mobile Content

Sanjoy Malik . . . . . . President/CEO
Jeff Cagle . . . . . . CFO
Dale Gonzalez . . . . . . CTO
Jay Sheth . . . . . . Executive VP, Business Development
Len Emmick . . . . . . Sr. VP, Sales
Alfredo Narez . . . . . . VP, Marketing

AIRBORNE ENTERTAINMENT

3575 St. Laurent, Ste. 750
Montreal, PQ H2X 2T7, Canada
PHONE 514-289-9111
FAX 514-289-9494
EMAIL . . . . . . info@airborne-e.com
WEB SITE . . . . . . www.airborne-e.com

TYPES	Mobile Content
DEVELOPMENT	Mobileyes
UPCOMING RELEASES	Maxim Score Wars - Family Guy Freakin Slider - Ishido - TonemakerDJ - Family Guy Air Griffin - Maxim Slider
COMMENTS	Creating ringtones and wallpapers for Robotech

Garner Bornstein . . . . . . CEO
Andrew Zeidel . . . . . . COO
Bessy Ziannis . . . . . . CFO
Andy Nulman . . . . . . CMO
Dennis McFern . . . . . . CTO
Nancie Wight . . . . . . Executive VP, Carrier Relations
Marc Alloul . . . . . . VP, International/M&A
Ion Valaskakis . . . . . . VP, Brand Relations & Commercial Development

ALAMEDA FILMS

Avenida Presidente Masaryk 490
Tercer Piso, Colonia Polanco-Palmitas
Mexico City CP 11560, Mexico
PHONE 52-551-055-2333
FAX 52-555-280-8952
EMAIL . . . . . . daniel.birman@alamedafilms.com
WEB SITE . . . . . . www.alamedafilms.com

TYPES	Documentaries - Features
CREDITS	The Crime of Father Amaro - El Callejon de Los Milagros - The Red Queen: A Mayan Mystery - Birth of a Passion

Alfredo Ripstein . . . . . . CEO
Daniel Birman Ripstein . . . . . . Sr. VP

ALCHEMY ENTERTAINMENT

9229 Sunset Blvd., Ste. 720
Los Angeles, CA 90069
PHONE 310-278-8889
FAX 310-278-8822

TYPES	Direct-to-Video/DVD - Features - Internet Content - Mobile Content - Music Videos - TV Series
HAS DEAL WITH	Lionsgate
DEVELOPMENT	Overnight (Lionsgate) - Ironman (Kingsgate) - Untitled Race Project (Lionsgate) - Benny Blanco (Independent)
COMMENTS	Shares ongoing Lionsgate deal with LL Cool J

Jason Barrett . . . . . . Manager/Producer
Annie Foonberg . . . . . . Jr. Manager
Angie Edgar . . . . . . Assistant/Creative Executive
Stephanie Hughes . . . . . . Office Manager

ALCON ENTERTAINMENT, LLC

10390 Santa Monica Blvd., Ste. 250
Los Angeles, CA 90025

PHONE	310-789-3040
FAX	310-789-3060
TYPES	Features - TV Series
HAS DEAL WITH	Warner Bros. Pictures
PROVIDES DEAL TO	Rocklin Entertainment
DEVELOPMENT	P.S. I Love You - The Whole Pemberton Thing - Brothers in Arms - Hong Kong Phooey - Wimpy
PRODUCTION	One Missed Call
CREDITS	The Wicker Man - 16 Blocks - The Sisterhood of the Traveling Pants - Love Don't Cost a Thing - Chasing Liberty - My Dog Skip - Dude, Where's My Car? - Insomnia - The Affair of the Necklace - Lost and Found - Racing Stripes
SUBMISSION POLICY	No unsolicited submissions

Broderick Johnson . . . Co-President/Co-Founder
Andrew A. Kosove . . . Co-President/Co-Founder
Scott Parish . . . CFO/Sr. VP
Steven P. Wegner . . . Sr. VP, Development
Yolanda Cochran . . . VP, Physical Production
Jamie Wager . . . VP, TV
Chris Alexander . . . VP, Operations & Administration
Al Cuenca . . . Director, IT & New Media
Jennifer Petruniak . . . Director, Marketing & Publicity
Bob Newport . . . Controller
Jesse Israel . . . Creative Executive
Carl Rogers . . . Executive Assistant to Messrs. Kosove & Johnson
Zambak Tukan . . . Executive Assistant to Messrs. Kosove & Johnson
Scott Briggs . . . Executive Assistant to Mr. Parish
Joel Veenstra . . . Executive Assistant to Mr. Wegner
Elizabeth Colagiovanni . . . Executive Assistant to Ms. Cochran
Erin Okada . . . Development Assistant
Chad Clark . . . Corporate Accountant
Thomas Dagnino . . . Office Runner

ALEXANDER/ENRIGHT & ASSOCIATES

201 Wilshire Blvd., 3rd Fl.
Santa Monica, CA 90401

PHONE	310-458-3003
FAX	310-393-7238
TYPES	Made-for-TV/Cable Movies - TV Series
CREDITS	More Sex & The Single Mom (Lifetime) - Confessions of An American Bride (Lifetime) - Perfect Romance (Lifetime) - Rain - Our Son the Matchmaker - Point Last Seen - Family Pictures - Two Babies: Switched at Birth - Outside the Law (Columbia TriStar) - Bad Dogs (Animal Planet) - Sex & the Single Mom (Lifetime)

Les Alexander . . . Executive Producer
Don Enright . . . Executive Producer
Andrea Baynes . . . Executive Producer
Tami Gunby . . . Director, Administration
Miles Tanter . . . Development Associate

A-LINE PICTURES

9 Desbrosses St., 2nd Fl.
New York, NY 10013

PHONE	212-609-0939
FAX	212-609-0938
EMAIL	info@a-linepictures.com
WEB SITE	www.a-linepictures.com
TYPES	Features
DEVELOPMENT	Dangerous Doses - Bel Canto - The Magician's Assistant - The Master Builder
CREDITS	Capote - Monsoon Wedding
SUBMISSION POLICY	No unsolicited screenplays

Caroline Baron . . . Producer
Anthony Weintraub . . . Director/Producer
Joel Spitalnik . . . Assistant to Caroline Baron & Anthony Weintraub

ALLIANCE ATLANTIS

ALLIANCE ATLANTIS

1543 Seventh St., 3rd Fl.
Santa Monica, CA 90401

PHONE	310-899-8000/416-967-1174
FAX	310-899-8100
WEB SITE	www.allianceatlantis.com
TYPES	Animation - Documentaries - Features - Made-for-TV/Cable Movies - TV Series
CREDITS	Life with Judy Garland: Me and My Shadows - When Billie Beat Bobby - Haven - eXistenZ - The Sweet Hereafter - Sunshine - Joan of Arc - Nuremberg - CSI - CSI: Miami - CSI: NY - Bowling for Columbine
COMMENTS	Toronto office: 121 Bloor St. East, Ste. 1500, Toronto, ON M4W 3M5, Canada

Rose Marie Vega . . . Sr. VP, Distribution, Latin America
Janine Coughlin . . . Sr. VP, Content, International Distribution
Jennifer Bennett . . . VP, Merchandising & Licensing, Entertainment Group
Annemarie Sulatycky . . . VP, Business & Legal Affairs, Entertainment Group

ALTITUDE ENTERTAINMENT

8265 Sunset Blvd., Ste. 205
Los Angeles, CA 90046

PHONE	323-230-9539
FAX	818-710-1477
EMAIL	kyle@altitudeentertainment.com
WEB SITE	www.altitudeentertainment.com
TYPES	Direct-to-Video/DVD - Documentaries - Features - Made-for-TV/Cable Movies - Reality TV - TV Series
DEVELOPMENT	Fifty Dead Men Walking - Trapped - The Phoenix - Tijuana - Red Jungle - The Town That Came A-Courtin'
PRE-PRODUCTION	Veritas - World Renovation (Pilot)
POST PRODUCTION	Hipcooks (Pilot)
UPCOMING RELEASES	Little Athens
COMPLETED UNRELEASED	Fear Within - Fault - Moondance
CREDITS	Scorched
COMMENTS	No unsolicited submissions

Kyle Lundberg . . . CEO/Producer
Michael Benson . . . VP, Production
Genevieve Symons . . . Creative Executive

ALTURAS FILMS
2017 Pacific Ave., Ste. 6
Venice, CA 90291
PHONE .310-315-1380
FAX .310-822-7565
EMAIL .info@alturasfilms.com
WEB SITE .www.alturasfilms.com
TYPES Commercials - Documentaries - Features - Internet Content - Mobile Content - Music Videos
PRE-PRODUCTION Texas Lullaby - Lucy 212 - 2.2 - Lost Chord

Marshall Rawlings .CEO
Aldo LaPietra .Producer
Nancy Gaelen .Business Affairs

AM PRODUCTIONS & MANAGEMENT
8899 Beverly Blvd., Ste. 713
Los Angeles, CA 90048
PHONE .310-275-9081
FAX .310-275-9082
TYPES Features - Made-for-TV/Cable Movies - TV Series

Ann-Margret .No Title
Engelbert Humperdinck .No Title
Roger Smith .No Title
Alan Margulies .No Title
Kristine Ronquillo .Executive Administrator

AMBASSADOR ENTERTAINMENT INC.
PO Box 1522
Pacific Palisades, CA 90272
PHONE .310-584-1000
FAX .310-496-3140
EMAIL .spe@earthlink.net
TYPES Specials - TV Series
CREDITS Cheech Marin & Friends Live from South Beach - Chapel of Love - Return to Sin City: A Tribute to Gram Parsons - Chicago and Earth, Wind & Fire Live at the Greek Theatre - Farm Aid 20th Anniversary Concert

Albert Spevak .President

AMBUSH ENTERTAINMENT
8271 Melrose Ave., Ste. 207
Los Angeles, CA 90046
PHONE .323-951-9197
FAX .323-951-9998
WEB SITE .www.ambushentertainment.com
SECOND WEB SITE .www.dandbfilm.com
TYPES Features - Made-for-TV/Cable Movies - TV Series
DEVELOPMENT Number One Son - Yummy - Point of Faith - Party Favors
PRE-PRODUCTION Expecting
POST PRODUCTION Unearthed
CREDITS The OH in Ohio - Dead & Breakfast - The Squid and the Whale
SUBMISSION POLICY By referral only

Miranda Bailey .Partner/Producer
Francey Grace .Partner/Producer
Matthew Leutwyler .Partner/Producer/Director/Writer
Jun Tan .Partner/Producer
Julie Sandor .Producer/Development Executive
Amanda Hartrey .Executive Assistant

AMC
200 Jericho Quadrangle
Jericho, NY 11753
PHONE .516-803-3000
WEB SITE .www.amctv.com
TYPES Documentaries - Miniseries - TV Series
CREDITS Hustle - Sunday Morning Shootout - Movies 101 - Celebrity Charades - Broken Trail (Miniseries)
COMMENTS TV Cable Network; Series and documentaries about movies and movie culture

Joshua Sapan .President/CEO, Rainbow Media Holdings LLC
Ed Carroll .President, Rainbow Entertainment Services
Gregg Hill .President, Rainbow Network Sales
Robert Sorcher .Executive VP, Programming, Packaging & Production
Todd Green .Sr. VP, Affiliate Marketing, Rainbow Network Sales
Harold Gronenthal .Sr. VP, Acquisitions
Judi Lopez .Sr. VP, Eastern Region, Rainbow Network Sales
Ed Palluth .Sr. VP, Southern Region, Rainbow Network Sales
Linda Schupack .Sr. VP, Marketing
Theano Apostolou .VP, Consumer Public Relations
Matthew Frankel .VP, Corporate Communications
Kurt Greves .VP, Affiliate Advertising, Rainbow Network Sales
Tom Halleen .VP, Scheduling & Acquisitions
Gina Degnan Hughes .VP, Advertising
Christina Wayne .VP, Scripted Series & Movies
Jeremy Elice .Director, Scripted Series & Movies
Alison Hoffman .Director, Advertising

AMERICAN BLACKGUARD, INC.
PO Box 680686
Franklin, TN 37068-0686
PHONE .615-599-4032
EMAIL .contact@americanblackguard.com
SECOND EMAIL .contact@claystafford.com
WEB SITE .www.americanblackguard.com
SECOND WEB SITE .www.claystafford.com
TYPES Animation - Commercials - Direct-to-Video/DVD - Documentaries - Features - Internet Content - Made-for-TV/Cable Movies - Music Videos - Specials - TV Series
CREDITS Michael - Patterns of Power - A Ziegfield Extravaganza - We Are Family - What's the Story - New Horizons in Bonsai - Esquire Travel Guides - Tell Me Why

Clay Stafford .Producer/Director/Writer
Eddie Lightsey .Sr. Publicist
Phillip Lacy .Production/Post Coordinator

AMERICAN WORK
9 Desbrosses St., 2nd Fl.
New York, NY 10013
PHONE 212-905-2325
FAX 212-905-2329
TYPES: Features
HAS DEAL WITH: Radar Pictures
DEVELOPMENT: Jeff the Demon (New Line) - Amnesia (Paramount) - ID Crisis (Warner Bros.)

Scot Armstrong . . . . . Writer/Director/Producer
Ravi Nandan . . . . . VP, Development
Lindsay Gelfand . . . . . Assistant

AMERICAN ZOETROPE
1641 N. Ivar Ave.
Los Angeles, CA 90028
PHONE 323-460-4420
FAX 323-460-4459
WEB SITE . . . . . www.zoetrope.com
TYPES: Documentaries - Features
DEVELOPMENT: On the Road - Cavemen in the Hedges - The Girls' Guide to Hunting and Fishing - Black Stallion Revolts - Jeepers Creepers 3 - Twin Study - Anything for Money - When God Dips - You
PRODUCTION: On the Road Documentary
POST PRODUCTION: Youth Without Youth
UPCOMING RELEASES: The Good Shepherd - Marie Antoinette
CREDITS: Wind - CQ - The Virgin Suicides - Jeepers Creepers 1&2 - Lost in Translation - Kinsey - Sleepy Hollow - Jack - Don Juan DeMarco - The Rain People - THX 1138 - Hearts of Darkness: A Filmmaker's Apocalypse - Bram Stoker's Dracula - The Rainmaker - Apocalypse Now - The Conversation
SUBMISSION POLICY: Accepts submissions at submissions@zoetrope.com

Bobby Rock . . . . . Sr. VP, Film Production & Development
Giselle Galper . . . . . Legal Counsel
Brendan Kenney . . . . . Manager, Creative Affairs
Liz Eckerling . . . . . Assistant to Francis Ford Coppola

AMICUS ENTERTAINMENT LIMITED
8899 Beverly Blvd., #702
Los Angeles, CA 90048
PHONE 310-247-2201
FAX 310-247-2230
TYPES: Features - Made-for-TV/Cable Movies
PRE-PRODUCTION: Clown - Stuck
SUBMISSION POLICY: No unsolicited submissions, phone calls or resumes

Robert Katz . . . . . Producer
Julie G. Moldo . . . . . VP, Development

AMP'D MOBILE
1925 S. Bundy Dr.
Los Angeles, CA 90025
PHONE 310-575-2500
FAX 310-575-2501
EMAIL . . . . . pr@ampdmobile.com
WEB SITE . . . . . www.ampd.com
TYPES: Internet Content - Mobile Content
HAS DEAL WITH: MTV Networks - Universal Music Group
DEVELOPMENT: International Federation of Competitive Eating - Amp'd Investigates - Hot Dish - Extreme Makeover: Homeless Edition - Movie Review - Hollywood & Vine - The Daily Wad - Iron Lunch Lady - WTF America
PRE-PRODUCTION: Lil' Bush - America's Greatest Fan - WPFF - Mexican Crazy Show - Tattoo Tales
PRODUCTION: Swing Shift - Z-List - Bush: Stinky or Sweet - Venice Beach - Moto Mark's Round Table - Red Carpet Treatment
CREDITS: Ultimate Fight Night Live (Spike TV)
SUBMISSION POLICY: Submit via email to jcohen@ampdmobile.com or brian@ampdmobile.com
COMMENTS: Collaborative partnership with Logo, Orchard, Spike TV, Bunim Murray, LivePlanet, Donick Cary, Break.com & QD3 Productions

Peter Adderton . . . . . CEO
Bill Stone . . . . . COO
Doug Dobie . . . . . CMO
Seth Cummings . . . . . Sr. VP, Content
Larry Mattera . . . . . Sr. VP, Music
David Sypniewski . . . . . Sr. Director, Content Marketing
Jodi Lederman . . . . . Public Relations

***AND THEN PRODUCTIONS**
120 Broadway, Ste. 200
Santa Monica, CA 90401
PHONE 310-260-7073/310-260-7064
FAX 310-260-7060
TYPES: Features - TV Series
DEVELOPMENT: The Other Guy - Miss Captivity (Universal) - 36 - Mount Pleasant

David Duchovny . . . . . Principal
Téa Leoni . . . . . Principal
Susanna Jolly . . . . . Executive VP
Eric Knight . . . . . Assistant

ANDELL ENTERTAINMENT
10877 Wilshire Blvd., Ste. 2200
Los Angeles, CA 90024
PHONE 310-954-4890
FAX 310-954-4881
TYPES: Features
PRE-PRODUCTION: State of Play - Electric God
CREDITS: Millions - Piccadilly Jim - Safe Men

Andrew Hauptman . . . . . Chairman/CEO
Ellen Bronfman Hauptman . . . . . Partner/Sr. VP, Creative
Tracy Falco . . . . . Sr. VP, Production
Bret Magpiong . . . . . Sr. VP, Business Affairs
Jennifer Gerber . . . . . Assistant
Lisbeth Vitallo-Hook . . . . . Assistant

CRAIG ANDERSON PRODUCTIONS
9696 Culver Blvd., Meralta Plaza, Ste. 208
Culver City, CA 90232
PHONE .310-841-2555
FAX .310-841-5934
EMAIL .info@cappix.com
WEB SITE .www.cappix.com
TYPES Features - Made-for-TV/Cable Movies - TV Series
PROVIDES DEAL TO Beth Grossbard Productions
CREDITS On Golden Pond - Songs in Ordinary Time - The Piano Lesson - The Ballad of Lucy Whipple - Midwives - True Women - The Christmas Shoes - O Pioneers! - Sally Hemings - Wilder Days - Meltdown - For the Love of a Child - The Christmas Blessing

Craig Anderson .Executive Producer
Beth Grossbard .Executive Producer
Gary Goldberger .Executive Producer
Kerry Bailey .Creative Executive
Dani DeJesus .Director, Development

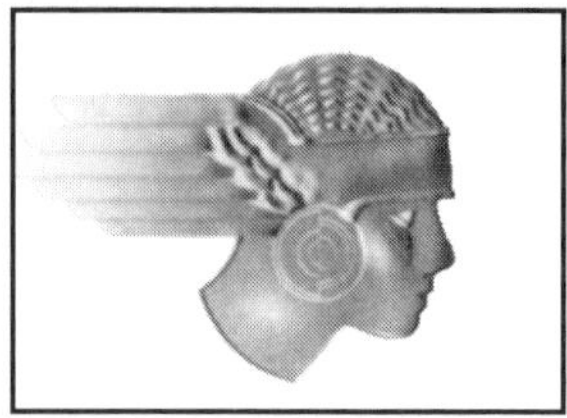

ANGELIKA
PO Box 4956
New York, NY 10185
PHONE .212-410-9404/213-840-6224
FAX .213-477-2004
EMAIL .barney@angelikafilm.com
WEB SITE .www.angelikafilm.com
TYPES Documentaries - Features - Made-for-TV/Cable Movies - TV Series
DEVELOPMENT Angelika TV Channel - All Ivy (Feature)
PRE-PRODUCTION WBway (Series)
PRODUCTION Another Deep Breath (Feature)
CREDITS Streetwise - Too Much Sleep - Metro Angelika (Cablevision)
COMMENTS A division of Crimson Screen Partners

Angelika Saleh .President
Barney Oldfield .General Manager
David Maquiling .VP, Production
Thomas Bannister .VP, Distribution

ANGRY FILMS, INC.
1416 N. La Brea Ave.
Hollywood, CA 90028
PHONE .323-802-1715
FAX .323-802-1720
WEB SITE .www.donmurphy.net
TYPES Features - TV Series
DEVELOPMENT Deadman - Iron Man - Torso
PRODUCTION Transformers
POST PRODUCTION Shoot Em Up
CREDITS Double Dragon - The League of Extraordinary Gentlemen - Bully - Natural Born Killers - Apt Pupil - Permanent Midnight - From Hell

Don Murphy .Producer
Susan Montford .Producer
Dianne Bloom .Executive Assistant

ANIMAL PLANET
c/o Discovery Networks, U.S.
One Discovery Pl.
Silver Spring, MD 20910-3354
PHONE .240-662-2000
FAX .240-662-1845
EMAIL .firstname_lastname@discovery.com
WEB SITE .www.discovery.com
TYPES Documentaries - TV Series
CREDITS Backyard Habitat - Corwin's Quest - Get Out There! - Horse Power - Planet's Funniest Animals - The Crocodile Hunter - Jane Goodall - K9 Karma

Maureen Smith .Executive VP/General Manager
David Doyle .VP, Production & Development
Patricia Kollappallil .VP, Communications
Dan Russell .VP, Programming

ANIMUS FILMS
914 Hauser Blvd.
Los Angeles, CA 90036
PHONE .323-571-3302
FAX .323-571-3361
EMAIL .info@animusfilms.com
WEB SITE .www.animusfilms.com
TYPES Documentaries - Features - TV Series
DEVELOPMENT Beautiful Exile - Corporate Executioner - The Credenza - Cut Throat City - Fire on the Mountain - Homecoming - Life of a King - The Man Who Knew Infinity - The Passion of Danny Burke - the Peabody Sisters - The Pride of Bismarck - Wonderful
CREDITS Year of the Bull

Jim Young .Producer

***ANONYMOUS CREATORS PRODUCTIONS**
8306 Wilshire Blvd., Ste. 1222
Beverly Hills, CA 90211
PHONE .323-578-2652
FAX .323-913-0467
EMAIL .info@anonymousecreators.com
WEB SITE .www.anonymouscreators.com
TYPES Animation - Commercials - Direct-to-Video/DVD - Documentaries - Features - Internet Content - Mobile Content - Music Videos - Reality TV - TV Series
DEVELOPMENT Speedline - Gallery - Pearl - Heartstruck
PRODUCTION Lifestylin' (Pilot)
POST PRODUCTION An Ocean Apart (Documentary)
COMPLETED UNRELEASED Glorybox (Documentary) - Out the Box (Pilot)
CREDITS Au Pair Chocolate

Allen Dam .Producer
Janine Giaime .Producer
Benson McGrath .Producer
Kevin Lee .New Media Director
Steven Lee .Consultant, Programming
Andrew Shiozaki .Consultant, Video Game/Interactive

ANTIDOTE INTERNATIONAL FILMS, INC.
200 Varick St., Ste. 502
New York, NY 10014
PHONE .646-486-4344
FAX .646-486-5885
EMAIL .info@antidotefilms.com
WEB SITE .www.antidotefilms.com
TYPES Features
DEVELOPMENT The Kids Are Alright - Macbeth - The Knockout Artist - Famous Long Ago - Sarah
POST PRODUCTION The Last Winter
COMPLETED UNRELEASED The Hawk Is Dying
CREDITS Mysterious Skin - High Art - Wendigo - Limon - Laurel Canyon - Thirteen - Chain
SUBMISSION POLICY No unsolicited material

Jeffrey Levy-Hinte .Producer
Mike Andrus .Head, Development
Takeo Hori .Director, Operations
James Debbs .Production Supervisor
Marcus Grundahl .Assistant to Mr. Levy-Hinte

AOL MEDIA NETWORKS
75 Rockefeller Plaza, 6th Fl.
New York, NY 10019
PHONE .212-652-6400
WEB SITE .www.aol.com
SECOND WEB SITE .www.aim.com
TYPES Internet Content - Mobile Content - Specials
HAS DEAL WITH Mark Burnett Productions
DEVELOPMENT The Biz - Project Freshman - Gold Rush! (Mark Burnett Productions)
CREDITS Live 8 on AOL - AOL Music Sessions
COMMENTS West Coast office: 331 N. Maple Dr., Beverly Hills, CA 90210; Additional deals with Katalyst Films, In2TV, Network LIVE and TMZ

Jonathan Miller .Chairman/CEO
Ted Leonsis .Vice Chairman
Jim Bankoff .Executive VP, Original Programming & Products
Kevin Conroy .Executive VP, AOL Media Networks
Michael Wolfson .VP, Creative Development & Production
Jordan Kurzweil .VP, AOL Productions
James Luria .Director, Creative Development
Andre Mika .Director, Productions

APARTMENT 3B PRODUCTIONS
10250 Constellation Blvd., Ste. 2064
Los Angeles, CA 90067
PHONE .310-449-3478
FAX .310-449-3923
TYPES Features - TV Series
DEVELOPMENT Don't Tell My Mother - Scrawl - Selling Time - Truce - F+ - Charlie Chan - The Gentleman (TV) - Hexxx - Rizzle Pizzle Sizzle - Two Minutes to Midnight - Man Without a Gun - Orbit (Fox 2000) - Selling Time - Inferno (Spyglass) - Tammi Chase (Warner Independent) - A Family Affair (New Line)
COMMENTS No unsolicited submissions

Jennifer Klein .Producer
Pooneh Zandazma .Creative Executive

APATOW PRODUCTIONS
2900 W. Olympic Blvd., Ste. 141
Santa Monica, CA 90404
PHONE .310-255-7026
FAX .310-255-7025
TYPES Features - TV Series
DEVELOPMENT Forgetting Sarah Marshall
PRE-PRODUCTION Drillbit Taylor
PRODUCTION Knocked Up
CREDITS Film: Talladega Nights: The Ballad of Ricky Bobby - The 40 Year-Old Virgin - Anchorman: The Legend of Ron Burgundy - The Cable Guy - Celtic Pride - Heavyweights; TV: Undeclared - Freaks and Geeks - The Larry Sanders Show - The Ben Stiller Show
SUBMISSION POLICY No unsolicited submissions

Judd Apatow .Writer/Director/Producer
Andrew Cohen .Associate Producer
Andrew Epstein .Assistant to Judd Apatow

APOSTLE
568 Broadway, #301
New York, NY 10012
PHONE .212-541-4323
FAX .212-541-4330
WEB SITE .www.apostlenyc.com
TYPES Features - TV Series
HAS DEAL WITH Sony Pictures Entertainment
CREDITS Features: Blow - Monument Avenue; TV: Rescue Me (FX) - The Job (ABC)

Denis Leary .Actor/Director/Producer
Jim Serpico .President, Motion Pictures & TV
Bartow Church .Producer/Manager
Tom Sellitti .Creative Executive
Adrienne O'Riain .Director, Development
Anna Urban .Executive Assistant to Denis Leary
Steve Hochmuth .Assistant to Denis Leary
Maurice Singer .Assistant to Producers

APPIAN WAY
9255 Sunset Blvd., Ste. 615
West Hollywood, CA 90069
PHONE .310-300-1390
FAX .310-300-1388
TYPES Features
HAS DEAL WITH Warner Bros. Pictures
DEVELOPMENT Drunken Angel - The Chancellor Manuscript - Blink - Kite - The Infiltrator
PRODUCTION Blood Diamonds
POST PRODUCTION Gardener of Eden
CREDITS The Aviator - The Assassination of Richard Nixon

Leonardo DiCaprio .Owner
Bradford Simpson .President, Production
Franklin Leonard .Development Executive
Sarah Shepard .Development Executive

APPLE & HONEY FILM CORP.
9190 W. Olympic Blvd., Ste. 363
Beverly Hills, CA 90212
PHONE .310-556-5639
WEB SITE .www.awardwinningfilms.com
TYPES Features - Made-for-TV/Cable Movies
DEVELOPMENT Hint of Rain - Larry and Elvis
CREDITS My Life as a Dog - The Quarrel - American Hero

David Brandes .Producer

APPLESEED ENTERTAINMENT, LLC

4125 Hood Ave., #104
Burbank, CA 91505
PHONE .818-718-6000
FAX .818-556-5610
EMAIL .info@appleseedent.com
WEB SITE .www.appleseedent.com

TYPES	Animation - Documentaries - Features - Made-for-TV/Cable Movies - TV Series
DEVELOPMENT	Run Away Home - Dress Blues - Untitled Leroy Walker Story - Gus: A Dog's Story
PRE-PRODUCTION	Daybreak (Feature)
PRODUCTION	Reptile Chronicles (Pilot)
POST PRODUCTION	The Legend of Secret Pass: Behind the Scenes
COMPLETED UNRELEASED	One Line - Mothers Be Good
CREDITS	Nickel & Dime - Cruel But Necessary - Good Morning, Vietnam - Without a Clue - What Are We Doing to Our Children? - Dying with Dignity - Not a Question of Courage - Hope Ranch - Cupid's Prey
SUBMISSION POLICY	Queries accepted through agent, attorney or from published/produced writers

Lynne Moses .Partner
Ben Moses .Partner

LOREEN ARBUS PRODUCTIONS, INC.

8075 W. Third St., Ste. 410
Los Angeles, CA 90048
PHONE .323-930-1244
FAX .323-930-0186
EMAIL .arbusprod@arbusprod.com
SECOND EMAIL .jayme@arbusprod.com

TYPES	Documentaries - New Media - Reality TV - Specials - Syndication - TV Series
CREDITS	Case Closed - In the Name of Love - Crimes of Passion - Forgive or Forget
COMMENTS	Emphasis on nonfiction series, movies, specials

Loreen Arbus .President/Executive Producer
Jayme Brown .Assistant to President/Projects Coordinator/Office Manager
Brett Sales .Assistant to the President

ARCHER ENTERTAINMENT

140 W. 22nd St., Ste. 7-B
New York, NY 10011
PHONE .212-741-2200
FAX .212-741-9575
WEB SITE .www.archerent.com

TYPES	Documentaries - Features - Made-for-TV/Cable Movies - TV Series
DEVELOPMENT	Marga
PRE-PRODUCTION	Flyin' V - She Needed Me
PRODUCTION	New York City Serenade - American Widow
POST PRODUCTION	Gray Matters
COMPLETED UNRELEASED	The Warrior Class
CREDITS	Boys Don't Cry - Dark Harbor - Nola - You Can Count on Me
SUBMISSION POLICY	Query letter with SASE; Include synopsis and bio

Rachel Peters .Producer/Principal
Meredith Petty .Director, Development

MARK ARCHER ENTERTAINMENT

c/o New Hollywood Studios
1910 St. Joe Center Rd., Ste. 22
Fort Wayne, IN 46825
PHONE .260-399-4379
EMAIL .archer@newhollywoodonline.com

TYPES	Direct-to-Video/DVD - Documentaries - Features
PRODUCTION	Paper Dolls: Chapter One
CREDITS	New Hope - In the Company of Men - American Reel - Joe Bonamassa: A New Day Yesterday Live - Night Shift (Series)

Mark Archer .President/CEO

ARDEN ENTERTAINMENT

12034 Riverside Dr., Ste. 200
North Hollywood, CA 91607
PHONE .818-985-4600
FAX .818-985-3021
EMAIL .admin@ardenentertainment.com
WEB SITE .www.ardenentertainment.com

TYPES	Documentaries - Specials - TV Series
PRODUCTION	Growing Up (Animal Planet) - Cosmic Signals (TV Land) - K9 Karma (Animal Planet) - Extreme Surgery (TLC)
CREDITS	Growing Up Grizzly 1&2 - Another Way of Seeing Things - Lord of the Rings: Behind the Scenes - A Quiet Revolution - Mob Scene - King Kong TV Specials

Dan Arden .President
Jim Cirigliano .Supervising Producer
Shari Dunn .Director, Development

ARDUSTRY ENTERTAINMENT

9255 Sunset Blvd., Ste. 1000
West Hollywood, CA 90069
PHONE .310-281-0070
FAX .310-281-0050
EMAIL .info@ardustry.com
WEB SITE .www.ardustry.com

TYPES	Animation - Direct-to-Video/DVD - Features - Reality TV - TV Series
DEVELOPMENT	Francois
POST PRODUCTION	Orphan King
CREDITS	Guide to Recognizing Your Saints
SUBMISSION POLICY	No unsolicited material
COMMENTS	Deal with Speakeasy Comics

Peter D. Sahagen .Chairman
Gary Reeves .Vice-Chairman

ARJAY ENTERTAINMENT

1627 Pontius Ave., Ste. 100
Los Angeles, CA 90025
PHONE 310-481-2282
FAX 310-481-2287
EMAIL . . . . . . info@arjayentertainment.com
WEB SITE . . . . . . www.arjayentertainment.com

TYPES	Direct-to-Video/DVD - Internet Content - Mobile Content - Reality TV - Specials
DEVELOPMENT	The Ultimate Weekend
UPCOMING RELEASES	The Young Hollywood Awards 2006
CREDITS	Breakthrough of the Year Awards 2005 - The Young Hollywood Awards 2005 - Above the Line Beauty - The Red Carpet - VIP Access

R.J. Williams . . . . . . CEO
Bob Williams . . . . . . Producer
Mark Mitchell . . . . . . Producer
James Larson . . . . . . VP, Development
Leandra Jones . . . . . . VP, Production
Michael Vann . . . . . . VP, Post Production

ARLINGTON ENTERTAINMENT, INC.

10866 Wilshire Blvd., Ste. 850
Los Angeles, CA 90024
PHONE 310-481-7190
FAX 310-481-7191

TYPES	Direct-to-Video/DVD - Made-for-TV/Cable Movies - Miniseries - TV Series
DEVELOPMENT	Tyburn's Tales of Terror - The Aftermath - The Bloody Millennium
PRE-PRODUCTION	The Moorgate Legacy
POST PRODUCTION	Persecution (1973, Restoration) - Legend of the Werewolf (1975, Restoration)
CREDITS	Masks of Death - Murder Elite - One Way Ticket to Hollywood - The Ghoul (1974, Restoration)
SUBMISSION POLICY	Unsolicited submissions via recognized talent agent/agency only
COMMENTS	UK office: Cippenham Ct., Cippenham Ln., Cippenham, Nr Slough, Berkshire SL1 5AU, United Kingdom

Anthony Palladino . . . . . . President
Kevin Francis . . . . . . Executive VP
Annette Pearse . . . . . . VP/Administrator
Bernard Thomas . . . . . . VP/Controller
Gillian Garrow . . . . . . Story & Research Editor

ARMADA PICTURES

1691 Woods Dr.
Los Angeles, CA 90069
PHONE 323-656-1746
FAX 323-656-1034
EMAIL . . . . . . info@armada-pictures.com

TYPES	Features
DEVELOPMENT	Family of the Year
POST PRODUCTION	Drive Thru - Plague
UPCOMING RELEASES	Drum - Tamara
CREDITS	One Point O - The Quiet American - The Wedding Planner - Blow Dry - Nurse Betty - Where the Money Is - The Crow: Salvation - Clay Pigeons - The Innocent - The Dead - Paris, Texas

Chris Sievernich . . . . . . President
Yarek Danielak . . . . . . VP, International Distribution
Matt Milich . . . . . . VP, Production
Jenny Baek . . . . . . Creative Executive

ARMAGH FILMS, INC.

PO Box 17593
Beverly Hills, CA 90209
PHONE 310-395-8053
FAX 310-395-8063
EMAIL . . . . . . tim@armaghfilms.com
WEB SITE . . . . . . www.armaghfilms.com

TYPES	Features - Miniseries
DEVELOPMENT	Seeing Other Women
PRE-PRODUCTION	Lighthouse
COMPLETED UNRELEASED	How to Rob a Bank - The Plague
SUBMISSION POLICY	Unsolicited material will not be accepted

Tim O'Hair . . . . . . Producer

*ARRAMIS FILMS

8619 17th NE
Seattle, WA 98115
PHONE 323-572-0158
FAX 206-782-8351
EMAIL . . . . . . rafael@arramisfilms.com
WEB SITE . . . . . . www.arramisfilms.com

TYPES	Features
DEVELOPMENT	Devil's Villa
CREDITS	Ultimate Force

Rafael Primorac . . . . . . President
John Hicks . . . . . . VP/General Counsel

ARS NOVA

511 W. 54th St.
New York, NY 10019
PHONE 212-489-9800
FAX 212-489-1908
EMAIL . . . . . . info@arsnovanyc.com
WEB SITE . . . . . . www.arsnovanyc.com

TYPES	Features - Theatre - TV Series
HAS DEAL WITH	NBC Universal Television Studio
CREDITS	Judy Gold's 25 Questions for a Jewish Mother - Thick as Thieves - Lobby Hero - God Said, "Ha!" - Julia Sweeney in the Family Way

Jon Steingart . . . . . . Partner/Producer
Jenny Wiener . . . . . . Partner/Producer
Jason Eagan . . . . . . Producer
Jillian Apfelbaum . . . . . . Assistant to Producer

*ARTICLE 19 FILMS
380 Lafayette St., Ste. 303
New York, NY 10003
PHONE .212-777-1987
FAX .212-777-2585
EMAIL .info@article19films.com
WEB SITE .www.article19films.com
TYPES Documentaries - Features
PRODUCTION Bling: A Planet Rock - Cry Haiti
UPCOMING RELEASES Lockdown, USA
CREDITS Last Party 2000

Filippo Bozotti .Producer
Rebecca Chaiklin .Producer
Michael Skolnik .Producer
Roslyn Waldron-Harding .Associate Producer

THE ARTISTS' COLONY
256 S. Robertson Blvd., Ste. 1500
Beverly Hills, CA 90211
PHONE .310-720-8300
TYPES Documentaries - Features - Made-for-TV/Cable Movies - TV Series
DEVELOPMENT Isabella & the Monsters - Bohemian Heart
PRE-PRODUCTION Caravaggio - Waking Up the Day - Phinney's Life
PRODUCTION Arnold Newman
CREDITS Heroes - The Tenants - Snow Falling on Cedars - `Til the End of Time - Shattered Image - A Girl, Three Guys and a Gun - Tidal Wave - 12

Lloyd A. Silverman .Producer
P.J. Koll .VP, Development
Steve Grill .Director, Development (NY)
David Donnelly .Creative Executive
Firoze Salimi .Creative Executive

ARTISTS PRODUCTION GROUP (APG)
2601 Colorado Ave.
Santa Monica, CA 90404
PHONE .310-300-2400
FAX .310-300-2424
TYPES Features - TV Series
DEVELOPMENT Tom Clancy's Splinter Cell - Without Remorse - Rainbow Six - Red Rabbit - Teeth of the Tiger - Tom Clancy's Ghost Recon - The Brazilian - Conquest of Mexico - Nightmare Creatures
CREDITS Timeline - Godsend - Sidewalks of New York - You Stupid Man - A Gentleman's Game
SUBMISSION POLICY Through agents only

Chris George .Development Executive
Vanessa Marcello .Development Executive
Bryce Johnson .Business & Legal Affairs

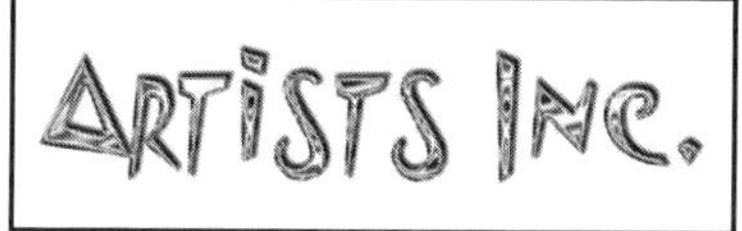

ARTISTS, INC.
5777 W. Century Blvd., 10th Fl.
Los Angeles, CA 90045
PHONE .323-960-1111
EMAIL .info@artistsinc.org
WEB SITE .www.artistsinc.org
TYPES Animation - Commercials - Direct-to-Video/DVD - Features - Music Videos
DEVELOPMENT Secret of Mandora - Ultimate Berzerkers - Syd Pollock's Indianapolis Clowns
PRE-PRODUCTION Pet Peeves
PRODUCTION Code Runners
CREDITS The Rugrats Movie - Rugrats Go Wild! - The Wild Thornberrys Movie - Rugrats in Paris - We're Back - UPN Blockbuster Shockwave Theater

Thad Weinlein .Executive Producer
Andrea Eisen .No Title
Beth Fraikorn .No Title
Reuben Langdon .No Title
Steven Sears .No Title
Mary Wall .No Title

ASCENDANT PICTURES
9350 Civic Center Dr., Ste. 110
Beverly Hills, CA 90210
PHONE .310-288-4600
FAX .310-288-4601
WEB SITE .www.ascendantpictures.com
TYPES Features
DEVELOPMENT American Knight - Grounded - The Run - Race for the Sky - Future Force X - Who's Your Caddy?
PRE-PRODUCTION Outlander - Blackwater Transit
CREDITS Lucky Number Sleven - Ask the Dust - The Big White - The Jacket - Lord of War - Wing Commander - Half Past Dead - The Punisher

Chris Roberts .Partner/Co-CEO
Christopher Eberts .Partner/Co-CEO
Kia Jam .Partner/COO
John Schimmel .President, Production
Jodi Heaston .Director, Development
Nicole Haeussermann .Production Coordinator
Sheila Kerrigan .Production Executive

ASGAARD ENTERTAINMENT

9320 Wilshire Blvd., Ste. 202
Beverly Hills, CA 90212
PHONE . . . 310-274-2825
FAX . . . 310-774-3919
EMAIL . . . info@asgaardentertainment.com
WEB SITE . . . www.asgaardentertainment.com

TYPES	Features
DEVELOPMENT	La Prima Famiglia - Celestial Clockwork - Providence - Broken Hearts
PRE-PRODUCTION	Untitled Military - The First Vampire
PRODUCTION	Together Again for the First Time
POST PRODUCTION	Everybody Wants to Be Italian
CREDITS	Unrest
SUBMISSION POLICY	Agency represented or requested submissions only
COMMENTS	Also finances films

Jason Todd Ipson . . . Principal
James Huntsman . . . Principal
Jaime Ipson Burke . . . Production/Development

ASIS PRODUCTIONS

316 N. Rossmore Ave., Ste. 400
Los Angeles, CA 90004
PHONE . . . 310-890-5527

TYPES	Features - Made-for-TV/Cable Movies
DEVELOPMENT	The Giver - Keller - The Moon in Two Windows
CREDITS	American Heart - Hidden in America

Jeff Bridges . . . President
Neil Koenigsberg . . . Executive

ASYLUM ENTERTAINMENT

7920 W. Sunset Blvd., 2nd Fl.
Los Angeles, CA 90046
PHONE . . . 310-696-4600
FAX . . . 310-696-4893
WEB SITE . . . www.asylument.com

TYPES	Documentaries - Features - Reality TV - Specials - TV Series
DEVELOPMENT	Murderer's Row (HBO)
UPCOMING RELEASES	Story of My Life (ABC) - Island Fever (MTV)
CREDITS	Beyond the Glory (FSN) - Fearless (OLN) - The Family Makers (TLC) - The Gift (TLC) - Love Is in the Heir (E!) - The Sports List (FSN) - Anything to Win (GSN) - In Focus (FSN) - A Date with Anna Kournikova (ESPN) - American Gangster (BET)
SUBMISSION POLICY	See Web site
COMMENTS	Talent management; Music publishing; Consulting group; Post production facility

Steve Michaels . . . President/CEO
Eric M. Johnson . . . Executive VP/CFO
Jonathan Koch . . . Executive Producer
Frank Sinton . . . Executive Producer
Tiffany Reis . . . VP, Production & Operations
Shelley Storm . . . Director, Production & Operations
Amy Manchester . . . Director, Development
Erin Copen . . . Development Executive
Sam Hartley . . . Post Production Manager

THE ASYLUM

1012 N. Sycamore Ave.
Los Angeles, CA 90038
PHONE . . . 323-850-1214
FAX . . . 323-850-1218
WEB SITE . . . www.theasylum.cc

TYPES	Direct-to-Video/DVD - Features
DEVELOPMENT	Vampire Wars
PRE-PRODUCTION	Oddities
POST PRODUCTION	9/11 Report
UPCOMING RELEASES	Pirates of Treasure Island - Snakes on a Train
CREDITS	King of the Lost World - Shapeshifter - Dead Men Walking - Frankenstein - Beast of Bray Road - H.G. Wells' War of the Worlds - Bram Stroker's Way of the Vampire - King of the Ants - Death Valley: The Revenge of Bloody Bill - Evil Eyes
SUBMISSION POLICY	Scripts: email David Michael Latt at productions@theasylum.cc; Completed films: rossi@theasylum.cc
COMMENTS	International sales and distribution

David Michael Latt . . . Partner, Production
David Rimawi . . . Partner, Acquisitions
Sherri Strain . . . Partner, Sales & Distribution
Amanda Rossi . . . Director, Acquisitions
Rick Walker . . . Distribution & Operations

ATLAS ENTERTAINMENT

9200 Sunset Blvd., 10th Fl.
Los Angeles, CA 90069
PHONE . . . 310-786-4900
FAX . . . 310-777-2185

TYPES	Features
CREDITS	Idlewild - Batman Begins - The Brothers Grimm - The Upside of Anger - 12 Monkeys - Fallen - City of Angels - Three Kings - Scooby Doo 1&2 - Bulletproof Monk

Charles Roven . . . Producer/Partner (310-786-4935)
Allen Shapiro . . . President/Partner (310-786-4940)
Alex Gartner . . . Producer/Partner (310-786-8105)
Ted MacKinney . . . CFO (310-786-4911)
Alan Glazer . . . Executive VP (310-786-4929)
Gloria Fan . . . VP, Development & Production (310-786-4914)
Joe Palmer . . . Assistant to Mr. Roven (310-786-4935)
Pierre Parisot . . . Assistant to Mr. Roven (310-786-4935)
Alexis Cohen . . . Assistant to Mr. Shapiro (310-786-4944)
Nick Miller . . . Assistant to Mr. Gartner (310-786-8105)
Mary Cybriwsky . . . Assistant to Mr. Glazer (310-786-4931)
Tina Jones . . . Assistant to Ms. Fan (310-786-8917)

ATMAN ENTERTAINMENT

335 N. Maple Dr., Ste. 354
Beverly Hills, CA 90210
PHONE . . . 310-246-7719

TYPES	Features - Made-for-TV/Cable Movies - TV Series
DEVELOPMENT	Lambs of God - I'd Like to Teach the World to Sing in Perfect Cantonese - Mark Leech Project - Evidence of Harm - Nancy Wake
CREDITS	Fight Club - Under Suspicion

Ross Grayson Bell . . . Producer
Matt Valenti . . . Creative Executive

ATMOSPHERE ENTERTAINMENT MM, LLC
9107 Wilshire Blvd., Ste. 650
Beverly Hills, CA 90210
PHONE 310-860-0310
FAX 310-860-0410
TYPES — Features - Made-for-TV/Cable Movies - Reality TV - TV Series
DEVELOPMENT — Killing Demons - Dating Nick McBride - Books of Magic - Ride Down Mt. Morgan - Chasing the Dime - Interior Decorators - Revelation
PRE-PRODUCTION — The Spiderwick Chronicles - Piranha
POST PRODUCTION — 300
COMPLETED UNRELEASED — Full of It
CREDITS — Taking Lives - Godsend - Land of the Dead

Mark Canton . . . . . Chairman/CEO
Steve Barnett . . . . . Executive VP, Motion Picture Development & Production
David Hopwood . . . . . Director, Film & TV Development
Frazier . . . . . VP, Administration

ATOMIC CARTOONS, INC.
1125 Howe St., #250
Vancouver, BC V6Z 2K8, Canada
PHONE 604-734-2866
FAX 604-734-2869
EMAIL . . . . . info@atomiccartoons.com
WEB SITE . . . . . www.atomiccartoons.com
TYPES — Animation - Commercials - Direct-to-Video/DVD - TV Series
DEVELOPMENT — Kitty Kazoodle - Big City Birds - Jett Set - The Misfits - Secret Agent Band - Soulforge - Dr. Ferocious
CREDITS — Atomic Betty - Captain Flamingo

Trevor Bentley . . . . . CEO/VP, Co-Production
Rob Davies . . . . . VP, Business & Creative Development
Mauro Casalese . . . . . Sr. Director/VP, Production
Jeffery Agala . . . . . Director
Ridd Sorensen . . . . . Director
Paddy Gillen . . . . . Production Manager
Olaf Miller . . . . . BG Designer, Art Director
Scott Davies . . . . . Accountant/Coordinator

AUTOMATIC PICTURES, INC.
5225 Wilshire Blvd., Ste. 525
Los Angeles, CA 90036
PHONE 323-935-1800
FAX 323-935-8040
EMAIL . . . . . automaticpictures@hotmail.com
WEB SITE . . . . . www.automaticpictures.net
SECOND WEB SITE . . . . . www.lookingglasswars.com
TYPES — Animation - Features - Made-for-TV/Cable Movies - New Media - TV Series
DEVELOPMENT — The Season - The Looking Glass Wars
CREDITS — There's Something About Mary - Wicked

Frank Beddor . . . . . Producer
Liz Cavalier . . . . . Creative Executive
Greg Cook . . . . . Product Development
Nate Barlow . . . . . Assistant to Frank Beddor

THE AV CLUB
2629 Main St., #211
Santa Monica, CA 90405
PHONE 310-396-1165
TYPES — Features
CREDITS — The OH in Ohio

Amy Salko Robertson . . . . . Partner
Billy Kent . . . . . Partner

AVALANCHE! ENTERTAINMENT
11041 Santa Monica Blvd., Ste. 511
Los Angeles, CA 90025
PHONE 310-477-1464
FAX 310-552-0549
TYPES — Animation - Documentaries - Features - Internet Content - Mobile Content - Reality TV - TV Series
POST PRODUCTION — For Love of Liberty
CREDITS — Free for All (Showtime Series) - MTV's Campus Cops - She's All That - On the Line - Get Over It - American Psycho 2 - Jekyll Island - The Story of Darrell Royal - MTV's He's the Mayor

Richard Hull . . . . . President

AVALON TELEVISION, INC.
5619 W. Fourth St., Ste. 7
Los Angeles, CA 90036
PHONE 323-930-6010/44-207-598-8000
FAX 323-930-6018/44-207-598-7300
WEB SITE . . . . . www.avalon-usa.com
TYPES — Direct-to-Video/DVD - Reality TV - TV Series
HAS DEAL WITH — Regency Television
PRODUCTION — Greg Behrendt Reality Project (ABC)
POST PRODUCTION — Mystery Bros. (Regency/Fox)
CREDITS — Kelsey Grammer Presents: The Sketch Show - Greg Behrendt Is Uncool
COMMENTS — UK office: 4A Exmoor St., London W10 6BD, United Kingdom

Jon Thoday . . . . . CEO/Managing Director (UK)
Richard Allen-Turner . . . . . Managing Director (UK)
David Martin . . . . . President
Dan Lubetkin . . . . . Manager, Development

AVENUE PICTURES
10202 W. Washington Blvd., David Lean Bldg., Rm. 119
Culver City, CA 90232
PHONE .310-244-6868
FAX .310-244-6869
TYPES — Features - Made-for-TV/Cable Movies - TV Series
HAS DEAL WITH — John Calley Productions - Fox Television Studios - Sony Pictures Entertainment
DEVELOPMENT — The Grays - Rembrandt's Shadow - The Collector - Quitting Texas - Cities of the Plain - A Life in the Day of Tom Rowan - The Solace of Leaving Early - The Moviegoer - Beautiful
PRE-PRODUCTION — Sex & Death 101 - Untitled Ruth Reichl Project (HBO)
CREDITS — Mindhunters - The Merchant of Venice - Closer - Short Cuts - The Player - Restoration - Drugstore Cowboy - Wayward Son - Wit - Path to War - Normal - Angels in America

Cary Brokaw .Chairman/CEO
Aaron Geller .Executive VP/Head, Production
Judy Geletko .Controller
Edward Vaisman .No Title

AWOUNDED KNEE
c/o Homestead Editorial
48 W. 25th Fl., 9th Fl.
New York, NY 10010
PHONE .212-255-4440
FAX .212-255-4494/212-229-1847
EMAIL .info@awkfilms.com
WEB SITE .www.awkfilms.com
SECOND WEB SITE .www.homesteadedit.com
TYPES — Features
DEVELOPMENT — Two Plus Two - Dead, Dead - One Dead Man
PRE-PRODUCTION — Jacky Peek
UPCOMING RELEASES — Noise
CREDITS — The Lucky Ones - Beyond the Ashes - Ash Tuesday - Noise

Lance Doty .Principal
Sam Welch .No Title

THE AXELROD/EDWARDS COMPANY
5555 Melrose Ave., B Annex 1
Los Angeles, CA 90038
PHONE .323-956-3705
FAX .323-862-0079
TYPES — Features - Made-for-TV/Cable Movies - Reality TV - TV Series
HAS DEAL WITH — CBS Paramount Network Television
CREDITS — Dave's World - Can't Hurry Love - Late Bloomer - Brother's Keeper - Movie Stars - Manhattan Man - Against the Wall - The Revenge - Some of My Best Friends - Hollywood Babylon - Sex, Love & Secrets (UPN)

Jonathan Axelrod .Executive Producer
Kelly Edwards .Executive Producer
Michael Klein .Assistant

*BABY COW PRODUCTIONS LTD.
77 Oxford St.
London W1D 2ES, United Kingdom
PHONE .44-20-7399-1267
FAX .44-20-7399-1262
WEB SITE .www.babycow.co.uk
TYPES — Features - TV Series
HAS DEAL WITH — NBC Universal Television Studio
DEVELOPMENT — Nighty Night (Showtime)
CREDITS — Snow Cake - Tristram Shandy: A Cock and Bull Story - 24 Hour Party People - The Sketch Show

Steve Coogan .Managing Director
Henry Normal .Managing Director

BACK LOT PICTURES
1351 N. Genesee Ave.
Los Angeles, CA 90046
PHONE .323-876-1057
TYPES — Features
DEVELOPMENT — The Funnies - The Changeling - Señor Dracula - Untitled Crowhurst Project - Crossing - The Kitchen Boy - Immortal
PRE-PRODUCTION — Sunshine Cleaning - Wonderful World
CREDITS — Hollywoodland - The Omen - Eternal Sunshine of the Spotless Mind - The Ice Harvest
SUBMISSION POLICY — Send query letter via US Mail; Release required prior to submissions; No unsolicited material; No calls or faxes

Glenn Williamson .Producer

BAD BOY FILMS
1710 Broadway
New York, NY 10019
PHONE .212-381-2057
FAX .212-381-1599
WEB SITE .www.badboyonline.com
TYPES — Direct-to-Video/DVD - Features - Reality TV - TV Series
HAS DEAL WITH — MTV Networks
CREDITS — Making the Band 2 (MTV) - Diddy Runs the City (MTV) - Bad Boys of Comedy

Sean Combs .CEO
Anthony Maddox .VP

BAD HAT HARRY PRODUCTIONS
4000 Warner Blvd., Bldg. 81, Ste. 200
Burbank, CA 91522
PHONE .818-954-4043
FAX .818-954-4053
TYPES — Features - Miniseries - TV Series
HAS DEAL WITH — ABC Entertainment Television Group - Warner Bros. Pictures
DEVELOPMENT — U Want Me 2 Kill Him? - Something Happened - Trick or Treat - Secret Service
CREDITS — Film: Superman Returns - X-Men 1&2 - Apt Pupil - Burn - Public Access - The Usual Suspects; TV: The Science of Superman - Look Up in the Sky: The Amazing Story of Superman - House - The Triangle (Sci Fi)

Bryan Singer .Director/Producer
Alex Garcia .Director, Development
Marc Berliner .Development Executive
Jason Taylor .Production Executive

BAD ROBOT PRODUCTIONS

500 S. Buena Vista, Production Bldg., Rm. 361
Burbank, CA 91521
PHONE .818-560-5789
TYPES TV Series
HAS DEAL WITH Paramount Pictures - Warner Bros. Television Production
CREDITS 6 Degrees - What About Brian - Lost - Alias
COMMENTS Moving at press time

J.J. Abrams .No Title
Bryan Burk .Executive VP

THE BADHAM COMPANY

16830 Ventura Blvd., Ste. 300
Encino, CA 91436
PHONE .818-990-9495
FAX .818-981-9163
EMAIL .development@badhamcompany.com
WEB SITE .www.badhamcompany.com
TYPES Features - Made-for-TV/Cable Movies - TV Series
DEVELOPMENT The Parish Files
CREDITS Blind Justice - Evel Knievel (TNT/MOW) - Nick of Time - Stakeout 1&2 - War Games - The Jack Bull
SUBMISSION POLICY Through registered agents only
COMMENTS Feature representation: Robert Lazar, ICM; Cable TV representation: Jill Gillett, ICM; Manager: Todd Harris, 310-276-7884; PR: A&K Public Relations, allison_raven-scroft@yahoo.com or kbadham@earth-link.net

John Badham .Director/Producer

BARNET BAIN FILMS

4250 Wilshire Blvd.
Los Angeles, CA 90010
PHONE .323-656-8829
TYPES Features - Made-for-TV/Cable Movies
DEVELOPMENT Ilium - Illusions - La Magdalena
CREDITS What Dreams May Come - Quantum Project - The Linda McCartney Story - Homeless to Harvard - Jesus - Celestine Prophecy
COMMENTS Deal with Sightsound Technologies

Barnet Bain .Producer

JOHN BALDECCHI PRODUCTIONS

10202 W. Washington Blvd., David Lean Bldg., Ste. 333
Culver City, CA 90232
PHONE .310-244-8232
FAX .310-244-0005
TYPES Features - Made-for-TV/Cable Movies
HAS DEAL WITH Sony Pictures Entertainment
DEVELOPMENT Hot Wheels - The Scared Guys - Delilah - Argonauts - RPM - Return to Castle Wolfenstein
CREDITS Ultraviolet - The Mexican - Stark Raving Mad - Simon Birch - Deep Rising - The Adventures of Huck Finn - Oliver Twist (TV)

John Baldecchi .Producer
Keith Dinielli .Creative Executive
Rich Silverman .Manager
Kevin Rosenberg .Story Editor

BALDWIN ENTERTAINMENT GROUP, LTD.

3000 Olympic Blvd., Bldg. 1, Ste. 2510
Santa Monica, CA 90404
PHONE .310-453-9277
FAX .310-453-9254
WEB SITE .www.baldwinent.com
TYPES Documentaries - Features - Theatre - TV Series
PROVIDES DEAL TO Nick Grillo Productions
DEVELOPMENT Luna - Mandrake - Atlas Shrugged - Rat's Tale - Jackie Robinson/Branch Rickey Project - Custer Battles - 1:30 Train - Death Sentence
CREDITS Ray - Sahara - Swimming Upstream - Mystery, Alaska - Sudden Death - From the Hip - Billy Galvin - The Cellar - The Patriot - Resurrection - Spellbinder - Gideon - Danny Deckchair - Game of Their Lives
SUBMISSION POLICY No unsolicited submissions

Howard Baldwin .Producer
Karen Baldwin .Producer
Stuart Benjamin .No Title
Eric Mitchell .No Title
Todd Slater .Executive VP
Nick Morton .Executive VP
Nick Ruta .Executive VP, Business Affairs
Nathaniel Baldwin .Creative Executive
Erin Enslin .Administrative Assistant
Johnathon McFadden .Executive Assistant to Howard Baldwin & Karen Baldwin

BALLYHOO, INC.

c/o Mandalay Pictures
6738 Wedgewood Pl.
Hollywood, CA 90068
PHONE .323-874-3396
EMAIL .michaelbesman1@aol.com
TYPES Features - TV Series
DEVELOPMENT Jump (Mandalay/Universal) - The Last Game of the Season (Mandalay) - Da Vinci's Mother (Fox Searchlight) - Larry
PRE-PRODUCTION Georgia Rule (Morgan Creek)
POST PRODUCTION Careless (Friday Night Entertainment)
CREDITS Seven Years in Tibet - Bounce - The Opposite of Sex - About Schmidt
SUBMISSION POLICY No unsolicited material

Michael Besman .Producer

BANG ZOOM! ENTERTAINMENT
1100 N. Hollywood Way
Burbank, CA 91505
PHONE 818-295-3939
FAX 818-295-3999
EMAIL ....info@bangzoomentertainment.com
WEB SITE ....www.bangzoomentertainment.com
TYPES Animation - Direct-to-Video/DVD - Documentaries - Features - TV Series
DEVELOPMENT Kill Me Softly - Untitled Anime-Style Feature - Attack of the Killer Worms from Outer Space
PRODUCTION Anime TV (Pilot) - Adventures in Voice Acting
UPCOMING RELEASES Karas (Film Roman) - Eureka Seven (Cartoon Network) - IGPX (Cartoon Network)
CREDITS Encore: Vandread; Cartoon Network: Samurai Champloo - Rurouni Kenshin - Witch Hunter Robin - Scryed; G4/TechTV: Last Exile - Gad Guard - Gungrave; Showtime: Versus; MTV: Heatguy J
COMMENTS Specialize in Anime; Focus on voice-over and localization

Eric P. Sherman ....President
Kaeko Sakamoto ....VP/Casting Director
Megumi Kunisada ....Production Coordinator
Mami Okada ....Associate Producer
Patrick Rodman ....Chief Engineer
Mark Fujita ....Creative Director
Kevin Patzelt ....Engineer/Sound Design
Lisa Marie Cisneroz ....Executive Assistant

BANKABLE PRODUCTIONS
6310 San Vicente Blvd., Ste. 505
Los Angeles, CA 90048
PHONE 323-934-4308
FAX 323-934-4387
EMAIL ....inquiries@bankableprods.com
WEB SITE ....www.bankableprods.com
TYPES Features - Made-for-TV/Cable Movies - Reality TV - TV Series
CREDITS America's Next Top Model - The Tyra Banks Show
SUBMISSION POLICY By agent or manager only

Tyra Banks ....Executive Producer
Carolyn London ....VP, Creative Affairs
Bradford Sisk ....Production Executive
Lisa Momberger ....Executive Assistant to Ms. Banks
Daphne Butts ....Executive Assistant to Carolyn London

BANYAN PRODUCTIONS
13101 Washington Blvd., Ste. 238
Los Angeles, CA 90066
PHONE 310-566-7158/215-928-1414
FAX 310-566-7159/215-928-9944
EMAIL ....corporate@banyanprod.com
WEB SITE ....www.banyan.com
TYPES Reality TV - Syndication - TV Series
CREDITS Trading Spaces - Ambush Makeover - Perfect Proposal - A Makeover Story - Design Invasion - Epicurious - Birth Day
COMMENTS East Coast office: 530 Walnut St., Ste. 276, Philadelphia, PA 19106

Jeanne McHale Waite ....CEO
Tom Farrell ....COO
Dave Bowers ....VP/CFO
Linda Calabrese Kane ....VP/Director, Operations
Susan Cohen-Dickler ....Executive Producer
Ray Murray ....Executive Producer
Jan Dickler ....Executive Producer
Benjamin Ringe ....Director, Development

BANYAN TREE FILMS
1 Worth St., 2nd Fl.
New York, NY 10013
PHONE 212-966-1135
FAX 212-966-1125
TYPES Features
CREDITS City of Ghosts
SUBMISSION POLICY No unsolicited submissions

Matt Dillon ....Principal
Joe Revitte ....Producer

ALAN BARNETTE PRODUCTIONS
100 Universal City Plaza, Bldg. 2352, Ste. 101
Universal City, CA 91608
PHONE 818-733-0993/818-733-1074
FAX 818-733-3172
EMAIL ....dabarnette@aol.com
TYPES Features - Made-for-TV/Cable Movies - Miniseries - TV Series
DEVELOPMENT The Roxy - The Franchise (NFL) - Alfred Hitchcock and the Making of Psycho (Focus) - Execution Live (ABC)
CREDITS Faith of My Fathers (A&E) - Resurrection - Sliders - The Equalizer - Off Limits - Broken Cord - Extreme - Seeing Double

Alan Barnette ....Executive Producer
Aaron Sandler ....Director
Nancy Mosher Hall ....Development

BARNHOLTZ ENTERTAINMENT

23480 Park Sorrento, Ste. 217-A
Calabasas, CA 91302
PHONE .818-591-1900
FAX .818-591-5960
EMAIL .bbarnholtz@aol.com
SECOND EMAIL .barnholtzacquisitions@hotmail.com

TYPES	Features - Internet Content - Made-for-TV/Cable Movies
DEVELOPMENT	Ed Gein
POST PRODUCTION	The Calling - The Devil Within
UPCOMING RELEASES	Heebie Jeebies - 12 Days of Christmas Eve - Satanic - After Sundown - Ball and Chain - Harvest of Fear - Haunted Highway - Chasing Christmas - Twisted Sisters
CREDITS	Red Neck Comedy Round Up - Mangler Reborn - Paranoid - They Are Among Us - The Off Season - Ghostwatcher 1&2 - The Slaughterhouse Massacre - Chronicle of the Raven - Dead Doll - The Rebel Rousers - The Bunker - Ball and Chain - Little Boy Blue - Hallowed - Latino Kings of Comedy
SUBMISSION POLICY	No unsoliticited material
COMMENTS	Also distributes

Barry Barnholtz .President/CEO
Kate Barnholtz .CFO
Matthew Fladell .Sr. VP, Business Affairs
Melvin Butters .Director, Acquisitions
Will Santa Cruz .Supervisor, Post Production
Deborah Templeton .Delivery Manager
Liana Bryer .Executive Assistant

BARNSTORM FILMS

73 Market St.
Venice, CA 90291
PHONE .310-396-5937
FAX .310-450-4988
EMAIL .tony@barnstormfilms.com

TYPES	Features - Made-for-TV/Cable Movies - TV Series
DEVELOPMENT	The Possum Trot Cloggers (New Line) - Walkaway Joe - Step-Ball-Change - The Untitled Hip-Hop Nanny Project - Come & Go Molly Snow
CREDITS	Taxi Driver - Untamed Heart - My Bodyguard - Five Corners - The Sting - Harlan County War - In the Time of the Butterflies - Last Call - The Fixer
SUBMISSION POLICY	Query letter with synopsis

Tony Bill .Producer/Director
Helen Bartlett .Producer

BARRACUDA PRODUCTIONS

5512 Lemona Ave.
Sherman Oaks, CA 91411
PHONE .818-749-3729
EMAIL .tvmovies@aol.com

TYPES	Made-for-TV/Cable Movies - TV Series
DEVELOPMENT	Dancing on the Edge of the Roof (TNT) - Ship on Fire (CBS) - I'll Be You (Oxygen)
PRODUCTION	Peter the Great
CREDITS	Hello Sister, Goodbye Life - Betty La Fea - Danger Beneath the Sea - King and Country - The Chris Isaak Show - A Tale of Two Wives - Off Season - Rough Air - Shake Rattle & Roll - Seconds to Spare - A Mother Waits (Lifetime)
SUBMISSION POLICY	No unsolicited mail, calls or faxes; Email only; Queries completed scripts only

Marc B. Lorber .Producer
Molly Marks .Creative Assistant

BARWOOD FILMS

321 W. 78th St., Ste. 1-A
New York, NY 10024
PHONE .212-787-4151
FAX .212-787-7418
EMAIL .lilycor@aol.com

TYPES	Documentaries - Features - Made-for-TV/Cable Movies - TV Series
DEVELOPMENT	Mendel's Dwarf
CREDITS	Serving in Silence - Prince of Tides - The Mirror Has Two Faces - Yentl - Reel Models: The 1st Women in Film - Varian's War - What Makes a Family - The Living Century

Barbra Streisand .Owner/Actress/Producer/Director
Cis Corman .President
Gina Biscotti .Development Assistant

BATES ENTERTAINMENT

895-1/2 S. Lucerne Blvd.
Los Angeles, CA 90005
PHONE .323-936-6117

TYPES	Documentaries - Features - Made-for-TV/Cable Movies - TV Series
DEVELOPMENT	Whacked! - Hot Property - The Butler Did It - Second Hand - Catching Hell - The Enthusiast - Sick Day - Werenation
PRE-PRODUCTION	Holy War - Kid Bang - 3 Stones Back - White Hot - Slasher Basher
PRODUCTION	Fallen (ABC Family)
CREDITS	Last Time I Committed Suicide - Kingdom Come - Fall Time
SUBMISSION POLICY	Submit query letter in writing; No unsolicited scripts

Edward J. Bates .Producer
Rochelle Bates .Producer

BATTLE PLAN PRODUCTIONS
500 S. Buena Vista St., Old Animation Bldg., 3rd Fl.
Burbank, CA 91521
PHONE .818-560-2616
FAX .818-560-1991
TYPES Features - TV Series
HAS DEAL WITH Touchstone Television
DEVELOPMENT The Cell Game - Soul of the Age - Triumph - The Contractor
PRODUCTION Resurrecting the Champ
POST PRODUCTION Flyboys
CREDITS Film: The Jacket - Deterrence - The Contender - 4 Second Delay; TV: Commander-in-Chief - Line of Fire

Marc Frydman .President/Producer
Rod Lurie .President/Producer/Writer/Director
James Spies .Producer
Alan Goss .Assistant to Rod Lurie
Peter Rawlinson .Assistant to Marc Frydman

THE BAUER COMPANY
9720 Wilshire Blvd., Mezzanine
Beverly Hills, CA 90212
PHONE .310-247-3880
FAX .310-247-3881
TYPES Features - Made-for-TV/Cable Movies - Miniseries - TV Series

Martin R. Bauer .Producer
Tom Demko .Producer
Mario Garcia .Executive Assistant

BAUER MARTINEZ ENTERTAINMENT
10250 Constellation Blvd., 3rd Fl.
Los Angeles, CA 90067
PHONE .310-843-0464
FAX .310-843-0460
EMAIL .mail@bauermartinez.com
SECOND EMAIL .bmstudios1@aol.com
WEB SITE .www.bauermartinez.com
TYPES Features
PROVIDES DEAL TO Forest Park Pictures
CREDITS Modigliani

Philippe Martinez .CEO
Drew Larner .Vice Chairman
Karinne Behr .President
Corrie Rothbart .COO
Steven Break .VP, Development & Acquisitions
Nabil Sedeak .VP, Accounting & Finance
Hugh Spurling .Head, Business Affairs
Martin J. Barab .General Counsel

CAROL BAUM PRODUCTIONS
8899 Beverly Blvd., Ste. 721
Los Angeles, CA 90048
PHONE .310-550-4575
FAX .310-550-2088
TYPES Features - Made-for-TV/Cable Movies - Theatre - TV Series
DEVELOPMENT Grace (Fox 2000) - Naomi Foner - Slammer (Revolution) - The Cell Game (Showtime) - Tynan (Royal Shakespeare Company) - Challenger
COMPLETED UNRELEASED You Kill Me
CREDITS Sexual Life - Carolina - Fly Away Home - Father of the Bride - Dead Ringers - Kicking & Screaming - My First Mister - IQ - The Good Girl
SUBMISSION POLICY No unsolicited submissions

Carol Baum .Producer

SUZANNE BAUMAN PRODUCTIONS
21901 Velicata St.
Woodland Hills, CA 91364
PHONE .818-348-4342
EMAIL .filmforthought@aol.com
WEB SITE .www.filmforthought.com
TYPES Documentaries - Features - TV Series
DEVELOPMENT Ladies of the Canyon - In the Time of Roses - Edge of the Bonfire - Circling the Drain
PRODUCTION River of Dreams - What the Soul Sees
CREDITS The Writing Code - Shadow of Afghanistan - Jackie: Behind the Myth - Animal Adventures - La Belle Epoque - Suleyman the Magnificent

Suzanne Bauman .Producer/Director
Toni Pace Carstenson .Producer
Ryan Burroughs .Director, Development

BAY FILMS
631 Colorado Ave.
Santa Monica, CA 90401
PHONE .310-319-6565
FAX .310-319-6570
TYPES Commercials - Features
CREDITS Pearl Harbor - Armageddon - The Rock - Bad Boys 1&2 - The Island

Michael Bay .Director/Producer
Matthew Cohan .VP, Development
Joli Eberhart .Executive Assistant to Michael Bay
Edward Albolote .Assistant
Danielle Zloto .Assistant

BAYONNE ENTERTAINMENT
11200 Chalon Rd.
Los Angeles, CA 90049
PHONE .310-889-9222
FAX .310-889-9323
TYPES Features - Made-for-TV/Cable Movies - Miniseries - Reality TV - TV Series
HAS DEAL WITH Lionsgate
DEVELOPMENT V
COMPLETED UNRELEASED Simply Irresistible (VH1)
CREDITS Minding the Store - Crossroads (Feature) - Dancing at the Harvest Moon (MOW) - Dean Koontz's Black River (MOW) - Blow Out (Bravo) - Brave New Girl (ABC Family)

Rob Lee .Producer
Geoff Talley .Assistant

BAZMARK, INQ.
2 Darley St.
Darlinghurst NSW 2010, Australia
PHONE .61-2-9361-6668
FAX .61-2-9361-6667
EMAIL .reception@bazmark.com
WEB SITE .www.bazmark.com
TYPES Features
HAS DEAL WITH Twentieth Century Fox
CREDITS Moulin Rouge - Romeo + Juliet - Strictly Ballroom - La Bohème
SUBMISSION POLICY No unsolicited material or phone calls

Baz Luhrmann .President
Amanda Luhrmann .COO
Catherine Martin .VP

BBC FILMS

BBC FILMS

Grafton House
379 Eusten Rd., 4th Fl.
London NW1 3AU, United Kingdom
PHONE .44-207-765-0251
FAX .44-207-765-0278
WEB SITE .www.bbc.co.uk/bbcfilms/

TYPES: Features - TV Series
DEVELOPMENT: Eastern Promises - Boy Soldier - Payback
POST PRODUCTION: Dragnet
UPCOMING RELEASES: The History Boys - Life 'n' Lyrics - Red Road - Fast Food Nation
CREDITS: Film: Mrs. Henderson Presents - Match Point - Millions - Stage Beauty - Masked & Anonymous - Dirty Pretty Things - Iris - Billy Elliot - My Summer of Love - The Life and Death of Peter Sellers - The Mighty Celt - A Cock and Bull Story - Glastonbury; TV: The Catherine Tate Show - Little Britain

David Thompson .Head, BBC Films
Susy Liddell .Head, Production
Emma Broughton .Development Executive
Luke Alkin .Development Producer
Ruth Caleb .Producer/Executive Producer
Christine Langan .Producer/Executive Producer
Jamie Laurenson .Development Producer
Joe Oppenheimer .Development Producer
Anne Pivcevic .Producer/Executive Producer
Jane Hawley .Production Executive
Michael Wood .Production Executive
Alexei Boltho .Commercial Executive
Kenton Allen .Head, Comedy Talent
Isabel Begg .Head, Business & Legal Affairs
Jane Wright .Head, Business & Commercial Affairs

BBC WORLDWIDE AMERICAS

4144 Lankershim Blvd., Ste. 200
North Hollywood, CA 91602
PHONE .818-299-9715
FAX .818-299-9761
WEB SITE .www.bbc.co.uk

TYPES: Features - Made-for-TV/Cable Movies - Miniseries - TV Series
HAS DEAL WITH: Sony Pictures Television
CREDITS: Dancing with the Stars - The Office - State of Play - The Grid

Mark Thompson .Director General
Jana Bennett .Director, TV
George McGhee .Controller, Program Acquisitions
Paul Telegdy .Sr. VP, Programming & Co-Productions
Susanna Pollack .VP, Children's Business Development
Guy Phillips .Manager, Reality & Gameshow
Jeremy Whitham .Manager, Drama & Comedy

BEACON

A Division of Holding Pictures
120 Broadway, Ste. 200
Santa Monica, CA 90401
PHONE .310-260-7000
FAX .310-260-7050
WEB SITE .www.beaconpictures.com

TYPES: Features
HAS DEAL WITH: Walt Disney Pictures/Touchstone Pictures
DEVELOPMENT: Mount Pleasant - Who Killed Daniel Pearl Adaptation - Confession of an Economic Hitman - Havana Room - Legends - Serial - 74 Gallons - Outrider - Mardi Gras Project
PRODUCTION: The Water Horse
POST PRODUCTION: PU-239
CREDITS: The Guardian - Firewall - For Love of the Game - The Commitments - Air Force One - A Thousand Acres - End of Days - The Hurricane - Bring It On - Family Man - Thirteen Days - Spy Game - The Emperor's Club - Tuck Everlasting - Open Range - Raising Helen - Ladder 49 - A Lot Like Love

Armyan Bernstein .Chairman
Charlie Lyons .CEO
Ted Howells .CFO
Zanne Devine .President, Production
Suzann Ellis .Executive VP, Development & Production
Christian McLaughlin .Executive VP, Development & Production
Nancy Rae Stone .Executive VP, Production
Gregory R. Schenz .VP, Business & Legal
Jun Oh .VP, Business & Legal Affairs
Jason Sachs .VP, Financial Planning
Cynthia Hahn .Director, Business Affairs Administration

JUNE BEALLOR PRODUCTIONS

100 Universal City Plaza, Bldg. 6147
Universal City, CA 91608
PHONE .818-777-9000
FAX .818-866-2222

TYPES: Documentaries - Features - Made-for-TV/Cable Movies - Reality TV - TV Series
CREDITS: Survivors of the Holocaust - The Lost Children of Berlin - The Last Days
SUBMISSION POLICY: No unsolicited material

June Beallor .Producer/Director
Susan M. Baker .VP

THE BEDFORD FALLS COMPANY
409 Santa Monica Blvd., PH
Santa Monica, CA 90401
PHONE . . . 310-394-5022
FAX . . . 310-394-5825
TYPES Features - TV Series
HAS DEAL WITH ABC Entertainment Television Group - Warner Bros. Pictures
POST PRODUCTION The Blood Diamond
CREDITS The Last Samurai - Traffic - Once and Again - Dangerous Beauty - Shakespeare in Love - I Am Sam - Legends of the Fall - thirtysomething
SUBMISSION POLICY Query letters only

Edward Zwick . . . Executive Producer/Writer/Director (310-394-2697)
Marshall Herskovitz . . . Executive Producer/Writer/Director (310-394-5355)
Richard Solomon . . . President (310-394-5643)
Troy Putney . . . Creative Executive to Mr. Zwick
Joshua Gummersall . . . Creative Executive to Mr. Herskovitz
Ryan F. Coleman . . . Creative Executive to Mr. Herskovitz
David Passman . . . Creative Executive to Mr. Solomon
Julian Milam . . . St. Lunatic

BEECH HILL FILMS
330 W. 38th St., Ste. 1405
New York, NY 10018
PHONE . . . 212-594-8095
FAX . . . 212-594-8118
TYPES Features - TV Series
DEVELOPMENT The Tricky Part - Drift
PRE-PRODUCTION Raritan Valley Line - Run, Fat Boy, Run - Untitled Tom Fontana Project
UPCOMING RELEASES Jimmy
CREDITS A Hole in One - Our Song - Face

Alexa L. Fogel . . . Producer
Joseph Infantolino . . . Producer
Brendan Mason . . . Director, Production

BELISARIUS PRODUCTIONS
c/o Sunset Gower Studios
1438 N. Gower St., Box 25, Bldg. 35, 4th Fl.
Los Angeles, CA 90028
PHONE . . . 323-468-4500
FAX . . . 323-468-4599
TYPES TV Series
HAS DEAL WITH CBS Paramount Network Television
CREDITS N.C.I.S. - Quantum Leap - Magnum, P.I. - JAG - Last Rites - First Monday
COMMENTS A division of Viacom

Donald P. Bellisario . . . Executive Producer/Director/Writer
Chas. Floyd Johnson . . . Co-Executive Producer
John C. Kelley . . . Co-Executive Producer/Writer
Mark Horowitz . . . Co-Executive Producer
David Bellisario . . . Producer
Avery Drewe . . . Producer
Julie Watson . . . Coordinating Producer
Susan Hollander . . . Script Coordinator
Steven Binder . . . Story Editor
David North . . . Story Editor
Patty Sachs . . . Executive Assistant to Mr. Bellisario
Brian Napleton . . . Second Assistant to Mr. Bellisario
Debra Mayfield . . . Executive Assistant to Mr. Johnson

DAVE BELL ASSOCIATES
3211 Cahuenga Blvd. West
Los Angeles, CA 90068
PHONE . . . 323-851-7801
FAX . . . 323-851-9349
EMAIL . . . dbamovies@aol.com
TYPES Documentaries - Features - Made-for-TV/Cable Movies - TV Series
DEVELOPMENT The Proud & Few - Tinker - Tunnel Rats - Bikini Zombie Warrior - Tell Dolly Parton I Love Her
CREDITS Deep Red - Long Walk Home - Do You Remember Love? - Nadia - Just a Dream - Asylum - Skinheads

David L. Bell . . . President
Ted Weiant . . . Director, Motion Pictures
Fred Putman . . . Director, TV
Kitty Stallings . . . Creative Associate

BELLADONNA PRODUCTIONS
118 W. 22nd St., 3rd Fl
New York, NY 10011
PHONE . . . 212-807-0108
FAX . . . 212-807-6263
EMAIL . . . cordelia@belladonna.bz
WEB SITE . . . www.belladonna.bz
TYPES Commercials - Documentaries - Features - Music Videos
UPCOMING RELEASES A Guide to Recognizing Your Saints
CREDITS Transamerica - L.I.E. - Sue

Rene Bastian . . . Producer
Linda Moran . . . Producer
Cordelia Stephens . . . Head, Development

BELL-PHILLIP TV PRODUCTIONS, INC.
7800 Beverly Blvd., Ste. 3371
Los Angeles, CA 90036-2188
PHONE . . . 323-575-4138
FAX . . . 323-655-8760
TYPES TV Series
CREDITS The Bold and the Beautiful

Lee Phillip Bell . . . Co-Creator
Bradley Bell . . . Executive Producer/Head Writer
Ron Weaver . . . Sr. Producer
Rhonda Friedman . . . Supervising Producer
Cynthia J. Popp . . . Producer
Adam Dusevoir . . . Associate Producer

LAWRENCE BENDER PRODUCTIONS
8530 Wilshire Blvd., Ste. 500
Beverly Hills, CA 90211
PHONE . . . 323-951-4600
FAX . . . 323-951-4601
TYPES Features - TV Series
HAS DEAL WITH Nickelodeon Movies
DEVELOPMENT The Five Ancestors - Holy Cow - Addicks (HBO) - Pumped (VH1) - Normal State (UPN) - Flirt (UPN) - Friendly Skies (Fox) - The Beatles in America (TNT) - Heroes Anonymous (Sci Fi) - Video Village - Tank McNamara (Amuse Entertainemt) - Terri: The Truth

Lawrence Bender . . . Producer/Partner
Karen Barber . . . Producer
Kevin Brown . . . Production
Janet Jeffries . . . Development
Jason Olin . . . Development
Ariana Harris . . . Assistant to Mr. Bender
Justin Jacquemotte . . . Assistant to Mr. Brown
Zac Minor . . . Second Assistant to Mr. Bender

BENDERSPINK
110 S. Fairfax Ave., Ste. 350
Los Angeles, CA 90036
PHONE .323-904-1800
FAX .323-904-1802
EMAIL .info@benderspink.com
WEB SITE .www.benderspink.com
TYPES Features - TV Series
HAS DEAL WITH fox 21 - New Line Cinema
DEVELOPMENT Curve - Urban Townie - Y: The Last Man - We're the Millers - R-5 - This Bill Smith - Bob the Musical - Ride Along - The Guy Not Taken - The Ghouly Boys - Major Movie Star - All Boxed Up - Torrente - Power and Glory - Burt Dickenson: The Most Powerful Magician on Planet Earth - 99 Problems - The Adventures of Luther Arkwright
POST PRODUCTION The Butterfly Effect 2
UPCOMING RELEASES Full of It
CREDITS Just Friends - Red Eye - A History of Violence - Monster-In-Law - The Ring 1&2 - American Pie 1-3 - Cats & Dogs - Final Destination - Cheats - The Butterfly Effect - Blind Horizon

Chris Bender .Executive
J.C. Spink .Executive
Charlie Gogolak .Executive
Brian Spink .Executive
Jill McElroy .Executive
Jake Weiner .Executive
Courtney Kivowitz .Executive
Christian Donatelli .Executive
Julie Plec .Executive
Mason Novick .Executive
Dave Brown .Executive
Cory Hebenstreit .Executive
Jon Silk .Executive
Tom Boardman .Assistant
Andrea Castro .Assistant
Peter Collins .Assistant
Amber DeFrancis .Assistant
Neal Flaherty .Assistant
Langley Perer .Assistant
Matthew Reis .Assistant
Jonathan Tuckerman .Assistant
Amanda Potts .Assistant

HARVE BENNETT PRODUCTIONS
PO Box 825
Culver City, CA 90232-0825
PHONE .310-306-7198
FAX .310-306-7598
TYPES Animation - Features - Made-for-TV/Cable Movies - Miniseries - TV Series
CREDITS Star Trek II: The Wrath of Khan - Star Trek III: The Search for Spock - Star Trek IV: The Voyage Home - Star Trek V: The Final Frontier - Rich Man, Poor Man - A Woman Called Golda - The Jesse Owens Story - The Mod Squad - The Six Million Dollar Man - The Bionic Woman
SUBMISSION POLICY No unsolicited material

Harve Bennett .Executive Producer/Writer
Marianne Tyler .VP, Development

BERLANTI PRODUCTIONS
500 S. Buena Vista St., Old Animation Bldg., 2D-10
Burbank, CA 91521
PHONE .818-560-4846
TYPES Features - TV Series
HAS DEAL WITH Touchstone Television
DEVELOPMENT Bridge and Tunnel
CREDITS The Broken Hearts Club - Everwood - Jack & Bobby

Greg Berlanti .Writer/Producer
Melissa Berman .Head, Development
Carl Ogawa .Assistant to Greg Berlanti
Lakesha Walker .Assistant to Melissa Berman

RICK BERMAN PRODUCTIONS
5555 Melrose Ave., Cooper Bldg., Ste. 232
Los Angeles, CA 90038
PHONE .323-956-5037
FAX .323-862-1076
TYPES Features - Syndication - TV Series
HAS DEAL WITH CBS Paramount Network Television
CREDITS Star Trek: The Next Generation - Star Trek: Insurrection - Star Trek: Deep Space Nine - Star Trek: First Contact - Star Trek: Voyager - Enterprise - Star Trek: Nemesis

Rick Berman .Executive Producer
Ellie Hannibal .Sr. VP, Development
Doug Mirabello .Assistant to Mr. Berman
Lou Bottino .Production Assistant to Mr. Berman

BET NETWORKS
One BET Plaza, 1235 W St. NE
Washington, DC 20018-1211
PHONE .202-608-2000/818-655-6700
FAX .202-608-2631/818-655-6770
WEB SITE .www.bet.com
TYPES Animation - Direct-to-Video/DVD - Documentaries - Features - Made-for-TV/Cable Movies - Reality TV - Specials - Theatre - TV Series
DEVELOPMENT Season of the Tiger - Meet the Faith - Next Level: Vince Young - DMX: Soul of a Man - Keyshia Cole: The Way It Is - Black Book Diaries - American Gangster - Hotwyred - The Black Carpet - Iron Ring - Beef: The Series
CREDITS College Hill - BET Comedy Awards - 106 & Park - Rap City - ComicView - Spring Bling - Celebration of Gospel - BET Walk of Fame - BET Awards Show - Coming to the Stage - Ultimate Hustler - REMIXED! - Star Time Keyshia Cole
SUBMISSION POLICY Agency referrals only to Robyn Lattaker-Johnson
COMMENTS West Coast production studio: 4024 Radford Ave., R&D Bldg., 4th Fl., Studio City, CA 91604

Robert L. Johnson .Founder
Debra L. Lee .Chairman/CEO
Reginald Hudlin .President, Entertainment
Louis Carr .President, Advertising Media Sales
Scott Mills .Executive VP/CFO
Paxton Baker .Executive VP, BET Digital Networks & BET Event Productions
Raymond Goulbourne .Executive VP, Advertising Media Sales
Nina Henderson Moore .Executive VP, News & Public Affairs
Stephen Hill .Executive VP, Entertainment & Music Programming
(Continued)

BET NETWORKS (Continued)
Kelli Richardson Lawson . . . . .Executive VP, Corporate Marketing
Byron Marchant . . . . .Executive VP/General Counsel/CAO
Byron Phillips . . . . .Executive VP, Entertainment
Michael Pickrum . . . . .Executive VP, BET Interactive LLC
Darrell Walker . . . . .Executive VP, Business Affairs
Michael D. Armstrong . . . . .Sr. VP, BET International
Matthew Barnhill . . . . .Sr. VP, Market Research
Quinton Bowman . . . . .Sr. VP, Human Resources
Denys Cowan . . . . .Sr. VP, Animation
John Gordon . . . . .Sr. VP, Finance/Controller
Donovan Gordon . . . . .Sr. VP, Affiliate Sales & Marketing
Michael Lewellen . . . . .Sr. VP, Corporate Communications
Robyn Lattaker-Johnson . . . . .VP, Development/Original Programming
Tom Reynolds . . . . .VP/Chief of Staff
Endyia Kinney-Sterns . . . . . . .Director, Development/Original Programming
Kevin Morrison . . . . .Director, Development/Original Programming
Shirley Salomon . . . . .Director, Production

BIG BEACH
41 Great Jones St., 5th Fl.
New York, NY 10012
PHONE 212-473-5800
FAX 212-473-5805
EMAIL . . . . .info@bigbeachfilms.com
WEB SITE . . . . .www.bigbeachfilms.com
TYPES Features
CREDITS Sherrybaby - Little Miss Sunshine - Everything Is Illuminated - Duane Hopwood
SUBMISSION POLICY No unsolicited submissions

Marc Turtletaub . . . . .Partner
Jeb Brody . . . . .Partner
Peter Saraf . . . . .Partner
Sara Pollack . . . . .Production Executive
Emily McMaster . . . . .No Title
Noelle Griffis . . . . .No Title

***BIG CATTLE PRODUCTIONS**
4370 Tujunga Ave., Ste. 130
Studio City, CA 91604
PHONE 818-506-7200
FAX 818-506-7333
EMAIL . . . . .bigcattlemail@bigcattleprod.com
TYPES Features - TV Series
HAS DEAL WITH NBC Universal Television Studio
DEVELOPMENT The Center (Lifetime) - Blink (Sci Fi) - Flint (TBS) - Morningside Heights (NBC) - Evil (CW) - Plato's Retreat
PRE-PRODUCTION Hunting Rabbets (USA)
CREDITS Lovespring (Lifetime)
SUBMISSION POLICY No unsolicited submissions

Eric McCormack . . . . .President
Michael C. Forman . . . . .President, Development & Production
Julia Nickerson . . . . .Development

BIG LIGHT PRODUCTIONS
500 S. Buena Vista St., Animation Bldg., #2A-10
Burbank, CA 91521-1711
PHONE 818-560-4782
EMAIL . . . . .questions@biglight.com
WEB SITE . . . . .www.biglight.com
TYPES Features - TV Series
HAS DEAL WITH ABC Entertainment Television Group - Touchstone Television
DEVELOPMENT Star Chamber (20th Century Fox)
PRE-PRODUCTION Amped (Fox 21/Spike TV)
CREDITS The Night Stalker - The X-Files - Robbery Homicide Division - Millenium - The Lone Gunmen

Frank Spotnitz . . . . .Producer
Jana Fain . . . . .Director, Development

BIG PIX INC.
c/o Murphy & Kress
2401 Main St.
Santa Monica, CA 90405
PHONE 310-396-7000
FAX 310-396-2690
TYPES Animation - Direct-to-Video/DVD - Documentaries - Features - Made-for-TV/Cable Movies - Syndication - TV Series
CREDITS MacGyver - Legend - Stargate SG-1

Michael Greenburg . . . . .President

BIGEL ENTERTAINMENT
9701 Wilshire Blvd., Ste. 1100
Beverly Hills, CA 90212
PHONE 310-278-9400
FAX 310-278-2220
WEB SITE . . . . .www.bigelentertainment.com
TYPES Features - Internet Content - Reality TV - TV Series
DEVELOPMENT Break - The Host - Pork Pie - Never Change - Play Dates
CREDITS Loverboy - Devour - The Money Shot - Black and White - Two Girls and a Guy - Giving It Up - Harvard Man - Empire - The Last Producer - Lost Junction
SUBMISSION POLICY No unsolicited submissions

Daniel Bigel . . . . .CEO
Stephanie Striegel . . . . .Head, Development

STU BILLETT PRODUCTIONS
6922 Hollywood Blvd., Ste. 300
Hollywood, CA 90028
PHONE 323-957-6300
FAX 323-461-0253
WEB SITE . . . . .www.peoplescourt.com
TYPES Reality TV - TV Series
CREDITS People's Court

Stu Billett . . . . .Executive Producer

BLACK & WHITE PRODUCTIONS
100 Universal City Plaza, Bldg. 4113
Universal City, CA 91608
PHONE 818-777-0999
FAX 818-733-2651
TYPES Features
HAS DEAL WITH Universal Pictures
DEVELOPMENT Death Ray - Yes Man - Them
CREDITS Nacho Libre

Jack Black . . . . .Principal
Mike White . . . . .Principal
Ben Cooley . . . . .Development
Ben LeClair . . . . .Development
Rebecca Robinson . . . . .Executive Assistant

BLACK FOLK ENTERTAINMENT
2533 N. Beachwood Dr.
Los Angeles, CA 90068
PHONE 323-466-3828
FAX 323-466-3821
EMAIL . . . . .john@blackfolkfilms.com
TYPES Direct-to-Video/DVD - Features - TV Series
PRE-PRODUCTION Places You'll Go - When Love Calls - Scorn
CREDITS Ride Salley Ride - A Fare to Remember

John Salley . . . . .CEO
Sandra Rabbin . . . . .Executive Assistant to CEO

BLACK SHEEP ENTERTAINMENT

c/o The Lot
1041 N. Formosa Ave., Formosa Bldg., Ste. 4
West Hollywood, CA 90046
PHONE .310-347-6066
FAX .310-424-7117
EMAIL .development@blacksheepent.com
TYPES Features - TV Series
DEVELOPMENT To Forsake All Others - Ride Share - Breaking Irish - The Blood Room - Hello, My Name Is...
PRE-PRODUCTION Fifty-Two
PRODUCTION Hooking Up
CREDITS The Cottonwood - It Had to Be You - The Big Gig
SUBMISSION POLICY No unsolicited material

Steven Feder .Owner/Writer/Producer/Director
Jay Beeber .Director, Development & Acquisitions
Mark Groubert .Development Executive

BLACKFRIARS BRIDGE

9200 Sunset Blvd., Ste. 820
Los Angeles, CA 90069
PHONE .310-402-5161
FAX .310-246-4424
TYPES Features - TV Series
DEVELOPMENT Death and Dishonor - Against All Enemies - Honeymoon with Harry
PRODUCTION The Black Donnellys (NBC)
CREDITS Crash

Paul Haggis .Producer
Laurence Becsey .Producer
Gian Sardar .No Title
Janie Sakura Guevara .No Title

BLEIBERG ENTERTAINMENT

9454 Wilshire Blvd., Ste. 200
Beverly Hills, CA 90212
PHONE .310-273-0003
FAX .310-273-0007
EMAIL .info@bleibergent.com
WEB SITE .www.bleibergent.com
TYPES Animation - Features - Mobile Content
DEVELOPMENT Kirot
PRE-PRODUCTION Adam Resurrected
UPCOMING RELEASES Disaster!
COMPLETED UNRELEASED Love & Dance - Frozen Days
SUBMISSION POLICY No unsolicited material

Ehud Bleiberg .Producer/CEO
Roman Kopelevich .VP, Worldwide Sales
Shannon Banal .VP, Operations
Nicholas Donnermeyer .Executive Assistant

BLOODWORKS, LLC

c/o The Steel Company
9220 Sunset Blvd., Ste. 212
Los Angeles, CA 90069
PHONE .310-861-1715
FAX .310-861-1715
EMAIL .info@bloodworks.net
WEB SITE .www.bloodworks.net
TYPES Animation - Direct-to-Video/DVD - Documentaries - Features - Reality TV
DEVELOPMENT White Zombies - Lil' Barber Shop of Horrors - The Sung Gym Gang - Bathory
PRE-PRODUCTION 2001 Maniacs: Beverly Hellbillys
PRODUCTION After Dark
COMPLETED UNRELEASED Through the Moebius Strip - Hood of Horror
CREDITS 2001 Maniacs

Christopher Tuffin .Managing Partner
Glenn Cadrez .Partner
Jonathan McHugh .Producer

*BLOSSOM FILMS

10201 W. Pico Blvd., Bldg. 45
Los Angeles, CA 90035
PHONE .310-369-5359
TYPES Documentaries - Features - Theatre
HAS DEAL WITH Twentieth Century Fox - Twentieth Century Fox - Fox 2000
DEVELOPMENT The Bachelorette Party - Headhunters - Untitled Simon Kinberg Project
SUBMISSION POLICY No unsolicited submissions

Nicole Kidman .Producer
Per Saari .Producer

BLT PRODUCTIONS LTD.

2339 Columbia St., Ste. 203
Vancouver, BC V5Y 3Y3, Canada
PHONE .604-873-6559
FAX .604-873-0122
EMAIL .blt@intergate.ca
WEB SITE .www.bltproductions.ca
TYPES Animation - Made-for-TV/Cable Movies - Miniseries - TV Series
PRODUCTION Last Chance Café (Made-for-TV Movie)
CREDITS A Wrinkle in Time (ABC) - Gene Roddenberry's Andromeda

Josanne B. Lovick .President

BLUE BAY PRODUCTIONS

1119 Colorado Ave., Ste. 100
Santa Monica, CA 90401
PHONE .310-440-9904
TYPES Features
DEVELOPMENT Short List - Ed's Dead - Soundbite - To Be True - Guy Island
PRE-PRODUCTION Never Say Die
CREDITS American Dreamz - In Good Company - Big Momma's House - Wild Things - Dunston Checks In

Rodney Liber .Producer
Rebecca Hedrick .Producer's Assistant

BLUE PRINT

43-45 Charlotte St.
London W1T 1RS, United Kingdom
PHONE .44-20-7580-6915
FAX .44-20-7580-6934
TYPES Features
PRODUCTION Wind Chill (Revolution/Section Eight) - Becoming Jane

Peter Czernin .Producer
Graham Broadbent .Producer

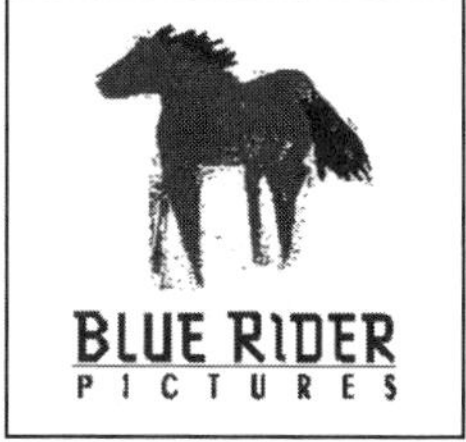

BLUE RIDER PICTURES

2801 Ocean Park Blvd., #193
Santa Monica, CA 90405
PHONE .310-314-8405
FAX .310-314-8402
EMAIL .info@blueriderpictures.com
WEB SITE .www.blueriderpictures.com
TYPES Direct-to-Video/DVD - Documentaries - Features - Made-for-TV/Cable Movies - Reality TV - TV Series
DEVELOPMENT Jaco - The Conspirator - Damien of Molokai
CREDITS Shergar - Silverwolf - Call of the Wild - Hide and Seek - Behind the Red Door - Around the World in 80 Days - Witchboard - The Incredible Mrs. Ritchie - Asylum - Back in the Day
SUBMISSION POLICY No unsolicited material

Jeff Geoffray .Producer/Partner
Walter Josten .Producer/Partner
Brian Castillo .Development

BLUE SKY STUDIOS

44 S. Broadway, 17th Fl.
White Plains, NY 10601
PHONE .914-259-6500
FAX .914-259-6499
WEB SITE .www.blueskystudios.com
TYPES Animation - Features
HAS DEAL WITH Twentieth Century Fox Animation
DEVELOPMENT Dr. Seuss' Horton Hears a Who
CREDITS Ice Age 1&2 - Robots
SUBMISSION POLICY No unsolicited submissions

Chris Wedge .President
Lisa Fragner .Head, Feature Development
Christina Witoshkin .Creative Executive
Ed Corcoran .Development Assistant

BLUE STAR PICTURES

2900 W. Olympic Blvd., Ste. 140
Santa Monica, CA 90404
PHONE .See Below
FAX .310-255-7020
TYPES Features - Made-for-TV/Cable Movies - TV Series
HAS DEAL WITH Sony Pictures Entertainment
DEVELOPMENT Holmes & Watson - My Tutor - Unfinished Country - Bachelor Party 2 - 50 Million - Mr. Lucky - I Hate Valentine's Day - Big Brothers - Harold
PRE-PRODUCTION The Burrowers - Bangkok Dangerous - Daddy Day Camp
POST PRODUCTION The Messengers
COMPLETED UNRELEASED The Hard Easy
CREDITS Darkness Falls - Little Black Book - Dawn Anna Story (TV)

William Sherak .Producer (310-255-7018)
Jason Shuman .Producer (310-255-7019)
Rhiannon Meier .Director, Development (310-255-7047)
Kathryn Floro .Assistant (310-255-7021)

BLUE TULIP PRODUCTIONS

631 Wilshire Blvd., Ste. 4-C
Santa Monica, CA 90401
PHONE .310-458-2166
FAX .310-458-2188
EMAIL .contact@bluetulipprod.com
TYPES Animation - Commercials - Features - Made-for-TV/Cable Movies - Miniseries - Reality TV - TV Series
DEVELOPMENT The Un-Dead - Meg - Stopping Power
CREDITS Speed - Twister - SLC Punk - Minority Report - Equilibrium - Lara Croft Tomb Raider: The Cradle of Life
SUBMISSION POLICY Through agency only

Jan De Bont .Producer/Director
Christopher Stanley .Associate Producer

BLUEBIRD HOUSE

2003 El Cerrito, Ste. 1
Los Angeles, CA 90068
PHONE .323-876-3555
TYPES Features - Made-for-TV/Cable Movies - TV Series
DEVELOPMENT A Day in the Life - Bandits (Remake) - On the Bright Side
CREDITS Disturbing the Peace - Iron Jawed Angels (HBO)
SUBMISSION POLICY No unsolicited submissions

Laura McCorkindale .Producer/Writer
Zoë Levy .Assistant

BLUELINE PRODUCTIONS

212 26th St., Ste. 295
Santa Monica, CA 90402
PHONE .310-319-2421
TYPES Features - Made-for-TV/Cable Movies - TV Series
CREDITS Flight 93 - Faith of My Fathers - Virginia's Run - Saving Jessica Lynch - The Personals - Bat 21 - El Diablo - Nightbreaker - The Last Days of Frankie the Fly - Youngblood

Peter Markle .Director/Producer/Writer
Melinda Culea .Producer

BLUEPRINT ENTERTAINMENT
1801 Century Park East, Ste. 1910
Los Angeles, CA 90067
PHONE 310-407-0960/416-531-8585
FAX 310-407-0961/416-588-7276
EMAIL ....info@blueprint-corp.com
WEB SITE ....www.blueprint-corp.com
TYPES: Animation - Made-for-TV/Cable Movies - Miniseries - Reality TV - TV Series
DEVELOPMENT: Til Death Do Us Part (Court TV/Global Television) - Class (The N/Global Television)
PRODUCTION: Noah's Arc (Logo) - Iggy Arbuckle (Teletoon)
UPCOMING RELEASES: Absolution (Lifetime) - The Road to Christmas (Lifetime)
CREDITS: Cradle of Lies (Lifetime) - Crazy for Christmas (Lifetime) - Gospel of Deceit (Lifetime) - Whistler (The N/CTV) - Chasing Freedom (Court TV/CBC) - Kenny vs. Spenny (GSN/CBC) - Man in the Mirror: The Michael Jackson Story (VH1) - Impossible Heists (Court TV/Discovery Channels International) - Shoebox Zoo (CBBC/CBC/BBC Kids) - Playing House (Lifetime)
SUBMISSION POLICY: No unsolicited submissions
COMMENTS: Toronto office: 6 Pardee Ave., Ste. 104, Toronto, ON, M6K 3H5, Canada

Noreen Halpern ....Co-President
John Morayniss ....Co-President
Jeff Lynas ....Sr. VP
Ira Pincus ....Executive Producer
Lael McCall ....Consultant, Development & Production
John Robinson ....Head, Business & Legal Affairs
Elizabeth Madariaga ....Director, Development
Jesse Ikeman ....Finance/Business Affairs
Shari Cohen ....Legal Affairs
Anne Marie Sorrenti ....Legal Affairs
Anna Salim ....Operations Coordinator
Paul Bullock ....Executive Assistant
Melissa Williamson ....Executive Assistant

BLUEPRINT FILMS
77 Mercer St., Ste. 2N
New York, NY 10012
PHONE 212-625-0530
FAX 212-625-0533
TYPES: Features
HAS DEAL WITH: Initial Entertainment Group
DEVELOPMENT: The Bachelorette Party (Fox) - Headhunters (Fox 2000/New Regency) - Quality of Life Report (Warner Bros.)
PRE-PRODUCTION: Southbound
CREDITS: The Aviator - Gangs of New York - First Born

Rick Schwartz ....Producer
Talia Osteen ....Executive Assistant

BLUMHOUSE PRODUCTIONS
5555 Melrose Ave., Chevalier Bldg., Ste. 205
Los Angeles, CA 90038
PHONE 323-956-8855
FAX 323-862-1141
TYPES: Features - TV Series
HAS DEAL WITH: Paramount Pictures
PROVIDES DEAL TO: ROOM 101, Inc.
DEVELOPMENT: Five Men Who Broke My Heart - Rex Mex - Tooth Fairy - My Korean Deli - Manhattan Brave - Sweet and Vicious - The Washingtonienne
PRE-PRODUCTION: Accidental Husband - The Inheritance
POST PRODUCTION: Graduation
UPCOMING RELEASES: Griffin & Phoenix (Gold Circle) - The Fever (HBO) - The Darwin Awards (MGM)
CREDITS: Hysterical Blindness (HBO) - Hamlet - Easy Six - Stagedoor
SUBMISSION POLICY: No unsolicited material

Jason Blum ....Producer
Tracy Underwood ....Executive VP
Michael Falbo ....Creative Executive
Christine Walby ....Assistant to the Producer

BOBKER/KRUGER FILMS
1416 N. La Brea Ave.
Hollywood, CA 90028
PHONE 323-802-1567
FAX 323-802-1597
TYPES: Features
HAS DEAL WITH: Universal Pictures
DEVELOPMENT: In a Dark Wood - Dream House - Night and Day You Are the One - Zoo
UPCOMING RELEASES: Blood & Chocolate
CREDITS: The Brothers Grimm - The Skeleton Key

Daniel Bobker ....Producer
Ehren Kruger ....Writer/Producer
Dave Massey ....Rising Executive
Jessica Shulman ....Rising Executive
Oscar Torres ....Rising Executive

STEVEN BOCHCO PRODUCTIONS
3000 Olympic Blvd., Ste. 1310
Santa Monica, CA 90404
PHONE 310-566-6900
FAX 310-566-6901
TYPES: TV Series
HAS DEAL WITH: Touchstone Television
CREDITS: Commander In Chief - Over There - Blind Justice - NYPD Blue

Steven Bochco ....Chairman/CEO
Dayna Kalins Bochco ....President
Craig Shenkler ....CFO/VP, Finance
Caroline James ....VP, Production
Yemaya Royce ....Director, Media Relations

BODEGA BAY PRODUCTIONS, INC.
PO Box 17338
Beverly Hills, CA 90209-3338
PHONE 310-273-3157
TYPES: Features - TV Series
PRE-PRODUCTION: Stone of Destiny
CREDITS: Celebrity Island Videos - The Last Best Sunday - Bill & Ted's Excellent Adventure - Purpose

Michael S. Murphey ....Producer

BOGNER ENTERTAINMENT, INC.
269 S. Beverly Dr., Ste. 8
Beverly Hills, CA 90212
PHONE 818-505-6688
EMAIL . . . . jsbogner@aol.com
TYPES — Direct-to-Video/DVD - Features - Made-for-TV/Cable Movies - TV Series
PRODUCTION — Trailer Park of Terror - Kid Midnight - Soccer Mom
CREDITS — Supercross - Popstar - Conan: Red Nails - The Retrievers - Hansel and Gretel - Miracle Dogs - The Santa Trap - Motocross Kids - Red Riding Hood

Jonathan Bogner . . . . Producer/President

BOKU FILMS
1438 N. Gower St., Box 36
Hollywood, CA 90028
PHONE 323-993-7979
FAX 323-993-7978
TYPES — Features - TV Series
DEVELOPMENT — Babycakes - The Walker - Maps to the Stars
CREDITS — Six Feet Under - Woman on Top - Further Tales of the City - More Tales of the City - Thursday - My So-Called Life
SUBMISSION POLICY — No unsolicited material

Alan Poul . . . . Producer
John Flavin . . . . Assistant to Alan Poul

BOLD FILMS
6464 Sunset Blvd., Ste. 800
Los Angeles, CA 90028
PHONE 323-769-8900
FAX 323-769-8954
WEB SITE . . . . www.boldfilms.com
TYPES — Features
POST PRODUCTION — Bobby
COMPLETED UNRELEASED — Come Early Morning - Slingshot
CREDITS — Mini's First Time
COMMENTS — Financing

Gary Michael Walters . . . . President
Michael Litvak . . . . Executive Producer
David Lancaster . . . . Producer
Donald Bruce . . . . VP, Finance
Paul Salamoff . . . . VP, Production
Garrick Dion . . . . Director, Development
Grant McFadden . . . . Assistant to Gary Michael Walters
Aaron Rottinghaus . . . . No Title

BONA FIDE PRODUCTIONS
8899 Beverly Blvd., Ste. 804
Los Angeles, CA 90048
PHONE 310-273-6782
FAX 310 273 7821
TYPES — Documentaries - Features
HAS DEAL WITH — MTV Films - Paramount Pictures
DEVELOPMENT — Nebraska - The Only Living Boy in New York - Adult World - Baster - The Rug Merchant - Boomerang
POST PRODUCTION — Little Children
CREDITS — Little Miss Sunshine - Bee Season - Cold Mountain - Election - King of the Hill - Crumb - The Wood - Jack the Bear - I Am Trying to Break Your Heart - Pumpkin - The Ice Harvest

Albert Berger . . . . Producer
Ron Yerxa . . . . Producer
Carlo Martinelli . . . . Development
Ken Furer . . . . Assistant

BONEYARD ENTERTAINMENT
863 Park Ave., Ste. 11-E
New York, NY 10021
PHONE 212-628-8600
FAX 212-628-8615
EMAIL . . . . boneyardentertainment@gmail.com
TYPES — Documentaries - Features - Made-for-TV/Cable Movies - Reality TV - Specials - TV Series
DEVELOPMENT — The Illustrating Man - Puck - Timmy Moves In - VC 3
CREDITS — Illtown - Niagara, Niagara - Sling Blade - Henry Fool - The 24 Hour Woman - Frogs for Snakes - The Bumblebee Flies Anyway - Greenfingers - Go Further

Daniel J. Victor . . . . President/CEO
Richard M. Victor . . . . Executive VP

bonne pioche

BONNE PIOCHE
22, Avenue Jean Aicard
Paris 75011, France
PHONE 33-1-4929-4600/212-219-9692
FAX 33-1-4929-9300
EMAIL . . . . bonnepioche@bonnepioche.fr
SECOND EMAIL . . . . wu@bonnepioche.fr
WEB SITE . . . . www.bonnepioche.fr
TYPES — Features
HAS DEAL WITH — Warner Independent Pictures
DEVELOPMENT — Amen Birdmen: Across the Atlantic - World Almanac - The Search for Roald Amundsen - Reverse Exploration - The Mole - Lascaux: Prehistoric Skies - The Mystery of the Virgin of Guadalupe
PRE-PRODUCTION — Paris 2010: The Great Flood
PRODUCTION — Kabul Soccer - Fox and the Child
CREDITS — March of the Penguins
COMMENTS — East Coast address: 451 Greenwich St., 2nd Fl., New York, NY 10013; Deal with Wild Bunch

Yves Darondeau . . . . Producer
Christophe Lioud . . . . Producer
Emmanuel Priou . . . . Producer
Claire Barrau . . . . No Title
Jean-Christophe Barret . . . . No Title
Amandine Henrion . . . . No Title
Dorothée Lachaud . . . . No Title
Laurence Liakhoff . . . . No Title
Laurence Picollec . . . . No Title
Linda Saetre . . . . No Title (NY)

BOB BOOKER PRODUCTIONS
11811 W. Olympic Blvd.
Los Angeles, CA 90064
PHONE 831-626-6505
FAX 831-626-6505
EMAIL . . . . bbooker@earthlink.net
TYPES — Direct-to-Video/DVD - Reality TV - Syndication - TV Series
CREDITS — Out of This World - Anything for a Laugh - Foul-Ups, Bleeps & Blunders - America's Funniest Foul-Ups (ABC)

Bob Booker . . . . CEO
Laura Booker . . . . VP

BOXX COMMUNICATIONS, LLC
3685 Motor Ave., Ste. 120
Los Angeles, CA 90034
PHONE . . . 310-287-1285
FAX . . . 310-287-1218
EMAIL . . . info@boxxcommunications.tv
SECOND EMAIL . . . info@boxx.tv
WEB SITE . . . www.boxxcommunications.tv
SECOND WEB SITE . . . www.boxx.tv
TYPES: Commercials - Direct-to-Video/DVD - Documentaries - Features - Made-for-TV/Cable Movies - Music Videos - Reality TV - TV Series
DEVELOPMENT: Traffic Jam (Game Show) - Eat This! (Reality) - X-Treme Team Racing (Game Show) - Retro Bill Safety Series (Direct-to-Video/DVD)
POST PRODUCTION: First Night Documentary
UPCOMING RELEASES: Knock-Knock
COMPLETED UNRELEASED: The Jim Rose Experience (Direct-to-Video/DVD)
CREDITS: Shattered Bits - Liquid News (BBC) - The Jim Rose Twisted Tour (Travel Channel)

Scott Noe . . . No Title
Jeff Watts . . . No Title
Mark Walker . . . No Title
Scott Walker . . . No Title
Tamara Brinkman . . . No Title
Richard Brooker . . . No Title
Brendan Cusack . . . No Title
Jeremy Pfeiffer . . . No Title
Gretel Roenfeldt . . . No Title
Neil Rubbert . . . No Title

BOZ PRODUCTIONS
1822 Camino Palmero
Los Angeles, CA 90046-2202
PHONE . . . 323-876-3232
EMAIL . . . bozenga@sbcglobal.net
TYPES: Features - Reality TV - TV Series
DEVELOPMENT: Stan Helsing - Da Miracle - Gotcha! - Wannabes - Potter's Field - Time Jumpers - As Time Goes By - Mischief Night - Pete - Becoming Ursula - Tiny's Treasure - Gossip - Hollywood Now
POST PRODUCTION: National Lampoon's Reel Movie Review Show
UPCOMING RELEASES: Prey - Turistas
CREDITS: Soul Plane - Scary Movie - A Light in the Darkness - Everything's Jake

Bo Zenga . . . Writer/Director/Producer
Hilary Swett . . . Assistant to Mr. Zenga

DAVID BRADY PRODUCTIONS
4499 Bath Rd., Unit 901
Amherstview, ON K7N 1A6, Canada
PHONE . . . 613-389-7884/613-484-9675
FAX . . . 613-389-5726
EMAIL . . . development@davidbradyproductions.com
WEB SITE . . . www.davidbradyproductions.com
TYPES: Documentaries - Features - Made-for-TV/Cable Movies - TV Series
DEVELOPMENT: Global Force - CANUSA Lodge - Heaven Bound
PRE-PRODUCTION: Extreme Beats - The Pagan Christ
CREDITS: Features: You Wish - The Grey Fox - Till Death Do Us Part - Dixie Lanes; TV: Around the World with Tippi - Counter Force - Singles Court - Life After Death

David Brady . . . President
Milt Avruskin . . . VP, Co-Production/Distribution
Deborah Kimmett . . . VP
Michael Wheeler . . . Director, Development
Bonnie K. Marshall . . . Production Coordinator

BRAGA PRODUCTIONS
c/o Paramount Pictures
5555 Melrose Ave., Hart Bldg., Ste. 205
Los Angeles, CA 90038
PHONE . . . 323-956-5799
FAX . . . 323-862-8503
TYPES: Animation - Direct-to-Video/DVD - Documentaries - Features - Made-for-TV/Cable Movies - TV Series
HAS DEAL WITH: CBS Entertainment - CBS Paramount Network Television
CREDITS: Threshhold (CBS) - Star Trek: Enterprise - Star Trek: Voyager - Star Trek: The Next Generation - Star Trek: Generations - Star Trek: First Contact - Mission: Impossible 2 - Lara Croft: Tomb Raider - Real Time
SUBMISSION POLICY: No unsolicited material
COMMENTS: Interactive games

Brannon Braga . . . President
Terry Matalas . . . VP, Production & Development

BRAINSTORM MEDIA
280 S. Beverly Dr., Ste. 208
Beverly Hills, CA 90212
PHONE . . . 310-285-0812
FAX . . . 310-285-0772
WEB SITE . . . www.brainmedia.com
TYPES: Direct-to-Video/DVD - Documentaries - Features - Made-for-TV/Cable Movies - TV Series
DEVELOPMENT: Beyond Sherwood Forest
CREDITS: Engaged to Kill - Banshee - Android Apocalypse - Kid Cop - Little Men (Feature) - The Truth About Lying - Little Men (Series) - 3-Way - The Stranger I Married - Crimson Force
SUBMISSION POLICY: No submissions without written or verbal approval
COMMENTS: US distributor, sales agent and co-financier

Meyer Shwarzstein . . . President
Trisha Robinson . . . Executive VP
Susan Kahn . . . Controller
Amy Henderson . . . Production Coordinator/Office Manager
Jenelle Szelest . . . Administrative Assistant

BRANCATO/SALKE PRODUCTIONS
500 S. Buena Vista St., Old Animation Bldg. 1E, Ste. 6
Burbank, CA 91521
PHONE .818-560-1520
FAX .818-560-2004
TYPES Features - TV Series
HAS DEAL WITH Touchstone Television
CREDITS Film: Hoodlum - Species 2 - Stealing Harvard; TV: North Shore - Tru Calling - Boomtown - Crossing Jordan - First Wave - X-Files

Chris Brancato .Writer/Producer
Albert J. Salke .Producer
Tara Flynn .Assistant

BRANDMAN PRODUCTIONS
2062 N. Vine St., Ste. 5
Los Angeles, CA 90068
PHONE .323-463-3224
TYPES Features - Made-for-TV/Cable Movies - TV Series
POST PRODUCTION Sea Change
UPCOMING RELEASES Death in Paradise
CREDITS Jesse Stone: Death in Paradise - Night Passage - Robert B. Parker's Stone Cold (CBS) - Walking Shadow - Crossfire Trail - The Heidi Chronicles - Small Vices - Last Stand at Saber River - Alone - Monte Walsh

Michael Brandman .President
Joanna Miles .VP
Miles Brandman .VP, Development
Anita Gnan .No Title

BRAUN ENTERTAINMENT GROUP, INC.
280 S. Beverly Dr., Ste. 500
Beverly Hills, CA 90212
PHONE .310-888-7727
FAX .310-888-7726
EMAIL .braunent@aol.com
WEB SITE .www.braunentertainmentgroup.com
TYPES Features - Made-for-TV/Cable Movies - TV Series
UPCOMING RELEASES A Girl Like Me: The Gwen Araujo Story
CREDITS Amber Frey: Witness for the Prosecution - Edges of the Lord - Tour of Duty - Lethal Vows - Abducted: A Father's Love - Menendez: Killing in Beverly Hills

Zev Braun .President/Executive Producer
Philip M. Krupp .Executive VP/Producer
Jess I. Place .Development Assistant

DAVID BRAUN PRODUCTIONS
2530 Wilshire Blvd., 3rd Fl.
Santa Monica, CA 90403-4616
PHONE .310-453-0089
TYPES Features - Made-for-TV/Cable Movies - TV Series
DEVELOPMENT Wild Thing - MythQuest 2 - Erebus & Terror
CREDITS MythQuest (PBS) - Blind Judgment - Labyrinth: A Life of Kafka - No Good Deed
SUBMISSION POLICY No unsolicited material

David Braun .Producer
Peter Zinner .VP, Production
Melissa Bulnes .Development/Research

BRAVE NEW FILMS
1948 N. Van Ness Ave.
Los Angeles, CA 90068
PHONE .323-962-9913
FAX .323-962-9903
TYPES Direct-to-Video/DVD - Features - Made-for-TV/Cable Movies - TV Series
DEVELOPMENT Fairmount Fours - Last Year's River - The Minority Quarterback - A Providence Romance
PRODUCTION Ten Inch Hero
CREDITS The Lesser Evil - Route 9 - Black Point

David Mackay .Producer/Director
Mark Witsken .Producer

BRAVERMAN PRODUCTIONS, INC.
3000 Olympic Blvd.
Santa Monica, CA 90404
PHONE .310-264-4184
FAX .310-388-5885
EMAIL .info@braverman.com
WEB SITE .www.bravermanproductions.com
TYPES Commercials - Direct-to-Video/DVD - Documentaries - Features - Reality TV
DEVELOPMENT Masquerade
PRODUCTION American Pit Bull
POST PRODUCTION I Remember Me
UPCOMING RELEASES Curtain Call (New Day Films) - Homeless in Paradise (New Day Films)
CREDITS Abused (A&E) - Extremely Out of Control (Discovery) - Prison Medical (Discovery) - Making Marines - Prison Boot Camp - Season of the Grizzly (Animal Planet) - Sextuplets (Discovery) - When Planes Go Down (Discovery) - Biography of Oscar® (A&E) - Broken Wings (History Channel) - Debutantes (A&E) - Yellowstone Bison (Animal Planet) - Love Behind Bars (Discovery)

Chuck Braverman .Executive Producer/Director
Marilyn Braverman .Producer/Camera/Sound
Alex Braverman .Producer/Cameraman
Rob King .Post Production Supervisor
Katrina Markel .Development Executive
Ash Hansen .Editor/Graphics

BRAVO
30 Rockefeller Plaza, Ste. 8-E
New York, NY 10112
PHONE 212-664-4444/818-840-4444
WEB SITE . . . . www.bravotv.com

TYPES	Documentaries - Features - Made-for-TV/Cable Movies - Reality TV - TV Series
DEVELOPMENT	Surprise - Can We Dish? - War of the Wives - Heads Up - The Inn Crowd - Top Decorator - Three of Hearts: A Post-Modern Family
CREDITS	Blow Out - Inside the Actors Studio - Project Runway - Queer Eye - Celebrity Poker Showdown - Kathy Griffin: My Life on the D-List - Tabloid Wars - Million Dollar Listing - Top Chef - Workout
COMMENTS	West Coast office: 3000 W. Alameda Ave., Burbank, CA 91523; Includes Brilliant But Cancelled and Trio; Additional Web sites: www.brilliantbutcancelled.com, www.triotv.com and www.outzonetv.com

Lauren Zalaznick . . . . President, Bravo & TRIO Networks
Todd Saypoff . . . . CFO, Bravo & TRIO Networks
Frances Berwick . . . . Executive VP, Programming & Production
Andrew Cohen . . . . Sr. VP, Production & Programming
Lisa Hsia . . . . Sr. VP, New Media & Special Projects
Jason Klarman . . . . Sr. VP, Marketing & Brand Strategy
Marietta Hurwitz . . . . VP, BravoTV.com
Amy Introcaso-Davis . . . . VP, Production & Development
Jerry Leo . . . . VP, Strategic Program Planning & Scheduling
David O'Connell . . . . VP, Production
David Serwatka . . . . VP, Programming & Production
Kris Slava . . . . VP, Digital Content & Acquisitions
Amelie Tseng . . . . VP, Publicity, Bravo & TRIO Networks
Justin Reichman . . . . Creative Director, On-Air Promotion
Christian Barcellos . . . . Director, Packaging & Production
Joe Brown . . . . Director, Program Research
Allison Clarke . . . . Director, Advertising Sales
Thordis Howard . . . . Director, Production & Operations
Eli Lehrer . . . . Director, Development
Brenda Lowry . . . . Director, Bravo Publicity
Nora Grudman . . . . Sr. Manager, Bravo Publicity
Carolyn Hommel . . . . Manager, Program Planning & Scheduling
Bonita Lynch . . . . Press Manager, Bravo Publicity
Mark Scholnick . . . . Manager, Programming
Torrey Bell . . . . Sr. Writer-Producer/Manager, New Media Integration
Dru Libby . . . . Coordinator, Bravo Publicity
Mary Somers . . . . Coordinator, Bravo Publicity

PAULETTE BREEN PRODUCTIONS
6920 Texhoma Ave., Ste. 100
Van Nuys, CA 91406
PHONE 818-342-0228
FAX 818-342-0228

TYPES	Features - Made-for-TV/Cable Movies - Miniseries - TV Series
DEVELOPMENT	Nightwatch - A Father Condemned - Stranger Beside Me - Too High a Price - Recluse - The Jean Hertel Story - Wild About Harry - Campbell and Lee - Working Girls
PRE-PRODUCTION	Dynamite - Tomorrow Doesn't Count - Regrets
POST PRODUCTION	Changing Times - For the People
COMPLETED UNRELEASED	High End - Commitment
CREDITS	83 Hrs. - Separated by Murder - Abducted: A Father's Love - The Stranger Within - Down Will Come Baby - Haven - A Dry Spell

Paulette Breen . . . . President/Producer
Randall Sanders . . . . VP, Creative Affairs
Tye Bennett . . . . Legal Affairs
Kathy Page . . . . Creative Assistant/Office Administration
Marvin Rich . . . . Executive Assistant

THE BREGMAN ENTERTAINMENT GROUP
1950 Sawtelle Blvd., Ste. 360
West Los Angeles, CA 90025-7014
PHONE 213-833-6207
EMAIL . . . . buddybregman@comcast.net
WEB SITE . . . . www.buddybregman.com

TYPES	Features - Made-for-TV/Cable Movies - Miniseries - Music Videos - Specials - Theatre - TV Series
DEVELOPMENT	All of Me: The Billie Holiday-Lester Young Encounters - Evil Shadows - The Brazilian Bombshell - Happy Street (TV Series) - The Trial of Ezra Pound - Euro-Central (Feature/TV Series) - Runway (Miniseries)
PRE-PRODUCTION	What's New - Fast Break - Garbo - City of Masks - 1st Black Playboy Bunny
CREDITS	Wandering Minstrel Show (Feature) - Fraud Squad (ABC) - Pros & Cons (ABC MOW) - Ain't Misbehavin' (NBC) - American Civil War/Saga of the Wild West/Chicago in the Roaring Twenties (BBC) - Circus of the Stars 2 (CBS) - Newport Jazz Festival (NBC) - Fair Weather Friends (CBC) - Great American Music Celebration (20th Century Fox) - International Cabaret (BBC) - Sun Power (ABC) - Capone: The Musical (Theatre)
COMMENTS	Deal with International Filmed Entertainment, LLC

Buddy Bregman . . . . Producer/Director/Writer
Marie de Puthod . . . . Writer/Director/Producer

BREGMAN PRODUCTIONS
240 E. 39th St., Ste. 47-B
New York, NY 10016
PHONE 212-421-6161/818-954-9988
FAX 212-842-1775/818-954-9989
EMAIL . . . . . bregmanproductions@sbcglobal.net
TYPES Features
DEVELOPMENT The Pajama King - The Gold Coast - The Domestic - Moe Snyder - Tapping the Source - Dead and Alive
CREDITS The Bone Collector - Sea of Love - Scarface - Serpico - Dog Day Afternoon - Carlito's Way 1&2 - The Four Seasons - The Seduction of Joe Tynan - Nothing to Lose

Martin Bregman . . . . . Producer
Michael Bregman . . . . . Writer/Director
Michael Klawitter . . . . . Producer

*THE BREMER GOFF COMPANY
14361 Ocean Ave., Ste. 900
Santa Monica, CA 90401
PHONE 310-656-4500
TYPES Features - Made-for-TV/Cable Movies - Reality TV - TV Series
DEVELOPMENT What to Expect When You're Expecting (CBS) - 10 Stupid Things Women Do to Mess Up Their Lives (CBS) - Tales of Two Wives (Lifetime)
UPCOMING RELEASES Inventing Mark Twain
CREDITS CyberSeduction: His Secret Life (Lifetime) - More Than Meets the Eye (Lifetime)

Michael Bremer . . . . . Executive Producer
Paul Goff . . . . . Executive Producer

*BRIDGE FILMS, LLC
149 South Barrington Ave., #762
Los Angeles, CA 90049-3310
PHONE 310-472-0780
FAX 310-472-4781
EMAIL . . . . . mriklin@bridgefilms.com
WEB SITE . . . . . www.bridgefilms.com
TYPES Features
COMMENTS Remakes

Matt Riklin . . . . . Principal

BRIGHTLIGHT PICTURES, INC.
3500 Cornett Rd.
Vancouver, BC V5M 2H5, Canada
PHONE 604-453-4710
FAX 604-453-4711
EMAIL . . . . . info@brightlightpictures.com
WEB SITE . . . . . www.brightlightpictures.com
TYPES Features - Made-for-TV/Cable Movies - TV Series
POST PRODUCTION American Venus - White Noise 2: The Light - Dungeon Siege - Whisper
COMPLETED UNRELEASED The Long Weekend
CREDITS Feature: Slither - Alone in the Dark - White Noise - House of the Dead - Going the Distance - Alienated - Severed - Punch; TV: Saved
COMMENTS Also finances projects

Stephen Hegyes . . . . . Producer
Shawn Williamson . . . . . Producer
Karyn Edwards . . . . . VP, Legal & Business Affairs
Jonathan Shore . . . . . VP, Distribution & Post Production
Brad Van Arragon . . . . . VP, Production
Mary Quinn . . . . . Director, Development
Marilyn Liu . . . . . Corporate Controller
Jane Grimston . . . . . Paralegal

(Continued)

BRIGHTLIGHT PICTURES, INC. (Continued)
Denise Bonney . . . . . Legal Assistant to Karyn Edwards
Dani Elias . . . . . Assistant to Stephen Hegyes
Margo MacPherson . . . . . Assistant to Shawn Williamson
Krista Kelloway . . . . . Assistant to Brad Van Arragon
Aisla Webster . . . . . Assistant to Jonathan Shore

BRILLSTEIN-GREY ENTERTAINMENT
9150 Wilshire Blvd., Ste. 350
Beverly Hills, CA 90212
PHONE 310-275-6135
FAX 310-275-6180
TYPES Features - TV Series
HAS DEAL WITH Touchstone Television
CREDITS According to Jim (ABC) - Jake in Progress (ABC) - The Showbiz Show with David Spade (Comedy Central) - Real Time with Bill Maher (HBO)

Bernie Brillstein . . . . . Founding Partner/Consultant
Jonathan Liebman . . . . . CEO
Cynthia Pett-Dante . . . . . Partner
David Zwarg . . . . . CFO
Peter Traugott . . . . . President, Brillstein-Grey Television
Sandy Wernick . . . . . Sr. Executive VP
Becky Clements . . . . . Executive VP, Brillstein-Grey Television
Marc Gurvitz . . . . . Executive VP
Amy Weiss . . . . . Executive VP, Business Affairs
Mike Marks . . . . . VP, Brillstein-Grey Television
Geoff Cheddy . . . . . Manager
JoAnne Colonna . . . . . Manager
Naren Desai . . . . . Manager
Todd Diener . . . . . Manager
Kassie Evashevski . . . . . Literary Manager
Colton Gramm . . . . . Manager
Mary Putnam Greene . . . . . Manager
Lee Kernis . . . . . Manager
Aleen Keshishian . . . . . Manager
Jai Khanna . . . . . Manager
Andrea Pett-Joseph . . . . . Manager
Margaret Riley . . . . . Literary Manager
Tim Sarkes . . . . . Manager
Ezekiel Steiner . . . . . Literary Manager
Danny Sussman . . . . . Manager

JOHN BRISTER FILMS
1211 Sunset Plaza Dr., Ste. 413
Los Angeles, CA 90069
PHONE 310-652-3800
FAX 310-652-3801
EMAIL . . . . . info@johnbrister.com
WEB SITE . . . . . www.johnbrister.com
TYPES Direct-to-Video/DVD - Features - Made-for-TV/Cable Movies - TV Series
DEVELOPMENT Voice of Treason - Hockey Dog - Rudy's Run - Gravity - Untitled U-Boat Project - First Mouse - Ship of Souls - Stealing Signs
PRE-PRODUCTION Soccer Dog: America - Marty
CREDITS Shooting Gallery - In Enemy Hands - Rocket's Red Glare - Soccer Dog 1&2
SUBMISSION POLICY See Web site

John H. Brister . . . . . President
Erik Mountain . . . . . Sr. VP, Development

BRISTOL BAY PRODUCTIONS

1888 Century Park East, Ste. 1400
Los Angeles, CA 90067
PHONE .310-887-1000
FAX .310-887-1001
TYPES Features
HAS DEAL WITH Walden Media
DEVELOPMENT Charm School - Untitled Sean Hayes Project - The Desmond Doss Story - All's Faire in Love - Parent Wars - Untitled Texas Hold 'Em Family Comedy - The Great Buck Howard
CREDITS Sahara - Swimming Upstream - Danny Deckchair - Ray - A Sound of Thunder - The Game of Their Lives
COMMENTS Parent company is Anschutz Film Group

Cary Granat .President, Anschutz Film Group
David Weil .CEO, Anschutz Film Group
Jess Wittenberg .COO
Francesca Lindley .CFO
Chris DeMoulin .Executive VP, Marketing
Doug Jones .Sr. VP, Physical Production
Jackie Levine .Sr. VP, Production
Jim Meenaghan .Sr. VP, Buisness & Legal Affairs
Frank Smith .Sr. VP, Buisness & Legal Affairs
Gordon Tichell .Sr. VP, Finance/Controller
Lindsay Fellows .VP, Music
Mylan Stepanovich .VP, Physical Production
Jonas Thaler .VP, Post Production
Jay Galston .VP, Finance & Strategic Planning
Tommy Finkelstein .Director, Buisness & Legal Affairs
Bonnie Solomon .Creative Executive

BRITISH LION

5302 Ethel Ave.
Sherman Oaks, CA 91401
PHONE .818-789-9112/44-1753-651-700
FAX .818-789-2901/44-1753-656-844
WEB SITE .www.britishlionfilms.com
TYPES Features - Made-for-TV/Cable Movies
DEVELOPMENT Puccini - Duel of Kings - Blithe Spirit - Cowboys for Christ
CREDITS The Third Man - A Man for All Seasons - Don't Look Now - The Wicker Man - Lady Jane - Turtle Diary
COMMENTS UK office: Pinewood Studios, Pinewood Rd., Iver Heath, Bucks SLO ONH, United Kingdom

Peter R. E. Snell .Chairman/CEO
Toni Pinnolis .VP (LA)

BROAD STROKES ENTERTAINMENT

3575 Cahuenga Blvd. West, Ste. 360
Los Angeles, CA 90068
PHONE .323-874-1648
FAX .323-874-1650
TYPES Features - Internet Content - Made-for-TV/Cable Movies - TV Series
PRE-PRODUCTION In Tune
CREDITS The Longshot (Hallmark Channel) - Little Sister - Teen Steam - Below Utopia - Safesearching.com

Lin Milano .Producer
Vanessa Torres .Producer
Scott Fuchs .Webmaster

BROADWAY VIDEO

1619 Broadway, Brill Bldg., 9th Fl.
New York, NY 10019
PHONE .212-265-7600
WEB SITE .www.broadwayvideo.com
TYPES Animation - Documentaries - Features - New Media - TV Series
HAS DEAL WITH NBC Universal Television Studio
CREDITS Saturday Night Live - Kids in the Hall - Night Music - Late Night with Conan O'Brien
COMMENTS Audio/video post production, graphics, duplication; Distribution

Lorne Michaels .Chairman
Jack Sullivan .CEO

BROADWAY VIDEO ENTERTAINMENT

c/o Paramount Studios
5555 Melrose Ave., Dressing Room Bldg., Ste. 105
Los Angeles, CA 90038-3197
PHONE .323-956-5655 (Film)/818-777-6450 (TV)
TYPES Features - TV Series
HAS DEAL WITH NBC Universal Television Studio - Paramount Pictures
DEVELOPMENT After Hailey (A Michaels Goldwyn Production)
PRE-PRODUCTION Hot Rod (A Michaels Goldwyn Production)
CREDITS Wayne's World - A Night at the Roxbury - Superstar - Kids in the Hall - Lady's Man - Mean Girls - Tommy Boy - Black Sheep - Enigma
SUBMISSION POLICY No unsolicited submissions
COMMENTS Subsidiary of Broadway Video; TV office: 100 Universal City Plaza, John Ford Bldg., Ste. 3A, Universal City, CA 91608

Lorne Michaels .Chairman
JoAnn Alfano .President, TV
Jill Messick .President, Features
Jack Sullivan .CEO
Andrew Singer .VP, TV
Hilary Marx .Creative Executive, Features
Peggy Powers .Development Assistant, Features

BROKEN LIZARD INDUSTRIES

4000 Warner Blvd., Bldg. 139, Rm. 102
Burbank, CA 91522
PHONE .818-954-5600
FAX .818-954-5620
WEB SITE .www.brokenlizard.com
TYPES Features
HAS DEAL WITH Warner Bros. Pictures
DEVELOPMENT Nutcracker - Ambulance Chasers
POST PRODUCTION Beerfest
CREDITS Club Dread - Puddle Cruiser - Super Troopers

Jay Chandrasekhar .No Title
Julia Dray .Producer
Kevin Heffernan .No Title
Steve Lemme .No Title
Richard Perello .No Title
Paul Soter .No Title
Erik Stolhanske .No Title
Aaron Behl .Assistant
Brian Nossokoff .Assistant
Jenny Weatherholtz .Assistant

BROKEN ROAD PRODUCTIONS
2900 W. Olympic Blvd.
Santa Monica, CA 90404
PHONE . . . . See Below
FAX 310-255-7211
TYPES: Features - TV Series
HAS DEAL WITH: Revolution Studios
DEVELOPMENT: Common Enemy - Henchman vs. Sidekick - Last Resort - Big Bosoms and Square Jaws: The Biography of Russ Meyer, King of the Sex Film - Secure - Amigos - Unsportsmanlike Conduct - Jack and Jill
PRE-PRODUCTION: Next - Mr. Blandings Builds His Dream House - Wichita
POST PRODUCTION: Next
CREDITS: Zoom
SUBMISSION POLICY: No unsolicited submissions

Todd Garner . . . . Producer (310-255-7210)
Ben Haber . . . . No Title (310-255-7013)
Sean Robins . . . . No Title (310-255-7014)
Jayne Polousky . . . . No Title (310-255-7212)

BROOKLYN FILMS
3815 Hughes Ave.
Culver City, CA 90232-2715
PHONE 310-841-4300
FAX 310-204-3464
TYPES: Features - Made-for-TV/Cable Movies - Miniseries - TV Series
DEVELOPMENT: The Understudy - Henry & Ella - Second World - Redbird Christmas
POST PRODUCTION: 88 Minutes
COMPLETED UNRELEASED: 60 Minute Man (Pilot) - Land of the Blind
CREDITS: Sky Captain and the World of Tomorrow - Uprising (Miniseries) - Things You Can Tell Just by Looking at Her - Red Corner - Up Close & Personal - The War - Fried Green Tomatoes - Boomtown
SUBMISSION POLICY: Submit through agent only

Jon Avnet . . . . Director/Producer (310-841-4300)
Carol Chacamaty . . . Executive VP, Finance/Administration (310-841-4307)
Marsha Oglesby . . . . . . Sr. VP, Development & Production (310-841-4316)
Jason Abril . . . . Director, Development (310-841-4353)

BROOKLYN MEDIA
1827 N. Sierra Bonita Ave.
Los Angeles, CA 90046
PHONE 323-851-5585
FAX 323-969-8285
EMAIL . . . . jzelin@mac.com
TYPES: Features
HAS DEAL WITH: Yari Film Group (YFG)
DEVELOPMENT: Killing Pablo - Sushi Girl - Underground - Hank Sloan - Mystery Ball

Jason Zelin . . . . Partner
Finley Glaize . . . . VP, Development & Production

BROOKSFILMS LIMITED
c/o Culver Studios
9336 W. Washington Blvd.
Culver City, CA 90232
PHONE 310-202-3292
FAX 310-202-3225
TYPES: Features - Theatre
CREDITS: The Producers (Feature) - The Fly 1&2 - Frances - The Elephant Man - My Favorite Year - The Producers (Theatre)

Mel Brooks . . . . President
Leah Zappy . . . . VP, Production Services
Felicia Flick . . . . Assistant to Mel Brooks

BROOKWELL McNAMARA ENTERTAINMENT

BROOKWELL MCNAMARA ENTERTAINMENT, INC.
c/o Raleigh Studios
1600 Rosecrans Ave., Bldg. 6A, 3rd Fl.
Manhattan Beach, CA 90266
PHONE 310-727-3353
FAX 310-727-3354
WEB SITE . . . . www.bmetvfilm.com
TYPES: Direct-to-Video/DVD - Features - Made-for-TV/Cable Movies - TV Series
PROVIDES DEAL TO: MarVista Entertainment
DEVELOPMENT: Better Watch Out - Pope Jack - Daytona Cabbie - Gagsters
PRE-PRODUCTION: Cake - Dance Revolution - Super Slumber Party
POST PRODUCTION: Beyond the Break
CREDITS: The Cutting Edge: Going for the Gold - Raise Your Voice - That's So Raven - Even Stevens - The Even Stevens Movie - Race to Space - The Trial of Old Drum - Treehouse Hostage - Wild Grizzly

Sean McNamara . . . . Producer/Writer/Director
David Brookwell . . . . Producer/Writer/Director
David Buclow . . . . President, Development
Steve Ecclesine . . . . President, Production

BONNIE BRUCKHEIMER PRODUCTIONS
12439 Magnolia Blvd., Ste. 217
Valley Village, CA 91607
PHONE 818-761-0270
TYPES: Features - Made-for-TV/Cable Movies
CREDITS: Divine Secrets of the Ya-Ya Sisterhood - For the Boys - Man of the House - That Old Feeling - Beaches
SUBMISSION POLICY: No unsolicited material

Bonnie Bruckheimer . . . . Producer

JERRY BRUCKHEIMER FILMS & TELEVISION

1631 10th St.
Santa Monica, CA 90404
PHONE . . . 310-664-6246
FAX . . . 310-664-6276
WEB SITE . . . www.jbfilms.com
TYPES: Features - Reality TV - TV Series
HAS DEAL WITH: Walt Disney Pictures/Touchstone Pictures - Warner Bros. Television Production
DEVELOPMENT: Beware the Night
PRODUCTION: Pirates of the Caribbean 3
CREDITS: Features: Glory Road - National Treasure - King Arthur - Veronica Guerin - Pirates of the Caribbean 1&2 - Bad Boys 1&2 - Kangaroo Jack - Pearl Harbor - Remember the Titans; TV: The Amazing Race - CSI - CSI: NY - CSI: Miami - Cold Case - Without a Trace - Close to Home - Justice

Jerry Bruckheimer . . . Producer/Chairman/CEO
Mike Stenson . . . President
Jonathan Littman . . . President, TV
Chad Oman . . . President, Production
KristieAnne Reed . . . Executive VP, TV
Kim Metcalf . . . Sr. VP, TV
Melissa Reid . . . Sr. VP, Production
Diane Drummond . . . VP, Special Projects
Pat Sandston . . . Producer/Director, Post Production
Mike Azzolino . . . Director, TV
Charles Vignola . . . Director, Development
Kellie Urdang . . . Director, Human Resources
John Campbell . . . Creative Executive
Yelena Chak . . . Manager, TV
Tami Goldman . . . Post Production Coordinator
Jeremiah Steen . . . Facilities Manager
Robbie Salter . . . Assistant to KristieAnne Reed

THE BUBBLE FACTORY

8840 Wilshire Blvd., 3rd Fl.
Beverly Hills, CA 90211
PHONE . . . 310-358-3000
FAX . . . 310-358-3299
TYPES: Features
CREDITS: The Pest - A Simple Wish - For Richer or Poorer - Playing Mona Lisa - Flipper - McHale's Navy - Stinkers - That Old Feeling - A Fate Totally Worse Than Death

Sid Sheinberg . . . Partner
Bill Sheinberg . . . Partner
Jon Sheinberg . . . Partner
Wendy Brennan . . . Manager, Contract Administration
Joe Carrabba . . . Executive Assistant to J. Sheinberg
Melanie Chapman . . . Executive Assistant to S. Sheinberg
Caryn Santoro . . . Building & Administration
Diane Moser . . . Building & Administration
Leigth Mitcheltree . . . Executive Assistant

BUCKAROO ENTERTAINMENT

c/o Sony Pictures Entertainment
10202 W. Washington Blvd., David Lean Bldg., Ste. 100
Culver City, CA 90232
PHONE . . . 310-244-4646
TYPES: Features
HAS DEAL WITH: Sony Pictures Entertainment
DEVELOPMENT: The Wee Free Men - 20,000 Leagues Under the Sea (Remake)

Josh Donen . . . Partner
Sam Raimi . . . Partner
Russell Hollander . . . Production Executive
Ryan Carroll . . . Assistant to Josh Donen
Aaron Lam . . . Assistant to Sam Raimi

BUENA VISTA MOTION PICTURES GROUP

500 S. Buena Vista St.
Burbank, CA 91521-0001
PHONE . . . 818-560-1000
WEB SITE . . . www.disney.com
TYPES: Animation - Features
PROVIDES DEAL TO: Scott Rudin Productions
SUBMISSION POLICY: No unsolicited materials accepted
COMMENTS: Includes Walt Disney Pictures/Touchstone Pictures

Richard Cook . . . Chairman, The Walt Disney Studios
John Lasseter . . . Chief Creative Officer, Walt Disney Animation Studios/ Principal Creative Advisor, Walt Disney Imagineering
Ed Catmull . . . President, Pixar & Walt Disney Animation Studios
Mark Zoradi . . . President, Walt Disney Motion Pictures Group
Oren Aviv . . . President, Production, Walt Disney Pictures
Alan Bergman . . . President, The Walt Disney Studios
Thomas Schumacher . . . President, Disney Theatrical Productions, Ltd.
Chuck Viane . . . President, Buena Vista Pictures Distribution
Bruce Hendricks . . . President, Motion Picture Production, Walt Disney Pictures
Mitchell Leib . . . President, Music & Soundtracks, Walt Disney Pictures & Television & Buena Vista Music Group
Jeffrey Miller . . . President, Worldwide Post Production & Operations, The Walt Disney Studios
Steve Bardwil . . . Executive VP, Legal Affairs, The Walt Disney Studios
Bernardine Brandis . . . Executive VP, Business & Legal Affairs, The Walt Disney Studios
Scott Holtzman . . . Executive VP, Music Affairs, Buena Vista Motion Pictures Group
Glen Lajeski . . . Executive VP, Music Creative/Marketing, Buena Vista Motion Pictures Group
Phil Lofaro . . . Producer, Walt Disney Feature Animation
Andrew Milstein . . . Executive VP, Walt Disney Feature Animation
Phillip E. Muhl . . . Executive VP, Business & Legal Affairs, Walt Disney Pictures
Jason T. Reed . . . Executive VP, Production, Buena Vista Motion Pictures Group
Marcia Ross . . . Executive VP, Feature Casting, Buena Vista Motion Pictures Group
Doug Carter . . . Sr. VP, Business Affairs, Buena Vista Motion Pictures Group
Tim Engel . . . Sr. VP, Walt Disney Feature Animation
Brad Epstein . . . Sr. VP, Production, Buena Vista Motion Pictures Group
Michele Gazica . . . Sr. VP, Participations & Residuals, Walt Disney Pictures & Television
Steven W. Gerse . . . Sr. VP, Business & Legal Affairs, Buena Vista Motion Pictures Group
Whitney Green . . . Sr. VP, Production, Buena Vista Motion Pictures Group
Robert W. Johnson . . . Sr. VP, Labor Relations, Walt Disney Worldwide Services
Jerry Ketcham . . . Sr. VP, Motion Picture Production, Walt Disney Studios
Sylvia J. Krask . . . Sr. VP, Music Business & Legal Affairs, Buena Vista Motion Pictures Group
Bob Lambert . . . Sr. VP, Worldwide New Technology & Development, The Walt Disney Company
Alan Levey . . . Sr. VP/General Manager, Disney Theatrical Productions, Ltd.
David McCann . . . Sr. VP, Walt Disney Pictures Theatrical Production
Donna Morong . . . Sr. VP, Feature Casting, Buena Vista Motion Pictures Group
Duncan Orrell-Jones . . . Sr. VP, Finance & Planning, Walt Disney Feature Animation
Marjorie Randolph . . . Sr. VP, Human Resources & Administration, The Walt Disney Studios

(Continued)

BUENA VISTA MOTION PICTURES GROUP (Continued)

Art Repola . . . . .Sr. VP, Visual Effects & Production, Walt Disney Pictures
Dennis Rice . . . . .Sr. VP, Publicity, Buena Vista Pictures Marketing
Paul Steinke . . . . .Sr. VP, Production Finance, Walt Disney Pictures
Brigham Taylor . . . . .Sr. VP, Production, Buena Vista Motion Pictures Group
Heidi Trotta . . . . .Sr. VP, Communications, The Walt Disney Studios
Kal Walthers . . .Sr. VP, Business Affairs, Buena Vista Motion Pictures Group
John Blas . . . . .VP, Animation Creative Services, Walt Disney Motion Pictures Group
Kristin Burr . . . . .VP, Development & Production, Buena Vista Motion Pictures Group
Kaylin Frank . . . . .VP, Creative Music & Soundtracks, Walt Disney Pictures & Television
Gail Goldberg . . . .VP, Feature Casting, Buena Vista Motion Pictures Group
Stephanie Harris . . . . .VP, Credits & Title Administration, Buena Vista Motion Pictures Group
Iya Labunka . . . . .VP, Motion Picture Production, Buena Vista Motion Pictures Group
Stephanie Mangano . . . . .VP, Casting Administration, Walt Disney Pictures & Television
Paige Olson . . . . .VP, Business & Legal Affairs, Buena Vista Motion Pictures Group
Doug Short . . . . .VP, Production, Buena Vista Motion Pictures Group
Calvin Tindal . . . . .VP, Motion Picture Production Resources, Walt Disney Pictures
Jonathan Treisman . . . . . .VP, Development, Walt Disney Feature Animation
Monica Zierhut . . . .VP, Music Production, Walt Disney Pictures & Television
LouAnne Brickhouse . . . . .Director, Production, Buena Vista Motion Pictures Group

BUENA VISTA TELEVISION

500 S. Buena Vista St.
Burbank, CA 91521-0001
PHONE 818-560-1000
WEB SITE . . . . .www.bvtvmarketing.com
TYPES Mobile Content - TV Series
CREDITS Live with Regis and Kelly - Who Wants To Be A Millionaire - Ebert & Roeper
COMMENTS Unsolicited materials not accepted; Media please call Kim Harbin for password to access site

Janice Marinelli .President, Buena Vista Television
Jed Cohen . . .Executive VP/General Sales Manager, Buena Vista Television
Lloyd Komesar . . . .Executive VP, Strategic Research, Buena Vista Television
Howard Levy . . . . .Executive VP, Ad Sales, Buena Vista Television (NY)
Sal Sardo . . . . .Executive VP, Marketing, Buena Vista Television
Gwynne Thomas . . . . .Executive VP, Programming, Buena Vista Productions
Michael Thornton . . . . .Executive VP, Business & Legal Affairs, Buena Vista Television
Dan Cohen . . .Sr. VP/General Manager, Buena Vista Pay TV & Distribution
Jim Engleman . .Sr. VP, Ad Sales Midwest, Buena Vista Television (Chicago)
Jared Goetz . . . . . .Sr. VP, Southeast Sales, Buena Vista Television (Atlanta)
Norman Lesser . . . . .Sr. VP, Ad Sales East, Buena Vista Television (NY)
David McLeod . . . . . .Sr. VP/General Sales Manager, Midwest, Buena Vista Television (Chicago)
Chris Oldre . . . . .Sr. VP, Eastern Sales, Buena Vista Television (NY)
Irv Schulman . . . .Sr. VP, Advertising Sales & Marketing, Buena Vista Television
Roni Selig . . . . . . .Sr. VP, Current Programming & East Coast Development, Buena Vista Productions
Jennie Born . . . . .VP, National Promotions, Buena Vista Television
Sandra Brewer . . . . .VP, Affiliate Relations, Buena Vista Television
Blake Bryant . . . . .VP, Creative Services, Buena Vista Television
Steve Calandra . . . .VP, Ad Sales Research Marketing, Buena Vista Television
Helen Faust . . .VP, Operations & Sales Development, Buena Vista Television
George Gubert . . . . .VP, Research, Buena Vista Television
Kim Harbin . . . . .VP, Publicity, Buena Vista Television
Jimmy Lee . . . . .VP, Print Advertising, Buena Vista Television
Eddie Meister . . . . . .VP, Operations, Ad Sales, Buena Vista Television (NY)

(Continued)

BUENA VISTA TELEVISION (Continued)

Steven Orr Jr. . . . . . . .VP, Southwest Region, Buena Vista Television (Dallas)
Michael Patterson . . . . .VP, Business Affairs, Buena Vista Television
Ann Lewis Roberts . . . . .VP, Development, Buena Vista Productions
Christopher Stefanidis . . . . .VP, Distribution
Carlos Torres . . . . .VP, Production, Buena Vista Productions
Bill Webb . . . . .VP, Eastern Region Sales, Buena Vista Television (NY)

BULL'S EYE ENTERTAINMENT

11900 Olympic Blvd, Ste. 730
Los Angeles, CA 90064
PHONE 310-979-7117
FAX 310-979-0370
TYPES Features - TV Series
HAS DEAL WITH Sony Pictures Television
DEVELOPMENT TV: The Group (Sony TV/Touchstone) - Crash (Series) - The Guy Next Door (Touchstone) - Chicken or Beef? (Fox) - The Ant Hines Project (CBS/UPN) - Surveillance
CREDITS Employee of the Month - The Illusionist - Crash - Thumbsucker

Tom Nunan . . . . .Partner
Cathy Schulman . . . . .Partner
Lee Kramer . . . . .Executive Assistant to Cathy Schulman

BUNGALOW 78 PRODUCTIONS

c/o The Walt Disney Company
500 S. Buena Vista St., Old Animation Bldg. 1-E, Ste. 9
Burbank, CA 91521
PHONE 818-560-4878
FAX 818-560-4448
TYPES Features - TV Series
HAS DEAL WITH ABC Entertainment Television Group - Touchstone Television
CREDITS A Minute with Stan Hooper - Coach - Catch Me If You Can - Patch Adams - Romy & Michelle's High School Reunion

Barry Kemp . . . . .Executive Producer/Writer
Nikki Reed . . . . .Development Executive
Jill Bowles . . . . .Assistant to Mr. Kemp

BUNIM/MURRAY PRODUCTIONS, INC.

6007 Sepulveda Blvd.
Van Nuys, CA 91411
PHONE 818-756-5100/818-756-5253
FAX 818-756-5140
WEB SITE . . . . .www.bunim-murray.com
TYPES Direct-to-Video/DVD - Documentaries - Features - Made-for-TV/Cable Movies - Reality TV - TV Series
DEVELOPMENT Summer Share (ABC)
CREDITS The Scholar - The Simple Life - Starting Over (Syndication) - Born to Diva - The Real Cancun - The Real World - Road Rules - The Real World/Road Rules Challenge - Class Reunion (MOW) - Making the Band - Love Cruise: The Maiden Voyage - The Rebel Billionaire: Branson's Quest for the Best

Jonathan Murray . . . . .Chairman
Joey Carson . . . . .CEO
Scott Freeman . . . . .Sr. VP, Current Programming & Development
Gil Goldschein . . . . .Sr. VP, Business & Legal Affairs
Joachim Blunck . . . . .Sr. VP, Digital Content
Sasha Alpert . . . . .VP, Casting

(Continued)

BUNIM/MURRAY PRODUCTIONS, INC. (Continued)

Fabian Andre . . . . . VP, Business Development
Joyce Corrington . . . . . VP, Creative Affairs
Randy Dugan . . . . . VP, Finance & Administration
Jeff Jenkins . . . . . VP, Creative Affairs
Kevin Lee . . . . . VP, Creative Affairs
Bart Peele . . . . . VP, Operations
Mark Raudonis . . . . . VP, Post Production
Dave Stone . . . . . VP, Music
Stacey O'Donnell . . . . . Director, Human Resources
Saul Friedman . . . . . Executive Coordinator

BURLEIGH FILMWORKS

22287 Mulholland Hwy., Ste. 129
Calabasas, CA 91302
PHONE 818-224-4686
FAX 818-223-9089
EMAIL . . . . . steve.burleigh@burleighfilmworks.com

TYPES	Features - Made-for-TV/Cable Movies - TV Series
DEVELOPMENT	The Horse's Mouth - Gravelwalk - Stretch - Hannah and the Queen of Halloween - Riot Song - Rezmurs
CREDITS	Edge of America - Execution of Justice - Bereft
SUBMISSION POLICY	Query by email

Stephen Burleigh . . . . . Producer
Kelly Ford . . . . . Director, Development

MARK BURNETT PRODUCTIONS

640 N. Sepulveda Blvd.
Los Angeles, CA 90049
PHONE 310-903-5400

TYPES	Internet Content - Mobile Content - Reality TV - TV Series
PROVIDES DEAL TO	AOL Media Networks
DEVELOPMENT	On the Lot
PRE-PRODUCTION	Gold Rush!
CREDITS	Rock Star - The Contender - Survivor - The Apprentice - Martha - The Restaurant - The Casino - Commando Nanny

Mark Burnett . . . . . No Title
Conrad Riggs . . . . . No Title

BURNSIDE ENTERTAINMENT, INC.

1136 S. Cloverdale Ave.
Los Angeles, CA 90019
PHONE 323-934-1095/212-727-7665
EMAIL . . . . . mail@burnsideentertainment.com
WEB SITE . . . . . www.burnsideentertainment.com

TYPES	Features - TV Series
DEVELOPMENT	Transition Man - The Home Field - The Outlands - The Lease Is Up - I'll Meet You at the Signing of the Decleration of Independence
PRE-PRODUCTION	With Friends Like These...
CREDITS	Overnight Sensation - Piñero - Radio Inside - I Love You, I Love You Not - Tony and Tina's - Bella - Bernard and Doris - The Opinion Maker

Glen Trotiner . . . . . Producer/Director/Partner
Seth William Meier . . . . . Producer/Partner
Eddie Micallef . . . . . Producer
Scott Stevens . . . . . Assistant to Seth William Meier

BURNT ORANGE PRODUCTIONS

710 W. Fifth St.
Austin, TX 78701
PHONE 512-232-5943
FAX 512-322-9195
WEB SITE . . . . . www.burntorangeproductions.com

TYPES	Features
DEVELOPMENT	Austin Angel - The Marfa Lights
POST PRODUCTION	Homo Erectus - Elvis and Anabelle
UPCOMING RELEASES	The Quiet
COMPLETED UNRELEASED	The Cassidy Kids
SUBMISSION POLICY	No unsolicited submissions

Carolyn Pfeiffer . . . . . Producer
Gregory Collins . . . . . Development
Sam Marshall . . . . . Director, Finance
Andy Alexander . . . . . Jr. Finance Analyst

BURRUD PRODUCTIONS

468 N. Camden Dr., 2nd Fl.
Beverly Hills, CA 90210
PHONE 310-860-5158
EMAIL . . . . . info@burrud.com
WEB SITE . . . . . www.burrud.com

TYPES	Documentaries - Features - TV Series
PRE-PRODUCTION	Women on Death Row 2
PRODUCTION	Black Widow Women - Munchausen Moms - Working Women
UPCOMING RELEASES	Bling
CREDITS	Weird Worlds - Beyond Bizarre - Strange Travels - Mysteries Within - Yoga for Kids - Vegas Cops - Vegas Challenge - Mutter Museum - Shark Chasers - Mostly True Stories - Vegas Dealers - Mardi Gras Cops - Multiples, Multiples - Whales Tales - Million Dollar Blackjack - Other Side of the Cell - Women on Death Row - Two Funny: Cotter & Louise
SUBMISSION POLICY	No unsolicited submissions

John Burrud . . . . . President/CEO
Stanley H. Green . . . . . Executive VP, Business Affairs
Shannon Mead . . . . . VP, Administration

AL BURTON PRODUCTIONS

555 Laurel Ave.
San Mateo, CA 94401
PHONE 650-348-3463
EMAIL . . . . . alburton22@aol.com

TYPES	TV Series
PRE-PRODUCTION	Scott Baio Project - Bethany Hamilton Story - The Oscar Levant Story
PRODUCTION	Sundays and Show Tunes - Ben Stein Project
CREDITS	Alvin Toffler's Beyond Futureshock - The New Lassie - Charles in Charge - Win Ben Stein's Money - Turn Ben Stein On - World Poker Tour

Al Burton . . . . . Executive Producer
Phillip Weldele . . . . . Producer/Director, Development

TIM BURTON PRODUCTIONS

8033 Sunset Blvd., Ste. 7500
West Hollywood, CA 90046
PHONE .310-300-1670
FAX .310-300-1671
WEB SITE www.timburton.com

TYPES: Animation - Commercials - Features - Music Videos
PRE-PRODUCTION: Sweeney Todd - Believe It or Not
CREDITS: Charlie and the Chocolate Factory - Corpse Bride - Mars Attacks! - Ed Wood - The Nightmare Before Christmas - Edward Scissorhands - Batman - Batman Returns - Beetlejuice - Big Fish - Pee Wee's Big Adventure - Planet of the Apes - Sleepy Hollow
SUBMISSION POLICY: No unsolicited submissions

Tim Burton .Director/Producer
Derek Frey .Producer

BUSBOY PRODUCTIONS

436 W. 45th St., 3rd Fl.
New York, NY 10036
PHONE .212-262-6165
FAX .212-262-6177

TYPES: Features - TV Series
HAS DEAL WITH: Comedy Central
DEVELOPMENT: Sports Fan (Spike TV) - Comedy Love Call (Comedy Central)
CREDITS: The Colbert Report

Jon Stewart .Executive Producer
Ben Karlin .Executive Producer
Richard Korson .Head, Development & Production
Chris McShane .Development

BUSHWACKER PRODUCTIONS

1201 W. Fifth St., Ste. M270
Los Angeles, CA 90017
PHONE .213-534-3145
FAX .213-534-3114

TYPES: Made-for-TV/Cable Movies - Reality TV - TV Series
HAS DEAL WITH: Touchstone Television
DEVELOPMENT: Deer Park - The War Room - Monogamy - NY Hotel - Borrowed Lives - Untitled Dee Johnson Project - Untitled Amy Sohn Project
PRODUCTION: Try My Life (Style)
CREDITS: In Case of Emergency (ABC) - Hope & Faith - Threat Matrix - War Stories - Haunted - The Education of Max Bickford
SUBMISSION POLICY: No unsolicited material accepted

Emile Levisetti .Producer
Caitlin McGinty .Assistant

BUTCHERS RUN FILMS

1041 N. Formosa Ave., Santa Monica Bldg., East 200
West Hollywood, CA 90046
PHONE .323-850-2703
FAX .323-850-2741

TYPES: Features - Miniseries
DEVELOPMENT: The Running Kind
CREDITS: A Family Thing - The Man Who Captured Eichmann - The Apostle - A Shot at Glory - Assassination Tango - Broken Trail

Robert Duvall .Actor/Producer/Director
Rob Carliner .Producer/Manager

BYRUM POWER & LIGHT

PO Box 1211
Redding, CT 06875
PHONE .310-428-2049

TYPES: Features - TV Series
CREDITS: Duets - The Razor's Edge - Heart Beat - Mahogany - Inserts - Middle Ages - South of Sunset - Winnetka Road
SUBMISSION POLICY: No unsolicited material

John Byrum .Writer/Director
Karin Reznack-Byrum .No Title

C2 PICTURES

c/o Cinergi Pictures Entertainment, Inc.
2308 Broadway
Santa Monica, CA 90404
PHONE .310-315-6000
FAX .310-828-0443

TYPES: Animation - Direct-to-Video/DVD - Features - Made-for-TV/Cable Movies - Miniseries - TV Series
DEVELOPMENT: Terminator 4 - Evermere - Trapped - The Sarah Connor Chronicles - The Wall - Audition - Ramses - No Quarter Given - Jonathan Livingston Seagull
POST PRODUCTION: Children of Glory
CREDITS: Basic Instinct 2 - Terminator 3 - I Spy - Die Hard 3 - Total Recall - Evita - Star Gate - Rambo 1-3 - Jacob's Ladder - Angel Heart
SUBMISSION POLICY: No unsolicited submissions accepted

Mario Kassar .Co-CEO
Andrew Vajna .Co-CEO
James Middleton .Sr. VP, Production & Development
Joel Michaels .Production Executive

CAFE PRODUCTIONS

6503 W. Sixth St., Ste. 200
Los Angeles, CA 90048
PHONE .323-653-8433

TYPES: Commercials - Documentaries - Features - Made-for-TV/Cable Movies - Music Videos
CREDITS: Goodbye Casanova - Milwaukee, Minnesota - Neighborhood Watch - Gung Fu - Fun - Out in Fifty - Milo

Jeff Kirshbaum .Producer/Owner
Graeme Whifler .Writer/Director

CAIRO/SIMPSON ENTERTAINMENT, INC.

10800 Wilkins Ave.
Los Angeles, CA 90024
PHONE .310-470-9309
EMAIL cairosimpsonent@earthlink.net

TYPES: Documentaries - Features - Made-for-TV/Cable Movies - Miniseries - Reality TV - TV Series
CREDITS: Mayday - Elvis (Miniseries) - The Jackie Gleason Story - The Pilot's Wife - Price of a Broken Heart - Perfect Body - What We Did That Night - Vanished Without a Trace - Her Deadly Rival - Twisted Desire - Lucky 7 - Infidelity - Brooke Ellison Story

Judy Cairo .Producer/Partner
Michael Simpson .Producer/Partner

CALDERA/DE FANTI ENTERTAINMENT

PO Box 402, 1954 N. Hillhurst Ave.
Los Angeles, CA 90027
PHONE .323-906-9500
FAX .323-906-9555
TYPES Animation - Features - Made-for-TV/Cable Movies - Miniseries - TV Series
DEVELOPMENT Locas - A Little Lower Than the Angels - Giants - Diego - Quincera - Answer to My Prayer
PRE-PRODUCTION Dragonfire (TV)
CREDITS Selena - The Disappearance of Garcia Lorca - 3 Blind Mice

Carolyn Caldera-De Fanti .Producer
Jean-Luc De Fanti .Producer
Rebecca Randall .Executive Assistant

CALLAHAN FILMWORKS

3800 Barham Blvd., Ste. 500
Los Angeles, CA 90068
PHONE .323-878-0645
FAX .323-878-0649
TYPES Features - TV Series
HAS DEAL WITH Twentieth Century Fox Television
DEVELOPMENT Starship Dave - The Refs - Shazam! - Get Smart

Peter Segal .Director/Producer
Michael Ewing .Producer

JOHN CALLEY PRODUCTIONS

10202 W. Washington Blvd., David Lean Bldg., Ste. 119
Culver City, CA 90232
PHONE .310-244-7777
FAX .310-244-4070
TYPES Features - Miniseries
HAS DEAL WITH Sony Pictures Entertainment
PROVIDES DEAL TO Avenue Pictures
DEVELOPMENT Angels & Demons - Fear of Flying - The Jane Austen Book Club - Against All Enemies - The Scorpion's Gate - Skinny Dip - The Company (TNT)
CREDITS The Da Vinci Code - Closer
SUBMISSION POLICY No unsolicited submissions

John Calley .Chairman/CEO/Producer
Lisa Medwid .VP
Erica Hagen .Executive Assistant to Mr. Calley

CAMDEN PICTURES

944 Lincoln Blvd.
Santa Monica, CA 90403
PHONE .310-458-3906
EMAIL .producer@camdenpictures.com
WEB SITE .www.camdenpictures.com
TYPES Documentaries - Features
DEVELOPMENT Magic Matt - Chiller - Mischief Night
UPCOMING RELEASES No Limit: A Search for the American Dream on the Poker Tournament Trail
CREDITS Men in Scoring Position

Susan Genard .Producer
Timothy Rhys .Screenwriter/Director

CAMELOT ENTERTAINMENT GROUP, INC.

2020 Main St., Ste. 990
Irvine, CA 92614
PHONE .949-777-1090
FAX .949-777-1091
EMAIL .rpatwell@camelotfilms.com
SECOND EMAIL .mellis@camelotfilms.com
WEB SITE .www.camelotfilms.com
TYPES Direct-to-Video/DVD - Features - Made-for-TV/Cable Movies - TV Series
DEVELOPMENT Victims - The Cauldron - The Only Game in Town - 1st Rule of Survival - Hail to the Thief - Drop the Elephant - Untitled Horror Project
CREDITS Saved! - He Is My Brother - One Down, Two to Go

Robert P. Atwell .Chairman/President/CEO
Michael Ellis .COO
George Jackson .CFO
Craig Kitchens .VP, Production
Jane Olmstead .Director
Rounsevelle Schaum .Director
Patrick Winn .Production Executive
Susan Sanchez .Administrator

CAMELOT PICTURES

CAMELOT PICTURES

451 Greenwich St., 2nd Fl.
New York, NY 10013
PHONE .212-609-9393/323-651-2427
FAX .212-609-9394
WEB SITE .www.camelot-pictures.com
TYPES Features - Made-for-TV/Cable Movies - TV Series
DEVELOPMENT Revelation - Brothel - David, Lolly, Donny and Dan - Sensibilidad - Leave 'em Laughing - Marlene - Untitled Adam Niskar Project - The Waking - Chasing the Sleeper Cell - Fantastic Voyage - Extended Family - Ahab's Wife - Gander
POST PRODUCTION Margaret
CREDITS Garden State - Beyond Borders - S.W.A.T.
SUBMISSION POLICY No unsolicited submissions
COMMENTS West Coast office: 8330 W. Third St., Los Angeles, CA 90048

Gary Gilbert .President
Jordan Horowitz .Development/Production Executive

COLLEEN CAMP PRODUCTIONS

6310 San Vicente Blvd., Ste. 510
Los Angeles, CA 90048
PHONE .323-932-2530
FAX .323-932-2534
EMAIL .asst@ccprods.com
TYPES Features - TV Series
DEVELOPMENT Lady Gold - The Alibi Club - Karma - The War Magician - Napoleon - Bread and Butter - Parent Wars
CREDITS An American Rhapsody - HBO Creature Features

Colleen Camp .Producer (colleen@ccprods.com)
Darin Pfeiffer .Creative Executive (darin@ccprods.com)
Aram Siruni .Assistant (asst@ccprods.com)

CANARY FILMS
180 Varick St., Ste. 1002
New York, NY 10014
PHONE .212-741-0406
FAX .212-741-0424
WEB SITE www.canaryfilms.net
TYPES Features
DEVELOPMENT Dispatches from the Cold
PRE-PRODUCTION Never Forever
POST PRODUCTION Chapter 27 - Beautiful Ohio
UPCOMING RELEASES Beer League
CREDITS Twelve and Holding

Brian Bell .Partner
Jenny Schweitzer .Partner

CANNELL STUDIOS
7083 Hollywood Blvd., Ste. 600
Hollywood, CA 90028
PHONE .323-465-5800
FAX .323-856-7390
WEB SITE www.cannell.com
TYPES Features
DEVELOPMENT The A-Team - King Con - The Greatest American Hero - 21 Jump Street - Wiseguy - Runaway Heart - Love at First Sight - The Viking Funeral
PRODUCTION The Yellow Wood - Inferno
UPCOMING RELEASES It Waits - Demon Hunter - The Garden - Left in Darkness - The Tooth Fairy

Stephen J. Cannell .Chairman of the Board/Producer
Michael Dubelko .President/Producer
Daisy Marco .CFO/Producer
Theresa Peoples .Creative Executive
Kathy Ezso .Assistant to Mr. Cannell

REUBEN CANNON PRODUCTIONS
5225 Wilshire Blvd., Ste. 526
Los Angeles, CA 90036
PHONE .323-939-3190
FAX .323-939-7793
EMAIL reubcan@aol.com
TYPES Features - Made-for-TV/Cable Movies - TV Series
DEVELOPMENT Daddy's Little Girl
CREDITS Features: Madea's Family Reunion - Down in the Delta - Get on the Bus - Woman Thou Art Loosed - Love Don't Cost a Thing - Diary of a Mad Black Woman; Made-for-TV/Cable Movie: Dancing in September (HBO)

Reuben Cannon .Producer/Casting Director
Kim Williams .Casting Director

MAJ CANTON PRODUCTIONS
655 Oxford Ave.
Venice, CA 90291-4724
PHONE .310-823-1917
TYPES Made-for-TV/Cable Movies - Reality TV - TV Series
CREDITS Wife, Mother, Murderer - A Mother's Revenge
COMMENTS Author, *Complete Guide to TV Movies & Miniseries 1984-2005*

Maj Canton .Producer

CAPITAL ARTS ENTERTAINMENT
17941 Ventura Blvd., Ste. 205
Encino, CA 91316
PHONE .818-343-8950
WEB SITE www.capitalarts.com
TYPES Direct-to-Video/DVD - Features - Made-for-TV/Cable Movies - TV Series
DEVELOPMENT On the Twelfth Day of Christmas - War Games 2 - Punisher 2
PRE-PRODUCTION Perfect Christmas
PRODUCTION PDR
POST PRODUCTION Rogue
CREDITS Peaceful Warrior - Happy Endings - American Pie: Band Camp - The Devil's Rejects - The Prince and Me 1&2 - The Cookout - Beethoven's 5th - Casper Meets Wendy - Route 9 - Addams Family Reunion - After the Storm - Time Cop 2 - All I Want

Mike Elliott .Partner
Rob Kerchner .Partner
Pamela Eisen .Development
Joe Genier .Production
Karen Gorodetzky .Production
Kristen Morton .Production
Jan Kikumoto .Post Production
Paul Di Franco .Music

ANNE CARLUCCI PRODUCTIONS
9200 Sunset Blvd., PH 20
Los Angeles, CA 90069
PHONE .310-550-9545
FAX .310-550-8471
EMAIL acprod@sbcglobal.net
TYPES Features - Made-for-TV/Cable Movies - TV Series
DEVELOPMENT Female Intelligence (CBS) - Fat Chance (Lifetime) - Debbie Smith Project (Lifetime)
PRE-PRODUCTION Circle of Friends (Lifetime)
UPCOMING RELEASES Fatal Trust (Lifetime) - Flirting with Danger (Lifetime)
CREDITS Donato and Daughter - Sex & Mrs. X - The Soul Collector - When Husbands Cheat - Dangerous Evidence - Sublet - Not Our Son - Unforgivable - Out of Sync - Guilt by Association - Dangerous Child - Going for Broke - Forbidden Secrets
SUBMISSION POLICY Query letter with SASE
COMMENTS Deal with Lifetime Television & Incendo Media

Anne Carlucci .Executive Producer
Stacey Pantazis .Creative Executive
Robyn Snyder .VP, Development & Production

CARRIE PRODUCTIONS, INC.
2625 Alcatraz Ave., Ste. 243
Berkeley, CA 94705
PHONE .510-450-2500
FAX .510-450-2506
TYPES Features - TV Series
CREDITS Buffalo Soldiers - Freedom Song - America's Dream - Just a Dream
SUBMISSION POLICY No unsolicited submissions
COMMENTS Affiliated with Robey Theatre Company

Danny Glover .Executive Producer
Sarisa Middelton .VP
Karen Bolt .Development Executive

CARSEY-WERNER FILMS
12001 Ventura Pl., 6th Fl.
Studio City, CA 91604
PHONE 818-299-9600
FAX 818-299-9650
WEB SITE . . . . www.carseywerner.com

TYPES	Features
DEVELOPMENT	Get 'Em Wet
PRODUCTION	The Brothers Solomon
POST PRODUCTION	Let's Go to Prison
CREDITS	That '70s Show - Grounded for Life - 3rd Rock from the Sun - Roseanne - The Cosby Show - Grace Under Fire - A Different World - Cybill

Marcy Carsey . . . . Partner/Executive Producer
Tom Werner . . . . Partner/Executive Producer
Bob Dubelko . . . . Co-President/COO
Matt Berenson . . . . President, CW Films
James Kraus . . . . President, CW Domestic Television Distribution
Herb Lazarus . . . . President, CW International Television Distribution
Rochelle Gerson . . . . Executive VP, Business Affairs
Bret Sarnoff . . . . Executive VP, Finance/CFO
Norma Acland . . . . General Counel
Janet Bonifer . . . . VP, Marketing/Creative Services
Bill McCarthy . . . . VP, Research

CARSON DALY PRODUCTIONS
3500 W. Olive Ave., Ste. 330
Burbank, CA 91505
PHONE 818-827-7123
FAX 818-827-7124

TYPES	TV Series
HAS DEAL WITH	MTV Networks - NBC Universal Television Studio
DEVELOPMENT	Tall and Small - Ground Control (Sci-Fi)
PRE-PRODUCTION	Cyberhood (NBC)
CREDITS	Last Call with Carson Daly

Carson Daly . . . . Principal
Marianne Hayden . . . . COO
Ruth Caruso . . . . Head, Development

CARSON SIGNATURE FILMS, INC.
10 Universal City Plaza, 20th Fl.
Universal City, CA 91608
PHONE 818-753-2333
FAX 818-753-2310

TYPES	Commercials - Direct-to-Video/DVD - Documentaries - Features - Made-for-TV/Cable Movies - Reality TV - Specials - TV Series
DEVELOPMENT	Mean Streets - Jesus in Cowboy Boots - Untitled Paint Ball Project
PRE-PRODUCTION	Blue Mountain
CREDITS	ESPN2 Special - In the Company of Spies
SUBMISSION POLICY	Query only, no unsolicited submissions

Beaux Carson . . . . President
Darby Connor . . . . Sr. VP

THE THOMAS CARTER COMPANY
3000 W. Olympic Blvd.
Santa Monica, CA 90404
PHONE 310-264-3990
EMAIL . . . . tcc.film@verizon.net

TYPES	Features - Made-for-TV/Cable Movies - TV Series
DEVELOPMENT	The Marcus Dixon Story (Paramount) - Freedom House (Warner Bros.) - Carlisle (HBO) - Jackie Robinson (Fox Searchlight)
CREDITS	Features: Coach Carter - Save the Last Dance - Metro - Swing Kids; Cable Movies: Don King: Only in America - Five Desperate Hours - The Uninvited - Trapped in a Purple Haze - Ali: An American Hero

Thomas Carter . . . . President
Jennifer Buchwald-Paletz . . . . Manager, Development

CARTOON NETWORK
1050 Techwood Dr. NW
Atlanta, GA 30318
PHONE 404-885-2263
FAX 404-885-4312
WEB SITE . . . . www.cartoonnetwork.com

TYPES	Animation - Features - Internet Content - Mobile Content - TV Series
DEVELOPMENT	Re-Animated (Original Movie) - Teen Titans - Fantastic Four (Animated)
CREDITS	Squirrel Boy - Class of 3000 - Camp Lazlo - Hi Hi Puffy Ami Yumi - The Life & Times of Juniper Lee - The Grim Adventures of Billy and Mandy - Foster's Home for Imaginary Friends - My Gym Partner's a Monkey - Ben 10 - The Powerpuff Girls Movie - Megas XLR - Star Wars: Clone Wars - Samurai Jack
COMMENTS	Includes Toonami Jetstream, broadband service for viewing Cartoon Network programs

Jim Samples . . . Executive VP/General Manager, Cartoon Network Worldwide
Kim McQuilken . . . . Executive VP, Kids Advertising Sales & Marketing, Cartoon Network Enterprises
Michael Ouweleen . . . . Sr. VP, Development & Creative Direction
Bob Higgins . . . . Sr. VP, Programming
Sam Register . . . . Sr. VP, Development
Dennis Adamovich . . . . Sr. VP, Marketing
Mark Norman . . . . Sr. VP, Business Operations & General Manager, Boomerang
Gary Albright . . . . Sr. VP, Creative Services
John Friend . . . . Sr. VP, Cartoon Network Enterprises
Phyllis Ehrlich . . . . Sr. VP, Promotions
Brian Miller . . . . Sr. VP/General Manager, Cartoon Network Studios
Jennifer Pelphrey . . . . VP, Production, Cartoon Network Studios
Stacey Isenhour . . . . VP, Research
Marc Buhaj . . . . VP, Programming
Pola Changnon . . . . VP, On-Air/Executive Producer, Program Production
Khaki Jones . . . . VP, Programming
Terry Kalagian . . . . VP, Programming
James Anderson . . . . VP, Public Relations
Paul Condolora . . . Sr. VP/General Manager, Cartoon Network New Media
Keith Crofford . . . . VP, Production, Adult Swim
Josh Feldman . . . . VP, Ad Sales & Marketing
Christina Miller . . . VP, US Consumer Products, Cartoon Network Enterprises
Ramsey Naito . . . . VP, Longform Development
Heather Kenyon . . . . Sr. Director, Original Development
Jim Babcock . . . . Director, Public Relations
Rick Blanco . . . . Director, Hardline Design

(Continued)

CARTOON NETWORK (Continued)

Deena Boykin . . . . Director, Retail Development
Daria Cronin . . . . Director, Softline Design
Courtenay Palaski . . . . Director, Public Relations
Joseph Swaney . . . . Director, Public Relations
Rob Renzetti . . . . Supervising Producer
Craig McCracken . . . . Executive Consultant, Animated Shorts

CASTLE ROCK ENTERTAINMENT

335 N. Maple Dr., Ste. 135
Beverly Hills, CA 90210-3867
PHONE 310-285-2300
FAX 310-285-2345
EMAIL . . . . first.lastname@castle-rock.com
WEB SITE . . . . www.castle-rock.com

TYPES	Features
HAS DEAL WITH	Warner Bros. Pictures
PROVIDES DEAL TO	Reiner/Greisman
DEVELOPMENT	Faith Buffalo - Friends with Benefits - Cincinnati Kid
PRODUCTION	Music and Lyrics By
POST PRODUCTION	Chaos Theory - Fracture - Mostly Martha - For Your Consideration
COMPLETED UNRELEASED	In the Land of Women
CREDITS	Two Weeks Notice - Before Sunrise - The Polar Express - Before Sunset - Miss Congeniality - A Few Good Men - Misery - The Shawshank Redemption - Seinfeld - The Green Mile - When Harry Met Sally...
SUBMISSION POLICY	Must be submitted by a Writer's Guild signatory agent or lawyer

Rob Reiner . . . . Producer/Director
Martin Shafer . . . . Chairman/CEO
Liz Glotzer . . . . President, Castle Rock Pictures
Andrew Scheinman . . . . Producer/Director
Kristine Hrycun . . . . Sr. Projects Coordinator

CASTLEBRIGHT STUDIOS

10 Universal City Plaza, 20th Fl.
Universal City, CA 91608
PHONE 818-753-2319
FAX 818-753-2310
EMAIL . . . . info@castlebrightstudios.net

TYPES	Animation - Features
DEVELOPMENT	Stonehenge: Rise of the Druids - Elements - Sidetrack and the Traits - The Toothfairy
COMMENTS	Screenplay development; Comic book development and publishing

Jay Douglas . . . . Principal/Producer
Nav Gupta . . . . Principal/Producer
Heather Kenealy . . . . Comic Book Department
Julie Cook . . . . Creative Executive
Crystal Dizol . . . . Development
Claire Rose Bernard . . . . Development
Jasmine Grace . . . . Creative Affairs
Christina DeRosa . . . . Public Relations
Heather Shay . . . . Office Manager
Andrew Sandler . . . . Assistant to Mr. Douglas
Danella Lucioni . . . . Assistant to Mr. Gupta

CATALAND FILMS

555 W. 25th St., 4th Fl.
New York, NY 10001
PHONE 212-989-5995/818-954-5600
FAX 212-989-5505/818-954-5620
EMAIL . . . . richp@cataland.com
WEB SITE . . . . www.cataland.com

TYPES	Animation - Documentaries - Features - TV Series
DEVELOPMENT	Time Riders - Greek Road - Baby Maker
POST PRODUCTION	Brooklyn Rules - Rodeo Clowns
CREDITS	Club Dread - Super Troopers - Puddle Cruiser - Way Off Broadway - Preaching to the Choir - Beerfest
COMMENTS	West Coast address: c/o Broken Lizard Industries, 4000 Warner Blvd., Bldg. 139, Rm. 102, Burbank, CA 91522

Richard Perello . . . . No Title
Phil Cottone . . . . No Title

CATAPULT FILMS

832 Third St., Ste. 303
Santa Monica, CA 90403-1155
PHONE 310-395-1470

TYPES	Documentaries - Features - Made-for-TV/Cable Movies
DEVELOPMENT	The Inventors of Sex - Outerberlin - Laundry - Traces
CREDITS	Inferno - Bride of the Wind (Paramount Classics) - Love Object (Content/Pressman Films) - Mr. Rock 'N Roll
SUBMISSION POLICY	No unsolicited submissions

Lawrence Levy . . . . Producer
Lisa Josefsberg . . . . Producer

CATCHLIGHT FILMS

4216-3/4 Glencoe Ave.
Marina del Rey, CA 90292
PHONE 310-827-3797
FAX 310-827-2533
EMAIL . . . . mailbox@catchlightfilms.com
WEB SITE . . . . www.catchlightfilms.com

TYPES	Commercials - Direct-to-Video/DVD - Documentaries - Features - Music Videos
DEVELOPMENT	Satana - My Necropolis - Remains - Black Mountain - Transgressions - Black Tulip - The Daily Grind
CREDITS	Heart of the Beholder - Songs for the City of Angels - Rings - Amy's Orgasm - World Festival of Sacred Music: The Americas - In the Weeds - Break a Leg

Arnon Manor . . . . Producer
Jeanette Volturno . . . . Producer
Rick Osako . . . . Producer

CATES/DOTY PRODUCTIONS

10920 Wilshire Blvd., Ste. 830
Los Angeles, CA 90024
PHONE 310-208-2134

TYPES	Features - Specials - TV Series
CREDITS	Absolute Strangers - Call Me Anna - The Academy Awards® - Tom Clancy's Net Force - Innocent Victims - Confessions: Two Faces of Evil

Gilbert Cates . . . . Producer/Director
Dennis Doty . . . . Producer
Peggy Griffin . . . . Associate Producer

CATFISH PRODUCTIONS

23852 Pacific Coast Hwy., Ste. 313
Malibu, CA 90265
PHONE 310-456-6175
FAX 310-456-5276
EMAIL .....catfishprods@aol.com
TYPES: Commercials - Documentaries - Features - Made-for-TV/Cable Movies - Miniseries - TV Series
DEVELOPMENT: The Back Up Guy - Waking Up Driving - The Handyman - Jury of Her Peers - The Dress - Popcorn - Campaign!
PRE-PRODUCTION: Luther
COMPLETED UNRELEASED: The Blind Guy
CREDITS: Walk the Line - Marriage of Convenience - The Stars Fell on Henrietta - The Absolute Truth - A Passion for Justice - Blackout - Dr. Quinn, Medicine Woman: The Movie - Murder in the Mirror - Submerged - Enslavement: The True Story of Fanny Kemble - Disease of the Wind
SUBMISSION POLICY: No unsolicited screenplays or books; Fax or email one-page queries only; Finished films OK

James Keach .....Actor/Producer/Director
Jane Seymour .....Actress/Producer
Nick Hippisley Coxe .....Sr. VP, Production, PCH Films
Molly Hassel .....Production, PCH Films
Richard Keith .....Development/Production
Debra Pearl .....Development/Production

CATTLEYA

Via Della Frezza, 59
Rome 00186, Italy
PHONE 39-06-367-201
FAX 39-06-367-2050
EMAIL .....info@cattleya.it
WEB SITE .....www.cattleya.it
TYPES: Features
DEVELOPMENT: Perfect Skin - At a Glance
PRE-PRODUCTION: I Want You
PRODUCTION: My Brother Is an Only Child - Commediasexi
UPCOMING RELEASES: N: Napoleon and Me - The Missing Star - Black Sea - Flying Lessons
CREDITS: Don't Move - I'm Not Scared - The Missing Star - Don't Tell - Crime Novel
SUBMISSION POLICY: No unsolicited submissions

Riccardo Tozzi .....President
Giovanni Stabilini .....CEO
Marco Chimenz .....Executive VP
Gina Gardini .....Producer
Francesca Longardi .....Head, Development

*CBS CORPORATION

51 W. 52nd St.
New York, NY 10019
PHONE 212-975-4321
WEB SITE .....www.cbs.com
TYPES: TV Series

Sumner Redstone .....Chairman of the Board
Leslie Moonves .....President/CEO, CBS Corporation
David Poltrack .....President, CBS Vision/Executive VP/Chief Research Officer, CBS Corporation
Anthony Ambrosio .....Executive VP, Human Resources & Administration, CBS Corporation
Louis Briskman .....Executive VP/General Counsel
Carl Folta .....Executive VP/Office of the Chairman
Martin Franks .....Executive VP, Planning, Policy & Government Relations
Fred Reynolds .....Executive VP/CFO
Gil Schwartz .....Executive VP, CBS Corporate Communications
Martin Shea .....Executive VP, Investor Relations
Chris Ender .....Sr. VP, CBS Communications Group
Susan Gordon .....Sr. VP/Corporate Controller/Chief Accounting Officer
Joseph Ianniello .....Sr. VP, Finance/Treasurer
Richard Jones .....Sr. VP/General Tax Counsel
Joanna Massey .....Sr. VP, Communications, West Coast, CBS Corporation
Dana McClintock .....Sr. VP, CBS Communications Group
Angie Straka .....Sr. VP/Deputy Counsel/Secretary, CBS Corporation
Beth Feldman .....VP, CBS Communications Group
Bryce N. Harlow II .....VP, Government Relations
Shannon Jacobs .....VP, CBS Communications Group

CBS ENTERTAINMENT

7800 Beverly Blvd.
Los Angeles, CA 90036-2188
PHONE 323-575-2345/212-975-4321
WEB SITE .....www.cbs.com
TYPES: Made-for-TV/Cable Movies - Reality TV - TV Series
COMMENTS: East Coast office: 51 W. 52nd St., 6th Fl., New York, NY 10019; Includes internet channel Innertube

Leslie Moonves .....President/CEO, CBS Corporation
Nancy Tellem .....President, CBS Paramount Network Television Entertainment Group
Nina Tassler .....President, CBS Entertainment
Larry Kramer .....President, CBS Digital Media
Kelly Kahl .....Sr. Executive VP, Programming Operations
Deborah Barak .....Executive VP, Business Affairs, CBS Paramount Network Television Entertainment Group
Peter Golden .....Executive VP, Talent & Casting
Ghen Maynard .....Executive VP, Alternative Programming & Entertainment Content for New Media
Jack Sussman .....Executive VP, Specials, Music & Live Events
Wendi Trilling .....Executive VP, Comedy Development
Bela Bajaria .....Sr. VP, Movies & Miniseries
Barbara Bloom .....Sr. VP, Daytime Programs
David Brownfield .....Sr. VP, Current Programming
Chris Ender .....Sr. VP, CBS Communications Group
Joanna Massey .....Sr. VP, Communications, West Coast, CBS Corporation
Laverne McKinnon .....Sr. VP, Drama Development
Roni Mueller .....Sr. VP, Business Affairs
Gary Silver .....Sr. VP, Business Affairs
Eric Steinberg .....Sr. VP, West Coast Research
Lucy Cavallo .....VP, Casting
Francis Cavanaugh .....VP, Photography, West Coast
Karen Church .....VP, Casting
Nancy Daniels .....VP, Alternative Series Development
Chris Davidson .....VP, Current Programs
Christina Davis .....VP, Drama Series Development

(Continued)

CBS ENTERTAINMENT (Continued)

Vincent P. Favale . . . . .VP, Late Night Programs, East Coast
Beth Feldman . . . . .VP, CBS Communications Group
Phil Gonzales . . . . .VP, Communications
Amy Herzig . . . . .VP, Casting, East Coast
Alix Jaffe . . . . .VP, Current Programs
Andy Kubitz . . . . .VP, Scheduling & Program Planning
Lisa Leingang . . . . .VP, Development, East Coast
Sidney H. Lyons . . . .VP, Business Affairs, Longform Contracts & Acquisitions
David Marko . . . . .VP, Miniseries & Movies
Edy Mendoza . . . . .VP, Comedy Development
Richard J. Mensing Jr. . . . . .VP, Daytime Programs, East Coast
Ian Metrose . . . . .VP, Talent Relations & Special Events
Anne R. Nelson . . . . .VP, Business Affairs
Shannon O'Connor . . . . .VP, Miniseries & Movies
Fern Orenstein . . . . .VP, Casting
Julie Pernworth . . . . .VP, Comedy Development
Cyriac Roeding . . . . .VP, Wireless, CBS Digital Media
Jodi Roth . . . . .VP, Specials
Sam Semon . . . . .VP, Business Affairs
Pamela Soaper . . . . .VP, Current Programs
Joan Yee . . . . .VP, Sponsor Programming, Movies & Miniseries
Robert Zotnowski . . . . .VP, Drama Series Development
Cindy Badell-Slaughter . . . . .Director, Music Operations
Carolyn Ceslik . . . . .Director, Children's Programs, East Coast
Dorian Hannaway . . . . .Director, Late Night Programming, West Coast
Sandy Varo . . . . .Director, Alternative Series
Greg Harris . . . . .Director, Current Programs
Alison Rinzel . . . . .Director, Daytime Casting, East Coast
Margot Wain . . . . .Director, Daytime Programs, West Coast
Cynthia Brown . . . . .Director, Business Affairs
Joel Goldberg . . . . .Director, Business Affairs
Travis Pierson . . . . .Director, Business Affairs
Christopher T. Ryan . . . . .Director, Business Affairs
Roger Senders . . . . .Director, Business Affairs

CBS NEWS

524 W. 57th St.
New York, NY 10019
PHONE 212-975-4321
WEB SITE . . . . .www.cbsnews.com
CREDITS The Early Show - The Saturday Early Show - CBS Morning News - CBS Evening News - 60 Minutes - 48 Hours Mystery - Sunday Morning - Face the Nation - Up to the Minute

Sean McManus . . . . .President
John Frazee . . . . .Sr. VP, News Services
Linda Mason . . . . .Sr. VP, Standards & Special Projects
Margery Baker-Riker . . . . .VP, CBS News Productions
Steve Friedman . . . . .VP, Morning Broadcasts
Paul Friedman . . . . .VP, News
Sandra Genelius . . . . .VP, Communications
Frank Governale . . . . .VP, Operations
Janet Leissner . . . . .VP/Washington Bureau Chief
James McKenna . . . . .VP, Finance & Administration
Harvey Nagler . . . . .VP, CBS Radio News
Jennifer Siebens . . . . .VP/London Bureau Chief
Rome Hartman . . . . .Executive Producer, CBS Evening News

CBS PARAMOUNT INTERNATIONAL TELEVISION

5555 Melrose Ave.
Los Angeles, CA 90036
PHONE 323-956-5000
FAX 323-862-2217
WEB SITE . . . . .www.cbscorporation.com
TYPES TV Series
COMMENTS Syndication Pay/Cable TV; News; Formats game shows; Comedy; Drama; Reality; Sales offices in Canada, France, London, Australia, Miami, New York, Italy, Japan

Armando Nuñez Jr. . . . . .President, CBS Paramount International Television
Susan Akens . . . . .Executive VP, Business Affairs
Joe Lucas . . . . .Executive VP, Sales & Marketing
Barry Chamberlain . . . . .Sr. VP, Sales
Isis Moussa . . . . .Sr. VP, Marketing
Mina Patel . . . . .Sr. VP, Sales Strategy & Operations
Cece Braun . . . . .VP, Finance
Sean Cleary . . . . .VP/Managing Director, Asia Pacific
Scott Michels . . . . .VP, Sales Operations & Administration, New York
Giovanni Pedde . . . . .VP, European Operations, Rome
Bruce Swanson . . . . .VP/General Manager, Canada
Stephen Tague . . . . .VP, European Sales
Jennifer Weingroff . . . . .VP, Communications
Richard Yannich . . . . .VP, International Operations
Catherine Molinier . . . . .Managing Director, France
Stephanie Pacheco .Managing Director, Latin America
Mie Horasawa . . . . .Director, Sales, Northeast Asia

CBS PARAMOUNT NETWORK TELEVISION

CBS Studios
4024 Radford Ave.
Studio City, CA 91604
PHONE 818-655-5000
WEB SITE . . . . .www.cbsparamount.com
TYPES Made-for-TV/Cable Movies - Miniseries - Specials - TV Series

Nancy Tellem . . . . .President, CBS Paramount Network Television Entertainment Group
David Stapf . . . . .President, CBS Paramount Network Television
Maria Crenna . . . . .Executive VP, CBS Paramount Network Television
Deborah Barak . . . . .Executive VP, Business Affairs, CBS Paramount Network Television Entertainment Group
Kevin Berg . . . . .Executive VP, Production, CBS Paramount Network Television Entertainment Group
John A. Wentworth . . . . . . .Executive VP, Communications, CBS Paramount Television
David Karnes . . . . .Executive VP, Legal, CBS Paramount Network Television
Lauri Metrose . . . .VP, Communications, CBS Paramount Network Television
Brian Banks . . . . .Sr. VP, Comedy Development, CBS Paramount Network Television
Glenn Geller . . .Sr. VP, Current Programs, CBS Paramount Network Television
Sheila Guthrie . . .Sr. VP, Talent & Casting, CBS Paramount Network Television
Hal Harrison . . . . .Sr. VP, Post Production, CBS Paramount Network Television
Dan Kupetz . . . . . .Sr. VP, Business Affairs, CBS Paramount Network Television
Julie McNamara . . . . .Sr. VP, Drama Development, CBS Paramount Network Television
Roni Mueller . . . . .Sr. VP, TV Music, CBS Paramount Network Television
Kate Adler . . . .VP, Comedy Development, CBS Paramount Network Television
Francisco Arias . . . .VP, Business Affairs, CBS Paramount Network Television
Jocelyn Freid . . . . .VP, Current Programming, CBS Paramount Network Television
Jennifer Grisanti . . . . .VP, Current Programming, CBS Paramount Network Television
Bridget Hegarty . . . . .VP, Current Programming, CBS Paramount Network Television
David Lavin . . . . . .VP, Business Affairs, CBS Paramount Network Television
Marilyn Loncar . . . . . . .VP, Production, CBS Paramount Network Television
Bryan Seabury . . . . .VP, Drama Development, CBS Paramount Network Television

CBS PARAMOUNT WORLDWIDE TELEVISION DISTRIBUTION
5555 Melrose Ave.
Los Angeles, CA 90038-3197
PHONE 323-956-5000
WEB SITE . . . . . www.cbsparamount.com
TYPES Syndication - TV Series

Joel Berman . . . .President, CBS Paramount Worldwide Television Distribution
Armando Nuñez . . . . . . .President, CBS Paramount International Television
John Nogawski . . . . . President, CBS Paramount Domestic TV
Greg Meidel . . . . . .President, Programming, CBS Paramount Domestic TV
Terry Wood . . . . . . .President, Creative Affairs & Development, King World Productions & CBS Paramount Domestic TV
Marc Hirsch . . . . .President, CBS Paramount Advertising Services (NY)
Mark Dvornik . . . . . .Executive VP/General Sales Manager, CBS Paramount Domestic TV
Scott Koondel . . . . .Executive VP, Distribution, CBS Paramount Domestic TV
Reed Manville . . . . . .Executive VP, International Channels, CBS Paramount Worldwide Pay TV
Michael Mischler . . .Executive VP, Marketing, CBS Paramount Domestic TV
Bruce Pottash . . . . . .Executive VP, Business & Legal Affairs, CBS Paramount Domestic TV
Bob Sheehan . . . .Executive VP, Finance & Business Affairs, CBS Paramount Domestic TV
John A. Wentworth . . . .Executive VP, Communications, CBS Paramount TV
Dawn Abel . . . . . . .Sr. VP, Research, CBS Paramount Worldwide Television Distribution
Brad Hart . . . . .Sr. VP, Programming & Production, CBS Paramount Domestic TV
Kathy Samuels . . . . .Sr. VP, Programming, CBS Paramount Domestic TV

CBS SPORTS
51 W. 52nd St.
New York, NY 10019
PHONE 212-975-4321
WEB SITE . . . . . www.cbs.com
SECOND WEB SITE . . . . . www.cbssportsonline.com
TYPES TV Series

Sean McManus . . . . . President
Tony Petitti . . . . . Executive VP/Executive Producer
Ken Aagaard . . . . . Sr. VP, Operations & Production Services
Michael L. Aresco . . . . . Sr. VP, Programming
Robert Correa . . . . . Sr. VP, Programming
Arthur Harris . . . . . VP, Broadcast Operations
Martin L. Kaye . . . . . VP, Finance
LeslieAnne Wade . . . . . VP, Communications

CECCHI GORI PICTURES
11990 San Vicente Blvd., Ste. 300
Los Angeles, CA 90049
PHONE 310-442-4777
FAX 310-442-9507
EMAIL . . . . . dcaplan@cgpusa.com
WEB SITE . . . . . www.cecchigoripictures.com
TYPES Features
DEVELOPMENT Il Sorpasso - Taming Ben Taylor - Ferrari - Numbers - Everybody's Fine - Silence - The Cyclone
CREDITS Alexander - Il Postino - The Starmaker - Mediterraneo - Life Is Beautiful - Canone Inverso - Il Mio West - Ciao Professore - Everybody's Fine - House of Cards - Man Trouble - A Bronx Tale - Night in The City - Seven - From Dusk Till Dawn
SUBMISSION POLICY Solicited projects only
COMMENTS Motion picture development; Italian distribution and production

Gianni Nunnari . . . . . President
Craig J. Flores . . . . . VP, Business & Legal Affairs
Nathalie Peter-Contesse . . . . . VP, Creative Affairs
David Caplan . . . . . Creative Assistant

CENTROPOLIS ENTERTAINMENT
1445 N. Stanley Ave., 3rd Fl.
Los Angeles, CA 90046
PHONE 323-850-1212
FAX 323-850-1201
TYPES Features
PRODUCTION 10,000 B.C.
POST PRODUCTION Welcome to America
CREDITS Universal Soldier - Stargate - Independence Day - Godzilla - The Patriot - The Visitor - The 13th Floor - The Day After Tomorrow
SUBMISSION POLICY No unsolicited submissions

Roland Emmerich . . . . . Partner
Ute Emmerich . . . . . Partner
Michael Wimer . . . . . Partner
Aaron Boyd . . . . . Creative Executive
Kirstin Winkler . . . . . Executive Assistant
Shawna Hoppes . . . . . Assistant to Producer
Sarah Koplin . . . . . Assistant to Producer

CFP PRODUCTIONS
5555 Melrose Ave., Lucy Bungalow 105
Los Angeles, CA 90038
PHONE 323-956-8866
FAX 323-862-2445
WEB SITE . . . . . www.cfpproductions.com
TYPES Features
HAS DEAL WITH Paramount Pictures
DEVELOPMENT Fashionistas - Area 51 - Diamond Life: Confessions of a Master Jewel Thief - Fear and Respect - How to Get a Guy in 10 Days - How to Tell He's Not the One in 10 Days (Paramount) - The Thing About Jane Spring (Paramount) - The Other Billy Drake
CREDITS The Out-of-Towners - How to Lose a Guy in 10 Days

Christine Peters . . . . . Producer
Bradford Smith . . . . . President
Randy Tat . . . . . Executive VP
Petersen Harris . . . . . Creative Executive

STOKELY CHAFFIN PRODUCTIONS
1416 N. La Brea Ave.
Hollywood, CA 90028
PHONE 323-802-1790/310-497-5074
FAX 480-247-5323
TYPES Features - TV Series
HAS DEAL WITH New Line Cinema
DEVELOPMENT Bridge & Tunnel - Dream House - Guilty Pleasure - Sleight of Mind - Wild Horses
CREDITS Snakes on a Plane - Held Up - Soul Survivors - Freddy vs. Jason - Sweet Home Alabama - I Know What You Did Last Summer - Out of Time - The Rat Pack - Volcano

Stokely Chaffin . . . . . Producer
David Steinberg . . . . . Director, Development
David Reed . . . . . Development Assistant

CHAMELEON ENTERTAINMENT
1617 Broadway, Ste. 3000
Santa Monica, CA 90403
PHONE 310-401-6270
FAX 310-401-6177
WEB SITE ....www.chameleonent.com
SECOND WEB SITE ....www.povfilms.com
TYPES Commercials - Mobile Content - Music Videos - Reality TV
COMPLETED UNRELEASED Remix (Pilot) - Adventures in the C League (Pilot)
CREDITS Pulled Over (E!/Style) - Taildaters (MTV) - Burned (MTV)

Damon Harman ....CEO/Executive Producer
Jon Nixon ....VP, Production
Nathan Rotmensz ....VP, Post Production
Joan Vento-Hall ....Business Affairs

CHANTICLEER FILMS
5914 Foothill Dr.
Los Angeles, CA 90068
PHONE 323-462-4705
FAX 323-462-1603
EMAIL ....yona@aol.com
TYPES Animation - Documentaries - Features - Made-for-TV/Cable Movies - TV Series
DEVELOPMENT Turning Points
CREDITS Going to the Mat - Down Came a Black Bird - Tru Confessions - On the Edge - Directed by... - Lush Life

Jana Sue Memel ....President/Producer/Director
Mindi Memel ....Executive Assistant

CHARLES BROS.
c/o Paramount Television
5555 Melrose Ave., Shulberg Bldg., Ste. 317
Los Angeles, CA 90038-3197
PHONE 323-956-5962
FAX 323-862-3407
TYPES TV Series
HAS DEAL WITH CBS Paramount Network Television
CREDITS Cheers - Will & Grace
COMMENTS Moving at press time

James Burrows ....Executive Producer/Director
Glen Charles ....Executive Producer
Les Charles ....Executive Producer

CHARLES FLOYD JOHNSON PRODUCTIONS
c/o Sunset Gower Studios
1438 N. Gower St., Bldg. 35, Ste. 451
Los Angeles, CA 90028-3197
PHONE 323-468-4520
FAX 323-468-4517
TYPES TV Series
HAS DEAL WITH CBS Paramount Network Television
CREDITS The Rockford Files - Quantum Leap - Magnum PI - JAG - First Monday - N.C.I.S.

Chas. Floyd Johnson ....Executive Producer
Anne Burford ....VP, Development
Debra Mayfield ....Assistant to Mr. Johnson
Austin Grady ....Second Assistant to Mr. Johnson

CHARLOTTE STREET FILMS
9701 Wilshire Blvd., 10th Fl.
Beverly Hills, CA 90212
PHONE 310-601-7150
FAX 310-388-5366
TYPES Animation - Features - Made-for-TV/Cable Movies - TV Series
DEVELOPMENT The Franchise - Pastime
CREDITS Tim Burton's Corpse Bride - Slacker Cats - Boyer Bros. - Nightbreaker - A Chance of Snow - Mortal Sins - Marilyn & Bobby - Da - No Means No - Babies Having Babies

Jeffrey Auerbach ....Producer
Gabrielle Ginter ....Assistant

CHARTOFF PRODUCTIONS
1250 Sixth St., Ste. 101
Santa Monica, CA 90401
PHONE 310-319-1960
FAX 310-319-3469
TYPES Animation - Features - Made-for-TV/Cable Movies
DEVELOPMENT The Man Who Stole the Mona Lisa - Ender's Game - The Tutor - Nothing But the Blues
CREDITS Rocky 1-5 - Raging Bull - Straight Talk - The Right Stuff - In My Country

Robert Chartoff ....CEO
Lynn Hendee ....President
Lori Imbler Vernon ....Production Associate

CHERRY ROAD FILMS, LLC
1460 Fourth St., Ste. 212
Santa Monica, CA 90401
PHONE 310-458-6550
FAX 310-458-6510
EMAIL ....info@cherryroadfilms.com
WEB SITE ....www.cherryroadfilms.com
TYPES Features
HAS DEAL WITH Warner Independent Pictures
DEVELOPMENT Solitaire - Money for Nothing - Manhattan Loverboy - Forget About It - Spring Break in Bosnia - Iraqi Convoy Project - White Noise
PRE-PRODUCTION Dark Reaches - Illegal Superman
COMPLETED UNRELEASED Southland Tales
CREDITS Eulogy - Mail Order Wife - The L.A. Riot Spectacular

Kendall Morgan ....President/Producer
Bo Hyde ....CEO/Co-Founder
Tommaso Fiacchino ....VP, Development & Acquisitions

CHEYENNE ENTERPRISES
406 Wilshire Blvd., 2nd Fl.
Santa Monica, CA 90401
PHONE 310-455-5000
TYPES Features - TV Series
DEVELOPMENT The Tourist - Timber Falls
PRE-PRODUCTION Black Water Transit
CREDITS Features: Just My Luck - 16 Blocks - Hostage - Tears of the Sun - The Crocodile Hunter: Collision Course - Hart's War - Bandits; TV: Scarlett (Pilot) - Touching Evil - Gary the Rat
SUBMISSION POLICY Does not accept unsolicited material

Arnold Rifkin ....No Title
Marjorie Shik ....No Title
Martha Haight ....No Title
Todd Shotz ....No Title
Justin Hamann ....No Title

CHIC PRODUCTIONS

1228 Venice Blvd., Ste. 499
Los Angeles, CA 90066
PHONE .310-391-2152/310-551-2060
FAX .310-857-6412
EMAIL .steve@chicproductions.com
WEB SITE .www.chicproductions.com
TYPES Made-for-TV/Cable Movies - Miniseries - Reality TV - TV Series
HAS DEAL WITH Shoreline Entertainment, Inc.
DEVELOPMENT Duty Calls - The Fourth Realm - Dr. Jekyll & Mr. Hyde - MK-8 - Ice Moon Europa - Cyber Guy - Book Crooks - Mirror Lake - Locked In - Last Meals - Random Acts - Daytona Dog
PRE-PRODUCTION Backwards in High Heels - Telegraph Hill
CREDITS Film: Marylyn Hotchkiss Ballroom Dancing - Charm School; TV: The Engagement Ring (TNT)

Steve Chicorel .Executive Producer
Jessica Miller .Executive Assistant/Production Coordinator
Taoyun Fu .Assistant

CHICAGOFILMS

101 Fifth Ave., 8th Fl.
New York, NY 10003
PHONE .212-645-3000
FAX .212-645-3014
TYPES Features - TV Series
CREDITS The Last Good Time - Parents - Gosford Park - Celebrity Charades - Hopeless Pictures (Animated)

Bob Balaban .Actor/Director/Producer
Peter Duchan .Director, Development

CHICK FLICKS

116 N. Robertson Blvd., Ste. 400
Los Angeles, CA 90048
PHONE .310-967-6541
FAX .310-657-2836
TYPES Features - Made-for-TV/Cable Movies
HAS DEAL WITH New Line Cinema
DEVELOPMENT Drop Dead Fred - Daddy's Girl - I Love You Again - This Perfect Day - The Politician's Wife - The Harder They Come - Gridiron Girls - Callas Hurricane Season - Eleanor and Colette - Bad Hair Day - Stories I Couldn't Tell When I Was a Pastor - Ellis Jump
POST PRODUCTION Broken Bridges
CREDITS Raise Your Voice (New Line) - Murder Without Conviction (Hallmark Channel)
SUBMISSION POLICY Only through representation

Sara Risher .President

CHINA FILM GROUP

25 Xin Wai St.
Beijing 100088, China
PHONE .86-106-2268-023
TYPES Features
DEVELOPMENT The Promise
CREDITS Kung Fu Hustle - Together

Han Sanping .Vice Chairman
Yang Buting .CEO
Zhongqiang Jin .General Manager
Tiejun Mu .Director

CHIODO BROS. PRODUCTIONS, INC.

110 W. Providencia Ave.
Burbank, CA 91502
PHONE .818-842-5656
FAX .818-848-0891
EMAIL .klowns@chiodobros.com
WEB SITE .www.chiodobros.com
TYPES Animation - Direct-to-Video/DVD - Documentaries - Features - Made-for-TV/Cable Movies - TV Series
DEVELOPMENT Innards - The Italian Odyssey - Alien X-Mas - It Came Upon a Midnight Clear
PRE-PRODUCTION The Trail of the Screaming Forehead
CREDITS Team America (Paramount Pictures) - Elf (Animation) - Killer Klowns from Outer Space - The Crayon Box - The Amazing Live Sea Monkeys - Clay (Disney Channel)
COMMENTS Main title and stop motion animation

Stephen Chiodo .Director/Development
Edward Chiodo .Producer/Development
Charles Chiodo .Designer/Development
Roger Medanich .Production Manager

CHOTZEN/JENNER PRODUCTIONS

1608 N. Cahuenga Blvd., Ste. 381
Hollywood, CA 90028
PHONE .323-465-9877
FAX .323-460-6451
TYPES Features - Made-for-TV/Cable Movies - TV Series
HAS DEAL WITH Jaffe/Braunstein Films, LLC
DEVELOPMENT A Shred of Love
CREDITS My Father's Shadow - The Rosa Parks Story - Lies He Told - Prison of Secrets - Matter of Justice - Murder in the Mirror

Yvonne Chotzen .Producer/Partner
William Jenner .Producer/Partner
Dominique Azusa .Development

CHRIS/ROSE PRODUCTIONS

3131 Torreyson Pl.
Los Angeles, CA 90046
PHONE .323-851-8772
FAX .323-851-0662
TYPES Features - Made-for-TV/Cable Movies - TV Series
PRE-PRODUCTION Singing in the Comeback Choir - An Accidental Friendship (Lifetime)
CREDITS The Crossing - Down in the Delta - Kingfish - Hide in Plain Sight - Queen of the Stardust Ballroom - Autobiography of Miss Jane Pittman
SUBMISSION POLICY By agent or legal representative only

Robert W. Christiansen .Executive Producer
Rick Rosenberg .Executive Producer

CHUBBCO FILM CO.

1416 N. La Brea Ave.
Hollywood, CA 90028
PHONE .323-802-1886
FAX .310-451-4825
TYPES Features - Made-for-TV/Cable Movies
DEVELOPMENT Unthinkable - Garage Band - Eight Pieces for Josette - Glass Gun - A Hustler's Wife
PRE-PRODUCTION Trust
UPCOMING RELEASES Banshee
COMPLETED UNRELEASED Believe in Me
CREDITS To Sleep With Anger - Hoffa - The Crow - Eve's Bayou - Dark Blue - Pootie Tang - Everyday People
SUBMISSION POLICY No queries

Caldecot Chubb .Producer
Kerry Russell .Associate

CIDER MILL PRODUCTIONS

c/o Walt Disney Pictures
500 S. Buena Vista St., Animation C16
Burbank, CA 91521
PHONE .818-560-8016
FAX .818-560-4487
TYPES Features
HAS DEAL WITH Walt Disney Pictures/Touchstone Pictures
DEVELOPMENT Dead in the Water - Again
CREDITS Out of Time - Catch That Kid - Annapolis

Damien Saccani .Producer
Bridget Humphrey .VP, Development

THE CIELO GROUP, INC.

396 Washington St., Ste. 110
Wellesley, MA 02481
PHONE .617-784-8837
FAX .617-323-6579
EMAIL .info@cielo-group.com
WEB SITE .www.cielo-group.com
TYPES Mobile Content
COMMENTS Distribution channels include Jamster

Dean Macri .President/CEO
Steven Feldman .Marketing, VP

CINE MOSAIC

130 West 25th St., Ste. 12A
New York, NY 10001
PHONE .212-625-3797/212-625-3819
FAX .212-625-3571
WEB SITE .www.cinemosaic.net
TYPES Features
HAS DEAL WITH HBO Films
DEVELOPMENT The Outcasts of 19 Schuyler Place - Diamond, Louisiana - The Impressionist - The Probable Future - I Know Where Bruce Lee Lives - A Gesture Life - Chaos - Fela Kuti: Music is the Weapon - Ruthie & Connie - The Silent Twins - Virtual Love
UPCOMING RELEASES The Namesake
CREDITS Vanity Fair
SUBMISSION POLICY No unsolicited material

Lydia Dean Pilcher .President/Producer (ldp@cinemosaic.net)
Thomas De Napoli .Production/Creative Executive (td@cinemosaic.net)

CINECITY PICTURES

1925 Century Park East, 5th Fl.
Los Angeles, CA 90067
PHONE .310-559-7410
FAX .310-559-7452
EMAIL .cinecity@cinecity.com
TYPES Features
CREDITS Bopha!

Lawrence Taubman .Producer
Stacy Katz .Director, Development

CINÉGROUPE

1151, Alexandre-DeSève
Montréal, PQ H2L 2T7, Canada
PHONE .514-524-7567
FAX .514-849-9846
EMAIL .distribution@cinegroupe.com
SECOND EMAIL .info@cinegroupe.com
WEB SITE .www.cinegroupe.com
TYPES Animation - Direct-to-Video/DVD - Features - Internet Content - Made-for-TV/Cable Movies - Miniseries - Mobile Content - TV Series
DEVELOPMENT Porgy & Bass - Splish, Splash
CREDITS Tripping the Rift - What's with Andy? - P3K: Pinocchio 3000 - 11 Somerset - Seriously Weird - Pig City - Galidor: Defenders of the Outer Dimension - Sagwa: The Chinese Siamese Cat - Mega Babies - Lion of Oz - Charlie Jade
SUBMISSION POLICY Email an outline with financial structure to distribution@cinegroupe.com
COMMENTS Seeking creative projects in animation or live action with CGI

Jacques Pettigrew .President/CEO (Montréal)
Michel Lemire .Executive VP/Creative Affairs (Montréal)
Marie-Christine Dufour .Executive VP, Pre-Sales, Distribution, & Marketing
Andrew Makarewicz .VP, Documentary Acquisitions & Co-Productions (amakarewicz@cinegroupe.ca)

CINEMA 21 GROUP

140 Butterfly Ln.
Montecito, CA 93108
PHONE .805-565-5754/212-203-6123
FAX .805-565-5795
EMAIL .pl@cinema21group.com
WEB SITE .www.peterlance.com
TYPES Documentaries - Features - Miniseries - TV Series
PRE-PRODUCTION Triple Cross
CREDITS Blackjack - First Degree Burn - Missing Persons - The Stingray: Lethal Tactics of the Sole Survivor - JAG - Crime Story - Wiseguy - Miami Vice - The Sentinel - 1000 Years for Revenge - The Riverman - Cover Up
COMMENTS Also publishes Cinema 21 Books

Peter Lance .Writer/Producer
Travis Payne .Co-Producer

CINEMA LIBRE STUDIO

8328 De Soto Ave.
Canoga Park, CA 91304
PHONE .818-349-8822
FAX .818-349-9922
EMAIL .info@cinemalibrestudio.com
WEB SITE .www.cinemalibrestudio.com

TYPES	Direct-to-Video/DVD - Documentaries - Features
DEVELOPMENT	Mundo Mata - World Debt (Documentary)
PRODUCTION	Phenom
POST PRODUCTION	Tre - Driving to ZigZigland
UPCOMING RELEASES	America: Freedom to Facism - My First Wedding
COMPLETED UNRELEASED	Conventioneers - Heads N' TailZ
CREDITS	Giuliani Time - Through the Fire - The Future of Food - Uncovered: The War on Iraq - World Order (Somewhere in Africa) - Heavy Metal 2000 - St. Patrick's Day - Outfoxed: Rupert Murdoch's War on Journalism - Fish Without a Bicycle - Soldier's Pay - Unconstitutional: The War on Our Civil Liberties - Unprecedented: The 2004 Presidential Election - McLibel
SUBMISSION POLICY	Query first via email
COMMENTS	Distributor (US and International); Post production services for independent filmmakers

Philippe Diaz .Producer/Owner
Kindra Ruocco .Studio Operations/Project Analysis
Nicole Ballivian .International Sales
Beth Portello .Business Development/Marketing
Rick Rosen .Legal/Business Affairs
Richard Castro .Distribution, Theatrical
Khadijah Rashid .Distribution, Theatrical & DVD
Arik Treston .Distribution, DVD

CINEMA SEVEN PRODUCTIONS

c/o Carnegie Hall
154 W. 57th St., Ste. 112
New York, NY 10019
PHONE .212-315-1060/310-247-1444
FAX .212-315-1085/310-247-1477
EMAIL .cin7prod@aol.com

TYPES	Features
PRE-PRODUCTION	The Madman's Tale
CREDITS	Opa! - Where Eagles Dare - Angel Heart - The Long Goodbye - Harper - Farewell, My Lovely - Equus - The Missouri Breaks
COMMENTS	West Coast office: 144 S. Beverly Dr., Ste. 407, Beverly Hills, CA 90212; UK office: Pinewood Studios, Pinewood Rd., Iver Heath, Bucks SL0 0NH, United Kingdom, phone: 44-1-753-656-825

Elliott Kastner .President
Dillon Kastner .Producer (LA)
George Pappas .Sr. VP
James Deyarmin .VP, Business Affairs
Pasquale Botta .Head, Production (NY)
Julius Ortiguero .Head, Production (LA)

CINEMA-ELECTRIC INC.

6634 Sunset Blvd.
Los Angeles, CA 90028
PHONE .213-388-4260
FAX .323-464-0699
EMAIL .info@cinemaelectric.com
WEB SITE .www.cinemaelectric.com

TYPES	Mobile Content
CREDITS	Portable Hollywood - Smashbrain - Portable Vinyl

Josh Kaye .Co-President (joshk@cinemaelectric.com)
Adam Levin .Co-President (alevin@cinemaelectric.com)
Sherry Wang .Producer (sherryw@cinemaelectric.com)

CINEMAGIC ENTERTAINMENT

9229 Sunset Blvd., Ste. 610
West Hollywood, CA 90069
PHONE .310-385-9322
FAX .310-385-9347
WEB SITE .www.cinemagicent.com

TYPES	Animation - Direct-to-Video/DVD - Documentaries - Features - Internet Content - Made-for-TV/Cable Movies - Miniseries - Mobile Content - Reality TV - TV Series
DEVELOPMENT	Features: Virtua Fighter - Pacific Edge - Shenmue 2 - Halloween (Animation) - Sudden Death - Kill for Hire - Ballerz - There Goes the Neighborhood - Pee Wee Football - Blood Diamonds - For a Good Time Call - The Chunnel - Nuclear Football - Death Book - Sure Death - Oh My God - The Mask of the Black Death - Pacific Edge; TV: Spy vs Spy - The Duel - The Rap - Celebrity Chef - Chef's Table - Destination Unknown - The Smoking Room - S.I.S. - There Goes The Neighborhood - Tuner Shootout - SuperKart - Crank Call
PRE-PRODUCTION	Maid of Honor
CREDITS	Shenmue - Gedo - Fatal Blade - The Yakuza Way - New York Cop - Distant Justice - Sweet Evil - Silencer

Simon Tse .Founder/Producer
Bradley Hong .Founder/Producer
Lee Cohen .VP, Development
Joy Park .Creative Executive
Ayu White .Assistant

CINESON PRODUCTIONS INC.

4519 Varna Ave.
Sherman Oaks, CA 91423
PHONE .818-501-8246
FAX .818-501-3647

TYPES	Documentaries - Features
CREDITS	The Lost City - The Man From Elysian Fields - The Ties That Bind - Just the Ticket - For Love or Country: The Arturo Sandoval Story - Cachao...Como Su Ritmo No Hay Dos

Andy Garcia .Producer/Director

CINETIC

555 W. 25th St.
New York, NY 10001

PHONE .212-204-7979
FAX .212-204-7980
EMAIL .office@cineticmedia.com
WEB SITE .www.cineticmedia.com

TYPES	Direct-to-Video/DVD - Documentaries - Features - TV Series
CREDITS	The Ground Truth - Little Miss Sunshine - Wordplay - A Prairie Home Companion - Quinceanera - A Scanner Darkly - The Notorious Bettie Page - Before Sunset - Bowling for Columbine - Boys Don't Cry - Capturing the Friedmans - The Company - Control Room - Everything Is Illuminated - Far From Heaven - Fog of War - The Machinist - Mad Hot Ballroom - Murderball - Napoleon Dynamite - Spellbound - The Station Agent - Super Size Me - Supertroopers - Waking Life - Where the Truth Lies - Why We Fight - Brick - The Heart of the Game - On a Clear Day - Sketches of Frank Gehry - Water

Janet Brown .No Title
Liesl Copland .No Title
Eric Heidenreich .No Title
John Horowitz .No Title
Chris Horton .No Title
Matt Littin .No Title
Robert Nathan .No Title
Dana O'Keefe .No Title
Ani Pandit .No Title
Julia Rogawski .No Title
John Sloss .No Title

CINEVILLE LLC

3400 Airport Ave.
Santa Monica, CA 90405

PHONE .310-397-7150
FAX .310-397-7155
EMAIL .info@cineville.com
WEB SITE .www.cineville.com

TYPES	Direct-to-Video/DVD - Documentaries - Features
DEVELOPMENT	William Faulkner's The Hound - William Faulkner's Wild Palms - The Beauty of Jane
PRE-PRODUCTION	Grin
PRODUCTION	Hoop Realities
POST PRODUCTION	G.I. Jesus
UPCOMING RELEASES	Surviving Eden
CREDITS	Gas, Food Lodging - The Crew - Swimming with Sharks - Cafe Society - Hurlyburly - The Affair - The Whole Wide World - Mi Vida Loca - Steal Me - Mrs. Palfrey at the Claremont
SUBMISSION POLICY	Email queries
COMMENTS	Distribution deal with Universal Pictures International

Carl Colpaert .Co-Principal
Christoph Henkel .Co-Principal
Lee Caplin .Partner
Gina Carollo .Sr. VP
Frederic Demey .Marketing
Robert Mercado .Assistant, New Media
Sarah Wachel .Assistant

CIRCLE OF CONFUSION PRODUCTIONS

8548 Washington Blvd.
Culver City, CA 90232

PHONE .310-253-7777/718-275-1012
FAX .310-253-9065/718-997-0521
WEB SITE .www.circleofconfusion.com

TYPES	Animation - Features - Internet Content - TV Series
HAS DEAL WITH	CBS Paramount Network Television
DEVELOPMENT	Cable Day (Paramount) - Shadow 19 (Warner Bros.) - Outcast (Universal) - Hammer of the Gods (New Regency) - The House at Awful End (Warner Bros.) - The Psycho (Universal) - Jinx (Universal) - Driving While Dead (Lionsgate) - Magic Kingdom for Sale - Sold! (Universal) - Reaper (Media 8) - Invincible (Paramount) - Invasion (Universal) - Split (CBS Paramount) - We Are Family (Fox) - Straight & Narrow (New Regency) - Extinction (Sony) - The Suffering (MTV Films) - Fantastic Planet (Paramount) - Straight Outta Compton (New Line)
PRE-PRODUCTION	The Heir (Shoreline)
PRODUCTION	Senseless (Matador) - Weapons (Fred Films)
UPCOMING RELEASES	S&Man (HDNet)
COMPLETED UNRELEASED	Ultra (CBS Pilot)
SUBMISSION POLICY	See Web site
COMMENTS	East Coast office: 107-23 71st Rd., Ste. 300, Forest Hills, NY 11375

Lawrence Mattis .Partner
David Alpert .Partner
David Engel .Partner
Ashley Berns .Manager
David Mattis .Manager
John Orlando .Manager
Noah Rosen .Manager
Kemper Donovan .Coordinator
Barrett Korerat .Assistant
Bryan Millard .Assistant

CITY ENTERTAINMENT

266-1/2 S. Rexford Dr.
Beverly Hills, CA 90212

PHONE .310-273-3101
FAX .310-273-3676

TYPES	Animation - Documentaries - Features - Internet Content - Made-for-TV/Cable Movies - Reality TV - TV Series
HAS DEAL WITH	Lionsgate
DEVELOPMENT	Timothy Leary (Miramax) - Jon Dos Passos' U.S.A. - A Band of Angels - Exodus 1947 - Broadway Joe - Howard Street - A Doll's House: The Secret Life of Barbie's Mom - Banana Republic (Showtime) - The Joy Goddess (HBO) - Papillon (NBC/Lionsgate) - Sandra Bernhard Show (Logo) - Women in Arms (Lifetime) - D-Day (CBS/Lionsgate) - Georgia O'Keefe (HBO) - Korshak (CBS)
UPCOMING RELEASES	The Hoax
CREDITS	Dead Men Can't Dance - Introducing Dorothy Dandridge (HBO) - Dodson's Journey (CBS) - The Pentagon Papers (FX) - And Starring Pancho Villa as Himself (HBO)
SUBMISSION POLICY	No unsolicited material
COMMENTS	Deal is with Lionsgate Television

Joshua D. Maurer .President/Executive Producer
Alixandre Witlin .President/Executive Producer
Amanda Hernandez .Assistant

CITY LIGHTS MEDIA GROUP

6 E. 39th St.
New York, NY 10016
PHONE .212-679-4400
FAX .212-679-3819
WEB SITE .www.citylightsmedia.com

TYPES	Commercials - Direct-to-Video/DVD - Documentaries - Features - Made-for-TV/Cable Movies - Music Videos
DEVELOPMENT	Interrupted
PRODUCTION	The Ten
CREDITS	The Descent - Tamara - A Dirty Shame - Torn Apart - A Generation Apart - Unforgotten
SUBMISSION POLICY	Email information with subject heading: re: project

Danny Fisher .CEO
Jack Fisher .President, City Lights Productions
David Noll .President, TV Division
Michael Cohen .VP, Production & Development
Michael Krupat .VP, TV Development
Irad Eyal .VP, TV Production
Marcus Lansdell .Director, Motion Picture Development

CIVILIAN PICTURES

5225 Wilshire Blvd., Ste. 202
Los Angeles, CA 90036
PHONE .323-857-6880
FAX .323-938-3229
EMAIL .info@civilian.com
WEB SITE .www.civilian.com

TYPES	Features
COMPLETED UNRELEASED	Rock the Bells

Barry Poltermann .President
Carrie Heckman .VP, Marketing
Wrye Martin .VP, Production
John Murphy .VP, Operations

CJ Entertainment

CJ ENTERTAINMENT AMERICA

1801 Century Park East, Ste. 520
Los Angeles, CA 90067
PHONE .310-557-3050
FAX .310-557-3469
WEB SITE .www.cjent.co.kr/ccp/e_p_list.asp

TYPES	Features - Music Videos
DEVELOPMENT	Black House
PRE-PRODUCTION	Daddy, Mary and I - Hwaryohan Hyuga - Sex is Zero 2 - Keanom Moksori - Ilbeonga eui Kijeok
PRODUCTION	My Tutor Friend 2
POST PRODUCTION	Ghost Theater - Life is Cool
UPCOMING RELEASES	Like a Virgin - SIM's Family - Miyeol - Righteous Ties - Fly Daddy Fly - Tazza - Cruel Winter Blues - Lump of Sugar - Hanbando - August Rush - I'm a Cyborg - The Restless
COMPLETED UNRELEASED	Sweet Troublemaker
CREDITS	Family Matters - My Scary Girl - Romance - A Dirty Carnival - Forbidden Quest - Sympathy for Lady Vengeance - The Greatest Expectation - Typhoon - Mapado: The Isle of Fortune

Ted Kim .Executive VP
Richard Jun .VP, Business Affairs & Development
Hai-young Yun .VP, Public Relations/Marketing

CLARITY PICTURES, LLC

1107 Fair Oaks Ave., Ste. 155
South Pasadena, CA 91030
PHONE .877-868-8298
EMAIL .info@claritypictures.net
WEB SITE .www.claritypictures.net

TYPES	Animation - Commercials - Documentaries - Features - Made-for-TV/Cable Movies - New Media - TV Series
DEVELOPMENT	The Legend of Black Peter
PRE-PRODUCTION	Forever Quest (Documentary) - Devil's Peak
CREDITS	Hiding in Plain Sight (Documentary) - 18 Shades of Dust - Love & Action in Chicago - Wish You Were Dead - Perfect Romance (Lifetime) - The Clique
SUBMISSION POLICY	Email query letter

David Basulto .President/Producer/Director
Loren Basulto .Producer/Director
Ryan Carty .Development
Allison Saucy .New Media

DICK CLARK PRODUCTIONS, INC.

9200 Sunset Blvd., Ste. 601
Los Angeles, CA 90069
PHONE .310-786-8900
FAX .310-777-2187
WEB SITE .www.dickclarkproductions.com

TYPES	Made-for-TV/Cable Movies - Specials - TV Series

Dick Clark .Chairman/CEO
Jules Haimovitz .Vice-Chairman
Francis La Maina .President/COO
Brian Pope .Sr. VP, Business Affairs
Mike Richards .Sr. Development Executive/Producer
Maria Higgins .Sr. VP, Contoller
Barry Adelman .Sr. VP, Creative Affairs
Mike Mahan .Sr. VP, Corporate Development
Mona Metwalli .VP, Business Affairs
Karen Smith .VP, Clearance/Director, International Distribution
Maria E. Hernandez .Director, Business Affairs

CLASS 5 FILMS
200 Park Avenue South, 8th Fl.
New York, NY 10003
PHONE 917-414-9404
TYPES Documentaries - Features - Miniseries
HAS DEAL WITH Universal Pictures
DEVELOPMENT Muscle - Buffalo for the Broken Heart - Motherless Brooklyn - Undaunted Courage - Fear Itself - Soldier of the Great War - Sugar Mommies
CREDITS The Painted Veil - Down in the Valley - The Yunan Great Rivers Expedition
SUBMISSION POLICY No unsolicited submissions

Edward Norton .....Producer/Actor/Director/Writer
Stuart Blumberg .....Producer/Writer/Director
Jim Norton .....Producer/Director
Bill Migliore .....Producer
Robyn Nickerson .....Executive Assistant
Silvana Tropea .....Executive Assistant

CLASS IV PRODUCTIONS
c/o Warner Bros.
4000 Warner Blvd., Bldg. 138, Rm. 1201
Burbank, CA 91522
PHONE 818-954-7206/818-954-2796
FAX 818-954-6315
TYPES TV Series
HAS DEAL WITH Warner Bros. Television Production
CREDITS Related - Reunion

Steve Pearlman .....Executive Producer
Andrew Plotkin .....Executive Producer

CLEAR PICTURES ENTERTAINMENT INC.
12400 Ventura Blvd., Ste. 306
Studio City, CA 91604
PHONE 818-980-5460
FAX 818-980-4716
EMAIL .....elizfowler@aol.com
TYPES Features - Made-for-TV/Cable Movies - TV Series
DEVELOPMENT First Seal - Homestead - Half-Life - Nice Girls Don't Get the Corner Office (Paramount)
PRE-PRODUCTION Blood Trail - Beyond the River
POST PRODUCTION Making Change
CREDITS Devil's Knot (USA Network) - Frontera Street (Lifetime)
COMMENTS A Division of Elizabeth Fowler Management

Elizabeth Fowler .....President
Paula Smith .....CFO/Executive VP, Business Development
Jenny Rankin .....Assistant

PATRICIA CLIFFORD PRODUCTIONS
PO Box 1166
Malibu, CA 90265
PHONE 310-317-1195
FAX 310-317-1485
TYPES Features - Made-for-TV/Cable Movies - TV Series
CREDITS Ambulance Girl - Secret Life of Zoey - Hysteria: The Def Leppard Story - Warden of Red Rock - To Dance with the White Dog - A Husband, a Wife and a Lover - The Elizabeth Smart Story - Pop Rocks
SUBMISSION POLICY No unsolicited material

Patricia Clifford .....Producer

CMT: COUNTRY MUSIC TELEVISION
330 Commerce St.
Nashville, TN 37201
PHONE 615-335-8400/310-752-8248
WEB SITE .....www.cmt.com
TYPES Made-for-TV/Cable Movies - Music Videos - TV Series
DEVELOPMENT Foxworthy's Big Night Out - Broken Bridges (CMT Films)
UPCOMING RELEASES CMT Greatest Moments - Unsung Stories
CREDITS CMT Most Wanted Live - Top 20 Countdown - Inside Fame - CMT Total Release - 100 Greatest Songs of Country Music - Controversy - Cowboy U - 40 Greatest Men of Country Music - 40 Greatest Women of Country Music - CMT Outlaws - CMT Insider - Trick My Truck - CMT Music Awards - Crossroads - The Ultimate Coyote Ugly Search
COMMENTS West Coast office: 2600 Colorado Ave., Santa Monica, CA 90404; Includes broadband channel CMT Loaded

Van Toffler .....President, MTV Networks Group
Brian Graden .....President, Entertainment MTV Networks Group
James Hitchcock .....Sr. VP, Creative & Marketing
Brian Philips .....Executive VP/General Manager
Paul Villadolid .....VP, Programming & Development
Lewis Bogach .....VP, Programming Development & Production
Sarah Brock .....VP, Production
Lisa Chader .....VP, Press
Martin Clayton .....VP/General Manager, CMT.com
Suzanne Norman .....VP, Finance
Jennifer Ortega .....VP, Business & Legal Affairs
Chris Parr .....VP, Music & Talent
John C. Feld .....Director, Development
John Fitzgerald .....Director, Development
Melanie Moreau .....Director, Development
Nicole Raffanello .....Director, Development
Laurissa Ryan .....Director, Music & Talent Development
Richard Van Syckle .....Director, Development

CNBC

Global Headquarters
900 Sylvan Ave.
Englewood Cliff, NJ 07632

PHONE . . . 201-735-2622
FAX . . . 201-735-3200
WEB SITE . . . www.nbcumv.com/cnbc

TYPES: TV Series
CREDITS: CNBC's High Net Worth - Conversations With Michael Eisner - Mad Money - On The Money - The Big Idea with Donny Deutsch - The Suze Orman Show - Tim Russert - Worldwide Exchange - Squawk Box - Squawk on the Street - Morning Call - Power Lunch - Street Signs - Closing Bell - Kudlow and Company
COMMENTS: News Bureaus: Midtown Manhattan, Chicago, Los Angeles, Palo Alto, London and Singapore; CNBC is wholly owned by NBC Universal

Mark Hoffman . . . President, CNBC
Jeremy Pink . . . President/CEO, CNBC Asia Pacific
David M. Zaslav . . . President, NBC Universal Cable, Domestic Television & New Media Distribution
Christy Rupert-Shibata . . . CFO
Lauren Donovan . . . Sr. VP/General Counsel, CNBC & NBC Cable
Robert Fouthorap . . . Sr. VP, Advertising Sales
Thomas Clendenin . . . VP, Marketing
Scott Drake . . . VP, Management Information Technology
Steve Fastook . . . VP, Engineering & Technology
Kevin Goldman . . . VP, Public Relations
Nikki Gonzalez . . . VP, Human Resources
Susan Krakower . . . VP, Strategic Programming & Development
Glen Rochkind . . . VP, Business News
Elisabeth Sami . . . VP, Global Business Development
Susan DeBaun . . . Quality Leader
Josh Howard . . . Head, Documentaries

COBBLESTONE FILMS

PO Box 34370
Los Angeles, CA 90034

PHONE . . . 310-404-5959
EMAIL . . . development@cstonefilms.com

TYPES: Features - Made-for-TV/Cable Movies - TV Series
DEVELOPMENT: Wings of an Angel - The Bone Yard - The Fairchild File - Achilles Heel - Sparrow on the Roof - Marlboro Man
CREDITS: One Against the Wind - Dalva - A Home for the Holidays
SUBMISSION POLICY: Query letters and submissions by email only

Ben Adler . . . Producer
Jacqui Adler . . . Producer

CODE ENTERTAINMENT

9229 Sunset Blvd., Ste. 615
Los Angeles, CA 90069

PHONE . . . 310-772-0008
FAX . . . 310-772-0006
WEB SITE . . . www.neverlandfilms.com

TYPES: Features - TV Series
DEVELOPMENT: Challenger - Dreams of a Dying Heart
PRE-PRODUCTION: Spring Breakdown
POST PRODUCTION: You Kill Me
UPCOMING RELEASES: The Gravedancers - Behind the Mask
CREDITS: Edmond - Bigger Than the Sky - Noel - 50 First Dates - Debs - Barbershop - Scorched - Drowning Mona - Cowboy Up - Palmetto - A Brother's Kiss - The L Word (TV Series)

Bart Rosenblatt . . . Producer
Al Corley . . . Producer
Eugene Musso . . . Producer
Larry Kennar . . . Producer/Literary Management
Rogers Hartmann . . . Partner
Rick Berg . . . Literary Management
Sarah Jane Wilde . . . Literary Management
Jason Babiszewski . . . Director, Development
Kim Olsen . . . VP, Production Services
Karen Irvin . . . Story Editor
Christopher Marlon . . . Literary Management Assistant
Nick Miller . . . Literary Management Assistant

COLEBROOK ROAD, INC.

2045 S. Barrington Ave.
Los Angeles, CA 90025

PHONE . . . 310-445-2020/310-351-1916
FAX . . . 310-445-9191
WEB SITE . . . www.colebrookroad.com

TYPES: Features
DEVELOPMENT: Rogue Elements - The Trouble With Jerry
CREDITS: Behind Enemy Lines - Flight of the Phoenix
SUBMISSION POLICY: No unsolicited submissions

T. Alex Blum . . . Producer/President

THE COLLECTIVE

9100 Wilshire Blvd., Ste. 700W
Beverly Hills, CA 90212

PHONE . . . 310-288-8181
FAX . . . 310-888-1555

TYPES: Animation - Direct-to-Video/DVD - Features - Internet Content - Made-for-TV/Cable Movies - Reality TV - TV Series
DEVELOPMENT: Untitled Drake & Josh Feature
PRODUCTION: The Education of Charlie Banks
CREDITS: One on One (UPN) - Wild 'n' Out - Big Momma's House 2

Michael Green . . . Manager/Partner
Sam Maydew . . . Manager/Partner
Jeff Golenberg . . . Manager/Partner
Aaron Ray . . . Manager/Partner
Max Burgos . . . Manager
Aron Giannini . . . Manager
Michael Goldman . . . Manager
Adam Griffin . . . Manager
Allan Grifka . . . Manager
Rob Kahane . . . Manager
Shaun Redick . . . Manager
Alexis Nicholls . . . Office Manager
Angela Bures . . . Assistant
Cary Degraff . . . Assistant
Kristin Fine . . . Assistant
Solomon Hinton . . . Assistant
Kottie Kreischer . . . Assistant
Brett Ruttenberg . . . Assistant
Gary Binkow . . . Venture Partner
Rachel Acker . . . Venture Associate

THE COLLETON COMPANY

20 Fifth Ave., Ste. 13-F
New York, NY 10011
PHONE 212-673-0916
FAX 212-673-1172
TYPES Features - Made-for-TV/Cable Movies - TV Series
DEVELOPMENT Prep - Present Value - Pledged - Ferry Tales - After Hailey
UPCOMING RELEASES Dexter (Showtime) - The Painted Veil (WIP)
CREDITS Renaissance Man - Riding in Cars With Boys - Live from Baghdad

Sara Colleton .....President
Kelly Moulton .....Assistant to Sara Colleton

COLOMBY FILMS

2110 Main St., Ste. 302
Santa Monica, CA 90405
PHONE 310-399-8881
FAX 310-392-1323
WEB SITE .....www.colombyfilms.com
TYPES Features - Made-for-TV/Cable Movies - TV Series
DEVELOPMENT Unstoppable - Ghost of a Chance - Another Kind of Justice - The Great Day In Glenbrook - Into the Fire - Monk - Blue Monday
CREDITS Body Shots (New Line) - Breakdown - One Good Cop

Harry Colomby .....No Title
Cam Roberts .....Development/Acquisitions

COLOSSAL ENTERTAINMENT

PO Box 461010
Los Angeles, CA 90046
PHONE 323-656-6647
EMAIL .....clsslent@aol.com
TYPES Features - Made-for-TV/Cable Movies - TV Series
DEVELOPMENT U.N. - Comeback Queen - Party Girls (Animated Series) - Rich Deceiver (Fox 2000) - Back to Africa (Universal)
PRODUCTION In God's Country - The Condemned (Lionsgate/WWE Films)
CREDITS Eight Days to Live - The Call of the Wild - Anya's Bell

Graham Ludlow .....Producer/Writer
Art Hamilton .....Development Assistant

COLUMBIA PICTURES

A Sony Pictures Entertainment Company
10202 W. Washington Blvd.
Culver City, CA 90232
PHONE 310-244-4000
FAX 310-244-2626
WEB SITE .....www.spe.sony.com
TYPES Features
PROVIDES DEAL TO Michael De Luca Productions - Gittes, Inc. - The Mark Gordon Company - The Hal Lieberman Company - Out of the Blue . . . Entertainment - Outlaw Productions - Phoenix Pictures - Spyglass Entertainment Group - Wonderland Sound and Vision - Laura Ziskin Productions
COMMENTS Includes Columbia TriStar Motion Picture Group; See also Sony Pictures

Amy Pascal .....Chairman, Motion Picture Group, SPE
Gareth Wigan .....Vice Chairman, CTMPG
Bob Osher .....COO, CPMPG
Doug Belgrad .....President, Production
Ben Feingold .....President, CTMPG, SPHE, DVD Distribution
Matt Tolmach .....President, Production
Gary Martin .....President, Columbia Production Administration & SPS Operations
Ken Munekata .....President, SPE-Japan
Paul Smith .....President, Worldwide Theatrical Operations, CTMPG
Lia Vollack .....President, Worldwide Music
Robert Geary .....Sr. Executive VP, Business Affairs & Operations
Andrew Gumpert .....Sr. Executive VP, Business Affairs
Peter Iacono .....Sr. Executive VP, Local Language Productions
Amy Baer .....Executive VP, Production
Elizabeth Cantillon .....Executive VP, Production
Andrea Giannetti .....Executive VP, Production
James Honore .....Executive VP, Post Production
Elvis Mitchell .....Executive Production Consultant (NY)
Deborah Schindler .....Executive Production Consultant (NY)
Pete Corral .....Sr. VP, Production Administration
Ronni Coulter .....Sr. VP, Business Affairs
Samuel Dickerman .....Sr. VP, Production
Lori Furie .....Sr. VP, Production
Andy Given .....Sr. VP, Production Administration
Jonathan Krauss .....Sr. VP, Production
Pam Kunath .....Sr. VP, Business Affairs, CTMPG
John Levy .....Sr. VP, Business Affairs
Stefan Litt .....Sr. VP/CFO, CTMPG
Eileen Lomis . .Sr. VP, Worldwide Theatrical Financial Administration, CTMPG
Iona Macedo .....Sr. VP, European Production
Pilar McCurry .....Sr. VP, Music Creative Affairs
Russ Paris .....Sr. VP, Post Production
Raul Perez .....Sr. VP, Music Administration
Masao Takiyama .....Sr. VP, SPE-Japan
Mark Wyman .....Sr. VP, Business Affairs
Al Barton .....VP, Digital Cinema
Debra Grieco Bergman .....VP, Production Administration
Shannon Gaulding .....VP, Production
Jordi Gazull .....VP, European Production, Spain
Jonathan Kadin .....VP, Production
Patricia Kendig .....VP, Worldwide Theatrical Research, CTMPG
Donald Kennedy .....VP, Music Licensing
Larry Kohorn .....VP, Music Business Affairs
Adam Moss .....VP, Production Administration
Karen Moy .....VP, Story Department
Rachel O'Connor .....VP, Production
Thomas Stack .....VP, Business Affairs Contract Administration
Rita Zakrzewski .....VP, Music Publishing

COMEDY ARTS STUDIOS
2500 Broadway, Ste. 400
Santa Monica, CA 90404
PHONE .310-382-3677
FAX .310-382-3170
TYPES TV Series
HAS DEAL WITH HBO Entertainment
CREDITS Everybody Loves Raymond - The Mind of the Married Man - The HBO Comedy Festival

Stu Smiley .Owner/Executive Producer
Leslie Patent .Director, Development
Adam Gordon .Assistant

COMEDY CENTRAL
1775 Broadway, 10th Fl.
New York, NY 10019
PHONE .212-767-8600/310-407-4700
FAX .212-767-8592 (Press)/310-407-4797
WEB SITE .www.comedycentral.com
TYPES Animation - Internet Content - Mobile Content - Reality TV - TV Series
PROVIDES DEAL TO Busboy Productions - Parallel Entertainment, Inc.
UPCOMING RELEASES MotherLoad Shows: Live-Action: Honest - Good God - Baloonheads - Live at Gotham; Animated: Baxter & McGuire - Time Travelers
CREDITS The Colbert Report - The Showbiz Show with David Spade - Mind of Mencia - Distraction - Drawn Together - Reno 911! - Chappelle's Show - The Daily Show with Jon Stewart - South Park - Freak Show - Comedy Central Presents - American Lives (Working Title) - Naked Trucker & T-Bones - Dog Bites Man - Blue Collar Comedy Tour: One for the Road
COMMENTS West Coast office: 2049 Century Park East, Ste. 4170, Los Angeles, CA 90067; Includes MotherLoad, broadband video channel

Doug Herzog .President/CEO
John Cucci .COO, Comedy Central, Spike TV & TV Land
Chris Pergola .CFO
Lauren Corrao .Executive VP, Original Programming & Development
Tony Fox .Executive VP, Corporate Communications
Michele Ganeless .Executive VP/General Manager
David Bernath .Sr. VP, Programming
Mitch Fried .Sr. VP, Promotion Marketing
Jeff Lucas .Sr. VP, Ad Sales
Elizabeth Porter .Sr. VP, Specials & Talent
Peter Risafi .Sr. VP, Brand Creative
Jim Sharp .Sr. VP, Development & Original Programming, West Coast
Lou Wallach .Sr. VP, Development & Original Programming, East Coast
Joella West .Sr. VP/General Counsel, Business & Legal Affairs
Steve Albani .VP, Corporate Communications
Debbie Beiter .VP, Production, On-Air Promotions
Brian Bloodgood .VP, West Coast Ad Sales
Eric Blume .VP, Studio Relations & Production
Val Boreland .VP, Program & Promotion Scheduling
Aileen Budow .VP, Corporate Communications
Kelleigh Dulany .VP, Promotion Marketing
Zoe Friedman .VP, Current Programming, West Coast
Glenn Ginsburg .VP, Interactive Ad Sales
Genise Jackson .VP, Business & Legal Affairs

(Continued)

COMEDY CENTRAL (Continued)
Debbie Kirsh .VP, Operations, Production
Lynne Levey .VP, Ad Sales (Midwest)
Beth Lewand .VP, Digital Media
Gary Mann .VP, Development, West Coast
Gary Merrifield .VP, National Ad Sales
Patty Newberger .VP, Comedy Central Films
Bob Pederson .VP, On-Air Creative
Kendrick Reid .VP, On-Air Design
Robert Stein .VP, Production
Bobby Amirshahi .Director, Corporate Communications
Dave Koga .Director, Development, West Coast
Renata Luczak .Director, Corporate Communications
Marie Raubicheck .Director
Aaron Rothman .Director, Development, East Coast
Margaret Yuspa .Director, Development, West Coast
Lee Barden .Controller
Seth Cohen .Manager, Comedy Development
Mary Ann Minster .Manager
Dan Powell .Manager, Development, East Coast
Jenni Runyan .Manager
William Oh .Counsel, Business Affairs
Thomas Mouscardy .Executive Assistant

COMEDY TIME
8737 Venice Blvd., Ste. 101
Los Angeles, CA 90034
PHONE .310-287-1617
FAX .310-287-2056
EMAIL .info@comedy-time.com
WEB SITE .www.comedy-time.com
TYPES Mobile Content
CREDITS Ultimate Wingman - Free Stylin' - Roscoe, the Party Dog - Rock with Earl - LA Writer
COMMENTS Produces made-for-mobile stand up comedy and original episodic programming; Deals with Sprint, MobiTV, Amp'd, Real Networks, AOL and Roo Networks

David Goldman .CEO
Michael Goldman .President
Todd Piper .CTO
Bob Fisher .Sr. VP, Live Entertainment
Kara Jullian .Head, Talent
R. Michael Crill .Director
Mike Jaglin .Director, Development

COMIC BOOK MOVIES, LLC/BRANDED ENTERTAINMENT/ BATFILM PRODUCTIONS

333 Crestmont Rd.
Cedar Grove, NJ 07009
PHONE . . . 973-857-6172/310-460-3222
FAX . . . 973-857-6174
EMAIL . . . info@comicbookmovies.net
WEB SITE . . . www.comicbookmovies.net
TYPES — Animation - Direct-to-Video/DVD - Documentaries - Features - TV Series
DEVELOPMENT — Young Santa - Mysterians - Shazam! - Way of the Rat - The Spirit - Constantine 2 - Black Cat - Ruse - Batman
CREDITS — Batman Begins - Constantine - Batman 1-4 - Where on Earth Is Carmen Sandiego? - Three Sovereigns for Sarah - Dinosaucers - Robin Cook's Harmful Intent - Batman: Mystery of the Batwoman - National Treasure - Batman Meets Dracula - Batman Beyond: Return of the Joker
SUBMISSION POLICY — No unsolicited submissions
COMMENTS — West Coast office: 1601 Cloverfield Blvd., South Tower, 2nd Fl., Santa Monica, CA 90404

Jack Roberts . . . CEO/President (Comic Book Movies, LLC)
Michael Uslan . . . President & Producer (Branded Entertainment)/ CCO & Producer (Comic Book Movies, LLC)
F.J. DeSanto . . . Sr. VP, Production (Branded Entertainment/ Comic Book Movies, LLC)
Nate Hicks . . . Sr. VP, Finance (Comic Book Movies, LLC)
Chad Sugerman . . . VP, Development (Branded Entertainment/ Comic Book Movies, LLC)
David Uslan . . . VP, Creative Affairs (Branded Entertainment/ Comic Book Movies, LLC)

COMPLETION FILMS

445 Hamilton Ave., Ste. 1102
White Plains, NY 10601
PHONE . . . 718-693-2057
FAX . . . 718-693-2054
EMAIL . . . kcameron@completionfilms.com
TYPES — Features - Made-for-TV/Cable Movies
HAS DEAL WITH — Focus Features/Rogue Pictures
DEVELOPMENT — Razor Wire - The Vow
CREDITS — Sometimes in April
SUBMISSION POLICY — No unsolicited material

Kisha Imani Cameron . . . Producer

CON ARTISTS PRODUCTIONS

808 Wilshire Blvd., 4th Fl.
Santa Monica, CA 90401
PHONE . . . 310-434-7300
FAX . . . 310-434-7377
TYPES — Documentaries - Made-for-TV/Cable Movies - Miniseries - TV Series
DEVELOPMENT — Flory - Baghdad Boys
POST PRODUCTION — Carrier
CREDITS — Complete Savages - Kevin Hill - Clubhouse - Dive From Clausen's Pier - Evel Knievel
COMMENTS — A division of Icon Productions

Nancy Cotton . . . President
Larry Gilbert . . . Director, Development
Christine Ryan . . . Coordinator

CONCEPT ENTERTAINMENT

334-1/2 N. Sierra Bonita Ave.
Los Angeles, CA 90036
PHONE . . . 323-937-5700
EMAIL . . . enquiries@conceptentertainment.biz
WEB SITE . . . www.conceptentertainment.biz
TYPES — Features - Made-for-TV/Cable Movies - TV Series
DEVELOPMENT — Mississippi Birding - The Next Step - Tag - Crimes of Produce - Dead Letters - Fuego - Market Forces - Man Camp
UPCOMING RELEASES — Material Girls - The Big White

David Faigenblum . . . Producer/Manager
Melissa Goddard . . . Producer/Manager
Karina Wilson . . . Creative Executive/Manager

CONCORDE-NEW HORIZONS

11600 San Vicente Blvd.
Los Angeles, CA 90049
PHONE . . . 310-820-6733
FAX . . . 310-207-6819
WEB SITE . . . www.newhorizonspix.com
TYPES — Direct-to-Video/DVD - Features - TV Series
CREDITS — Bloodfist 2050 - DinoCroc - Barbarian - The Killer Within Me - When Eagles Strike - Slaughter Studios - The Arena - Vital Parts - Kyoko - The Phantom Eye - Born Bad - Club Vampire - Alien Avengers II - Detonator - Desert Thunder - Spacejacked - Under Oath - Black Scorpion II: Aftershock - Don't Sleep Alone - Eruption

Roger Corman . . . Principal

CONCRETE ENTERTAINMENT

468 N. Camden Dr., Ste. 200
Beverly Hills, CA 90210
PHONE . . . 310-860-5611
FAX . . . 310-860-5600
TYPES — Features - TV Series
PRODUCTION — Queen B (Pilot)
CREDITS — Braceface - Excess Baggage

Alicia Silverstone . . . Actress/Producer
Carolyn Kessler . . . Manager/Producer

CONCRETE PICTURES

One Bala Ave.
Bala Cynwyd, PA 19004
PHONE . . . 610-668-8662
FAX . . . 610-668-8664
EMAIL . . . drew@concretepictures.com
WEB SITE . . . www.concretepictures.com
TYPES — Animation - Commercials - Direct-to-Video/DVD - Documentaries - Features - Music Videos - Reality TV - TV Series
UPCOMING RELEASES — Journeys of the Heart: Peru
CREDITS — Cherish - One - Tear It Down - Dream with Fishes

Jeff Boortz . . . President
Miles Dinsmoor . . . Sr. VP
Drew Fleming . . . Sr. VP
Bob Lowery . . . VP, Business Development
Michele Pew . . . Executive Producer/Writer
Richard Rice . . . Director, New Media
Janet Bess . . . Director, Development

CONSTANTIN FILM DEVELOPMENT, INC./ CONSTANTIN TELEVISION

9200 Sunset Blvd., Ste. 800
Los Angeles, CA 90069
PHONE .310-247-0300/49-89-44446-0
FAX .310-247-0305/49-89-444460-666
WEB SITE .www.constantin-film.com

TYPES	Features
PROVIDES DEAL TO	Impact Pictures
DEVELOPMENT	Fantastic Four 2
PRODUCTION	Resident Evil: Extinction
POST PRODUCTION	DOA: Dead or Alive - Skinwalkers - Perfume
CREDITS	Resident Evil 1&2 - The House of the Spirits - Last Exit to Brooklyn - The Name of the Rose - Smilla's Sense of Snow - Downfall
COMMENTS	New TV division: Constantin Television; European office: Feilitzschstrasse 6, D-80802 Munich, Germany

Bernd Eichinger .No Title
Lisa Kregness .No Title
Robert Kulzer .No Title
Marsha Metz .No Title
Martin Moszkowicz .No Title
Johannes Schlichting .No Title
Kerstin Schmidbauer .No Title
Robin von der Leyen .No Title

CONTENTFILM

1337 3rd St. Promenade, Ste. 302
Santa Monica, CA 90401
PHONE .310-576-1059/44-207-851-6500
FAX .310-576-1859/44-207-851-6506
WEB SITE .www.contentfilm.com

TYPES	Features
CREDITS	The King - Thank You For Smoking - Undertow - Never Die Alone - The Cooler - The Guys - The Hebrew Hammer - Party Monster - Love Object
COMMENTS	London office: 19 Heddon St., London W1B 4BG, United Kingdom

John Schmidt .President/CEO (NY)
Rick Kwak .Head, Business & Legal Affairs (LA)
Jamie Carmichael .Managing Director (London)
Harry White .Sales Manager (LA)
Judith Baugin .Head, International Marketing (London)

CONTRAFILM

1531 N. Cahuenga Blvd.
Los Angeles, CA 90028
PHONE .323-467-8787
FAX .323-467-7730

TYPES	Features - TV Series
HAS DEAL WITH	New Line Cinema
DEVELOPMENT	Baywatch - Choke - Conrail - Bob the Musical - Date School - Dead Asleep - Interman - Solace - Stompanato - The Missing Link - 20 Times a Lady - Fulton - Sleepwalker - Scared Straight - Crusader
PRODUCTION	Journey to the Center of the Earth
POST PRODUCTION	The Number 23
CREDITS	The Guardian - The Exorcism of Emily Rose - 11:14 - After the Sunset - The Wild

Beau Flynn .Producer
Tripp Vinson .Producer
Lisa Zambri .Director, Development
Gitty Daneshvari .Director, Development
Julie Benson .Story Editor/Assistant to Tripp Vinson
Max Dionne .Assistant to Gitty Daneshvari & Lisa Zambri
Maryn Silverberg .Assistant to Beau Flynn

CONUNDRUM ENTERTAINMENT

325 Wilshire Blvd., Ste. 201
Santa Monica, CA 90401
PHONE .310-319-2800
FAX .310-319-2808

TYPES	Features
HAS DEAL WITH	Twentieth Century Fox
DEVELOPMENT	Three Stooges - The Valet
PRE-PRODUCTION	Seven Day Itch
CREDITS	The Ringer - Fever Pitch - Stuck on You - Shallow Hal - Osmosis Jones - Me, Myself & Irene - There's Something About Mary - Dumb & Dumber - Kingpin

Peter Farrelly .No Title
Bobby Farrelly .No Title
Bradley Thomas .No Title
Mark Charpentier .No Title
Clemens Franek .No Title
Kevin Barnett .No Title
Ellen Dumouchel .No Title
Tom Kocsis .No Title
Kris Meyer .No Title

COOKIE JAR ENTERTAINMENT

4500 Wilshire Blvd., 1st Fl.
Los Angeles, CA 90010
PHONE .323-937-6244
FAX .323-939-8933
EMAIL .nmartin@thecookiejarcompany.com
WEB SITE .www.thecookiejarcompany.com

TYPES	Animation - Direct-to-Video/DVD - Internet Content - TV Series
CREDITS	The Doodlebops - Caillou - Arthur - Gerald McBoing Boing
COMMENTS	Toronto office: 266 King St. W., Ste. 301, Toronto, ON, M5V 1H8, phone: 416-977-3238, fax: 416-977-6071; Montréal office: 1055 Rene Levesque E., Ste. 900, Montréal, PQ, H2L 4S5, phone: 514-843-7070, fax: 514-843-6773

Michael Hirsh .CEO (Toronto)
Toper Taylor .President/COO (LA)
Lesley Taylor .Executive VP, Production (Montréal)
Fonda Snyder .Sr. VP, Development (LA)
Ken Locker .Sr. VP, Digital Media (LA)
Jim Weatherford .Sr. VP, Asia (Tokyo)
Kelly Elwood .Sr. VP, Marketing (Toronto)
John Vandervelde .Sr. VP, Finance
John Gildea .Sr. VP, Consumer Products (Rhode Island)
Carrie Dumont .VP, Business Affairs
Jean Gauvin .Creative Director
Hally Bayer .Director, Business Development, Digital Media

COOPER'S TOWN PRODUCTIONS

302A W. 12th St., Ste. 214
New York, NY 10014
PHONE .212-255-7566
FAX .212-255-0211
EMAIL .info@cooperstownproductions.com
WEB SITE .www.cooperstownproductions.com

TYPES	Features
DEVELOPMENT	One Split Second
CREDITS	Capote
SUBMISSION POLICY	No unsolicited material

Philip Seymour Hoffman .Partner
Davien Littlefield .Partner
Emily Ziff .Partner
Sara Murphy .Assistant

COQUETTE PRODUCTIONS
8105 W. 3rd St.
West Hollywood, CA 90048
PHONE 323-801-1000
FAX 323-801-1001
TYPES — Features - TV Series
HAS DEAL WITH — Touchstone Television
DEVELOPMENT — Dirt Squirrel (Series) - Lowlifes (TBS); Features: Untitled Paramount Comedy - The Last Ride of Cowboy Bob - Untitled Documentary
PRODUCTION — The Tripper - Dirt (F/X)
COMPLETED UNRELEASED — Talk Show Diaries - Mid-Nightly News
CREDITS — Mix It Up - Daisy Does America
SUBMISSION POLICY — No unsolicited material

Courteney Cox-Arquette . . . . . No Title
David Arquette . . . . . No Title
Thea Mann . . . . . No Title
Jayme Lemons . . . . . No Title
Jeff Bowland . . . . . No Title

THE CORE
14724 Ventura Blvd., PH
Sherman Oaks, CA 91403
PHONE 818-986-8040
FAX 818-986-8041
EMAIL . . . . . core@coreentertainment.biz
TYPES — Features - Reality TV - Syndication - TV Series
CREDITS — Hollywood Tonight - The New Tom Green Show - The Man Show - Loveline - Open Mike - My House/My Rules - Happy as I Can Be - On Target - Mike MacDonald Christmas - Freddy Got Fingered - Stealing Harvard
COMMENTS — Formerly Siddons & Associates and Lapides Entertainment Organization; Music

Howard Lapides . . . . . President
Bill Siddons . . . . . President
Andrew Lear . . . . . VP, Comedy & Development
Jackie Stern . . . . . VP/Manager
Toni Profera . . . . . Manager
Jordan Yousem . . . . . Manager
Kesila Childers . . . . . Associate Manager
Danielle Gary . . . . . Office Manager
Barbra Frederick . . . . . Executive Assistant

CORNICE ENTERTAINMENT
421 S. Beverly Dr., 8th Fl.
Beverly Hills, CA 90212
PHONE 310-279-4080
FAX 310-789-4791
TYPES — Features - TV Series
POST PRODUCTION — You Kill Me
CREDITS — Highwaymen

Michael E. Marcus . . . . . Owner

ROBERT CORT PRODUCTIONS
1041 N. Formosa Ave., Admin. Bldg., Ste. 196
West Hollywood, CA 90046
PHONE 323-850-2644
FAX 323-850-2634
TYPES — Direct-to-Video/DVD - Features - Made-for-TV/Cable Movies
UPCOMING RELEASES — Save the Last Dance 2: Stepping Up
CREDITS — Save the Last Dance - Runaway Bride - Mr. Holland's Opus - Harlan County War - Against the Ropes - Something the Lord Made
SUBMISSION POLICY — No unsolicited submissions

Robert Cort . . . . . Producer
Scarlett Lacey . . . . . VP, Production
Eric Hetzel . . . . . VP, Production
Kim Rasser . . . . . Creative
Gabe Reiter . . . . . Assistant

CORYMORE ENTERTAINMENT
9171 Wilshire Blvd., Ste. 400
Beverly Hills, CA 90210
PHONE 310-274-7891
FAX 310-274-7892
EMAIL . . . . . dena@corymore.com
TYPES — Made-for-TV/Cable Movies - TV Series
CREDITS — South by Southwest - Mrs. Pollifax - Murder She Wrote - Mrs. 'Arris Goes to Paris - Positive Moves - Mrs. Santa Claus - A Story to Die For - The Last Free Man

Angela Lansbury . . . . . Actress/Producer
Anthony Shaw . . . . . Director/Producer

COSGROVE-MEURER PRODUCTIONS
4303 W. Verdugo Ave.
Burbank, CA 91505
PHONE 818-843-5600
FAX 818-843-8585
TYPES — Features - Made-for-TV/Cable Movies - TV Series
UPCOMING RELEASES — Caffeine
CREDITS — Unsolved Mysteries - The Inheritance - Karroll's Christmas - Buffalo Dreams - Yesterday's Children - Ball in the House

John Cosgrove . . . . . CEO
Terry Meurer . . . . . President
Stuart Schwartz . . . . . VP, Reality Development
Jo Levi . . . . . Feature Development
Christine Lenig . . . . . Assistant to T. Meurer & J. Cosgrove

COSSETTE PRODUCTIONS
8899 Beverly Blvd., Ste. 100
Los Angeles, CA 90048
PHONE 310-278-3366
FAX 310-278-6587
TYPES — Specials - Theatre - TV Series
CREDITS — BET Awards Show - BET Walk of Fame - Grammy Awards - Latin Grammy Awards - The Civil War - The Scarlet Pimpernel - The Will Rogers Follies

John Cossette . . . . . President

COURT TV NETWORKS
600 Third Ave.
New York, NY 10016
PHONE .212-973-2800
FAX .212-973-3210
WEB SITE .www.courttv.com
TYPES Direct-to-Video/DVD - Documentaries - Made-for-TV/Cable Movies - Reality TV - Specials - TV Series
PROVIDES DEAL TO KLS Communications, Inc.
CREDITS LA Forensics - Haunting Evidence - Video Justice - Parco, P.I. - Beach Patrol: Miami - Dominick Dunne's Power, Privilege and Justice - Catherine Crier Live - Hollywood Heat

Art Bell .President/COO
Darren Campo .Sr. VP, Programming Strategy & Research
Brian Compare .VP, Programming & Market Research
Mary Corigliano .Sr. VP, Marketing
Marlene Dann .Executive VP, Daytime, News Programming
Debbie D'Arinzo .VP, Financial Planning & Strategy
Mark Fichandler .VP, Documentary Development & International Co-Production
Ira Fields .Executive VP/CFO
Ed Hersh .Executive VP, Current Programming & Specials
Doug Jacobs .Executive VP/General Counsel, Legal & Business Affairs
Marc Juris .General Manager, Programming & Marketing
Ilene Kennedy .VP, Online Analytics & Development
Scoot MacPherson .Executive VP, Corporate & Government Affairs
Eric Neuhaus .Director, Talent Development, Primetime Entertainment
Debbie Paitchel .Director, Legal & Business Affairs
Jennifer Randolph .VP, Organizational Development
Ed Simicich .VP, Finance
Tim Sullivan .Sr. VP, Daytime Programming
Andy Verderame .Sr. VP, Creative Services

CINDY COWAN ENTERTAINMENT, INC.
8265 Sunset Blvd., Ste. 205
Los Angeles, CA 90046
PHONE .323-822-1082
FAX .323-822-1086
EMAIL .info@cowanent.com
WEB SITE .www.cowanent.com
TYPES Features - TV Series
DEVELOPMENT Untitled Thriller - 27 - Sweat (TV)
PRE-PRODUCTION Sleight of Hand
CREDITS Dr. T & the Women - Very Bad Things - Savior - Little City - The Florentine - Changing Habits - Scorched

Cindy Cowan .President
Atlanta Treloar .No Title

CRAFTSMAN FILMS
6565 Sunset Blvd., Ste. 412
Los Angeles, CA 90028
PHONE .323-465-2500
TYPES Features - TV Series
DEVELOPMENT The Ch'o-Do Incident - Star Trek Feature
CREDITS Homeland Security

Kerry McCluggage .Producer
Sebastian Twardosz .VP, Development
Kimberly Koenen .Executive Assistant

CRANE WEXELBLATT ENTERTAINMENT
6061 Galahad Dr.
Malibu, CA 90265
PHONE .310-457-4821
FAX .310-457-3888
EMAIL .twomoguls@aol.com
TYPES Features - Made-for-TV/Cable Movies - TV Series
DEVELOPMENT Ticker - Darby Sabini - The Raven (Pebble Hut) - Widow Claire (Sandcastle/ Footprints/Unity Productions) - Untitled NASCAR Series - Bleeders (Pebble Hut)
CREDITS Lily Dale - The Passion of Ayn Rand - One-Eyed King

Peter Crane .Producer/Director
Linda Curran Wexelblatt .Producer

CRAVE FILMS
3312 Sunset Blvd.
Los Angeles, CA 90026
PHONE .323-669-9000
FAX .323-669-9002
WEB SITE .www.cravefilms.com
TYPES Features
DEVELOPMENT Cartel - Convoy - Righteous Kill - Fallen Angel
UPCOMING RELEASES Harsh Times
CREDITS Dark Blue - Training Day - The Fast and the Furious - U-571 - The Patriot - S.W.A.T.
SUBMISSION POLICY No unsolicited submissions; Through agency or management company only

David Ayer .President
Roberta "Ro" Gorski .Sr. VP, Production/Producer
Joe Caston .Intern

CRAVEN/MADDALENA FILMS
11846 Ventura Blvd., Ste. 208
Studio City, CA 91604
PHONE .818-752-0197
FAX .818-752-1789
TYPES Features - Made-for-TV/Cable Movies - TV Series
DEVELOPMENT The Waiting - Home - Last House on the Left
CREDITS The Breed - The Hills Have Eyes - Red Eye - Cursed - Scream 1-3 - Music of the Heart

Wes Craven .Director/Producer
Marianne Maddalena .President/Producer
Cody Zwieg .VP
Carly Feingold .Assistant to Mr. Craven
Tara Billik .Assistant to Ms. Maddalena

CRAZYDREAMS ENTERTAINMENT
51 Los Altos Rd.
Orinda, CA 94563
PHONE .925-253-9525/925-698-4388
FAX .925-253-0406
EMAIL .randy@crazydreams.com
WEB SITE .www.crazydreams.com
TYPES Animation - Commercials - Features - Made-for-TV/Cable Movies
DEVELOPMENT Room 6 - Saving Trinity - The Magi
PRODUCTION Towards Darkness
UPCOMING RELEASES The Sasquatch Dumpling Gang
CREDITS Confession - All You Need - Changing Hearts - Hunt for Justice
SUBMISSION POLICY See Web site

Randy Holleschau .CEO
Jeff Johnson .CFO
Craig Anderson .VP, Production
Daniel Wright .VP, Development

CREANSPEAK PRODUCTIONS LLC
120 S. El Camino Dr., Ste. 100
Beverly Hills, CA 90212
PHONE 310-273-8217
EMAIL . . . . assistant@creanspeak.com
WEB SITE . . . . www.creanspeak.com

TYPES	Animation - Direct-to-Video/DVD - Documentaries - Features - Made-for-TV/Cable Movies - Reality TV - TV Series
DEVELOPMENT	Last Night - The Statue Game - Monster Mania - Once Was Lost
PRE-PRODUCTION	1/9 - One Step Beyond - Live Life
PRODUCTION	Cover
POST PRODUCTION	Black Irish
UPCOMING RELEASES	God on the Mic
COMPLETED UNRELEASED	Screaming Cocktail Hour
CREDITS	Film: Prey for Rock & Roll - False Start; TV: Gagsters! - Doctors of Rock
SUBMISSION POLICY	See Web site

Kelly Crean . . . . President/CEO
Gwen Field . . . . Head, Production
Jon H. Freis, Esq. . . . . VP, Business Affairs
Aaron Schmidt . . . . Development
Sara Rostami . . . . Assistant

CREATIVE CAPERS ENTERTAINMENT
2233 Honolulu Ave.
Montrose, CA 91020
PHONE 818-552-2290
WEB SITE . . . . www.creativecapers.com

TYPES	Animation - Direct-to-Video/DVD - Features - Internet Content - Mobile Content - TV Series
DEVELOPMENT	The Studman Bros. - TIKIS - Frank
PRODUCTION	AOL Super Buddies - AOL 3D Web Games
CREDITS	Bionicle: Web of Shadows - Nightmare Ned (ABC) - Sitting Ducks (Cartoon Network) - Bionicle: Mask of Light (Lego/Miramax) - Bionicle: Legends of Metru-Nui
SUBMISSION POLICY	No unsolicited material

Sue Shakespeare . . . . Producer/Partner
Terry Shakespeare . . . . Producer/Director/Partner
David Molina . . . . Producer/Director/Partner

*CREATIVE COALITION
1322 2nd St., Ste. 22
Santa Monica, CA 90401
PHONE 310-458-6900
FAX 310-458-0300

TYPES	Features - TV Series
CREDITS	Stardust - The Hollow Men - Spyder Games - The Andy Dick Show - Jackass: The Movie - Virgin Chronicles - Back to Norm

Norman Siderow . . . . CEO

CREATIVE DIFFERENCES
11846 Ventura Blvd., Ste. 204
Studio City, CA 91604
PHONE 818-432-4200
FAX 818-763-2485
WEB SITE . . . . www.creatvdiff.com

TYPES	Reality TV - TV Series
PROVIDES DEAL TO	Rive Gauche Entertainment
CREDITS	Anything to Win

Erik Nelson . . . . Producer
Robert Wise . . . . Producer

CREATIVE IMPULSE ENTERTAINMENT
8383 Wilshire Blvd., Ste. 923
Beverly Hills, CA 90211
PHONE 661-268-1920

TYPES	Features - Made-for-TV/Cable Movies - TV Series
DEVELOPMENT	Cult - Urban Arcan - In the Blood - U.S.P.D.
CREDITS	The Triangle - Farscape - Alien Nation - SeaQuest DSV - Fear

Rockne S. O'Bannon . . . . Executive Producer/Writer/Director
Dorthea Christiansen . . . . Assistant to Mr. O'Bannon

CREATURE ENTERTAINMENT
11766 Wilshire Blvd., Ste. 1610
Los Angeles, CA 90025
PHONE 310-278-9013
FAX 310-278-8933
EMAIL . . . . creatureent@aol.com

TYPES	Features

Milla Jovovich . . . . Partner/Producer
Chris Brenner . . . . Partner/Producer

CROSSROADS FILMS
136 W. 21st St., 7th Fl.
New York, NY 10011
PHONE 212-647-1300
FAX 212-647-9090
WEB SITE . . . . www.xroadsfilms.com

TYPES	Features - Music Videos - TV Series
PRODUCTION	Snow Angels
CREDITS	A Love Song for Bobby Long - Igby Goes Down - The Big Split - Jawbreaker

Dan Landau . . . . Partner
Camille Taylor . . . . Partner
Paul Miller . . . . Head, Production

CRPI ENTERTAINMENT
19200 Von Karman Ave., Ste. 400
Irvine, CA 92612
PHONE 949-887-9291
FAX 949-706-7147

TYPES	Made-for-TV/Cable Movies - TV Series
CREDITS	Celine Dion: The Concert - Celine Dion: The Colour of My Love - Lilith Fair: Sarah McLachlan & Friends - Golden Will: The Silken Laumann Story

Carol Reynolds . . . . President/Executive Producer
David McCarthy . . . . Executive VP

CRYSTAL LAKE ENTERTAINMENT, INC.
4420 Hayvenhurst Ave.
Encino, CA 91436
PHONE 818-995-1585

TYPES	Features - TV Series
PRE-PRODUCTION	Last House on the Left - Crystal Lake Chronicles
CREDITS	Freddy vs. Jason - Terminal Invasion - Deep Star Six - My Boyfriend's Back - House - Friday the 13th - Jason X - Extreme Close-Up

Sean S. Cunningham . . . . Producer/Director
Geoff Garrett . . . . Creative Executive

CRYSTAL SKY PICTURES, LLC

10203 Santa Monica Blvd.
Los Angeles, CA 90067

PHONE 310-843-0223
FAX 310-553-9895
EMAIL ....sales@crystalsky.com
WEB SITE ....www.crystalsky.com

TYPES	Features
DEVELOPMENT	Deathlok - Tekken - Castlevania - Bratz
PRE-PRODUCTION	Doomsday
PRODUCTION	Big Stan
UPCOMING RELEASES	Ghost Rider
CREDITS	Baby Geniuses 1&2 - The Musketeer
COMMENTS	Producing partner: Jon Voight Entertainment; Management division: Artists Only Management

Hank Paul ....Co-Chairman
Dorothy Koster ....Co-Chairman
Steven Paul ....Chairman/CEO
Benedict Carver ....President, Crystal Sky Pictures, LLC
Joe Inga ....President, Crystal Sky Finance, LLC
Travis Mann ....VP, Business Affairs
Jodea Bloomfield ....Sales & Marketing Manager
Daniel Diamond ....International Sales Consultant

CRYSTAL SPRING PRODUCTIONS, INC.

9713 Santa Monica Blvd.
Beverly Hills, CA 90210

PHONE 310-550-2720
FAX 310-550-2701
EMAIL ....mail@crystalspringproductions.com

TYPES	Animation - Direct-to-Video/DVD - Documentaries - Features - Made-for-TV/Cable Movies - New Media - Reality TV - Syndication - TV Series
CREDITS	Welcome to Hollywood - The Last Game - RAAM: Race Across America (NBC)
COMMENTS	Projects in development in all media

Jim Lampley ....Producer
Bree Walker Lampley ....Producer
Stephen Ricci ....Producer
Brian Haynes ....Producer

CSM COMMUNICATIONS

154 Bell Canyon Rd.
Bell Canyon, CA 91307-1109

PHONE 818-883-7891
FAX 818-883-7895
EMAIL ....lh@csmcommunications.com
WEB SITE ....www.csmcommunications.com

TYPES	Direct-to-Video/DVD - Documentaries - Internet Content - Made-for-TV/Cable Movies - Miniseries - Mobile Content - Music Videos - Reality TV - Specials - TV Series
PRE-PRODUCTION	A2S - Lottery Winners - Global Classrooms for Peace: South Africa, Jordan, Brazil - World Music Movement: Brazil, South Africa, Malaysian Borneo
PRODUCTION	World Music Festival Initiative - Global Classrooms for Peace: Brazil, China, South Africa
POST PRODUCTION	Global Classrooms for Peace: Fiji, Philippines
UPCOMING RELEASES	Blue
CREDITS	The Restaurant - Survivor - KSI - The Casino - SPWMF - WWR - Extreme Expeditions
COMMENTS	Live Events; Representation: Les Abel, 310-820-7717

Lori Hall ....Executive Producer
John Feist ....Executive Producer
Krystyna Clarke ....Sr. Producer/Director

CUBE VISION

2900 W. Olympic Blvd.
Santa Monica, CA 90404

PHONE 310-255-7100
FAX 310-255-7163
WEB SITE ....www.icecube.com

TYPES	Animation - Features - Music Videos - Reality TV - TV Series
HAS DEAL WITH	Dimension Films - The Weinstein Company
PRE-PRODUCTION	Are We Done Yet?
UPCOMING RELEASES	Friday (Animated)
CREDITS	Black.White. (FX) - Barbershop: The Series - Friday - Next Friday - Friday After Next - Barbershop 1&2 - All About the Benjamins - Are We There Yet?

Ice Cube ....Partner
Matt Alvarez ....Partner
John Hayes ....No Title
David Hebenstreit ....No Title
Jerry Sandoval ....No Title
Nancy Leiviska ....Executive Assistant to Ice Cube

CURB ENTERTAINMENT

3907 W. Alameda Ave.
Burbank, CA 91505

PHONE 818-843-8580
FAX 818-566-1719
EMAIL ....eweber@curb.com
WEB SITE ....www.curbentertainment.com

TYPES	Features
UPCOMING RELEASES	Devil on the Mountain
CREDITS	Tough Luck - Pipe Dream - Pressure - Mexico City - Oxygen - The Proposal - Wedding Bell Blues - Kill Me Later - Zoe - Out of Line - Water's Edge - The Untold
SUBMISSION POLICY	Submit synopsis, attachments and budget

Carole Curb ....President
Ildi Toth Davy ....Executive Director/Head, Sales
Eddie Francis ....Acquisitions

CURIOUS PICTURES

440 Lafayette St., 6th Fl.
New York, NY 10003

PHONE 212-674-1400
FAX 212-674-0081
EMAIL ....shows@curiouspictures.com
WEB SITE ....www.curiouspictures.com

TYPES	Animation - Commercials - Direct-to-Video/DVD - Features - Made-for-TV/Cable Movies - Music Videos - Specials - TV Series
DEVELOPMENT	Slap - The Pull - Trash - Artopia - Gluey - Smart World - Spamazon
CREDITS	Little Einsteins - Codename: Kids Next Door (Cartoon Network) - Sheep in the Big City (Cartoon Network) - A Little Curious (HBO Family) - Avenue Amy (Oxygen) - The Offbeats (Nickelodeon) - Mattel DTVs
SUBMISSION POLICY	Not looking for new projects at this time

Steve Oakes ....President/Director
Susan Holden ....CFO
Richard Winkler ....Partner/Executive Producer
Jon Paley ....Managing Director, DCODE

CURRENT ENTERTAINMENT

9200 Sunset Blvd., 10th Fl.
Los Angeles, CA 90069
PHONE .310-786-8975
WEB SITE .www.currentent.com

TYPES	Features
POST PRODUCTION	Rogue
COMPLETED UNRELEASED	Chaos
CREDITS	DOA: Dead or Alive - Unleashed - Kiss of the Dragon - The One - Invincible - The Transporter 1&2

Steven Chasman .CEO/Producer/Manager
Samantha Hazen .No Title

CURRENT TV, LLC

118 King St.
San Francisco, CA 94107
PHONE .415-995-8200
FAX .415-995-8201
EMAIL .info@current.tv
WEB SITE .www.current.tv

SUBMISSION POLICY	See Web site
COMMENTS	News, information and lifestyle; 70% original programming, 30% viewer created content

Al Gore .Chairman
Joel Hyatt .CEO
Steven Blumenfeld .CTO
Mark Goldman .COO
David Neuman .President, Programming
Anne Zehren .President, Sales & Marketing
Joanna Drake-Earl .President, Online Studio
Gayle Allen .Sr. VP, Programming & Scheduling
Jason Meil .Sr. VP, Original Programming & Acquisitions
Karl Carter .VP, Marketing & Vanguard Ideas
Frank Lentz .VP, Creative Affairs
Herndon Graddick .Producer/Manager, News
Laura Ling .Producer/Manager, Vanguard Journalism
Rawley Valverde .Lead Producer
Davis Powers .Talent Executive, Music
Ellen Rydzewski .Talent Executive, Film & TV
Mike Bunnell .Director, Production & Scheduling
Madeleine Smithberg .Creative Consultant/Executive Producer
Ashley Kaplan .Associate Producer

C/W PRODUCTIONS

c/o Paramount Pictures
5555 Melrose Ave.
Hollywood, CA 90038
PHONE .323-956-8199
FAX .323-862-1250

TYPES	Features
HAS DEAL WITH	Paramount Pictures
DEVELOPMENT	The Fall of the Warrior King
CREDITS	Mission: Impossible 1-3 - Without Limits - The Others - Vanilla Sky - The Last Samurai - Shattered Glass - Elizabethtown

Paula Wagner .Producer
Don Granger .No Title
Darren Miller .No Title
Jeff Buitenveld .No Title
Chrissie McLean .No Title
Alison Peck .No Title
Arik Ruchim .No Title
Alisa Starler .No Title
Dan Sullivan .No Title

THE CW

3300 W. Olive Ave.
Burbank, CA 91505
PHONE .818-954-6000
WEB SITE .www.cwtv.com

TYPES	Reality TV - TV Series
DEVELOPMENT	Southern Comfort - Aliens in America - Untitled Girl Band Project
CREDITS	Veronica Mars - Runaway - Reba - 7th Heaven - Gilmore Girls - America's Next Top Model - Beauty and the Geek - One Tree Hill - Smallville - Supernatural - WWE SmackDown! - Everybody Hates Chris - All of Us - Girlfriends - The Game - Hidden Palms

Dawn Ostroff .President, Entertainment
John Maatta .COO
Kim Fleary .Executive VP, Comedy
Rick Haskins .Executive VP, Marketing & Brand Strategy
Mitch Nedick .Executive VP/CFO
Michael Roberts .Executive VP, Current Programming
Thom Sherman .Executive VP, Drama Development
Jennifer Bresnan .Sr. VP, Alternative Programming
Eric Cardinal .Sr. VP, Research
Rick Mater .Sr. VP, Broadcast Standards
Betsy McGowan .Sr. VP/General Manager, Children's Programming
Lori Openden .Sr. VP, Talent & Casting
Elizabeth Tumulty .Sr. VP, Network Distribution
Paul McGuire .Head, Publicity

*CYAN PICTURES

410 Park Ave., 15th Fl.
New York, NY 10022
PHONE .212-274-1085/415-593-5929
EMAIL .info@cyanpictures.com
WEB SITE .www.cyanpictures.com

TYPES	Features
POST PRODUCTION	Underground - Premium
CREDITS	I Love Your Work
COMMENTS	Also distributes; West coast office: 182 Howard St., Ste. 513, San Francisco, CA 94105

Joshua Newman .CFO
Rob Barnum .Executive VP
Scott Bromley .Sr. VP
Josh Pincus .VP, Finance
Nathan Peterson .Operations Manager

CYPRESS FILMS, INC.
630 Ninth Ave., Ste. 415
New York, NY 10036
PHONE .212-262-3900
FAX .212-262-3925
EMAIL .linserra@cypressfilms.com
WEB SITE .www.cypressfilms.com
TYPES Features
PRE-PRODUCTION Escalate
POST PRODUCTION The Lost City of New York (Short)
CREDITS EvenHand - Cherry - Julian Po
SUBMISSION POLICY See Web site for guidelines

Jon Glascoe .Executive Producer/Writer
Joseph Pierson .Director/Producer
Tim Bohn .Writer/Director
Lovisa Inserra .Development

CYPRESS POINT PRODUCTIONS
3000 Olympic Blvd.
Santa Monica, CA 90404
PHONE .310-315-4787
FAX .310-315-4785
EMAIL .cppfilms@earthlink.net
TYPES Made-for-TV/Cable Movies - Miniseries - Reality TV
DEVELOPMENT Joe Namath Story - Jack Johnson - Dr. West
UPCOMING RELEASES Wildfires
CREDITS Nuremberg - 44 Minutes: Shootout in North Hollywood - Out of the Ashes - The Mystery of Natalie Wood - See Arnold Run - Four Minutes

Gerald W. Abrams .Chairman
Michael Waldron .Director, Development

DAKOTA NORTH ENTERTAINMENT/DAKOTA FILMS
4133 Lankershim Blvd.
North Hollywood, CA 91602
PHONE .818-760-0099
FAX .818-760-1070
EMAIL .info@dakotafilms.com
WEB SITE .www.dakotafilms.com
TYPES Direct-to-Video/DVD - Features - Made-for-TV/Cable Movies - Reality TV - TV Series
PRE-PRODUCTION Beacher's Madhouse
PRODUCTION Celebrity Autobiography: In Their Own Words - Just for Laughs - Wyclef Jean in America - Flight of the Conchords
CREDITS Reel Comedy - Run Ronnie, Run - Tenacious D - Oscar's Opening Film Sequence - MTV's Movie Awards Film - Mr. Show with Bob and David - The Best Commercials You've Never Seen - The Lemur - Viva La Bam (MTV) - Real Comedy (Comedy Central) - 20: Entertainment Weekly's Movie Specials
SUBMISSION POLICY No unsolicited material

Troy Miller .Producer/Director
Tracey Baird .Producer
Tally Barr .Producer, Development
Lisa Valenzuela .Office Manager

DALAKLIS-MCKEOWN ENTERTAINMENT, INC.
1750 Berkeley St.
Santa Monica, CA 90404
PHONE .310-460-0200
FAX .310-460-0202
EMAIL .production@dmetv.net
WEB SITE .www.dmetv.net
TYPES Documentaries - Reality TV - Specials - TV Series
POST PRODUCTION Ready for the Weekend Movies (USA Network) - Before & Afternoon Movies (USA Network)
CREDITS Insider's List (Fine Living) - How Stars Get Hot 4 - Rob & Amber Get Married (CBS) - Merge 3 (Lifetime) - 10 Perfect Summer Getaways (Fine Living) - All Access: Fleetwood Mac, Josh Groban, Clay Aiken, Lenny Kravitz, Joey McIntyre (VH1) - Babyface: Face2Face - Music Paradise - Intimate Portrait: Young Hollywood - Lisa Marie Presley - Porn to Rock - MERGE (Lifetime) - Ultimate Guide to Greece (Travel) - Instant Wedding (Lifetime) - Soapography (SoapNet)

Charles Dalaklis .President/Executive Producer
Theresa McKeown .VP/COO/Executive Producer
Bob Asher .VP, Creative Affairs
Jim Bianco .Executive in Charge of Production
Colin Whelan .Producer
Rob Canter .Executive in Charge of Post Production
Greg Ashamana .Accounting Supervisor
Jennifer Faitro .Coordinator, Product Placement
Jay Moehring .Production Coordinator

THE SEAN DANIEL COMPANY
5555 Melrose Ave., Swanson Bldg., Ste. 200
Los Angeles, CA 90038-3197
PHONE .323-956-4855
FAX .323-862-1618
TYPES Features - Made-for-TV/Cable Movies - TV Series
HAS DEAL WITH Paramount Pictures
DEVELOPMENT Ripley's Believe It or Not - Untitled College Humor Project
SUBMISSION POLICY Does not accept queries

Sean Daniel .Producer
Jennifer Moyer .Producer/Executive VP, Development
Andrea Chu .Development
Ryan Coleman .Assistant

LEE DANIELS ENTERTAINMENT
39 W. 131st St., Ste. 2
New York, NY 10037
PHONE .646-548-0930
FAX .646-548-9883
EMAIL .info@leedanielsentertainment.com
WEB SITE .www.leedanielsentertainment.com
TYPES Features
DEVELOPMENT Push - ICED - Izzy's Yearbook
PRE-PRODUCTION Tennessee
UPCOMING RELEASES Shadowboxer
CREDITS Monster's Ball - The Woodsman
SUBMISSION POLICY Send loglines/query letters to Nova Smith; No submissions without signed company release form

Lee Daniels .Producer/Director/CEO
David Robinson .CFO/Head, International Sales
Lisa Cortés .Sr. VP, Production
Nova Smith .VP, Development
Asger Hussain .Manager, Worldwide Distribution

DANJAQ, LLC

c/o Colorado Center
2400 Broadway St., Ste. 310
Santa Monica, CA 90404
PHONE . . . 310-449-3185
FAX . . . 310-449-3189

TYPES	Features
HAS DEAL WITH	Metro-Goldwyn-Mayer Studios, Inc. (MGM)
PRODUCTION	Casino Royale
CREDITS	The James Bond Films - Chitty Chitty Bang Bang
SUBMISSION POLICY	No unsolicited material

Michael Wilson . . . President
David Pope . . . CEO
Barbara Broccoli . . . VP, Production/Development

DARK HORSE ENTERTAINMENT

8425 W. Third St., Ste. 400
Los Angeles, CA 90048
PHONE . . . 323-655-3600
WEB SITE . . . www.darkhorse.com

TYPES	Animation - Direct-to-Video/DVD - Features - TV Series
DEVELOPMENT	Criminal Macabre - Damn Nation - Grendel - Hellboy 2 - Rex Mundi - R.I.P.D.
PRE-PRODUCTION	30 Days of Night
CREDITS	The Mask - Time Cop - Mystery Men - Hellboy - Alien vs. Predator
SUBMISSION POLICY	No unsolicited material or calls
COMMENTS	Comic books; Interactive games

Mike Richardson . . . President/Producer
Chris Tongue . . . Creative Executive

DARK TRICK FILMS

421 N. Beverly Dr., Ste. 280
Beverly Hills, CA 90210
PHONE . . . 310-274-3600
FAX . . . 310-274-3670

TYPES	Features
DEVELOPMENT	Schooled
CREDITS	National Lampoon's Van Wilder

Ryan Reynolds . . . Partner
Jonathon Komack Martin . . . Partner
Jeremy Martin . . . No Title
Brian Winterton . . . Assistant to Jonathon Komack Martin

DARKWOODS PRODUCTIONS

c/o Venturelli, Cary & Co.
301 E. Colorado Blvd., Ste. 705
Pasadena, CA 91101
PHONE . . . 323-454-4580
FAX . . . 323-454-4581

TYPES	Features - TV Series
HAS DEAL WITH	NBC Entertainment - Paramount Pictures
DEVELOPMENT	Foreign Babes in Beijing
CREDITS	The Green Mile - The Shawshank Redemption - Black Cat Run - The Salton Sea - The Majestic - Collateral
SUBMISSION POLICY	No unsolicited submissions

Frank Darabont . . . Director/Writer/Producer/Partner
Anna Garduño . . . President, Production/Partner
Denise Huth . . . VP, Production
Juan Francisco . . . Assistant to Frank Darabont
Jessica Gieseke . . . Assistant to Anna Garduño

ALAN DAVID MANAGEMENT

8840 Wilshire Blvd.
Beverly Hills, CA 90211
PHONE . . . 310-358-3155
FAX . . . 310-358-3256
EMAIL . . . adavid@planbproductions.net

TYPES	Features - Reality TV - TV Series
CREDITS	Ghost Hunters (Sci Fi) - The Ultimate Fighter (Spike) - The Cut (CBS)
SUBMISSION POLICY	No unsolicited ideas or scripts

Alan David . . . President
Miriam Kravitz . . . Assistant

DAVIS ENTERTAINMENT COMPANY

150 S. Barrington Pl.
Los Angeles, CA 90049
PHONE . . . 310-556-3550
FAX . . . 310-556-3688/310-889-8008

TYPES	Features - Made-for-TV/Cable Movies - TV Series
HAS DEAL WITH	Twentieth Century Fox
DEVELOPMENT	The Mistaken - Andrew Henry's Meadow - Selling Time
PRE-PRODUCTION	Alien vs. Predator 2
PRODUCTION	Norbit
POST PRODUCTION	Eragon
CREDITS	When a Stranger Calls - Flight of the Phoenix - Fat Albert - I, Robot - Garfield 1&2 - Daddy Day Care - Behind Enemy Lines - Dr. Dolittle 1-3 - Grumpy Old Men 1&2 - Out to Sea - Predator 1&2 - The Chamber - Waterworld - The Firm - Asteroid - Heartbreakers - Life or Something Like It - First Daughter - Alien vs. Predator
COMMENTS	Business office: 10201 W. Pico Blvd., Ste. 31-301, Los Angeles, CA 90035; TV fax: 310-889-8011

John A. Davis . . . Chairman (310-556-3550)
Derek Dauchy . . . President, Production (310-889-8006)
Robbie Brenner . . . President, Davis Entertainment Classics (310-889-8015)
Brooke Brooks . . . Executive VP (310-556-3550)
Brian D. Manis . . . Executive VP, Production (310-889-8012)
Dallas Jackson . . . Head, DJ Classicz (310-889-8016)
Amy Palmer . . . VP, TV (310-889-8005)
Will Stubbs . . . Director, Development (310-889-8007)
Garth Friedrich . . . Creative Executive (310-889-8009)
Erik Stone . . . Story Editor (310-889-8013)
Richard McConaghey . . . Assistant/Creative Executive (310-369-3031)
Chris Tipton . . . Assistant to Brian Manis (3108898013)
Jon Cohen . . . Assistant to Robbie Brenner (310-889-8014)
Alex Deas . . . Assistant to John Davis (310-889-8002)
Shannon Gregory . . . Assistant to Amy Palmer & Garth Friedrich (310-889-8003)

DAYBREAK PRODUCTIONS
3000 W. Olympic Blvd., Bldg. 5, Ste. 2121
Santa Monica, CA 90404
PHONE .310-264-4202
FAX .310-264-4222
TYPES Features - TV Series
DEVELOPMENT Spy Hunter - Hitman - Herobear
CREDITS Waterworld - Field of Dreams - The Rocketeer - Die Hard 1&2 - October Sky - The Girl Next Door

Charles Gordon .Producer
James Abraham .No Title

DC COMICS
1700 Broadway
New York, NY 10019
PHONE .212-636-5400
TYPES Features

Paul Levitz .President/Publisher
Patrick Caldon .Executive VP, Finance & Operations
Richard Bruning .Sr. VP/Creative Director
Daniel DiDio .Sr. VP/Executive Editor
Stephanie Fierman .Sr. VP, Sales & Marketing
Lillian Laserson .Sr. VP/General Counsel, DC Comics
Paula Lowitt .Sr. VP, Business & Legal Affairs
Gregory Noveck .Sr. VP, Creative Affairs
Cheryl Rubin .Sr. VP, Brand Management
Karen Berger .VP/Executive Editor, Vertigo
Georg Brewer .VP, Design & Retail Product Development
Chris M. Caramalis .VP, Finance
Teresa Cunningham .VP/Managing Editor
John Cunningham .VP, Marketing
John J. Ficarra .VP/Editor, MAD Magazine
Alison Gill .VP, Manufacturing
Richard R. Johnson .VP, Book Trade Sales
Hank Kanalz III .VP/General Manager, WildStorm
John Nee .VP, Business Development/General Manager, WildStorm
Jeffrey Trojan .VP, Business Development, DC Direct
Bob Wayne .VP, Sales & Marketing
Jim Lee .Editorial Director, WildStorm

DINO DE LAURENTIIS COMPANY
100 Universal City Plaza, Bungalow 5195
Universal City, CA 91608
PHONE .818-777-2111
FAX .818-866-5566
TYPES Features - TV Series
DEVELOPMENT ALX
POST PRODUCTION Young Hannibal: Behind the Mask - The Last Legion - Decameron: Angels & Virgins
CREDITS Breakdown - Bound - U-571 - Hannibal - Red Dragon
SUBMISSION POLICY No unsolicited material

Dino De Laurentiis .Producer
Martha De Laurentiis .President/Producer
Stuart Boros .Business Affairs
Roberta Shintani .Corporate Affairs
Lorenzo De Maio .Production & Development
Eddie Wacek .Development
Pamela Pickering .International Sales & Marketing

DE LINE PICTURES
c/o Warner Bros.
4000 Warner Blvd., Bldg. 66, #147
Burbank, CA 91522
PHONE .818-954-5200
FAX .818-954-5430
TYPES Features
HAS DEAL WITH Warner Bros. Pictures
DEVELOPMENT Guardians of Ga 'Hoole - Lonny the Great - Fool's Gold - Phantom Tollbooth - Home School - Penetration - Invisible World - Fraud Prince - Jetsons - Phantom Tollbooth - Brad Cutter Ruined My Life...Again
CREDITS The Stepford Wives - Without a Paddle - The Italian Job - Domestic Disturbance
SUBMISSION POLICY No unsolicited submissions

Donald De Line .Producer
Jennifer Berman .Executive VP (818-954-5298)
Andrew Haas .Sr. VP (818-954-5205)
Ed Walton .Creative Executive (818-954-5209)

MICHAEL DE LUCA PRODUCTIONS
c/o Columbia Pictures
10202 W. Washington Blvd., Astaire Bldg., Ste. 3028
Culver City, CA 90232
PHONE .See Below
FAX .310-244-0449
TYPES Features
HAS DEAL WITH Columbia Pictures
DEVELOPMENT Ten Bears - Around the World in 80 Dates - Soulmates - Embedded - Moneyball - The Game - 102 Minutes - Priest - This Present Darkness - Already Dead - I Am Vanessa Delgado - Button Man - How to Survive a Robot Uprising - Drug of Choice - Dracula Year Zero
UPCOMING RELEASES Ghost Rider
CREDITS Zathura
SUBMISSION POLICY No unsolicited submissions

Michael De Luca .Producer (310-244-4990)
Josh Bratman .Development Executive (310-244-4916)
Alissa Phillips .Development Executive (310-244-4918)
Zach Schiff-Abrams .Development Executive (310-244-4915)
Lauren Abrahams .Assistant to Alissa Phillips (310-244-4914)
Kristen Detwiler .Assistant to Mike De Luca (310-244-4990)
Bryan Haas .Assistant to Josh Bratman (310-244-4964)
Ersin Pertan .Assistant to Zach Schiff-Abrams (310-244-4631)

DE PASSE ENTERTAINMENT
5750 Wilshire Blvd., Ste. 640
Los Angeles, CA 90036
PHONE .323-965-2590
FAX .323-934-2548
TYPES Features - Made-for-TV/Cable Movies - Miniseries - Specials - TV Series
DEVELOPMENT Addicted (de Passe/Zane Entertainment)
CREDITS Black Movie Awards - Showtime at the Apollo - Essence Awards - NAACP Image Awards - Cheaters - Buffalo Girls - The Jacksons: An American Dream - Lonesome Dove - Sister Sister - The Smart Guy - The Temptations (Miniseries)
SUBMISSION POLICY No unsolicited submissions

Suzanne de Passe .Chairman/CEO
Suzanne Coston .President
Rose Caraet .Director, Creative Affairs

DEACON ENTERTAINMENT
100 Universal City Plaza, Bldg. 2352, Rm. A-103
Universal City, CA 91608
PHONE 818-733-0814
FAX 818-866-7852
WEB SITE . . . . www.deaconent.com
TYPES Features
HAS DEAL WITH Focus Features/Rogue Pictures
DEVELOPMENT Lost Boys of Sudan (Paramount) - Abaddon's Gate (Gold Circle) - Welfare Queen (Focus) - Panther 21 (Focus) - Chainmail (Gold Circle)
PRE-PRODUCTION This Christmas (Screen Gems)
UPCOMING RELEASES Whisper
CREDITS Undercover Brother - Double Tap (HBO) - One Flight Stand (HBO)
SUBMISSION POLICY No unsolicited material

Damon Lee . . . . Producer
Jennifer Pfautch . . . . Creative Executive

DEEP RIVER PRODUCTIONS
100 N. Crescent Dr., Ste. 350
Beverly Hills, CA 90210
PHONE 310-432-1800
FAX 310-432-1803
TYPES Features
HAS DEAL WITH Paramount Pictures
PRE-PRODUCTION Don't Send Help - Starship Dave
CREDITS Little Miss Sunshine - Dr. Dolittle - Courage Under Fire - Laws of Attraction - Big Momma's House 1&2

David T. Friendly . . . . Partner
Marc Turtletaub . . . . Partner
Laura Hopper . . . . No Title
Felipe Linz . . . . Creative Executive

DEJA VIEW PRODUCTIONS LTD.
96 Oak Park Ave.
Toronto, ON M4C 4M3, Canada
PHONE 416-963-8171
EMAIL . . . . denneJon@aol.com
TYPES Features - Made-for-TV/Cable Movies
CREDITS Land of the Dead - Dawn of the Dead - High Crimes - The Flintstones in Viva Rock Vegas - Pacific Heights - Short Circuit

Dennis E. Jones . . . . Producer/Line Producer

DEPARTURE STUDIOS
10 Universal City Plaza, Ste. 2000
Universal City, CA 91608
PHONE 818-753-2322
FAX 818-753-2332
EMAIL . . . . info@departurestudios.com
WEB SITE . . . . www.departurestudios.com
TYPES Features
CREDITS Come Early Morning - Mini's First Time - The Shooting Gallery - The Heart Is Deceitful Above All Things - This Girl's Life - I Love Your Work - Northfork

Damon Martin . . . . Producer
Chad Troutwine . . . . Producer
Charlotte Chatton . . . . Director, Development
David Mack . . . . Director, Sales & Marketing
Brad Whitcomb . . . . Executive Assistant

DESTINY PICTURES
1423 Second St., Ste. 411
Santa Monica, CA 90401
PHONE 310-656-1034
EMAIL . . . . destinypictures@hotmail.com
TYPES Direct-to-Video/DVD - Features - Made-for-TV/Cable Movies - TV Series
DEVELOPMENT Psyche 9
PRE-PRODUCTION It Ain't New Yawk - Zygote
CREDITS The Perfect Tenant - The Perfect Nanny
SUBMISSION POLICY Email queries only

Mark Castaldo . . . . Producer

DETOUR
PO Box 13351
Austin, TX 78711
PHONE 512-322-0031
TYPES Features
CREDITS A Scanner Darkly - Bad News Bears - Before Sunset - Dazed and Confused - Slacker

Richard Linklater . . . . Producer/Director/Writer

DEUTSCH/OPEN CITY FILMS
122 Hudson St., 5th Fl.
New York, NY 10013
PHONE 212-255-0500
FAX 212-255-0455
EMAIL . . . . docinquiries@opencityfilms.com
WEB SITE . . . . www.opencityfilms.com
TYPES Features
DEVELOPMENT Infinite Jest - Preist's Grotto - Twins Study - Chess - Probate - The Lady - The Toothpaste Millionaire
UPCOMING RELEASES Awake
CREDITS The Assassination of Richard Nixon - Three Seasons - Down to You - The Guys - Welcome to the Dollhouse - Lovely and Amazing - Series 7 - Coffee and Cigarettes

Jason Kliot . . . . Co-President/Co-Founder/Producer
Joana Vicente . . . . Co-President/Co-Founder/Producer
Courtney Andrialis . . . . Head, Development
Lauren Lillie . . . . Assistant to Co-Presidents

DFZ PRODUCTIONS
9465 Wilshire Blvd., Ste. 930
Beverly Hills, CA 90212
PHONE 310-274-5735
FAX 310-273-9217
TYPES Animation - Features - TV Series
DEVELOPMENT Get Low - Regression - State of Affairs - Goosetown - Hold My Hand - Voice From the Stone - Liberty Lane
CREDITS Road to Perdition
COMMENTS Financing deal with Firstar Productions

Dean Zanuck . . . . Producer

VIN DI BONA PRODUCTIONS

12233 W. Olympic Blvd., Ste. 170
Los Angeles, CA 90064
PHONE .310-442-5600
FAX .310-442-5605
WEB SITE .www.vdbp.com
SECOND WEB SITE .www.afv.tv
TYPES Reality TV - TV Series
CREDITS America's Funniest People - The "I Do" Diaries Presents: Wacky Wedding Videos - America's Funniest Videos - Meet the Marks - Sherman Oaks - Show Me the Funny - Extraordinary World of Animals - That's Funny
COMMENTS Distribution through Hollywood Licensing, LLC

Vin Di Bona .Chairman
Tammy Treglia .Co-Chairman, Hollywood Licensing
Peter J. Schankowitz .President, Worldwide Development
Dawn Friedman .Executive VP, Business & Legal Affairs
Cara Di Bona .VP, Corporate
Janet Ghio .VP, Human Resources
Sharon Arnett .VP, Post Production
Scott Jackson .Director, Development
Yolanda Seabourne .Director, Licensing & New Media, Hollywood Licensing
Jeff Foster .Manager, Development

DI BONAVENTURA PICTURES, INC.

5555 Melrose Ave., Dressing Room Bldg., Ste. 112
Los Angeles, CA 90038
PHONE .323-956-5454
FAX .323-862-2288
TYPES Documentaries - Features - TV Series
HAS DEAL WITH Paramount Pictures
DEVELOPMENT Trudain Rising - Convoy - Deceit - Me & Olivia - King Tut - By Any Means Necessary
PRE-PRODUCTION 1408
PRODUCTION Stardust - Shooter - Transformers
CREDITS Derailed - Four Brothers - Constantine - Doom

Lorenzo di Bonaventura .President/Producer
Mark Vahradian .President, Production
Erik Howsam .Sr. VP, Production
David Ready .VP, Production
Toni Kalmacoff .Creative Executive
Edward Fee .Development Assistant
Samantha Kolker .Development Assistant
Linda Pianigiani .Development Assistant

DI NOVI PICTURES

3110 Main St., Ste. 220
Santa Monica, CA 90405
PHONE .310-581-1355
FAX .310-399-0499
TYPES Features - TV Series
HAS DEAL WITH Warner Bros. Pictures
DEVELOPMENT The Food of Love - Jetsons - Maid of Dishonor - Nights in Rodanthe - Larklight - Vaporetto 13
POST PRODUCTION Lucky You
CREDITS The Sisterhood of the Traveling Pants - Practical Magic - Little Women - Ed Wood - Edward Scissorhands - Batman Returns - A Walk to Remember - The District - What a Girl Wants - Message in a Bottle - Catwoman - New York Minute - Eloise at the Plaza - Eloise at Christmas Time
SUBMISSION POLICY No unsolicited material

Denise Di Novi .Producer
Alison Greenspan .President
Clark Wells .Director, Development
Maureen Poon Fear .Assistant to Denise Di Novi
Lauren Gordon .Assistant to Alison Greenspan
Trevor Ryan .Assistant to Clark Wells

LOUIS DIGIAIMO & ASSOCIATES, LTD.

214 Sullivan St., Ste. 2-C
New York, NY 10012
PHONE .212-253-5510
FAX .212-253-5540
EMAIL .l.digiaimo@att.net
TYPES Features - Made-for-TV/Cable Movies - TV Series
DEVELOPMENT Hit #29 - The Booster - No Lights, No Sirens - Fort Pit - Untitled Exorcist Cop Project - America
PRE-PRODUCTION Nebraska Fish & Game
CREDITS Donnie Brasco - An Everlasting Piece - Falcone - Dinner Rush - The 24th Day
COMMENTS Also casting director

Lou DiGiaimo .Producer
Lou DiGiaimo Jr. .Producer
Russ Lyster .Producer/Manager

DIGITAL DOMAIN, INC.

300 Rose Ave.
Venice, CA 90291
PHONE .310-314-2800
FAX .310-314-2888
WEB SITE .www.digitaldomain.com
TYPES Commercials - Features - Music Videos
COMMENTS No unsolicited material

Michael Bay .Co-Chair
John Textor .Co-Chair
Carl Stork .CEO
C. Brad Call .President/COO
Ed Ulbrich .Sr. VP, Commercial Production
Yvette Macaluso .VP, Finance
Molly Hansen .VP/General Counsel

DIGITAL RANCH PRODUCTIONS

14110 Riverside Dr.
Sherman Oaks, CA 91423
PHONE .818-817-9690
FAX .818-817-9699
WEB SITE .www.digitalranch.tv
TYPES Commercials - Direct-to-Video/DVD - Documentaries - New Media - Reality TV - Syndication - TV Series
CREDITS Russell Simmons Presents Hip Hop Justice - Mail Call - Shifting Gears - Dangerous Missions - Modern Marvels - James Bond's Gadgets - The Investigators
COMMENTS Representation: Peter Hankwitz Production & Management

Robert Kirk .Executive Producer
Robert Lihani .Executive Producer
Valarie Sheldon .Director, Business Affairs

DIMENSION FILMS

c/o The Weinstein Company
345 Hudson St., 13th Fl.
New York, NY 10014
PHONE 646-862-3400
FAX 917-368-7000
WEB SITE . . . . www.weinsteinco.com
SECOND WEB SITE . . . . www.twcpublicity.com
TYPES Direct-to-Video/DVD - Features
PROVIDES DEAL TO Cube Vision - Platinum Dunes - Trancas International Films
DEVELOPMENT Quebec - Piranha - Devil's Knot
PRE-PRODUCTION Castlevania
UPCOMING RELEASES Sin City 2 - Superhero! - Rogue - Grind House - Black Christmas - 1408
CREDITS Pulse - DOA: Dead or Alive - School for Scoundrels - Wolf Creek - Sin City - Cursed - Bad Santa - The Others - Scream 1-3 - Scary Movie 1-4 - Spy Kids 1-3 - The Adventures of Shark Boy & Lava Girl in 3-D - The Brothers Grimm - The Reaper
COMMENTS Second address: 375 Greenwich St., New York, NY 10013, phone: 212-941-3800, fax: 212-941-3949

Bob Weinstein . . . . Co-Chairman (NY)
Richard Saperstein . . . . President, Production (LA)
Andrew Kramer . . . . Executive VP, Business & Legal Affairs (NY)
Sanjeev Lamba . . Executive VP, Marketing & New Media Development (NY)
Matthew Stein . . . . Sr. VP, Production (NY)
Tracy McGrath . . . . Sr. VP, Physical Production (LA)
Liz Biber . . . . Sr. VP, Publicity (LA)
Lumumba Mosquera . . . . Sr. VP, Business & Legal Affairs (NY)
Sarah Sobel . . . . Sr. VP, Business & Legal Affairs (NY)
Katrina Wolfe . . . . VP, Production & Casting (NY)
Rachel Levy . . . . VP, Motion Picture Music (LA)

DISCOVERY CHANNEL

c/o Discovery Networks, U.S.
One Discovery Pl.
Silver Spring, MD 20910-3354
PHONE 240-662-2000
FAX 240-662-1845
EMAIL . . . . firstname_lastname@discovery.com
WEB SITE . . . . www.discovery.com
TYPES Documentaries - TV Series
CREDITS American Chopper - Dirty Jobs - Cash Cab - Monster Garage - Myth Busters - Perfect Disaster - Stunt Junkies

Jane Root . . . . Executive VP/General Manager, Discovery Channel, The Science Channel & Military Channel
Tom Bettag . . . . Executive Producer, Discovery Channel
Elizabeth Hillman . . . . VP, Communications, Discovery Channel
Ted Koppel . . . . Managing Editor, Discovery Channel

DISCOVERY HEALTH CHANNEL

c/o Discovery Networks, U.S.
One Discovery Pl.
Silver Spring, MD 20910-3354
PHONE 240-662-2000
FAX 240-662-1845
EMAIL . . . . firstname_lastname@discovery.com
WEB SITE . . . . www.discovery.com
TYPES Documentaries - TV Series
CREDITS Dr. G: Medical Examiner - Dr. Drew - Impact: Stories of Survival - Mystery Diagnosis - Plastic Surgery: Before & After

Eileen O'Neill . . . . Executive VP/General Manager, Discovery Health Channel & FitTV
Toni Egger . . . . VP, Program Development, Discovery Health Channel
Reenie Kuhlman . . . . Director, Communications

DISCOVERY NETWORKS, U.S.

One Discovery Pl.
Silver Spring, MD 20910-3354
PHONE 240-662-2000
FAX 240-662-1845
EMAIL . . . . firstname_lastname@discovery.com
WEB SITE . . . . www.discovery.com
TYPES Documentaries - Miniseries - Reality TV - Specials - TV Series
COMMENTS Animal Planet, Discovery Channel, Discovery Channel Beyond, Discovery HD Theater™, Discovery en Español, Discovery Health Channel, Discovery Home Channel, Discovery Kids Channel, Discovery Kids en Español, Discovery Times Channel, Discovery Travel & Living, Discovery Mobile, Military Channel, FitTV, The Science Channel, TLC, Travel Channel, Travel Channel Beyond, Turbo

John S. Hendricks . . . Founder/Chairman, Discovery Communications, Inc.
Judith A. McHale . . . . President/CEO, Discovery Communications, Inc.
Billy Campbell . . . . President, Discovery Networks, U.S.
Clark Bunting . . . . President, Discovery Networks U.S. Production
Frank Rosales . . . . President, Discovery Commerce
Donald Baer . . . . Sr. Executive VP, Strategy & Development
Mark Hollinger . . . Sr. Executive VP, Corporate Operations & General Counsel
Pandit Wright . . . . Sr. Executive VP, Human Resources & Administration
David Abraham . . . . Executive VP/General Manager, TLC & Discovery Home Channel
Steve Burns . . . . Executive VP/Chief Science Editor, Discovery Networks U.S. Production
Ken Dice . . . . Executive VP, Marketing, Discovery Networks, U.S.
Marjorie Kaplan . . . . Executive VP/General Manager, Discovery Kids Channel
David Leavy . . . . Executive VP, Corporate Affairs & Communications
Eileen O'Neill . . . . Executive VP/General Manager, Discovery Health Channel & FitTV
Jane Root . . . . Executive VP/General Manager, Discovery Channel, The Science Channel & Military Channel
Maureen Smith . . . . Executive VP/General Manager, Animal Planet
Carole Tomko . . . . Executive VP, Discovery Networks U.S. Production
Patrick Younge . . . . Executive VP/GM, Discovery Travel Media
Christian Drobnyk . . . . Sr. VP, Programming & Development, TLC

(Continued)

DISCOVERY NETWORKS, U.S. (Continued)

Jim McKairnes . . . . .Sr. VP, Scheduling & Program Planning, Discovery Networks, U.S.
Luis Silberwasser . . . . .Sr. VP/General Manager, US Hispanic Networks
Sarita Smith . . . . .Sr. VP, Research
Evan Sternschein .Sr. VP, National Advertising Sales
Douglas Craig . . . . .VP, Programming, Discovery On Demand
Joseph Czarkowski . . . . .VP/National Sales Manager
David Doyle . . . . .VP, Production & Development, Animal Planet
Toni Egger . . . . .VP, Program Development, Discovery Health Channel
Joan Harrison . . . . .VP, Development, TLC
Roger Henry . . . . .VP, Programming, The Science Channel
Maria Kennedy . . . . .VP, Advertising Sales, Direct Response
Michael Klein . . . . .VP, Production, Lifestyle Programming Genre, Discovery Networks, U.S.
Bill Margol . . . . .VP, Production, Travel Programming Genre, Discovery Networks, U.S.
David McKillop . . . . .VP, Production, Factual Programming Genre, Discovery Networks, U.S.
Allan Navarrete . . .VP, U.S. Hispanic Networks Distribution, Affiliate Sales & Marketing, Discovery Networks, U.S.
Joe Paglino . . . . .VP, Advertising Sales, Discovery Networks, U.S.
Dan Russell . . . . .VP, Programming, Animal Planet
Chris Schembri .VP, Media Planning & Partnerships
Bill Smee . . . . .VP, Production, Current Affairs Programming Genre, Discovery Networks, U.S./Acting General Manager, Discovery Times Channel
Donald Thoms . . . . . . .VP, Production, Health/Fitness Programming Genre, Discovery Networks, U.S.
Michael Weber . . . . .VP, Advertising Sales, Western Region, Discovery Networks, U.S.
Mark Sonnenberg . . . . .Head, West Coast Entertainment
Ted Koppel . . . . .Managing Editor, Discovery Channel
Tom Bettag .Executive Producer, Discovery Channel

DISNEY ABC CABLE NETWORKS GROUP

3800 W. Alameda Ave.
Burbank, CA 91505
PHONE 818-569-7500
WEB SITE . . . . .www.disneychannel.com
SECOND WEB SITE . . . . .www.abcfamily.com
TYPES Animation - Made-for-TV/Cable Movies - New Media - TV Series
COMMENTS Additional Web sites: www.jetix.tv, www.soapnet.com, www.toondisney.go.com

Anne Sweeney . . . . .Co-Chair, Disney Media Networks/President, Disney-ABC Television Group
Rich Ross . . . . .President, Disney Channel Worldwide
Gary K. Marsh . . . . . .President, Entertainment, Disney Channel Worldwide
Paul Lee . . . . .President, ABC Family
Deborah Blackwell . . . . .Executive VP/General Manager, SOAPnet
Jewell Engstrom . . .Executive VP/CFO, Disney ABC Cable Networks Group
Eleo Hensleigh . . . . . . .Chief Marketing Officer/Executive VP, Marketing & Brand Strategy, Disney-ABC Television Group
Frederick Kuperberg . . . . .Executive VP, Business & Legal Affairs, Disney ABC Cable Networks Group
Laura Nathanson . . . . .Executive VP, National Sales, Disney ABC Cable Networks Group
Vincent H. Roberts . . . .Executive VP, Technology & Operations, Disney ABC Cable Networks Group
Mark Silverman . . . . .Sr. VP/General Manager, Disney ABC Cable Networks Group
Adam Bonnett . . . . .Sr. VP, Original Programming, Disney Channel
Jill Casagrande . . . . .Sr. VP, Worldwide Programming Strategy, Disney Channel Worldwide
Scott Garner . . . . .Sr. VP, Programming, Disney ABC Cable Networks Group
Michael Healy . .Sr. VP, Original Movies, Disney ABC Cable Networks Group
Susette Hsiung . . . . . .Sr. VP, Production, Disney ABC Cable Networks Group
Kate Jeurgens . . . . .Sr. VP, Programming & Development, ABC Family
Nancy Kanter . . . . .Sr. VP, Programming, Disney Channel
Jeffrey R. Lai . . . . .Sr. VP, Legal Affairs, Disney ABC Cable Networks Group
Patti McTeague . . . . .Sr. VP, Children's Communications, Disney-ABC Television Group
Meredith Metz . . . .Sr. VP, Creative Affairs, Walt Disney Television Animation
Nicole Nichols . . . . . . .Sr. VP, Entertainment Communications, Disney-ABC Television Group
Julie Piepenkotter . . . .Sr. VP, Research, Disney ABC Cable Networks Group
Mark Rejtig . . . . .Sr. VP, ABC Family

(Continued)

DISNEY ABC CABLE NETWORKS GROUP (Continued)

John Rood . . . . .Sr. VP, Marketing, ABC Family
Lisa Salamone . . . . . . .Sr. VP, Production, Walt Disney Television Animation
Adina Savin . . .Sr. VP, Business Affairs, Disney ABC Cable Networks Group
Tricia Wilber . . . . .Sr. VP, Advertising Sales & Promotions, Disney Cable Networks Group
Tom Zappala . . . . .Sr. VP, Acquisitions & Scheduling, ABC Family
Jeff Brustrom . . . . .VP, Live-Action Series, Disney Channel
Donna Ebbs . . . . .VP, Original Movies
Lynn Finley . . .VP, Broadcast Operations, Disney ABC Cable Networks Group
Karen Holm . . . . .VP, Legal Affairs, Disney ABC Cable Networks Group
Kelly Pena . . . . .VP, Research, Disney ABC Cable Networks Group
Chris Ryan . . . . .VP, Business Affairs, Disney ABC Cable Networks Group

THE WALT DISNEY COMPANY

500 S. Buena Vista St.
Burbank, CA 91521
PHONE 818-560-1000
WEB SITE . . . . .www.thewaltdisneycompany.com
TYPES Features

Robert Iger . . . . .President/CEO
George Bodenheimer . . . . .Co-Chairman, Disney Media Networks/ President, ESPN, Inc. & ABC Sports/ Chairman, ESPN Board of Directors
Anne Sweeney . . . . .Co-Chair, Disney Media Networks/President, Disney-ABC Television Group
Bob Cavallo . . . . .Chairman, Buena Vista Music Group
Richard Cook . . . . .Chairman, The Walt Disney Studios
Andrew Mooney . . . . .Chairman, Disney Consumer Products
James Rasulo . . . . .Chairman, Walt Disney Parks & Resorts
John Lasseter . . . . .Chief Creative Officer, Walt Disney Animation Studios/ Principal Creative Advisor, Walt Disney Imagineering
Andy Bird . . . . .President, Walt Disney International
Ed Catmull . . . . .President, Pixar & Walt Disney Animation Studios
Steve Wadsworth . . . . .President, Walt Disney Internet Group
Alan N. Braverman . . . . .Sr. Executive VP/General Counsel/Secretary
Thomas O. Staggs . . . . .Sr. Executive VP/CFO
Zenia Mucha . . . . .Executive VP, Corporate Communications
Brent Woodford . . . . .Sr. VP/Planning & Control

***DISNEY ONLINE**

A Division of Walt Disney Internet Group
5161 Lankershim Blvd.
North Hollywood, CA 91601
PHONE 818-623-3200
FAX 818-623-3554
WEB SITE . . . . .www.disney.com
SECOND WEB SITE . . . . .www.familyfun.com
TYPES Internet Content - Mobile Content
CREDITS Pirates of the Caribbean Online - Playhouse Disney Preschool Time Online - Disney's Game Café

Paul Yanover . . . . .Executive VP/Managing Director, Disney Online
Brad Davis . . . . .VP, Advertising Sales & Marketing, Disney Online
Robert Gonzales . . . . .VP, Production Operations, Disney Online
Steve Parkis . . . . .VP, Premium Products, Disney Online
Jodie Resnick . . . . . . .VP, Agency Services, The Walt Disney Internet Group
Dan Sherlock . . . . .VP, Movies.com
Emily Smith . . . . .VP, FamilyFun.com

WALT DISNEY PICTURES/TOUCHSTONE PICTURES
SEE Buena Vista Motion Pictures Group

WALT DISNEY TELEVISION ANIMATION
500 S. Buena Vista St.
Burbank, CA 91521
PHONE .818-560-0560
WEB SITE www.disney.com
TYPES Animation - TV Series
SUBMISSION POLICY Unsolicited materials not accepted

Mark Kenchelian . Sr. VP, Business & Legal Affairs
Meredith Metz . Sr. VP, Creative Affairs
Lisa Salamone . Sr. VP, Production
Joanna Spak . Sr. VP, Finance & Planning
Mike Moon . VP, Animated Series, Disney Channel
Jay Stutler . VP, Music Production
Andy Schoentag . Executive Director, Digital Production & Technology

DISNEY-ABC TELEVISION GROUP
500 S. Buena Vista St.
Burbank, CA 91521
PHONE .818-460-7777
TYPES Animation - New Media - TV Series

Anne Sweeney . Co-Chair, Disney Media Networks/President, Disney-ABC Television Group
Eleo Hensleigh . Chief Marketing Officer/Executive VP, Marketing & Brand Strategy, Disney-ABC Television Group
Brian Frons . President, Daytime, Disney-ABC Television Group
Albert Cheng . Executive VP, Digital Media, Disney-ABC Television Group
Kevin Brockman . Sr. VP, Communications, Disney-ABC Television Group
Nicole Nichols . Sr. VP, Entertainment Communications, Disney-ABC Television Group
Sharon Williams . Sr. VP, Communications Resources, Disney-ABC Television Group
Patti McTeague . Sr. VP, Children's Communications, Disney-ABC Television Group
Julie Hoover . VP, Corporate Communications, Disney-ABC Television Group
Kenneth C. Estenson . VP, Office of the President, Disney-ABC Television Group
Robert Mendez . Sr. VP, Diversity, Disney-ABC Television Group

DISNEYTOON STUDIOS
500 S. Buena Vista St.
Burbank, CA 91521-3418
PHONE .818-560-5000
WEB SITE www.disney.com
TYPES Animation - Direct-to-Video/DVD - Features
SUBMISSION POLICY Unsolicited materials not accepted

Sharon Morrill . President, DisneyToon Studios
Brian Snedeker . Sr. VP, Production
Matt Walker . Sr. VP, Music
Karen Ferguson . VP, Production
Susan Kirch . VP, Creative
Amir Nasrabadi . VP, Finance & Operations
Brett Swain . VP, Music
Steve Swofford . VP, Post Production & Editorial
Elizabeth Wolfe . VP, Publicity
Jamie Thomason . Voice Casting & Dialogue Director
Sossi Bilanjian . Executive Director, Finance
Jennifer Blohm . Director, Production
Dawn Ernster-Rivera . Director, Animation Resources (Recruiting)
Brad Kleinerman . Director, Human Resources
Stephen Toback . Director, Studio Technology
Emily Hache . Manager, Creative Affairs
Dan Soulsby . Supervisor, Casting

DIY NETWORK
9721 Sherrill Blvd.
Knoxville, TN 37932
PHONE .865-694-2700
FAX .865-342-3483
WEB SITE www.diynetwork.com
TYPES Internet Content - TV Series
UPCOMING RELEASES 10 Things You Must Know - Project Paradise - Wasted Spaces - Home Made Easy - Uncommon Threads - B. Original
CREDITS Barkitecture - DIY to the Rescue - Grounds for Improvement - Scrapbooking - Kitchen Renovations - Bath Renovations - Classic Rides - Best Built Home - Garden Sense - Tricked Out - Material Girls - From Junky to Funky - Creative Juice - Stylelicious - Dirt on Gardening
COMMENTS TV and online network providing step-by-step, do-it-yourself instructions and demonstrations

Bob Baskerville . President
Kathleen Finch . Sr. VP/General Manager
Robyn Ulrich . Sr. VP, Marketing & Public Relations
Freddy James . VP, Programming
Jeff Sears . VP, Creative Services
Gary McCormick . Director, Public Relations
Phillip Williams . Director, DIYnetwork.com

DNA FILMS
15 Greek St., 1st Fl.
London W1D 4DP, United Kingdom
PHONE .44-207-292-8700
FAX .44-207-292-8701
EMAIL .info@dnafilms.com
WEB SITE .www.dnafilms.com

TYPES	Features
HAS DEAL WITH	Twentieth Century Fox - Searchlight Pictures
PRODUCTION	28 Weeks Later
POST PRODUCTION	Sunshine - Notes on a Scandal - The History Boys - Last King of Scotland
CREDITS	28 Days Later
SUBMISSION POLICY	No unsolicited material

Andrew Macdonald .Partner
Allon Reich .Partner
Tanya Phegan .Development
Carey Berlin .Development
Leah Clarke .Assistant to Andrew Macdonald

DOMINANT PICTURES
10201 W. Pico Blvd., Bldg. 43
Los Angeles, CA 90064
PHONE .310-369-0707

TYPES	Features - TV Series
HAS DEAL WITH	Twentieth Century Fox
DEVELOPMENT	Pay the Girl (Paramount) - Beached (Fox 2000)
CREDITS	John Tucker Must Die (Fox) - Surviving Christmas - Charlie's Angels 1&2 - Private Parts - The Brady Bunch Movie - Dr. Dolittle - The Late Shift - 28 Days - Can't Hardly Wait - I Spy

Betty Thomas .Owner/Director
Ben Spector .Executive
Angelina Burnett .Assistant to Betty Thomas

DONALDSON/SANDERS ENTERTAINMENT
1640 S. Sepulveda Blvd., Ste. 530
Los Angeles, CA 90025
PHONE .310-689-9811
FAX .310-689-9801

TYPES	Features - Internet Content - Made-for-TV/Cable Movies - Miniseries - Mobile Content - Reality TV - Specials - TV Series
DEVELOPMENT	Outcast (Universal Pictures) - Fallen 2&3 (ABC Family) - Sleeper (Warner Bros.) - The Caan Game (NBC)
PRE-PRODUCTION	Jumper (New Regency)
POST PRODUCTION	December Boys (Village Roadshow)
CREDITS	Fallen (ABC Family)

Peter Donaldson .Partner
Jay Sanders .Partner

THE DONNERS' COMPANY
9465 Wilshire Blvd., Ste. 430
Beverly Hills, CA 90212
PHONE .310-777-4600

TYPES	Animation - Features - TV Series
DEVELOPMENT	Labor Day - 12 Days of Christmas - Hotel for Dogs - Cirque du Freak - Sam & George - Science Fiction - The Secret Life of Bees
POST PRODUCTION	Unaccompanied Minors
CREDITS	16 Blocks - She's the Man - Timeline - Lethal Weapon 1-4 - Maverick - Free Willy 1-3 - Ladyhawke - Dave - Volcano - Conspiracy Theory - You've Got Mail - Any Given Sunday - X-Men 1-3 - Constantine
SUBMISSION POLICY	No unsolicited submissions

Richard Donner .No Title (310-777-6730)
Lauren Shuler Donner .No Title (310-777-6725)
Jack Leslie .President (310-777-6720)
Dantram Nguyen .Creative Executive (310-777-6735)
Kathy Liska .Office Manager/Assistant to Ms. Shuler (310-777-6725)
Cece Neber .Assistant to Mr. Donner (310-777-6730)
Jack Dubnicek .Assistant to Ms. Shuler (310-777-6725)
Derek Hoffman .Assistant to Mr. Donner (310-777-6735)

DOOZER
c/o Scrubs
12629 Riverside Dr., 3rd Fl.
Valley Village, CA 91607
PHONE .818-623-1880, x104/818-840-6072

TYPES	TV Series
HAS DEAL WITH	NBC Universal Television Studio
DEVELOPMENT	Nobody's Watching (WB) - Confessions of a Dog - Untitled Brian Regan Project
CREDITS	Scrubs - Spin City - Clone High

Bill Lawrence .Executive Producer/Creator
Eren Celeboglu .Assistant

BONNY DORE PRODUCTIONS
10940 Wilshire Blvd., Ste. 1600
Los Angeles, CA 90024
PHONE .310-443-4189
FAX .310-443-4190
EMAIL .bonnyinc@aol.com

TYPES	Animation - Direct-to-Video/DVD - Documentaries - Features - Internet Content - Made-for-TV/Cable Movies - Miniseries - Mobile Content - Music Videos - Reality TV - Specials - Theatre - TV Series
CREDITS	Captive - Sins - Glory, Glory! - The Jill Ireland Story - Rainbow Warrior - First Impressions - 1/2 Hour Comedy Hour

Bonny Dore .President/Executive Producer

CHRIS DORR PRODUCTIONS
156 S. Irving Blvd.
Los Angeles, CA 90004
PHONE .323-610-6557
FAX .323-461-3419
EMAIL .cdorr@earthlink.net

TYPES	Features - Made-for-TV/Cable Movies - Mobile Content
DEVELOPMENT	The Dennis Littkey Story - Stella's Choice - No Transfer
CREDITS	Clay Pigeons - Where the Money Is - The Deal (Sony/Showtime)
COMMENTS	Consultant to motion picture investment companies and mobile communications companies seeking content

Christopher Dorr .Producer
Matt Rosen .VP, Development

DOUBLE EDGE ENTERTAINMENT
15233 Ventura Blvd., PH 9
Sherman Oaks, CA 91403
PHONE .818-205-9898
FAX .818-205-9797
EMAIL .jmazalian.dee@gmail.com
WEB SITE .www.doubleedgeentertainment.com
TYPES Animation - Features
DEVELOPMENT Dark Reaches - Book of the Dead - 900 Sacramento - Children of Huang Shi
PRODUCTION Chasing the Dragon
UPCOMING RELEASES Sledge: The Untold Story
CREDITS Mail Order Wife

Bob Sheng .Co-Founder/CEO
Alan Lee .Co-Founder/COO
Nina Yang .Co-Founder/President/Producer
Stanley Tong .Producer/Director
Steve Yang .VP, Production
Josh Mazalian .Office Coordinator

DOUBLE FEATURE FILMS
9465 Wilshire Blvd., Ste. 950
Beverly Hills, CA 90212
PHONE .310-887-1100
FAX .310-887-1110
TYPES Features
HAS DEAL WITH Paramount Pictures
COMPLETED UNRELEASED Freedom Writers - Reno 911: Miami
CREDITS World Trade Center - Be Cool - Garden State - Skeleton Key

Michael Shamberg .Co-Chair
Stacey Sher .Co-Chair
Carla Santos Shamberg .Executive VP
Karen Willaman .COO/CFO
Josh Rothstein .Creative Executive

DOUBLE NICKEL
ENTERTAINMENT

DOUBLE NICKEL ENTERTAINMENT
c/o Warner Bros.
1325 Avenue of the Americas, 30th Fl.
New York, NY 10019
PHONE .212-636-5488/310-859-1035
FAX .212-636-5487
TYPES Features - Made-for-TV/Cable Movies - Reality TV - TV Series
HAS DEAL WITH Warner Bros. Pictures - Warner Bros. Television Production
PROVIDES DEAL TO Foremost Films
DEVELOPMENT Allison's Automotive Repair Manual - As Luck Would Have It - The Mission - Standing on the Moon - The Set (Warner Bros. Television) - I'm Fine (Paramount) - I, Paparazzi - Dead Already - The Diagnosis - Follow You Down - Red - Tranquility
PRE-PRODUCTION Peter
PRODUCTION Untitled Makeover Show
UPCOMING RELEASES The Flock
COMMENTS West Coast office: 311 N. Robertson Blvd., Ste. 385, Beverly Hills, CA 90211

Jenette Kahn .Producer/Partner (NY & LA)
Adam Richman .Producer/Partner (NY & LA) (212-636-5112)
Jen Kelly .Producer (LA) (310-859-1064)
Jeffrey Belkin .Producer (NY) (212-636-4205)
Jeremy Platt .Producer (LA) (310-859-1035)
Michael O'Shea .Assistant to the Partners (NY) (212-636-5486)

JEAN DOUMANIAN PRODUCTIONS
595 Madison Ave., Ste. 2200
New York, NY 10022
PHONE .212-486-2626
FAX .212-688-6236
TYPES Features - Made-for-TV/Cable Movies - Theatre - TV Series
DEVELOPMENT Film: Godspeed - Fly'n V - Schoolgirl Figure; Off-Broadway: The Great American Trailer Park Musical
CREDITS Film: Everyone Says I Love You - Deconstructing Harry - The Spanish Prisoner - Sweet and Lowdown - Small Time Crooks - Celebrity - Mighty Aphrodite - Women Talking Dirty - All the Real Girls - Bullets Over Broadway; Off-Broadway: Dinah Was - Things You Shouldn't Say Past Midnight - Fuddy Meers - What the Butler Saw - Bat Boy; Broadway: Frankie & Johnny - Amour - Jumpers - Democracy

Jean Doumanian .President
Kimberly Jose .VP
Stephen Lancellotti .Director, Development
Patrick Daly .Executive Assistant

JEFF DOWD & ASSOCIATES
3200 Airport Ave., Ste. 1
Santa Monica, CA 90405
PHONE .310-572-1500
FAX .310-572-1501
EMAIL .jeffdowdassist@aol.com
WEB SITE .www.jeffdowd.com
TYPES Features
DEVELOPMENT One: The Gary Davis Story - Nifty
PRE-PRODUCTION Voices - The Secret Life of Huckleberry Finn - Ghost Country - Struck - The Thought Gang
UPCOMING RELEASES Subject Two
CREDITS Neil Young's Greendale - Better Luck Tomorrow - Kissing Jessica Stein - Scratch - Fern Gully - Zebrahead - Dream with the Fishes - Smiling Fish & Goat on Fire - Metallica: Some Kind of Monster - The Cockettes - Going Upriver: The Long War of John Kerry - The Thing About My Folks
COMMENTS Producer's representative

Jeff Dowd .President

DREAM ENTERTAINMENT, INC.

8489 W. Third St.
Los Angeles, CA 90048
PHONE .323-655-5501
FAX .323-655-5603
EMAIL .dream@dreamentertainment.net
WEB SITE .www.dreamentertainment.net
TYPES Direct-to-Video/DVD - Features
DEVELOPMENT Masquerade - First Class Affair
PRODUCTION Max the Toad
COMPLETED UNRELEASED Disaster!
CREDITS According to Spencer - Girl Fever - 100 Girls - More Dogs Than Bones - Monster Man - The Manor - Amnesia - Baja - Lover Girl - The Pass - Soft Kill - Spree - Three Women

Yitzhak Ginsberg .President/Producer
Nolan Pielak .President, International Distribution
Marcia Matthew .VP, Finance
Silke Wolz .Director, Business Affairs

DREAMWORKS ANIMATION SKG

1000 Flower St.
Glendale, CA 91201
PHONE .818-695-5000
FAX .818-695-3510
WEB SITE .www.dreamworksanimation.com
TYPES Animation - Features
DEVELOPMENT Rex Havoc - Route 66 - It Came From Earth! - How to Train Your Dragon - Punk Farm
PRE-PRODUCTION Kung Fu Panda - Madagascar 2
PRODUCTION Flushed Away - Shrek the Third - Bee Movie
CREDITS Over the Hedge

Jeffrey Katzenberg .CEO
Ann Daly .COO
Lewis Coleman .President
Kris Leslie .CFO
Terry Press .Head, Marketing
Kristine Belson .Head, Development
Nancy Bernstein .Head, Production
Bill Damaschke .Head, Creative Production & Development
Bob Feldman .Head, Corporate Communications
Anne Globe .Head, Worldwide Consumer Products & Promotions
Jane Hartwell .Head, Global Production
John Batter .Head, Studio Operations
Katherine Kendrick .General Counsel

DREAMWORKS SKG

100 Universal City Plaza
Universal City, CA 91608
PHONE .818-733-7000
WEB SITE .www.dreamworks.com
TYPES Animation - Features - TV Series
HAS DEAL WITH NBC Universal Television Studio - Paramount Pictures
PROVIDES DEAL TO Aardman Animations - Ember Entertainment Group - Jason Hoffs Productions - ImageMovers - Kurtzman/Orci - The Montecito Picture Company - Neal Street Productions Ltd. - Red Hour Films - The Zanuck Company
DEVELOPMENT Heartbreak Kid - Lincoln
PRE-PRODUCTION Things We Lost in the Fire - Kite Runner
PRODUCTION Transformers - Disturbia - Blades of Glory - Norbit; TV: On the Lot
POST PRODUCTION Dreamgirls
UPCOMING RELEASES Flags of Our Fathers - Perfume
CREDITS Dreamer - Red Eye - The Last Kiss - The Island - Madagascar - Shark Tale - Collateral - The Terminal - Anchorman - Almost Famous - American Beauty - A.I. - A Beautiful Mind - Catch Me If You Can - Cast Away - EuroTrip - Gladiator - Minority Report - Old School - The Ring 1&2 - Road to Perdition - Saving Private Ryan - Seabiscuit - Shrek 1&2 - Win a Date with Tad Hamilton - Surviving Christmas - Just Like Heaven - She's the Man
COMMENTS New York office: 650 Madison Ave., 22nd Fl., New York, NY 10022, phone: 212-588-6229, fax: 212-588-6233

David Geffen .Co-Principal
Jeffrey Katzenberg .Co-Principal
Steven Spielberg .Co-Principal
Stacey Snider .Co-Chairman/CEO
Justin Falvey .Co-Head, TV
Darryl Frank .Co-Head, TV
Ann Daly .Head, Feature Animation
Adam Goodman .Head, Theatrical Production
David Beaubaire .Theatrical Production
Kira Goldberg .Theatrical Production
Marc Haimes .Theatrical Production
Jeremy Kramer .Theatrical Production
Andrea McCall .Theatrical Production/Head, Story Department
Steven Molen .Theatrical, Physical Production
Mark Sourian .Theatrical Production
Jonathan Berry .Creative Executive, TV
Lisa Hamilton .Feature Development, Literary (Universal City)
Sara Roby .Feature Development, Literary (NY)
Leslee Feldman .Head, Casting
Jack Bleck .Head, Theatrical Business Affairs
A.J. Brandenstein .Theatrical Business Affairs
Brian Edwards .General Counsel
Jamie Kershaw .Animation Business/Legal Affairs
Alison Lima .Animation Business/Legal Affairs
Rich Shuter .TV Business Affairs
Deborah Chiaramonte .Legal Affairs

DREYFUSS/JAMES PRODUCTIONS

c/o The Lot
1041 N. Formosa Ave., Formosa Bldg., Rm 200
West Hollywood, CA 90046

PHONE 323-850-3140
FAX 323-850-3141
TYPES Features - Made-for-TV/Cable Movies - TV Series
UPCOMING RELEASES The Forest
CREDITS Quiz Show - Mr. Holland's Opus - Having Our Say

Richard Dreyfuss . . . . .Owner/Executive Producer
Judith James . . . . .Owner/Executive Producer
Greg Szimonisz . . . . .VP, Development

DRIVEN ENTERTAINMENT

PO Box 491085
Los Angeles, CA 90049

PHONE 310-980-2882
EMAIL . . . . .driven@drivenentertaiment.com
WEB SITE . . . . .www.driventertainment.com
TYPES Features - Music Videos - TV Series
PRE-PRODUCTION One Republic
CREDITS Sunday with Simon - Cravings - The Ringbearer - God Is Watching Over You - The Chickilu Ya-Yas - Every 15 Minutes
SUBMISSION POLICY No unsolicited submissions

Celeste Wade . . . . .Producer
Laura Hudson . . . . .Producer

DULY NOTED

5225 Wilshire Blvd., Ste. 403
Los Angeles, CA 90036

PHONE 323-525-1855
EMAIL . . . . .info@dulynotedinc.com
WEB SITE . . . . .www.dulynotedinc.com
TYPES Features - Made-for-TV/Cable Movies
HAS DEAL WITH HBO Films
DEVELOPMENT Bobby Zero - My Place in the Horror - Polish Bar - Strangers in the Snow - American Way
PRE-PRODUCTION Exactly Like You
POST PRODUCTION Rocket Science
CREDITS Real Women Have Curves - Stranger Inside - Everyday People - In the Cut

Effie Brown . . . . .Producer
Nicole Colombie . . . . .Production Executive

E! NETWORKS

5750 Wilshire Blvd.
Los Angeles, CA 90036

PHONE 323-954-2400
FAX . . . . .323-954-2662 (PR)
WEB SITE . . . . .www.eonline.com
TYPES Documentaries - Reality TV - Specials - TV Series
PROVIDES DEAL TO Ryan Seacrest Productions
DEVELOPMENT Starveillance
UPCOMING RELEASES Series: The Carters - 7 Deadly Hollywood Sins - Sexiest; Specials: Forbes 100 Richest Celebrities - Uncovered: Hidden Lives of Miss USA
CREDITS The Simple Life: 'Til Death Do Us Part - 101 Series - E! News - E! True Hollywood Story - Dr. 90210 - The Girls Next Door - E! Original Specials - #1 Single - The Chelsea Handler Show - The Simple Life - The Soup - The Daily 10 - Last Bride Standing: To Have and to Hold - Rise of the Geeks

Ted Harbert . . . . .President/CEO
Steve Dolcemaschio . . . . .Executive VP, Finance & Business Operations
Neil Baker . . . . .Sr. VP, Sales & Distribution
Lisa Berger . . . . .Sr. VP, Programming Development
Howard Bolter . . . . .Sr. VP, Network & Production Operations
Salaam Coleman-Smith . . . . .Sr. VP, Programming
Brad Fox . . . . .Sr. VP, Affiliate Relations
Sarah Goldstein . . . . .Sr. VP, Publicity & Media Relations
Jay James . . . . .Sr. VP, Development
Sheila K. Johnson . . . . .Sr. VP, Business Operations & General Counsel
Alex Maggioni . . . . .Sr. VP, Original Programming & Series Development
Jeff Mayzurk . . . . .Sr. VP, Technology
Kevin McClellan . . . . .Sr. VP, International
Cyndi McClellan . . . . .Sr. VP, Research & Program Strategy
John Najarian . . . . .Sr. VP, New Media
Barry Nugent . . . . .Sr. VP, Talent Development & Casting
Jeff Shore . . . . .Sr. VP, Production
David Walkley . . . . .Sr. VP, Human Resources
Frank Albano . . . . .VP, Operations
Steven Blue . . . . .VP, Production Management
Ann Lewis . . . . .VP/Executive Producer
Susan Lierle . . . . .VP, Business & Legal Affairs
Bill McLean . . . . .VP, New Media
Betsy Rott . . . . .VP, Current Programming
Gary Snegaroff . . . . .VP, Current Programming
Peggy Jo Abraham . . . . .Executive Producer, E! News
Steve Tseckares . . . . .Executive Producer, Programming
Jennifer Danska . . . . .Director, Talent Development
Jerri Howell . . . . .Director, Current Programming
Rachel Karzen . . . . .Director, Development
Karyn Wulbrun . . . . .Director, Talent
Adrian Seto . . . . .Sr. Manager, New Media (Asia)
Hayley Lozitsky . . . . .Coordinator, Programming Development
Donna Scavella . . . . .News Producer

E ENTERTAINMENT, LLC

1201 W. Fifth St., Ste. M-250
Los Angeles, CA 90017
PHONE .213-534-3446
FAX .213-534-3463
WEB SITE .www.e3ent.net

TYPES	Animation - Direct-to-Video/DVD - Features - Made-for-TV/Cable Movies
DEVELOPMENT	The Virgin - Future Force - No Alternative - The Roman - The Sailmaker - The Jar by the Door
PRE-PRODUCTION	The Mermaids Singing - The Fat Man
POST PRODUCTION	Black Box
COMPLETED UNRELEASED	Dizzyland
CREDITS	Morning - The Last Supper - Campfire Tales - Photographing Fairies - Kiss the Girls - Apple Jack
COMMENTS	Business and legal affairs consulting

Don Schneider .Principal
Larry Weinberg .Principal

EALING STUDIOS

Ealing Green
London W5 5EP, United Kingdom
PHONE .44-208-567-6655
FAX .44-208-758-8658
EMAIL .info@ealingstudios.com
WEB SITE .www.ealingstudios.com

TYPES	Features
CREDITS	Alien Autopsy - Click - The Importance of Being Earnest
SUBMISSION POLICY	See Web site for submission requirements

Barnaby Thompson .Head of Studio
James Spring .Managing Director, Film & TV
Jeremy Pelzer .Studio Director
Sophie Meyer .Head, Development
Nic Martin .Development Executive

EARS XXI

6565 Sunset Blvd.
Los Angeles, CA 90028
PHONE .323-469-8500/323-469-9800
FAX .323-469-3400
EMAIL .info@earsxxi.com
WEB SITE .www.earsxxi.com

TYPES	Animation - Commercials - Direct-to-Video/DVD - Documentaries - Features - Internet Content - Miniseries - Mobile Content - Reality TV - Specials - TV Series
DEVELOPMENT	Biker Chef - Black Stallion - MacBeth - Duck Duck Goose - Big Bad Voodo Mama - Breeze Ave.
CREDITS	HD American Portraits - The Creature of the Sunny Side Up Trailer Park - G-Men from Hell - Gunfighter - Palmer's Pick-up - Bel Air
COMMENTS	Digital films; Formerly PlasterCITY Productions

Christopher Coppola .President
Adrienne-Stout Coppola .VP
Nicholas Paine .Head, Production
Bill L. Watson .Head, Development & Marketing

EARTHVIEW INC.

200 N. Continental Blvd., 2nd Fl.
El Segundo, CA 90245
PHONE .310-577-9381
FAX .310-577-9473

TYPES	Reality TV
CREDITS	The Amazing Race

Bertram van Munster .Executive Producer/Director
Elise Doganieri .Co-Executive Producer

EARTHWORKS FILMS

13527 Contour Dr.
Sherman Oaks, CA 91423
PHONE .818-990-2261
FAX .818-990-2265
EMAIL .maflorio@pacbell.net

TYPES	Documentaries - Features - TV Series
DEVELOPMENT	S.O.S. (United Nations) - December's Boudoir: Laura Nyro Documentary
CREDITS	Broken Rainbow - Tibet: Cry of the Snow Lion

Maria Florio .President
Victoria Mudd .VP

EAST OF DOHENY/LEXINGTON ROAD PRODUCTIONS

9014 Melrose Ave.
Los Angeles, CA 90069
PHONE .310-248-4880/212-957-5510
FAX .310-248-4990/212-957-5511
EMAIL .info@eastofdoheny.com
WEB SITE .www.eastofdoheny.com

TYPES	Direct-to-Video/DVD - Documentaries - Features - Theatre - TV Series
DEVELOPMENT	Stuffed: Adventures of a Restaurant Family - Secret Letters - Flipped - Pool Boy
PRE-PRODUCTION	Grey Gardens: Behind the Scenes
UPCOMING RELEASES	Grey Gardens (Broadway)
CREDITS	Features: A Time for Dancing - Siegfried & Roy: The Magic Box (IMAX) - Men with Guns; Theater: 'Night Mother (Broadway) - The Good Body (Broadway) - Napoleon: The Musical - The Full Monty - Art - Cressida (West End, London) - Flower Drum Song (Los Angeles) - The Sweet Smell of Success - Big River - Match - Not About Nightingales (Broadway) - Chitty Chitty Bang Bang (Broadway)
SUBMISSION POLICY	Agent submissions only
COMMENTS	East Coast office: 321 W. 44th St., Ste. 603, New York, NY 10036

Lou Gonda .Partner
Kelly Gonda .Partner
Harvey Gettleson .CFO
Tracey Trench .Producer/Executive VP, Film
Beth Williams .Producer/Executive VP, Theatre (NY)
Kimberly Guidone .VP, Development, Film
David Hamlin .Head, Pico Playhouse
Anastasia Barzee .Creative Executive, Theatre (NY)
Anne-Elisa Schaffer .Story Editor
Marcia Johnson .Executive Assistant to Kelly Gonda
Aimee Barneburg .Development Assistant
Rachel Murch .Production Assistant (NY)
Alena Kastin .Receptionist (NY)

THE EBERSOLE-HUGHES COMPANY

1427 Sanborn Ave.
Los Angeles, CA 90027
PHONE . . . 323-666-4911
WEB SITE . . . www.ebersolehughes.com

TYPES	Features - Made-for-TV/Cable Movies - TV Series
DEVELOPMENT	Out There
PRE-PRODUCTION	Oceanside
PRODUCTION	Desire: Art of Betrayal
CREDITS	Desire: Table for Three - Hot Chicks - Stranger Inside - The New Women - Straight Right - Death in Venice, CA - Hubby/Wifey
SUBMISSION POLICY	No unsolicited scripts or treatments; No email inquiries

P. David Ebersole . . . Writer/Director/Producer (323-666-4911)
Todd Hughes . . . Writer/Director/Producer (323-666-0313)
Tristen Tuckfield . . . Assistant

ECHELON ENTERTAINMENT WORLD DISTRIBUTION & PRODUCTION

1725 Victory Blvd.
Glendale, CA 91201
PHONE . . . 818-500-1640
FAX . . . 818-500-1644
EMAIL . . . info@echelonent.com
WEB SITE . . . www.echelonent.com

TYPES	Animation - Direct-to-Video/DVD - Documentaries - Features - Miniseries - TV Series
DEVELOPMENT	Bad Kitty - El Destino - Bordergate - Deep Blue - Grim's Day Off
PRE-PRODUCTION	Latin Comics
CREDITS	Our Italian Husband (Theatrical) - Maniacts (Video/MTI) - A Light in the Forest (Ardustry)
SUBMISSION POLICY	Name talent only; Send query letter with SASE or submit online
COMMENTS	Theatrical releasing company: Newmark/Echelon Entertainment Group; DVD/Video label: Singa Home Entertainment

Eric Louzil . . . President/CEO
Gloria Morrison . . . President, Development & Acquisitions
Matthew Mueller . . . Sr. VP, Acquisitions
Derrick Anunciation . . . VP, International Sales
Lewei Duan . . . VP, Domestic & International Sales
Matthew Moon . . . VP, International Sales
Diane Ramirez . . . VP, Accounting & Client Relations
Jacqueline Plaza . . . Director, Press Relations
Yoonah Yim . . . Post Production
Harold Golingay . . . Art Director
Ellen Roongcharoen . . . Sales Assistant
Jennifer Ward . . . DVD Fulfillment

ECHO LAKE PRODUCTIONS

421 S. Beverly Dr., 8th Fl.
Beverly Hills, CA 90212
PHONE . . . 310-789-4790
FAX . . . 310-789-4791
EMAIL . . . contact@echolakeproductions.com
WEB SITE . . . www.echolakeproductions.com

TYPES	Direct-to-Video/DVD - Features - Made-for-TV/Cable Movies - Miniseries - TV Series
DEVELOPMENT	Helen - Montana 1948 - Devil to Pay - City Island - Son of a G Man - Summer - Viagra Falls - 105 Degrees and Rising - Dust Brothers - Echo - You Kill Me - Standoff
POST PRODUCTION	Kerala
UPCOMING RELEASES	Water - Twelve & Holding
COMPLETED UNRELEASED	Dreamland
CREDITS	The Big Empty - Things Behind the Sun - Thirteen Conversations About One Thing - Levity - La Ciudad
SUBMISSION POLICY	No unsolicited submissions

Doug Mankoff . . . President
Andrew D. Spaulding . . . Executive VP
Jessica Stamen . . . VP, Development
Amotz Zakai . . . VP, Production

ABRA EDELMAN PRODUCTIONS

16170 Kennedy Rd.
Los Gatos, CA 95032
PHONE . . . 408-356-2804
FAX . . . 408-358-6593

TYPES	Direct-to-Video/DVD - Features - Made-for-TV/Cable Movies - TV Series
UPCOMING RELEASES	Behind Enemy Lines 2
CREDITS	Just Ask My Children - Air Bud 1&2 - Dungeons & Dragons - Some Girls - Loving Lulu - Bulletproof Heart - Underworld - Changing Habits - According to Spencer - Snap Judgment

Abra Edelman . . . Producer

THE EDELSTEIN COMPANY

500 S. Buena Vista St., Animation Bldg., Ste. 2D4
Burbank, CA 91521-1740
PHONE . . . 818-560-3884
FAX . . . 818-560-4949

TYPES	Features - Made-for-TV/Cable Movies - Miniseries - TV Series
HAS DEAL WITH	Touchstone Television
CREDITS	Desperate Housewives - Threat Matrix - Hope and Faith (Pilot)

Michael Edelstein . . . Principal
Maher Jafari . . . Director, Development
Chris Loveall . . . Manager, Development
Brad Margolis . . . Development Assistant

EDEN ROCK MEDIA, INC.
c/o Henson-Chaplin Lot
1416 N. La Brea Ave.
Hollywood, CA 90028
PHONE . . . 323-802-1718
FAX . . . 323-802-1832
WEB SITE . . . www.edenrockmedia.com
TYPES: Features - Miniseries
DEVELOPMENT: Solace - Berlin - Waiting 2 - Paddington Project
PRODUCTION: Mr. Brooks
CREDITS: Features: Waiting - Incident at Loch Ness - Strange Bedfellows - Till Human Voices Wake Us - Slap Her, She's French - Maedchen, Maedchen (German Language) - Love and a Bullet - Coming Soon - Judas Kiss - Splittsville - The Alarmist; TV: Have No Fear: The Life of John Paul II - USA's Cannonball Run 2001
SUBMISSION POLICY: No unsolicited submissions

Thomas Augsberger . . . Producer
Jana Augsberger . . . Development

EDKO FILMS LTD.
1212, Tower II, Admiralty Centre
18 Harcourt Rd.
Hong Kong , China
PHONE . . . 852-2529-3898
EMAIL . . . edkofilm@hkstar.com
WEB SITE . . . www.edkofilm.com.hk
TYPES: Features
DEVELOPMENT: Untitled Zhang Yimou Project
CREDITS: Fearless - Riding Alone for Thousands of Miles - House of Flying Daggers - Windstruck - Hero - Springtime in a Small Town - Crouching Tiger, Hidden Dragon

Bill Kong . . . Executive Director

EDMONDS ENTERTAINMENT
1635 N. Cahuenga Blvd., 5th Fl.
Los Angeles, CA 90028
PHONE . . . 323-860-1550
FAX . . . 323-860-1537
WEB SITE . . . www.edmondsentertainment.com
TYPES: Features - Reality TV - TV Series
DEVELOPMENT: Welfare Queen
CREDITS: Lil' Kim: Countdown to Lockdown - Soul Food (Feature) - Hav Plenty - Light It Up - Punks - Soul Food (Series) - Maniac Magee - College Hill (Reality Series/BET)
SUBMISSION POLICY: No unsolicited material

Tracey E. Edmonds . . . President/CEO
Kenneth "Babyface" Edmonds . . . President/CEO
Seth Rappaport . . . Director, Creative Affairs
Emerlynn Lampitoc . . . Manager, TV

RALPH EDWARDS PRODUCTIONS
6922 Hollywood Blvd., Ste. 300
Hollywood, CA 90028
PHONE . . . 323-462-2212
FAX . . . 323-461-1224
EMAIL . . . info@ralphedwards.com
WEB SITE . . . www.ralphedwardsproductions.com
TYPES: Animation - Direct-to-Video/DVD - Reality TV - Syndication - TV Series
CREDITS: Truth or Consequences - People's Court - Annabelle's Wish - This Is Your Life

Barbara Dunn-Leonard . . . President
James B. Pollock . . . Vice Chairman
Gary Edwards . . . Executive VP
John Couch . . . VP, Business Affairs

RONA EDWARDS PRODUCTIONS/ES ENTERTAINMENT
264 S. La Cienega Blvd., Ste. 1052
Beverly Hills, CA 90211
PHONE . . . 323-466-3013
FAX . . . 323-467-1258
TYPES: Documentaries - Features - Made-for-TV/Cable Movies - Reality TV - TV Series
DEVELOPMENT: Blind Trust - Johnny Got His Gun - The Passion of Dalton Trumbo - Passing Grade - Cold Peace - Last Verdict - The Birbal Tales - Creative Differences
CREDITS: The Companion - One Special Victory - I Know What You Did - Out of Sync - Der Murder Meiner Mutter
COMMENTS: Literary Consultants - Co-Authors: *I Liked It, Didn't Love It: Screenplay Development from the Inside Out*

Rona Edwards . . . Producer
Monika Skerbelis . . . Producer, ES Entertainment (310-278-4484)

DAVID EICK PRODUCTIONS
100 Universal City Plaza, Bldg. 2372A, Ste. E
Universal City, CA 91608
PHONE . . . 818-777-7567
FAX . . . 818-733-2522
TYPES: Miniseries - TV Series
CREDITS: Battlestar Galactica (Series) - Battlestar Galactica (Miniseries) - Cover Me - The Agency - Spy Game - American Gothic - Hercules: The Legendary Journeys

David Eick . . . President
James Halpern . . . Creative Executive

EIGHTH SQUARE ENTERTAINMENT
606 N. Larchmont Blvd., Ste. 307
Los Angeles, CA 90004
PHONE . . . 323-469-1003
FAX . . . 323-469-1516
TYPES: Features - Made-for-TV/Cable Movies - Theatre - TV Series
PRE-PRODUCTION: Before the Devil Knows You're Dead
CREDITS: Psycho Beach Party - I'll See You in My Dreams - Lehi's Wife
SUBMISSION POLICY: No unsolicited material

Jeff Melnick . . . No Title
Janette Jensen "JJ" Hoffman . . . No Title

EL DORADO PICTURES
725 Arizona Ave., Ste. 404
Santa Monica, CA 90401
PHONE . . . 310-458-4800
FAX . . . 310-458-4802
WEB SITE . . . www.alecbaldwin.com
TYPES: Features - Made-for-TV/Cable Movies - Miniseries - TV Series
PRE-PRODUCTION: Lymelife - The Mentor
CREDITS: The Confession - Nuremberg - State and Main - Second Nature

Alec Baldwin . . . Producer
Tiffany Nishimoto . . . Producer
Summer Grindle . . . Assistant to Mr. Baldwin

EL NORTE PRODUCTIONS

1201 Olympic Blvd.
Santa Monica, CA 90404
PHONE 310-396-5937
EMAIL ....bmjelnorte@hotmail.com

TYPES	Documentaries - Features - TV Series
DEVELOPMENT	Zapata - Bordertown - Tattooed Soldier
CREDITS	American Tapestry - El Norte - Mi Familia - Selena - Why Do Fools Fall in Love? - American Family (PBS)
SUBMISSION POLICY	No unsolicited submissions

Gregory Nava ....CEO/Producer
Barbara Martinez Jitner ....President/Producer

ELECTRIC ENTERTAINMENT

1438 N. Gower St., Box 24
Los Angeles, CA 90028
PHONE 323-817-1300
FAX 323-467-7155
WEB SITE ....www.electric-entertainment.com

TYPES	Documentaries - Features - Internet Content - Made-for-TV/Cable Movies - Miniseries - TV Series
DEVELOPMENT	Carrier - Ghosting - One Little Problem - Alcott & Diana - Anthem - The Isobar Run - The Librarian 3: Curse of the Judas Chalice
POST PRODUCTION	The Librarian 2
UPCOMING RELEASES	Flyboys
CREDITS	Who Killed the Electric Car? - Universal Soldier - Stargate - Eight Legged Freaks - Independence Day - Godzilla - The Patriot - The Visitor - Cellular - The Librarian (TNT) - The Triangle (Sci Fi)
SUBMISSION POLICY	No unsolicited submissions
COMMENTS	Distribution deal with MGM

Dean Devlin ....President
Marc Roskin ....Partner
Kearie Peak ....Partner
Rachel Olschan ....Partner
Josh Jacobs ....Assistant to Rachel Olschan
Rebecca Kirsch ....Assistant to Marc Roskin
Matthew Urofsky ....Assistant to Kearie Peak

ELEMENT FILMS

7966 Beverly Blvd., 3rd. Fl.
Los Angeles, CA 90048
PHONE 323-330-8000
FAX 323-330-8001

TYPES	Features
HAS DEAL WITH	Lionsgate
PRODUCTION	Mr. Brooks
POST PRODUCTION	The Last Time
UPCOMING RELEASES	Freshman Orientation - Five Fingers
CREDITS	Waiting - Evil Remains - Beautiful Country - Wonderland - Washington Heights - Prey for Rock and Roll - A Midsummer Night's Rave - Home of Phobia - Down in the Valley
COMMENTS	No unsolicited material

Sam Nazarian ....Owner
Adam Rosenfelt ....President/Partner
Marc Schaberg ....COO
John Fremes ....President, Element Films International
Julie Dangel ....Executive, Production & Development
Lorraine Evanoff ....Director, Finance
Scarlett Pettyjohn ....Director, Business & Legal Affairs
Chris Kulikowski ....Supervisor, Post Production
Shane McCloskey ....No Title
Katie McMillan ....Executive Assistant

*ELEVATION FILMWORKS

609 Greenwich St., Ste. 401A
New York, NY 10014
PHONE 212-430-5090
FAX 212-430-5099
EMAIL ....info@elevationfilmworks.com
WEB SITE ....www.elevationfilmworks.com

TYPES	Features
DEVELOPMENT	The Woody - Human Capital
PRE-PRODUCTION	Gracie
POST PRODUCTION	Morirse Esta en Hebreo - First Born
UPCOMING RELEASES	Sherrybaby
COMPLETED UNRELEASED	Forgiveness
CREDITS	Angela - Santitos - Personal Velocity - Casa De Los Babys - The Ballad of Jack and Rose - King of the Corner - Duane Hopwood
SUBMISSION POLICY	No unsolicited submissions

Lemore Syvan ....Founder/Producer
Iliana Nikolic ....Head, Production
Lauren Elmer ....Post Production Supervisor
April Lo ....Development
Jessica Lustgarten ....Assistant to Producer

ELIXIR FILMS

8033 Sunset Blvd., Ste. 867
West Hollywood, CA 90046
PHONE 323-517-7525
WEB SITE ....www.elixirfilms.com

TYPES	Features
CREDITS	Long Way Round - Wake Up and Smell the Coffee - The Good Thief - Where the Red Fern Grows
SUBMISSION POLICY	No unsolicited submissions

David Alexanian ....Producer
Alexis Alexanian ....Producer
Josh Zetumer ....Assistant to Producer

ELKINS ENTERTAINMENT
8306 Wilshire Blvd., PMB 3643
Beverly Hills, CA 90211-2382
PHONE .323-932-0400
FAX .323-932-6400
EMAIL .info@elkinsent.com

TYPES	Animation - Direct-to-Video/DVD - Documentaries - Features - Made-for-TV/Cable Movies - Theatre - TV Series
HAS DEAL WITH	Showtime Networks Inc.
DEVELOPMENT	The Huntsman - Romeo & Juliet - Cat's Cradle - The Timothy Leary Story - The Challenger - Asphalt Prophets
POST PRODUCTION	For the Love of Liberty
CREDITS	Steve McQueen: The Essence of Cool - A Doll's House - Richard Pryor Live - A New Leaf - Inside - In His Father's Shoes - Oh! Calcutta! - Golden Boy - Father for Charlie - Sex, Censorship and the Silver Screen - Stander - Pippin - Alice's Restaurant
COMMENTS	Syndication; Management; Deal with The Mark Taper Forum

Hillard Elkins .President/Producer/Manager
Sandi Love .VP/Manager
Diana Nunez .Assistant

EMBASSY ROW LLC
435 W. 19th St. 2nd Fl.
New York, NY 10011
PHONE .212-627-3439
FAX .212-905-0672

TYPES	Features - Reality TV - TV Series
HAS DEAL WITH	ABC Entertainment Television Group - ESPN Original Entertainment (EOE) - Sony Pictures Television
CREDITS	Who Wants to be a Millionaire? - Wife Swap - First Descent

Michael Davies .Chairman

EMBER ENTERTAINMENT GROUP
11718 Barrington Court, Ste. 116
Los Angeles, CA 90049
PHONE .310-230-9759
FAX .310-589-4850
EMAIL .eeg.bronson@verizon.net

TYPES	Features - TV Series
HAS DEAL WITH	DreamWorks SKG
DEVELOPMENT	The Man from U.N.C.L.E. - The Girl from U.N.C.L.E. - Thirty Minutes or Less - Wolverines - Celebrity Charities Television - The Unseen - Forbidden Planet (DreamWorks)
CREDITS	Permanent Record - The Night Before

Lindsay Dunlap .Producer
T.S. Goldberg .President, Physical Production
J.A. Keller .Finance
J.A. McGuire .Finance (UK)

EMERALD CITY PRODUCTIONS, INC.
c/o Stankevich-Gochman, LLP
9777 Wilshire Blvd., Ste. 550
Beverly Hills, CA 90212
PHONE .310-859-8825
FAX .310-859-8830

TYPES	Features
DEVELOPMENT	City of the Beasts
PRODUCTION	The Water Horse
CREDITS	Little Fish - World's Fastest Indian - Lord of the Rings Trilogy - The Matrix - Face/Off - The Fan - Rapa Nui - Wilder Napalm - China Moon - Dick Tracy - Child's Play - Peggy Sue Got Married - The Cotton Club
SUBMISSION POLICY	No unsolicited submissions

Barrie M. Osborne .Producer

EMERGING PICTURES
245 W. 55th St., 4th Fl.
New York, NY 10019
PHONE .212-245-6767
FAX .212-202-4984
EMAIL .inquiries@emergingpictures.com
WEB SITE .www.emergingpictures.com

TYPES	Documentaries - Features - Made-for-TV/Cable Movies
DEVELOPMENT	Love, Marriage and Marilyn Monroe - Master and Margarita - Nickel and Dimed
PRODUCTION	For Real
POST PRODUCTION	Superheroes
UPCOMING RELEASES	Amu - Beauty Remains - Tony and Tina's Wedding - Red Doors - Bullrider
COMPLETED UNRELEASED	The Forgotten - Brothel - In the Blood - Sex & Sushi - The Actress - Rome & Jewel
CREDITS	Twelve - Killing Time - The Lucky Ones - Way Past Cool - This Old Cub - Relative Evil - The Game of Their Lives
SUBMISSION POLICY	See Web site

Ira Deutchman .CEO
Barry Rebo .Chairman
Giovanni Cozzi .President
Josh Green .VP, Distribution

EMMETT/FURLA FILMS

8530 Wilshire Blvd., Ste. 420
Beverly Hills, CA 90211
PHONE 310-659-9411
FAX 310-659-9412

TYPES — Animation - Features - Reality TV
HAS DEAL WITH — Millennium Films
DEVELOPMENT — Terror Train - Micronauts - Room Service - Second World - Untitled Red Sonja Feature
PRE-PRODUCTION — Day of the Dead - The Code - Husk - Microwave Park - Brilliant - Rambo 4
POST PRODUCTION — The King of California - Home of the Brave - The Rin Tin Tin Story
UPCOMING RELEASES — Lonely Hearts
COMPLETED UNRELEASED — Borderland - The Contract - 88 Minutes
CREDITS — The Wicker Man - 16 Blocks - The Tenants - Edison - The Amityville Horror - A Love Song for Bobby Long - Wonderland - Narc - Half Past Dead - Good Advice - Speedway Junky
SUBMISSION POLICY — No unsolicited submissions

Randall Emmett . . . . Producer/Co-Chair
George Furla . . . . Producer/Co-Chair
Stanley Tepper . . . . CFO
M. Dal Walton III . . . . Executive VP, Development & Business Affairs
Nick Reimond . . . . Development Executive
Dina Oxenberg . . . . Executive Assistant to Producers
Melissa Smith . . . . Executive Assistant to Executive VP
Jason Maddoch . . . . Second Assistant to Producers

EMOTIONAL PICTURES CORPORATION

285 W. Broadway, Ste. 330
New York, NY 10013
PHONE 212-941-7200, x208
EMAIL . . . . sara@emot.tv
WEB SITE . . . . www.emotionalpictures.com

TYPES — Commercials - Documentaries - Specials - TV Series
CREDITS — Uncovered: Hidden Lives of Miss USA (E! Entertainment Networks) - Gastineau Girls (E!/True Entertainment) - Room Raiders (Granada/MTV) - Total Access 24/7 (ABC Family) - Growing Up Gotti: My Dinner with Peter (GRB/A&E) - Growing Up Gotti: A Very Gotti Christmas (GRB/A&E) - *NYSNC & Britney Spears: Your #1 Video Requests...And More! (Jive) - Evanescence: Anywhere But Home (DVD) - Janet Jackson: Damita Jo (DVD)

Sara Nichols . . . . President/Executive Producer

EMPIRE PICTURES INCORPORATED

1900 Blue Heights Dr.
Los Angeles, CA 90069
PHONE 323-656-4075
FAX 323-656-7772

TYPES — Animation - Features - Made-for-TV/Cable Movies - Miniseries - TV Series
DEVELOPMENT — Veronica - I Know That You Know - Art Con - High Maintenance - Amazing Sea Monkeys - The McCrearys
PRE-PRODUCTION — Quail Hollow
CREDITS — The Big White - John Tucker Must Die - Keys to Tulsa - Bandits - The Last Seduction

Michael Birnbaum . . . . President/Producer

*ENDEMOL USA LATINO

4040 NE Second Ave.
Miami, FL 33137
PHONE 305-576-4949
FAX 305-576-4980

TYPES — Reality TV - TV Series
CREDITS — Vas O No Vas (Telemundo Network)

Stephanie Fisch . . . . Sr. VP
Rosalind Rodriguez . . . . Executive Assistant

ENDEMOL USA, INC.

9255 Sunset Blvd., Ste. 1100
Los Angeles, CA 90069
PHONE 310-860-9914
FAX 310-860-0073
WEB SITE . . . . www.endemol.com

TYPES — Reality TV - TV Series
CREDITS — I Want to Be a Hilton - Big Brother - Fear Factor - Spy TV - Performing As... - The People's Champions - Anything for Love - Extreme Makeover: Home Edition - Todd TV - The Next Great Champ - Deal or No Deal
SUBMISSION POLICY — No unsolicited material

David Goldberg . . . . President
Peter Bazalgette . . . . CCO
Laura Armstrong . . . . Sr. VP, Scripted Development
Lisa Higgins . . . . Sr. VP, Production
Caroline Baumgard . . . . VP, Development
Ira Chartoff . . . . VP, Finance & Administration
Robert Smith . . . . VP, Programming
Jon Vlassopulos . . . . VP, Business Development, Digital Media & Strategic Planning
Brandie Tucker . . . . Interactive Producer
Jon Lawrence . . . . Interactive Producer, Mobile
Sara Auspitz . . . . Director, Programming
Tina Hoover . . . . Director, Production
Joerg Bachmaier . . . . Director, Business Development & Strategic Planning, Digital Media
Benson Berro . . . . Controller
Codessa Gill . . . . Manager, Development
Cynthia Stockhammer . . . . Manager, Programming & Development
Tamra Barcinas . . . . Coordinator, Development/Talent
Shannon Herlihy . . . . Manager, Production
Rebecca Lane . . . . Coordinator, Development

ENDGAME ENTERTAINMENT

c/o The Lot
1041 N. Formosa Ave., Admin. Bldg., Ste. 195
Los Angeles, CA 90046
PHONE .323-850-2747
FAX .323-850-2754
WEB SITE .www.endgameentertainment.com

TYPES: Animation - Documentaries - Features - Made-for-TV/Cable Movies - Theatre - TV Series
PRE-PRODUCTION: I'm Not There
POST PRODUCTION: Solstice
UPCOMING RELEASES: Lies and Alibis
COMPLETED UNRELEASED: The Best Man - Beowulf & Grendel - The Battleground
CREDITS: Stay Alive - Proof - Lord of War - Harold & Kumar Go to White Castle - Hotel Rwanda - White Noise - The Year of the Yao; Broadway: Hairspray - The Producers - Stomp - Little Shop of Horrors

James D. Stern .CEO
Douglas E. Hansen .COO
Julia Eisenman .President, Production (323-850-2738)
Cindy Kirven .Sr. VP, Finance & Business Affairs (323-850-2795)
Christopher C. Chen .Producer (323-850-2715)
Adam Del Deo .Producer (323-850-2765)
Eleanor Nett .Production Executive (323-850-2732)
Lucas Smith .Creative Executive (323-850-2753)
Jared Morell .Assistant to Mr. Stern
Nicholas Anglewicz .Assistant to Mr. Hansen & Ms. Kirven
Bryan Okamoto .Assistant to Mr. Del Deo

ENERGY ENTERTAINMENT

999 N. Doheny Dr., Ste. 711
Los Angeles, CA 90069
PHONE .310-274-3440
WEB SITE .www.energyentertainment.com

TYPES: Features
DEVELOPMENT: Planet Terry (New Line) - Pan (New Line) - Prom (Lionsgate) - Spin (Spyglass) - Wimpy (Alcon/WB) - Rapid (Columbia) - Bachelorette (Universal) - Isis (Grammnet/Paramount)
POST PRODUCTION: The Number 23 (New Line)
COMMENTS: Also a management company

Brooklyn Weaver .Owner/Manager
Adam Marshall .Manager
Jake Wagner .Manager

PETER ENGEL PRODUCTIONS

1438 N. Gower, Bldg. 48
Hollywood, CA 90028
PHONE .323-993-7324
FAX .323-993-7330

TYPES: Reality TV - TV Series
CREDITS: Last Comic Standing - All About Us - City Guys - USA High - One World - Malibu, CA - Saved by the Bell: The New Class - Hang Time
COMMENTS: No unsolicited material

Peter Engel .Chairman/CEO
Hannah Pinter .Executive Assistant to Peter Engel

ENPOCKET

31 St. James Ave., Ste. 920
Boston, MA 02116
PHONE .617-262-7001
FAX .617-262-7085
EMAIL .usa.sales@enpocket.com
WEB SITE .www.enpocket.com

TYPES: Mobile Content

Mike Baker .CEO

ENSEMBLE ENTERTAINMENT

10474 Santa Monica Blvd., Ste. 380
Los Angeles, CA 90025
PHONE .310-882-8900
FAX .310-882-8901

TYPES: Animation - Direct-to-Video/DVD - Documentaries - Features - Made-for-TV/Cable Movies - Miniseries - TV Series
DEVELOPMENT: Party Animals - Cola Wars - Above Kansas - Screams & Shadows - Thomasina - San Diablo - Antibodies - U.I.S.A.
PRE-PRODUCTION: The Snow Goose
CREDITS: The Poseidon Adventure - The Ties That Bind - Slaves to the Underground - Mr. Bill Presents
SUBMISSION POLICY: Faxes only; No phone calls
COMMENTS: Management and production company

Jon Brown .Partner
Jeffrey Thal .Partner
Orlando Alegret .Assistant to Jon Brown
Patti Cummings .Assistant to Jeffrey Thal

ENTERAKTION STUDIOS

Sound City Center Stage
15466 Cabrito Rd.
Van Nuys, CA 91406
PHONE .818-994-5494
FAX .818-994-5794
EMAIL .info@enteraktion.com
WEB SITE .www.enteraktion.com

TYPES: Animation - Direct-to-Video/DVD - Documentaries - Features - New Media - Syndication - TV Series
PRE-PRODUCTION: The Neighborhood
PRODUCTION: Los Opolis - The Kernies
POST PRODUCTION: Kidsline - 14 Stories
CREDITS: Denial - We Dare You - Mismatch - House to House - The Arrival (CD-ROM)
COMMENTS: Computer animation and development of CG content

Tom Walsh .CEO/Producer/Director/Co-Chairman
Ronald Hilton .Co-Chairman
Adriana Walsh .Executive VP
Chris Goger .VP, Production
Jerry Smith .Director, Digital/CGI
Paulina Guth .Animation Coordinator

ENTERTAINMENT STUDIOS, INC.

9903 Santa Monica Blvd., Ste. 418
Beverly Hills, CA 90212
PHONE .310-277-3500
FAX .310-277-3511
EMAIL .info@entertainmentstudios.com
WEB SITE .www.entertainmentstudios.com
SECOND WEB SITE .www.es.tv
TYPES Direct-to-Video/DVD - Documentaries - Specials
CREDITS The American Athlete - Automotive Vision.TV - Beautiful Homes & Great Estates - Designers, Fashions & Runways - Destination Stardom - Entertainers with Byron Allen - Every Woman - Global Business People - Kickin' It with Byron Allen - Latin Lifestyles - Recipe TV Featuring the World's Greatest Chefs - Urban Style - Travel in Style - The Writer's Book Club; Specials: We Have a Dream - Feel the Beat - Happy Holidays America
COMMENTS Magazine format shows

Byron Allen .Chairman/CEO/Executive Producer
Deborah Mitchell .President, Home Entertainment
Carolyn Folks .Executive Producer
Joan Robbins .Co-Producer/Sr. VP, Talent
Barry Illovitch .Executive in Charge of Production
Stu Stringfellow .President, Domestic Television Distribution
Tom Devlin .President, International Television Sales & Distribution
Mike Espinosa .Editor
Dave Bogosian .Producer
Michelle Hanson .Producer
Jennifer Lucas .Producer
Aaron Wiener .Producer
Kristine Eckert .Producer

ENTITLED ENTERTAINMENT

606 N. Larchmont Blvd., Ste. 100
Los Angeles, CA 90004
PHONE .323-469-9000
FAX .323-469-9008
WEB SITE .www.entitledentertainment.com
TYPES Features - Theatre
DEVELOPMENT Getting Blue - Well Done, Pear Danube! - The Next Rainy Day
UPCOMING RELEASES The L.A. Riot Spectacular - Aurora Borealis
COMPLETED UNRELEASED Tom 51
CREDITS Illusion - Thirteen Conversations About One Thing - Levity - Long Day's Journey Into Night (Broadway)
SUBMISSION POLICY No unsolicited submissions

James Burke .Partner
Scott Disharoon .Partner
Laura Citrano .VP

ENTPRO, INC.

1015 Gayley Ave., Ste. 1149
Los Angeles, CA 90024-3424
PHONE .310-440-4829
TYPES Features - Made-for-TV/Cable Movies - Theatre
DEVELOPMENT Six Dance Lessons in Six Weeks
CREDITS TV: Rescue Me - False Witness - A Friendship in Vienna - The Sisters; Theatre: Six Dance Lessons in Six Weeks

Richard Alfieri .Writer/Producer
Arthur Allan Seidelman .Director/Producer
Joseph Eastwood .Development

EPIC LEVEL ENTERTAINMENT, LTD.

12413 Ventura Ct, Ste. 300
Studio City, CA 91604
PHONE .818-752-6800
FAX .818-752-6814
EMAIL .info@epiclevel.com
WEB SITE .www.epiclevel.com
TYPES Animation - Direct-to-Video/DVD - Documentaries - Features - Made-for-TV/Cable Movies - Reality TV - TV Series
DEVELOPMENT M.I.T.H. - The Barrow - Dinoverse - Sonja Blue - Vampire: The Masquerade - World of Darkness
PRE-PRODUCTION Masters of Fantasy (TV Series) - Dungeons & Dragons III (Warner Bros.)
PRODUCTION Dungeons & Dragons: Dragonlance (Paramount)
POST PRODUCTION The Gamers II: Dorkness Rising
UPCOMING RELEASES Southland Tales
COMPLETED UNRELEASED Xombie (Animated)
CREDITS Dungeons & Dragons: The Elemental Might - Dungeons & Dragons: Wrath of the Dragon God

John Frank Rosenblum .Producer
Michael Zoumas .Producer
Cindi Rice .Producer

EPIDEMIC PICTURES & MANAGEMENT

1635 N. Cahuenga Blvd., 5th Fl.
Hollywood, CA 90028
PHONE .323-468-1800
FAX .323-468-1803
TYPES Features - Reality TV - TV Series
DEVELOPMENT 32 and Single - Slay the Bully - A Girl's Guide to Hunting and Fishing
PRE-PRODUCTION Cabrini Gardens
CREDITS King's Ransom - Go for Broke - Higher Ed - Thicker Than Water - Kitchen Privileges

Darryl Taja .Producer/Manager

EPIGRAM ENTERTAINMENT

13636 Ventura Blvd., #508
Sherman Oaks, CA 91423
PHONE .818-461-8937/914-325-2999
FAX .818-461-8919
EMAIL .flashforward@sbcglobal.net
TYPES Direct-to-Video/DVD - Features - Made-for-TV/Cable Movies - TV Series
POST PRODUCTION Love Comes to the Executioner
CREDITS Fools Rush In - Spy Hard - Heart of the Storm

Doug Draizin .Partner
Val McLeroy .Partner
Ellen Baskin .Producer/Development, West Coast
Ellen Feig .Producer/Development, East Coast
Paula Price .Assistant

EPIPHANY PICTURES, INC.
10625 Esther Ave.
Los Angeles, CA 90064
PHONE 310-815-1266/310-452-0242
FAX 310-815-1269/310-452-7542
EMAIL .....firstname@ephiphanypictures.com
SECOND EMAIL .....submissions@ephiphanypictures.com
WEB SITE .....www.epiphanypictures.com
SECOND WEB SITE .....www.roadkingsthemovie.com
TYPES Direct-to-Video/DVD - Documentaries - Features - Made-for-TV/Cable Movies - TV Series
DEVELOPMENT Blood, Gold and Sky - Behind the Lines - Mayor Daley: American Pharaoh - American Standard - Cigars, Cars (and Guitars) - Caveman Robot - Deep Creek - Candy War - On Your Toes
PRE-PRODUCTION Sweet Home Chicago - Everlasting
CREDITS Phenomenon: The Lost Archives (PBS) - Picture Windows (Showtime) - Rosemary - Road Kings (Lionsgate)
SUBMISSION POLICY Will supply release with script request; Email queries
COMMENTS Deal with Windy City Productions & Transformational Entertainment & Media

Scott JT Frank .....Producer/Director (scott@epiphanypictures.com)
Dan Halperin .....Producer/Director (310-452-0242, dan@epiphanypictures.com)
John Kennedy .....Director, Development
Carly Rose Jackson .....Development (carlyr@epiphanypictures.com)
Gene Grarut .....Reader
Chris Ann Jay .....Reader
Samson Kellman .....Reader
Cynthia Myron .....Reader
Bernadette Nath .....Reader
Shannon Russell .....Reader

EPITOME PICTURES, INC.
220 Bartley Dr.
Toronto, ON M4A 1G1, Canada
PHONE 416-752-7627
FAX 416-752-7837
EMAIL .....info@epitomepictures.com
WEB SITE .....www.epitomepictures.com
SECOND WEB SITE .....www.degrassi.tv
TYPES TV Series
DEVELOPMENT The Degrassi Feature
CREDITS Degrassi: The Next Generation - Degrassi Junior High - Degrassi High - Instant Star - Riverdale

Linda Schuyler .....CEO/Executive Producer
Stephen Stohn .....President/Executive Producer

STEFANIE EPSTEIN PRODUCTIONS
427 N. Canon Dr., Ste. 214
Beverly Hills, CA 90210
PHONE 310-385-0300
FAX 310-385-0302
EMAIL .....joeseprods@aol.com
TYPES Features - Made-for-TV/Cable Movies - TV Series
DEVELOPMENT Shore Leave - What Men Want Most - Postal Police - Babygate - Vanishing Act - The Russell Girl
CREDITS Audrey's Rain - Abduction of Innocence - A Boyfriend for Christmas (Hallmark) - Searching for David's Heart (ABC Family)

Stefanie Epstein .....Producer
Joseph Frankel .....Creative Executive

ESCAPE ARTISTS II
c/o Sony Pictures
10202 W. Washington Blvd., Astaire Bldg., 3rd Fl.
Culver City, CA 90232
PHONE 310-244-8833
FAX 310-244-2151
EMAIL .....firstname_lastname@spe.sony.com
TYPES Features - TV Series
HAS DEAL WITH Sony Pictures Entertainment
DEVELOPMENT Diary - Need - Nautica - Knowing - Chad Schmidt
POST PRODUCTION The Pursuit of Happyness
CREDITS The Weather Man - Antwone Fisher - A Knight's Tale - Alex and Emma

Steve Tisch .....Partner/Producer (310-244-6612)
Todd Black .....Partner/Producer (310-244-8683)
Jason Blumenthal .....Partner/Producer (310-244-8670)
David Bloomfield .....Executive VP, Business & Legal Affairs (310-244-6631)
Kim Skeeters .....VP, Administration & Finance (310-244-6619)
Lance Johnson .....Director, Development (310-244-5053)
Chris Coggins .....Creative Assistant (310-244-8659)
Lacy Boughn .....Assistant to Steve Tisch (310-244-6620)

ESPARZA-KATZ PRODUCTIONS
1201 W. 5th St.
Los Angeles, CA 90017
PHONE 213-534-3845
FAX 213-534-3846
TYPES Features - Made-for-TV/Cable Movies - TV Series
CREDITS Walkout - Gods and Generals - Avenging Angel - Selena - Gettysburg - Rough Riders - The Cisco Kid - The Milagro Beanfield War - The Disappearance of Garcia Lorca - Introducing Dorothy Dandridge
SUBMISSION POLICY No unsolicited submissions or phone calls

Moctesuma Esparza .....Producer
Robert Katz .....Producer
Luis Guerrero .....Executive Assistant

ESPERANTO FILMS
443 Greenwich St., 5th Fl.
New York, NY 10013
PHONE 212-219-7610
FAX 212-334-5478
TYPES Features
HAS DEAL WITH Warner Bros. Pictures
DEVELOPMENT Mexico 68 - The History of Love
POST PRODUCTION Pan's Labyrinth
CREDITS Crónicas - The Devil's Backbone - The Assassination of Richard Nixon - Temporada de Patos (Warner Independent)
SUBMISSION POLICY No unsolicited submissions

Alfonso Cuarón .....Producer
Frida Torresblanco .....President, Production
Carlos Cuarón .....Creative Executive
Juan Tovar .....Development Coordinator
Mandy Goldberg .....Development Executive/Production Coordinator

ESPN ORIGINAL ENTERTAINMENT (EOE)

ESPN Plaza
Bristol, CT 06010
PHONE 860-766-2000/212-916-9200
FAX 860-766-2415
EMAIL . . . . footage@espn.com
WEB SITE . . . . www.espn.com
SECOND WEB SITE . . . . www.abcsports.com

TYPES — Documentaries - Reality TV - TV Series
PROVIDES DEAL TO — Embassy Row LLC - Mango Tree Pictures - MRB Productions, Inc.
DEVELOPMENT — Once in a Lifetime: The Extraordinary Story of the New York Cosmos - Bonds on Bonds - Ruffian - The Bronx is Burning
CREDITS — Through the Fire (Documentary) - Teammates - Battle of the Gridiron Stars - ESPN Bowling Night - Timeless - It's the Shoes - All Muscle with Funkmaster Flex - Monster Shark Tournament - Tilt - I'd Do Anything - Hustle - ESPN New Year's Eve - 3 - Stump the Schwab - Playmakers - Pardon the Interruption - The Junction Boys - Dream Job - ESPYs - World Series of Poker - Streetball - A Season on the Brink - The Season - Around the Horn - Chopper Nation - Truck Stop - Import Racers - Bound for Glory - Full Ride - Knight School - Four Minutes - Quite Frankly with Stephen A. Smith - City Slam - 2 Live Stews - Free Agent - U.S. Paintball Championship - World Series of Darts
COMMENTS — Sports programming; Business offices: 605 Third Ave., 8th Fl., New York, NY 10158: Executive offices: 77 West 66th St., New York, NY 10023

George Bodenheimer . . . . President, ESPN, Inc. & ABC Sports/ Co-Chairman, Disney Media Networks
Ed Erhardt . . . . President, ESPN/ABC Sports Customer Marketing & Sales
Ben Pyne . . . . President, Disney & ESPN Networks Affiliate Sales & Marketing
Steve Anderson . . . . Executive VP, Production & Technical Operations
Christine Driessen . . . . Executive VP/CFO
Ed Durso . . . . Executive VP, Administration
Chuck Gerber . . . . Executive VP, Collegiate Sports
Salil Mehta . . . . Executive VP, ESPN Enterprises
Chuck Pagano . . . . Executive VP, Technology
John Skipper . . . . Executive VP, Content
John Walsh . . . . Executive VP/Executive Editor
Norby Williamson . . . . Executive VP, Studio & Remote Productions
Russell Wolff . . . . Executive VP/Managing Director, ESPN International
Rick Alessandri . . . . Sr. VP, Consumer Products
Len DeLuca . . . . Sr. VP, Programming Acquisitions
Jed Drake . . . . Sr. VP/Executive Producer, Remote Producer
Bob Eaton . . . . Sr. VP/Managing Editor, Studio Production
Rosa Gatti . . . . Sr. VP, Communications & Corporate Outreach
Manish Jha . . . . Sr. VP/General Manager, Emerging Media & Data Services
John Kosner . . . . Sr. VP, ESPN New Media
Chris LaPlaca . . . . Sr. VP, Communications
Jodi Markley . . . . Sr. VP, International Production, ESPN Classic & ESPNEWS
John Papanek . . . . Sr. VP/Editorial Director
Geoff Reiss . . . . Sr. VP, EOE Programming
Ron Semiao . . . . Sr. VP, ESPN Original Entertainment
John Wildhack . . . . Sr. VP, Programming Acquisitions & Strategy
Joan Lynch . . . . Executive Producer, ESPN Original Entertainment
Dan Weinberg . . . . Executive Producer, Media Packaging
Brian Robinson . . . . VP, Development, ESPN Original Entertainment
Ron Wechsler . . . . VP, Development, ESPN Original Entertainment
John Zehr . . . . VP, Product Development, ESPN Mobile

ETERNITY PICTURES, INC.

7421 Beverly Blvd., Ste. 9
Los Angeles, CA 90036
PHONE 323-932-9939
FAX 323-932-9949
EMAIL . . . . production@eternitypictures.com

TYPES — Features
DEVELOPMENT — The Courier - Sinners
CREDITS — Jeepers Creepers - Deuces Wild - The Contender - If You Only Knew - Afterglow - Cookie's Fortune - Laws of Deception - Shaded Places - Detour - The Virgin Suicides - Partners - Enemies of Laughter

Willi E. Baer . . . . Producer
Carmen M. Miller . . . . Producer
Zana Fong . . . . Assistant to Ms. Miller & Mr. Baer

EUPHORIA ENTERTAINMENT

1505 Fourth St., Ste. 220
Santa Monica, CA 90401
PHONE 310-576-7500
FAX 310-576-7501
EMAIL . . . . euphoriafilm@aol.com

TYPES — Animation - Documentaries - Features - Made-for-TV/Cable Movies - Miniseries - Reality TV - TV Series
DEVELOPMENT — Our House (TNT/Johnson & Johnson) - The Trade - Golden Gate - John Doe - Blood Dreams - The Man Who Saved the World
COMMENTS — News and information programming

Gary Kessler . . . . Producer/Writer
Herman Miller . . . . Development

EUROPACORP FILMS

137 Rue du Faubourg, St. Honore
Paris 75008, France
PHONE 33-153-830303
FAX 33-153-830340

TYPES — Animation - Features
DEVELOPMENT — Arthur and the Minimoys
POST PRODUCTION — Bandidas - The Secret - Love and Other Disasters
CREDITS — The Transporter - Wasabi - The Messenger: The Story of Joan of Arc - The Fifth Element - La Femme Nikita - Kiss of the Dragon - The Dancer

Luc Besson . . . . Producer/Director
Virginie Silla . . . . Producer

THE ROBERT EVANS COMPANY

c/o Paramount Studios
5555 Melrose Ave., Lubitsch Bldg., Ste. 117
Los Angeles, CA 90038-3197
PHONE 323-956-8800
FAX 323-862-0070

TYPES — Direct-to-Video/DVD - Features - TV Series
HAS DEAL WITH — Paramount Pictures
DEVELOPMENT — Stan Lee's Foreverman - Stranger at the Palazzo - The Myth - Nice Girls Don't Get the Corner Office - Mailman - Triggerfish - Wedding Season - Cain & Able - Don Juan Con - Love Is...
CREDITS — Kid Notorious - Chinatown - The Saint - The Godfather - How to Lose a Guy in 10 Days

Robert Evans . . . . Chairman
Alicia Allain . . . . President

EVERGREEN FILMS, LLC
1515 Palisades Dr., Ste. N
Pacific Palisades, CA 90272
PHONE .310-573-9978
FAX .310-573-1137
EMAIL .fran@evergreenfilms.com
WEB SITE .www.evergreenfilms.com
TYPES Animation - Commercials - Documentaries - TV Series
PRODUCTION Faces of Earth
CREDITS Red Flag: Thunder at Nell's - Alien Planet - Science of Star Wars - When Dinos Roamed America - Before We Ruled the Earth - International Space Station - Weather X - Dinosaur Planet (Discovery)

Pierre de Lespinois .Director
Fran LoCascio .Executive Producer
John Copeland .Producer
Peter Crabbe .Writer

EVERYMAN PICTURES
3000 W. Olympic Blvd., Ste. 1500
Santa Monica, CA 90404
PHONE .310-264-4211
FAX .310-264-4212
TYPES Features - Reality TV - TV Series
HAS DEAL WITH Universal Pictures
DEVELOPMENT Elling - Utopia Street - Niagara - Used Guys - Smother - The Party - My Out-Sourced Life
CREDITS The Hitchhiker's Guide to the Galaxy - Meet the Fockers - Fifty First Dates - Mystery, Alaska - Meet the Parents - Austin Powers 1-3 - American Candidate (Showtime)
SUBMISSION POLICY No unsolicited material

Jay Roach .Chairman/CEO
Jennifer Perini .President
Carrye Gilliland .Creative Executive
Rheanna Bates .Story Editor
Zeynep Coskan .Development Assistant
Christopher Godfrey .Assistant to Jay Roach
Erica Graham .Assistant to Jennifer Perini

EVOLUTION
3310 W. Vanowen St.
Burbank, CA 91505
PHONE .818-260-0300
FAX .818-260-1333
WEB SITE .www.evolutionusa.com
TYPES Direct-to-Video/DVD - Documentaries - Made-for-TV/Cable Movies - Reality TV - TV Series
PRODUCTION Movie Surfers (Disney Channel) - Yo Momma (MTV) - Adam Carolla Project (TLC) - That Ying Yang Thing (TLC) - Beach Patrol (Court TV) - Surprise Party (Bravo Pilot)
CREDITS He's a Lady (TBS) - Clean Sweep (TLC) - Boy Meets Boy (Bravo) - Fear Factor - Big Brother - Bug Juice (Disney Channel) - Gay Weddings (Bravo) - 10 Years Younger - Search for the World's Greatest Kid Magician (Disney Channel) - Bands Reunited (VH1) - Flab to Fab (VH1) - Switched (ABC Family)
SUBMISSION POLICY No unsolicited pitches
COMMENTS Promos

Douglas Ross .President
Greg Stewart .CFO
Kathleen French .Sr. VP, Production
Dean Minerd .Sr. VP
Bryan Hale .VP, Development
Alex Baskin .Manager, Development

EVOLUTION ENTERTAINMENT
901 N. Highland Ave.
Los Angeles, CA 90038
PHONE .323-850-3232
FAX .323-850-0521
TYPES Features - TV Series
POST PRODUCTION Saw 3 - Silence - Catacombs
CREDITS Bull Durham - Set It Off - John Q - The Sandlot - Love Don't Cost a Thing - Saw 1&2 - Two and a Half Men - Love Inc.
COMMENTS Twisted Pictures (Genre production division)

Mark Burg .Partner/Producer
Oren Koules .Partner/Producer
Carl Mazzocone .Head, Production
Troy Begnaud .Director, Development
Stephen Gates .Head, Literary
Evan Corday .Literary
Brad Kaplan .Literary
Stephen Marks .Literary
Chris Ridenhour .Literary
Andrew Wilson .Literary
Laina Cohn .Talent
Tiffany Kuzon .Talent
Scott Zimmerman .Talent
Chad Cole .Production
Justine Stevenson .Office Manager
Zach Brandler .Assistant
Emily Bugg .Assistant
Irma Esquibel .Assistant
Jared Ferrie .Assistant
Jason Mirch .Assistant
Oubansack Pouiphanvongxay .Assistant

EVOLVING PICTURES ENTERTAINMENT
3151 Cahuenga Blvd. West, Ste. 110
Hollywood, CA 90068
PHONE .323-850-3380
FAX .323-850-3395
EMAIL .evolvingpictures@yahoo.com
WEB SITE .www.evolvingpicturesentertainment.com
TYPES Animation - Direct-to-Video/DVD - Features - Reality TV - TV Series
DEVELOPMENT Mod Monster Pary - Necroscope - Sadako
COMPLETED UNRELEASED Detention - The Mechanik
CREDITS Mystery, Alaska - Gideon - Resurrection - Time Served - Spincycle - Where's Angelo?

Jeff Beltzner .President
Jean Pierre Pereat .VP
Jack Gilardi Jr. .No Title
Peter E. Jackson .No Title

EXILE ENTERTAINMENT
732 El Medio Ave.
Pacific Palisades, CA 90272
PHONE .310-573-1523
FAX .310-573-0109
EMAIL .exile_ent@yahoo.com
TYPES Documentaries - Features
DEVELOPMENT Mississippi Mud - Cowboy Cupid Mephisto's Bridge - The Fifth Woman - Steal a Pencil for Me - Freedom Nevada - Mountains of Madness - The Mentor
PRE-PRODUCTION Babylon A.D. (Fox)
UPCOMING RELEASES The Alibi
CREDITS Cowboy Del Amor - Modigliani - American Wake - Gothika - Blueberry
SUBMISSION POLICY Email only

Gary Ungar .Producer
Tyler Ruggeri .Assistant

EXXCELL ENTERTAINMENT, INC./EXXCELL FILMS

PO Box 1740
Ojai, CA 93024
PHONE .805-640-9430
FAX .805-640-6584
WEB SITE .www.exxcell.com
SECOND WEB SITE .www.dianeladd.com
TYPES Documentaries - Features - Made-for-TV/Cable Movies - Miniseries - TV Series
DEVELOPMENT Hot Water Biscuits - White on Rice - Last of the Bad Girls - Kicks - High Maintenance-Swordsman of Brooklyn - Chasing Roger Maris
PRE-PRODUCTION Two Rebels with a Cause - Woman Inside
POST PRODUCTION Whispers in the Wind (Documentary)
CREDITS Mrs. Munck
COMMENTS Offices in Austin, TX

Robert C. Hunter .Chairman/CEO
Diane Ladd .President/Actress/Director/Writer
C. Scott Alsop .Associate Producer
Fredrick A. Kleberg .Development Associate
Rita Claggett .Assistant to Diane Ladd
John McKnight .Assistant to Robert Hunter
Bonnie White .Personal Assistant

*EYE IN THE SKY ENTERTAINMENT

4204 Tracy St.
Los Angeles, CA 90027
PHONE .323-644-1709/323-387-0366
EMAIL .koornick@yahoo.com
TYPES Direct-to-Video/DVD - Documentaries - Features - Music Videos
DEVELOPMENT Over the Edge of the World - The Flyer Hold-Up - Untitled Philip K. Dick Biopic - All the Best Ones Are Taken - System Failure
PRODUCTION Next

Jason Koornick .Producer

EYE ON THE BALL FILMS, INC.

PO Box 46877
Los Angeles, CA 90046
PHONE .323-935-0634
EMAIL .keepyoureye@aol.com
WEB SITE .www.yareli.com
SECOND WEB SITE .www.sergioarau.com
TYPES Animation - Features - Music Videos
DEVELOPMENT Plan B
CREDITS A Day Without a Mexican - El Muro

Sergio Arau .Writer/Producer/Director/Musician
Yareli Arizmendi .Writer/Producer/Actress

EYEWORKS TOUCHDOWN

3000 W. Olympic Blvd., Ste. 1368
Santa Monica, CA 90404
PHONE .310-449-4095
FAX .310-449-4096
WEB SITE .www.touchdowntv.com
TYPES Reality TV
UPCOMING RELEASES The Ultimate Coyote Ugly Search (CMT)

Julie Christie .Executive Producer
Stacey Schuman .Line Producer

FACE PRODUCTIONS/JENNILIND PRODUCTIONS

335 N. Maple Dr., Ste. 175
Beverly Hills, CA 90210
PHONE .310-205-2746
FAX .310-285-2386
TYPES Documentaries - Features - Made-for-TV/Cable Movies - Miniseries - TV Series
HAS DEAL WITH HBO Entertainment
DEVELOPMENT Apres Vous (Warner Bros.) - Have a Nice Day (New Line)
CREDITS Analyze That - America's Sweethearts - 61* - Forget Paris - Analyze This - Mr. Saturday Night - City Slickers 1&2 - My Giant
SUBMISSION POLICY No unsolicited submissions

Billy Crystal .Actor/Writer/Director
Cheryl Bloch .Sr. VP, Development, TV (310-888-3588)
Samantha Sprecher .VP, Development, Features (310-285-2375)
Liz Goumas .Development Assistant (310-205-2746)
Carol Sidlow .Assistant to Mr. Crystal

FADE IN FILMS

287 S. Robertson Blvd., Ste. 467
Beverly Hills, CA 90211
PHONE .310-275-0287
EMAIL .inquiries@fadeinonline.com
WEB SITE .www.fadeinonline.com
TYPES Features
PRODUCTION An American Crime - Untitled Frank Baldwin Project
CREDITS Clay Pigeons
COMMENTS A division of Fade In Publishing Group, Inc.

Audrey Kelly .President/Producer
Heather Millerton .No Title

FAIR DINKUM PRODUCTIONS

PO Box 49914
Los Angeles, CA 90049
PHONE .310-260-2122
TYPES Features - TV Series

Henry Winkler .Actor/Executive Producer/Director

FALLOUT

3100 Airport Ave.
Santa Monica, CA 90405
PHONE .310-572-6027
FAX .310-572-6029
EMAIL .fofilms@aol.com
WEB SITE .www.falloutent.com
TYPES Commercials - Features - Music Videos - TV Series
DEVELOPMENT For the Love of Joey - Diamond Salvation
CREDITS Tapeheads - Car 54, Where Are You? - Posse - Desperate But Not Serious - My Dinner With Jimi

Bill Fishman .Chairman
Sundae .Executive Producer
Jim Fishman .Writer/Producer

FARRELL PAURA PRODUCTIONS, LLC
500 S. Buena Vista St., Animation Bldg., Ste. 2-C
Burbank, CA 91521-1700
PHONE 818-560-3000
FAX 818-560-4070
TYPES — Features - TV Series
HAS DEAL WITH — The Walt Disney Company
DEVELOPMENT — Film: Lust for Life (WDP) - Rescued (WDP) - Valentine's Day (WDP) - Infantile (MGM/Sony) - Playing It Straight (Sony); TV: Saints of Newport Beach (Touchstone)

Joseph Farrell ....CEO
Catherine Paura ....CEO
Barry Isaacson ....Executive VP, Production
Wayne Kline ....VP, Liaison Office of Production/Research
Palmer Emmitt ....Director, Development
Paul Jackson ....Executive Assistant
Eric Seppala ....Executive Assistant

FARRELL/MINOFF PRODUCTIONS
14011 Ventura Blvd., Ste. 401
Sherman Oaks, CA 91423
PHONE 818-789-5766
FAX 818-789-7459
TYPES — Direct-to-Video/DVD - Documentaries - Features - Made-for-TV/Cable Movies - TV Series
DEVELOPMENT — The Wrong Man - Terri: The Truth
CREDITS — Dominick & Eugene - Sins of the Mind - Patch Adams

Mike Farrell ....Actor/Producer/Director
Marvin Minoff ....Producer

THE PHIL FEHRLE COMPANY
16857 Escalon Dr.
Encino, CA 91436
PHONE 818-981-6553
TYPES — Features - Made-for-TV/Cable Movies
DEVELOPMENT — Short Ends - Date Expectations - Baker's Dozen
PRE-PRODUCTION — Parachute Lies
CREDITS — Thomas and the Magic Railroad - The Secret of Roan Inish - The Whipping Boy - Curaçao - The Little Kidnappers - Thomas and Friends (Children's Series) - Jack and the Pack (Children's Series)
SUBMISSION POLICY — Accepted only after telephone inquiry; All submissions must be accompanied by standard release form
COMMENTS — Smart, character-based specialty films for the independent market; No tent-pole movies

Jim Ferhrle ....Executive Producer/CEO
Phil Fehrle ....Producer
Marieke Fehrle ....Associate Producer

THE FELDMAN COMPANY
c/o The Lot
1041 N. Formosa Ave., Writers Bldg., Rm. 315
West Hollywood, CA 90046
PHONE 323-850-2503
FAX 323-850-2506
WEB SITE ....www.thefeldmancompany.com
TYPES — Features - Made-for-TV/Cable Movies - TV Series
DEVELOPMENT — Karski: How One Man Tried to Stop the Holocaust - Cookie - The Temps - Plane Insanity
COMPLETED UNRELEASED — Moose Mating - Planet Parenthood
CREDITS — Trash
COMMENTS — Management

Todd Feldman ....Producer
Ann Reilly ....Assistant

EDWARD S. FELDMAN COMPANY
520 Evelyn Place
Beverly Hills, CA 90210
PHONE 310-246-1990
EMAIL ....esfeldco@aol.com
SECOND EMAIL ....winshipper@aol.com
TYPES — Features
DEVELOPMENT — East Side Story
CREDITS — K-19: The Widowmaker - 102 Dalmatians - The Truman Show - The Doctor - Witness - Green Card - Forever Young - 101 Dalmatians

Ed Feldman ....President/Producer
Winship Cook ....Producer

ZACHARY FEUER FILMS
c/o Maverick
9348 Civic Center Dr., 3rd Fl.
Beverly Hills, CA 90210
PHONE 310-729-2110
FAX 310-820-7535
TYPES — Features - Made-for-TV/Cable Movies - TV Series
DEVELOPMENT — Mort the Dead Teenager - Chicky Baby Sweets - A Penny Earned - All Ages Night - Nothing but Net - The Lost Painting - The Lightning Field
PRODUCTION — All Ages Night
CREDITS — All the Queen's Men - Texas Cheerleader Murdering Mom

Zachary Feuer ....Producer/President

ADAM FIELDS PRODUCTIONS
8899 Beverly Blvd., Ste. 821
West Hollywood, CA 90048
PHONE 310-859-9300
FAX 310-859-4795
TYPES — Features
DEVELOPMENT — Russ Meyer Project - Wanted: Dead or Alive - NY Dive - What a Man's Gotta Do - Josiah's Canon - The Retriever - Gumball - Fire & Rain
CREDITS — Donnie Darko - Brokedown Palace - Ravenous - Money Train - Great Balls of Fire - Johnny Be Good - Vision Quest - Whoopee Boys

Adam Fields ....President
Robert Gonzalez ....Creative Executive

FIERCE ENTERTAINMENT, LLC

8306 Wilshire Blvd., #904
Beverly Hills, CA 90211
PHONE .310-860-1174
FAX .310-860-9446/310-362-8643
EMAIL .info@fierce-entertainment.com
WEB SITE .www.fierce-entertainment.com
TYPES Direct-to-Video/DVD - Documentaries - Features - Made-for-TV/Cable Movies - Miniseries - Reality TV - TV Series
PRODUCTION Hip Hop Revolution
POST PRODUCTION Rogue
CREDITS American Soldiers - Shadows in the Sun - Marvel's Man-Thing (Sci Fi) - To Kill a King - Carolina

Christopher Petzel .CEO
Steve Emmerson .Coordinator, Acquisitions

FIFTY CANNON ENTERTAINMENT, LLC

c/o ICM
8942 Wilshire Blvd.
Beverly Hills, CA 90211
PHONE .310-550-4000
FAX .310-550-4100
TYPES Features - TV Series
CREDITS Traffic - Huff
COMMENTS UK office: Oxford House, 76 Oxford St., London W1D 1BS, United Kingdom

Mike Newell .Chairman
Cameron Jones .President
William Butler-Sloss .VP
Esther Douglas .Head, Development & Production (UK)
Alex Hayes .Story Editor

FILBERT STEPS PRODUCTIONS

9 Desbrosses St., 2nd Fl.
New York, NY 10013
PHONE .212-246-2301
FAX .212-246-2285
EMAIL .info@filbertsteps.com
WEB SITE .www.filbertsteps.com
TYPES Features
DEVELOPMENT Scorpions in a Bottle - Down the Dirt Road - Murdering Michael Malloy - The Disappearance of Daniel Klein
CREDITS Runaway - Two Family House - Forever Fabulous

Alan Klingenstein .No Title
David Viola .No Title
Robb Badlam .No Title
Jessica Scott .No Title

FILM & MUSIC ENTERTAINMENT, LTD. (F&ME)

25 Noel St.
London W1F 7DE, United Kingdom
PHONE .44-207-434-6607
FAX .44-207-434-6673
EMAIL .info@fame.uk.com
WEB SITE .www.fame.uk.com
TYPES Features
DEVELOPMENT Cassandra at the Wedding - White Lightnin' - Killer on the Road - Reykjavik Whale Watching Massacre - A Gathering of Foes - Whodunnit - Victim of the Aurora
PRE-PRODUCTION Rent Boy!
PRODUCTION Bathory by Juraj - Dark Side of the Earth - Quest for a Heart
POST PRODUCTION Mystery of the Wolf
COMPLETED UNRELEASED Anastezsi - Son of Man
CREDITS Loving Glances - Cold Light - Niceland - Strings - Guy X - The Headsman - Eleven Men Out - Call of the Toad - Murk - My Brother Is a Dog - Deathwatch - Under the Stars - Falcons - Border Post
SUBMISSION POLICY No unsolicited scripts

Mike Downey .Producer/Managing Director
Zorana Piggott .Producer/Head, Production
Sam Taylor .Producer/Head, Production
Hannah Longbottom .Coordinator

FILM 44

12233 W. Olympic Blvd., Ste. 352
Los Angeles, CA 90064
PHONE .310-689-2929
FAX .310-689-2928
TYPES Features - TV Series
HAS DEAL WITH Universal Pictures
DEVELOPMENT Film: Truck 44 - Bran Mak Morn - The Mission - Absent Hearts - The Losers; TV: Trap Team
PRE-PRODUCTION Lars and the Real Girl - The Kingdom
UPCOMING RELEASES PU-239
CREDITS Film: Friday Night Lights - Very Bad Things - The Rundown - Bad Santa - The Ladykillers - Intolerable Cruelty; TV: Friday Night Lights - Wonderland
SUBMISSION POLICY Via Endeavor Agency

Peter Berg .Partner
John Cameron .Partner
Sarah Aubrey .Partner
Maria Williams .Director, Development
Justin Levy .VP, Television
Polly Auritt .Assistant to Peter Berg
Braden Aftergood .Assistant to John Cameron & Sarah Aubrey

FILM BRIDGE INTERNATIONAL
1316 Third Street Promenade, Ste. 105
Santa Monica, CA 90401
PHONE .310-656-8680
FAX .310-656-8683
EMAIL .contact@filmbridgeinternational.com
WEB SITE .www.filmbridgeinternational.com
TYPES Features - Made-for-TV/Cable Movies
DEVELOPMENT Disaster at Sea
PRE-PRODUCTION Deadly Exchange - Angel Makers - Beast of Bataan - Freezer Burn
CREDITS Lying in Wait - Beyond the Summit - Splitsville - Velocity of Gary - Say Nothing - Big Spender
SUBMISSION POLICY No unsolicited material

Ellen S. Wander .No Title
Lori Mathison .No Title
Amanda Seward .No Title

FILM CRASH
1433 Yale St., Ste. D
Santa Monica, CA 90404
PHONE .310-315-1821
WEB SITE .www.filmcrash.com
TYPES Features - TV Series
POST PRODUCTION My Little Hollywood (Feature)
COMPLETED UNRELEASED The Deep and Dreamless Sleep (Feature)
CREDITS Thanatos and Eros: A Monster Love Story - The Technical Writer - Kicked in the Head (Universal) - The Headhunter's Sister - Rhythm Thief - The Lost Words - Spare Me - Sex and the City (HBO) - Popular (Disney) - Dead Last (Warner Bros.)
SUBMISSION POLICY Not accepting submissions at this time
COMMENTS New York office: 336 West End Ave., Ste. 16F, New York, NY 10023

Matthew Harrison .Partner
Karl Nussbaum .Partner
Scott Saunders .Partner
Daniel Blumberg .Producer

*THE FILM DEPARTMENT
4000 Warner Blvd., Bldg. 66
Burbank, CA 91522
PHONE .818-954-4015
FAX .818-954-4284
TYPES Features
HAS DEAL WITH Warner Bros. Pictures

Mark Gill .Producer
Amanda Coplan .Development Executive
Allison Rayne .Development Executive

FILM FARM
3204 Pearl St.
Santa Monica, CA 90405
PHONE .310-450-5838
TYPES Features - TV Series
DEVELOPMENT Picasso at the Lapin Agile - Naked High - Out of Gas - The Saints and Sinners of Okay County - The Bra
PRE-PRODUCTION Nim's Island - Tangerine
CREDITS The Vagina Monologues - Corrina, Corrina - The Search for Signs of Intelligent Life in the Universe - Traveller - Off the Lip - Prayer of the Roller Boys
SUBMISSION POLICY No unsolicited submissions

Paula Mazur .Writer/Producer
Robert Mickelson .Director/Producer
Eric Rogge .Assistant to Paula Mazur

FILM GARDEN ENTERTAINMENT, INC.
6727 Odessa Ave.
Van Nuys, CA 91406
PHONE .818-783-3456
FAX .818-752-8186
WEB SITE .www.filmgarden.tv
TYPES Documentaries - Reality TV - Specials - TV Series
PRE-PRODUCTION Fantasy Weddings
POST PRODUCTION The Message
CREDITS Secret World Of - Crash Test - Body Challenge Hollywood - A Wedding Story - Murder Reopened - Women in Blue - Wild on the Set - Discovery Health Body Challenge - Two for Las Vegas - Ultimate Ten - Mysteries of Mating - Total Zoo - Adoption Stories - Tailgate Party - Calorie Commando - Your Reality Checked - Taste of America - Insider's List - Popularity Contest

Nancy Jacobs Miller .President/Executive Producer
Michelle Van Kempen .Executive VP/Executive Producer
Amanda Crane .Co-Executive Producer
Craig Golin .Executive in Charge of Production
Toni Gray .Director, Operations

FILM ROMAN, INC.
2950 N. Hollywood Way, 3rd Fl.
Burbank, CA 91505
PHONE .818-748-4000
FAX .818-748-4613
WEB SITE .www.filmroman.com
TYPES Animation - Commercials - Direct-to-Video/DVD - Features - Internet Content - Made-for-TV/Cable Movies - Miniseries - Mobile Content - Music Videos - Specials - TV Series
DEVELOPMENT The Mask Reanimated - Ty the Tasmanian Tiger
PRODUCTION Stan Lee Presents: Condor - Stan Lee Presents: Mosaic - Stan Lee Presents: Ringo Starr - Harry Connick Jr.'s The Happy Elf - Rob Zombie's El Superbeasto - Me, Eloise - Wow! Wow! Wubzy! - Spawn - Hellboy
CREDITS The Simpsons - King of the Hill - Johnny Tsunami - Mission Hill - The Oblongs - X-Men - Family Guy - Free for All - Tripping the Rift
SUBMISSION POLICY See Web site
COMMENTS An IDT Entertainment company; Visual effects; Internet/Web development

John W. Hyde .CEO
Scott Greenberg .COO/President
Mike Wolf .Sr. VP, Production Animation
Sidney Clifton .Executive VP, Creative Development
Kevin Van Hook .VP/General Manager, Forum Visual Effects
Carin Davis .VP, Business Development/Visual Effects & Commercials

FILMCOLONY
465 S. Sycamore Ave.
Los Angeles, CA 90036
PHONE .323-933-4670
FAX .323-933-4674
TYPES Features - Made-for-TV/Cable Movies
DEVELOPMENT The Fourth Hand - Solomon Grundy - Mr. Vertigo - Paper Man - The Words
PRODUCTION The Nanny Diaries - Mr. Magorium's Wonder Emporium
POST PRODUCTION Killshot - Journey to the End of the Night
CREDITS Finding Neverland - Levity - The Bourne Identity - The Cider House Rules - She's All That - Hurlyburly - Jackie Brown - Pulp Fiction - Reservoir Dogs

Richard N. Gladstein .President/Producer

FILMENGINE
9220 Sunset Blvd., Ste. 301
West Hollywood, CA 90069
PHONE .310-205-9500
FAX .310-205-9580
TYPES Direct-to-Video/DVD - Features - TV Series
DEVELOPMENT Untitled Joe Carnahan/Will Wright Project - The Butterfly Effect (TV) - Wish You Were Here - The Rum Diary - The Whale Hunter - The Other Side of Simple
PRE-PRODUCTION Seasons of Dust
POST PRODUCTION The Butterfly Effect 2
COMPLETED UNRELEASED The Cleaner
CREDITS Lucky Number Slevin - The Butterfly Effect - O - Cheaters - The Real Cancun - Raise Your Voice

Anthony Rhulen .No Title
A.J. Dix .No Title
Rich Stirling .No Title
Mike Stirling .No Title

FILMFOUR
124 Horseferry Rd.
London SW1P 2TX, United Kingdom
PHONE .44-207-306-5190/44-207-306-5515
FAX .44-207-306-8369/44-207-306-8368
TYPES Features
DEVELOPMENT On Beauty
CREDITS Touching the Void - Once Upon a Time in the Midlands - Dead Man's Shoes - The Motorcycle Diaries - Enduring Love - The League of Gentleman's Apocalypse - Me and You and Everyone We Know

Peter Carlton .Executive
Tess Ross .Head, FilmFour & Drama

FILMS BY JOVE
23852 Pacific Coast Hwy., Ste. 308
Malibu, CA 90265
PHONE .310-589-2496
FAX .310-589-2407
EMAIL .filmsbyjove@earthlink.net
WEB SITE .www.russiananimation.com
TYPES Animation - Features - TV Series
CREDITS Cheburashka - Animated Soviet Propaganda - Mikhail Baryshnikov's Stories from My Childhood - The Jungle Book - Fairy Tales from Faroff Lands: The Animated Classic Showcase
SUBMISSION POLICY No submissions
COMMENTS Distribution

Joan Borsten .Principal
Oleg Vidov .Principal
Sergei Vidov .Sales

FILMSMITH
707 Strand St., Ste. 5
Santa Monica, CA 90405
PHONE .310-260-8866
FAX .310-392-0828
EMAIL .filmsmith@mac.com
TYPES Features
PRODUCTION E.L. Doctoro's Jolene
CREDITS Mrs. Palfrey at the Claremont - Drum - One Point 0 - Welcome to Hollywood - The Price of Air - Wildflowers - Sleep Easy, Hutch Rimes - Glam - French Exit - Birds of Prey

Zachary Matz .Producer

FILMSTREET, INC.
8306 Wilshire Blvd., Ste. 331
Beverly Hills, CA 90211
PHONE .323-935-5707
EMAIL .filmstreetinc@yahoo.com
TYPES Direct-to-Video/DVD - Features - Made-for-TV/Cable Movies - Reality TV - TV Series
DEVELOPMENT Face the Music - Fish & Chips
CREDITS Midnight Witness - Conversations in Limbo
SUBMISSION POLICY No unsolicited submissions

Peter Foldy .Writer/Producer/Director
Palmerston Hughes .Creative Assistant

FINE LIVING
9721 Sherrill Blvd.
Knoxville, TN 37932
PHONE .865-694-2700
FAX .865-342-3483
WEB SITE .www.fineliving.com
TYPES TV Series
DEVELOPMENT America: Toast to Toast
PRODUCTION Windshield America - Mixer - Healthy Half Hour - Zero to Hero
CREDITS Wandering Golfer - Thirsty Traveler - Opening Soon - Born American - Best for Less - Fantasy Camp - 10 Perfect Summer Getaways - Simply Wine with Andrea Immer - Radical Sabbatical - Genuine Article - The Great Adventure
COMMENTS Original lifestyle programming

Chad Youngblood .General Manager
Robyn Ulrich .Sr. VP, Marketing, Emerging Networks
Kent Takano .VP, Programming & Production
Gary McCormick .Director, Public Relations

WENDY FINERMAN PRODUCTIONS
10202 W. Washington Blvd.
Culver City, CA 90232
PHONE 310-244-8800
FAX 310-244-8488
TYPES Features - Made-for-TV/Cable Movies
HAS DEAL WITH Sony Pictures Entertainment
DEVELOPMENT Everything Changes - One for the Money - P.S. I Love You
POST PRODUCTION Devil Wears Prada
UPCOMING RELEASES Surrender, Dorothy
CREDITS FairyTale: A True Story - Stepmom - Forrest Gump - The Fan - Sugar & Spice - Drumline

Wendy Finerman . . . . . Producer
Lisa Zupan . . . . . VP (310-244-8144)

FIREBRAND PRODUCTIONS
1524 Riverside Dr.
Burbank, CA 91506
PHONE 818-955-5711
FAX 818-955-5158
TYPES Features - Made-for-TV/Cable Movies - TV Series
DEVELOPMENT Out of the Rough
CREDITS The Good Old Boys - A Slight Case of Murder - Four Eyes & Six Guns - The New Adventures of Spin and Marty: Suspect Behavior - Just Ask My Children

Salli Newman . . . . . Producer
Gina DeMasters . . . . . Assistant to Ms. Newman

FIRM FILMS
9465 Wilshire Blvd., 6th Fl.
Beverly Hills, CA 90212
PHONE 310-860-8000
FAX 310-860-8100
TYPES Animation - Documentaries - Features - Reality TV - TV Series
HAS DEAL WITH Twentieth Century Fox
DEVELOPMENT Vandal - Hell House Outreach - The Runaway - First Sunday - Max Payne - Alice - Trespasser - Bombing Harvey - The Lies of Locke Lamora - Bachelor Boys - X-Girls
COMPLETED UNRELEASED Come Early Morning
CREDITS After the Sunset - The Exorcism of Emily Rose

Julie Yorn . . . . . Head, Film & TV Production
Marc Gordon . . . . . Head, Development

FIRM TELEVISION
9465 Wilshire Blvd., 6th Fl.
Beverly Hills, CA 90212
PHONE 310-860-8000
FAX 310-860-8126
TYPES Documentaries - Made-for-TV/Cable Movies - Miniseries - Reality TV - TV Series
DEVELOPMENT Turf (USA) - Sheriff Luke (ABC) - The Bounty (A&E)
PRODUCTION Comanche Moon (CBS)
CREDITS Campus Confidential (ABC Family) - Criss Angel Mindfreak (A&E) - Freddie (ABC)
COMMENTS A division of Firm Films

Paul Frank . . . . . Executive Producer/Head, Firm Television
Cheryl Mulingbayan . . . . . Manager, TV Development
Laurie Ferneau . . . . . Coordinator, TV Development

FIRST LOOK PICTURES
8000 Sunset Blvd., East PH
Los Angeles, CA 90046
PHONE 323-337-1000
FAX 323-337-1037
TYPES Features
PRODUCTION An American Crime
POST PRODUCTION Smiley Face
COMPLETED UNRELEASED A Guide to Recognizing Your Saints
CREDITS The Proposition - Wassup Rockers - Underworld - Wicker Park - Madhouse
SUBMISSION POLICY No unsolicited material

Henry Winterstern . . . . . Chairman/CEO
Bill Lischak . . . . . President
Ruth Vitale . . . . . President, First Look Pictures
J. Beck . . . . . Head, Acquisitions/Production
Kevin Turen . . . . . Head, Production/Development
Richard Shore . . . . . Sr. VP, Business Affairs/Legal
Jonathan Christodoro . . . . . VP, Finance & Corporate Development

PRESTON STEPHEN FISCHER COMPANY
13078 Mindanao Way, PH 313
Marina del Rey, CA 90292
PHONE 310-578-9587
FAX 310-823-3548
EMAIL . . . . . psfco@aol.com
TYPES Made-for-TV/Cable Movies - Miniseries - TV Series
CREDITS Raines - Wildfire (ABC Family Pilot) - Talking to Heaven - Intensity - Las Vegas (Pilot) - War Stories - Countdown (Pilot) - World of Trouble (NBC Pilot)
COMMENTS Produces TV Pilots

Preston Fischer . . . . . Producer

FISHER PRODUCTIONS
269 S. Wilton Pl.
Los Angeles, CA 90004
PHONE 323-692-0991
FAX 323-692-0981
EMAIL . . . . . rickafilms@aol.com
TYPES Features - Made-for-TV/Cable Movies - Miniseries - Theatre - TV Series
CREDITS New Suit - Family Sins - Stepsister from the Planet Weird - Follow Your Heart - In Broad Daylight
SUBMISSION POLICY No unsolicited material

Ricka Fisher . . . . . Executive Producer

FIVE MILE RIVER FILMS, LTD.
104 Rowayton Ave., 2nd Fl.
Rowayton, CT 06853
PHONE 203-855-1141
FAX 203-855-7552
WEB SITE . . . . . www.fivemileriverfilms.com
TYPES Documentaries - Made-for-TV/Cable Movies - TV Series
DEVELOPMENT David
CREDITS Have No Fear: The Life of John Paul II (ABC) - Nicholas' Gift

Lorenzo Minoli . . . . . Producer
Alyssa Nollman . . . . . Office Manager

FIVE SISTERS PRODUCTIONS

171 Pier Ave., Ste. 207
Santa Monica, CA 90405
PHONE 310-712-5443
WEB SITE . . . . www.fivesistersproductions.com

TYPES	Commercials - Features - TV Series
DEVELOPMENT	Blackjack Boot Camp (Series)
POST PRODUCTION	The Happiest Day of His Life
CREDITS	Just Friends - Temps - Manna from Heaven
SUBMISSION POLICY	No submissions

Maria Burton . . . . Producer/Director
Jennifer Burton . . . . Producer/Writer
Ursula Burton . . . . Producer/Actor
Gabrielle C. Burton . . . . Producer/Director
Charity Burton . . . . Producer
Roger Burton . . . . Co-Producer
Gabrielle B. Burton . . . . Co-Producer/Writer

FLAME VENTURES LLC

1416 N. La Brea Ave.
Los Angeles, CA 90028
PHONE 323-802-1700
FAX 323-802-1709

TYPES	Animation - Direct-to-Video/DVD - Features - Internet Content - Made-for-TV/Cable Movies - Mobile Content - Reality TV - TV Series
PRE-PRODUCTION	The Believers - Unstable Fables
PRODUCTION	Sublime
UPCOMING RELEASES	Rest Stop
CREDITS	24 (FBC) - NASCAR Drivers: 360 (F/X) - Frankenstein - Rock Me Baby - Sports Night - The PJ's - Mulholland Drive - Felicity - Wonderland - The Beast - Bad Girl's Guide - South Beach (UPN) - The Gift (Sci Fi) - Yoga Now (Infomercial)
COMMENTS	Transactional television

Tony Krantz . . Chairman/CEO, Flame Television LLC & Flame Ventures LLC
Lowell Mate . . . . President, Flame Television LLC
Rita Safady . . . . Director, Flame Ventures LLC
Rebecca McGill . . . . Director, Creative Affairs, Flame Television LLC
Zack Sherman . . . . Manager, Creative Affairs, Flame Ventures LLC
Cory Calhoun . . . . Assistant to Tony Krantz
Reece Pearson . . . . Assistant to Lowell Mate

FLASHPOINT ENTERTAINMENT

1318 San Ysidro Dr.
Beverly Hills, CA 90210
PHONE 310-205-6300

TYPES	Features - TV Series
DEVELOPMENT	Huntington
PRE-PRODUCTION	The Bourne Ultimatum
PRODUCTION	Fan - Demania
CREDITS	The Bourne Identity - The Bourne Supremacy
SUBMISSION POLICY	No unsolicited material

Andrew R. Tennenbaum . . . . Producer

FLAVOR UNIT ENTERTAINMENT

155 Morgan St.
Jersey City, NJ 07302
PHONE 201-333-4883
FAX 201-333-0728

TYPES	Features
HAS DEAL WITH	Focus Features/Rogue Pictures
DEVELOPMENT	Welfare Queen
CREDITS	Beauty Shop - The Cookout - Bringing Down the House - Queen Latifah Show

Sha-Kim Compere . . . . CEO
Queen Latifah . . . . CEO
Sandy Tate . . . . Executive Assistant to Sha-Kim Compere

FLORENTINE FILMS

59 Maple Grove Rd., PO Box 613
Walpole, NH 03608
PHONE 603-756-3038
FAX 603-756-4389
WEB SITE . . . . www.florentinefilms.com

TYPES	Documentaries
PRODUCTION	America's Best Idea: Our National Parks
POST PRODUCTION	The War
CREDITS	Thomas Jefferson - Lewis and Clark - Baseball - The Civil War - Jazz - Mark Twain - The Shakers: Hands to Work, Hearts to God - Empire of the Air: The Men Who Made Radio - Huey Long - Unforgivable Blackness: The Rise and Fall of Jack Johnson

Ken Burns . . . . President/Producer/Director
Lynn Novick . . . . Producer
Paul Barnes . . . . Producer/Supervising Film Editor
Dayton Duncan . . . . Producer/Writer
Geoffrey C. Ward . . . . Writer
Erik Ewers . . . . Editor
Craig Mellish . . . . Editor/Field Producer
Sarah Botstein . . . . Co-Producer
Aileen Silverstone . . . . Associate Producer
Susanna Steisel . . . . Associate Producer
Pam Baucom . . . . Coordinating Producer

FLOWER FILMS, INC.

4000 Warner Blvd., Bungalow 3
Burbank, CA 91522
PHONE 818-954-5840
FAX 818-954-5830

TYPES	Features
HAS DEAL WITH	Warner Bros. Pictures
DEVELOPMENT	He's Just Not That Into You - He Loves Me
PRODUCTION	Music and Lyrics By
CREDITS	Fever Pitch - Fifty First Dates - Charlie's Angels: Full Throttle - Duplex - Never Been Kissed - Charlie's Angels - Olive, the Other Reindeer - Donnie Darko
SUBMISSION POLICY	By agent or manager only

Drew Barrymore . . . . Partner
Nancy Juvonen . . . . Partner
Chris Miller . . . . VP, Production
Gwenn Stroman . . . . VP, Development
Ember Truesdell . . . . Development

FLYING A STUDIOS, INC.

28537 Conejo View Dr.
Agoura Hills, CA 91301
PHONE 818-706-3456
FAX 818-706-3416
EMAIL . . . . dave@flyingastudios.com
SECOND EMAIL . . . . kathy@flyingastudios.com
WEB SITE . . . . www.flyingastudios.com

TYPES	Direct-to-Video/DVD - Features - Made-for-TV/Cable Movies - TV Series
DEVELOPMENT	Destination West - Untarnished Valor - The Little Lady in Pants - Blood Brew
PRE-PRODUCTION	Witness in the Shadows
COMPLETED UNRELEASED	My Friends Call Me Moose (Direct-to-Video/DVD)
CREDITS	Frequent Flyer

Dave Berthiaume . . . . President (818-519-0705)
Kathy Leitch . . . . VP, Development
James Talbott . . . . VP, Business Affairs (310-980-4690)

FOCUS FEATURES

FOCUS FEATURES/ROGUE PICTURES

A Division of Universal Pictures
100 Universal City Plaza
Universal City, CA 91608

PHONE . . . 818-777-1000/212-539-4000
WEB SITE . . . www.focusfeatures.com
SECOND WEB SITE . . . www.roguepictures.com

TYPES	Direct-to-Video/DVD - Features
PROVIDES DEAL TO	Completion Films - Deacon Entertainment - Flavor Unit Entertainment - Intrepid Pictures - Primary Productions - Random House Films - Vertigo Entertainment
DEVELOPMENT	Rogue: Driver - Balls of Fury; Focus: The Husband - Curveball - The Attack - Julia Project - Eastern Promises - Lust, Caution
UPCOMING RELEASES	Focus: Something New - On a Clear Day
CREDITS	Focus: Scoop - The Constant Gardener - Broken Flowers - Vanity Fair - The Motorcyle Diaries - Eternal Sunshine of the Spotless Mind - Ned Kelly - Sylvia - Swimming Pool - Lost in Translation - 8 Women - Far from Heaven - The Pianist - The Guys - The Shape of Things - 21 Grams - The Door in the Floor - Brick; Rogue: Seed of Chucky - Assault on Precinct 13 - Shaun of the Dead - Unleashed - Dave Chappelle's Block Party
SUBMISSION POLICY	Unsolicited submissions not accepted
COMMENTS	East Coast office: 65 Bleecker St., 3rd Fl., New York, NY 10012

James Schamus . . . CEO
Andrew Karpen . . . President, Focus Features/Co-President, Rogue Pictures
Andrew Rona . . . Co-President, Rogue Pictures
John Lyons . . . President, Production, Focus Features
David Brooks . . . President, Marketing
Alison Thompson . . . President, International Sales & Distribution (London)
Jack Foley . . . President, Theatrical Distribution
Adriene Bowles . . . Executive VP, Publicity & Marketing
Linda Ditrinco . . . Executive VP, Sales
Avy Eschenasy . . . Executive VP, Strategic Planning, Business Affairs & Acquisitions
Steve Flynn . . . Executive VP, Marketing
Jonathan King . . . Executive VP, Production
Adrienne Biddle . . . Sr. VP, Production
Donna Dickman . . . Sr. VP, Publicity
Jane Evans . . . Sr. VP, Physical Production
Howard Meyers . . . Sr. VP, Business Affairs
Teresa Moneo . . . Sr. VP, European Production
Jill Morris . . . Sr. VP, Production
Heta Paarte . . . Sr. VP, International Marketing & Publicity
Jason Resnick . . . Sr. VP, Acquisitions
Kahli Small . . . Sr. VP, Production
Tim Spencer . . . Sr. VP, International Sales
Gordon Ampel . . . VP, Operations
Susan Anderson . . . VP, Finance
Myles Bender . . . VP, Creative Advertising
David Bloch . . . VP, Advertising
Eric Carr . . . VP, Exhibitor Marketing
Timothy Collins . . . VP, Business Affairs
Jim Donlon . . . VP, Western Division Sales
Blair Green . . . VP, Creative Advertising
Deette Kearns . . . VP, Publicity
Peter Kujawski . . . VP, International Sales
Paulette Osorio . . . VP, Publicity
Jeffrey Roth . . . VP, Post Production
Rob Wilkinson . . . VP, Research
V.J. Carbone . . . Director, National Publicity (NY)
David Gerson . . . Creative Executive (Focus)
Paul Getto . . . Creative Executive (Rogue)
Harlan Gulko . . . Director, National Publicity (LA)
Alex Heineman . . . Creative Executive (Rogue)
Nicole Quenqua . . . Sr. Publicist

FOOD NETWORK

75 Ninth Ave.
New York, NY 10011

PHONE . . . 212-398-8836
FAX . . . 212-997-0997
EMAIL . . . msmith@foodnetwork.com
WEB SITE . . . www.foodnetwork.com

TYPES	Reality TV - TV Series
PROVIDES DEAL TO	Weller/Grossman Productions
UPCOMING RELEASES	Throwdown with Bobby Flay - Two for the Road - Nigella Feasts - Paula's Cooking Party - Healthy Appetite with Ellie Krieger - Limited Series: Feasting on Asphalt - The Next Food Network Star 2: Winner Show
CREDITS	Unwrapped - Iron Chef America - Emeril Live - Roker on the Road - Challenge - 30 Minute Meals - Tasty Travels - Good Eats - Everyday Italian - Paula's Home Cooking - Food Network Challenge
COMMENTS	Programs that celebrate food and the people who love food

Brooke Bailey Johnson . . . President
Bob Tuschman . . . Sr. VP, Programming & Production
Michael Smith . . . Sr. VP, Marketing & Creative Services
Susie Fogelson . . . VP, Marketing
Greg Neal . . . VP, Creative Services
Charles Nordlander . . . VP, Primetime Programming
Allison Page . . . VP, Programming
Bruce Seidel . . . VP, Acquisitions & Program Planning

FOOTHILL ENTERTAINMENT, INC.

1231 State St., Ste. 206
Santa Barbara, CA 93101

PHONE . . . 805-965-4488
FAX . . . 805-965-1168
EMAIL . . . info@foothillentertainment.com
WEB SITE . . . www.foothillentertainment.com

TYPES	Animation - Direct-to-Video/DVD - Documentaries - Features - Made-for-TV/Cable Movies - TV Series
DEVELOPMENT	Yuri - Iconicles - Me & My Shadow - Wings of Angels - Kiz & Tel - Gododo - Vessels - Kid Kaiju - Boxing Bobbies and Boy - Snapper - Special Delivery - Food Chain - Tutu Lulu
POST PRODUCTION	Little Monsters - Animal Stories - My Little Fox - Toy Warrior - Wish-A-Roo Park
CREDITS	Barney - Monkeez - Uncle Marvin - The Dress-Up Box - Batfink - Rarg - Elysium - Milton the Monster
COMMENTS	Children's and family entertainment

Gregory B. Payne . . . CEO
Jo Kavanagh-Payne . . . President
Jill Monther . . . Marketing Coordinator
Shane Welch . . . Executive Assistant
Natalie Wagner . . . Marketing Assistant

BONNIE FORBES PRODUCTIONS

6725 Sunset Blvd., Ste. 280
Hollywood, CA 90028
PHONE . . . 323-606-4403
EMAIL . . . bonnie@fortress-ent.com
TYPES Direct-to-Video/DVD - Documentaries - Features - Made-for-TV/Cable Movies - Reality TV - TV Series
HAS DEAL WITH Fortress Entertainment
DEVELOPMENT Features: Robbers - Bull; TV: The Susan Powter Show - Fisticops (Reality)
CREDITS Time to Say Goodbye (Lifetime)
SUBMISSION POLICY No unsolicited material
COMMENTS Options book rights

Bonnie Forbes . . . CEO/Producer

*FOREMOST FILMS

205 West End Ave., Ste. 11-G
New York, NY 10023
PHONE . . . 646-662-0829
EMAIL . . . jeff@foremostfilms.com
TYPES Animation - Features
HAS DEAL WITH Double Nickel Entertainment
DEVELOPMENT Omelette O'Neil - Semper Fido
SUBMISSION POLICY Query via email only; No phone calls
COMMENTS Second office: 1325 Avenue of the Americas, 30th Fl., New York, NY 10019

Jeffrey Belkin . . . President/Producer
Mindy Finkelstein . . . Development Assistant

FORENSIC FILMS, INC.

1 Worth St., 2nd Fl.
New York, NY 10013
PHONE . . . 212-966-1110
FAX . . . 212-966-1125
EMAIL . . . forfilm@aol.com
TYPES Features
DEVELOPMENT Up - Jack Marlow Steals - The Maid's Room - In the Forest There Is Every Kind of Bird
PRE-PRODUCTION Cry of the Owl - The Babysitters
POST PRODUCTION A Crime
UPCOMING RELEASES Off the Black
CREDITS Idlewild - Raising Victor Vargas - Clean - Undefeated - Gummo - Demonlover - What Happened Was - First Love, Last Rights - Joe the King - Julien Donkey-Boy - Chasing Sleep - The Chateau - King of the Jungle - Saving Face
SUBMISSION POLICY Send query first

Scott Macaulay . . . Producer
Robin O'Hara . . . Producer

FORESIGHT UNLIMITED

2934-1/2 Beverly Glen Circle, Ste. 900
Bel Air, CA 90077
PHONE . . . 310-275-5222
FAX . . . 310-275-5202
EMAIL . . . info@foresight-unltd.com
TYPES Features - Miniseries
DEVELOPMENT War & Peace
PRE-PRODUCTION Twist of Fate
POST PRODUCTION Captivity
COMMENTS Production, development, financing, and distribution

Mark Damon . . . CEO
Tamara Stuparich De La Barra . . . VP, Production & Acquisitions
Larry Chan . . . Executive Assistant to CEO
Scott Collette . . . Assistant to VP, Production & Acquisitions

FOREST PARK PICTURES

8228 Sunset Blvd., Ste. 208
West Hollywood, CA 90046
PHONE . . . 323-848-2942
FAX . . . 323-650-8511
EMAIL . . . aimee@forestparkpictures.com
TYPES Animation - Features - Reality TV - TV Series
HAS DEAL WITH Bauer Martinez Entertainment
DEVELOPMENT Small Town Odds - Poker Night - Man on Third - Analog
PRE-PRODUCTION Crash Bandits
CREDITS Shattered Glass

Tove Christensen . . . Partner
Hayden Christensen . . . Partner
Peter Michels . . . VP, Commercial Production/TV Development
Aimée Barth . . . Creative Executive

FORT HILL PRODUCTIONS

4000 Warner Blvd., Bldg. 138, Ste. 1102
Burbank, CA 91522
PHONE . . . 818-954-7575
FAX . . . 818-954-6412
TYPES Documentaries - Features - TV Series
HAS DEAL WITH Warner Bros. Television Production
DEVELOPMENT A Moveable Feast - Calumet - The Good Soldier - Summertime
PRE-PRODUCTION The Watch
SUBMISSION POLICY No unsolicited submissions

Matt LeBlanc . . . Actor/Producer
John Goldstone . . . Producer
Halla Timon . . . Coordinator

FORTIS FILMS

8581 Santa Monica Blvd., Ste. 1
West Hollywood, CA 90069
PHONE . . . 310-659-4533
TYPES Features - TV Series
HAS DEAL WITH Warner Bros. Pictures
CREDITS Practical Magic - Hope Floats - Making Sandwiches - Trespasses - Gun Shy - Miss Congeniality 1&2 - Two Weeks' Notice - The George Lopez Show

Sandra Bullock . . . Actor/Producer
Maggie Biggar . . . VP, Production
Lillian Dean . . . VP, Development
Bryan Moore . . . Office Manager

FORTRESS ENTERTAINMENT

6725 Sunset Blvd., Ste. 280
Hollywood, CA 90028
PHONE . . . 323-467-4700
FAX . . . 323-467-6425
EMAIL . . . info@fortress-ent.com
WEB SITE . . . www.fortress-ent.com
TYPES Documentaries - Features - Made-for-TV/Cable Movies - Reality TV - TV Series
PROVIDES DEAL TO Bonnie Forbes Productions
DEVELOPMENT The Secret Diary of Adrian Mole - Bull - Syrup - Midnight Man - The Road Back - The Lighthouse at the End of the World - Franco - The Joy of Funerals - Robbers
POST PRODUCTION PDR
CREDITS Battleground
SUBMISSION POLICY No unsolicited submissions
COMMENTS Financing, development and production

Brett Forbes . . . Executive Producer/Partner
Patrick Rizzotti . . . Executive Producer/Partner
Ben Weiss . . . Creative Executive

FORWARD ENTERTAINMENT
9255 Sunset Blvd., Ste. 805
Los Angeles, CA 90069
PHONE 310-278-6700
FAX 310-278-6770
TYPES Features - TV Series
DEVELOPMENT Then She Found Me
CREDITS Judging Amy - The Wishing Tree - Ride the Wind - Summer's End - Fever - Due East

Connie Tavel ....Partner
Vera Mihailovich ....Partner
Adrianne Sandoval ....Assistant to Ms. Tavel

FORWARD PASS, INC.
12233 W. Olympic Blvd., Ste. 340
Los Angeles, CA 90064
PHONE 310-207-7378
TYPES Features - TV Series
PRE-PRODUCTION The Kingdom
CREDITS Miami Vice - Collateral - Ali - The Last of the Mohicans - Manhunter - Thief - Drug Wars - Heat - Jericho Mile - The Insider

Michael Mann ....Writer/Producer/Director

DAVID FOSTER PRODUCTIONS
4401 Wilshire Blvd., 2nd Fl.
Los Angeles, CA 90010
PHONE 323-965-0902
FAX 323-965-0962
EMAIL ....fosterflicks@aol.com
TYPES Features - Miniseries
DEVELOPMENT The Thing (Miniseries) - The Upturned Stone - Legacy - Powder Blue - Don Quixote - Twisted
CREDITS McCabe & Mrs. Miller - Running Scared - Short Circuit 1&2 - The Mask of Zorro - The River Wild - The Getaway (Original & Remake) - The Thing - Collateral Damage - Hart's War - The Core - The Fog

David Foster ....Producer
Laura Terry ....Creative Executive
Chris Sobolewski ....Development Assistant
Brian Wilson ....Development Assistant
Jillian Glantz ....Assistant
Ryan Heppe ....No Title

FOUNDATION ENTERTAINMENT
3272 Motor Ave., Ste. G
Los Angeles, CA 90034
PHONE 310-204-4686
FAX 310-204-4603
WEB SITE ....www.foundent.com
SECOND WEB SITE ....www.visionboxmedia.com
TYPES Features - Theatre - TV Series
DEVELOPMENT Watermark - Cousin Ginny - Morningstar
CREDITS The Umbilical Brothers' THWAK! - The Basketball Diaries - Daybreak - Swing Kids - Foxfire - Tortilla Soup - Charlotte Sometimes - Teddy Bears' Picnic
SUBMISSION POLICY Synopses only, unless solicited

John Manulis ....President
Randy Weiss ....Director, Development & Production

FOUR BOYS FILMS
500 S. Buena Vista St., Animation Bldg., 2F-3-4, MC 1763
Burbank, CA 91521
PHONE 818-560-1230
FAX 818-560-1225
EMAIL ....fourboysfilms@sbcglobal.net
TYPES Documentaries - Features - Made-for-TV/Cable Movies - Theatre - TV Series
HAS DEAL WITH ABC Entertainment Television Group
DEVELOPMENT Wendover Whale - Mother's Day - Affairs of Men - Enslaved by Ducks
POST PRODUCTION Amazing Grace
CREDITS The Bituminous Coal Queens of Pennsylvania - The Engagement Ring - And So to Bedlam...
SUBMISSION POLICY No unsolicited submissions
COMMENTS Produced series of telefilms in partnership with 1A Productions and BBC; Representation, UTA; Partnership with the Play Company and Edgemar Center for the Arts

David Hunt ....President/CEO
Patricia Heaton ....VP
Anna Kim ....Director, Development

FOX 21
1847 Centinela Ave.
Santa Monica, CA 90404
PHONE 310-315-7890
FAX 310-315-7878
TYPES TV Series
PROVIDES DEAL TO Benderspink - Katalyst
DEVELOPMENT StandOffish
PRE-PRODUCTION Fountain of Youth - Amped
CREDITS Saved - Free Ride - Beauty & The Geek - Kelsey Grammer's Sketch Show

Jane Francis ....Sr. VP
Brett Weitz ....VP, Creative Affairs
Shaleen Desai ....Director, Creative Affairs
Marci Wiseman ....Consultant, Business Affairs
Brad Holcman ....Coordinator, Creative Affairs
Scott McAboy ....Consultant, Production
Susan Edelist ....Business Affairs
Colin McFadden-Roan ....Business Affairs

FOX ATOMIC
10201 W. Pico Blvd., Bldg. 99
Los Angeles, CA 90035
PHONE 310-369-4402
FAX 310-369-2359
TYPES Features - Internet Content - Mobile Content
PROVIDES DEAL TO OZLA Pictures, Inc.

John Hegeman ....COO
Peter Rice ....President
Duncan MacDonald ....Sr. VP, Promotions
Lawrence Grey ....VP, Production
Jake Zim ....VP, Online
Jeff Arkuss ....Director, Production
Eric Lieb ....Director, Digital Promotions

FOX BROADCASTING COMPANY

10201 W. Pico Blvd.
Los Angeles, CA 90035
PHONE . . . 310-369-1000/212-556-2400
WEB SITE . . . www.fox.com
TYPES Specials - TV Series
PROVIDES DEAL TO Heel & Toe Films
COMMENTS Mailing address: PO Box 900, Beverly Hills, CA 90213

K. Rupert Murdoch . . . Chairman/CEO, News Corporation
Peter Chernin . . . Chairman/CEO, The Fox Group/President & COO, News Corporation
Tony Vinciquerra . . . President/CEO, Fox Networks Group
Peter Liguori . . . President, Entertainment
Ed Wilson . . . President, Fox Television Network
Jon Nesvig . . . President, Sales
Andrew Setos . . . President, Engineering Fox Group
Lee Bartlett . . . Executive VP, Business Affairs
Preston Beckman . . . Executive VP, Strategic Program Planning
Mike Darnell . . . Executive VP, Specials & Alternative Programming
Joe Earley . . . Executive VP, Publicity, Corporate Communications & Creative Services
Craig Erwich . . . Executive VP, Programming
Jon Hookstratten . . . Executive VP, Network Distribution
Del Mayberry . . . Executive VP, Finance & Administration
Marcia Shulman . . . Executive VP, Casting
Kathy Atkinson . . . Sr. VP, Finance
Melva Benoit . . . Sr. VP, Research
Nicole Bernard . . . Sr. VP, Broadcast Standards & Practices
Karen Fox . . . Sr. VP, Business Affairs
Kary McHoul Gatens . . . Sr. VP, Alternative Programming
Ted Gold . . . Sr. VP, Drama Development
Scott Grogin . . . Sr. VP, Corporate Communications
Missy Halperin . . . Sr. VP, Talent Relations
Bob Huber . . . Sr. VP, Casting
Susan Levison . . . Sr. VP, Comedy Development
George Oswald . . . Sr. VP, Creative Services
Donna Redier-Linsk . . . Sr. VP, Business Affairs
Marcy Ross . . . Sr. VP, Current Programming
Tom Sheets . . . Sr. VP, Special Programming
Minna Taylor . . . Sr. VP, Legal Affairs
Mitsy Wilson . . . Sr. VP, Diversity Development
Todd Yasui . . . Sr. VP, Latenight Programming
Ciro Abate . . . VP, Network Distribution
Gerald Alcantar . . . VP, Diversity Development
Amy Christopher . . . VP, East Coast Casting
Jonathan Davis . . . VP, Comedy Development
Kathy Edrich . . . VP, Business Affairs
Wenda Fong . . . VP, Alternative Programming
Kristen Guertin Graham . . . VP, Talent Relations
Sabrina Bonet Ishak . . . VP, Alternative Programming & Specials
Elissa Johansmeier . . . VP, Publicity & Corporate Communications
MJ LaVaccare . . . VP, Scheduling
Pauline O'Con . . . VP, Drama Casting
Alan Rust . . . VP, Creative Services
Stefani Relles . . . VP, Creative Writer Development
Russell Rothberg . . . VP, Current Programming
Shannon Ryan . . . VP, Entertainment Publicity
Jonathan Wax . . . VP, Drama Development
Jason Clark . . . Executive Director, Publicity
Todd Adair . . . Director, Publicity
Jill Hudson Bell . . . Director, Publicity
Kim Fitzgerald Kurland . . . Director, Publicity
Suzanna Makkos . . . Director, Current Programming
Beth Miyares . . . Director, Current Programming
Anne Schwarz . . . Director, Scheduling
Yvette Urbina . . . Director, Current Programming
Alexandra Gillespie . . . Manager, Publicity
Joshua Governale . . . Manager, Publicity
James Oh . . . Manager, Current Programming
Michael Roach . . . Manager, Publicity

*FOX CABLE NETWORKS

10201 W. Pico Blvd.
Los Angeles, CA 90035
PHONE . . . 310-369-1000
WEB SITE . . . www.foxcable.com
TYPES Reality TV - TV Series
COMMENTS Includes FX, Fox Movie Channel, National Geographic Channel, Fox Reality, FUEL TV, Fox Sports Networks (fifteen owned and operated regional sports networks), SPEED, Fox Soccer Channel, Fox College Sports and Fox Sports en Español

Anthony Vinciquerra . . . President/CEO, Fox Networks Group
Lindsay Gardner . . . President, Affiliate Sales & Marketing
John Landgraf . . . President, FX Networks (FX & Fox Movie Channel)
Laureen Ong . . . President, National Geographic Channel US
Bob Thompson . . . President, Fox Sports Networks
Randy Freer . . . COO, Fox Sports Networks
David Lyle . . . COO/General Manager, Fox Reality
Mike Hopkins . . . Executive VP, Affiliate Sales & Marketing
Michael Lang . . . Executive VP, Business Development & Strategy, Fox Networks Group
Hunter Nickell . . . Executive VP/General Manager, SPEED
David Rone . . . Executive VP/General Manager, Fox College Sports
David Sternberg . . . Executive VP, Emerging Networks/General Manager, FUEL TV, Fox Soccer Channel & Fox Sports en Español
Rita Tuzon . . . Executive VP, Business & Legal Affairs/General Counsel
Kelly Cline . . . Sr. VP, Production, Business & Legal Affairs
Tony Carey . . . VP, Production, Business & Legal Affairs
Will Flannery . . . VP, Advanced Services

FOX MOBILE ENTERTAINMENT

10201 W. Pico Blvd.
Los Angeles, CA 90035
PHONE . . . 310-369-1000
TYPES Internet Content - Mobile Content
CREDITS 24: Conspiracy - Prison Break: Proof of Innocence
COMMENTS Offers mobile content through Mobizzo

Lucy Hood . . . President
Mitch Feinman . . . Sr. VP
Leighton Webb . . . VP, International Wireless (London)
Miriam Holzman . . . Executive Director
Craig Vaughan . . . Executive Director, Business Development
Adam Wilensky . . . Director, Media Services
Chris Packard . . . Assistant to Mitch Feinman

FOX NEWS CHANNEL

1211 Avenue of the Americas
New York, NY 10036
PHONE . . . 212-301-3000
WEB SITE . . . www.foxnews.com
SECOND WEB SITE . . . www.foxnewsaffiliates.com
TYPES TV Series
CREDITS The O'Reilly Factor - Hannity & Colmes - The Fox Report with Shepard Smith - On the Record with Greta Van Susteren
COMMENTS News Programming

Roger Ailes . . Chairman, Fox Television Stations/Chairman/CEO, Fox News
Bill Shine . . . Sr. VP, Programming
Irena Briganti . . . VP, Media Relations
Jeremy Steinberg . . . VP, Digital Media

FOX REALITY

1440 S. Sepulveda Blvd.
Los Angeles, CA 90025
PHONE . . . 310-689-1500
FAX . . . 310-689-1560
EMAIL . . . firstname.lastname@fox.com
WEB SITE . . . www.foxreality.com
TYPES: Internet Content - Mobile Content - Reality TV - TV Series
UPCOMING RELEASES: Castaway - There's Something About Miriam - Driving School
CREDITS: Reality Remix - Solitary - American Idol Extra

David Lyle . . . COO/General Manager
Bob Boden . . . VP, Programming
Ed Skolarus . . . VP, Business Operations
Lorey Zlotnick . . . VP, Marketing
Mandel Ilagan . . . Director, Programming & Production
Melissa Rudman . . . Director, Scheduling, Acquisitions & Operations
Noel Siegel . . . Director, Development
Marisa Aronoff . . . Coordinator, Production & Development

FOX SPORTS NETWORK

10201 W. Pico Blvd., Bldg. 101
Los Angeles, CA 90035
PHONE . . . 310-369-1000
WEB SITE . . . www.foxsports.com
TYPES: TV Series
CREDITS: The Best Damn Sports Show Period - Beyond the Glory
COMMENTS: National and regional sports networks providing 24-hour sports and entertainment programming

Bob Thompson . . . President
Randy Freer . . . COO
George Greenberg . . . Executive VP, Programming & Production
David Rone . . . Executive VP, Network Development & Rights Acquisitions
Read Jackson . . . Sr. VP, Programming & Production
Michael Feller . . . VP, Programming
David Leepson . . . VP, Development
Jeremy Langer . . . Director, Scheduling
Doug Levy . . . Director, Production & Operations

FOX TELEVISION STUDIOS

10201 W. Pico Blvd., Bldg. 41
Los Angeles, CA 90035
PHONE . . . 310-369-1000
FAX . . . 310-369-7378
WEB SITE . . . www.fox.com
SECOND WEB SITE . . . www.newscorp.com
TYPES: Made-for-TV/Cable Movies - TV Series
PROVIDES DEAL TO: Avenue Pictures - Fuse Entertainment - Grand Productions, Inc. - Key Creatives, LLC - KLS Communications, Inc. - Landscape Entertainment - MobiTV - The Shuman Company
CREDITS: Wedding Album - Talkshow with Spike Feresten - Duets - The Shield - Flight 93 - The Girls Next Door - Inked; Through Regency Television: Help Me Help You - Windfall
COMMENTS: Scripted and non-scripted TV series; Documentary programming

Angela Shapiro-Mathes . . . President, Fox Television Studios
David Madden . . . Executive VP, Scripted Programming
Holly Jacobs . . . Executive VP, Alternative Development
Regina DiMartino . . . Executive VP, Global Marketing
Jerry Longarzo . . . Executive VP, Business & Legal Affairs
Chris Ottinger . . . Executive VP, Fox TV Studios International
Lisa Demberg . . . Sr. VP, Scripted Programming
Marney Hochman Nash . . . Sr. VP, Scripted Programming
Bob Lemchen . . . Sr. VP, Fox Television Studios, Physical Production
Leslie Oren . . . Sr. VP, Publicity & Corporate Communications
Edward Sabin . . . Sr. VP, Business Affairs & Business Development
Hayley Babcock . . . Sr. VP, Fox World
Cheryl Buysse Lynch . . . VP, Business & Legal Affairs
Stefanie Henning . . . Sr. VP, Global Marketing & New Media
Mindy Moore . . . VP, Alternative Development
Cathy Veisel . . . VP, Alternative Development
Naomi Martinez . . . VP, Finance & Administration
Stacy Kreisberg . . . VP, Business & Legal Affairs
Laurie Howarter . . . VP, Physical Production, Alternative Development
Dean Barnes . . . Director, Post Production
Stephanie Van Hoff . . . Director, Alternative Development
Gabriel Marano . . . Manager, Scripted Programming

THE FOXBORO COMPANY, INC.

222 E. 44th St., 4th Fl.
New York, NY 10017
PHONE . . . 212-450-7970
FAX . . . 212-450-7977
EMAIL . . . tfci@aol.com
TYPES: Direct-to-Video/DVD - Features - Made-for-TV/Cable Movies - Reality TV - Theatre
DEVELOPMENT: Master Harold...and the Boys
CREDITS: In the Presence of Mine Enemies - A Town Has Turned to Dust - Jane Doe - After the Storm
COMMENTS: Unscripted series and specials

Nelle Nugent . . . President
Kenneth Teaton . . . Sr. VP, Creative Affairs & Production
Matt Alesevich . . . Development Assistant

FR PRODUCTIONS

2980 Beverly Glen Circle, Ste. 200
Los Angeles, CA 90077
PHONE 310-470-9212
FAX 310-470-4905
EMAIL . . . . . frprod@earthlink.net

TYPES — Features
DEVELOPMENT — Reel Boys - The Black Stallion Revolts - Tre Belle Donne - Cody & Roger - Texas Boys
PRE-PRODUCTION — Master Class - Street of Dreams - Rounding Third
PRODUCTION — Expired - 5-25-77
POST PRODUCTION — Marie-Antoinette - Youth Without Youth
CREDITS — Lost in Translation - The Young Black Stallion - Black Stallion - Barfly - The Godfather 2&3 - Apocalypse Now - The Secret Garden - Town and Country - The Virgin Suicides - The Conversation - The Outsiders

Fred Roos . . . . . Producer/President
Kara Mazzola . . . . . Director, Development

FRANZKE ENTERTAINMENT INC.

6206 Langden Ave.
Van Nuys, CA 91411
PHONE 818-414-0245
FAX 818-373-4846
EMAIL . . . . . davidfranzke@yahoo.com

TYPES — Reality TV - TV Series
DEVELOPMENT — Karma - The Company - Stunting
CREDITS — The Replacement (TBS Pilot) - Lovitz Says (CBS) - You're Not the Man I Married (Lifetime) - Punk'd (MTV) - Granted (MTV) - Jamie Kennedy Experiment (WB) - Brainiac (WB) - Little Monsters (NBC)

David Franzke . . . . . Executive Producer/CEO

FRAZIER | CHIPMAN ENTERTAINMENT

11825 Laurelwood Dr., Ste. 6
Studio City, CA 91604
PHONE 818-980-9104
FAX 240-282-8892
EMAIL . . . . . info@frazierchipman.com
WEB SITE . . . . . www.frazierchipman.com

TYPES — Commercials - Documentaries - Features - Made-for-TV/Cable Movies - Music Videos - Reality TV - TV Series
PRE-PRODUCTION — Last Dying Breath
CREDITS — One Door Down - Money Trouble - The Zeros - Eriq Music Videos: Here with Me Tonight - Vibe

Garett Chipman . . . . . President/Director/Producer
Kelly Frazier . . . . . President/Executive Producer
Ehrich Van Lowe . . . . . VP, Production

FREDERATOR STUDIOS

231 W. Olive Ave.
Burbank, CA 91502
PHONE 818-736-3606
FAX 818-736-3850
EMAIL . . . . . hey@frederator.kz
WEB SITE . . . . . www.frederator.kz

TYPES — Animation - TV Series
HAS DEAL WITH — Nickelodeon/MTVN Kids & Family Group
PRODUCTION — Random! Cartoons (Nickelodeon) - Wow Wow Wubbzy! (Nick Jr.)
CREDITS — Oh Yeah! Cartoons - ChalkZone - The Fairly OddParents - My Life as a Teenage Robot - The Nicktoons Network Animation Festival

Fred Seibert . . . . . President
Eric Homan . . . . . VP, Creative Affairs
Kevin Kolde . . . . . Producer
Melissa Wolfe . . . . . Development Coordinator

JACK FREEDMAN PRODUCTIONS

1093 Broxton Ave., Ste. 228
Los Angeles, CA 90024
PHONE 310-208-2200
EMAIL . . . . . freedmanfilms@aol.com

TYPES — Features - Made-for-TV/Cable Movies - TV Series
UPCOMING RELEASES — The Christmas Card (Hallmark Channel)
CREDITS — Killers in the House - Mother's Boys - Toy Soldiers - Body Parts

Jack Freedman . . . . . President
Patricia Herskovic . . . . . Chairman of the Board

JOEL FREEMAN PRODUCTIONS, INC.

15323 Weddington St., Ste. 102
Sherman Oaks, CA 91411
PHONE 818-995-1189
FAX 818-995-1638
EMAIL . . . . . jprods@pacbell.net
WEB SITE . . . . . www.joelfreemanproductions.com

TYPES — Features - Made-for-TV/Cable Movies - TV Series
DEVELOPMENT — Air Med - Romantics, Misfits & Fools - Woof - Maternal Instinct - A Choice of Weapons - The Sun Stalker - Monte - Jappath, Prince of Dore - Ducktail
CREDITS — The Heart Is a Lonely Hunter - Shaft - Love at First Bite - The Octagon - Soapdish

Joel Freeman . . . . . Producor

FRELAINE
c/o Paramount Pictures
5555 Melrose Ave., Lasky Bldg., Stes. 107 & 108
Los Angeles, CA 90038-3197
PHONE 323-956-4830
FAX 323-862-1619
TYPES Features
DEVELOPMENT John Carter of Mars - County Sheriff - Untitled CollegeHumor.com Feature - Ivanhoe - Straw Man - The Mummy 3 - Ripley's Believe It or Not!
CREDITS Intolerable Cruelty - The Scorpion King - The Mummy 1&2 - A Simple Plan - Mallrats - Tombstone - Dazed and Confused - Raising Arizona

Jim Jacks .....Producer (323-956-4830)
Alyson Madigan .....Creative Executive (323-956-4826)
Natasha Espiedra .....Assistant

FREMANTLEMEDIA

FREMANTLE PRODUCTIONS LATIN AMERICA
5200 Blue Lagoon Dr., Ste. 200
Miami, FL 33126
PHONE 305-267-0821
FAX 305-267-0459
WEB SITE .....www.fremantlemedia.com
TYPES Reality TV - TV Series

Carlos Gonzales .....Managing Director
Tomas Gonzalez .....General Manager
Jack Alfandary .....VP, Licensing & New Business Development
Carole Bardasano .....VP, Marketing & Sales
Linda McLoughlin .....Legal
Flavia Da Matta .....Territory Manager, Brazil
Arturo Perez .....Controller
Renata Jabali .....Production Coordinator
Jenny Llano .....Sales & Marketing Assistant

FREMANTLEMEDIA NORTH AMERICA
2700 Colorado Ave., Ste. 450
Santa Monica, CA 90404
PHONE 310-255-4700
FAX 310-255-4800
EMAIL .....firstname.lastname@fremantlemedia.com
WEB SITE .....www.fremantlemedia.com
TYPES Direct-to-Video/DVD - Internet Content - Mobile Content - Reality TV - Specials - TV Series
PROVIDES DEAL TO Krasnow Productions - Nasser Entertainment Group
PRE-PRODUCTION Bianca
CREDITS American Inventor - America's Got Talent - The Janice Dickinson Modeling Agency - Gameshow Marathon - American Idol 1-5 - The Price Is Right - Family Feud - Game Shows Gone Bananas - Canadian Idol - The Swan - Complex Malibu - How Clean Is Your House? 1&2 - Distraction 1&2 - Your Face or Mine - Sex Inspectors - Property Ladder 1&2 - Love on the Rocks
COMMENTS Drama, alternative, game shows

Cecile Frot-Coutaz .....CEO/Executive Producer, American Idol (310-255-4779)
Eugene Young .....Chief Creative Officer (310-255-4770)
David Shall .....Executive VP, Business & Legal Affairs, General Counsel (310-255-4729)
Tracy Verna .....Sr. VP, Programming Development (310-255-4723)
Dan Goldberg .....Sr. VP, Current Programming (310-255-4739)
Gaby Johnston .....Sr. VP, Entertainment (310-255-4722)

(Continued)

FREMANTLEMEDIA NORTH AMERICA (Continued)
Jennifer Mullin .....Sr. VP, Development (310-255-4875)
Steve Tao .....Sr. VP, Scripted Programming (310-255-4880)
Julie Uribe .....Sr. VP, Programming Development (310-255-4724)
Ted Haimes .....Executive Producer, Alternative Programming (310-255-4707)
Stuart Krasnow .....Executive Producer, Krasnow Productions (310-255-4824)
James Sunderland .....Executive Producer, Unscripted Programming (310-255-4767)
Ken Warwick .....Executive Producer, American Idol (323-575-8015)
Jill Schwartz .....VP, Alternative Programming Development (310-255-4764)
Andy Felsher .....VP, Development/Executive Producer, Price Is Right Live (310-255-4785)
Stefanie Gelinas .....VP, Strategy (310-255-4744)
David Johnson .....VP, Production (310-255-4732)
Suzanne Lopez .....VP, Business & Legal Affairs (310-255-4796)
Paul Reaney .....Director, Development (310-255-4714)
Joseph Scavetta .....Director, Business & Legal Affairs (310-255-4750)
Nigel Caaro-Evans .....Manager, Acquisitions & Programming Development (310-255-4715)
Dave Luce .....Manager, Documentary & Lifestyle Acquisitions (310-255-4858)
Kathryne Gadarian .....Manager, Development (310-255-4787)

FRESH PAINT
1414 Second St., #103
Santa Monica, CA 90401
PHONE 310-656-4300
FAX 310-656-4309
TYPES Features - TV Series
HAS DEAL WITH Sony Pictures Entertainment
DEVELOPMENT Charlie Ravioli - Ghost Parents - Queen and Country - If the Shoe Fits - Naked Man - The Craving
POST PRODUCTION Catch & Release

Jenno Topping .....Producer
Joshua Siegel .....Director, Development
Robyn Shwer .....Assistant to Jenno Topping

FRESH PRODUCE FILMS
306 N. Mansfield Ave.
Los Angeles, CA 90036
PHONE 323-934-5500
FAX 323-933-6463
EMAIL .....mpfp2002@yahoo.com
TYPES Features - Made-for-TV/Cable Movies - TV Series
DEVELOPMENT Cease Fire - The Crystal Skull - Karaoke King
COMPLETED UNRELEASED Prisoner
CREDITS Z Channel: A Magnificent Obsession (IFC) - Amos and Andrew - Still Breathing - Kill the Man - Twin Falls Idaho - Cherry Falls - Wild Iris - Expert Witness (CBS)

Marshall Persinger .....President/Producer
Jon Montepare .....Director, Development

FRIED FILMS
12233 W. Olympic Blvd., Ste. 150
Los Angeles, CA 90064
PHONE 310-689-2460
TYPES Features
PROVIDES DEAL TO Daniel Fried Productions
DEVELOPMENT In the Dark - Damned
POST PRODUCTION Weapons
CREDITS The Man - Collateral - Two Can Play That Game - Boondock Saints - Winchell - Black Cat Run - Godzilla - Only You - Rudy - So I Married an Axe Murderer

Rob Fried .....Producer
Matt Brutocao .....Director, Development

DANIEL FRIED PRODUCTIONS
12233 W. Olympic Blvd., Ste. 150
Los Angeles, CA 90064
PHONE . . . 310-689-2460
EMAIL . . . info@dfprods.com
WEB SITE . . . www.dfprods.com
TYPES Features - Made-for-TV/Cable Movies - TV Series
HAS DEAL WITH Fried Films
CREDITS O - Illusion

Daniel Fried . . . Producer

BUDD FRIEDMAN DIGITAL
8454 Magnolia Dr.
Los Angeles, CA 90046
PHONE . . . 323-848-9268
EMAIL . . . skippywithnuts@earthlink.net
WEB SITE . . . www.buddfriedman.com
TYPES Documentaries - Internet Content - Reality TV - TV Series
CREDITS 40 Years of Laughter at the Improv (NBC) - Comedians Unleashed (Animal Planet) - National Lampoon's Funny Money (GSN)
COMMENTS Web venture: ijoke.tv

Budd Friedman . . . Founder/CEO
Marc Price . . . Partner/Producer

CHUCK FRIES PRODUCTIONS, INC.
1880 Century Park East, Ste. 213
Los Angeles, CA 90067
PHONE . . . 310-203-9520
FAX . . . 310-203-9519
TYPES Direct-to-Video/DVD - Features - Made-for-TV/Cable Movies - Theatre - TV Series
DEVELOPMENT The Flying Nun - Petals on the Wind - Chicken and the Cheerleader - The Big Ride - Woman on the Ledge 2 - Screamers 2: Survival Instinct
CREDITS Screamers - Deadly Web - Troop Beverly Hills
SUBMISSION POLICY No unsolicited submissions
COMMENTS Fries Film Company, Inc.; Fries Enterprises, Inc.; Avanti Enterprises

Charles W. Fries . . . Chairman/President/CEO
Pete Riesenberg . . . Director, Development
Ava Fries . . . President, Avanti Enterprises

FRONT STREET PICTURES, INC.
2-210 555 Brooksbank Ave.
North Vancouver, BC V7J 3S5, Canada
PHONE . . . 604-983-5262
FAX . . . 604-983-5162
WEB SITE . . . www.frontstreetprods.com
TYPES Features - Made-for-TV/Cable Movies - TV Series
DEVELOPMENT Cherry Blossoms - Cape Breton Road
PRODUCTION Open Season - Sisters - Anna's Storm
POST PRODUCTION Past Tense - Obsession - Scare Tactics - Murder on Spec
CREDITS The Deal - We Don't Live Here Anymore - Hush - Personal Effects

Harvey Kahn . . . Producer/Partner
Ruth Epstein . . . Producer/Partner
Jonas Goodman . . . Producer
Jaye Gazeley . . . Production Manager/Line Producer
Marc Stevenson . . . Production Supervisor
Costa Vassos . . . Unit Manager

FULL PICTURE
915 Broadway, 20th Fl.
New York, NY 10010
PHONE . . . 212-627-0001/310-860-0505
FAX . . . 212-627-1110/310-860-0163
WEB SITE . . . www.fullpic.com
TYPES Reality TV - TV Series
DEVELOPMENT Project Jay - The Model
CREDITS Project Runway
COMMENTS West Coast address: 517 N. Robertson Blvd., Ste. 200, Los Angeles, CA 90048

Jane Cha . . . Producer
Desiree Gruber . . . Producer

FULLER FILMS, INC.
625 Santa Clara Ave.
Venice, CA 90291
PHONE . . . 310-450-5280
TYPES Features - Theatre - TV Series
PRE-PRODUCTION Noise
UPCOMING RELEASES Basic Instinct 2 - Crazy Dog
CREDITS The Believer - K Street - Internal Affairs - Deep Cover
SUBMISSION POLICY Send query letter to Paul De Souza

Henry Bean . . . Writer/Director/Producer
Leora Barish . . . Writer/Director/Producer
Paul De Souza . . . Producer

FUNNYBOY FILMS

FUNNY BOY FILMS
346 N. Detroit St.
Los Angeles, CA 90036
PHONE . . . 323-993-0000
FAX . . . 323-954-0440
EMAIL . . . 411@funnyboyfilms.com
WEB SITE . . . www.funnyboyfilms.com
SECOND WEB SITE . . . www.adamandstevemovie.com
TYPES Documentaries - Features - TV Series
DEVELOPMENT Elliot Loves - Sex Crime Panic
CREDITS Adam & Steve - Latter Days

Kirkland Tibbels . . . President & CEO/Producer
George Bendele . . . Vice President, Development/Producer
Darryl Anderle . . . CFO/Co-Producer
Johnny Ortez . . . Accounting & Operations

FURST FILMS
8954 W. Pico Blvd., 2nd Fl.
Los Angeles, CA 90035
PHONE . . . 310-278-6468
FAX . . . 310-278-7401
EMAIL . . . info@furstfilms.com
TYPES Features - Made-for-TV/Cable Movies - TV Series
DEVELOPMENT Occupational Hazards - The Girl in the Park - The Precious Few - Rain Falls - Daybreakers
POST PRODUCTION First Snow
UPCOMING RELEASES The Woods
CREDITS The Matador - The Cooler - Owning Mahowny - Blue Ridge Fall - Everything Put Together

Sean Furst . . . Producer
Bryan Furst . . . Producer
Shauna Phelan . . . Creative Executive

FURTHUR FILMS

100 Universal City Plaza, Bldg. 1320, Ste. 1-C
Universal City, CA 91608
PHONE . . . 818-777-6700/212-333-1421
FAX . . . 818-866-1278/212-333-8163
TYPES Features
CREDITS Sentinel - It Runs in the Family - The In-Laws - Swimfan - Don't Say a Word - One Night at McCool's
COMMENTS East Coast office: 825 Eighth Ave., 30th Fl., New York, NY 10019

Michael Douglas . . . Producer
Robert Mitas . . . Executive VP (LA)
Allen Burry . . . Publicist (LA)
Angela Congelose . . . Controller (LA)
James LaVigne . . . VP, Development & Production
Diana Lopez . . . (LA)
Alec Nunez . . . (LA)

FUSE ENTERTAINMENT

1041 N. Formosa Ave., Formosa Bldg., Ste. 197
West Hollywood, CA 90046
PHONE . . . 323-850-3873
FAX . . . 323-850-3874
TYPES Features - Reality TV - TV Series
HAS DEAL WITH Fox Television Studios

Mikkel Bondesen . . . President/Manager
David Levine . . . Producer
Richard Demato . . . Manager
Alex Goldstone . . . Manager
Bethany Stirdivant . . . Manager
Ryan Lewis . . . Manager
Tyler Rose . . . Coordinator
William Thompson . . . Receptionist

FX

FX

2121 Avenue of the Stars, 19th Fl.
Los Angeles, CA 90067
PHONE . . . 310-369-1000
FAX . . . 310-969-4688
WEB SITE . . . www.fxnetworks.com
TYPES Made-for-TV/Cable Movies - Reality TV - TV Series
CREDITS The Shield - Nip/Tuck - Rescue Me - Over There - Thief - Starved - It's Always Sunny in Philadelphia - 30 Days - NASCAR Drivers: 360 - Black. White.

John Landgraf . . . President/General Manager
Kelly Cline . . . Executive VP, Business & Legal Affairs
Nick Grad . . . Executive VP, Original Programming
Chuck Saftler . . . Executive VP, Programming
Stephanie Gibbons . . . Executive VP, Marketing & On-Air Promotions
Bruce Lefkowitz . . . Executive VP, Advertising Sales
Guy Sousa . . . Executive VP, Advertising Sales
Steve Leblang . . . Sr. VP, Strategic Planning & Research
John Solberg . . . Sr. VP, Public Relations
Matt Cherniss . . . Sr. VP, Original Programming, Drama & Comedy Series Development
Eric Schreier . . . Sr. VP, Original Programming, Current Series, Alternative Programming & Limited Series
Sean Riley . . . Sr. VP, Affiliate Sales
Tony Carey . . . VP, Production, Business & Legal Affairs
Sally Daws . . . VP, Marketing
John Varvi . . . VP, On-Air Promotions
Roslyn Bibby . . . Director, Public Relations
Clayton Krueger . . . Manager, Comedy & Drama Development

G4 TV

12100 W. Olympic Blvd., Ste. 200
Los Angeles, CA 90064
PHONE . . . 310-979-5000
FAX . . . 310-979-5091
EMAIL . . . info@g4tv.com
WEB SITE . . . www.g4tv.com
TYPES Documentaries - Internet Content - Specials - TV Series
CREDITS TV Series: Star Trek 2.0 - Cheat! - Fastlane - Formula D - X-Play - Cinematech - Electric Playground - Filter - Attack of the Show! - G4's Training Camp - Street Fury - Formula D; Documentaries: Icons
COMMENTS Cable and satellite TV network; Video gaming, technology and lifestyle programming

Neal Tiles . . . President
Dale Hopkins . . . COO
John Rieber . . . Sr. VP, Production
Alan Duke . . . Sr. VP, Business & Legal Affairs
Scott Bantle . . . Sr. VP, Creative Services
Gil Breakman . . . VP, Finance
Julie Fields . . . VP, Marketing
Lauren de la Fuente . . . VP, Marketing Solutions
Laura Civiello . . . VP, Program Acquisitions & Development
Robert Liuag . . . VP, Research
Joshua Krane . . . VP, Interactive
Rob Hause . . . VP, Broadcast Operations
Soheila Ataei . . . VP, Human Resources

GALÁN ENTERTAINMENT

523 Victoria Ave.
Venice, CA 90291
PHONE . . . 310-823-2822
FAX . . . 310-823-7361
EMAIL . . . info@galanent.com
WEB SITE . . . www.galanent.com
TYPES Documentaries - Made-for-TV/Cable Movies - Reality TV - TV Series
HAS DEAL WITH NBC Universal Television Studio
DEVELOPMENT The Swan 3 - Body of Desire
CREDITS The Swan 1&2

Nely Galán . . . CEO
Diana R. Mogollon . . . Director, Development

GALLANT ENTERTAINMENT

4565 Sherman Oaks Ave., Ste. 3
Sherman Oaks, CA 91403
PHONE . . . 818-461-8900
FAX . . . 818-461-8999
EMAIL . . . gallantent@aol.com
TYPES Direct-to-Video/DVD - Documentaries - Features - Made-for-TV/Cable Movies - TV Series
DEVELOPMENT The Lighthouse
CREDITS Journeys Below the Line - 10 Attitudes - Stompin' at the Savoy - Bionic Ever After

Michael O. Gallant . . . President/Producer
Geoffrey Going . . . Production Coordinator

GAMBIT PICTURES

c/o Warner Bros.
4000 Warner Blvd.
Burbank, CA 91522
PHONE . . . 818-954-3100
TYPES Features
HAS DEAL WITH Warner Bros. Pictures
DEVELOPMENT Marco Polo

George Nolfi . . . Writer/Producer
Michael Hackett . . . Producer
Rebecca Brooks . . . Development Executive

GARLIN PICTURES, INC.
11640 Woodbridge St., Ste. 106
Studio City, CA 91406
PHONE .310-488-9092
FAX .818-506-7122
EMAIL .garlinpic@hotmail.com
TYPES Features - Made-for-TV/Cable Movies - Reality TV - TV Series
DEVELOPMENT My Brother Ernesto - The Gathered - Disneyland 2 Miles - The Seven Wonders of Sassafras Springs - Absence - Wise Kids - Safe Passage - Mandie - Cheer Fever
PRE-PRODUCTION My Brother's Fiancee's Sister - Night Train - Dreamgirl - Sue Me - Untitled Comedy (Regency)
POST PRODUCTION Kickin' It Old School - Broken
UPCOMING RELEASES Relative Strangers - The Godfather of Green Bay
COMPLETED UNRELEASED I Will Survive
CREDITS Starlets - Malibu's Most Wanted - Tough Luck - The Jamie Kennedy Experiment - Living with Fran

Brian R. Etting .Producer/Director
Josh Etting .Producer/Writer

GENERATE
1545 26th St., 2nd Fl.
Santa Monica, CA 90404
PHONE .310-255-0460/310-255-0461
WEB SITE .www.generatela.com
TYPES Direct-to-Video/DVD - Documentaries - Features - Internet Content - Made-for-TV/Cable Movies - Miniseries - Mobile Content - Reality TV - Specials - TV Series
HAS DEAL WITH MTV Networks

Jordan Levin .Partner
Kara Welker .Partner
Dave Rath .Partner
Mike Karz .Partner
Pete Aronson .Partner
Andy Corren .Manager
Josh Weinstock .Creative Executive, Film
Terra Hoster .Management
Ivana Ma .TV
Cori Monger .Management
Josh Goldenberg .Film

GENERATION ENTERTAINMENT
533 Canal St., Ste. 5E
New York, NY 10013
PHONE .212-966-1444
TYPES Features - TV Series
DEVELOPMENT Love & Ambition - Racing Time - Paranoia - The Crossing - The Tuckersville Mafia - Jack & Addie
CREDITS The Photographer - Mugshots: Dr. Richard Sharpe - Mugshots: Robert Blake
SUBMISSION POLICY Query by fax only

Jeremy Stein .Producer/Writer/Director
Potter Lewis .Director, Development

GENREBEND PRODUCTIONS, INC.
233 Wilshire Blvd., 4th Fl.
Santa Monica, CA 90401
PHONE .310-917-1064
FAX .310-917-1065
TYPES Features - Made-for-TV/Cable Movies - New Media - TV Series
HAS DEAL WITH Warner Bros. Television Production
CREDITS Supernatural - Tarzan - Without a Trace - Band of Brothers - Smallville - Millennium - The X-Files

David Nutter .Director/President
Tom Lavagnino .Writer/VP, Creative Affairs

GERBER PICTURES
9465 Wilshire Blvd., #318
Beverly Hills, CA 90212
PHONE .310-385-5880
FAX .310-385-5881
TYPES Animation - Direct-to-Video/DVD - Documentaries - Features - Made-for-TV/Cable Movies - TV Series
HAS DEAL WITH Warner Bros. Pictures
DEVELOPMENT The Fix-Up - Major Movie Star - Void Moon
PRODUCTION Beerfest
CREDITS A Very Long Engagement - Juwanna Man - James Dean - Queen of the Damned - What a Girl Wants - The In-Laws - Grind - The Dukes of Hazzard

Bill Gerber .President
Taylor Latham .Director, Development (310-385-1416)
Carrie Gillogly .Assistant to Taylor Latham (310-385-9369)
Jay Polidoro .Assistant to Bill Gerber (310-385-9606)

GHOST HOUSE PICTURES
315 S. Beverly Dr., Ste. 216
Beverly Hills, CA 90212
PHONE .310-785-3900
FAX .310-785-9176
TYPES Features
DEVELOPMENT Siren
PRE-PRODUCTION 30 Days of Night
POST PRODUCTION The Grudge 2 - Rise - The Messengers
CREDITS Boogeyman - The Grudge
SUBMISSION POLICY Via representation only
COMMENTS Partnership with Mandate Pictures

Sam Raimi .Director/Executive Producer
Robert Tapert .Executive Producer
Michael Kirk .VP, Development/Producer
J.R. Young .Creative Executive/Producer
Bill Hamm .Television Executive
Grant Curtis .Production Executive
Ben Ketai .Archiving
Shannon Lugger .Assistant to Mr. Tapert
David Pollison .Assistant

GHOST ROBOT

373 Broadway, Ste. F-3
New York, NY 10013

PHONE 212-343-0900
FAX 212-898-1119
EMAIL .....man@ghostrobot.com
WEB SITE .....www.ghostrobot.com
TYPES: Animation - Commercials - Documentaries - Features - Music Videos
DEVELOPMENT: Kingston - Demon at the Wheel - Kumiko: The Treasure Hunter
PRE-PRODUCTION: Against the Current
POST PRODUCTION: Cropsey - Dr. Bronner's Magic Soapbox
UPCOMING RELEASES: Road
COMPLETED UNRELEASED: Choking Man
CREDITS: Hell House - Breath Control - The Federation of Black Cowboys

Zachary Mortensen .....Producer
Tommy Pallotta .....Producer
Joshua Zeman .....Producer
Mark De Pace .....Producer, Music Videos

LEEZA GIBBONS ENTERPRISES (LGE)

7257 Beverly Blvd., Ste. 218
Los Angeles, CA 90036

PHONE 323-634-0581
FAX 323-634-0582
TYPES: Made-for-TV/Cable Movies - Reality TV - Specials
CREDITS: The Michael Essany Show - MTV's Verdict - Leeza - Intimate Portrait of JFK Jr. - Straight from the Heart - The Teen Files - E! Specials: Hollywood Youth - Gay Hollywood - Celebrities and Their Causes - Leeza Gibbons Hollywood Confidential - Leeza Live
SUBMISSION POLICY: No unsolicited submissions
COMMENTS: Radio; Leeza Gibbons Memory Foundation

Leeza Gibbons .....CEO
Vincent J. Arcuri .....Creative Executive
Bobby Xydis .....Creative Executive
Rick Bradley .....Marketing, Licensing & Endorsements
Leslie Garson .....Publicity & PR

GIGANTIC PICTURES

16065 Jeanne Lane
Encino, CA 91436

PHONE 310-488-1195
EMAIL .....giganticpictures@hotmail.com
TYPES: Features
DEVELOPMENT: Wait and See Annie Lee - Illegitimate - Icon - Emergence - Cajun Night Before Christmas
POST PRODUCTION: Deep Winter
UPCOMING RELEASES: Dishdogz
CREDITS: Thick as Thieves

Glenn Zoller .....Producer

GILLEN & PRICE

4016 W. 62nd St.
Los Angeles, CA 90043

PHONE .....See below
TYPES: Features - TV Series
DEVELOPMENT: Peking Moon - The Unknowns
CREDITS: Under Suspicion - Fried Green Tomatoes - Mercy Point
SUBMISSION POLICY: Unsolicited material will not be read and will be destroyed upon receipt

Anne Marie Gillen .....Producer (323-294-5449)
Jody Price .....Producer (323-655-8047)

ROGER GIMBEL PRODUCTIONS, INC.

1675 Old Oak Rd.
Los Angeles, CA 90049

PHONE 310-459-3838
FAX 310-459-6940
TYPES: Features - Made-for-TV/Cable Movies - Miniseries - Specials
DEVELOPMENT: Synanon - Rachel Carson (Silent Spring)
CREDITS: The Amazing Howard Hughes - Montana - Chernobyl: The Final Warning - Murder Between Friends - The Perfect Mother

Roger Gimbel .....President/Executive Producer
Connie Dobson .....Development Associate

GINTY FILMS INTERNATIONAL

483 Euclid Ave.
Toronto, ON M6G 2T1, Canada

PHONE 416-992-5438/416-944-0475
FAX 416-924-3229
EMAIL .....rwginty@aol.com
WEB SITE .....www.robertginty.com
TYPES: Commercials - Direct-to-Video/DVD - Features - Made-for-TV/Cable Movies - Music Videos - TV Series
DEVELOPMENT: Green Shadows - White Whale - Robyn Hood - The Cotton Club Murders - Elaine & Bill: Portrait of a Marriage - Mrs. Warren's Profession - Elvis and Red - Churchill at Harrow
PRE-PRODUCTION: Mrs. Judy
PRODUCTION: A Clockwork Orange: The Musical
CREDITS: China Beach - Dream On - Early Edition - Fame L.A. - Charmed - V.I.P. - Exterminator 3 - Nash Bridges - Xena - Honey, I Shrunk the Kids - MTV's 2gether - Tracker
COMMENTS: Irish Theatre Art Center (New York/Dublin/London); Deals with The Irish Film Board, RTE (Ireland), Stage 5 Productions (Rome), Cinecitta Studios (Rome) and Ardmore Studios (Dublin)

Robert Ginty .....Producer/Director/CEO
Cindy Brace .....Company Representative (Paris)
Suzanne Depoe .....Company Representative (Toronto)

GIRAFFE PRODUCTIONS

10202 W. Washington Blvd., David Lean Bldg., Ste. 321
Culver City, CA 90232
PHONE .310-244-2230
FAX .310-244-0972
EMAIL .giraffeprods@aol.com
WEB SITE .www.jaymohrlive.com
TYPES Features - Reality TV - TV Series
HAS DEAL WITH Sony Pictures Television
DEVELOPMENT Diamond - East of Cielo - Get Got - Dude Food - Primal - Velcro
PRE-PRODUCTION Lonely Street
CREDITS Mohr Sports (ESPN) - Last Comic Standing 1-2 (NBC) - Last Comic Standing: Battle of the Best

Jay Mohr .President
Cori Fry Hengst .VP

GITTES, INC.

c/o Columbia Pictures
10202 W. Washington Blvd., Poitier Bldg., Ste. 1200
Culver City, CA 90232-3195
PHONE .310-244-4333
FAX .310-244-1711
TYPES Features
HAS DEAL WITH Columbia Pictures
DEVELOPMENT The Chet Baker Project - The Ladies' Man
CREDITS Little Nikita - Breaking In - Goin' South - About Schmidt - The Girl Next Door

Harry Gittes .Producer
Edward C. Wang .Director, Development (310-244-4334)

GLATZER PRODUCTIONS

c/o Villains
9247 Alden Dr.
Beverly Hills, CA 90210
PHONE .310-888-8900
TYPES Features - TV Series
PRE-PRODUCTION The Death of Harry Tobin
POST PRODUCTION The Underdog
CREDITS In the Weeds (Series) - The Grave - Deceiver - In the Weeds (Feature) - Blue Ridge Fall
COMMENTS Deal with Villains

Peter Glatzer .Producer
Emerson Bruns .Business Affairs
Beau J. Genot .Post Production

GO GIRL MEDIA

11733 Montana Ave., Ste. 107
Los Angeles, CA 90049
PHONE .310-472-8910
FAX .310-691-8519
EMAIL .info@gogirlmedia.com
WEB SITE .www.gogirlmedia.com
TYPES Features - Made-for-TV/Cable Movies - Reality TV - TV Series
DEVELOPMENT TV: My Mother's a Bitch! (Fox Studios) - The New York Dog (Cosgrove Muerer) - Cracked (Fox Studios) - Pat Allen's I Do... I Don't; Film: The Edge of the Moon (Michelle Manning Productions) - Cutting The Rose (Fox Studios/MOW)
CREDITS Dance Revolution (CBS) - Cake (CBS) - Gagsters! (Brookwell/McNamara) - Back in the Day (Pilot/Film Roman) - Doggie Style (Pilot/Lifetime) - It's Just a Movie (Pilot/E!)
COMMENTS Deals with Brookwell McNamara and Fox Television Studios; Second address: 9062 Hayvenhurst Ave., North Hills, CA 91343

Susie Singer Carter .Partner/Producer/Writer
Laura Keats .Partner/Producer/Director
Don Priess .Writer/Co-Executive VP, Creative & Production
Deborah Zimmerly .VP, Development
Joey Singer .Executive Assistant

GO GO LUCKEY PRODUCTIONS

1918 Main St., Ste. 200
Santa Monica, CA 90405
PHONE .310-314-3900
FAX .310-314-3990
EMAIL .gogoluckey@gogoluckey.com
WEB SITE .www.gogoluckey.com
TYPES Commercials - Direct-to-Video/DVD - Documentaries - Features - Made-for-TV/Cable Movies - Miniseries - Music Videos - Reality TV - Specials - TV Series
CREDITS Laguna Beach (MTV) - Roller Girls (A&E)

Gary Auerbach .Producer
Julie Auerbach .Producer

GO TIME ENTERTAINMENT

3981 Weslin Ave.
Sherman Oaks, CA 91423
PHONE 818-681-1677
FAX 818-981-7986
TYPES — TV Series
DEVELOPMENT — The Breakroom - Str8 Up - King Arthurs Courts
CREDITS — Let's Bowl (Comedy Central) - Victory Tonight (GSN) - The Sportsman's News (OLN)

Tim Scott . . . . Executive Producer/Director
Nick Schenk . . . . Executive Producer/Writer

THE GOATSINGERS

177 W. Broadway, 2nd Fl.
New York, NY 10013
PHONE 212-966-3045
FAX 212-966-4362
TYPES — Features
CREDITS — The Grey Zone - Three Seasons

Harvey Keitel . . . . President
Michael Cawley . . . . Assistant to Harvey Keitel

GOEPP CIRCLE PRODUCTIONS

c/o JLL Management, Inc.
1601 Cloverfield Blvd., 2nd Fl., South Tower
Santa Monica, CA 90404
PHONE 310-460-3095
FAX 310-460-3293
TYPES — Features - TV Series
COMPLETED UNRELEASED — The Librarian 2
CREDITS — The Thunderbirds - Clockstoppers - Dying to Live - Roswell - Star Trek: Insurrection - Star Trek: First Contact

Jonathan Frakes . . . . Director/Producer

gk productions
Goff-Kellam Productions

GOFF-KELLAM PRODUCTIONS

8491 Sunset Blvd., Ste. 1000
West Hollywood, CA 90069
PHONE 323-656-2001
FAX 323-656-1002
EMAIL . . . . goffkellam@aol.com
WEB SITE . . . . www.goffkellam.com
TYPES — Features
DEVELOPMENT — Deprivation - Teen Bitch - Conjurer
CREDITS — Kartenspieler - Children of the Struggle - Roberta Loved - Seventy - Heavy Put-Away - Girl Play - Dropped - Out at the Wedding

Gina G. Goff . . . . Producer
Laura A. Kellam . . . . Producer
Mark D'Onofrio . . . . Assistant

FREDERIC GOLCHAN PRODUCTIONS

c/o Radar Pictures
10900 Wilshire Blvd., 14th Fl.
Los Angeles, CA 90024
PHONE 310-208-8525/310-854-3030
FAX 310-208-1764
EMAIL . . . . fgfilm@aol.com
TYPES — Animation - Features
HAS DEAL WITH — Radar Pictures
DEVELOPMENT — White Skin - Family Values - Divorce Club - Fandorin
PRE-PRODUCTION — Bad Dog - The Way the Dead Love - Claire - Intimate Strangers - Rififi - Perfect Crime
PRODUCTION — Chaos Theory
CREDITS — In the Deep Woods - Kimberly - Intersection - Quick Change - The Associate - Dream Date

Frederic Golchan . . . . President
Jeronimo Beccar Varela . . . . Assistant
Megan McClelland . . . . Assistant

GOLD CIRCLE FILMS

9420 Wilshire Blvd., Ste. 250
Beverly Hills, CA 90212
PHONE 310-278-4800
FAX 310-278-0885
EMAIL . . . . info@goldcirclefilms.com
WEB SITE . . . . www.goldcirclefilms.com
TYPES — Features
HAS DEAL WITH — Universal Pictures
PROVIDES DEAL TO — Lloyd Entertainment - Safran Company
DEVELOPMENT — Rizzle, Pizzle, Sizzle - Sanctum - The Waiting - The Winged Boy - Forsaken - Town Creek - A Haunting in Connecticut - The Puritan - Cold Hand in Mine - Cougars - Family Portrait - Soundless - The Push - Angel Heart - Anvil
PRE-PRODUCTION — My Sassy Girl - Quail Hollow - How I Met My Boyfriend's Dead Fianceé
POST PRODUCTION — Griffin and Phoenix - Because I Said So - White Noise 2
UPCOMING RELEASES — Whisper
CREDITS — Slither - My Big Fat Greek Wedding - White Noise - The Wedding Date - Poolhall Junkies - The Man from Elysian Fields

Paul Brooks . . . . President
Scott Niemeyer . . . . CFO
Jeff Levine . . . . Head of Production
Joanna Jones . . . . Sr. VP, Post Production & Worldwide Distribution
Zak Kadison . . . . Sr. VP, Production
Adam Mehr . . . . Sr. VP, Business Affairs
Brad Kessll . . . . Production Executive
Nikki Levy . . . . Creative Executive
Kevin Waehner . . . . Story Editor
Guy Danella . . . . Assistant to Zak Kadison

GOLDCREST FILMS INTERNATIONAL, INC.

1240 N. Olive Dr.
Los Angeles, CA 90069
PHONE 323-650-4551/44-207-437-8696
FAX 323-650-3581/44-207-437-4448
EMAIL ......mailbox@goldcrestfilms.com
WEB SITE ......www.goldcrest.org

TYPES: Animation - Features - Made-for-TV/Cable Movies
POST PRODUCTION: Elvis and Anabelle
CREDITS: To End All Wars - Space Truckers - No Way Home - Rock-A-Doodle - Black Rainbow - Clockwatchers
COMMENTS: UK office: 65/66 Dean St., London W1D 4PL, United Kingdom; East Coast office: 799 Washington St., New York, NY 10014, phone: 212-243-4700

John Quested ......Chairman (NY)
Stephen R. Johnston ......President (LA)
Nick Quested ......Director
Tony Murphy ......Sr. VP, Business Affairs (London)
Abigail Walsh ......Sales Executive (London)
Seth Carmichael ......Director, Acquistions
Wayne Godfrey ......Acquisitions & Development Coordinator (London)
Susan England ......Production & Acquisitions (LA)

GOLDENRING PRODUCTIONS

11271 Ventura Blvd., Rm. 506
Studio City, CA 91604
PHONE 818-508-7425
FAX 818-508-7428

TYPES: Features - Made-for-TV/Cable Movies - Miniseries - TV Series
DEVELOPMENT: I Know That You Know (Landscape Pictures) - Mad Men (Fox Searchlight) - Neighborhood Watch (Lifetime)
CREDITS: Fatal Desire - Pizza My Heart - On the Second Day of Christmas - My First Mister - Widows - Heart of a Stranger - I Do, But I Don't

Jane Goldenring ......President
Ethan Ambado ......Development

THE GOLDSTEIN COMPANY

1644 Courtney Ave.
Los Angeles, CA 90046
PHONE 310-659-9511
FAX 775-637-6684

TYPES: Features
DEVELOPMENT: The Art of Breaking Glass - Blue Tears
PRE-PRODUCTION: The Other Side of Simple
CREDITS: The Mothman Prophecies - Ringmaster - Under Siege - Pretty Woman - The Hunted

Gary W. Goldstein ......Producer
Sandra Tomita ......Associate Producer
Catherine Wachter ......Development

JOHN GOLDWYN PRODUCTIONS

5555 Melrose Ave., Chevalier Bldg., 1st Fl.
Los Angeles, CA 90038
PHONE 323-956-5054
FAX 323-862-0055

TYPES: Animation - Features - Made-for-TV/Cable Movies
HAS DEAL WITH: Paramount Pictures
DEVELOPMENT: The Italian Job 2 - Sebastian Knight - Untitled Williamsburg Project - The Secret Life of Walter Mitty - Armored - City of Water - The Nightmarist - I'm Not There: Suppositions of Being Bob Dylan - Present Value - Prep - Senior Week - After Hailey (A Michaels Goldwyn Production)
PRE-PRODUCTION: Hot Rod
UPCOMING RELEASES: Dexter (Pilot/Showtime)

John Goldwyn ......President/Producer
John Hodges ......Director, Creative Affairs
Eliza Dyson ......Assistant

GOOD GAME

4000 Warner Blvd., Bldg. 34, Ste. 101
Burbank, CA 91522
PHONE 818-954-3414
FAX 818-954-3415

TYPES: Made-for-TV/Cable Movies - TV Series
HAS DEAL WITH: Warner Bros. Television Production

Lauren Graham ......President
Kathy Ebel ......VP
Matt Warshauer ......Development Associate

GOOD KOP FILMS

1720-1/2 Whitley Ave.
Los Angeles, CA 90028
PHONE 323-462-0500
FAX 323-462-6024

TYPES: Features
UPCOMING RELEASES: Idiocracy

Elysa Koplovitz ......Producer
Lizzy Klein ......Creative Executive

THE GOODMAN COMPANY

8491 Sunset Blvd., Ste. 329
Los Angeles, CA 90069
PHONE 323-655-0719
EMAIL ......ilyssagoodman@sbcglobal.net

TYPES: Features - Reality TV - TV Series
DEVELOPMENT: Fashion Academy - Little Green Men - The Yoga Mamas
PRE-PRODUCTION: Jeremy Thatcher, Dragon Hatcher
POST PRODUCTION: Love and Other Dilemmas
COMPLETED UNRELEASED: The Hidden Realm - Mall or Nothing
CREDITS: A Cinderella Story - Moolah Beach - Summer of the Monkeys

Ilyssa Goodman ......President/Producer

GOOGLE INC.

1600 Amphitheatre Parkway
Mountain View, CA 94030
PHONE 650-253-0000
FAX 650-253-0001
WEB SITE ......www.google.com

TYPES: Internet Content - Mobile Content
CREDITS: Google Video Releases: Waterborne - Aardvark'd: 12 Weeks with Geeks

Joanna Shields ......European Director, Syndication & Partnerships
Jennifer Feiken ......Director, Video & Multimedia Search Partnerships, Google Video
Chris Sacca ......Business Development

THE MARK GORDON COMPANY

12200 W. Olympic Blvd., Ste. 250
Los Angeles, CA 90064

PHONE .310-943-6401
FAX .310-943-6402

TYPES	Features - Made-for-TV/Cable Movies - TV Series
HAS DEAL WITH	Columbia Pictures - Touchstone Television
CREDITS	The Day After Tomorrow - The Patriot - Saving Private Ryan - Speed - Criminal Minds - Grey's Anatomy
SUBMISSION POLICY	No unsolicited material

Mark Gordon .Principal/Producer
Deborah Spera .President, TV
Lawrence Inglee .Executive VP, Features
Josh McLaughlin .Executive VP, Features
Lindsey Liberatore .Creative Executive
Jordan Wynn .Creative Executive
Jae Kim .Director, TV Development
Jennifer Mancino .Assistant to Mark Gordon
Allyson Seeger .Assistant to Mark Gordon
Christina Johnson .Assistant to Deborah Spera
Michelle Lee .Assistant to Lawrence Inglee
Tito Ortiz .Assistant to Josh McLaughlin
Carlos Tower .Assistant to Jae Kim

DAN GORDON PRODUCTIONS

1927 Meadow View Ct.
Thousand Oaks, CA 91362

PHONE .805-496-2566
WEB SITE .www.zaki.yc.edu

TYPES	Documentaries - Features - TV Series
DEVELOPMENT	Isabella V. - Little War of Our Own - Samurai Girl - Just Play Dead - Mafia Cop
PRODUCTION	Oklahoma City
CREDITS	The Hurricane - Passenger 57 - Wyatt Earp - Murder in the First - The Assignment - Gotcha
SUBMISSION POLICY	No unsolicited submissions

Dan Gordon .Writer/Producer
Matt O'Neill .VP

*GORDONSTREET PICTURES

2241 N. Cahuenga Blvd.
Los Angeles, CA 90068

PHONE .323-467-6267
FAX .323-467-0438
EMAIL .info@gordonstreetpictures.com

TYPES	Commercials - Direct-to-Video/DVD - Documentaries - Features - Made-for-TV/Cable Movies - TV Series
DEVELOPMENT	All I've Got
PRE-PRODUCTION	Brothers Bloom
UPCOMING RELEASES	Nomad - Conversations with Other Women - Relative Strangers
CREDITS	Brick - Dancing at the Blue Iguana - Kill Me Later - Black & White - Wedding Bell Blues - Tough Luck - Stranger Than Fiction - Long Time Since - Zoe - For Hire - Rave Review - Power 98 - Partners in Crime
COMMENTS	IFC Image Campaign 2002/2003; Promos

Ram Bergman .Producer
Raymond Izaac .Development

*GORILLA PICTURES

2000 W. Olive Ave.
Burbank, CA 91506

PHONE .818-848-2198
FAX .818-848-2232
EMAIL .info@gorillapictures.net
WEB SITE .www.gorillapictures.net

TYPES	Animation - Documentaries - Features
DEVELOPMENT	Alien Olympics
CREDITS	The Last Sentinel - Soft Target - X-Treme Fighter - The Legend of Sasquatch - Kickin' Back in the USSR
SUBMISSION POLICY	No unsolicited submissions

Bill J. Gottlieb .CEO
Don Wilson .Executive VP, Development
Brenda Arson .Director, Operations
Dustin Harrison .Director, Post Production
Lidia Jay .Director, Sales
Judy Lea .Manager, Marketing

GOTHAM ENTERTAINMENT GROUP

99 John St., Ste. 1609
New York, NY 10038

PHONE .443-269-1405
FAX .801-439-6998
EMAIL .newyork@gothamcity.com
SECOND EMAIL .losangeles@gothamcity.com
WEB SITE .www.gothamcity.com

TYPES	Animation - Direct-to-Video/DVD - Features - Made-for-TV/Cable Movies - Reality TV - TV Series
DEVELOPMENT	Howard Stern's Porky's - Smokey Bear - The Funky Monkeys
CREDITS	Goodbye Lover (Warner Bros.) - The Blood Oranges (Lionsgate)
SUBMISSION POLICY	See Web site

Eric Kopeloff .Partner
Joel Roodman .Partner

THE GOTHAM GROUP, INC.

9255 Sunset Blvd., Ste. 515
Los Angeles, CA 90069
PHONE .310-285-0001
FAX .310-285-0077
TYPES: Animation - Direct-to-Video/DVD - Features - Internet Content - Made-for-TV/Cable Movies - Miniseries - TV Series
DEVELOPMENT: Features: A Great and Terrible Beauty - The Spiderwick Chronicles - Creature Tech - Redwall - The Princess and the Pauper; TV: A Pretty Good Life - Charlie & Chunk - Stormriders
PRE-PRODUCTION: Creature Comforts (TV)
SUBMISSION POLICY: No unsolicited material
COMMENTS: Management/production company representing book authors, directors, producers, screenwriters and TV writers in addition to its own production slate

Ellen Goldsmith-Vein .President/CEO/Producer
Julie Kane-Ritsch .Partner/Manager/Producer
Lindsay Williams .Manager/Producer
Peter McHugh .Manager/Producer
Eddie Gamarra .Manager
Ronak Kordestani .Manager
Michael Bracken .Business Affairs
Julie Nelson .Accounting
Dmitri M. Johnson .Manager Trainee
Chad Steers .Manager Trainee
Timothy I. Stevenson .Manager Trainee
Carrie Van Hoy .Assistant

GOTV NETWORKS

14144 Ventura Blvd, Ste. 300
Sherman Oaks, CA 91423
PHONE .818-933-2100
FAX .818-704-9386
EMAIL .info@gotvnetworks.com
SECOND EMAIL .content@gotvnetworks.com
WEB SITE .www.gotvnetworks.com
TYPES: Mobile Content
UPCOMING RELEASES: Primped
CREDITS: Hip Hop Official - ALTitude - GoTV Superchannel - Diva - Laugh Riot - Sports Edge
SUBMISSION POLICY: Contact by email

David Bluhm .CEO
Thomas Ellsworth .COO
Elizabeth Brooks .Executive VP, Marketing
Daniel Tibbets .Executive VP, GoTV Studios
Eric Wilson .Executive VP, Technology

GRACIE FILMS

c/o Sony Pictures Entertainment
10202 Washington Blvd., Poitier Bldg.
Culver City, CA 90232
PHONE .310-244-4222
FAX .310-244-1530
TYPES: Animation - Features - TV Series
HAS DEAL WITH: Sony Pictures Entertainment
PRODUCTION: The Simpsons Movie
CREDITS: Spanglish - Riding in Cars with Boys - What About Joan? - As Good as It Gets - Big - Bottle Rocket - Broadcast News - Jerry Maguire - The Simpsons

James L. Brooks .Producer/Writer/Director
Richard Sakai .President
Julie Ansell .President, Motion Pictures
Denise Sirkot .Executive VP

GRADE A ENTERTAINMENT

149 S. Barrington Ave., Ste. 719
Los Angeles, CA 90049
PHONE .310-358-8600
FAX .310-919-2998
EMAIL .development@gradeaent.com
TYPES: Features - Made-for-TV/Cable Movies - TV Series
DEVELOPMENT: Miracle Cars - Midnight Voices - Granny - Magic Kingdom for Sale - The Five Ancestors - Untraceable
CREDITS: Captain Ron - It Takes Two - A Chance of Snow

Andy Cohen .Producer/Manager

MICHAEL GRAIS PRODUCTIONS

395 S. Topanga Canyon Blvd.
Topanga, CA 90290
PHONE .310-455-2699/310-277-9393
WEB SITE .www.michaelgrais.com
TYPES: Features - Made-for-TV/Cable Movies - TV Series
DEVELOPMENT: Jawbone - Manticore - Void Moon - Lakeshore Drive - Lisa P.I. (Series) - The Network (Series) - Homeward Bound - Poltergeist: In the Shadows - Border War - The Prince of Peru - Heartland - Lost Girls - The 13th Juror (Series) - Interns
PRE-PRODUCTION: Winter Heat
CREDITS: Poltergeist 1&2 - Marked for Death - Stephen King's Sleepwalkers - Great Balls of Fire - Who Killed Atlanta's Children? - The Immortal (Series) - Cool World - Visitors from the Unknown (Miniseries) - Death Hunt

Michael Grais .Writer/Producer/Director
Judy Fox .Manager/Producer

GRAMMNET PRODUCTIONS

c/o Paramount Pictures
5555 Melrose Ave., Wilder Bldg., Ste. 114
Los Angeles, CA 90038-3197
PHONE ....323-956-5455 (TV)/323-956-5840 (Features)
FAX ....323-862-2284 (TV)/323-862-1433 (Features)

TYPES Animation - Features - TV Series
HAS DEAL WITH CBS Paramount Network Television
DEVELOPMENT Inner Bitch - Isis - The Case of the Halloween Hangman - Honeymoon in Hell - You're Not the Boss of Me
PRODUCTION Girlfriends - Medium (NBC)
CREDITS The Game (CW) - Kelsey Grammer Salutes Jack Benny - Fired Up - The Innocent - Girlfriends - Gary the Rat - In-Laws - World Cup Comedy - The Sketch Show (FOX)
SUBMISSION POLICY No unsolicited material
COMMENTS Features office: 5555 Melrose Ave., Wilder Bldg., Ste. 116, Los Angeles, CA 90038-3197

Kelsey Grammer ....Actor/Producer/CEO (323-956-5547)
Steve Stark ....President (323-956-5455)
Jessica Hochman ....Director, Feature Development (323-956-5832)
Melanie Grodanz ....Manager, TV Development (323-956-5420)
Chris Maul ....Manager, Programming (323-956-5423)
Xochitl L. Olivas ....Production Manager (323-956-5547)
Tiffani Copeland ....Features Assistant (323-956-5832)
Danny Warren ....Assistant to Steve Stark (323-956-5455)

GRAN VIA PRODUCTIONS

1888 Century Park East, 14th Fl.
Los Angeles, CA 90067
PHONE 310-859-3060

TYPES Features - TV Series
HAS DEAL WITH CBS Entertainment - CBS Paramount Network Television - Walden Media
DEVELOPMENT Spring Break in Bosnia - Steinbeck's Point of View
POST PRODUCTION How to Eat Fried Worms
COMPLETED UNRELEASED The Wendell Baker Story
CREDITS Chronicles of Narnia: The Lion, the Witch and the Wardrobe - The Notebook - The Alamo - The Rookie - Moonlight Mile - Dragonfly - The Banger Sisters - Galaxy Quest - My Dog Skip - Donnie Brasco - A Little Princess - Bugsy - Rain Man - Good Morning, Vietnam; TV: Love Monkey - The Guardian
SUBMISSION POLICY No unsolicited submissions

Mark Johnson ....No Title
Tom Williams ....No Title
Bryan Seabury ....No Title
Melissa Bernstein ....No Title
Michelle Cates ....No Title

GRANADA AMERICA

15303 Ventura Blvd., Ste. C800
Sherman Oaks, CA 91403
PHONE 818-455-4600
FAX 818-455-4700

TYPES Made-for-TV/Cable Movies - Miniseries - Reality TV - TV Series
PRODUCTION But Can They Sing? (VH1)
POST PRODUCTION The Ron Clark Story
CREDITS Hit Me Baby One More Time (NBC) - Hell's Kitchen (Fox) - Nanny 911 (Fox) - Celebrity Fit Club (VH1) - Scent of Murder - Second Nature - Rush of Fear - Rudy: The Rudy Giuliani Story - Maiden Voyage - Identity Theft - The Twelve Days of Christmas - I'm a Celebrity: Get Me Out of Here (ABC) - Airline (A&E) - Room Raiders (MTV) - Dallas SWAT (A&E) - First 48 (A&E) - Ultimate Tree House (Discovery) - House of Dreams (A&E) - Caught! (Court TV)

David Gyngell ....CEO
Emily Brecher ....CFO
Katrina Moran ....Executive VP, Digital Media Division
Charles Tremayne ....Executive VP, East Coast
Sam Zoda ....Executive VP, West Coast
Jody Brockway ....Sr. VP, Scripted Development
Craig McNeil ....Sr. VP, Scripted Production
David Polakoff ....Sr. VP, Finance & Business Development
Curt Northrup ....Sr. VP, Non-Scripted Development
Ivan Garel-Jones ....Sr. VP, Business Affairs
Patrice Andrews ....Sr. VP, Production & Operations
Nick Oakley ....Director, Development (LA)
Pami Shamir ....Director, Development (NY)

GRAND PRODUCTIONS, INC.

10201 W. Pico Blvd., Bldg. 51
Los Angeles, CA 90035
PHONE 310-369-5027
FAX 310-969-3142

TYPES Features - Made-for-TV/Cable Movies - TV Series
HAS DEAL WITH Fox Television Studios
DEVELOPMENT Mi Familia - Cat's Cradle - Golden Hour - Dad (NBC) - Chasing Gold (WB Network) - Urban Arcana (Sci Fi) - Paradise Salvage (Spike) - The Kelly & Craig Perkins Story (TNT)
PRE-PRODUCTION Grace (Pilot)
PRODUCTION The Sante & Kenny Kimes Project
CREDITS Any Day Now - Beauty - A Song from the Heart - The Round Table - Leaving L.A. - Adventure, Inc. - An Unexpected Love - John Grisham's The Street Lawyer
SUBMISSION POLICY No unsolicited material

Gary A. Randall ....President/Owner
Alex Sapot ....Director, Development

GRAY ANGEL PRODUCTIONS

74 Market St.
Venice, CA 90291
PHONE 310-581-0010
FAX 310-396-0551

TYPES Features
CREDITS Bastard Out of Carolina - Agnes Browne

Anjelica Huston ....President
Jaclyn Bashoff ....Director, Development

*GRAYMARK PRODUCTIONS INC.

101 N. Robinson Ave., Ste. 920
Oklahoma City, OK 73102
PHONE .405-601-5300
FAX .405-601-4550
EMAIL .megan@graymark.net
WEB SITE .www.graymarkproductions.com
TYPES Direct-to-Video/DVD - Features
POST PRODUCTION Fingerprints
COMPLETED UNRELEASED Soul's Midnight - Surveillance - The Hunt

Gray Fredrickson .COO
John Simonelli .CEO
Mark Kidd .CFO
Amy Briede .Executive Assistant
Megan Slump .Executive Assistant

GRB ENTERTAINMENT

c/o Michael Branton
13400 Riverside Dr., Ste. 300
Sherman Oaks, CA 91423
PHONE .818-728-7600
FAX .818-728-7601
EMAIL .mbranton@grbtv.com
WEB SITE .www.grbtv.com
TYPES Made-for-TV/Cable Movies - Reality TV - Specials - TV Series
DEVELOPMENT Rumble
PRODUCTION Intervention (A&E) - Tuckerville (TLC) - Untold Stories of the ER (TLC) - Flight Attendant School (Travel) - Guardian Angels, MD (TLC) - Full Force Nature (The Weather Channel)
CREDITS Growing Up Gotti (A&E) - Princes of Malibu - Expeditions to the Edge - Invasion Iowa - Next Action Star - Cannonball Run - Travel Scams & Rip-Offs Revealed - World of Wonder - Movie Magic
COMMENTS International distribution; Unscripted drama and comedy; Incredible clip shows

Gary R. Benz .President
Michael Branton .Executive VP, Creative Affairs
Mark Rains .Sr. VP, Production
Brant Pinvidic .VP, Development

GREASY ENTERTAINMENT

2422-B Wilshire Blvd.
Santa Monica, CA 90403
PHONE .310-586-2300
FAX .310-586-2336
TYPES Animation - Features - TV Series
HAS DEAL WITH Universal Pictures
DEVELOPMENT Loudermilk

Dan Heder .Co-President
Doug Heder .Co-President
Jon Heder .Co-President
Darren Everitt .Executive Assistant

SARAH GREEN FILM CORP.

451 Greenwich St., 7th Fl.
New York, NY 10013
PHONE .646-214-7929
FAX .646-214-7920
EMAIL .sgfilmcorp@prodigy.net
TYPES Features
DEVELOPMENT Wise Child - Monopolis - The City - Beauty - Okefenokee
CREDITS The New World - Frida - State and Main - Girlfight - The Winslow Boy - The Spanish Prisoner - The Secret of Roan Inish - Havana Nights - City of Hope - Passion Fish - Oleanna
SUBMISSION POLICY No unsolicited material

Sarah Green .Producer
Ivan Bess .Associate Producer

GREENESTREET FILMS

9 Desbrosses St., 2nd Fl.
New York, NY 10013
PHONE .212-609-9000
FAX .212-609-9099
EMAIL .general@gstreet.com
WEB SITE .www.greenestreetfilms.com
TYPES Documentaries - Features
DEVELOPMENT The Invisible Woman - The Townie - Gary the Tennis Coach
PRODUCTION Tenderness - Bill
POST PRODUCTION Unknown
UPCOMING RELEASES A Prairie Home Companion - Yes - Slow Burn - Once in a Lifetime - Awake - The Pleasure of Your Company
CREDITS Romance & Cigarettes - Piñero - Just a Kiss - The Chateau - A Price Above Rubies - Illuminata - Company Man - I'm Not Rappaport - Lisa Picard Is Famous - In the Bedroom - Swimfan - Uptown Girls

John Penotti .President/Founding Partner
Fisher Stevens .Creative Director/Founding Partner
Ariel Veneziano .President, Greenestreet International
Tim Williams .Head, Production
Vicki Cherkas .Head, Legal & Business Affairs
Rich Glassey .Manager, Production
Annie Marter .Head, Development
Crystal Bourbeau .Manager, International
Amanda Essick .Assistant to John Penotti
Matt Portner .Assistant, Development

ROBERT GREENWALD PRODUCTIONS

10510 Culver Blvd.
Culver City, CA 90232-3400
PHONE .310-204-0404
FAX .310-204-0174
WEB SITE .www.rgpinc.com
TYPES Direct-to-Video/DVD - Documentaries - Features - Made-for-TV/Cable Movies - Reality TV - TV Series
POST PRODUCTION A Christmas Wedding
CREDITS Augusta, Gone - Trump Unauthorized - Murder in the Hamptons - Wal-Mart: The High Cost of Low Price - The Book of Ruth - Redeemer - Steal This Movie - Audrey Hepburn - Deadlocked - Blonde - Livin' for Love: The Natalie Cole Story - The Crooked E. - Uncovered - The Dead Will Tell - Plain Truth - Beach Girls

Robert Greenwald .Producer/Director
Philip Kleinbart .Producer/Executive VP
Alys Shanti .Producer/Sr. VP
Tracy Fleischman .Assistant to Robert Greenwald
Matt Graham .Assistant to Alys Shanti

GREENWOOD AVENUE ENTERTAINMENT

2004 Palisades Dr.
Pacific Palisades, CA 90272
PHONE 310-454-9984
FAX 310-454-9984
EMAIL . . . . dwyercat@aol.com
SECOND EMAIL . . . . davesprod@aol.com
TYPES Direct-to-Video/DVD - Documentaries - Made-for-TV/Cable Movies - Syndication - TV Series
CREDITS Deep Diver: Tiger Shark Odyssey - Baywatch - Thunder in Paradise - Avalon: Beyond the Abyss - Wildfire

David W. Hagar . . . . Executive Producer/Director
Cathy Dwyer . . . . Executive Producer

THE GREIF COMPANY

9233 W. Pico Blvd., Ste. 218
Los Angeles, CA 90035
PHONE 310-385-1200
FAX 310-385-1207
WEB SITE . . . . www.greifcompany.com
TYPES Documentaries - Features - Made-for-TV/Cable Movies - Reality TV - TV Series
PRE-PRODUCTION Marlon Brando Documentary
PRODUCTION Gene Simmons Family Jewels
UPCOMING RELEASES Funny Money
CREDITS Monday Night Mayhem - Word of Honor - Walker: Texas Ranger - Keys to Tulsa - Baby for Sale - Heaven's Prisoners - Meet Wally Sparks - The Maddening - Steve McQueen: The Essence of Cool - Intimate Portraits - A&E Biography - Headliners & Legends
SUBMISSION POLICY No unsolicited material

Leslie Greif . . . . President/Executive Producer/Director/Writer
Joanne Rubino . . . . Executive in Charge of Production
Mimi Freedman . . . . Producer/Director
Tavis Larkham . . . . Assistant to Mr. Greif

GREYSTONE TELEVISION AND FILMS

5200 Lankershim Blvd., Ste. 800
North Hollywood, CA 91601
PHONE 818-762-2900
FAX 818-762-1626
EMAIL . . . . info@greystonetv.com
WEB SITE . . . . www.greystonetv.com
TYPES Direct-to-Video/DVD - Documentaries - Features - Reality TV - TV Series
CREDITS TR: An American Lion - Wild West Tech (Series) - Fine Living: Breathing Room - American Presidency - Spirit of Yosemite - Wild Wheels (Series) - Alexander - A&E Biography (Various)

Craig Haffner . . . . President/CEO
Donna E. Lusitana . . . . President, Greystone Television
Shinaan Krakowsky . . . . COO/General Counsel
Rick Brookwell . . . . CFO/Corporate Counsel

MERV GRIFFIN ENTERTAINMENT

130 S. El Camino Dr.
Beverly Hills, CA 90212
PHONE 310-385-2700
FAX 310-385-2728
WEB SITE . . . . www.merv.com
TYPES Features - Made-for-TV/Cable Movies - Reality TV - Specials - TV Series
CREDITS The Merv Griffin Show - Jeopardy - Wheel of Fortune - Dance Fever - The Ainsley Harriott Show - The Christmas List - Click! - Men Are from Mars, Women Are from Venus - Murder at the Cannes Film Festival - Inside the Osmonds - Gilda Radner: It's Always Something - Shade

Merv Griffin . . . . Chairman
Lawrence Cohen . . . . President/CEO
Ron Ward . . . . Executive VP
Jim Bradley . . . . TV Development
Ray Brune . . . . TV Development
Ernest Chambers . . . . Film & TV Development
Candace Farrell . . . . Film & TV Development
Tony Griffin . . . . Film & TV Development
Audrey Loggia . . . . Film & TV Development
Andrew Yani . . . . TV Development

NICK GRILLO PRODUCTIONS

3000 Olympic Blvd., Bldg. 1, Ste. 2510
Santa Monica, CA 90404
PHONE 310-453-1351
FAX 310-453-9254
TYPES Features - Made-for-TV/Cable Movies - TV Series
HAS DEAL WITH Baldwin Entertainment Group, Ltd.
DEVELOPMENT Custer/Battles - Nothing Like It in the World - Defender of the People - Orangeburg Massacre - Honor for Sale - The Culture of Heroin - High Flyer - Manifest Destiny - Cuba Libre
CREDITS Gods and Generals - Deacons for Defense - Conviction

Nick Grillo . . . . President/Producer

GRINNING DOG PICTURES

GreeneStreet Film Center
9 Desbrosses St., 2nd Fl.
New York, NY 10013
PHONE 609-922-1960
FAX 239-590-9988
EMAIL . . . . connie@grinningdogpictures.com
WEB SITE . . . . www.grinningdogpictures.com
TYPES Documentaries - Reality TV - TV Series
DEVELOPMENT Jail Journey - The OSI Files - The Postcard Geisha - Cowboy: The Life of a Legend - Bogie & Me: A Beautiful Friendship - Precious Cargo - Pro Bono
PRODUCTION Map of the Missing (Documentary) - Colby's Story: Pink Means Fatality (Documentary)
CREDITS Wolfman: Myth & Science - Jessica Savitch Bio - The Curse of Tutankhamun - Medical Detectives - Forensic Files - Science Frontiers
COMMENTS Feature length IMAX films in development with series attached; Florida address: 9080 Spring Mountain Way, Fort Myers, FL 33908

Connie Bottinelli . . . . CEO/Executive Producer
Gary Parker . . . . Writer

GRISHAM FILMS USA
477 E. Freehold Rd.
Freehold, NJ 07728
PHONE 917-887-8851
EMAIL ....esavia@grishamfilms.com
WEB SITE ....www.grishamfilms.com
TYPES Commercials - Documentaries - Features - Made-for-TV/Cable Movies - TV Series
DEVELOPMENT The Gucci Wars - Further Lane - Seven Five Nine - Angel on My Shoulder
CREDITS Cuban Fire - The Big Bang

Emile Savia ....Producer

ALLISON GRODNER PRODUCTIONS, INC.
12925 Riverside Dr., 4th Fl.
Sherman Oaks, CA 91423
PHONE 818-325-6900
FAX 818-379-4720/818-379-4722
TYPES Documentaries - Reality TV
UPCOMING RELEASES Get This Party Started - My Other Life
CREDITS Brat Camp (ABC) - Situation: Comedy (Bravo) - Minding the Store (TBS) - The Road to Stardom with Missy Elliott (UPN) - Big Brother 2-7 (CBS) - Blow Out (Bravo) - The Family (ABC) - DNA: Guilty or Innocent - Flipped - The Teen Files - Rescue 911 - Scared Straight! - The Story of Santa Claus - Scared Straight! 20 Years Later - Family Business 1-4 (Showtime)
SUBMISSION POLICY No unsolicited material

Allison Grodner ....Executive Producer
Jeff Anderson ....Executive in Charge of Production
Charisma Sieras ....Assistant to Allison Grodner

DAN GRODNIK PRODUCTIONS
1180 S. Beverly Dr., Ste. 700
Los Angeles, CA 90035
PHONE 310-271-7698/310-503-8455
FAX 323-927-1614
EMAIL ....grodzilla@earthlink.net
SECOND EMAIL ....dgrodnik_assistant@yahoo.com
TYPES Features - Made-for-TV/Cable Movies - TV Series
HAS DEAL WITH Genius Products, Inc.
PRE-PRODUCTION Something in the Pipes
PRODUCTION Camille
UPCOMING RELEASES Bobby
CREDITS Come Early Morning - Mini's First Time - Blue Demon - Who Is Cletis Tout? - National Lampoon's Christmas Vacation - Powder
SUBMISSION POLICY Email dgrodnik_assistant@yahoo.com

Daniel L. Grodnik ....Producer
Wendy Moore ....Creative Director

GROOVE MOBILE
3 Riverside Dr.
Andover, MA 01810
PHONE 978-683-5882
FAX 978-683-5248
EMAIL ....info@groovemobile.net
WEB SITE ....www.groovemobile.net
TYPES Mobile Content

Adam Sexton ....Vice President

GROSS ENTERTAINMENT
500 S. Buena Vista St., Old Animation Bldg., Rm. 3B-8
Burbank, CA 91521-1850
PHONE 818-560-8117
FAX 818-560-8180
EMAIL ....nick.nicolella@abc.com
TYPES Features - Reality TV - TV Series
HAS DEAL WITH Touchstone Television
DEVELOPMENT Fired Up - Napoleon (ABC)
PRODUCTION Day Break (ABC) - Twenty Questions (ABC)
POST PRODUCTION Across the Universe (Revolution Studios)
COMPLETED UNRELEASED Neighbors (ABC) - Sherman's March (ABC)
CREDITS Joe Somebody - Bronx Cheers
SUBMISSION POLICY No unsolicited material

Matthew Gross ....President
Nicholas Nicolella ....Development

KEN GROSS MANAGEMENT
7720 Sunset Blvd., 2nd Fl.
Los Angeles, CA 90046
PHONE 323-512-2999
FAX 323-512-2699
EMAIL ....kgmla@pacbell.net
TYPES Direct-to-Video/DVD - Features - Made-for-TV/Cable Movies - Miniseries - TV Series
DEVELOPMENT A Christmas Wish - Slow Emergencies - The Dreyfus Affair - Guys - The Deal
CREDITS When Angels Come to Town - Murder at Midnight - A Town Without Christmas - Stealing Sinatra - Finding John Christmas
COMMENTS Also manages writers, directors and producers

Kenneth H. Gross ....President/Producer/Manager
Daryl DePollo ....VP, Development

BETH GROSSBARD PRODUCTIONS
9696 Culver Blvd., Ste. 208
Culver City, CA 90232
PHONE 310-841-2555/818-758-2500
FAX 310-841-5934
EMAIL ....bethgcap@aol.com
SECOND EMAIL ....bgpix@sbcglobal.net
TYPES Features - Made-for-TV/Cable Movies - Miniseries - TV Series
HAS DEAL WITH Craig Anderson Productions
DEVELOPMENT The Angels of Morgan Hill - The Christmas Hope - Untouchable - Joey Pigza - The Frank Barnaba Story
CREDITS Black Widower - The Christmas Blessing - Mind Over Murder - Meltdown - The Christmas Shoes - Passion & Prejudice - Range of Motion - No One Could Protect Her
SUBMISSION POLICY Query with treatment

Beth Grossbard ....Executive Producer
Jessica Roach ....Development Associate

GROSSBART KENT PRODUCTIONS
9255 Sunset Blvd., Ste. 500
Los Angeles, CA 90069
PHONE 310-275-5800
FAX 310-275-5818
TYPES: Features - Syndication - TV Series
CREDITS: Unforgivable - Any Mother's Son - The Preppie Murder - The Alison Gertz Story - Personally Yours - Heartless

Jack Grossbart ....President/Executive Producer
Linda L. Kent ....Sr. VP, Development
Scott Sablosky ....Executive Assistant

GROSSO JACOBSON COMMUNICATIONS CORP.
1801 Avenue of the Stars, Ste. 911
Los Angeles, CA 90067
PHONE 310-788-8900/212-644-6909
FAX 310-788-8914/212-355-3178
TYPES: Documentaries - Features - Made-for-TV/Cable Movies - Miniseries - Reality TV - Specials - TV Series
DEVELOPMENT: Untitled A&E Limited Series - Untitled HBO Special
POST PRODUCTION: Kings of South Beach (A&E)
CREDITS: Mary Higgins Clark Movies: Remember Me (CBS) - While My Pretty One Sleeps (Family Channel) - Let Me Call You Sweetheart (Family Channel) - Moonlight Becomes You (Family Channel) - Loves Music - Loves to Dance (PAX) - Pretend You Don't See Her (PAX) - You Belong to Me (PAX)- Haven't We Met Before (PAX) - All Around the Town (PAX) - Lucky Day (PAX); Baker's Dozen (CBS) - Johnny Garage (CBS) - Night Heat (CBS) - Hot Shots (CBS) - Diamonds (CBS) - Counterstrike (USA) - True Blue (NBC) - A Family for Joe (NBC) - Top Cops (CBS) - Secret Service (NBC) - Juvenile Justice (Syndicated/New World) - The Big Easy (USA) - Judgment Day (HBO) - Out of the Darkness (CBS) - Trackdown: Finding the Goodbar Killer (NBC) - Gunfighters (Syndicated/Tribune) - All American Girl: Mary Kay Letourneau (USA) - Lost in Death Valley (CBS) - Diary of a Teenage Shoplifter (CBS) - Pee Wee's Playhouse (ABC) - The French Connection's 30th Anniversary Special (FOX) - Mug Shot (Court TV)
COMMENTS: East Coast office: 767 Third Ave., 27th Fl., New York, NY 10017; Toronto office: 373 Front St. East, Toronto, Ontario M5A 1G4, Canada

Sonny Grosso ....Co-Chairman/Executive Producer (NY)
Lawrence S. Jacobson ....Co-Chairman/Executive Producer (LA)
Clay Kahler ....Executive Producer (LA)
Keith Johnson ....Sr. VP, Development (NY)
Christina Avis Krauss ....Development & Casting (NY)
Lena Saban ....Controller (NY)

GROSS-WESTON PRODUCTIONS
10560 Wilshire Blvd., Ste. 801
Los Angeles, CA 90024
PHONE 310-777-0010
FAX 310-777-0016
EMAIL ....gross-weston@sbcglobal.net
TYPES: Direct-to-Video/DVD - Features - Made-for-TV/Cable Movies - Miniseries - TV Series
DEVELOPMENT: Rat Dog Dick - All the Good Ones Are Married (Lifetime) - The Fountainhead (Paramount/Warner Bros.) - Untitled Screen Gems Feature
CREDITS: Stranger Game (Lifetime) - Encrypt (Sci Fi) - Decoy (Hearst) - Little John (CBS) - Hallmark Billionaire Boys Club (NBC) - Children of Times Square (ABC) - Have You Seen My Son (ABC) - Can of Worms (Disney Channel) - Invisible Child (Lifetime) - Big & Hairy (Showtime) The Spree (Showtime) - A Place for Annie (Hallmark Hall of Fame)
SUBMISSION POLICY: From agent or lawyer, or with a release form

Marcy Gross ....Executive Producer
Ann Weston ....Executive Producer

GROUNDSWELL PRODUCTION
9350 Wilshire Blvd., Ste. 324
Beverly Hills, CA 90212
PHONE 323-850-3530
TYPES: Features
DEVELOPMENT: The Mysteries of Pittsburgh - Trust - Marc Pease Experience
CREDITS: The Illusionist - The Family Stone - Sideways - House of Sand and Fog - Thirteen - The Guru - 40 Days and 40 Nights - Second String

Michael London ....CEO
Bruna Papandrea ....President, Production
Khristina Kravas ....VP
Juliana Farrell ....Creative Executive
Elizabeth Grave ....Executive Assistant
Lucy Shapiro ....Executive Assistant
Eric Borja ....Executive Assistant

*THE GROUP ENTERTAINMENT
115 W. 29th St., #1102
New York, NY 10001
PHONE 212-868-5233
FAX 212-504-3082
EMAIL ....info@thegroupentertainment.com
SECOND EMAIL ....scripts@thegroupentertainment.com
TYPES: Documentaries - Features - Music Videos - TV Series
DEVELOPMENT: Moustache - Bodies of Water - The Adventures of Power
PRE-PRODUCTION: I Do and I Don't
PRODUCTION: Water
COMPLETED UNRELEASED: Pagans - Sweet Land - Findlove - Just Like the Son - American Cannibal
SUBMISSION POLICY: Email query first

Gill Holland ....Partner/Producer
Matt Parker ....Partner/Producer
Kyle Luker ....Partner/Manager
Cymbre Walk ....Partner/Director, Development
Raymond DeMarco ....Managing Partner
Mike Morley ....Managing Partner
Carly Hugo ....No Title

GRYPHON FILMS
13042 Rose Ave.
Los Angeles, CA 90066
PHONE 310-861-5383
WEB SITE ....www.gryphonfilms.com
TYPES Features
DEVELOPMENT The Cloak and the Breach - Steele's Island - Call of Cthulhu - Five Generations of Jerks - House of Shadows - Parallel Kiss
CREDITS The Cooler - Lady Jayne Killer

Robert Gryphon ....Chairman/Executive Producer
Brett Morrison ....President/Producer
Wil Forbis ....Genre Development

GSN
A Sony Pictures/Liberty Media Company
2150 Colorado Ave.
Santa Monica, CA 90404
PHONE 310-255-6800
FAX 310-255-6810
WEB SITE ....www.gsn.com
TYPES Documentaries - Internet Content - Mobile Content - Specials - TV Series
DEVELOPMENT Your Worst Nightmare - That's the Question
PRODUCTION 50 Greatest Game Shows of All Time
POST PRODUCTION High Stakes Poker 2 - World Series of Blackjack 3
UPCOMING RELEASES Chain Reaction - Fame Game
COMMENTS The Network for Games; Casino shows; Game shows; Interactive programming

Rich Cronin ....President/CEO
Brent Willman ....CFO, Finance
Jan Hatcher ....Sr. VP, Distribution
Dena Kaplan ....Sr. VP, Marketing
Michael Kohn ....Sr. VP, Business & Legal Affairs
Chris Raleigh ....Sr. VP, Advertising Sales
John P. Roberts ....Sr. VP, Digital Media & Interactive Entertainment
Dave Andrews ....VP, Production, Interactive Entertainment
Kevin Belinkoff ....VP, Programming
Joel Chiodi ....VP, Promotions & Marketing
Zig Gauthier ....VP, Original Programming
Linnea Hemenez ....VP, Creative Services
David Primuth ....VP, Research
Cindy Ronzoni ....VP, Publicity & Corporate Communications
Sabri Sansoy ....VP, Technology, Interactive Entertainment
Ryan Tredinnick ....VP, Operations
Michael Bevan ....Executive Director, Development
Rich Fineza ....Executive Director, Research

GUARDIAN ENTERTAINMENT, LTD.
71 Fifth Ave., 5th Fl.
New York, NY 10003
PHONE 212-727-4729/845-647-7369
EMAIL ....guardian@guardianltd.com
WEB SITE ....www.guardianltd.com
TYPES Animation - Commercials - Direct-to-Video/DVD - Features - Made-for-TV/Cable Movies - Mobile Content - Music Videos - Reality TV - TV Series
DEVELOPMENT Deeper Shade of Blue - Untitled Superhero Film Series
PRODUCTION 90 MPH: Down a Dead End Street - Teen Jesus (Animated) - Twist the Cap: A Tale of Redemption
POST PRODUCTION Gun for Hire
COMPLETED UNRELEASED Behind the Game - BlackFist
CREDITS Untitled Dane Cook Project - Retaliation - Looks Like Another Brown Trouser Job - Out of the Darkness - Anne B. Real
COMMENTS High Definition co-production with Sony; Deal with Metroscope Entertainment; West Coast office: 1701 S. La Cienega Blvd., Los Angeles, CA 90035; Also Post Production facility

Richard Miller ....CEO/Executive Producer
Clem Turner ....VP, Business Development/General Counsel
Peter Benson ....Treasurer
David Oltman ....Line Producer
Richard Thomson ....Composer
Rene Fidz ....Sr. Editor
Scott Benson ....Editor
Daniel Wright ....UMD Editor

***G-UNIT TELEVISION & FILMS**
PO Box 1500
New York, NY 10116
PHONE 212-359-3000
FAX 212-359-3019
TYPES Direct-to-Video/DVD - Documentaries - Features - Internet Content - Music Videos
DEVELOPMENT Live Bet

Curtis "50 Cent" Jackson ....CEO/President
Sha Money XL ....President
Nikki Martin ....VP
Derick Prosper ....A&R
Sheena Curry ....Manager

GUNN FILMS

500 S. Buena Vista St., Old Animation Bldg., Ste. 3-A7
Burbank, CA 91521
PHONE 818-560-6156
FAX 818-842-8394

TYPES	Features - TV Series
HAS DEAL WITH	Walt Disney Pictures/Touchstone Pictures
DEVELOPMENT	Untitled Viking Project - Spaulding Gets Nothing - Maid of Honor - All Access - South China Sea - Candleshoe - Snow and the Seven - Welcome to the Doghouse - Off the Chain - Society Girl - College Roadtrip - Escape to Witch Mountain - Lady Marian - Dear God, It's Me Rod - The Lighthouse
CREDITS	Freaky Friday - The Haunted Mansion - The Country Bears - Sky High
SUBMISSION POLICY	No unsolicited submissions

Andrew Gunn . . . . Producer
Ann Marie Sanderlin . . . . President (818-560-6284)
Amy Stenftenagel . . . . Creative Exectuive
Marc Brunswick . . . . Assistant to Ann Marie Sanderlin
Erin Westerman . . . . Assistant to Andrew Gunn

THE GURIN COMPANY

11846 Ventura Blvd., Ste. 303
Studio City, CA 91604
PHONE 818-623-9393
FAX 818-623-9595

TYPES	Mobile Content - Reality TV - Specials - TV Series
DEVELOPMENT	Test the Nation - Fred Silverman Project - What Kids Really Think - Fort Boyard - The Burundis - The Arena - Race to the Summit
PRE-PRODUCTION	Fox New Years 2006 - USOC 2008
PRODUCTION	Lingo - Miss Universe 2006
CREDITS	Fox New Years Eve Live 2005 - USOC 2006 - Candid Camera - World's Most Dangerous Stunts - Weakest Link - Lingo - Voice of a Child - Only Joking - Twenty One - Now or Never - On Thin Ice - KISS Live - Miss USA - Miss Universe - Miss Teen USA - Queen for a Day - Survival Test - Settle the Score - Test the Nation - Women Rock - US Olympics Hall of Fame 2004 - All New 3's a Crowd - When Cameras Cross the Line - Extreme World Records

Phil Gurin . . . . President
Troy Norton . . . . Producer
Andrew Simonian . . . . Director, Development
Marc Jansen . . . . Creative Consultant
Jordan Goodman . . . . Post Production Supervisor
Erika Gardner . . . . Assistant, Phil Gurin
Kristi Stossel . . . . Reception

GUY WALKS INTO A BAR

7421 Beverly Blvd., Ste. 4
Los Angeles, CA 90036
PHONE 323-930-9935/212-941-1509
FAX 323-930-9934/212-941-1557
EMAIL . . . . info@guywalks.com
WEB SITE . . . . www.guywalks.com

TYPES	Features - TV Series
HAS DEAL WITH	Paramount Pictures
DEVELOPMENT	Number One Girl - Dillinger - The Retreat - The Manny - The User - Starship Dave - Wild About Harry - It's Not You, It's Me - Camp Sachem - Mean Streak - Oxley's Road
CREDITS	Elf - Out of Time
SUBMISSION POLICY	No unsolicited material

Todd Komarnicki . . . . Partner/Producer
Jon Berg . . . . Partner/Producer
Matthew Weinberg . . . . Manager/Executive
Ross Siegel . . . . Director, Development
Heather Zicko . . . . Assistant to Todd Komarnicki
Adam Friedberg . . . . Assistant to Matthew Weinberg
Andy Tunnicliffe . . . . Assistant to Jon Berg

H. BEALE COMPANY

PO Box 5356
Beverly Hills, CA 90209
PHONE 310-278-1762
FAX 310-278-6971

TYPES	Features - Made-for-TV/Cable Movies - Syndication - TV Series
CREDITS	Bladesquad - Beggars and Choosers

Lilly Tartikoff . . . . President

H2F ENTERTAINMENT

9000 Sunset Blvd., Ste. 710
West Hollywood, CA 90069
PHONE 310-275-3750
FAX 310-275-3770

TYPES	Features - TV Series
DEVELOPMENT	Wulf - Gotta Dance - The Chump - Man Crush - 5-0 - Camp Sachem - Cox Blocker - Faded Stars - Super Movie - Untitled Sports Movie Parody
POST PRODUCTION	Whisper
CREDITS	Sorority Boys - Waiting

Chris Fenton . . . . Partner
Walter Hamada . . . . Partner
Jason Hendrixson . . . . No Title
George Allicon . . . . No Title
Alison Black . . . . No Title
Ed Corrado . . . . No Title
Jessica Ehimika . . . . No Title
Max Kramer . . . . No Title

H2O MOTION PICTURES
8549 Hedges Pl.
Los Angeles, CA 90069
PHONE 323-654-5920/44-207-240-5656
FAX 323-654-5923/44-207-240-5647
EMAIL .....h2o@h2omotionpictures.com
WEB SITE www.h2omotionpictures.com

TYPES	Features
DEVELOPMENT	Capa - His Majesty's Pleasure - People Who Knock on the Door - Running Wild
POST PRODUCTION	Opium-Diary of a Madwoman
UPCOMING RELEASES	Big Nothing
CREDITS	Fateless - Formula 51 - Max - Owning Mahowny - eXistenZ - Sunshine

Andras Hamori .....Producer

HAFT ENTERTAINMENT
38 Gramercy Park North, #2C
New York, NY 10010
PHONE 212-586-3881
FAX 212-459-9798
EMAIL .....haft11@hotmail.com

TYPES	Direct-to-Video/DVD - Documentaries - Features - Made-for-TV/Cable Movies - Reality TV - Specials - TV Series
PRE-PRODUCTION	Journey Home - Fate
PRODUCTION	MADTV - Climb Higher
CREDITS	Make Your Fortune Online (PBS) - Eulogy - The Singing Detective - Dead Poets Society - Emma - Pirates of Silicon Valley - Tigerland - Jakob the Liar - The Third Miracle - Hocus Pocus - Last Dance - Beyond Therapy
SUBMISSION POLICY	Published works or screenplays through representation only

Steven Haft .....Producer
Jennifer Chiurco .....Development

HALF SHELL ENTERTAINMENT
145 Bay St., Unit 11
Santa Monica, CA 90405
PHONE 310-314-7672
EMAIL .....info@halfshellent.com
WEB SITE .....www.halfshellent.com

TYPES	Direct-to-Video/DVD - Documentaries - Features - Internet Content - TV Series
HAS DEAL WITH	National Lampoon
DEVELOPMENT	Stud: Adventures in Breeding - Art Imitates Life - Back to Paradise

Mark Burrell .....Partner
James DeJulio .....Partner
Rob Salvatore .....Partner

HALLMARK HALL OF FAME PRODUCTIONS, INC.
12001 Ventura Pl., Ste. 300
Studio City, CA 91604
PHONE 818-505-9191
FAX .....818-505-9842/818-505-8379 (Production)

TYPES	Made-for-TV/Cable Movies
PRE-PRODUCTION	Candles on Bay Street
POST PRODUCTION	The Valley of Light
CREDITS	In from the Night - Silver Bells - Riding the Bus with My Sister - A Painted House - Blackwater Lightship - Back When We Were Grown-Ups - Magic of Ordinary Days - The Water Is Wide
SUBMISSION POLICY	All material to be submitted by film professionals or accompanied by Hallmark release
COMMENTS	2-hour TV dramas; Post production fax: 818-505-9394; Development fax: 818-505-0776

Dennis Sullivan .....L.A. Coordinator

HAND PICKED FILMS
2893 Sea Ridge
Malibu, CA 90265
PHONE 310-456-3444
FAX 310-456-1166
EMAIL .....michel@romanoshaneproductions.com
WEB SITE .....www.romanoshaneproductions.com

TYPES	Animation - Direct-to-Video/DVD - Features - Made-for-TV/Cable Movies - Specials - TV Series
HAS DEAL WITH	National Lampoon
DEVELOPMENT	Leonardo - Black Belt Club - Bye Pass Gang - Hot House - I, Robot 2 - Too Good to Be True - Fixed - The Life Story of Buddha - Happily Ever After
PRE-PRODUCTION	Band on the Run - The Italian - Paranoia - Saint Louis Blues - The Otherside
PRODUCTION	The Lodge
COMPLETED UNRELEASED	Badland - Statistics
CREDITS	Catch Me If You Can - North Fork - Stealing Time - The Lost Treasures of the Titanic - Dracula: Live from Transylvania - I, Robot
COMMENTS	Co-financing; Foreign Sales; Co-Productions

Anthony Romano .....Co-President/Producer
Michel Shane .....Co-President/Producer

HANDPRINT ENTERTAINMENT
1100 Glendon Ave., Ste. 1000
Los Angeles, CA 90024

PHONE	310-481-4400
FAX	310-481-4419
TYPES	Features - TV Series
DEVELOPMENT	Wedding Daze (Media 8) - Sanford and Son (Columbia Pictures)
CREDITS	The Tyra Banks Show (UPN) - Fresh Prince of Bel Air - Above the Rim - Booty Call - The Fighting Temptations - Monster - Maid in Manhattan

Benny Medina . . . Partner
Jeff Pollack . . . Partner
Evan Weiss . . . Manager/Head, TV Development
Michael Baum . . . Manager
Jill Littman . . . Manager
Jean Kwolek . . . Jr. Manager, Music
Melissa Ruderman . . . Jr. Manager, Music

PETER HANKWITZ PRODUCTION & MANAGEMENT
14110 Riverside Dr.
Sherman Oaks, CA 91423

PHONE	818-943-2283
FAX	818-337-7444
EMAIL	info@hankwitz.com
WEB SITE	www.hankwitz.com
TYPES	Documentaries - Features - TV Series
CREDITS	Film: Gallipoli (Documentary) - The Hitties (Documentary); TV: The Investigators: Deadly Lessons - America's Crime Writers: Murder They Wrote - The Investigators: A Day to Die For - Russell Simmons Presents Hip Hop Justice - Safety Challenge: Buyer Beware - A Dangerous Game - Lover's Leap

Peter Hankwitz . . . Executive Producer
Hali Simon . . . Head, Corporate Communications
Seth Baron . . . Assistant to Peter Hankwitz

HARBOR LIGHTS PRODUCTIONS
8634 Oak Park Ave.
Northridge, CA 91325

PHONE	818-993-5255
FAX	818-993-5266
TYPES	Documentaries - Features - Made-for-TV/Cable Movies - Reality TV - TV Series
DEVELOPMENT	Prison Runners
CREDITS	White Squall - Titanic - Nervous Ticks - Race for Glory - All's Fair

Rocky Lang . . . Writer/Producer/Director

HARDING & ASSOCIATES
c/o Dave Harding
11846 Ventura Blvd., Ste. 204
Studio City, CA 91604

PHONE	818-432-4200
TYPES	Documentaries - Features - Reality TV - Specials - TV Series
PRODUCTION	After the Attack - Science of the Bible - Made in America - Unsolved History - Leonard Cohen
CREDITS	Grizzly Man - Second Verdict - Celebrity Undercover - A Century of Living - Yes, Virginia - Secrets Revealed - World's Most Dangerous... - Anything to Win

Dave Harding . . . Executive Producer

HARDING-KURTZ ENTERTAINMENT
9946 St. Marys Circle
Cowan Heights, CA 92705

PHONE	714-997-8807/310-962-8644
FAX	714-394-2676
EMAIL	gary@harding-kurtz.com
TYPES	Features - Made-for-TV/Cable Movies - Reality TV - TV Series
DEVELOPMENT	The Spike Girls (MOW/Disney Channel) - Dia de los Muertos (Feature/Zalman King Co./CFQ Films) - XtraOrdinary (Reality/Dick Clark Prods.) - Trashy Lingerie (Reality/New Line TV) - The Crew (TV/Humble Journey Films) - The Frank Sinatra Story (MOW/Big Purple Prods.)
PRODUCTION	Curb Appeal (USA) - Gallup Extreme Hidden Video (TLC) - Testing 101(TLC)

Gary Kurtz . . . Producer
Dave Harding . . . Producer
Steve Gerbson . . . Producer
Peter Zasuly . . . Producer

DEAN HARGROVE PRODUCTIONS
10202 W. Washington Blvd.
Culver City, CA 90232

PHONE	310-244-8383
FAX	310-244-0303
TYPES	TV Series
HAS DEAL WITH	Sony Pictures Television
CREDITS	Matlock - Diagnosis Murder - Perry Mason Movies

Dean Hargrove . . . Executive Producer
Doris Stockstill . . . Executive Assistant to Mr. Hargrove

HARMS WAY PRODUCTIONS
4000 Warner Blvd., Bldg. 17, Rm. 111
Burbank, CA 91522

PHONE	818-954-2160
FAX	818-954-7033
TYPES	Features - TV Series
HAS DEAL WITH	John Wells Productions
DEVELOPMENT	Dreams of a Dying Heart
CREDITS	Duma - White Oleander - The Good Thief - Third Watch - The West Wing

Kristin Harms . . . Producer
Matt Billingsly . . . Creative Executive (818-954-3295)

HARPO FILMS, INC.

345 N. Maple Dr., Ste. 315
Beverly Hills, CA 90210
PHONE .310-278-5559/312-633-1000

TYPES	Features - Made-for-TV/Cable Movies - TV Series
HAS DEAL WITH	ABC Entertainment Television Group - The Walt Disney Company
CREDITS	Their Eyes Were Watching God - Beloved - Before Women Had Wings - The Wedding - David & Lisa - Tuesdays with Morrie - Amy & Isabelle
SUBMISSION POLICY	No unsolicited material
COMMENTS	Chicago office: 110 N. Carpenter St., Chicago, IL 60607

Oprah Winfrey .Chairman/CEO
Kate Forte .President
Scott Stein .Business Affairs & Operations
Melody Fowler .Director, Development
Eileen Lee .Production
Lisa Halliday .Media & Corporate Relations
Carolyn McGuinness .Executive Assistant to President
Shannon Thompson .Assistant to President & Eileen Lee
Todd Davis .Office Manager
Mark Durel .Assistant to Scott Stein
Briana Newton .Assistant to Melody Fowler

THE HARRIS COMPANY

17605 Belinda St.
Encino, CA 91316
PHONE .818-981-3211
FAX .818-981-3271
EMAIL .info@theharriscompany.com

TYPES	Direct-to-Video/DVD - Documentaries - Features - Made-for-TV/Cable Movies - Miniseries - TV Series
DEVELOPMENT	1000 Clowns - Batya - Black Orpheus - The Girl with the Golden Gun - Possessed - Alex - Chevalier and Antoinette - Kevin Approaches - Freedom Rocks (Documentary)
PRE-PRODUCTION	Run - A Hole in the Earth - Chevalier and Antoinette - 'Till Death Do Us Part
COMPLETED UNRELEASED	Conversations with Other Women
CREDITS	Film: Crash - A Good Night to Die - I'll Remember April - A Woman's a Helluva Thing - Gods & Monsters - Twilight of the Golds - Maze; TV: Family Law - EZ Streets - The Black Donnellys

Mark R. Harris .CEO
Dan Harris .Creative Director
Jon Rowland .Office Manager
Suzanne Joskow .Executive Assistant

HART SHARP ENTERTAINMENT, INC.

575 Broadway, 6th Fl.
New York, NY 10012
PHONE .212-475-7555
FAX .212-475-1717
WEB SITE .www.hartsharp.com
SECOND WEB SITE .www.hartsharpvideo.com

TYPES	Features - Made-for-TV/Cable Movies - Theatre
DEVELOPMENT	God of Driving - Achates McNeil - Evening - Revolutionary Road - Two Guys from Verona - Women's Maintenance Club - Breakfast with Tiffany
UPCOMING RELEASES	The Night Listener
CREDITS	Proof - Dark Harbor - Boys Don't Cry - You Can Count on Me - Lift - Nicholas Nickleby - Undefeated - Just Another Story - P.S. - A Home at the End of the World
SUBMISSION POLICY	No unsolicited submissions

Jeffrey Sharp .President
Michael Hogan .COO
Robert Kessel .Head, Production
Nina Wolarsky .Director, Development
Luke Parker Bowles .Production Executive
Natsu Furuichi .Assistant to Robert Kessel

THE HATCHERY

4751 Wilshire Blvd., 3rd Fl.
Los Angeles, CA 90010
PHONE .323-549-4392
FAX .323-549-9836

TYPES	Animation - Direct-to-Video/DVD - Features - Made-for-TV/Cable Movies - Miniseries - TV Series
PROVIDES DEAL TO	Janicek-Marino Creative
DEVELOPMENT	Christmas in Canaan - Gifted Hands - The Great Brain - The Freak - Maryoku Yummy - Dan Vs.... - Sushi Pack - Boys Lost at Sea - V.C. Andrews - Jekyll & Hyde - Shock Treatment
PRE-PRODUCTION	R.L. Stine Presents The Haunting Hours
PRODUCTION	Care Bears Movie - Twisted Whiskers Shorts
CREDITS	Balderdash (PAX) - Young Blades (PAX) - Benji Off the Leash

Bruce Stein .Co-CEO
Margaret Loesch .Co-CEO
Dan Angel .Partner/Executive Producer
Sean Gorman .VP, Development

HAZY MILLS PRODUCTIONS

4024 Radford Ave., Ste. 289
Studio City, CA 91604
PHONE .818-655-5000

TYPES	Animation - Features - Made-for-TV/Cable Movies - Miniseries - Reality TV - TV Series
HAS DEAL WITH	CBS Paramount Network Television
DEVELOPMENT	Broken News (TBS) - Reckless (SCI FI) - Untitled Walden Media Project - Big Shot (Showtime)
CREDITS	Situation: Comedy - Under Exposed
SUBMISSION POLICY	No unsolicited material

Sean Hayes .No Title
Todd Milliner .No Title
Michele Craig .No Title
Matt Bankston .No Title

HBO DOCUMENTARIES & FAMILY

1100 Avenue of the Americas
New York, NY 10036
PHONE 212-512-1000
WEB SITE . . . . www.hbo.com
TYPES Documentaries
CREDITS America Undercover - Capturing the Friedmans - Pandemic: Facing Aids - Murder on a Sunday Morning - In Memoriam, New York City, 9/11/01 - Spellbound

Sheila Nevins . . . . President, HBO Documentary & Family
Nancy Abraham . . . . VP, HBO Documentary Films
Lisa Heller . . . . VP, HBO Documentary Films
John Hoffman . . . . VP, HBO Documentary Films
Dolores Morris . . . . VP, HBO Family

HBO ENTERTAINMENT

2500 Broadway, Ste. 400
Santa Monica, CA 90404
PHONE 310-382-3000/212-512-1000
WEB SITE . . . . www.hbo.com
TYPES TV Series - TV Specials
PROVIDES DEAL TO Chase Films - Comedy Arts Studios - Face Productions/Jennilind Productions - Leverage Entertainment - Pretty Matches Productions - Q Media Partners - Red Board Productions - Simmons/Lathan - Studios International - SUperFInger Entertainment
CREDITS The Comeback - Deadwood - Entourage - Carnivàle - K Street - Six Feet Under - Curb Your Enthusiasm - Sex and the City - The Sopranos - The Wire - Lucky Louie
COMMENTS East Coast office: 1100 Avenue of the Americas, New York, NY 10036

Chris Albrecht . . . . Chairman/CEO, HBO, Inc.
Carolyn Strauss . . . . President, HBO Entertainment
Michael Lombardo . . . . Executive VP, Business Affairs, Production & Program Operations
Susan Ennis . . . . Sr. VP, Planning & Operations, Original Programming & Films (NY)
Nancy Geller . . . . Sr. VP, HBO Entertainment (NY)
Michael Hill . . . . Sr. VP, Production
Bruce Richmond . . . . Sr. VP, Production
Russell Schwartz . . . . Sr. VP, Business Affairs
Casey Bloys . . . . VP, Comedy Series
Jada Miranda . . . . VP, Comedy Series
Mike Garcia . . . . VP, Drama Series
David Goodman . . . . VP, Business Affairs
Lisa Pongracic . . . . VP, Business Affairs
Nina Rosenstein . . . . VP, HBO Entertainment (NY)
Beth White . . . . VP, Business Affairs
Gina Balian . . . . Director, HBO Entertainment

HBO FILMS

2500 Broadway, Ste. 400
Santa Monica, CA 90404
PHONE 310-382-3000
WEB SITE . . . . www.hbo.com/films
TYPES Features - Made-for-TV/Cable Movies - Miniseries
PROVIDES DEAL TO Cine Mosaic - Duly Noted
PRE-PRODUCTION Taking Chance - A Dog Year
PRODUCTION Life Support
POST PRODUCTION PU-239 - Starter for Ten - Longford
UPCOMING RELEASES Angel Rodriguez - Tsunami
COMPLETED UNRELEASED As You Like It - Rocket Science
CREDITS Walkout - Mrs. Harris - The Notorious Bettie Page - Warm Springs - Empire Falls - The Girl in the Cafe - Angels in America - American Splendor - Maria Full of Grace - The Life and Death of Peter Sellers - Lackawanna Blues - Sometimes in April - Yesterday - Elizabeth I
COMMENTS Premium cable movies; Picturehouse theatricals

Colin Callender . . . . President
Dennis O'Connor . . . . Executive VP, Marketing, Picturehouse
Kary Antholis . . . . Sr. VP, Development & Production, Miniseries
Jeffrey Guthrie . . . . Sr. VP/Sr. Counsel (West Coast Programming)
Glenn Whitehead . . . . Sr. VP, Business Affairs & Production
Janet Graham Borba . . . . VP, Production
Carrie Frazier . . . . VP, Casting
Cynthia Davis Kanner . . . . VP, Post Production
Sam Martin . . . . VP, Development & Production
John Murchison . . . . VP, Development & Production, Miniseries
Maud Nadler . . . . VP, Independent Films
Jay Roewe . . . . VP, Production
Jenni Sherwood . . . . VP, Development & Production
Molly Wilson . . . . VP/Chief Counsel (West Coast Programming)
Suzanne Young . . . . VP, Business Affairs
Amy Berman . . . . Director, Casting
Elaine Chin . . . . Director, Development & Production
Mark Hoerr . . . . Director, Post Production
Mark Levenstein . . . . Director, Production
Ginny Nugent . . . . Director, Production
Pam Winn . . . . Director, Post Production
Holly Schiffer Zucker . . . . Director, Post Production
Maria Zuckerman . . . . Director, Development & Production
Donna Pearlmutter Reichman . . . . Production Manager
Dottie Simmons . . . . Creative Operations Manager
Matt Bass . . . . Story Editor
Jennifer Altobell . . . . Creative Associate
Marc Thomas King . . . . Coordinator
Karin Wholey . . . . Production Coordinator

HBO MEDIA VENTURES

2500 Broadway, Ste. 400
Santa Monica, CA 90404
PHONE 310-382-3000/212-512-1000
WEB SITE . . . . www.hbo.com
TYPES Internet Content - Mobile Content

Jim Moloshok . . . . President, Media Ventures
Carmi Zlotnik . . . . Executive VP, New Media Programming

HDNET
2909 Taylor St.
Dallas, TX 75226
PHONE .214-651-1446/888-919-HDTV
WEB SITE .www.hd.net
TYPES TV Series
DEVELOPMENT Art Mann Presents
CREDITS Original Series: HDNet World Report - True Music - HDNet Concert Series - Bikini Destinations - Get Out! - Face 2 Face with Roy Firestone - Higher Definition: Live Sports Programming: HDNet Boxing - The HDNet Horse Racing Challenge
COMMENTS National television network broadcasting all programming in highest-quality format of high-definition television; Denver office: 2400 N. Ulster St., Denver, CO 80238, phone: 303-542-5600

Mark Cuban .Chairman/President
Terdema Ussery .CEO
Philip Garvin .COO/General Manager
Elisabeth Glass .General Manager, HDNet Movies
Darrell Ewalt .Executive Producer, Sports
Dave Green .Executive Producer, Documentaries
Evan Haiman .Executive Producer, Music & Entertainment
Michael Adrian .Producer
Hank Lena .Producer/Director
Dan Myers .Producer, Sports
Pat O'Connor .Producer/Director, Sports
David Butler .Assistant Producer, Sports
Katie Gladstone .Director, Programming, HDNet Movies
Tiffany Comstock .Programming Coordinator, HDNet Movies

HDNET FILMS
122 Hudson St., 5th Fl.
New York, NY 10013
PHONE .212-255-0626
FAX .212-255-0602
EMAIL .hdinquiries@hdnetfilms.com
WEB SITE .www.hdnetfilms.com
TYPES Features
DEVELOPMENT This Is the Strokes
PRODUCTION Hunter S. Thompson - Broken English - Mr. Untouchable - Surfwise - American Swing: The Rise and Fall of Plato's Retreat - Spalding Gray: The Last Monologue
POST PRODUCTION Quid Pro Quo - Diggers - S&Man
UPCOMING RELEASES The Architect
COMPLETED UNRELEASED Fay Grim
CREDITS One Last Thing - Bubble - The War Within - Enron: The Smartest Guys in the Room - Herbie Hancock: Possibilities
COMMENTS Digital features

Jason Kliot .Co-President/Producer
Joana Vicente .Co-President/Producer
Chris Matson .Head, Business Affairs
Gretchen McGowan .Head, Production
Laird Adamson .Head, International Sales
Chris Edwards .Head, Post Production
Quentin Little .Director, Development
Steve Holmgren .Office Manager
Courtney Andrialis .1st Assistant to Jason Kliot & Joana Vicente
Lauren Lillie .2nd Assistant to Jason Kliot & Joana Vicente
Virginia Williams .Production Assistant

THE HECHT COMPANY
3607 W. Magnolia, Ste. L
Burbank, CA 91505
PHONE .310-989-3467
EMAIL .hechtco@aol.com
TYPES Features - Made-for-TV/Cable Movies - TV Series
DEVELOPMENT Cops - Finding Normal - 2GFC
CREDITS First, Last and Deposit - King of the Ants - Edmond

Duffy Hecht .Producer

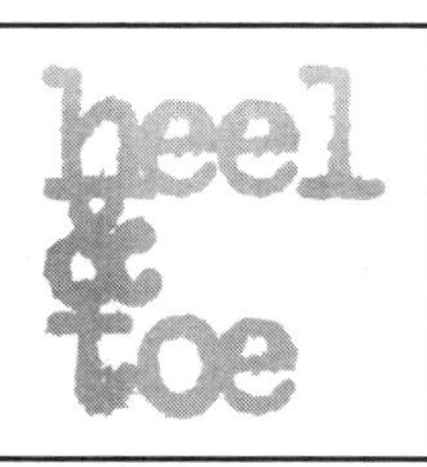

HEEL & TOE FILMS
2058 Broadway
Santa Monica, CA 90404
PHONE .310-264-1866
FAX .310-264-1865
TYPES Features - TV Series
HAS DEAL WITH Fox Broadcasting Company
UPCOMING RELEASES The Good German
CREDITS House - Quiz Show - Donnie Brasco - Homicide: Life on the Street - Gideon's Crossing - Sum of All Fears - Disclosure

Paul Attanasio .Writer/Executive Producer
Katie Jacobs .Executive Producer
Andrew Avner .Executive Assistant to Paul Attanasio
Lindsey Jaffin .Executive Assistant to Katie Jacobs
Ellen Shapiro .Special Projects Coordinator

HELLA GOOD MOVING PICTURES
PO Box 97
Venice, CA 90294
PHONE . . . 310-488-9478
EMAIL . . . hella-good@earthlink.net

TYPES	Animation - Features - TV Series
DEVELOPMENT	The Watsons (One Ho/Sony/CBS) - The Marx Brothers (Jersey/Universal) - Fenwick's Suit (Fox 2000) - Sleepless Beauty - King of Crash - Waxing Macabre - Taxi Dog (Radar/Warner) - Guardian Angels - Creation - Notorious - On the Table - Elephants - Sexploitation - Dry Fire (Parkway/HBO) - The Search - Sunbunrt Angels
PRE-PRODUCTION	The Other Side - Surveillance
UPCOMING RELEASES	Statistics
CREDITS	The Reunion - Murder at the Cannes Film Festival - Shelter Island - Macabre Theatre (KDOC) - Napoleon Dynamite
SUBMISSION POLICY	No unsolicited material
COMMENTS	Partnership with Film Star Pictures (310-365-5558)

David Michaels . . . Writer/Producer/Director
Jory Weitz . . . Producer/Casting
Chris Douridas . . . President, Music
Kent Harper . . . Writer/Producer
Chloe Kromwell . . . Assistant to David Michaels

PAUL HELLER PRODUCTIONS
1666 N. Beverly Dr.
Beverly Hills, CA 90210
PHONE . . . 310-275-4477
FAX . . . 310-275-4714
EMAIL . . . pheller@earthlink.net
WEB SITE . . . home.earthlink.net/~pheller/

TYPES	Documentaries - Features - Made-for-TV/Cable Movies - New Media
DEVELOPMENT	Enter the Dragon Prequel - Bloodrite - O.B.E. (Out of Body Experience) - In High Places
PRODUCTION	Skirball Cultural Center Exhibits: Kaleidoscope Theatre: Traditions
CREDITS	Withnail & I - David & Lisa - My Left Foot - The Annihilation of Fish - Enter the Dragon - The First Monday in October
COMMENTS	Museum audio and video; Skirball Cultural Center: New Exhibits; Hong Kong Museum of History; US Department of State: New Exhibits; Science Center of Iowa

Paul Heller . . . Producer
Kathy Zebrowski-Heller . . . President
Michael Peters . . . Development/Editor

ROSILYN HELLER PRODUCTIONS
2237 Nichols Canyon Rd.
Los Angeles, CA 90046
PHONE . . . 323-876-2820
EMAIL . . . rozheller@aol.com

TYPES	Features - Made-for-TV/Cable Movies
PRE-PRODUCTION	Am I Up or Am I Down? - The Defiant
UPCOMING RELEASES	Trade
CREDITS	Ice Castles - Beans of Egypt, Maine - Who's That Girl? - American Heart
SUBMISSION POLICY	No unsolicited material

Rosilyn Heller . . . President/Producer

HELL'S KITCHEN LTD.
21 Mespil Rd.
Dublin 4, Ireland
PHONE . . . 3531-667-5599
FAX . . . 3531-667-5592
EMAIL . . . hellskit@iol.ie

TYPES	Features
CREDITS	Get Rich or Die Tryin' (Paramount/MTV) - Laws of Attraction - In America - Bloody Sunday - On the Edge - Borstal Boy - Agnes Browne - The Boxer - Some Mother's Son - In the Name of the Father

Jim Sheridan . . . Director/Producer
Arthur Lappin . . . Managing Director/Producer
Niamh Nolan . . . Production Executive

HENDERSON PRODUCTIONS, INC.
4252 Riverside Dr.
Burbank, CA 91505
PHONE . . . 818-955-5702

TYPES	Features - Theatre
CREDITS	The Princess Diaries 1&2 - Raising Helen - The Twilight of the Golds - Exit to Eden - Young Doctors in Love - Frankie and Johnny - Laverne & Shirley - Happy Days - Pretty Woman - Beaches
SUBMISSION POLICY	No unsolicited submissions
COMMENTS	Founder of the Falcon Theatre

Garry Marshall . . . Producer/Director

THE JIM HENSON COMPANY

1416 N. La Brea Ave.
Hollywood, CA 90028

PHONE 323-802-1500/212-794-2400
FAX 323-802-1825/212-570-1147
WEB SITE . . . . . www.henson.com

TYPES	Animation - Commercials - Direct-to-Video/DVD - Features - Internet Content - Made-for-TV/Cable Movies - Miniseries - Mobile Content - Music Videos - Reality TV - Specials - Theatre - TV Series
HAS DEAL WITH	The Walt Disney Company - HIT Entertainment - Sony Pictures Entertainment
DEVELOPMENT	Astroboy - The Moon and the Sun - Thumb - Time Dogs - King of the Elves - Neverwhere - Parasyte - The Tatooed Map - The Witch's Children - Varjak Paw
PRE-PRODUCTION	Power of the Dark Crystal - Unstable Fables - Late Night Buffet
COMPLETED UNRELEASED	Frances
CREDITS	MirrorMask - Farscape: The Peacekeeper Wars - Good Boy! - Farscape (Series) - Mopatop's Shop - Jim Henson's The Hoobs - Jim Henson's Animal Jam - Bambaloo - Five Children & It - The Muppets' Wizard of Oz
SUBMISSION POLICY	No unsolicited submissions

Lisa Henson . . . . . Co-CEO
Brian Henson . . . . . Co-CEO
Peter Schube . . . . . President/COO
Laurie Don . . . . . Sr. VP, Worldwide Financial Operations
Joe Henderson . . . . . Sr. VP, Worldwide Administration
Jason Lust . . . . . Sr. VP, Feature Films
Michael R. Polis . . . . . Sr. VP, Marketing, Home Entertainment
Eric Poticha . . . . . Sr. VP, Television
Dan Scharf . . . . . VP, Business & Legal Affairs
Nicole Goldman . . . . . Head, Publicity
Halle Stanford . . . . . Head, Children's Television

HERE! NETWORKS

10990 Wilshire Blvd., PH
Los Angeles, CA 90024

PHONE 310-806-4298
FAX 310-806-4268
EMAIL . . . . . info@heretv.com
WEB SITE . . . . . www.heretv.com

TYPES	Animation - Direct-to-Video/DVD - Documentaries - Features - Internet Content - Made-for-TV/Cable Movies - Mobile Content - Reality TV - Specials - TV Series
DEVELOPMENT	Nijinsky - Ice Blues: A Donald Strachey Mystery - The Becky Snow Show - Lesbian Sex and Sexuality - Buddy's World
PRE-PRODUCTION	Ryan's Life - In the Name of Love - Second Chance
POST PRODUCTION	Birch & Co.: Howard Dean
UPCOMING RELEASES	Race You to the Bottom - Mr. Leather - ShowBusiness - Queens - Aurora Borealis - Cut Sleeve Boys - Unconscious - Poster Boy - Shock to the System: A Donald Strachey Mystery - Deadly Skies
CREDITS	Merci Docteur Rey - Yes Nurse! No Nurse! - Callas Forever - Beautiful Boxer - Straight Jacket - Naked Fame - Sex, Politics & Cocktails - April's Shower - Tides of War - here! Together - here! Family - here! Comedy Presents: Kate Clinton - Dante's Cove - Third Man Out: A Donald Strachey Mystery - here! Comedy Presents: Margaret Cho - John Waters Presents Movies That Will Corrupt You
SUBMISSION POLICY	No unsolicited material or calls; Query letters accepted

Paul Colichman . . . . . Founder & CEO
Stephen P. Jarchow . . . . . Founder & CEO
Andrew Tow . . . . . COO
Karen Flischel . . . . . Executive VP/General Manager
Eric Feldman . . . . . Executive VP, Programming & Operations
Mark Reinhart . . . . . Executive VP, Acquisitions & Distribution
Maria Dwyer . . . . . Sr. VP, Distribution Sales & Marketing
Stephen Macias . . . . . Sr. VP, Corporate & Marketing Communications
Joan Danto . . . . . Sr. VP, Business & Legal Affairs
Dan Gelfand . . . . . VP, Promotional Marketing
Meredith Kadlec . . . . . VP, Original Programming
John Mongiardo . . . . . VP, Operations
Andy Vecchione . . . . . VP, Finance
Michael Dubin . . . . . Director, Programming
Josh Rosenzweig . . . . . Director, Corporate & Marketing Communication
Jonathan Aubry . . . . . Manager, Corporate & Marketing Communications
Matt Chun . . . . . Online Marketing Manager
John Dexter . . . . . Manager, Operations
Brian Goldman . . . . . Manager, Creative Affairs
Andrea Krauss . . . . . Manager, Administration
Dennis Alfrey . . . . . Coordinator, Operations
Billy Cogar . . . . . Development Coordinator
Sara Logue . . . . . Coordinator, Interactive Programming
Lindsay Marsak . . . . . Marketing Coordinator

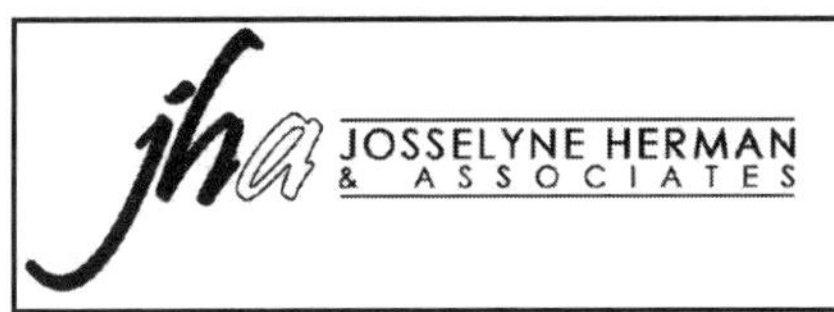

JOSSELYNE HERMAN & ASSOCIATES/ MOVING IMAGE FILMS

345 E. 56th St., Ste. 3-B
New York, NY 10022
PHONE .212-355-3033/323-244-4979
FAX .212-937-5270
EMAIL .info@jhermanassociates.com
SECOND EMAIL .producerofdreams@aol.com
WEB SITE .www.movingimagefilms.com
SECOND WEB SITE .www.jhamanagement.com
TYPES Commercials - Direct-to-Video/DVD - Documentaries - Features - Made-for-TV/Cable Movies - Music Videos - Reality TV - Specials - TV Series
DEVELOPMENT The Junket - Roller Queen - Chicks with Schticks - Girls on the Run - The Little Prince - Kids Cooking with Comedy - Olivia - The Mail Room - Urban Family Slate
PRE-PRODUCTION Prop Master Diaries - Pup Culture
PRODUCTION Madness is Catching
POST PRODUCTION The Pack
COMPLETED UNRELEASED Tollbooth - The Making of...
CREDITS They're Just My Friends - A&E Biography - Anne B. Real - Caged - Choice Cinema - Bob's Workshop - Consensus - Kat Man Doo Asks You - Video Active - College All Stars - Mind Over Matter with Harry Lorayne

Josselyne Herman-Saccio .Owner/Producer
Michael Saccio .Producer
Harvey Herman .Director
Chelsey Ball .New Talent Division
Elaine Herman .Casting Director

HEYDAY FILMS

4000 Warner Blvd., Bldg. 81, Rm. 207
Burbank, CA 91522
PHONE .818-954-3004/44-207-836-6333
FAX .818-954-3017/44-207-836-6444
TYPES Features - TV Series
HAS DEAL WITH Warner Bros. Pictures
DEVELOPMENT Helium - Yucatan - The Mighty Flynn - We're the Millers - All My Life for Sale - Dogs of Babel - Bill from My Father - Yes Man - Have Spacesuit, Will Travel - Unique - Half Magic - Odyssey - On the Nature - Moon Is a Harsh Mistress - Supercar - The History of Love - The Exec - The Curious Incident of the Dog in the Night Time - A Long Way Down - The Giants of Groil
PRE-PRODUCTION The Dionaea House
PRODUCTION Harry Potter and the Order of the Phoenix
CREDITS Threshold (CBS) - Harry Potter 1-4 - Ravenous - Daytrippers
SUBMISSION POLICY No unsolicited submissions
COMMENTS UK office: 5 Denmark St., London, WC2H 8LP, United Kingdom

David Heyman .Producer
Rosie Alison .Executive (UK)
Ali Bell .Executive (LA)
Tiffany Daniel .Executive (LA)
Marc Rosen .Executive (LA)
Rachel Godfrey .Development Assistant
Rachel Hargreaves-Heald .Development Assistant

BRYAN HICKOX PICTURES, INC.

1120 Hideaway Dr. North
Jacksonville, FL 32259
PHONE .904-509-4790
FAX .904-230-4162
EMAIL .b.hickox@comcast.net
TYPES Direct-to-Video/DVD - Documentaries - Features - Made-for-TV/Cable Movies - Reality TV - TV Series
DEVELOPMENT Feature: Wrong Turn - Tidings of Comfort and Joys; TV: Greatest Performances
PRE-PRODUCTION Profiles in Character
PRODUCTION Freedom in Prison
POST PRODUCTION Who Will Cry for My People?
CREDITS The Painting - Take Back Hollywood - Spring Fling - Safe Harbor - Ride - Stand for What Is Right - Sudden Terror: The Hijacking of School Bus #17 - CCPD - Family Reunion

S. Bryan Hickox .Producer/Owner
Joanne Kraemer .CFO
Michael Stark .Casting
Terry VanderWier .Casting

HIGH HORSE FILMS

100 Universal City Plaza, Bldg. 2128, Ste. E
Universal City, CA 91608
PHONE .323-939-8802
FAX .323-939-8832
TYPES Features - TV Series
HAS DEAL WITH CBS Entertainment
CREDITS CSI: Crime Scene Investigation - Keep the Change - Hard Promises - Baby It's You

William Petersen .Actor/Producer
Cynthia Chvatal .Producer
Laurel Dibble .Assistant

HIGHWAY 9 FILMS

5721 Buckingham Pkwy., Ste. B
Culver City, CA 90230
PHONE .310-410-6750
FAX .310-410-9447
EMAIL .info@highway9films.com
WEB SITE .www.highway9films.com
TYPES Animation - Direct-to-Video/DVD - Documentaries - Features - Reality TV - TV Series
DEVELOPMENT Flash Bang - Mountain of Fire - Phobophobia - Bloody Knuckles
COMPLETED UNRELEASED Farewell Bender
CREDITS Bobby Jones: Stroke of Genius - The Climb - Road to Redemption
COMMENTS Formerly Revel Entertainment

Jason "Bear" Behrman .Producer/Partner
Mellany Behrman .Producer/Partner

S. HIRSCH COMPANY, INC./SEEMORE FILMS

15456 Ventura Blvd., Ste. 300
Sherman Oaks, CA 91403
PHONE .818-990-1212
FAX .818-990-1824
EMAIL .info@shirschco.com
TYPES Features - Reality TV - TV Series
DEVELOPMENT The Loose End - Revenge of the Wannabes - Seville Communion - The Crumley Chronicles - Hail Mary
COMMENTS Acquisitions consulting

Steven Hirsch .President/CEO
Darius Kapfer .Partner
Darren Brandl .Sr. VP

THE HISTORY CHANNEL

235 E. 45th St.
New York, NY 10017
PHONE .212-210-1400
FAX .212-907-9481
WEB SITE .www.history.com
TYPES Documentaries - Internet Content - Mobile Content - Specials - TV Series
PROVIDES DEAL TO Weller/Grossman Productions
DEVELOPMENT Engineering an Empire - Dogfights - Ancient Discoveries; Specials: True Caribbean Pirates - Desperate Crossing: The Untold Story of the Mayflower - The Exodus Decoded - Race to the South Pole - Inside the Volcano - The Dark Ages - The States; History International: Tales of the Living Dead - Drive-Thru History
UPCOMING RELEASES 10 Days That Unexpectedly Changed America - Washington the Warrior - Mega Disasters - Mega Movers - The Revolution - The Sahara - Where Did It Come From? - Lost Worlds - How William Shatner Changed The World - American Eats - True Caribbean Pirates - Return of the Pirates
CREDITS Lincoln - Declassified - Titanic's Final Moments: Missing Pieces - Save Our History: Alaska - Rome: Engineering an Empire - The Real Tomb Hunters - Digging for the Truth - Man, Moment, Machine - Shootout! Mail Call - Deep Sea Detectives - Modern Marvels
SUBMISSION POLICY No unsolicited proposals

Abbe Raven .President & CEO, AETN
Daniel Davids .President, The History Channel, USA
Charles Maday .Sr. VP, Programming
Michael Mohamad .Sr. VP, Marketing
Beth Dietrich .VP, Historical Programming
Peter Gaffney .VP, Program Acquisitions & Scheduling
Carl Lindahl .VP, Historical Programming
Susan Werbe .VP, Historical Programming
Dolores Gavin .Director, Historical Programming
Peggy Kim .Director, Historical Programming
Marc Etkind .Director, Historical Programming
Andrew Weissberg .Director, Program Scheduling & Acquisitions

HIT ENTERTAINMENT

1133 Broadway, Ste. 1520
New York, NY 10010
PHONE .212-463-9623
FAX .212-463-9626
WEB SITE .www.hitentertainment.com
TYPES Animation - Direct-to-Video/DVD - Features - Made-for-TV/Cable Movies - Specials - TV Series
PROVIDES DEAL TO The Jim Henson Company
CREDITS Thomas & Friends - Pingu - Barney & Friends® - Bob the Builder™ - Angelina Ballerina™ - Thomas and the Magic Railroad

Bruce Steinberg .CEO
Patricia Wyatt .President, HIT North America
Peter Byrne .Executive VP, International Licensing Merchandising & Home Entertainment
Alison Homewood .Executive VP, Worldwide Television Distribution (London)
Jamie Cygielman .Sr. VP, Consumer Products
Claudia Scott-Hansen .VP, US Distribution
Rick Glankler .VP, Licensing
Veronica Hart .Director, Hard Lines
Jennifer Zivic .Director, Soft Lines

HOCK FILMS, INC.

133 W. 19th St., 10th Fl.
New York, NY 10011
PHONE .212-337-3292
FAX .212-337-8522
WEB SITE .www.hockfilms.com
TYPES Features - TV Series
CREDITS Through the Fire (Documentary Feature) - Streetball (ESPN Series)

Jonathan Hock .President/Producer/Director
Phil Aromando .Producer

GARY HOFFMAN PRODUCTIONS

3931 Puerco Canyon Rd.
Malibu, CA 90265
PHONE .310-456-1830
EMAIL .garyhofprods@charter.net
TYPES Features - Made-for-TV/Cable Movies - TV Series
CREDITS Bastard Out of Carolina - Soul of the Game - Bonnie & Clyde: The True Story - The Fitzgeralds & the Kennedys - WWIII - The Big Heist - National Lampoon's Thanksgiving Reunion

Gary Hoffman .Producer/President
Ann Ryan .Development

JASON HOFFS PRODUCTIONS

c/o DreamWorks SKG
100 Universal City Plaza, Bungalow 5171
Universal City, CA 91608
PHONE .818-733-9926
TYPES — Features
HAS DEAL WITH — DreamWorks SKG
DEVELOPMENT — Argonauts - Escape Artists - Brats - Traded - Pretty Ugly - Hot Wheels
CREDITS — The Terminal
SUBMISSION POLICY — No unsolicited submissions

Jason Hoffs .Producer
Ira Napoliello .Development Executive (818-733-9927)
Gailor Large .Story Editor (818-733-9909)

HOLLYWOOD EAST ENTERTAINMENT, INC.

900 Wheeler Rd., Ste. 225
Hauppauge, NY 11788
PHONE .631-584-4371
FAX .631-584-4365
WEB SITE .www.hollywoodeast.tv
TYPES — Commercials - Documentaries - Music Videos - Reality TV - Specials - TV Series
CREDITS — Unique Whips - Hollywood East
SUBMISSION POLICY — No unsolicted material; Query first
COMMENTS — Additional deal with the Speed Channel

Corey Damsker .President/Executive Producer
Steve Hillebrand .VP/Executive Producer
Jessica Iaccarino .Supervising Producer
Barry Shapiro .Line Producer
Scott Speed .Music Supervisor

HOLLYWOOD GANG PRODUCTIONS, LLC

11990 San Vicente Blvd., Ste. 300
Los Angeles, CA 90049
PHONE .310-442-4777
FAX .310-442-9507
WEB SITE .www.hollywoodgangproductions.com
TYPES — Features
DEVELOPMENT — 11 Minutes - Il Sorpasso - Taming Ben Taylor - The Good Guys - Silence - Marco Polo - Plastic - Ferrari - Ronin - A Pure Formality - Hannibal the Conqueror
PRE-PRODUCTION — Conquistador
POST PRODUCTION — 300
UPCOMING RELEASES — The Departed - N.
CREDITS — Alexander - Seven - A Bronx Tale - Night in the City - From Dusk Till Dawn - Romeo and Juliet Get Married
SUBMISSION POLICY — Solicited projects only

Gianni Nunnari .President
Craig J. Flores .VP, Business & Legal Affairs
Nathalie Peter-Contesse .VP, Creative Affairs
David Caplan .Creative Assistant

HOME & GARDEN TELEVISION (HGTV)

9721 Sherrill Blvd.
Knoxville, TN 37932
PHONE .865-694-2700
FAX .865-531-1588
WEB SITE .www.hgtv.com
TYPES — TV Series
PROVIDES DEAL TO — Weller/Grossman Productions
UPCOMING RELEASES — Home to Stay - Takeover My Makover - HGTV Design Star - What's Your Sign? Design - I Want That! Tech Toys - Hidden Potential - Haulin' House - Over Your Head
CREDITS — Mission: Organization - Designers' Challenge - Decorating Cents - Designed to Sell - Divine Design - Curb Appeal - Design on a Dime - House Hunters - reDesign - That's Clever! - Cash in the Attic
SUBMISSION POLICY — See Web site; Production companies have access to http://resourcedirectory.hgtv.com, exclusively for the purpose of submitting story ideas, guest or product information and location/event descriptions for potential programming use

Judy Girard .President
Michael Dingley .Sr. VP, Programming/Content Strategy
Melissa Sykes .Sr. VP, Programming
Mary Ellen Iwata .VP, Development
Andy Singer .VP, Original Programming
Maddie Henri .Programming
Gabriella Messina .Programming
Bill Myers .Programming
Amy Quimby .Programming
Laura Sillars .Programming

HOMERUN ENTERTAINMENT, INC.

5800 Hannum Ave., Ste. B
Culver City, CA 90230
PHONE .310-338-1500
FAX .310-338-1490
WEB SITE .www.homerunent.com
TYPES — Commercials - Documentaries - Internet Content - Reality TV - TV Series
UPCOMING RELEASES — Bid Whist Party Throw Down (TV One) Can You Dig It (TV One) - Best Built Home (DIY) - RV Roadtrips (DIY)
CREDITS — Kitchen & Bath 2006 - Best Practices - Best Built Home: Keytesville - Celebrity Hobbies - Jewelry Making - Blueprint for Home Building - Be Your Own Contractor - Weekend Gardening - Weekend Landscaping - The Best Of... - Food Finds - Top 5 Food & Wine Adventures - Homes of the Wine Country - Line on Design - Bid Whist Party Throwdown - Can You Dig It

Barry Gribbon .Executive Producer/CEO/Founder
Jennifer Gribbon .General Manager/Founder
Steve Plutte .Coordinating Producer

HOPE ENTERPRISES, INC.
135 W. Magnolia Blvd., Ste. 301
Burbank, CA 91502
PHONE 818-841-2020
FAX 818-841-2028
EMAIL . . . . .hei@bobhope.com
WEB SITE . . . . .www.bobhope.com
TYPES Documentaries - TV Series
DEVELOPMENT Various Bob Hope Projects
CREDITS Bob Hope Archives
COMMENTS Company established by Bob Hope in 1946

Linda Hope . . . . .Producer/Writer
Jim Hardy . . . . .Post Production Supervisor/Editor/Archivist

HOPSCOTCH PICTURES
616 N. Robertson Blvd., Ste. B
Los Angeles, CA 90069
PHONE 310-358-0630
FAX 310-358-0631
TYPES Features - Made-for-TV/Cable Movies - TV Series
CREDITS My First Mister

Sukee Chew . . . . .Manager/Producer
Jeff Holland . . . . .Manager

HORSEPOWER ENTERTAINMENT
4063 Radford Ave., Ste. 206
Studio City, CA 91604
PHONE 818-506-4300
TYPES Features - Reality TV - TV Series
DEVELOPMENT No Fear (Independent)
PRE-PRODUCTION Dreadnaught (Columbia)
CREDITS The Fog - The Core (Paramount) - The Emperor's Club (Universal)

Cooper Layne . . . . .Writer/Producer
Tina Velvet . . . . .Creative Executive

*HOUSE OF ROCK PRODUCTIONS, INC.
902 Wapello St.
Altadena, CA 91001
PHONE 626-296-0822/626-379-4582
FAX 626-296-0872
EMAIL . . . . .hansinla@mac.com
TYPES Music Videos - Reality TV - Specials - TV Series
PRE-PRODUCTION BZN: The Final Tour

Hans van Riet . . . . .CEO

HUMBLE JOURNEY FILMS
7656 W. Sunset Blvd.
Los Angeles, CA 90046
PHONE 323-882-6376
FAX 323-882-6386
TYPES Features - Made-for-TV/Cable Movies - Miniseries - Reality TV - TV Series
HAS DEAL WITH CBS Paramount Network Television
DEVELOPMENT Features: Beneath a Marble Sky - Mama's Boys; TV: 25 to Life - Ice - Damage Control - The Four Next Door
CREDITS Crazy as Hell - Rebound - Mind Prey - Psalms from the Underground - The Salton Sea
SUBMISSION POLICY No unsolicited submissions

Eriq La Salle . . . . .No Title
Butch Robinson . . . . .No Title
Terri Feldman Lubaroff . . . . .No Title
Glendon Palmer . . . . .No Title
Ben Roberts . . . . .No Title
Chika Chukudebelu . . . . .No Title
Mark Lilico . . . . .No Title

PETER HYAMS PRODUCTIONS, INC.
1453 Third Street Promenade, Ste. 315
Santa Monica, CA 90401-2397
PHONE 310-393-1553
FAX 310-393-1554
TYPES Features - TV Series

Peter Hyams . . . . .Director/Writer
Marc Protzel . . . . .Director, Development

HYDE PARK ENTERTAINMENT
14958 Ventura Blvd., Ste. 100
Sherman Oaks, CA 91403
PHONE 818-783-6060
FAX 818-783-6319
TYPES Features
HAS DEAL WITH The Walt Disney Company - Twentieth Century Fox
DEVELOPMENT Death Sentence - Asylum
PRODUCTION Premonition
CREDITS Shopgirl - Dreamer - Bringing Down the House - Raising Helen - Walking Tall - Moonlight Mile - Bandits - Original Sin - AntiTrust

Ashok Amritraj . . . . .Chairman/CEO
Lisa Wilson . . . . .President, Hyde Park International
Patrick Aiello . . . . .Sr. VP, Hyde Park Entertainment
Caroline Raufi . . . . .Sr. VP, Business & Legal Affairs
Joe D'Angelo . . . . .VP, Finance
Vicki Rocco . . . . .Director, Finance
Alex Van Fleet . . . . .Assistant to Ashok Amritraj

HYPERION STUDIO
6725 Sunset Blvd., Ste. 240
Hollywood, CA 90028
PHONE 323-871-0022
FAX 323-871-0044
WEB SITE . . . . .www.hyperionpictures.com
TYPES Animation - Direct-to-Video/DVD - Features - Made-for-TV/Cable Movies - TV Series
PRE-PRODUCTION Dinner Music
PRODUCTION The Proud Family Movie 2
UPCOMING RELEASES Marigold
CREDITS Film: The Proud Family Movie - Playing by Heart - Brave Little Toaster - Bebe's Kids; TV: Da Boom Crew - The Proud Family

Tom Wilhite . . . . .President
Willard Carroll . . . . .Co-Owner/Writer/Director/Producer
Bruce Smith . . . . .Executive Producer/Director
Chris Young . . . . .Producer/Director
Peter Sandvoss . . . . .Writer/Producer
Steve Sandvoss . . . . .Writer/Producer
J.P. White . . . . .Writer/Producer
Stiles White . . . . .Writer/Producer
Christian Mills . . . . .Producer
Michele L. Jennings . . . . .Producer/Development

HYPNOTIC
12233 W. Olympic Blvd., Ste. 350
Los Angeles, CA 90064
PHONE . . . 310-806-6930
FAX . . . 310-806-6931
WEB SITE . . . www.hypnotic.com
TYPES: Commercials - Features - TV Series
HAS DEAL WITH: NBC Universal Television Studio
DEVELOPMENT: 22 Birthdays (CBS) - Vaporetto 13
CREDITS: Heist (NBC) - Cry Wolf - The O.C. - Terry Tate: Office Linebacker - The Bourne Identity - The Bourne Supremacy - Mail Order Wife
SUBMISSION POLICY: No unsolicited material

David Bartis . . . CEO
Doug Liman . . . Vice Chairman
Gene Klein . . . VP, Development
Cristina Wildzumas . . . Office Manager

I.E. PRODUCTIONS, INC.
6404 Wilshire Blvd., Ste. 1505
Los Angeles, CA 90048
PHONE . . . 516-524-5817
FAX . . . 213-559-8306
EMAIL . . . bbutterflyeagle@aol.com
SECOND EMAIL . . . smrosenfelt@earthlink.net
TYPES: Documentaries - Features - Made-for-TV/Cable Movies - TV Series
DEVELOPMENT: Mustang Sally - Stranglehold - Oh Soul e Mio - Whatever It Takes
PRE-PRODUCTION: Kingz
CREDITS: Valley of the Heart's Delight - Kids in America - Lenny the Wonder Dog - The Californians - Smoke Signals - Home Alone - Mystic Pizza

Scott Rosenfelt . . . Producer/Director
B. Billie Greif . . . Writer/Producer

IAC/INTERACTIVECORP
152 W. 57th St., 42nd Fl.
New York, NY 10019
PHONE . . . 212-314-7300
FAX . . . 212-632-9656
WEB SITE . . . www.iac.com
TYPES: Internet Content - Mobile Content

Barry Diller . . . Chairman/CEO
Doug Lebda . . . President/COO
Victor Kaufman . . . Vice Chairman
Michael Jackson . . . President, TV Programming Division
Greg Blatt . . . Executive VP/General Counsel/Secretary

ICON PRODUCTIONS, LLC
808 Wilshire Blvd., 4th Fl.
Santa Monica, CA 90401
PHONE . . . 310-434-7300
FAX . . . 310-434-7377
TYPES: Features - TV Series
PROVIDES DEAL TO: Rive Gauche Entertainment
DEVELOPMENT: A Great and Terrible Beauty - Push - Peace Out
PRODUCTION: Apocolypto
POST PRODUCTION: Seraphim Falls
CREDITS: Maverick - Hamlet - Braveheart - Payback - What Women Want - We Were Soldiers - The Passion of the Christ - Clubhouse - Complete Savages - Paparazzi - The Singing Detective

Bruce Davey . . . President
Mark Gooder . . . President, Film Acquisitions
Vicki Christianson . . . COO
Stefanie Huie . . . VP, Features

THE IDEA FACTORY
15335 Morrison St., #325
Sherman Oaks, CA 91403
PHONE . . . 818-510-3283
FAX . . . 818-510-3286
EMAIL . . . darryl@tiftv.com
TYPES: Documentaries - Features - Made-for-TV/Cable Movies - Mobile Content - Reality TV - Specials - TV Series
COMPLETED UNRELEASED: Can't Stop Dancing
CREDITS: God or the Girl (A&E) - Bound for Glory (ESPN) - Freedom House (Warner Bros.) - This Is Sevareid (Revolution/Imagine)

Stephen David . . . Executive Producer/Partner
Darryl M. Silver . . . Executive Producer/Partner

IDEAL ENTERTAINMENT, INC.
8787 Shoreham Dr., Ste. 1206
Los Angeles, CA 90069
PHONE . . . 323-939-3399
FAX . . . 323-939-3009
EMAIL . . . info@ideal-entertainment.com
TYPES: Animation - Features - TV Series
PRODUCTION: NFL 3D
POST PRODUCTION: U2 3D
CREDITS: Curious George - All Access: Front Row. Backstage. LIVE! (IMAX) - Richie Rich - The Big Brass Ring - Chick Corea: Rendezvous in New York
COMMENTS: IMAX films; Music-related films; 3D films; East Coast office: 150 E. 18th St., Ste. 11M, New York, NY 10003

Jon Shapiro . . . President/Producer
Peter Shapiro . . . Co-President/Producer

IDENTITY FILMS
100 Universal City Plaza, Bungalow 4144
Universal City, CA 91608
PHONE . . . 818-733-3378
FAX . . . 818-733-5424
TYPES: Features
HAS DEAL WITH: Universal Pictures
DEVELOPMENT: Nerd Camp - The Optimist - The Book of Leo - Coxblocker
PRE-PRODUCTION: Gary the Tennis Coach
POST PRODUCTION: Trainwreck - Mr. Woodcock
UPCOMING RELEASES: Southland Tales

Seann William Scott . . . Producer
Graham Larson . . . Producer
Danny Bress . . . Executive Assistant to Seann William Scott
Eric Loy . . . Executive Assistant to Graham Larson

IDT ENTERTAINMENT
2950 N. Hollywood Way, 3rd Fl.
Burbank, CA 91505
PHONE 818-748-4000/973-438-1000
FAX 818-748-4613
WEB SITE ....www.idtentertainment.com
TYPES Animation - Features - TV Series
PRODUCTION Everyone's Hero
CREDITS Masters of Horror

Morris Berger ....CEO
Jerry Davis ....CCO, Animated Features
Nick Foster ....CTO
Neil Braun ....President, Feature Films & TV
Janet Healey ....President, Animation
Amorette Jones ....Executive VP, Marketing
Bob Turner ....Executive VP, Animation Finance
Paul Campbell ....Sr. VP, Publicity & Promotion (NJ)
Marc DeBevoise ....Sr. VP, Business Development & Strategy (NJ)
Chris McGurk ....Sr. Advisor, New Ventures

IFM FILM ASSOCIATES, INC.
1328 E. Palmer Ave.
Glendale, CA 91205
PHONE 818-243-4976
FAX 818-550-9728
EMAIL ....contact@ifmfilm.com
WEB SITE ....www.ifmfilm.com
TYPES Direct-to-Video/DVD - Features - Made-for-TV/Cable Movies - TV Series
DEVELOPMENT Patrick - Thirst - Islanders
PRE-PRODUCTION Sally Marshall Is Not an Alien (Series)
UPCOMING RELEASES Look @ Me - Brothers - Bachelor Party Massacre
CREDITS Sally Marshall Is Not an Alien (Feature) - The Whole of the Moon - The Hit
SUBMISSION POLICY Synopsis only; No unsolicited scripts

Antony I. Ginnane ....President
Ann Lyons ....Executive VP
Anthony J. Lyons ....VP, International
David Makhlout ....Director, International Sales
Patrick Cochran ....Executive Assistant

IMAGERIES ENTERTAINMENT
2815 Coldwater Canyon Dr.
Beverly Hills, CA 90210
PHONE 310-278-7297
FAX 310-278-5085
TYPES Features - Made-for-TV/Cable Movies - TV Series
DEVELOPMENT The Tension Ring - Elixir - Ripple
PRE-PRODUCTION North of Sunset - Behind the Glass - Straight Ballin'
POST PRODUCTION Captivity
COMPLETED UNRELEASED The Water Giant - Jeckyl & Hyde
CREDITS Eyes of the Beholder - Men of Respect - Friday the 13th Part VII - Curse of the Forty-Niner - The New Adventures of Pippi Longstocking - A Light in the Forest

Gary Mehlman ....Producer/Partner
Alexandra Mehlman ....Producer
John Buechler ....Writer/Director/Partner

IMAGI SERVICES (USA)
15760 Ventura Blvd., Ste. 823
Encino, CA 91436
PHONE 818-986-3988
FAX 818-986-3288
EMAIL ....mikearnold@imagius.com
WEB SITE ....www.imagi.com.hk
TYPES Animation - Direct-to-Video/DVD - Features - TV Series
PRE-PRODUCTION Gatchaman
PRODUCTION Teenage Mutant Ninja Turtles - Cat Tale - Highlander
CREDITS Zentrix - Father of the Pride
COMMENTS Deal with Madhouse Studios and Davis/Panzer Productions

Thomas K. Gray ....President/CEO
Galen Walker ....Executive VP/COO
Michael J. Arnold ....Manager, Foreign Sales

IMAGINARIUM ENTERTAINMENT GROUP
723 Ocean Front Walk
Venice, CA 90291
PHONE 310-314-6400
FAX 310-388-5855
WEB SITE ....www.imaginariumeg.com
TYPES Documentaries - Features - TV Series
DEVELOPMENT A Rhinestone Alibi (Paramount) - American Empire: A Documentary - Wicked West (Dark Woods Prods.) - Nano - Moosebend Dispatch - Rose and the Americans - The Instigators - Untitled Cindy McCreery/Julie Richardson Dramedy - The Chosen (Dark Woods Prods.) - To Beat Hell - Sacrifice (Fortress)
PRE-PRODUCTION Appetite - Starry Night
CREDITS Collateral

Julie Richardson ....Producer/Founding Partner
Nathan Holtz ....Producer/Founding Partner
Paul Rubenfeld ....Staff

IMAGINATION PRODUCTIONS, INC.
6300 Wilshire Blvd., Ste. 1460
Los Angeles, CA 90048
PHONE 310-471-3456
WEB SITE ....www.imagination-productions.com
TYPES Animation - Features - Internet Content - Made-for-TV/Cable Movies - Specials - TV Series
DEVELOPMENT High Alert - Humor Me - Boomertown - Take My Life, Please! - Larry Gelbart's Power Failure - Plenty of Money & You
CREDITS The Don's Analyst - National Lampoon's Favorite Deadly Sins - Public Enemy #2 - Larry Gelbart's Mastergate - The Ratings Game - Likely Stories

David Jablin ....Executive Producer/Director
Michael Barrie ....Producer
Jim Mulholland ....Producer

IMAGINE

IMAGINE ENTERTAINMENT
9465 Wilshire Blvd., 7th Fl.
Beverly Hills, CA 90212
PHONE 310-858-2000
FAX 310-858-2020
WEB SITE .....www.imagine-entertainment.com
TYPES Features
HAS DEAL WITH Universal Pictures
PRE-PRODUCTION American Gangster
CREDITS The Da Vinci Code - Inside Man - Curious George - Fun with Dick and Jane - Flight Plan - Cinderella Man - Friday Night Lights - A Beautiful Mind - 8 Mile

Brian Grazer .....Chairman
Ron Howard .....Chairman
Karen Kehela Sherwood .....Co-Chairman, Imagine Films
Michael Rosenberg .....President, Entertainment
Jim Whitaker .....President, Production
Robin Barris .....Executive VP, Administration & Operations
Kim Roth .....Executive VP, Motion Pictures
David Bernardi .....Sr. VP, Motion Pictures
Erica Huggins .....Sr. VP, Motion Pictures
Sarah Bowen .....VP, Motion Pictures
Christy Sterling .....VP, Finance
Anna Culp .....Director, Development
Brad Grossman .....Executive in Charge of Special Projects
Chris Wade .....Creative Executive
Leah Estrin .....Story Editor

IMAGINE TELEVISION
9465 Wilshire Blvd., 7th Fl.
Beverly Hills, CA 90212
PHONE 310-858-2000
FAX 310-858-2011
TYPES Miniseries - Reality TV - Specials - TV Series
HAS DEAL WITH Twentieth Century Fox Television
CREDITS Friday Night Lights - Shark - Saved - 24 - Arrested Development

Brian Grazer .....Chairman
Ron Howard .....Chairman
David Nevins .....President
Skip Chasey .....Executive VP, Business Affairs
Robin Gurney .....Executive VP, Development
Erin Nowocinski .....VP, Current Programming
Bianca Chern .....Manager, Development
Elio Chavez Jr. .....Coordinator, Business Affairs

IMAX CORPORATION
3003 Exposition Blvd.
Santa Monica, CA 90404
PHONE 310-255-5500
FAX 310-315-1759
WEB SITE .....www.imax.com
TYPES Animation - Documentaries - Features
DEVELOPMENT Surfari
CREDITS Magnificent Desolation: Walking on the Moon - NASCAR 3D - Harry Potter and the Prisoner of Azkaban: The IMAX Experience - Matrix Revolutions: The IMAX Experience - Matrix Reloaded: The IMAX Experience - Apollo 13: The IMAX Experience - Space Station 3D - Star Wars: Attack of the Clones - Santa vs. the Snowman 3D
COMMENTS Large format

Greg Foster .....Chairman/President, Filmed Entertainment
Meg Wilson .....Sr. VP, Filmed Entertainment
Phil Groves .....VP, Film Distribution & Development

IMG MEDIA
McCormack House
Burlington Ln.
London W4 2TH, United Kingdom
PHONE 44-208-233-5300
FAX 44-208-233-5301
WEB SITE .....www.imgworld.com
TYPES Direct-to-Video/DVD - Documentaries - TV Series
DEVELOPMENT Colour of War: In Their Own Words - Chef vs. USA
PRE-PRODUCTION War of the Wives - Timewatch - Take It or Leave It - Celebrity Darts - Hidden Camera
PRODUCTION Trendwatch
UPCOMING RELEASES The Mind of a Demon
COMPLETED UNRELEASED I'd Do Anything - E-Force
CREDITS All Star Cup - Chef vs. Britain - Sport Matters - Victory in Europe in Colour - Christopher Reeve: Keeping Hope in Motion - Adolf Hitler in Colour - 2006 Academy Awards® (Sky One UK) - UKTV Sport - England vs. Germany: The Legends - African Nations Cup
COMMENTS 40 offices worldwide; Represents independent producers and its own productions in the areas of factual, entertainment and sports

Ted Forstmann .....Chairman/CEO
Alastair Waddington .....CCO/Executive VP
Michel Masquelier .....Executive VP/Head, Acquisitions & Distribution Worldwide
Robb Dalton .....President/Head, TV & New Media, North America
Barry Frank .....Vice Chairman
Martin Baker .....Commercial Director
Felix Alvarez-Garmon .....Sr. VP, Operations (Miami)
David Bulhack .....Sr. VP/General Sales Manager, Syndication
Hillary Mandel .....Sr. VP, Programming & Development
Greg Carroll .....VP, West Coast Sales
Linda Lieberman .....VP, East Coast Sales
Bob Massie .....Head, Entertainment
John Morris .....Head, Sales & Acquisitions, Factual & Entertainment
Jake Smith .....Account Executive
Allison Cozzini .....Syndication Assistant

IMPACT PICTURES

9200 Sunset Blvd., Ste. 800
Los Angeles, CA 90069
PHONE 310-247-1803
TYPES Features
HAS DEAL WITH Constantin Film Development, Inc./Constantin Television
DEVELOPMENT Driver
PRODUCTION Resident Evil 3
UPCOMING RELEASES DOA: Dead or Alive
CREDITS Resident Evil 1&2 - Mortal Kombat - Soldier - Event Horizon

Paul W.S. Anderson . . . . Producer/Writer
Jeremy Bolt . . . . Producer
Damon Chua . . . . VP/General Manager
Sarah Crompton . . . . Assistant to Paul W.S. Anderson
Judy Goldberg . . . . Assistant to Jeremy Bolt

IN CAHOOTS

4024 Radford Ave., Editorial Bldg. 2, Ste. 7
Studio City, CA 91604
PHONE 818-655-6482
FAX 818-655-8472
EMAIL . . . . incahootsprod@aol.com
TYPES Features - TV Series
CREDITS The Bernie Mac Show - The Office - Malcolm in the Middle - Sexual Life
SUBMISSION POLICY No unsolicited material

Ken Kwapis . . . . Director/Producer
Alex Beattie . . . . Producer
Rebecca Rajkowski . . . . Assistant

INCOGNITO ENTERTAINMENT

9440 Santa Monica Blvd., Ste. 302
Beverly Hills, CA 90210
PHONE 310-246-1500
FAX 310-246-0469
TYPES Features - Reality TV - TV Series
CREDITS Three to Tango - Morning - Freeway 2 - Modern Vampires

Lawrence Abramson . . . . Owner/CEO
Andrew Howard . . . . Executive
Brian Klinsport . . . . Development

THE INDEPENDENT FILM CHANNEL (IFC)

200 Jericho Quadrangle
Jericho, NY 11753
PHONE 516-803-4500
FAX 516-803-4506
EMAIL . . . . info@ifctv.com
WEB SITE . . . . www.ifctv.com
TYPES Documentaries - Features - Made-for-TV/Cable Movies - TV Series
UPCOMING RELEASES The Minor Accomplishments of Jackie Woodman - The Business
CREDITS Original Programming: Independent Spirit Awards - Greg the Bunny - Hopeless Pictures - The Festival - Dinner for Five - The Henry Rollins Show - At the IFC Center - Wanderlust (Documentary); Film Strands: Samurai Saturdays - Escape From Hollywood - Pulp Indies - Film Fanatic Fridays - Cinema Red Mondays - Fabulous! The Story of Queer Cinema - I'm Boricua, Just So You Know! - This Film Is Not Yet Rated

Joshua Sapan . . . . President/CEO, Rainbow Programming Holdings LLC
Ed Carroll . . . . President, Rainbow Entertainment Services
Gregg Hill . . . . President, Rainbow Network Sales
Evan Shapiro . . . . Executive VP/General Manager
Jennifer Caserta . . . . Sr. VP, Marketing
Todd Green . . . . Sr. VP, Affiliate Marketing, Rainbow Network Sales
Harold Gronenthal . . . . Sr. VP, Acquisitions
Alan Klein . . . . Sr. VP, Partnerships & Licensing
Judi Lopez . . . . Sr. VP, Eastern Region, Rainbow Network Sales
Ed Palluth . . . . Sr. VP, Southern Region, Rainbow Network Sales
Alison Bourke . . . . VP, Original Programming
Debbie DeMontreux . . . . VP, Original Series & Events
Matthew Frankel . . . . VP, Corporate Communications
Elektra Gray . . . . VP, Consumer Public Relations
Lisa Penha . . . . VP, Event Marketing
Rachel Smith . . . . Director, Development & Production, Original Series

INDIGENT

135 W. 26th St., 5th Fl.
New York, NY 10001
PHONE 212-929-7711
FAX 212-929-7722
WEB SITE . . . . www.indigent.net
TYPES Features
POST PRODUCTION Flakes - Starting Out in the Evening
CREDITS Lonesome Jim - Sorry, Haters - November - Final - Chelsea Walls - Women in Film - Tape - Ten Tiny Love Stories - Tadpole - Personal Velocity - Kill the Poor - Pieces of April - Pizza - Land of Plenty

Gary Winick . . . . Producer/Director
John Sloss . . . . Attorney
Jake Abraham . . . . Producer

INDIGO FILMS
155 Redwood Dr., Ste. 250
San Rafael, CA 94903
PHONE .415-444-1700
FAX .415-444-1720
EMAIL .info@indigofilms.com
WEB SITE .www.indigofilms.com
TYPES Documentaries - Reality TV - TV Series
PRE-PRODUCTION UFO Files
PRODUCTION Cash & Treasures - Hunt for John W. Booth - Mega-Structures - The Plot to Kill...
POST PRODUCTION U.S.S. Constellation
CREDITS Twister Sisters - Vampire Secrets - Supercoasters
COMMENTS Los Angeles office: 11901 Santa Monica Blvd., Ste. 329, Los Angeles, CA 90025

David M. Frank .President
Rosemary Wall .Supervising Producer
Laurie Brian .Series Producer
Katie Gilbert .Producer
Kim Hawkins .Series Producer
Chris Leavell .Series Producer
Julie Nelson .Producer
Josh Rosen .Producer
Diana Zaslaw .Producer

INDUSTRIAL LIGHT & MAGIC (ILM)
PO Box 29909
San Francisco, CA 94129
PHONE .415-746-3000
FAX .415-746-3015
WEB SITE .www.ilm.com
COMMENTS VFX Studio

Chrissie England .President
Mark Miller .VP/Sr. Executive, Production

INDUSTRY ENTERTAINMENT PARTNERS
955 S. Carrillo Dr., 3rd Fl.
Los Angeles, CA 90048
PHONE .323-954-9000
FAX .323-954-9009
TYPES Features - TV Series
CREDITS Masters of Science Fiction - Masters of Horror - 25th Hour - The Player - sex, lies, and videotape - Drugstore Cowboy - The Yards - Fifteen Minutes - Requiem for a Dream - Quills - Becker (CBS) - Live from Baghdad (HBO) - War Stories (NBC)
SUBMISSION POLICY WGA-registered material by industry referral only
COMMENTS Also produces TV anthologies

Keith Addis .Feature/TV Production/Manager
Eryn Brown .Feature/TV Production/Manager
Sandra Chang .Feature/TV Production/Manager
Andrew Deane .Feature/TV Production/Manager
Dianne Fraser .Feature/TV Production/Manager
Helena Heyman .Feature/TV Production/Manager
Ira Liss .Feature/TV Production
Brad Mendelsohn .Manager
Lauren Rothstein .Feature/TV Production/Manager
Rosalie Swedlin .Feature/TV Production/Manager
John Baldasare .Feature/TV Production/Manager
Ben Browning .Production Executive
Adam Goldworm .Production Executive/Manager

*INFINITUM NIHIL
c/o IEG
3000 W. Olympic Blvd., Bldg. 2
Santa Monica, CA 90404
PHONE .310-273-6700
WEB SITE .www.infinitum-nihil.com
TYPES Features
HAS DEAL WITH Initial Entertainment Group
DEVELOPMENT Happy Days - The Bomb in My Garden - A Long Way Down
PRE-PRODUCTION Shantaram
SUBMISSION POLICY No unsolicited submissions or calls

Johnny Depp .Principal
Christi Dembrowski .President
Jason Forman .No Title
Sam Sarkar .Director, Development
Jeff Taplin .Creative Executive
Norman Todd .Creative Executive

*INFINITY FEATURES ENTERTAINMENT
319 Main St.
Vancouver, BC V6A 259
PHONE .604-899-1077
FAX .605-899-1027
EMAIL .info@infinityfeatures.net
WEB SITE .www.infinityfeatures.net
TYPES Features - TV Series
DEVELOPMENT The Magician's Wife - Rule of Thumb - The Ancient One - Mantis - Gala Dali - The Miracle Life of Edgar Mint
PRE-PRODUCTION Push - Stone of Destiny
POST PRODUCTION Butterfly on a Wheel
CREDITS Capote - Just Friends - Saved - Snow Walker - Dead Heat
SUBMISSION POLICY Unsolicited material not accepted
COMMENTS Deals with Icon Entertainment International and Capitol Films; Company has mandate to support writer/driven packages

William Vince .Producer
Rob Merilees .Producer
Michael Potkins .Producer
Dave Valleau .Executive Producer
Lyn Vince .Executive Producer
Erin Haskett .Development Executive
Jared Valentine .Development Executive
Rob LaBelle .Television Executive
Pete Valleau .Project Manager

INFINITY MEDIA, INC.
8000 Sunset Blvd., Ste. B310
Los Angeles, CA 90046
PHONE .323-848-8966
FAX .323-848-8727
EMAIL .info@infinitymediainc.com
WEB SITE .www.infinitymediainc.com
TYPES Features
DEVELOPMENT Gravy - Winalota Cash - Mike the Bike
POST PRODUCTION P.D.R.
UPCOMING RELEASES Bug - Ripley Under Ground
CREDITS Just Friends - Capote - The Woods - The Cave - The Devil's Rejects - Saved! - Confidence - Evelyn - Dead Heat - Frailty - The Human Stain - The Snow Walker - The Final Cut
SUBMISSION POLICY Submit brief synopsis via email

Michael Ohoven .Producer/CEO

INFRONT PRODUCTIONS

c/o Debbee Klein/The Paradigm Agency
360 N. Crescent Dr., North Bldg.
Beverly Hills, CA 90210

PHONE 310-288-8000

TYPES	Features - Theatre - TV Series
HAS DEAL WITH	Touchstone Television
DEVELOPMENT	Film: Voting Under the Influence; TV: The Catch (Touchstone/The CW) - Love Like Crazy (Warner Bros.); Theatre: Bang Zoom
CREDITS	Film: The Honeymooners (Paramount); TV: Mad About You - Good Advice - Two Guys and a Girl - Roseanne - Davis Rules - Simon - Soap - Fame
SUBMISSION POLICY	All submissions through the Paradigm Agency

Danny Jacobson . . . . .Writer/Producer
Marc Brener . . . . .Producer

INITIAL ENTERTAINMENT GROUP

3000 W. Olympic Blvd., Bldg. 2, Ste. 1550
Santa Monica, CA 90404

PHONE 310-315-1722
FAX 310-315-1723

TYPES	Features
HAS DEAL WITH	Warner Bros. Pictures
PROVIDES DEAL TO	Blueprint Films - Infinitum Nihil
DEVELOPMENT	The Accidental Husband - A Long Way Down - Southbound - Shantaram - Bangkok Dangerous
PRODUCTION	Next
POST PRODUCTION	First Born - Gardener of Eden
UPCOMING RELEASES	The Departed
CREDITS	The Ballad of Jack and Rose - The Aviator - Gangs of New York - Ali - The Dangerous Lives of Altar Boys - Traffic - Dr. T & the Women - Desert Saints - Joe the King - Savior - Little City - Montana - An Unfinished Life
COMMENTS	Specializes in international distribution

Graham King . . . . .President/CEO
Eric Christenson .President, Sales & Distribution
Colin Cotter . . . . .COO
Schuyler Ha . . . . .Sr. VP, Marketing & Publicity
James Putt . . . . .Sr. VP, Post Production Services
Julie Roach . . . . .Sr. VP, Business & Legal Affairs
Jennifer Wachtell . . . . .Sr. VP, Creative Affairs
Alexa Faigen . . . . .Director, Development
Heather Vye . . . . .Director, Business Affairs

INTEGRATED FILMS & MANAGEMENT

1154 N. Wetherly Dr.
Los Angeles, CA 90069

PHONE 310-247-9655
FAX 310-247-9855

TYPES	Features - Made-for-TV/Cable Movies - TV Series
DEVELOPMENT	Meet John Doe - The Liberty (FX Studios) - Haunting in Connecticut (Gold Circle) - Rin Tin Tin - Terror Train (Nu Image) - Hooking Up
PRE-PRODUCTION	The Yellow Wood (Spyglass)
POST PRODUCTION	Borderland
CREDITS	Tamara - The Amityville Horror

Andy Trapani . . . . .Principal
Brendan Bragg . . . . .Creative Executive
Chris Winvick . . . . .Creative Executive

INTERLOPER FILMS

6063 W. Sunset Blvd.
Hollywood, CA 90028

PHONE 323-461-2444
FAX 323-461-6744
EMAIL . . . . .info@interloperfilms.com
WEB SITE . . . . .www.interloperfilms.com

TYPES	Documentaries - Music Videos
CREDITS	DIG!

Ondi Timoner . . . . .Director/Producer
Vasco Nunes . . . . .Co-Producer
Jeff Frey . . . . .Co-Producer
Civan Gur-Arieh . . . . .Production Coordinator

INTERMEDIA

INTERMEDIA FILM EQUITIES USA, INC.

9242 Beverly Blvd., Ste. 201
Beverly Hills, CA 90210

PHONE 310-777-0007/44-207-593-1630
FAX 310-777-0008/44-207-593-1639
EMAIL . . . . .info@intermediafilm.com
WEB SITE . . . . .www.intermediafilm.com

TYPES	Features
DEVELOPMENT	Prodigy - Killer's Game - Sleepwalker - Number One Girl - The Frog King - DJ - Abyssinia - In the Heart of the Sea - Baghdad Blog - Shelter - Adenaline - Heavy Metal Thunder - Jolt - Phenomenum
PRE-PRODUCTION	Magicians - Stopping Power - One Missed Call - Spring Break in Bosnia
POST PRODUCTION	Breach
CREDITS	RV - The Quiet American - K-19: The Widowmaker - Basic Instinct 2 - If Only - Terminator 3 - Alexander - Mindhunters - Suspect Zero - Adaptation - Dark Blue - The Life of David Gale - K-Pax - Nurse Betty - The Wedding Planner - Iris - Sliding Doors - Playing by Heart - Hilary and Jackie
SUBMISSION POLICY	No unsolicited submissions
COMMENTS	London office: Unit 12 Enterprise House, 1-2 Hatfields, London SE1 9PG, United Kingdom

Martin Schuermann . . . . .Chairman
Scott Kroopf . . . . .President, Motion Picture Group
Noel Lohr . . . . .General Counsel
Gavin James . . . . .Managing Director, UK Operations (London)
Linda Benjamin . . . . .Executive VP, Business & Legal Affairs
Robert Lacy . . . . .Sr. VP, Controller
Tony Alessi . . . . .VP, Film Finance
Steve Freedman . . . . .VP, Production & Finance
Ollie Madden . . . . .VP/Head, UK Production & Development (London)
Saeed Daeenejad . . . . .VP, Operations
Alison Haskovec . . . . .VP, Creative
Mark Austin . . . . .Distribution & Finance Coordinator
Ryan Lane . . . . .Legal Affairs Coordinator
Laura K. Miller . . . . .Business Affairs Coordinator

INTERNATIONAL ARTS ENTERTAINMENT
8899 Beverly Blvd., Ste. 800
Los Angeles, CA 90048
PHONE .310-550-6760
FAX .310-550-8839
EMAIL .info@internationalartsentertainment.com
TYPES Features - TV Series
DEVELOPMENT Untitled Disney/Dudi Appleton & Jim Keeble Comedy - Untitled Sebastian Junger Project - My Fat Brother - Untitled Garrett & Ward Project - Clowns & Heroes
COMPLETED UNRELEASED Bookies
CREDITS Fever Pitch - High Fidelity - Donnie Brasco - Best Laid Plans - 200 Cigarettes - My Little Eye - Pushing Tin - A Good Woman
SUBMISSION POLICY No unsolicited submissions
COMMENTS Overall deal with Studio Hamburg

Alan Greenspan .Owner/Producer
Robyn Morrison .Creative Executive

INTERNATIONAL TELEVISION GROUP (ITG) - EPIX FILMS
1322 Second St.
Santa Monica, CA 90401
PHONE .310-656-9100
FAX .310-656-9104
EMAIL .info@epixfilms.com
WEB SITE .www.epixfilms.com
TYPES Commercials - Features - Music Videos - TV Series
DEVELOPMENT 8 Ball Chicks
CREDITS Cat on a Hot Tin Roof - Uncle Wally's General Store

Lou LaMonte .President/Executive Producer
Ish Muniz .Head, Music Video Division/Executive Producer
Teresa Campbell .VP, Production & Development

INTERSCOPE/SHADY/AFTERMATH FILMS
c/o Paramount Pictures
5555 Melrose Ave.
Los Angeles, CA 90035
PHONE .323-956-5989
FAX .323-862-2169
TYPES Features
HAS DEAL WITH Paramount Pictures - Paramount Vantage/Paramount Classics
CREDITS Get Rich or Die Tryin' - 8 Mile
COMMENTS Full-service production company specializing in pop-culture related genres, combined with a musical element

Jimmy Iovine .Producer
Paul Rosenberg .Producer
Stuart Parr .Producer
Gene Kirkwood .Producer
Rick Heller .Development Coordinator

INTREPID PICTURES
3000 W. Olympic Blvd., Bldg. 4, Ste. 2266
Santa Monica, CA 90404
PHONE .310-264-3995
FAX .310-264-3996
EMAIL .info@intrepid-pictures.com
TYPES Features
HAS DEAL WITH Focus Features/Rogue Pictures
DEVELOPMENT Kid Bang - Black Tide - Four Horsemen - Prodigy - Chance in Hell - If She Only Knew - Orphans - The Ridge Boys - Park Narcs - The Djinn - Laws Of Nature - Jinxing Barry Gluck
UPCOMING RELEASES The Return
CREDITS Waist Deep - Auto Focus - The Badge - Bark
SUBMISSION POLICY No unsolicited material

Trevor Macy .Principal
Marc Evans .Principal
Jonathan Fischer .CFO
Katherine Brown .VP, Development
Kasey Adler .Assistant to Jonathan Fischer
Ryan Beeman .Assistant to Marc Evans
Anil Kurian .Assistant to Trevor Macy
Arielle Singh .Assistant to Katherine Brown

INTUITION PRODUCTIONS
1635 Cahuenga Dr., 5th Fl.
Los Angeles, CA 90028
PHONE .323-464-1682
FAX .323-962-2081
EMAIL .intuitionamy@yahoo.com
TYPES Features - Made-for-TV/Cable Movies - Miniseries - TV Series
DEVELOPMENT House of Pain (Arclight)
PRE-PRODUCTION The Adoption Project (Lifetime) - Passengers (Mandate Pictures/Sony) - Stranded (Sony) - Untitled Robert Altman Project (Picturehouse) - Happy Maisy Coleman (20th Century Fox)
CREDITS Film: The Stepford Wives (Paramount) - Three to Tango (Warner Bros.) - After the Rain (Capella International); TV: Summer of '77 (UPN) - In the Company of Spies (Showtime) - Harlan County War (Showtime) - Point of Origin (HBO) - Mafia Doctor (CBS) - It Must Be Love (CBS) - Spy Girl (NBC)

Keri Selig .President/Producer
Amy Ficken .Creative Executive

INVENTURE ENTERTAINMENT
609 Fifth Ave., 4th Fl.
New York, NY 10017
PHONE .212-735-8418
FAX .212-208-4324
EMAIL info@inventureentertainment.com
WEB SITE .www.inventureentertainment.com
TYPES Features - TV Series
DEVELOPMENT Righteous Kill - Dream Racer
PRE-PRODUCTION Liquor
CREDITS Inside Man - Novocaine

Daniel Rosenberg .Principal
Brad Harris .Development Executive

INVITATION ENTERTAINMENT
100 Wilshire Blvd., Ste. 750
Santa Monica, CA 90401
PHONE .310-584-8100
FAX .310-584-8101
TYPES Features - Miniseries - TV Series
DEVELOPMENT The Other Side of Silence - Destined to Witness: Growing Up Black in Nazi Germany - Freeway Ricky Ross
PRE-PRODUCTION Momo (TNT Miniseries)
CREDITS Jane Doe

Judah Hertz .No Title
Ron Samuels .No Title

ION MEDIA NETWORKS, INC.
601 Clearwater Park Rd.
West Palm Beach, FL 33401
PHONE .561-659-4122
WEB SITE .www.ionmedia.tv
TYPES Reality TV - TV Series
CREDITS America's Most Talented Kids - Balderdash - Cold Turkey - Doc - It's a Miracle - Lie Detector - Model Citizens - On the Cover - Second Verdict - Shop 'Til You Drop - Sue Thomas: F.B. Eye - World Cup Comedy - Xtreme Fakeovers - Young Blades
COMMENTS Formerly Paxson Communications Corporation

Brandon Burgess .CEO
Dean Goodman .President/COO
Richard Garcia .Sr. VP/CFO
Adam Weinstein .Sr. VP/Secretary/Chief Legal Officer
Steve Friedman .President, Cable
Doug Barker .President, Broadcast Distribution & Southern Region
Steve Appel .President, Sales & Marketing
Stacey Nagel .Sr. VP, Programming & Strategic Planning
Leslie Monreal .Director, Public Relations

IRIDIUM ENTERTAINMENT
151 West 25th St., Ste. 12F
New York, NY 10001
PHONE .212-366-4790
FAX .212-366-4795
EMAIL .brent@iridiument.com
TYPES Features
DEVELOPMENT The Prince of Providence
PRODUCTION The Education of Charlie Banks
CREDITS Brooklyn Rules - The Door in the Floor - I'll Sleep When I'm Dead - Outside Providence - A Shot at Glory

Michael Corrente .Producer
Marisa Polvino .Producer

IRISH DREAMTIME
3110 Main St., Ste. 200
Santa Monica, CA 90405
PHONE .310-449-3411
FAX .310-586-8138
TYPES Features
HAS DEAL WITH Metro-Goldwyn-Mayer Studios, Inc. (MGM)
POST PRODUCTION Butterfly on a Wheel
CREDITS The Matador - Laws of Attraction - Evelyn - The Thomas Crown Affair (1999) - The Match - The Nephew
SUBMISSION POLICY No unsolicited material

Pierce Brosnan .Producer/Partner
Beau St. Clair .Producer/Partner
Angelique Higgins .Executive VP, Development
Amanda Scarano .Production Executive
Chris Charalambous .Creative Executive

IRONWORKS PRODUCTION
295 Greenwich St., Ste. 391
New York, NY 10007
PHONE .212-486-9829
FAX .212-486-9829
EMAIL .ironworksproductions@pobox.com
TYPES Direct-to-Video/DVD - Documentaries - Features - TV Series
DEVELOPMENT Lions & Foxes - Home Swap - Joyful Noise - 1-900 - Salon - Psychic Tea Party - In Darwin's Footsteps
PRE-PRODUCTION Blind Date
PRODUCTION Interview
CREDITS Trust - Curse of the Starving Class - Side Streets - Island of the Dead

Bruce Weiss .President
Isa Freeling .Executive VP, Development

IS OR ISN'T ENTERTAINMENT
8391 Beverly Blvd., Ste. 125
Los Angeles, CA 90048
PHONE .310-248-2000
TYPES TV Series
HAS DEAL WITH NBC Universal Television Studio
CREDITS All In (NBC Pilot) - The Commuters (CBS Pilot) - The Comeback (HBO) - My Life Incorporated (CBS Pilot) - Beck and Call (UPN Pilot)

Lisa Kudrow .Partner
Dan Bucatinsky .Partner
Rebecca Stay .Sr. VP, Development
Nicole Tocantins .Development Associate

*ISBE PRODUCTIONS
c/o Paradigm
360 N. Crescent Dr.
Beverly Hills, CA 90210
PHONE .310-287-0357
TYPES Animation - Features - Made-for-TV/Cable Movies - Miniseries - Reality TV - TV Series

Teri Hatcher .President
Jennifer Glassman .Sr. VP

ISHTAR FILMS
11333 Moorpark St., Ste. 460
Studio City, CA 91602
PHONE . . . 800-428-7136/818-985-0567
FAX . . . 818-753-0040
EMAIL . . . ishtarfilms@sbcglobal.net
WEB SITE . . . www.ishtarfilms.com
TYPES — Documentaries - Made-for-TV/Cable Movies
DEVELOPMENT — Locked Out: Sex Discrimination in Corporate America
PRODUCTION — The Art of Aging
POST PRODUCTION — Untitled May Sarton Project
CREDITS — Berenice Abbott: A View of the 20th Century - Votes for Women - Thistle Hotel - A Ring of Endless Light (Disney)
COMMENTS — Independent filmmakers; Distributor; Documentaries for educational and TV release

Martha Wheelock . . . President
Marita Giovanni . . . Associate

ITHAKA

ITHAKA
4553 Glencoe Ave., Ste. 320
Marina del Rey, CA 90292
PHONE . . . 310-314-9585/310-314-9588
FAX . . . 310-581-7374
EMAIL . . . bpope@lionsgate.com
SECOND EMAIL . . . aweiner@lionsgate.com
TYPES — Features - Made-for-TV/Cable Movies - Reality TV - Theatre - TV Series
HAS DEAL WITH — Lionsgate
DEVELOPMENT — Truth Machine - Amarillo Slim - Iced - Manhattan Monologue Slam
PRE-PRODUCTION — Party Boys - Man and Wife - The Rabbit Factory - Bumper
PRODUCTION — The Take
POST PRODUCTION — Hedonism
UPCOMING RELEASES — Penny Dreadful - Bondage
CREDITS — Mail Order Wife - What's Not to Love? (Showtime)

Andrew Weiner . . . Producer
Braxton Pope . . . Producer
Justin Steel . . . Assistant

IXTLAN
1207 Fourth St., PH 1
Santa Monica, CA 90401
PHONE . . . 310-395-0525
FAX . . . 310-395-1536
TYPES — Features
CREDITS — Alexander - Born on the Fourth of July - JFK - Nixon - Any Given Sunday - Heaven and Earth - Salvador - The People vs. Larry Flynt - Comandante - The Corruptor - Assassinated - Gravesend - Killer - Freeway - Indictment: The McMartin Trial - The New Age - The Joy Luck Club - Wild Palms - Zebrahead - South Central - Iron Maze - Blue Steel - Reversal of Fortune
SUBMISSION POLICY — No unsolicited material

Oliver Stone . . . Writer/Director
Suzie Gilbert . . . No Title
Rob Wilson . . . No Title

J.K. LIVIN PRODUCTIONS
238 S. Lasky Dr.
Beverly Hills, CA 90212
PHONE . . . 310-556-0079
FAX . . . 310-556-1995
TYPES — Documentaries - Features - TV Series
HAS DEAL WITH — New Line Cinema
DEVELOPMENT — Dear Delilah (Paramount) - Arrested Development (New Line Cinema) - Dirty Little Secret (Paramount) - Johnny Diamond (Imagine); Independent: Bone Game - Surfer Dude - River Road - The Grackle
CREDITS — Sahara (Paramount) - Hands on a Hard Body (Documentary)

Matthew McConaughey . . . Producer/Partner
Gus Gustawes . . . COO
Mark Gustawes . . . President, Production
Anita Ferry . . . Executive Assistant

J2 pictures
J2 TV

J2 PICTURES/J2TV
11684 Ventura Blvd., 968
Studio City, CA 91604
PHONE . . . 818-980-8114
FAX . . . 818-980-8115
WEB SITE . . . www.j2tv.com
TYPES — Features - Reality TV - TV Series
DEVELOPMENT — Jerry Garcia Project - Doris Payne Project
UPCOMING RELEASES — Romance & Cigarettes
CREDITS — Filthy Rich: Cattle Drive
SUBMISSION POLICY — No unsolicited submissions

Justin Berfield . . . Partner/Actor/Producer
Jason Felts . . . Partner/Writer/Producer
Rebecca Farrell . . . No Title

JACK ANGEL PRODUCTIONS INC.
2044 Stanley Hills Dr.
Los Angeles, CA 90046
PHONE . . . 323-650-3392
EMAIL . . . jackangelprods@aol.com
TYPES — Features - Made-for-TV/Cable Movies - TV Series
DEVELOPMENT — Illusion - Phrackers - Forensic Nurse - Young at Heartless
CREDITS — Roswell - Dying to Live

Lisa J. Olin . . . Producer

JACKHOLE INDUSTRIES
6834 Hollywood Blvd., Ste. 400
Los Angeles, CA 90028
PHONE . . . 323-860-5760
TYPES — Made-for-TV/Cable Movies - Reality TV - TV Series
CREDITS — The Andy Milonakis Show - Jimmy Kimmel Live

Jimmy Kimmel . . . Partner
Adam Carolla . . . Partner
Daniel Kellison . . . Producer
Doug DeLuca . . . Producer

TOM JACOBSON PRODUCTIONS
c/o Paramount Pictures
5555 Melrose Ave., Hart Bldg., Rm. 100
Los Angeles, CA 90038-3197
PHONE 323-956-5040
TYPES Features - TV Series
HAS DEAL WITH Paramount Pictures
DEVELOPMENT Family Time - Black Monday

Tom Jacobson . . . . .President/Producer
Monnie Wills . . . . .VP, Production
Oliver Obst . . . . .Director, Development
Lynsey Jones . . . . .Development Associate
Leslie Kolb . . . . .Assistant

JAFFE/BRAUNSTEIN FILMS, LLC
12301 Wilshire Blvd., Ste. 110
Los Angeles, CA 90025
PHONE 310-207-6600
TYPES Made-for-TV/Cable Movies - TV Series
PROVIDES DEAL TO Chotzen/Jenner Productions
DEVELOPMENT Beyond The Sound of Music - Back in Action - Keeping Faith - Wonderland - Flory - Somebody's Somneone - Lost & Found
PRE-PRODUCTION The Party Never Stops
POST PRODUCTION Wildfires
UPCOMING RELEASES Not Everyone Else
CREDITS Touch the Top of the World - 10.5 Apocalypse - Nero Wolfe (A&E) - 100 Centre Street (A&E) - The Rosa Parks Story - It's Always Something: The Gilda Radner Story - Sounder - Martha, Inc. - 10.5 - Word of Honor - Undercover Christmas - Evel Knievel - The Brooke Ellison Story - Elvis - Faith of My Fathers - The Engagement Ring
SUBMISSION POLICY Must have representation by an agent or lawyer

Michael Jaffe . . . . .Partner
Howard Braunstein . . . . .Partner
John Hassig . . . . .Business Affairs Attorney
Carole Parker . . . . .Business Affairs Associate
Lynn Delaney . . . . .Assistant to Mr. Jaffe
Victor Boutrous . . . . .Production & Development Coordinator

JAFFILMS, LLC
745 Fifth Ave., Ste. 1604
New York, NY 10151
PHONE 212-262-4700
FAX 212-223-0615
TYPES Features
DEVELOPMENT Don Juan Zimmerman - Crossing to Safety - Madness
CREDITS Goodbye, Columbus - School Ties - Bad Company - Four Feathers - I Dreamed of Africa - Madeline - The Accused - Fatal Attraction - Kramer vs. Kramer - Taps

Stanley R. Jaffe . . . . .Producer
Bob Jaffe . . . . .Producer
Megan Cannan .Assistant to Stanley R. Jaffe (NY)

JANICEK-MARINO CREATIVE
600 Ogden St.
Denver, CO 80218
PHONE 303-860-0070/818-754-1792
FAX 303-837-8451
EMAIL . . . . .cre8vtv@aol.com
WEB SITE . . . . .www.janicekmarino.com
TYPES Animation - Commercials - Direct-to-Video/DVD - Documentaries - Features - Internet Content - Mobile Content - Reality TV - Specials - TV Series
HAS DEAL WITH Buena Vista Home Entertainment - The Walt Disney Company - The Hatchery
DEVELOPMENT Jack and the Box
PRE-PRODUCTION Family Tree - Little Hot Rods
COMPLETED UNRELEASED Baby Einstein - Baby's First Movies - Muppet Spotlight (Disney Pilot)
CREDITS Mymo's My Gym Adventures - Baby Einstein's Meet the Orchestra - Baby on the Go - Baby Neptune - Ancient Secrets of Life - Winnie the Pooh/Book of Pooh Documentary - ABC TGIF - Baby Einstein Videos - ABC Specials - Baby Einstein's Numbers Nursery - Baby McDonald - Baby Noah - Baby Monet
SUBMISSION POLICY No unsolicited submissions
COMMENTS Specializes in branding and children's programming; Representation: Innovative Artists, Marcia Hurwitz, phone: 310-656-5144; Rita Cahill 310-556-2712

Jim Janicek . . . . .Partner/Executive Producer
Len Marino . . . . .Partner/Executive Producer
Jane Pahl . . . . .Production Manager

JANUARY FILMS
c/o Serendipity Point Films
9 Price St.
Toronto, ON M4W 1Z1, Canada
PHONE 416-967-7071
FAX 416-960-8656
TYPES Features - TV Series
CREDITS Being Julia - Ararat - Where the Truth Lies - G-Spot (TV Series)

Julia Rosenberg . . . . .Producer
Tyler Levine . . . . .Assistant to Ms. Rosenberg

JANUS FILMS, LLC
265 E. 66th St., Ste. 16-A
New York, NY 10021
PHONE 212-396-9209
FAX 212-327-0541
WEB SITE . . . . .www.janusfilms.net
TYPES Features
DEVELOPMENT By Grand Central Station I Sat Down and Wept - Change
COMPLETED UNRELEASED Romance & Cigarettes
CREDITS Kart Racer - Among Giants - Investigating Sex - Advice from a Caterpillar - Top of the Foodchain - The Incredible Mrs. Ritchie

Jana Edelbaum . . . . .President
Robin Gold . . . . .Development Executive

JARET ENTERTAINMENT
6973 Birdview Ave.
Malibu, CA 90265
PHONE .310-589-9600
FAX .310-589-9602
WEB SITE .www.jaretentertainment.com
TYPES Documentaries - Features - TV Series
DEVELOPMENT The Push
PRE-PRODUCTION The Cold
CREDITS 10 Things I Hate About You
COMMENTS Also publishes

Seth Jaret .CEO/Producer
Adam Jaret .Creative Executive

MELINDA JASON COMPANY
c/o IPG
9200 Sunset Blvd., Ste. 820
Los Angeles, CA 90069
PHONE .310-402-5156
TYPES Features - Made-for-TV/Cable Movies - TV Series
DEVELOPMENT Sweet Talk (Love Spell) - We Make Your Dreams Come True (Fox TV/Mark Gordon)
PRE-PRODUCTION Secrets (Showtime/Mark Gordon/Love Spell)
PRODUCTION Untitled Dramedy (Paramount)
CREDITS The First Power - Eve of Destruction - Body of Evidence - Killer
SUBMISSION POLICY No unsolicited submissions
COMMENTS Also literary manager and producer with IPG (Intellectual Property Group)

Melinda Jason .President

JAY & TONY SHOW PRODUCTIONS
12925 Riverside Dr., 4th Fl.
Sherman Oaks, CA 91423
PHONE .818-325-6938
WEB SITE .www.jayandtonyshow.com
TYPES Reality TV - TV Series
CREDITS Tuesday Night Book Club (CBS) - Tourgasm - Raising the Roofs - Welcome to the Neighborhood - R U the Girl (UPN) - Family Business (Showtime)

Jay Blumenfield .Producer
Tony Marsh .Producer

JBE PRODUCTIONS
15445 Ventura Blvd., Ste. 110
Sherman Oaks, CA 91403
PHONE .818-981-8833
FAX .818-981-8412
TYPES Features - Made-for-TV/Cable Movies - Reality TV - TV Series
DEVELOPMENT Untitled Reality Series (New Line) - Trailer Park Cinderella (New Line) - Up & Down Guys (GRB) - Trading Up (Broadway Video)
POST PRODUCTION Let Bob Do It (Nick at Nite)
CREDITS Agent Cody Banks 1&2 (MGM) - Bob Patterson (ABC) - On Edge (MGM Home Video)

Jenny Birchfield-Eick .Producer

JCS ENTERTAINMENT II
48 Brandermill Dr.
Henderson, NV 89052
PHONE .310-963-2927
FAX .310-943-1909
EMAIL .jc@jcsent.com
TYPES Documentaries - Made-for-TV/Cable Movies - Reality TV - TV Series
DEVELOPMENT The Challengers - Coco Chanel (MOW) - Earth Angels - The Barn - Phyllis Sharon Kirkland Story (MOW)
CREDITS Best in Show - America's Greatest Pets - Ripley's Believe It or Not - Stay the Night - Something Borrowed/Blue - P.S.I. for Teens (Documentary)

JC Shardo .Executive Producer/President
Lisa Ferrell .Director, Development

JEFF WALD ENTERTAINMENT
1467 Chastain Pkwy. West
Pacific Palisades, CA 90272
PHONE .310-459-0168
FAX .310-459-8230
TYPES Features - Reality TV - TV Series
DEVELOPMENT The Playboy Interviews - The Ruth Bowen Story - Playoff - The Power of Joy (George Foreman) - George Foreman Biopic - Rampart Scandal (HBO)
CREDITS Behind Bars - Back to School '92 - Opposing Force - Kenny Rogers Classical Weekend - Helen Reddy Special - The Contender (NBC) - Pensacola - Two Days in the Valley - Beyond Gang Lines - The Gong Show - The All New Dating Game - The Newlywed Game - Quiz Kids Challenge - El Show De Paul Rodriguez - Switched at Birth - Elvis: The Tribute - The Roseanne Show

Jeff Wald .Chairman
Kelly Newby .President
Josie Lamberth .Development Executive
Amy Cheong .Assistant to Mr. Wald

JERSEY FILMS
PO Box 491246
Los Angeles, CA 90049
PHONE .310-477-7704
FAX .310-550-3210
TYPES Features
POST PRODUCTION Freedom Writers
CREDITS Along Came Polly - Erin Brockovich - Man on the Moon - Living Out Loud - Out of Sight - Gattaca - Feeling Minnesota - Sunset Park - Get Shorty - Reality Bites - Pulp Fiction - Hoffa - 8 Seconds

Danny DeVito .No Title
Nikki Allyn Grosso .Business Manager

JIBJAB MEDIA INC.
209 Ashland Ave.
Santa Monica, CA 90405
PHONE .800-777-3874
FAX .310-664-1972
EMAIL .support@jibjab.net
WEB SITE .www.jibjab.com
TYPES Animation - Internet Content - Mobile Content
CREDITS This Land - 2-0-5 - Big Box Mart - Second Term - Good to Be in D.C. - Nasty Santa - Ahnuld for Governor - Matzah!!
SUBMISSION POLICY No unsolicted submissions; Accepted through agents only
COMMENTS Includes JokeBox, an online social networking service

Gregg Spiridellis .CEO/Co-Founder
Evan Spiridellis .Design/Co-Founder
Daman Petta .CTO
Hanh Rohan .VP, Operations
Aaron Simpson .VP, Interactive
Lydia Antonini .Director, Development

THE JINKS/COHEN COMPANY
c/o Paramount Pictures
5555 Melrose Ave., Swanson Bldg., Ste. 215
Los Angeles, CA 90038
PHONE .323-956-8411
FAX .323-862-2220
TYPES Features - TV Series
HAS DEAL WITH Paramount Pictures - Warner Bros. Television Production
CREDITS The Forgotten - American Beauty - Big Fish - Down with Love

Dan Jinks .Producer
Bruce Cohen .Producer
Matt Moore .Executive VP, Production
Sam Hansen .Director, Development
Bree Tichy .Creative Executive
Adam Hendricks .Assistant to Mssrs. Moore & Hansen
Timothy Rogier .Assistant to Mssrs. Jinks & Cohen

JOADA PRODUCTIONS, INC.
1437 Rising Glen Rd., Ste. H23
Los Angeles, CA 90069
PHONE .310-652-6263
FAX .310-652-2995
EMAIL .joadaproductions@cs.com
TYPES Features - Made-for-TV/Cable Movies
DEVELOPMENT Bring Her Back Alive - Game Point - Miss Chatelaine - Lipstick City
CREDITS Grizzly Adams and the Legend of Dark Mountain - Secrets of a Small Town - Sheba Baby - Grizzly - The Guardian - Predator - Lovely but Deadly - Just Before Dawn - The Manitou - Day of the Animals - Abby
COMMENTS Owns and operates Hollywood Writers Studio; Ongoing development deals with Atlantis-Visions Entertainment, Nassau & PDC, Toronto

David Sheldon .Producer/CEO
Joan McCall .President, Production & Development
Boyd Aug .VP, Business Affairs
Ed Roberts .Director, Development
China Winston .Creative Executive
William Meringoff .Director, Marketing

JOEL FILMS
11718 Gwynne Ln.
Los Angeles, CA 90077
PHONE .310-476-4041/310-880-9692
FAX .310-889-0060
EMAIL .joelfilms@aol.com
TYPES Features - Theatre
DEVELOPMENT Film: Unfit - Taxi Boy - Alone (Empty World) - Tiger and the Snow - Sicario 2 (S2); Theatre: La Leccion
PRE-PRODUCTION A Distant Place
PRODUCTION Un-Authorized
CREDITS El Don - A Step Forward (Punto y Raya) - Devil Gold - Glue Sniffer - Sicario (Assassins for Hire) - Agony - Pedro Navaja - Borrowed Land - The Big World

Joseph Novoa .Director/Producer
Elia Schneider .Director/Producer
Joel Novoa .Director/Producer
Santiago Rindel .Producer
Isabel N. Meneses .International Relations
Rafael Schneider .Associate Producer
Ibi Schneider .Associate Producer
Gaby Rindel .Associate
Romina Stambouli .Press
Fornando Butazzoni .Writer
Rosa Clemente .Writer
Henry Herrera .Writer

JOHN FOGEL ENTERTAINMENT GROUP
969 Hilgard Ave.
Los Angeles, CA 90024
PHONE 310-441-5906/310-208-1969
EMAIL .... jafent@aol.com
TYPES — Features
DEVELOPMENT — The Only Living Boy in New York (Sony) - Protection (20th Century Fox) - Switcheroo (Revolution) - Second Time Around (DreamWorks) - 7th Game (MGM/UA) - Contingency - The Trust List
COMMENTS — Develops high-concept feature screenplays from seed to studio sale

John Fogel .... Producer
Mickey Groom .... Director, Development (mgroom_jafent@earthlink.net)
Andy Kravetz .... Reader

JOHNENELLY PRODUCTIONS
4000 Warner Blvd., Bldg. 139, Rm. 207
Burbank, CA 91522
PHONE 818-954-6445
FAX 818-954-6449
TYPES — Features - Made-for-TV/Cable Movies - Miniseries - Reality TV - TV Series
HAS DEAL WITH — Warner Bros. Television Production
CREDITS — Mary Christmas

John Schneider .... Producer/Owner
Ellen Aaronson .... VP, Development
Nathan Miller .... Director, Development

BRIDGET JOHNSON FILMS
1416 N. La Brea Ave.
Hollywood, CA 90028
PHONE 323-802-1749
TYPES — Features - Made-for-TV/Cable Movies
DEVELOPMENT — Smart People - An American Love Story - Meet John Trow - The Basic Eight - Weetzie Bat - Grasping the Sparrow's Tail - American Hostage
CREDITS — Ice Princess - As Good as It Gets - Riding in Cars with Boys - Joy Ride - Jerry Maguire
SUBMISSION POLICY — No unsolicited material

Bridget Johnson .... Producer

DON JOHNSON PRODUCTIONS
9663 Santa Monica Blvd., Ste. 278
Beverly Hills, CA 90210
PHONE 310-246-1452
FAX 310-601-7272
TYPES — Features - TV Series
CREDITS — In the Company of Darkness - The Horatio Alger Awards - The Marshall - Nash Bridges - Word of Honor
SUBMISSION POLICY — No unsolicited material

Don Johnson .... CEO/Executive Producer
J.B. Moresco .... Production Executive

TONY JONAS PRODUCTIONS
c/o The Management Group
9100 Wilshire Blvd., Ste. 400W
Beverly Hills, CA 90212
PHONE 310-736-8844
TYPES — Features - Miniseries - TV Series
CREDITS — Empire - Queer as Folk - Leap Years - Lost at Home
SUBMISSION POLICY — No unsolicited material

Tony Jonas .... President
Darin Wymer .... Development Assistant

JOSEPHSON ENTERTAINMENT
10201 W. Pico Blvd., Bldg. 50
Los Angeles, CA 90035
PHONE 310-369-7501
FAX 310-969-0898
TYPES — Features - TV Series
HAS DEAL WITH — Twentieth Century Fox - Twentieth Century Fox Television
DEVELOPMENT — They Came From Upstairs
PRODUCTION — Enchanted

Barry Josephson .... Producer
Danica Radovanov .... VP, Production
Alex Young .... Creative Executive
Josh Levy .... Assistant to Barry Josephson

JPH PRODUCTIONS
3469 Wonder View Pl.
Los Angeles, CA 90068
PHONE 323-874-7254
TYPES — Features - Made-for-TV/Cable Movies - TV Series
DEVELOPMENT — Dirty (Series) - Hype (Series) - Love and Money (Series)
CREDITS — Popumentary (Series) - Unauthorized (VH1) - Rockstrology - Legalese - Truth or Consequences, NM

J. Paul Higgins .... Producer/Writer

JT ENTERTAINMENT
14804 Greenleaf St.
Sherman Oaks, CA 91403
PHONE 818-788-7608
FAX 818-788-7612
EMAIL .... info@papajoefilms.com
TYPES — Features - Reality TV - TV Series
DEVELOPMENT — Hunt for Heroes - Condemned - Untitled Jerry Garcia Project - Creepers - The Island - Woman's Murder Club - Nightbird
PRE-PRODUCTION — Austin Brown Show
PRODUCTION — Employee of the Month
CREDITS — Newlyweds - Ashlee Simpson Show - Nick and Jessica Variety Hour - Nick and Jessica Family Christmas - Nick and Jessica: Tour of Duty - Filthy Rich - Score

Joe Simpson .... CEO
Erin Alexander .... VP, Development/Production
Richard Channer .... Office Manager
Ike Lee .... Executive Assistant
Adam Blain .... Assistant to Joe Simpson

JTN PRODUCTIONS
13743 Ventura Blvd., Ste. 200
Sherman Oaks, CA 91423
PHONE .818-789-5891
FAX .818-789-5892
EMAIL .staff@jtnproductions.com
WEB SITE .www.jtnproductions.com
TYPES Documentaries - Made-for-TV/Cable Movies - Miniseries - Reality TV - Specials - TV Series
PRE-PRODUCTION Unlikely Neighbors - Worse Than War
PRODUCTION The Jewish Americans
POST PRODUCTION The Hidden Wisdom of Our Yearnings with Irwin Kula
CREDITS PBS: Exodus & Freedom - A Chanukah Celebration - A Passover Celebration - Simple Wisdom with Irwin Kula - New Jewish Cuisine - No Safe Place - The 92nd Street Y Presents - Alef...Bet...Blast-off! - HomeStyles
SUBMISSION POLICY Does not accept unsolicited submissions

Jay Sanderson .CEO
David Kukoff .VP, Creative Affairs
Harvey Lehrer .VP, Production

JUDGE-BELSHAW ENTERTAINMENT, INC.
4655 Kingswell Ave., Ste. 208
Los Angeles, CA 90027
PHONE .323-662-3365
FAX .323-662-3313
EMAIL .mail@judgebelshaw.com
WEB SITE .www.judgebelshaw.com
TYPES Features - TV Series
DEVELOPMENT The Patient - The Bride Stripped Bare - Below the Beltway
CREDITS Actual Jokes (HBO) - Urban Myths (Hypnotic) - Shanahan's Army (CBS) - Office Party (HBO) - Ratchet (Feature)
SUBMISSION POLICY No unsolicited materials accepted

George Belshaw .Partner
Jonathan Judge .Partner

JUNCTION ENTERTAINMENT
500 S. Buena Vista St., Animation Bldg., Ste. 1-B
Burbank, CA 91521-1616
PHONE .818-560-2800
FAX .818-841-3176
TYPES Features - TV Series
HAS DEAL WITH The Walt Disney Company
DEVELOPMENT Fraternity Brothers - Princess and the Pauper - Tucker Ames - Suspect Behavior
CREDITS Instinct - Phenomenon - While You Were Sleeping - The Kid - National Treasure - Jericho

Jon Turteltaub .Producer/Director
Karim Zreik .VP, Development
Dan Shotz .Director, Development
David Spiegelman .Assistant
Patrick Wymore .Assistant

JUNCTION FILMS
9615 Brighton Way, Ste. M110
Beverly Hills, CA 90210
PHONE .310-246-9799
FAX .310-246-3824
TYPES Features - Reality TV - TV Series
DEVELOPMENT Untitled Matthew Bright Project
PRE-PRODUCTION The Possibility of Fireflies - The Harvester
POST PRODUCTION Normal Adolescent Behavior - Second in Command - Toyman
UPCOMING RELEASES Razor's Edge - Snuff Movie - Incubus - Hard Luck
CREDITS The Method - Blessed - Seven Seconds - The Kid and I - Tiptoes - Case of Evil - Freeway - Trees Lounge - Love & Sex - Barb Wire - Monster - Tron

Brad Wyman .Producer
Donald Kushner .Producer
Daniel Weisinger .Creative Executive

JUPITER ENTERTAINMENT
419 Erin Dr.
Knoxville, TN 37919
PHONE .865-588-2626
FAX .865-588-2202
EMAIL .info@jupiterent.com
WEB SITE .www.jupiterent.com
TYPES Documentaries - Reality TV - Specials - TV Series
PRE-PRODUCTION Who Knew? - Jewelry TV
PRODUCTION The Human Weapon - Crime Wave
POST PRODUCTION Tools - Lock Up - Katrina
CREDITS City Confidential - Snapped - Relentless - Modern Marvels - Biography - Hands on History - King of the Jungle - Roller Jam - Power Privilege & Justice - Empires of Industry

Stephen Land .President/Executive Producer
Geoffrey Proud .VP, Production/Executive Producer
Zak Weisfeld .VP, Development
Robert Twilley .Director, Operations
Sharla Wertz .Director, Business Affairs
Deborah Dawkins .Supervising Producer
Patrick Leigh-Bell .Supervising Producer
Cindy Robinson .Supervising Producer
David Wallach .Supervising Producer

JURIST PRODUCTIONS
215 W. 20th St.
New York, NY 10011
PHONE .212-627-4660
FAX .212-242-9056
TYPES Documentaries - Features - Made-for-TV/Cable Movies - TV Series
CREDITS Without Warning: Terror in the Towers - Stolen from the Heart (CBS)

Madelon Rosenfeld .Producer/President
Ira Block .VP

JUST SINGER ENTERTAINMENT
4242 Tujunga Ave.
Studio City, CA 91604
PHONE .818-506-2400
FAX .818-506-2409
TYPES Features - Made-for-TV/Cable Movies - Miniseries - TV Series
DEVELOPMENT Halloweentown: The Musical
PRODUCTION Halloweentown 4: Witch University
POST PRODUCTION How My Personal Private Journal Became a Bestseller
CREDITS Go Figure - The Luck of the Irish - Halloweentown 1-3 - Jackie, Ethel, Joan: Women of Camelot - Double Teamed - Right on Track - One Minute Soaps - Crimes of Fashion - Now You See It - Cow Belles
SUBMISSION POLICY Through signatory reps only

Sheri Singer .Executive Producer/Owner
Meghan Hooper .Director, Development

K2 PICTURES, INC.
27 W. 20th St., Ste. 801
New York, NY 10011
PHONE .212-741-1900, x12
FAX .212-741-9101
EMAIL .info@k2pictures.com
WEB SITE .www.k2pictures.com
TYPES Documentaries - Music Videos - Specials - TV Series
DEVELOPMENT Heroes and Villains - Moving Day
PRODUCTION Untitled Ernest Withers Film
CREDITS Classic Now (ESPN Classic) - Same Sex America (Showtime) - NCAA Town Hall Special (ESPN) - Pete Rose on Trial (ESPN) - Festival Dailies 2005 (Sundance)

Robert F. Katz .Producer
Jay Peterson .Producer
Chris Ryan .Producer

KADOKAWA PICTURES USA
15165 Ventura Blvd., Ste. 310
Sherman Oaks, CA 91403
PHONE .818-455-8440
FAX .818-455-8439
TYPES Animation - Features - TV Series
DEVELOPMENT Adrift - Gamera - Isola - One Missed Call - Voyeur
SUBMISSION POLICY No unsolicited submissions
COMMENTS Publishing; US division of Kadokawa Japan

Jennie Lew Tugend .Producer
Lauren C. Weissman .Producer
Danielle Reardon .Creative Executive
Elizabeth Kushman .Director, Development
Golan Ramras .Director, Development

KAHN POWER PICTURES
818 N. Doheny Dr., Ste. 1003
West Hollywood, CA 90069
PHONE .310-550-0770/310-550-8708
FAX .310-550-6292
EMAIL .iampower007@gmail.com
SECOND EMAIL .ikpower@pacbell.net
WEB SITE .www.artists4film.com
TYPES Documentaries - Features - Made-for-TV/Cable Movies - Miniseries
CREDITS Elvis (CBS, Miniseries) - Gia - Stalin - Fatherland - Roswell - White Mile - Buffalo Soldiers - Out of the Gate: The Sirr Parker Story - Hot Spot - The Dead Hollywood Mom's Society - Traffic (Miniseries) - Open House
SUBMISSION POLICY No unsolicited submissions

Derek Power .Chairman
Ilene Kahn Power .President/Executive Producer (310-550-8708)
Jeremy Kahn .New Media
Steve Fantasia .Management Associate

KANDOR ENTERTAINMENT
10061 Riverside Dr., Ste. 849
Toluca Lake, CA 91602
PHONE .818-721-2171
WEB SITE .www.kandor.tv
TYPES Reality TV - Specials - TV Series
DEVELOPMENT Style Spies - Dinner Music - Moving In - Live the Game - Green Grrl - Go to Hell
PRE-PRODUCTION Mecha Man (MTV2)
UPCOMING RELEASES Gears of War: The Race to E3 (MTV2)
CREDITS The Entertainer (E! Networks)

Lee Brownstein .Executive Producer

KANPAI PICTURES
7807 Sunset Blvd.
Los Angeles, CA 90046
PHONE .323-883-0725
EMAIL .mail@kanpaipictures.com
WEB SITE .www.kanpaipictures.com
TYPES Animation - Documentaries - Features - Reality TV - Specials - TV Series
CREDITS But Can They Sing? (VH1) - Channel 101 (FX Pilot) - Gordian (Sci Fi Animated Pilot) - Osbourne Family Christmas Special (MTV) - Under Exposed (Bravo Pilot) - My VH1 Music Awards 2000/2001 - VH1 Fashion Awards 2000 - VH1 ILL-ustrated - WB Presents Teen People's What's Next - Women in Hollywood (AMC Special)

Jay Karas .Executive Producer/Director
Andee Kuroda .Executive Producer/Director
Kalia Waits-Smith .Executive Assistant/Production Coordinator

KAPLAN/PERRONE ENTERTAINMENT, LLC
10202 W. Washington Blvd., Astaire Bldg., Ste. 3024
Culver City, CA 90232
PHONE .310-244-6681
FAX .310-244-2151
TYPES Features - TV Series
DEVELOPMENT Knowing - Dead Asleep
CREDITS You, Me and Dupree (Universal)

Aaron Kaplan .No Title
Sean Perrone .No Title
Justin Killion .No Title

KAREEM PRODUCTIONS
20434 S. Santa Fe Ave., Ste. 194
Long Beach, CA 90810
PHONE .310-762-1001
FAX .310-639-2055
TYPES Documentaries - Features - Mobile Content - Theatre
PRODUCTION On the Shoulders of Giants
COMMENTS Theatrical agent, Mike Eisenstadt, phone: 323-939-1188

Kareem Abdul-Jabbar .President
Deborah Morales .Business Manager

MARTY KATZ PRODUCTIONS
23852 Pacific Coast Hwy., #297
Malibu, CA 90265
PHONE .310-589-1560
FAX .310-589-1565
EMAIL .martykatzproductions@earthlink.net
WEB SITE .www.martykatzproductions.com
TYPES Features
DEVELOPMENT Valentine's Day Massacre: A Love Story - Little Tokyo - Walk on Water
CREDITS The Great Raid - Man of the House - Lost in America - Mr. Wrong - Reindeer Games - Impostor - The Four Feathers

Marty Katz .Producer
Tiffany Tiesiera .VP, Development & Production
Campbell Katz .Director, Development

JON KATZMAN PRODUCTIONS
c/o CBS Studio Center
4024 Radford Ave., Bungalow 5
Studio City, CA 91604
PHONE .818-655-5322
FAX .818-655-8410
TYPES Features - Made-for-TV/Cable Movies - TV Series
CREDITS You're Killing Me - Bio-Dome - Redemption (FX) - The Man in the Mirror: The Michael Jackson Story (VH1)

Jon Katzman .President/Executive Producer
Craig Gore .Creative Executive

THE KAUFMAN COMPANY
15030 Ventura Blvd., Ste. 510
Sherman Oaks, CA 91403
PHONE .818-223-9840
EMAIL .info@thekaufmancompany.com
WEB SITE .www.thekaufmancompany.com
TYPES Features - Made-for-TV/Cable Movies - TV Series
DEVELOPMENT Billy Liar - The Last Safari - The Owen Hart Story - Appointment with Dr. Death
CREDITS Return to the Batcave - Surviving Gilligan's Island - Run the Wild Fields - Jewel

Paul A. Kaufman .Executive Producer

KCET
4401 Sunset Blvd.
Los Angeles, CA 90027
PHONE .323-953-5258/323-666-6500
FAX .323-953-5496
WEB SITE .www.kcet.org
TYPES Documentaries - Made-for-TV/Cable Movies - Miniseries - Reality TV - TV Series
CREDITS PBS Hollywood Presents: The Gin Game, Copenhagen, Collected Stories - Senior Year - Chasing the Sun - John Glenn: An American Hero - Tavis Smiley

Al Jerome .President
Mare Mazur .Sr. VP, Programming & Production
Karen Robinson Hunte .Executive Director, Program Development
Joyce Campbell .Director, Production

KDD PRODUCTIONS, LLC
156 S. Irving Blvd.
Los Angeles, CA 90004
PHONE .323-461-3379
TYPES Documentaries - Features - Made-for-TV/Cable Movies - TV Series
DEVELOPMENT The Infamous Harris Boys (Hearst/Lifetime) - Guilty
CREDITS Hostile Hallways (Documentary) - Scattering Dad (CBS) - Somebody's Daughter (ABC) - Special Bulletin (NBC) - Under Siege (NBC) - Anya's Bell (CBS) - Blackout (NBC) - Cold Sassy Tree (TNT) - Crazy in Love (TNT) - Devil's Child (ABC) - Nickel & Dimed (Showtime)
SUBMISSION POLICY No unsolicited material

Karen Danaher-Dorr .Executive Producer
Lynne Bover .VP, Development

KECKINS PROJECTS, LTD.
c/o Attorney Allen Arrow/Shugett and Arrow
111 W. 57th St.
New York, NY 10107
PHONE .212-645-0049
FAX .212-645-0049
EMAIL .keckinsprojects@aol.com
TYPES Features - Made-for-TV/Cable Movies - TV Series
DEVELOPMENT The Man Who Loved Movies - The Other Woman - Timed Out Credentials
PRE-PRODUCTION The Hive - 12 Hours
CREDITS The Simian Line - Northern Lights - Parallel Lives - Everybody Wins - Chantilly Lace - Playing for Time - End of Summer - Second Serve - Mayflower - Looking Up - Prisoner Without a Name, Cell Without a Number - Sweet Bird of Youth - Hard Hat and Legs - The Royal Romance of Charles and Diana - Liberace: Behind the Music - Prospera
SUBMISSION POLICY No unsolicited material

Linda Yellen .Director/Writer
Martin Yellen .Executive VP
Karen Monaco .Director, Development
Robert Snyder .Director, Development
Martin Mathews .Production Executive
Lydia Rodriguez .Production
Renee Rivas .Development
Jennifer Woolf .Development
Samantha Levin .Development

KEEP CLEAR
c/o The Independent Group, LLC
8721 Sunset Blvd., Ste. 105
Los Angeles, CA 90069
PHONE 310-854-2300
FAX 310-854-2304
TYPES — Made-for-TV/Cable Movies - Miniseries - Reality TV - Specials - TV Series
HAS DEAL WITH — TV Guide Channel
DEVELOPMENT — The Craze (FitTV) - The Stylist (TV Guide Channel) - Raptors (Animation/Live Action Series)

Melissa Rivers .... Producer/Partner
Steven Jensen .... Manager/Partner

KELLER ENTERTAINMENT GROUP
c/o Micheline Keller
1093 Broxton Ave., Ste. 246
Los Angeles, CA 90024
PHONE 310-443-2226
FAX 310-443-2194
EMAIL .... maxkeller@kellerentertainment.com
WEB SITE .... www.kellerentertainment.com
TYPES — Features - Made-for-TV/Cable Movies - TV Series
DEVELOPMENT — The Woodpecker Waltz - The Atlantis Conspiracy - Soccer Mom - Bed Bugs
PRE-PRODUCTION — Wyland's World (TV) - Tug of War (Feature)
COMPLETED UNRELEASED — Bug Spreaders (Short Film)
CREDITS — Conan - Tarzan - Acapulco Heat - Summer of Fear - Women of Valor - Kent State - Dreams of Gold - A Summer to Remember - Swimsuit - Betrayed By Innocence - Grambling's White Tiger - Deadly Blessing - Conspiracy: The Trial of the Chicago 8 - Casey's Gift: For the Love of a Child

Max Keller .... Chairman/CEO
Micheline Keller .... President
David Keller .... Director, Development
Alex King .... Administrator

DAVID E. KELLEY PRODUCTIONS
1600 Rosecrans Ave., Bldg. 4-B
Manhattan Beach, CA 90266
PHONE 310-727-2200
TYPES — Features - TV Series
HAS DEAL WITH — Twentieth Century Fox Television
CREDITS — Boston Legal - The Law Firm - The Practice - Boston Public - The Brotherhood of Poland, New Hampshire - girls club - Ally McBeal - Snoops - Chicago Hope - Picket Fences - Mystery, Alaska - Lake Placid

David E. Kelley .... CEO/Writer/Executive Producer
Rick Silverman .... COO
Bob Breech .... President, Development
Veronica Wilson .... General Counsel
Neely Swanson .... VP, Development
Stacey M. Luchs .... VP, Media Relations & Publicity

THE KENNEDY/MARSHALL COMPANY
619 Arizona Ave.
Santa Monica, CA 90401
PHONE 310-656-8400
FAX 310-656-8430
TYPES — Features
HAS DEAL WITH — Universal Pictures
COMMENTS — Large Format

Frank Marshall .... Producer/Director
Kathleen Kennedy .... Producer
Mary Radford .... Assistant to Frank Marshall
Elyse Klaits .... Assistant to Kathleen Kennedy
Gregg Taylor .... Sr. VP, Development
Tara Grace .... Creative Executive
Kyle Schmidt .... Office Manager
Mike Schneider .... Story Editor

KENNETH JOHNSON PRODUCTIONS
4461 Vista Del Monte Ave.
Sherman Oaks, CA 91403
PHONE 818-905-5255
FAX 818-905-6114
EMAIL .... kennycjohnson@aol.com
TYPES — Features - Made-for-TV/Cable Movies - TV Series
DEVELOPMENT — V: The Second Generation (NBC/Warner Bros.) - Dead & Breakfast (Hoodwinked Prods.)
CREDITS — The Incredible Hulk (TV) - Bride of the Incredible Hulk - Alien Nation (Six TV Movies) - The Liberators - Shadow Chasers - Hot Pursuit - V

Kenneth Johnson .... Writer/Director/Executive Producer
Susan Appling .... VP

KENWRIGHT USA/BILL KENWRIGHT LTD.
1501 Broadway, Ste. 1401
New York, NY 10036
PHONE 212-221-0200/44-207-446-6200
FAX 212-764-5423
TYPES — Features - Theatre
CREDITS — Die Mommie Die - The Purifiers - Zoe - Don't Go Breaking My Heart

Bill Kenwright .... No Title
Dante Di Loreto .... No Title

DIANA KEREW PRODUCTIONS
2036 Hillsboro Ave.
Los Angeles, CA 90034
PHONE 310-838-3931
TYPES — Features - Made-for-TV/Cable Movies - Miniseries - TV Series
HAS DEAL WITH — Sony Pictures Television
DEVELOPMENT — The Franco Magnani Story (Feature) - The Joy of Funerals (Feature) - Lab257 (ABC) - In Search of the Dead Zone (A&E)
PRODUCTION — Untiled ABC Project
CREDITS — Fatal Contact: Bird Flu in America (ABC) - The Hunt for the BTK Killer (CBS) - Surrender, Dorothy (CBS) - The Perfect Husband: The Laci Peterson Story (USA) - Hitler: The Rise of Evil (CBS) - When Billie Beat Bobby - Stepsister from Planet Weird - Fifteen and Pregnant - Paris Trout - Ed McBain's 87th Precinct - Crossed Over - Jenifer
SUBMISSION POLICY — No unsolicited submissions

Diana Kerew .... Producer

THE KERNER ENTERTAINMENT COMPANY
469 St. Pierre Rd.
Los Angeles, CA 90077
PHONE .310-815-5100
FAX .310-446-9503
TYPES: Features - TV Series
PRODUCTION: Charlotte's Web
CREDITS: Snow Dogs - Inspector Gadget - When a Man Loves a Woman - George of the Jungle - Fried Green Tomatoes - Less Than Zero - Mighty Ducks 1-3
SUBMISSION POLICY: No unsolicited submissions

Jordan Kerner .President
Paul Neesan .Executive VP
Dorothy Davis .Office Manager

KETCHAM FILMS
610 Santa Monica Blvd.
Santa Monica, CA 90401
PHONE .310-656-0070
EMAIL .ketchamfilms@aol.com
TYPES: Features - Made-for-TV/Cable Movies - TV Series
CREDITS: The Hurricane - I Accuse

John Ketcham .Producer

KEY CREATIVES, LLC
9595 Wilshire Blvd., Ste. 800
Beverly Hills, CA 90212
PHONE .310-273-3004
FAX .310-273-3006
TYPES: Features - TV Series
HAS DEAL WITH: Fox Television Studios
COMMENTS: Also management company

Ken Kamins .Chairman/CEO
Mark Yaloff .Controller
Jonathan Weber .Assistant to Ken Kamins

KEYLIGHT ENTERTAINMENT GROUP
425 Park Avenue South, 19th Fl.
New York, NY 10016
PHONE .212-725-2090
FAX .212-725-1588
TYPES: Features
DEVELOPMENT: Miss Pettigrew Lives for a Day - Coal - Apes and Angels - The Music Lesson - Second Chance
CREDITS: Finding Neverland
SUBMISSION POLICY: No unsolicited material

Nellie Bellflower .President
Michael Mislove .VP, Development
Jane McCanny .Development

KEYSTONE ENTERTAINMENT, INC.
23410 Civic Center Way, Ste. E-9
Malibu, CA 90265
PHONE .310-317-4883
FAX .310-317-4903
EMAIL .films@keypics.com
WEB SITE .www.keypics.com
TYPES: Features
UPCOMING RELEASES: Air Buddies
CREDITS: Chestnut: Hero of Central Park - Spymate 2 - Tooth Fairy - Air Bud 1-5 - The Duke - MVP - Final Cut - Underworld - Bulletproof Heart - MXP 3

Michael Strange .President
Robert Vince .Producer
Anna McRoberts .Producer

KILLER FILMS, INC.
380 Lafayette St., Ste. 202
New York, NY 10003
PHONE .212-473-3950
FAX .212-473-6152
WEB SITE .www.killerfilms.com
TYPES: Features
HAS DEAL WITH: John Wells Productions
DEVELOPMENT: The Lonely Doll - Urinetown - Potential - The PeeWee Herman Story - Goat - Kimberly Akimbo
PRE-PRODUCTION: Then She Found Me - I'm Not There - Savage Grace - White & Rice
PRODUCTION: An American Crime
UPCOMING RELEASES: Infamous
CREDITS: Mrs. Harris - The Notorious Bettie Page - A Dirty Shame - A Home at the End of the World - The Company - Far from Heaven - One Hour Photo - Hedwig and the Angry Inch - Boys Don't Cry - The Grey Zone - Storytelling - Safe - I Shot Andy Warhol - Camp - Party Monster - Happiness - The Safety of Objects - Velvet Goldmine
SUBMISSION POLICY: No unsolicited material or queries
COMMENTS: West Coast office: 4000 Warner Blvd., Bldg. 1, Burbank, CA 91522-0001

Christine Vachon .Principal/Producer
Pamela Koffler .Principal/Producer
Katie Roumel .Principal/Producer
Jocelyn Hayes .Producer
Charles Pugliese .Creative Executive
Ramsey Fong .Business Affairs
Yee Yeo Chang .Assistant to Producer

SIDNEY KIMMEL ENTERTAINMENT
9460 Wilshire Blvd., Ste. 500
Beverly Hills, CA 90212
PHONE .310-777-8818
FAX .310-777-8892
TYPES: Features
DEVELOPMENT: The Radioactive Boy Scout - American Gothic - To Love or Die - Flag Day - Accordion
PRE-PRODUCTION: Marriage - Lars and the Real Girl - Kite Runner
PRODUCTION: Death at a Funeral - Charlie Bartlett - Talk to Me
POST PRODUCTION: Breach
UPCOMING RELEASES: Copying Beethoven - Alpha Dog - Trust the Man
COMPLETED UNRELEASED: Neverwas - Griffin and Phoenix
CREDITS: United 93 - The Emperor's Club - 9-1/2 Weeks

Sidney Kimmel .Chairman/CEO
Alan Salke .Vice Chairman
Jim Tauber .President
Mark Lindsay .President, Kimmel International
William Horberg .President, Production
Mark Kristol .President, Marketing & Distribution
Richard Lewis .CFO
Stephanie Kluft .Executive VP, Publicity
Holly Becker .Sr. VP, Production
Joshua Deighton .Sr. VP, Production
Nicholas Hanks .Sr. VP, Business & Legal Affairs
Scott Nicolaides .Sr. VP, Production
Victor Teran .VP, Production
Aaron Merrell .Director, Production
Anne Schmidt .Manager, Marketing & Publicity
Jodi Hildebrand .Creative Executive
Jennifer Welch .Production Coordinator
Monique Jones .Controller
Rachel Gandin .Assistant, Jim Tauber
Lisa Garvey .Assistant, William Horberg
Andy Jurgensen .Assistant, Scott Nicolaides

KINETIC FILMWORKS

6660 Sunset Blvd., Ste. L193
Hollywood, CA 90028
PHONE .323-462-6355
EMAIL .kineticfilmworks@aol.com
WEB SITE .www.kineticfilmworks.com
TYPES Direct-to-Video/DVD - Features
DEVELOPMENT The Last Horror Picture Show - Death Dragon
CREDITS Frostbiter - Hellblock 13 - Head Cheerleader, Dead Cheerleader
SUBMISSION POLICY Email queries only (no attachments); No drop-offs
COMMENTS Also provides finishing funds

Gary Jones .Producer/Partner
Jeff Miller .Producer/Partner

KINETIC PICTURES

8324 Fountain Ave., Ste. A
Los Angeles, CA 90069
PHONE .323-654-0530
FAX .323-988-2142
WEB SITE .www.kineticpictures.com
TYPES Features - Made-for-TV/Cable Movies - TV Series
CREDITS A Season on the Brink - Beer Money - Prancer Returns - Clive Barker's Saint Sinner - Deathlands

Joshua Butler .Partner
Chet Fenster .Partner

KING WORLD PRODUCTIONS, INC.

2401 Colorado Ave., Ste. 110
Santa Monica, CA 90404
PHONE .310-264-3300/212-315-4000
FAX .310-264-3301
WEB SITE .www.kingworld.com
TYPES TV Series
CREDITS Rachael Ray - Wheel of Fortune - Jeopardy! - The Oprah Winfrey Show - Dr. Phil - Inside Edition - CSI: Crime Scene Investigation - CSI: Miami - CSI: NY - Everybody Loves Raymond - MarketWatch Weekend - Bob Vila - Mr. Food
COMMENTS East Coast office: 1700 Broadway, 32nd & 33rd Fls., New York, NY 10019

Roger King .CEO, CBS Enterprises & King World Productions, Inc.
Robert V. Madden .COO, CBS Enterprises
Joe DiSalvo .President, Domestic TV Sales, King World Productions, Inc.
Steven R. Hirsch .President, King World Media Sales
Terry Wood .President, Creative Affairs & Development
John A. Wentworth .Executive VP, Communications
Michael Auerbach .Sr. VP, King World Media Sales
Jonathan Birkhahn .Sr. VP, Business Affairs, CBS Enterprises & King World Productions, Inc.
Moira Coffey .Sr. VP, Research
Stephen Hackett .Sr. VP/Regional Sales Manager, Southwest Division (Dallas)
Randall C. Hanson .Sr. VP, Sales, West (LA)
(Continued)

KING WORLD PRODUCTIONS, INC. (Continued)

John Holdridge .Sr. VP, Regional Sales Manager, Southeast Division (Atlanta)
Steve LoCascio .Sr. VP/CFO, CBS Enterprises & King World Productions, Inc.
Delilah Loud .Sr. VP, Advertising & Promotion
Patsy Bundy .VP, Contract Administration
Chris Carson .VP, Advertising & Promotion
Dale Casterline .VP, Western Sales, King World Media Sales
Rich Cervini .VP, Operations
Bob Cole .VP, Eastern Sales, King World Media Sales
Lucy Denny-Gardner .VP, Creative Services Finance & Special Projects
Bill Hague .VP, Sales, Midwest Division (Chicago)
Alex Ignon .VP, Marketing & Promotion
Robin King .VP, Midwest Sales, King World Media Sales
Veronika Lineberry .VP, Creative Services, West Coast
Sylvester Russo .VP/Controller
Ken Starkey .VP, Operations, King World Media Sales
Lee Villas .VP, Northeast Sales (NY)

KINTOP PICTURES

7955 W. Third St.
Los Angeles, CA 90048
PHONE .323-634-1570
TYPES Features
DEVELOPMENT The Walker
CREDITS The Mistress of Spices - Bride and Prejudice
COMMENTS Partnership with Ingenious Media

Deepak Nayar .Producer

DAVID KIRSCHNER PRODUCTIONS

400 S. June St.
Los Angeles, CA 90020
PHONE .323-939-0230
FAX .323-930-0753
EMAIL .dkps@pacbell.net
TYPES Animation - Features - Made-for-TV/Cable Movies - Miniseries - TV Series
DEVELOPMENT santaKid
PRODUCTION Miss Potter
POST PRODUCTION Martian Child
CREDITS Curious George - An American Tail 1-4 - Hocus Pocus - Titan A.E. - Bride of Chucky - Frailty - The Flintstones - Secondhand Lions - 5 Days to Midnight (Miniseries) - Seed of Chucky
SUBMISSION POLICY No unsolicited material

David Kirschner .Producer/President
Corey Sienega .Producer/VP, Production & Development
Nick Shaheen .Story Editor

SAM KITT/FUTURE FILMS

11271 Ventura Blvd., #275
Studio City, CA 91604
PHONE .310-499-4817
FAX .818-985-9755
EMAIL .info@futurefilms.net
TYPES Features - Made-for-TV/Cable Movies
DEVELOPMENT Cherry - Closer Than You Think - Fabulation - Harlem Little League - Little Man - Luke's Inferno - Mr. Baby - Oscar Micheaux Story - Ron Morris Story - Sauce - The House That Jack Built
CREDITS The Best Man - Love and Basketball - 3 A.M. - Good Fences - Sucker Free City

Sam Kitt .Producer

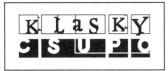

KLASKY CSUPO, INC.

1238 N. Highland Blvd.
Hollywood, CA 90038
PHONE .323-468-2600
WEB SITE www.klaskycsupo.com
TYPES Animation - Commercials - Direct-to-Video/DVD - Features - Internet Content - Mobile Content - TV Series
CREDITS The Wild Thornberrys Movie - The Rugrats Go Wild - Stressed Eric - Rugrats - The Wild Thornberrys - Rocket Power - As Told by Ginger - Duckman - The Simpsons - The Rugrats Movie - Rugrats in Paris: The Movie
COMMENTS Tone Casualties Records

Gabor Csupo .Co-Chairman
Arlene Klasky .Co-Chairman
John Andrews .Sr. VP, Commercials & Internet
Alexandra Booke .Sr. VP, TV
Michael McGahey .Sr. VP, Feature Film
Brandon Scott .VP, Creative Affairs

KLS COMMUNICATIONS, INC.

5430 Oakdale Ave.
Woodland Hills, CA 91364
PHONE .818-887-0308
FAX .818-887-0257
EMAIL .lschiller@klscomm.com
WEB SITE .www.klscomm.com
TYPES Documentaries - Features - Made-for-TV/Cable Movies - Miniseries - Reality TV - TV Series
HAS DEAL WITH Court TV Networks - Fox Television Studios
DEVELOPMENT Why America Slept (Showtime) - First Hours (CBS) - Henry Lee Series (Court TV)
UPCOMING RELEASES Court TV: JonBenet Ramsey - Anatomy of a Cold Case
CREDITS Miniseries: Master Spy (CBS) - American Tragedy (CBS) - Peter the Great (NBC) - The Executioner's Song (NBC); MOW: Double Jeopardy (CBS) - The Plot to Kill Hitler (CBS) - Marilyn, The Untold Story (ABC) - Hey I'm Alive (ABC) - Perfect Murder, Perfect Town (CBS) - Trace Evidence (Court TV)

Lawrence Schiller .President

KOMUT ENTERTAINMENT

4024 Radford Ave., Editorial 1
Studio City, CA 91604
PHONE .818-655-5563
FAX .818-655-8479
TYPES TV Series
HAS DEAL WITH Warner Bros. Television Production
CREDITS Twins - Four Kings - Will & Grace - Good Morning, Miami - The Stones - Boston Common

David Kohan .Producer
Max Mutchnick .Producer
Heather Hicks .Executive Assistant
Melissa Strauss .Executive Assistant

THE KONIGSBERG-SMITH COMPANY

7919 Sunset Blvd., 2nd Fl.
Los Angeles, CA 90046
PHONE .323-845-1000
FAX .323-845-1020
EMAIL .konigsbergsmith@pacbell.net
TYPES Features - Made-for-TV/Cable Movies - Miniseries
CREDITS The Last Don - Titanic - Bella Mafia - Like Mother, Like Son: The Strange Story of Sante and Kenny Kimes - Caught in the Act

Frank Konigsberg .No Title
Drew Smith .No Title
Neal Doherty .No Title

KONWISER BROTHERS

4547 Morro Dr.
Woodland Hills, CA 91364
PHONE .818-887-0502
FAX .818-992-7706
EMAIL .kern@konwiserbros.com
SECOND EMAIL .kip@konwiserbros.com
WEB SITE .www.konwiserbros.com
TYPES Animation - Commercials - Direct-to-Video/DVD - Documentaries - Features - Made-for-TV/Cable Movies - Reality TV - Theatre - TV Series
DEVELOPMENT The Last Game (Feature)
PRE-PRODUCTION Repo (Feature) - On the Shoulders of Giants (Documentary) - The Company: Bay of Pigs - Kidnapped
UPCOMING RELEASES Kings of South Beach - Burton/Mandalay Snowboard feature documentary
COMPLETED UNRELEASED Shanghai Kiss
CREDITS Island Heat: Stranded (Lifetime) - Island Heat: Vanished (Lifetime) - Island Heat: Break In (Lifetime) - White Space (NBC) - Animal (DEJ) - Crossover (Showtime) - Dallas 362 (ThinkFilm) - Smile (Universal/Screen Media) - Back in the Day (DEJ/Blockbuster) - Miss Evers' Boys - On Hallowed Ground - Focus - The Wash - Maze - Quest for Nutrition - The Last Game (Documentary)

Kip Konwiser .Partner
Kern Konwiser .Partner

KOPELSON ENTERTAINMENT

1900 Avenue of the Stars, Ste. 500
Los Angeles, CA 90067
PHONE .310-407-1500
FAX .310-407-1501
TYPES Features - Made-for-TV/Cable Movies - Miniseries - TV Series
DEVELOPMENT Killing on Carnival Row - Witch Hunters - Strangers on a Train - Decoy - In the Navy
CREDITS Don't Say a Word - A Perfect Murder - U.S. Marshals - Devil's Advocate - Eraser - Seven - Outbreak - The Fugitive - Falling Down - Platoon - Twisted

Arnold Kopelson .Producer/Co-Chairperson/President (310-407-1522)
Anne Kopelson .Producer/Co-Chairperson (310-407-1532)
Sherryl Clark .President (310-407-1540)
Evan Kopelson .Sr. VP, TV (310-407-1560)
Ryan Engle .Director, Development (310-407-1535)
Hedi Jalon .Story Editor (310-407-1570)
Kevin Jarzynski .Story Editor (310-407-1533)
Megan Close .Executive Assistant to Anne Kopelson
Jill Latham .Executive Assistant to Arnold Kopelson

ROBERT KOSBERG PRODUCTIONS
c/o Nash Entertainment
1438 N. Gower St., Box 10
Hollywood, CA 90028
PHONE . . . 323-468-4513
FAX . . . 530-483-3257
WEB SITE . . . www.moviepitch.com
TYPES — Animation - Features - Internet Content - Made-for-TV/Cable Movies - Reality TV - Specials - TV Series
DEVELOPMENT — Surrender Dorothy (Warner Bros.) - The Hardy Men (Fox 2000) - Teacher of the Year (New Line) - Sherlock's Secretary (Walden) - Untitled Alien Project (Warner Bros.) - Falling Awake (Warner Bros.) - Time of Their Lives (Universal) - Santa Paws (Vanguard)
CREDITS — Commando - In the Mood - Man's Best Friend - Twelve Monkeys - Mr. Personality

Robert Kosberg . . . Producer
Jane Lawton Moore . . . Director, Development

KRAININ PRODUCTIONS, INC.
25211 Summerhill Ln.
Stevenson Ranch, CA 91381
PHONE . . . 661-259-9700
EMAIL . . . krainin@comcast.net
WEB SITE . . . www.kraininproductions.com
TYPES — Documentaries - Features - Made-for-TV/Cable Movies - Miniseries - Specials
DEVELOPMENT — TV Movies: The Bulger Brothers; Features: Why Dean Drank - Tube Wars - Lovers, Liars, and Thieves - Ota Benga - Jerry Lewis - The Good Fight - Rubitsky
CREDITS — To America - Disaster at Silo 7 - George Wallace - Quiz Show - John Glenn: Return of the Hero - Something the Lord Made

Julian Krainin . . . Producer/Director/President
Joel Adams . . . Development Executive
Jason Hart . . . Special Projects
Martha Wineblatt . . . Production & Development
Todd Philips . . . TV & Feature Development

THE JONATHAN KRANE GROUP
8033 W. Sunset Blvd., Rm. 6750
Hollywood, CA 90046
PHONE . . . 323-650-0942
FAX . . . 323-650-9132
WEB SITE . . . www.kraneonproducing.com
TYPES — Features
CREDITS — Look Who's Talking - Chocolate War - Michael - Blind Date - Face/Off - The General's Daughter - Swordfish - Domestic Disturbance

Jonathan D. Krane . . . Producer/CEO/Chairman

KRASNOFF FOSTER PRODUCTIONS
c/o Sony Pictures Television
10202 W. Washington Blvd., Poitier Bldg., Ste. 3206
Culver City, CA 90232
PHONE . . . 310-244-3282
TYPES — Features - TV Series
HAS DEAL WITH — Sony Pictures Television
DEVELOPMENT — Once and Future King
UPCOMING RELEASES — Ghost Rider

Russ Krasnoff . . . Producer
Gary Foster . . . Producer
Stephanie Shapiro . . . Sr. VP, TV
Rikki Lea Bestall . . . Director, Feature Development
Heather Hawley . . . Development Executive
Michael Palmer . . . Development Executive

KRASNOW PRODUCTIONS
c/o FremantleMedia North America
2700 Colorado Ave., Ste. 450
Santa Monica, CA 90404
PHONE . . . 310-255-4824
FAX . . . 310-255-4804
TYPES — Reality TV - TV Series
HAS DEAL WITH — FremantleMedia North America
COMPLETED UNRELEASED — Gameshow Marathon - Psychic at Large
CREDITS — The Janice Dickinson Modeling Agency - Average Joe - Dog Eat Dog - The Weakest Link - The Martin Short Show

Stuart Krasnow . . . Executive Producer
Garrett Jacobs . . . Manager, Development
Damon Lewis . . . Executive Assistant

SID & MARTY KROFFT PICTURES CORPORATION
c/o CBS Studio Center
4024 Radford Ave., Bldg. 5, Ste. 102
Studio City, CA 91604
PHONE . . . 818-655-5314
FAX . . . 818-655-8235
TYPES — Features - TV Series
DEVELOPMENT — Land of the Lost - H.R. Pufnstuf (Feature) - Bugaloos (TV) - Middle Age Crazy (TV)
CREDITS — Family Affair (WB) - Land of the Lost - Electrawoman and Dynagirl

Marty Krofft . . . President
Sid Krofft . . . Executive VP
Deanna Pope . . . Finance

FRED KUEHNERT PRODUCTIONS
1601 Hilts Ave., #2
Los Angeles, CA 90024
PHONE . . . 310-470-3363
TYPES — Direct-to-Video/DVD - Features
DEVELOPMENT — Sicilian Love Story - Free Falling - Thunder Mountain - Rest Stop
PRE-PRODUCTION — Termite
CREDITS — The Fallen Ones - Buddy Holly Story - Grey Night - Cold Night Into Dawn - Cypress Edge - Beneath Loch Ness
COMMENTS — Financial consulting; Producer's representative; Expert witness

Fred T. Kuehnert . . . Managing Partner
Robert Birmingham . . . Partner/Producer
Billy Verkin . . . Partner/Producer
Sandra Chouinard . . . Executive Assistant

KURTZMAN/ORCI
c/o DreamWorks SKG
100 Universal Plaza, Bldg. 5171
Universal City, CA 91608
PHONE 818-733-9645

TYPES	Features - TV Series
HAS DEAL WITH	DreamWorks SKG
DEVELOPMENT	Nightlife - 2:22 - Eagle Eye - The Proposal - Red Cell - Amazon - The Forger - Star Trek
PRE-PRODUCTION	Transformers
CREDITS	Alias - Hercules: The Legendary Journeys - Xena: Warrior Princess - Jack of All Trades

Alex Kurtzman . . . . Producer/Writer
Roberto Orci . . . . Producer/Writer
Pete Chiarelli . . . . President (818-733-6986)

THE KUSHNER-LOCKE COMPANY
280 S. Beverly Dr., Ste. 205
Beverly Hills, CA 90212
PHONE 310-275-7508
FAX 310-275-7518

TYPES	Features - Direct-to-Video/DVD - TV Series
CREDITS	Pinocchio (New Line) - Andre (Paramount) - Brave Little Toaster 1-3 (Disney) - Gun (ABC) - Freeway 1&2 - Harvard Man - Basil - Whole Wide World - Picking Up the Pieces - Ringmaster - Harts of the West (CBS)

Alice Neuhauser . . . . Responsible Officer

L.I.F.T. PRODUCTIONS
365 Canal St., Ste. 3170
New Orleans, LA 70130
PHONE 504-565-5438/504-733-5438
FAX 504-565-5411/504-212-4857
EMAIL . . . . catherine@lift-la.com
WEB SITE . . . . www.lift-la.com

TYPES	Commercials - Direct-to-Video/DVD - Documentaries - Features - Made-for-TV/Cable Movies - Miniseries - Music Videos - Reality TV - TV Series
POST PRODUCTION	Not Like Everyone Else - Mr. Brooks - Road House 2: Last Call - Life Is Not a Fairy Tale - Premonition
UPCOMING RELEASES	P.D.R. - Factory Girl - Bug
COMPLETED UNRELEASED	Five Fingers - Last Time - Ruffian
CREDITS	Evil Remains - Home of Phobia - Faith of My Fathers - Elvis - The Brooke Ellison Story - Miracle Run - Frankenstein - Vampire Bats - Locusts - The Dead Will Tell - For One Night - Infidelity - The Madam's Family: The Truth About the Canal Street Brothel
SUBMISSION POLICY	No unsolicited submissions

Malcolm Petal . . . . CEO
Kimberly Anderson . . . . COO
Debbie Sarjeant . . . . VP, Film & TV Development
Catherine Shreves . . . . VP, Marketing & Publicity
Edith Leblanc . . . . Executive in Charge of Production
Christian Froude . . . . Production Supervisor
Dan Seekman . . . . Production Supervisor
Welch Lambeth . . . . Director, Transportation
Jon Tower . . . . Director, Human Resources
Kolie Wegner . . . . Director, Accounting & Business Affairs

THE LADD COMPANY
9465 Wilshire Blvd., Ste. 910
Beverly Hills, CA 90210
PHONE 310-777-2060
FAX 310-777-2061

TYPES	Features
DEVELOPMENT	Tortoise and the Hare - A Dream of Red Mansions - The First Force - Deathline
PRE-PRODUCTION	Gone Baby Gone
CREDITS	Chariots of Fire - Blade Runner - The Right Stuff - Police Academy - Braveheart - An Unfinished Life

Alan Ladd Jr. . . . . President
Natasha Klibansky . . . . VP, Development (310-777-2064)

DAVID LADD FILMS
PO Box 69947
West Hollywood, CA 90069
PHONE 310-858-0550
FAX 310-858-5917
EMAIL . . . . info@davidladdfilms.com
WEB SITE . . . . www.davidladdfilms.com

TYPES	Features - Miniseries - TV Series
DEVELOPMENT	Man on Third - Godspeed Lawrence Mann - How to Steal $100 Million - The Year The Gypsies Came - Treasure in the Badlands
CREDITS	The Serpent and the Rainbow - The Mod Squad - Hart's War - A Guy Thing
SUBMISSION POLICY	No unsolicited submissions

David Ladd . . . . President
Madelon Smith . . . . Director, Development
Patrick Mullen . . . . Creative Executive

LAIKA ENTERTAINMENT
1400 NW 22nd Ave.
Portland, OR 97210
PHONE 503-225-1130
FAX 503-226-3746
EMAIL . . . . ask_us@laika.com
WEB SITE . . . . www.laika.com

TYPES	Animation - Commercials - Features - Music Videos
DEVELOPMENT	The Wall and the Wing - Here Be Monsters
PRE-PRODUCTION	Jack & Ben's Animated Adventure
PRODUCTION	Coraline
CREDITS	The PJs - Gary & Mike

Dale Wahl . . . . CEO/President
Henry Selick . . . . Supervising Director, Entertainment
Dan Philips . . . . VP/Head, Production
Lourri Hammack . . . . President, Commercial Division
Al Cubillas . . . . VP/Head, Technology
Kirk Kelley . . . . Creative Director
Jan Johnson . . . . Co-Executive Producer
Helen Kalafatic . . . . Producer
Mike Cacheula . . . . Director
Dan Casey . . . . Director, Digital Productions
Fiona Kenshole . . . . Director, Scouting Operations
Jorgen Klubien . . . . Director, Story Development
Mary Sandell . . . . Director, Production
Erin Baldwin . . . . Controller
Anita Peters . . . . Human Resources Manager

LAKESHORE ENTERTAINMENT GROUP LLC

9268 W. Third St.
Beverly Hills, CA 90210
PHONE 310-867-8000
FAX 310-300-3015
WEB SITE ....www.lakeshoreentertainment.com

TYPES	Features
HAS DEAL WITH	Paramount Pictures
DEVELOPMENT	Lucky Stars - Serpentine - R.S.V.P. - Dying Animal - The Ugly Truth - American Pastoral - Ivanhoe - The Straight Man - School Spirit - Detention - Janis - Kingdom Come - Train - Barking Orders - Lincoln Lawyer - Excite Loves Vita - Midnight Train - Untraceable - Feast of Love
POST PRODUCTION	Blood & Chocolate - The Covenant - The Dead Girl
UPCOMING RELEASES	The Last Kiss - Crank
CREDITS	Aeon Flux - The Exorcism of Emily Rose - She's The Man - Undiscovered - Cave - Million Dollar Baby - Underworld 1&2 - The Human Stain - Wicker Park - The Mothman Prophecies - The Gift - Autumn in New York - Runaway Bride - Arlington Road - The Last Kiss

Tom Rosenberg ....Chairman/CEO
Gary Lucchesi ....President, Lakeshore Entertainment
Eric Reid ....COO
Marc Reid ....CFO
Richard Wright ....Executive VP/Head, Production
Robert Benun ....Sr. VP, Business & Legal Affairs
Jennifer Brooks ....Director, Business & Legal Affairs
Toby Midgen ....Director, Business & Legal Affairs
Robert McMinn ....Sr. VP, Development
Virginia Longmuir ....Sr. VP, International Business, Legal Affairs & Operations
Andre Lamal ....VP, Physical Production
Renee Mancuso ....VP, Finance
Christine Buckley ....VP, Music, Business & Legal Affairs
Bic Tran ....VP, Acquistions & Co-Productions
Kjose Elliott ....Office Manager
Vicki Roker ....Executive Assistant to Mssrs. Benun, Brooks & Midgen
Kate Schriver ....Assistant to Tom Rosenberg
Scott Herbst ....Assistant to Gary Lucchesi
Malvena Walker ....Assistant to Virginia Longmuir
Max Smerling ....Assistant to Eric Reid
Thomas Beatty ....Assistant to Richard Wright

LANCASTER GATE ENTERTAINMENT

4702 Hayvenhurst Ave.
Encino, CA 91436
PHONE 818-995-6000
FAX 818-905-8164

TYPES	Documentaries - Features - Made-for-TV/Cable Movies
DEVELOPMENT	Tough Cookie - Sumo Mouse
CREDITS	Secret Cutting - December - Grumpy Old Men - Grumpier Old Men - Angel Flight Down - The Four Chaplains: Sacrifice at Sea

Richard C. Berman ....Producer
Brian K. Schlichter ....Executive VP, Development & Production

DAVID LANCASTER PRODUCTIONS

3356 Bennett Dr.
Los Angeles, CA 90068-1704
PHONE 323-874-1415
FAX 323-372-3930
EMAIL ....laninco@earthlink.net

TYPES	Features
DEVELOPMENT	Legion
POST PRODUCTION	Smiley Face
UPCOMING RELEASES	Wes Craven's The Breed
CREDITS	Hollow Man 2 - Riding the Bullet - A Love Song for Bobby Long - 'Night Mother - Sadness of Sex - Loving Jezebel - Don't Look Under the Bed - Federal Protection - Borderline - Pavement - Consequence - Blast - Infinite Darkness
SUBMISSION POLICY	Query letters accepted; No unsolicited material or drop-offs

David Lancaster ....Producer
Garrick Dion ....Director, Development
Paul J. Salamoff ....VP, Production
Karri O'Reilly ....Production Consultant

LANCE ENTERTAINMENT, INC.

9107 Wilshire Blvd., Ste. 625
PHONE 310-888-3494
FAX 310-859-7173
EMAIL ....pierre@lance-ent.com

TYPES	Features - Made-for-TV/Cable Movies
PRE-PRODUCTION	Framed for Murder - Christie's Revenge
PRODUCTION	Demons from Her Past
POST PRODUCTION	The Rival
CREDITS	A Killer Upstairs - A Woman Hunted - The Perfect Nanny - The Perfect Wife - Yesterday's Children - Blind Obsession - Rain - Living with Fear - Seduced by a Thief - Internal Affairs - Platoon - Deep Cover - Scanners - The Perfect Husband - Stranger at the Door - Murder in My House - The Perfect Marriage - Maid of Honor - The Perfect Neighbor - Saving Emily
SUBMISSION POLICY	No unsolicited submissions

Pierre David ....President
Noel Zanitsch ....Creative Affairs & Production
David DeCrane ....Creative Affairs & Production
Kendall Nowlin ....Marketing Coordinator
Tippi Thomas ....Associate

THE LANDSBURG COMPANY
PO Box 49920
Los Angeles, CA 90049-0920
PHONE 310-889-7112
FAX 310-889-7116
TYPES Features - Specials - TV Series
CREDITS Living Dolls: The Making of a Child Beauty Queen (HBO) - The Lottery (NBC) - Country Justice (CBS) - If Someone Had Known (NBC) - A Mother's Right: The Elizabeth Morgan Story (ABC)
SUBMISSION POLICY No unsolicited material

Alan Landsburg ....Chairman/CEO
Howard Lipstone ....President/COO
Diane Skwarek ....Manager, Business Affairs

LANDSCAPE ENTERTAINMENT
9465 Wilshire Blvd., Ste. 308
Beverly Hills, CA 90212
PHONE 310-248-6200
FAX 310-248-6300
TYPES Features - Made-for-TV/Cable Movies - TV Series
HAS DEAL WITH Fox Television Studios
DEVELOPMENT 92 Minutes - I Know That You Know What I Know - The Hypnotist - Man on a Train - Fly on the Wall - The McCrearys - High T - Barry & Stan Gone Wild - Man in Uniform - Bodyguard of Lies - Fearless Pearsons - Animated American - Au Pair - Failan - Leisureworld
PRE-PRODUCTION The Crusaders - Quail Hollow
POST PRODUCTION Mr. Woodcock
CREDITS John Tucker Must Die - Sleepover - Medical Investigation
SUBMISSION POLICY No unsolicited material

Bob Cooper ....Chairman/CEO
Michael Nash ....Sr. VP, Production & Development
Orin Woinsky ....Sr. VP, Production & Development
Connie Cochran ....VP, Finance & Operations
Brian Truman ....Story Editor
Vince Damato ....Development Assistant
Brandon Jones ....Assistant to Mr. Cooper
Monica Sandstede ....Assistant to Mr. Cooper

LIZ SELZER LANG PRODUCTIONS
2801 Ocean Park Blvd., Ste. 215
Santa Monica, CA 90405
PHONE 310-745-0414
FAX 310-745-0413
EMAIL ....lizlangprods@aol.com
TYPES Features - Made-for-TV/Cable Movies - Miniseries - Reality TV - TV Series
DEVELOPMENT Infernal Affairs (CBS) - Manner Manor (Nick @ Nite/TV Land)
CREDITS Blonde (CBS/Miniseries) - The Natalie Cole Story (NBC) - Steal This Movie (Lionsgate) - The Day Lincoln Was Shot (TNT)
SUBMISSION POLICY Via agents only

Liz Selzer Lang ....Executive Producer

LANGLEY PRODUCTIONS
1111 Broadway
Santa Monica, CA 90401
PHONE 310-449-5300
FAX 310-449-5330
WEB SITE ....www.cops.com
TYPES Documentaries - Features - Reality TV - TV Series
UPCOMING RELEASES Video Justice
CREDITS Code 3 - Anatomy of Crime - Cops - Reality Check - Vampire Clan - Dogwatch - Wildside - Tiptoes
SUBMISSION POLICY Through representation only

John Langley ....President/Executive Producer/Director/Writer
Doug Waterman ....Supervising Producer, Cops
Elie Cohn ....Producer, Features
Karen Hori ....VP, TV Production
Morgan Langley ....Film & TV Development

LARCO PRODUCTIONS, INC.
2111 Coldwater Canyon
Beverly Hills, CA 90210
PHONE 323-350-5455
TYPES Animation - Features - Theatre - TV Series
COMPLETED UNRELEASED XIS
CREDITS Masters of Horror - Cellular - Captivity - Phone Booth - Invasion of Privacy - Original Gangstas - Guilty as Sin - Body Snatchers - Best Seller - The Invaders (TV Series) - Q - Private Files of J. Edgar Hoover - It's Alive - God Told Me To - Bone
SUBMISSION POLICY No unsolicited mail or calls accepted

Larry Cohen ....Writer/Producer/Director
Jill Gatsby ....VP, Development/Producer

LARGER THAN LIFE PRODUCTIONS
100 Universal City Plaza, Bldg. 5138
Universal City, CA 91608
PHONE 818-777-4004
FAX 818-866-5677
TYPES Animation - Features
HAS DEAL WITH Universal Pictures
DEVELOPMENT Creature from the Black Lagoon - The Deal (aka Bye-Bye Brooklyn) - Zero Game - Vegas 55 (aka Moulin Rouge) - One Part Sugar
PRE-PRODUCTION Tale of Despereaux
CREDITS Pleasantville - Seabiscuit
SUBMISSION POLICY No unsolicited submissions

Gary Ross ....Writer/Director/Principal
Allison Thomas ....Producer
Robin Bissell ....Producer

LARKIN-GOLDSTEIN PRODUCTION
1750 Berkeley St.
Santa Monica, CA 90404
PHONE 310-460-0200
FAX 310-460-0202
EMAIL ....info@larkingoldstein.com
TYPES — Features - Made-for-TV/Cable Movies - Miniseries - Reality TV - TV Series
UPCOMING RELEASES — Wildfires
CREDITS — 44 Minutes - Caesars 24/7 - Behind the Camera: The Charlie's Angels Story - Murder in the Heartland

Michael G. Larkin ....Producer/Partner
Michael R. Goldstein ....Producer/Partner

LASALLEHOLLAND
141 W. 28th St., Ste. 300
New York, NY 10001
PHONE 212-541-4443
FAX 212-563-9655
EMAIL ....scripts@lasalleholland.com
WEB SITE ....www.lasalleholland.com
TYPES — Documentaries - Features - Music Videos - TV Series
DEVELOPMENT — Between the Cracks - Achoo Baby - The Bill Hicks Story - The Wright Brothers - Aurelia
PRE-PRODUCTION — Down Bleecker
POST PRODUCTION — Just Like the Son - Mentor - Nicky's Game
COMPLETED UNRELEASED — Southern Belles - Pagans - Sweet Land - Find Love
CREDITS — Loggerheads - Martin and Orloff - Hurricane Streets - Spring Forward - Desert Blue - Bobby G. Can't Swim - Spin The Bottle - Dear Jesse - Shooting Vegetarians - Remembering Sex - Revolution #9

Lillian LaSalle ....Partner
Nadav Manham ....Business Development

RICK LASHBROOK FILMS
PO Box 17858
Beverly Hills, CA 90209
PHONE 310-406-0802
FAX 310-406-0902
EMAIL ....rlfilms@aol.com
TYPES — Features
DEVELOPMENT — The Duelist
POST PRODUCTION — How to Rob a Bank
UPCOMING RELEASES — Unknown
CREDITS — Kissing a Fool - Trading Favors

Rick Lashbrook ....Producer
Darby Parker ....Producer (310-666-1779)

LAST STRAW PRODUCTIONS
4000 Warner Blvd., Bldg. 133, Ste. 209
Burbank, CA 91522
PHONE 818-954-1064
FAX 818-954-1081
TYPES — Documentaries - Features - Made-for-TV/Cable Movies - Reality TV - TV Series
HAS DEAL WITH — Warner Bros. Television Production

Anthony LaPaglia ....President/Executive Producer
JJ Jamieson ....Executive VP/Executive Producer
Natalie Stevenson ....VP, Production
Douglas Reid ....Manager, Development

THE LATE BLOOMER COMPANY, LTD.
56 W. 56th St., 3rd Fl.
New York, NY 10019
PHONE 212-247-4945
FAX 212-247-4945
EMAIL ....lejen@verizon.net
TYPES — Animation - Documentaries - Features - Made-for-TV/Cable Movies - Miniseries - TV Series
DEVELOPMENT — Daddy's Girl - Overtones - Mr. Black and the Woman in White - Don't Ask, Don't Tell - The Protector - The Electra Conspiracy - The Englishman's Gospel - Lady Crusaders - Lovers' Leap - Whispers on the Wind - The Color of Music - Socks - Where the Buffalo Roam
CREDITS — Out of the Ashes (Showtime) - Skeezer (NBC) - The Legend of Walks Far Woman (NBC) - Playing with Fire (NBC) - Runaway Father (CBS)
SUBMISSION POLICY — Query letters for books and screenplays via email only; Include logline and synopsis
COMMENTS — Member: PGA, ATAS

Lee Levinson ....Partner/Producer
Jena Levinson ....Partner/Producer

LATHAM ENTERTAINMENT
3200 Northline Ave., Ste. 210
Greensboro, NC 27408
PHONE 336-315-1440
FAX 336-315-1450
EMAIL ....info@lathamentertainment.com
WEB SITE ....www.lathamentertainment.com
TYPES — Direct-to-Video/DVD - Features - TV Series
CREDITS — The Original Kings of Comedy - The Queens of Comedy - P Diddy's Bad Boys of Comedy
SUBMISSION POLICY — No unsolicited submissions

Walter Latham ....President/Producer

LATIN HOLLYWOOD FILMS
2934-1/2 Beverly Glen Circle, Ste. 262
Bel Air, CA 90077
PHONE 310-441-5454
EMAIL ....latinafilm@aol.com
WEB SITE ....www.kikikiss.com
TYPES — Documentaries - Features - TV Series
DEVELOPMENT — The Gloria Trevi Story (Keller World) - Exonerating Evidence (Lalu Prouctions) - The Other Side of the Rainbow - Kiki's Late Nite
CREDITS — Dominican Baseball with Manny Mota (Documentary) - Salsa Desde Hollywood - Kiki Desde Hollywood - The Effects of Vicodin in Hollywood - Hot Tamales Live!
SUBMISSION POLICY — No unsolicited submissions
COMMENTS — Latin themes for the general market; Hollywood segments for BBC and international markets; AOL coverage of Latin Grammys; La Musica.com; Deal with Western International Syndication; Deal with Universal Pay-Per-View/On Demand

Christian "Kiki" Melendez ....CEO/Executive Producer
David Baum ....Partner
Lupe Ontiveros ....Producer
Anthony Lopez ....Head Writer
John Berry ....International Sales
Lillian Casares ....Promotions & Marketing
Sandy Fairall ....Development
Adriano Serafini ....Development
Nancy Tiballi ....Talent Coordinator

LATITUDE TELEVISION LLC

2001 Wilshire Blvd., Ste. 320
Santa Monica, CA 90403
PHONE .310-828-2124
FAX .310-828-4556
TYPES Animation - Documentaries - Features - Internet Content - Made-for-TV/Cable Movies - Mobile Content - Reality TV - TV Series

Gregory Coote .Producer
Edward Olson .Producer
Robert Lundberg .Development Coordinator

LAUGH FACTORY ENTERTAINMENT

8001 Sunset Blvd.
West Hollywood, CA 90046
PHONE .323-848-2800/212-586-7829
FAX .323-848-2810
WEB SITE .www.laughfactory.com
TYPES Features - Made-for-TV/Cable Movies - TV Series
CREDITS Rocket Man

Jamie Masada .Owner/President
Shawn Ullman .Business Deveopment
Andrea Nittoli .Executive Assistant to Jamie Masada

LAUNA NEWMAN PRODUCTIONS (LNP)

10390 Wilshire Blvd., Ste. 1114
Los Angeles, CA 90022
PHONE .310-288-8383
EMAIL .minsonw@aol.com
TYPES Documentaries - New Media - Reality TV - Syndication - TV Series
HAS DEAL WITH ABC Entertainment Television Group
DEVELOPMENT Happy Hour
POST PRODUCTION Kids R Funny
CREDITS I Survived a Disaster 1-4

Launa Newman-Minson .Executive Producer
Eric Fleming .Sr. VP, Development
Whitney Minson .VP, Development

LAUNCHPAD PRODUCTIONS

4335 Van Nuys Blvd., Ste. 339
Sherman Oaks, CA 91403
PHONE .310-502-1113
EMAIL .queries@launchpadprods.com
TYPES Features
DEVELOPMENT Colin's Needle - Stacked
PRODUCTION Disfigured
CREDITS Hard Candy - Big Momma's House 1&2 - Here on Earth
SUBMISSION POLICY Query email only

David W. Higgins .Producer

ANDREW LAUREN PRODUCTIONS

36 E. 23rd St., Ste. 6-F
New York, NY 10010
PHONE .212-475-1600/323-822-1343
FAX .212-529-1095
EMAIL .query@andrewlaurenproductions.com
WEB SITE .www.andrewlaurenproductions.com
TYPES Documentaries - Features
DEVELOPMENT Capture the Flag - Cast of Shadows - Consolation - Creative Differences - Live Bait - Untitled Noah Baumbach Project
CREDITS The Squid and the Whale - G
COMMENTS All inquiries should be directed to the New York office; West Coast office: 1355 N. Laurel Ave., Ste. 7, Los Angeles, CA 90046

Andrew Lauren .CEO
Jennifer Dana .VP, Development & Production
David D'Alessio .Director, Development & Production
Ariana Jackson .Creative Executive
Nathan Hayashigawa .Development Coordinator (LA)
Art Heller .Development Coordinator (NY)

ROBERT LAWRENCE PRODUCTIONS

1810 14th St., #203
Santa Monica, CA 90404
PHONE .310-399-2762
FAX .310-452-0479
TYPES Features
DEVELOPMENT Hombre - The Interrogator - Jane Austen's Guide to Dating - Gates of Fire - Chavez Ravine - Aztlan
CREDITS Mozart & the Whale - The Last Castle - Rock Star - Clueless - Rapid Fire - A Kiss Before Dying - Die Hard: With a Vengeance - Down Periscope

Robert Lawrence .No Title
Robb Aguirre .No Title

LEFRAK PRODUCTIONS

50 W. 57th St., 7th Fl.
New York, NY 10019
PHONE .212-541-9444
FAX .212-974-8205
TYPES Documentaries - Features - Made-for-TV/Cable Movies - New Media - TV Series
DEVELOPMENT 100 Days of Darkness - Betrayal.com - Liz Holtzman: Nazi Hunter (Doc)
CREDITS Miss Rose White - Mi Vida Loca - The Infiltrator - Shot Through the Heart - Life of the Party - Student Seduction

Francine LeFrak .President
Sean Cassels .VP, Development
Caitlen Rubino-Bradway .Assistant

LEGENDARY PICTURES

4000 Warner Blvd., Bldg. 76
Burbank, CA 91522
PHONE .818-954-1940
FAX .818-954-3884
WEB SITE .www.legendarypictures.com
TYPES Features
HAS DEAL WITH Warner Bros. Pictures

Thomas Tull .Chairman/CEO
William Fay .President, Physical Production
Larry Clark .CFO/COO
John Jashni .CCO
Scott Mednick .Chief Marketing Executive
Marlin Prager .VP, Finance
Alysia Cotter .VP, Creative Affairs

ARNOLD LEIBOVIT ENTERTAINMENT

PO Box 33544
Santa Fe, NM 87594
PHONE 505-989-1887
WEB SITE ....www.scifistation.com
TYPES Animation - Features - TV Series
DEVELOPMENT The Time Machine (Miniseries) - Untitled Arnold Leibovit Comedy - Dr. Lao
CREDITS The Time Machine - Puppetoon Movie - Fantasy Film Worlds of George Pal
COMMENTS Puppetoon animation studios

Arnold Leibovit ....Producer/Director
Barbara Schimpf ....VP, Production

THE JERRY LEIDER COMPANY

11661 San Vicente Blvd., Ste. 505
Los Angeles, CA 90049
PHONE 310-820-3161
FAX 310-820-4323
EMAIL ....gjleider@pacbell.net
TYPES Features - Made-for-TV/Cable Movies - TV Series
DEVELOPMENT Two Blind Mice - I Love You Again - Face of War - Peck - Wild Thing - This Perfect Day - Politician's Wife
PRODUCTION MythQuest
CREDITS Mayday - Confessions of a Teen Aged Drama Queen - Coast to Coast - Cadet Kelly - My Favorite Martian - Trucks - Payne

Jerry Leider ....President
Gerald Rubin Esq. ....Legal Affairs

LEISURE TIME ENTERPRISES

9785 Santa Monica Blvd.
Beverly Hills, CA 90210
PHONE 310-360-1144
FAX 310-360-1145
TYPES Direct-to-Video/DVD - Features - Made-for-TV/Cable Movies - Miniseries - Reality TV - Specials - TV Series
DEVELOPMENT Hell's Angels (Fox) - Barbarella (Warner Bros.)
PRODUCTION Cheaper by the Dozen 2
CREDITS Cheaper by the Dozen - Wakin' Up in Reno - One False Move - One Night Stand - Mr. Magoo - Telling Lies in America - Keep Your Eyes Open - The Mod Squad

Ben Myron ....Partner
Al Uzielli ....Partner
David Simmer ....VP, Production

LEMON SKY PRODUCTIONS, INC.

2282 El Contento Dr.
Los Angeles, CA 90068
PHONE 323-957-9620
FAX 323-957-9699
TYPES Features - TV Series
DEVELOPMENT Nine Dead - Unlucky in Love - Perfect Scandal - Malik
UPCOMING RELEASES The Last Kiss
CREDITS Shopgirl - Wicker Park - Lemon Sky - Living in Oblivion - The Real Blonde - Double Whammy

Marcus Viscidi ....President
Adam Ellison ....VP, Development
John Parker ....VP, Finance

MALCOLM LEO PRODUCTIONS

6536 Sunset Blvd.
Hollywood, CA 90028
PHONE 323-464-4448
FAX 323-462-1428
EMAIL ....malcolmleoprods@aol.com
WEB SITE ....www.malcolmleoproductions.com
TYPES Direct-to-Video/DVD - Documentaries - Features - TV Series
DEVELOPMENT Jerry Garcia - American Cool - The Secret Life of Rock 'n' Roll
PRE-PRODUCTION Sound of the Cities - Hollywood Palace
CREDITS This Is Elvis - Rock 'n' Roll Moments - Rolling Stone Anniversary - Beach Boys: An American Band (DVD) - Brady Bunch Reunion - Happy Days Reunion - Rock 'n' Roll Christmas - Will Rogers Look Back in Laughter - Cole Porter Red, Hot & Blue
COMMENTS Deal with NBD-TV; Archive licensing source footage for film, TV, music, pop culture, rock'n'roll

Malcolm Leo ....Executive Producer/Director
David Fairfield ....Development/Editorial
Rodney Merrick ....Librarian/Research

LETNOM PRODUCTIONS

423 W. 55th St., 2nd Fl.
New York, NY 10019
PHONE 212-830-0350
FAX 212-262-4608
TYPES Features - Reality TV - TV Series
COMMENTS West Coast office: 6725 W. Sunset Blvd., Ste. 350, Los Angeles, CA 90028

Montel Williams ....Principal
Nancy Goldman ....VP, Development (NY)
Jennifer Roe Reyes ....VP, Development (LA)
Eric Hanson ....Director, Development (NY)
Guy Rocourt II ....Director, Development (LA)

LETT/REESE INTERNATIONAL PRODUCTIONS

1910 Bel Air Rd.
Los Angeles, CA 90077
PHONE 310-472-7387
FAX 310-476-5043
EMAIL ....lettreese@earthlink.net
TYPES Animation - TV Series
DEVELOPMENT Post Scripts - Mahalia & Me - Galtalk.net
CREDITS The Secret Path (CBS) - Anya's Bell (CBS) - The Moving of Sophia Myles (CBS)

Franklin Lett ....Chairman/CEO
Della Reese-Lett ....Vice Chairman
Frank T. Lett III ....Producer
Billie E. Hall ....Assistant to Chairman

LEVEL 1 ENTERTAINMENT

9100 Wilshire Blvd., Ste. 503 East
Beverly Hills, CA 90212

PHONE	310-777-7600
FAX	310-777-7608
TYPES	Features
DEVELOPMENT	Games of the Hangman - Angel City Bullet - Nobody's Safe - Bad Dogs - NASCAR Cabbie - How to Win Back Your High School Sweetheart - Putt Putt
POST PRODUCTION	Strange Wilderness
CREDITS	Grandma's Boy
SUBMISSION POLICY	No unsolicited material

Edward L. Milstein . . . . . Co-Chairman/CEO
Bill Todman Jr. . . . . . Co-Chairman/CEO
Paul Schwake . . . . . COO
Erin Newell . . . . . Production Executive
Mark Stein . . . . . Development Executive
Lyna Cunningham . . . . . Executive Assistant

THE LEVINSON/FONTANA COMPANY

185 Broome St.
New York, NY 10002

PHONE	212-206-3585
FAX	212-206-3581
WEB SITE	www.tomfontana.com
SECOND WEB SITE	www.levinson.com
TYPES	Made-for-TV/Cable Movies - TV Series
CREDITS	The Bedford Diaries (WB) - Homicide: Life on the Street - Oz - The Beat - The Jury - Strip Search (HBO) - Shot in the Heart (HBO)
SUBMISSION POLICY	Through agent only

Barry Levinson . . . . . Executive Producer/Director/Writer
Tom Fontana . . . . . Executive Producer/Writer
James Finnerty . . . . . Executive Producer
Kevin Deiboldt . . . . . Assistant to Mr. Fontana
Kyle Bradstreet . . . . . Assistant to Mr. Fontana

ZANE W. LEVITT PRODUCTIONS/ZETA ENTERTAINMENT

3422 Rowena Ave.
Los Angeles, CA 90027

PHONE	213-399-2001
TYPES	Features
PRE-PRODUCTION	Tres Cruzados
CREDITS	Blast - Montana - Guncrazy - Shiloh - Amityville - Fist of the North Star - Liquid Dreams - The Big Squeeze - One Good Turn - Mortuary Academy - Out of the Dark - A Sea Apart - Puerta Vallarta Squeeze
SUBMISSION POLICY	No unsolicited emails accepted

Zane W. Levitt . . . . . Writer/Producer/Director
Rowena Murphy . . . . . CEO/Producer
Paul Chramosta . . . . . Producer
Lynn Mason . . . . . Production Associate/Talent Consultant

LICHT ENTERTAINMENT CORPORATION

132 S. Lasky Dr., Ste. 200
Beverly Hills, CA 90212

PHONE	310-205-5500
FAX	310-205-5590
TYPES	Features - Made-for-TV/Cable Movies - TV Series
CREDITS	Idle Hands - The Cable Guy - Waterworld - Spinning Boris (Showtime)

Andrew Licht . . . . . Producer
Kent Bennett . . . . . Creative Assistant

*LIDDELL ENTERTAINMENT

606 N. Larchmont Blvd., Ste. 202
Los Angeles, CA 90004

PHONE	323-461-8600
FAX	323-461-8611
TYPES	Features - TV Series
DEVELOPMENT	Zoe August - Bridge and Tunnel
PRE-PRODUCTION	Terese Raquin
CREDITS	Barfuss - Jack and Bobby - Book of Love - Everwood - The Broken Hearts Club - Go - Under Heaven - Cosmo's Tale - Delivered - Telling Lies in America - Traveller

Mickey Liddell . . . . . Producer
Jennifer Hilton . . . . . Director, Development
Alison Small . . . . . Assistant

BARBARA LIEBERMAN PRODUCTIONS

c/o Robert Greenwald Productions, Inc.
10510 Culver Blvd.
Culver City, CA 90232

PHONE	310-204-0404
FAX	310-204-0174
WEB SITE	www.rgpinc.com
TYPES	Features - Made-for-TV/Cable Movies - Miniseries - TV Series
CREDITS	Trump Unauthorized - Murder in the Hamptons - The Dead Will Tell - Ann Rule Presents The Stranger Beside Me - Gleason - Obsessed - Fever - And Never Let Her Go - Til Death Us Do Part

Barbara Lieberman . . . . . Executive Producer
Nathaniel McCullagh . . . . . Director, Development

THE HAL LIEBERMAN COMPANY

c/o Sony Pictures Entertainment
10202 W. Washington Blvd., Robert Young Bldg., Ste. 3200
Culver City, CA 90232

PHONE	310-244-4744
FAX	310-244-1944
TYPES	Features
HAS DEAL WITH	Columbia Pictures
DEVELOPMENT	Before
PRE-PRODUCTION	Vacancy
POST PRODUCTION	Bridge to Terabithia
CREDITS	Terminator 3 - Around the World in 80 Days - U-571 - The Jackal

Hal Lieberman . . . . . Producer
Michael Converse . . . . . Director, Development
Brian Paschal . . . . . Director, Development
Shashwata Catterjee . . . . . Story Analyst
Debbie Levy . . . . . Assistant/Office Manager

LIFETIME TELEVISION (LOS ANGELES)
2049 Century Park East, Ste. 840
Los Angeles, CA 90067
PHONE . . . 310-556-7500
WEB SITE . . . www.lifetimetv.com
TYPES Made-for-TV/Cable Movies - Reality TV - TV Series
DEVELOPMENT Scripted Series: Angela's Eyes - Bianca: Journey to Paradise; Unscripted Series: Alessandra - Off the Leash - Lisa Williams; Original Movies: Nora Roberts MOWs - Karaoke Queens
CREDITS Lovespring International - The Fantasia Barrino Story: Life is Not a Fairy Tale - The Mermaid Chair - Dawn Anna - Odd Girl Out - Human Trafficking - Missing - Ambulance Girl - Beach Girls - The Dive from Claussen's Pier - Cheerleader Nation - Face the Family

Susanne Daniels . . . President, Entertainment
Louise Henry Bryson . . President, Distribution & Affiliate Business Development & Executive VP/General Manager, Lifetime Movie Network
Maria Grasso . . . Sr. VP, Series Development
Colleen McCormick . . . Sr. VP, Production
Jessica Samet . . . Sr. VP, Reality Programming
Neil Schubert . . . Sr. VP, Publicity
Libby Beers . . . VP, Original Movies
Lucia Cottone . . . VP, Series Development & Current Programming
Marianne Goode . . . VP, Music
Arturo Interian . . . VP, Original Movies
Rick Jacobs . . . VP, Talent
Joey Plager . . . VP, Original Movies
Colette Shelton . . . VP, Reality Programming
David Hillman . . . Executive Director, Programming
Julie Stern . . . Executive Director, Production
Mark Petulla . . . Director, Production
Tracy Speed . . . Director, Publicity
Sean Boyle . . . Manager, Programming
Sara Isaacson . . . Manager, Casting
Jennifer Jenkins . . . Manager, Original Movies
Megan Tantillo . . . Manager, Publicity
Elizabeth Wise . . . Manager, Original Movies
Brian Wright . . . Manager, Series Programming
Kannie Yu . . . Manager, Publicity

LIFETIME TELEVISION (NEW YORK)
Worldwide Plaza, 309 W. 49th St.
New York, NY 10019
PHONE . . . 212-424-7000
WEB SITE . . . www.lifetimetv.com
TYPES Made-for-TV/Cable Movies - Reality TV - TV Series
COMMENTS Studio address: 111 Eighth Ave., New York, NY 10011

Betty Cohen . . . President/CEO
Lynn Picard . . . President, Ad Sales/General Manager, Lifetime Television
James Wesley . . . CFO/Executive VP, Finance
Tim Brooks . . . Executive VP, Research
Pat Langer . . . Executive VP, Business & Legal Affairs/Human Resources
Gerry Logue . . . Executive VP, Executive Creative Director
Martha Pease . . . Executive VP, Marketing & Enterprise Development
Dan Suratt . . . Executive VP, Digital Media & Business Development
Meredith Wagner . . . Executive VP, Public Affairs
Leslie Glenn-Chesloff . . . Sr. VP, Acquisitions, Planning & Scheduling
Frank DeRose . . . VP, Scheduling & Acquisitions
Ron Plante . . . VP, Strategic Planning & Scheduling
Renee Presser . . . VP, Standards & Practices
Allison Wallach . . . VP, Original Programming

LIGHT RENEGADE ENTERTAINMENT, INC.
8383 Wilshire Blvd., Ste. 510
Beverly Hills, CA 90211
PHONE . . . 323-653-0076
FAX . . . 323-653-6005
EMAIL . . . info@lightrenegade.com
WEB SITE . . . www.lightrenegade.com
TYPES Features
DEVELOPMENT Absolution - Thunderwalk - Men Are Dogs - Spike the Heat - Aloha, Where Are You? - The Socialites - Rockin' the Suburbs - Dark House
CREDITS Stonebrook
SUBMISSION POLICY No unsolicited calls or faxes; Email queries only

Dinah Perez . . . President
Byron Thompson . . . Director, Development

LIGHTHOUSE ENTERTAINMENT
409 N. Camden Dr., Ste. 202
Beverly Hills, CA 90210
PHONE . . . 310-246-0499
FAX . . . 310-246-0899
EMAIL . . . ssiebert@lighthousela.com
SECOND EMAIL . . . asst@lighthousela.com
TYPES Features - Made-for-TV/Cable Movies - TV Series
DEVELOPMENT The Lion's Share - Tooth Fairy
POST PRODUCTION One Way to Valhalla
CREDITS The Darwin Awards - A Good Woman (Lionsgate) - Bigger Than the Sky - Cherish - Gridlock'd - Fun - The Rookie

Steven Siebert . . . Producer/Manager
Rahul Chatterjee . . . Assistant

LIGHTHOUSE PRODUCTIONS
120 El Camino Dr., Ste. 212
Beverly Hills, CA 90212
PHONE . . . 310-859-4923
FAX . . . 310-859-7511
EMAIL . . . lighthouseprods@gmail.com
TYPES Animation - Direct-to-Video/DVD - Features - TV Series
DEVELOPMENT Tropic of Night - The Paradise
POST PRODUCTION Mimzy
CREDITS The Flamingo Kid - The Sting - Close Encounters of the Third Kind - Taxi Driver - Mimic - Impostor
SUBMISSION POLICY No unsolicited submissions; Synopses only via fax, mail or email

Michael Phillips . . . Producer/President
Juliana Maio . . . Producer (310-859-2309)
John Frank Rosenblum . . . Producer (310-859-0670)
Magdalena Sikorska . . . Director, Development

LIGHTSTONE ENTERTAINMENT, INC.
1257 S. Orange Grove
Los Angeles, CA 90019
PHONE .323-939-3555
FAX .323-939-7523
EMAIL .lightstonefilms@hotmail.com
WEB SITE .www.lightstoneentertainment.com
TYPES Commercials - Features - Music Videos - TV Series
DEVELOPMENT Bullfighter - Dragster - Goliath - Bounty
CREDITS 3000 Miles to Graceland - Lowball - Chix on Flix (New Media) - Venus & Vegas - Love & Suicide - The Unseen

Demian Lichtenstein .President
Jesse Guma .Director, Development
Miklos Wright .Creative Development
David Coplan Schneider .Development

LIGHTSTORM ENTERTAINMENT
919 Santa Monica Blvd.
Santa Monica, CA 90401
PHONE .310-656-6100
FAX .310-656-6102
TYPES Features
HAS DEAL WITH Twentieth Century Fox
CREDITS Strange Days - Titanic - Aliens - Abyss - The Terminator - T2 - True Lies - Solaris - Dark Angel (TV)
SUBMISSION POLICY No unsolicited material

James Cameron .Chairman/CEO
Jon Landau .Partner

LINKLETTER/KRITZER
8484 Wilshire Blvd., Ste. 205 & 210
Beverly Hills, CA 90211
PHONE .310-702-5356/323-655-5696
FAX .310-394-7076
EMAIL .producedby@aol.com
WEB SITE .www.eddiekritzer.com
TYPES Direct-to-Video/DVD - Documentaries - Features - Internet Content - Made-for-TV/Cable Movies - Miniseries - Mobile Content - Reality TV - Specials - TV Series
DEVELOPMENT The New Kids Say the Darndest Things (VH1) - The Nuremberg Interviews - 6 Weeks to a Hollywood Body - Television Week - Movie Call - Gmen & Gangsters (Mandeville Films) - A Season in the Heartland
CREDITS Rockline (Radio) - Hits of Beverly Hills 90210 (Radio) - Animals Are People Too (Pax) - Callanetics (Universal Home Video) - High Voltage (KDP Productions) - Kids Say the Darndest Things (CBS/Syndication) - False Witness (NBC) - Shattered: If Your Kid's on Drugs (USA/Universal Home Video) - How Do They Do That? with Ed McMahon (Radio) - Rock Around the World (Radio)
COMMENTS Created/produced Rockline; Founded Global Satellite Network; Radio; EKP Productions offices: 101 California Ave., Ste. 307, Santa Monica, CA 90403

Art Linkletter .Partner
Eddie Kritzer .Partner

LION EYES ENTERTAINMENT
12210-1/2 Nebraska Ave.
Los Angeles, CA 90025
PHONE .310-943-4354
TYPES Features - TV Series
DEVELOPMENT Shi - Paper Dragon - W.A.S.P. - Subterranean
CREDITS White Squall - Thelma & Louise - The Browning Version - Trapped - 1492: Conquest of Paradise

Mimi Polk Gitlin .Producer/President
Richard Gitlin .Producer
Patrick Walmsley .Story Editor/Assistant to Mimi Polk Gitlin

LION ROCK PRODUCTIONS
2120 Colorado Ave., Ste. 225
Santa Monica, CA 90404
PHONE .310-309-2980
FAX .310-309-6151
TYPES Animation - Features - TV Series
CREDITS Paycheck - The Big Hit - Face/Off - Broken Arrow - Windtalkers - Bulletproof Monk - Mission: Impossible 2

John Woo .Director/Producer
Terence Chang .Producer
Caroline Macaulay .Executive VP
Suzanne Zizzi .Sr. VP
Lori Tilkin .VP, Animation
Kim Woo .Animation Executive
Brittany Philion .Executive Assistant to Mr. Woo
Todd Weinger .Assistant to Mr. Chang
Tom W. Metz III .Assistant to Ms. Macaulay & Ms. Zizzi
Angeles Woo .Assistant to Mr. Woo

LION TELEVISION U.S.
1831 Stanford St.
Santa Monica, CA 90404
PHONE .310-566-6285/212-206-8633
FAX .310-566-6284/212-206-8636
EMAIL .liontvla@liontv.us
WEB SITE .www.liontv.co.uk
TYPES Documentaries - Made-for-TV/Cable Movies - Reality TV - TV Series
CREDITS Cash Cab - History Detectives - It Takes a Thief - Sheer Dallas - Texas S.W.A.T. - The Perfect Dress - Days That Shook the World - Ape to Man - Secrets of the First Emperor
COMMENTS East Coast office: 304 Hudson St., 5th Fl., New York, NY 10013

Tracy Green .Executive VP (LA)
Tony Tackaberry .Executive VP (NY)
Adam Steinman .Director, Development (NY)
Hilary Rushnell .Manager, Development (LA)

LIONSGATE

LIONSGATE

2700 Colorado Ave.
Santa Monica, CA 90404
PHONE .310-255-3700
FAX .310-255-3870
EMAIL .general-inquiries@lgf.com
WEB SITE .www.lionsgate.com
TYPES Animation - Direct-to-Video/DVD - Documentaries - Features - Made-for-TV/Cable Movies - TV Series
PROVIDES DEAL TO Alchemy Entertainment - Bayonne Entertainment - City Entertainment - Element Films - Ithaka - Panamax Films - Sobini Films
DEVELOPMENT Rogue - PDR - Skinwalkers - The Prom - Daddy's Little Girl - Midnight Meat Train - Kid Delicious - Addicted - Stir of Echoes: The Dead Speak
UPCOMING RELEASES Bug
CREDITS Features: Employee of the Month - Madea's Family Reunion - Larry the Cable Guy: Health Inspector - Lord of War - La Mujer de Mi Hermano - Crash - Akeelah and the Bee - Hostel - Saw II - Saw - Diary of a Mad Black Woman - Open Water - The Punisher™ - Waiting - Fahrenheit 9/11 - Monster's Ball - Grizzly Man; Television: The Dead Zone™ - Missing - Wildfire - Weeds
COMMENTS Programming agreement with Nine Network (Australia)

Jon Feltheimer .CEO
Mark Amin .Vice Chairman
Michael Burns .Vice Chairman
Steve Beeks .President, Lionsgate
Jim Keegan .CFO
Wayne Levin .General Counsel/Executive VP, Corporate Operations
Kevin Beggs .President, Lionsgate Television Programming & Production
Peter Block .President, Acquisitions & Co-Productions
Stephanie Denton .President, International Film Sales
Jay Faires .President, Music & Publishing
Nick Meyer .President, International
Tom Ortenberg .President, Theatrical Films
Michael Paseornek .President, Productions
Steve Rothenberg .President, Domestic Theatrical Distribution
Sarah Greenberg .Co-President, Theatrical Marketing
Tim Palen .Co-President, Theatrical Marketing
Sandra Stern .COO, Television
John Dellaverson .Executive VP
James Gladstone .Executive VP, Business & Legal Affairs
Gary Goodman .Executive VP, TV Production
Jed Grossman .Executive VP, Home Entertainment Sales/Distribution
Ken Katsumoto .Executive VP, Family Entertainment
Robert Melnik .Executive VP, Business Affairs, Lionsgate Films Development & Production
Anne Parducci .Executive VP, Family Entertainment & Marketing
Ron Schwartz .Executive VP/General Manager, Home Entertainment
Bob Wenokur .Executive VP, Post Production
Marni Wieshofer .Executive VP, Corporate Development
Peter Wilkes .Sr. VP, Investor Relations & Executive Communications
Adam Bialow .Sr. VP, International Business & Legal Affairs
Jason Constantine .Sr. VP, Acquisitions & Co-Productions
Jon Ferro .Sr. VP, TV
Joel High .Sr. VP, Music & Contracts
Wendy Jaffe .Sr. VP, Acquisitions/Business & Legal Affairs
Jim Jenkins .Sr. VP, Legal
J. David Nonaka .Sr. VP, Business & Legal Affairs
Carl Pedregal .Sr. VP, Feature Post Production
Mike Polydoros .Sr. VP, Exhibitor Relations
Erika Schimik .Sr. VP, Media & Research
Donna Sloan .Sr. VP, Lionsgate Films Production

(Continued)

LIONSGATE (Continued)

David Spitz .Sr. VP, Domestic Theatrical Distribution
Barbara Wall .Sr. VP, Television, Program Development & Current Programming
Craig Cegielski .VP, International Programming & Sales
Malik Ducard .VP, Home Entertainment Acquisitions & Business Development
Shyama Friedenson .VP, International Marketing
Elizabeth Kim .VP, International Sales
Ally Lattman .VP, Development, TV
Erik Nelson .VP, Documentaries
Michael Rathauser .VP, Marketing
John Sacchi .VP, Productions
Adrian Sexton .VP, Digital Media
Dave Shankwiler .VP, Participation & Residuals
Danny St. Pierre .VP, Distribution Services
Charlyn Ware .VP, Legal Affairs & Contracts Administration
Arturo Chavez .Director, Spanish Language Programming

JAMES LIPTON PRODUCTIONS

159 E. 80th St.
New York, NY 10021
PHONE .212-535-9500
FAX .212-772-1126
TYPES TV Series
CREDITS Inside the Actors' Studio

James Lipton .Writer/Producer

LIQUID THEORY

8981 Sunset Blvd., Ste. 102
Los Angeles, CA 90069
PHONE .310-276-1094
FAX .310-276-1093
EMAIL .info@liquid-theory.com
WEB SITE .www.liquid-theory.com
TYPES Animation - Commercials - Music Videos - Reality TV - Specials - TV Series
HAS DEAL WITH MTV Networks - Spike TV
PRODUCTION Scream Awards (Spike TV)
CREDITS All That Rocks (MTV2) - Call to Greatness (MTV) - 2006 People's Choice Awards - Video Game Awards (Spike TV) - MTV News Re-Launch - MTV XBox Special - MTV Video Music Awards - MTV Movie Awards - MTV Reality Awards - Spike Likes Movies - Roger That (Spike TV) - VH1 Big in '03 Awards - VH1 Fashion Awards - GQ Awards - MusiCares: Person of the Year - Rock and Roll Hall of Fame Ceremony - 52 Most Irresistible Women (Spike TV) - People's Choice Awards
SUBMISSION POLICY By mail only

Austin Reading .President
Julie Kellman Reading .President
Kiana Perry .Administrative Assistant

THE LITTLEFIELD COMPANY

c/o Touchstone Television
500 S. Buena Vista St., Mail Code 1835
Burbank, CA 91521
PHONE .818-560-2280
FAX .818-560-3775
TYPES TV Series
HAS DEAL WITH Touchstone Television
CREDITS Love Inc. (UPN) - Keen Eddie (Fox) - Like Family (WB) - Do Over (WB) - Foody Call (Style)
SUBMISSION POLICY No unsolicited material

Warren Littlefield .Principal
Andrew Bourne .Sr. VP, Development
Patricia Mann .Executive Assistant to Warren Littlefield
Janelle Young .Assistant to Andrew Bourne

GEORGE LITTO PRODUCTIONS, INC.
c/o Warner Bros.
4000 Warner Blvd., Bldg. 146, Rm. 101
Burbank, CA 91522
PHONE .818-954-1627
FAX .818-954-6584
TYPES Features
DEVELOPMENT Playing Through - Hawaii Five-0 - M.I.C.E. - Any Four Women Could Rob the Bank of Italy - Accidental Soldier
CREDITS Over the Edge - Dressed to Kill - Kansas - Blow Out - Obsession - The Crew - Thieves Like Us - Drive In - Night Game
SUBMISSION POLICY Through agents only

George Litto .CEO/Owner
Andria Litto .Partner/President
Linda Lee .Executive Assistant

***LIVE ANIMALS**
5711 W. Adams Blvd.
Los Angeles, CA 90016
PHONE .310-280-0635
FAX .310-280-0377
EMAIL .alex@liveanimals.net
WEB SITE .www.liveanimals.net
TYPES Commercials - Documentaries - Miniseries - Music Videos - Reality TV - Specials - TV Series
DEVELOPMENT SK8HOP - The Coe Show - On the Record
PRE-PRODUCTION CMT Outlaws 2006
CREDITS CMT 2006 Music Awards - Key Art Awards 2006

Audrey Morrisey .Producer

LIVEPLANET
2644 30th St., Ste. 101
Santa Monica, CA 90405
PHONE .310-664-2400
FAX .310-664-2401
EMAIL .info@liveplanet.com
WEB SITE .www.liveplanet.com
TYPES Documentaries - Features - Made-for-TV/Cable Movies - Mobile Content - Reality TV - TV Series
HAS DEAL WITH The Walt Disney Company - Touchstone Television
DEVELOPMENT Liberty - The Divorcees - Solace - Aftermath - Tron 2.0 - Nowhere Men - Hero - Big Nasty - Fan Club: Reality Baseball
PRE-PRODUCTION Running the Sahara (Documentary)
PRODUCTION Gone, Baby, Gone
UPCOMING RELEASES Feast
CREDITS Gears of War: The Race to E3 - American Wedding - Project Greenlight 1-3 - Push, Nevada - The Core - Emperor's Club - American Pie 1&2 - Joy Ride - Stolen Summer - Best Laid Plans - Matchstick Men - The Battle of Shaker Heights - The Entertainer - First Descent - Phone Tag (Amp'd)
SUBMISSION POLICY No unsolicited material

Matt Damon .Founder
Ben Affleck .Founder
Sean Bailey .Founder/Producer
Larry Tanz .CEO/President
Marc Joubert .Sr. VP, Development & Production
Keith Quinn .Sr. VP, Development & Production
Daniel Pipski .Sr. VP, Production
Dennis De Nobile .Manager, Development & Production
Justin Springer .Story Editor

***LJ FILM**
25-11 Nonhyun-dong, Gangnam-gu
Seoul 135-814, Korea
PHONE .82-2-3444-4143
FAX .82-2-3444-6858
WEB SITE .www.ljfilm.com
TYPES Features
DEVELOPMENT Julia Project (Focus Features)

Seung-jae Lee .CEO/President
So-Hee Kim .Managing Director/Producer (fanta@ljfilm.com)
Cindy Rhyu .Assistant Manager (cindy@ljfilm.com)
Ji-Yeon Kim .Coordinator (jiyeon@ljfilm.com)

LLOYD ENTERTAINMENT
9420 Wilshire Blvd., Ste. 250
Beverly Hills, CA 90212
PHONE .310-278-4800
FAX .310-278-4254
TYPES Features - TV Series
HAS DEAL WITH Gold Circle Films
DEVELOPMENT Diary - Lake Powell - Nina Simone Biopic - Viagra Falls - Smoke - Carlisle - Elisabeth Kublerross
PRE-PRODUCTION Seether
CREDITS Cellular - Mermaids - Freddy Got Fingered - Drop Zone - The Butcher's Wife - Fires Within
SUBMISSION POLICY No unsolicited submissions

Lauren Lloyd .Producer/Literary Manager
Jessica Wiltgen .Story Editor/Talent Management

LMNO PRODUCTIONS
15821 Ventura Blvd., Ste. 320
Encino, CA 91436
PHONE .818-380-8000
FAX .818-995-5544
WEB SITE .www.lmnotv.com
TYPES Documentaries - Reality TV - TV Series
PROVIDES DEAL TO Rive Gauche Entertainment
DEVELOPMENT Double or Nothing
CREDITS Medical Fraud Investigators - Babies: Special Delivery - Amazing Medical Stories - I Wanna Be a Soap Star (SoapNet) - Wickedly Perfect (CBS) - Fire Me Please (CBS) - Over Your Head (HGTV) - What's With That House? (HGTV) - Anatomy of a Giant (Discovery Health) - National Body Challenge (Discovery Health)

Eric Schotz .President/CEO/Executive Producer
Bill Paolantonio .Executive VP, Creative Affairs/Executive Producer
Andrew Suser .Sr. VP/General Counsel
Lisa Bourgoujian .Sr. VP, Cable Group
Ed Horwitz .Sr. VP, Production
Larry Goldman .VP, Corporate Communications
Kevin Kappock .VP, Development
Ruth Rivin .VP, Special Projects

MIKE LOBELL PRODUCTIONS
9477 Lloydcrest Dr.
Beverly Hills, CA 90210
PHONE .310-274-2147
TYPES Features
PRE-PRODUCTION Gambit
CREDITS Striptease - It Could Happen to You - The Freshman - Honeymoon in Vegas - White Fang - Journey of Natty Gann - Tears of the Sun

Mike Lobell .Producer
Janet Chiarabaglio .Assistant to Mike Lobell

PETER LOCKE PRODUCTIONS
846 Woodacres Rd.
Santa Monica, CA 90402
PHONE .310-395-3433
FAX .310-458-1241
EMAIL .peter@peterlocke.net
TYPES Direct-to-Video/DVD - Features - Made-for-TV/Cable Movies - TV Series
PRE-PRODUCTION The Hills Have Eyes II (Atomic Fox) - Diced Pinocchio (New Line) - Andre (Paramount) -
CREDITS Brave Little Toaster 1-3 (Disney) - Divorce Court - First & Ten (HBO) - Gun (ABC) - Freeway - Harvard Man - Basil - Whole Wide World - Picking Up the Pieces

Peter Locke .President
Nanette Munro .Assistant

LOGO
1633 Broadway, 5th Fl.
New York, NY 10019
PHONE .212-654-3005
FAX .212-654-4772
WEB SITE .www.logoonline.com
TYPES TV Series
DEVELOPMENT Wisecrack - Tickled Pink - Open Bar - Surfer Girls - Bob and Rose - Simply Sketch - U.S. of ANT - Rick and Steve - Slink - The Rules: A Lesbian Survival Guide - Heartland - The Big Gay Show - The Service - Sordid Lives: The Series - That Gay Ghost - Reconnection
CREDITS 10 Count - Hearsay - First Comes Love; LOGOmotion: Noah's Arc (Seasons 1&2) - Buzz - Trip Out - CBS News on Logo
COMMENTS Includes LOGOmotion (Streaming Channel)

Brian Graden .President, Entertainment, Music Group (MTV, VH1, MTV2, CMT) & Logo
Lisa Sherman .Sr. VP/General Manager
Kristin Frank .Sr. VP, Multiplatform Distribution & Marketing
Eileen Opatut .Sr. VP, Original Programming
David Bittler .VP, Communications & Public Affairs
Steven Fisher .VP, Communications & Public Affairs
Joanne Jacobson .VP, Business Development & Operations
Marc Leonard .VP, Programming & Scheduling
Dave Mace .VP, Original Programming
Tom Watson .VP, Ad Sales
Emily Spitale .Sr. Publicist

LONDINE PRODUCTIONS
1626 N. Wilcox Ave., Ste. 480
Hollywood, CA 90028-6273
PHONE .310-281-7540
FAX .310-822-9025
EMAIL .cassiusii@aol.com
TYPES Commercials - Direct-to-Video/DVD - Features - Internet Content - Made-for-TV/Cable Movies - Mobile Content - Music Videos - TV Series
DEVELOPMENT Runnin' Down Crenshaw - Mall Crazy - Bugs
PRE-PRODUCTION At the Movies - Rhythm of the Night
CREDITS D.C. Cab - House Party 4 - High Frequency - You Got Served
SUBMISSION POLICY By email only
COMMENTS Internet streaming video; Produced more than 70 music videos that have aired on MTV and BET

Cassius Vernon Weathersby .President/Producer
Nadine Weathersby .VP/Producer
Joshua Weathersby .VP

LONE STAR FILM GROUP
335 N. Maple Dr., Ste. 127
Beverly Hills, CA 90210
PHONE .310-285-0700
FAX .310-388-0960
EMAIL .lsfg@lonestarfilmgroup.com
TYPES Features
POST PRODUCTION Chaos Theory - The Savages
SUBMISSION POLICY No unsolicited submissions
COMMENTS Financing

Fred Westheimer .CEO
Erica Westheimer .Executive in Charge of Production

LONETREE ENTERTAINMENT
23852 Pacific Coast Hwy., Ste. 741
Malibu, CA 90265
PHONE .310-589-6016
FAX .310-589-1506
EMAIL .lonetreez@aol.com
TYPES Animation - Direct-to-Video/DVD - Documentaries - Features - Made-for-TV/Cable Movies - TV Series
DEVELOPMENT Patient No. 1 - The War Magician - Soul Catchers - Hard Evidence - Lone Justice - Earth on Fire
PRE-PRODUCTION The Equalizer - The Vixens - Paradise
PRODUCTION The Naked Truth - Twilight Heroes
POST PRODUCTION Chi-Chian
CREDITS The Ghost - Code of the Dragon
SUBMISSION POLICY No unsolicited submissions

Tony Eldridge .President/Producer
Michele Barbera .Producer
Roger Davis .Producer
Michelle Browning .Development
Victoria Woodbeck-Natkin .Development
Ian Austin .Development
Ellen Fitzmaurice .Development
Stephanie Rutten .Project Coordinator
Rob Lee .Development Assistant

LONGBOW PRODUCTIONS

PO Box 240
Van Nuys, CA 91408-0240
PHONE 818-907-8140
TYPES Direct-to-Video/DVD - Documentaries - Features - Made-for-TV/Cable Movies - Miniseries - Reality TV - Specials - Syndication
DEVELOPMENT Smoke & Mirrors - The Battle of Hastings - Mt. Weather
PRE-PRODUCTION World Champions
POST PRODUCTION Hollywood Hold 'Em
CREDITS Secret Cutting - The Summer of Ben Tyler - A Private Matter - A League of Their Own - The Last Brickmaker in America - Forever & Always
SUBMISSION POLICY Via mail only

Bill Pace . . . . . Partner (x10)
Ronnie D. Clemmer . . . . . Partner (x26)
Richard Kughn . . . . . Partner (x0)
Herman Hong . . . . . Technological Operations (x31)

LONGFELLOW PICTURES

250 Hudson St., 10th Fl.
New York, NY 10013
PHONE 212-431-5550
FAX 212-431-5822
EMAIL . . . . . longfellow@mindspring.com
TYPES Direct-to-Video/DVD - Features
DEVELOPMENT Bettie Ann Waters - House of Lords - Four and Twenty Blackbirds - Ten Point Bold - Bathing Suits
UPCOMING RELEASES Slowburn
COMPLETED UNRELEASED Meeting Resistance
CREDITS Princess Caraboo - The Prince of Tides - The Rachel Papers - Curtain Call - Town and Country - Rough Magic - Nights at O'Rear's - The Emperor's Club - Stars Above the City
SUBMISSION POLICY No unsolicited material

Rachael Horovitz . . . . . Producer
Andrew Karsch . . . . . Producer/President
Abigail Spindel . . . . . Assistant

*L'ORANGE

5225 Wilsire Blvd., Ste. 524
Los Angeles, CA 90036
PHONE 323-938-3220
FAX 323-938-3229
EMAIL . . . . . jesse@lorangestudios.com
WEB SITE . . . . . www.lorangestudios.com
TYPES Documentaries - Features - Internet Content - Mobile Content
CREDITS The Life of Reilly - Mud, Blood and Beer - Last Call Poker

Robert Fagan . . . . . Owner
Wrye Martin . . . . . Owner
Jesse Trott . . . . . Owner

LYNN LORING PRODUCTIONS

2313 Canyonback Rd.
Los Angeles, CA 90049
PHONE 310-472-5050
FAX 310-476-2828
EMAIL . . . . . lynn3939@aol.com
TYPES Direct-to-Video/DVD - Features - Made-for-TV/Cable Movies - Miniseries - New Media - Syndication - TV Series
DEVELOPMENT I Love You Tomorrow
CREDITS Mr. Mom - Best Little Girl in the World - Taking Gary Feldman

Lynn Loring . . . . . President/Executive Producer
Brett Tracy . . . . . Creative Assistant

LOTUS PICTURES

10810 Via Verona St.
Los Angeles, CA 90077
PHONE 310-440-5681
FAX 310-440-5682
EMAIL . . . . . lotuspics@aol.com
TYPES Features - Made-for-TV/Cable Movies
DEVELOPMENT Jinetera - The Haole Substitute - The Rig - Tark the Shark - Binion Murder Story
PRE-PRODUCTION Baywatch (Feature) - Young at Heart - A Dream of Mansions
CREDITS Tranced - Blacktop - Legacy - Bandits - Baywatch (TV) - Stateside - Downtown: A Street Tale - The Circle

Michele Berk . . . . . Owner/Producer
Joseph Salemi . . . . . VP, Production
Sidney Kiwitt . . . . . Business Affairs

LOVE SPELL ENTERTAINMENT

500 S. Buena Vista St., Animation 1-E, Rm. 24
Burbank, CA 91521
PHONE 818-560-5376
FAX 818-560-6430
TYPES Features - TV Series
HAS DEAL WITH Touchstone Television
DEVELOPMENT Film: Secrets - 13 Seconds - She Had Brains, a Body and the Ability to Make Men Love Her; TV: Angry Little Girls
CREDITS Ghost Whisperer - If Only

Jennifer Love Hewitt . . . . . President
Matt Ferrone . . . . . Creative Executive

LUCASFILM LTD.

PO Box 29901
San Francisco, CA 94129
PHONE 415-623-1000
WEB SITE . . . . . www.lucasfilm.com
TYPES Animation - Features - TV Series
PRODUCTION Clone Wars (Animated TV Series)

George Lucas . . . . . Chairman
Micheline Chau . . . . . President/COO, Lucasfilm Ltd.
Jim Ward . . President, LucasArts/VP, Marketing & Distribution, Lucasfilm Ltd.
Cliff Plumer . . . . . CTO
Gail Currey . . . . . VP/General Manager, Lucasfilm Animation
Chris Kubsch . . . . . General Manager, Lucasfilm Animation Co. Singapore
Catherine Winder . . . . . Executive Producer
Dave Filoni . . . . . Supervising Director
Rob Coleman . . . . . Director, Animation & Development
Philip Stamp . . . . Director, Animation, Lucasfilm Animation Co. Singapore
Henry Gilroy . . . . . Episodic Development

LUCID PICTURES
7024 Hawthorn Ave., Ste. 200
Los Angeles, CA 90028
PHONE .323-466-7448
TYPES Features
DEVELOPMENT Love Her Madly - With Love, Brendan - My Clementine - Bright Midnight
PRE-PRODUCTION Vinyl
CREDITS A Perfect Little Man - Fix - A Test of Will (Short Film)

Richard Zelniker .Writer/Director/Producer
Tram Nguyen Zelniker .Writer
Jannie Penvari .Assitant to Richard Zelniker

LUCKY CROW FILMS
4335 Van Nuys Blvd., Ste. 355
Sherman Oaks, CA 91403
PHONE .818-783-7529/818-990-8030
FAX .818-783-7594
EMAIL .luckycrowfilms@aol.com
WEB SITE .www.indieproducer.net
TYPES Direct-to-Video/DVD - Documentaries - Features - Made-for-TV/Cable Movies - Reality TV
DEVELOPMENT Flight - God Box - Blood from Stones - The J Allen Hynek Story - My Date With... - Just Visiting - Ian the Vampire
PRE-PRODUCTION Why Beulah Shot Her Pistol in the Baptist Church - It's Good to Be King
CREDITS My Date with Drew - Agent Cody Banks 1&2 - The Usual Suspects (Special Edition DVD) - Mercy Streets - Perfect Romance - Final Table Poker with Phil Gordon - Short Game Golf with Jim Furyk & Fred Funk
SUBMISSION POLICY Query letters accepted via email
COMMENTS Affiliated with Indieproducer.net

Kerry David .Producer
Jon Gunn .Producer/Director

LUMINAIR ENTERTAINMENT
112 S. Sangamon St., Ste. 301
Chicago, IL 60607
PHONE .312-491-8380
FAX .312-491-8381
EMAIL .george@luminair.com
WEB SITE .www.luminair.com
TYPES Commercials - Direct-to-Video/DVD - Documentaries - Features - TV Series
DEVELOPMENT Wesley Wizard
PRE-PRODUCTION Driving a Bargain
COMPLETED UNRELEASED Boxboarders!
CREDITS 3D Mania: Encounter in the 3rd Dimension - Piaf: Her Story...Her Songs (Lionsgate) - Forever Young with Bill Frank - Mexico: One Plate at a Time

George Elder .President/Executive Producer
Scott Dummler .Producer/Director
Jeremy Pinkwater .Producer
Daniel Elder .Producer
Elizabeth Elder .Business Manager

LUMINOUS ENTERTAINMENT
36 Breeze Ave., Ste. 3
Venice, CA 90291
PHONE .323-931-3700
TYPES Features
DEVELOPMENT A Thousand Days - Untitled Action Project
COMPLETED UNRELEASED Guarding Eddy
CREDITS Admissions - Twin Falls Idaho - Still Breathing - Kill the Man - Cherry Falls - The Breed - Wild Iris

Annette Vait .Producer
Joyce Schweickert .Executive Producer

LUNA RAY FILMS
2018 N. Vine St.
Los Angeles, CA 90068
PHONE .213-353-4900
FAX .213-210-4876
TYPES Features - Made-for-TV/Cable Movies
DEVELOPMENT Maker of Saints
CREDITS A Huey P. Newton Story - God's Waiting List - Justice

Steven Adams .Partner
Bob L. Johnson .Partner
Roger Guenveur Smith .Partner

LUNARIA FILMS
2922 Second St., Ste. E
Santa Monica, CA 90405-5433
PHONE .310-450-5917
FAX .310-943-6947
EMAIL .lunariafilms@mindspring.com
TYPES Features - Made-for-TV/Cable Movies - TV Series
DEVELOPMENT Saint-Ex - John Steinbeck's Travels with Charley - Where War Lives - The Sunday Wife - Breathing Recommended - Sing Fat and the Imperial Duchess of Woo - The Star Detective Agency - Foreign Affairs - Rope Trick - Vulture's Row - Where Are the Carriers?
CREDITS Kicking & Screaming - Black Circle Boys - The Only Thrill - Vig - Lakeboat - 'Til Death

Erin E. Martin .Producer

DAN LUPOVITZ PRODUCTIONS
1501 S. Holt Ave.
Los Angeles, CA 90035
PHONE .310-276-4923
TYPES Features - Made-for-TV/Cable Movies - TV Series
PRODUCTION Death Defying Acts
CREDITS Simpatico - Search and Destroy - The Velocity of Gary - Mrs. Cage - Late for Dinner

Dan Lupovitz .Producer
Randy Albelda .Head, Development

A.C. LYLES PRODUCTIONS, INC.

c/o Paramount Pictures
5555 Melrose Ave., Hart Bldg., Rm. 409
Hollywood, CA 90038-3197

PHONE .323-956-5819
TYPES: Features - TV Series
CREDITS: Deadwood (HBO) - Conversations with the President - The Last Day - Dear Mr. President - Here's Boomer - Buckskin - Arizona Bushwhackers - Fort Utah - Hostile Guns - Red Tomahawk - Waco - Johnny Reno - Apache Uprising - Town Tamer - Black Spurs - Young Fury - Stage to Thunder Rock - Law of the Lawless

A.C. Lyles .Executive Producer

THE TOM LYNCH COMPANY

9100 Wilshire Blvd., Ste. 345, East Tower
Beverly Hills, CA 90212

PHONE .310-724-6900
FAX .310-282-9176
WEB SITE .www.tomlynchco.com
TYPES: Animation - Direct-to-Video/DVD - Documentaries - Features - Made-for-TV/Cable Movies - Reality TV - Specials - TV Series
PRODUCTION: Class of 3000
CREDITS: Red Sneakers - The Jersey - Journey of Allen Strange - 100 Deeds for Eddie McDowd - Night Tracks - Kids Inc. - Secret World of Alex Mack - Caitlin's Way - Just Deal - Skate - Scout's Safari - Romeo! - South of Nowhere - The Team

Thomas W. Lynch .CEO/Writer/Executive Producer/Director
Gary Stephenson .President
Jonas Agin .Sr. VP
Andy Fiedler .Production Supervisor
David Hail .Executive Assistant

M3 TELEVISION

4111 W. Alameda Ave., Ste. 101
Burbank, CA 91505

PHONE .818-558-3633
EMAIL .info@m3television.com
WEB SITE .www.m3television.com
TYPES: Commercials - Direct-to-Video/DVD - Internet Content - Music Videos - TV Series
HAS DEAL WITH: Disney ABC Cable Networks Group
PRODUCTION: Disney 365 - JETIX @
CREDITS: ESPN Hollywood - Entertainment Tonight - ET on MTV - ET on VH1 - ET Weekend
COMMENTS: EPKs, PSAs and promos

Andy Meyers .Producer/Writer/Director
Roman Perez .Editor/Producer/Director
Brad Baruh .Director, Publicity Production

MACARI/EDELSTEIN FILMS

112 N. Mansfield Ave.
Los Angeles, CA 90036

PHONE .323-938-7007/323-936-1967
TYPES: Features
DEVELOPMENT: Kung Fu High School - Manila Bay (Disney) - Le Trou - The Big Blow (Scott Free/Fox Production) - The Imagined (Fox) - Resurrection (Disney) - Balls of Courage (Universal) - Adrift (Dimension) - Fracture
PRE-PRODUCTION: Shelter (InterMedia) - Amusement (New Line) - No Place Like Home - Cold Hand in Mine
COMPLETED UNRELEASED: The Invisible
CREDITS: The Ring 1&2 - Mulholland Drive - The Straight Story - Lumiere Campaign

Neal Edelstein .Producer
Mike Macari .Producer

MACEDON MEDIA, INC.

5001 Alta Canyada Rd.
La Canada, CA 91011

PHONE .818-790-7862
EMAIL .williams@macedonmedia.com
WEB SITE .www.macedonmedia.com
TYPES: Features - Made-for-TV/Cable Movies - Theatre - TV Series
PRE-PRODUCTION: Pools - Double-Edged Sword
CREDITS: Two Divorced Guys in a Bar - What Girls Learn - Papa's Angels - Mr. & Mrs. Smith (Series) - The Bachelor's Baby - Prowler - Escanaba in 'da Moonlight - Super Sucker - Chicken Man - Reality Check (Series)
SUBMISSION POLICY: All inquiries by phone or email to Barry Williams only

Tom Spiroff .President/CEO/Producer/Director
Barry Williams .VP, Production
Allison Forgey .Executive Assistant to Tom Spiroff

MACGILLIVRAY FREEMAN FILMS

PO Box 205
Laguna Beach, CA 92652

PHONE .949-494-1055
FAX .949-494-2079
WEB SITE .www.macfreefilms.com
TYPES: Documentaries
DEVELOPMENT: Space Journey
PRODUCTION: Water Planet - The Alps
POST PRODUCTION: Hurricane on the Bayou
CREDITS: Greece: Secrets of the Past - Mystery of the Nile - Everest - Dolphins - The Living Sea - To Fly! - Coral Reef Adventure - Top Speed
COMMENTS: IMAX Documentaries

Greg MacGillivray .President/Producer/Director

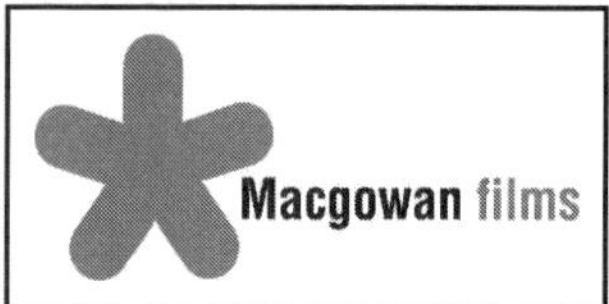

*MACGOWAN FILMS
402 Bourke St.
Surry Hills, Sydney NSW 2010, Australia
PHONE 61-2-9357-7366
FAX 61-2-9357-1566
EMAIL . . . . info@macgowanfilms.com
WEB SITE . . . . www.macgowanfilms.com
TYPES — Features - TV Series
DEVELOPMENT — South Solitary - Cold Harvest - Fat Tuesday - Something Happened
PRE-PRODUCTION — Death Defying Acts
CREDITS — The Rage in Placid Lake - Risk - Two Hands - Lillian's Story

Marian Macgowan . . . . Producer
Celia Richards . . . . Assistant

MAD CHANCE
9021 Melrose Ave., Ste. 202
West Hollywood, CA 90069
PHONE 310-285-2077
FAX 310-285-2078
WEB SITE . . . . www.madchance.com
TYPES — Features
DEVELOPMENT — Get Smart - Diva - Hergatory - Fellini Black and White - Killer's Game - Pre-Astronauts - Fleming - Rodney on the Roq - Time and a Half - The Handyman - Only Human - While I'm Dead...Feed the Dog - Wardogs - The Great Mordecai Moustache Mystery - I Love You Phillip Morris - Ash - IQ 83 - Swell - Dramarama - Welcome Back Kotter - Cleopatra Jones - Dirty Little Secret
CREDITS — Catch That Kid - Confessions of a Dangerous Mind - Death to Smoochy - Cats and Dogs - Panic - Space Cowboys - Lucky Numbers - 10 Things I Hate About You - Bound - Assassins - The Astronaut's Wife

Andrew Lazar . . . . Producer
Bethany Bilsky . . . . Creative Executive

*MADHOUSE ENTERTAINMENT
8484 Wilshire Blvd., Ste. 640
Beverly Hills, CA 90211
PHONE 310-587-2200
FAX 323-782-0491
EMAIL . . . . query@madhouseent.net
TYPES — Features - Reality TV - TV Series
DEVELOPMENT — Town Creek (WB) - Closed for the Holidays (Paramount) - Forget About It (New Line) - Monkey's Paw (Mandate) - Odd Jobs (ABC Family) - Christmas Every Day (ABC Family)
POST PRODUCTION — First Snow
SUBMISSION POLICY — Email queries; Unsolicited material will be returned unread
COMMENTS — Formerly Kustom Entertainment

Robyn Meisinger . . . . Partner/Manager/Producer
Adam Kolbrenner . . . . Partner/Manager/Producer
Trevor Stewart . . . . Story Editor
Chris Cook . . . . Associate Manager

MADISON ROAD ENTERTAINMENT
9200 Sunset Blvd., Ste.325
Los Angeles, CA 90069
PHONE 310-858-1100
FAX 310-858-1104
EMAIL . . . . info@madisonroad.com
WEB SITE . . . . www.madisonroad.com
TYPES — Animation - Direct-to-Video/DVD - Features - Reality TV - Specials
PROVIDES DEAL TO — Once A Frog Productions
DEVELOPMENT — 50 Jobs (E!) - Holidaze (Animation)
CREDITS — Treasure Hunters (NBC)

Tom Mazza . . . . Partner
Jak Severson . . . . Partner
Dan Thorman . . . . Partner
John Bronson . . . . Partner
Danica Krislovich . . . . Sr. VP, Programming
Michael Jaffa . . . . VP, Business & Legal Affairs
Chris Ceccarelli . . . . Director, Development

GUY MAGAR FILMS
11288 Ventura Blvd., Ste. 400-B
Studio City, CA 91604
PHONE 323-692-7140
FAX 323-876-9809
EMAIL . . . . filmmaking@actioncut.com
WEB SITE . . . . www.actioncut.com
TYPES — Direct-to-Video/DVD - Features - Made-for-TV/Cable Movies - TV Series
DEVELOPMENT — Encounter from Beyond - The Offspring - Justice Denied - Bounty Hunter
PRE-PRODUCTION — Dagger in the Heartland
CREDITS — Children of the Corn: Revelation - Dark Avenger - Showdown - Stepfather 3 - Retribution
SUBMISSION POLICY — No unsolicited submissions

Guy Magar . . . . Director/Writer/Producer

MAGIC LIGHT PICTURES
Pinewood Studios, Pinewood Rd.
Iver Buckinghamshire SLO 0NH, United Kingdom
PHONE .44-175-365-2778
FAX .44-175-365-5043
EMAIL .michael@magiclightpictures.com
TYPES Animation - Features
CREDITS Sparkle - Chicken Run - The Heart of Me - The Lawless Heart - Alive and Kicking - Touch of Pink - Wallace & Gromit: The Curse of the Were-Rabbit
SUBMISSION POLICY Unsolicited submissions not accepted
COMMENTS Comedy; Family

Martin Pope .Producer
Michael Rose .Producer

MAGNET MANAGEMENT
6380 Wilshire Blvd., Ste. 1606
Los Angeles, CA 90048
PHONE .See Below
FAX .323-658-8636
EMAIL .magnetasst@magnetmanagement.com
TYPES Features
DEVELOPMENT The Tingler

Jennie Frankel .Producer/Manager (323-658-8123)
Bob Sobhani .Producer/Manager (323-658-8210)
Mitch Solomon .Producer (323-456-0556)
Zach Tann .Producer/Manager (323-658-8095)
Chris Mills .Manager, Television (323-658-8706)
Michelle Markowitz .Assistant (323-456-0275)

MAGNETIC FILM
310 N. Stanley Ave.
Los Angeles, CA 90036
PHONE .310-384-3000
TYPES Features - Reality TV
DEVELOPMENT The Four Jacks - The Diameter of the Bomb - T.U.F.F. - Contact Sport
PRE-PRODUCTION Symmetry of Broken Things
CREDITS The United States of Leland

Bernie Morris .CEO/Producer
Bryan Meyers .Creative Executive
Susie Rosen .Executive Assistant

MICHAEL MAILER FILMS
443 Greenwich St., Ste. 3-A
New York, NY 10013
PHONE .212-999-6767
FAX .212-542-2540
EMAIL .trish@michaelmailerfilms.com
WEB SITE .www.michaelmailerfilms.com
TYPES Direct-to-Video/DVD - Features - Made-for-TV/Cable Movies - TV Series
DEVELOPMENT The Genesis Code - The Night Job - Neanderthal - Nothing to Declare - Break Point - Widow's Walk - The Ledge - Detour - Nantucket
POST PRODUCTION Kettle of Fish
CREDITS Loverboy - Devour - The Money Shot - Black and White - Two Girls and a Guy - Giving It Up - Harvard Man - Empire - The Last Producer - Lost Junction
SUBMISSION POLICY No unsolicited submissions

Michael Mailer .President
Trish Gonnella .Creative Executive

MAIN LINE PICTURES
7920 Sunset Blvd., Ste. 250
Los Angeles, CA 90046
PHONE .323-851-5555
WEB SITE .www.mainlinepictures.com
TYPES Features
DEVELOPMENT The Back Nine - Above and Beyond: The USS Indianapolis Story - Built with a Name
CREDITS Boxing Helena - Body Count - Good Advice - Run Ronnie Run! - Three Amigos (TV) - Dumb and Dumberer - Chasing Farrah (TV)

James Schaeffer .Chairman
Carl Mazzocone .President
Liz Hecht-Ward .Controller

MAINLINE RELEASING
301 Arizona Ave., Ste. 400
Santa Monica, CA 90401
PHONE .310-255-1200
FAX .310-255-1201
WEB SITE .www.mainlinereleasing.com
TYPES Direct-to-Video/DVD - Documentaries - Features - Made-for-TV/Cable Movies - Theatre
PRODUCTION Are You Scared?
POST PRODUCTION The Harvest
CREDITS Indiscreet - Wild Things 2&3 - Single White Female - The Psych

Rich Goldberg .President
Marc Greenberg .President
Tannaz Anisi .Sr. VP, International Sales
Joe Dickstein .Sr. VP, Marketing & Acquisitions
Marc Bienstock .Sr. VP, Production
Kelley Cauthen .VP, Post Production

MAKEMAGIC PRODUCTIONS
8489 W. Third St., Ste. 1044
Los Angeles, CA 90048
PHONE .323-653-3108
FAX .323-653-3144
EMAIL .ddavid@makemagicproductions.com
WEB SITE .www.makemagicproductions.com
TYPES Features
DEVELOPMENT Bite Me... A Love Story - The John Mack Story - Dining with Dick - The Card Game
PRE-PRODUCTION A Good American

Denise David Williams .President/Producer
Chris Duarte .Development
Jill Carty .Executive Assistant
Michelle Franklin .Assistant

MALOOF PRODUCTIONS

315 S. Beverly Dr., Ste. 211
Beverly Hills, CA 90212
PHONE .310-551-3111
FAX .310-284-9043
WEB SITE www.maloofproductions.com

TYPES	Features - Reality TV - TV Series
DEVELOPMENT	The Rucker - All the King's Men - Big Biazarro
PRE-PRODUCTION	Bullrun
UPCOMING RELEASES	Feast
COMPLETED UNRELEASED	Untitled HBO/Section Eight NBA Project
SUBMISSION POLICY	No unsolicited material
COMMENTS	Maloof Television/Maloof Motion Pictures/ Maloof Music

Phil Maloof .Owner/Chairman
Gavin Maloof .Owner
Joe Maloof .Owner
George Maloof .Owner
Adrienne Maloof .Owner
Andrew Jameson .President
Ben Pratt .Director, Development
W. Jay Moore .Creative/Adminstrative Executive

MALPASO PRODUCTIONS

c/o Warner Bros.
4000 Warner Blvd., Bldg. 81
Burbank, CA 91522-0811
PHONE .818-954-3367
FAX .818-954-4803

TYPES	Features
HAS DEAL WITH	Warner Bros. Pictures
POST PRODUCTION	Red Sun, Black Sand - Flags of Our Fathers
CREDITS	Million Dollar Baby - Mystic River - The Bridges of Madison County - Bird - Unforgiven - Space Cowboys

Clint Eastwood .Producer/Actor/Director
Robert Lorenz .Producer
Joel Cox .Film Editor

MANAGED PASSION FILMS

PO Box 491202
Los Angeles, CA 90049
PHONE .310-777-8860
FAX .310-777-8864
EMAIL .mgdpassion@aol.com

TYPES	Direct-to-Video/DVD - Features - Made-for-TV/Cable Movies
DEVELOPMENT	Three Wild Ones - Rainmaker - The Looters
CREDITS	The Hungry Bachelors Club - Deadly Little Secrets

Kimberly Becker .President

MANAGEMENT 360

9111 Wilshire Blvd.
Beverly Hills, CA 90210
PHONE .310-272-7000
FAX .310-272-0070

TYPES	Features - TV Series
HAS DEAL WITH	Warner Bros. Pictures
DEVELOPMENT	The Infiltrator

Suzan Bymel .Partner
Guymon Casady .Partner
Eric Kranzler .Partner
Evelyn O'Neill .Partner
Daniel Rappaport .Partner
David Seltzer .Partner
William Choi .Manager
Darin Friedman .Manager
Doug Johnson .Manager
Peter Kiernan .Manager
Nicole King .Manager
Bradley Lefler .Manager
Christie Smith .Manager
Lainie Stolhanske .Manager
Ben Forkner .Production

MANDALAY PICTURES

4751 Wilshire Blvd., 3rd Fl.
Los Angeles, CA 90010
PHONE .323-549-4300
FAX .323-549-9832

TYPES	Features - Made-for-TV/Cable Movies - TV Series
HAS DEAL WITH	Universal Pictures

Peter Guber .Chairman/CEO
Paul Schaeffer .Vice Chairman/COO
Randy Hermann .CFO/Executive VP
Shelly Riney .Executive VP, Corporate Operations
Elizabeth Guber Stephen .Executive VP, Motion Picture Production
Peter Strauss .Executive VP
David Zelon .Executive VP, Motion Picture Production
Michelle DiRaffaele .Sr. VP, Motion Picture Administration
Adam Stone .Creative Executive
Brian Spain .Director, Accounting & Administration

MANDALAY SPORTS ACTION ENTERTAINMENT & MANDALAY INTEGRATED MEDIA ENTERTAINMENT

4751 Wilshire Blvd., 3rd Fl.
Los Angeles, CA 90010
PHONE .323-549-4300
FAX .323-549-9844
WEB SITE .www.mandalay.com

TYPES	Documentaries - Features - Internet Content - Made-for-TV/Cable Movies - Mobile Content - Reality TV - Specials - TV Series
DEVELOPMENT	Five Seconds (Feature) - Our Father (Feature) - Rabbi Paul (Feature) - The Heart of the Man (Feature)
PRE-PRODUCTION	The Third Miracle - Running the Sahara (Documentary)
POST PRODUCTION	For Right or Wrong (AKA Burton Snowboards Feature Documentary)
COMPLETED UNRELEASED	Wonders of the World Music Series (TV)
CREDITS	Burton Snowboard US Open Special (TV) - White Space - Jason Roberts' Taste (TV) - First Daughter - Shutter Speed - First Target - WCW Superstar Series - Go for It (ABC Family) - First Shot - MIA Solved (History Channel) - The Quest for Nutrition (Discovery)
COMMENTS	Branded entertainment; Integrated Media

David G. Salzberg .President
Christian Tureaud .Producer
Martin Trejo .Producer
Joshua Cotten .Director, Development
Chris Mehl .Office Manager

MANDATE PICTURES

8750 Wilshire Blvd., Ste. 300E
Beverly Hills, CA 90211
PHONE .310-360-1441
FAX .310-360-1447
EMAIL .info@mandatepictures.com

TYPES: Features
PROVIDES DEAL TO: Three Strange Angels, Inc.
DEVELOPMENT: Jonestown Suckernucks - Dibbuck Box - Monkey's Paw - Passengers - Year of Wonders - The Ghouly Boys
PRE-PRODUCTION: Strangers - Juno
PRODUCTION: 30 Days of Night
POST PRODUCTION: Mr. Magorium's Wonder Emporium - Stranger Than Fiction - Rise - The Messengers - The Grudge 2
CREDITS: Boogeyman - The Grudge - Harold and Kumar Go to White Castle

Joe Drake .President (310-300-2062)
Nathan Kahane .President, Motion Pictures (310-300-2053)
Brian Goldsmith .CFO/Executive VP, Operations (310-300-2057)
Mali Kinberg .Sr. VP/Head, International Sales & Distribution (310-300-2071)
Helen Lee Kim .Director, International Sales (310-300-2080)
Kelli Konop .VP, Physical Production (310-300-2066)
Scott Coleman .VP, Production (310-300-2061)
Drew Crevello .VP, Production (310-300-2068)
Rob McEntegart .Executive VP, Business Affairs (310-300-2078)
John Biondo .VP, Business & Legal Affairs (310-300-2049)
Dan Freedman .VP, Business & Legal Affairs (310-300-2047)
Meredith Grindlinger .Director, Business & Legal Affairs (310-300-2048)
Jack Schuster .VP, Post Production & Worldwide Servicing (310-300-2054)
Brent Jack .Sr. VP, International Marketing (310-300-2056)
Andrew Boyd .Director, International Marketing (310-300-2052)
Jim Miller .Director, Development (310-300-2073)
Mikhail Nayfeld .Director, Television Development
Delphine Perrier .Director, Legal Affairs & Contract Administration (310-300-2051)
Jennie Yamaki .Director, Physical Production (310-300-2065)
Stephanie Phillips .Director, Publicity (310-300-2045)
Matthew Milam .Story Editor (310-300-2081)
Patricia Rivera .Human Resources/Operations Manager (310-300-2060)
Abigail Schirmann .Sales Coordinator (310-300-2077)
Jennifer Regan .Contract Administrator (310-300-2079)
Alex Valhouli .Executive Assistant to Joe Drake (310-300-2063)
Monika Ramnath .Executive Assistant to Brian Goldsmith (310-300-2058)
Daniel Duka .Executive Assistant to Scott Coleman & Jim Miller (310-300-2069)
Lynne Richardson .Executive Assistant to Rob McEntegart (310-300-2083)
Sibyl Chen .Executive Assistant to Mali Kinberg (310-300-2075)
Mary Lee .Executive Assistant to Nathan Kahane (310-300-2055)

MANDEVILLE FILMS

500 S. Buena Vista St., Animation Bldg., 2-G
Burbank, CA 91521-1783
PHONE .See Below
FAX .818-842-2937

TYPES: Features - TV Series
HAS DEAL WITH: The Walt Disney Company - Touchstone Television
DEVELOPMENT: Swiss Family Robinson - Traitor - The Fighter - The Ghost - Cellmates - Dad Knap - Never Happened - Topper - Jungle Cruise
UPCOMING RELEASES: Five Fingers
CREDITS: Eight Below (Disney) - Shaggy Dog - Mr. Wrong - The Other Sister - George of the Jungle - The Negotiator - Ryan Caufield - Bandits - Bringing Down the House - Antitrust - What's the Worst That Could Happen? - Monk - Raising Helen - The Last Shot - Walking Tall - Beauty Shop

David Hoberman .CEO/Partner (818-560-4077)
Todd Lieberman .President/Partner (818-560-4113)
Albert Page .VP, Development (818-560-7903)
Jenny Marchick .Creative Executive (818-560-7237)
Kim Meade .Executive Assistant to David Hoberman (818-560-4077)
Genevieve Gonzalez-Turner .Assistant to Todd Lieberman (818-560-4113)
Shauna Zomek .Office Assistant (818-560-7662)

MANDOKI PRODUCTIONS, INC.

c/o Keller E. Vandernorth Inc.
1133 Broadway, Ste. 911
New York, NY 10010
PHONE .212-741-0202
FAX .212-633-6317

TYPES: Animation - Commercials - Features
CREDITS: Innocent Voices - Trapped - Gaby: A True Story
SUBMISSION POLICY: Submissions not accepted
COMMENTS: Call office for current on-set address

Luis Mandoki .Director/Producer/Writer
Rebecca Husain .Writer/Development

MANDY FILMS

9201 Wilshire Blvd., Ste. 206
Beverly Hills, CA 90210
PHONE .310-246-0500
FAX .310-246-0350

TYPES: Features - Made-for-TV/Cable Movies - TV Series
DEVELOPMENT: Wonder Woman - The Sleeping Detective - First Ghost - Blackwater - Out of My Head
CREDITS: Sleeping with the Enemy - War Games - Distinguished Gentleman - Double Jeopardy - Charlie's Angels 1&2 - Ground Zero

Leonard Goldberg .President
Amanda Goldberg .VP, Development/Production
Jaime Toporovich .Executive Assistant to Leonard Goldberg
Julie Johnsen .Executive Assistant to Amanda Goldberg

*MANGO TREE PICTURES
438 Crestwood Rd.
Fairfield, CT 06824
PHONE 203-259-7771/203-470-1620
EMAIL .... nadine@willstaeger.com
WEB SITE .... www.willstaeger.com
TYPES Features - Made-for-TV/Cable Movies - Reality TV - TV Series
HAS DEAL WITH ESPN Original Entertainment (EOE)
DEVELOPMENT Painkiller - Public Enemy - Burst - Escape
PRE-PRODUCTION Warrior
CREDITS Playmakers - Tilt - 3 - The Junction Boys

Will Staeger .... Producer/Partner
Nadine Staeger .... Producer/Partner

THE MANHATTAN PROJECT, LTD.
1775 Broadway, Ste. 410
New York, NY 10019-1903
PHONE 212-258-2541
FAX 212-258-2546
TYPES Features - Made-for-TV/Cable Movies - Theatre
DEVELOPMENT Appointment in Samarra - Renato's Luck - Peace Like a River
CREDITS Dirty Rotten Scoundrels (Theatre) - Jaws - The Verdict - The Player - Deep Impact - Chocolat - Along Came a Spider - A Few Good Men - Sweet Smell of Success (Theatre) - Mr. Goldwyn (Theatre) - Framed (TV)

David Brown .... Owner/Producer
Kit Golden .... President, Production (212-258-2543)
Doris Wood .... Executive Assistant to David Brown

THE MANHEIM COMPANY
23852 Pacific Coast Hwy., Ste. 924
Malibu, CA 90265
PHONE 310-456-7272
FAX 310-456-3790
TYPES Features - Made-for-TV/Cable Movies - TV Series
CREDITS Dirty Pictures - Leap of Faith - Roe vs. Wade - Zooman

Michael Manheim .... President

MANIFEST FILM COMPANY
2525 Main St., Ste. 206
Santa Monica, CA 90405
PHONE 310-899-5554
FAX 310-452-4403
EMAIL .... info@manifestfilms.com
TYPES Features - Made-for-TV/Cable Movies - New Media - TV Series
CREDITS High Crimes - The People vs. Larry Flynt - The Joy Luck Club - Zero Effect - The Weight of Water

Janet Yang .... President/Producer

MANIFESTOVISION
63 W. 17th St., Ste. 5-A
New York, NY 10011
PHONE 212-966-7686
FAX 212-675-2009
EMAIL .... info@manifestovision.com
WEB SITE .... www.manifestovision.com
TYPES Commercials - Features - TV Series
DEVELOPMENT Black Butterflies (Feature) - Blu Tomato (TV)
UPCOMING RELEASES Come Away with Me (Feature)
CREDITS Acts of Worship - Perfume - Hostage

Nadia Leonelli .... CEO
Fredrik Sundwall .... CEO
Rob Feld .... Head, Production

JAMES MANOS PRODUCTIONS, INC.
5410 Wilshire Blvd., Ste. 602
Los Angeles, CA 90036
PHONE 323-857-1630
FAX 323-857-1465
TYPES Features - Made-for-TV/Cable Movies - TV Series
CREDITS Apollo 11 - The Ditchdigger's Daughters - The Positively True Adventures of the Alleged Texas Cheerleader Murdering Mom - The Sopranos (College Episode) - The Shield - Dexter

James Manos Jr. .... Writer/Producer
Michelle Trump .... Director, Creative Affairs

MAPLE SHADE FILMS
c/o Warner Bros.
4000 Warner Blvd., Bldg. 138. Rm. 1203
Burbank, CA 91522
PHONE 818-954-3137
TYPES Features
HAS DEAL WITH Warner Bros. Pictures
CREDITS Racing Stripes - Insomnia - A Walk to Remember - Three Kings - Catwoman

Ed McDonnell .... President
Carolyn Manetti .... VP, Production

LAURENCE MARK PRODUCTIONS
c/o Columbia Pictures
10202 W. Washington Blvd., Poitier Bldg., Ste. 3111
Culver City, CA 90232
PHONE 310-244-5239
TYPES Features - Theatre - TV Series
HAS DEAL WITH Sony Pictures Entertainment
DEVELOPMENT Twist of Fate - Salem - Sammy - Honeymoon
POST PRODUCTION Dreamgirls - The Lookout
CREDITS Last Holiday - I, Robot - Finding Forrester - Riding in Cars with Boys - As Good as It Gets - Romy & Michele's High School Reunion - Jerry Maguire - Anywhere But Here - Center Stage - The Object of My Affection - Hanging Up - Simon Birch - Working Girl

Laurence Mark .... President/Producer
David Blackman .... Sr. VP, Production (310-244-5236)
Brian Schornak .... Director, Development (310-244-3965)
Petra Alexandria .... Production Office Manager (310-244-3962)
Judy Faulkner .... Story Analyst
Chad Ahrendt .... Assistant to Laurence Mark
Kathryn Oden .... Assistant to Laurence Mark
Marcele Kutkauskaite .... Assistant to Lis Peery

THE MARSHAK/ZACHARY COMPANY
8840 Wilshire Blvd., 1st Fl.
Beverly Hills, CA 90211
PHONE .310-358-3191
FAX .310-358-3192
EMAIL .marshakzachary@aol.com
TYPES Direct-to-Video/DVD - Features - Made-for-TV/Cable Movies - Reality TV - TV Series
CREDITS Tiptoes - Tie That Binds - Carriers - For All Time
SUBMISSION POLICY Referral only

Darryl Marshak .Producer/Manager
Susan Zachary .Producer/Manager
Mitch Clem .Manager
Alan W. Mills .Associate

MARTHA STEWART LIVING OMNIMEDIA, INC.
11 W. 42nd St.
New York, NY 10036
PHONE .212-827-8000
FAX .212-827-8204
WEB SITE .www.marthastewart.com
TYPES TV Series
CREDITS MARTHA - Everyday Food

Martha Stewart .Founder
Susan Lyne .President/CEO
Sheraton Kalouria .President, TV
Gael Towey .Chief Creative Officer
Jill Boulet-Gercourt .VP, Marketing Broadcasting
Richard Clafin .VP, Broadcasting Programming
Rob Dauber .Co-Executive Producer, MARTHA

MARTIN CHASE PRODUCTIONS
500 S. Buena Vista St.
Burbank, CA 91521-1757
PHONE .818-560-3952
TYPES Direct-to-Video/DVD - Features - Made-for-TV/Cable Movies - TV Series
HAS DEAL WITH Walt Disney Pictures/Touchstone Pictures
DEVELOPMENT Just Wright - I'd Tell You, But Then I'd Have to Kill You
PRE-PRODUCTION Fast Girls
CREDITS Missing - The Sisterhood of the Traveling Pants (Warner Bros.) - The Princess Diaries 1&2 (Disney) - Missing (Lifetime) - The Cheetah Girls (Disney Channel) - Rodgers & Hammerstein's Cinderella (ABC)
SUBMISSION POLICY No unsolicited submissions

Debra Martin Chase .President/Producer
Gaylyn Fraiche .VP

MARTIN/STEIN PRODUCTIONS
1528 N. Curson Ave.
Los Angeles, CA 90046
PHONE .323-851-4870
TYPES TV Series
DEVELOPMENT Affluenza (Showtime)
COMPLETED UNRELEASED Mindy & Brenda (WB Pilot)
CREDITS The Scholar (ABC) - The Downer Channel
SUBMISSION POLICY No unsolicited material

Steve Martin .Partner/Executive Producer
Joan Stein .Partner/Executive Producer

MARVEL STUDIOS, INC.
9242 Beverly Blvd., Ste. 350
Beverly Hills, CA 90210
PHONE .310-550-3100
FAX .310-285-9825
WEB SITE .www.marvel.com
TYPES Animation - Direct-to-Video/DVD - Features - TV Series
DEVELOPMENT Ant Man - Captain America - Nick Fury - Thor - Punisher 2 - Wolverine - Magneto - Deathlok - Gargoyle - Namor: The Sub-Mariner
PRE-PRODUCTION Iron Man - The Incredible Hulk
PRODUCTION Feature: Fantastic Four 2 - Iron Man - Dr. Strange; DVD Animated TV: Fantastic Four
POST PRODUCTION Ghost Rider - Spider-Man 3
UPCOMING RELEASES DVD Animated Feature: Ultimate Avengers 2
CREDITS Fantastic Four - Daredevil - Spider-Man 1&2 - X-Men 1-3 - Punisher - Blade 1-3 - Hulk - Elektra; TV: X-Men Evolution; DVD: Ultimate Avengers - Blade (TV)
SUBMISSION POLICY No unsolicited submissions
COMMENTS Stan Lee, Chairman Emeritus

Avi Arad .Creative Advisor
Michael Helfant .President/COO
Kevin Feige .President, Production
Tim Rothwell .President, Worldwide Consumer Products Media Group
Ari Arad .Executive VP, Production
Eric Rollman .Executive VP, Home Entertainment & TV Production
Michael E. Marshall .Sr. VP, Business & Legal Affairs
Ron Hohauser .Sr. VP, Finance & Operations
Craig Kyle .VP, Creative Development, Animation
Ames Kirshen .VP, Interactive
Mark Rhodes .VP, Retail Development
Jeremy Latcham .Creative Executive
Jana Haney .Creative/Marketing Coordinator
Kyla Kraman .Executive Assistant to Avi Arad
Stephen Broussard .Executive Assistant to Kevin Feige & Ari Arad
Steve Grantowitz .Executive Assistant to Michael Helfant
Joshua Fine .Executive Assistant to Craig Kyle

NIKI MARVIN PRODUCTIONS, INC.
8919 Harratt St., Ste. 304
Los Angeles, CA 90069
PHONE .310-274-6320
FAX .310-274-3890
TYPES Documentaries - Features - Made-for-TV/Cable Movies - TV Series
CREDITS A Nightmare on Elm Street 3: Dream Warriors - Buried Alive 1&2 - The Shawshank Redemption - Private Islands - Flying High - Inside Dallas

Niki Marvin .Producer/Director/Writer

MARVISTA ENTERTAINMENT

12519 Venice Blvd.
Los Angeles, CA 90066
PHONE .310-737-0950
FAX .310-737-9115
EMAIL .info@marvista.net
WEB SITE .www.marvista.net

TYPES	Features - Made-for-TV/Cable Movies - TV Series
HAS DEAL WITH	Brookwell McNamara Entertainment, Inc.
PRODUCTION	Past Sins
COMPLETED UNRELEASED	Instant Message - Night of Terror - Beyond the Break - Disaster Zone: Volcano in NY
CREDITS	Absolute Zero - Love Thy Neighbor - Disaster Zone - Volcano in New York - Inhabited - Lost at Home - Terminal Error - Trapped: Buried Alive
COMMENTS	Includes MarVista Home Entertainment, US DVD label, seeking product for home video market and worldwide sales

Joseph Szew .President/CEO
Michael Jacobs .President, Production & Distribution
Fernando Szew .Managing Director/COO
George Port .Executive VP
Tom Emma .VP, Business Affairs
Zac Reeder .Head, Acquisitions
Carol Holdsworth .Sales & Marketing
JJ Lopez .Distribution Supervisor
Sue Sprecher .Sales
Anoosh Tertzakian .Office Manager

TIMOTHY MARX PRODUCTIONS, INC.

17177 Adlon Rd.
Encino, CA 91436
PHONE .818-789-4344

TYPES	Documentaries - Features - Made-for-TV/Cable Movies - TV Series
DEVELOPMENT	Thorpe Project - Say Hey - Henry the Steinway
CREDITS	Justice (Fox) - Invasion - Neil Simon's The Goodbye Girl (TNT) - Arli$$ - Citizen X - Passed Away - Smooth Talk - Entourage (HBO)

Timothy Marx .Producer

MASE/KAPLAN PRODUCTIONS, INC.

5314 Wortser Ave.
Sherman Oaks, CA 91401
PHONE .213-304-5267

TYPES	Features - Made-for-TV/Cable Movies - TV Series
CREDITS	Red Shoe Diaries - Strangers - She's So Lovely - Buffalo '66 - Dark Prince - John Q. - The Notebook - Raise Your Voice - Alpha Dog
SUBMISSION POLICY	No unsolicited submissions

Avram Butch Kaplan .Producer

MATADOR PICTURES

12021 Wilshire Blvd., Ste. 117
Los Angeles, CA 90025
PHONE .310-472-6220/44-20-7025-8028
FAX .310-472-6223/44-20-7504-8555
EMAIL .info@matadorpictures.com
WEB SITE .www.matadorpictures.com

TYPES	Features
POST PRODUCTION	Senseless
UPCOMING RELEASES	The Wind That Shakes the Barley - Voodoo Lagoon - Dark Corners - Cargo
CREDITS	Ae Fond Kiss... - Ashes and Sand - Chaos and Cadavers - Mad Dogs and Englishmen - The Fall - Dead Funny - Mortal Kombat - Princess in Love - Another Life - Ten Minutes Older: The Trumpet - Ten Minutes Older: The Cello
SUBMISSION POLICY	No unsolicited material
COMMENTS	UK office: 18 Soho Square, London, W1D 3QL, United Kingdom

Lauri Apelian .Producer/Partner (LA)
Nigel Thomas .Producer/Partner (UK)
Charlotte Walls .Associate Producer (UK)

THE MATTHAU COMPANY, INC.

11661 San Vicente Blvd., Ste. 609
Los Angeles, CA 90049
PHONE .310-454-3300
WEB SITE .www.matthau.com

TYPES	Commercials - Features - Made-for-TV/Cable Movies - Music Videos - Reality TV - TV Series
DEVELOPMENT	Freaky Deaky - Joy - Double Trouble - The Desert Fox - Picasso Blue Period
POST PRODUCTION	Her Minor Thing
CREDITS	Hanging Up - Mrs. Lambert Remembers Love - The Grass Harp - Grumpier Old Men - The Marriage Fool - Dennis the Menace - Doin' Time on Planet Earth

Charles Matthau .President
Lana Morgan .Director, Creative Affairs
Sam Levin .Director, Business Affairs
Jeff Bullard .Director, Technology
Ashley Anderson .Creative Executive
Jessica Cooper .Business Affairs
Reuben Sack .Story Editor

SCOTT MAURO ENTERTAINMENT, INC.

8436 W. Third St., Ste. 650
Los Angeles, CA 90048
PHONE .323-951-9970
FAX .323-951-9971
EMAIL .shmauro@aol.com

TYPES	Specials
PRODUCTION	Princess Grace Awards
CREDITS	16th & 17th Annual Producers Guild Awards - Independence Day, July 4th Special 2 (ABC) - The Seventh & Eighth Annual Soap Opera Update Awards (Lifetime) - Rosemary Clooney's Golden Anniversary: An All Star Salute (A&E) - The Whimsical World of Oz (PBS) - Night of 100 Stars (NBC) - Grand Opening of Disney/MGM Studios (NBC)
COMMENTS	TV Specials only; Cable, network and syndication

Scott Mauro .President/Producer
Brian Fitzmorris .Production Manager
Stuart Weissman .Production Manager
Worth Howe .Associate

MAVERICK FILMS
331 N. Maple Dr., 3rd Fl.
Beverly Hills, CA 90210
PHONE 310-276-6177
FAX 310-276-9477

TYPES	Direct-to-Video/DVD - Features - Made-for-TV/Cable Movies - Miniseries - Reality TV - TV Series
DEVELOPMENT	Percy Jackson and the Lightning Thief - One Giant Leap (MOW) - Twilight - The Whale - Deep Cover (Series)- That Gay Ghost (Series) - Untitled Us Weekly Project (Series) - Exposed (Series) - San Rafael (Series)
PRE-PRODUCTION	Stepfather - The Stanford Prison Experiment
PRODUCTION	My Sassy Girl - Lowlife (Series) - Untitled Rolling Stone Project (Series)
UPCOMING RELEASES	Material Girls
COMPLETED UNRELEASED	Sam's Lake - Cruel World
CREDITS	Turn It Up - Agent Cody Banks 1&2 - 30 Days Until I'm Famous - Chasing Christmas

Madonna . . . . Principal/Producer
Guy Oseary . . . . Principal/Producer
Mark Morgan . . . . CEO/President
Brent Emery . . . . Sr. VP, Development
Tara Pirnia . . . . Producer
Michael Rosenberg . . . . President, TV
Michele Zieger . . . . Producer
Rachel Rothman . . . . Producer
Eric Thompson . . . . Producer
Jennifer Chambers . . . . Director, TV Development
Naomi Beaty . . . . Creative Executive

MAYA PICTURES
1201 W. 5th St., Ste. T-210
Los Angeles, CA 90017
PHONE 213-534-3845
FAX 213-534-3846

TYPES	Features - Made-for-TV/Cable Movies - Miniseries
DEVELOPMENT	Rain of Gold - Two Badges
CREDITS	Walkout
SUBMISSION POLICY	No phone calls; Latino directors from backgrounds including film, music videos, commercials and TV series will be considered

Moctesuma Esparza . . . . CEO/Producer
Kimberly Myers . . . . Producer
Tery Lopez . . . . Development
Tonantzin Esparza . . . . Development
Luis Guerrero . . . . Executive Assistant

MAYHEM PICTURES
725 Arizona Ave., Ste. 302
Santa Monica, CA 90401
PHONE 310-393-5005
FAX 310-393-5017

TYPES	Features - TV Series
HAS DEAL WITH	Walt Disney Pictures/Touchstone Pictures
DEVELOPMENT	The Feynman Chronicles
PRODUCTION	Daddy's Girl
CREDITS	Invincible - The New Guy - The Rookie - Miracle

Mark Ciardi . . . . Producer
Gordon Gray . . . . Producer
Victor Constantino . . . . Sr. VP, Production & Development
Megan McNichol . . . . Assistant

***THE MAYHEM PROJECT**
1041 N. Formosa Ave., Formosa Bldg. 106
West Hollywood, CA 90046
PHONE 323-850-3850
FAX 323-850-3860
EMAIL . . . . mayhem@themayhemproject.com
WEB SITE . . . . www.themayhemproject.com

TYPES	Features
DEVELOPMENT	Sanctuary - Again - Smoke - Free Runner - Duane Adler Dance Project
PRE-PRODUCTION	Clock Tower

Anthony Mosawi . . . . Chairman/CEO
Brad Luff . . . . Production President
Paul Doble . . . . Production Executive
Jennifer Rogers . . . . Production Executive
Alison Abaro . . . . Operations

MBST ENTERTAINMENT, INC.
345 N. Maple Dr., Ste. 200
Beverly Hills, CA 90210
PHONE 310-385-1820
FAX 310-385-1834

TYPES	Features - Theatre - TV Series
DEVELOPMENT	Modern Bride - Prodigy - Ghostwalker - The Club - Ride Along - Finishing School
CREDITS	The Greatest Game Ever Played - Arthur - Throw Momma from the Train - Good Morning, Vietnam - Krippendorf's Tribe - Angie - Freddy Got Fingered - Sorority Boys - The Last Shot

Larry Brezner . . . . Partner
David Steinberg . . . . Partner
Stephen Tenenbaum . . . . Partner
Jonathan Brandstein . . . . No Title
Meegan Kelso . . . . No Title
Andrew D. Tenenbaum . . . . No Title

MEDIA 8 ENTERTAINMENT

1875 Century Park East, Ste. 2000
Los Angeles, CA 90067
PHONE .310-226-8300
FAX .310-226-8350
WEB SITE www.media8entertainment.com
TYPES Features
DEVELOPMENT Wedding Daze - Challenger - The Ramen Girl
PRE-PRODUCTION Reaper
UPCOMING RELEASES Man About Town - Lovewrecked
CREDITS Running Scared - The Upside of Anger - Monster - Havoc - 11:14 - Santa's Slay - Jungle Book - The Musketeer - The United States of Leland - Extreme Ops - FearDotCom - The Body - Eye of the Beholder
SUBMISSION POLICY No unsolicited submissions

Sammy Lee .Chairman of the Board
Stewart Hall .Producer/Board Member
Jenna Sanz-Agero .President
Jimmy Li .Sr. VP, Strategic & Financial Planning
Liz Mackiewicz .Sr. VP, Worldwide Distribution
Devin Cutler .VP, Finance & Controller
Tiffany Leclere .VP, Business & Legal Affairs
Audrey Delaney .Acquisitions & Development
Randy Dannenberg .Director, Creative Affairs
Philip Hall .Manager, Creative Affairs

MEDIA FINANCIAL INTERNATIONAL, LLC

4117-1/2 Radford Ave.
Studio City, CA 91604
PHONE .818-505-6635
FAX .818-505-6636
TYPES Features
CREDITS Next Stop Wonderland - National Lampoon's Van Wilder - Squeeze
COMMENTS Finance; Foreign sales

Ari Newman .President
Lee Beckett .Producer
Josh Blumenthal .Corporate Communications

MEDIA FOUR

8840 Wilshire Blvd., 2nd Fl.
Beverly Hills, CA 90211
PHONE .310-358-3288
FAX .310-358-3188
TYPES Features - Made-for-TV/Cable Movies - Specials - TV Series
DEVELOPMENT Julie Andrews/Carol Burnett Special
CREDITS Before They Were Stars - George - Whereabouts of Jenny

Steve Sauer .Founding Partner
Jane McKnight .Manager, Administration

MEDIA TALENT GROUP

9200 Sunset Blvd., Ste. 550
West Hollywood, CA 90069
PHONE .310-275-7900
FAX .310-275-7910
TYPES Features - TV Series
DEVELOPMENT Bitten - Hail Mary - Nevada Smith - Obsessed - Party Girl Chronicles - Savant - Old Days - Floyd Collins - Void Moon
POST PRODUCTION .45 - School for Scoundrels
CREDITS Film: Bad News Bears - Beyond Borders; TV: Going to California - Hope & Faith

Geyer Kosinski .Chairman/CEO
Tucker Tooley .Producer
Brad Marks .Manager/Producer
Chris Davey .Manager/Producer

MEDUSA FILM

1800 Avenue of the Stars, Ste. 470
Los Angeles, CA 90067
PHONE .310-553-7900/39-06-663-901
FAX .310-553-7901/39-06-6639-0450
EMAIL .infofilm@medusa.it
WEB SITE .www.medusa.it
TYPES Features
CREDITS Callas Forever - Remember Me, My Love - The Dreamers - Beyond Borders - The Triumph of Love - Malena - Tea With Mussolini - I Giorni Dell'Abbandono - The Consequences of Love - Oliver Twist - Last Kiss
SUBMISSION POLICY Cast and known director attached
COMMENTS European office: Via Aurelia Antica 422/424, Rome, 00165, Italy

Giampaolo Letta .CEO

MELEE ENTERTAINMENT

144 S. Beverly Dr., Ste. 402
Beverly Hills, CA 90212
PHONE .310-248-3931
FAX .310-248-3921
WEB SITE .www.melee.com
TYPES Features
DEVELOPMENT Viagra Falls
CREDITS Love Chronicles - You Got Served - Friday - I Got the Hook Up
SUBMISSION POLICY No unsolicited submissions

Bryan Turner .No Title
Scott Aronson .No Title
Christopher Dehau Lee .No Title
Michael Regen .No Title
Dani Dufresne .No Title
Mathieu Ratthe .No Title

BILL MELENDEZ PRODUCTIONS
13400 Riverside Dr., Ste. 201
Sherman Oaks, CA 91423-2501
PHONE 818-382-7382
FAX 818-382-7377
EMAIL . . . . . billmelprod@aol.com
WEB SITE . . . . . www.billmelendez.tv

TYPES	Animation - Commercials - Direct-to-Video/DVD - Features - TV Series
HAS DEAL WITH	ABC Entertainment Television Group - Paramount Home Entertainment
DEVELOPMENT	Kick the Football, Charlie Brown
PRE-PRODUCTION	Macy's Holiday Spot - MET Life Spot - The Wonderful World of Leprechauns (Feature)
COMPLETED UNRELEASED	He's a Bully, Charlie Brown
CREDITS	Knott's Berry Farm - A Charlie Brown Valentine - It's the Great Pumpkin, Charlie Brown - A Charlie Brown Christmas - A Charlie Brown Thanksgiving - Cathy - Garfield; Commercials: Met Life - McDonalds - Hallmark - Nissay Insurance - Calbee Cereals
COMMENTS	Peanuts characters worldwide; Distribution deal with Paramount Home Video

Bill Melendez . . . . . President
Warren Taylor . . . . . Production Coordinator/Line Producer
Sandy Arnold . . . . . Casting/Recording
Joanna Coletta . . . . . Office Manager, Budgets/Accounting

BARRY MENDEL PRODUCTIONS
100 Universal City Plaza, Bungalow 5163
Universal City, CA 91608
PHONE 818-733-3076
FAX 818-733-4070

TYPES	Features
HAS DEAL WITH	Universal Pictures
DEVELOPMENT	Appointment in Samarra
CREDITS	Munich - Serenity - The Life Aquatic with Steve Zissou - The Royal Tenenbaums - The Sixth Sense - Rushmore - Unbreakable

Barry Mendel . . . . . No Title
Neal Dusedau . . . . . No Title

MERCER FILM GROUP INC.
647 Camino de los Mares, Ste. 108-93
San Clemente, CA 92673
PHONE 323-462-4184
EMAIL . . . . . development@mercerfilm.tv
WEB SITE . . . . . www.mercerfilm.tv

TYPES	Features - Made-for-TV/Cable Movies - TV Series
DEVELOPMENT	Alex Clemente
CREDITS	Ambush of Ghosts - I Woke Up Early the Day I Died - The Gold Cup

Jennifer Arundale . . . . . President
Scott Arundale . . . . . Producer

MERCHANT-IVORY
250 W. 57th St., Ste. 1825
New York, NY 10107
PHONE 212-582-8049
FAX 212-459-9201
WEB SITE . . . . . www.merchantivory.com

TYPES	Commercials - Documentaries - Features - Internet Content - Made-for-TV/Cable Movies - Miniseries - Music Videos - Theatre - TV Series
DEVELOPMENT	The Playmaker - Giovanni's Room
PRE-PRODUCTION	Made in France
PRODUCTION	The City of Your Final Destination
CREDITS	The White Countess - Heights - Le Divorce - The Mystic Masseur - The Golden Bowl - Cotton Mary - A Soldier's Daughter Never Cries - The Proprietary - Jefferson in Paris - Slaves of New York - Maurice - Howards End - A Room with a View - Surviving Picasso - The Remains of the Day - The Bostonians - Merci Dr. Rey
SUBMISSION POLICY	No unsolicited material; Fax queries

James Ivory . . . . . President/Director
Richard Hawley . . . . . Executive VP/Producer/Director
Pierre Proner . . . . . Director, Production
Chiara Barlassina . . . . . Coordinator

METRO-GOLDWYN-MAYER STUDIOS, INC. (MGM)
10250 Constellation Blvd.
Los Angeles, CA 90067
PHONE 310-449-3000
WEB SITE . . . . . www.mgm.com

TYPES	Features - Made-for-TV/Cable Movies
PROVIDES DEAL TO	Danjaq, LLC - Irish DreamTime - The Robert Simonds Company - Winkler Films
UPCOMING RELEASES	DOA: Dead or Alive - Flyboys - Stormbreaker - Killshot - Bobby - Home of the Brave - Rocky Balboa - Miss Potter
CREDITS	Clerks II - Lucky Number Slevin - Capote - The Pink Panther - Into the Blue - The Woods - Soul Plane - Barbershop 1&2 - Walking Tall - Die Another Day - Windtalkers - Crocodile Hunter - Original Sin - Legally Blonde 1&2 - Hannibal - Heartbreakers - Autumn in New York - Antitrust - The Thomas Crown Affair - The World Is Not Enough - Supernova - Return to Me - Good Boy - Agent Cody Banks - Out of Time - DeLovely - Wicker Park

Harry E. Sloan . . . . . Chairman/CEO
Rick Sands . . . . . COO
Clark Woods . . . . . President, Domestic Theatrical Distribution
Jim Packer . . . . . President, Worldwide TV Distribution
Charles Cohen . . . . . Executive VP
Douglas Lee . . . . . Executive VP, Worldwide Digital Media Group
Scott Packman . . . . . Executive VP/General Counsel
Joe Patrick . . . . . Executive VP, Domestic Distribution
Jeff Pryor . . . . . Executive VP, Corporate Communications
Bruce Tuchman . . . . . Executive VP, MGM Networks

PATRICIA K. MEYER PRODUCTIONS
511 Hill St., Ste. 313
Santa Monica, CA 90405
PHONE .310-392-0422
FAX .310-264-3979
EMAIL .pk.meyer@verizon.net
TYPES: Features - Made-for-TV/Cable Movies - TV Series
CREDITS: The Women of Brewster Place - This Is My Life - Menu for Murder (CBS) - Beyond Suspicion (NBC) - The Other Woman (NBC) - Home Song - Take Me Home Again - The List (Short)

Patricia K. Meyer .Writer/Producer

MGA ENTERTAINMENT/MGA ENTERTAINMENT FILMS
16380 Roscoe Blvd.
Van Nuys, CA 91406-1221
PHONE .818-894-2525
FAX .818-221-4400
WEB SITE .www.mgae.com
TYPES: Animation - Commercials - Direct-to-Video/DVD - Features - TV Series
DEVELOPMENT: Bratz Babyz II - Bratz Musical Story Movie - Bratz Genie Magic II - Bratz Sportz - Live-Action Bratz Feature - Princess Twins
PRE-PRODUCTION: Bratz Fashion Pixiez - Bratz Kidz Sleep-Over Adventure
POST PRODUCTION: Alien Racers (Animated TV Series)
UPCOMING RELEASES: Bratz Passion for Fashion Diamondz (DVD) - Bratz Babyz (DVD)
CREDITS: Bratz Genie Magic - Bratz: The Video! Starrin' & Stylin' (DVD) - Bratz Rock Angelz (DVD) - Alien Racers: The Animated Series - Bratz: The Animated Series
SUBMISSION POLICY: Contact Jay Fukuto or Lisa Melbye

Isaac Larian .CEO, MGA Entertainment
Jay Fukuto .VP, Entertainment
Dave Malacrida .VP, Public & Media Relations
Lisa Melbye .Director, Entertainment
Rachel Griffin .Director, Public & Media Relations
Ken Kauffman .Advertising Executive

MICHAEL MELTZER PRODUCTIONS
12207 Riverside Dr., Ste. 208
Valley Village, CA 91607
PHONE .818-766-8339
TYPES: Direct-to-Video/DVD - Features - Made-for-TV/Cable Movies - TV Series
DEVELOPMENT: Tomorrow's Child - All Girl Band - Bite Me... A Love Story - Bad Road
PRE-PRODUCTION: Tooth and Nail
PRODUCTION: Dark Honeymoon
POST PRODUCTION: The Dread
UPCOMING RELEASES: Kalamazoo
CREDITS: Carnival of Souls - The Hidden - Up the Creek - Dead Heat
SUBMISSION POLICY: No unsolicited submissions

Michael L. Meltzer .Producer (melmax@aol.com)
Linda Smith .Associate

TERENCE MICHAEL PRODUCTIONS, INC.
421 Waterview St.
Playa del Rey, CA 90293
PHONE .310-823-3432
FAX .310-861-9093
EMAIL .tm@terencemichael.com
WEB SITE .www.terencemichael.com
TYPES: Features - Made-for-TV/Cable Movies - Reality TV
HAS DEAL WITH: MTV Networks
DEVELOPMENT: Super Sizemore
PRODUCTION: M.I.L.F.
COMPLETED UNRELEASED: Love for Rent
CREDITS: Never Again (Universal/Focus) - I Shot a Man in Vegas (Lakeshore) - If Lucy Fell (TriStar) - Wirey Spindell - Chill Factor (Warner) - 100 Girls (Lionsgate) - The Pact (Lifetime TV) - Going Greek (Showtime) - Duets (MTV) - Road to Ironman (NBC) - The Skateboard Show (WB) - According to Spencer (Lionsgate) - Mind the Gap (Showtime) - Family Business (Showtime)
SUBMISSION POLICY: Via email

Terence Michael .Producer
Jeanne Trepanier .Director, Development

MIDNIGHT SUN PICTURES
501 Colorado Ave., Ste. 206
Santa Monica, CA 90401
PHONE .310-440-5853
FAX .310-440-9167
WEB SITE .www.midnightsunpictures.com
TYPES: Features - TV Series
UPCOMING RELEASES: The Covenant
CREDITS: Die Hard 2 - Blast from the Past - Deep Blue Sea - Speechless - Cliffhanger - The Long Kiss Goodnight - T.R.A.X. - Driven - Mindhunters - Exorcist: The Beginning
SUBMISSION POLICY: No unsolicited material; Submit through representation only

Renny Harlin .Director/Producer
Nikki Stanghetti .Executive Assistant to Renny Harlin

MIKE'S MOVIES/MICHAEL PEYSER PRODUCTIONS
627 N. Las Palmas
Los Angeles, CA 90004
PHONE .323-462-4690
FAX .323-462-4699
TYPES: Animation - Documentaries - Features
DEVELOPMENT: Dragster - The Laundry Warrior - Florence - St. Vincent - Lover's Leap - Golden State - The Wedding Dress - Paris Trance - Orphan Train - The Flyer - Dot or Feather? - Miscommunication
CREDITS: Matilda - The Distinguished Gentleman - Big Business - Ruthless People - F/X Desperately Seeking Susan - The Purple Rose of Cairo - Hackers - Camp Nowhere - The Night We Never Met - SLC Punk! - Imagining Argentina

Michael Peyser .Producer
E. Nicholas Mariani .Director, Development

MILLENNIUM FILMS
6423 Wilshire Blvd.
Los Angeles, CA 90048
PHONE 310-388-6900
FAX 310-388-6901

TYPES	Features
PROVIDES DEAL TO	Emmett/Furla Films - Two Sticks Productions
DEVELOPMENT	Red Sonja
PRE-PRODUCTION	Rambo IV
PRODUCTION	Day of the Dead
POST PRODUCTION	The Death and Life of Bobby Z - 88 Minutes - Wicked Little Things - Journey to the End of the Night - Lonely Hearts
UPCOMING RELEASES	Home of the Brave
CREDITS	The Black Dahlia - The Wicker Man - 16 Blocks - Guinevere - How to Kill Your Neighbor's Dog - Replicant - Nobody's Baby - Undisputed - Prozac Nation - The Grey Zone - The Tenants - Endgame
SUBMISSION POLICY	No unsolicited material

Avi Lerner . . . . Co-Chairman/CEO
Danny Dimbort . . . . Co-Chairman/CEO
Trevor Short . . . . CFO
Joe Gatta . . . . Executive VP/Head
Boaz Davidson . . . . Head, Production & Creative Affairs
Ben Nedivi . . . . Creative Executive

MILLER/BOYETT PRODUCTIONS
268 W. 44th St., 4th Fl.
New York, NY 10036
PHONE 212-702-9779/212-702-8721
FAX 212-702-0899

TYPES	Theatre - TV Series
HAS DEAL WITH	Warner Bros. Television Production
CREDITS	Two of a Kind - Family Matters - Full House - Laverne & Shirley - Happy Days - Mork & Mindy - Perfect Strangers; Theater: A Year with Frog and Toad - Jumpers - Spamalot - Democracy - Fiddler on the Roof - The Pillowman - Drowsy Chaperone - History Boys
COMMENTS	Broadway and Off-Broadway; Musical Theatre; Robert Boyett Theatricals

Thomas L. Miller . . . . Executive Producer
Robert L. Boyett . . . . Executive Producer
Diane Murphy . . . . VP

MINDFIRE ENTERTAINMENT
3740 Overland Ave., Ste. E
Los Angeles, CA 90034
PHONE 310-204-4481
FAX 310-204-5882
WEB SITE . . . . www.mindfireentertainment.com

TYPES	Animation - Direct-to-Video/DVD - Features - Internet Content - Made-for-TV/Cable Movies - Miniseries - Mobile Content - Reality TV - Specials - TV Series
DEVELOPMENT	True Lust - The Night the Condom Broke - Marauder - Fear Effect
PRE-PRODUCTION	House of the Dead 3
POST PRODUCTION	Dead & Deader - Caught on Tape
UPCOMING RELEASES	Room 6 - The Thirst - The Darkroom - DOA: Dead or Alive
COMPLETED UNRELEASED	The Thirst
CREDITS	Free Enterprise - The Specials - The House of the Dead 1&2 - All Souls Day
COMMENTS	Includes Ray Harryhausen Presents projects

Mark Gottwald . . . . Chairman
Mark A. Altman . . . . CEO
Chuck Speed . . . . Sr. VP, Business Development & Business Affairs
Nick Stamos . . . . Line Producer
Aaron Ratner . . . . Post Production
Kim Stulwich . . . . Story Analyst

MIRAGE ENTERPRISES
9220 Sunset Blvd., Ste. 106
West Hollywood, CA 90069
PHONE 310-888-2830/44-207-284-5588
FAX 310-888-2825/44-207-284-5599

TYPES	Features
HAS DEAL WITH	The Weinstein Company
DEVELOPMENT	Turbulence - I Don't Know How She Does It - Bartimaeus - Shock Proof Sydney Skate - Colombian Gold - Liberty - The Ninth Life of Louis Drax - The Number One Ladies Detective Agency - Three Bad Men - Triage - The Resurrectionist - Story of You
POST PRODUCTION	Michael Clayton - Catch a Fire - Breaking and Entering - Margaret
CREDITS	Sketches of Frank Gehry - The Interpreter - Cold Mountain - Sliding Doors - The Talented Mr. Ripley - Random Hearts - Up at the Villa - Heaven - Blow Dry - Iris - Birthday Girl - The Quiet American
COMMENTS	UK office: Old Chapel Studios, 19 Fleet Rd., London NW3 2QR, United Kingdom

Sydney Pollack . . . . Producer/Director
Anthony Minghella . . . . Producer/Director
Laurie Webb . . . . VP, Development
Tim Bricknell . . . . Executive Assistant to Mr. Minghella
Caroline Harvey . . . . Creative Executive
Jenny McLaren . . . . Office Manager
Ralph Millero . . . . Assistant to Mr. Pollack
Donna Ostroff . . . . Executive Assistant to Mr. Pollack
Keri Wilson . . . . Creative Assistant to Mr. Pollack
Andrew Miller . . . . Executive/Development Assistant to Laurie Webb

MIRAMAX FILMS
161 Avenue of the Americas
New York, NY 10013-2338
PHONE 917-606-5500
FAX 917-606-5643
WEB SITE . . . . www.miramax.com

TYPES	Documentaries - Features
DEVELOPMENT	Becoming Jane - There Will Be Blood - The Lookout - No Country for Old Men - Gnomeo & Juliet - Timothy Leary: A Biography
UPCOMING RELEASES	Once in a Lifetime - The Night Listener
CREDITS	Kinky Boots - Keeping Up With the Steins - The Heart of the Game
COMMENTS	West Coast office: 8439 Sunset Blvd., West Hollywood, CA 90069, phone: 323-822-4100, fax: 323-822-4216

Daniel Battsek . . . . President
Keri Putnam . . . . President, Production
Emily Bear . . . . Executive VP, Publicity
Jason Cassidy . . . . Executive VP, Marketing
Michael Luisi . . . . Executive VP, Business & Legal Affairs
Linda Borgeson . . . . Sr. VP, Post Production
Jennifer Horowitz . . . . Sr. VP/Controller
Kristin Jones . . Sr. VP, Production, International Development & Acquisitions
Colleen Seldin . . . . Sr. VP, Worldwide Distribution & Operations
Elliot Slutzky . . . . Sr. VP/General Sales Manager
Christopher Brescia . . . . VP, Business Affairs & Delivery
Peter Lawson . . . . VP, Acquisitions
Rosalind Lawton . . . . VP, Business & Legal Affairs
Peter McPartlin . . . . VP, Business & Legal Affairs
Julie Daccord . . . . Director, Contracts Administration
Lindsay Nadler . . . . Sr. Manager, Human Resources

MIRANDA ENTERTAINMENT
7337 Pacific View Dr.
Los Angeles, CA 90068
PHONE 323-874-3600
FAX 323-851-5350
EMAIL .....clorenz1@aol.com

TYPES	Features - TV Series
PRODUCTION	Chlorine - Periphery Hammers On
COMPLETED UNRELEASED	Neverwas - Rise
CREDITS	Don't Come Knocking - Trapped - Harold and Kumar Go to White Castle - The Grudge - Boogeyman
SUBMISSION POLICY	No unsolicited materials

Carsten Lorenz .....Producer

THE MIRISCH CORPORATION
100 Universal City Plaza, Bldg. 1320, Ste. 2C
Universal City, CA 91608-1085
PHONE 818-777-1271
FAX 818-866-1422

TYPES	Animation - Features - Made-for-TV/Cable Movies - TV Series
CREDITS	In the Heat of the Night - The Magnificent Seven - Hawaii - Two for the Seesaw - Midway - Same Time Next Year

Walter Mirisch .....Producer
Bonnie Blume .....Assistant

MISHER FILMS
5555 Melrose Ave., Swanson Bldg.
Los Angeles, CA 90038
PHONE 323-956-8333
FAX 323-862-1111
WEB SITE .....www.misherfilms.com

TYPES	Features - TV Series
HAS DEAL WITH	ABC Entertainment Television Group - Paramount Pictures
DEVELOPMENT	The Day the World Came to Town (Universal) - Untitled Basketball Project (Paramount/MTV) - The Day I Turned Uncool (Paramount) - It Takes a Thief (Universal) - Life & Def (Paramount Classics) - The Clearing (Universal) - Closed Chambers (Universal) - Parents on Strike (Paramount) - Glory Days (Paramount) - It's Kind of Funny
PRE-PRODUCTION	Case No. 39 (Paramount)
CREDITS	The Scorpion King (Universal) - The Rundown (Universal) - The Interpreter (Universal)
SUBMISSION POLICY	No unsolicited submissions

Kevin Misher .....Producer/Owner
Patrick Baker .....President, Feature Development & Production
Andy Berman .....Director, Feature Development
Swanna MacNair .....Director, Feature Development
Tiffany Baker .....Manager, TV
Kevin Chang .....Creative Executive, Video/Interactive Department
Weston Cookler .....Assistant to Andy Berman & Swanna MacNair
Sarah Ezrin .....Assistant to Kevin Misher
Alice Pao .....Assistant to Patrick Baker

RENÉE MISSEL PRODUCTIONS
201 W. Eucalyptus, Ste. 4
Ojai, CA 93023
PHONE 310-463-0638
FAX 805-669-4511
EMAIL .....filmtao@aol.com

TYPES	Features
DEVELOPMENT	The Prodigal Spy - Rogue Scholar - Milarepa - Street Zen
CREDITS	Resurrection - Nell - Defenseless - The Main Event - Guy - My Man Adam

Renée Missel .....Producer
Bridget Stone .....Story Editor

MISSION ENTERTAINMENT
590 Madison Ave., 21st Fl.
New York, NY 10022
PHONE 646-403-9956
EMAIL .....info@missionnyc.com
SECOND EMAIL .....whatsthe411@vogelmediainc.com
WEB SITE .....www.missionnyc.com
SECOND WEB SITE .....www.vogelmediainc.com

TYPES	Animation - Commercials - Documentaries - Features - Music Videos
DEVELOPMENT	Speed Kills - Abaddon - Willing Suspension of Disbelief - 211: Master Thief (Shorts)
PRODUCTION	211: Master Thief (Video Game)
POST PRODUCTION	Untitled Patti Smith Documentary
CREDITS	Requiem for a Dream - Pi
SUBMISSION POLICY	No unsolicited submissions
COMMENTS	Also the Creative & Commercial Director for Vogel Media, Inc.; Takes on special assignments in industrial design, Web development and design, branded entertainment, video game design and development

M. Scott Vogel .....Director/Writer/Producer/Partner
Jordanna Vogel .....Producer/Manager/Partner

*MISTRE FILMS
3450 E. Thousand Oaks Blvd., Box No. 3422
Westlake Village, CA 91359-0422
PHONE 310-883-5330
EMAIL .....rogerellis@mistrefilms.com
WEB SITE .....www.mistrefilms.com

DEVELOPMENT	The Prince and the Fopper - Lust for Wife - Ghost Cow - Dial 90310 for Murder
PRE-PRODUCTION	Black Ties 'N White Trash (TNT)
COMMENTS	Investor financing for film projects

Roger R. Ellis .....Principal
Heather Ashley .....Executive Assistant
Kassie Hughes .....Executive Assistant

MM PRODUCTIONS
1351 Fourth St., Ste. 201
Santa Monica, CA 90401
PHONE 310-434-1477
FAX 310-434-1455

TYPES	Features
HAS DEAL WITH	MTV Films - Paramount Pictures
DEVELOPMENT	The Dirt
SUBMISSION POLICY	No unsolicited submissions

Michelle Manning .....Producer
William Gulliver .....Director, Development
Mitchell Krause .....Assistant to Ms. Manning

MOBILE STREAMS

416 Park Avenue South, Ste. 3F
New York, NY 10016
PHONE .212-679-7657
FAX .212-889-2623
EMAIL .team@mobilestreams.com
WEB SITE .www.mobilestreams.com
TYPES Animation - Mobile Content - Reality TV
POST PRODUCTION The G.R.I.T. Boys (Nexxt Mobile)

Simon Buckingham .CEO
Jitesh Sodha .CFO
Shawn Barber .COO, US
Robert Fleischer .Executive VP, Asia Pacific
Martyn McGoun .Executive VP, UK & Europe
Warren Platt .Executive VP, Global Business Development
Glenn D. Schmidt .Executive VP, Technology
Chris Coyle .VP, Content Acquisition & Devlopment

MOBITV

6425 Christie Ave., 5th Fl.
Emeryville, CA 94608
PHONE .510-450-5000
FAX .510-450-5001
EMAIL .fanmail@mobitv.com
WEB SITE .www.mobitv.com
TYPES Animation - Commercials - Features - Mobile Content - Music Videos - TV Series
HAS DEAL WITH Fox Television Studios - NBC Universal Television Studio - Universal Music Group
COMMENTS Additional deals with ITN Distribution Company, Sprint, Cingular, Alltel, Orange, BBC and 3 UK

Dr. Phillip Alvelda .Chairman/CEO
Jeff Annison .Co-Founder/VP, Engineering
Paul Scanlan .Co-Founder/COO
Jeff Bartee .VP, Content
Ray Derenzo .VP, Business Development, Europe
Jason Taylor .Director, Corporate Communications

MOBIUS INTERNATIONAL

5890 W. Jefferson Blvd.
Los Angeles, CA 90016
PHONE .310-202-9500
FAX .310-202-9505
EMAIL .info@mobiusinternational.com
TYPES Features
POST PRODUCTION Bordertown - .45
COMPLETED UNRELEASED The Wendell Baker Story - Chaos
CREDITS Laws of Attraction

David Bergstein .Chairman/CEO
Hans Turner .President/COO
Gil Fortis .VP, Development
Adam Church .Director, Film Services

MOD3PRODUCTIONS

10390 Wilshire Blvd., Ste. 1104
Los Angeles, CA 90024
PHONE .310-285-8036
WEB SITE .www.mod3productions.com
TYPES Direct-to-Video/DVD - Documentaries - Features - Reality TV - Specials - TV Series
DEVELOPMENT The ArchiTECHS (History Channel)
PRE-PRODUCTION The Box (Docu-Series) - Dukes of Hazzard Season 7 (DVD)
POST PRODUCTION Season of the Samurai (Documentary)
UPCOMING RELEASES Scary Movie 4 (DVD)
CREDITS MTV's Prom Date - Bible Code 1&2 - Agent Cody Banks 1&2 - Love and Action in Chicago - Wish You Were Dead - Hiroshima - In Search of Peace - Unlikely Heroes; DVD: Mary Tyler Moore Show Seasons 1&2 - Kung Fu Seasons 1-3 - The Thorn Birds Special Edition - The Dukes of Hazzard Seasons 1-6 - Growing Pains Season 1 - The Island - Cheyenne Season 1

Danny Gold .Partner
Matthew Asner .Partner
Bruce Levine .Producer

MODE OF 8

3520 Manhattan Ave.
Manhattan Beach, CA 90266
PHONE .310-545-4792
FAX .310-545-4892
EMAIL .info@modeof8.com
TYPES Animation - Documentaries - Features - Internet Content - Reality TV - TV Series
DEVELOPMENT Dollar Theater - Untitled Sci Fi Series - Show Me the Money - Untitled Hybrid Crime Series - Just Like the Real Thing Baby
COMPLETED UNRELEASED Defending Jesus
CREDITS Sorority Life 1-3 - Fraternity Life 1-2 - Soulmates - Instant Comedy with the Groundlings - The Outer Limits Phenomenon - Hollywood Digital Diaries

Catherin Finn .Executive Producer

MOFFITT-LEE PRODUCTIONS

c/o HBO
2500 Broadway Ave., Ste. 400
Santa Monica, CA 90404
PHONE .310-382-3469/310-382-3192
FAX .310-382-3529
CREDITS The Comedy Festival - US Comedy Arts Festival - Bill Maher: Victory Begins at Home (HBO) - George Carlin: 40 Years of Comedy - Dennis Miller: Citizen Arcane (HBO) - Comic Relief - Not Necessarily the News (HBO)

John Moffitt .Executive Producer
Pat Tourk Lee .Executive Producer

MOJO FILMS
500 S. Buena Vista St., Animation Bldg., Ste. 1D-13
Burbank, CA 91521
PHONE .818-560-8370
FAX .818-560-5045
TYPES Features - TV Series
HAS DEAL WITH Touchstone Television
DEVELOPMENT The Express (Universal) - Cage (New Regency) - The Counter Terrorist (MGM) - Talk Talk (Universal) - Worst Case (Universal)
PRODUCTION October Road (Touchstone/ABC)
CREDITS Runaway Jury - Don't Say a Word - Impostor - Kiss the Girls - Things to Do in Denver When You're Dead

Gary Fleder .President
Mary Beth Basile .VP, Production & Development
Allen Cary .Assistant to Mary Beth Basile
Timothy Meehan .Assistant to Gary Fleder

MONDO MEDIA
444 De Haro St., Ste. 201
San Francisco, CA 94107
PHONE .415-865-2700
FAX .415-865-2645
EMAIL .feedback@mondomedia.com
WEB SITE .www.mondomedia.com
TYPES Internet Content - Mobile Content
CREDITS Happy Tree Friends

John Evershed .Co-Founder/CEO
Deidre O'Malley .Co-Founder/Director, Business Affairs
Douglas Kay .CFO
Christina Chavez .Marketing & Licensing Director
Kenn Navarro .Co-Creator/Animation Director, Happy Tree Friends
Dean MacDonald .Creative Director
Andria Lo .eCommerce Manager
Christine Vilar .Web Manager

MONSTER PRODUCTIONS
c/o The New Post Group
6335 Homewood Ave.
Hollywood, CA 90028
PHONE .323-462-2300, x7288
FAX .323-462-0836
WEB SITE .www.comedyhell.com
SECOND WEB SITE .www.blairbitch.com
TYPES Commercials - Direct-to-Video/DVD - Features - Music Videos - TV Series
POST PRODUCTION Comedy Hell
CREDITS The Blair Bitch Project Starring Linda Blair
COMMENTS Additional Web site: www.nicbruno.com

Scott LaRose . . . .Executive Producer/Director/Writer (scott@blairbitch.com)
Jerry Diner . . . .Producer/Director, Development (jerrydiner@sbcglobal.net)

MONTAGE ENTERTAINMENT
2118 Wilshire Blvd., Ste. 297
Santa Monica, CA 90403-5784
PHONE .310-966-0222
FAX .310-966-0223
EMAIL .montage.ent@usa.net
TYPES Features - TV Series
CREDITS Caffeine - Mi Vida Loca - Gas, Food, Lodging - Red Letters - Poolhall Junkies - Bereft - Landslide

David Peters .Producer
Bill Ewart .Producer
Jim Mercurio .Director, Development

THE MONTECITO PICTURE COMPANY
1482 E. Valley Rd., Ste. 477
Montecito, CA 93108
PHONE .805-565-8590/310-247-9880
FAX .805-565-1893/310-247-9498
TYPES Features
HAS DEAL WITH DreamWorks SKG
DEVELOPMENT Over My Dead Body - Disturbia - Grand Theft Otto - Old School 2 - The Intern
PRODUCTION Disturbia - Trailer Park Boys
CREDITS Beethoven - Ghostbusters - Dave - Space Jam - Six Days Seven Nights - Private Parts - Road Trip - Evolution - Old School - Killing Me Softly - Eurotrip
COMMENTS Beverly Hills office: 9465 Wilshire Blvd., Ste. 920, Beverly Hills, CA 90212

Ivan Reitman .No Title
Tom Pollock .No Title
Joe Medjuck .No Title
Dan Goldberg .No Title
Ken Holdren .No Title
Jeffrey Clifford .No Title
Andrea Hirschegger .Assistant to Mr. Reitman
Jennie Reinish .Assistant to Mr. Pollock
Bill Kirchen .Assistant to Mr. Holdren
Karl Mefford .Assistant to Mr. Medjuck

MOONSTONE ENTERTAINMENT
PO Box 7400
Studio City, CA 91614
PHONE .818-985-3003
FAX .818-985-3009
TYPES Features
PRE-PRODUCTION Company of Heroes
UPCOMING RELEASES The Promise
CREDITS Together - Hotel - Dancing at the Blue Iguana - Pandaemonium - Twin Falls Idaho - Miss Julie - Cookie's Fortune - Afterglow - Digging to China - Toolbox Murders

Ernst "Etchie" Stroh .CEO
Yael Stroh .President
Luz Moretti .Executive VP
Greg Majerus .VP, Finance
Michael Grant .Director, Production & Marketing
Shahar Stroh .Director, Development & Acquisitions
Christine Meissner .Manager

MOORE/CRAMER PRODUCTIONS

427 N. Canon Dr., Ste. 215
Beverly Hills, CA 90210-4840
PHONE .310-276-5433
FAX .310-858-8299
EMAIL .info@moorecramer.com
WEB SITE .www.moorecramer.com

TYPES	Features - Made-for-TV/Cable Movies - Reality TV - TV Series
DEVELOPMENT	MotoXtreme - The Other Way Around - Chicago Picnic -Sanctuary - El Cid - Half Past High Noon (TV)
PRE-PRODUCTION	Hughes (Miniseries) - Hip-Hop Mogul Mamas (VH1 Reality TV)
CREDITS	Beverly Hills Brats - Second Chances
SUBMISSION POLICY	No unsolicited submissions

Terry Moore .Partner/Producer
Grant Cramer .Partner/Producer
Diego Del Pino .Development Executive

MORGAN CREEK PRODUCTIONS

10351 Santa Monica Blvd., Ste. 200
Los Angeles, CA 90025
PHONE .310-432-4848
FAX .310-432-4844
WEB SITE .www.morgancreek.com

TYPES	Features
HAS DEAL WITH	Universal Pictures
DEVELOPMENT	Georgia Rule - Touchback - Our Lady of the Ballpark
UPCOMING RELEASES	The Good Shepherd - Man of the Year
CREDITS	Two for the Money - Robin Hood: Prince of Thieves - Ace Ventura 1&2 - Major League 1-3 - Diabolique - Wild America - American Outlaws - True Romance - Young Guns 1&2

James G. Robinson .Chairman/CEO
Guy McElwaine .President
Howard Kaplan .CFO
David C. Robinson .Sr. VP, Production
Brian Robinson .Sr. VP, Worldwide Marketing
Chris Lytton .VP, Legal/Business Affairs
Gary Stutman .VP, Finance
Andy Fraser .Production Executive
Andy Bohn .Director, Development

MORNINGSTAR ENTERTAINMENT

350 N. Glenoaks Blvd., Ste. 300
Burbank, CA 91502
PHONE .818-559-7255
FAX .818-559-7551
EMAIL .mstar@morningstarentertainment.com
WEB SITE .www.morningstarentertainment.com

TYPES	Direct-to-Video/DVD - Documentaries - Miniseries - Reality TV - Specials - TV Series
PROVIDES DEAL TO	Rive Gauche Entertainment
DEVELOPMENT	The Hidden Bible - The Plumber - The Black Jet
PRE-PRODUCTION	Man Hunters - Ping Pong Diplomacy
POST PRODUCTION	Angel - The Book of the Dead
CREDITS	John Dillinger: Public Enemy #1 - Battleground: The Art of War - Rivals of Jesus - Knights Templar - Apocalypse - Great Battles - Airship with John Milius - Spec Ops with John Milius - Waterloo - Jesse James: Legend, Outlaw, Terrorist - Coasters of the West - Battleground: Alexander the Great - Lizzie Borden - Statue of Liberty - Stealth Secrets - Sports Century - Operation Thunderbolt - Super Surgery - Fire at Sea - I Survived! - The Texas Seven - The Enforcers - Chicago's Lifeline - Billy the Kid Unmasked - Theme Park Secrets - 160 lb. Tumor - 200 lb. Tumor - Crash - Future Air Power - Battleground - The Battle of the Bulge
COMMENTS	Specializes in high profile HD docudrama and docu-fiction programming based on true events and stories

Gary Tarpinian .President/CEO
Paninee Theeranuntawat .VP/Executive Producer
Mickey Frieberg .Agent, Features
Tim Evans .Supervising Producer
Dylan Tilley .Director, Development
Ken Lacheim .Business Affairs

JOHN MORRISSEY PRODUCTIONS

838 N. Doheny Dr., #901
Los Angeles, CA 90069
PHONE .310-550-1400
FAX .310-550-6886

TYPES	Features - Made-for-TV/Cable Movies
CREDITS	Prodigy - Havoc - American History X - What's the Worst That Could Happen? - Kingdom Come - Booty Call - The Badge - 11:14

John Morrissey .Producer

JEFF MORTON PRODUCTIONS

5027 Noeline Ave.
Encino, CA 91436
PHONE 310-467-1123
FAX 818-981-4152
EMAIL . . . . . scoutspence@mindspring.com
TYPES: Features - Made-for-TV/Cable Movies - TV Series
DEVELOPMENT: Bright Corners
CREDITS: The Winner - Jake in Progress - Elizabeth Smart Story - Oliver Beene - Caracara - Second Skin - Don't Look Under the Bed - Double Jeopardy - Firestarter

Jeff Morton . . . . . Producer

MOSAIC MEDIA GROUP

9200 Sunset Blvd., 10th Fl.
Los Angeles, CA 90069
PHONE 310-786-4900
FAX 310-777-2185
TYPES: Features - TV Series
DEVELOPMENT: Valiant - Afrosamurai - Season of the Witch - Get Smart - None of Her Business - The Art of Cool - Deep in the Heart of Texas
CREDITS: Idlewild - The Brothers Grimm - Batman Begins - Kicking & Screaming - Scooby-Doo 1&2
SUBMISSION POLICY: No unsolicited material

Allen Shapiro . . . . . President
Charles Roven . . . . . Partner
Jimmy Miller . . . . . Partner
Eric Gold . . . . . Partner
Ted MacKinney . . . . . CFO
Alan Glazer . . . . . Executive VP
George Gatins . . . . . VP, Production
Gloria Fan . . . . . VP, Production & Development
M. Riley . . . . . Creative Executive
Alex Ankeles . . . . . Creative Executive
Ilan Breil . . . . . Manager
Julie Darmody . . . . . Manager
John Elliot . . . . . Manager
David Fleming . . . . . Manager
Paul Nelson . . . . . Manager
Caryn Weingarten . . . . . Manager

MOSHAG PRODUCTIONS, INC.

c/o Mark Mower
1531 Wellesley Ave.
Los Angeles, CA 90025
PHONE 310-820-6760
FAX 310-820-6960
EMAIL . . . . . moshag@aol.com
TYPES: Features - TV Series
DEVELOPMENT: I Caught Flies for Howard Hughes - '57 Chicago - '46 Chicago - The Queen's Mark - Snowblind - The Greatest Game - Gallantyne - Unbridled - Fremantle - Jane Blonde - Found Money
PRE-PRODUCTION: The Payback All-Star Revue - The Family - Players - Wanted
CREDITS: Spun - Bully - The Bogus Witch Project (Trimark) - April's Shower

Mark Mower . . . . . Producer
Seth A. Miller . . . . . Producer
Edward Mejia . . . . . Executive Assistant

MOTION PICTURE CORPORATION OF AMERICA

1333 Second St., Ste. 210
Santa Monica, CA 90401
PHONE 310-319-9500
FAX 310-319-9501
WEB SITE . . . . . www.mpcafilm.com
TYPES: Direct-to-Video/DVD - Features - Made-for-TV/Cable Movies - Miniseries
PRE-PRODUCTION: Taking Chance
POST PRODUCTION: Pumpkinhead: Ashes to Ashes - Pumpkinhead: Dark Hell
UPCOMING RELEASES: The Hard Corps
CREDITS: Blast - National Lampoon Presents Barely Legal - Second in Command - Pavement - Consequence - Borderline - Undisputed - Boat Trip - Joe and Max - Dumb and Dumber - B.H. Ninja - Kingpin - Annie - The Breed - Stephen King's Riding the Bullet - Slipstream
SUBMISSION POLICY: No unsolicited material

Brad Krevoy . . . . . Chairman/CEO
Francisco Gonzalez . . . . . VP, International Sales & Marketing
Reuben Liber . . . . . VP, Production & Development
Mike Callaghan . . . . . Story Editor

Motion Picture Invest
Exclusive Private Placements

MOTION PICTURE INVEST

Emiliestr. 35
Hamburg 20259, Germany
PHONE 49-40-4319-3227
FAX 49-40-4319-3228
EMAIL . . . . . mpi@motionpictureinvest.com
WEB SITE . . . . . www.motionpictureinvest.com
TYPES: Features
POST PRODUCTION: Blood and Chocolate
COMPLETED UNRELEASED: Chestnut - Hero of Central Park
CREDITS: Dungeons & Dragons: Wrath of the Dragon God - The Boys and Girl from County Clare
COMMENTS: Finances and produces English language feature films

Wolfgang Esenwein . . . . . Founder & President

MOTION PICTURE PRODUCTION, INC.

3000 Olympic Blvd.
Santa Monica, CA 90404
PHONE .310-315-4720
FAX .310-315-4800

TYPES: Documentaries - Made-for-TV/Cable Movies - Reality TV - TV Series
PRODUCTION: Violent Earth (History Channel) - Untitled Pilot (History Channel)
UPCOMING RELEASES: Dragon's Triangle (History Channel) - Black Box Pilot Sightings (History Channel) - Deep Sea UFOs: Red Alert (History Channel)
CREDITS: Russian Roswell - Deep Sea UFOs 1&2 (History Channel) - Raising the Bar: America's Best Bar Chefs (Fine Living Network) - Cocktail Essentials (Fine Living Network) - Drive, She Said - Baggage - Max Knight: Ultra Spy (UPN) - Chameleon (UPN) - Virtual Nightmare (UPN) - Operation Sandman (UPN) - Lost in the Bermuda Triangle (UPN) - Primal Force (UPN)
SUBMISSION POLICY: No unsolicited submissions
COMMENTS: Scripted and non-scripted television programming

Jon Alon Walz .Executive Producer/Director
David Pavoni .Producer
Jeff Tober .Producer/Supervising Editor
Aaron Putnam .Editor
Edwin Zane .Development Consultant

MOTOR CITY FILMS

468 N. Camden Dr., Ste. 200
Beverly Hills, CA 90210
PHONE .310-860-5667

TYPES: Features - TV Series

Vondie Curtis Hall .Producer/Director
Monikka Starllworth .Assistant

THE MOTTOLA COMPANY

745 Fifth Ave., Ste. 800
New York, NY 10151
PHONE .212-471-4000
FAX .212-471-4090

TYPES: Internet Content - Mobile Content - Reality TV - TV Series
DEVELOPMENT: Queens Reigns Supreme: Fat Cat, 50 Cent and the Rise of the Hip-Hop Hustle - The Shop (MTV) - Vera Wang and the Entertainment Space (Buena Vista) - StarTomorrow

Tommy Mottola .President
Jeb Brien .Partner

MOVING PICTURES, DPI

11766 Wilshire Blvd., Ste. 500
Los Angeles, CA 90025
PHONE .310-288-5464
FAX .310-859-4728
WEB SITE .www.movingpicturesdp.com

TYPES: Animation - Direct-to-Video/DVD - Documentaries - Features - Made-for-TV/Cable Movies - Reality TV - TV Series
CREDITS: Maxim Hot 100 - Blender and VH1's 50 Most Awesomely Bad Songs - ESPN's All Maxim Team - Blender's Rockstar Wives and Girlfriends - Super Group - The Fabulous Life and Blender Present:
COMMENTS: Represents Maxim, Stuff, Blender and The Week magazines; Forthcoming Maxim Radio channel on Sirius Satellite Radio

Peter Jaysen .No Title
Andy Stevens .No Title

MOXIE FIRECRACKER FILMS

39 Lincoln Pl.
Brooklyn, NY 11217
PHONE .718-230-5111
FAX .718-230-5999
EMAIL .info@moxiefirecracker.com
WEB SITE .www.moxiefirecracker.com

TYPES: Documentaries
UPCOMING RELEASES: !
CREDITS: Yo Soy Boricua, Pa Que Tu Lo Sepas - The Homestead Strike - Street Fight - Nazi Officer's Wife - Girlhood - A Boy's Life - The Farm: Angola, USA - American Hollow - Different Moms - Epidemic Africa - Juvies - The Travelers - Up in Arms - All Kinds of Families - Healthy Start - Sixteen - Together: Stop Violence Against Women - Pandemic: Facing Aids - Indian Point: Imagining the Unimaginable - Xiara's Song

Liz Garbus .Producer/Director/Co-Owner
Rory Kennedy .Producer/Director/Co-Owner
Julie Gaither .Head, Production
Valerie Darmour .Assistant to Rory Kennedy
Matthew Justus .Assistant to Liz Garbus

MOZARK PRODUCTIONS

4024 Radford Ave., Bldg. 5, Ste. 104
Studio City, CA 91604
PHONE .818-655-5779
EMAIL .mozark@mptp.com

TYPES: Features - TV Series
DEVELOPMENT: 12 Miles of Bad Road
CREDITS: Woman of the House - Hearts Afire - Designing Women - Evening Shade - Emeril

Linda Bloodworth-Thomason .Executive Producer/Writer
Harry Thomason .Executive Producer/Director

MPH ENTERTAINMENT, INC.

1033 N. Hollywood Way, Ste. F
Burbank, CA 91505
PHONE .818-441-5040
FAX .818-441-5050
EMAIL .info@mphent.com
WEB SITE .www.mphent.com

TYPES: Direct-to-Video/DVD - Documentaries - Features - Made-for-TV/Cable Movies - Reality TV - TV Series
PROVIDES DEAL TO: Rive Gauche Entertainment
DEVELOPMENT: Rat Girl - Hometown Alcatraz
PRE-PRODUCTION: Deep Cover
CREDITS: Dog Whisperer with Cesar Millan - The Takedown - My Big Fat Greek Wedding - Founding Fathers - Sex in the 20th Century - The Nightclub Years - Lost Dinosaurs of Egypt - Founding Brothers - Inside Islam - In the Footsteps of Jesus - The Roswell Crash: Startling New Evidence - Tomb Raiders: Robbing the Dead - The New Roswell: Kecksberg Exposed - The True Story of Hannibal - The Search for John the Baptist - Run for Fun
SUBMISSION POLICY: No unsolicited submissions

Jim Milio .Co-Chair
Mark Hufnail .Co-Chair
Melissa Jo Peltier .Co-Chair
Bonnie Peterson .Sr. VP, Production
Juliana Weiss .Executive Assistant
Alleta Darby .Executive Assistant

MR. MUDD

5225 Wilshire Blvd., Ste. 604
Los Angeles, CA 90036
PHONE .323-932-5656
WEB SITE .www.mrmudd.com

TYPES: Documentaries - Features - Theatre - TV Series
CREDITS: Art School Confidential - The Libertine - Ghost World - The Dancer Upstairs - How to Draw a Bunny

John Malkovich .Producer/Director
Lianne Halfon .Producer
Russ Smith .Producer
Shannon Clark .No Title
Shelly Darden .No Title
E. Michael Stankevich .No Title

MRB PRODUCTIONS, INC.

311 N. Robertson Blvd., Ste. 513
Beverly Hills, CA 90211
PHONE .323-465-7676
FAX .323-962-6857
EMAIL .info@mrbproductions.com
WEB SITE .www.mrbproductions.com

TYPES: Commercials - Direct-to-Video/DVD - Features - Music Videos - New Media - Specials - TV Series
HAS DEAL WITH: ABC Sports - ESPN Original Entertainment (EOE)
CREDITS: Mattel - Bratz Dolls - Disney - Monday Night Football - ESPY Awards - Upperdeck - NFL Network - Sony - X-Games - DIRECTV

Matt R. Brady .Executive Producer
Mark Teitelman .Director
Brian O'Connell .Director
Jeremy Haft .Director
Rico Labbe .Director
Gary Califano .Director
Mike Wang .Director
Branson Veal .Director
Brenda Bank .Producer
Luke Watson .Producer
Michael Bennett .Head, Marketing

MSN ORIGINALS

c/o Microsoft/MSN
One Microsoft Way
Redmond, WA 98052-6399
PHONE .425-882-8080
FAX .425-936-7329
EMAIL .original@microsoft.com

TYPES: Internet Content
DEVELOPMENT: Fan Club: Reality Baseball
COMMENTS: Deal with BeJane to create original video programming and multiple deals to created original programming for broadband

Rob Bennett .General Manager, Entertainment & Video Services
Joe Michaels .Director, Business Development, Entertainment & Video Services

MSNBC
One MSNBC Plaza
Secaucus, NJ 07094
PHONE 201-583-5000
WEB SITE . . . . www.msnbc.com
TYPES Documentaries - Specials - TV Series
CREDITS Daytime: Imus in the Morning - MSNBC Live - The Most with Alison Stewart; Evening: Countdown with Keith Olbermann - Hardball with Chris Matthews - Scarborough Country - The Abrams Report - The Situation with Tucker Carlson; Headliners & Legends - MSNBC Investigates - MSNBC Special Presentations
COMMENTS News programming

Dan Abrams . . . . General Manager, MSNBC
Charlie Tillinghast . . . . President/CEO, MSNBC.com
Jeremy Gaines . . . . VP, Communications
Michael Rubin . . . . VP, Longform Programming
Susan Sullivan . . . . VP, News, Daytime Programming
Bill Wolff . . . . VP, Primetime Programming
Scott Hooker . . . . Sr. Executive Producer, Documentary Production & Development
Leslie Schwartz . . . . Director, Media Relations
Megan Kopf . . . . Manager, Media Relations

MSPOT
459 Hamilton Ave., 307
Palo Alto, CA 94301
PHONE 650-321-7000
FAX 650-321-7077
EMAIL . . . . info@mspot.com
WEB SITE . . . . www.mspot.com
TYPES Mobile Content
COMMENTS Sports programming

Daren Tsui . . . . Co-Founder/CEO

MTV FILMS
c/o Paramount Studios
5555 Melrose Ave., Modular Bldg., 2nd Fl.
Los Angeles, CA 90038
PHONE 323-956-8023
FAX . . . . 323-862-1386/323-862-8020 (Production)
WEB SITE . . . . www.mtv.com
TYPES Features
HAS DEAL WITH Paramount Pictures
PROVIDES DEAL TO Bona Fide Productions - MM Productions
DEVELOPMENT It's Kind of Funny - Born to Rock - The Warriors - The Suffering - The Dirt - Genius - Getting Up: Contents Under Pressure - Damn Nation - Valiant - The Wheelman - Adult World - Coxblocker - Psycho Funky Chimp - Rucker - The Tickles
PRODUCTION Freedom Writers - jackass 2 - Blades of Glory
CREDITS Aeon Flux - Get Rich or Die Tryin' - Murderball - Hustle & Flow - The Longest Yard - Napoleon Dynamite - Election - Original Kings of Comedy - Beavis & Butthead - Better Luck Tomorrow - Save the Last Dance - Varsity Blues - Orange County - The Wood - Fighting Temptations - Tupac: Resurrection - jackass: the movie - Martin Lawrence Live: Runteldat - Coach Carter

David Gale . . . . Executive VP (323-956-4390)
Troy Craig Poon . . . . Sr. VP, Acquisitions & Business Development (323-956-8005)
Momita Sengupta . . . . VP, Physical Production (323-956-8007)
Jason Weiss . . . . Sr. Director, Development (323-956-8320)
Carrie Beck . . . . Director, Development (323-956-8023)
Gregg Goldin . . . . Director, Development (323-956-3275)
Loretha Jones . . . . Head, DVD Division (323-956-1695)
Charlie Jordan Brookins . . . . Director, Development (323-956-8094)

MTV NETWORKS

1515 Broadway
New York, NY 10036
PHONE . . . 212-258-8000/310-752-8000
WEB SITE . . . www.mtv.com
TYPES Animation - Internet Content - Made-for-TV/Cable Movies - Mobile Content - Reality TV - TV Series
PROVIDES DEAL TO Amp'd Mobile - Bad Boy Films - Carson Daly Productions - Generate - Liquid Theory - Terence Michael Productions, Inc.
DEVELOPMENT Untitled Rolling Stone Project - Head and Body (Animated) - Rob & Big Black - Meet or Delete - Moves
CREDITS Fast Inc. - Blowin' Up - Cheyenne - The Hills - Tiara Girls - MTV Juvies - Two-A-Days - 8th and Ocean - Yo Mama - Call 2 Greatness - Score - Super Sweet 16 - Homewreckers - Real World/Road Rules Challenge - There and Back - The Andy Milonakis Show - MTV's Mashups - Laguna Beach - Next - Pimp My Ride - Punk'd - Making the Band - Real World - TRL - True Life - MTV's Cribs - MTV Movie Awards - MTV Video Music Awards - Making the Video - Made - The Reality Show - Bad Dads, Phat Mums - Parental Control - Nick Cannon Presents Wild'N Out - Wulffmorgenthaler (Mobisodic Series)
COMMENTS West Coast office: 2600 Colorado Ave., Santa Monica, CA 90404; Includes Xfire, online gaming site

Judith McGrath . . . Chairman/CEO, MTV Networks
Bill Roedy . . . Vice Chairman, MTV Networks Group/President, MTV Networks International
Brian Graden . . . President, Entertainment, MTV Music Group/President, Logo
Van Toffler . . . President, MTV Networks Music Group, Logo & MTV Films
Christina Norman . . . President, MTV
Michael J. Wolf . . . President/COO, MTV Networks
David Cohn . . . General Manager, MTV2
Stephen Friedman . . . General Manager, mtvU
Colette Chestnut . . . Executive VP/CFO, MTV Networks
Richard Eigendorff . . . Executive VP/COO, MTV Music Group & Logo
Alex R. Ferrari . . . Executive VP/COO, MTVN International
Bob Bakish . . . Executive VP, Operations, Viacom Enterprises
George Cheeks . . . Executive VP/General Counsel, MTVN, Business & Legal Affairs
Lois Curren . . . Executive VP, MTV Series Entertainment & Programming
Paul DeBenedettis . . . Executive VP, Multiplatform Programming, Content Strategy & Scheduling
Tony DiSanto . . . Executive VP, Series Development & Animation, MTV/Head, Programming, MTV2
Tina Exarhos . . . Executive VP, Marketing & Multiplatform Creative, MTV/MTV2/mtvU
David Gale . . . Executive VP, New Media & Specialty Film Content, MTV/Executive VP, MTV Films
JoAnne Adams Griffith . . . Executive VP, Human Resources, MTV Networks/Viacom
Nicholas Lehman . . . Executive VP, Strategy & Operations, Digital Music & Media/Interim Chief Digital Officer
Leslie Leventman . . . Executive VP, Creative Services, Special Events, Travel Management & Convention Planning
Sean Moran . . . Executive VP, MTV Brand Ad Sales
Nancy Newman . . . Executive VP, Strategy & Organizational Planning, MTV Music Group & Logo
Colleen Fahey Rush . . . Executive VP, Research, MTV Networks
John Shea . . . Executive VP, Sponsorship Development & Integrated Marketing, MTVN Music Group

(Continued)

MTV NETWORKS (Continued)

Sabrina Silverberg . . . Executive VP, Music Strategy & Relations
David Sirulnick . . . Executive VP, Multiplatform Production, News & Music
David Sussman . . . Executive VP/General Counsel, MTVN, Business & Legal Affairs
Denmark West . . . Executive VP, Strategy & Business Development
Jeffrey Yapp . . . Executive VP, Program Enterprises, MTV Music Group & Logo
Rod Aissa . . . Sr. VP, Talent & Series Development
Lucia Ballas-Traynor . . . Sr. VP/General Manager, MTV TR3S
Marnie Black . . . Sr. VP, MTV Communications
Anthony Dibari Jr. . . . Sr. VP, MTV Production
Amy Doyle . . . Sr. VP, Music & Talent
Nusrat Durrani . . . Sr. VP/General Manager, MTV World
Carol Eng . . . Sr. VP, MTV2 Programming & Development
Kathy Flynn . . . Sr. VP, Production Events, MTV & VH1
Salli Frattini . . . Sr. VP/Executive in Charge, MTV
Liz Gateley . . . Sr. VP, Series Development & Animation, MTV & MTV2
Catherine Houser . . . Sr. VP, Human Resources, West Coast Regional Operations
Jeannie Kedas . . . Sr. VP, Communications, MTVN Music Group
Chris Linn . . . Sr. VP, Production, Series Development & Animation, MTV & MTV2
Kevin Mackall . . . Sr. VP, On-Air Promotions
Tim Rosta . . . Sr. VP, Integrated Marketing
Michael Alex . . . VP, MTV News Digital
Peter Baron . . . VP, Label Relations
Robyn Demarco . . . VP, Programming & Scheduling, MTV/MTV2
Nina Diaz . . . VP, MTV News & Documentaries
Marshall Eisen . . . VP, MTV News & Documentaries
Carolyn Everson . . . VP, Advertising Sales, MTV, MTV2, mtvU, mtv.com
Andrew Hunter . . . VP, Network Development
Jesse Ignjatovic . . . VP, Music & Talent Development, MTV
Ross Martin . . . VP/Head, Programming, mtvU
Robin Reinhardt-Locke . . . VP, Studio Relations & Celebrity Talent
Lou Stellato . . . VP, MTV2 Production
Drew Tappon . . . VP, Series Development, MTV
Ariana Urbont . . . VP, MTV Communications
Ben White . . . VP, Digital Media, MTV
Lauren Dolgen . . . Director, MTV Series Development
Lauren Lazin . . . Executive Producer, MTVN

MTV NETWORKS LATIN AMERICA (MTVNLA)

1111 Lincoln Rd., 6th Fl.
Miami Beach, FL 33139
PHONE . . . 305-535-3700
WEB SITE . . . www.mtvla.com
SECOND WEB SITE . . . www.mundonick.com or www.vh1la.com
TYPES Animation - Documentaries - Internet Content - Mobile Content - Reality TV - Specials - TV Series
DEVELOPMENT MTV: Rock Dinner Series - Quiero Mis Quinces - Motorhome - MTV Docu AIDS: Nickelodeon: SKIMO

Pierluigi Gazzolo . . . Managing Director, MTVN Latin America
Scot McBride . . . COO, MTVN Latin America
Charlie Singer . . . Executive VP, Programming, Creative & Strategic Marketing, MTVN Latin America
Linda Alexander . . . Sr. VP, Corporate Communications & Public Affairs, MTVN Latin America
Sofia Ioannou . . . Sr. VP, Business & Legal Affairs, MTVN International & Latin America
Jose Tillan . . . Sr. VP, Music Programming & Talent Strategy, MTVN Latin America & MTVTr3s
Alina Vogtner . . . Sr. VP, Human Resources, MTVN International & Latin America
Alvaro Barros . . . VP, Distribution, MTVN Latin America
Noel Gladstone . . . VP, Research & Development, MTVN Latin America
Luis Goicouria . . . VP, New Media, MTVN Latin America
Josh Greenberg . . . VP, Programming & Creative Strategies, MTVN Latin America
Corinna Keller . . . VP, International Sales & Marketing Partnerships, MTVN Latin America
John Mafoutsis . . . VP, International Sales & Marketing Partnerships, MTVN Latin America
Tatiana Rodríguez . . . VP, Programming & Creative Strategies, Nickelodeon Latin America
Vicente Solis . . . VP, Programming & Creative Strategies, VH1 Latin America

MURPHY BOYZ PRODUCTIONS

270 Sparta Ave., Ste. 104
Sparta, NJ 07871
PHONE . . . 973-702-9000/973-702-9043
FAX . . . 973-702-1550
WEB SITE . . . www.murphyboyz.com

TYPES — Animation - Direct-to-Video/DVD - Documentaries - Features - Internet Content - Made-for-TV/Cable Movies - Mobile Content - Reality TV - Specials - TV Series
DEVELOPMENT — Heist Society - The Latin Comedy Review - Urban Ice - Trouble and In Love - Angel Starr
PRE-PRODUCTION — Soul Meets Jazz Tour
COMPLETED UNRELEASED — Big Black Comedy Show Vol. 5-8
CREDITS — Big Black Comedy Show Vol. 1-4 - Vampire in Brooklyn - Beverly Hills Cop 3 - Holy Man - Metro
COMMENTS — Looking for finished projects

Ray Murphy Jr. . . . Partner/Producer (ray@murphyboyz.com)
Bill Murphy . . . Partner/Producer (bill@murphyboyz.com)
Kim Taddeo . . . No Title (kim@murphyboyz.com)
Connie Adler-Galloway . . . No Title (connie@murphyboyz.com)

MUSE ENTERTAINMENT ENTERPRISES

3451 St-Jacques
Montréal, PQ H4C 1H1, Canada
PHONE . . . 514-866-6873/604-904-5615
FAX . . . 514-876-3911/604-904-5627
EMAIL . . . bpalik@muse.ca
WEB SITE . . . www.muse.ca

TYPES — Animation - Documentaries - Features - Made-for-TV/Cable Movies - Miniseries - TV Series
DEVELOPMENT — Delicious (Series) - The Deal (Feature) Love and War in Shanghai - (Miniseries) - Hiltons (Feature) - Thirty-Nine Steps - (Feature) - The Phoenix Files (Documentary Series) - Dad's in the Attic (Series) - Mysteries of Alfred Hedgehog (Animated Series) - Honest Blue Eyes (Series) - Frozen (MOW) - We're Open (Series) - Lonesome George (Documentary) I Thee Wed (MOW)
PRE-PRODUCTION — Durham County (Series) - Tipping Point (MOW)
PRODUCTION — The Wind in the Willows (MOW) - House Sitter (MOW) - Killer Wave (Miniseries)
POST PRODUCTION — The Flood (Miniseries) - Trace Evidence (MOW)
UPCOMING RELEASES — Answered by Fire (Miniseries)
COMPLETED UNRELEASED — The Fountain (Feature)
CREDITS — The Tournament (TV Series) - My Life and a Movie (2 Part Series) - Black Widower (Lifetime) - Apocalypse 10.5 - Human Trafficking (Miniseries) - Mind Over Murder (MOW) - Niagara Motel (Feature) - Murder in the Hamptons (Lifetime) - Silent Night (Hallmark) - Plain Truth (Lifetime) - Tales From the Neverending Story - The Butterfly Effect - 10.5 - Ice Bound - In the Name of the People (CBS) - Niagara Motel - This Is Wonderland - Recipe for a Perfect Christmas (MOW)

(Continued)

MUSE ENTERTAINMENT ENTERPRISES (Continued)

SUBMISSION POLICY — Unsolicited manuscripts only with release form

Michael Prupas . . . President
Irene Litinsky . . . President, Production (Montréal)
Betty Palik . . . Director, Communications
Jesse Prupas . . . Director, Development

MUSE PRODUCTIONS, INC.

15-B Brooks Ave.
Venice, CA 90291
PHONE . . . 310-306-2001
FAX . . . 310-574-2614
WEB SITE . . . www.musefilm.com

TYPES — Documentaries - Features
DEVELOPMENT — Leopard in the Sun - Killer Inside Me - London Fields - Going Down - Music for Torching - Veronika Decides to Die - Becoming Madame Mao - Heatstroke - Downloading Nancy
PRODUCTION — Hounddog
CREDITS — Edmond - The Heart Is Deceitful Above All Things - I Love Your Work - This Girl's Life - Tiptoes - Spun - Love, Liza - Bully - Freeway - Trees Lounge - Two Girls and a Guy - This World, Then the Fireworks - Girl - Buffalo '66 - The Virgin Suicides - American Psycho
SUBMISSION POLICY — No unsolicited submissions
COMMENTS — Interactive digital film

Chris Hanley . . . President
Roberta Hanley . . . Co-President
Rikki Jarrett . . . Office Manager

MUTUAL FILM COMPANY

8560 W. Sunset Blvd., Ste. 800
Los Angeles, CA 90069
PHONE . . . 310-855-7355
FAX . . . 310-855-7356
EMAIL . . . inquiries@mutualfilm.com
WEB SITE . . . www.mutualfilm.com

TYPES — Features - TV Series
DEVELOPMENT — The Authority - Lone Wolf and Cub - One Shot
CREDITS — Snakes on a Plane - Casanova - And Starring Pancho Villa as Himself - Timeline - Lara Croft Tomb Raider: The Cradle of Life - Paulie - Lara Croft: Tomb Raider - Saving Private Ryan - 12 Monkeys - The Patriot - Primary Colors - The Jackal - A Simple Plan - Man on the Moon - Wonder Boys - Virus
COMMENTS — Foreign distribution; Financing; International sales; Development

Gary Levinsohn . . . Principal
Edward Frumkes . . . Principal
Lesly Gross . . . VP, Operations & Administration
Libby Bancroft . . . Manager, Operations
Carlos Lopez . . . Assistant to E. Frumkes
Greg Rodgers . . . Assistant to G. Levinsohn
Robert Uyeda . . . Receptionist

MWG PRODUCTIONS
8075 W. Third St., Ste. 304
Los Angeles, CA 90048
PHONE .323-937-8313
FAX .323-937-5239
EMAIL .wynne9@aol.com
TYPES Documentaries - Features - Made-for-TV/Cable Movies - Miniseries - Reality TV - TV Series
DEVELOPMENT Hear My Testimony - Women in War
PRODUCTION The Haiti Project
CREDITS Nine - Alaska - American Veteran Awards 2001/2002
SUBMISSION POLICY Through representation only

Max Goldenson .President/Producer
Jeanette Estrem .Executive Assistant

***MY NETWORK TV**
c/o Fox Television Stations
1211 Avenue of the Americas, 7th Fl.
New York, NY 10036
PHONE .212-556-2400
TYPES TV Series
UPCOMING RELEASES Secret Obsessions - Fashion House - Desire

Roger Ailes . .Chairman, Fox Television Stations/Chairman/CEO, Fox News
Jack Abernethy .CEO, Fox Televisions Stations
Bob Cook .President/COO, Twentieth Television
Bob Cesa .Executive VP, Advertising Sales
Dave Barrington .Sr. VP/General Sales Manager, Advertising Sales
Peter Lops .VP

MYRIAD PICTURES
3015 Main St., Ste. 400
Santa Monica, CA 90405
PHONE .310-279-4000
FAX .310-279-4001
WEB SITE .www.myriadpictures.com
TYPES Documentaries - Features - Made-for-TV/Cable Movies - Miniseries - TV Series
DEVELOPMENT The Shadowchaser - Diva
PRE-PRODUCTION Death Defying Acts
PRODUCTION Dark Matter
POST PRODUCTION Copying Beethoven - Factory Girl - Partition
UPCOMING RELEASES Van Wilder 2: The Rise of Taj
COMPLETED UNRELEASED Comeback Season - The Moon & the Stars
CREDITS Little Fish - Trauma - The Deal - Kinsey - Eulogy - Jeeper Creepers 2 - The Good Girl - National Lampoon's Van Wilder - People I Know - Imagining Argentina
SUBMISSION POLICY Scripts through WGA recognized representatives only

Kirk D'Amico .President/CEO
Ann Dubinet .President, Distribution
Maxine Leonard .Executive VP, Marketing & Publicity
Elias Axume .VP, Post Production
Linda Sophie Chiu .Director, Development
Patrick Murray .Financial Consultant
Jennifer Sakurada .Director, Distribution & Production
Annie Domingo .Accounting Manager
James Hollis .Manager, Business Affairs
Matthew Smith .Manager, Development & Acquisitions
Evan Colfer .International Sales Assistant
Luiza Ricopero .Assistant to Kirk D'Amico

THE N
1633 Broadway, 7th Fl.
New York, NY 10019
PHONE .212-654-7707
WEB SITE .www.the-n.com
TYPES Animation - TV Series
DEVELOPMENT The Block - Whistler
PRODUCTION Makaha Surf
CREDITS South of Nowhere - Degrassi: The Next Generation - Instant Star - Radio Free Roscoe - O'Grady - Girls v. Boys - Best Friend's Date - Miracle's Boys - A Walk in Your Shoes
COMMENTS Network for teens; Programming arm of MTV Networks

Tom Ascheim .Executive VP/General Manager, Nickelodeon Television
Sarah Tomassi Lindman .VP, Programming & Production
Essie Chambers .VP, Development
Kenny Miller .VP, Programming & Production
Jill Greenberg Sands .VP, Talent & Casting, Nick Jr., Noggin & The N
Tanya Young .Manager, Development

NALA FILMS
126 N. Maple Dr.
Beverly Hills, CA 90210
PHONE .310-247-8500
FAX .310-388-0914
WEB SITE .www.nalafilms.com
TYPES Animation - Features
DEVELOPMENT La Magdalena - The Long Dark Train - Night of Light - Only Ever You
POST PRODUCTION The Air I Breathe - After Sex

Emilio Diez Barroso .CEO
Darlene Caamaño-Loquet .President, Production & Development
Ricardo Palacio .Creative Assistant/Office Manager

NAMESAKE ENTERTAINMENT
7608 West Hwy. 146, English Manor II, Ste. 100
Pewee Valley, KY 40056
PHONE .502-243-3185
FAX .502-243-3187
EMAIL .info@namesakeentertainment.com
WEB SITE .www.namesakeentertainment.com
TYPES Direct-to-Video/DVD - Features - Made-for-TV/Cable Movies - TV Series
DEVELOPMENT Nightbringer - All Hallows Eve
PRE-PRODUCTION House
POST PRODUCTION Thr3e
CREDITS Every Mother's Worst Fear - Left Behind - Can of Worms - Hangman's Curse - The Visitation
SUBMISSION POLICY Only solicited materials accepted

Joe Goodman .CEO/Producer
Bobby Neutz .COO/Producer
Kelly Neutz .VP, Development
Carol Pence .Production Coordinator
Doug Blahd .Controller
Holly McClure .Marketing & Promotion Director

NANAS ENTERTAINMENT

3963 Vista Linda Dr.
Encino, CA 91316
PHONE . . . 818-342-9800/310-385-1204
FAX . . . 818-342-1741/310-385-1207
EMAIL . . . nanasent1@aol.com
TYPES Features - Made-for-TV/Cable Movies - TV Series
DEVELOPMENT Pt. Thunder
CREDITS Funny Money - Looking for Comedy in the Muslim World - 2 Days in the Valley - Mother - Defending Your Life - The Muse - No Good Deed
COMMENTS Second office: 9233 W. Pico Blvd., #218, Los Angeles, CA 90035

Herb Nanas . . . Producer
Fran Messer . . . Office Manager

NASH ENTERTAINMENT

c/o Sunset Gower Studios
1438 N. Gower St., Box 10
Hollywood, CA 90028
PHONE . . . 323-993-7384
FAX . . . 323-993-7385
TYPES Features - Made-for-TV/Cable Movies - Miniseries - Reality TV - TV Series
DEVELOPMENT Film: Time of Their Lives (Universal) - Santa Paws (Vanguard) - To Wally Ward - Sherlock's Secretary (Walden Media) - Falling Awake (Warner Bros.) - Teacher of the Year (New Line)
UPCOMING RELEASES World's Most Amazing Videos (Spike)
CREDITS TV: Who Wants to Be a Superhero? (Sci-Fi) - For Love or Money (NBC) - Who Wants to Marry My Dad? (NBC) - Meet My Folks (NBC) - For Better or For Worse (TLC) - Totally Outrageous Behavior (Fox) - Outback Jack (TBS) - Wanna Come In? (MTV)

Bruce Nash . . . President/CEO
Robyn Nash . . . VP
Andrew Jebb . . . VP, Production
Robert Kosberg . . . Executive Producer, Features
Scott Satin . . . Executive Producer
Karen Nusbaum . . . Executive Assistant to the President/Director, Corporate Events
Geoff Skinner . . . Development Executive
Jo Sharon . . . Development Executive
Jennifer Dougherty . . . Assistant to the President

NASSER ENTERTAINMENT GROUP

11350 Ventura Blvd., Ste. 101
Studio City, CA 91604
PHONE . . . 818-505-8030
EMAIL . . . nassent@pacbell.net
WEB SITE . . . www.moviesfortv.com
SECOND WEB SITE . . . www.animalworldnetwork.com
TYPES Direct-to-Video/DVD - Documentaries - Made-for-TV/Cable Movies - Miniseries - Reality TV - Specials - TV Series
HAS DEAL WITH FremantleMedia North America
PRODUCTION Amber Alert
CREDITS The Suspect - A Stranger to Love - Father's Choice - Forever Love - Last Brickmaker in America - Hostage Negotiator
COMMENTS Also Distributes

Jack Nasser . . . President
Steve Pine . . . CFO
Joe Nasser . . . VP
Rita Saigh . . . Accounting
Christina Debeenie . . . Assistant

NATIONAL GEOGRAPHIC FEATURE FILMS

9100 Wilshire Blvd., Ste. 401E
Beverly Hills, CA 90212
PHONE . . . 310-858-5800
FAX . . . 310-858-5801
WEB SITE . . . www.nationalgeographic.com
TYPES Documentaries - Features - Made-for-TV/Cable Movies - TV Series
DEVELOPMENT Undaunted Courage - Endurance - On the Wing - Zulu Wave - Krakatoa - Across the Medicine Line
CREDITS Kekexili: Mountain Patrol - March of the Penguins - The Story of the Weeping Camel - K-19: The Widowmaker - Snow Dogs - Forbidden Territory: Stanley's Search for Livingstone

Adam Leipzig . . . President
Kenna Jones . . . Development
Laura Lodin . . . Development
Kattie Evans . . . Acquistions
Jessica Ponte . . . Office Coordinator

*NATIONAL GEOGRAPHIC GIANT SCREEN FILMS & SPECIAL PROJECTS

M St., 6th Fl.
1145 17th St., N.W.
Washington, DC 20036-4688
PHONE . . . 202-857-7665
FAX . . . 202-775-6517

Lisa Truitt . . . President
Leslie Ann Aldridge . . . Production Coordinator
Erica Immucci . . . Manager, Film Production
Antonietta Monteleone . . . Manager, Distribution
Derek Threinen . . . Director, Film Marketing, Outreach, & Corporate Relations
Ashley Howard . . . Intern

NATIONAL GEOGRAPHIC KIDS' PROGRAMMING & PRODUCTION

9100 Wilshire Blvd., Ste. 401E
Beverly Hills, CA 90212
PHONE . . . 310-858-5225
FAX . . . 310-858-5801
TYPES Animation - TV Series
COMMENTS Primarily chidren's and family programming; Pre-school through tween

Donna Friedman Meir . . . President
Tara Sorenson . . . VP, Development
Michael Karsh . . . Manager, Current Series & Development
Andy Riddle . . . Sr. Administrative Assistant

NATIONAL LAMPOON
10850 Wilshire Blvd., Ste. 1000
Los Angeles, CA 90024
PHONE 310-474-5252/310-441-7810
FAX 310-474-1219
EMAIL . . . . .cora@nationallampoon.com
WEB SITE . . . . .www.nationallampoon.com
TYPES Animation - Direct-to-Video/DVD - Features - Internet Content - Made-for-TV/Cable Movies - Mobile Content - Reality TV - Specials - Theatre - TV Series
PROVIDES DEAL TO Half Shell Entertainment - Hand Picked Films
PRODUCTION Pledge This with Paris Hilton
UPCOMING RELEASES Totally Baked - Cattle Call
COMPLETED UNRELEASED Jake's Booty Call - Thanksgiving Reunion - Black Ball (DVD)
CREDITS Barely Legal - Adam & Eve - Blackball - Pucked - The Trouble with Frank with Bon Jovi - Gold Diggers - Van Wilder - Loaded Weapon 1 - Senior Trip - Vacation - Animal House
SUBMISSION POLICY No unsolicited material

Daniel S. Laikin . . . . .CEO
Douglas Bennett . . . . .President
Bruce Long . . . . .COO
Scott Rubin .Editor in Chief, Nationallampoon.com
Barry Layne . . . . .Executive VP

NBC ENTERTAINMENT
3000 W. Alameda Ave.
Burbank, CA 91523-0001
PHONE 818-840-4444/212-664-4444
WEB SITE . . . . .www.nbcuni.com
TYPES Made-for-TV/Cable Movies - TV Series - Reality TV
PROVIDES DEAL TO Darkwoods Productions

Jeff Zucker .CEO, NBC Universal Television Group
Jeff Gaspin . . . . .President, NBC Universal Cable Entertainment, Digital Content & Cross-Network Strategy
Kevin Reilly . . . . .President, NBC Entertainment
Marc Graboff . . . . .President, NBC Universal Television Group, West Coast
John Miller . . . . .President/Chief Marketing Officer, The NBC Agency
Vince Manze . . . . .President/Creative Director, The NBC Agency
Howard Averill . . . . .Executive VP/CFO, TV Group, West Coast
Katherine Pope . . . . .Executive VP, NBC Entertainment
Ted Frank . . . . .Executive VP, Entertainment Strategy & Programs, NBC Entertainment
Andrea Hartman . . . . .Executive VP/Deputy General Counsel, NBC
Marc Hirschfeld . . . . .Executive VP, Casting, NBC Entertainment
Rick Ludwin . . . . .Executive VP, Late Night & Primetime Series, NBC Entertainment
Rebecca Marks . . . .Executive VP, NBC Universal Television Group Publicity
Mitch Metcalf . . . . .Executive VP, Program Planning & Scheduling, NBC Entertainment
Jerry Petry . . . . .Executive VP, Administration, NBC Universal Television Group, West Coast
Beth Roberts . . . . .Executive VP, Business Affairs, NBC Universal Network & Cable Entertainment
Vivi Zigler . . . . .Executive VP, Current Programs, NBC Entertainment
Sumithra Barry . . . . .Sr. VP, NBC West Coach Program Research, NBC Entertainment
Thomas Cairns . . . . .Sr. VP, Human Resources
Jeff Ingold . . . . . .Sr. VP/Head, Comedy Development, NBC Entertainment
Katie O'Connell . . . . .Sr. VP, Drama Development, NBC Entertainment
Craig Plestis . . . . .Sr. VP, Alternative Programs & Development, NBC Entertainment

(Continued)

NBC ENTERTAINMENT (Continued)
Frank Radice . . . . .Sr. VP, Advertising & Promotion, The NBC Agency
Erin Gough Wehrenberg . . . . . . .Sr. VP, Current Series, NBC Entertainment
Grace Wu . . . . .Sr. VP, Casting, NBC Entertainment
Tom Alfieri . . . . .VP, Daytime Programs, NBC Entertainment
Carolyn Cassidy . . . . .VP, Current Series, NBC Entertainment
Chris Castallo . . . . .VP, Drama Development, NBC Entertainment
Jayson Dinsmore . . . . .VP, Alternative Programs, NBC Entertainment
Brian Dorfman . . . . .VP, Casting, NBC Entertainment
Greg Downey . . . . .VP, Network & Branded Entertainment Business Affairs, NBC Entertainment
Jane Greenstein . . . . .VP, Comedy Development, NBC Entertainment
Nate Kirtman . . . . .VP, NBC Universal Television Group Publicity
Annamarie Kostura . . . . .VP, Daytime Programs, NBC Entertainment
Wendy Luckenbill . . . . .VP, Publicity, Daytime, Alternative & Specials
Jennifer McNamara . . . . .VP, Casting, NBC Entertainment (NY)
Jennifer O'Connell . . . . .VP, Alternative Programs, NBC Entertainment
Renate Radford . . . . .VP, Comedy Development, NBC Entertainment
Ray Slay . . . . .VP, Photography & New Media
Erin Underhill . . . . .VP, Current Series
Scott Williams . . . . .VP, Program Research, NBC Entertainment
Kevin Fitzgerald . . .Head, NBC Universal Digital Media Distribution Group
Michael Weisman . . . .Executive Producer, NBC Universal Television Group
Meredith Ahr . . . . . .Director, Alternative Programming, NBC Entertainment
Nick Bernstein . . . . .Director, Late Night & Primetime Series
Edwin Chung . . . . .Director, Current Series, NBC Entertainment
Jeanette Eliot . . . . .Director, Events & Operations, NBC Entertainment
Rachel Filippelli . . . . .Director, Current Series, NBC Entertainment
Jamie French . . . . .Director, Primetime Series, NBC Entertainment
Mary Ann Wolf . . . . .Director, Current Series, NBC Entertainment
Marina Nieto . . . . .Programming Associate, Drama Development, NBC Entertainment

NBC NEWS
30 Rockefeller Plaza
New York, NY 10112
PHONE 212-664-4444
WEB SITE . . . . .www.msnbc.com
TYPES Documentaries - News
CREDITS Dateline NBC - Meet the Press - NBC Nightly News with Brian Williams - NBC Nightly News, Weekend Edition - The Chris Matthews Show - Today - Today, Weekend Edition

Jeff Zucker .CEO, NBC Universal Television Group
Steve Capus . . . . .President, NBC News
David Verdi . . . . .VP, NBC News
Alex Wallace . . . . .VP, NBC News
Jim Bell . . . . .Executive Producer, Today
David Corvo . . . . .Executive Producer, Dateline NBC
John Reiss .Executive Producer, NBC Nightly News
Mark Lukasiewicz . . . . .VP, Digital Media, NBC News
Elena Nachmanoff . . . . .VP, Talent Development, NBC News
Lloyd Siegel . . . . .VP, News Partnerships, NBC News
Doug Vaughan . . . . .VP, Special Programs, NBC News
Jeff Gralnick . . . . .Consultant, Internet & Technology
Allison Gollust . . . . .Sr. VP, NBC News Communications
Cheryl Gould . . . . .Sr. VP, NBC News
Phil Griffin . . . . .Sr. VP, NBC News/Executive in Charge of MSNBC
Barbara Levin . . . .Sr. Director, NBC News Communications, Nightly News, Meet the Press, Specials & Politics
Lauren Kapp . . . . .Director, NBC News Communications, Today
Jenny Tartikoff . .Press Manager, NBC News Communications, Dateline NBC
Megan Kopf . . . . .Publicist, NBC News Communications, Weekend Today, The Chris Matthews Show
Lauren Skowronski . . . . .Coordinator, NBC News

NBC SPORTS

30 Rockefeller Plaza
New York, NY 10112
PHONE ... 212-664-4444/212-664-2014
FAX ... 212-664-6035
WEB SITE ... www.nbcuni.com
TYPES New Media - TV Series
COMMENTS Sports programming

Dick Ebersol ... Chairman, NBC Universal Sports & NBC Olympics
Kenneth Schanzer ... President, NBC Sports
Gary Zenkel ... President, NBC Olympics/Executive VP, Strategic Partnerships, NBC Sports
David Neal ... Executive VP, NBC Olympics/Executive Producer, NBC Sports
Peter Diamond ... Sr. VP, Programs, NBC Olympics
Jonathan D. Miller ... Sr. VP, Sports Programming
Perkins Miller ... Sr. VP, Digital Media, NBC Universal Sports & Olympic
Mike McCarley ... VP, Communications & Marketing, NBC Universal Sports & Olympics
Kevin Monaghan ... VP, New Business Development, New Media, NBC Sports
Brian Walker ... Director, NBC Sports
Alana Russo ... Manager, NBC Sports
Lindsay Fitz ... Publicist, NBC Sports

NBC UNIVERSAL CABLE ENTERTAINMENT

3000 W. Alameda Ave.
Burbank, CA 91523-0001
PHONE ... 818-840-4444/818-777-1000
WEB SITE ... www.nbcuni.com
TYPES TV Series
COMMENTS Additional office: 100 Universal City Plaza, Universal City, CA 91608

Randel A. Falco ... President/COO, NBC Universal Television Group
David M. Zaslav ... President, NBC Universal Cable, Domestic Television & New Media Distribution
Jeff Gaspin ... President, NBC Universal Cable Entertainment, Digital Content & Cross-Network Strategy
Bonnie Hammer ... President, USA & Sci Fi Networks
Lauren Zalaznick ... President, Bravo & TRIO Networks
Bridget Baker ... Executive VP, Cable Distribution, NBC Universal Cable
Dave Howe ... Executive VP/General Manager, Sci Fi Channel
Mark Stern ... Executive VP, Original Programming, Sci Fi Channel
Henry Ahn ... Sr. VP, Affiliate Sales, NBC Universal Cable
Andrew Cohen ... Sr. VP, Programming & Production, Bravo
Mark Hotz ... Sr. VP, Marketing, NBC Universal Cable
Jason Klarman ... Sr. VP, Marketing, TRIO
Jean-Briac Perrette ... Sr. VP, New Media/CFO
Jennifer Skorlich ... Sr. VP, Cable Publicity & NBC Late Night
Thomas Vitale ... Sr. VP, Programming & Original Movies, Sci Fi Channel
Erica Conaty ... VP, Marketing, NBC Universal Cable
Brian Hunt ... VP, Local Ad Sales, Promotions & National Accounts, NBC Universal Cable
Megumi Ikeda ... VP, Strategic Initiatives & New Media
Ron Lamprecht ... VP, New Media
Lynette Pinto ... VP, Marketing, NBC Universal Cable
Kris Slava ... VP, Digital Content & Acquisitions

NBC UNIVERSAL CORPORATE

3000 W. Alameda Ave.
Burbank, CA 91523-0001
PHONE ... 818-840-4444/818-777-1000
WEB SITE ... www.nbcuni.com
TYPES Features - TV Series
COMMENTS Additional office: 100 Universal City Plaza, Universal City, CA 91608

Bob Wright ... Vice Chairman/Executive Officer, GE & Chairman/CEO
Beth Comstock ... President, NBC Universal Digital Media & Market Development
John Eck ... President, Technical Operations & Integration
Ron Meyer ... President/COO, Universal Studios
Peter Naylor ... President, NBC Universal Digital Media Sales
Keith Turner ... President, NBC Universal Sales & Marketing
Alan Wurtzel ... President, Research & Media Development, NBC
Marc J. Saperstein ... Sr. Executive VP, Human Resources & Communications
Lynn Calpeter ... Executive VP/CFO
Bruce Campbell ... Executive VP, Business Development
Rick Cotton ... Executive VP/General Counsel
John Damiano ... Executive VP, Affiliate Relations
Jay Linden ... Executive VP, NBC Universal Strategic Partnership Group
Paula Madison ... Executive VP, Diversity
H. David Overbeeke ... Executive VP/CIO
Cory Shields ... Executive VP, Corporate Communications, NBC Universal
Eileen Whelley ... Executive VP, Human Resources
Cindy Gardner ... Sr. VP, Internal Communications, NBC Universal & Corporate Affairs, Universal Studios
Kathy Kelly-Brown ... Sr. VP, Corporate Communications & Media Relations
Deborah Thomas ... Sr. VP, Entertainment Publicity
Salil Dalvi ... VP, Digital Media, NBC Universal
Yolanda Foster ... VP, Programming & Promotions, Telemundo Cable

NBC UNIVERSAL TELEVISION STUDIO

100 Universal City Plaza
Universal City, CA 91608
PHONE ... 818-840-4444/818-777-1000
WEB SITE ... www.nbcuni.com
TYPES Made-for-TV/Cable Movies - Miniseries - Reality TV - Specials - TV Series
PROVIDES DEAL TO 40 Acres & A Mule Filmworks, Inc. - Ars Nova - Baby Cow Productions Ltd. - Big Cattle Productions - Broadway Video - Broadway Video Entertainment - Carson Daly Productions - Doozer - DreamWorks SKG - Galán Entertainment - Hypnotic - Is Or Isn't Entertainment - MobiTV - Principato-Young Entertainment - Raines - Reveille, LLC - Superb Entertainment - Tapestry Films, Inc. - Tollin/Robbins Productions - Upright Citizens Brigade - Wolf Films, Inc.
COMMENTS Late night, daytime, longform and specials; Additional offices: 3000 W. Alameda Ave., Burbank, CA 91523-0001

Jeff Zucker ... CEO, NBC Universal Television Group
Angela Bromstad ... President, NBC Universal Television Studio
Jerry DiCanio ... Executive VP, Production
Charles Engel ... Executive VP, Programming
Rick Olshansky ... Executive VP, Business Affairs
Andy Warren ... Executive VP/CFO
Curt King ... Sr. VP, Publicity, Marketing & Corporate Communications
Laura Lancaster ... Sr. VP, Drama & Cable Programming
Shelley McCrory ... Sr. VP, Comedy Programming
Nancy Perkins ... Sr. VP, Casting
Gina Girolamo ... VP, Comedy Programming
Steven O'Neill ... VP, Casting
Elisa Roth ... VP, Drama Programming
Richard Rothstein ... VP, Cable Programming
Vernon Sanders ... VP, Comedy Programming
Jennifer Turner ... VP, Drama Programming
Lauren Stein ... Director, Drama
Joe Chandler ... Manager, Comedy Programming
Dana Dubois ... Manager, Primetime Series
Jonathan Koa ... Manager, Drama

NEAL STREET PRODUCTIONS LTD.

26-28 Neal St., 1st Fl.
London WC2H 9QQ, UK
PHONE 44-207-240-8890
FAX 44-207-240-7099
EMAIL ....post@nealstreetproductions.com
WEB SITE ....www.nealstreetproductions.com
TYPES Features - Theatre
HAS DEAL WITH DreamWorks SKG
PRODUCTION Things We Lost in the Fire
POST PRODUCTION Starter for Ten
CREDITS Jarhead
SUBMISSION POLICY No unsolicited material

Sam Mendes ....Producer/Director
Pippa Harris ....Producer/Director
Caro Newling ....Director

NEIGHBORS ENTERTAINMENT

3348 Overland Ave.
Los Angeles, CA 90034
PHONE 310-815-8182
FAX 310-815-9977
TYPES Features - Made for TV/Cable Movies - TV Series
DEVELOPMENT How To Murder Your Wife - Point, North Dakota - In Hiding - State of the Union - MVP - Avon Calling - Seven Year Itch - Adventures in Marriage
CREDITS Em & Me

Tim Misenhimer ....Producer/Partner
George Unger ....Producer/Partner
David Wiggins ....Producer/Partner
Jim Langlois ....Director/Partner

NELVANA COMMUNICATIONS, INC.

A Corus Entertainment Company
7920 Sunset Blvd., Ste. 402
Los Angeles, CA 90046
PHONE 323-850-9380/416-588-5571
FAX 323-850-9381
WEB SITE ....www.nelvana.com
SECOND WEB SITE ....www.corusent.com
TYPES Animation - Direct-to-Video/DVD - Features - TV Series
CREDITS The Backyardigans - Babar - Franklin - Rolie-Polie-Olie - Cardcaptors - Medabots - Beyblade - Braceface - Cyberchase - Miss Spider's Sunnypatch Kids - George Shrinks - The Berenstain Bears
COMMENTS Toronto office: 32 Atlantic Ave., Toronto, ON M6K 1X8, Canada

Doug Murphy ....Executive VP, Business Development (Toronto)
Scott Dyer ....Executive VP, Production & Development (Toronto)
Irene Weibel ....VP, Development
Christie Dreyfuss ....VP, Development

NEO ART & LOGIC

8315 Beverly Blvd.
Los Angeles, CA 90048-2607
PHONE 323-653-6007
FAX 323-653-0409
WEB SITE ....www.neoartandlogic.com
TYPES Documentaries - Features - TV Series
DEVELOPMENT Does Anybody Here Remember When Hanz Gubentstein Invented Time Travel? - Perfect Ghost
POST PRODUCTION He Was a Quiet Man
UPCOMING RELEASES Feast
CREDITS Pulse - Wes Craven's Dracula 2000 1-3 - The Prophecy: Uprising - Trekkies 1&2
SUBMISSION POLICY Via Web site

Joel Soisson ....Partner/Producer
Mike Leahy ....Partner/Producer
W.K. Border ....Partner/Producer
Simone DeCamargo ....Finance
Kirk Morri ....VP, Post Production
Courtney Balaker ....Development
Aaron Ockman ....Development
Teresa Zales ....Development

MACE NEUFELD PRODUCTIONS

9100 Wilshire Blvd., Ste. 517, East Tower
Beverly Hills, CA 90212
PHONE 310-401-6868
FAX 310-401-6866
TYPES Features - Made-for-TV/Cable Movies - Miniseries - TV Series
DEVELOPMENT Pathfinder - Seconds - Powers - Outrider - Ice Station Zebra - The Equalizer - Bielski Brothers - Silent Parade
CREDITS Sahara - The Saint - Clear and Present Danger - Patriot Games - The Hunt for Red October - The General's Daughter - The Sum of All Fears

Mace Neufeld ....Principal (310-401-6868)
Kel Symons ....VP, Development (310-401-6869)
Kathy Day ....Executive Assistant to Mr. Neufeld/Office Manager (310-401-6868)
Ryan Patterson ....Creative Executive (310-401-6862)

NEU-MAN-FILMS, INC.

21321 Lighthill Dr.
Topanga, CA 90290-4442
PHONE 818-346-9004
FAX 818-346-1023
EMAIL ....submissions@neumanfilms.com
TYPES Features - Made-for-TV/Cable Movies - Reality TV - TV Series
DEVELOPMENT Pandora - Rocked - Markers - Tempting Fate - Deadline
PRE-PRODUCTION The Apprenticeship of Tupac Shakur
POST PRODUCTION Hidden Adventures
CREDITS Under Siege 2 - Never Talk to Strangers - Sunstroke - Islanders - Across Apple Lake - Chill Factor
SUBMISSION POLICY Email synopsis only; Screenplays only by request via WGA agent or release form

Jeffrey R. Neuman ....President/Producer
Susan Clary ....Executive VP, Business Affairs

NEW AMSTERDAM ENTERTAINMENT, INC.

675 Third Ave., Ste. 2521
New York, NY 10017

PHONE	212-922-1930
FAX	212-922-0674
EMAIL	mail@newamsterdamnyc.com
WEB SITE	www.newamsterdamnyc.com
TYPES	Features - Made-for-TV/Cable Movies - TV Series
HAS DEAL WITH	Touchstone Television
DEVELOPMENT	Keller - Dune: The Lost Years - Dune Prequels - The Merciful Women - The Night Flier: Fear of Flying
CREDITS	Frank Herbert's Children of Dune - Dawn of the Dead (2004) - Pet Sematary - The Stand - The Vernon Johns Story - Frank Herbert's Dune - George A. Romero's Dawn of the Dead - George A. Romero's Martin
SUBMISSION POLICY	Fax one page queries, Attn: Mike Messina

Richard P. Rubinstein . . . . President
Michael Messina . . . . Sr. VP
Emily V. Austin-Bruns . . . . Director, Development & Distribution

NEW CITY PICTURES, INC.

1005 Cypress St.
Vancouver, BC V6J 3K6, Canada

PHONE	604-732-7677
FAX	604-732-7693
EMAIL	info@newcityfilms.com
WEB SITE	www.newcityfilms.com
SECOND WEB SITE	www.newcitypictures.net
TYPES	Features - Made-for-TV/Cable Movies
CREDITS	Mr. Rice's Secret - The Last Stop
COMMENTS	

Colleen Nystedt . . . . President
David Rockwell . . . . CFO
Christopher Courtney . . . . VP, Production
Quinn Bender . . . . Director, Development

NEW CONCORDE

11600 San Vicente Blvd.
Los Angeles, CA 90049

PHONE	310-820-6733
FAX	310-207-6816/310-207-8825
TYPES	Direct-to-Video/DVD - Features - Made-for-TV/Cable Movies - TV Series
DEVELOPMENT	Cyclops - Murder Big Business Style
POST PRODUCTION	Cry of the Winged Serpent - Crash Point
COMPLETED UNRELEASED	Asphalt Wars
CREDITS	Rage and Discipline - The Hunt for Eagle One - DinoCroc

Roger Corman . . . . President/CEO/Executive Producer
Julie Corman . . . . Sr. Executive VP/Executive Producer
Frank Moreno . . . . Vice Chairman
Catherine Corman . . . . Producer (NY)
Thomas Krentzin . . . . Executive VP
Frances Doel . . . . VP, Development
Max Yoshikawa . . . . VP, Finance
Germaine Simiens . . . . Director, Business Affairs

NEW CRIME PRODUCTIONS

555 Rose Ave.
Venice, CA 90291

PHONE	310-396-2199
FAX	310-396-4249
EMAIL	newcrime@aol.com
TYPES	Features
DEVELOPMENT	Pipe Dream - The Source - The Master and Margarita - Et Tu, Babe - Cosmic Banditos
POST PRODUCTION	Grace is Gone
CREDITS	Grosse Pointe Blank - The Jack Bull - High Fidelity - Never Get Outta the Boat

John Cusack . . . . Actor/Writer/Producer
Grace Loh . . . . President
Aurelie Levy . . . . Assistant to Mr. Cusack
Kevin Lawn . . . . Office Manager/Assistant to Ms. Loh

NEW DEAL PRODUCTIONS

9830 Wilshire Blvd.
Beverly Hills, CA 90212

PHONE	323-299-2183
TYPES	Features
HAS DEAL WITH	Universal Pictures
PRODUCTION	Illegal Tender
CREDITS	Black Snake Moan - Hustle and Flow
SUBMISSION POLICY	No unsolicited submissions

John Singleton . . . . Director/Producer/Writer

NEW ENGLAND PRODUCTIONS, INC.

3430 Barry Ave.
Los Angeles, CA 90066-2002

PHONE	310-390-6567
FAX	310-397-3070
TYPES	Features - Made-for-TV/Cable Movies - TV Series
CREDITS	Desperate Housewives - Motocrossed - Medusa's Child - King of the World - Out of Darkness - Metro - James Dean - Live from Baghdad - Threat Matrix

George W. Perkins . . . . Producer

NEW GENERATION FILMS, INC.

304 N. Edinburgh Ave.
Los Angeles, CA 90048

PHONE 323-655-7705/323-655-7702
FAX 323-655-7706
EMAIL . . . .ngf@newgenerationfilmsinc.com
WEB SITE . . . .www.newgenerationfilmsinc.com

TYPES — Animation - Direct-to-Video/DVD - Features - TV Series
DEVELOPMENT — Hana's Ring - M
PRE-PRODUCTION — Booty and the Beast - Dookie
PRODUCTION — Oy Vey, My Son Is Gay! - Gunga Din
CREDITS — Crime & Punishment - Death Game - Days of Love - The Return from India - Open Heart
COMMENTS — Also distributes

Evgeny Afineevsky . . . .Co-Chairman/President/Producer
Igor Zektser . . . .CFO/VP, Business Affairs/Producer
Svetlana Anufrieeva . . . .Executive VP/Producer
Victor Freilich . . . .VP, Production/Producer
Leslie Borodi . . . .VP, Finance/Producer
Alfred Soultan . . . .VP, Development/Producer
Alexander Walker Jr. . . . .General Counsel
Alexander Walker III . . . .VP, Legal Affairs
Alexander H. Vinnitski . . . .VP, Marketing/Producer
Lance K.R. Kawas . . . .Development/Producer

NEW LINE CINEMA

116 N. Robertson Blvd., Ste. 200
Los Angeles, CA 90048

PHONE 310-854-5811/212-649-4900
FAX 310-659-2459/212-649-4966
WEB SITE . . . .www.newline.com

TYPES — Features - Made-for-TV/Cable Movies - TV Series
PROVIDES DEAL TO — Benderspink - Stokely Chaffin Productions - Chick Flicks - Contrafilm - j.k. livin productions - Rat Entertainment/Rat TV - Storyline Entertainment - Temple Hill Productions
DEVELOPMENT — Hairspray - The Golden Compass - Inkheart - Rush Hour 3 - Love in the Time of Cholera - Pride and Glory - Be Kind Rewind
UPCOMING RELEASES — The Texas Chainsaw Massacre: The Beginning - Little Children - Tenacious D in The Pick of Destiny - The Nativity Story - The Number 23 - Mimzy
CREDITS — Snakes on a Plane - Final Destination 3 - Wedding Crashers - Monster-in-Law - The Lord of the Rings Trilogy - Elf - The Notebook - A History of Violence
COMMENTS — East Coast office: 888 Seventh Ave., 20th Fl., New York, NY 10106

Robert K. Shaye . . . .Co-Chairman/Co-CEO
Michael Lynne . . . .Co-Chairman/Co-CEO
Rolf Mittweg . .President/COO, New Line Worldwide Distribution & Marketing
Toby Emmerich . . . .President, New Line Productions
Stephen D. Abramson . . . .CFO

(Continued)

NEW LINE CINEMA (Continued)

Stephen L. Einhorn . . . .President, New Line Home Entertainment
Camela Galano . . . .President, New Line International Releasing, Inc.
Jim Rosenthal . . . .President, New Line Television
Russell Schwartz . . . .President, New Line Domestic Marketing
David Tuckerman . . . .President, New Line Domestic Theatrical Distribution
Erik Holmberg . . . .Co-President, Physical Production
Paul Prokop . . . .Co-President, Physical Production
Paul B. Broucek . . . .President, Music
Benjamin Zinkin . .Sr. Executive VP, Business & Legal Affairs/General Counsel
Judd Funk . . . .Sr. Executive VP, Business & Legal Affairs
Karen S. Zimmer . . . .Sr. Executive VP, Information Systems
Michael Spatt . . . .Sr. Executive VP, Finance
Richard Brener . . . .Sr. Executive VP, Production
David Imhoff . . . .Sr. Executive VP, Worldwide Licensing & Merchandising
David Spiegelman . .Sr. Executive VP, Domestic TV Distribution & Marketing
Kent Alterman . . . .Executive VP, Production
Jayne Bieber . . . .Executive VP, TV Production
Carolyn Blackwood . . . .Executive VP, Business Affairs & Co-Production
Laura Carrillo . . . .Executive VP, Creative Advertising
Diane Charbanic . . . .Executive VP, Media & Co-Op Advertising
David Eichler . . . .Executive VP/Controller
Erik Ellner . . . .Executive VP, Business & Legal Affairs
Teri Fournier . . . .Executive VP, Business & Legal Affairs
Elissa Greer . . . .Executive VP, Field Publicity & Promotions
Susannah Juni . . . .Executive VP, Participation & Contract Accounting
Mark S. Kaufman . . . .Executive VP, Production & Theater
Christina Kounelias . . .Executive VP, Publicity & Corporate Communications
Jon Kroll . . . .Executive VP, Original Programming (TV)
Raymond J. Landes . . . .Executive VP, Finance & Reporting
Jody A. Levin . . . .Executive VP, Film Post Production
Jason Linn . . . .Executive VP, New Line Records
Andrew Matthews . . . .Executive VP, Finance & International Affairs/ Sr. VP, Business & Legal Affairs
Steve Miller . . . .Executive VP, Creative Advertising
Jacqueline R. Moskow . . . .Executive VP, Finance & Reporting
Bob Mott . . . .Executive VP, International Finance & Administration
Nestor Nieves . . . .Executive VP, International Sales
Mark Ordesky . . . .Executive VP, New Line Productions
Gordon Paddison . . . .Executive VP, New Media Marketing
Julie A. Shapiro . . . .Executive VP, Business & Legal Affairs (TV)
Lori Silfen . . . .Executive VP, Music/Sr. VP, Business & Legal Affairs
Lance Still . . . .Executive VP, National Promotions
Craig Alexander . . . .Sr. VP, Business & Legal Affairs
Dana M. Belcastro . . . .Sr. VP, Physical Production
Katherine Beyda . . . .Sr. VP, Physical Production
Cale Boyter . . . .Sr. VP, Development
Kathy Busby . . . .Sr. VP, Production
Clare Anne Conlon . . . .Sr. VP, National Publicity
Jon Davidson . . . .Sr. VP, Production Finance
Bobby L. Doyle . . . .Sr. VP, International Post Production
Leon Dudevoir . . . .Sr. VP, Physical Production
Susie Farris . . . .Sr. VP, Casting
Sara Frith . . . .Sr. VP, Business & Legal Affairs
John Giraldo . . . .Sr. VP/Assistant Controller
Kevin Kasha . . . .Sr. VP, Acquisitions & Programming
Brent Kaviar . . . .Sr. VP, Post Production
Warren Lenard . . . .Sr. VP, Technology & Network Services
Lita Parker . . . .Sr. VP, Human Resources
Robert Pini . . . .Sr. VP, Corporate Communications
Joshua Ravetch . . . .Sr. VP, Production
Lauren A. Ritchie . . . .Sr. VP, Visual Effects
Ron Signorotti . . . .Sr. VP, Participation & Contracts
Tim Stevens . . . .Sr. VP, Administration
Guy Stodel . . . .Sr. VP, Acquisitions
Kelli Turner . . . .Sr. VP, Business Development
Derek Arleta . . . .VP, Business & Legal Affairs
Erica Beier . . . .VP, Production Services
Jack Deutchman . . . .VP, Feature Post Production
Emily Glatter . . . .VP, Production Administration
Keith Goldberg . . . .VP, Production & Development
Phil Goore . . . .VP, Business & Legal Affairs
Scott Kanyuck . . . .VP, Business & Legal Affairs
Kevin Kertes . . . .VP, Music Promotions
Virginia Martino . . . .VP, Business Affairs
Susan Nezami . . . .VP, Business & Legal Affairs
Eric Reynolds . . . .VP, Post Production
Sara D. Romilly . . . .VP, Feature Post Production
Frank Salvino . . . .VP, Feature Post Production
Michele Weiss . . . .VP, Development & Production

(Continued)

NEW LINE CINEMA (Continued)

Jeff Katz . . . . . Director, Development
Candice McDonough . . . . Director, Publicity & Corporate Communications
Luke Ryan . . . . . Director, Development
Sam Brown . . . . . Creative Executive
Michael Disco . . . . . Creative Executive
Daryl Freimark . . . . . Story Editor
Campbell McInnes . . . . . Story Editor
Jonna Smith . . . . . Executive Assistant to Robert K. Shaye
Terry Stewart . . . . . Executive Assistant to Michael Lynne

NEW LINE TELEVISION

888 Seventh Ave.
New York, NY 10106
PHONE 212-649-4900/310-854-5811
FAX 212-956-1936/310-659-2459
WEB SITE . . . . . www.newline.com
TYPES Made-for-TV/Cable Movies - Reality TV - TV Series
CREDITS Blade - Kitchen Confidential - Amish in the City - The Twilight Zone
COMMENTS West Coast office: 116 N. Robertson Blvd., Ste. 710, Los Angeles, CA 90048

Jim Rosenthal . . . . . President, New Line Television
David Spiegelman . . Sr. Executive VP, Domestic TV Distribution & Marketing
David Imhoff . . . . . Sr. Executive VP, Worldwide Licensing & Merchandising
Jon Kroll . . . . . Executive VP, Original Programming
Jayne Bieber . . . . . Executive VP, Production
Julie A. Shapiro . . . . . Executive VP, Business & Legal Affairs
Frank A. Buquicchio . . . . . Sr. VP, TV & Ancillary Accounting
Robin Seidner D'Elia . . . . . Sr. VP, National TV Promotions & Marketing
Randi Goodman . . . . . Sr. VP, Domestic Licensing & Merchandising
Christine Menna . . . . . Sr. VP, Video-on-Demand Sales & Marketing
Nevin Shalit . . . . . Sr. VP, New Media Projects
Sydney Levin . . . . . VP, Alternative Programming
Brendan Kelly . . . . . VP, TV Business Administration
Lori Huck . . . . . VP, Creative Affairs
Ed Bolkus . . . . . VP, Product Development & Merchandising
Mark Costa . . . . . VP, Production
John Mayo . . . . . VP, Creative Services for Licensing & Merchandising
Lourdes Arocho . . . . . Director, International Licensing & Merchandising
Erin Cristall . . . . . Director, Alternative Programming
Jaret Keller . . . . . Manager, East Coast TV Development
Aisha Corpas . . . . . Coordinator, New Line Television
Melissa Genson . . . . . Coordinator, National TV Promotions & Marketing
Tara Halper . . . . . Coordinator, Worldwide Licensing & Merchandising
Caroline Kaam . . . . . Coordinator, Video-on-Demand, Sales & Marketing
Lauren Wohl . . . . . Coordinator, New Line Television

NEW REDEMPTION PICTURES

3000 W. Olympic Blvd., Bldg. 3, Ste. 1437
Santa Monica, CA 90404
PHONE 310-315-4820
FAX 310-315-4821
TYPES Features - Made-for-TV/Cable Movies - Reality TV - TV Series
DEVELOPMENT Untitled Ultimate Fighting Project - Glad All Over - Jersey
POST PRODUCTION The Death and Life of Bobby Z
COMPLETED UNRELEASED Safe & Sound (Reality Pilot)
CREDITS Point of Origin - 15 Minutes - Don King: Only in America - 2 Days in the Valley - The Ryan White Story - The Preppy Murder - Daddy - Stoned - A Father's Revenge

John Herzfeld . . . . . Writer/Director/Producer
Adrian Vina . . . . . Assistant to Mr. Herzfeld

NEW REGENCY PRODUCTIONS

SEE Regency Enterprises

NEW SCREEN CONCEPTS, INC.

84 W. Park Pl.
Stamford, CT 06901
PHONE 203-961-0670
FAX 203-961-0831
WEB SITE . . . . . www.newscreenconcepts.com
TYPES Reality TV
CREDITS Body Human 2000 Series - Yearbook - I Am Your Child - Siegfried & Roy - Brazelton on Parenting - Houston Medical (ABC) - Extreme Makeover

Charles Bangert . . . . . Chairman
Louis Gorfain . . . . . President
Hank O'Karma . . . . . Producer/Director
Janis Biewend . . . . . Producer
David Lee . . . . . Associate Producer
Edna Calastro . . . . . Finance/Business Affairs
Becka Slade . . . . . Editor
Vic Zimet . . . . . Editor

NEW WAVE ENTERTAINMENT

2660 W. Olive Ave.
Burbank, CA 91505
PHONE 818-295-5000
FAX 818-295-8026
EMAIL . . . . . mmeadows@nwe.com
WEB SITE . . . . . www.nwe.com
TYPES Direct-to-Video/DVD

Mike Meadows . . . . . President, Home Entertainment

NEW WAVE ENTERTAINMENT

2660 W. Olive Ave.
Burbank, CA 91505
PHONE 818-955-5240
FAX 818-955-5299
WEB SITE . . . . . www.nwe.com
TYPES Direct-to-Video/DVD - Features - Internet Content - Made-for-TV/Cable Movies - Mobile Content - TV Series
DEVELOPMENT Power Trip - Cougars - Dr. Father - Bird - Dates from Hell
PRODUCTION The Condemned
CREDITS I Married a Princess (Lifetime) - The Wade Robson Project - Hot Spot: The Roosevelt Hotel (E!)
COMMENTS Recently launched El Estudio, producing original Spanish-language content for US market

Mara Jacobs . . . . . Head, Production
Branon Coluccio . . . . . Creative Executive
Gary Lister . . . . . Co-Creative Director, El Estudio
Jeff Myers . . . . . Co-Creative Director, El Estudio
Scott Potter . . . . . Story Editor

NEW WAVE MANAGEMENT

2660 W. Olive Ave.
Burbank, CA 91505
PHONE 818-295-5000
FAX 818-295-5099
EMAIL . . . . bkatz@nwe.com
WEB SITE . . . . www.nwe.com

TYPES: Features - Reality TV - TV Series
DEVELOPMENT: 24 Dates in 24 Hours - Backstage at the Comedy Club - Black Sheep - Laughter Unleashed - Spiritually Speaking - Then & Now - American Roasts - King of Magic - The Wild Life
PRODUCTION: America's Dirtiest Comics - Cooked - One Night Stand-Up - Out of Bounds - Sports Comedy Stand-Up Show - Vivian Lives - New Wave Comedy Series
CREDITS: U.S. of ANT (Logo)- Tourgasm - Last Comic Standing - I Married a Princess - National Lampoon Live - Everybody Hates Bobcat - Hurt Burt - Supermarket - Trash To Cash - Mohr Sports - Welcome to New York - Hype - Action - Spiral

Barry Katz . . . . No Title
Brian Volk-Weiss . . . . No Title
Mark Rousso . . . . Manager
Julie Ayers . . . . Executive Assistant
Laura Dunkelgrun . . . . Executive Assistant
Elizabeth Holmes . . . . Executive Assistant

VINCENT NEWMAN ENTERTAINMENT

8840 Wilshire Blvd., 3rd Fl.
Beverly Hills, CA 90211
PHONE 310-358-3050
FAX 310-358-3289
EMAIL . . . . vnentertainment@aol.com

TYPES: Features - TV Series
DEVELOPMENT: Features: Paradise Lost - Son of Al Qaeda - Night for Day - Kingdom Come - Bluesman - Untitled Abdurachman Khadr Project; TV: Hot Property
PRE-PRODUCTION: Untitled ESPN Project - We're the Millers
CREDITS: A Man Apart - Poolhall Junkies - Sol Goode

Vincent Newman . . . . No Title
Joe Rohrlich . . . . Development
Nancy Lanham . . . . Associate

PETER NEWMAN PRODUCTIONS, INC.

799 Washington St., Ste. 201
New York, NY 10014
PHONE 212-897-3949/212-897-3979
FAX 212-624-1737
EMAIL . . . . pnproduction@aol.com

TYPES: Features - TV Series
DEVELOPMENT: Veeck as in Wreck - Strom Thurmond's Daughter
PRE-PRODUCTION: Janis Joplin
CREDITS: The Squid and the Whale - Smoke - The Secret of Roan Inish - Swimming to Cambodia - Lord of the Flies

Peter Newman . . . . President
Chelsea Horenstein . . . . Production Executive

NEWMARKET CAPITAL GROUP

202 N. Canon Dr.
Beverly Hills, CA 90210
PHONE 310-858-7472
FAX 310-858-7473
EMAIL . . . . info@newmarketcap.com
WEB SITE . . . . www.newmarketfilms.com

TYPES: Features
CREDITS: Memento - The Mexican - Topsy-Turvy - Cruel Intentions - Stark Raving Mad - Donnie Darko - The Skulls - Real Women Have Curves - Spun
SUBMISSION POLICY: Accepted from WGA registered agents only

Chris Ball . . . . Partner/Co-Founder
William Tyrer . . . . Partner/Co-Founder
Rene Cogan . . . . CFO
Aaron Ryder . . . . Production
John Crye . . . . Development
Robert Fyvolent . . . . Business Affairs

NEXT ENTERTAINMENT

3500 W. Olive Ave., Ste. 600
Burbank, CA 91505
PHONE 818-972-0077
FAX 818-972-0349

TYPES: Reality TV - TV Series
HAS DEAL WITH: ABC Entertainment Television Group - Warner Horizon Television
CREDITS: Hostel - The Bachelor - The Bachelorette - Million Dollar Mysteries - Public Property (Pilot) - Smartest Kid in America - Before They Were Stars - Real Funny - World's Worst Drivers - High School Reunion - The Real Gilligan's Island - Ryan & Trista's Wedding

Mike Fleiss . . . . President/Executive Producer (818-972-0122)
Scott Einziger . . . . Co-Executive Producer (818-972-0193)
Lisa Levenson . . . . Co-Executive Producer (818-972-0045)
Tawnya Brown . . . . Executive Assistant (818-972-0122)
Nikki Pattison . . . . Executive Assistant (818-972-0815)

NEXT WEDNESDAY

15900 Riverside Dr. West, #4A
New York, NY 10032
PHONE 347-523-9214
FAX 206-203-3369
EMAIL . . . . mskalski@earthlink.net

TYPES: Documentaries - Features - TV Series
DEVELOPMENT: In a Country of Mothers
PRE-PRODUCTION: The Visitor
POST PRODUCTION: Fur
COMPLETED UNRELEASED: The Hawk Is Dying
CREDITS: Chain - Mysterious Skin - The Jimmy Show - Trick - The Myth of Fingerprints - Wonderland - The Brothers McMullen - The Lifestyle - The Station Agent
SUBMISSION POLICY: No unsolicited material

Mary Jane Skalski . . . . Producer

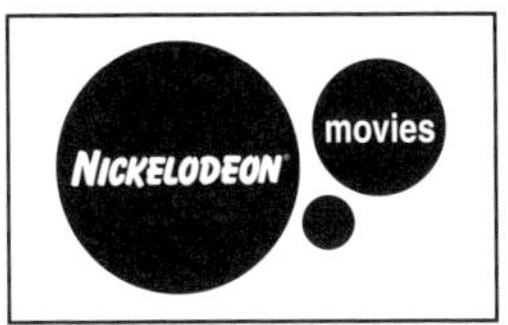

NICKELODEON MOVIES

c/o Paramount Studios
5555 Melrose Ave., Lubitsch Annex, Ste. 119
Los Angeles, CA 90038

PHONE 323-956-8650
FAX 323-862-1663
WEB SITE . . . . www.nick.com

TYPES	Animation - Direct-to-Video/DVD - Features
HAS DEAL WITH	Paramount Pictures
PROVIDES DEAL TO	Lawrence Bender Productions
DEVELOPMENT	Angus - Thongs & Full Frontal Snogging - The Hit - Little Wing - The Five Ancestors - Camp Couture - Fire Breather - Drift House - Legend of the Rings
PRE-PRODUCTION	The Spiderwick Chronicles
PRODUCTION	Charlotte's Web
CREDITS	Nacho Libre - Yours, Mine and Ours - The SpongeBob SquarePants Movie - Lemony Snicket's A Series of Unfortunate Events - Barnyard - The Wild Thornberrys Movie - Hey Arnold! The Movie - Clockstoppers - Jimmy Neutron: Boy Genius - Rugrats in Paris - Snow Day - The Rugrats Movie - Good Burger - Harriet the Spy - Rugrats Go Wild
SUBMISSION POLICY	No unsolicited material
COMMENTS	East Coast office: 1515 Broadway, 38th Fl., New York, NY 10036, phone: 212-258-7550, fax: 212-846-1873

Julia Pistor . . . . Executive VP, Nickelodeon Movies
Michelle Raimo . . . . Sr. VP, Production
Damon Ross . . . . VP, Nickelodeon Movies
Mani Beil . . . . Creative Executive, Development
Brandon Brito . . . . Director, Development
Brad Ong . . . . Director, Marketing
Q Beck . . . . Development/Production
Jain Yu . . . . Development/Production
Michael Zermeno . . . . Marketing
Daniel Rothbart . . . . Executive Assistant, Development
Natasha Stephan . . . . Executive Assistant, Development

NICKELODEON/MTVN KIDS & FAMILY GROUP

1515 Broadway, 38th Fl.
New York, NY 10036

PHONE 212-258-7500
WEB SITE . . . . www.nick.com or www.nickatnite.com
SECOND WEB SITE . . . . www.tvland.com or www.nickjr.com

TYPES	Animation - Direct-to-Video/DVD - Features - TV Series
PROVIDES DEAL TO	Frederator Studios - Worldwide Biggies
DEVELOPMENT	The Darlene Westgor Project (Nickelodeon) - I Pity the Fool (TV Land) - Back to the Grind (TV Land)
PRODUCTION	It Ain't Right
UPCOMING RELEASES	Nick at Nite/TV Land: At the Poocharelli's - Boomers Know Best; Nickelodeon: Tak and the Power of JuJu - The Little JJ Show
CREDITS	Live Action: Just for Kicks - Drake & Josh - The Amanda Show - Ned's Declassified School Survival Guide - Romeo! - Unfabulous - Zoey 101 - My First Time; Animation: Avatar - All Grown Up - The Backyardigans - Jimmy Neutron - CatScratch - Go, Diego, Go! - The Fairly OddParents - Hey Arnold! - The Wild Thornberrys - As Told by Ginger - Rocket Power - Dora the Explorer - Oswald - Little Bill - Blue's Clues - SpongeBob SquarePants - Rugrats - Wonder Pets - The X's
COMMENTS	Includes Nick at Nite and TV Land; TurboNick is a broadband video platform allowing kids to watch full length shows online at any time: www.turbonick.com; West Coast offices: 2600 Colorado Ave., Santa Monica, CA 90404, phone: 310-752-8000; 231 Olive Ave., Burbank, CA 91502, phone: 818-736-3000

Cyma Zarghami . . . . President, Nickelodeon, MTVN Kids & Family Group
Larry Jones . . . . President, Nick at Nite/TV Land
Leigh Anne Brodsky . . . President, Nickelodeon & Viacom Consumer Products
Keith Dawkins . . . . General Manager, Nicktoons Networks
Tom Ascheim . . . . Executive VP/General Manager, Nickelodeon Television
Marjorie Cohn . . . . Executive VP, Original Programming & Development, Nickelodeon
Pam Kaufman . . . . Executive VP, Marketing & Worldwide Partnerships, Nickelodeon
Sarah Kirshbaum Levy . . . . Executive VP, Strategy & Business Operations
Dan Martinsen . . . Executive VP, Corporate Communications, Nickelodeon/MTVN Kids & Family Group
Andra Shapiro . . . . Executive VP/General Counsel, Nickelodeon
Steve Youngblood . . . . Executive VP, Digital Media, Nickelodeon
Brown Johnson . . . . Executive Creative Director, Preschool TV/Nickelodeon
Jaclyn Rann Cohen . . . . Sr. VP, Programming & Acquisitions, Nick at Nite/TV Land
Jim Davey . . . . Sr. VP, Global Consumer Products, Marketing & Planning
Alison Dexter . . . . Sr. VP, Operations & Planning, Nickelodeon
Amy Friedman . . . . Sr. VP, Development/Creative Director, Nickelodeon Digital Television
Ron Geraci . . . . Sr. VP, Research
Steve Grieder . . . . Sr. VP, Nickelodeon International
Russell Hicks . . . . Sr. VP, Creative Resources, Nick/Nick at Nite/TV Land
Paula Kaplan . . . . Sr. VP, Talent, MTV Networks/Nickelodeon
Angela Leaney . . . . Sr. VP, Brand Communications, Nickelodeon Digital Television
Sal Maniaci . . . . Sr. VP, Development & Production, Nick at Nite/TV Land
Melissa Polaner . . . Sr. VP, Law & Business Affairs, MTV Networks/Nickelodeon
Marianne Romano . . . . Sr. VP, Communications, Nickelodeon

(Continued)

NICKELODEON/MTVN KIDS & FAMILY GROUP (Continued)

Kim Rosenblum . . . . .Sr. VP, Creative, Nick at Nite/TV Land
Maureen Taxter . . . . .Sr. VP, Retail & New Business Development
Paul Ward . . . . .Sr. VP, Communications, Nick at Nite/TV Land
Laura Wendt . . . . . .Sr. VP, Research & Planning, Nick/Nick at Nite/TV Land
Marsha E. Williams . . . . .Sr. VP, Research & Planning, Nickelodeon
Lee Tsu Aries . . . . .VP, Animation Productions, Nickelodeon
Jules Borkent . . . . .VP, Programming, Nickelodeon International
Kristen Buckley . . . . .VP, Programming
Eric Coleman . . . . .VP, Animation Development & Production, Nickelodeon Animation Studios
Jodi Davis . . .VP, Communications, Nickelodeon Preschool & Nickelodeon Digital Television
Michael D. Gaylord . . . . .VP, Online
Tanya Giles . . . . .VP, Research & Planning, Nick at Nite/TV Land
Nina Hahn . . . . .VP, International Development (London)
Eddie Hill . . . . .VP, Marketing, Nick Movies
Shari Howard . . . . .VP, Sponsored Promotions, TV Land
Steve Keller . . . .VP, Live-Action Development, Nickelodeon Animation Studios
Sharon Chazin Lieblein . . . . .VP, Talent & Casting
Samantha Maltin . . . . .VP, Business Development, Promotions & Marketing
Adina Pitt . . . . .VP, Acquisitions, Nickelodeon & Nicktoons
Jaclyn Rann-Cohen . . . . .VP, Programming, Nick at Nite/TV Land
Vanessa Reyes-Smith . . . . .VP, Communications, Nick at Nite/TV Land
Ned Sands . . . . .VP/Director, Sales, Western Region
Jill Greenberg Sands . . . . .VP, Talent & Casting
Radha Subramanyam . . . . .VP, Research & Planning, Nickelodeon Digital Television
Shelly Sumpter . . . . .VP, Talent, MTV Networks/Nickelodeon
Mark Taylor . . . . .VP/General Manager, Nicktoons Animation Studios
Kim Killilea . . . . .Sr. Director, Photography, Nickelodeon, Nick at Nite, TV Land, Nick Digital Television
Nicole Mazer . . . . .Sr. Director, Animation Publicity, Nickelodeon
Jennifer Musselman . . . . .Sr. Director, Communications, Nickelodeon
Joanna Roses . . . . .Sr. Director, Corporate Communications, Nickelodeon
Peter Gal . . . . .Director, Animation Development, Nickelodeon Animation Studios
Keirsten Wanamaker . . .Manager, Photography, Nickelodeon, Nick at Nite, TV Land, Nick Digital Television
Margo Zinberg . . . . .Manager, Communications, Nickelodeon
Thamar Romero . . . . . .Publicist, Corporate Communications, Nickelodeon

NIGHTSTAR PRODUCTIONS, INC.

1256 Devon Ave.
Los Angeles, CA 90024
PHONE 310-271-2402
EMAIL . . . . .lgoldst963@aol.com

TYPES	Features - Made-for-TV/Cable Movies - Reality TV - TV Series
CREDITS	Augusta, Gone (Lifetime) - Disappearance (TBS) - Sharing the Secret (CBS/MOW) - Evolution's Child (USA) - Can't Touch This: The MC Hammer Story (VH1)
COMMENTS	Emphasis on true stories, uplifting comedies and drama, and inspirational movies that are a testament to the human spirit; Interest in teen-related stories; Only books and completed screenplays

Laurie Goldstein . . . . .Executive Producer

NINE YARDS ENTERTAINMENT

8530 Wilshire Blvd., Ste. 550
Beverly Hills, CA 90211
PHONE 310-289-1088
FAX 310-289-1288

TYPES	Features - Made-for-TV/Cable Movies - TV Series
COMMENTS	Also a management company

Larry Schapiro . . . . .Producer/Manager
Matt Luber . . . . .Producer/Manager
Alex Cole . . . . .Manager
Steve Crawford . . . . .Manager
Ben Feigen . . . . .Manager/Producer
Jamie Freed . . . . .Manager
Kiran Maguire . . . . .Manager
Stephanie Moy . . . . .Assistant to Matt Luber
Katie Henderson . . . . .Assistant to Ben Feigen
Dianne Kamin . . . . .Assistant to Jamie Freed & Steve Crawford

NITELITE ENTERTAINMENT

205 E. 16th St., #4F
New York, NY 10003
PHONE 310-271-1774

TYPES	Features - Internet Content - Made-for-TV/Cable Movies - Miniseries - Reality TV - Specials - Theatre - TV Series
CREDITS	Dynasty: The Making of a Guilty Pleasure (ABC) - Beautiful Girl (ABC Family) - The Legend of Butch & Sundance (NBC) - Living with the Dead (CBS) - The Perfect Getaway - Nightmare in Big Sky Country - Cheaters (HBO) - Behind the Camera: The Unauthorized Story of Three's Company (NBC)

Greg Gugliotta . . . . .Executive Producer

NOBLE HOUSE ENTERTAINMENT, INC.

c/o Big Time Picture Co.
12210-1/2 Nebraska Ave., Ste. 22
Los Angeles, CA 90025
PHONE 310-943-4378
FAX 310-826-0071
EMAIL . . . . .info@thescriptbroker.com
WEB SITE .www.noblehouseentertainment.com
SECOND WEB SITE .www.thescriptbroker.com

TYPES	Direct-to-Video/DVD - Features - Made-for-TV/Cable Movies - Reality TV
DEVELOPMENT	Untitled Jonathan Lipnicki Project - Truth? or Dare! - Against the Wind - The Other Side of Innocence
PRE-PRODUCTION	East of NY - Scar Lover - Untitled Animation Feature
COMPLETED UNRELEASED	Death House
CREDITS	The Substitute 1&2 - Peacock Blues (Showtime) - Tell About the South (PBS) - Not Afraid to Laugh (Video) - What's the Big Idea? Writing Award Winning Shorts (DVD) - Tattoo U (FX) - Funny You Should Ask (WNEZ Talk Show) - The Insider's Guide to Film Financing (DVD)
SUBMISSION POLICY	No unsolicited submissions; Release form required

Devorah Cutler-Rubenstein . . . . .President
Laura Scheiner . . . . .VP, Development
Andrew Shepherd .Director, Sales & Promotions
Trey Green . . . . .Creative Executive

NOGGIN

1633 Broadway, 7th Fl.
New York, NY 10019
PHONE .212-654-7707
WEB SITE .www.noggin.com

TYPES	Animation - TV Series
CREDITS	Jack's Big Music Show - Connie the Cow - Oobi - Miffy and Friends - 64 Zoo Lane - Tweenies - Play With Me Sesame
COMMENTS	Commercial-free educational TV network to help children gain curricular knowledge in thematic blocks of shows; Preschool TV series

Tom Ascheim .Executive VP/General Manager, Nickelodeon Television
Sarah Lindman .VP, Programming & Production
Kenny Miller .VP, Programming & Production
Jill Greenberg Sands .VP, Talent & Casting, Nick Jr., Noggin & The N
Tanya Young .Manager, Development

NORSEMEN TELEVISION PRODUCTIONS, LLC

4705 Laurel Canyon Blvd., Ste. 400
Valley Village, CA 91607
PHONE .818-753-3100
FAX .818-753-3101
EMAIL .generalinfo@norsemen.tv
WEB SITE .www.norsemen.tv

TYPES	Commercials - Documentaries - Features - Made-for-TV/Cable Movies - Reality TV - TV Series
DEVELOPMENT	Knight Lights
PRODUCTION	Saturday Night Solution (Court TV) - Bringing Home Baby (TLC)
COMMENTS	Promos

Mike Sears .Chairman/CEO
Seth Blair .Executive in Charge of Production
Mark Rosello .CFO
Michelle Davis .VP, Development
Jeff Berk .VP, Production
Diane Eaton .Supervising Producer, SNS
Todd Lachniet .Producer, SNS
Scott Young .Post Production Supervisor
Murray Oden .Head Writer
Eric Smith .Writer, SNS
Ray Klein .Director, Operations, Knight Lights
Mark Henderson .Legal Affairs

NORTH BY NORTHWEST ENTERTAINMENT

903 W. Broadway
Spokane, WA 99201
PHONE .509-324-2949
FAX .509-324-2959
EMAIL .kbeatty@nxnw.net
SECOND EMAIL .moviesales@nxnw.net
WEB SITE .www.nxnw.net

TYPES	Commercials - Direct-to-Video/DVD - Documentaries - Features - Made-for-TV/Cable Movies
DEVELOPMENT	Stuck in Neutral - River Sorrow - Pink Butterfly
UPCOMING RELEASES	End Game - The Cutter
CREDITS	Mel - The Basket - Hangman's Curse - Touched - The Big Empty - Whacked - The Choke - Shadow of Fear - The Making of the Passion of the Christ
SUBMISSION POLICY	Via Web site only
COMMENTS	Also distributes

Rich Cowan .CEO
Tay Voye .General Manager
Brad Harlan .CFO
Kim Beatty .VP, Development
Juan Mas .Production Supervisor

NORTHSOUTH PRODUCTIONS

134 W. 26th St., Ste. 710
New York, NY 10001
PHONE .212-414-8670
FAX .212-414-8668
EMAIL .info@northsouth.tv
WEB SITE .www.northsouth.tv

TYPES	Documentaries - Internet Content - Reality TV - TV Series
PRODUCTION	Big Spender (A&E) - Bride vs. Bride (WE) - Evolution Of... (Discovery) - Try My Life (Style) - What Makes It Tick (FineLiving)
CREDITS	Million Dollar Agents - In a Fix - A Wedding Story (TLC) - Make Room for Baby - Unzipped: Teen Sex in America - Price of Ecstacy (Discovery Health) - Skin Sculptors (TLC) - Get Packing (Travel)

Mark Hickman .Executive Producer
Charlie DeBevoise .Executive Producer
Amy Rapp .Director, Development
Gary Carr .VP, Production
Brian Hopkins .VP, Programming

NORTHSTAR ENTERTAINMENT

4315 Coldwater Canyon Ave., Ste. 9
Studio City, CA 91604
PHONE .818-762-1010
WEB SITE .www.bryanmichaelstoller.com

TYPES	Direct-to-Video/DVD - Features - Specials - TV Series
DEVELOPMENT	Paul's Intergalactic Adventure - Second Chance - Home of the Angels - The Dragon's Candle - Island Girl - They Cage the Animals at Night
PRODUCTION	Filmmaking for Dummies
UPCOMING RELEASES	Light Years Away
CREDITS	Undercover Angel - The Random Factor - Turn of the Blade - American Comedy Awards - Animal Crackers - Dragon Fury 2 - Miss Castaway & the Island Girls
SUBMISSION POLICY	No unsolicited calls

Bryan Michael Stoller .President

NOVA PICTURES
6496 Ivarene Ave.
Los Angeles, CA 90068
PHONE .323-462-5502
EMAIL .pbarnett@novapictures.com
WEB SITE .www.novapictures.com
TYPES Commercials - Features - Made-for-TV/Cable Movies - New Media - Reality TV - TV Series
DEVELOPMENT Couch Potato Make-Over - Enemy at Large - To Have and to Hold - Hollywood Marine
COMPLETED UNRELEASED Extreme Marine
CREDITS Extraordinary Visitor - The Yellow Badge of Courage - The Life and Times of Charlie Putz
SUBMISSION POLICY Submit synopsis via email
COMMENTS PSAs; Member: PGA, ATAS

Peter J. Barnett .Producer
Chris Debiec .Line Producer

NUANCE PRODUCTIONS
4049 Radford Ave.
Studio City, CA 91604
PHONE .818-754-5484
FAX .818-754-5485
TYPES Features - Made-for-TV/Cable Movies - TV Series
HAS DEAL WITH CBS Paramount Network Television
DEVELOPMENT I Did Not Know That - Untitled Car Dealership Pilot
PRODUCTION Love Bites (TBS) - Links (Amazon)
CREDITS Mad About You - The Thing About My Folks
SUBMISSION POLICY No unsolicited submissions

Paul Reiser .Partner
Craig Knizek .Producer
Stacey Bunch .Associate

NUMENOREAN FILMS
12930 Ventura Blvd., Ste. 820
Studio City, CA 91604
PHONE .818-763-3797
FAX .818-980-5170
EMAIL .daguys@pacificnet.net
TYPES Direct-to-Video/DVD - Features - Made-for-TV/Cable Movies - TV Series
DEVELOPMENT Inferno - Bad Karma - Dead Again - Stealing Tomorrow - The Green - Tokyo Ghost Story
COMPLETED UNRELEASED The Insatiable
CREDITS Point Blank - TNT - The Immortal - Race Against Time - HBO Creature Features: The Spider

Cary Solomon .Producer/Director
Chuck Konzelman .Producer/Director
Carol Smith .Office Manager

NUYORICAN
1100 Glendon Ave., Ste. 920
Los Angeles, CA 90024
PHONE .310-943-6600
FAX .310-943-6609
TYPES Features - Reality TV - Specials - TV Series
DEVELOPMENT Carmen - Dance Lessons - Billy Two Sugars
PRODUCTION Moves
POST PRODUCTION Untitled Reggaeton Project - Bordertown - El Cantante
CREDITS Beyond the Runway (MTV) - Borrow My Crew (MTV) - South Beach (UPN)
SUBMISSION POLICY No unsolicited material

Jennifer Lopez .Principal
Simon Fields .Producer
Aida Bernal .Managing Director, Special Projects
Matt Robertson .Director, Development
Jonathan Barry .Assistant to Simon Fields

O ENTERTAINMENT
31878 Camino Capistrano, Ste. 101
San Juan Capistrano, CA 92675
PHONE .949-443-3222
FAX .949-443-3223
EMAIL .info@oent.net
WEB SITE .www.oentertainment.com
SECOND WEB SITE .www.oent.com
TYPES Animation - Direct-to-Video/DVD - Features - Made-for-TV/Cable Movies - TV Series
PRODUCTION Dirk Derby the Wonder Jockey
CREDITS Bruce Almighty - Barnyard - Patch Adams - Kung Pow: Enter the Fist - The Adventures of Jimmy Neutron: Boy Genius - Santa vs. The Snowman - Thumbs - The O-Show

Steve Oedekerk .Producer/Writer/Director
Paul Marshal .Producer
Bruce Devan .Producer
Salvy Maleki .Development Associate
Leryn Doggett .Development Research
Linda Sweigart .Story Analyst

O.N.C. ENTERTAINMENT INC.
10202 W. Washington Blvd., David Lean Bldg., Ste. 430
Culver City, CA 90232
PHONE .310-244-4555
FAX .310-244-4550
TYPES Direct-to-Video/DVD - Documentaries - Features - Made-for-TV/Cable Movies - Miniseries - Mobile Content - Specials - TV Series
HAS DEAL WITH Sony Pictures Entertainment
DEVELOPMENT Gary the Tennis Coach
CREDITS Yours, Mine & Ours - L.A. Confidential - A Time to Kill - The Man Who Knew Too Little - Empire Records - Carpool - Dangerous Beauty - Murder at 1600 - Goodbye Lover - The Sunchaser - Copycat - Bogus

Michael G. Nathanson .President/CEO
Peter Morgan .Sr. VP
Julie Duffell .Director, Management & Affairs
Devin Arbiter .Assistant to Peter Morgan
Sean Dryke .Assistant

LYNDA OBST PRODUCTIONS

c/o Paramount Pictures
5555 Melrose Ave., Bldg. 210
Hollywood, CA 90038

PHONE 323-956-8744
FAX 323-862-2287
WEB SITE . . . . .www.lyndaobst.com

TYPES	Features - Made-for-TV/Cable Movies - TV Series
HAS DEAL WITH	Paramount Pictures
DEVELOPMENT	Adventures in Babysitting
PRE-PRODUCTION	How to Tell He's Not the One in 10 Days (Paramount)
CREDITS	How to Lose a Guy in 10 Days - Sleepless in Seattle - The Fisher King - One Fine Day - Contact - Hope Floats - The Siege - The '60s - Someone Like You - Abandon

Lynda Obst . . . . .Producer
Billy Rosenberg . . . . .VP, Development
Saskia Young . . . . .Director, Development
Taylor Kephart . . . . .Story Editor
Sadath Garcia . . . . .Office Manager
Rachel Abarbanell . . . . .Assistant to Lynda Obst

OCEAN PICTURES

c/o Jim Berkus/UTA
9560 Wilshire Blvd.
Beverly Hills, CA 90212

PHONE 847-266-9530

TYPES	Features
DEVELOPMENT	Unititled Harold Ramis/Owen Wilson Project
CREDITS	Ice Harvest - Analyze That - Analyze This - Bedazzled - Groundhog Day - Caddyshack - Multiplicity - National Lampoon's Vacation

Harold Ramis . . . . .Director/Writer/Producer
Laurel Ward . . . . .Development/Production
Suzanne Herrington . . . . .Development/Production
Pam Kasper . . . . .Assistant to Harold Ramis

ODD LOT ENTERTAINMENT

368 N. La Cienega Blvd.
Los Angeles, CA 90048-1925

PHONE 310-652-0999
FAX 310-652-0718
EMAIL . . . . .info@oddlotent.com

TYPES	Features
DEVELOPMENT	Family Pictures - Lavender Hill Mob - The Reckoning - The Spirit - Trap for Cinderella - Return to Sender - A House Divided - Sensibilidad - Imaginary Larry
POST PRODUCTION	Wanted: Undead or Alive - The Horror Chronicles: Living Hell - The Horror Chronicles: Buried Alive - The Girls' Guide to Hunting and Fishing
CREDITS	Hooligans - Mean Creek - The Wedding Planner - Ricochet River - Hostile Intent - Simple Justice
SUBMISSION POLICY	Accepts solicited material from WGA signatories only

Gigi Pritzker . . . . .CEO/Partner
Deborah Del Prete . . . . .COO/Partner
Laura Ivey . . . . .Executive VP, Business Affairs, Operations & Finance
Linda McDonough . . . . .Executive VP, Production & Development
Brian O'Shea . . . . .Executive VP, Worldwide Sales
Natalya Petrosova . . . . .VP, Finance
Eryl Woodlief . . . . .Director, Development
Sara Kutney . . . . .Creative Executive
Michael Urann . . . . .International Distribution Coordinator
Marcie Friedman . . . . .Assistant to Gigi Pritzker
Joe Kleinberg . . . . .Assistant to Linda McDonough
Chris Ranta . . . . .Assistant to Laura Ivey
Steve Bocsi . . . . .2nd Assistant to Deborah Del Prete

OFFSPRING ENTERTAINMENT

500 S. Buena Vista St.
Burbank, CA 91521

PHONE 818-560-5645
FAX 818-560-5642

TYPES	Features - TV Series
DEVELOPMENT	Jack of All Trades - All's Fare in Love - Flight Risk - Topper - The Fiancé - The Other Guy - Overparenting - The Last Lap - Nut Jobs - Al and Gene
PRE-PRODUCTION	Hairspray
POST PRODUCTION	Premonition
CREDITS	Step Up - The Wedding Planner - Bringing Down the House - A Walk to Remember - The Pacifier - Cheaper By the Dozen 2

Adam Shankman . . . . .Director/Partner
Jennifer Gibgot . . . . .Producer/Partner
Matthew Mizel . . . . .VP, Production (818-560-6017)
Jim Badstibner . . . . .Assistant to Adam Shankman
Bryan Kalfus . . . . .Assistant to Jennifer Gibgot
Michael Simkin . . . . .Assistant to Matthew Mizel

SAM OKUN PRODUCTIONS, INC.

6607 Orange St.
Los Angeles, CA 90048
PHONE .323-655-2424
TYPES Animation - Documentaries - Features - Made-for-TV/Cable Movies - Miniseries - Reality TV - TV Series
DEVELOPMENT Gym Ratz (TV) - Rich Deceiver (20th Century Fox) - Swimming to Atlantis - Rendezvous in Black - Blood-Sucking Shrinks - Burger Kings - Psycho Ball - Project Breakdown
POST PRODUCTION The Secret Life of Super Fans (Documentary)
CREDITS Anya's Bell - The Call of the Wild

Sam Okun .Chairman/Producer
Ron Hart .VP, Literary Acquisitions
Constantine Yeallourides .Director, Development
Arlene Pachasa .Assistant to Sam Okun

OLD DIME BOX PRODUCTIONS, INC.

1999 N. Sycamore Ave., Ste. 503
Los Angeles, CA 90068
PHONE .323-876-1282
TYPES Documentaries - Features - Made-for-TV/Cable Movies - TV Series
CREDITS Escape: Human Cargo - Creating the Future
SUBMISSION POLICY No unsolicited faxes or emails

Anne E. Curry .President/Producer/Writer
Aaron H. Sanchez .Consultant
Elizabeth Common .Executive Assistant

OLD SCHOOL PICTURES, LLC

12438 Houston St.
Valley Village, CA 91607
PHONE .323-640-2258
EMAIL .johnsavs@sbcglobal.net
TYPES Direct-to-Video/DVD - Features - Made-for-TV/Cable Movies - TV Series
DEVELOPMENT Trancas - The Warning
PRE-PRODUCTION Science of Seduction - The Take
POST PRODUCTION Bondage - Beautiful Dreamer - On the Doll
UPCOMING RELEASES Venice Underground
CREDITS Wicked Prayer - Partners - Normal Life - Deceiver - Girl - The Suburbans - Beyond City Limits - Con Express - Sand - Sin - Lucky 13
SUBMISSION POLICY No unsolicited material

John Saviano .President/Producer

LIN OLIVER PRODUCTIONS

8271 Beverly Blvd.
Los Angeles, CA 90048
PHONE .323-782-1495
FAX .323-782-1892
EMAIL .info@linoliverproductions.com
WEB SITE .www.linoliverproductions.com
TYPES Animation - Direct-to-Video/DVD - Features - Made-for-TV/Cable Movies - Theatre - TV Series
DEVELOPMENT Wayside School - Hank Zipzer: The Television Series - Bingo and Bongo - Hip and Hop - Cool Times
CREDITS Harry & the Hendersons - Corduroy - Trumpet of the Swan - Finding Buck McHenry - Aliens Ate My Homework
COMMENTS Children's TV and publishing; Family feature films

Lin Oliver .Producer/Executive
Kim Turrisi .Director, Development

OLMOS PRODUCTIONS, INC.

c/o The Walt Disney Company
500 S. Buena Vista St.
Old Animation Bldg., 1G2, Code 1675
Burbank, CA 91521
PHONE .818-560-8651
FAX .818-560-8655
TYPES Documentaries - Features - Made-for-TV/Cable Movies - TV Series
HAS DEAL WITH ABC Entertainment Television Group
CREDITS Walkout - American Family - Roosters - American Me - It Ain't Love - Americanos - Stand and Deliver - Lives in Hazard

Edward James Olmos .President
Nick Athas .Producer
Bodie James Olmos .VP, Creative Development
Perla Aboulache .Office Manager

OMNIBUS

5007 Arundel Dr.
Woodland Hills, CA 91364
PHONE .818-716-7043
TYPES Features - Made-for-TV/Cable Movies - Reality TV - TV Series
DEVELOPMENT Beached (20th Century Fox) - Mickey (TNT)
PRODUCTION Persons Unknown (Lionsgate/Showtime)
CREDITS Cousin Bette - Sports Night (TV) - Speaking of Sex - The Crash of Flight 323 (TV) - The Court (TV)

Rob Scheidlinger .Producer/President

ON STILTS PRODUCTIONS

9699 N. Hayden Rd., Ste. 108, PMB 233
Scottsdale, AZ 85258-5808
PHONE .310-391-6053/480-991-2142
EMAIL .osp14@aol.com
TYPES Features - Made-for-TV/Cable Movies - Theatre
CREDITS An Affectionate Look at Fatherhood (NBC) - Miss Evers' Boys (HBO) - On Promised Land (Disney Channel) - Mercy Mission: The Rescue of Flight 771 (NBC)

Peter Stelzer .Producer

ONCE A FROG PRODUCTIONS

9200 W. Sunset Blvd., Ste. 325
Los Angeles, CA 90069
PHONE .310-432-6630
FAX .310-858-1104
TYPES Features - Made-for-TV/Cable Movies - TV Series
HAS DEAL WITH Madison Road Entertainment
CREDITS American Dreams (NBC) - My Life Is a Sitcom (ABC)

Jonathan Prince .Executive Producer/Writer/Director
Pamela K. Bruce .VP, Development
Brian Casey .Assistant to Jonathan Prince

ONCE UPON A TIME FILMS, LTD.

2314 Michigan Ave.
Santa Monica, CA 90404-3930
PHONE 310-582-1220
FAX 310-582-0098
EMAIL . . . . oncupnatim@aol.com

TYPES	Features - Made-for-TV/Cable Movies - TV Series
COMPLETED UNRELEASED	The Legend of Butch & Sundance (NBC) - Behind the Camera: The Unauthorized Story of Diff'rent Strokes (NBC)
CREDITS	Broken Trail (AMC) - Fighting the Odds: The Marilyn Gambrell Story (Lifetime) - Behind the Camera: The Unauthorized Story of Diff'rent Strokes - Murder at the Presidio - Confessions of a Sociopathic Social Climber (Oxygen) - Cool Money (USA) - Rapid Fire: The Norco Bank Robbery (USA) - Behind the Camera: The Unauthorized Story of Mork & Mindy - Dynasty: The Making of a Guilty Pleasure (ABC) - Call Me: The Rise and Fall of Heidi Fleiss (USA) - Beautiful Girl (ABC Family) - On Thin Ice (Lifetime) - Behind the Camera: The Unauthorized Story of Three's Company (NBC)

Stanley M. Brooks . . . . Executive Producer
Scott W. Anderson . . . . Producer
Damian Ganczewski . . . . Producer
Fernando Alessandri . . . . Producer
Nimo Mathenge . . . . Manager, Production
Huy Luong . . . . Assistant to Mr. Brooks
Aaron Slavick . . . . Runner/Production Assistant

ONE STEP PRODUCTIONS

12188 Laurel Terrace Dr.
Studio City, CA 91604-3644
PHONE 818-762-1624
FAX 818-763-1955
EMAIL . . . . judy@jchaikin.com
WEB SITE . . . . www.onestepproductions.com

TYPES	Documentaries - Features - Made-for-TV/Cable Movies
PRODUCTION	The Girls in the Band
CREDITS	Legacy of the Hollywood Blacklist (PBS) - Stolen Innocence (CBS) - Los Pastores (PBS) - Cotillion '65
SUBMISSION POLICY	No unsolicited material

Judy Chaikin . . . . Executive Producer
Loren Stephens . . . . Co-Executive Producer

ONE VOICE ENTERTAINMENT, INC.

14926 Moorpark St., Ste. 101
Sherman Oaks, CA 91403
PHONE 310-203-1526

TYPES	Features - TV Series
DEVELOPMENT	Mama Got Back - Dead Beats - Kool Media Bounce - Record Men - Under Pressure
COMPLETED UNRELEASED	Elegies - Storm Warning - AEIOU Sometimes Y
CREDITS	I Witness (aka God's Witness)
COMMENTS	Representation: Liz Robinson, phone: 310-446-1466; Amy Schiffman, Gersh Agency, phone: 310-274-6611

Robert Ozn . . . . Writer/Producer

OPEN ROAD FILMS

6815 W. Willoughby Ave., Ste. 205
Los Angeles, CA 90038
PHONE 323-464-6034
FAX 323-464-6049
EMAIL . . . . openroadfilms@yahoo.com

TYPES	Commercials - Direct-to-Video/DVD - Documentaries - Features - Music Videos - TV Series
DEVELOPMENT	Bold Native - La Milagrosa - Lucid - WKYD 78 - Sibling Rivalry - Kid Saves the Day - The Scene - The Art of War
POST PRODUCTION	Rock the Bells - Middle of Nowhere
COMPLETED UNRELEASED	The Last Stand
CREDITS	Beef 1&2 - Thug Angel - The Freshest Kids
SUBMISSION POLICY	No unsolicited material read without submission agreement; Email for guidelines

Casey Suchan . . . . Producer/Director
Denis Henry Hennelly . . . . Producer/Director

ORCHARD FILMS

119 W. 23rd St., Ste. 409
New York, NY 10011
PHONE 212-229-3770
FAX 212-229-3772
WEB SITE . . . . www.orchardfilms.com

TYPES	Documentaries - Reality TV - TV Series
DEVELOPMENT	The Last Word
PRODUCTION	Indie Sex 2 (IFC)
UPCOMING RELEASES	Fabulous! The Story of Queer Cinema (IFC)
CREDITS	In the Company of Women (IFC) - Chasing the Crown (WE) - Love Files (WE) - Hope in a Jar (A&E) - Indie Sex: Taboos (IFC) - Miss America (PBS) - Who Is Alan Smithee? (AMC) - Are You Comfortable? (IFC Pilot)
SUBMISSION POLICY	No unsolicited submissions

Lesli Klainberg . . . . Producer/Director
Chandra Simon . . . . Producer
Tammie Rhee . . . . Associate Producer
Dave Donnars . . . . Assistant

ORIGINAL FILM

11466 San Vicente Blvd.
Los Angeles, CA 90049

PHONE	310-575-6950
FAX	310-575-6990
TYPES	Direct-to-Video/DVD - Features
HAS DEAL WITH	Sony Pictures Entertainment - Sony Pictures Television
DEVELOPMENT	Nightlife - Curve - The Unprofessionals - Man with the Football - Skip Tracer - Wimpy - R.I.P.D. - Untitled Eloping Comedy
PRE-PRODUCTION	The Prom
PRODUCTION	Evan Almighty - Vantage Point
POST PRODUCTION	Gridiron Gang
COMPLETED UNRELEASED	I Know What You Did Last Summer (Direct-to-Video)
CREDITS	The Fast and the Furious 3: Tokyo Drift - Click - Stealth - XXX 1&2 - S.W.A.T. - 2 Fast 2 Furious - Not Another Teen Movie - The Fast and the Furious - Cruel Intentions 1&2 - I Know What You Did Last Summer 1&2 - Blue Streak - The Rat Pack - Saving Silverman - Urban Legend 1&2 - Torque - Out of Time - Juice - Volcano - Sweet Home Alabama
SUBMISSION POLICY	No unsolicited material

Neal Moritz . . . . Owner/Producer
Elizabeth Buraglio . . . . Production Executive
Amanda Cohen . . . . Production Executive
Toby Jaffe . . . . Production Executive
Tania Landau . . . . Production Executive
Ori Marmur . . . . Production Executive
Vivian Cannon . . . . Head, TV
Mehrak Easley . . . . Assistant to Ms. Cannon
Jeff Fierson . . . . Assistant to Mr. Marmur
Jen Levett . . . . Assistant to Ms. Cohen
Alex Mircheff . . . . Assistant to Ms. Landau
Jeni Mulein . . . . Assistant to Mr. Moritz
Jon Oakes . . . . Assistant to Mr. Jaffe
Jonas Barnes . . . . Production Assistant

ORIGINAL PRODUCTIONS

308 W. Verdugo Ave.
Burbank, CA 91502

PHONE	818-295-6966
FAX	818-295-6923
WEB SITE	www.originalproductions.com
TYPES	Reality TV - Specials - TV Series
CREDITS	The Messengers - Monster Garage - Deadliest Catch - Ballroom Bootcamp - Boom! - Monster Nation - Wing Nuts - Biker Build-Off - Plastic Surgery: Before & After
COMMENTS	Culture series

Thom Beers . . . . CEO/Executive Producer
Tim Beers . . . . CFO
Ernie Avila . . . . COO/VP, Business Affairs
George Puckhaber . . . . VP, Production
Philip Segal . . . . Executive VP, Entertainment
Stuart Swezey . . . . VP, Development
Amy Procop . . . . Executive Assistant to Thom Beers
Jay Bennett . . . . Development
Brandon Killion . . . . Development

THE ORPHANAGE

6725 Sunset Blvd., Ste. 220
Hollywood, CA 90028

PHONE	323-469-6700/415-561-2570
FAX	323-469-6701/415-561-2575
EMAIL	sari@theorphanage.com
WEB SITE	www.theorphanage.com
TYPES	Animation - Commercials - Features - Made-for-TV/Cable Movies - Miniseries - Music Videos - TV Series
DEVELOPMENT	Power of the Dark Crystal - Blackwater - City of Darkness - The Madman's Kiss - Twenty First Century Blues - Prodigy - Blackdeer - Dust - Legion - The Elementals - Untitled Teen Horror Project
POST PRODUCTION	Griffin and Phoenix - Mimzy - Dungeon Siege - Night at the Museum
UPCOMING RELEASES	The Host
CREDITS	Superman Returns - Ten Tiny Love Stories (Lionsgate)
COMMENTS	High-end VFX; San Francisco office: c/o The Presidio, 39 Mesa St., Ste. 201, San Francisco, CA 94129

Paul Grimshaw . . . . VP, Orphanage Commercials
Marc Sadeghi . . . . VP, Feature Post & VFX
Carsten Sorenson . . . . CEO
Scott Stewart . . . . Co-Founder
Jonathan Rothbart . . . . Co-Founder/Sr. VFX Supervisor
Stuart Maschwitz . . . . CTO
Sari Stewart . . . . Assistant, Production & Development
Brian Stone . . . . Assistant, Feature Post & VFX

OUT OF THE BLUE . . . ENTERTAINMENT

c/o Sony Pictures Entertainment
10202 W. Washington Blvd., Astaire Bldg., Ste. 1200
Culver City, CA 90232-3195

PHONE	310-244-7811
FAX	310-244-1539
EMAIL	info@outoftheblueent.com
WEB SITE	www.outoftheblueent.com
TYPES	Features
HAS DEAL WITH	Columbia Pictures
DEVELOPMENT	The Governess - The Toy - I Dream of Jeannie
PRE-PRODUCTION	Water's Edge
CREDITS	Akeelah and the Bee - Mr. Deeds - Master of Disguise - Big Daddy - Deuce Bigalow
SUBMISSION POLICY	By agent or entertainment lawyer only

Sid Ganis . . . . No Title
Alex Siskin . . . . No Title
Mandy Safavi . . . . No Title
Carlo Eugster . . . . No Title
Mike Johnson . . . . No Title
Joyce San Pedro . . . . No Title

OUTERBANKS ENTERTAINMENT

9000 Sunset Blvd., Ste. 1001
Los Angeles, CA 90069
PHONE .310-858-8711
FAX .310-858-6947
EMAIL .firstname@outerbanks-ent.com
TYPES Features - TV Series
HAS DEAL WITH The Weinstein Company
DEVELOPMENT Her Leading Man - Retribution
PRODUCTION Hidden Palms (CW)
CREDITS Cursed - Backwater - Scream 1&2 - Dawson's Creek - I Know What You Did Last Summer - Wasteland - Glory Days - Halloween: H20

Kevin Williamson .President
Alexis Bayoud .Creative Executive
Mike Costa .Assistant to Kevin Williamson

OUTLAW PRODUCTIONS

c/o Sony Pictures Entertainment
10202 W. Washington Blvd., Sidney Poitier Bldg., Ste. 3214
Culver City, CA 90232
PHONE .310-244-3445
FAX .310-244-1139
WEB SITE .www.outlawfilm.com
TYPES Features - TV Series
HAS DEAL WITH Columbia Pictures
DEVELOPMENT DJ - Season in Central Park - Wanna-be - Shanghai - 27 Dresses - Lost Boys - Space Between - Lucid - Iron Curtain
POST PRODUCTION Breach
UPCOMING RELEASES The Santa Clause 3
CREDITS Phat Girlz - The Santa Clause 1&2 - National Security - Training Day - Gossip - Ready to Rumble - Three to Tango - Addicted to Love - Don Juan DeMarco - sex, lies and videotape - The Opposite Sex - The Thing About My Folks
SUBMISSION POLICY No unsolicited submissions

Deb Newmyer .Producer
Michael Glassman .VP, Production & Development
Luke Sandler .Story Editor

THE OVER THE HILL GANG

578 Washington Blvd., Ste. 214
Marina del Rey, CA 90292
PHONE .310-578-2040
FAX .310-388-4617
EMAIL .tvproduc@att.net
TYPES Commercials - Features - Made-for-TV/Cable Movies - Miniseries - Mobile Content - Music Videos - Reality TV - TV Series
HAS DEAL WITH Liberation Entertainment Inc.
DEVELOPMENT The Great Christmas Train Robbery - David Chicken - Skagel Time
CREDITS Sir Arthur Conan Doyle's The Lost World (Seasons 1-4)
COMMENTS Deal with Digital Acquisitions Corp.

Peter Bergmann .Executive Producer
Arnold Soloway .Executive Producer
Todd Makler .CFO

OVERBROOK ENTERTAINMENT

450 N. Roxbury Dr., 4th Fl.
Beverly Hills, CA 90210
PHONE .310-432-2400
FAX .310-432-2401
TYPES Features - TV Series
HAS DEAL WITH Sony Pictures Entertainment
DEVELOPMENT Tonight, He Comes - Monster Hunter - It Takes a Thief - Greenbacks
PRE-PRODUCTION I Am Legend
UPCOMING RELEASES The Pursuit of Happyness
CREDITS Ali - All of Us (Series) - I, Robot - Hitch - Saving Face - ATL
COMMENTS Soundtracks; Music

Will Smith .Partner
James Lassiter .Partner
Joe Pichirallo .Film Executive
Tracey Nyberg .Creative Executive
Haroon Saleem .Creative Executive
Dawn Thomas .Creative Executive
Jana Babatunde-Bey .General Manager
Omarr Rambert .A&R Executive, Music
Miguel Melendez .Music Management

OXYGEN MEDIA

75 Ninth Ave.
New York, NY 10011
PHONE .212-651-2000/323-860-3500
FAX .212-651-2099/323-860-3505
WEB SITE .www.oxygen.com
TYPES Features - Internet Content - Made-for-TV/Cable Movies - Reality TV - Specials - TV Series
DEVELOPMENT Angry Little Girls - Ivana Young Man (Special) - Fight Girls - Once More With Feeling - Capitol Hill Girls - Tease - Bastards! - Identical - Nicky Velvet - Robin Hudson Mysteries - Serial - Sexy Justice; Original Movies: MK Ultra - The Pact - Blindsided
CREDITS Banshee - The Janice Dickinson Modeling Agency - Breaking Up With Shannen Doherty - Oprah: After the Show - Girls Behaving Badly - Nice Package - Good Girls Don't - Naked Josh - Talk Sex with Sue Johanson - Campus Ladies - Mo'Nique's Fat Chance - Nighty Night
COMMENTS Cable and Internet network; West Coast office: 6650 Romaine Ave., Lot D, Bldg. 40, Hollywood, CA 90038

Geraldine Laybourne .Founder/CEO
Marcy Carsey .Co-Founder/Partner
Tom Werner .Co-Founder/Partner
Oprah Winfrey .Co-Founder
Lisa Gersh .COO/President
Kassie Canter .CCO
Debby Beece .President, Programming
Geoffrey Darby .President, Production & Convergence
Daniel Taitz .Chief Administrative Officer/General Counsel
Cynthia Ashworth .Sr. VP, Marketing
Mary Jeanne Cavanaugh .Sr. VP, Advertising Sales
Julie Insogna .Sr. VP, Talent Relations & Music Programming
Brigitte McCray .Sr. VP, Programming (NY)
Aaron Meyerson .Sr. VP, Development & Production
Elizabeth Cullen .VP, Program Acquisitions & Co-Production
Nikki Donen .VP, Development
Kristen Connolly Vadas .VP, West Coast Development (LA)
Stephanie Ziev .VP, Development (NY)
Nicole De Fusco .Manager, Development

*OZLA PICTURES, INC.
1800 Camino Palmero St.
Los Angeles, CA 90046
PHONE .323-876-0180
FAX .323-876-0189
EMAIL .ozla@ozla.com
WEB SITE .www.takaichise.com/ozla
TYPES Features - TV Series
HAS DEAL WITH Fox Atomic - Regency Television
DEVELOPMENT The Entity - Yomi - Infection - Premonition - Shutter - Creep-Show - Siren
POST PRODUCTION The Grudge 2
CREDITS The Grudge - American Yakuza - No Way Back - Crying Freeman - Ringu 1&2 - Ringu 0: Birthday - Honogurai Mizu No Soko Kara - Ju-On 1&2
SUBMISSION POLICY Accepted through and agent or lawyer only
COMMENTS US and Japanese productions; Production offices in Los Angeles and Tokyo, Japan

Take Ichise .Producer
Hiroko Stanhope .Executive Assistant to Take Ichise
Mihoko Bunker .Office Assistant
Yuko Sakurai .Office Assistant

PACIFICA INTERNATIONAL FILM & TV CORPORATION
PO Box 8329
Northridge, CA 91327
PHONE .818-831-0360
FAX .818-831-0352
EMAIL .pacifica@pacifica.la
TYPES Features
DEVELOPMENT Turn - Cop on a Mission - Bambi and Her Pink Gun - Lady Zatoichi - Django
PRE-PRODUCTION Phone
CREDITS Eight Below - The Ring
COMMENTS Actively developing Asian remakes

Christine Iso .Producer
Andra St. Ivanyi .Acquisition & Production
Lori Stillman .Finance
Shirley Alovera .Acquisition & Production Assistant

GEORGE PAIGE ASSOCIATES, INC.
13101 Washington Blvd., Ste. 215
Los Angeles, CA 90066
PHONE .310-397-1746
FAX .310-397-1748
EMAIL .info@gpaent.com
WEB SITE .www.gpaent.com
TYPES Animation - Direct-to-Video/DVD - Documentaries - Features - Made-for-TV/Cable Movies - Specials - TV Series
DEVELOPMENT The Nutty Professor (Animated)
CREDITS Fueled - Gilda Radner's Greatest Moments - Martin & Lewis - Abbott & Costello Meet Jerry Seinfeld - The Three Stooges 75th Anniversary (NBC) - TV's Greatest Sidekicks

George Paige .President
James Tumminia .Producer

PALOMAR PICTURES
155 N. Anita Ave.
Los Angeles, CA 90049
PHONE .310-440-3494
FAX .310-440-9565
EMAIL .ad@palomarpics.com
TYPES Documentaries - Features - TV Series
DEVELOPMENT Brothers - Elling - The Knockout Artist - Dark Highway - The Feathermen
PRE-PRODUCTION The Devil in the White City - The Good Heart
UPCOMING RELEASES Zidane: A 21st Century Portrait - A Little Trip to Heaven - Destricted - Screaming Masterpiece (Documentary)
CREDITS Pretty Persuasion - K-19: The Widowmaker - The Weight of Water - Arlington Road - Basquiat - Kalifornia - Red Rock West - Candyman - Wild at Heart - Madonna: Truth or Dare
SUBMISSION POLICY No unsolicited materials

Joni Sighvatsson .CEO/Producer
Jay Burnley .Director, Development
Aditya Ezhuthachan .Story Editor

PANAMAX FILMS
2000 Ponce de Leon Blvd., Ste. 500
Coral Gables, FL 33134
PHONE .305-421-6336
FAX .305-421-6389
EMAIL .info@panamaxfilms.com
WEB SITE .www.panamaxfilms.com
TYPES Features
HAS DEAL WITH Lionsgate
DEVELOPMENT Reggaeton - La Mujer de Mi Hermano
SUBMISSION POLICY No unsolicited submissions; Must be submitted through professional representation
COMMENTS New York office: Greenestreet Film Center, 9 DesBrosses St., 2nd Fl., New York, NY 10013

James M. McNamara .Founder/Chairman
Benjamin Odell .Head, Creative Development

PANDEMONIUM
100 N. Crescent Dr., Ste. 125
Beverly Hills, CA 90210
PHONE .310-385-4088
FAX .310-385-4232
TYPES Features
HAS DEAL WITH Walt Disney Pictures/Touchstone Pictures
DEVELOPMENT Desmond Doss - Torso
PRE-PRODUCTION Coraline
CREDITS Dark Water - The New World

Bill Mechanic .President/CEO
Suzanne Warren .VP, Production
Raquel Rubio .Contract Administrator

PANTHEON ENTERTAINMENT CORP.

3576 Dixie Canyon Ave.
Sherman Oaks, CA 91423
PHONE 213-891-2670
WEB SITE . . . . .www.hometown.aol.com/absuger
TYPES — Features - Made-for-TV/Cable Movies
POST PRODUCTION — Premonition
COMPLETED UNRELEASED — Grilled
CREDITS — Love Kills - Working Trash - Kimberly - Basic Training - Payoff - Spiders - Prozac Nation - Undisputed - Ballistic - Boat Trip - The Whole Ten Yards - Johnson Family Vacation - Shopgirl

Andrew Sugerman . . . . .Producer
Britta Ziegert . . . . .VP/CFO

PARADIGM STUDIO

2701 Second Avenue North
Seattle, WA 98109
PHONE 206-282-2162/877-282-2162
FAX 206-283-6433
EMAIL . . . . .info@paradigmstudio.com
WEB SITE . . . . .www.paradigmstudio.com
SECOND WEB SITE . . . . .www.iconsamongus.com
TYPES — Documentaries - Features - TV Series
DEVELOPMENT — You Don't Know About Me - The Wild
PRODUCTION — Icons Among Us: Jazz in the Present Tense (Documentary Series)
CREDITS — Around the Fire
COMMENTS — Development deal with Jeff Dowd & Associates; Los Angeles office: 3200 Airport Ave., Ste. 1, Santa Monica, CA 90405, phone: 310-915-9700, fax: 310-572-1501; www.aroundthefire.com

John Comerford . . . . .President
B Dahlia . . . . .Manager
Lance Rosen . . . . .Director, Business Affairs

PARADOX PRODUCTIONS, INC.

801 Tarcuto Way
Los Angeles, CA 90077
PHONE 310-440-8133
FAX 310-472-6467
EMAIL . . . . .doubledox@aol.com
TYPES — Features - TV Series
PRODUCTION — Welcome to the Jungle Gym (CBS/Warner Bros. Pilot)
CREDITS — Miss Congeniality 2: Armed and Fabulous - The Santa Clause - Home Improvement - Roseanne - L.A. Law - Jungle 2 Jungle - Joe Somebody - thirtysomething - George Lopez Show - Freddie (ABC)

John Pasquin .Director/President

PARALLEL ENTERTAINMENT, INC.

9255 Sunset Blvd., Ste. 1040
Los Angeles, CA 90069
PHONE 310-279-1123
FAX 310-279-1147
WEB SITE . . . . .www.parallelentertainment.com
TYPES — Direct-to-Video/DVD - Features - Specials
HAS DEAL WITH — Comedy Central - Paramount Home Entertainment
DEVELOPMENT — Bait Shop - The Crossing - Never Give Up - Witless Protection
PRE-PRODUCTION — Delta Farce
PRODUCTION — Foxworthy's Big Night Out (CMT)
COMPLETED UNRELEASED — Henry Cho: What's That Clickin' Noise? (Comedy Central) - Russell Peters: One Hour Special (Comedy Central) - Ralphie May "Girth of a Nation" One Hour Special (Comedy Central)
CREDITS — Kathleen Madigan: In Other Words - Larry the Cable Guy: Health Inspector - Blue Collar TV - Blue Collar Comedy Tour Rides Again - Blue Collar Comedy Tour: The Movie - Blue Collar Comedy Tour: One for the Road
SUBMISSION POLICY — Does not accept unsolicited submissions

J.P. Williams . . . . .Owner/Manager
Jessica Williams . . . . .Assistant to J.P. WIlliams
Ken Madson . . . . .Manager
Maggie Houlehan . . . . .Manager
Kimberly Lollar . . . . .Associate
Alan Blomquist . . . . .Producer
Jennifer Novak . . . . .Development

PARAMOUNT DIGITAL MEDIA GROUP

5555 Melrose Ave.
Los Angeles, CA 90038-3197
PHONE 323-956-4444
WEB SITE . . . . . www.paramount.com
TYPES Internet Content - Mobile Content

Tom Lesinski . . . . . President

PARAMOUNT PICTURES

5555 Melrose Ave.
Los Angeles, CA 90038-3197
PHONE 323-956-5000
FAX 323-862-1204
WEB SITE . . . . . www.paramount.com
TYPES Features
PROVIDES DEAL TO Bad Robot Productions - Blumhouse Productions - Bona Fide Productions - Broadway Video Entertainment - C/W Productions - The Sean Daniel Company - Darkwoods Productions - Deep River Productions - di Bonaventura Pictures, Inc. - Double Feature Films - DreamWorks SKG - The Robert Evans Company - John Goldwyn Productions - Guy Walks Into a Bar - Interscope/Shady/Aftermath Films - Tom Jacobson Productions - The Jinks/Cohen Company - Lakeshore Entertainment Group LLC - Misher Films - MTV Films - Nickelodeon Movies - Lynda Obst Productions - Paramount Vantage/Paramount Classics - Plan B Entertainment - Revelations Entertainment - Southern Cross the Dog - Trunity, a Mediar Company, a Division of True Mediar, a Unity Corpbopoly - Watermark Productions
UPCOMING RELEASES Barnyard - Zodiac - Charlotte's Web - Untitled World Trade Center Project
CREDITS Nacho Libre - Mission: Impossible III - Elizabethtown - Get Rich or Die Tryin' - The Weather Man - War of the Worlds - Bad News Bears - Four Brothers - The Honeymooners - Yours, Mine and Ours - Aeon Flux - Last Holiday - Failure to Launch

Brad Grey . . . . . Chairman, CEO, Paramount Pictures Corporation
Gail Berman . . . . . President, Paramount Pictures
Frederick Huntsberry . . . . . COO
Rob Moore . . . . . President, Marketing, Distribution & Home Entertainment
John Lesher . . . . . President, Paramount Vantage/Paramount Classics
Kelley Avery . . . . . President, Worldwide Home Entertainment
Tom Lesinski . . . . . President, Digital Media Group
Mark Badagliacca . . . . . Executive VP/CFO
Daniel Ferleger . . . . . Executive VP, Paramount Pictures
Paul Neinstein . . . . . Executive VP, Business Affairs

PARAMOUNT PICTURES PRODUCTION DIVISION

5555 Melrose Ave.
Los Angeles, CA 90038-3197
PHONE 323-956-5000
WEB SITE . . . . . www.paramount.com
TYPES Features

Allison Shearmur . . . . . Co-President, Production
Brad Weston . . . . . Co-President, Production
Mark Bakshi . . . . . President, Feature Production Management Worldwide
Burt Berman . . . . . President, Music Division
Pamela Abdy . . . . . Executive VP, Production
Marty Cohen . . . . . Executive VP, Post Production
Ben Cosgrove . . . . . Sr. VP, Production
Michael Hill . . . . . Sr. VP, Production Finance
Alexandra Koch-Stone . . . . . Sr. VP, Feature Production Management
Gail Levin . . . . . Sr. VP, Features Casting
Dan Levine . . . . . Sr. VP, Production
Mark Miner . . . . . Sr. VP, Story Department
Sara Spring . . . . . Sr. VP, Feature Production Management
Linda Springer . . . . . Sr. VP, Music Production
Marc Evans . . . . . VP, Production
Matt Jackson . . . . . VP, Production
Lee E. Rosenthal . . . . . VP, Feature Production Management
Brian Wensel . . . . . VP, Production Finance
John Wiseman . . . . . VP, Post Production
Tian Lan . . . . . Production Representative (China)
Dede Nickerson . . . . . Production Representative (China)
Clark Randt . . . . . Production Representative (China)

PARAMOUNT VANTAGE/PARAMOUNT CLASSICS

5555 Melrose Ave., Marathon Bldg., 4th Fl.
Los Angeles, CA 90038
PHONE 323-956-5000
FAX . . . . . 323-862-1212 (Acquisitions)
WEB SITE . . . . . www.paramountclassics.com
TYPES Features
HAS DEAL WITH Paramount Pictures
PROVIDES DEAL TO Interscope/Shady/Aftermath Films
DEVELOPMENT The Dirt
PRODUCTION Untitled Pastor Brothers Project (Vantage) - A Mighty Heart (Vantage)
POST PRODUCTION Untitled Noah Baumbach Project (Vantage) - There Will Be Blood (Vantage) - Year of the Dog (Vantage) - No Country for Old Men (Vantage)
UPCOMING RELEASES Babel (Vantage) - Black Snake Moan (Classics)
CREDITS An Inconvenient Truth (Classics)

John Lesher . . . . . President
Megan Colligan . . . . . Executive VP, Publicity & Promotions
Jeffrey Freedman . . . . . Executive VP, Business Affairs & Operations
Amy Israel . . . . . Executive VP, Production & Acquisitions
Georgia Kacandes . . . . . Executive VP, Physical Production
Rob Schulze . . . . . Executive VP, Distribution
Matt Brodlie . . . . . Sr. VP, Production & Acquisitions
Guy Endore-Kaiser . . . . . Sr. VP, Creative Advertising
Mark Geller . . . . . Sr. VP, Media
Geoff Stier . . . . . Sr. VP, Production & Development
Ralph Bertelle . . . . . VP, Physical Production
Louise DeCordoba . . . . . VP, Production Finance
Dave Dunbar . . . . . VP, Distribution, East Coast
Berenice Fugard . . . . . VP, Acquisitions & Co-Productions
Steve Garrett . . . . . VP, Distribution, West Coast
Kevin Grayson . . . . . VP, Distribution Central
Chad Hamilton . . . . . VP, Production
Andrew Lin . . . . . VP, Interactive Marketing
Dee Poku . . . . . VP, International Marketing
John Wiseman . . . . . VP, Post Production
Rachel Eggebeen . . . . . Creative Executive
Joe Matukewicz . . . . . Director, Acquisitions
Gretchen Stresemann . . . . . Director, Marketing
Ben Cotner . . . . . Manager, Acquisitions
Adam Kassan . . . . . Manager, Production

PARASKEVAS STUDIOS
157 Tuckahoe Lane
Southampton, NY 11968
PHONE 631-287-1665
EMAIL . . . . .jrkroll@mac.com
WEB SITE . . . . .www.thegreenmonkeys.com
SECOND WEB SITE . . . . .www.thecheapshow.com
TYPES Animation - Direct-to-Video/DVD - Features - TV Series
DEVELOPMENT Leo Spats Ratcatcher - Cartoon Diner - Red Moon Beach - Wacky Shellhammer - Nibbles O'Hare
PRE-PRODUCTION Green Monkeys - Jerolemon Street (Nelvana) - Untitled Paraskevas Series (Cookie Jar)
CREDITS The Cheap Show (Plum TV) - Maggie and the Ferocious Beast - Marvin the Tap Dancing Horse - Kids From Room 402 - The Tangerine Bear

Michael Paraskevas . . . . .Producer
Betty Paraskevas . . . . .Producer

PARIAH
6030 Wilshire Blvd., Ste. 301
Los Angeles, CA 90036
PHONE 310-276-3500
FAX . . . . .323 -556-2118
TYPES Features - Internet Content - Mobile Content - Reality TV - Specials - TV Series
HAS DEAL WITH Sony Pictures Entertainment
PRE-PRODUCTION Angriest Man in Suburbia (Pilot) - More, Patience (Pilot) - sexLIFE (HBO) - My Boys (TBS)
POST PRODUCTION Primevil
UPCOMING RELEASES Population 436
CREDITS Super Ex-Girlfriend - Thief - Revelations - Curb Your Enthusiasm - Gilmore Girls - Stir of Echoes - Panic Room - Hack - The Ortegas - P.I. - Secret Window - Sports Illustrated Swimsuit Model Search - Showbiz Show with David Spade - Emily's Reasons Why Not - Little Manhattan

Gavin Polone . . . . .Owner
Jamie Tarses . . . . .Partner
Kathy Landsberg . . . . .VP, Physical Production
Amanda Klein . . . . .VP, Development - Film

PARK EX PICTURES
1001, rue Lenoir, Ste. B 2-37
Montréal, PQ H4C 2Z6, Canada
PHONE 514-933-4133
FAX 514-933-3199
EMAIL . . . . .info@parkexpictures.ca
WEB SITE . . . . .www.parkexpictures.ca
TYPES Features - Made-for-TV/Cable Movies - TV Series
CREDITS Bon Cop/Bad Cop (Feature) - Twist (Feature) - Choice: The Henry Morgentaler Story (CTV) - Varian's War (Showtime) - Bonanno (Showtime) - P.T. Barnum (A&E) - More Tales of the City (Showtime) - One Dead Indian (CTV)

Kevin Tierney . . . . .President
Pierre Larouche . . . . .Assistant to the Producer

PARKCHESTER PICTURES
8750 Wilshire Blvd., Ste. 301
Beverly Hills, CA 90211
PHONE 310-289-5988
TYPES Animation - Features - TV Series
HAS DEAL WITH CBS Entertainment
DEVELOPMENT Home Before Daylight: My Life on the Road with the Grateful Dead - Six Dance Lessons in Six Weeks
PRODUCTION As Seen Through These Eyes (Documentary)
CREDITS Speak - The Best Little Thief in the World - Bereft - Baadasssss!

Jerry Offsay . . . . .President
Amy Duzinski . . . . .Film Development
David Gadarian . . . . .TV Development
Judy Margolin . . . . .Executive Assistant

PARKWAY PRODUCTIONS
7095 Hollywood Blvd., Ste. 1009
Hollywood, CA 90028
PHONE 323-874-6207
TYPES Documentaries - Features - Internet Content - TV Series
CREDITS Bewitched - Cinderella Man - Riding in Cars with Boys - The Preacher's Wife - Awakenings - Renaissance Man - A League of Their Own - Big

Penny Marshall . . . . .Director/Producer
Richard D. Tucci . . . . .Executive Assistant to Ms. Marshall
Terry Trahan . . . . .Assistant to Ms. Marshall
Nicole Cassidy . . . . .Assistant to Ms. Marshall (NY)

PARTICIPANT PRODUCTIONS
335 N. Maple Dr., Ste. 245
Beverly Hills, CA 90210
PHONE 310-550-5100
FAX 310-550-5106
EMAIL . . . . .info@participantproductions.com
WEB SITE . . . . .www.participantproductions.com
TYPES Documentaries - Features
PROVIDES DEAL TO Edward Saxon Productions (ESP)
DEVELOPMENT Evidence of Harm - Nancy Wake - The Legacy of Luna
PRODUCTION C7
POST PRODUCTION Fast Food Nation
UPCOMING RELEASES American Gun
CREDITS The World According to Sesame Street - An Inconvenient Truth - American Gun - Syriana - North Country - Good Night, and Good Luck - Arna's Children

Jeff Skoll . . . . .Founder/CEO
Ricky Strauss . . . . .President
Chris Salvaterra . . . . .Executive VP, Creative Affairs & Production
Jeff Ivers . . . . .Executive VP, Finance & Business Affairs
Diane Weyermann . . . . .Executive VP, Documentary Production
Meredith Blake . . . . .Executive VP, Corporate & Community Affairs/ President, Participant Foundation
Lisa Day . . . . .VP, Corporate & Community Affairs
Jodi Zuckerman . . . . .VP, Creative Affairs
Nate Moore . . . . .Director, Development
Courtney Sexton . . . . .Director, Documentaries
Amber Offutt . . . . .Creative Executive
Amanda Garrison . . . . .Marketing Coordinator
Peter Schiessel . . . . .Consultant

*PARTIZAN

7083 Hollywood Blvd., Ste. 401
Los Angeles, CA 90028
PHONE .323-468-0123
FAX .323-468-0129
WEB SITE .www.partizan.com
TYPES Features - Music Videos
DEVELOPMENT Be Kind Rewind - The Science of Sleep - Scum
COMMENTS New York office: 73 Spring St., #503, New York, NY 10012, phone: 212-388-0123, fax: 212-625-2040; London office: 40/2 Lexington St., London W1F 0LN United Kingdom, phone: 44-207-851-0200, fax: 44-207-851-0249; Paris office: 10 Rue Vivienne, Paris, 75002 France; phone: 331-5345-0123, fax: 331-5345-0124

Georges Bermann .Chairman/Executive Producer (Paris)
Frederic Genest .Executive Producer (Paris)
Franck Montillot .Executive Producer (Paris)
Madeleine Sanderson .Executive Producer (London)
Sheila Stepanek .CEO/Executive Producer (LA)
Jeff Pantaleo .Executive Producer, Music Videos (LA)
Aurelia Grossmann .Head, Music Video (Paris)
Sasha Nixon .Head, Music Video (London)

P.A.T. PRODUCTIONS

10202 W. Washington Blvd., David Lean Bldg., Ste. 230
Culver City, CA 90232
PHONE .310-244-8881
FAX .310-244-1210
EMAIL .patprod@spe.sony.com
WEB SITE .www.patsajakgames.com
TYPES Animation - Features - Internet Content - Mobile Content - Reality TV - TV Series
HAS DEAL WITH Sony Pictures Television
CREDITS Games: Blackjack Bowling - Run for the Money; Animation: Leo the Late Bloomer - Space Case - Merry Christmas, Space Case; Live Action: Angus and the Ducks - Pat Sajak's American League Ballpark Tour - Pat Sajak's National League Ballpark Tour
SUBMISSION POLICY No unsolicited submissions accepted

Pat Sajak .President
David S. Williger .Executive VP
Gary Templeton .Director, Development
Gwen Klemann .Executive Assistant, Development

PATCHETT KAUFMAN ENTERTAINMENT

8621 Hayden Pl.
Culver City, CA 90232
PHONE .310-838-7000
FAX .310-838-8430
TYPES Direct-to-Video/DVD - Features - Made-for-TV/Cable Movies - Miniseries - Reality TV - Specials
DEVELOPMENT In the Line of Duty: The Texas Seven (MOW)
CREDITS Dean Koontz's Mr. Murder - In the Line of Duty - Franchise - The Betty Broderick Story - Miracle in the Woods
COMMENTS Stage and executive offices for production

Tom Patchett .Chairman
Kenneth Kaufman .President/COO
Debra Cannold .VP, Production Services
Brian McKeaney .Director, Development

PATHFINDER PICTURES, LLC

801 Ocean Front Walk, Ste. 7
Venice, CA 90291
PHONE .310-664-1500
FAX .310-664-0400
EMAIL .info@pathfinderpictures.com
WEB SITE .www.pathfinderpictures.com
TYPES Features
DEVELOPMENT Father of Spin - Heartbeat
PRE-PRODUCTION Halfs - Basic Jane - Moon Colony
CREDITS Until the Night - You've Got Spam - Shadow Fury - Yellow - Double Deception - Tweeked
COMMENTS Also distributes

Taka Arai .Producer
Gregory Hatanaka .Executive Producer/Director
Kaido Yamada .Executive Producer
Jeff Milne .Operations
Norith Soth .Development
T.L. Young .Marketing

PATRIOT PICTURES, LLC

9065 Nemo St.
West Hollywood, CA 90069
PHONE .310-274-0745
FAX .310-274-0925
WEB SITE .www.patriotpictures.com
TYPES Features - TV Series
DEVELOPMENT Rip - Shelter - Stealing Cars - Wagner Mistress of Avaria - Vampire Hunter - Magnificat - Stick It - Holy Cross - White House Secret Service - Gang Impact Team - Junior Black Mafia
PRE-PRODUCTION Gabriella - Unforsaken - Crenshaw Blvd. - All Women Are Born Cruel
CREDITS Material Girls - Lord of War
SUBMISSION POLICY Via website: www.unionpatriotcapital.com/submission

Michael Mendelsohn .Chairman/CEO
Julia Lillis .Comedy Development
Carli Posner .Executive Assistant
Ravi Malhotra .No Title

PAULIST PRODUCTIONS

17575 Pacific Coast Hwy.
Pacific Palisades, CA 90272-1057
PHONE .310-454-0688
FAX .310-459-6549
EMAIL .paulistmail@paulistproductions.org
WEB SITE .www.paulistproductions.org
TYPES Direct-to-Video/DVD - Documentaries - Features - Made-for-TV/Cable Movies - TV Series
DEVELOPMENT The Fourth Wiseman (Animated) - Brother Fire - Beautiful Miracles - Soul of a Nation - The Last Valentine
PRODUCTION Forgiveness
CREDITS Insight - Yoga Prayer - Let's Go to Mass/Let's Go to Church - Saints Preserved - Stigmata - St. Peter - The Twelve Apostles - Romero - Healing & Prayer - The Fourth Wiseman - Juggler of Notre Dame - Entertaining Angels: The Dorothy Day Story - Judas: Traitor or Friend - The Jesus Experience - Visions of the Virgin - Joseph, the Silent Saint - The Apostle Paul - We Are the Children - Prophecies of Iraq - Prophecies of Israel - James, Brother of Jesus

Father Frank Desiderio, C.S.P. .President
Enid N. Sevilla .General Manager/Financial Officer
Joseph Kim .VP, Business Affairs
Barbara Gangi .Director, Development/Producer

DANIEL L. PAULSON PRODUCTIONS
9056 Santa Monica Blvd., Ste. 203-A
West Hollywood, CA 90069
PHONE .310-278-9747
FAX .310-278-9751
EMAIL .dlpprods@sbcglobal.net
TYPES Documentaries - Features - Made-for-TV/Cable Movies - Reality TV - TV Series
CREDITS Sunset Park - Passenger 57 - Comes a Horseman - A Cooler Climate - Saving Jessica Lynch
SUBMISSION POLICY Email queries to dlpprods@hotmail.com

Daniel L. Paulson .President
Steve A. Kennedy .Director, Administration
Whitney Oliver .Development Assistant
Jenny Lewis .Development Assistant

PAYASO ENTERTAINMENT
5555 Melrose Ave., Haggar Bldg., Ste. 233
Hollywood, CA 90038
PHONE .323-956-3822/818-509-1730
FAX .323-862-2148
EMAIL .yvettey@usa.net
WEB SITE .www.payasoentertainment.com
SECOND WEB SITE .www.thelatindivasofcomedy.com
TYPES Direct-to-Video/DVD - Features - Made-for-TV/Cable Movies - TV Series
DEVELOPMENT Don't Look Back - Dead Warrior's Song - Another 15 Minutes - Slob
PRE-PRODUCTION The Original Latin Divas of Comedy - The Original Latino Comedy Slam
COMPLETED UNRELEASED The Alex Reymundo Show *Hick-Spanics*
CREDITS The Original Latin Kings of Comedy

Scott Montoya .Producer
Yvette Yates .Development Executive/Producer

PBS
2100 Crystal Dr.
Arlington, VA 22202-3785
PHONE .703-739-5000
FAX .703-739-0775
WEB SITE .www.pbs.org
TYPES Documentaries - Reality TV - TV Series
UPCOMING RELEASES Branson Jubilee
CREDITS American Experience - American Masters - Antiques Roadshow - ExxonMobil Masterpiece Theatre - Frontline - Independent Lens - Mister Rogers' Neighborhood - The NewsHour with Jim Lehrer - NOVA - Now with Bill Moyers - Reading Rainbow - Wall Street Week with Fortune - Washington Week - Great Performances - Nature; Children's Programming: Arthur - Barney - Between the Lions - Clifford the Big Red Dog - Reading Rainbow - Sesame Street - Teletubbies - Zoom

Paula Kerger .President/CEO
Wayne Godwin .COO
John Boland .Chief Content Officer
John F. Wilson .Sr. VP/Co-Chief Programming Executive
Pat Hunter .Sr. VP, Programming Services
Katherine Lauderdale .Sr. VP/General Counsel

(Continued)

PBS (Continued)
Lesli Rotenberg .Sr. VP, Brand Management, Promotion & Media Relations
Judy Braune .VP, Brand Management & Promotion
Steven Gray .VP, Program Scheduling & Editorial Managent
Paul Greco .VP/Deputy General Counsel
Mary Kadera .VP, Education
Gustavo Sagastume .VP, Programming Services, South
Lea Sloan .VP, Media Relations
Elizabeth Suarez .VP, Development
Gwen Wood .VP, Distribution Services
Stephanie Aaronson .Sr. Director, Media Relations
Sylvia Bennett .Sr. Director, Fundraising Programming
Caryn Ginsberg .Sr. Director, Programming Operations & Communications
Sandy Heberer .Sr. Director, Primetime Programming
John Ruppenthal .Sr. Director, Creative Services
Allison Winshell .Sr. Director, Primetime Programming
Dawn Ciccone .Director, Consumer Products
Cynthia Jackson .Director, Operations & Distribution Services
Lauren Kalos .Director, Program Operations
Sarah Melville .Director, Program Management

PEACE ARCH ENTERTAINMENT GROUP INC.
407-124 Merton St.
Toronto, ON M4S 2Z2, Canada
PHONE .416-487-0377
FAX .416-487-6141
EMAIL .info@peacearch.com
WEB SITE .www.peacearch.com
TYPES Documentaries - Features - Made-for-TV/Cable Movies - TV Series
HAS DEAL WITH Showtime Networks Inc.
PRE-PRODUCTION The Mod - Maneater - Harm's Way - Stillborn - Grizzly
PRODUCTION The Tudors - Off Road - Bottom Feeder
POST PRODUCTION Troubled Waters - U.K.M. - Dead Mary
COMPLETED UNRELEASED Heartstopper - Warriors of Terra - 5ive Girls - The Last Sect
CREDITS Absolon - Belly of the Beast - Crime Spree - Detention - The Keeper - The Limit - Partners in Action - Animal Miracles - Campus Vets - Whistler Stories - Raven in the Sun - Heroines - The Good Shepherd - Nature Unleashed: Avalanche, Earthquake, Fire, Tornado, Volcano - Direct Action - Hollywood Flies - Prisoners of Age - Shadows in the Sun - Our Fathers
SUBMISSION POLICY No unsolicited materials accepted

Gary Howsam .CEO
John Flock .President
Mara Di Pasquale .CFO/COO
Lewin Webb .President, Peace Arch Motion Pictures Inc.
Michael Taylor .President, Peach Arch Television
Blair Reekie .President, The Eyes Project Development Corporation
Penny Wolf .Executive VP, International Sales & Marketing
Mark Balsam .Head, US Distribution

PEARL PICTURES
10956 Weyburn Ave., Ste. 200
Los Angeles, CA 90024
PHONE .310-443-7773
FAX .310-443-7753
EMAIL .info@pearlpics.com
TYPES Features - Miniseries - Reality TV - TV Series
DEVELOPMENT Assuming Room Temperature - The Line - Full Cleveland - A Fan's Notes
PRE-PRODUCTION Mother's Little Helpers
CREDITS A Chance of Snow - Liberty Stands Still - 10.5 Apocalypse
COMMENTS Production and management

Gary Pearl .No Title
J.J. Feldman .No Title

PECULIAR FILMS
15332 Antioch St., #14
Pacific Palisades, CA 90272
PHONE .310-230-0851
WEB SITE .www.peculiarfilms.com
TYPES Animation - Direct-to-Video/DVD - Features - TV Series
DEVELOPMENT Thornley and Oswald - Fool That I Am - Paranoid
PRE-PRODUCTION Hard Hearts
CREDITS Permanent Midnight - Fight Club
SUBMISSION POLICY No unsolicited submissions

Jim Uhls .Producer/Writer
Yalda Tehranian Uhls .Producer

PEIRCE PICTURES
c/o Tory Metzger, CAA
9830 Wilshire Blvd.
Beverly Hills, CA 90212
PHONE .323-655-0606
TYPES Features
DEVELOPMENT Silent Star (DreamWorks) - Childhood's End (Beacon)
PRODUCTION Stop-Loss (Paramount)
CREDITS Boys Don't Cry
SUBMISSION POLICY Through Tory Metzger/CAA

Kimberly Peirce .Director/Writer/Producer
Reid Carolin .Director, Development

PENN STATION ENTERTAINMENT
2013 S. Westgate Ave.
Los Angeles, CA 90025
PHONE .310-207-2501
FAX .310-207-2192
TYPES Features
HAS DEAL WITH Twentieth Century Fox

Dean Georgaris .Principal/Producer/Screenwriter (310-207-2501)
Michael Aguilar .Principal/Producer (310-207-2501)
Kimberly Barton .Development Assistant (310-207-2190)
Sara Gunther .Development Assistant (310-207-2191)

ZAK PENN'S COMPANY
6240 W. Third St., Ste. 421
Los Angeles, CA 90036
PHONE .323-939-1700
FAX .323-930-2339
TYPES Features
HAS DEAL WITH Twentieth Century Fox
DEVELOPMENT Mother's Day - Clan of the 7th Circle
PRODUCTION The Grand
CREDITS Incident at Loch Ness - X-Men 2-3 - PCU - Osmosis Jones - Behind Enemy Lines - Last Action Hero - Antz
SUBMISSION POLICY No unsolicited submissions

Zak Penn .Writer/Producer/Director
Lance Stockton .VP, Production
Mike Chamoy .Development Executive

PERISCOPE ENTERTAINMENT, LLC
2340 Kenilworth Ave.
Los Angeles, CA 90039
PHONE .323-953-8930
FAX .323-953-4720
WEB SITE .www.periscopeentertainment.com
TYPES Documentaries - Features - TV Series
DEVELOPMENT Cornboy - Laughs Take a Holiday - One Last Thing - The Dating Lives of Butch and Daisy - London Fields
PRE-PRODUCTION August - Werewolf Hunters of the Midwest
POST PRODUCTION Untitled King of Hearts Documentary
COMPLETED UNRELEASED Lying
SUBMISSION POLICY No unsolicited material

David Guy Levy .President/CEO
Gregory Leonarczyk .Sr. VP
Penny Margara .Human Resources
Ryle Eddings .Executive Assistant

PERMUT PRESENTATIONS
9150 Wilshire Blvd., Ste. 247
Beverly Hills, CA 90212
PHONE .310-248-2792
FAX .310-248-2797
TYPES Features - TV Series
DEVELOPMENT The Desmond Doss Story - Allegiance - Kings for a Day - The Sam Kinison Story - Money to Burn - Friends Again - Blind Sided - Julia Pastrana - Rewind - Youth in Revolt
PRODUCTION Charlie Bartlett
CREDITS Face/Off - Eddie - Dragnet - Blind Date - Double Take - Consenting Adults - Three of Hearts - Richard Pryor Live in Concert - DysFunktional Family

David Permut .Producer/President
Steven A. Longi .VP, Production
Matthew Hals .Development Associate

***PERRY FILMS**
135 W. 29th St., #703
New York, NY 10001
PHONE 212-989-2880
FAX 212-989-3262
WEB SITE . . . . . www.perryfilms.com
TYPES Documentaries - Specials - TV Series
UPCOMING RELEASES The Drug Years (VH1 & The Sundance Channel)
CREDITS And You Don't Stop: 30 Years of Hip Hop (VH1) - John Hammond: From Bessie Smith to Bruce Springsteen (PBS American Masters) - Motown 40 (ABC) - Imagining America: Icons of 20th Century Art (PBS)

Dana Heinz Perry . . . . . Producer/Director
Hart Perry . . . . . Producer/Director

PERSISTENT ENTERTAINMENT
8000 Sunset Blvd., 3rd Fl., East PH
Los Angeles, CA 90046
PHONE 323-337-1055
FAX 323-337-1079
EMAIL . . . . . mail@persistent-ent.com
WEB SITE . . . . . www.persistent-ent.com
TYPES Features - Made-for-TV/Cable Movies - TV Series
DEVELOPMENT Passengers - Deep in the Valley - High Stakes
POST PRODUCTION The Beautiful Ordinary
UPCOMING RELEASES Freshman Orientation - Walker Payne
COMPLETED UNRELEASED Southland Tales
CREDITS The Sisters - An Unfinished Life - Auggie Rose - The Amati Girls - Starf*cker - The Alarmist - September Tapes

Matthew Rhodes . . . . . Producer
Judd Payne . . . . . Producer
Jim Dominello . . . . . Creative Executive
Nick Myles . . . . . Assistant

PETERS ENTERTAINMENT
23852 Pacific Coast Highway, #383
Malibu, CA 90265
PHONE 310-317-6832
FAX 310-317-6835
EMAIL . . . . . jon@petersentertainment.com
TYPES Features
CREDITS Superman Returns - Ali - My Fellow Americans - Wild Wild West - Batman 1-4 - Rain Man - Money Train - Rosewood - A Star Is Born - Caddyshack - Missing - Eyes of Laura Mars - The Color Purple - This Boy's Life

Jon Peters . . . . . Chairman
Ronnie Grigg . . . . . President

DANIEL PETRIE JR. & COMPANY
18034 Ventura Blvd., Ste. 445
Encino, CA 91316
PHONE 818-708-1602
FAX 818-774-0345
WEB SITE . . . . . www.danielpetriejrandcompany.com
TYPES Features - Made-for-TV/Cable Movies - Reality TV - TV Series
DEVELOPMENT Legacy - Beverly Bonds - Warning Signs - Claim the Earth
PRE-PRODUCTION Ashes to Ashes - Magic Castle
CREDITS Framed (TNT) - In the Army Now - Toy Soldiers - Turner & Hooch - Beverly Hills Cop - Dead Silence - The 6th Day

Dan Petrie Jr. . . . . . Director/Writer/Producer
Rick Dugdale . . . . . Producer/Director of Development/VP

D. PETRIE PRODUCTIONS, INC.
13201 Haney Pl.
Los Angeles, CA 90049
PHONE 310-394-2608
FAX 310-395-8530
TYPES Features - Made-for-TV/Cable Movies - TV Series
DEVELOPMENT The Merchant of Death - Stray Hearts
CREDITS The Song of the Lark - Echo of Thunder - Captive Heart - Getting Out - Caroline - Foxfire - Love Is Never Silent - License to Kill - The Perfect Tribute

Dorothea G. Petrie . . . . . Executive Producer/Producer
June Petrie . . . . . Producer/Co-Producer
John Cockrell . . . . . Associate Producer

STEPHEN PEVNER, INC.
382 Lafayette St., 8th Fl.
New York, NY 10003
PHONE 212-674-8403
FAX 212-529-3692
EMAIL . . . . . stephen@stephenpevnerinc.com
TYPES Features - Theatre
CREDITS In the Company of Men - Your Friends & Neighbors - Nurse Betty - Possession - Bash

Stephen Pevner . . . . . Producer
Peet R. Abernethy . . . . . Development Executive

PFEFFER FILM
c/o Walt Disney Studios
500 S. Buena Vista Blvd., Animation Bldg., Ste. 2F-8
Burbank, CA 91521
PHONE 818-560-3177
FAX 818-843-7485
TYPES Features
HAS DEAL WITH Walt Disney Pictures/Touchstone Pictures
DEVELOPMENT Temping Fate - Hell on Wheels - Pants on Fire - Matrophobia - Marine Electric - Varjak Paw - The Last Lap - The First Man - Princess Bootcamp - Deep in the Heart of Texas
CREDITS Crazy/Beautiful - Malice - Grand Avenue - A Civil Action - The Horse Whisperer - A Few Good Men

Rachel Pfeffer . . . . . Producer
Asha Kurian . . . . . VP
Lindy Louis . . . . . Story Editor
Jeff Lane . . . . . Development Assistant

PHASE TWO PRODUCTIONS
c/o Twentieth Century Fox
10201 W. Pico Blvd., Bldg. 80, Rm. 12
Los Angeles, CA 90035
PHONE 310-369-8555
FAX 310-369-8980
TYPES Animation - TV Series
HAS DEAL WITH Twentieth Century Fox Television
DEVELOPMENT Moonbeamers
SUBMISSION POLICY No unsolicited submissions

Sandy Grushow . . . . . President
Jono Golding . . . . . Director, Development
Robyn Harwood . . . . . Assistant, Sandy Grushow

THE TODD PHILLIPS COMPANY
4000 Warner Blvd., Bldg. 66
Burbank, CA 91522
PHONE 818-954-6000
TYPES Documentaries - Features
HAS DEAL WITH Warner Bros. Pictures
UPCOMING RELEASES School For Scoundrels
CREDITS Road Trip - Old School - Starsky & Hutch

Todd Phillips ....Director/President
Daniel Goldberg ....Producer
Scott Budnick ....Executive VP, Production
Annette Savitch ....Director, Development
Josh Gold ....Creative Executive
Natalie Borlaug ....Executive Assistant
Joseph Garner ....Executive Assistant
Benjamin Sachs ....Executive Assistant

PHOENIX PICTURES
10202 W. Washington Blvd., Frankovich Bldg.
Culver City, CA 90232
PHONE 310-244-6100
FAX 310-842-7530
WEB SITE ....www.phoenixpictures.com
TYPES Direct-to-Video/DVD - Features - Made-for-TV/Cable Movies - TV Series
HAS DEAL WITH Columbia Pictures
DEVELOPMENT Ditch the Bitch - Black Autumn - The Last Voyage of the Demeter - Destination Unknown - Pig Blood Blues - Kid Mayor - The Understudy - To the Ends of the Earth - Mile Zero - The Girl Who Loved Tom Gordon - Fantasy Freak - The Moon Is a Harsh Mistress - Brass Wall - The Nightmare of Hugo Bearing - The Damnation Game - Florida Road Kill - Already Dead
PRODUCTION License to Wed - Resurrecting the Champ
POST PRODUCTION Zodiac - Miss Potter - Pathfinder
CREDITS All the King's Men - In My Country - Stealth - Basic - The Thin Red Line - The People vs. Larry Flynt - Urban Legend

Mike Medavoy ....Chairman/CEO (310-244-6106)
Arnold Messer ....President/COO (310-244-6101)
Christopher Trunkey ....Executive VP/CFO (310-244-6382)
Brad Fischer ....Sr. VP, Production (310-244-6540)
Rochel Blachman ....Sr. VP, Business Affairs (310-244-4134)
Louis Phillips ....Executive VP, Physical Production/Post Production (310-244-6455)
David Thwaites ....VP, Production (310-244-6815)
Anne Rodman ....Executive, Development (310-244-3542)
Ken Rosen ....Story Editor (310-244-8576)

*PICTUREHOUSE
597 Fifth Ave., 7th Fl.
New York, NY 10017
PHONE 212-303-1700/310-246-7600
FAX 212-421-1163/310-279-1052
WEB SITE ....www.picturehouse.com
TYPES Features
PRODUCTION The Ice at the Bottom of the World - Gracie - Mongol
POST PRODUCTION Silk
UPCOMING RELEASES Fur - Pan's Labyrinth - Starter for Ten - PU239
CREDITS A Prairie Home Companion - Rock School - Last Days - The Chumscrubber - The Thing About My Folks - A Cock and Bull Story - Ushpizin - The Notorious Bettie Page
COMMENTS West Coast office: 9000 Sunset Blvd., Ste. 1204, Los Angeles, CA 90069

Bob Berney ....President
Robert Schwartz ....COO
Marian Koltai-Levine ....Executive VP, Marketing
Dennis O'Connor ....Executive VP, Marketing
John Lange ....Sr. VP/Co-General Sales Manager
Bill Thompson ....Sr. VP/Co-General Sales Manager
Sara Rose ....Sr. VP, Acquisitions
Nina Baron ....Sr. VP, National Publicity
Jennifer Stott ....Sr. VP, National Publicity & Promotion
Molly Albright ....VP, Creative Advertising
Tom Hassell ....VP, Distribution
Mary Ann Hult ....VP, National Publicity
Crystal King ....VP, Marketing Operations
Dan Lange ....VP, Distribution
Elizabeth Brambilla ....Manager, Field Operations/Promotion
Veronica Bufalini ....Director, Publicity (West Coast)
Vicky Eguia ....Director, Corporate Communications & West Coast Field Operations
Lia Bozonelis ....Coordinator, Marketing
Erin Hildebrand ....Lead Executive Assistant to Bob Berney

PIE TOWN PRODUCTIONS
5433 Laurel Canyon Blvd.
North Hollywood, CA 91607
PHONE 818-255-9300/312-229-1400
FAX 818-255-9333/312-229-1401
EMAIL ....pietown@pietown.tv
WEB SITE ....www.pietown.tv
TYPES Documentaries - Reality TV - TV Series
CREDITS Designed to Sell - Homes Across America - Weekend Warriors - House Hunters - Design on a Dime - Designers' Challenge - Landscapers' Challenge - reDesign - National Open House - Take Over My Makeover - My House Is Worth What? - Design In a Day
SUBMISSION POLICY No unsolicited submissions
COMMENTS Chicago office: 1438 W. Kinzie St., Ste. 300, Chicago, IL 60622

Tara Sandler ....Executive Producer
Jennifer Davidson ....Executive Producer
Scott Templeton ....Executive Producer
Eric Black ....VP, Programming
Greg Spring ....VP, Development
Dana Besnoy ....Director, Post Production
Samantha Leonard ....Executive in Charge of Production
Stina Thomas ....Post Production Supervisor
Betsy Allman ....Co-Executive Producer
Peter Field ....Supervising Producer
Drew Hallman ....Supervising Producer
Margaret Hussey ....Supervising Producer

(Continued)

PIETOWN PRODUCTIONS (Continued)

Vicky Landin . . . . Supervising Producer
Jim Lichtenstein . . . . Supervising Producer
Kim Pflieger . . . . Supervising Producer
Andrea Pilat . . . . Supervising Producer
Sharon G. Riley . . . . Supervising Producer
Stacy Schneider . . . . Supervising Producer
Beth Suskind . . . . Supervising Producer
Roberta White . . . . Supervising Producer
Jake Gibson . . . . Lead Field Producer

PIERCE WILLIAMS ENTERTAINMENT

1531 14th St.
Santa Monica, CA 90404
PHONE 310-656-9440
FAX 310-656-9441
EMAIL . . . . georgia@piercewilliams.com
TYPES: Features - Reality TV
DEVELOPMENT: Surrender - Desert Run - Distortion - The Zero - Theorem - The Canyon - Beverly Hills - House of Doors - Glass Hive
PRE-PRODUCTION: Run - Sleeping Detective - All the Little Things - Illumination; TV: Cooler TV Show - Evilseek - Malice in Sunderland - Victim
UPCOMING RELEASES: Running Scared
COMPLETED UNRELEASED: Chaos
CREDITS: The Cooler - In Enemy Hands
SUBMISSION POLICY: Query letter via email
COMMENTS: Manager

Michael Pierce . . . . Partner
Mark C. Williams . . . . Partner

PILGRIM FILMS & TELEVISION, INC.

4730 Woodman Ave., Ste. 300
Sherman Oaks, CA 91423
PHONE 818-728-8800
FAX 818-728-8810
TYPES: Documentaries - Features - Reality TV - TV Series
CREDITS: Survivor 1-3 - Worst-Case Scenario (TBS) - CIA Secrets (Discovery) - Cupid (CBS) - American Chopper (Discovery) - American Hot Rod (Discovery) - American Casino (Discovery) - Ghost Hunters (SCI FI/NBC) - Guilty or Innocent (Discovery) - Southern Steel (Discovery) - The Cut (CBS) - The Ultimate Fighter (Spike) - Strip Search (VH1) - Dry Dock (Travel Channel) - Dirty Jobs (Discovery) - Firehouse USA: Boston (Discovery)

Craig M. Piligian . . . . Owner/Executive Producer
Kathleen Burns Rohr . . . . VP, Production

PILLER/SEGAN

7025 Santa Monica Blvd.
Hollywood, CA 90038
PHONE 323-464-6201
FAX 323-464-6529
TYPES: Features - Made-for-TV/Cable Movies - TV Series
DEVELOPMENT: Sweet Revenge - Burke - Thief River Falls
COMPLETED UNRELEASED: Bickford Shmeckler's Cool Ideas
CREDITS: TV: Wildfire (ABC Family) - The Dead Zone (USA) - Star Trek: Voyager - Star Trek: Deep Space Nine - Star Trek: The Next Generation; Features: Swimfan - Bones - Star Trek: Insurrection - Saving Private Ryan - Broken Arrow - Speed - Boondock Saints - Shark Tale

Shawn Piller . . . . Producer/Writer
Lloyd Segan . . . . Producer
Adam Fratto . . . . VP, Development & Production
Suzanne Bradley . . . . Associate
Brian Millikin . . . . Associate

PINK SLIP PICTURES

1314 N. Coronado St.
Los Angeles, CA 90026
PHONE 213-483-7100
FAX 213-483-7200
EMAIL . . . . pinkslip@earthlink.net
TYPES: Features - TV Series
DEVELOPMENT: Red Hollow - Windfall - Case of the Halloween Hangman - The Tucker Max Show
PRE-PRODUCTION: Capture the Flag - The Crossing - Snakebite
CREDITS: All You've Got - The Bumblebee Flies Anyway - Bring It On - Tuck Everlasting
SUBMISSION POLICY: No unsolicited material

Karen Firestone . . . . Producer
Max Wong . . . . Producer

PINK SNEAKERS PRODUCTIONS

1000 Colour Pl.
Apopka, FL 32703
PHONE 407-464-2080
FAX 407-464-2801
EMAIL . . . . info@pinksneakers.net
WEB SITE . . . . www.pinksneakers.net
TYPES: Documentaries - Reality TV - TV Series
DEVELOPMENT: Untitled Paul Wall Series
PRODUCTION: My Big Fat Fabulous Wedding (VH1)
CREDITS: Tiara Girls (MTV) - Hogan Knows Best (VH1) - Inside/Out (VH1) - I Want a Famous Face (MTV) - Cribs (MTV) - True Life (MTV) - Ultrasound (MTV) - Britney Spears: In the Zone (ABC)

Kimberly Cowin . . . . President/Executive Producer
John Ehrhard . . . . VP, Development
Susan Janis-Mashayekhi . . . . VP, Production
Sarah Griffith . . . . Director, TV Production Development
Jeff Doden . . . . Production Coordinator
Padra Sanchez . . . . Executive/Production Assistant
Angela Webster . . . . Executive/Production Assistant

PIRANHA PICTURES, INC.
347 W. 36th St., 15th Fl.
New York, NY 10018
PHONE .212-216-9470
FAX .212-216-9317
EMAIL .info@piranhapix.com
WEB SITE .www.piranhapix.com
TYPES Animation - Commercials - Direct-to-Video/DVD - Features - Made-for-TV/Cable Movies - Mobile Content - Music Videos
DEVELOPMENT Untitled Sony Pictures Project
PRE-PRODUCTION Places of Greater Safety - J.B. Project
UPCOMING RELEASES Bull Trouble
COMPLETED UNRELEASED UN Emergency
CREDITS Dead Beat - Breaking Up - An Occasional Hell - Scorpion Spring - The Obit Writer
SUBMISSION POLICY See Web site for electronic release

George Moffly .Producer
Alyssa St. Vincent .Producer
David Starobin .Development

THE PITT GROUP
9465 Wilshire Blvd., Ste. 470
Beverly Hills, CA 90212
PHONE .310-246-4800
FAX .310-275-9258
TYPES Features - Made-for-TV/Cable Movies - TV Series
DEVELOPMENT The First Stone - Four Horsemen - Glen Sherley - Engaged Encounter
POST PRODUCTION Spinning Into Butter (Whitsett Hill)
CREDITS Hollywood Homicide - Carolina

Lou Pitt .President
Ryan Vernon .Creative Executive
Steve Desmond .Assistant to Mr. Pitt
Whitney Piro .Assistant

PIXAR ANIMATION STUDIOS
1200 Park Ave.
Emeryville, CA 94608
PHONE .510-752-3000
FAX .510-752-3151
WEB SITE .www.pixar.com
TYPES Animation - Features
UPCOMING RELEASES Ratatouille
CREDITS Cars - One Man Band - Finding Nemo - Mike's New Car - Monsters, Inc. - For the Birds - Toy Story 1&2 - A Bug's Life - Geri's Game - Tin Toy - Red's Dream - Luxo Jr. - Knickknack - Boundin' - The Incredibles
COMMENTS Feature and short film computer animation

Steven P. Jobs .Chairman
Robert Iger .CEO
Dr. Edwin E. Catmull .President
John Lasseter .Executive VP, Creative
Lois Scali .Executive VP/General Counsel

PLAN B ENTERTAINMENT
9150 Wilshire Blvd., Ste. 350
Beverly Hills, CA 90212
PHONE .310-275-6135
FAX .310-275-5234
TYPES Documentaries - Features - Made-for-TV/Cable Movies
HAS DEAL WITH Paramount Pictures
DEVELOPMENT True Story - Glass Castle - Undaunted Courage - Shantaram - The Sparrow - Black Hole - The Every Boy - World War Z - Chasing Vermeer - A Mighty Heart
POST PRODUCTION The Assassination of Jesse James - Running with Scissors
CREDITS Troy - Charlie & the Chocolate Factory
SUBMISSION POLICY No unsolicited submissions or phone calls

Dede Gardner .President
Jeremy Kleiner .Executive
Kassie Evashevski .Executive
Tendo Nagenda .Executive

PLANET GRANDE PICTURES
23440 Civic Center Way, Ste. 104
Malibu, CA 90265
PHONE .310-317-1545
FAX .310-317-0256
WEB SITE .www.planetgrande.tv
TYPES Animation - Documentaries - Reality TV - Specials - TV Series
DEVELOPMENT Name that Tune (Sony) - Bordertown (FX) - Alaska Air Rescue (Discovery) - Texas Rangers (History Channel)
POST PRODUCTION A Day in the Life of Television (CBS) - World Series of Black Jack (GSN)
CREDITS InStyle Celebrity Weddings 2006 - The Andy Griffith Show Reunion: Back to Mayberry - Breaking the News - Deadwood Mysteries - InStyle Celebrity Weddings 2001-2005 - InStyle Celebrity Moms - On the Edge of Our Seats: TV's Greatest Moments (NBC)

John Watkin .Owner
Eamon Harrington .Owner
Rosa Gonzalez .Production Controller
Kim Naumann .Executive Assistant to Owners/Office Manager

PLATFORM ENTERTAINMENT
128 Sierra St.
El Segundo, CA 90245
PHONE .310-322-3737
FAX .310-322-3729
WEB SITE .www.platformpictures.com
TYPES Features
PRE-PRODUCTION Brew - Milton
CREDITS Dante's View - Morgan's Ferry - The Job - The Hollow (ABC Family) - The Hard Easy

Daniel Levin .Producer
Larry Gabriel .Producer
Scott Sorrentino .Producer
Andrew Kassov .Production
Garrett Wheeler .Production

PLATINUM DUNES

631 Colorado Ave.
Santa Monica, CA 90401
PHONE .310-394-9200
FAX .310-319-6570
TYPES Features
HAS DEAL WITH Dimension Films
DEVELOPMENT The Birds - Superstition - The Horsemen - Lunatic - The Surrogate - Molly's World - Friday the 13th
PRODUCTION The Hitcher
POST PRODUCTION The Texas Chainsaw Massacre: The Beginning
CREDITS The Texas Chainsaw Massacre - The Amityville Horror
SUBMISSION POLICY No unsolicited submissions

Michael Bay .Partner
Andrew Form .Partner
Brad Fuller .Partner
Lisa Greenblatt .Creative Executive

PLATINUM STUDIOS, LLC

9744 Wilshire Blvd., Ste. 210
Beverly Hills, CA 90212
PHONE .310-276-3900
FAX .310-276-2799
EMAIL .info@platinumstudios.com
WEB SITE .www.platinumstudios.com
TYPES Animation - Features - Mobile Content - TV Series
DEVELOPMENT Million $ Heroes - Cowboys & Aliens - Nathan Never - Trace of Chalk - Mal Chance - Blackjack - Unique - Dark Fringe - Atlantis Rising - Final Orbit - Ghost Bullet - Book of Mercury - Ghosting - Seen (Gold Circle) - Dylan Dog - Bone Hill - Play Dead - The Whisper King - Magdalena - Meet the Haunteds (NBC) - Killing Demons
PRE-PRODUCTION Witchblade - The Darkness
CREDITS Men in Black - Night Man - Ultraforce (Animated Series) - Jeremiah
COMMENTS Sponsoring deals with Col. John Alexander, Karen Brown, Fog Studios, Handheld Games, Hexagon Comics and Blue Shift Inc.

Scott Mitchell Rosenberg .Chairman/CEO
Brian Altounian .COO
Randy Greenberg .Head, Marketing & Licensing
Aaron Severson .Director, Development
Lee Nordling .Executive Editor
Gerry Kline .Business Development & Licensing
Georges Elias .President, Wireless/Mobile Content Division
William Louis Widmaier .President, New Media Online Content Division
Richard Marincic .Creative Executive
Meredith Berg .Story Editor
Calvin Chow .IT Manager/Database Programmer
Daniel Forcey .Manager, Marketing & Communications
Jina Jones .Assistant to Richard Marincic
David Koll .Assistant to Scott Mitchell Rosenberg
Tim Monson .Second Assistant to Scott Mitchell Rosenberg
Sid Davis .Submissions Editor
Malissa Wise .Bookkeeper

MARC PLATT PRODUCTIONS

100 Universal City Plaza, Bungalow 5184
Universal City, CA 91608
PHONE .818-777-8811/818-777-1201 (Production)
FAX .818-866-6353
TYPES Features - Made-for-TV/Cable Movies - Miniseries - Theatre - TV Series
HAS DEAL WITH ABC Entertainment Television Group - Universal Pictures
DEVELOPMENT The Red Star - Scott Pilgrim's Precious Little Life - Good Grief - Wanted - Love & Other Impossible Pursuits - Phillipa Schuyler - Legends - Charlie St. Cloud - Nappily Ever After - The Dark Is Rising - The Book of Leo - The Power of Duff - Dusty Springfield - Marla Ruzicka - Drive - A Child's Game
PRODUCTION Three Days of Rain (Theatre) - Wicked (Theatre)
POST PRODUCTION Untitled History Project
CREDITS Once Upon a Mattress - Empire Falls - The Perfect Man - Legally Blonde 2: Red, White & Blonde - Josie and the Pussycats - Legally Blonde - Honey; Theatre: Wicked

Marc Platt .No Title (818-777-1122)
Joey Levy .No Title (818-777-7866)
Adam Siegel .No Title (818-777-9544)
Nicole Brown .No Title (818-777-5705)
Jared LeBoff .No Title (818-777-9961)
Nik Mavinkurve .No Title (818-777-2598)
Chris Kuhl .No Title (818-777-9549)

PLAYBOY ENTERTAINMENT GROUP, INC.

2706 Media Center Dr.
Los Angeles, CA 90065
PHONE .323-276-4000
FAX .323-276-4505
EMAIL .mkalinowski@playboy.com
WEB SITE .www.playboy.com
TYPES Documentaries - Reality TV - Specials - TV Series

Jim Griffiths .Sr. Executive VP, Playboy Enterprises/President, PEGI
Ned Nalle .President, Programming
Sol Weisel .Executive VP, Production & Operations
Seth Chasin .Sr. VP, Business Planning & Analysis
Alexandra Shepard .Sr. VP, Business & Legal Affairs
Michael Sprouse .Sr. VP, Marketing
Tom Furr .VP, On Air Promotion
Mark Mauceri .VP, Programming
Dan Smith .VP, Production
Catherine Zulfer .VP/Controller

PLAYTIME PRODUCTIONS

311 N. Robertson Blvd., Ste. 283
Beverly Hills, CA 90211
PHONE .310-203-1360/212-664-5499
FAX .413-778-2150/253-650-3470
TYPES Animation - Features - TV Series
COMMENTS Second office: Raleigh Studios, 5400 Melrose Ave., Los Angeles, CA 90038; New York office: 30 Rockefeller Plaza, 6th Fl., New York, NY 10010

Brett A. Liebman .Producer/Writer
Danny Goldwyn .VP, Production
Sarah Levinson .Production Executive
Annie Simon .Development Executive
Abbie Brooks .Development Executive/Animation
Tom Hilman .Executive Assistant
Jessica Kasdan .Executive Assistant

*PLAYTONE PRODUCTIONS

PO Box 7340
Santa Monica, CA 90406
PHONE 310-394-5700
TYPES — Animation - Documentaries - Features - Miniseries - Reality TV - Theatre - TV Series
PRE-PRODUCTION — Charlie Wilson's War - The Great Buck Howard - Where the Wild Things Are - City of Ember - John Adams - The Pacific
CREDITS — The Ant Bully - Starter for Ten - Big Love - Band of Brothers - Magnificent Desolation: Walking on the Moon 3-D - The Polar Express - My Big Fat Greek Wedding - Neil Young: Heart of Gold

Tom Hanks . . . . . Partner
Gary Goetzman . . . . . Partner
Diana Choi . . . . . Head, Development
Steven Shareshian . . . . . Head, Production
Kirk Saduski . . . . . Development Executive
Miura Smith-Kite . . . . . Development Executive
Peter Friedlander . . . . . Production Executive
Eric Paulson . . . . . Production Executive
Patrick Roscoe . . . . . Creative Executive
Bo Stevenson . . . . . Production Associate
Tory Haljun . . . . . Executive Assistant
Eric Quijano . . . . . Executive Assistant
Julie Shimer . . . . . Executive Assistant
Stefanie Berk . . . . . Executive Assistant

PLOTPOINT, INC.

12600 Kling St.
Studio City, CA 91604
PHONE 818-509-9464
TYPES — Animation - Features - TV Series
CREDITS — Handy Manny - Rugrats - Lazytown

Rick Gitelson . . . . . Producer

PLUM PICTURES

141 Fifth Ave., Ste. 8N
New York, NY 10010
PHONE 212-529-5820
FAX 212-529-5824
EMAIL . . . . . plumpic@plumpic.com
WEB SITE . . . . . www.plumpic.com
TYPES — Documentaries - Features - TV Series
DEVELOPMENT — Golden - Laws of Motion - Turkey in the Straw - Jimbo - Cache - Hipster's Handbook
PRE-PRODUCTION — Watching the Detectives
POST PRODUCTION — Dedication - Grace Is Gone
CREDITS — The Baxter - Lonesome Jim

Celine Rattray . . . . . Producer
Galt Niederhoffer . . . . . Producer
Daniela Taplin Lundberg . . . . . Producer
Carina Alves . . . . . Development

PLUS ENTERTAINMENT, INC.

20 W. 23rd St., 3rd Fl.
New York, NY 10010
PHONE 212-206-8160
FAX 212-206-8168
EMAIL . . . . . info@plusentertainment.net
WEB SITE . . . . . www.plusentertainment.net
SECOND WEB SITE . . . . . www.shoutthemodmusical.com
TYPES — Features - Made-for-TV/Cable Movies - Reality TV - Theatre
DEVELOPMENT — Matt & Ben: The Movie
PRE-PRODUCTION — Silence! The Musical - Untitled Spalding Grey Project
CREDITS — Shout! The Mod Musical - Bat Boy: The Musical - Macbeth in Manhattan - Chaos Theory - Dark Tides - Perfect Lies (The Last Lie) - Fountain of Death; Theatre: Matt & Ben - Listen to My Heart: The Songs of David Friedman - Johnny Guitar: The Musical - Bat Boy: The Musical
SUBMISSION POLICY — Via agent, attorney or signed release form

Victoria Lang . . . . . Co-President
Pier Paolo Piccoli . . . . . Co-President
Jared Fine . . . . . Director, Project Development

POETRY & PICTURES INC.

13366 Huston St., Ste. C
Sherman Oaks, CA 91423
PHONE 818-788-9900
FAX 818-788-9902
EMAIL . . . . . doug@dougclaybourne.com
WEB SITE . . . . . www.dougclaybourne.com
TYPES — Documentaries - Features
DEVELOPMENT — Finding the Heart of America - The Carolers - The Cruelest Winter - Looking for Grandpa - Mined - 3 Marys
PRE-PRODUCTION — Saving Trinity
CREDITS — North Country - Duma - Every Twenty One Seconds - The Fast and the Furious - The Mask of Zorro - Jack - Money Train - Mr. Baseball - D2: The Mighty Ducks - Hearts of Darkness: A Filmmaker's Apocalypse - The War of the Roses - Rumble Fish
SUBMISSION POLICY — No unsolicited material
COMMENTS — Ongoing deal with Film 7

Doug Claybourne . . . . . Producer
Laura Napier . . . . . Producer/Director/Writer

POINT ROAD, INC.

1041 N. Formosa Ave., Writer's Bldg., Ste. 9
West Hollywood, CA 90046
PHONE 323-850-2670
TYPES — Features
HAS DEAL WITH — Twentieth Century Fox
DEVELOPMENT — All the Men in the Sea
CREDITS — The Omen 666 - Flight of the Phoenix - Behind Enemy Lines
SUBMISSION POLICY — No unsolicited submissions

John Moore . . . . . No Title
Peter Veverka . . . . . No Title

MARTIN POLL FILMS, LTD.

PO Box 17137
Beverly Hills, CA 90209-3137
PHONE 323-876-8873/212-223-2881
FAX 323-876-8892/212-223-2897
TYPES Features - Made-for-TV/Cable Movies - TV Series
CREDITS Nighthawks - The Lion in Winter - Diana, Her True Story

Martin Poll . . . . . President/Producer
Shirley Mellner . . . . . Executive VP, Creative
Adam Cohen . . . . . VP, Creative
Aliana Scurlock . . . . . Executive Assistant

POLLYWOG ENTERTAINMENT, INC

PO Box 2969
Beverly Hills, CA 90213
PHONE 323-651-5005
FAX 323-651-5851
EMAIL . . . . . pollywog@andydick.com
WEB SITE . . . . . www.andydick.com
SECOND WEB SITE . . . . . www.circlesfromthecenter.com
TYPES Commercials - Direct-to-Video/DVD - Documentaries - Features - Music Videos - Reality TV - Theatre - TV Series
DEVELOPMENT Untitled Andy Dick Film - Daphne Aguilera Film
COMPLETED UNRELEASED Danny Roane: First Time Director (Feature)
CREDITS The Andy Dick Show (MTV) - The Assistant (MTV)

Andy Dick . . . . . Director/Producer/Actor (323-651-5005)
Marshall Cook . . . . . Director/Producer/Editor (323-356-5796)
Shawn Geer . . . . . Director/Editor/Web Design (310-498-4409)

THE POLSON COMPANY

391 S. Madison Ave.
Pasadena, CA 91101
PHONE 626-405-0080
FAX 626-795-9039
TYPES Features - Made-for-TV/Cable Movies - TV Series
CREDITS Go Toward the Light - The Christmas Box - The Christmas Wish - Going Home - The Last Dance - Miss Lettie and Me - Secret Santa - Not My Kid - Baby Girl Scott - A Message from Holly - Guess Who's Coming for Christmas - This Child Is Mine - A Place to Be Loved

Beth Polson . . . . . Executive Producer
Leah Goodman . . . . . Development

PAUL POMPIAN PRODUCTIONS, INC.

5093 Van Alden
Tarzana, CA 91356
PHONE 310-966-1616
FAX 310-694-3776
TYPES Documentaries - Features - Made-for-TV/Cable Movies - Reality TV - TV Series
DEVELOPMENT The Last Apprentice
CREDITS Swimming Upstream - The Watcher

Paul Pompian . . . . . Producer
John Burrows . . . . . VP, Production
Polly Middleton . . . . . VP, Development

POOR BOYS PRODUCTIONS

900 N. Western Ave.
Los Angeles, CA 90029
PHONE 818-445-2147
FAX 323-375-0383
EMAIL . . . . . poorboysprod@yahoo.com
TYPES Animation - Features - Made-for-TV/Cable Movies - TV Series
DEVELOPMENT The Upturned Stone - Baldur's Gate - Savage
CREDITS The Fog

Shane Riches . . . . . Producer
Mark Cartier . . . . . Producer
Victor Riches . . . . . Creative Executive

POPULAR ARTS ENTERTAINMENT, INC.

2006 W. Olive Ave.
Burbank, CA 91506
PHONE 818-562-6366
FAX 818-562-6373
EMAIL . . . . . contactus@populararts.com
WEB SITE . . . . . www.populararts.com
TYPES Animation - Direct-to-Video/DVD - Documentaries - Internet Content - Mobile Content - Reality TV - Specials - TV Series
DEVELOPMENT Lassie (PBS)
PRE-PRODUCTION Fresh (Food/Lifestyle)
PRODUCTION Famous (Syndicated) - Cine News (Syndicated) - Are We There Yet? with Steve Natt (Fine Living)
CREDITS Where Did It Come From? (History Channel) - Going Wild with Jeff Corwin - Dr. Katz - Entertainment News Service - The Jeff Corwin Experience - Mondo Magic (A&E) - Famous (A&E Biography)
SUBMISSION POLICY Must sign waiver

Gordon (Tim) Braine . . . . . Co-CEO/Executive Producer
Kevin Meagher . . . . . Co-CEO/Executive Producer
Marc Wolloff . . . . . Executive in Charge

PORCHLIGHT ENTERTAINMENT

11777 Mississippi Ave.
Los Angeles, CA 90025
PHONE 310-477-8400
FAX 310-477-5555
EMAIL . . . . . info@porchlight.com
WEB SITE . . . . . www.porchlight.com
TYPES Animation - Direct-to-Video/DVD - Features - Made-for-TV/Cable Movies - New Media - TV Series
PRODUCTION Four Eyes
CREDITS Tutenstein - Night of the Twisters - Adventures from the Book of Virtues - Wild Grizzly - Jay Jay the Jet Plane - Treehouse Hostage - The Trial of Old Drum - The Brainiacs.com

Bruce D. Johnson . . . . . President/CEO
William T. Baumann . . . . . Executive VP/CFO/COO
Joe Broido . . . . . Sr. VP, Filmed Entertainment
Fred Schaefer . . . . . Sr. VP/Producer, Children's Programming
Caren Shalek . . . . . Sr. VP, Consumer Products
Adam Wright . . . . . Sr. VP, Worldwide Sales
Mark Young . . . . . Sr. VP, Animation Production
Katherine Kaufman . . . . . VP, International & Home Video Sales
Peggy Lisberger . . . . . VP, Business Affairs
David Bynder . . . . . Director, Marketing & Promotions
Jeffrey Engelen . . . . . Director, International Licensing
Kimberly Healy . . . . . Director, Sales & Acquisitions
Laura Hoffman . . . . . Director, International Sales
Stanley Malone . . . . . Director, International Servicing
Rene Rodman . . . . . Director, Licensing
Todd Bartoo . . . . . Coordinator, Distribution
Anja Bosch . . . . . Coordinator, Marketing & Sales

PORT MAGEE PICTURES, INC.
c/o E! Networks
5750 Wilshire Blvd.
Los Angeles, CA 90036
PHONE .323-692-6455
FAX .323-954-2620
EMAIL .danriley@portmageepictures.com
SECOND EMAIL .peterjclark@portmageepictures.com
TYPES Documentaries - Features - Made-for-TV/Cable Movies - Reality TV - TV Series
DEVELOPMENT The Peter Fitzpatrick Story - Traitors Among Us - Tangled Web - A Kind Man and a Good Lover - Dr. Nookie 911
PRE-PRODUCTION My Fractured Life
POST PRODUCTION The Battalion
COMPLETED UNRELEASED Probies
CREDITS 50 Best Chick Flicks - What Hollywood Taught Us About Sex - It's So Over - Glamour's Biggest Fashion Dos and Don'ts - The 5th Wheel - Kid Stuff - Ex-treme Dating - Lloyd & Lee - E!'s 101 Reasons the 90's Ruled - E!'s 101 Best Kept Hollywood Secrets - The Ultimate Hollywood Blonde - 101 Most Awesome Moments in Entertainment - 50 Wicked Women of Primetime - 50 Outrageous TV Moments - 50 Hottest Vegas Moments - 40 Celebrity Weddings and a Funeral - 50 Steamiest Southern Stars - Child Stars: All Grown Up - Craziest TV Moments
SUBMISSION POLICY No phone calls

Dan Riley .Partner
Peter J. Clark .Partner

***POTBOILER PRODUCTIONS**
9 Greek St.
London W1D 4DQ, United Kingdom
PHONE .44-207-734-7372
FAX .44-207-287-5228
EMAIL .abbie@potboiler.co.uk
TYPES Features
CREDITS The Constant Gardener - Vera Drake - De-Lovely - Man About Dog

Simon Channing-Williams .Producer
Gail Egan .Producer

P.O.V. COMPANY
3033 Three Springs Dr.
Westlake Village, CA 91361
PHONE .818-707-2644
FAX .818-707-3557
TYPES Features - Made-for-TV/Cable Movies - TV Series
CREDITS Runaway - Four Minutes - American Tragedy - Two Against Time - A Town Without Christmas - Glory & Honor - The Love Letter - The Kennedys of Massachusetts - Double Platinum - The Virginian - Falcone - Fallen Angel - The Reagans - 3: The Dale Earnhardt Story - One Tree Hill (Pilot) - Four Minutes

Lynn Raynor .Producer

POW! ENTERTAINMENT
9440 Santa Monica Blvd., Ste. 620
Beverly Hills, CA 90210
PHONE .310-275-9933
FAX .310-285-9955
WEB SITE .www.powentertainment.com
TYPES Animation - Direct-to-Video/DVD - Features - Made-for-TV/Cable Movies - Mobile Content - Reality TV - TV Series
DEVELOPMENT Tigress - Thunder Rider - Alexa - Stripperella - Double Man - Nightbird - Earth Walker - Heroes at Large - Demons - Time Trap - Nick Ratchet - J.J. Armes/Hooked - The Cougar - Superhero Christmas
PRE-PRODUCTION Ringo Starr - Harpies - Forever Man
PRODUCTION El Condor - Mosaic
POST PRODUCTION Who Wants to Be a Superhero?
UPCOMING RELEASES Lightspeed

Stan Lee .Chief Creative Officer
Gill Champion .Chief Operating Officer
Arthur Lieberman .Chief Business Affairs
Junko Kobayashi .Chief Financial Officer
Michael Kelly .Chief Executive Assistant, Stan Lee
Yuka Kobayashi .Chief Executive Assistant, Gill Champion

POWER UP
419 N. Larchmont Blvd., Ste. 283
Los Angeles, CA 90004
PHONE .323-463-3154
EMAIL .joinpowerup@aol.com
WEB SITE .www.power-up.net
TYPES Features - TV Series
DEVELOPMENT 2005 Film Grant Program
POST PRODUCTION Itty Bitty Titty Committee
CREDITS Stuck - Breaking Up Really Sucks - Chicken Night - Fatal Instinct - Under the Hula Moon - To Kill For - In Search of Holden Caulfield - Fly Cherry - Give or Take an Inch - D.E.B.S. - Little Black Boot - Intent - The Nearly Unadventurous Life of Zoe Caudwalder - Starcrossed - Billy's Dad is a Fudgepacker - Prom-troversy

Stacy Codikow .Producer/Writer
Lisa Thrasher .Executive VP, Production & Distribution
Kevin Vermilion .VP
Chris Thrasher .Development

PRACTICAL PICTURES

5900 Wilshire Blvd., Ste. 404
Los Angeles, CA 90036

PHONE 323-456-0422/323-456-0423
FAX 323-456-0191

TYPES	Features - TV Series
DEVELOPMENT	Henry's List of Wrongs (New Line) - All You Can Eat (New Line) - Final Destination 4 - Westward - Hawaiian Dick (New Line) - Lafayette Terrace (AMC)
CREDITS	Replikate - Final Destination 1-3 - American Pie 1-3 - Cats & Dogs - The Big Hit
SUBMISSION POLICY	No unsolicited material; Queries only from agented sources

Craig Perry ... Producer
Sheila Hanahan Taylor ... Producer

PRECIS PRODUCTIONS, INC.

333 Washington Blvd., #13
Marina del Rey, CA 90292

PHONE 310-614-6263
FAX 310-823-7602
EMAIL info@precisproductions.com
WEB SITE www.precisproductions.com

TYPES	Animation - Internet Content - Reality TV - Specials - TV Series
PRODUCTION	Precistv.com
CREDITS	The Biggest Loser - The Surreal Life - Girls Behaving Badly - 5th Wheel - Blind Date
SUBMISSION POLICY	No unsolicited submissions

Bradford Schultze ... Executive Producer
Larry Struber ... Executive Producer

EDWARD R. PRESSMAN FILM CORPORATION

1648 N. Wilcox Ave.
Hollywood, CA 90028

PHONE 323-871-8383/646-383-4664
FAX 323-871-1870/212-489-2103
WEB SITE www.pressman.com

TYPES	Features - TV Series
DEVELOPMENT	The Monkey Wrench Gang - The Hill - Rhapsody - The Man Who Knew Infinity: A Life of the Genius Ramanujan - Little Green Men
PRODUCTION	The Mutant Chronicles
POST PRODUCTION	Sisters
CREDITS	Owning Mahowny - City Hall - The Crow - Conan - Reversal of Fortune - Wall Street - Two Girls and a Guy - Black & White - American Psycho - Thank You for Smoking - The Cooler - The King - Beautiful Country
COMMENTS	East Coast address: 149 Wooster St., 2nd Fl., New York, NY 10012

Edward R. Pressman ... CEO/Chairman
Alessandro Camon ... Head, Production (LA)
Jon Katz ... Head, Business Affairs (NY)
Blanca Camacho ... COO (LA)
Steve Hora ... Creative Executive (LA)
Sarah Ramey ... Creative Executive (NY)

PRETTY DANGEROUS FILMS

1315 Main St.
Venice, CA 90291

PHONE 310-581-0382
FAX 310-496-1329
WEB SITE www.prettydangerousfilms.com

TYPES	Features
DEVELOPMENT	Dropback - Together Twins - Bad Company - Conrail
PRE-PRODUCTION	Thieves
PRODUCTION	Cosmic Radio
POST PRODUCTION	Chasing 3000 - The Fifth Commandment
CREDITS	Edmond - The Nickel Children - The Curse of El Charro - The Heart Is Deceitful Above All Things - The Drone Virus - The Falls - Dark Justice - 7 Mummies

Ryan R. Johnson ... President/CEO
Kevin Ragsdale ... Co-Founder/CFO

PRETTY MATCHES PRODUCTIONS

1100 Avenue of the Americas, G14, Ste. 39
New York, NY 10036

PHONE 212-512-5755
FAX 212-512-5716

TYPES	Documentaries - Features - Made-for-TV/Cable Movies - Miniseries - TV Series
HAS DEAL WITH	HBO Entertainment
DEVELOPMENT	Washingtonienne
CREDITS	Sex and the City

Sarah Jessica Parker ... President
Alison Benson ... Producer
Benjamin Stark ... Director, Development

PRETTY PICTURES

100 Universal City Plaza, Bldg. 2352-A, 3rd Fl.
Universal City, CA 91608

PHONE 818-733-0926
FAX 818-866-0847

TYPES	Features - TV Series
DEVELOPMENT	The Danish Girl - Nic's Way - Celia
PRE-PRODUCTION	Dem - Number Thirteen
CREDITS	Kinsey - The Shape of Things - Nurse Betty - Donnie Brasco - Quiz Show - Homicide: Life on the Street
SUBMISSION POLICY	No unsolicited submissions

Gail Mutrux ... Producer
Lisa Bellomo ... Sr. VP, Production
Charlie Kimball ... Assistant to Gail Mutrux

PRIMARY PRODUCTIONS

227 W. 17th St., 3rd Fl.
New York, NY 10011

PHONE 212-620-4582

TYPES	Features
HAS DEAL WITH	Focus Features/Rogue Pictures
DEVELOPMENT	Untitled Thriller (Rogue Pictures)

Amy Kaufman ... Founder/Producer
Cecilia Morelli ... Creative Executive

PRIMETIME PICTURES
8730 Sunset Blvd., Ste. 470
Los Angeles, CA 90069
PHONE 310-855-1235
FAX 310-855-1245
EMAIL .....info@primetime-pictures.com
WEB SITE .....www.primetime-pictures.com
TYPES Direct-to-Video/DVD - Features - Made-for-TV/Cable Movies
DEVELOPMENT The Devil's Highway - Autopsy
PRE-PRODUCTION Microwave Park
COMPLETED UNRELEASED Cruel World

Kelsey Howard .....President
Todd Nealy .....Executive VP
Eric Maloney .....Assistant

PRINCIPAL ENTERTAINMENT
1964 Westwood Blvd., Ste. 400
Los Angeles, CA 90025
PHONE 310-446-1466/212-997-9191
FAX 310-446-1566/212-997-9280
TYPES Features
DEVELOPMENT Mistral - Heart of the Atom - Against the Current - Living and Breathing - Sober Buddies - Nutjobs - Juggernaut
PRODUCTION Death at a Funeral
COMPLETED UNRELEASED Five Fingers
CREDITS The Last Time I Committed Suicide - Outreach (Pilot) - The Killing Yard - Monster Island (MTV) - The Hebrew Hammer
COMMENTS Personal management; East Coast office: 130 W. 42nd St., Ste. 614, New York, NY 10036

Estelle Lasher .....Principal
Marsha McManus .....Principal
Elizabeth Robinson .....Principal
Meg Mortimer .....Principal
Larry Taube .....Principal
Josh Kesselman .....Manager/Producer
Danny Sherman .....Manager/Producer
Jill Kaplan .....Manager
Stacey McLaughlin .....Manager
Geoff Silverman .....Manager
Michael Smith .....Manager
Lauren Egber .....Associate (LA)
MIke Escott .....Associate (LA)
Colin Wilhm .....Associate (NY)
Josh Taylor .....Associate (NY)

PRINCIPATO-YOUNG ENTERTAINMENT
9465 Wilshire Blvd., Ste. 880
Beverly Hills, CA 90212
PHONE 310-274-4474
FAX 310-274-4108
TYPES Features - TV Series
HAS DEAL WITH NBC Universal Television Studio - Twentieth Century Fox
DEVELOPMENT Dad Can't Lose - Making Daddy a Man - Untitled Will Arnett Project (Universal) - Worst Friends (Warner Bros.) - Man Wedding - The Ambassador
POST PRODUCTION You Are Going to Prison
CREDITS Campus Ladies (Oxygen) - Wet Hot American Summer - Reno 911 (Series)

Peter Principato .....Partner (310-274-4130)
Paul Young .....Partner (310-274-4424)
Ted Bender .....Manager (310-274-4457)
E. Brian Dobbins .....Manager (310-274-2294)
Allen Fischer .....Manager (310-274-4180)
David Gardner .....Manager (310-274-4677)
Dave Rosenthal .....Manager (310-432-5962)
Joel Zadak .....Manager (310-274-2970)

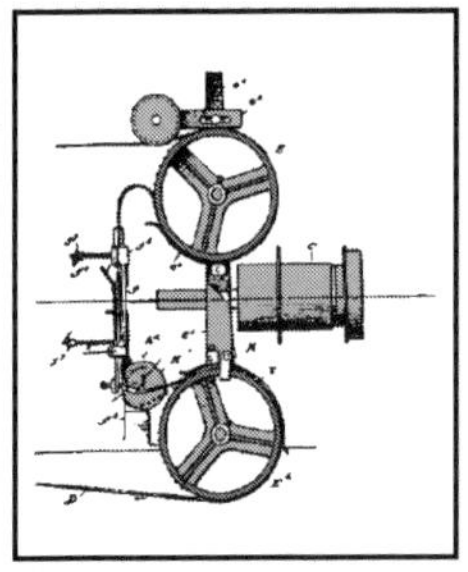

PRODUCTION LOGISTICS, INC.
c/o Louis G. Friedman
204 White Oak Rd.
Santa Ynez, CA 93460
PHONE 805-688-9440/310-738-8338
EMAIL .....productionlogistics@msn.com
WEB SITE .....www.geocities.com/ProductionLogistics
TYPES Features
DEVELOPMENT Reading, Writing, & Relativity or How I Learned to Displace Matter and Raise the Dead Before Breakfast - The Other Road
CREDITS Accepted - Into the Blue - Kicking & Screaming - American Wedding - Blue Crush - American Pie - The Third Wheel - Slackers - How High - Titanic - Starship Troopers - Return of the Jedi - Hexed - Raiders of the Lost Ark
COMMENTS Member of the DGA and PGA

Louis G. Friedman .....Executive Producer

PRODUCTION PARTNERS, INC.
4421 Riverside Dr., Ste. 206
Burbank, CA 91505
PHONE 818-556-5065
FAX 818-556-5069
EMAIL .....contact@productionpartners.com
WEB SITE .....www.productionpartners.com
TYPES Features - TV Series
POST PRODUCTION Caroline Rhea Special - Joan Rivers Special - Paula Poundstone Special
CREDITS TV Series: Fat Actress - Curb Your Enthusiasm; Comedy Specials: Ben Stiller's Wake Up Your Smile - Chris Rock: Bigger & Blacker - Chris Rock: Bring the Pain - Adam Sandler: What the Hell Happened to Me? - Kathy Griffin: The D List - Bill Maher: Be More Cynical - David Spade: Take the Hit - Chris Rock: Big Ass Jokes

Sandy Chanley .....Executive Producer
Tom Bull .....Producer
Keith Truesdell .....Director

PROGRAM PARTNERS
818 Hampton Dr.
Venice, CA 90291
PHONE 310-399-4499
FAX 310-399-6336
EMAIL .....info@programpartners.com
WEB SITE .....www.programpartners.com
TYPES Made-for-TV/Cable Movies - Reality TV - TV Series

Ritch Colbert .....Partner (ritch@programpartners.com)
Josh Raphaelson .....Partner (josh@programpartners.com)
David Hutchinson ...Business Development (hutch@programpartners.com)
Chad MacDonald .....Research & Sales
Jay Wheeler .....Sales
Theophilus Lacey .....Executive Assistant

PROMETHEUS ENTERTAINMENT
6430 Sunset Blvd., Ste. 1450
Culver City, CA 90028
PHONE . . . 323-769-4000
FAX . . . 323-769-4060
EMAIL . . . scott.hartford@prometheuspix.com
TYPES Documentaries - Made-for-TV/Cable Movies - Reality TV - TV Series
CREDITS Look, Up in the Sky! - The Science of Superman - The Girls Next Door - Hollywood Science - Star Wars: Empire of Dreams

Kevin J. Burns . . . President
Scott Hartford . . . Executive VP, Development & Production
Jenny Krochmal . . . Executive Assistant to President/VP, Development & Production

PROSPECT PICTURES
8332 Melrose Ave., 2nd Fl.
West Hollywood, CA 90069
PHONE . . . 323-653-9300
FAX . . . 323-653-9301
WEB SITE . . . www.prospectpictures.com
TYPES Documentaries - Features - Theatre - TV Series
DEVELOPMENT Stalker: A Love Story - Time After Time - Something Blue - You're Amazing
PRE-PRODUCTION Barry Munday
PRODUCTION Surfwise
CREDITS My Baby's Daddy - Rock the House - Pretty Persuasion - Rock of Ages

Matthew Weaver . . . Partner
Marcos Siega . . . Partner
Carl Levin . . . Partner
Markus Goerg . . . Director, Development
Chris Losnegard . . . Development Assistant
Morgan Schechter . . . Development Assistant

proteus®

PROTEUS
1101 15th St., NW, Ste. 1010
Washington, DC 20005
PHONE . . . 202-452-6800
FAX . . . 202-452-6866
WEB SITE . . . www.proteus.com
TYPES Internet Content - Mobile Content
COMMENTS New York office: 575 Lexington Ave., Ste. 400, New York, NY 10022; West Coast office: 1411 Fifth St., Ste. 400, Santa Monica, CA 90401

Kenneth Krushel . . . CEO
Jeff Lee . . . President
Russell Kagan . . . Managing Director
Eric Ashman . . . Director, Technology
Sunil Doshi . . . Director, Creative Services
Michael Maleski . . . Director, Account Management
Jaspreet Singh . . . Director, Distribution Services
Guy Vidra . . . Director, Content Strategy

PROTOZOA PICTURES
438 W. 37th St., Ste. 5-G
New York, NY 10018
PHONE . . . 212-244-3369
FAX . . . 212-244-3735
TYPES Animation - Features - TV Series
HAS DEAL WITH Universal Pictures
DEVELOPMENT Flicker - Lone Wolf & Cub - Song of Kali - The Hunt
UPCOMING RELEASES The Fountain
CREDITS Pi - Requiem for a Dream - Below

Darren Aronofsky . . . Partner
Eric Watson . . . Partner
Ari Handel . . . President
Mark Heyman . . . Director, Development
Nicole Romano . . . Staff

PROUD MARY ENTERTAINMENT
433 N. Camden Dr., Ste. 600
Beverly Hills, CA 90210
PHONE . . . 310-288-1886
FAX . . . 310-288-1801
EMAIL . . . proudmaryent@earthlink.net
TYPES Animation - Direct-to-Video/DVD - Features - Made-for-TV/Cable Movies - Miniseries - Reality TV - TV Series
DEVELOPMENT The Informant (Spike) - Kicking Ash - Amazing Grace (Fox) - The Higher the Hair the Closer to Heaven (Showtime) - Trick'd (MTV) - Girl from Impanema - The Patient - Zoom Suit
PRE-PRODUCTION When a Man Falls in the Forest
CREDITS Caught in the Act - Full Metal Racket - The Princess & the Marine (NBC) - Downtown: A Street Tale

Mary L. Aloe . . . Producer/Executive Producer
Robert J. Halvorson . . . VP, Production
Amyn Bhai . . . Development
Jude Hinajosa . . . Development
Mary Robinson . . . Development

PTERODACTYL PRODUCTIONS INC.
2541 Canyon Oak Dr.
Los Angeles, CA 90068
PHONE . . . 323-469-5778
TYPES Direct-to-Video/DVD - Features - TV Series
DEVELOPMENT Neal Adams' Knighthawk - Marmaduke - Heathcliff the Cat - Love & Terror
CREDITS Sabrina, the Teenage Witch - Doom Runners - Forever Knight

Ivan Cohen . . . Partner (323-461-6167)
Barney Cohen . . . Partner

Q MEDIA PARTNERS
2 Connecticut St.
San Francisco, CA 94107
PHONE 415-252-2868
EMAIL ....info@qmediapartners.com
WEB SITE ....www.qmediapartners.com
TYPES — Direct-to-Video/DVD - Internet Content - Made-for-TV/Cable Movies - Mobile Content - Reality TV - TV Series
HAS DEAL WITH — HBO Entertainment - Touchstone Television

Peter Calabrese ....Chairman/CEO
Alan Sternfeld ....Executive VP, Sales & Program Development
Kim Swann ....Executive VP, Development
David Mekles ....VP, Development (Los Angeles)
Golareh Safarian ....VP, Development (San Francisco)
Elizabeth Morse ....Director, Development
Erik Nordby ....Director, Development
George Thelen ....Executive Assistant, Development

QED INTERNATIONAL
9595 Wilshire Blvd., Ste. 800
Beverly Hills, CA 90212
PHONE 310-273-3004
FAX 310-273-3006
WEB SITE ....www.qedintl.com
TYPES — Features
DEVELOPMENT — Just a Pilgrim - Cul De Sac - Second Wife - The Killer's Game
PRE-PRODUCTION — Spring Break in Bosnia - Stopping Power

Bill Block ....CEO
Paul Hanson ....COO
Kimberly Fox ....Sr. VP, Worldwide Sales
Elliot Ferwerda ....VP, Production
Tatyana Joffe ....VP, International Distribution
Nicolina Liddi ....Coordinator, Worldwide Sales
Mark Yaloff ....Controller
Heather Montgomery ....Assistant to CEO

QUINTA COMMUNICATIONS USA
3000 Olympic Blvd.
Santa Monica, CA 90404
PHONE 310-264-3978
FAX 310-264-3979
TYPES — Features
DEVELOPMENT — Toyer
POST PRODUCTION — Decameron - The Last Legion - Young Hannibal: Behind the Mask
UPCOMING RELEASES — Chromophobia - The Kite
CREDITS — Femme Fatale - Avenging Angelo - Ballistic: Ecks vs. Sever - Boys on the Run - Pirates
COMMENTS — Distributor; Paris office: Quinta Communications S.A., 16 Avenue Hoche, Paris 75008, France, phone: 331-4076-0454, fax: 331-4076-0455

Tarak Ben Ammar ....Chairman (Paris)
Paul Rosenblum ....President (LA)
Brigitte Segal ....Legal & Business Affairs (LA)

QVF INC.
629 Eastern Ave., Bldg. A, Ste. 102
Toronto, ON M4M 1E4, Canada
PHONE 416-406-6528
FAX 416-406-1207
EMAIL ....general@qvfinc.com
WEB SITE ....www.qvfinc.com
TYPES — Documentaries - Features - Made-for-TV/Cable Movies - TV Series
DEVELOPMENT — Strange Boy - The Venitian - Hominids - Push - Goldrush - Inferno
PRE-PRODUCTION — IDS/Quill
CREDITS — Johnny 2.0 (Feature) - Daydream Believers - The Monkees Story (MOW); TV: Sue Thomas: F.B.Eye - Doc - Twice in a Lifetime - The Stranger I Married - Doomstown

Patricia Curmi ....No Title
Susan Murdoch ....No Title
Deborah Nathan ....No Title

QWERTY FILMS
42-44 Beak St.
London W1F 9RH, United Kingdom
PHONE 44-207-440-5920
TYPES — Features
UPCOMING RELEASES — The Amateurs - Severance - Alien Autopsy
CREDITS — Stage Beauty - I Heart Huckabees - Kinsey - The Order - Being John Malkovich - Kalifornia - Wild at Heart

Michael Kuhn ....Chairman

RADAR PICTURES
10900 Wilshire Blvd., Ste. 1400
Los Angeles, CA 90024
PHONE 310-208-8525
FAX 310-208-1764
WEB SITE ....www.radarpictures.com
TYPES — Animation - Features - TV Series
PROVIDES DEAL TO — American Work - Frederic Golchan Productions
DEVELOPMENT — Hot Plastic (Focus) - Emerald City - The Gifted - The Know It All - In Search of Captain Zero - Twelve - Heartbreak Kid (DreamWorks) - Zooport (Universal) - Jeff the Demon (New Line) - Amnesia (Paramount) - Lucky's Last Stand - Seven Day Itch
CREDITS — Waist Deep - Amityville Horror - The Last Samurai - Pitch Black - Runaway Bride - Jumanji - Mr. Holland's Opus - Texas Chainsaw Massacre - Three Men and a Baby - Revenge of the Nerds - Bill & Ted's Excellent Adventure - The Hand that Rocked the Cradle - Cocktail
SUBMISSION POLICY — No unsolicited submissions

Ted W. Field ....Chairman/CEO
David Boyle ....COO
Joe Rosenberg ....Executive VP/Producer
Sharon Steinhauser ....Coordinator, Business & Legal Affairs
Davida Heller ....Creative Executive
Mike Weber ....Creative Executive
Francesca DeLaurentis ....Development Coordinator

RADIANT PRODUCTIONS
914 Montana Ave., 2nd Fl.
Santa Monica, CA 90403
PHONE .310-656-1400
FAX .310-656-1408
TYPES Features - Made-for-TV/Cable Movies
HAS DEAL WITH Warner Bros. Pictures
CREDITS Avenger (TNT) - Poseidon (Warner Bros.) - Troy - The Perfect Storm - Air Force One - Outbreak - In the Line of Fire - Das Boot - The Agency

Wolfgang Petersen .Director/Producer (310-656-1401)
Kimberly Miller .President, Production/Producer (310-656-1404)
Rachel Walens .Creative Executive (310-656-1407)
Barbara Huber .Assistant to Mr. Petersen (310-656-1401)

THE RADMIN COMPANY
9201 Wilshire Blvd., Ste. 102
Beverly Hills, CA 90210
PHONE .310-274-9515
FAX .310-274-0739
EMAIL .info@radmincompany.com
SECOND EMAIL .queries@radmincompany.com
TYPES Features - TV Series
DEVELOPMENT One Neck
CREDITS The Next Best Thing - The Fantasticks - Twisted
SUBMISSION POLICY Fax or email

Linne Radmin .Producer
Becky Zoshak .Creative Executive
Ben Stebor .Story Editor
David Langford .Story Department

RAFELSON MEDIA
10713 Burbank Blvd.
North Hollywood, CA 91601
PHONE .818-753-9300
FAX .818-753-9966
WEB SITE .www.rafelson.com
SECOND WEB SITE .www.stratmediagroup.com
TYPES Animation - Commercials - Direct-to-Video/DVD - Documentaries - Features - Made-for-TV/Cable Movies - Music Videos - Reality TV - Theatre - TV Series
CREDITS A Midsummer Night's Rave (Feature) - Afterthoughts (Bravo/TV Series) - Heart of the Beholder (Feature)

Peter Rafelson .President/CEO
Michael Brooks .Head, Production
Wyatt Peabody .Director, Operations
Brad Houshour .Label Manager

RAFFAELLA PRODUCTIONS, INC.
14320 Ventura Blvd., Ste. 617
Sherman Oaks, CA 91423
PHONE .310-472-0466
FAX .310-471-6315
TYPES Direct-to-Video/DVD - Features - Made-for-TV/Cable Movies - Miniseries - TV Series
DEVELOPMENT Prototype - MacGyver (Feature) - Smoke and Mirrors - Spotted in France - Seven Extraordinary Things - Mama Day - Little Man
POST PRODUCTION The Last Legion
CREDITS Prancer Returns - Daylight - Dragonheart 1&2 - Dragon: Bruce Lee Story - Uprising - Sky Captain and the World of Tomorrow
SUBMISSION POLICY No unsolicited material

Raffaella De Laurentiis .President/Producer
Hester Hargett-Aupetit .Executive VP/Co-Producer

RAINBOW FILM COMPANY/RAINBOW RELEASING
9165 Sunset Blvd., Ste. 300
Los Angeles, CA 90069
PHONE .310-271-0202
FAX .310-271-2753
EMAIL .lester310@earthlink.net
WEB SITE .www.rainbowreleasing.com
TYPES Features
CREDITS Going Shopping - Deja Vu - Mistress - Eating - Last Summer in the Hamptons - Love After Love - New Year's Day
COMMENTS Also distributes; Deal with Revere Entertainment, London

Henry Jaglom .President
Sharon Lester Kohn .VP, Distribution

RAINFOREST FILMS
2141 Powers Ferry Rd., Ste. 300
Marietta, GA 30067
PHONE .770-960-8733
FAX .770-953-0848
EMAIL .staff@rainforest-films.com
WEB SITE .www.rainforestproductions.com
TYPES Features
PRODUCTION Steppin'
CREDITS The Gospel - Puff, Puff, Pass

William Packer .Producer
Rob Hardy .Director/Producer

RAINSTORM ENTERTAINMENT, INC.
15821 Ventura Blvd., Ste. 515
Encino, CA 91436
PHONE .818-784-7500
FAX .818-981-4618
EMAIL .gregg@rainstormentertainment.com
SECOND EMAIL .steve@rainstormentertainment.com
WEB SITE .www.rainstormentertainment.com
TYPES Documentaries - Features
DEVELOPMENT The Green Falcon - Juggernaut - Frost Bites - Vlad the Impaler - In the Face of Jinn
POST PRODUCTION Big Bad Wolf
UPCOMING RELEASES F*CK (Documentary)
COMPLETED UNRELEASED Red, White, Black and Blue
CREDITS Terror Tract - The Big Empty
SUBMISSION POLICY Treatments only; No scripts unless through agency

Steven G. Kaplan .President/Producer
Gregg L. Daniel .Creative Affairs/Producer

PEGGY RAJSKI PRODUCTIONS
918 Alandele Ave.
Los Angeles, CA 90036
PHONE .323-634-7020
FAX .323-634-7021
EMAIL .rajskip@aol.com
TYPES Documentaries - Features
DEVELOPMENT Film: Two Night Stand - Baggage - Urban Paranoia; TV: Trevor
CREDITS Bee Season - Home for the Holidays - Used People - Little Man Tate - Matewan - The Brother from Another Planet - The Scoundrel's Wife - The Grifters - Eight Men Out

Peggy Rajski .Producer/Director

RANDOM HOUSE FILMS
1745 Broadway
New York, NY 10019
PHONE 212-782-9000
WEB SITE .....www.randomhouse.com
SECOND WEB SITE .....www.focusfeatures.com
TYPES Features
HAS DEAL WITH Focus Features/Rogue Pictures
DEVELOPMENT The Attack - Curveball - The Husband

Peter Gethers .....President
Valerie Cates .....Executive Story Editor
Claudia Herr .....Executive Story Editor

RANDWELL PRODUCTIONS
185 Pier Ave., Ste. 103
Santa Monica, CA 90405
PHONE 310-396-0966
FAX 310-396-0963
EMAIL .....randwellprods@yahoo.com
WEB SITE .....www.randwell.com
TYPES Features - Made-for-TV/Cable Movies
CREDITS The Pact - Profoundly Normal - Amelia Earhart: The Final Flight - See You in My Dreams - Two Mothers for Zachary - Lies My Mother Told Me

Randy Robinson .....President/Executive Producer
Christina Wanke .....Assistant

RAT ENTERTAINMENT/RAT TV
9255 Sunset Blvd., Ste. 310
Los Angeles, CA 90069
PHONE 310-228-5000
FAX 310-860-9251
TYPES Features - TV Series
HAS DEAL WITH New Line Cinema
DEVELOPMENT Blue Blood
UPCOMING RELEASES The Cleaner
CREDITS X-Men: The Last Stand - After the Sunset - Red Dragon - Rush Hour 1&2 - The Family Man - Money Talks

Brett Ratner .....Director/Producer/Chairman
Jay Stern .....President
John Cheng .....Head, Feature Development
Anita S. Chang .....Executive Assistant to Mr. Ratner
Frank Slesinski .....Office Manager/Executive Assistant to Mr. Stern
Winston Pear .....Assistant to Mr. Cheng

RAYGUN PRODUCTIONS
6565 Sunset Blvd., Ste. 416
Hollywood, CA 90028
PHONE 323-993-0080
FAX 323-993-0088
TYPES Features
POST PRODUCTION The Prestige
UPCOMING RELEASES The Return
COMPLETED UNRELEASED The TV Set
CREDITS Memento - Donnie Darko - The Mexican - The Amateurs

Aaron Ryder .....Producer
Carolyn Harris .....Creative Executive
Beatrice Springborn .....Assistant

RDF MEDIA
440 Ninth Ave., 11th Fl.
New York, NY 10001
PHONE 212-404-1463
FAX 212-404-1423
WEB SITE .....www.rdfmedia.com
TYPES Reality TV - TV Series
CREDITS Wife Swap (ABC) - Survival of the Richest (The WB) - Gene Simmons Rock School (VH1) - Junkyard Wars (TLC) - Faking It (TLC)
COMMENTS London office: The Gloucester Building, Kensington Village, Avonmore Rd., London, W14 8RF, phone: 44-20-7013-4000, fax: 44-20-7013-4001

Chris Coelen .....CEO
Tony Yates .....COO
Stephen Lambert .....CCO
Kirk Schenck .....President/General Counsel
Teresa Watkins .....Joint Head, Development
Greg Goldman .....Executive VP, Development & Current Series
Simon Rockwell .....Executive Producer
Wendy Roth .....Executive VP, New York Office
Brian Lenard .....Manager, Development

REASON PICTURES
9155 W. Sunset Blvd.
West Hollywood, CA 90069
PHONE 310-691-1020
FAX 310-691-1022
WEB SITE .....www.reasonpictures.com
TYPES Documentaries - Features
DEVELOPMENT Marching Powder - A Nation of Lords - The Futurist - The Messenger
PRE-PRODUCTION The World 2006 - Americas

Ben Goldhirsh .....CEO
Chris Koch .....No Title
Bristol Baughan .....No Title
Zach Miller .....No Title
Noella Boudart .....No Title
Dan Mitchell .....No Title
Kenneth Garcia .....No Title

RECORDED PICTURE COMPANY
24 Hanway St.
London W1T 1UH, United Kingdom
PHONE 44-207-636-2251
FAX 44-207-636-2261
EMAIL .....rpc@recordedpicture.com
WEB SITE .....www.recordedpicture.com
TYPES Features
CREDITS Fast Food Nation - Sexy Beast - The Last Emperor - Rabbit Proof Fence - Stealing Beauty - The Brave - Crash - Beseiged - All the Little Animals - Brother - The Cup - The Triumph of Love - The Dreamers - Young Adam - Tideland

Jeremy Thomas .....Producer/Chairman
Peter Watson .....CEO/Business Affairs
Stephan Mallman .....COO/Finance
Alexandra Stone .....Sr. VP/Head, Development
Hercules Bellville .....Head, Development
Florence Larsonneur .....Business Affairs Executive
Richard Mansell .....Business Affairs Executive
Matthew Baker .....Acquisitions & Development Executive
Stuart Cooke .....Company Accountant
Karin Padgham .....Executive Assistant to Jeremy Thomas
Alainee Kent .....Assistant to Alexandra Stone
Mel Reynard .....Assistant to Peter Watson & Stephan Mallman
Amelie Turgis .....Assistant to Stuart Cooke

RED BIRD PRODUCTIONS

3623 Hayden Ave.
Culver City, CA 90232
PHONE .310-202-1711
TYPES Features - Theatre - TV Series
DEVELOPMENT Behind the Glass - I Sought My Brother
PRE-PRODUCTION Pepito's Story
CREDITS Amistad - Out of Sync - Cool Women - Dancing in the Wings (Theatre) - Pepito's Story (Theatre)

Debbie Allen .President/Actor/Director/Producer

RED BOARD PRODUCTIONS

3000 W. Olympic, Bldg. 4, Ste. 1200
Santa Monica, CA 90404
PHONE .310-264-4285
FAX .310-264-4286
TYPES TV Series
HAS DEAL WITH HBO Entertainment
DEVELOPMENT John from Cincinatti - Untitled Bill Clark Project
CREDITS Big Apple - Deadwood

David Milch .Executive Producer/Writer
Zack Whedon .Assistant to Mr. Milch

RED DOG ENTERTAINMENT

3130 Wilshire Blvd., Ste. 150
Santa Monica, CA 90403
PHONE .310-909-1117/212-603-1818
FAX .310-453-3448/212-603-1889
EMAIL .info@reddogentertainment.com
WEB SITE .www.reddogentertainment.com
TYPES TV Series
CREDITS SOS: Coast Guard Rescue - Fit Nation - Prisoner of Iraq? - The Wrong Man (Court TV)

Michael Schlossman .Producer
Jeanne Dresp .Executive Director, Production Management
Greg Kanaan .Director, Programming

RED DOOR FILMS/ DAVID POULSHOCK PRODUCTIONS, INC.

2211 NW Front, Ste. 209
Portland, OR 97209
PHONE .503-872-9280
FAX .503-872-9281
EMAIL .reel@reddoorfilms.com
WEB SITE .www.reddoorfilms.com
TYPES Commercials - Direct-to-Video/DVD - Features - TV Series
DEVELOPMENT The Head Table - Wee Sing Singalings - The Fix
COMPLETED UNRELEASED The Wonderful World of Wooleycat
CREDITS Wee Sing in Sillyville - Wee Sing Under the Sea - The Wee Sing Train - Wee Sing in the Marvelous Musical Mansion Wee Sing in the Big Rock Candy Mountains - Wee Sing's Best Christmas Ever! - The Head Table (Pilot)

David Poulshock .President/CEO
Ryan Crisman .Producer

RED HEN PRODUCTIONS

3607 W. Magnolia, Ste. L
Burbank, CA 91505
PHONE .818-563-3600
FAX .818-787-6637
EMAIL .goridich@aol.com
TYPES Direct-to-Video/DVD - Features - Made-for-TV/Cable Movies
DEVELOPMENT The Thing on the Doorstep - Cops - Horror 101 - Ladies Night
PRE-PRODUCTION Stuck
CREDITS Edmond - King of the Ants - Dagon - Space Truckers - The Wonderful Ice Cream Suit - Honey I Blew Up the Kid - Honey, I Shrunk the Kids - Fortress - Re-Animator
SUBMISSION POLICY Send a brief synopsis
COMMENTS Looking for low budget horror projects

Stuart Gordon .Director/Writer/Producer
Stuart Ortiz .Assistant

RED HOUR FILMS

629 N. La Brea
Los Angeles, CA 90036
PHONE .323-602-5000
TYPES Features
HAS DEAL WITH DreamWorks SKG
DEVELOPMENT Used Guys - The Persuaders - Big Wave
PRODUCTION Blades of Glory
POST PRODUCTION Tenacious D in The Pick of Destiny
CREDITS Duplex - Zoolander - Dodgeball - Starsky and Hutch
SUBMISSION POLICY No unsolicited material

Ben Stiller .Writer/Director/Producer
Stuart Cornfeld .Producer
Lara Breay .VP, Develpment
Patrick Dain .Story Editor
Samantha Lloyd .Assistant to Ben Stiller
Erica Palm .Second Assistant to Ben Stiller
Charlie Ward .Assistant to Stuart Cornfeld

RED OM FILMS, INC.

c/o Engelman and Company
156 5th Ave., Ste. 711
New York, NY 10010
PHONE .212-645-9222
FAX .212-645-9333
TYPES Documentaries - Features - Made-for-TV/Cable Movies - Reality TV - TV Series
CREDITS Felicity: An American Girl Adventure - Mona Lisa Smile - Stepmom - Maid in Manhattan
SUBMISSION POLICY No unsolicited submissions

Julia Roberts .Actor/Producer

RED STROKES ENTERTAINMENT

9465 Wilshire Blvd., Ste. 319
Beverly Hills, CA 90212
PHONE .310-786-7887
FAX .310-786-7827
TYPES Features - TV Series
CREDITS Call Me Claus (TNT)

Garth Brooks .Talent/Producer
Lisa Sanderson .CEO/Producer/Partner
Anka Brazzell .Executive Assistant

RED WAGON ENTERTAINMENT
c/o Sony Pictures Studios
10202 W. Washington Blvd., Hepburn Bldg.
Culver City, CA 90232-3195
PHONE .310-244-4466
FAX .310-244-1480
TYPES Animation - Direct-to-Video/DVD - Features - TV Series
HAS DEAL WITH Sony Pictures Entertainment
DEVELOPMENT The Manny - The Chancellor Manuscript - The Historian - Tokyo Suckerpunch - American Caesar - Lone Ranger - Flint - Hannibal - Don't Ask - Uprising - Fertig - Dreadnought - Sammy's Hill - Gidget - Bye Bye Birdie - Hell Week - Seven Year Switch - St. George & the Dragon
CREDITS Hollow Man 1&2 - RV - Memoirs of a Geisha - Jarhead - Stuart Little 1-3 - Bewitched - Wolf - Working Girl - The Craft - Girl, Interrupted - Gladiator - Spy Game - Stuart Little (HBO Animated Series) - Peter Pan - Win a Date with Tad Hamilton

Douglas Wick .Producer
Lucy Fisher .Producer
Rachel Shane .Executive VP, Creative Affairs
Emily Cummins .Executive VP, Production
Tia Maggini .Creative Executive
Steven Puri .Creative Executive
Leigh Evans .Assistant
Meghan Snyder .Assistant
Haj Chenzira-Pinnock .Assistant
Conor Copeland .Assistant
Brandi Jackson .Assistant
Andrei Klibansky .Assistant
Megan Moran .Assistant
Bridget Tyler .Assistant

MARIAN REES ASSOCIATES
12400 Ventura Blvd., Box 225
Studio City, CA 91604
PHONE .818-508-5599
FAX .818-508-8012
EMAIL .vantageave4@yahoo.com
TYPES Features - Made-for-TV/Cable Movies
DEVELOPMENT Film: Bet Me - Lighthouse at the End of the World - Meant to Be - Doña Ana's Funeral; TV: Maggie and Mark - Just Breathe
CREDITS In Pursuit of Honor (HBO) - Miss Rose White - Decoration Day - Love Is Never Silent (Hallmark) - Ruby Bridges (Wonderful World of Disney) Is There Life Out There? (CBS) - Papa's Angels (CBS) - Keeping the Promise (CBS) - ExxonMobil Masterpiece Theatre: The American Collection

Marian Rees .CEO/Executive Producer
Anne Hopkins .President/Executive Producer
Dyan Austin Conway .VP, Business Affairs/Development

REGAN
10100 Santa Monica Blvd., 10th Fl.
Los Angeles, CA 90067
PHONE .310-228-1010
FAX .310-228-3430
EMAIL .regan@harpercollins.com
WEB SITE .www.reganbooks.com
TYPES Animation - Direct-to-Video/DVD - Documentaries - Features - Internet Content - Made-for-TV/Cable Movies - Miniseries - Mobile Content - Reality TV - Specials - Theatre - TV Series
DEVELOPMENT Citizen Vince - I Know This Much is True - Straight Up & Dirty - Post Secret - D.S.I. - Howtoons - Round-Up Saloon - The Assistants - The Dive - The Day the World Came to Town
CREDITS Microserfs - The Other Man - Growing Up Gotti
COMMENTS New York Office: 10 E. 53rd St., 18th Fl., New York, NY 10022, phone: 212-207-7474, fax: 212-207-7973

Judith Regan .President/Publisher

REGENCY®

REGENCY ENTERPRISES
10201 W. Pico Blvd., Bldg. 12
Los Angeles, CA 90035
PHONE .310-369-8300
FAX .310-969-0470
WEB SITE .www.newregency.com
TYPES Features
HAS DEAL WITH Twentieth Century Fox
PRODUCTION Dallas - Jumper
POST PRODUCTION Deck the Halls - The Fountain - Firehouse Dog
CREDITS My Super Ex-Girlfriend - Date Movie - Mr. & Mrs. Smith - Guess Who - Man on Fire - Daredevil - Unfaithful - Big Momma's House 1&2 - Fight Club - L.A. Confidential - The Client - Entrapment - A Time to Kill - Heat - City of Angels

Arnon Milchan .Producer
David Matalon .President/CEO
Sanford Panitch .President, Filmed Entertainment
Louis Santor .Executive VP/CFO
Adam Schroeder .Executive VP, Production
William S. Weiner . .Executive VP, Business & Legal Affairs/General Counsel
Thomas Imperato .Executive VP/Head, Physical Production
Kara Francis .Executive VP, Production
Robert S. Corzo .Sr. VP, Finance/Chief Accounting Officer
Elissa Loparco .Sr. VP, Post Production
Alexa Amin .VP, Production
Michael H. Brown .VP, Marketing
Alexandra Milchan-Lambert .VP
Jonathan Ruiz .VP, Production
Heidi Sherman .Creative Executive
Alexandra Sundell .Creative Executive
Tal Almog .Story Associate
Chad Freet .Production Administrator

REGENCY TELEVISION

10201 W. Pico Blvd., Bldg. 12
Los Angeles, CA 90035
PHONE . . . 310-369-7593
FAX . . . 310-969-1339
TYPES — TV Series
PROVIDES DEAL TO — Avalon Television, Inc. - OZLA Pictures, Inc.
CREDITS — Malcolm in the Middle - The Bernie Mac Show - Windfall - Help Me Help You

Robin Schwartz . . . President
Stephanie Levine . . . Sr. VP (x7580)
Joanna Klein . . . VP (x3655)
Andrea Shay . . . VP (x7525)
Stacy Fung . . . Director (x7524)
Larry Sullivan . . . Manager (x7336)

REGENT

10990 Wilshire Blvd., PH
Los Angeles, CA 90024
PHONE . . . 310-806-4288
FAX . . . 310-806-4268
EMAIL . . . info@regententertainment.com
WEB SITE . . . www.regententertainment.com
TYPES — Features - Made-for-TV/Cable Movies - TV Series
DEVELOPMENT — Dante's Cove 4-6 - Ice Blues - Ice Spiders - Nuclear Hurricane
PRE-PRODUCTION — Second Chance - Urgency
CREDITS — Snowman's Pass - Chupacabra: Dark Seas - Secret Lives - Pit Fighter - The Sisterhood - Witches of the Caribbean - Found - Third Man Out - Blind Injustice - Deadly Skies - Killer Bash - Tides of War - Fatal Reunion - Brittanic - Gen-Y Cops - Gods & Monsters - I'll Remember April - Nostradamus - Hot Zone - Terror Peak - Tom & Viv - Cave In - Tornado Warning - Paradise Virus - A Good Night to Die - The Brotherhood 1-3 - Wolves of Wall Street - Dante's Cove - Too Cool for Christmas - Home for the Holidays - Chasing Christmas - Air Force 2
COMMENTS — Produces 12-18 TV/Cable movies per year

Stephen P. Jarchow . . . Chairman/CEO
Paul Colichman . . . President
Jeff Schenck . . . President, Regent Studios LLC
Gene L. George . . . President, Regent World Wide Sales, LLC
John Lambert . . . President, Regent Releasing, LLC

TIM REID PRODUCTIONS, INC.

One New Millennium Dr.
Petersburg, VA 23805-8907
PHONE . . . 804-957-4200
FAX . . . 804-862-1200
EMAIL . . . daphne@nmstudios.com
WEB SITE . . . www.nmstudios.com
SECOND WEB SITE . . . www.timreidproductions.com
TYPES — Commercials - Direct-to-Video/DVD - Documentaries - Features - TV Series
PRE-PRODUCTION — Raw Passion (Feature) - Legacy of a People (Documentary)
CREDITS — American Legacy Television (Syndicated Series) - About Sarah - Linc's (Showtime Series) - For Real (Feature) - Asunder (Feature) - Paul Mooney: Analyzing White America (DVD)
SUBMISSION POLICY — No unsolicited submissions

Tim Reid . . . President
Daphne Reid . . . VP

REINER/GREISMAN

335 N. Maple Dr., Ste. 135
Beverly Hills, CA 90210
PHONE . . . 310-285-2300
TYPES — Features
HAS DEAL WITH — Castle Rock Entertainment
DEVELOPMENT — The Bucket List
CREDITS — A Few Good Men - The American President - When Harry Met Sally... - Soap Dish - Alex and Emma

Rob Reiner . . . Director/Producer (310-285-2328)
Alan Greisman . . . Producer (310-205-2766)
Pam Jones . . . Assistant to Rob Reiner (310-285-2352)

RELATIVITY MEDIA LLC

8899 Beverly Blvd., Ste. 510
West Hollywood, CA 90048
PHONE . . . 310-859-1250
FAX . . . 310-859-1254
TYPES — Features
DEVELOPMENT — Morgan's Summit
PRE-PRODUCTION — Conquistador
CREDITS — Land of the Dead
COMMENTS — Film financier

Ryan Kavanaugh . . . CEO
Lynwood Spinks . . . COO
Aaron Michiel . . . VP, Business Affairs
Eva Quiroz . . . Executive
Gale Hansen . . . Creative Executive
Andrew Marcus . . . Finance Executive

RELEVANT ENTERTAINMENT GROUP

144 S. Beverly Dr., Ste. 400
Beverly Hills, CA 90212
PHONE . . . 310-246-1212/212-431-0001
FAX . . . 310-246-1250/212-213-2453
TYPES: Animation - Direct-to-Video/DVD - Features - Miniseries - Reality TV - Theatre - TV Series
DEVELOPMENT: Tortoise and Hippo
COMMENTS: East Coast office: 450 Park Avenue South, 3rd Fl., New York, NY 10016

Michael Menchel . . . Partner/Manager (LA)
Jonathan Baruch . . . Partner/Manager (LA)
Rick Dorfman . . . Partner/Manager (NY)
Michael Prevett . . . Manager (LA)
Gina Rugolo . . . Manager (LA)
Beth Stine . . . Manager (LA)
Steve Whitney . . . Manager (LA)
Lorraine De Leon . . . Assistant (LA)
Alfredo LaMont . . . Assistant (LA)
Roman Ortega-Cowan . . . Assistant (LA)
Ali Hart . . . Assistant (NY)

RENAISSANCE PICTURES

315 S. Beverly Dr., Ste. 216
Beverly Hills, CA 90212
PHONE . . . 310-785-3900
FAX . . . 310-785-9176
TYPES: Direct-to-Video/DVD - Features - TV Series
CREDITS: Evil Dead - Hard Target - A Simple Plan - The Gift - Hercules - Xena - Cleopatra 2525 - Jack of All Trades - Spider-Man

Sam Raimi . . . Director/Executive Producer
Robert Tapert . . . Executive Producer
Michael Kirk . . . VP, Development/Producer
J.R. Young . . . Producer, Creative Executive
Grant Curtis . . . Production Executive
Bill Hamm . . . TV Executive
Ben Ketai . . . Archiving
Shannon Lugger . . . Assistant to Mr. Tapert
David Pollison . . . Assistant

RENEGADE 83

5700 Wilshire Blvd., 6th Fl.
Los Angeles, CA 90046
PHONE . . . 323-954-9077
FAX . . . 323-954-9075
EMAIL . . . info@renegade83.com
WEB SITE . . . www.renegade83.com
TYPES: Reality TV - TV Series
DEVELOPMENT: Cover Girl - The Complete Asshole's Guide to Life - Carson's Cyberhood
CREDITS: Blind Date - The 5th Wheel - The Surreal Life - The 4400

David Garfinkle . . . Partner
Jay Renfroe . . . Partner
Maira Suro . . . Head, Scripted TV
Michelle Letarte . . . VP, Production
Christine Grund . . . Director, Development

RENEGADE ANIMATION, INC.

116 N. Maryland Ave., Lower Level
Glendale, CA 91206
PHONE . . . 818-551-2351
FAX . . . 818-551-2350
EMAIL . . . marva.sutton@renegadeanimation.com
WEB SITE . . . www.renegadeanimation.com
SECOND WEB SITE . . . www.renegadecartoons.com
TYPES: Animation - Commercials - TV Series
DEVELOPMENT: Who Stole Santa's Sack?
CREDITS: Captain Sturdy: Back in Action - Captain Sturdy: The Originals - Hi Hi Puffy Amiyumi
SUBMISSION POLICY: By query letter only
COMMENTS: Flash animation

Darrell Van Citters . . . President/Director
Ashley Q. Postlewaite . . . VP/Executive Producer
Darin McGowan . . . Director, Development

RENFIELD PRODUCTIONS

c/o The Lot
1041 N. Formosa Ave., Writer's Bldg., Ste. 321
West Hollywood, CA 90046
PHONE . . . 323-850-3905
FAX . . . 323-850-3907
EMAIL . . . markalan@renfieldproductions.net
TYPES: Features - New Media - TV Series
CREDITS: Looney Tunes: Back in Action - Gremlins 1&2 - Innerspace - Deceived - Matinee - 2nd Civil War - Small Soldiers

Michael Finnell . . . Producer/President
Joe Dante . . . Director
T. L. Kittle . . . Director, Development
Mark Alan Brown . . . Creative Executive

REVEILLE, LLC

100 Universal City Plaza, Bungalow 5180/5170
Universal City, CA 91608
PHONE . . . 818-733-1218/212-413-5515
FAX . . . 818-733-3303/212-413-6554
TYPES: Documentaries - Features - Reality TV - Syndication - TV Series
HAS DEAL WITH: NBC Universal Television Studio
DEVELOPMENT: Betty
CREDITS: The Restaurant - Coupling - Nashville Star 1-3 - Blow Out 1&2 - Adrenaline X - The Office - The Biggest Loser - 30 Days - Date My Mom - America's Most Useless Teen - The Club - Betty Le Fea - The Tudors - The Hoax (NBC) - Bound for Glory - The Maloof Touch - Brother Voodoo
COMMENTS: East Coast office: 1230 Sixth Ave., 20th Fl., New York, NY 10020

Benjamin Silverman . . . CEO
Charles Steenveld . . . Executive VP, Business Affairs
Howard Owens . . . Sr. VP, Creative Affairs/International Distribution
Christopher Grant . . . VP/Head, International Distribution & Creative Affairs
Mark Koops . . . VP, Creative Affairs & Distribution
Teri Weinberg . . . VP, Comedy & Drama
Todd Cohen . . . Creative Executive

REVELATIONS ENTERTAINMENT

1221 2nd St., 4th Fl.
Santa Monica, CA 90401
PHONE .310-394-3131
FAX .310-394-3133
EMAIL .info@revelationsentertainment.com
WEB SITE .www.revelationsentertainment.com

TYPES: Features - Made-for-TV/Cable Movies - TV Series
HAS DEAL WITH: Paramount Pictures
DEVELOPMENT: Rendezvous with RAMA - 761st Tank Battalion Project - The True Confessions of Charlotte Doyle - The Jazz Ambassadors - Surprise! - Harry and the Butler - The Feast of Love
PRE-PRODUCTION: The Code - Charlotte Doyle
POST PRODUCTION: 10 Items or Less
CREDITS: Along Came a Spider - Bopha! - Mutiny - Under Suspicion - Levity
COMMENTS: Includes Digital Revelations division; Morgan Freeman's publicist: Donna Lee, 5727 Canoga Ave., Ste. 144, Woodland Hills, CA 91367, phone: 800-523-3155, fax: 818-610-7498

Morgan Freeman .President/Actor/Producer
Lori McCreary .CEO/Producer
Kelly Mendelsohn .NY Division/Producer
Tracy Mercer .VP, Development
Kelley Sims .Manager, Production
Ryan Dornbusch .Story Editor
Jill Goularte .Project Manager
Angela Miller .Assistant to Lori McCreary
Kenji Yasutake .Office Manager
Geanne Frank .Business Consultant
Stuart Hammer .Business Manager
Meg Madison .Production Photographer

REVOLUTION STUDIOS

2900 W. Olympic Blvd.
Santa Monica, CA 90404
PHONE .310-255-7000/212-243-2900
EMAIL .info@revolutionstudios.com
WEB SITE .www.revolutionstudios.com

TYPES: Features
HAS DEAL WITH: Sony Pictures Entertainment
PROVIDES DEAL TO: Broken Road Productions - Team Todd
COMMENTS: East Coast office: 145 W. 57th St., 19th Fl., New York, NY 10019

REYNOLDS ENTERTAINMENT

2938 Oakhurst Ave.
Los Angeles, CA 90034
PHONE .310-836-9000
FAX .310-836-9292
EMAIL .info@reynoldsent.com
WEB SITE .www.reynoldsent.com

TYPES: Features - Made-for-TV/Cable Movies
DEVELOPMENT: Greensleeves
PRE-PRODUCTION: Deafening
POST PRODUCTION: Fly Boys - Five Fingers
CREDITS: Soul Assassin - Retroactive - Silent Hearts - Princess of Thieves - The Unsaid

Kelley Feldsott Reynolds .Partner
Patrick F. Reynolds .Partner
John Caire .Writer/Director
Ra'uf Glasgow .Writer/Director
Jackie Feldman .Assistant, Development/Acquisitions

RHI ENTERTAINMENT

1325 Avenue of the Americas, 21st Fl.
New York, NY 10019
PHONE .212-977-9001
FAX .212-977-9049
WEB SITE .www.rhifilms.com

TYPES: Direct-to-Video/DVD - Made-for-TV/Cable Movies - Miniseries
PRE-PRODUCTION: Time's Eye
PRODUCTION: Marco Polo - Son of the Dragon - The Last Templar - Hogfather
UPCOMING RELEASES: Blackbeard - The Ten Commandments - Final Days of Planet Earth
CREDITS: King of Texas - Dinotopia - Noah's Ark - Alice in Wonderland - Cleopatra - Arabian Nights - Animal Farm - Temptations - Merlin - Snow White - Prince Charming - Snow Queen - The Lion in Winter - Dream Keeper - Mitch Albom's The Five People You Meet in Heaven - Earthsea - Hercules - The Poseidon Adventure
COMMENTS: West Coast distribution office: 4201 Wilshire Blvd., Ste. 304, Los Angeles, CA 90010

Robert Halmi Sr. .Chairman
Robert Halmi Jr. .President/CEO
Peter von Gal .Executive VP/COO
Tony Guido .Executive VP, Legal & Business Affairs
Janet Jacobson .Executive VP, Co-Production Programming
Lynn Holst .Sr. VP, Development
Kelly Coogan Swanson .Sr. VP, Marketing

RHINO FILMS
10501 Wilshire Blvd., Ste. 814
Los Angeles, CA 90024
PHONE .310-441-6557
FAX .310-474-4749
WEB SITE .www.rhino.com
TYPES Animation - Documentaries - Features
PRODUCTION Project Street - Fields of Fuel
CREDITS Ivans Xtc. - Fear and Loathing in Las Vegas - Why Do Fools Fall in Love? - Plump Fiction - What We Do Is Secret - Pick Up the Mic - Shriek If You Know What I Did Last Friday the 13th

Stephen Nemeth .President
Andy Wombwell .VP

RICE & BEANS PRODUCTIONS
30 N. Raymond, Ste. 605
Pasadena, CA 91103
PHONE .626-792-9171
FAX .626-792-9171
EMAIL .vin88@pacbell.net
TYPES Animation - Features - Internet Content - Made-for-TV/Cable Movies - TV Series
UPCOMING RELEASES Wendy Wu: Homecoming Warrior (Disney Channel Movie)
CREDITS In the House - Night Court - Roc - Growing Pains - Married with Children - Empty Nest - Between Brothers - The Steve Harvey Show - Greetings from Tucson - Ned's Declassified School Survival Guide (Nickelodeon) - American Dragon: Jake Long (Disney Channel)

Vince Cheung .Writer/Producer
Ben Montanio .Writer/Producer

RICHCREST ANIMATION STUDIOS
333 N. Glenoaks Blvd., Ste. 300
Burbank, CA 91502
PHONE .818-846-0166
FAX .818-846-6074
EMAIL .crest@crestindia.com
WEB SITE .www.crestindia.com
TYPES Animation
DEVELOPMENT Sylvester and the Magic Pebble

Seema Ramanna .Managing Director
A.K. Madhavan .CEO
Vinayak Purohit .CFO
Terry Noss .VP, Production, RichCrest Animation (Burbank)
Krishna Prasad .Head, Technology

RIVE GAUCHE ENTERTAINMENT
15442 Ventura Blvd., Ste. 101
Sherman Oaks, CA 91403
PHONE .818-784-9912
FAX .818-784-9916
EMAIL .sales@rgitv.com
WEB SITE .www.rgitv.com
TYPES Direct-to-Video/DVD - Documentaries - Features - Internet Content - Made-for-TV/Cable Movies - Miniseries - Mobile Content - Reality TV - Specials - TV Series
HAS DEAL WITH Creative Differences - Icon Productions, LLC - LMNO Productions - Morningstar Entertainment - MPH Entertainment, Inc.
DEVELOPMENT The Hot Gates
PRE-PRODUCTION Flight of the Tibetan Antelope
PRODUCTION Faces of Earth - Beyond the Badge
POST PRODUCTION Dino Lab
UPCOMING RELEASES Wild Weddings 2 - Sports Disasters 6
COMPLETED UNRELEASED The Long March - Alien Autopsy Redux - 101 More Things Removed from the Human Body - After the Attack - The Chain: From I.D. to Impact - A Face for Yulce - Obese at 16: A Life in the Balance - Science of the Bible - Iraq: Front-line ER
COMMENTS Film Library includes Dead Rail, Helix and Metamorphosis

Jon Kramer .Chairman
Mark Rafalowski .Chief Operating Officer
Jennifer Smith .Sr. Vice President, Co-Productions
Dorothy Crompton .Sr. Vice President, Sales
Christiane Nicolini-Glazer .VP, Sales
Jeff Houser .VP, Sales
Sharon Beverly .Manager, Worldwide Operations

RIVER ONE FILMS
220 E. 10th St., Ste. 2-R
New York, NY 10003
PHONE .917-748-6834
EMAIL .riveronefilms@yahoo.com
TYPES Features - Made-for-TV/Cable Movies
DEVELOPMENT The Member - Guest - La Boda Negra - Blue Lips - Miss Christina
PRE-PRODUCTION Spring Break Chain Gang - A Tale of Two Horses
COMPLETED UNRELEASED Sunburn
CREDITS Tumbleweeds - The Jack Bull - Watch It

Thomas J. Mangan IV .President

RIVER ROAD ENTERTAINMENT
1901 Avenue of the Stars, 2nd Fl.
Los Angeles, CA 90067
PHONE .310-461-1491
FAX .310-461-1490
WEB SITE .www.riverroadentertainment.com
TYPES Animation - Documentaries - Features
POST PRODUCTION Into the Wild - C7
COMPLETED UNRELEASED Fur
CREDITS A Prairie Home Companion - Brokeback Mountain - Madonna: I'm Going to Tell You a Secret
SUBMISSION POLICY No unsolicited materials or calls

Robin Schorr .Head, Creative Production
Frank Hildebrand .Head, Production
Teodora Kerkeniakova .Director, Production & Development

RIVERROCK ENTERTAINMENT GROUP

3974 Cloverleaf St.
Westlake Village, CA 91362
PHONE .805-496-4624
FAX .805-496-0915
WEB SITE .www.riverrockentertainmentgroup.com
TYPES Documentaries - Features - TV Series
DEVELOPMENT Staying Fat for Sarah Byrnes - The Style of Integrity: Martin Ritt

Martina Ritt .Owner/Producer/Director

RKO PICTURES, LLC

1875 Century Park East, Ste. 2140
Los Angeles, CA 90067
PHONE .310-277-0707/212-644-0600
FAX .310-226-2490/212-644-0384
EMAIL .info@rko.com
WEB SITE .www.rko.com
TYPES Animation - Direct-to-Video/DVD - Documentaries - Features - Made-for-TV/Cable Movies
DEVELOPMENT Devil & Miss Jones - Beyond a Reasonable Doubt
PRE-PRODUCTION Are We Done Yet?
CREDITS Mighty Joe Young - The Magnificent Ambersons - Milk & Money - A Holiday Affair - Ritual
COMMENTS East Coast office: 3 E. 54th St., 12th Fl., New York, NY 10022

Ted Hartley .Chairman/CEO
Dina Merrill .Vice Chairman
Kevin Cornish .VP, Development

ROBERTS/DAVID FILMS, INC.

100 Universal City Plaza, T6139
Universal City, CA 91608
PHONE .818-733-2143
FAX .818-733-1551
WEB SITE .www.robertsdavidfilms.com
TYPES Features
DEVELOPMENT Patti Astor's Fun Gallery - Main/Street
UPCOMING RELEASES Dark Ride - Danika
CREDITS Strangers with Candy - Plump Fiction - Eastside - Poor White Trash - Outta Time - Extreme Dating
SUBMISSION POLICY Accepted from agents and managers; Query letters; Unsolicited submissions not accepted

Lorena David .Partner
Mark Roberts .Partner
Max Velez .Creative Executive

AMY ROBINSON PRODUCTIONS

101 Fifth Ave., 8th Fl., Ste. 8R
New York, NY 10003
PHONE .212-645-9811
FAX .212-645-9810
TYPES Features
DEVELOPMENT Julie & Julia - Lessons for Bennie Blanco - The Mirror - The Deep Blue Goodbye
CREDITS Game 6 - When Zachary Beaver Came to Town - Chilly Scenes of Winter - With Honors - Once Around - Running on Empty - Drive Me Crazy - For Love of the Game - Autumn in New York - From Hell - White Palace - Baby It's You - After Hours

Amy Robinson .Producer
Jesse Patrone-Werdiger .Director, Development

ROCKET ENTERTAINMENT

16 Fleet St., #2
Venice, CA 90292
PHONE .310-612-6767
TYPES Features - Internet Content - Mobile Content - TV Series
CREDITS The Lather Effect - Boogeyman - Terry Tate: Office Linebacker - Save Virgil - George Lucas in Love

Gary Bryman .Producer

ROCKET PICTURES LIMITED

1 Blythe Rd.
London W14 0HG, United Kingdom
PHONE .44-207-603-9530
FAX .44-207-348-4830
HAS DEAL WITH Walt Disney Pictures/Touchstone Pictures
DEVELOPMENT Gnomeo & Juliet
PRODUCTION It's a Boy Girl Thing

Elton John .Chairman
David Furnish .Producer
Steve Hamilton-Shaw .Producer
Ed King .Development Executive

ROCKET SCIENCE LABORATORIES

8441 Santa Monica Blvd.
West Hollywood, CA 90069
PHONE .323-802-0500
FAX .323-802-0599
EMAIL .rsl@rocketsciencelabs.com
TYPES Documentaries - Features - Made-for-TV/Cable Movies - Reality TV - TV Series
CREDITS Trading Spouses - Renovate My Family - My Big Fat Obnoixous Fiance - Joe Millionaire 1&2 - Married by America - M*A*S*H: 30th Anniversary - Temptation Island 1&2 - Images of Life: Photographs That Changed the World

Jean-Michel Michenaud .Partner/Executive Producer
Chris Cowan .Partner/Executive Producer
Charles Duncombe .Head, Production
Tracy Geyer .Production Supervisor
David Stone .Sr. Director, Development
Michael S. Wood .Director, New Business Development

*ROCKLIN ENTERTAINMENT
10390 Santa Monica Blvd., Ste. 200
Los Angeles, CA 90025
PHONE 310-789-3066
FAX 310-789-3060
TYPES Features - TV Series
HAS DEAL WITH Alcon Entertainment, LLC
DEVELOPMENT Kid Cannabis (HBO/Picturehouse) - The Puritan (Gold Circle Films) - Untitled Michael Anthony Snowden Project (with Bob Yari Productions) - Con Ed (Alcon Entertainment)

Nicole Rocklin . . . . .Producer/President

STAN ROGOW PRODUCTIONS
3000 Olympic Blvd., Bldg. 3, Rm. 1436
Santa Monica, CA 90404
PHONE 310-264-4199
TYPES Features - Made-for-TV/Cable Movies - TV Series
CREDITS Nowhere Man - The Defenders - Nowhere to Hide - Shannon's Deal - Middle Ages - Lizzie McGuire - State of Grace - Darcy's Wild Life - Twenty-Nine Down

Stan Rogow . . . . .Executive Producer

AL ROKER PRODUCTIONS
250 W. 57th St., Ste. 1525
New York, NY 10019
PHONE 212-757-8500
FAX 212-757-8513
EMAIL . . . . .info@alroker.com
WEB SITE . . . . .www.alrokerproductions.com
TYPES TV Series
DEVELOPMENT Uncovered: Hidden Lives of Miss USA
CREDITS Roker on the Road - Al Roker Investigates - Recipe for Success - An Honor Deferred (The History Channel) - Celebrity Food Fight

Al Roker . . . . .CEO
Lisa Sharkey . . . . .President
Victoria Bert . . . . .VP, Development & Production
Tracie Brennan . . . . .VP, Operations
Laura Shur . . . . .General Counel

PHIL ROMAN ENTERTAINMENT
4450 Lakeside Dr., Ste. 250
Burbank, CA 91505
PHONE 818-985-1200
FAX 818-985-2668
EMAIL . . . . .sales@romanent.com
WEB SITE . . . . .www.philromanent.com
TYPES Animation - Direct-to-Video/DVD - Features - TV Series
CREDITS Howdi Gaudi - Atomic Betty - Grandma Got Run Over by a Reindeer - Christmas in Gaudinia
COMMENTS Develops and consults on features for the US, Mexico and Russia

Phil Roman . . . . .President/CEO

*ROOM 101, INC.
5555 Melrose Ave., Chevalier Bldg., Ste. 205
Los Angeles, CA 90038
PHONE 323-956-3038
FAX 323-862-1141
TYPES Features
HAS DEAL WITH Blumhouse Productions
DEVELOPMENT Home (Craven/Maddalena Films) - The Drowning Man (Intermedia) - In Darkness Waiting (Gold Circle Films) - Family Portrait (Gold Circle Films)
PRE-PRODUCTION The Inheritance (Leonard Hill) - 100 Feet (Grand Illusions)
POST PRODUCTION White Noise 2 (Gold Circle Films)

Steven Schneider . . . . .Producer

ROOM 9 ENTERTAINMENT
10635 Santa Monica Blvd., Ste. 320
Los Angeles, CA 90025
PHONE 310-475-3700
FAX 310-475-3707
EMAIL . . . . .info@room9entertainment.com
WEB SITE www.room9entertainment.com
TYPES Features
DEVELOPMENT Slipping - Genuine Fake - Queen Lara
CREDITS Thank You for Smoking
COMMENTS Unsolicited material not accepted

David Sacks . . . . .CEO
Daniel Brunt . . . . .VP, Development & Production
Michael Newman . . . . .VP, Creative Affairs
Adam Zadikoff . . . . .Assistant

ROPE THE MOON PRODUCTIONS
421 N. Rodeo Dr.
Beverly Hills, CA 90210
PHONE 310-276-9559
FAX 310-276-9449
TYPES Documentaries - Features - Made-for-TV/Cable Movies
CREDITS Grand Champion - In a Whisper

Amanda Micallef . . . . .Producer
Lawren Sunderland . . . . .Creative Executive
Julie Cannon . . . . .Director, Development, TV

ALEX ROSE PRODUCTIONS, INC.
8291 Presson Pl.
Los Angeles, CA 90069
PHONE 323-654-8662
FAX 323-654-0196
TYPES Features - TV Series
DEVELOPMENT The Wonder 5 - Greased - I'm Pretty Sure I Might Have a Fear of Committment - Wu Sen - Kiss the Frog
CREDITS Film: The Other Sister - Exit to Eden - Frankie & Johnny - Quigley Down Under - Overboard - Nothing in Common - Norma Rae - Big Wednesday; TV: Nothing in Common (Series) - Just Us Kids
SUBMISSION POLICY Accepts query letters

Alexandra Rose . . . . .President
Shiva Baum . . . . .Development

ROSEMONT PRODUCTIONS INTERNATIONAL, LTD.
8424-A Santa Monica Blvd., Ste. 809
West Hollywood, CA 90069
PHONE .818-597-1661
FAX .818-597-8523
TYPES Made-for-TV/Cable Movies - TV Series
POST PRODUCTION The Company
CREDITS The Winning Season - Door to Door - Purgatory - The Secret Garden - What Love Sees - High Noon - For All Time - The Wool Cap - Into the West (Miniseries) - Riders of the Purple Sage

Norman Rosemont .Executive Producer
David A. Rosemont .Executive Producer

ZVI HOWARD ROSENMAN PRODUCTIONS
635-A Westbourne Dr.
Los Angeles, CA 90069
PHONE .310-659-2100
EMAIL .bigzr@aol.com
TYPES Documentaries - Features - Made-for-TV/Cable Movies - TV Series
DEVELOPMENT Downsizing - Eagle's Wings - Ten Good Men - Park Avenue Ghost - Life of an Honest Man - Gloria & Doria Gray - Trapped - Grace Metallious - Trophy Boys - Crim Law
PRE-PRODUCTION Breakfast with Scott - American Neurotic - Monster of Longwood - Cat 'n Mouse - Slammer - John From Cincinatti (TV)
POST PRODUCTION You Kill Me
CREDITS Noel - The Family Man - Father of The Bride - Gross Anatomy - Shining Through - A Stranger Among Us - Resurrection - Sparkle - The Main Event - Tidy Endings - True Identity - Straight Talk - Common Threads - The Celluloid Closet - Paragraph 175 - Bond Girls Are Forever - My First Mister - Virginia Hill - Killer Bees - Isn't It Shocking? - Pink Triangle - All Together Now - Death Scream - Lost Angels

Zvi Howard Rosenman .President

GAY ROSENTHAL PRODUCTIONS
1438 N. Gower St., Box 16
Hollywood, CA 90028
PHONE .323-468-3300
FAX .323-468-3301
TYPES Documentaries - Reality TV - Specials - TV Series
PRODUCTION Little People, Big World
CREDITS TV's Most Unexpected Moments (TV Land) - Face the Family (Lifetime) - Little People, Big World (TLC) - Jackpot Diaries (A&E) - Lost Weekend (Travel Channel) - TV's Most Memorable Weddings (NBC) - Child Stars: Then and Now (NBC) - VH1's Behind the Music - Inside TV Land - TNN's Fame for 15 - NBC's 20 Years of Must See TV - Friends Season Finale Special - Frasier Season Finale Special - TV's Most Memorable Moments (TV Land)

Gay Rosenthal .President/Executive Producer
Paul Barrosse .Executive Producer
Nicholas Caprio .Executive VP, Programming & Production
Jonna Walsh .Production Manager
Robyn Olson .Finance
Troy Combs .Development Coordinator
Jen Sims .Production Coordinator

ROSENZWEIG FILMS
6399 Wilshire Blvd., Ste. 510
Los Angeles, CA 90048
PHONE .323-782-6888
FAX .323-782-6967
TYPES Features - Made-for-TV/Cable Movies - TV Series
DEVELOPMENT Darksiders - Where's the Party At? - The Reincarnation of Peter Proud
CREDITS Windtalkers - Phoenix - Dumb and Dumber - The War at Home - Threesome

Alison Rosenzweig .Producer
Aimee Morono .Director, Development

ROSEROCK FILMS
4000 Warner Blvd., Bldg. 81, Ste. 215-A
Burbank, CA 91522
PHONE .818-954-7528
TYPES Direct-to-Video/DVD - Features
DEVELOPMENT Unsportsmanlike Conduct
POST PRODUCTION Thou Shalt Laugh

Hunt Lowry .No Title
Stacy Cohen .No Title (818-954-7438)
Patty Reed .No Title (818-954-7673)

HEIDI ROTBART MANAGEMENT
1810 Malcolm Ave., Ste. 207
Los Angeles, CA 90025
PHONE .310-470-8339/310-880-7656
FAX .310-446-8610
EMAIL .hrotbartmgt@aol.com
TYPES Reality TV - TV Series
DEVELOPMENT Untitled Carlos Alazraqui Project - Untitled Sam Lloyd Project
COMMENTS Specializes in the Hispanic market

Heidi Rotbart .Partner/President
Lori Morrison .Assistant to Heidi Rotbart

JOE ROTH TELEVISION
c/o CBS Center Studios
4024 Radford Ave., Bungalow 9
Studio City, CA 91604
PHONE .818-655-7266
FAX .818-655-8319
TYPES TV Series
HAS DEAL WITH CBS Paramount Network Television

Nina Lederman .President
Miri Tyler .Coordinator

ROTH/ARNOLD PRODUCTIONS
3000 Olympic Blvd., Ste. 1302
Santa Monica, CA 90404
PHONE .310-449-4075
FAX .310-449-4074
TYPES Features
DEVELOPMENT Christmas in Connecticut - The Bastard McSwain - Handle With Care - Drillbit Taylor - The Perfesser
CREDITS Grosse Pointe Blank - Unstrung Heroes - Benny & Joon - Forces of Nature - America's Sweethearts - 13 Going on 30

Donna Arkoff Roth .Principal (310-449-4075)
Susan Arnold .Principal (310-449-4075)
Desi Van Til .VP, Development (310-449-4073)
Eric Rosen .Development (310-449-4072)

ROUGH DIAMOND PRODUCTIONS

1424 N. Kings Rd.
Los Angeles, CA 90069
PHONE .323-848-2900
FAX .323-848-8142

TYPES	Features
DEVELOPMENT	Confidence Game - Lola Montez - Jumper - Wavelength - Senior Will - The Trust List - Sexual Healing
PRE-PRODUCTION	Summerhill
CREDITS	I Witness - Blast - Merchant of Venice - Slipstream - Riding the Bullet - Stander - Temptation - The Set Up - Past Perfect - A Matter of Trust - A Breed Apart - Detour - The Contaminated Man - In Pursuit - Styx - The Shipment - Greenmail - Pavement - Consequence

Julia Verdin .President/Partner/Producer
Bill Kravitz .President, Production

ROUGH DRAFT STUDIOS

209 N. Brand Blvd.
Glendale, CA 91203
PHONE .818-507-0491
FAX .818-507-0486
WEB SITE .www.roughdraftstudios.com

TYPES	Animation - Features - TV Series
DEVELOPMENT	Nancy Stellar (Cartoon Network)
PRODUCTION	The Simpsons Movie
CREDITS	Drawn Together (Comedy Central) - Futurama (Fox) - Baby Blues (WB) - The Maxx (MTV) - Star Wars Clone Wars (Cartoon Network/Lucasfilm Ltd.)
COMMENTS	Animation studio, specializing in the blend of traditional and computer animation

Gregg Vanzo .President
Claudia Katz .Producer/Partner
Rich Moore .Director/Partner
Scott Vanzo .Director, CGI/Partner

ROUNDTABLE ENTERTAINMENT

5300 Melrose Ave., Ste. E-331
Los Angeles, CA 90038
PHONE .323-769-2567
FAX .323-769-2568

TYPES	Features - TV Series
HAS DEAL WITH	Twentieth Century Fox Television
DEVELOPMENT	Features: Counter Clockwise - Fear Itself - What Happens in Vegas... - Broken Records; TV: Mr. & Mrs. Doe - The Score - Darkside - Blue Blood - Ballroomba - Philtopia
PRE-PRODUCTION	Superfan
CREDITS	Features: 13 Going on 30 - What Women Want - Urban Legend 1&2 - The Wishing Tree - Summer's End; TV: The Mountain - Jake 2.0 - The Chronicle - Popular

Gina Matthews .Partner/Producer
Grant Scharbo .Partner/Producer
Laura Davis .Story Editor

RUBICON

4028 Lamarr Ave.
Culver City, CA 90232
PHONE .310-204-0444
FAX .310-280-3807
EMAIL .jmorgan@infinnity.com
SECOND EMAIL .pfinn@infinnity.com
WEB SITE .www.infinnity.com

TYPES	Commercials - Reality TV - TV Series
PRODUCTION	Starface (GSN)
CREDITS	Instant Comedy with the Groundlings (FX) - National Lampoon's Funny Money (GSN) - SOULmates (HBO Feature)
COMMENTS	Formerly In-Finn-Ity Productions, Inc.

Pat Finn .Executive Producer
Dustin Hauptman .Producer
Jana Morgan .VP, Development
Greg Reimink .Editor

RUBY-SPEARS PRODUCTIONS

3500 W. Olive Ave., Ste. 300
Burbank, CA 91505
PHONE .818-840-1234
FAX .818-885-6251
EMAIL .rsproductions@earthlink.net
WEB SITE .www.rubyspears.com

TYPES	Animation - Features - TV Series
DEVELOPMENT	The Arm - The Super Ts - Super Racing Frogs - Skysurfer Strike Force...The Movie - Jack Kirby's SpaceDevils
CREDITS	Rumpelstiltskin - Jirimpimbira - Slammin' Sammy: The Sammy Sosa Story - Skysurfer Strike Force
SUBMISSION POLICY	No unsolicited submissions
COMMENTS	Animation consultants; Production services

Joseph Ruby .President/Executive Producer
Kenneth Spears .VP/Executive Producer

THE RUDDY MORGAN ORGANIZATION, INC./ ALBERT S. RUDDY PRODUCTIONS

1180 S. Beverly Dr., Ste. 700
Los Angeles, CA 90035
PHONE .310-247-2140
FAX .310-278-9978
EMAIL .andremorgan@ruddymorgan.com

TYPES	Features - TV Series
DEVELOPMENT	The Rape of Nanking - Pound for Pound - Wanted Dead or Alive - Point Thunder - One Nation - Mr. Ed - Last Kind Word Blues - Terry and the Pirates - Waiting - Airborne
POST PRODUCTION	Camille
COMPLETED UNRELEASED	Flatland
CREDITS	Million Dollar Baby - The Longest Yard - Perhaps Love - White Countess - Cloud Nine - Farewell to the King - Bad Girls - Impulse - Ladybugs - The Godfather - Canonball Run - The Scout - Heaven's Prisoners - Mr. Magoo - Walker: Texas Ranger - Martial Law - Running Mates
COMMENTS	Shanghai-based Hweilai Studio in China

Al Ruddy .Producer
Andre Morgan .Producer
Cynthia Perez-Brown .Staff
Alana Ribble .Staff

SCOTT RUDIN PRODUCTIONS

c/o Paramount Pictures
5555 Melrose Ave., DeMille Bldg., Ste. 100
Los Angeles, CA 90038
PHONE 323-956-4600/212-704-4600
FAX 323-869-8557

TYPES	Features
HAS DEAL WITH	Buena Vista Motion Pictures Group
DEVELOPMENT	Green Eyes
CREDITS	Iris - The Royal Tenenbaums - The Hours - Zoolander - The First Wives Club - Clueless - The Firm - In and Out - The Truman Show - Sleepy Hollow - Wonder Boys - Shaft - South Park: Bigger, Longer & Uncut - The School of Rock
COMMENTS	East Coast office: 120 W. 45th St., 10th Fl., New York, NY 10036

Scott Rudin . . . . . Producer (NY)
Mark Roybal . . . . . President (LA)
John Delaney . . . . . VP (NY)
Michael Ellenberg . . . . . Director, Development (LA) (323-956-4662)
Dan Kois . . . . . Director, Development (NY)
Mira Shin . . . . . Creative Executive
Sam Cassel . . . . . Story Editor (LA)
James Queen . . . . . Executive Assistant to Scott Rudin (NY)
Danny Roman . . . . . Assistant to Scott Rudin (LA)

RUNAWAY PRODUCTIONS

7336 Santa Monica Blvd., #751
West Hollywood, CA 90046
PHONE 310-801-0885
FAX 562-856-8109
WEB SITE . . . . . www.runawayproductions.tv

TYPES	Commercials - Direct-to-Video/DVD - Features
DEVELOPMENT	Bloodline
PRE-PRODUCTION	Bill Shakespeare - October 30th - Last Call at Murray's
POST PRODUCTION	The Wedding Video
CREDITS	Look @ Me - The Mailman - Interviewing Norman - The Appointment
SUBMISSION POLICY	Via email

Linda Palmer . . . . . Producer/Writer
Todd Wade . . . . . Producer/Director

RUPERT PRODUCTIONS, INC.

3760 Grandview Blvd.
Los Angeles, CA 90066
PHONE 310-390-9360
FAX 310-390-9620
EMAIL . . . . . ooglerupe@aol.com
WEB SITE . . . . . www.bizazzmedia.com

TYPES	Direct-to-Video/DVD - Documentaries - Features - Internet Content - Music Videos - Reality TV
DEVELOPMENT	Happy Faces - A Simple Road - Community Property
PRE-PRODUCTION	Roseto, Roseto
PRODUCTION	Teamwork - Four Weeks in May (Rahal/Letterman Racing/Danica Patrick)
CREDITS	Nowhere Land - Electra Glide in Blue - Last Dragon - Wolfen - Snakes and Ladders - Liar, Liar - NASCAR's Victory Lane (Foxsports Net) - The Squeeze - Happy Birthday Gemini - Jaws 3-D - Much Ado About Nothing
COMMENTS	Deal with Bizazz Media

Rupert Hitzig . . . . . President
Tony Kucenski . . . . . Production
Mickey Friedman . . . . . Account Executive

S PICTURES, INC.

4420 Hayvenhurst Ave.
Encino, CA 91436
PHONE 818-995-1585
FAX 818-995-1677
EMAIL . . . . . chuck.simon@stoneworkstv.com
WEB SITE . . . . . www.stoneworkstv.com

TYPES	Direct-to-Video/DVD - Documentaries - Features - Made-for-TV/Cable Movies - Miniseries - Reality TV - Specials - TV Series
DEVELOPMENT	The Biz - Kingpins - Palm Beach
PRE-PRODUCTION	Dead on the Bone - Stealing Tennessee - Celebrity Bowling
CREDITS	Hallelujah Gospel - Count Basie, Carnegie Hall - Terminal Invasion (Sci Fi) - Control Factor (Sci Fi)
SUBMISSION POLICY	Release required
COMMENTS	Producer's representative for worldwide distribution

Chuck Simon . . . . . President/Producer
Seth Brown . . . . . Director, Development

SACHS JUDAH PRODUCTIONS

500 S. Buena Vista St., Old Animation Bldg., Ste. 3E5
Burbank, CA 91521
PHONE 818-560-5435
FAX 818-560-5013

TYPES	Features - TV Series
HAS DEAL WITH	Touchstone Television
CREDITS	What About Brian (ABC) - Life as We Know It - Pranks - Undeclared - Freaks & Geeks - Just Shoot Me - Platonically Incorrect (Pilot)

Jeff Judah . . . . . Partner/Executive Producer
Gabe Sachs . . . . . Partner/Executive Producer
Niki Savage . . . . . Creative Executive

ALAN SACKS PRODUCTIONS, INC.

11684 Ventura Blvd., Ste. 809
Studio City, CA 91604
PHONE 818-752-6999
FAX 818-752-6985
EMAIL . . . . . asacks@pacbell.net

TYPES	Documentaries - Features - Made-for-TV/Cable Movies - Specials - Theatre - TV Series
DEVELOPMENT	Down to Earth - Welcome Back, Kotter (Feature) - Rock Camp - The Club
PRODUCTION	Lenny Bruce (In His Own Words) - Zipper Theater, NYC
CREDITS	Pixel Perfect - The Color of Friendship - Smart House - The Other Me - You Wish - Welcome Back, Kotter - Thrashin' - Cowboy Poetry

Alan Sacks . . . . . Producer

SACRED DOGS ENTERTAINMENT, LLC

311 N. Robertson Blvd., #249
Beverly Hills, CA 90211

PHONE .323-656-6900
FAX .949-487-9759
EMAIL .info@sacreddogs.com
SECOND EMAIL .publicity@sacreddogs.com
WEB SITE .www.sacreddogs.com
SECOND WEB SITE .www.victorytischlerblue.com

TYPES	Documentaries - Features - Made-for-TV/Cable Movies - Music Videos - Reality TV - Specials - TV Series
HAS DEAL WITH	Showtime Networks Inc.
DEVELOPMENT	Lupino
PRE-PRODUCTION	The Bee Gees: Chateau D'Herouville Revisited - Wonder When You'll Miss Me
UPCOMING RELEASES	Naked Under Leather - The Equus Project
COMPLETED UNRELEASED	Lockout
CREDITS	Edgeplay: A Film About the Runaways - Leather Forever
SUBMISSION POLICY	Agent submissions or legal representation only; No unsolicited submissions

Victory Tischler-Blue .Producer/Director
P. Arden Brotman .Executive Producer
Dwina Murphy-Gibb .Executive Producer
Chris Green .Assistant

*SAFRAN COMPANY

9420 Wilshire Blvd., #250
Beverly Hills, CA 90212

PHONE .310-278-1450
FAX .310-278-0885

HAS DEAL WITH	Gold Circle Films
DEVELOPMENT	Anvil
PRE-PRODUCTION	How I Met My Boyfriend's Dead Fianceé

Peter Safran .Producer
Tom Drumm .Manager
Ben Brown .Assistant to Peter Safran

SALTIRE ENTERTAINMENT

3733 Motor Ave., Ste. 204
Los Angeles, CA 90034

PHONE .323-525-0023
FAX .323-417-4962
EMAIL .info@saltireent.com
WEB SITE .www.saltireent.com

TYPES	Features
DEVELOPMENT	The Three Investigators: Terror Castle - Stone of Destiny
COMPLETED UNRELEASED	The Three Investigators: The Mystery of Skeleton Island
CREDITS	One of the Hollywood Ten - The Conclave
SUBMISSION POLICY	No unsolicited submissions

Stuart Pollok .Producer

SALTY FEATURES

104 W. 14th St., 4th Fl.
New York, NY 10011

PHONE .212-924-1601
FAX .212-924-2306
EMAIL .info@saltyfeatures.com
WEB SITE .www.saltyfeatures.com

TYPES	Features
DEVELOPMENT	Valparaiso - Signs of Life - The Brutal Language of Love - Finn at the Blue Line - Martyr's Crossing
PRODUCTION	Inner Life of Martin Frost
CREDITS	Boys Don't Cry - Rhinoceros Eyes - My Architect - Evergreen
SUBMISSION POLICY	No unsolicited submissions

Eva Kolodner .Producer
Yael Melamede .Producer
Jen Dougherty .Office Manager

SAMOSET, INC./SACRET, INC.

127 Broadway, Ste. 220
Santa Monica, CA 90401

PHONE .310-458-1618
FAX .310-458-9020

TYPES	Features - Made-for-TV/Cable Movies - TV Series
DEVELOPMENT	Untitled JSY Military Series (Showtime) - Untitled TNT Pilot
CREDITS	Bronx County - Sirens - Orleans - Texarkana - VR5 - Romero - Testament - China Beach - Thanks of a Grateful Nation - Level 9 - King of the World - Champions - Rumor of War - Keys - Pentagon Papers - The West Wing - Deceit (Lifetime)
SUBMISSION POLICY	No unsolicited submissions
COMMENTS	Published nonfiction memoir titled *Remains: Non-Viewable*

John Sacret Young .Writer/Director/Producer
Jacqueline Lookofsky .CFO

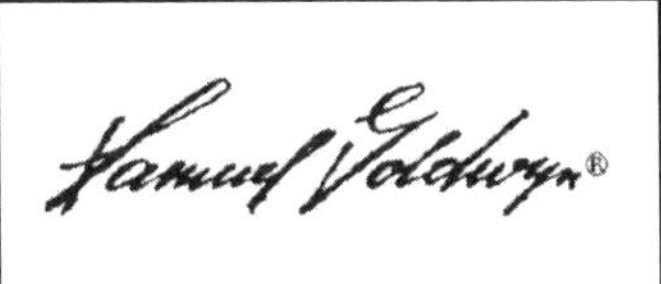

SAMUEL GOLDWYN FILMS
9570 W. Pico Blvd., Ste. 400
Los Angeles, CA 90035
PHONE .310-860-3100/212-367-9435
FAX .310-860-3195/212-367-0853
WEB SITE .www.samuelgoldwynfilms.com
TYPES Features
DEVELOPMENT Goshawk Squadron - The Secret Life of Walter Mitty - He Loves Me, He Loves Me Not
UPCOMING RELEASES Sleeping Dogs Lie
CREDITS The Squid and the Whale - Super Size Me - Raising Victor Vargas - El Crimen Del Padre Amaro - Master and Commander - Man from Elysian Fields - Madness of King George - Much Ado About Nothing - Big Night - What the #$*! Do We Know? - Rosenstrasse - Walk on Water - Wah Wah
SUBMISSION POLICY No unsolicited material; By agent or manager only
COMMENTS East Coast office: 1133 Broadway, Ste. 926, New York, NY 10010

Samuel Goldwyn Jr. .Chairman of the Board/CEO
Meyer Gottlieb .President
Peter Goldwyn .VP, Acquisitions (NY)
Shane Starr .Development/Acquisitions
Rorri Feinstein .Manager, Contract Adminstration
Jennifer Wright .Development & Acquisitions

SAMUELSON PRODUCTIONS

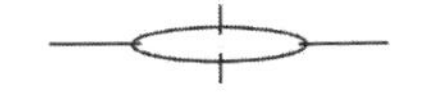

SAMUELSON PRODUCTIONS LIMITED
10401 Wyton Dr.
Los Angeles, CA 90024-2527
PHONE .310-208-1000/44-207-439-4900
FAX .310-208-2809/44-207-439-4901
EMAIL .petersam@who.net
SECOND EMAIL .mjwsam@aol.com
WEB SITE .www.stormbreaker.com
SECOND WEB SITE .www.oscarwilde.com
TYPES Features
DEVELOPMENT Ockham's Razor - The Art of Bellydancing - China Punk - Mickey & Me
PRODUCTION Alex Rider 2
CREDITS Wilde - Revenge of the Nerds - Tom & Viv - Turk 182 - Arlington Road - Dog's Best Friend - The Commissioner - Gabriel and Me - Playmaker - The Gathering - Things to Do Before You're 30 - The Libertine - Chromophobia - Stormbreaker - Man in the Chair - The Last Time
SUBMISSION POLICY No unsolicited submissions
COMMENTS Deal with Isle of Man Film; See also www.starlight.org; London office: 13 Manette St., London, W1V 5LB United Kingdom

Peter Samuelson .No Title (US)
Marc Samuelson .No Title (UK)
Saryl Hirsch .Controller (US)
Jessica Parker .Associate Producer (UK)
Victoria Parr .Producer's Assistant (US)
Renato Celani .Assistant (UK)

SANDCASTLE 5 PRODUCTIONS
545 W. 45th St., 9th Fl.
New York, NY 10036
PHONE .212-489-8778
TYPES Features
CREDITS A Prairie Home Companion - The Company - Gosford Park - Dr. T & The Women - Cookie's Fortune - Afterglow - Kansas City - Prêt-à-Porter - Mrs. Parker and the Vicious Circle

Robert Altman .Director/Producer

SANDER/MOSES PRODUCTIONS, INC.
500 S. Buena Vista St.
Burbank, CA 91521-1657
PHONE .818-560-4500
FAX .818-560-8777
EMAIL .info@sandermoses.com
WEB SITE .www.sandermoses.com
TYPES Features - Internet Content - Made-for-TV/Cable Movies - Miniseries - Reality TV - Specials - TV Series
HAS DEAL WITH Touchstone Television
DEVELOPMENT Dark Thoughts - The Surgeon - Cadie & Serafina
CREDITS Ghost Whisperer (CBS) - Frankenstein - For the People - Profiler - The Beast - How to Marry a Billionaire - Brimstone - Ali: An American Hero - Chasing The Dragon - New York News - Stolen Babies - I'll Fly Away - D.O.A. - Everybody's All American
COMMENTS Internet Programming

Ian Sander .Executive Producer/Writer/Director
Kim Moses .Executive Producer/Writer/Director
Rey Amaya .Development Executive
Stephanie Neifing .Executive Assistant

SANFORD/PILLSBURY PRODUCTIONS
708 Euclid St.
Santa Monica, CA 90402
PHONE .310-486-9006
FAX .310-393-5013
TYPES Features - Made-for-TV/Cable Movies
POST PRODUCTION Quid Pro Quo
CREDITS Desperately Seeking Susan - River's Edge - Eight Men Out - And the Band Played On - How to Make an American Quilt - The Love Letter

Sarah Pillsbury .Producer
Midge Sanford .Producer

SANITSKY COMPANY
9200 Sunset Blvd., Ste. 430
Los Angeles, CA 90069
PHONE .310-274-0120
FAX .310-274-1455
TYPES Made-for-TV/Cable Movies - TV Series
CREDITS Robert Ludlum's The Hades Factor (CBS) - The Pennsylvania Miners' Story (ABC) - Blessings (CBS) - Open House (CBS) - Riding the Bus with My Sister (CBS) - A Very Married Christmas (CBS)

Larry Sanitsky .President

SAPHIER PRODUCTIONS
4245 Valley Meadow Rd.
Encino, CA 91436
PHONE . . . 818-501-3531
FAX . . . 818-995-6554
EMAIL . . . psaphier@mindspring.com
TYPES Features - TV Series
DEVELOPMENT Creation - Chippendales - Amateur Night at the Apollo - Sequestered - Dixie Mafia
CREDITS Black Dog - Scarface - Eddie Macon's Run - Four Seasons (TV)

Peter Saphier . . . Principal

SARABANDE PRODUCTIONS
715 Broadway, Ste. 210
Santa Monica, CA 90401
PHONE . . . 310-395-4842
TYPES Features - Made-for-TV/Cable Movies - Miniseries - TV Series
CREDITS Thief - Saved - Birdy - Bring on the Night - Mad Love - Nothing Sacred - Thicker Than Blood - Nightjohn - Baby - The Wedding Dress

David Manson . . . President
Arla Sorkin Manson . . . Executive VP
Aaron Graff . . . Director, Development
Charlotte Stoudt . . . Director, Development

ARTHUR SARKISSIAN PRODUCTIONS
9336 W. Washington Blvd., Bldg. K
Culver City, CA 90232
PHONE . . . 310-385-1486
FAX . . . 310-385-1171
TYPES Features - TV Series
DEVELOPMENT Starring Vic - Defiant Ones - Red Circle - El Cid - Red Sun - Christmas Robbers - Champagne - You Must Remember This - Again - Weddingville - Street - Between the Covers - Two Lucky People - Seven Day Soldiers - Bellboy - Back to School - Untitled Ralph Lamb Project - Dirty Rotten Scoundrels - Fortune Cookie - Thieves - Prince Test - The Perfect Target
PRODUCTION Rush Hour 3 - How to Rob a Bank
CREDITS Rush Hour 1&2 - Last Man Standing - While You Were Sleeping - Wanted Dead or Alive

Arthur Sarkissian . . . Producer
Nadine Maybruck . . . Creative Executive
Parker Morris . . . Development Assistant

SATURN FILMS
9000 Sunset Blvd., Ste. 911
West Hollywood, CA 90069
PHONE . . . 310-887-0900
FAX . . . 310-248-2965
TYPES Documentaries - Features - TV Series
DEVELOPMENT 1,000 Words - The Dance
PRE-PRODUCTION Bangkok Dangerous
PRODUCTION The Dresden Files (TV)
POST PRODUCTION Next
UPCOMING RELEASES Wicker Man
CREDITS Sonny - Shadow of the Vampire - The Life of David Gale - Family Man - National Treasure - Lord of War

Nicolas Cage . . . CEO/Producer
Norm Golightly . . . President/Producer
Seth Schur . . . VP, Development
Matt Summers . . . Story Editor/Assistant to Norm Golightly
Rolly Lee . . . Assistant to Nicolas Cage
Michael Davison . . . Assistant to Nicolas Cage

EDWARD SAXON PRODUCTIONS (ESP)
335 North Maple Dr., Ste. 354
Beverly Hills, CA 90210
PHONE . . . 310-246-7700
FAX . . . 310-388-1797
WEB SITE . . . www.saxonproductions.net
TYPES Animation - Documentaries - Features - Made-for-TV/Cable Movies - TV Series
HAS DEAL WITH Participant Productions
CREDITS Fast Food Nation - Adaptation - The Truth About Charlie - Beloved - Mandela - That Thing You Do! - Philadelphia - The Silence of the Lambs - Married to the Mob

Ed Saxon . . . Producer
Steven Kung . . . Story Editor

SCARAB PRODUCTIONS
PO Box 4617
North Hollywood, CA 91617-0617
PHONE . . . 818-766-6418
TYPES Animation - Features - TV Series
DEVELOPMENT Goosetown - Borrowed Time - Just My Luck - Little Legends - The Jester's Son - The Amazing Henry
CREDITS Cats Don't Dance - Disney's House of Mouse - Disney's 101 Dalmations (Series)
SUBMISSION POLICY No unsolicited material

Rick Schneider . . . Producer/Writer/Director
Terry Notary . . . Producer
Jason Lethcoe . . . Writer
Elizabeth Del Sol . . . Assistant

PAUL SCHIFF PRODUCTIONS
10202 W. Washington Blvd., Astaire Bldg., Ste. 2310
Culver City, CA 90232
PHONE . . . 310-244-5454
TYPES Features - TV Series
HAS DEAL WITH Sony Pictures Entertainment
DEVELOPMENT The Air I Breathe - You Are Here - Numb
CREDITS Date Movie - Maid in Manhattan - My Cousin Vinny - Young Guns 1&2 - Rushmore - Black Knight - Mona Lisa Smile - Walking Tall

Paul Schiff . . . President/Producer
Tai Duncan . . . VP, Production
Andrew Bernstein . . . Creative Executive

GEORGE SCHLATTER PRODUCTIONS
8321 Beverly Blvd.
Los Angeles, CA 90048
PHONE . . . 323-655-1400
FAX . . . 323-852-1640
EMAIL . . . gsgsp@aol.com
TYPES Specials - TV Series
CREDITS 15 Years of the American Comedy Awards - Laugh In - Real People - Sinatra: 80 Years My Way - AFI Life Achievement in Honor of Dustin Hoffman - AFI Life Achievement in Honor of Harrison Ford - Muhammad Ali 60th Birthday Celebration - HBO Tribute to Las Vegas Founders of Comedy - Inaugural Ceremonies for President George Bush 2001 & 2005

George Schlatter . . . Executive Producer
Maria S. Schlatter . . . Co-Producer
Donn Hoyer . . . Co-Producer
Gary Necessary . . . Executive in Charge of Production
Suzzanne Stangel . . . Production Manager
Marta Lee . . . Assistant to George Schlatter
Nathan Golden . . . Accounting
Gunther Schiff . . . Attorney

SCHOLASTIC ENTERTAINMENT
557 Broadway
New York, NY 10012-3999
PHONE .212-389-3964
FAX .212-389-3887
EMAIL .slauchaire@scholastic.com
WEB SITE .www.scholastic.com

TYPES	Animation - Features - TV Series
DEVELOPMENT	The Golden Compass
PRE-PRODUCTION	His Dark Materials
CREDITS	Goosebumps - Indian in the Cupboard - The Magic School Bus - Clifford the Big Red Dog - Dear America - Horrible Histories - Clifford's Really Big Movie - Maya and Miguel - Clifford: Puppy Days

Deborah Forte .President
Juliet Blake .Sr. VP, TV Programming
Martha Atwater .VP, Special Projects

JOEL SCHUMACHER PRODUCTIONS
1149 N. Gower St., Ste. 247
Los Angeles, CA 90038
PHONE .323-785-2274

TYPES	Features
CREDITS	Batman & Robin - A Time to Kill - Batman Forever - 8mm - Flawless - Tigerland - Bad Company - Phone Booth - Veronica Guerin - Phantom of the Opera
SUBMISSION POLICY	No unsolicited submissions

Joel Schumacher .Owner
Eli Richbourg .Associate Producer
Tony Barger .Executive Assistant to Joel Schumacher

FAYE SCHWAB PRODUCTIONS/MMA, INC.
9461 Charleville Blvd., Ste. 367
Beverly Hills, CA 90212
PHONE .310-278-4738
FAX .310-278-5006
EMAIL .fayeschwab@aol.com
WEB SITE .www.fayeschwab.com

TYPES	Features - Made-for-TV/Cable Movies - TV Series
DEVELOPMENT	Red Lips, White Lies - The Machinist - PO Box 134 - The Cut-Out Man - Higher - Jay J. Armes - Betrayal - The Seduction Diet - Visions - The Puzzle - Waiting for Shade - On the Money - As Time Goes By
CREDITS	The Morning After - Chattahoochee - Demolition Man - Love Comes Softly (Hallmark)

Faye Schwab .President/Producer
Stephanie Seidan .Director, Development

SCHWARTZ & COMPANY, INC.
1223 Wilshire Blvd., Ste. 283
Santa Monica, CA 90403
PHONE .310-394-8227
FAX .310-394-7871
EMAIL .bill@schwartzcompany.com
WEB SITE .www.schwartzcompany.com

TYPES	Animation - Direct-to-Video/DVD - Documentaries - Features - Made-for-TV/Cable Movies - Miniseries - Reality TV - Specials - TV Series
DEVELOPMENT	The Secret of Zack's Gullwing - The Secret of the Little Mermaid - The Secret of the Scariest Monsters - The Secret of the Little Princess - The Secret of Captain's Courageous
UPCOMING RELEASES	Puff the Magic Dragon - Puff in the Land of Mr. Nobody - Dorothy in the Land of Oz - Sam Kinison Comedy Collection - Rodney Dangerfield Collection
COMPLETED UNRELEASED	The Singing Princess with Julie Andrews - Happily Ever After
CREDITS	Puff the Magic Dragon - Puff in the Land of Mr. Nobody - Dorothy in the Land of Oz - The HBO Sam Kinison Comedy Collection - The Lenny Bruce Performance - Jim Breuer Heavy Metal Comedy - Little Shop of Horror - Night of the Living Dead - Reefer Madness - The Three Stooges - A Christmas Story - Shirley Temple Collection - Plan Nine From Outer Space - Sherlock Holmes Collection - The Howard Hughes: The Real Aviator (Documentary) - Bob Hope's Funniest Moments - Terror on the Titanic - Man of the Year - Snow White & the Magic Mirror - Young Pocahontas - Moses: Egypt's Great Prince - Secret of Anastasia - Secret of Mulan - Operation Dalmation: The Big Adventure, Kathy Ireland Exercise Videos - Rachel Hunter Exercise Videos

William A. Schwartz .CEO
Sabrina Bassman .Director, Research

STEVEN SCHWARTZ PRODUCTIONS, INC.
4058 Tilden Ave.
Culver City, CA 90232
PHONE .310-839-2100

TYPES	Features - TV Series
CREDITS	Critical Care - 100 Centre Street - The Practice - A Raisin in the Sun - Likely Stories
SUBMISSION POLICY	No unsolicited submissions

Steven Schwartz .Writer/Producer
Nicki Miller .Director, Development

SCI FI CHANNEL

30 Rockefeller Center, 21st Fl.
New York, NY 10112

PHONE .212-664-4444/818-777-1000
FAX .212-703-8533/818-866-1420
WEB SITE .www.scifi.com
SECOND WEB SITE .www.nbcuni.com

TYPES — Animation - Documentaries - Features - Internet Content - Made-for-TV/Cable Movies - Miniseries - Mobile Content - Reality TV - TV Series

DEVELOPMENT — Dresden Files - The Butterfly Effect - The Bridge - Nine Lives - Motel Man - Those Who Walk in Darkness - Untitled Michael Douglas Project - Time Tunnel - 3:52 - Urban Arcana - Tomorrow's Child - Heroes Anonymous - Dallas in Wonderland - Dresden Files - The Thing - What If? - The Gift - Amazing Screw-On Head - Barbarian Chronicles - Seriously Baffling Mysteries - The End - Winney - Sci Fi Investigates - Chariots of the Gods (Miniseries) - Motel Man - Snap - Caprica

CREDITS — Battlestar Galactica - Stargate SG-1 - Stargate: Atlantis - Ghost Hunters - Eureka - Who Wants to Be a Superhero?

COMMENTS — West Coast office: 100 Universal City Plaza, Bldg. 1440, 14th Fl., Universal City, CA 91608; Includes Sci Fi Pulse (Broadband Video Channel)

Bonnie Hammer .President, Sci Fi Channel & USA Network
Dave Howe .Executive VP/General Manager
Mark Stern .Executive VP, Original Programming
Thomas Vitale .Sr. VP, Acquisitions, Scheduling & Programming Planning
Craig Engler .Sr. VP, scifi.com & Sci Fi Magazine
Sallie Schoneboom .Sr. VP, Public Relations
Adam Stotsky .Sr. VP, Marketing & Creative
Tahira Batti-McClure .VP, Operations, Sci Fi Channel & USA Network
Bill Brennan .VP, Publicity
Blake Calloway .VP, Brand Marketing
Gunilla DeSanto .VP, Production & Project Management
Russell Friedman .VP, Production & Sci Fi Programming
Roger Guillen .VP, Creative
Nora O'Brien .VP, Original Programming
Tony Optican .VP, Development & Current Programming
Chris Regina .VP, Programming
Erik Storey .VP, Development
Rob Swartz .VP, Alternative Programming
Matthew Chiavelli .Multimedia Director
Marlon Jackson .Web Director
Shara Zoll .Project Director

SCOTT FREE PRODUCTIONS

614 N. La Peer Dr.
West Hollywood, CA 90069

PHONE .310-360-2250
FAX .310-360-2251

TYPES — Documentaries - Features - Made-for-TV/Cable Movies - TV Series

HAS DEAL WITH — CBS Entertainment - CBS Paramount Network Television - Twentieth Century Fox

DEVELOPMENT — Hell's Angel - Warriors - Wolf Brother - New Mexico - Orpheus - The Company (TNT) - Penetration - All Lit Up - The Killing Sea

POST PRODUCTION — A Good Year - The Assassination of Jesse James

CREDITS — Domino - In Her Shoes - Kingdom of Heaven - Numb3rs (TV) - Man on Fire - Black Hawk Down - The Gathering Storm - Crimson Tide - Thelma & Louise - Enemy of the State - Gladiator - Tristan & Isolde

COMMENTS — Interactive games

Ridley Scott .Co-Chairman
Tony Scott .Co-Chairman
Michael Costigan .President
David Zucker .President, TV
Erin Upson .VP
Anne Lai .VP
Alan Trezza .Creative Executive
Jordan Sheehan .Executive Assistant to Ridley Scott
Tom Moran .Executive Assistant to Tony Scott
Blake Smith .Executive Assistant to David Zucker
Jennah Dirksen .Executive Assistant to Anne Lai & Erin Upson
Maresa Pullman .Executive Assistant to Michael Costigan

SCOUT PRODUCTIONS

1040 N. Las Palmas Ave., Bldg. 26W
Los Angeles, CA 90038

PHONE .323-860-8575/617-782-7722
FAX .323-860-8576/617-782-7799
EMAIL .info@scoutvision.com
WEB SITE .www.scoutvision.com

TYPES — Documentaries - Features - Reality TV - TV Series

CREDITS — How to Get the Guy - The Fog of War - Session 9 - Dead Dog - Private Lies - Mr. Death - Six Ways to Sunday - Home Before Dark - Never Met Picasso - First Person (IFC/Bravo) - Queer Eye - Knock First - Queer Eye for the Straight Girl - Ding Dong Feng Shui

David Collins .Principal
Michael Williams .Principal
David Metzler .Executive Producer/CCO
Joel K. Savitt .Sr. VP, Production
Tina Elmo .VP, Branded Entertainment

SCREEN DOOR ENTERTAINMENT

15223 Burbank Blvd.
Sherman Oaks, CA 91411
PHONE .818-781-5600
FAX .818-781-5601
WEB SITE .www.sdetv.com
TYPES Internet Content - Reality TV - Specials - TV Series
DEVELOPMENT Women in Football
PRE-PRODUCTION Sold!
CREDITS Stylelicious - Uncommon Threads - Craft Lab - Insider's Garden - Seasoned Gardener - Room by Room - Outer Spaces - Knitty Gritty - The Look for Spring - Family Fun TV
SUBMISSION POLICY No phone calls
COMMENTS Additional Web sites: www.craftlab.tv, www.uncommonthreads.tv, www.styleicious.tv, www.knittygritty.com

Joel Rizor .President/Executive Producer
Nicole W. Block .Line Producer
M. Alessandra Ascoli .Director, Development & Programming
Kevin Mercier .Post Production Supervisor
David Shikiar .Director, Production

SCREEN GEMS

A Sony Pictures Entertainment Company
10202 W. Washington Blvd.
Culver City, CA 90232
PHONE .310-244-4000
TYPES Features

Clinton Culpepper .President
Marc Weinstock .Executive VP, Marketing
Gilbert Dumontet .Sr. VP, Production
Gary Hirsch .Sr. VP, Business Affairs
Pam Kunath .Sr. VP, Business Affairs
Eric Paquette .Sr. VP, Production
Scott Strauss .Sr. VP, Production
Michael Helfand .VP, Business Affairs
Nicholas Phillips .VP, Production

SE8 GROUP

505 N. Robertson Blvd.
Los Angeles, CA 90048
PHONE .310-285-6090
FAX .310-285-6097
TYPES Features
CREDITS Dead Fish - The Contender - Nil by Mouth

Douglas Urbanski .Producer
Gary Oldman .Actor/Producer

RYAN SEACREST PRODUCTIONS

5750 Wilshire Blvd., 4th Fl.
Los Angeles, CA 90036
PHONE .323-954-2400
WEB SITE .www.ryanseacrest.com
TYPES TV Series
HAS DEAL WITH E! Networks

Ryan Seacrest .Producer
Eliot Goldberg .Sr. VP, Production & Development

SEASIDE PRODUCTIONS

9229 W. Sunset Blvd., Ste. 850
Los Angeles, CA 90069
PHONE .310-275-3288
FAX .310-275-3270
TYPES Animation - Features

India Osborne .Producer
Kevin Curry .Creative Executive

SEED PRODUCTIONS

c/o Twentieth Century Fox
10201 W. Pico Blvd., Bldg. 52, Rm. 101
Los Angeles, CA 90035
PHONE .310-369-1900
TYPES Features - Theatre - TV Series
HAS DEAL WITH Twentieth Century Fox
DEVELOPMENT If You Could See Me Now - Wolverine - Drive - Fed X - The Tourist - Rebound Guy
COMMENTS Additional offices on Fox lot in Sydney, Australia

Hugh Jackman .Producer/Actor (310-369-7660)
Deborra-lee Furness .Director/Actress (310-369-7660)
John Palermo .Producer/Partner (310-369-7660)
Amanda Schweitzer .Creative Executive (310-369-1920)
Alexandra Ducocq .Assistant to Hugh Jackman & John Palermo (310-369-7660)

SEGUE PRODUCTIONS, INC.

11150 Santa Monica Blvd., Ste. 1200
Los Angeles, CA 90025
PHONE .310-312-1828
FAX .310-231-7014
TYPES Features
CREDITS Restoration - Ransom

Kip Hagopian .Chairman/President
Pat Papero .Executive Assistant

SEKRETAGENT PRODUCTIONS

1608 Argyle Ave.
Los Angeles, CA 90028
PHONE .323-462-9900
FAX .323-462-9911
WEB SITE .www.sekretagents.com
TYPES Animation - Features - TV Series
DEVELOPMENT Sleeping Beauty (Sony) - The Wind in the Willows (Disney) - The Dogs of Babel (Focus Features) - Son of the Gun (Fox Searchlight) - The Hunt (Universal)
UPCOMING RELEASES The Plague (Armada)
COMMENTS Owns S2 Filmed Entertainment, Inc.; Deal with Ubisoft

Andrew J. Levitas .Producer
Corey May .Producer
Dooma Wendschuh .Producer
Margo Klewans .Producer
Tim Bowden .VP, Operations
Matt Smith .Development Assistant

DYLAN SELLERS PRODUCTIONS
4000 Warner Blvd.
Burbank, CA 91522
PHONE .818-954-4929
FAX .818-954-4190
TYPES Features - TV Series
HAS DEAL WITH Warner Bros. Pictures
DEVELOPMENT Hateship, Friendship, Courtship, Loveship, Marriage - All In - Palm Fitness - The Greatest Escape - The Jailhouse Lawyer - The Pool Guy - Mainline
PRE-PRODUCTION The Expendables - Kung Fu Kids - Fishing For Moonlight - Neopets - To Live And Drive In LA - Continuing Ed - Something Borrowed - Unemployed
CREDITS A Cinderella Story - Passenger 57 - The Paper - The Replacements - Valentine - Agent Cody Banks 1&2 - Out to Sea - Black Sash - Music of Chance - Big Bully - The Amazing Panda Adventure

Dylan Sellers .Producer/President
Jesse Ehrman .Senior Director, Development
Neal Dodson .Director, Development

***SENART FILMS**
133 West Broadway, 5th Fl.
New York, NY 10013
PHONE .212-406-9610
FAX .212-406-9581
EMAIL .info@senartfilms.com
WEB SITE .www.senartfilms.com
TYPES Documentaries - Features
COMPLETED UNRELEASED Bonneville
CREDITS The War Tapes - The Station Agent - The Fog of War - Stevie
SUBMISSION POLICY No unsolicited manuscripts

Robert May .Producer
Lauren Timmons .Story Editor
Anastasia Kousakis .Assistant to Robert May

***SENATOR ENTERTAINMENT, INC.**
5254 Melrose Ave.
Hollywood, CA 90038
PHONE .323-871-4447
FAX .323-871-4448
EMAIL .info@senatorentertainment.com
WEB SITE .www.senator.de
TYPES Features

Marco Weber .President/CEO
Vanessa Coifman .Executive VP, Production

SENZA PICTURES
349 Broadway, 3rd Fl.
New York, NY 10013
PHONE .212-334-3577
FAX .212-334-3565
EMAIL .submission@senzapix.com
WEB SITE .www.senzapix.com
TYPES Commercials - Features - Internet Content - Mobile Content - Music Videos - Reality TV - TV Series
CREDITS Our Italian Husband - Double Exile
SUBMISSION POLICY Submit logline or brief description via email

Brandi Savitt .President/Producer
Amie Castaldo .Director, Development
Anne Takahashi .Assistant

SERAPHIM FILMS
1606 Argyle Ave.
Hollywood, CA 90028
PHONE .310-717-4737
WEB SITE .www.clivebarker.com
TYPES Direct-to-Video/DVD - Features - New Media - TV Series
DEVELOPMENT Thief of Always - Dread - Abarat - Damnation Game - Coldheart Canyon - Tortured Souls - Demonik - New York Ressurection - Pig Blood Blues
PRE-PRODUCTION Midnight Meat Train
POST PRODUCTION The Plague
CREDITS Saint Sinner - Salome - The Forbidden - Nightbreed - Candyman 1&2 - Lord of Illusions - Hellraiser 1-4 - Gods & Monsters

Clive Barker .President
Joe Daley .Executive VP, Production
Anthony DiBlasi .VP, Production

SERENADE FILMS
2901 Ocean Park Blvd., Ste. 217
Santa Monica, CA 90405
PHONE .310-452-3335
FAX .310-452-0108
EMAIL .serenadefilms@aol.com
TYPES Features
CREDITS Game 6 - Twelve and Holding - The Great New Wonderful
COMMENTS Email synopsis for script submission consideration

Leslie Urdang .Producer/Partner
Michael Nozik .Producer/Partner
Geoffrey Linville .Director, Production
J.P. Impastato .Post Production Assistant

SERENDIPITY POINT FILMS
9 Price St.
Toronto, ON M4W 1Z1, Canada
PHONE .416-960-0300
FAX .416-960-8656
WEB SITE .www.serendipitypoint.com
TYPES Features - TV Series
PRODUCTION Fugitive Pieces
CREDITS Where the Truth Lies - Being Julia - The Statement - Ararat - Men With Brooms - Sunshine - eXistenZ
SUBMISSION POLICY No unsolicited material

Robert Lantos .Producer
Mark Musselman .Head, Business & Legal Affairs
Wendy Saffer .Head, Publicity & Marketing
Aida Tannyan .Head, Finance
Cherri Campbell .Assistant to Mr. Lantos

SERENDIPITY PRODUCTIONS, INC.
15260 Ventura Blvd., Ste. 1040
Sherman Oaks, CA 91403
PHONE .818-789-3035
FAX .818-789-0213
EMAIL .serendipityprod@earthlink.net
WEB SITE .home.earthlink.net/~danheffner
TYPES Direct-to-Video/DVD - Features - Made-for-TV/Cable Movies
DEVELOPMENT Saw 4
PRODUCTION Saw 3
CREDITS Saw 1&2 - Anonymous Rex - Highway 395 - Holy Matrimony - The Good Mother - George of the Jungle 2

Daniel Jason Heffner .Producer/Principal

SESAME WORKSHOP

One Lincoln Plaza, 4th Fl.
New York, NY 10023
PHONE .212-595-3456
FAX .212-875-6114
WEB SITE www.sesamestreet.com
SECOND WEB SITE www.sesameworkshop.org
TYPES Animation - TV Series
CREDITS Sesame Street - Dragon Tales - Sagwa, the Chinese Siamese Cat

Gary E. Knell . President/CEO
Melvin Ming . COO
Lewis Bernstein . Executive VP, Education, Research & Outreach
Terry Fitzpatrick . Executive VP, Distribution
Susan Kolar . Executive VP/CAO
Liz Nealon . Executive VP, Creative Director
Sherrie Rollins Westin . Executive VP/CMO
Daniel Victor . Executive VP, Global Strategy
Jennifer Monier-Williams . VP, International TV Distribution & Sales
Jamie Greenberg . VP, Philanthropic Development
Anita Stewart . VP, Corporate Sponsorship

SEVEN ARTS PICTURES

6310 San Vicente Ave., Ste. 510
Los Angeles, CA 90048
PHONE .323-634-0990
FAX .323-634-1061
WEB SITE www.7artspictures.com
TYPES Direct-to-Video/DVD - Features
PRE-PRODUCTION The Winter Queen
PRODUCTION Nine Miles Down
POST PRODUCTION Noise - Deal
COMPLETED UNRELEASED Captivity
CREDITS Another 9-1/2 Weeks - Shattered Image - The Hustle - Naked Movie - Never Talk To Strangers - An American Rhapsody - The Believer - Johnny Mnemonic - No Good Deed - I'll Sleep When I'm Dead - Stander - Shooting Gallery - Asylum

Peter M. Hoffman . President/CEO
Susan Hoffman . Producer
Daniel Diamond . Consultant
Kate Hoffman . Executive VP
Justin Kelly . VP, Business Affairs
Erik Smith . VP, Finance & Operations
Sandra Staggs . Marketing Executive
Linda Silverthorn . Executive Assistant to President
Eric Min . Executive Assistant

SEVEN SUMMITS PICTURES & MANAGEMENT

8906 W. Olympic Blvd., Garden Level
Beverly Hills, CA 90211
PHONE .310-550-6777
FAX .310-550-0606
TYPES Direct-to-Video/DVD - Documentaries - Features - Made-for-TV/Cable Movies - TV Series
DEVELOPMENT Brother Bill - Echoes - Lovers Are Not People - Roads - Free Love - Earthquake Weather - Flight Risk
PRE-PRODUCTION Justice
CREDITS Grandview USA - Zandalee - Linguini Incident - Hollywood Palms - Penn & Teller's Sin City Spectacular - Pros and Cons of Breathing

William Blaylock . Producer/Manager
Sarah Jackson . Producer/Manager
Paul Canterna . Producer/Manager
Nicolas Bernheim . Manager
David Shojai . Assistant

SHADOWCATCHER ENTERTAINMENT

800 Fifth Ave., Ste. 4100
Seattle, WA 98104
PHONE .206-328-6266
FAX .206-447-1462
EMAIL kate@shadowcatcherent.com
TYPES Features - Made-for-TV/Cable Movies - Theatre
DEVELOPMENT 69 - The High Road - The Probable Future - Zulu Wave - The All of It - The Calling - Inside Passage - Blind Man's Bluff
PRODUCTION The American Pastime
POST PRODUCTION Outsourced
CREDITS Game 6 - The Skeleton Key - Smoke Signals - The Book of Stars - Getting to Know You

David Skinner . Executive Producer
Tom Gorai . Producer
Kate Wickstrom . No Title

SHADY ACRES ENTERTAINMENT

c/o Universal Pictures
100 Universal City Plaza, Bldg. 6111
Universal City, CA 91608
PHONE .818-777-4446
FAX .818-866-6612
TYPES Features - TV Series
HAS DEAL WITH Touchstone Television - Universal Pictures
DEVELOPMENT The Company
PRE-PRODUCTION I Now Pronounce You Chuck and Larry
PRODUCTION Evan Almighty
CREDITS Accepted - Bruce Almighty - Liar Liar - Patch Adams - The Nutty Professor - Dragonfly - 8 Simple Rules
SUBMISSION POLICY No unsolicited submissions

Michael Bostick . No Title
Greta Bramberg . No Title
Ginny Durkin . No Title
Dagan Handy . No Title
Anderson Hopkins . No Title
Kathy Jones . No Title
Alex Kerr . No Title
Amanda Morgan Palmer . No Title
Tom Shadyac . No Title
Buffy Shutt . No Title
Glenda Storm . No Title
Lalo Vasquez . No Title
Jason Wilson . No Title
Jordan Wolfe . No Title

ARNOLD SHAPIRO PRODUCTIONS

c/o CBS Studio Center
4024 Radford Ave.
Studio City, CA 91604
PHONE .818-655-6872
FAX .818-655-8396
EMAIL aspproductions@aol.com
WEB SITE www.arnoldshapiroproductions.com
CREDITS Brat Camp (ABC) - Situation: Comedy (Bravo) - Minding the Store (TBS) - The Road to Stardom with Missy Elliott (UPN) - Big Brother 2-7 (CBS) - Blow Out (Bravo) - The Family (ABC) - DNA: Guilty or Innocent - Flipped - The Teen Files - Rescue 911

Arnold Shapiro . Executive Producer
Rickey Ackerman . Director, Finance
Joy Mariano . Assistant to Arnold Shapiro

THE SHEPHARD/ROBIN COMPANY

c/o Raleigh Studios
5300 Melrose Ave., Ste. 225E
Los Angeles, CA 90038
PHONE 323-871-4412
FAX 323-871-4418
TYPES TV Series
HAS DEAL WITH Warner Bros. Television Production
PRE-PRODUCTION State of Mind (Lifetime)
CREDITS The Closer (TNT) - Popular - Brutally Normal - Bailey's Mistake (ABC MOW) - Nip/Tuck (FX) - The D.A. (ABC)
SUBMISSION POLICY No unsolicited submissions

Greer Shephard ....Executive Producer/Owner
Michael Robin ....Executive Producer/Owner

JON SHESTACK PRODUCTIONS

409 N. Larchmont Blvd.
Los Angeles, CA 90004
PHONE 323-468-1113
FAX 323-468-1114
TYPES Animation - Features - TV Series
HAS DEAL WITH Warner Bros. Pictures
DEVELOPMENT Piano Lessons - Skyport - Stolen Season - Boss Go Home - The Theory of Everything - Egyptology - Escape from Planet Earth
PRE-PRODUCTION Dan in Real Life
CREDITS Waiting - Air Force One - The Last Seduction - Firewall

Jon Shestack ....Producer
Ginny Brewer ....Production Executive
Jeremy Stein ....Production Executive

SHOE MONEY PRODUCTIONS

4000 Warner Blvd., Bldg. 138, Rm. 1101
Burbank, CA 91522
PHONE 818-954-2682
FAX 818-954-1660
EMAIL ....shoemoney@warnerbros.com
TYPES Features - TV Series
HAS DEAL WITH Warner Bros. Television Production
UPCOMING RELEASES Studio 60
CREDITS Invasion - Jack & Bobby - The West Wing

Thomas Schlamme ....Executive Producer/Director
AJ Marcantonio ....Executive
Julie De Joie ....Executive
Paula Hallin ....Assistant to Thomas Schlamme

SHOOT THE MOON PRODUCTIONS

9 Desbrosses St., 2nd Fl.
New York, NY 10013
PHONE 212-609-0590
FAX 212-609-0594
WEB SITE ....www.dkcnews.com
TYPES Documentaries - Features - TV Series
POST PRODUCTION Love Is in the Air
CREDITS The Boys of 2nd Street Park - Ring of Fire: The Emile Griffith Story - Viva Baseball

Dan Klores ....President/Producer
Jake Bandman ....Associate Producer
Libby Geist ....Associate Producer

SHORE VIEW ENTERTAINMENT

10880 Wilshire Blvd., Ste. 1100
Los Angeles, CA 90024
PHONE 323-956-2002
FAX 310-234-5484
TYPES Made-for-TV/Cable Movies - TV Series
CREDITS The 4400

Perry Simon ....President/Executive Producer

SHORELINE ENTERTAINMENT, INC.

1875 Century Park East, Ste. 600
Los Angeles, CA 90067
PHONE 310-551-2060
FAX 310-201-0729
EMAIL ....info@shorelineentertainment.com
SECOND EMAIL ....macy@shorelineentertainment.com
WEB SITE ....www.shorelineentertainment.com
TYPES Direct-to-Video/DVD - Documentaries - Features - Made-for-TV/Cable Movies - Reality TV - TV Series
PROVIDES DEAL TO Chic Productions
DEVELOPMENT Fuel - Under Uruguay
PRE-PRODUCTION Hank & Mike
PRODUCTION Senseless - The Signal
POST PRODUCTION Barstool Words - Shadow Puppets - Dark Corners - The Dread - The Fifth Patient - Voodoo Lagoon - The Guardians - Shadow Walkers - Everything's Gone Green - Weirdsville
UPCOMING RELEASES Marilyn Hotchkiss' Ballroom Dancing & Charm School - Kalamazoo - Swimmers
COMPLETED UNRELEASED Constellation
CREDITS Stinger - Alien Incursion - The Man from Elysian Fields - Price of Glory - Lakeboat - Dark Asylum - The Godson - Detour - Flight of Fancy - Tail Sting - The Visit - The King's Guard - A Matter of Trust - Glengarry Glen Ross

Morris Ruskin ....President
Sam Eigen ....Director, World-Wide Distribution
Steve Chicorel ....Head, Marketing
Chad Leslie ....Director, Acquisitions
Steve Macy ....Manager
Brian Sweet ....Sales Manager
Rachel Dufresne ....Market & Fesitval Coordinator
Chelsea Miller ....Sales

SHOWTIME INDEPENDENT FILMS

1633 Broadway
New York, NY 10019
PHONE 212-708-1600/310-234-5200
FAX 310-234-5393
WEB SITE ....www.sho.com
TYPES Features
CREDITS Same Sex America - After Innocence - Baadasssss! - Home Front
COMMENTS West Coast office: 10880 Wilshire Blvd., Ste. 1600, Los Angeles, CA 90024

Robert Greenblatt ......President, Entertainment, Showtime Networks Inc.
Matthew Duda ....Executive VP, Program Acquisitions, Planning & Distribution, Showtime Networks Inc.

SHOWTIME NETWORKS INC.

1633 Broadway
New York, NY 10019
PHONE 212-708-1600/310-234-5200
WEB SITE ....www.sho.com
TYPES Documentaries - Made-for-TV/Cable Movies - Miniseries - Specials - TV Series
PROVIDES DEAL TO Elkins Entertainment - Peace Arch Entertainment Group Inc. - Sacred Dogs Entertainment, LLC
DEVELOPMENT Big Shot
UPCOMING RELEASES The Tudors
CREDITS The L Word - Masters of Horror - Penn & Teller: Bullshit! - Family Business - Weeds - Brotherhood - Sexual Healing - Sleeper Cell - Dexter - The Underground
COMMENTS West Coast office: 10880 Wilshire Blvd., Ste. 1600, Los Angeles, CA 90024

Matthew C. Blank ....Chairman/CEO (NY)
Robert Greenblatt ....President, Entertainment (LA)
Melinda Benedek ....Executive VP, Business Affairs (LA)
Matthew Duda ....Executive VP, Program Acquisitions & Planning (LA)
Gary Levine ....Executive VP, Original Programming (LA)
Richard Licata ....Executive VP, Entertainment Public Relations & Corporate Communications (LA)
Michael Rauch ....Executive VP, Production (LA)
Joan Boorstein ....Sr. VP, Creative Affairs (LA)
Tim Delaney ....Sr. VP, Production Operations (NY)
Gary Garfinkel ....Sr. VP, Program Acquisitions (LA)
Danielle Gelber ....Sr. VP, Original Programming (LA)
Pearlena Igbokwe ....Sr. VP, Original Programming (LA)
Beth Klein ....Sr. VP, Talent & Casting, Showtime/Viacom (LA)
Carol Mechanic ....Sr. VP, Programming (LA)
Frank Pintauro ....Sr. VP/General Manager, Red Group (NY)
Marica Chacona ....VP, Program Scheduling (NY)
Nikki Ferraro ....VP, Talent Relations & Special Events (LA)
Anne Kurrasch ....VP, Business Affairs (LA)
John Moser ....VP, Original Programming (NY)
Jamie Padnos ....VP, Program Planning (LA)
Judith Pless ....VP, International Business Development (NY)
Vince Porter ....VP, Production (LA)
Tom Christie ....Sundance Channel (NY)

SHUKOVSKY ENGLISH ENTERTAINMENT

4605 Lankershim Blvd., Ste. 510
North Hollywood, CA 91602
PHONE 818-763-9191
FAX 818-763-9878
TYPES Features - TV Series
CREDITS Murphy Brown - Love & War - Double Rush - The Louie Show - Ink - Living in Captivity

Diane English ....Writer/Executive Producer
Joel Shukovsky ....Executive Producer
Mark Mascolo .....Executive Assistant to Diane English & Joel Shukovsky

THE SHUMAN COMPANY

3815 Hughes Ave., 4th Fl.
Culver City, CA 90232
PHONE 310-841-4344
FAX 310-204-3578
TYPES Features - TV Series
HAS DEAL WITH Fox Television Studios
CREDITS Sweethearts - Kissing Miranda
COMMENTS Manager

Lawrence Shuman ....No Title
Marc Sternberg ....No Title
David Wolthoff ....No Title
A.B. Fischer ....No Title

SHUTT-JONES PRODUCTIONS

100 Universal City Plaza, Bldg. 6111, Ste. 100
Universal City, CA 91608
PHONE 818-777-9619
FAX 818-866-5006
TYPES Direct-to-Video/DVD - Features - TV Series
DEVELOPMENT Madame President - One Nation Under Bob - Love in the Driest Season
CREDITS Blue Crush
SUBMISSION POLICY No unsolicited material

Buffy Shutt ....Producer
Kathy Jones ....Producer
Lalo Vasquez ....Creative Executive

SIERRA CLUB PRODUCTIONS

21550 Oxnard St., Ste. 300
Woodland Hills, CA 91367
PHONE 818-224-6640
WEB SITE ....www.sierraclub.org/scp
TYPES Documentaries - Features - TV Series
DEVELOPMENT Voices of the American Earth
UPCOMING RELEASES On the Brink: Solutions to Global Warming
CREDITS Sierra Club Chronicles - Ansel Adams: A Documentary Film - Vertical Frontier - Refuge at Risk - Lethal Swarms: Killer Bees

Adrienne Bramhall ....Executive Producer

SIGNATURE PICTURES
8285 Sunset Blvd., Ste. 7
Los Angeles, CA 90046
PHONE .323-848-9005
FAX .323-908-9305
EMAIL .james@signaturepictures.com
WEB SITE .www.signaturepictures.com
TYPES Direct-to-Video/DVD - Features
DEVELOPMENT On One Side of the Ring - The Shooter - Napoleon and Betsy
PRE-PRODUCTION Hurricane Chaser
POST PRODUCTION Til Death
COMPLETED UNRELEASED The Black Dahlia
CREDITS Triumph of the Spirit - Tristan & Isolde - Imaginary Heroes - Hairy Tale - The Lords of Dogtown - Extreme Ops - The Musketeer - Maximum Risk - Time Cop - Double Team - The Body - Feardotcom - Spartan - Island on Bird Street - Sound of Thunder
SUBMISSION POLICY No unsolicited materials

Moshe Diamant .Producer
Illana Diamant .Producer
Rene Gil-Besson .Production Executive
James Portolese .Development Executive

SILLY ROBIN PRODUCTIONS
500 S. Buena Vista St.
Burbank, CA 91521
PHONE .818-560-8585
FAX .818-560-3320
TYPES Features - TV Series
HAS DEAL WITH Touchstone Television
DEVELOPMENT Once Upon a Time, Inc. (Showtime) - Untitled Touchstone Project (FOX) - Bunny Bunny (HBO Films) - The Ambassador (Robert Cort Productions)
CREDITS 700 Sundays (Broadway) - Saturday Night Live - Curb Your Enthusiasm - The Story of Us - It's Garry Shandling's Show (Creator) - Dragnet - North - The Please Watch the Jon Lovitz Special (Fox)
COMMENTS Stageplays, novels, magazine fiction, essays

Alan Zweibel .Writer/Producer/Director
John Robertson .Director, Development

SILVER DREAM PRODUCTIONS
1499 Huntington Dr., Ste. 506
South Pasadena, CA 91030
PHONE .626-799-3880
FAX .626-799-5363
EMAIL .luoyan@silverdreamprods.com
TYPES Features - Miniseries
DEVELOPMENT Merchant of Shanghai - Bamboo Circle - Madam Goldenflower - The White Mandarin
CREDITS Pavillion of Women

Luo Yan .Actress/Producer
Diana Chin .Assistant

SILVER LION FILMS
701 Santa Monica Blvd.
Santa Monica, CA 90401
PHONE .310-393-9177
FAX .310-458-9372
WEB SITE .www.silverlionfilms.com
TYPES Animation - Features - Made-for-TV/Cable Movies - TV Series
DEVELOPMENT The Cup - Resolution - Nekkid Cowboy - Legends - Two Men and a Moving Truck - The Doomsday Plan - Raven's Crossing - Sea of Cortez
PRODUCTION Marco Polo
CREDITS Club Dread - Caught in the Act - Flashfire - The Air Up There - Pure Luck - Steel Dawn - Flipper - Gunmen - McHale's Navy - One Man's Hero - Crocodile Dundee in L.A. - Man on Fire

Lance Hool .Producer/Director
Conrad Hool .Producer
Chase Mellen .VP, Business Affairs
Belinda White .Production Coordinator
Azalia Mendoza .Executive Assistant

SILVER NITRATE PICTURES
12268 Ventura Blvd.
Studio City, CA 91604
PHONE .818-762-9559
FAX .818-762-9177
EMAIL .reception@silvernitrate.net
WEB SITE .www.silvernitrate.net
TYPES Animation - Direct-to-Video/DVD - Features - Theatre
DEVELOPMENT Small Apartments - Bats 2 - Harvey Richards: Lawyer for Children
PRODUCTION Big Stan
CREDITS Dirty - London - Rampage: The Hillside Strangler Murders - FrankenFish - Dead Birds - Nightstalker

Barry Booker .Executive Producer
Sundip Shah .Executive Producer
Ash Shah .Producer

SILVER PICTURES

c/o Warner Bros.
4000 Warner Blvd., Bldg. 90
Burbank, CA 91522-0001
PHONE .818-954-4490
FAX .818-954-3237

TYPES	Features - Reality TV - TV Series
HAS DEAL WITH	Warner Bros. Pictures - Warner Bros. Television Production
DEVELOPMENT	Mama's Boys - Swamp Thing - Fully Automatic - Wonder Woman - Speed Racer - Superfly - Dodging Bullets - The Brave One - Time and Again - Shadow 19 - Altered Carbon - Sgt. Rock - Bad Deeds - Logan's Run; Dark Castle: Bad Ronald - I Saw What You Did - The Dirty Dozen (Remake)
POST PRODUCTION	The Visiting - The Reaping
CREDITS	V for Vendetta - House of Wax - Kiss Kiss, Bang Bang - Veronica Mars - Predator 1&2 - The Matrix 1-3 - Die Hard 1&2 - Lethal Weapon 1-4 - Action - Tales from the Crypt - Cradle 2 the Grave - Gothika - Next Action Star
COMMENTS	Dark Castle Entertainment is part of Silver Pictures

Joel Silver .Chairman
Steve Richards .COO
Gerard Bocaccio .President, TV
Susan Levin .Executive VP, Production
Adam Kuhn .VP, Finance
Navid McIlhargey .VP, Development
Erik Olsen .VP, Development
David Gambino .Director, Development
Sara Harmelin .Creative Executive, TV

CASEY SILVER PRODUCTIONS

506 Santa Monica Blvd., Ste. 322
Santa Monica, CA 90401
PHONE .310-566-3750
FAX .310-566-3751

TYPES	Features - TV Series
DEVELOPMENT	Rebels - Cruel & Unusual - Area 52 - Stud - Party Animals - Work to Ride - Big Bad Wolf - The Highwaymen - The Monkey King
CREDITS	Gigli - Hidalgo - Ladder 49
SUBMISSION POLICY	Through agent or attorney only

Casey Silver .Chairman
Afshin Ketabi .VP
Fleming Brooks .Director, Operations
Matthew Reynolds .Creative Executive

SILVERLINE ENTERTAINMENT, INC.

22837 Ventura Blvd., Ste. 205
Woodland Hills, CA 91364
PHONE .818-225-9032
FAX .818-225-9053
EMAIL .admin@silverlineentertainment.com
WEB SITE .www.silverlineentertainment.com

TYPES	Direct-to-Video/DVD - Features - Made-for-TV/Cable Movies
DEVELOPMENT	Deadline
CREDITS	Lethal

Leman Cetiner .CEO/Producer
Axel Munch .President/Producer
Robert Yap .VP, Development & Distribution

THE FRED SILVERMAN COMPANY

1648 Mandeville Canyon Rd.
Los Angeles, CA 90049
PHONE .310-471-4676
FAX .310-471-6536
EMAIL .fsprods@aol.com

TYPES	TV Series
CREDITS	Diagnosis Murder - Perry Mason - Matlock - In the Heat of the Night - 21 - Father Dowling Mysteries - Jake & the Fatman

Fred Silverman .President
Linsey Hubbard .Development Executive

SILVERS/KOSTER PRODUCTIONS, INC.

353 S. Reeves Dr., PH
Beverly Hills, CA 90212
PHONE .310-991-4736
FAX .310-284-5797
EMAIL .skfilmco@aol.com
WEB SITE .www.silvers-koster.com

TYPES	Animation - Commercials - Direct-to-Video/DVD - Features - Made-for-TV/Cable Movies - Music Videos - Reality TV - TV Series
DEVELOPMENT	The Adventures of Mutt and Jeff - Man with a Mission - Love Slave - Mr. Beautiful
PRE-PRODUCTION	Invisible Kids
PRODUCTION	Perfect Partners
UPCOMING RELEASES	Mustang Sally
CREDITS	Hugo Pool - Dead End - My Gardner - Meet Me in Miami

Tracey Silvers .Chairman
Iren Koster .President
Karen Corcoran .VP, Development
Louis Koyatch .VP, Finance

THE GENE SIMMONS COMPANY

PO Box 16075
Beverly Hills, CA 90210
PHONE .310-859-1694
FAX .310-859-2631
EMAIL .genesimmonsco@aol.com

TYPES	Animation - Direct-to-Video/DVD - Features - Reality TV - Syndication - TV Series
CREDITS	Film: Detroit Rock City; TV: My Dad the Rock Star (Nickelodeon) - Mr. Romance (Oxygen) - Gene Simmons' Rock School (VH1) - Gene Simmons' Family Jewels (A&E)
SUBMISSION POLICY	No unsolicited material

Gene Simmons .Producer

SIMMONS/LATHAN

6100 Wilshire Blvd., Ste. 1111
Los Angeles, CA 90048
PHONE .323-634-6400
FAX .323-634-1904
WEB SITE .www.simmonslathan.com

TYPES	Features
HAS DEAL WITH	HBO Entertainment
PRE-PRODUCTION	The Unsuccessful Thug
CREDITS	Run's House
COMMENTS	Offers Def on Demand (Video on Demand Service)

Russell Simmons .Producer
Stan Lathan .Producer

THE ROBERT SIMONDS COMPANY

1999 Avenue of the Stars, Ste. 2350
Los Angeles, CA 90067
PHONE .310-789-2200
FAX .310-201-5998

TYPES: Features
UPCOMING RELEASES: License to Wed
CREDITS: The Pink Panther - The Shaggy Dog - Herbie: Fully Loaded - Cheaper by the Dozen - Yours, Mine & Ours - Just Married - The Water Boy - Big Daddy - The Wedding Singer - Half Baked - Happy Gilmore - Billy Madison - Problem Child 1&2

Robert Simonds .Producer
Kim Zubick .President
Julie Valine .Assistant to Bob Simonds
Lindsey Ames .Assistant to Kim Zubick

SIMSIE FILMS/MEDIA SAVANT PICTURES

1977 Coldwater Canyon Dr.
Beverly Hills, CA 90210
PHONE .310-271-0777/310-273-8217
FAX .310-271-7439
EMAIL .simsie@earthlink.net

TYPES: Features - Made-for-TV/Cable Movies - Mobile Content - Reality TV
DEVELOPMENT: Water's Edge - Ordinary Miracles - The End of the Real World - Wi-Fi - Champagne - Full Cleveland - Spacey Movie
PRE-PRODUCTION: Oceanside
CREDITS: Patti Rocks - Reflections on a Crime - Mortal Passions - Young Blades - Charlton Heston Presents the Bible
SUBMISSION POLICY: Via email query only
COMMENTS: Development deal with Fun Little Movies, LLC

Gwen Field .Partner
Christopher Sepulveda .Assistant

SINGLE CELL PICTURES

1016 N. Palm Ave.
West Hollywood, CA 90069
PHONE .310-360-7600
FAX .310-360-7011

TYPES: Features - TV Series
CREDITS: Velvet Goldmine - Being John Malkovich - Freak City - Thirteen Conversations About One Thing - Saved!

Michael Stipe .Producer
Sandy Stern .Producer
Raj Hundal .Assistant

*SINOVOI ENTERTAINMENT

1317 N. San Fernando Blvd., Ste. 393
Burbank, CA 91504
PHONE .818-562-6404
FAX .818-567-0104
EMAIL .sinovoientertainment@yahoo.com

TYPES: Documentaries - Features - Made-for-TV/Cable Movies - TV Series
DEVELOPMENT: Three Kisses
CREDITS: When a Man Falls in a Forest - Cabin Fever 2 - Full Circle

Maxwell Sinovoi .Executive Producer
Lana Sinovoi .Producer/Writer
Vivi Farella .Producer/Director, Acquisitions

*SIROCCO MEDIA

269 S. Beverly Dr., Ste. 697
Beverly Hills, CA 90212
PHONE .310-651-0810
EMAIL .info@siroccomedia.com

TYPES: Direct-to-Video/DVD - Features - Reality TV - TV Series
DEVELOPMENT: Refocus (Reality TV)
PRE-PRODUCTION: Rosa
POST PRODUCTION: Bobby
COMPLETED UNRELEASED: Mini's First Time
CREDITS: The Elevator (HBO) - The Theory of the Leisure Class (Vanguard Cinema)
SUBMISSION POLICY: No unsolicited material or calls

Athena Ashburn .Co-Founder/Producer/Writer
Matthew Ashburn .Co-Founder/Producer/Director

SITTING DUCKS PRODUCTIONS

2578 Verbena Dr.
Los Angeles, CA 90068
PHONE .323-461-2095
EMAIL .sittingducks@earthlink.net

TYPES: Animation - Direct-to-Video/DVD - Features - Made-for-TV/Cable Movies - New Media - TV Series
DEVELOPMENT: Noah's Blimp - Mambo - Nelvana - Katchoo - Cookie Jar
CREDITS: Sitting Ducks (Cartoon Network) - The Mouse and Monster (UPN) - The Santa Claus Brothers (Disney Channel)

Michael Bedard .Executive Producer
Elizabeth Daro .Executive Producer

SITV

3030 Andrita St., Bldg. A
Los Angeles, CA 90065
PHONE .323-256-8900
FAX .323-256-9888
WEB SITE .www.sitv.com

TYPES: Internet Content - Mobile Content - Reality TV - Specials - TV Series
PRE-PRODUCTION: Jammin - Flor N' Tell - Styleyes Miami
UPCOMING RELEASES: Dating Factory - Heir Time - Road Dogz
CREDITS: The Brothers Garcia (Series) - Funny Is Funny - Café Olé - Latino Laugh Festival - The Drop - Across the Hall - Inside Joke - Urban Jungle - Not So Foreign Filmmaker Showcase - Unacceptable Behavior - Styleyes - The Rub
SUBMISSION POLICY: Must contact Development Manager for submission release form and to schedule an appointment
COMMENTS: Original programming for 18-34 Latino and multicultural

Michael Schwimmer .CEO
Leo Perez .COO
Ed Leon .Sr. VP, Production/Acting Head, Programming & Production
Steve Levin .Sr. VP, Advertising/Sales
Rori Peters .Sr. VP, Affiliate Sales
Albert Chavez .VP, Finance
Eyal Shemtov .VP, Series Development & Current Programmig
Danny Ohman .Executive in Charge of Production
Dolly Romero .Sr. Manager, Development
Marlen Landin .Production Manager

SIXTH WAY PRODUCTIONS
1107 N. El Centro Ave.
Los Angeles, CA 90038
PHONE .323-466-7222
FAX .323-924-5822
EMAIL .info@sixthwayproductions.com
WEB SITE .www.sixthwayproductions.com
TYPES Direct-to-Video/DVD - Documentaries - Features - Music Videos - TV Series
UPCOMING RELEASES Live at the El Rey
COMPLETED UNRELEASED DVD: Joe Rogan Live - Zach Galifianakis Live - Feature: Suffering Man's Charity
CREDITS The Comedians of Comedy (Comedy Central Series) - Comedians of Comedy: The Movie (Netflix/Showtime) - Bette Midler (Epic) - Fiona Apple (Music Video)

DJ Paul .Partner/President
Inman Young .Line Producer
Jeff Crocker .Development
Sarah Holzgraf .Assistant to DJ Paul

SKY NETWORKS
9220 Sunset Blvd., Ste. 230
West Hollywood, CA 90069
PHONE .310-860-2740
FAX .310-860-2471
WEB SITE .www.sky.com
TYPES TV Series
CREDITS Threshold - The 4400 - Battlestar Galactica

Ben Boyer .No Title
Rebecca Siegel .No Title

SKYLARK ENTERTAINMENT, INC.
12405 Venice Blvd., Ste. 237
Los Angeles, CA 90066
PHONE .310-390-2659
TYPES Features - Made-for-TV/Cable Movies - TV Series
DEVELOPMENT Blue Mountain
CREDITS Empire (ABC) - Anacondas: The Hunt for the Blood Orchid - The Linda McCartney Story - Steal This Movie - Election - Orgazmo - Deadlocked - Blonde - Super Fire - Blood Crime - The Lucille Ball Story

Jacobus Rose .President/Producer

SKYLINE PICTURES, LLC
237 N. Windsor Blvd.
Los Angeles, CA 90004
PHONE .323-464-1770
FAX .323-464-4577
EMAIL .info@skylinepix.com
SECOND WEB SITE .www.skylinepix.com
TYPES Features - Made-for-TV/Cable Movies
DEVELOPMENT Not Forgotten
PRE-PRODUCTION Del Rio
CREDITS Basic - The 7th Coin
SUBMISSION POLICY No unsolicited material

Dror Soref .Producer/Director

SKYZONE ENTERTAINMENT
Parker Plaza
400 Kelby St., 17th Fl.
Fort Lee, NJ 07024
PHONE .201-613-8160
FAX .201-613-8046
EMAIL .info@skyzonemobile.com
WEB SITE .www.skyzonemobile.com
TYPES Mobile Content

James Wee .CEO
Richard Park .COO
Neil Haldar .VP, Content Programming & Strategy

***SLEUTH**
900 Sylvan Ave.
One CNBC Plaza
Englewood Cliffs, NJ 07632
PHONE .201-735-3600
FAX .201-735-3630
WEB SITE .www.sleuthchannel.com
TYPES TV Series
COMMENTS Cable channel dedicated to popular crime, mystery and suspense genres

Jeff Gaspin .President, NBC Universal Cable Entertainment, Digital Content & Cross-Network Strategy
David M. Zaslav .President, NBC Universal Cable & Domestic TV & New Media Distribution
Dan Harrison .Sr. VP, Emerging Networks, NBC Universal Cable Entertainment

SLING MEDIA
901 Mariners Island Blvd., Ste. 300
San Mateo, CA 94404
PHONE .650-293-8000
FAX .650-378-4422
WEB SITE .www.slingmedia.com
TYPES Mobile Content
COMMENTS Mobile distribution via Slingbox

Blake Krikorian .Co-Founder/CEO
Jason Krikorian .Co-Founder/VP, Business Development
Bhupen Shah .Co-Founder/VP, Engineering
Brian Jaquet .Public Relations Director

SLINGSHOT MEDIA
4751 Wilshire Blvd., 3rd Fl.
Los Angeles, CA 90010
PHONE .323-549-4300
FAX .323-549-4314
EMAIL .info@slingshot-media.com
WEB SITE .www.slingshot-media.com
TYPES Internet Content

C.J. Bowden .Partner
David Fisch .Partner
Lori Macias .Partner

SLIPNOT! PRODUCTIONS/SPG

3762 Willow Crest Ave.
Studio City, CA 91604
PHONE 818-753-5965
FAX 818-753-0569
EMAIL . . . . slipnotspg@aol.com
SECOND EMAIL . . . . spghomevideo@aol.com
WEB SITE . . . . www.spghomevideo.com
TYPES: Commercials - Direct-to-Video/DVD - Documentaries - Features - Made-for-TV/Cable Movies - Music Videos - Reality TV - TV Series
DEVELOPMENT: Curveball - Delinquent - Double Jointed
CREDITS: Awakening - The Pros and Cons of Breathing - Breaking Point - Point Blank - Out of Time - Love Crimes - Murder by Numbers - Stay on Point - Narcosys - Evicted - LA Rules
SUBMISSION POLICY: Contact before submitting
COMMENTS: Film and video distribution

David Penn . . . . Writer/Producer
Scott Simons . . . . Writer/Producer
Michael Stahlberg . . . . Writer/Director

SMART ENTERTAINMENT

9348 Civic Center Dr., Mezzanine
Beverly Hills, CA 90210
PHONE 310-205-6090
FAX 310-205-6093
EMAIL . . . . john@smartentla.com
WEB SITE . . . . www.smartentertainmentla.com
SECOND WEB SITE . . . . www.smartentla.com
TYPES: Animation - Direct-to-Video/DVD - Features - Internet Content - Made-for-TV/Cable Movies - Miniseries - Mobile Content - Specials - TV Series
DEVELOPMENT: The Family Guy Movie (FOX) - Man Scout (New Line) - No Pain, No Gain (Warner Bros.) - Trap Door (New Line) - The First Bastard (Miramax) - Not a Pretty Woman (Fox) - The Race (MGM) - Labor Day Mason (Beacon) - Get Me Roman Faraday (DreamWorks) - House Breakers (DreamWorks) - Incurable (Fox Atomic)
PRE-PRODUCTION: Arctic Station (GSN) - The Kenny Hotz Show
PRODUCTION: Game Show on Ice (Sony) - Man Scout
POST PRODUCTION: Blades of Glory (Dreamworks/Paramount)
CREDITS: The Ringer - First to Go - Married to It - Bingo - Anger Management - My Boss's Daughter
COMMENTS: Comedy, thrillers, horror, game shows; Jacobs Entertainment: Personal management for writers, directors and animators

John Jacobs . . . . President
Colin O'Reilly . . . . Manager
Zac Unterman . . . . Story Editor

SMG PRODUCTIONS

9200 Sunset Blvd., Ste. 918
Los Angeles, CA 90069
PHONE 310-777-8200
FAX 310-777-8205
EMAIL . . . . info@slamdancemedia.com
WEB SITE . . . . www.slamdancemedia.com
TYPES: Direct-to-Video/DVD - Features - Made-for-TV/Cable Movies - Miniseries - Reality TV - TV Series
HAS DEAL WITH: Touchstone Television
PRE-PRODUCTION: Housewives of Comedy
CREDITS: Final Justice - My Little Assassin - An American Daughter - Santa Who? - Brimstone

Robert Schwartz . . . . CEO
Peter Baxter . . . . President
George Ketvertis . . . . Executive VP
Janine Jones . . . . Sr. VP, Development
Anna Barber . . . . VP
Heather Allyn . . . . Director, Development
Karen Laverty . . . . Assistant

A. SMITH & CO. PRODUCTIONS

9911 W. Pico Blvd., Ste. 250
Los Angeles, CA 90035
PHONE 310-432-4800
FAX 310-551-3085
EMAIL . . . . info@asmithco.com
WEB SITE . . . . www.asmithco.com
TYPES: Reality TV - Specials - TV Series
PRODUCTION: Hell's Kitchen 2
CREDITS: Hell's Kitchen - The Swan 1&2 - I'm Still Alive! - Mad Mad House - Paradise Hotel - Come Home Alive - You Gotta See This! - Pat Croce: Moving In

Arthur Smith . . . . CEO
Kent Weed . . . . President
Sean Atkins . . . . Executive VP
Mariana Manela . . . . Director, Development

GARY SMITH COMPANY

1001 Colorado Ave.
Santa Monica, CA 90401
PHONE 323-871-1200
FAX 323-464-8075
TYPES: Features - Made-for-TV/Cable Movies - Specials
DEVELOPMENT: Mendel's Dwarf - The Match
PRODUCTION: AFI's 100 Years...100 Cheers
CREDITS: AFI Awards - Tony Awards - Emmy Awards - AFI 100 Years

Gary Smith . . . . Executive Producer
Zack Smith . . . . Director, Development
Jeffrey M. Moskowitz . . . . Coordinator, Production

*SMOKE HOUSE

c/o Warner Bros.
4000 Warner Blvd., Bldg. 15
Burbank, CA 91522
PHONE 818-954-4840
FAX 818-954-4860
TYPES: Features - TV Series
HAS DEAL WITH: Warner Bros. Pictures - Warner Bros. Television Production

George Clooney . . . . Partner
Grant Heslov . . . . Partner
Abby Wolf-Weiss . . . . President (Television)
Nina Wolarsky . . . . VP, Development (Features)
Rachna Patel . . . . Assistant to Mr. Heslov

SNAPDRAGON FILMS, INC.
23852 Pacific Coast Hwy., Ste. 373
Malibu, CA 90265
PHONE . . . 310-456-0101
FAX . . . 310-456-7504
EMAIL . . . bpalef@earthlink.net
TYPES Documentaries - Features - Made-for-TV/Cable Movies - New Media - TV Series
DEVELOPMENT Wired for Sound (Feature)
CREDITS Marvin's Room - Cemetery Club - Parents - Moonstruck

Bonnie Palef . . . Director/Producer/Writer
Michael Stellman . . . Producer's Assistant

SNEAK PREVIEW ENTERTAINMENT, INC.
6705 Sunset Blvd., 2nd Fl.
Hollywood, CA 90028
PHONE . . . 323-962-0295
FAX . . . 323-962-0372
EMAIL . . . indiefilm@sneakpreviewentertain.com
WEB SITE . . . www.sneakpreviewentertain.com
TYPES Features - Made-for-TV/Cable Movies - TV Series
DEVELOPMENT Arrow Man - The Secret Lives of Dorks - Three Faces of Evie
PRE-PRODUCTION Queer Fear
POST PRODUCTION Beautiful Loser
COMPLETED UNRELEASED The Civilization of Maxwell Bright
CREDITS Phat Girlz - When Do We Eat? - Circuit - Relax...It's Just Sex - Twin Falls Idaho - Tollbooth - The Clean and Narrow - Scorchers - Bird of Prey - Fast Sofa
COMMENTS Talent management

Steven J. Wolfe . . . Chairman/CEO/Producer
Josh Silver . . . Manager/Producer
Michael J. Roth . . . Manager/Producer
Scott Hyman . . . Production Executive
Anne McDermott . . . Manager, Literary
Gints Krastins . . . Accountant
Adrian Pellereau . . . Office Manager

SNOWFALL FILMS/WINDCHILL FILMS
2321 W. Olive Ave., Ste. A
Burbank, CA 91506
PHONE . . . 818-558-5917 (Snowfall)/818 985-9715 (Windchill)
FAX . . . 818-842-4112 (Snowfall)/818-985-1178 (Windchill)
WEB SITE . . . www.snowfallfilms.com
SECOND WEB SITE . . . www.windchillfilms.com
TYPES Features - Made-for-TV/Cable Movies
DEVELOPMENT Portal - Scouts Honour - A Dead Man in Deptford - Chaperone - Miracle Journey - The Lisa Aguilar Story
POST PRODUCTION Seance
CREDITS Candy Stripers - Undertaking Betty - Jericho Mansions - Bailey's Billions - The Heart Is Deceitful Above All Things

Suzanne Lyons . . . Producer
Kate Robbins . . . Producer

*SOAPNET
3800 W. Alameda Ave.
Burbank, CA 91505
PHONE . . . 818-569-7500
FAX . . . 818-566-7402
WEB SITE . . . www.soapnet.com
TYPES Internet Content - Mobile Content - Reality TV - Specials - TV Series
CREDITS Soapography - One Minute Soaps - SOAPnet's Live From the Red Carpet of the Daytime Emmys - I Wanna Be a Soap Star

Deborah Blackwell . . . Executive VP/General Manager
Sherri York . . . Sr. VP, Marketing
Claire Zrimc . . . Sr. VP, Program Planning, Scheduling & Acquisitions
Mary Ellen Di Prisco . . . VP, Original Programming
Jori Petersen . . . VP, Media Relations
Kate Nelson . . . Business Director

SOBINI FILMS
2700 Colorado Ave., Ste. 510B
Santa Monica, CA 90404
PHONE . . . See Below
FAX . . . 310-255-5110
WEB SITE . . . www.sobini.com
TYPES Features
HAS DEAL WITH Lionsgate
DEVELOPMENT Julia Pastrana - Dark Sister - Blackwell's Island - Speechless - Prey - Eliza Graves
CREDITS Streets of Legend - Framed - The Prince & Me 1&2 - Peaceful Warrior
SUBMISSION POLICY No unsolicited submissions

Mark Amin . . . Producer/Chairman (310-255-5111)
Ron Safinick . . . CFO
Cami Winikoff . . . President (310-255-5115)
Ira Singerman . . . VP, Production (310-225-5104)
James Masi . . . Project Manager
Jill Courtemanche . . . Attorney (310-255-5122)
Tyler Boehm . . . Administrative Assistant (310-255-5121)
Joe Abramo . . . Administrative Assistant

SOLARIS
5555 Melrose Ave., B Annex 2
Los Angeles, CA 90038
PHONE . . . 323-956-8899
FAX . . . 323-862-2266
WEB SITE . . . www.solarisentertainment.com
TYPES Documentaries - Features - TV Series
HAS DEAL WITH CBS Paramount Network Television
DEVELOPMENT Born to Rock (MTV Films) - Parents on Strike - Clark and Lewis - The Third Witch
PRODUCTION Pride and Glory - Superheroes
CREDITS Miracle - Tumbleweeds - The Slaughter Rule - The Specimen - Mule Skinner Blues - My Generation - Murphy's Dozen (TV)
SUBMISSION POLICY No unsolicited materials

Gregory O'Connor . . . Producer/Writer
Gavin O'Connor . . . Producer/Director/Writer
Josh Fagin . . . Development Director
Briegh Morrison . . . Executive Assistant/Office Manager

SOLO ENTERTAINMENT GROUP
14 Beverly Park
Beverly Hills, CA 90210
PHONE 310-205-6262
FAX 310-205-6264
TYPES — Documentaries - Features - TV Series
DEVELOPMENT — Hunted Hunter - Gene Pool - Itz - Purple Land - The Keep
CREDITS — American Psycho - Rollerball - Igby Goes Down - Hansel & Gretel - Historias Minimas - Dude, Where's the Party?

Christian Halsey Solomon .....President/CEO
Lee Solomon .....Executive VP/COO
Lucas Jarach .....VP, Sales & Acquisitions

SOLO ONE PRODUCTIONS
8205 Santa Monica Blvd., Ste. 1279
Los Angeles, CA 90046-5912
PHONE 323-658-8748
FAX 323-658-8749
EMAIL .....solo1productions@aol.com
TYPES — Features - Made-for-TV/Cable Movies - TV Series
DEVELOPMENT — Baby Einstein (Disney) - Sound and Fury - The Decorators
CREDITS — What the #$*! Do We Know!? - Where the Truth Lies - Eddie's Million Dollar Cookoff

Marlee Matlin .....Actress/Producer
Jack Jason .....Producer

ANDREW SOLT PRODUCTIONS
9121 Sunset Blvd.
Los Angeles, CA 90069
PHONE 310-276-9522
FAX 310-276-0242
EMAIL .....edsshow@aol.com
WEB SITE .....www.sofaentertainment.com
TYPES — Specials - TV Series
CREDITS — CBS @ 75 - The NBC 75th Anniversary Special - NBC's 50 Years of Late Night - CBS Funny Flubs & Screw-ups - The History of Rock 'n' Roll - The Best of Ed Sullivan - First 50 Years of CBS - The Hunt for Amazing Treasure - D.J. Games

Andrew Solt .....Producer/Writer/Director
Greg Vines .....Sr. VP, Production
Brian Legrand .....VP, Business Affairs
Beatrice McMillian .....VP, International Sales & Clip Licensing

THE SOMMERS COMPANY
204 Santa Monica Blvd., Ste. A
Santa Monica, CA 90401
PHONE 310-917-9200
FAX 310-917-5036
EMAIL .....info@sommerscompany.com
WEB SITE .....www.sommerscompany.com
TYPES — Features - TV Series
HAS DEAL WITH — Universal Pictures
DEVELOPMENT — Goosebumps - Airborn - The Big Love - Magic Kingdom For Sale - Proximity Effect - The Argonauts - Flame Over India - Flash Gordon - Who Was Claire Jallu? - Delaware McChood - Zooport - When Worlds Collide - Mummy 3
CREDITS — Van Helsing - The Mummy - The Mummy Returns - The Scorpion King - The Jungle Book - Huck Finn - Deep Rising
SUBMISSION POLICY — No unsolicited submissions

Stephen Sommers .....Chairman
Robert Ducsay .....President, Production
Matthew Stuecken .....VP, Development
Jennifer Ceballos .....Story Editor
Ryan Landels .....Assistant to Mr. Ducsay
Andy Camagna .....Assistant
Dikran Ornekian .....Assistant to Mr. Stuecken

SONY BMG FEATURE FILMS
550 Madison Ave., 19th Fl.
New York, NY 10022
PHONE 212-833-8000
TYPES — Documentaries - Features
DEVELOPMENT — Reggaeton - The Man Who Knew Infinity: A Life of the Genius Ramanujan
COMPLETED UNRELEASED — The Sasquatch Dumpling Gang
SUBMISSION POLICY — No unsolicited projects

Sofia Sondervan .....Sr. VP, Feature Films
Patrick Russell .....Director, Production & Acquisitions
Jane Han .....Executive Assistant

SONY ONLINE ENTERTAINMENT
8958 Terman Court
San Diego, CA 92121
PHONE 858-577-3100
FAX 858-577-3200
WEB SITE .....www.sonypictures.com
TYPES — Features - New Media

John Smedley .....President
Adam Joffe .....CTO
John Needham .....CFO/Sr. VP, Finance
Russell Shanks .....COO
Torrie Dorrell .....Sr. VP, Sales, Marketing & Entertainment
Donald Vercelli .....Sr. VP, Sales
Ken Dopher .....VP, Finance
Chris Yates .....VP, Technology, Platform

SONY PICTURES ANIMATION

9050 W. Washington Blvd.
Culver City, CA 90232
PHONE 310-840-8000
FAX 310-840-8100
WEB SITE . . . . . .www.spe.sony.com
TYPES Animation - Features
COMMENTS Feature digital animation

Penney Finkelman Cox . . . . . .Executive VP
Sandra Rabins . . . . . .Executive VP
Nate Hopper . . . . . .Sr. VP, Development
Barbara Zipperman . . . . . .Sr. VP, Business Affairs
Andrea Miloro . . . . . .VP, Animation

SONY PICTURES DIGITAL

3960 Ince Blvd.
Culver City, CA 90232
PHONE 310-840-8676
FAX 310-840-8390
WEB SITE . . . . . .www.spe.sony.com
TYPES Features

Yair Landau . . . . . .President, Sony Pictures Digital
Ira Rubenstein . . . . . .Executive VP, Digital Sales & Marketing
Don Levy . . . . . .Sr. VP, Media Relations
Emmanuelle Borde . . . . . .VP, Digital Sales & Marketing
Becky Chaires . . . . . .VP, Marketing
Eric Gaynor . . . . . .VP, Business & Legal Affairs
Shalom Mann . . . . . .VP, Game Studio
Scott Nourse . . . . . .VP, Production
Bill Sanders . . . . . .VP, Programming
Jerome Schmitz . . . . . .VP, Marketing
Jason Spivak . . . . . .VP, Distribution
Michael Wayne . . . . . .VP, Strategic Alliances

SONY PICTURES ENTERTAINMENT

10202 W. Washington Blvd.
Culver City, CA 90232
PHONE 310-244-4000
FAX 310-244-2626
WEB SITE . . . . . .www.spe.sony.com
TYPES Features - TV Series
PROVIDES DEAL TO 360 Pictures/FGM Entertainment - Apostle - Avenue Pictures - John Baldecchi Productions - Blue Star Pictures - Buckaroo Entertainment - John Calley Productions - Escape Artists II - Wendy Finerman Productions - Fresh Paint - Gracie Films - The Jim Henson Company - Laurence Mark Productions - O.N.C. Entertainment Inc. - Original Film - Overbrook Entertainment - Pariah - Red Wagon Entertainment - Revolution Studios - Paul Schiff Productions - Trilogy Entertainment Group - Winkler Films
COMMENTS See also Columbia Pictures

Michael Lynton . . . . . .Chairman/CEO, SPE
Amy Pascal . . . . . .Chairman, Motion Picture Group/Vice Chairman, SPE
Jeff Blake . . . . . .Vice Chairman, SPE/Chairman, Worldwide Marketing & Distribution, CTMPG
Yair Landau . . . . . .Vice Chairman, SPE/President, Sony Pictures Digital
Beth Berke . . . . . .Executive VP/Chief Administrative Officer
Charlie Falcetti . . . . . .Executive VP, Corporate Finance
David Hendler . . . . . .Executive VP/CFO
Leah Weil . . . . . .Executive VP/General Counsel
Simon Baker . . . . . .Sr. VP/Corporate Treasurer
Karen L. Halby . . . . . .VP
Joseph Chianese . . . . . .Assistant Secretary
Jared Jussim . . . . . .Assistant Secretary
Stephanie Roth . . . . . .Assistant Secretary

SONY PICTURES IMAGEWORKS

A Sony Pictures Entertainment Company
9050 W. Washington Blvd.
Culver City, CA 90232
PHONE 310-840-8000
FAX 310-840-8100
WEB SITE . . . . . .www.imageworks.com
TYPES Animation - Features - New Media - TV Series
COMMENTS See also Sony Pictures Digital Entertainment; Full-service visual effects and digital animation

Tim Sarnoff . . . . . .President
Debbie Denise . . .Executive VP/Executive Producer, Production Infrastructure
Jenny Fulle . . . . . .Executive VP/Executive Producer, Production
Thomas Hershey . . . . . .Sr. VP, Operations
George Joblove . . . . . .Sr. VP/CTO
Stanley Szymanski . . . . . .Sr. VP, Digital Production
Barry Weiss . . . . . .Sr. VP, Animation Production
Mae Turner-Moody . . . . . .VP, Digital Operations
Alberto Velez . . . . . .VP, Systems Engineering
William Villarreal . . . . . .VP, Technical Operations

SONY PICTURES TELEVISION

A Sony Pictures Entertainment Company
10202 W. Washington Blvd.
Culver City, CA 90232
PHONE . . . 310-244-4000
WEB SITE . . . www.sonypicturestelevision.com
TYPES Made-for-TV/Cable Movies - Reality TV - TV Series
PROVIDES DEAL TO 25C Productions - BBC Worldwide Americas - Bull's Eye Entertainment - Embassy Row LLC - Giraffe Productions - Dean Hargrove Productions - Diana Kerew Productions - Krasnoff Foster Productions - Original Film - P.A.T. Productions - Darren Star Productions - Storyline Entertainment - von Zerneck-Sertner Films - Warrior Poets

Steve Mosko . . . President
John Weiser . . . President, Distribution
Jamie Erlicht . . . Co-President, Programming & Production
Zackary Van Amburg . . . Co-President, Programming & Production
Jeanie Bradley . . . Executive VP, Programming
Amy Carney . . . Executive VP, Advertiser Sales & Operations
Richard Frankie . . . Executive VP, Business Operations
Edward Lammi . . . Executive VP, Production
Don Loughery . . . Executive VP, Strategic Operations
Steve Maddox . . . Executive VP, Syndication Sales
David Mumford . . . Executive VP, Planning & Operations
Robert Oswaks . . . Executive VP, Marketing
John Rohrs Jr. . . . Executive VP, Eastern Region
Helen Verno . . . Executive VP, Movies & Miniseries
Jeff Wolf . . . Executive VP, Syndication Sales
Glenn Adilman . . . Sr. VP, Comedy Development
Paula Askanas . . . Sr. VP, Media Relations/Promotions
Francine Beougher . . . Sr. VP, Distribution Operations
Bryan Bowles . . . Sr. VP, Pay TV
Flory Bramnick . . . Sr. VP, Strategic Sales Operations
Richard Burrus . . . Sr. VP, Advertiser Sales Strategy
Melanie Chilek . . . Sr. VP, Reality Programming
Alan Daniels . . . Sr. VP, Marketing
Sharon Hall . . . Sr. VP, Drama
Andy House . . . Sr. VP, Production
Eric Marx . . . Sr. VP, Domestic TV Product Status
Joanne Mazzu . . . Sr. VP, Business Affairs
J.R. McGinnis . . . Sr. VP, Business Affairs
John Morrissey . . . Sr. VP, Production
Winifred White Neisser . . . Sr. VP, Movies for TV & Miniseries
Doug Roth . . . Sr. VP, Research
Phil Squyres . . . Sr. VP, Technical Operations
Dawn Steinberg . . . Sr. VP, Talent & Casting
Joe Tafuri . . . Sr. VP, Ad Sales
Jeff Weiss . . . Sr. VP, Business Affairs, Syndication
Stewart Zimmerman . . . Sr. VP, Ad Sales
Gerette Allegra . . . VP, Programming
Grace Benn . . . VP, Development, Animation
Jason Clodfelter . . . VP, Drama Development
Ellen Cohen . . . VP, Business Affairs
Debra Curtis . . . VP, Current Programming
Jennifer Davidson . . . VP, Publicity
Andrew Deutscher . . . VP, Sales, Northeast Region
Sarah Finn . . . VP, Production
Doug Frederick . . . VP, Ad Sales
Christina Friedgen . . . VP, Post Production
Wayne Goldstein . . . VP, Ad Sales Research
Kerry Schmidt Hardy . . . VP, Development
Travis Howe . . . VP, Ad Sales
Melissa Kellner . . . VP, Development
Susan Law . . . VP, Ad Sales
Cynthia Lieberman . . . VP, Media Relations
Nina Louie . . . VP, Distribution Operations
Tresha Marshall . . . VP, Sales Administration
Tom Nikol . . . VP/Creative Director, Marketing
Deborah Norton . . . VP, Production
Kirk Olson . . . VP, Ad Sales
Margaret Paris . . . VP, Music Licensing
James Petretti . . . VP, Research
Tal Rabinowitz . . . VP, Development
Marti Rider . . . VP, Sales Southeast Region
Dick Roberts . . . VP, Marketing, Off-Network Programming

(Continued)

SONY PICTURES TELEVISION (Continued)

Kimi Serrano . . . VP, Southwest Region
Rick Sherrill . . . VP, TV Production
Eric Smith . . . VP, Western Region
Craig Smith . . . VP, Special Events
Charles Smolsky . . . VP, Business Affairs
John Spector . . . VP, Production
Karen Tatevosian . . . VP, Business Affairs
Andy Teach . . . VP, Network & Cable Research
Angela Turner . . . VP, Affiliate Marketing
Tom Warner . . . VP, Midwestern Region
John Westphal . . . VP, Development
Ed Zimmerman . . . VP, Media Production & Promotion

SONY PICTURES TELEVISION INTERNATIONAL

A Sony Pictures Entertainment Company
10202 W. Washington Blvd.
Culver City, CA 90232
PHONE . . . 310-244-4000
WEB SITE . . . www.sonypicturestelevision.com
TYPES Syndication - TV Series

Michael Grindon . . . President
Andy Kaplan . . . President, International Networks
John McMahon . . . President/Managing Director, Europe
Sean Chu . . . President/Representative Director, AXN-Japan
Steven Kent . . . Sr. Executive VP, International TV Production
Keith LeGoy . . . Executive VP, Distribution
Stuart Baxter . . . Sr. VP, European Distribution
Thanda Belker . . . Sr. VP, Sales Pay TV
Bob Billeci . . . Sr. VP, Technical Operations
Nathalie Civrais . . . Sr. VP, Southern European Production
Donna Cunningham . . . Sr. VP, Business Affairs, Production
Martha Eberts . . . Sr. VP, International Networks
Brendan Fitzgerald . . . Sr. VP, International Production
John Fukunaga . . . Sr. VP, Sales Planning
Ross Hair . . . Sr. VP, International Networks
Kim Hatamiya . . . Sr. VP, Sales & Marketing
Marie Jacobson . . . Sr. VP, Programming
Dan McCaffrey . . . Sr. VP, International Production
Fran McConnell . . . Sr. VP, Production
Todd Miller . . . Sr. VP, International Networks, Asia
Christoph Pachler . . . Sr. VP/CFO, SPTI
Ross Pollack . . . Sr. VP, Distribution, Asia
Antony Root . . . Sr. VP, International Production, Europe
T.C. Schultz . . . Sr. VP/Managing Director, Latin America
Michael Wald . . . Sr. VP, Pay TV Sales
Jason Wells . . . Sr. VP, Mobile Entertainment
Hui Keng Ang . . . VP, Finance, Distribution & Operations, International Networks
Klaudia Bermudez-Key . . . VP/General Manager, Ad Sales, Latin America
Mark Bluestone . . . VP/General Manager
Jiande Chen . . . VP/General Manager, Asia
Marco Cingoli . . . VP, Production & Distribution, Italy
Janet Tsai Dargan . . . VP, Business Affairs
Tom Davidson . . . VP, International Networks
Debbie Elbin . . . VP, Production, Russia
Rozanne Englehart . . . VP, Programming & Research
Jack Ford . . . VP/Managing Director, Australia
Atsushi Fukuda . . . VP, Business Development, Tokyo
Natalie Garcia . . . VP, Distribution & Production, Spain
Paul Gilbert . . . VP, International Program Development & Format Sales
Mark Gleeson . . . VP, Technical Operations
Danny Goldman . . . VP, Sales, London
Ann Harris . . . VP, Production
Shingo Ishiyama . . . VP/General Manager, Animax, Japan
Superna Kalle . . . VP, International Channels
Tom Keeter . . . VP, Marketing, London
James Kramer . . . VP, Production
Amy Larkowski . . . VP, Operations
Jeffrey Lerner . . . VP, International Production
Paul Littmann . . . VP, Pay-Per-View & Video-On-Demand
Ken Lo . . . VP, Business Affairs, Asia
Alexander Marin . . . VP/GM, Mexico
Arata Matsuhsima . . . VP, International Production
Angel Orengo . . . VP, Distribution, Latin American Sales
Ricky Ow . . . VP/General Manager, Singapore
Pamela Parker . . . VP, Business Affairs
Natalie Pratico . . . VP, Sales Planning & Administration

(Continued)

SONY PICTURES TELEVISION INTERNATIONAL (Continued)

Rick Rodriguez . . . . . VP, Production
Ron Sato . . . . . VP, Corporate Publicity
Dawn Schroeder-Telleson . . . . . VP, Channel Marketing
Allyson Terry-Goldsby . . . . . VP, Marketing
Jesus Torres . . . . . VP/General Manager, Latin America
Masaki Ushiroku . . . . . VP, TV Sales, SPE-Japan
Pietro Ventani . . . . . VP, Licensing, Hong Kong
Noemie Weisse . . . . . VP, Sales, France
Jamie Weissenborn . . . . . VP, Global Advertising Sales

SOUTH PRODUCTIONS, LLC

PO Box 240627
Honolulu, HI 96824-0627
PHONE 808-277-2531
FAX 808-373-7839
EMAIL . . . . . fsouth@hawaii.rr.com
WEB SITE . . . . . www.theartofstory.com
TYPES: Features - TV Series
CREDITS: Melrose Place - Hyperion Bay - Baywatch Hawaii - Almost Grown - Equal Justice - Models Inc. - Going to Extremes - Beaches - For the Boys - Man of the House
SUBMISSION POLICY: No unsolicited material

Frank South . . . . . Producer
Margaret South . . . . . Producer

SOUTH SIDE FILMS

26039 Mulholland Hwy.
Calabasas, CA 91302
PHONE 818-878-5748
FAX 818-878-5759
TYPES: Features - Made-for-TV/Cable Movies - TV Series
DEVELOPMENT: Archangel - Witless Protection - Next Day Delivery
CREDITS: Judas - Blind Fury - Vanishing Point - The Fixer - Crossfire Trail - Who Killed Atlanta's Children? - Christmas Rush - Red Water

Charles Robert Carner . . . . . Writer/Director
Debra Sharkey . . . . . Writer
Mark Shields . . . . . Storyboard Artist
John Lozano . . . . . Assistant

SOUTHERN CROSS THE DOG

c/o Paramount Pictures
5555 Melrose Ave., Gloria Swanson Bldg., Ste. 300
Los Angeles, CA 90038
PHONE 323-956-2080
FAX 323-862-2290
TYPES: Features
HAS DEAL WITH: Paramount Pictures
DEVELOPMENT: Maggie Lynn - Charley Price - Passport Diaries
CREDITS: Black Snake Moan - Something New - Hustle & Flow

Craig Brewer . . . . . Writer/Director/Producer
Stephanie Allain . . . . . Producer
Mike Farah . . . . . Director, Development
Erin Hagee . . . . . Assistant to Craig Brewer
Candice Cobette . . . . . Assistant to Stephanie Allain

SOUTHERN SKIES, INC.

1104 S. Holt Ave., Ste. 302
Los Angeles, CA 90035
PHONE 310-855-9833
FAX 310-855-0220
EMAIL . . . . . edman2000@comcast.net
TYPES: Features - Made-for-TV/Cable Movies - TV Series

Ed Markley . . . . . Producer

SOUTHPAW ENTERTAINMENT

1250 Sixth St., Ste. 305
Santa Monica, CA 90401
PHONE 310-587-3537
FAX 310-319-1897
TYPES: Features - Made-for-TV/Cable Movies - TV Series
DEVELOPMENT: PDR (Philadelphia Department of Recreation)
PRE-PRODUCTION: Windsor Road
PRODUCTION: August Rush
POST PRODUCTION: Take Off
CREDITS: Eulogy - House of D

Richard Barton Lewis . . . . . CEO
Corey Ackerman . . . . . VP, Development
Gaby Jerou . . . . . Director, Development

SPACEDOG

11111 Santa Monica Blvd., Ste. 2110
Los Angeles, CA 90025
PHONE 310-274-7650
EMAIL . . . . . contact@spacedoghouse.com
WEB SITE . . . . . www.spacedoghouse.com
TYPES: TV Series
DEVELOPMENT: Revved - Wight & Associates - Proximity Effect
UPCOMING RELEASES: The Covenant (Screen Gems)

Roger Mincheff . . . . . CEO
Dustin Callif . . . . . Managing Partner
Cosmo Jones . . . . . Creative Director
Regan Robinson . . . . . Director, Strategic Alliances
Annie Pham . . . . . Director, Marketing

SPARKY PICTURES

10040 Meritage Court
Sun Valley, CA 91352
PHONE 818 399 9209/818-632-4603
EMAIL . . . . . info@sparkypictures.com
TYPES: Animation - Direct-to-Video/DVD - Features
DEVELOPMENT: The Quarry - Extensions - Under the Weather - Dream Girl - All-Stars - Granted
POST PRODUCTION: Harbinger - Fall Out
CREDITS: Immortal
SUBMISSION POLICY: Unsolicited material not accepted

Walter Michael Bost . . . . . Partner/Producer
Liisa Kyle . . . . . Partner/Producer

SPICE FACTORY
14 Regent Hill
Brighton Sussex BN1 3ED, United Kingdom
PHONE .44-1273-739182
FAX .44-1273-749122
EMAIL .info@spicefactory.co.uk
WEB SITE .www.spicefactory.co.uk
TYPES Features
CREDITS Merchant of Venice - Undertaking Betty (aka Plots with a View) - Head in the Clouds - A Different Loyalty - Bridge Over San Luis Rey - Bollywood Queen - $teal - Strayed
SUBMISSION POLICY No unsolicited material accepted

Michael Lionello Cowan .Joint Managing Director
Jason Piette .Joint Managing Director
Taj Basunia .CFO
Lucy Shuttleworth .Head, Development
Alex Marshall .Head, Business Affairs

SPIKE TV
1775 Broadway
New York, NY 10019
PHONE .212-846-8000/310-407-1200
WEB SITE .www.spiketv.com
TYPES Animation - Documentaries - Made-for-TV/Cable Movies - Reality TV - Specials - TV Series
PROVIDES DEAL TO Liquid Theory
DEVELOPMENT Bull Run - Raising the Roofs - The Dudesons - Sports Fan - Journeys with George
UPCOMING RELEASES Scream 2006 - Guy's Choice Awards
CREDITS Ultimate Fighter Championship - King of Vegas - Pros vs. Joes - Video Game Awards (VGAs) - Blade: The Series - MXC - Total Non-Stop Wrestling
COMMENTS West Coast address: 2049 Century Park East, Ste. 4000, Los Angeles, CA 90067

Doug Herzog .President
John Cucci .COO
Kevin Kay .Executive VP/General Manager
Pancho Mansfield .Executive VP, Original Programming (LA)
Robert Friedman .Sr. VP, Programming
Jessica Heacock .Sr. VP, Affiliate Sales, MTVN
David Lawenda .Sr. VP, Ad Sales
Sharon Levy .Sr. VP, Alternative Programming (LA)
Casey Patterson .Sr. VP, Talent & Casting
Niels Schuurmans .Sr. VP, Branding
Dario Spina .Sr. VP, Marketing
Keith Brown .VP, Documentaries
Beth Coleman .VP, Ad Sales Research
John Griffin .VP, Programming
Bill McGoldrick .VP, Development (LA)
Laura Molen .VP/Director, Ad Sales
Debra Fazio .Sr. Director, Press
David Schwarz .Sr. Director, Press
Bobby Amirshahi .Director, Corporate Communications

SPIRIT HORSE PRODUCTIONS
6404 Wilshire Blvd., Box #1935
Los Angeles, CA 90048
PHONE .310-933-6250
FAX .310-388-0874
EMAIL .spirithorse@usa.com
WEB SITE .www.spirithorseusa.com
TYPES Animation - Commercials - Direct-to-Video/DVD - Documentaries - Features - Made-for-TV/Cable Movies - Music Videos - Reality TV - TV Series
DEVELOPMENT Undone - Cliff Monsters - Interstate 101 - Guppies
PRE-PRODUCTION The Butchering Ghost
PRODUCTION Pandemic
POST PRODUCTION The Raft
CREDITS Unnoticed - The Unit - Employee of the Month - Hidalgo - Russia's Polikarpov I-16 - Peter Hurd Sketching WWII - Operation Sethos
SUBMISSION POLICY Query first by email

Shari Hamrick .Producer (310-849-1957)
David Sean Stringer .Director
Matt Neely .Director, Development
Anthony R. Fiore Jr. .Business Affairs Liason
Greg Clayton .Spirit Horse Australia (61-7-5538-8903)

SPITFIRE PICTURES
9348 Civic Center Dr., Mezzanine
Beverly Hills, CA 90210
PHONE .310-300-9000
FAX .310-300-9001
EMAIL .info@spitfirepix.com
WEB SITE .www.spitfirepix.com
TYPES Documentaries - Features
PRODUCTION My Generation: Who's Still Who (Documentary)
CREDITS No Direction Home: Bob Dylan - The Quiet American - K-19 - Adaptation - K-PAX - The Life of David Gale - National Security - Sliding Doors - Hilary and Jackie - Iris - Enigma - The Wedding Planner - Masked & Anonymous - Terminator 3

Guy East .Principal (UK)
Nigel Sinclair .Principal (LA)
Tobin Armbrust .President
Alex Brunner .VP (LA)
Ben Holden .Creative Executive (LA)
Paula Arnspiger .Executive Assistant to Nigel Sinclair (LA)
Edward Barlow .Executive Assistant to Guy East (UK)
Patrick Manasse .Creative Assistant (LA)
Annie Morse .Creative Assistant (LA)

SPRING CREEK PRODUCTIONS, INC.
335 N. Maple Dr., Ste. 209
Beverly Hills, CA 90210
PHONE .310-270-9000
FAX .310-270-9001
TYPES Features - Made-for-TV/Cable Movies
HAS DEAL WITH Warner Bros. Pictures
DEVELOPMENT A$$hole!: How I Got Rich & Happy by Not Giving a F#@% About You - Gaslight - Young Men & Fire
POST PRODUCTION The Blood Diamond - The Astronaut Farmer
CREDITS Rumor Has It - Monster-in-Law - Deliver Us From Eva - Iron Jawed Angels - Looney Tunes - Analyze This - Liberty Heights - The Perfect Storm - An Everlasting Piece - Bandits - Possession - Analyze That - Envy

Paula Weinstein .Producer
Len Amato .President (310-270-9080)
Jeffrey Levine .VP (310-270-9050)
Palak Patel .VP (310-270-9040)

SPYGLASS ENTERTAINMENT GROUP
10900 Wilshire Blvd., 10th Fl.
Los Angeles, CA 90024
PHONE . . . 310-443-5800
FAX . . . 310-443-5912
WEB SITE . . . www.spyglassentertainment.com
TYPES Direct-to-Video/DVD - Features - TV Series
HAS DEAL WITH Columbia Pictures - Touchstone Television
DEVELOPMENT Mute Witness - The Perfect Mile - Rat's Tale - Four Christmases - Baja 1000
PRODUCTION Balls of Fury - Underdog - Evan Almighty
POST PRODUCTION The Lookout - The Invisible
CREDITS Film: 8 Below - Memoirs of a Geisha - The Legend of Zorro - The Hitchhiker's Guide to the Galaxy - The Pacifier - Seabiscuit - Bruce Almighty - The Recruit - Shanghai Knights - The Count of Monte Cristo - The Sixth Sense - The Insider - Keeping the Faith

Gary Barber . . . Co-Chairman/CEO
Roger Birnbaum . . . Co-Chairman/CEO
Jonathan Glickman . . . President
Derek Evans . . . Executive VP, Production
Rebekah Rudd . . . Executive VP, Post Production
Karen Sortito . . . Executive VP, Worldwide Marketing
Jeffrey Chernov . . . Sr. VP, Physical Production
Cheryl Rodman . . . Sr. VP, Business & Legal Affairs
Erin Stam . . . VP, Production
Ivan Oyco . . . Director, Development
Kim Buttlar . . . Executive Director
Marlena Thomas . . . Executive Director

ST. AMOS PRODUCTIONS
3480 Barham Blvd., Ste. 108
Los Angeles, CA 90068
PHONE . . . 323-850-9872
TYPES Features - Made-for-TV/Cable Movies - TV Series
DEVELOPMENT Dillinger (Miniseries) - Meet Jane Doe (ABC) - Butterflies Are Free (CBS) - Mary Surratt - Saving Shakespeare - The Man That God Forgot - The Dog's Meow
CREDITS Jake in Progress (ABC) - The Beach Boys (ABC) - Grown Ups - Thieves (ABC) - The Virgin Chronicles (MTV) - Martin & Lewis (CBS)

John Stamos . . . Producer/Actor
Marc Aloxandcr . . . Producer/Writer/Development

STAMPEDE ENTERTAINMENT
3000 W. Olympic Blvd., Ste. 2222
Santa Monica, CA 90404
PHONE . . . 310-552-9977
EMAIL . . . info@stampede-entertainment.com
WEB SITE . . . www.stampede-entertainment.com
TYPES Features - TV Series
DEVELOPMENT Supernatural Law - Tremors 5
CREDITS City Slickers - Heart and Souls - Tremors 1-4 - Tremors (Series)

Nancy Roberts . . . Partner/Co-Chairman/CEO
S.S. Wilson . . . Partner/Co-Chairman
Brent Maddock . . . Partner
Greg Stevens . . . VP
Margaret Shields . . . No Title

STAR ENTERTAINMENT GROUP, INC.
13547 Ventura Blvd., Ste. 140
Sherman Oaks, CA 91423
PHONE . . . 818-988-2200
FAX . . . 818-988-2202
WEB SITE . . . www.findinghomemovie.com
TYPES Commercials - Features
DEVELOPMENT Shifting Sands - Young Warriors (Remake) - Memories of the Heart - Malibu High (Remake)
UPCOMING RELEASES Finding Home
CREDITS Young Warriors - Malibu High - Prima Donnas - Night Force - Don't Go Near the Park - The Great Skycopter Rescue - Lovely, but Deadly

Lawrence D. Foldes . . . Chairman
Victoria Paige Meyerink . . . President
Michael Sloan . . . Production Executive
Joe Kleinman . . . Director, Development
Sean Blodgett . . . Post Production Coordinator
Robert C. Rosen Esq. . . . Legal Counsel

STARBUCKS ENTERTAINMENT
2401 Utah Ave. South
Seattle, WA 98134
PHONE . . . 206-447-1575/800-782-7282
FAX . . . 206-447-0828
TYPES Features
CREDITS Akeelah and the Bee (A Starbucks Presentation) - Hail! Hail! Rock 'n' Roll (Home Video Release)
COMMENTS Additional offices in Los Angeles

Howard D. Schultz . . . Chairman
James L. Donald . . . President/CEO/Director
Ken Lombard . . . President, Entertainment
Michael Casey . . . Executive VP/CFO
Geoff Cottrill . . . VP, Marketing & Product
Don McKinnon . . . VP, Content Development
Alan Mintz . . . VP, Content Development
Tim Ziegler . . . Director, Content Development

DARREN STAR PRODUCTIONS
10202 W. Washington Blvd., Astaire Bldg., Ste. 2210
Culver City, CA 90232
PHONE .310-244-4000
FAX .310-244-0785
TYPES Features - TV Series
HAS DEAL WITH Sony Pictures Television
PRODUCTION Runaway (CW)
CREDITS Kitchen Confidential - Sex and the City - Miss Match - Grosse Pointe - The Street - Central Park West - Melrose Place - Beverly Hills, 90210

Darren Star .Producer/Writer (310-244-7898)
Susie Fitzgerald .Head, Development (310-244-7895)
Abram Hatch .VP (310-244-7876)
Meredith Barg .No Title (310-244-7813)
Elsa Jensen .Assistant to Abram Hatch (310-244-7876)
Erika Weinstein .Assistant to Susie Fitzgerald (310-244-7895)

STARRY NIGHT ENTERTAINMENT
975 Park Ave., Ste. 10-C
New York, NY 10028
PHONE .212-717-2750/818-895-4916
FAX .212-794-6150/818-895-8415
EMAIL .info@starrynightent.com
SECOND EMAIL .mailbox@starrynightent.com
WEB SITE .www.starrynightent.com
SECOND WEB SITE .www.starrynightentertainment.com
TYPES Features - TV Series
DEVELOPMENT Any Night - Leyendecker - A Severed Stage - Mothers and Sons - Two Hands
PRE-PRODUCTION Moscows
PRODUCTION Sherman's Way
CREDITS Rhapsody in Bloom - At First Sight - Two Guys Talkin' About Girls - Closer and Closer
COMMENTS West Coast office: 16931 Dearborn St., Northridge, CA 91343

Craig M. Saavedra .Partner (LA) (laoffice@starrynightent.com)
Michael Shulman .Partner (NY) (nyoffice@starrynightent.com)
Johnny Rowles .Creative Executive (LA) (johnny@starrynightent.com)

JANE STARTZ PRODUCTIONS, INC.
244 Fifth Ave., 11th Fl.
New York, NY 10001
PHONE .212-545-8910
FAX .212-545-8909
TYPES Animation - Direct-to-Video/DVD - Features - TV Series
DEVELOPMENT The Night Room - The Orphans Club - Lord of the Nutcracker Men - Judy Blume's Deenie - Wainscott Weasel - Princess Tales - The Tiger's Apprentice - Like Sisters on the Homefront - The Caterpillar Puzzle
PRE-PRODUCTION Mean Margaret
PRODUCTION The Last Day of Summer
CREDITS The Mighty - Indian in the Cupboard - The Magic Schoolbus - The Baby-Sitters Club - Tuck Everlasting - Ella Enchanted - We Are the Laurie Berkner Band

Jane Startz .President/Producer
Billy Mulligan .Director, Development

STATE STREET PICTURES
c/o Twentieth Century Fox
10201 W. Pico Blvd., Bldg. 52, Rm. 123
Los Angeles, CA 90064
PHONE .310-369-5099
FAX .310-369-8613
TYPES Features - TV Series
HAS DEAL WITH Twentieth Century Fox - Fox 2000
DEVELOPMENT College - My Ride with Gus - The Interrogator - Stephon's Corner - Ditch Day - Disco Sucks - Brandon T. Jackson Show - Bookies
CREDITS Feature: Beautyshop - Roll Bounce - Soul Food - Men of Honor - Barbershop 1&2; TV: Barbershop - Soul Food

Robert Teitel .Producer
George Tillman Jr. .Director
Rene Rigal .VP, Production & Development
Poppy Hanks .Director, Development
Chuck Hayward .Assistant to Producer
Ryan Jones .Assistant to VP
Jason Veley .Assistant to Director

***STATION 3**
9465 Wilshire Blvd., Ste. 335
Beverly Hills, CA 90212
PHONE .310-888-0082/212-245-3250
FAX .310-888-1848
TYPES Features - Made-for-TV/Cable Movies - Reality TV - TV Series
DEVELOPMENT Gardens of the Night - Killer Joe - Safety Glass

Edie Robb .Partner
R.D. Robb .Partner
Thomas Carter .Creative Executive
Kasra Ajir .Manager
Anne Woodward .Manager
Jill Stewart .Assistant
Vanessa Crase .Assistant

STEAMROLLER PRODUCTIONS, INC.
4117-1/2 Radford Ave.
Studio City, CA 91604
PHONE .818-505-6635
FAX .818-505-6636
EMAIL .steamrollerprod@aol.com
WEB SITE .www.stevenseagal.com
TYPES Direct-to-Video/DVD - Documentaries - Features - TV Series
DEVELOPMENT Under Siege 3 - Judas - Prince of Pistols
POST PRODUCTION Today You Die!
UPCOMING RELEASES Shadows of the Past - Harvester
CREDITS Black Dawn - Submerged - Into the Sun - The Glimmer Man - Fire Down Below - On Deadly Ground - Under Siege 1&2 - Above the Law - Steven Seagal's Aikido: The Path Beyond Thought - Exit Wounds - Half Past Dead - Out of Reach - Marked for Death - Mercenary
SUBMISSION POLICY Query via fax or mail first

Steven Seagal .CEO/Director/Writer/Producer/Actor
Phillip Goldfine .COO
Binh Dang .Production Executive
Tracy Irvine .Executive Assistant

THE HOWARD STERN PRODUCTION COMPANY

10 E. 44th St.
New York, NY 10017
PHONE .212-867-1200
FAX .212-867-2434

TYPES	Animation - Features - TV Series
DEVELOPMENT	Porky's - Rock 'n' Roll High School
PRODUCTION	Howard Stern: The High School Years (Spike TV)
CREDITS	The Howard Stern E! Show - Son of the Beach - Doomsday - The Howard Stern Radio Show
COMMENTS	Distribution deal with In Demand

Howard Stern .President
Don Buchwald .Agent
Mark Grande .Director, Development

SCOTT STERNBERG PRODUCTIONS

5254 Melrose Ave., Design Center, #401
Los Angeles, CA 90038
PHONE .323-960-4550
FAX .323-960-4555

TYPES	Documentaries - Reality TV - Specials - TV Series
PRODUCTION	That's the Question - Square-Off - My First Time
CREDITS	The Great Pretenders - Rock and Roll Jeopardy - Before They Were Stars - Sunday Morning Shootout

Scott Sternberg .Producer
Alison Powell .VP, Development
Brittany Dust .No Title

THE STEVENS COMPANY

c/o Jess Morgan & Company
5750 Wilshire Blvd., Ste. 590
Los Angeles, CA 90036-3697
PHONE .323-634-2400/202-416-7960
FAX .323-937-6532
EMAIL .newlibertydot@aol.com

TYPES	Documentaries - Features - Specials
DEVELOPMENT	American Requiem - Ghost of Jack Gilette - Chasing Rainbows
PRE-PRODUCTION	Kennedy Center Honors (CBS) - Christmas in Washington (TNT)
CREDITS	Thin Red Line - Kennedy Center Honors - Christmas in Washington - Sin
COMMENTS	East Coast office: JFK Center, Washington, DC 20566

George Stevens Jr. .Partner/Writer/Producer/Director
Michael Stevens .Partner/Writer/Producer/Director
Dottie McCarthy .Assistant to George Stevens Jr.

JOEL STEVENS ENTERTAINMENT

206 S. Brand Blvd.
Glendale, CA 91204
PHONE .818-509-5700
FAX .818-509-6734

TYPES	Features - Made-for-TV/Cable Movies - TV Series
DEVELOPMENT	David & the Devil - Liar - Yosemite National - Denmark: Hotel and Casino
CREDITS	Elvis & Me (ABC Miniseries)

Joel Stevens .President/CEO
John Will .Director, Development
Ian Baca .Talent & Development Associate

STICK FIGURE PRODUCTIONS

6 W. 18th St., 11th Fl.
New York, NY 10011
PHONE .212-277-3600
FAX .212-277-3611
EMAIL .stickfigureprod@aol.com
WEB SITE .www.stickfigureproductions.com

TYPES	Commercials - Documentaries - Features - Music Videos - Reality TV - TV Series
CREDITS	Loud Quiet Loud - What Remains - The Biz (AOL) - #1 Single - Amish in the City - Devil's Playground - Family Bonds - Slasher - The Cult of Cindy - Bounce: Behind the Velvet Rope - Willie Nelson: Still Is Still Moving - The Green Room

Steven Cantor .Director/Producer
Daniel Laikind .Executive in Charge of Development & Production
John Krasno .President
Matthew Galkin .VP, Development & Production
Pax Wassermann .Executive in Charge of Production
Joe Marino .Director, Development

STONE AND COMPANY ENTERTAINMENT

c/o Hollywood Center Studios
1040 N. Las Palmas Ave., Bldg. 1
Hollywood, CA 90038
PHONE .323-960-2599
FAX .323-860-3143
WEB SITE .www.stoneandcoent.com

TYPES	Animation - Documentaries - Reality TV - TV Series
CREDITS	1,000 Places to See Before You Die - Hijinks - The Mole - Celebrity Mole: Yucatan - The Joe Schmo Show - Fame - The Man Show - Shop 'til You Drop - Legends of the Hidden Temple - Oblivious - Ivana Young Man - American Dream Derby

Scott A. Stone .Principal
Jennifer Decker .Executive VP, Finance
Kevin Bloom .VP, Finance
Michael Frederick .VP, Development
Dan Helberg .VP, Business & Legal Affairs
Darren Kane .VP, Production
Rene Brar .Director, Development

STONE VILLAGE PICTURES, LLC

9200 Sunset Blvd., Ste. 520
West Hollywood, CA 90069
PHONE .310-402-5171
FAX .310-402-5172

TYPES	Features - TV Series
DEVELOPMENT	The Lincoln Lawyer - Tortilla Curtain - True Believer - Rififi - Ikiru - Risk Pool - Modoc - Vegas Heist - This Book Will Save Your Life
PRE-PRODUCTION	Love in the Time of Cholera
POST PRODUCTION	Penelope
COMPLETED UNRELEASED	Turistas
CREDITS	The Human Stain - Empire Falls - Las Vegas (NBC/DreamWorks)
COMMENTS	Books to movies

Scott Steindorff .Producer/President
Andrew Molasky .Partner
Danny Greenspun .Partner
Robin Greenspun .Partner
Michael Roban .COO/Head, Business Affairs
Scott LaStaiti .No Title
Valeska Ramet .No Title
Dylan Russell .No Title
Anne Quin-Harkin .No Title
Sara Geiger .No Title
Chris Peterson .No Title
Josh Mack .No Title
Ryan Michas .No Title

STONE VS. STONE

213 Rose Ave., The Firehouse, 2nd Fl.
Venice, CA 90291
PHONE .310-664-1999/212-334-8228

TYPES	Features - TV Series
CREDITS	Citizen X - The Negotiator - Gone in 60 Seconds
COMMENTS	Publishing company: Rugged Land Books, 401 West St., New York, NY 10014

Robert Stone .Producer/Writer
Webster Stone .Producer/Writer

STONEWORKS TELEVISION

4420 Hayvenhurst Ave.
Encino, CA 91436
PHONE .818-995-1585/310-475-3201
FAX .818-995-1677
WEB SITE .www.stoneworkstv.com

TYPES	Direct-to-Video/DVD - Documentaries - Made-for-TV/Cable Movies - Reality TV - Specials - TV Series
DEVELOPMENT	Shooters - Super Challenge - Untitled FBC Series - Billy Kindheart - Dead on the Bone - Divine Intervention
PRE-PRODUCTION	Palm Beach Project - Celebrity Kingpins - Stuntmen - Weekly World News
CREDITS	Terminal Invasion - Control Factor - Find a Fortune
SUBMISSION POLICY	No unsolicited submissions or drop-offs
COMMENTS	Development deal with FBC (Alternative Programming)

Chris Cusack .Partner/Producer
Chuck Simon .Partner/Producer

STORM ENTERTAINMENT

127 Broadway, Ste. 222
Santa Monica, CA 90401
PHONE .310-656-2500
FAX .310-656-2510
EMAIL .storment95@aol.com
WEB SITE .www.stormentertainment.com

TYPES	Documentaries - Features
PRE-PRODUCTION	Prisoners of the Sun - There Goes The Neighborhood
POST PRODUCTION	Lady Godiva Back in the Saddle - Outlanders
UPCOMING RELEASES	Heidi
COMPLETED UNRELEASED	These Foolish Things - Greyfriars Bobby - Played - Long Haul of A.I. Bezzerides (Documentary)
CREDITS	Modern Vampires - Hurlyburly - The Criminal - Fast Sofa - Big City Blues - Lovelife - Nevada - Glam - Heaven or Vegas
SUBMISSION POLICY	No unsolicited submissions

H. Michael Heuser .President/CEO
Kourosh Esmailzadeh .Director, International Distribution

*STORY AND FILM, INC.

2934-1/2 Beverly Glen Circle, Ste. 195
Los Angeles, CA 90077
PHONE .310-480-8833
EMAIL .info@storyandfilm.com
WEB SITE .www.storyandfilm.com

TYPES	Features - TV Series
DEVELOPMENT	Devil's Knot - Scanners - Children of the Roses
CREDITS	Monster - Behind the Smile - East of Havana
COMMENTS	No unsolicited material

Clark Peterson .Producer

STORYLINE ENTERTAINMENT

500 S. Buena Vista St., Old Animation Bldg., Ste. 3-C
Burbank, CA 91521
PHONE .818-560-2928
FAX .818-560-5145
EMAIL .info@storyline-entertainment.com
WEB SITE .www.storyline-entertainment.com

TYPES	Features - Made-for-TV/Cable Movies - TV Series
HAS DEAL WITH	New Line Cinema - Sony Pictures Television - Touchstone Television
DEVELOPMENT	If You Could See Me Now - The Bucket List
PRE-PRODUCTION	Hairspray
CREDITS	Empire - Chicago - The Music Man (ABC) - Annie - Footloose - The Beach Boys - The Three Stooges - Life with Judy Garland: Me and My Shadows - Martin and Lewis (CBS) - Lucy (CBS)

Craig Zadan .Executive Producer
Neil Meron .Executive Producer
Royce Bergman .Head, TV Development & Production
Travis Knox .Executive VP, Feature Development
Andrew Wang .Creative Executive, TV
Laine Bateman .Assistant to Mr. Zadan & Mr. Meron

STRIKE ENTERTAINMENT

3000 W. Olympic Blvd., Bldg. 5, Ste. 1250
Santa Monica, CA 90404
PHONE .310-315-0550
FAX .310-315-0560

TYPES	Features
HAS DEAL WITH	Universal Pictures
UPCOMING RELEASES	Let's Go to Prison - Children of Men
CREDITS	Slither - The Rundown - Dawn of the Dead - Bring It On Again

Marc Abraham .No Title
Tom Bliss .No Title
Eric Newman .No Title
Phil Altmann .No Title
Kristel Laiblin .No Title
Gabrielle Neimand .No Title
Mark Barclay .Assistant to Tom Bliss
Mary Browning .Assistant to Eric Newman
Jennifer Hoffmeister .Assistant to Marc Abraham

MEL STUART PRODUCTIONS, INC.

204 S. Beverly Dr., Ste. 109
Beverly Hills, CA 90212
PHONE .310-550-5872
FAX .310-550-5895
EMAIL .melfilm@aol.com
WEB SITE .www.melstuart.com

TYPES	Documentaries - Features - TV Series
UPCOMING RELEASES	The Hobart Shakespeare
CREDITS	Willy Wonka & the Chocolate Factory - Man Ray - Four Days in November - Running on the Sun - The Rise and Fall of the Third Reich - Wattsax - Ripley's Believe It or Not - W.S. Mervin: A Poet's View

Mel Stuart .President

STUDIOCANAL (US)

301 N. Canon Dr., Ste. 210
Beverly Hills, CA 90210
PHONE .310-247-0994/33-1-71-35-35-35
FAX .310-247-0998/33-1-71-35-11-98
WEB SITE .www.studiocanal.com

TYPES	Documentaries - Features
CREDITS	Unleashed - A Very Long Engagement - Notre Musique - Fear and Trembling - Bridget Jones: The Edge of Reason - Shaun of the Dead - Riding Giants - Love Actually - Vanilla Sky - Mulholland Drive - O Brother, Where Art Thou? - Central Station
COMMENTS	European office: Canal Eiffel, 1, Place du Spectacle, 92863 Issy les Moulineaux, France

Barbara DiNallo .No Title

STUDIOS INTERNATIONAL

9348 Civic Center Dr., Mezzanine
Beverly Hills, CA 90210
PHONE .310-300-9130
FAX .310-300-9098

TYPES	Features - Made-for-TV/Cable Movies - Miniseries - TV Series
HAS DEAL WITH	HBO Entertainment
CREDITS	Band of Brothers

Jennifer Jackson .No Title
Patrick Murray .No Title
Tony To .No Title

STYLE.

5750 Wilshire Blvd.
Los Angeles, CA 90036
PHONE .323-954-2400
FAX .323-954-2500/323-954-2662
WEB SITE .www.stylenetwork.com

TYPES	Reality TV - TV Series
DEVELOPMENT	Style Her Famous - Split Ends
CREDITS	Instant Beauty Pageant - Isaac - The Look for Less - Nigella Bites - You're Invited - Style Star - How Do I Look? - Clean House - Stripped - Whose Wedding Is It Anyway? - Modern Girl's Guide - Try My Life - My Celebrity Home - Trash to Treasure - Fashion Police
COMMENTS	Official channel for New York Fashion Week

Ted Harbert .President/CEO
Elaine Brooks .Sr. VP, Development
Salaam Coleman-Smith .Sr. VP, Programming

SUB ROSA PRODUCTIONS, INC.

8721 Santa Monica Blvd., Ste. 460
Los Angeles, CA 90069-4511
PHONE .323-650-4466
FAX .323-650-4448
EMAIL .sr@sub-rosa-productions.com
WEB SITE .www.sub-rosa-productions.com

TYPES	Features - Made-for-TV/Cable Movies - Mobile Content - Music Videos - Reality TV - TV Series
PRODUCTION	Floaters (TV Series) - Mundo Mario Lopez (Mobile Content) - All Acess with Kevin Mazur (Mobile Content)
UPCOMING RELEASES	2006 Tournament of Roses Parade (Mobile Content)
COMPLETED UNRELEASED	Built for Speed (Pilot)
CREDITS	Love at First Bite - Check Is in the Mail - How to Beat the High Cost of Living - People TV
SUBMISSION POLICY	No unsolicited submissions

Robin Krause .President/CEO/Producer
Karen G. Jackovich .President, Worldwide TV (914-833-2501)
Sherilyn Moore .Sr. VP, Development
Liz Amsden .VP, Production
Suzanne Cross .VP, Consumer Products
Charles Terry Goldstein Esq. .VP, Business Affairs
Ed Grosvenor .Chief IT/Consumer Products
Kit Westman .Head, Production
Jennifer Farrell .Head, Art Department
Jon Andersen .Creative Executive
Nikki Donahue .Creative Executive
A.D. Crane .Director, Operations
Tanya Sharma .Director, Online Marketing
Jarrett Widman .Director, New Media
Michelle Loparo .Development Assistant
Chris Cross .Assistant
Fleur Henry .Assistant

MIKE SULLIVAN PRODUCTIONS, INC.

2314 Michigan Ave.
Santa Monica, CA 90404-3930
PHONE .310-315-7315
FAX .310-582-0041
EMAIL .mikhsul@aol.com

TYPES	Direct-to-Video/DVD - Features - Made-for-TV/Cable Movies - Reality TV - TV Series
DEVELOPMENT	Mr. Carson's Opus - Forever Man - Penpals
COMPLETED UNRELEASED	Wannabe
CREDITS	Growing Pains - Just the Ten of Us - The Growing Pains Movie
SUBMISSION POLICY	No unsolicited materials

Mike Sullivan .President/Executive Producer
Paul Spadone .Sr. VP, Development
Craig Young .Director, Development

SUMMERLAND ENTERTAINMENT

17939 Chatsworth St., Ste. 260
Granada Hills, CA 91344
PHONE .818-368-3208
EMAIL .bruce@sumrland.com

TYPES	Features - Made-for-TV/Cable Movies - TV Series
DEVELOPMENT	The Girl from Hollywood - London, Texas - Pirates of Venus
CREDITS	MasterSpy: The Robert Hanssen Story - Trace Evidence - The Dream Team - Baywatch Nights - Nightmare Café - Fatal Memories - In the Heat of the Night - The Dirty Dozen - Police Story: The Freeway Killings - George Washington
SUBMISSION POLICY	No unsolicited material

Bruce A. Pobjoy .President/Producer
Brianne Michelle .VP, Development
Brooke Allison .Admistrative Assistant

SUMMERS ENTERTAINMENT

31708 Broad Beach Rd.
Malibu, CA 90265
PHONE .310-589-2189
FAX .310-457-1662
EMAIL .july4bu@charter.net

TYPES	Features - Miniseries
CREDITS	Slow Burn - Who Knew? - Stakeout 1&2 - Sandlot - Mystery Date - Vital Signs - Dogfight - DOA

Cathleen Summers .Producer

SUMMIT ENTERTAINMENT

1630 Stewart St., Ste. 120
Santa Monica, CA 90404
PHONE .310-309-8400/44-207-474-1724
FAX .310-828-4132/44-207-474-1725

TYPES	Features
DEVELOPMENT	Time Travel for Dummies - Untitled Doug Liman Project - Djinn - Nite - Countdown - Michael Clayton - Perfume - Miss Potter - Bridge to Terabithia
PRE-PRODUCTION	P2
POST PRODUCTION	Step up
UPCOMING RELEASES	The Alibi
CREDITS	Mr. & Mrs. Smith - Wrong Turn - Dot the I - Memento - Vanilla Sky

Patrick Wachsberger .President/CEO
Bob Hayward .COO
David Garrett .Executive VP (UK)
Erik Feig .President, Production & Acquisitions
Meredith Milton .Sr. Production Executive
Jean Song .Sr. Production Executive

SUNDANCE CHANNEL

1633 Broadway, 8th Fl.
New York, NY 10019
PHONE .212-654-1500
FAX .212-654-4738
EMAIL .feedback@sundancechannel.com
WEB SITE .www.sundancechannel.com

TYPES	Documentaries - TV Series
DEVELOPMENT	Change Agents
PRODUCTION	One Punk, Under God - Iconoclasts 2
POST PRODUCTION	The Hill
UPCOMING RELEASES	Swinging
CREDITS	The Drug Years (Documentary) - House of Boateng - The Human Behavior Experiments - Iconoclasts - Transgeneration - Slings and Arrows
COMMENTS	Programming includes multi-part documentary/docusoap, as well as hybrid/semi-scripted comedy and political satire projects

Larry Aidem .President/CEO
Stuart Benson .Executive VP/CFO
Laura Michalchyshyn .Executive VP, Programming & Marketing
Lynne Kirby .Sr. VP, Original Programming & Development
Samuel J. Paul .Director, Original Programming & Development

SUNLIGHT PRODUCTIONS
854-A Fifth St.
Santa Monica, CA 90403
PHONE 310-899-1522
FAX 310-899-1262
EMAIL . . . . info@sunlightproductions.com
WEB SITE . . . . www.sunlightproductions.com
TYPES Features - TV Series
POST PRODUCTION Reign O'er Me
CREDITS Man About Town - The Upside of Anger - The Search for John Gissing - The Mind of the Married Man (HBO) - Indian Summer - Crossing the Bridge - Londinium - The Sex Monster - Coupe de Ville
SUBMISSION POLICY Does not accept or read unsolicited submissions

Mike Binder . . . . Writer/Director/Actor
Jack Binder . . . . Producer
Rachel Zimmerman . . . . Co-Producer/Assistant to Mike Binder
Nat Dinga . . . . Assistant to the Producer

SUNRISE ENTERTAINMENT
4751 Wilshire Blvd., 3rd Fl.
Los Angeles, CA 90010
PHONE 323-549-4394
FAX 323-549-9821
TYPES Animation - Features - Made-for-TV/Cable Movies
DEVELOPMENT One of Us - The Year of Wonders - Tarzan - Books of Magic - Where's Waldo - Courtship of Eddie's Father - The Hookup Handbook
CREDITS Starsky and Hutch - Tomcats - The Family Man - Deep Blue Sea - Sweet Water - Mouse Hunt - The Mod Squad - Empire Records
SUBMISSION POLICY No unsolicited scripts

Alan Riche . . . . Partner
Peter Riche . . . . Partner
Jeanne Thompson . . . . Creative Executive
Michael Merlob . . . . Development Associate

SUNSET CANYON PRODUCTIONS
1120 E. Verdugo Ave.
Burbank, CA 91501
PHONE 818-559-2448
FAX 818-559-2481
EMAIL . . . . djc007x@earthlink.net
TYPES Features
CREDITS Stealing Sinatra (Showtime) - Neil Simon's The Goodbye Girl (TNT) - Comfort & Joy (Lifetime)

David J. Collins . . . . Executive Producer/Owner

SUNSWEPT ENTERTAINMENT
124 S. Lasky Dr., 1st Fl.
Beverly Hills, CA 90212
PHONE 310-859-1060
FAX 310-859-1070
TYPES Animation - Features
HAS DEAL WITH Twentieth Century Fox - Fox 2000
DEVELOPMENT Daniel Isn't Talking - The Book Thief - Percy Jackson - Jeremy Cabbage
CREDITS The Devil Wears Prada

Karen Rosenfelt . . . . President/Producer
Libby Shani . . . . Development Executive
Philip Hall . . . . Story Editor

SUNTAUR/ELSBOY ENTERTAINMENT
1581 N. Crescent Heights Blvd.
Los Angeles, CA 90046
PHONE 323-656-3800
EMAIL . . . . info@suntaurent.com
TYPES Documentaries - Features - Made-for-TV/Cable Movies - Miniseries - Theatre - TV Series
DEVELOPMENT TV: For Immediate Release (Sony TV); Features: Resurrection Men - Vamp Town (MM Productions) - The Party-Party (Infront Productions) - Impossible Dreams - The Steve Cabbler/Bali Bombing Story - Snow in April, Ray Qualey (Theatre) - Fish Out of Water (TV) - Red Xmas - Ushers - SpaGhetto Western
PRODUCTION Skills Like This
COMPLETED UNRELEASED Looking for Sunday
CREDITS On Thin Ice - A Force of One - The Octagon - Under One Roof (CBS, Series) - In Too Deep (Feature) - Maxie (Feature) - Laurel Avenue (HBO, Miniseries) - Grand Avenue (Miniseries) - Save the Dog (Disney Channel) - Casebusters
SUBMISSION POLICY No unsolicited material

Paul Aaron . . . . Writer/Producer/Director
James Waugh . . . . VP, Development
Matt Aldrich . . . . Development Assistant
Zac Sanford . . . . Assistant

SUPER DELICIOUS PRODUCTIONS
6121 Santa Monica Blvd., Ste. G
Los Angeles, CA 90038
PHONE 323-785-2660
FAX 323-785-2670
WEB SITE . . . . www.superdelicious.net
TYPES Commercials - Reality TV - TV Series
CREDITS MTV's The Reality Show - MTV's The '70s House - The Big Urban Myth Show - The Assistant (MTV)

Adam Cohen . . . . Principal
Cara Tapper . . . . Principal
Joanna Vernetti . . . . Principal
Jen Rowland . . . . Line Producer
Skye Wilson . . . . Production Manager
Phil Sternberg . . . . Executive Assistant

***SUPERB ENTERTAINMENT**
30 Rockefeller Plaza
New York, NY 10112
PHONE 212-664-3493
FAX 212-664-5450
EMAIL . . . . meryl.poster@nbcuni.com
TYPES Features - TV Series
HAS DEAL WITH NBC Universal Television Studio
DEVELOPMENT My Korean Deli (Feature) - Better Homes and Husbands (TV)

Meryl Poster . . . . Producer
Kate Schumaecker . . . . Director, Development
Jeanette Duffy . . . . Assistant

SUPERFINGER ENTERTAINMENT
2660 W. Olive Ave.
Burbank, CA 91505
PHONE .818-295-8013
FAX .818-295-5099
TYPES Animation - Documentaries - Features - Internet Content - Mobile Content - Reality TV - Specials - TV Series
HAS DEAL WITH HBO Entertainment
DEVELOPMENT Projects with New Wave Entertainment: Untitled Scripted Series for HBO - Lucked Out - Theatrical Stand-Up Concert Film Live from Boston Garden; Untitled Father & Son Film (Disney) - The Ex-Family (The Weinstein Company & New Wave Entertainment) - Dad Knap (Mandeville Pictures)
CREDITS Tourgasm - Vicious Circle

Dane Cook .President
Darryl McCauley .VP

RONALD SUPPA PRODUCTIONS, INC.
32063 Canterhill Pl.
Westlake Village, CA 91361-4817
PHONE .818-879-1383
EMAIL .rsprodinc@aol.com
TYPES Features - Reality TV
DEVELOPMENT Monty Cox's Killer Movie Animals
CREDITS Defense Play - Riding the Edge - Paradise Alley - Maui Heat

Ronald Suppa .Writer/Producer
Eric Harrington .VP, Development
Jolene Rae .VP, New Media

SWEENEY ENTERTAINMENT
8755 Lookout Mountain Ave.
Los Angeles, CA 90046
PHONE .323-822-3000
FAX .323-822-3020
TYPES Animation - Documentaries - Features - Made-for-TV/Cable Movies - TV Series
DEVELOPMENT Destiny - Camp Couture
CREDITS Wigstock: The Movie
SUBMISSION POLICY No unsolicited submissions

David Sweeney .Partner/Producer
Rob Schneider .Assistant

SYMBOLIC ACTION
11601 Wilshire Blvd., Ste. 750
PHONE .310-903-4949
FAX .310-903-4950
TYPES Animation - Direct-to-Video/DVD - Internet Content - Mobile Content

Dean Valentine .No Title
Scott Immergut .No Title
Colleen Lawler .No Title

SYMBOLIC ENTERTAINMENT
446 San Vicente Blvd., Ste. 106
Santa Monica, CA 90402
PHONE .310-899-1076/818-445-2521
EMAIL .cooper@symbolic-entertainment.com
SECOND EMAIL .jason@symbolic-entertainment.com
WEB SITE .www.symbolic-entertainment.com
TYPES Commercials - Features - Mobile Content - Music Videos
DEVELOPMENT Slow Motion Replay - Initial Intent - Dirty South
PRODUCTION Cosmic Radio
UPCOMING RELEASES Flourish
CREDITS The Beat - Zerophilia - The Nickel Children - Drone Virus

Jason Peterson .Executive Producer
BP Cooper .Executive Producer
Ian Bounds .Co-Producer
Logan Mulvey .Development

SYMPHONY PICTURES, INC.
6381 W. 80th Pl.
Los Angeles, CA 90045
PHONE .310-656-9040
FAX .310-656-9046
EMAIL .symphonypictures@sbcglobal.net
TYPES Features - Made-for-TV/Cable Movies - TV Series
DEVELOPMENT Factory Ride - Pegasus - Film School
PRE-PRODUCTION Warbirds
POST PRODUCTION Home of the Giants
CREDITS National Lampoon's Pucked - Seduced by a Thief - Clover Bend - Da - Nightbreaker - Judgment in Berlin - She Stood Alone: The Tailhook Scandal - Target Earth - Mickey and Dommy - Doomsday Man - Above Suspicion
SUBMISSION POLICY No unsolicited material

William R. Greenblatt .President
Tricia Pierce .Assistant to the Producer

SYNCHRONICITY PRODUCTIONS
6363 Santa Monica, 2nd Fl. West
Los Angeles, CA 90038
PHONE .310-246-1477/212-704-0515
FAX .310-274-1491
TYPES Animation - Documentaries - Features - Made-for-TV/Cable Movies - New Media - Syndication - Theatre - TV Series
CREDITS Holy Joe - In Pursuit of Honor - Element of Truth
COMMENTS East Coast office: 350 Fifth Ave., Ste. 2716, New York, NY 10118

Larry Peerce .No Title
Adam Peck .No Title

THE SYNDICATE

100 Universal City Plaza, Ste. 6148
Universal City, CA 91608
PHONE .818-733-2755
FAX .818-733-2754
EMAIL .info@syndicatela.com
WEB SITE .www.syndicatela.com
TYPES Direct-to-Video/DVD - Features - Reality TV
DEVELOPMENT Parallel - Cheerleader Island - In the Club
PRE-PRODUCTION Visioneers - Pawnhopping
CREDITS Pit Fighter - Unbeatable Harold - Chasing Ghosts - Ghost Game - Cult - Charlie
SUBMISSION POLICY No unsolicited submissions

James Henney .Partner
Henry Capanna .Partner
Scott Karp .Partner/Manager
Bryan Brucks .Manager
Ian Milne .Assistant to Mssrs. Capanna & Henney

TAE PRODUCTIONS/MEDEACOM PRODUCTIONS

4741 E. Palm Canyon Dr., Ste. 171
Palm Springs, CA 92264
PHONE .760-321-6683
FAX .760-328-3366
TYPES Direct-to-Video/DVD - Documentaries - Features - TV Series
DEVELOPMENT The Sun Is My Undoing - Warriors of the Rainbow: The Greenpeace Movie - Wealth & Power (PBS/KOCE) - Closer to Truth (Kuhn Foundation)
UPCOMING RELEASES The Directors/First Works (PBS/KOCE) - Terrorism: The Global War (Image Entertainment) - A Moment in Time (PBS/KOCE)
CREDITS Legendary Women (Image Entertainment) - Day of the Dead (Image Entertainment) - Harley-Davidson: The Spirit of America (PBS) - Operation Enduring Freedom (Lionsgate) - Crossing the Line (Lifetime) - Heaven & Earth (Warner Bros.) - Victory in the Desert: General Colin Powell (Lionsgate) - First Works 1&2 (Showtime/Rhino) - Princess Grace (ABC) - Terrorism: A World in Shadows (Series/The Discovery Channel)

Robert D. Kline .President/CEO
Stephanie Heredia .VP/Producer
Armando Diaz .VP, Production
Roger Diaz .VP, Internet
Johnnie Tidwell .Creative Affairs
Ann Kelly .Assistant to President/CEO

TAG ENTERTAINMENT, INC.

1333 2nd St., Ste. 240
Santa Monica, CA 90402
PHONE .310-260-3350
FAX .310-260-3351
EMAIL .info@tagentertainment.com
WEB SITE .www.tagentertainment.com
TYPES Features - Made-for-TV/Cable Movies
POST PRODUCTION Deal - Wild Stallion
CREDITS Supercross - No Place Like Home - Hansel & Gretel - Miracle Dogs 1&2 - The Santa Trap - Dumb Luck - The Retrievers - Castle Rock - Motocross Kids
COMMENTS Focus on family entertainment

Steve Austin .CEO/Chairman/Producer

TAGLINE PICTURES

9250 Wilshire Blvd., Ground Fl.
Beverly Hills, CA 90212
PHONE .310-595-1515
FAX .310-595-1505
TYPES Features - Made-for-TV/Cable Movies - TV Series
COMPLETED UNRELEASED Little Chenier
CREDITS Psych (USA) - Foster Hall (NBC)
SUBMISSION POLICY Must be submitted by agency
COMMENTS Management company is Thruline Entertainment

Chris Henze .No Title
J.B. Roberts .No Title
Ron West .No Title
Kelly Kulchak .President, Tagline Television
Sabrina Vito .Creative Executive
Willie Mercer .No Title

MARTIN TAHSE PRODUCTIONS

360 S. Burnside Ave., Ste. 5-L
Los Angeles, CA 90036
PHONE .323-965-5029
FAX .323-965-5039
EMAIL .nkhv@aol.com
TYPES Animation - Features - Made-for-TV/Cable Movies
DEVELOPMENT Make Someone Happy - The Boob Movie - You Don't Know Jack
CREDITS Kukla, Fran and Ollie - The Night Swimmers - Matters of the Heart - Words by Heart; Theatre: Oldest Living Confederate Widow Tells All

Martin Tahse .President
Michael Vodde .VP, Development

TAILFISH PRODUCTIONS

PO Box 491584
Brentwood, CA 90049
PHONE .310-453-4105
FAX .310-829-3908
EMAIL .kgolod@aol.com
TYPES Features - TV Series
DEVELOPMENT On Ice - Elevator - Body Brokers
PRE-PRODUCTION Earthbound
CREDITS Circus - Darkness Falls

James Gibb .Producer
Ksana Golod .Producer (310-289-0170, kgolod@aol.com)
Taylor Van Arsdale .Writer/Producer

TAILLIGHT TV
1223 17th Ave. South
Nashville, TN 37212
PHONE 615-385-1034
FAX 615-385-1024
EMAIL .....tomforrest@taillight.tv
WEB SITE .....www.taillight.tv
TYPES: Documentaries - Music Videos - Reality TV - Specials - TV Series
PRE-PRODUCTION: CMT Giants
PRODUCTION: CMT Cross Country - Toyota Summerfest Concert Series
CREDITS: 100 Greatest Duets of Country Music - Lynyrd Skynyrd's Super Bowl Saturday Night Special - CMT Music Awards Pre-Party - CMT Crossroads - 100 Greatest Songs of Country Music: The Concert - Most Wanted Live (Daily Live Show) - Keith Urban Spring Break Concert: Daytona Beach - LeAnn Rimes Live
COMMENTS: Specializes in televised live concerts and events, music documentaries and music videos

Tom Forrest .....President/Owner/Executive Producer
Chandra LaPlume .....VP/Owner/Executive Producer
Kristen Forrest .....Executive Producer
Elisa Sanders .....Head, Production
Koren Leamon .....Associate Producer/TV

TAKES ON PRODUCTIONS
1501 Broadway, #1614
New York, NY 10036
PHONE 212-354-4854
EMAIL .....takeson@mac.com
TYPES: Theatre - TV Series
CREDITS: Tracey Takes On - Tracey Ullman's Visible Panty Line - Ruby Romaine's Trailer Tales - Jerry Springer the Opera (Theatre)
COMMENTS: Distributor of 62 half-hour shows, 5 one-hour shows and 22 half-hour talk shows

Allan McKeown .....Chairman/CEO
Stephanie Cone Laing .....Producer

TALISMAN PACIFIC
20802 Hillside Dr.
Topanga, CA 90290
PHONE 310-455-2808/44-207-603-7474
FAX 44-207-602-7422
EMAIL .....talpacific@aol.com
TYPES: Features - TV Series
CREDITS: Rob Roy - Box of Moonlight - The Tic Code - The Secret Adventures of Jules Verne (TV)
COMMENTS: UK office: 5 Addison Pl., London W11 4RJ, United Kingdom

Steven Sherman .....No Title

TANNENBAUM COMPANY
c/o Warner Bros. Television
4000 Warner Blvd., Bldg. 146, Rm. 206
Burbank, CA 91522
PHONE 818-954-1113
FAX 818-954-7830
TYPES: Features - Reality TV - TV Series
HAS DEAL WITH: Warner Bros. Television Production
PRODUCTION: Delta Farce
CREDITS: Notes from the Underbelly - Two and a Half Men
SUBMISSION POLICY: No unsolicited material

Eric Tannenbaum .....Producer
Kim Tannenbaum .....Producer
Moe Jelline .....VP, Creative Affairs
Jason Wang .....Manager, Development
Lindsay Cohen .....Assistant to Eric Tannenbaum
Mike Dussault .....Assistant to Kim Tannenbaum

TAPESTRY FILMS, INC.
9328 Civic Center Dr., 2nd Fl.
Beverly Hills, CA 90210
PHONE 310-275-1191
FAX 310-275-1266
TYPES: Direct-to-Video/DVD - Features
HAS DEAL WITH: NBC Universal Television Studio - Twentieth Century Fox
DEVELOPMENT: Overtime - Electric God - Voodoo U. - A Horse's Tale - The Treehouse - Blowback - Schooled - Get a Life - Happy Campers - Great with Kids - Untitled David Dobkin - Paternity Leave
PRE-PRODUCTION: Employee of the Month
POST PRODUCTION: Van Wilder 2
CREDITS: Underclassman - Wedding Crashers - She's All That - The Wedding Planner - Pay It Forward - Serendipity - National Lampoon's Van Wilder - Point Break - A Kid in King Arthur's Court
COMMENTS: Includes newly formed TV division, Tapestry Television

Peter Abrams .....Producer/Partner
Robert L. Levy .....Producer/Partner
Andrew Panay .....Partner/Producer
Natan Zahavi .....Producer
Michael Schreiber .....VP, Development & Production
Terry Guerin .....Director, Literary Affairs (212-645-7114)
Sherwood Jones .....Post Production Supervisor
Alicia Hopkins .....Business Affairs
Katherine Blasband .....Creative Executive
Ted Boehm .....Development Assistant
Sarah Smith .....Assistant to Mr. Schreiber

TARYN PRODUCTIONS
431 S. Bedford Dr.
Beverly Hills, CA 90212
PHONE 323-525-2334
EMAIL .....mjblack/@aol.com
TYPES: Features - TV Series
CREDITS: Arli$$ - Major Dad - Black in Action
SUBMISSION POLICY: No unsolicited submissions

Bob Gold .....President
Mike Black .....Creative Executive
Larry Rudd .....Assistant

TAURUS ENTERTAINMENT COMPANY
c/o Hollywood Production Center
1149 N. Gower St., Ste. 250
Hollywood, CA 90038
PHONE 323-785-2500
FAX 323-785-2501
EMAIL . . . . taurusentco@yahoo.com
WEB SITE . . . . www.taurusec.com
TYPES — Direct-to-Video/DVD - Features - Made-for-TV/Cable Movies - Mobile Content - Theatre - TV Series
DEVELOPMENT — George Romero Presents Sharing Joy and Sorrow - Horror 103 - Creepshow 4
PRE-PRODUCTION — Children of the Lake
COMPLETED UNRELEASED — Creepshow 3
CREDITS — Killing Point - Mastermind - Morella - Hot Springs Hotel - Horror 101&102 - Lesson for an Assassin - Girls Fight Tonight - Museum of the Dead - Day of the Dead 2
COMMENTS — Also international distribution

Stanley E. Dudelson . . . . Chairman
James G. Dudelson . . . . President/CEO
Robert F. Dudelson . . . . President/CFO
Ana Clavell . . . . VP, Production & Post Production
Scott Dudelson . . . . Director, New Media
Stephen Kripner . . . . Director, Online Services
Cindy Stone . . . . Contracts Administration

TAYLOR MADE FILMS
1270 Stone Canyon Rd.
Los Angeles, CA 90077
PHONE 310-472-1763
FAX 310-472-8698
EMAIL . . . . tmadefilms@aol.com
TYPES — Documentaries - Features - TV Series
CREDITS — Moscow on the Hudson - Down and Out in Beverly Hills - The Tempest - Taking Care of Business - Moon Over Parador - Faithful

Geoffrey Taylor . . . . President/Producer

GRAZKA TAYLOR PRODUCTIONS
409 N. Camden Dr., Ste. 202
Beverly Hills, CA 90210
PHONE 310-246-1150
FAX 310-476-4186
EMAIL . . . . grazka@grazkat.com
TYPES — Documentaries - Features - Made-for-TV/Cable Movies
PRODUCTION — Forgiveness (Documentary)
CREDITS — Touched - The Burning Season - Tricks - The Operation - Voice in Exile - Rage - Mahalia Jackson - The Power and the Glory - Prophecies

Grazka Taylor . . . . Producer

MICHAEL TAYLOR PRODUCTIONS
2370 Bowmont Dr.
Beverly Hills, CA 90210
PHONE 213-821-3113/310-273-6040
FAX 213-740-3395/310-273-5698
EMAIL . . . . taycoprod@aol.com
TYPES — Features - Made-for-TV/Cable Movies - TV Series
DEVELOPMENT — Happy Holidays - Moving Elliott (Universal) - Once a Thief - Swiss Family Robinson - Warriors of Tsin - The Box - Before I Wake
PRE-PRODUCTION — Unforgettable
COMPLETED UNRELEASED — Copying Beethoven
CREDITS — Princess of Thieves - Instinct - Phenomenon 1&2 - The Hi-Line - Bottle Rocket - Mrs. Munck - Blue Steel - Hider in the House - Pursuit of D.B. Cooper - Last Embrace

Michael Taylor . . . . Producer
David Clawson . . . . Assistant
Yolanda Rodriguez . . . . Assistant

TBS
3500 W. Olive Ave., 15th Fl.
Burbank, CA 91505
PHONE 818-977-5500/404-827-1700
WEB SITE . . . . www.tbs.com
TYPES — Specials - TV Series
DEVELOPMENT — Late Night Buffet - My Thoughts Exactly
PRODUCTION — My Boys - 10 Items or Less
COMMENTS — Atlanta office: 1050 Techwood Drive NW, Atlanta, GA 30318

Mark Lazarus . . . . President, Turner Entertainment Group (Atlanta)
Steve Koonin . . . . Executive VP/COO, TBS & TNT (Atlanta)
Michael Wright . . . . Sr. VP, Original Programming, TBS & TNT (Burbank)
Sandra Dewey . . . . Sr. VP, Original Programming, TBS & TNT (Burbank)
Ken Schwab . . . . Sr. VP, Programming, TBS & TNT (Atlanta)
Nina Howie . . . . VP, Comedy Development, TBS (Burbank)
Lillah McCarthy . . . . VP, Series Programming, TBS & TNT (Burbank)
Sharon Byrens . . . . VP, Development , Sponsored Programming, TBS & TNT (Burbank)
David Hudson . . . . VP, Production & Production Finance, Sponsored Programming, TBS & TNT (Burbank)
Patrick Kelly . . . . VP, Business Affairs, TBS & TNT (Burbank)
Mark Taylor . . . . VP, Production, TBS & TNT (Burbank)
John Palmerton . . . . VP, Business Affairs, TBS & TNT (Burbank)
Bill Phillips . . . . VP, Production, TBS & TNT (Burbank)
Mary Lawler . . . . Sr. Director, Business Affairs, TBS & TNT (Burbank)
Martine Shahar . . . . Sr. Director, Business Affairs, TBS & TNT (Burbank)
Clinton Wilburn . . . . Director, Business Affairs (Burbank)
Gwenn Smith . . . . Director, Post Production & Production, TBS & TNT (Burbank)
Kristie Moomey . . . . Manager, Production & Post Production, TBS & TNT (Burbank)
Anne Smith . . . . Assistant to Mark Lazarus (Atlanta)
Priscilla Pierson . . . . Assistant to Steve Koonin (Atlanta)
Samantha Poverelli . . . . Assistant to Michael Wright (Burbank)
Lisa Clifton . . . . Assistant to Sandra Dewey (Burbank)
Barbara Lancaster . . . . Assistant to Ken Schwab (Atlanta)

TEAM TODD

c/o Revolution Studios
2900 W. Olympic Blvd.
Santa Monica, CA 90404
PHONE ....See Below
FAX 310-255-7222
TYPES Features - Made-for-TV/Cable Movies
HAS DEAL WITH Revolution Studios
DEVELOPMENT Finishing School - Unexplainables - The Ex Factor - Accidental Husband - A Taxonomy of Barnacles - The High Impact Infidelity Diet - Enlisted - Grandma Wars - 99 Problems
POST PRODUCTION Across the Universe
CREDITS Zoom - Prime - Must Love Dogs - Memento - Boiler Room - Austin Powers 1-3 - If These Walls Could Talk 1&2
SUBMISSION POLICY By referral only

Suzanne Todd ....Producer (310-255-7265)
Jennifer Todd ....Producer (310-255-7277)
Patrick Brennan ....Production Assistant
Christine Davila ....Production Assistant

TEITELBAUM ARTISTS GROUP

8840 Wilshire Blvd.
Beverly Hills, CA 90211
PHONE 310-358-3250
FAX 310-358-3251
TYPES Features - TV Series
DEVELOPMENT Untitled Rick Reynolds Project
PRE-PRODUCTION Bonjour, Monsieur Shlomi
PRODUCTION Happiness: A One Man Show
CREDITS Bonds of Love (CBS/MOW) - Valdez (NBC/Pilot) - Life...and Stuff (CBS) - Hacienda Heights (NBC/Pilot)

Mark Teitelbaum ....President
Cassandra Troy ....Assistant

TELEMUNDO NETWORK

2290 W. Eighth Ave.
Hialeah, FL 33010
PHONE 305-884-8200/800-688-8851
WEB SITE ....www.telemundo.com
SECOND WEB SITE ....telemundo.yahoo.com
TYPES Specials - TV Series
DEVELOPMENT Zorro: La Espada y la Rosa - Marina - Dame Chocolate - Madre Luna - Cuatro Rosas - Buena Fortuna - Vas o No Vas - Seguro y Urgente - El Gran Show
CREDITS Primetime: La Tormenta - Tierra de Pasiones - Corazón Partido - Decisiones: Casos Extraordinarios - Decisiones; Daytime: Cotorreando - 12 Corazones - Sra. León - Caso Cerrado - Laura - Al Rojo Vivo con María Celeste; News: Noticiero Telemundo - Sin Fronteras; Sports: Titulares Telemundo - Titulares y Más - Ritmo Deportivo - Boxeo Telemundo
COMMENTS Recently launched Estudios Mexicanos Telemundo (Production Studio in Mexico) and Palmas 26 (Broadcast TV); Novelas, News, Sports; West Coast office: 100 Universal City Plaza, City Walk Bldg. 4525, Ste. 2A, Universal City, CA 91608, phone: 818-622-4096

Don Browne ....President, Telemundo
Ibra Morales ....President, Telemundo Television Stations
Patricio Wills .....Head, Production, Telemundo/President, Telemundo-RTI
Macos Santana ....Head, Development, Telemundo
Ramón Escobar ....Sr. Executive VP, Entertainment
Jorge Hidalgo ....Sr. Executive VP, News & Sports
Antoinette Zel ....Sr. Executive VP, Network Strategy
Steven Mandala ...Sr. VP, Sales & Marketing, Telemundo & NBC Universal Networks
Peter Blacker ....Sr. VP, Digital Management
Millie Carrasquillo ....Sr. VP, Research
Glenn Dryfoos ....Sr. VP/General Counsel
Emilce Elgarresta ....Sr. VP, Entertainment Specials
Ann Gaulke ....Sr. VP, Affiliate Relations
Adriana Ibañez ....Sr. VP, Scheduling
Mimi Belt ....VP, Artistic Development
Joe Bernard ....VP, Network Sales, Mun2 Television
Berta Castaner ....VP, News, Telemundo Stations Group
Dennis Dunphy ....VP, Network Sales (Chicago)
Mike Gillespie ....VP, Network Sales (Dallas)
Gian Pablo Kates ....VP, Network Sales (Miami)
Sylvia Reed ....VP, Network Sales (LA)
Alfredo Richard ....VP, Corporate Communications
Gerardo Oyola ....Publicist, Sports & News
Elizabeth Sanjenis ....Publicist, Corporate News
Biana Toledo-Arencibia ....Web Editor, Telemundo Media Village

TELEPICTURES PRODUCTIONS

3500 W. Olive Ave., 10th Fl.
Burbank, CA 91505
PHONE .818-972-0777
WEB SITE .www.telepicturestv.com
TYPES TV Series
CREDITS The Tyra Banks Show - Showtime at the Apollo - Judge Mathis - ElimiDate - Extra - The Ellen DeGeneres Show - The People's Court - The Dr. Keith Ablow Show - TMZ.com

Jim Paratore .President
Hilary Estey-McLoughlin .Executive VP/General Manager
David M. Benavente .Sr. VP, Finance & Administration
David Decker .Sr. VP, Business & Legal Affairs
Lisa Hackner .Sr. VP, Development
Kevin Hamburger .Sr. VP, Production
Sheila Bouttier .VP, Programming
Brett Bouttier .VP, New Business & Sales Strategy
Chris Circosta .VP, Production
James V. Dorgan .VP, Business & Legal Affairs
Laura Danford Mandel .VP, Publicity
David McGuire .VP, Development
Vivienne Vella .VP, Legal & Business Affairs
David Zaccaria .VP/Creative Director, On-Air Promotions

TEMPEST ENTERTAINMENT

1920-1/2 N. Kenmore Ave.
Los Angeles, CA 90027
PHONE .323-653-1757
FAX .323-667-0525
EMAIL .info@tempestfinancing.com
WEB SITE .www.tempestfinancing.com
TYPES Animation - Features
DEVELOPMENT Northern Borders - Irene & Willie - Bacon - In Youth Is Pleasure
CREDITS Education of Little Tree - Chicken Run - Grey Owl - Snow in August
COMMENTS Deal with Allied Filmmakers

Lenny Young .President
Andrew Gould .Director, Development

TEMPESTA FILMS

c/o Starr and Co.
850 Third Ave.
New York, NY 10019
PHONE .212 787 5578
TYPES Features
DEVELOPMENT Mary Queen of Scots
POST PRODUCTION The Good Night
CREDITS Vanity Fair - Shakespeare in Love - Emma

Donna Gigliotti .Producer

TEMPLE HILL PRODUCTIONS

9255 Sunset Blvd., Ste. 801
Los Angeles, CA 90069
PHONE .310-270-4383
FAX .310-270-4395
TYPES Features
HAS DEAL WITH New Line Cinema
DEVELOPMENT Paper Wings
UPCOMING RELEASES Nativity
SUBMISSION POLICY No unsolicited submissions

Marty Bowen .Partner
Wyck Godfrey .Partner
Dena Twain .Assistant to Marty Bowen
Elek Hendrickson .Assistant to Wyck Godfrey

NANCY TENENBAUM FILMS

21 Wright St.
Westport, CT 06880
PHONE .203-221-6830
FAX .203-221-6832
EMAIL .ntfilms2@aol.com
SECOND EMAIL .shadygrove326@yahoo.com
TYPES Animation - Features
DEVELOPMENT The Winnowers - The Flip Side - The Bargain - The Truest Story of a Girl Ever Told - The Scary Boys
PRE-PRODUCTION Horror Hotel - Carsick - Life of the Party
CREDITS Meet the Fockers - Meet the Parents - The Daytrippers - Mac - The Rapture - sex, lies and videotape

Nancy Tenenbaum .President
Meredith Hall .Director, Development
Lyndsy Celestino .Assistant
Elke Pellicano .Assistant

TENTH PLANET PRODUCTIONS

833 N. La Cienega Blvd., Ste. 200
Los Angeles, CA 90069
PHONE .310-659-8001
FAX .310-659-8029
WEB SITE .www.tenthplanet.net
TYPES Specials
CREDITS Shelter from the Storm: A Concert for the Gulf Coast - Comedy Central Roast of Pamela Anderson - Dave Attell's Insomniac Tour - MTV Movie Awards - Pepsi SMASH - America: A Tribute to Heroes - Rock and Roll Hall of Fame Induction Ceremony - Countdown to Oscars® 2004 - The Nick and Jessica Variety Hour - Chris Rock: Never Scared - Ellen DeGeneres: Here and Now - An Evening with the Dixie Chicks - Super Bowl XXXVII Halftime Show - NFL Kickoff Live - A Very Special Christmas From Washington, DC - VH1 Fashion Awards

Joel Gallen .No Title
Peggy Yen .No Title
Charlotte Dunnam .No Title

TEOCALLI ENTERTAINMENT

6001 Creekwood Pass
Spring Branch, TX 78070
PHONE 830-228-5950
FAX 830-228-5904
WEB SITE ....www.needtovent.com
TYPES: Animation - Direct-to-Video/DVD - Documentaries - Features - Made-for-TV/Cable Movies - Specials - TV Series
DEVELOPMENT: Gaylord, The Penguin
UPCOMING RELEASES: False River
COMPLETED UNRELEASED: A Circle on the Cross
CREDITS: The Legend of Billy the Kid - The Radicals - The Top of the Bottom Half: An Evening with the Keeper of All Knowledge - Billy Galvin
SUBMISSION POLICY: No unsolicited submissions

Robert A. Nowotny ....President
Lynda Lorraine ....Development Executive

ARIELLE TEPPER PRODUCTIONS

1501 Broadway, Ste. 1301
New York, NY 10036
PHONE 212-944-9696
FAX 212-944-8999
EMAIL ....info@atpnyc.com
WEB SITE ....www.atpnyc.com
TYPES: Theatre
CREDITS: Feature: 30 Days; Theatre: SPAMALOT - The Pillowman - Democracy - A Raisin in the Sun - Jumpers - A Class Act - Hollywood Arms - The Last Five Years - Freak - Sandra Bernhard: I'm Still Here... Damn It! - James Joyce's The Dead - Harlem Song - Bounce - De La Guarda - Villa Villa - Goodnight Children Everywhere; London: Guys & Dolls - Mary Stuart

Arielle Tepper ....Producer
Holly Ferguson ....Executive Assistant to Arielle Tepper
Sarah Bagley ....Literary Assistant
Elisabeth Ford ....Office Manager

TERRA FIRMA FILMS

100 Universal City Plaza, Bungalow 5164
Universal City, CA 91608
PHONE 818-777-4457
FAX 818-733-4289
TYPES: Features
HAS DEAL WITH: Universal Pictures
CREDITS: American Pie 1&2 - American Wedding

Adam Herz ....Writer/Producer (818-777-5487)
Greg Lessans ....Co-President (818-777-9545)
Josh Shader ....Co-President (818-777-4771)
Craig Ferguson ....No Title (818-777-7197)

THIS IS THAT CORPORATION

435 W. 19th St., 4th Fl.
New York, NY 10011
PHONE 212-994-8455
TYPES: Documentaries - Features - Made-for-TV/Cable Movies
HAS DEAL WITH: Svensk Filmindustri, AB - Village Roadshow Pictures
DEVELOPMENT: The Children's March - Coup de Tat - The Fall of Rome - Florence - Fruitcake - I, Fatty - The Listener - Mondo Beyondo - Mothertrucker - Not Iris - The Passenger - The Russian Debutante's Handbook - The Second Wife - Sector 7 - A Slight Trick of the Mind - Untitled Todd Solondz Project - A Child's Book of True Crime - A Very Private Gentleman - Continental Drift - Adventureland - The City
PRODUCTION: Untitled Pastor Brothers Project - Untitled Alan Ball Project - Trainwreck: My Life as an Idiot - The Sleep Dealer - The Savages
UPCOMING RELEASES: Fay Grim
CREDITS: Fast Track - The Hawk Is Dying - The Devil & Daniel Johnson - Thumbsucker - The Door in the Floor - Eternal Sunshine of the Spotless Mind - 21 Grams - American Splendor - A Dirty Shame - Friends with Money
SUBMISSION POLICY: No unsolicited material

Ted Hope ....Partner/Producer
Anthony Bregman ....Partner/Producer
Anne Carey ....Partner/Producer
Diana Victor ....Partner/Head, Business Affairs
Stefanie Azpiazu ....Production/Creative Executive
Kara Blanchard ....Production/Creative Executive
Claire Pacacha ....Production/Creative Executive
Vinay Singh ....Director, Operations

LARRY THOMPSON ORGANIZATION

9663 Santa Monica Blvd., Ste. 801
Beverly Hills, CA 90210
PHONE 310-288-0700
FAX 310-288-0711
EMAIL ....ltbeverlyhills@aol.com
WEB SITE ....www.larrythompsonorg.com
SECOND WEB SITE ....www.projectriseandshine.com
TYPES: Features - Made-for-TV/Cable Movies - New Media - Reality TV - Syndication - TV Series
DEVELOPMENT: Project Rise & Shine
PRODUCTION: Celebrity Home Video - Little Girl Lost
CREDITS: Lucy & Desi: Before the Laughter - Crimes of Passion - The Woman He Loved - And the Beat Goes On: The Sonny & Cher Story - Murder in the Mirror - Iron Chef USA: Showdown in Las Vegas - A Date with Darkness: The Trial and Capture of Andrew Luster

Larry Thompson ....Chairman/CEO
Robert G. Endara II ....Director, Development
Kelly Thompson ....Director, Development

THOUSAND WORDS

110 S. Fairfax Ave., 3rd Fl.
Los Angeles, CA 90036
PHONE . . . . See below
FAX 323-936-4701
EMAIL . . . . info@thousand-words.com
WEB SITE . . . . www.thousand-words.com
TYPES: Features
DEVELOPMENT: The Missionary Position - The Edukators (Remake)
POST PRODUCTION: The Dog Problem
UPCOMING RELEASES: Right at Your Door
CREDITS: A Scanner Darkly - The Clearing - The United States of Leland - Waking Life - Requiem for a Dream - Saturn

Palmer West . . . . Co-President/Founder (323-936-4700)
Jonah Smith . . . . Co-President (323-936-4700)
Jesse Johnston . . . . Director, Development (323-936-4702)
Stephanie Lewis . . . . Creative Executive (323-936-4702)
Erin Hagerty . . . . Assistant (323-936-4700)

THREE STRANGE ANGELS, INC.

8750 Wilshire Blvd., Ste. 300 East
Beverly Hills, CA 90211
PHONE 310-601-2291
FAX 310-601-2298
TYPES: Features
HAS DEAL WITH: Mandate Pictures
UPCOMING RELEASES: Stranger Than Fiction
CREDITS: Nanny McPhee

Lindsay Doran . . . . Producer

THRESHOLD ENTERTAINMENT

1649 11th St.
Santa Monica, CA 90404
PHONE 310-452-8899
FAX 310-452-0736
EMAIL . . . . info@threshold-digital.com
WEB SITE . . . . www.thresholdentertainment.com
SECOND WEB SITE . . . . www.threshold-digital.com
TYPES: Animation - Commercials - Direct-to-Video/DVD - Features - TV Series
DEVELOPMENT: Mortal Kombat: Krusades - Pussy Cat Hustle - 6th Extinction
PRODUCTION: Food Fight!
CREDITS: Beowulf - Mortal Kombat 1-3
COMMENTS: Digital entertainment production

Larry Kasanoff . . . . Producer/Chairman/CEO
George Johnsen . . . . CTO
Joshua Wexler . . . . CIO
Kristy Scanlan . . . . VP, Development

THUNDER ROAD PICTURES

4000 Warner Blvd., Bldg. 81, Ste. 114
Burbank, CA 91522
PHONE 818-954-3130
FAX 818-954-3321
TYPES: Features - TV Series
HAS DEAL WITH: Warner Bros. Pictures
DEVELOPMENT: Sharky's Machine - Clash of the Titans (Remake) - Arrow - Untitled Bill Johnson Feature
UPCOMING RELEASES: We Are Marshall
CREDITS: Firewall - Alexander the Great - Welcome to Mooseport - Basic - K-19

Basil Iwanyk . . . . No Title
Mary Viola . . . . No Title
Viruna Cutler . . . . No Title
Erica Lee . . . . No Title
Rick Benattar . . . . No Title

THUNDERBIRD PICTURES

29120 Medea Ln., #1314
Agoura Hills, CA 91301
PHONE 310-962-8760
EMAIL . . . . thunderbirdpix@aol.com
TYPES: Documentaries - Features - TV Series
DEVELOPMENT: Untitled System of a Down Project
UPCOMING RELEASES: Screamers (BBC)
CREDITS: Naked Movie - Shadow Hours - Body and Soul - Champions

Peter McAlevey . . . . President

TIARA BLU FILMS

211 S. Spalding Dr., #103N
Beverly Hills, CA 90212
PHONE 310-282-8230
TYPES: Features - Made-for-TV/Cable Movies - Reality TV - TV Series
CREDITS: Take the Lead - After Hours with Daniel - Knights of the South Bronx (A&E) - Narc - Baseball Wives (HBO) - Very Bad Things - The Proposition - Operation Dumbo Drop - Separate Lives - Holy Matrimony - Body Language (HBO) - Hider in the House - Fear - Near Dark - The Kindred

Diane Nabatoff . . . . Producer

TIDEWATER ENTERTAINMENT, INC.

824 S. Wooster St., Ste. 104
Los Angeles, CA 90035
PHONE 310-855-9110
FAX 310-855-9110
EMAIL . . . . william_unger@hotmail.com
TYPES: Features - TV Series
DEVELOPMENT: No-Man's Land
CREDITS: Excellent Cadavers - Life Size - Crimson Tide - True Romance - The Fan

Bill Unger . . . . President

TIG PRODUCTIONS, INC.

4450 Lakeside Dr., Ste. 225
Burbank, CA 91505
PHONE 818-260-8707
FAX 818-260-0440
TYPES: Features
DEVELOPMENT: Horizon - A Little War of Our Own - Modoc
POST PRODUCTION: Mr. Brooks
CREDITS: Open Range - Thirteen Days - Dances with Wolves - The Bodyguard - Wyatt Earp - Message in a Bottle - Head Above Water - Encore Presentation: 500 Nations
SUBMISSION POLICY: Through agent only

Kevin Costner . . . . Partner
Robin Jonas . . . . Executive VP
Jasa Abreo . . . . Creative Executive

TIMELINE FILMS
9725 Culver Blvd.
Culver City, CA 90232-2739
PHONE 310-287-3702
FAX 310-287-1370
EMAIL . . . . . hugh@timelinefilms.com
WEB SITE . . . . . www.timelinefilms.com

TYPES	Documentaries
DEVELOPMENT	Pearl White - Uncle Tom's Cabin - Fire and Ice - City Builders - Hollywood Scandals of 1922 - Mermaids
POST PRODUCTION	Lionel Hampton
COMPLETED UNRELEASED	The Woman with the Hungry Eyes: The Life of Theda Bara
CREDITS	The Olive Thomas Collection - The Hidden Art of Hollywood - Captured on Film: True Story of Marion Davies - Clara Bow: Discovering the "It" Girl - Louise Brooks: Looking for Lulu - The DeMille Dynasty - Yosemite - Complicated Women (TCM)

Hugh Munro Neely . . . . . Owner/Producer
Andi Hicks . . . . . Producer
Francie Neely . . . . . Producer

THE STEVE TISCH COMPANY
10202 W. Washington Blvd., Astaire Bldg., 3rd Fl.
Culver City, CA 90232
PHONE 310-244-6612
FAX 310-204-2713

TYPES	Features
CREDITS	Long Kiss Goodnight - Forrest Gump - The Postman - American History X - Corrina, Corrina - Lock, Stock and Two Smoking Barrels - Snatch - Risky Business

Steve Tisch . . . . . Chairman (310-244-6612)
Kim Skeeters . . . . . VP, Administration & Finance (310-244-6619)
Lacy Boughn . . . . . Assistant to Steve Tisch (310-244-6620)

TLC
c/o Discovery Networks, U.S.
One Discovery Pl.
Silver Spring, MD 20910-3354
PHONE 240-662-2000
FAX 240-662-1845
EMAIL . . . . . firstname_lastname@discovery.com
WEB SITE . . . . . www.discovery.com

TYPES	Documentaries - TV Series
CREDITS	Trading Spaces - Miami Ink - Tuckerville - Overhaulin' - What Not to Wear - While You Were Out - Little People, Big World

David Abraham . . . . . Executive VP/General Manager, TLC & Discovery Home Channel
Christian Drobnyk . . . . . Sr. VP, Programming & Development, TLC
Kristin Brown . . . . . VP, Communications, TLC
Joan Harrison . . . . . VP, Development, TLC

TLC ENTERTAINMENT
c/o CBS Studio Center
4024 Radford Ave.
Studio City, CA 91604-2101
PHONE 818-655-6155
FAX 818-655-6254
EMAIL . . . . . tlc@tlcentertainment.com
WEB SITE . . . . . www.tlcentertainment.com

TYPES	Animation - Direct-to-Video/DVD - Features - TV Series
DEVELOPMENT	J-Files
POST PRODUCTION	Paloozaville
CREDITS	The Kids' Ten Commandments - McGee and Me! - Secret Adventures - The ALL NEW Captain Kangaroo - Mister Moose's Fun Time - The Christmas Lamb - The Legend of the Three Trees
SUBMISSION POLICY	No unsolicited material
COMMENTS	Focus on kids' and family entertainment

George Taweel . . . . . Co-Founder/Partner
Rob Loos . . . . . Co-Founder/Partner
Ryan Sandberg . . . . . Assistant to Producer

TMC ENTERTAINMENT
12200 W. Olympic Blvd., Ste. 470
Los Angeles, CA 90064
PHONE 310-806-4400
FAX 310-806-4401
EMAIL . . . . . contact@tmcent.tv
WEB SITE . . . . . www.tmcent.tv

TYPES	Animation - Documentaries - Miniseries - Reality TV - Specials - TV Series
DEVELOPMENT	The Route to Christianity - Noah's Arch - Future Quest - Loggers
CREDITS	Walking the Bible: A Journey by Land Through the Five Books of Moses - Zoo Diaries - The Invisible War - Curse of the Hope Diamond - Space Tech - Private Eyes: Undercover & Would You Believe It?
SUBMISSION POLICY	By email
COMMENTS	TMC Docs, distribution division; Production deal with Maya Vision International (UK)

Drew Levin . . . . . CEO
Tip McPartland . . . . . VP, Production & Development
Marc Kunis . . . . . VP/Controller

TOKYOPOP INC.

5900 Wilshire Blvd., Ste. 2000
Los Angeles, CA 90036
PHONE .323-692-6700
FAX .323-692-6701
EMAIL .susanh@tokyopop.com
WEB SITE .www.tokyopop.com

TYPES: Animation - Direct-to-Video/DVD - Features - TV Series
DEVELOPMENT: Pet Shop of Horrors - Mysterians - Lament of the Lamb - Bizenghast - Princess Ai - Peach Fuzz - @Large - Battle Vixens - Arm of Kanon - Juror 13 - I Luv Halloween - Samurai Girl - A Midnight Opera - The Dreaming
PRE-PRODUCTION: Priest
CREDITS: Rave Master - Reign: The Conqueror - Inital D - Street Fury - GTO - Brigadoon - Marmelade Boy - Spring & Chaos - Saint Tail - Vampire Princess Miyu

Stuart J. Levy .Chairman
John Parker .President/COO
Mike Kiley .Publisher
Bill Josey .General Counsel/VP, Business Affairs
Victor Chin .VP, Inventory Control
Steve Galloway .VP, Film & TV
Ron Klamert .VP, Production & Manufacturing
Susan Hale .Director, Public Relations
Jeremy Ross .Director, Editiorial

TOLLIN/ROBBINS PRODUCTIONS

4130 Cahuenga Blvd., Unit 305
Toluca Lake, CA 91602
PHONE .818-755-3000
FAX .818-766-8488
WEB SITE .www.tollinrobbins.com

TYPES: Documentaries - Features - TV Series
HAS DEAL WITH: Walt Disney Pictures/Touchstone Pictures - NBC Universal Television Studio
PRE-PRODUCTION: Wild Hogs
PRODUCTION: The Real Rocky (Doc)
CREDITS: Dreamer - Coach Carter - Hardwood Dreams - The Show - Big Fat Liar - Hardball - Summer Catch - Varsity Blues - Good Burger - Smallville - Inconceivable - Arli$$ - The Nick Cannon Show - The Nightmare Room - All That - The Amanda Show - What I Like About You - I'm with Her - One Tree Hill - The Perfect Score - Radio - Hardwood Dreams: Ten Years Later

Mike Tollin .Co-President/Executive Producer/Director
Brian Robbins .Co-President/Executive Producer/Director
Joe Davola .Executive Producer/Head, TV
Sharla Sumpter Bridgett .President, Film
Jonny Fink .Producer
Berna Levin .VP, Film Development
Lauren Wagner .Director, TV Development
Meghann Collins .Creative Executive, Film
Chip Bragg .Director, Operations
Gina Hall .Assistant to Mike Tollin
Ashley Jordan .Assistant to Brian Robbins
Andrew Stryker .Assistant to Joe Davola
Ivette Garcia .Assistant to Sharla Sumpter Bridgett
Alex Lafazia .Assistant, Features

TOMMY BOY FILMS

120 Fifth Ave., 7th Fl.
New York, NY 10011
PHONE .212-388-8300
FAX .212-388-8431
EMAIL .firstname.lastname@tommyboy.com

TYPES: Documentaries - Features - TV Series
CREDITS: We Are Family (Documentary) - Kung Faux, Volume 1-5
COMMENTS: Distribution deal with Koch Entertainment

Tom Silverman .Chairman
Mike Gomez .Production
Michael Newmann .General Manager
Linda Williams .Financial Controller

TOMORROW FILM CORPORATION

16250 Ventura Blvd., Ste. 400
Encino, CA 91436
PHONE .818-788-8776
FAX .818-788-8782
EMAIL .admin@tomorrowfilms.com
WEB SITE .www.tomorrowfilms.com

TYPES: Direct-to-Video/DVD - Features
DEVELOPMENT: New World Order - Turn and Earn
PRE-PRODUCTION: Wild - The Poker Club
POST PRODUCTION: Road House 2
CREDITS: The Third Wheel - Double Bang - Just the Ticket - Till Human Voices Wake Us - American Girl
SUBMISSION POLICY: Submit through an agent, literary manager or attorney

Yoram Pelman .President/Producer
Diane Miller .Director, Servicing
Alli Hartley .Director, Development
Azina Lulla .Director, Production

TOOLEY PRODUCTIONS

101 S. Robertson Blvd., Ste. 203
Los Angeles, CA 90048
PHONE .310-777-8733
FAX .310-777-8730
EMAIL .tooleyproduction@aol.com

TYPES: Features - Reality TV - TV Series
HAS DEAL WITH: CBS Paramount Network Television
DEVELOPMENT: Felon - The Courier - Mexicali - No Man's Land - Recoil - Rockdown - Silverfish; TV: The New West - Cutter (CBS) - PO (CBS)
PRE-PRODUCTION: Keep Coming Back - We're the Millers - Salvage
COMPLETED UNRELEASED: .45
CREDITS: Shadowboxer - A Man Apart - Blind Horizon - Poolhall Junkies - Sol Goode - In the Shadows - A Better Way to Die

Tucker Tooley .Producer
Christopher Wilhem .Creative Executive/Executive Assistant

TORNELL PRODUCTIONS

80 Varick St., Ste. 10C
New York, NY 10013
PHONE .212-625-2530/310-581-0422
FAX .212-625-2532/310-399-2901

TYPES: Features
DEVELOPMENT: August and Everything After - The Rigbys - Bad Dog - Carnivore
CREDITS: Igby Goes Down - Breakin' All the Rules - Jawbreaker - The Big Split - The Craft
SUBMISSION POLICY: No unsolicited material
COMMENTS: West Coast office: 149 Fraser Ave., Santa Monica, CA 90405

Lisa Tornell .Producer

TOTEM PRODUCTIONS
8009 Santa Monica Blvd.
Los Angeles, CA 90046
PHONE .323-650-4994
FAX .323-650-1961
TYPES Features
CREDITS Domino - Man on Fire

Tony Scott .Co-Chairman
Tom Moran .Executive Assistant to Mr. Scott
Jason Sterman .Assistant to Mr. Scott

TOUCHSTONE TELEVISION
c/o ABC Entertainment Television Group
500 S. Buena Vista St.
Burbank, CA 91521
PHONE .818-460-7777
WEB SITE .www.abc.com
SECOND WEB SITE .www.touchstonetvpress.com
TYPES Made-for-TV/Cable Movies - TV Series

Mark Pedowitz .President
Howard Davine .Executive VP
Julia Franz .Executive VP
Barry Jossen .Executive VP, Production
Keli Lee .Executive VP, Casting
Jeff Frost .Sr. VP, Business Affairs
Milinda McNeely .Sr. VP, Legal Affairs
Morgan Wandell .Sr. VP, Drama
Ayo Davis .VP, Casting
Channing Dungey .VP, Drama Series Development
Cheryl Foliart .VP, TV Music
Gary French .VP, Production
Jim Gaston .VP, Production
Audrey Gelb .VP, Production
Veronica Gentilli .VP, Business Affairs
Charissa Gilmore .VP, Media Relations
David Goldman .VP, Business Affairs
Jacqui Grunfeld .VP, Business Affairs
Kim Hershman .VP, Business Affairs
Joel Hopkins .VP, Production Finance
Roger Kirman .VP, Business Affairs
Brenda Kyle .VP, Production
Victoria LaFortune .VP, Production
Stephanie Leifer .VP, Current Programming
Stephanie Mangano .VP, Casting Administration
Karen Manne .VP, Research
Irwin Marcus .VP, Production, MOWs
Fera Mostow .VP/Counsel, Music
Phyllis Nelson .VP, Production
Bryan Noon .VP, Finance & Planning
Deborah O'Brien .VP, Contract Administration
Jodie Platt .VP, Comedy Series Development & Production
Steve Tann .VP, Current Series
Michael Villegas .VP, Post Production
Paula Warner .VP, Post Production
Alex Weinberger .VP, Comedy
Carlos Williams .VP, Business Affairs
Bruce Sandzimier .Post Production Executive
Brian Harvey .Executive Director, Drama Series
Betty LaBello .Executive Director, Contracts Administration
Sandi Logan .Executive Director, Casting
Michael McDonald .Executive Director, Drama Series Development
Nicole Norwood .Executive Director, Drama Series Development
Randi Chugerman .Director, Casting
Jean Hester .Director, Production Operations
Patrick Maguire .Director, Comedy Series
Kelly Sullivan .Director, Creative Research
Nancy Milo .Sr. Research Coordinator
Lisa Petraglia .Sr. Manager, Legal
Richard Ballering .Manager, Production
Morella Bello .Manager, Current Series
Liz Dickler .Manager, Drama Series & Alternative Programming
Sarah L. Hughes .Manager, Comedy Series
Lorelei Jeffers .Manager, Casting
Billy Murphy .Manager, Casting
John Villacorta .Manager, Casting

TOWER OF BABBLE ENTERTAINMENT
854 N. Spaulding Ave.
Los Angeles, CA 90046
PHONE .323-650-8754
FAX .323-822-0312
WEB SITE .www.towerofb.com
TYPES Features - TV Series
DEVELOPMENT The Kitchen - Hail to the Thief - Jack - American Storage
CREDITS Cry_Wolf

Beau Bauman .Writer/Producer
Jeff Wadlow .Writer/Director

TRANCAS INTERNATIONAL FILMS
1875 Century Park East, Ste. 1145
Century City, CA 90067
PHONE .310-553-5599
FAX .310-553-0536
WEB SITE .www.trancasfilms.com
TYPES Documentaries - Features - Made-for-TV/Cable Movies - Music Videos - Reality TV - TV Series
HAS DEAL WITH Dimension Films - The Weinstein Company
DEVELOPMENT Untitled Holt/Freeman Drama Series - Halloween 9 - Saladin & the Crusades - The Legend of Whisper Hollow
CREDITS Made in Brooklyn - The Halloween Movies - Lion of the Desert - The Message - Appointment with Fear - Free Ride - The Psychic Murders - Halloween: 25 Years of Terror
COMMENTS Diversified production, distribution and management company operating three core businesses: motion picture, television and studio facilities (Twickenham Film Studios, London, United Kingdom)

Malek Akkad .President, Production & Development
Bret D. McCartney .Sr. VP, Production & Development
Sammy Montana .Story Editor
George Newman .Story Editor
Christi Sinkus .Executive Assistant

TRAVEL CHANNEL
c/o Discovery Networks, U.S.
One Discovery Pl.
Silver Spring, MD 20910-3354
PHONE .240-662-2000
FAX .240-662-1845
WEB SITE .www.discovery.com
TYPES Documentaries - TV Series
CREDITS American Casinos - Flight Attendant School - Most Haunted - Made in America - No Reservations - World Poker Tour - Taste of America

Patrick Younge .Executive VP/GM, Discovery Travel Media
James Ashurst .VP, Communication
Bill Margol .VP, Production

TRAVELER'S REST FILMS
205 Washington Ave., Ste. 106
Santa Monica, CA 90403
PHONE 805-969-3379/310-395-9629
TYPES Features - TV Series
DEVELOPMENT Bury My Heart at Wounded Knee (HBO) - The Andromeda Strain (Sci Fi) - Alfred Hitchcock and the Making of Psycho (A&E)
CREDITS Faith of My Fathers (A&E) - Kojak (USA) - Firestarter: Rekindled - A&E's The Great Gatsby - The Darkling - Ghost Hunters (Sci Fi)

Tom Thayer ....President
Linda Messier ....Development Associate
Jenny Shapiro ....Assistant to Mr. Thayer

TREASURE ENTERTAINMENT
468 N. Camden Dr., Ste. 200
Beverly Hills, CA 90210
PHONE 310-860-7490
FAX 310-943-1488
EMAIL ....info@treasureentertainment.net
WEB SITE ....www.treasureentertainment.net
TYPES Commercials - Direct-to-Video/DVD - Documentaries - Features - Internet Content - Made-for-TV/Cable Movies - Mobile Content - Music Videos
DEVELOPMENT The Bloodwalkers - Move the Crowd - Prom Night - Los Coyotes
PRE-PRODUCTION High Midnight - It Ain't New Yawk
PRODUCTION Who Stole the Soul? (Doc)
UPCOMING RELEASES Rock Fresh (Doc)
COMPLETED UNRELEASED Cycles
CREDITS Personal Vendetta - Flintown Kids - Harsh Times
SUBMISSION POLICY No unsolicited submissions

Mark Heidelberger ....Co-Chairman/CEO
Jesse Felsot ....Co-Chairman/President
Ian Vishnevsky ....CFO
Kevin Asbell ....COO/General Counsel
Jonathan Hoffberg ....VP, Business Development
Andrew Yoo ....VP, Corporate Finance & Operations

TREE LINE FILM
1708 Berkeley St.
Santa Monica, CA 90404
PHONE 310-883-7220
FAX 310-883-7227
TYPES Features - TV Series
DEVELOPMENT The Rich Part of Life - The Sportswriter/Independence Day - 200 Block - 3:10 to Yuma/Contention - Mute Witness - Follow Me
CREDITS Walk the Line - The Sweetest Thing - Kate & Leopold - Girl, Interrupted - Things to Do in Denver When You're Dead - Beautiful Girls - Citizen Ruth - Kids - Wide Awake - Scream 1-3 - Cop Land - Identity
SUBMISSION POLICY No unsolicited accepted

Cathy Konrad ....Producer
James Mangold ....Writer/Director/Producer
Magnus Monroe ....Creative Executive
Adam Karasick ....Executive Assistant to James Mangold & Cathy Konrad

TREZZA ENTERTAINMENT
39 E. 78th St., Ste. 603
New York, NY 10021
PHONE 212-327-2218
FAX 212-327-2161
TYPES Documentaries - Features - Made-for-TV/Cable Movies
DEVELOPMENT My Pal Rinker - Piaf - What About Me?
PRE-PRODUCTION Headlong
PRODUCTION By Appointment - Terminal 4
CREDITS Pollock - Georgia

James Francis Trezza ....Producer
Gail Pellet ....Producer
Stephanie Vargas ....Producer
Barbara Turner ....Writer

TRIAGE ENTERTAINMENT
c/o John Bravakis
6701 Center Dr. West, #1111
Los Angeles, CA 90045
PHONE 310-417-4800
FAX 310-410-1544
EMAIL ....jbravakis@triageinc.com
WEB SITE ....www.triageinc.com
TYPES Animation - Documentaries - Internet Content - Mobile Content - Reality TV - Specials - TV Series
CREDITS Laffapalooza - Iron Chef America - Home for the Holidays - The Mentalist - Cowboy U - Scariest Places on Earth - Jamie Foxx: Unpredictable

Stu Schreiberg ....President
John Bravakis ....Executive VP
Steve Kroopnick ....Sr. VP
Matthew Marcus ....VP, Business & Creative Development
Stacy Hashimoto ....Production Executive
Myra Byrne ....Post Production Supervisor

TRIBECA PRODUCTIONS

375 Greenwich St., 8th Fl.
New York, NY 10013
PHONE . . . 212-941-4040
FAX . . . 212-941-4044
WEB SITE . . . www.tribecafilm.com
SECOND WEB SITE . . . www.tribecafilmfestival.org
TYPES: Features - Made-for-TV/Cable Movies - Miniseries - Reality TV - Theatre - TV Series
HAS DEAL WITH: Universal Pictures
DEVELOPMENT: Bridge and Tunnel - Sugar Kings - What Just Happened - Untitled Reality TV Project (Actual Reality/NBC)
POST PRODUCTION: The Good Shepherd
CREDITS: A Bronx Tale - Wag the Dog - Analyze This - Marvin's Room - Thunderheart - Rocky & Bullwinkle - Meet the Parents - About a Boy - Showtime - Analyze That - House of D - Meet the Fockers - Stage Beauty - Rent - We Will Rock You (Tribeca Theatrical Production)

Robert De Niro . . . Partner
Jane Rosenthal . . . Partner
Hardy Justice . . . VP, Development
Annie Armstrong . . . Executive Assistant to Jane Rosenthal
Samantha Bryant . . . Executive Assistant to Jane Rosenthal

TRIBUNE ENTERTAINMENT COMPANY

5800 Sunset Blvd., TEC Bldg., Ste. 10
Los Angeles, CA 90028
PHONE . . . 323-460-5800
FAX . . . 323-460-3858
WEB SITE . . . www.tribtv.com
TYPES: Reality TV - TV Series
CREDITS: Mutant X - Gene Roddenberry's Andromeda - Family Feud - Soul Train - Ron Hazelton's Housecalls - Pet Keeping with Mark Marrone - South Park - Marquee Movies - DIC Kids' Network - US Farm Report - American Idol Rewind
COMMENTS: Additional offices: 220 E. 42nd St., Ste. 400, New York, NY 10017, phone: 212-210-1000; 435 N. Michigan Ave., Ste. 1800, Chicago, IL 60611, phone: 312 222-4441

John Reardon . . . President, Tribune Broadcasting Company
David Berson . . . Sr. VP, Business Affairs (323-460-3802)
Clark Morehouse . . . Executive VP/General Manager (212-210-1060)
Donna Harrison . . . Sr. VP, Programming (323-460-3834)
Richard Inouye . . . Sr. VP, Finance & Administration (323-460-3852)
Steve Mulderrig . . . Sr. VP/General Sales Manager (212-210-1030)
Marc Schacher . . . Sr. VP, Programming & Development
Dick Bailey . . . VP, Midwest Advertising Sales (312-222-4412)
Cindy Connelly . . . VP, Advertising Sales (212-210-1024)
Taylor Fuller . . . VP, Southwestern Region (323-460-5316)
Lee Gonsalves . . . VP, Marketing & Creative Services (323-460-3972)
George NeJame . . . VP, Production & Operations (323-460-3894)

TRICOAST STUDIOS

1547 10th St.
Santa Monica, CA 90401
PHONE . . . 310-458-7707
FAX . . . 310-458-7701
EMAIL . . . tricoast@tricoast.com
WEB SITE . . . www.tricoast.com
TYPES: Commercials - Direct-to-Video/DVD - Documentaries - Features - Made-for-TV/Cable Movies - TV Series
DEVELOPMENT: 9 - Southern Comfort - Fast Willie - The Log
CREDITS: Features: The Pet - The Set Up - Escape from Atlantis - Madison - The Proposition - The Pact; TV: South of Nowhere; Direct-to-Video/DVD: Freestyle - Now That's Funny - Art of Knitting
COMMENTS: A full service independent studio, including distribution, marketing, production and post production facilities

Marcy Levitas Hamilton . . . CEO/President
Strath Hamilton . . . Executive Producer/Director
Martin Wiley . . . Executive Producer/Director
Jeff Willner . . . Sr. VP Production
Salina Farkas . . . Controller
Courtney Cross . . . Production Coordinator
Dale Tanguay . . . Visual Effects Supervisor
Blake Taylor . . . Visual Effects
Todd Beauchamp . . . DVD
Andrew Easterly . . . Editorial
Danielle Christine Smyer . . . Editorial
Mellany Boyd . . . Executive Assistant
Mike George . . . Studio Manager

TRICOR ENTERTAINMENT

1613 Chelsea Rd.
San Marino, CA 91108
PHONE . . . 626-282-5184
FAX . . . 626-282-5185
EMAIL . . . executiveoffices@tricorentertainment.com
WEB SITE . . . www.tricorentertainment.com
TYPES: Features - TV Series
UPCOMING RELEASES: The Devil & Daniel Webster
CREDITS: The Bridge of San Luis Rey - Extreme Days - The Amati Girls - Carlo's Wake - The Homecoming of Jimmy Whitecloud
SUBMISSION POLICY: Through major agencies or entertainment lawyers
COMMENTS: Also an international distributor and exhibitor

Craig Darian . . . Co-Chairman/CEO
Howard Kazanjian . . . Co-Chairman (818-763-0699)
William E. Wegner, Esq. . . . General Counsel

TRI-ELITE ENTERTAINMENT, LTD.

6100 Wilshire Blvd., Ste. 230
Los Angeles, CA 90048
PHONE .310-358-8300
FAX .310-358-8304
EMAIL .jhmmpa@sbcglobal.net
WEB SITE .www.thediversityawards.org

TYPES	Commercials - Direct-to-Video/DVD - Features - Made-for-TV/Cable Movies - Miniseries - Music Videos - Reality TV - Specials - TV Series
DEVELOPMENT	Hollywood Live - Annual Oscar Luncheon
CREDITS	The Annual Diversity Awards (The WB) - The American Society of Young Musicians - Cable Channel Awards - The Annual Spring House of Blues Benefit Concert & Awards

Jarvee Hutcherson .President/Executive Producer
Gordon Kenney .Producer/Development
Dionicio Virvez .Producer
Steve Gold .Business Affairs
Maggie Ngyman .Executive Assistant to President

TRIGGER STREET INDEPENDENT

799 Washington St.
New York, NY 10014
PHONE .212-897-3897
FAX .212-624-1704
WEB SITE .www.triggerstreetindependent.com

TYPES	Animation - Documentaries - Features - Reality TV - TV Series
DEVELOPMENT	Woody Allen is the Voice of Reason
POST PRODUCTION	Bernard and Doris - Mr. Gibb
UPCOMING RELEASES	The Sasquatch Dumpling Gang
COMMENTS	Also deals with Panasonic and Goldcrest Post

Adam Kassen .President/Writer/Director
Mark Kassen .President/Writer/Director
Mark Olsen .Director, Production & Development
Patrick Petrocelli .Executive Assistant

TRILLION ENTERTAINMENT, INC.

9465 Wilshire Blvd., Ste. 400
Beverly Hills, CA 90212
PHONE .310-601-2400
FAX .310-601-2401
EMAIL .sd@trillion-ent.com
WEB SITE .www.trillion-ent.com
SECOND WEB SITE .www.newsuitmovie.com

TYPES	Documentaries - Features
DEVELOPMENT	The Nazi Officer's Wife (Feature) - Bright Young Things - Friends & Lovers - The Gold of Malabar - The Porch
CREDITS	Joyride - The Item - Jane Bond (Short) - New Suit - The Nazi Officer's Wife (Documentary)

Laurent Zilber .Co-President
Christina Zilber .Co-President
Scott Duncan .Sr. VP, Operations
Kathryn Tyus-Adair .Sr. VP, Production
Ashley Bradley .Executive Assistant
Mailys Ann-Charlotte Suncic .Executive Assistant

TRILLIUM PRODUCTIONS, INC.

PO Box 1560
New Canaan, CT 06840
PHONE .203-966-5540
FAX .203-972-9175
EMAIL .trilliumct@aol.com

TYPES	Documentaries - Features - Made-for-TV/Cable Movies - TV Series
CREDITS	South Pacific - Sarah Plain and Tall 1-3 - Serving in Silence - Journey - Ballad of Lucy Whipple - Baby - Do You Mean There Are Still Real Cowboys? - Broken Hearts, Broken Homes
SUBMISSION POLICY	No unsolicited submissions accepted

Glenn Close .President
Nancy Evans .Executive Assistant

TRILOGY ENTERTAINMENT GROUP

1207 Fourth St., Ste. 400
Santa Monica, CA 90401
PHONE .310-656-9733
FAX .310-656-9730

TYPES	Features - TV Series
HAS DEAL WITH	Sony Pictures Entertainment
DEVELOPMENT	Music of the Spheres - Racing in the Streets - I Am Charlotte Simmons - Jones - Brown Eyed Girl - Sweet Smell of Success - Taj Mahal - If Not for You - Monster - Flying Tigers - An Infinity of Mirrors - Lighthouse - UFO - For the People - Between the Lines - Crusade - Black Ice - Allies
PRE-PRODUCTION	The Last Full Measure - Blood Crazy - Night-Shifts - Pushing Up Daisies - Eagles
CREDITS	The Dangerous Lives of Altar Boys - Robin Hood: Prince of Thieves - Backdraft - Blown Away - Moll Flanders - Larger Than Life - Tank Girl - The Kiss; TV: Outer Limits - The Magnificent Seven - The Twilight Zone - Carrie - Breaking News - Houdini
COMMENTS	Deal with MGM

Pen Densham .Partner
Neil Kaplan .Partner
John Watson .Partner
Bryan Flam .Development Executive, Features & TV
Nevin Densham .Creative Executive/Head, Development, Project X
Alex Daltas .Creative Executive
Julie Fitzgerald .Manager, Development
Howard Han .Creative Consultant
Jonathan Hughes .Creative Assistant

TRISTAR PICTURES

10202 W. Washington Blvd.
Culver City, CA 90232
PHONE .310-244-4000
FAX .310-244-2626
WEB SITE .www.spe.sony.com

TYPES	Features

Florence Grace .Sr. VP, Publicity
Danielle Misher .VP, Publicity

TROMA ENTERTAINMENT, INC.
733 Ninth Ave., Troma Bldg.
New York, NY 10019
PHONE .212-757-4555
FAX .212-399-9885
EMAIL .webmaster@troma.com
WEB SITE .www.troma.com
TYPES Direct-to-Video/DVD - Features - Internet Content - Mobile Content - Music Videos
DEVELOPMENT Schlock and Schlockability
POST PRODUCTION Poultrygeist
UPCOMING RELEASES Period Piece - Scarlet Moon - Lollilove - Touch Me in the Morning - Acting Out - Slaughter Party
CREDITS Toxic Avenger - Citizen Toxie - Terror Firmer - Sgt. Kabukiman NYPD - Tromeo & Juliet - Cannibal! The Musical - Rowdy Girls - Def by Temptation - Decampitated - Bloodsucking Freaks - Tales From the Crapper - Suicide - Trailer Town
SUBMISSION POLICY Email acquisitions@troma.com for info

Lloyd Kaufman .President
Michael Herz .VP
Jeremy Howell .VP, Sales

TRUNITY, A MEDIAR COMPANY, A DIVISION OF TRUE MEDIAR, A UNITY CORPBOPOLY
12910 Culver Blvd., Ste. A
Los Angeles, CA 90066
PHONE .310-306-8110
TYPES Features
HAS DEAL WITH Paramount Pictures
COMMENTS Entertainment solutions for a modern world

Trey Parker .CEO/Partner
Matt Stone .CEO/Partner
Anne Garefino .President
Jennifer Howell .Executive VP
Kurt Nickels .Creative Executive
Hannah Wachs .Executive Assistant

T-SQUARED PRODUCTIONS
3496 Wade St.
Los Angeles, CA 90066
PHONE .310-915-0055
TYPES Features - New Media - TV Series
CREDITS Kissing Miranda - Fried Green Tomatoes - Sweethearts - Kids World

Tom Taylor .Producer/Attorney

TUDOR MANAGEMENT GROUP
560 Broadway St., Ste. B
Venice, CA 90291
PHONE .310-401-2020
TYPES Features - Direct-to-Video/DVD - Made-for-TV/Cable Movies - TV Series
DEVELOPMENT Red Sneakers
CREDITS Getting Personal - The Fixer - Heads - Sahara - Next Door - BUGS

Marty Tudor .No Title
Mieke ter Poorten Berlin .No Title
Maria K. Aspinwall .No Title
Liberty Conboy .No Title

TULE RIVER FILMS
2801 W. Alameda Ave.
Burbank, CA 91505
PHONE .818-556-2666
FAX .818-556-2667
TYPES Features
DEVELOPMENT Rumble in the Jungle - Prodigal Son - Verdigris - Flight of the Falcon
PRE-PRODUCTION Downloading Nancy
CREDITS Black Cloud

David Moore .Producer
Igor Kovacevich .Producer

THE TURMAN INC. PICTURE COMPANY
12220 Dunoon Ln.
Los Angeles, CA 90049
PHONE .213-740-3307
FAX .213-745-6652
EMAIL .pstark@usc.edu
TYPES Features - Made-for-TV/Cable Movies
DEVELOPMENT The Best Man
CREDITS Kingdom Come - American History X - The River Wild - Running Scared - Short Circuit - Great White Hope - The Graduate - The Best Man - Pretty Poison
SUBMISSION POLICY No unsolicited material

Lawrence Turman .No Title
Richard Shepherd .No Title

TURNER ENTERTAINMENT GROUP
1050 Techwood Dr. NW
Atlanta, GA 30318-5604
PHONE .404-827-1500
WEB SITE .www.turner.com
TYPES Animation - Documentaries - Made-for-TV/Cable Movies - New Media - Syndication - TV Series - Reality TV

Philip Kent .Chairman/CEO, Turner Broadcasting System, Inc.
Terence McGuirk .Vice Chairman, TBS, Inc.
Mark Lazarus .President, Turner Entertainment Group, TBS, Inc.
Vicky Miller .Executive VP/CFO, TBS, Inc.
Kelly Regal .Executive VP, Corporate Communications & Human Resources, TBS, Inc.
Louise Sams .Executive VP/General Counsel, Turner Broadcasting System, Inc./President, Turner Broadcasting System International, Inc.
Jonathan Katz .Sr. VP, Program Planning & Acquisitions, TEG
Veronica Sheehan .Sr. VP, Network Operations, TEN
Shirley Powell .Sr. VP, Corporate Communications, TBS, Inc.
Terri Tingle .Sr. VP, Standards & Practices, TEN

TURNER NETWORK TELEVISION (TNT)

3500 W. Olive Ave., 15th Fl.
Burbank, CA 91505
PHONE 818-977-5500/404-827-1700
WEB SITE . . . . www.tnt.tv

TYPES: TV Series - Made-for-TV/Cable Movies - Limited Series
DEVELOPMENT: Heartland - Grace - Nightshades - Smoke & Mirrors - A Perfect Day - The Norms
PRE-PRODUCTION: The Company
UPCOMING RELEASES: The Librarian II: Return to King Solomon's Mines - Nightmares & Dreamscapes: From the Stories of Stephen King - The Ron Clark Story
CREDITS: The Closer - Saved - Into the West - The Wool Cap - The Librarian: Quest for the Spear - The Grid - Salem's Lot - The Winning Season - The Goodbye Girl - Door to Door - The 10th Annual SAG Awards - Engagement Ring - Avenger
COMMENTS: Atlanta office: 1050 Techwood Drive NW, Atlanta GA 30318

Mark Lazarus . . . . President, Turner Entertainment Group (Atlanta)
Steve Koonin . . . . Executive VP/COO, TBS & TNT (Atlanta)
Michael Borza . . . . Sr. VP, On-Air Creative, TBS & TNT (Atlanta)
Karen Cassell . . . . Sr. VP, Entertainment Publicity, TBS (Atlanta)
Michael Wright . . . . Sr. VP, Original Programming, TBS & TNT (Burbank)
Sandra Dewey . . . . Sr. VP, Original Programming, TBS & TNT (Burbank)
Ken Schwab . . . . Sr. VP, Programming, TBS & TNT (Atlanta)
Sharon Byrens . . . . VP, Development , Sponsored Programming, TBS & TNT (Burbank)
David Hudson . . . . VP, Production & Production Finance, Sponsored Programming, TBS & TNT (Burbank)
Patrick Kelly . . . . VP, Business Affairs, TBS & TNT (Burbank)
Sam Linsky . . . . VP, Original Programming, TNT (Burbank)
Lillah McCarthy . . . . VP, Series Programming, TBS & TNT (Burbank)
John Palmerton . . . . VP, Business Affairs, TBS & TNT (Burbank)
Bill Phillips . . . . VP, Production, TBS & TNT (Burbank)
Mark Taylor . . . . VP, Production, TBS & TNT (Burbank)
Mary Lawler . . . . Sr. Director, Business Affairs, TBS & TNT (Burbank)
Martine Shahar . . . . Sr. Director, Business Affairs, TBS & TNT (Burbank)
Gwenn Smith . . . . Director, Post Production & Production, TBS & TNT (Burbank)
Clinton Wilburn . . . . Director, Business Affairs, TBS & TNT (Burbank)
Lainie Gallers . . . . Manager, Original Programming (Burbank)
Kristie Moomey . . . . Manager, Production & Post Production, TBS & TNT (Burbank)
Lisa Clifton . . . . Assistant to Sandra Dewey (Burbank)
Barbara Lancaster . . . . Assistant to Ken Schwab (Atlanta)
Priscilla Pierson . . . . Assistant to Steve Koonin (Atlanta)
Samantha Poverelli . . . . Assistant to Michael Wright (Burbank)
Anne Smith . . . . Assistant to Mark Lazarus (Atlanta)

TURTLEBACK PRODUCTIONS, INC.

11736 Gwynne Ln.
Los Angeles, CA 90077
PHONE 310-440-8587
FAX 310-440-8903

TYPES: Features - Made-for-TV/Cable Movies - TV Series
POST PRODUCTION: Tenderness
CREDITS: The Brooke Ellison Story - Witness Protection - The Pentagon Wars - Remember WENN - Hell on Heels: The Battle of Mary Kay (CBS)

Howard Meltzer . . . . President/Executive Producer

TV GUIDE CHANNEL

6922 Hollywood Blvd., 11th Fl.
Hollywood, CA 90028
PHONE 323-817-4600/212-852-7500
FAX 323-817-4713/212-852-7323
WEB SITE . . . . www.tvguide.com

TYPES: Internet Content - Mobile Content - Specials - TV Series
PROVIDES DEAL TO: Keep Clear
CREDITS: Square Off - The 411 - Watch This - TV Watercooler - Idol Tonight - Reality Chat - Flicks - Infanity
COMMENTS: East Coast office: 1211 Avenue of the Americas, 28th Fl., New York, NY 10036

Rich Battista . . . . CEO, Gemstar & TV Guide Networks
Ryan O'Hara . . . . President, TV Guide Channel
Steve Shannon . . . . Executive VP/General Manager, Product Development
Richard Cusick . . . . Sr. VP/General Manager, Digital Media
Jack Carey . . . . Sr. VP, Operations
Matt Singerman . . . . Sr. VP, Programming & Production
Michael Starkenburg . . . . Sr. VP, Technology
Kristin Peace . . . . VP, Development
Dmitri Ponomarev . . . . VP, On Demand
Scott Woodward . . . . VP, Production
Paul Greenberg . . . . General Manager, TVGuide.com
Anita Devi-McConnell . . . . Executive Producer
Paul Adler . . . . Executive Producer
Lisa Frodsham . . . . Executive Producer
Nikki Kemezis . . . . Executive Producer
Eddie Delbridge . . . . Director, Live Events & Program Promotions
Robert Bentley . . . . Supervising Producer
Kristan Giordano . . . . Supervising Producer
Colin McLean . . . . Supervising Producer
Rick Saloomey . . . . Supervising Producer
Armando Villalpando . . . . Supervising Producer
Lisa Germani . . . . Sr. Talent Executive
Tricia Daniels . . . . Talent Executive
David Anderson . . . . On-Air Talent Coordinator

TV ONE, LLC

1010 Wayne Ave.
Silver Spring, MD 20910
PHONE 301-755-0400
EMAIL .....info@tv-one.tv
WEB SITE .....www.tvoneonline.com
TYPES — Specials - TV Series
DEVELOPMENT — Living It Up with Patti LaBelle - Turn Up the Heat with G. Garvin - TV One on One - TV One Access - Divine Restoration - Singletary Says
SUBMISSION POLICY — See Web site
COMMENTS — Program acquisition deal with Warner Bros. Domestic Cable Distribution

Alfred Liggins .....Chairman
Johnathan Rodgers .....CEO/President
Susan Banks .....Executive VP, Marketing & Creative Services
Bob Buenting .....Executive VP/CFO
Rose Catherine Pinkney .....Executive VP, Programming, Production & Development
Jay Schneider .....Executive VP, Operations
Karen Wishart .....Executive VP/General Counsel
Sitarah Pendleton .....Sr. VP, Programming & Production

TV REPAIR

857 Castac Pl.
Pacific Palisades, CA 90272
PHONE 310-459-3671
FAX 310-459-4251
EMAIL .....davidjlatt@earthlink.net
TYPES — TV Series
DEVELOPMENT — Adrift (CBS) - Belsky (F/X)
CREDITS — Citizen Baines (CBS) - EZ Streets - ATF - Under Suspicion - Hill Street Blues - Gramercy Park (ABC) - Girls on the Bus (ABC)

David J. Latt .....Producer/Writer

NORMAN TWAIN PRODUCTIONS

250 W. 54th St., Ste. 604
New York, NY 10019
PHONE 212-397-6605
FAX 212-397-6609
EMAIL .....ntprods@aol.com
TYPES — Features - Made-for-TV/Cable Movies - Theatre - TV Series
DEVELOPMENT — Scar - My Dog Tulip - Secret Order
POST PRODUCTION — Spinning Into Butter
COMPLETED UNRELEASED — Heaven's Fall
CREDITS — Boycott - Curveballs Along the Way - Lean on Me
SUBMISSION POLICY — Mail submissions to Tessa Mancini or Ellen Kelty

Norman Twain .....Producer
Ellen Kelty .....Development Associate
Tessa Mancini .....Development Associate

TWENTIETH CENTURY FOX

10201 W. Pico Blvd.
Los Angeles, CA 90035
PHONE 310-369-1000
WEB SITE .....www.fox.com
TYPES — Features
PROVIDES DEAL TO — 21 Laps Entertainment - Bazmark, Inq. - Blossom Films - Conundrum Entertainment - Davis Entertainment Company - Dominant Pictures - Firm Films - Hyde Park Entertainment - Josephson Entertainment - Lightstorm Entertainment - Penn Station Entertainment - Zak Penn's Company - Point Road, Inc. - Principato-Young Entertainment - Regency Enterprises - Scott Free Productions - Seed Productions - Tapestry Films, Inc. - Ralph Winter Productions, Inc.
UPCOMING RELEASES — Pathfinder - The Marine - Borat - Night at the Museum - The Perfect Creature - Fantastic Four 2
CREDITS — Fantastic Four - Cheaper By the Dozen 2 - X-Men: The Last Stand - The Omen - Garfield: A Tale of Two Kitties - John Tucker Must Die - Reno 911!
COMMENTS — Mailing address: PO Box 900, Beverly Hills, CA 90213

James Gianopulos .....Chairman
Tom Rothman .....Chairman
Robert Harper .....Vice Chairman, Fox Filmed Entertainment
Ted Gagliano .....President, Feature Post Production
Joe Hartwick .....President, Physical Production
Robert Kraft .....President, Fox Music, Inc.
Hutch Parker .....President, TCF
Steven Bersch .....COO, Fox Home Entertainment
Bob Cohen .....Executive VP, Legal Affairs
J.R. DeLang .....Executive VP, Studio Operations
Lisa Ellzey .....Executive VP, Production, TCF
Greg Gelfan .....Executive VP, Fox Filmed Entertainment
Dean Hallett .....Executive VP, Finance/CFO, FFE
Donna Isaacson .....Executive VP, Feature Talent
Deborah Liebling .....Executive VP, Production, TCF
Steve Plum .....Executive VP, Business Affairs
Mark Resnick .....Executive VP, Business Affairs
Gary D. Roberts .....Executive VP, Litigation
Emma Watts .....Executive VP, Production, TCF
Alex Young .....Executive VP, Production, TCF
Fred Baron .....Sr. VP, Physical Production
Fred Chandler .....Sr. VP, Post Production
Kimberly Cooper .....Sr. VP, Physical Production
Ted Dodd .....Sr. VP, Creative Affairs
Mike Hendrickson .....Sr. VP, Physical Production
Paul Hoffman .....Sr. VP, Business Affairs
Thomas Imperato .....Sr. VP, Physical Production
Christian Kaplan .....Sr. VP, Feature Casting
David Lux .....Sr. VP, Corporate Communications
Vanessa Morrison .....Sr. VP, Production, TCF
Victoria Rossellini .....Sr. VP, Production Finance & Business Affairs
Tony Safford .....Sr. VP, Acquisitions
David Starke .....Sr. VP, Physical Production
Steve Asbell .....VP, Production, TCF
Michael Heard .....VP, Physical Production
Peter Kang .....VP, Production, TCF
Tom Siegrist .....VP, Production, Fox Home Entertainment
Aaron Williams .....VP, Production Development Accounting
Mark O'Connor .....Director, Development, TCF
Marc Resteghini .....Director, Development, TCF

(Continued)

TWENTIETH CENTURY FOX (Continued)

Ray Strache .... Director, Acquisitions
Brehan Fitzgerald .... Manager, Feature Casting
Laura Lewis .... Creative Executive, TCF
Jason Young .... Creative Executive, TCF
Riley Kathryn Ellis .... Literary Scout, Young Adult & Children's

TWENTIETH CENTURY FOX - FOX 2000

10201 W. Pico Blvd., Bldg. 78
Los Angeles, CA 90035
PHONE 310-369-2000
FAX 310-369-4258
WEB SITE .... www.fox.com
TYPES: Features
PROVIDES DEAL TO: Blossom Films - State Street Pictures - Sunswept Entertainment - Zucker/Netter Productions
UPCOMING RELEASES: Flicka - A Good Year - Eragon
CREDITS: Fever Pitch - Roll Bounce - In Her Shoes - Walk the Line - The Family Stone - Aquamarine - The Devil Wears Prada

Elizabeth Gabler .... President, Production
Carla Hacken .... Executive VP, Production
Maria Faillace .... VP, Production
Rodney Ferrell .... VP, Production
Nick D'Angelo .... Creative Executive, Fox 2000
Amee McNaughton .... Creative Executive, Fox 2000
Erin Lindsey .... Creative Executive
Drew Reed .... Literary Consultant
Riley Kathryn Ellis .... Literary Scout, Young Adult & Children's

TWENTIETH CENTURY FOX - SEARCHLIGHT PICTURES

10201 W. Pico Blvd., Bldg. 38
Los Angeles, CA 90035
PHONE 310-369-4402
FAX 310-369-2359
WEB SITE .... www.foxsearchlight.com
TYPES: Features
PROVIDES DEAL TO: Ad Hominem Enterprises - DNA Films - Hard C
UPCOMING RELEASES: Trust the Man - The Last King of Scotland - The Namesake - Notes on a Scandal - I Think I Love My Wife
CREDITS: Little Miss Sunshine - Millions - Melinda and Melinda - Separate Lies - Bee Season - The Ringer - Night Watch - The Hills Have Eyes - Thank You For Smoking - Phat Girlz - Water
COMMENTS: East Coast office: 1211 Sixth Ave., 16th Fl., New York, NY 10036

Peter Rice .... President
Claudia Lewis .... President, Production
Stephen Gilula .... COO
Nancy Utley .... COO
Joseph De Marco .... Executive VP, Business Affairs
Matthew Greenfield .... Sr. VP, Production
Jill Gwen .... Sr. VP, Finance & Operations
Chris Maxwell .... Sr. VP, Legal Affairs
Liz Sayre .... Sr. VP, Physical Production
Jeremy Steckler .... Sr. VP, Production
Jamie Taylor .... Sr. VP, Legal Affairs
Zola Mashariki .... VP, Production
Nikki Scalise .... VP, Post Production
Jason Hargrove .... Creative Executive
Charlotte Koh .... Creative Executive
Cassidy Lange .... Assistant to Peter Rice

(Continued)

TWENTIETH CENTURY FOX - SEARCHLIGHT PICTURES (Continued)

Nicholas Dunlevy .... 2nd Assistant to Peter Rice
Liz Glotzbach .... Assistant to Jeremy Steckler & Matthew Greenfield
Veronica Lemcoff .... Assistant to Claudia Lewis
Vanessa Morelli .... Assistant to Zola Mashariki

TWENTIETH CENTURY FOX ANIMATION

10201 W. Pico Blvd., Bldg. 58
Los Angeles, CA 90035
PHONE 310-369-1000
FAX 310-369-3907
WEB SITE .... www.fox.com
TYPES: Animation - Features
PROVIDES DEAL TO: Blue Sky Studios
UPCOMING RELEASES: The Simpsons - Horton Hears a Who
CREDITS: Anastasia - Titan A.E. - Ice Age - Robots - Ice Age: The Meltdown

Christopher Meledandri .... President, Animation
John Cohen .... VP, Production
Lisa Fragner .... Head, Development, Blue Sky Studios

TWENTIETH CENTURY FOX TELEVISION

10201 W. Pico Blvd., Bldg. 88
Los Angeles, CA 90035
PHONE 310-369-1000
TYPES: TV Series
PROVIDES DEAL TO: Adelstein Productions - Callahan Filmworks - Imagine Television - Josephson Entertainment - David E. Kelley Productions - Dawn Parouse Productions - Phase Two Productions - Roundtable Entertainment - Watson Pond Productions
CREDITS: My Name Is Earl - Prison Break - How I Met Your Mother - Reba - 24 - The Simpsons - King of the Hill - American Dad - Family Guy - Boston Legal - Bones - The Unit - The Simple Life

Gary Newman .... President, Twentieth Century Fox Television
Dana Walden .... President, Twentieth Century Fox Television
Robert Barron .... CFO/Executive VP
Howard Kurtzman .... Executive VP, Business & Legal Affairs
Jennifer Nicholson-Salke .... Executive VP, Drama Development
Jim Sharp .... Executive VP, TV Production
Pam Baron .... Sr. VP, Business Affairs
Wendy Bartosh .... Sr. VP, Legal Affairs
Neal Baseman .... Sr. VP, Business Affairs
Sam Bramhall .... Sr. VP, Business Affairs
Jeffrey Glaser .... Sr. VP, Current Programming
Joel Hornstock .... Sr. VP, TV Production
Sharon Klein .... Sr. VP, Casting
Bruce Margolis .... Sr. VP, Production
Steven Melnick .... Sr. VP, Marketing & Media Relations
Sandra Ortiz .... Sr. VP, Business Affairs
Mark Pearson .... Sr. VP, Brand & Franchise Management
Quan Phung .... Sr. VP, Comedy Development
Chris Alexander .... VP, Media Relations
Lynn Barrie .... VP, Comedy Development
Carol Fahart .... VP, TV Music
Gary Hall .... VP, Post Production
Jonathan Harris .... VP, Legal Affairs
Beth Hoffman .... VP, Business Affairs
Jamila Hunter .... VP, Comedy Development
Eileen Ige .... VP, Production Accounting
Ann Johnson .... VP, Current Programming
Mark S. Johnson .... VP, Production
Lisa Katz .... VP, Drama Development
Geraldine Leder .... VP, Comedy Casting
Vibiana Molina .... VP, Business Affairs
Patrick Moran .... VP, Drama Development
Jacquie Perryman .... VP, Creative Music
Marci Proietto .... VP, TV Production
Lianne Siegel Shattuck .... VP, Current Programming
Steve Sicherman .... VP, Drama Development
Mike Walsh .... VP, Finance

(Continued)

TWENTIETH CENTURY FOX TELEVISION (Continued)

Nicholas Weinstock . . . . VP, Comedy Development
Jo Gard . . . . Executive Director, Production Accounting
Arlene Getman . . . . Director, Talent Relations
Casey Kyber . . . . Director, Marketing & Research
Stacey Levin . . . . Director, Current Programming
Tracey Raab . . . . Director, Media Relations
Alison Rothman . . . . Director, Comedy, TV Production Accounting
Dana Sharpless . . . . Director, Current Programming
Dana Shelburne . . . . Director, Current Programming
Amanda Tracey . . . . Director, Drama Development
Susannah Jeffers . . . . Sr. Counsel
James Dunn . . . . Counsel
Adriana Lemus . . . . Publicist, Media Relations
Brian Chambers . . . . Manager, Post Production
Grace Coffey . . . . Manager, Business Affairs Administration
Rick Glassman . . . . Manager, TV Production
Ward Hake . . . . Manager, Music
Alana Kleiman . . . . Manager, Casting
Jake Vonk . . . . Manager, Business Affairs
Mike D'Zurilla . . . . Coordinator, Production
Alissa Harris . . . . Coordinator, Post Production
Mandy Kaprall . . . . Coordinator, Current Programming
Gabe Nies . . . . Coordinator, Marketing & Media Relations
Rachel Speiser . . . . Coordinator, Comedy Development
Julie Wilson . . . . Coordinator, Casting
Traci Colwell . . . . Finance Administrator/Office Manager
Pam Smith . . . . Contract Administrator
Ryan Rappaport . . . . Sr. Paralegal, Business Affairs
Ron Part . . . . Production Supervisor

TWENTIETH TELEVISION

2121 Avenue of the Stars
Los Angeles, CA 90067
PHONE 310-369-1000/212-556-2400
FAX 310-369-1506
WEB SITE . . . . www.fox.com

TYPES	Reality TV - TV Series
CREDITS	Desire - Secret Obsessions - Cristina's Court - Geraldo at Large - Judge Alex - Divorce Court - Cops - King of the Hill - The Simpsons - Yes, Dear - Reba - The Bernie Mac Show - Dharma & Greg - Malcolm in the Middle - The Practice - Buffy the Vampire Slayer - The X-Files - Angel - 24
COMMENTS	East Coast office: 1211 Avenue of the Americas, 16th Fl., New York, NY 10036

Bob Cook . . . . President/COO
Paul Buccieri . . . . President, Programming
Joanne Burns . . . . Executive VP, Sales Marketing, Research & New Media
Bob Cesa . . . . Executive VP, Advertising Sales
Marisa Fermin . . Executive VP, Business & Legal Affairs/Business Development
Paul Franklin . . . . Executive VP/General Sales Manager, Broadcast
Steve MacDonald . . . . Executive VP/General Sales Manager, Basic Cable
Lori Bernstein-Baker . . Sr. VP, Business & Legal Affairs, Business Development
Stephen Brown . . . . Sr. VP, Programming & Development
Patrice Callahan . . . . Sr. VP, Business & Legal Affairs/Business Development
Ken Doyle . . . . Sr. VP, Sales, Eastern Region
Jim Gronfein . . . . Sr. VP, Advertising Sales
Elizabeth Herbst-Brady . . . . Sr. VP, Advertising Sales
Jerry Jameson . . . . Sr. VP, Sales, Western Region
Ken Lawson . . . . Sr. VP, Broadcast Sales, Central Region Manager
Michael Newson . . . Sr. VP, South Eastern & South Western Region Manager
Jodie Rea . . . . Sr. VP, Credit & Sales Admnistration
Bob Riordan . . . . Sr. VP, Advertising Sales, DirecTV
Matthew Rodriguez . . . . Sr. VP, Marketing & Creative
Cheri Vincent . . . . Sr. VP, Finance & Administration
Bruce Bower . . . . VP/Controller, Financial Reporting & Accounting

(Continued)

TWENTIETH TELEVISION (Continued)

Jodi Chisarick . . . . VP, Eastern Advertising Sales
Richard Dumont . . . . VP, Advertising & Promotion
Les Eisner . . . . VP, Media Relations
Steve Fish . . . . VP, Advertising Sales, DirectTV
Tannya Gast . . . . VP, Sales, Southwestern Region
Heather Hart-Smith . . . . VP, National Research
J.C. Kawalec . . . . VP, Advertising Sales, Los Angeles DirecTV
Shannon Keating . . . . VP, Domestic Distribution
Ken Kolb . . . . VP, Advertising Sales, DirecTV
Eileen O'Neill . . . . VP, Affiliate Relations
Scott Roth . . . . VP, Sales, Eastern Region
Larry Vanderbeke . . . . VP, Advertising Sales
Kevin Walsh . . . . VP, Broadcast Sales, Northeast Region
Craig Weakley . . . . VP, Sales, Western Region

TWILIGHT PICTURES, INC.

12400 Ventura Blvd., Ste. 735
Studio City, CA 91604
PHONE 877-255-2528/403-286-3248
FAX 403-286-3240
EMAIL . . . . twilight.pictures@shaw.ca
SECOND EMAIL . . . . info@twilight-pictures.com
WEB SITE . . . . www.twilight-pictures.com

TYPES	Direct-to-Video/DVD - Documentaries - Features - Made-for-TV/Cable Movies - Reality TV - TV Series
DEVELOPMENT	The Greatest of Them All - The Twilight Years - The Middle Child - Dirty Little Secrets - Gift of the Bambino - Bed Bugs
POST PRODUCTION	Great American Screenwriters
CREDITS	Features: Cheerful Tearful - Stone Coats - Check It Out (Six Part Series); Documentaries: Project Cougar - Suzuki's World
COMMENTS	Canada office: 3219 Collingwood Dr. NW, Calgary, AB, T2L 0R7, Canada

Signe Olynyk . . . . Writer/Producer
Lorene Lacey . . . . Associate Producer
Bob Schultz . . . . Associate Producer
Andrea Spiegel . . . . Development

TWISTED PICTURES

SEE Evolution Entertainment

TWO OCEANS ENTERTAINMENT GROUP

2017 Lemoyne St.
Los Angeles, CA 90026
PHONE 323-669-0824
FAX 323-669-0527
EMAIL . . . . twoceans@aol.com

TYPES	Animation - Documentaries - Features - Made-for-TV/Cable Movies - TV Series
DEVELOPMENT	Virginia Uribe Project
CREDITS	Sail Away (Discovery Kids) - Happily Ever After: Fairy Tales for Every Child (HBO) - Baby Monitor: Sound of Fear (USA Network) - Reading Your Heart Out (HBO) - Middle School Confessions (HBO)

Meryl Marshall-Daniels . . . . President/Executive Producer
Susan Whittaker . . . . Executive VP, Development/Executive Producer

TWO STICKS PRODUCTIONS

5650 Camellia Ave.
North Hollywood, CA 91601
PHONE . . . 323-822-2300
FAX . . . 818-757-1210/818-752-9321
EMAIL . . . richysal@aol.com

TYPES	Direct-to-Video/DVD - Features - Made-for-TV/Cable Movies
HAS DEAL WITH	Millennium Films
DEVELOPMENT	The Poison Rose - Framed - Manmade - Murdermaid - Pray for the Cardinal - The Last Loyalty - Harley, Wyoming - Hero Wanted - Daily Grind - OutKast - 7-10 Split
PRE-PRODUCTION	Amazon Kid - Homeland Security
PRODUCTION	White Lies
POST PRODUCTION	Final Move
UPCOMING RELEASES	End Game
CREDITS	Shadow of Fear - Larva - Enemies of Laughter - Deuces Wild - Skeleton Man - If You Only Knew - Detour - Matter of Trust - Den of Lions - Laws of Deception - Mel
SUBMISSION POLICY	Open
COMMENTS	Prefer projects with some attachments or partial financing

Richard Salvatore . . . Co-Chairman
David E. Ornston . . . Co-Chairman
Maggie Kretzmer . . . Head, Development
Merav Broder, Esq. . . . Legal Counsel
Sharla Tandler . . . Publicist
Jeff Leonard . . . Accounting

TYPE A FILMS

100 Universal City Plaza, Bldg. 1320, Ste. 2-E
Universal City, CA 91608
PHONE . . . 818-777-6222
FAX . . . 818-866-2866

TYPES	Features
HAS DEAL WITH	Universal Pictures
DEVELOPMENT	Sports Widow - Around the World in 80 Dates - The Reckoning - The Bell Witch
PRODUCTION	Penelope
CREDITS	Legally Blonde 2: Red, White & Blonde

Reese Witherspoon . . . Producer
Jennifer Simpson . . . President
Lauren Kisilevsky . . . VP
Pamela Palmer Doqui . . . Assistant to Reese Witherspoon
Rachel Murray . . . Assistant to Jennifer Simpson

UFLAND PRODUCTIONS

963 Moraga Dr.
Los Angeles, CA 90049
PHONE . . . 310-476-4520
FAX . . . 310-476-4891
EMAIL . . . ufland.productions@verizon.net

TYPES	Features - Made-for-TV/Cable Movies - Miniseries
CREDITS	Night and the City - The Last Temptation of Christ - Not Without My Daughter - Snow Falling on Cedars - One True Thing - Crazy/Beautiful
SUBMISSION POLICY	No unsolicited material; Through representation only

Mary Jane Ufland . . . Producer
Harry J. Ufland . . . Producer

UNDERGROUND FILMS

746 N. Citrus Ave.
Los Angeles, CA 90038
PHONE . . . 323-930-2588
FAX . . . 323-930-2334
WEB SITE . . . www.undergroundfilms.net

TYPES	Animation - Direct-to-Video/DVD - Documentaries - Features - Made-for-TV/Cable Movies - Miniseries - Theatre - TV Series
DEVELOPMENT	Tales From the Wishworks (Universal) - The Section - Venus Kincaid (Fox 2000) - Kiss the Bride Goodbye (Warner Bros.) - Destination Unknown - Black Autumn (Fox 2000) - Range Rats - Soccer Mom (New Line) - Pariah - Class Act (DreamWorks) - Touchback (Morgan Creek) - Coma
PRODUCTION	License to Wed (Warner Bros.)
POST PRODUCTION	Mary Christmas (ABC Family)
CREDITS	Zoom (Sony/Revolution) - Urban Legend 2
COMMENTS	Management division: Underground Management

Nick Osborne . . . Partner/Producer (323-930-2650, nick@undergroundfilms.net)
Trevor Engelson . . . Partner/Producer (323-930-2569, trevor@undergroundfilms.net)
William Lowery . . . VP (323-930-2435, william@undergroundfilms.net)
Liz Yeomans . . . Manager/Creative Executive (323-930-2588)

UNION ENTERTAINMENT

1337 Ocean Ave., Ste. B
Santa Monica, CA 90401
PHONE . . . 310-395-1040
FAX . . . 310-395-1065
WEB SITE . . . www.unionent.com

TYPES	Features
DEVELOPMENT	G.I. Spy - Lions, Tigers & Bears - Common Foe - Strange Eggs - Devil's Island - Priest - The Botanist's Trap - Khakee
PRODUCTION	Videogames: Crusty Demons - Darkness - Teen Titans - Ghostrider
CREDITS	Godsend
SUBMISSION POLICY	Solicited submissions only

Sean O'Keefe . . . President, Film
Richard Leibowitz . . . President, Games
Will Staples . . . VP, Film
Dan Jevons . . . Creative Executive, Games
Howard Bliss . . . Business & Legal Affairs
Rob Edgar . . . Manager, Games
Ethan Malykont . . . Graphic Designer

UNION SQUARE ENTERTAINMENT

9595 Wilshire Blvd., Ste. 900
Beverly Hills, CA 90212
PHONE . . . 310-300-8410
EMAIL . . . info@unionsquareent.com
WEB SITE . . . www.unionsquareent.com

TYPES	Features
CREDITS	
SUBMISSION POLICY	No unsolicited submissions
COMMENTS	Also finances

Jason Berk . . . Co-Chairman
Matt Lane . . . Co-Chairman

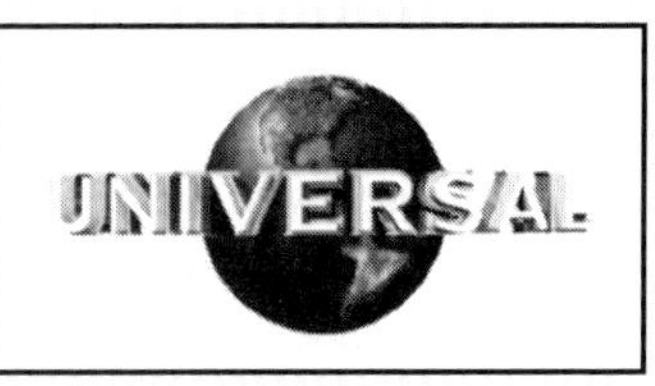

UNIVERSAL OPERATIONS GROUP

100 Universal City Plaza
Universal City, CA 91608
PHONE .818-777-1000
WEB SITE .www.universalstudios.com
TYPES Features

James Watters .President/General Manager
Michael J. Connor .Executive VP, Studio Operations & Administration
David Beanes .Sr. VP, Production Services
Michael Daruty .Sr. VP, Technical Operations
Chris Jenkins .Sr. VP, Sound Services
David Goldstein .VP, Post Production Engineering, Sound Services
Robert O'Neil .VP, Image Assets & Preservation
Tony Sanchez .VP, Special Projects Post Production
Ron Silveira .VP, Digital Video Services, Universal Studios Digital Services

UNIVERSAL PICTURES

100 Universal City Plaza
Universal City, CA 91608
PHONE .818-777-1000
WEB SITE .www.universalstudios.com
SECOND WEB SITE .www.nbcuni.com
TYPES Features - Animation
PROVIDES DEAL TO Black & White Productions - Bobker/Kruger Films - Class 5 Films - Everyman Pictures - Film 44 - Gold Circle Films - Greasy Entertainment - Identity Films - Imagine Entertainment - The Kennedy/Marshall Company - Larger Than Life Productions - Mandalay Pictures - Barry Mendel Productions - Morgan Creek Productions - New Deal Productions - Marc Platt Productions - Protozoa Pictures - Shady Acres Entertainment - The Sommers Company - Strike Entertainment - Terra Firma Films - Tribeca Productions - Type A Films - Vertigo Entertainment - Working Title Films - Yari Film Group (YFG)
UPCOMING RELEASES The Black Dahlia - Children of Men - Man of the Year - Let's Go to Prison - The Good Shepherd (Note: List of Projects Not Complete)

Marc Shmuger .Chairman
David Linde .Co-Chairman
Rick Finkelstein .Vice Chairman, Universal Pictures/Executive VP, Universal Studios
Donna Langley .President, Production
James D. Brubaker .President, Physical Production
James M. Horowitz .Co-President, Production/Executive VP
Adam Fogelson .President, Marketing
Eddie Egan .Co-President, Marketing
Craig Kornblau .President, Home Entertainment
David Kosse .President, Universal Pictures International, Marketing & Distribution
Kathy Nelson .President, Film Music
Nikki Rocco .President, Distribution
Peter Smith .President, International Home Entertainment
Frank Chiocchi .Executive VP, Creative Advertising
Peter Cramer .Executive VP, Production
Beth Goss .Executive VP, Universal Studios Consumer Products Group
Michael Joe .Executive VP
Michael Moses .Executive VP, Publicity
Glenn Ross .Executive VP/General Manager, Family Productions, USHE
Steve Scott .Executive VP, Music Publishing/Music Operations
Stephanie Sperber .Executive VP, Universal Studios Partnership
John Swallow .Executive VP, Production

(Continued)

UNIVERSAL PICTURES (Continued)

Holly Bario .Sr. VP, Production
Arturo Barquet .Sr. VP, Production Finance
Jeffrey Brauer .Sr. VP
Dylan Clark .Sr. VP, Production
Ellen Cockrill .Sr. VP, Animated Production, USHE
Philip Cohen .Sr. VP, Film Music
Suzanne Cole .Sr. VP, Media
Hollace Davids .Sr. VP, Special Projects
Thomas Emrey .Sr. VP/CFO, Home Entertainment
Andrew Fenady .Sr. VP, Physical Production
Chris Floyd .Sr. VP, Business Affairs
Harry Garfield .Sr. VP, Music Creative Affairs
Chuck Gaylord .Sr. VP, Market Research
Alissa Grayson .Sr. VP, Publicity
Julie Hutchison .Sr. VP, Casting
Patti Jackson .Sr. VP, Live Action Production, USHE
Bret Johnson .Sr. VP, Physical Production
Dan Martinez .Sr. VP, Finance & Accounting
Vivian Mayer .Sr. VP, Publicity, Home Entertainment
Greig McRitchie .Sr. VP, Post Production
Doug Neil .Sr. VP, Digital Marketing & Promotions
Gerald Pierce .Sr. VP, Technology
Tom Ruzicka .Sr. VP, Production, Universal Cartoon Studios
Syd Smith .Sr. VP, Universal Studios Partnership
Erica Steinberg .Sr. VP, Production
Jaime Stevens .Sr. VP, Universal Studios Partnership
Greg Sucherman .Sr. VP, Field Publicity & Promotions
Amy Thomases .Sr. VP, East Coast Publicity
Janice Trojan .Sr. VP, Universal Studios Partnership
Dan Wolfe .Sr. VP, Worldwide Creative Advertising Operations
Scott Bernstein .VP, Production
Bette Einbinder .VP, Stills Department
Teresa Johnson .VP, Publicity
Romy Kaufman .VP, Story Department
Jeffrey Kirschenbaum .VP, Production
Mark Markline .VP, International Publicity
Peter Oillataguerre .VP, Physical Production
Amanda Scholer .VP, Publicity

UNIVERSAL STUDIOS

100 Universal City Plaza
Universal City, CA 91608
PHONE .818-777-1000
WEB SITE .www.nbcuni.com
TYPES Features
COMMENTS Includes Universal Pictures, Universal Studios Home Entertainment, Consumer Products Group and Theme Parks

Ron Meyer .President/COO, Universal Studios
Rick Finkelstein .Vice Chairman, Universal Pictures/Executive VP, Universal Studios
Patti Hutton .CFO/Executive VP
Kenneth L. Kahrs .Executive VP, Human Resources
Maren Christensen .Executive VP/General Counsel
Cindy Gardner .Sr. VP, Internal Communications, NBC Universal & Corporate Affairs, Universal Studios
Keith Gorham .Sr. VP, Industrial Relations
Mark Wooster .Sr. VP, Legal Affairs
Nestor Barrero .VP, Employment Counsel
Stephanie Caprielian .VP, Labor Relations
Primo Custodio .VP, Human Resources
Karen Elliott .VP, Anti-Piracy Operations
Sheldon Kasdan .VP/Sr. Labor Counsel
Anne Nielsen .VP/Sr. Trademark Counsel
Ann O'Connor .VP, Government Affairs
Marc Palotay .VP, General Tax Counsel
William Phillips Jr. .VP, Labor & Legal Affairs
Crystal Wright .VP, Legal

UNPAINTED PICTURES

12400 Ventura Blvd., Ste. 171
Studio City, CA 91604
PHONE . . . 818-905-6672
EMAIL . . . unpaintedpix@aol.com
TYPES Features - Made-for-TV/Cable Movies
DEVELOPMENT Dance Parody (Carsey-Werner) - Stolen Wedding Video (Paramount)
CREDITS The Hot Chick - The Animal

Carr D'Angelo . . . Producer
Susan Avallone . . . Writer/Producer

UNTITLED ENTERTAINMENT

331 N. Maple Dr., 3rd Fl.
Beverly Hills, CA 90210
PHONE . . . 310-601-2100/212-777-1214
FAX . . . 310-601-2344/212-777-1165
TYPES Features - Theatre - TV Series
COMMENTS East Coast office: 23 E. 22nd St., 3rd Fl., New York, NY 10010

Jason Weinberg . . . Partner
Stephanie Simon . . . Partner
Guy Oseary . . . Partner
Beth Holden-Garland . . . Partner
Gene Parseghian . . . Partner (NY)
Johnnie Planco . . . Partner (NY)
Elise Konialian . . . VP (NY)
Jennifer Levine . . . Manager/Head, Literary
Laura Rister . . . Manager, Literary
Greg Clark . . . Manager
Mimi Di Trani . . . Manager
Evan Hainey . . . Manager
Jason Newman . . . Manager
Katie Rhodes . . . Manager
Danielle Thomas . . . Manager
Alissa Vradenburg . . . Manager
Brian Young . . . Manager
Sam Ireland . . . Assistant to Jason Weinberg
Rob Levy . . . Assistant to Jason Weinberg
Sarah Pura . . . Assistant to Jason Weinberg
Edward Resetar . . . Assistant to Jason Weinberg & Laura Rister
Jennifer Merlino . . . Assistant to Stephanie Simon
Angela Carbonetti . . . Assistant to Gene Parseghian
David Koth . . . Assistant to Beth Holden-Garland
Aynsley Armbrust . . . Assistant to Greg Clark & Mimi Di Trani
Dwight Armstrong . . . Assistant to Brian Young
Matt Barbee . . . Assistant to Alissa Vradenburg
Deanna Beckman . . . Assistant to Evan Hainey
Joe Biddix . . . Assistant to Jason Newman
Dafna DeBasc . . . Assistant to Danielle Thomas
Clara Kim . . . Assistant to Elise Konialian
Barbra Korn . . . Assistant to Johnnie Planco
Collin Mitchell . . . Assistant to Katie Rhodes
Erica Schillinger . . . Assistant to Jennifer Levine

UPRIGHT CITIZENS BRIGADE

5919 Franklin Ave.
Los Angeles, CA 90028
PHONE . . . 323-908-8702
FAX . . . 323-460-6185
EMAIL . . . la@ucbt.net
WEB SITE . . . www.ucbtheatre.com
TYPES Theatre - TV Series
HAS DEAL WITH NBC Universal Television Studio
CREDITS Asssscat - Comedy Death-Ray - Trapped in the Closet: A Panel Discussion - Pop & Politics with Jimmy Dore - F'ed Up & Illegal Videos - Rode Hard and Put Away Wet
SUBMISSION POLICY Send stage comedy submissions to seth@ucbt.net

Matt Besser . . . Owner
Amy Poehler . . . Owner
Ian Roberts . . . Owner
Matt Walsh . . . Owner
Susan Hale . . . Managing Director
Seth Morris . . . Artistic Director

URBAN ENTERTAINMENT

16133 Ventura Blvd., Ste. 700
Encino, CA 91436
PHONE . . . 818-377-7441
EMAIL . . . info@urbanent.com
TYPES Animation - Direct-to-Video/DVD - Features - TV Series
DEVELOPMENT Whitebread (New Line) - Diesel Debutantes (New Line) - Ralph (Universal) - Step in the Name of Love (MGM)
PRODUCTION Beanstalk in Brooklyn (Animated Feature)
CREDITS The Golden Blaze (Animated Feature) - Undercover Brother (Universal/Imagine)

Michael Jenkinson . . . CEO/Founder
Nichelle Protho . . . Sr. VP, Production & Development
Christopher Brown . . . Coordinator, Development & Production
Bryon Carson . . . Animation Director

USA NETWORK

30 Rockefeller Plaza, 21st Fl.
New York, NY 10112
PHONE . . . 212-664-4444/818-777-1000
FAX . . . 212-703-8582
WEB SITE . . . www.usanetwork.com
TYPES Made-for-TV/Cable Movies - Reality TV - TV Series
DEVELOPMENT eBaum's World - Peace Out - Starter Wife - Stuck in Paradise - Burn Notice - To Love and Die in L.A. - The Hamptons - Secrets of the Spa - Hunting Rabbets (with WWE Films) - The Last Tough Guy - Turf - The Capper - Crush
UPCOMING RELEASES US Open - Great American Christmas
CREDITS The 4400 - AFI Life Achievement Award - The Dead Zone - Monk - Nashville Star - Made in the USA - WWE Raw - Psych
COMMENTS West Coast office: 100 Universal City Plaza, Universal City, CA 91608

Bonnie Hammer . . . President
Catherine Dunleavy . . . CFO
Jeff Wachtel . . . Executive VP, Series & Longform
Richard W. Lynn . . . Executive VP, Business Affairs/General Counsel
Gordon Beck . . . Sr. VP, Production & Programming, Sports
Jane Blaney . . . Sr. VP, Programming, Acquisitions & Scheduling

(Continued)

USA NETWORK (Continued)

Jackie de Crinis . . . . Sr. VP, Original Series
Laurette Hayden . . . . Sr. VP, Movies & Miniseries
John Kelley . . . . Sr. VP, Communications, Publicity
Chris McCumber . . . . Sr. VP, Marketing & Brand Strategy
Christof Bove . . . . VP, Longform Programming
Lorenzo De Guttadauro . . . . VP/Creative Director
Jean Guerin . . . . VP, Publicity
Libby Hansen . . . . VP, Reality Programming
Kevin Landy . . . . VP, Programming/Sr. Producer, Golf
Alexandra Shapiro . . . . VP, Marketing & Brand Strategy

RENÉE VALENTE PRODUCTIONS

13547 Ventura Blvd., #195
Sherman Oaks, CA 91423
PHONE 310-472-5342
EMAIL . . . . valenteprod@aol.com

TYPES: Features - Made-for-TV/Cable Movies - TV Series
CREDITS: Hollywood Wives...The New Generation - A Storm in Summer (Showtime) - A Man Upstairs (CBS) - Poker Alice (CBS) - Around the World in 80 Days (NBC, Miniseries) - Contract on Cherry Street (NBC) - Blind Ambition (CBS)
SUBMISSION POLICY: Release must accompany; No email submissions accepted

Renée Valente . . . . Executive Producer

VALHALLA MOTION PICTURES

8530 Wilshire Blvd., Ste. 400
Beverly Hills, CA 90211
PHONE 310-360-8530
FAX 310-360-8531
EMAIL . . . . vmp@valhallapix.com

TYPES: Documentaries - Features - Made-for-TV/Cable Movies - TV Series
CREDITS: Aeon Flux - The Hulk - Dick - Terminator 1&2 - Aliens - Armageddon - Tremors - Dante's Peak - Clockstoppers - Water Dance - No Escape - Abyss - Safe Passage - Virus - The Punisher
SUBMISSION POLICY: No unsolicited submissions

Gale Anne Hurd . . . . CEO/Producer
Gary Ventimiglia . . . . President, Production
Julie Thomson . . . . CFO/Head, Business Affairs
Kevin Boyle . . . . Development Assistant
Michelle Reihel . . . . Assistant to Gale Anne Hurd

VANDERKLOOT FILM & TELEVISION

750 Ralph McGill Blvd. NE
Atlanta, GA 30312
PHONE 404-221-0236/404-688-3348
FAX 404-221-1057
EMAIL . . . . bv@vanderkloot.com
SECOND EMAIL . . . . bv@magicklantern.com
WEB SITE . . . . www.vanderkloot.com
SECOND WEB SITE . . . . www.magicklantern.com

TYPES: Commercials - Direct-to-Video/DVD - Documentaries - Features - TV Series
DEVELOPMENT: The Melungeons (Documentary) - The Chaldean Affair (Feature)
PRE-PRODUCTION: Flying the Secret Sky (Documentary)
UPCOMING RELEASES: The BIG Rescue
CREDITS: Cumberland: Island in Time - The BIG Adventure Series
COMMENTS: Little Mammoth Media (www.littlemammoth.com); Magick Lantern Post

William VanDerKloot . . . . President/Producer/Director
Jennifer Mador . . . . Director, Post Production
Jesenko Fazlagic Sr. . . . . Sr. Designer/Editor
James Powell . . . . Sr. Editor/Compositor
Nancy Rosette . . . . Symphony Editor/Compositor
Alphonso Dormun . . . . Designer/Editor
Bazyl Dripps . . . . Editor
Lisa Lewis . . . . Sales Manager, Post Production
Bridget Metzger . . . . Production Account Executive
Adrienne Watts . . . . Little Mammoth Sales Manager
Paul A. Johns . . . . Controller
Jeff Kinder . . . . Composer/Sound Designer
Rob Lansdowne . . . . Production Accountant

VANGUARD FILMS/VANGUARD ANIMATION

8703 W. Olympic Blvd.
Los Angeles, CA 90035
PHONE 310-360-8039
FAX 310-888-8012
WEB SITE . . . . www.vanguardfilms.com
SECOND WEB SITE . . . . www.vanguardanimation.com

TYPES: Animation - Features
DEVELOPMENT: Gnomes! - After Man - On the Road - Galaxy High - The Twits - Toad Trip - The Bob Marley Story - The Poppyfields - Santa Paws
PRE-PRODUCTION: Pet Boy - Gateway to the Gods - Space Chimps
COMPLETED UNRELEASED: Happily N'Ever After
CREDITS: Valiant - Seven Years in Tibet - Sarafina - Thin Blue Line - Shrek 1&2 - The Tuxedo
SUBMISSION POLICY: No unsolicited material

John H. Williams . . . . No Title
Margaret French Isaac . . . . No Title
Rob Moreland . . . . No Title
Venecia Duran . . . . No Title
Terry Botwick . . . . No Title
Jeremy Ross . . . . No Title
Brynne Orloski . . . . No Title

VANGUARD PRODUCTIONS
12111 Beatrice St.
Culver City, CA 90230
PHONE .310-306-4910
FAX .310-306-4910
EMAIL .vanguard.productions@verizon.net
TYPES Commercials - Direct-to-Video/DVD - Documentaries - Features - Made-for-TV/Cable Movies - Music Videos - Reality TV - TV Series
DEVELOPMENT The Lost Treasure - Border Lords - Kid Africa - Alpine Horror - Sea of Demons (Series) - Broken April - Regrettable Error
PRE-PRODUCTION They Also Served (Series)
CREDITS Alien Express - Dead Rail - We the People - The Bad Pack - Cross Dreams - Wanted - Closing the Deal - Route 666

Terence M. O'Keefe .Writer/Producer/Director
Bennett J. Fidlow .VP, Creative Affairs
Bruce Miyaki .VP, Development
Shirley Wang .Executive Assistant

VANTAGE ENTERPRISES, INC.
3724 Vantage Ave.
Studio City, CA 91604
PHONE .818-509-8967
TYPES Direct-to-Video/DVD - Documentaries - Features - Made-for-TV/Cable Movies - TV Series
POST PRODUCTION Brothers at War
CREDITS Hollywood's Best Kept Secrets - Convict Cowboy - The Lazarus Man - Black Fox - Orleans - National Desk - The Lot - Darkness at High Noon: The Carl Foreman Documents - American Valor
SUBMISSION POLICY No unsolicited submissions

Norman S. Powell .Partner
Ellen Levine .Partner

THE VAULT, INC.
1831 Centinela Ave., 2nd Fl.
Santa Monica, CA 90404
PHONE .310-315-0012
FAX .310-315-9322
TYPES Features
CREDITS The Last Supper - Campfire Tales - Panic - Perfect Opposites

Matt Cooper .Producer/Director/Writer
David Cooper .Executive Producer
Lori Miller .Producer

JOSEPH S. VECCHIO ENTERTAINMENT
811 Euclid Ave., Ste. #5
Santa Monica, CA 90403
PHONE .310-917-1515
EMAIL .jettv@aol.com
SECOND EMAIL .egcamerica@aol.com
TYPES Commercials - Direct-to-Video/DVD - Documentaries - Features - Internet Content - Made-for-TV/Cable Movies - Miniseries - Mobile Content - Reality TV - Specials - TV Series
DEVELOPMENT Fighting Black Lions - Night Magic - The Wanderer - Wild Card - In Deadly Earnest - Dante & the Debutante - Citizen X
PRE-PRODUCTION The Woods - Stranger in a Strange Land (Paramount)
CREDITS Oscar - Sunchaser
COMMENTS Entertainment Guidance Company: Consultation services for all aspects of the entertainment industry

Joseph S. Vecchio .Producer

*VEOH NETWORKS, INC.
7220 Trade St., Ste. 115
San Diego, CA 92121
PHONE .858-361-8468
FAX .858-695-6828
EMAIL .bizdev@veoh.com
WEB SITE .www.veoh.com
TYPES Internet Content - Mobile Content
COMMENTS Broadband entertainment specialist; New independent TV broadcasting system

Dmitry Shapiro .CEO
Dr. Ted Dunning .Chief Scientist
Arthur H. Bilger .Director
Todd Dagres .Director
Michael Eisner .Director
Dr. Pete Sealy .Advisor

VERDON-CEDRIC PRODUCTIONS
PO Box 2639
Beverly Hills, CA 90213
PHONE .310-274-7253
TYPES Features
SUBMISSION POLICY No unsolicited scripts

Sidney Poitier .Producer/Director/Writer/Actor

VERSUS
Two Stamford Plaza, 281 Tresser Blvd., 9th Fl.
Stamford, CT 06901
PHONE .203-406-2500
FAX .203-406-2530
EMAIL .info@olntv.com
WEB SITE .www.olntv.com
TYPES Commercials - Documentaries - Features - Internet Content - Reality TV - Specials - TV Series
COMMENTS Versus is a competitive sports network; Also produces VOD

Gavin Harvey .President
Kim Armor .CFO/Sr. VP, Business Development
Marc Fein .Sr. VP, Programming & Production
Martin Ehrlich .VP, Production & Executive Producer
Wendy McCoy .VP, Marketing
Victoria Quoss .VP, Programming, International & Strategic Planning
Amy Phillips .Director, Public Relations
Michael Winter .Director, Original Programming

VERTIGO ENTERTAINMENT
9348 Civic Center Dr., Mezzanine Level
Beverly Hills, CA 90210
PHONE .310-288-5160
FAX .310-278-5295
TYPES Features - TV Series
HAS DEAL WITH Focus Features/Rogue Pictures - Universal Pictures
DEVELOPMENT In-Utero - Chaos - The Eye - Old Boy - Addicted - Shutter - The Mission - Siren - Creepshow - Incurable - Anguish
PRE-PRODUCTION My Sassy Girl - Strangers
POST PRODUCTION The Grudge 2 - The Departed - The Visiting
CREDITS The Lake House - Eight Below - Dark Water - The Ring 1&2 - The Grudge

Roy Lee .Producer
Doug Davison .Producer
Sonny Mallhi .VP
Gabriel Mason .Director, Development
Irene Yeung .Creative Executive
Carly Norris .Story Editor

VH1
1515 Broadway
New York, NY 10036
PHONE .212-846-8000/310-752-8000
WEB SITE .www.vh1.com
TYPES Documentaries - Made-for-TV/Cable Movies - Reality TV - TV Series
PROVIDES DEAL TO 51 Minds Entertainment
CREDITS The World Series of Pop Culture - The Last Days of Lisa Lopes - so noTORIous - Best Week Ever - Bands Reunited - All Access - I Love The... - Driven - Fabulous Life Of - The Greatest - VH1 Goes Inside - Behind the Music - The Top 20 Countdown - True Spin - Super Secret TV Formulas - The Surreal Life - Celebrity Fit Club - Strange Love - (Inside) Out - Storytellers - Before They Were Rock Stars - My Fair Brady - Breaking Bonaduce - Hogan Knows Best - Motormouth - The Partridge Family - Totally Obsessed - Flavor of Love - Dingo Ate My Video (VH1 Mobile) - The Drug Years (Documentary)
COMMENTS West Coast office: 2600 Colorado Ave., Santa Monica, CA 90404

Judith McGrath .Chairman/CEO, MTV Networks
Van Toffler .MTV Networks Group President
Brian Graden .President, Entertainment, Music Group (MTV, VH1, MTV2, CMT) & Logo
Tom Calderone .General Manager
Michael Hirschorn .Executive VP, Original Programming & Production
Rick Krim .Executive VP, Talent & Music Programming
Colleen Fahey Rush .Executive VP, Research
Jim Ackerman .Sr. VP, Development & Production
Nigel Cox-Hagen .Sr. VP, Creative Consumer Marketing
Michele Megan Dix .Sr. VP, Music & Talent Develoment
Bruce Gillmer .Sr. VP, Music & Talent Relations
Maggie Malina .Sr. VP, VH1 Films & Scripted Series
Jeff Olde .Sr. VP, VH1 Production & Programming
Lee Rolontz .Sr. VP, VH1 Original Music Production
Eric Sherman . . .Sr. VP/General Manager, VH1 Classic/VH1 Digital Television
Ben Zurier .Sr. VP, Programming Strategy & Acquisitions
(Continued)

VH1 (Continued)
Brad Abramson .VP, Production & Programming
Stacy Alexander .VP, Casting, Talent & Creative Development
Alex Demyanenko .VP, West Coast Series Development
Michael Garvey .VP, Music Programming & Production, VH1 Classic
Matt Hanna .VP, Development
Brette Henne .VP, Corporate Communications
Jill Holmes .VP, West Coast Current Programming & Production
Tima Imm .VP, Digital Media & Music
Stella Stolper .VP, Talent & Creative Development
Danielle Woodrow .Sr. Director, Development, Original Movies & Scripted Series
Damla Dogan .Director, West Coast Series Development
Leah Horwitz .Director, Music & Talent Relations
Noah Pollack .Director, West Coast Series Development
David Allensworth .Manager, East Coast Programming & Development
Stacey Jenkins .Manager, East Coast Development
Kristen Kelly .Manager, West Coast Series Development
Jennifer Levy .Manager, West Coast Series Development
Claire McCabe . . .Executive Producer, West Coast Current Programming & Production

VIACOM ENTERTAINMENT GROUP
5555 Melrose Ave.
Los Angeles, CA 90038
PHONE .323-956-5000
TYPES Features - TV Series

Tom Freston .CEO
Mike Bartok .Executive VP, Legal & Business Affairs
Michael Dolan .Executive VP/CFO
James Bombassei .Sr. VP, Investor Relations
Wade Davis .Sr. VP, Mergers & Acquisitions

MARK VICTOR PRODUCTIONS
2932 Wilshire Blvd., Ste. 201
Santa Monica, CA 90403
PHONE .310-828-3339
FAX .310-828-9588
EMAIL .markvictorproductions@hotmail.com
TYPES Direct-to-Video/DVD - Features - Made-for-TV/Cable Movies - Reality TV - TV Series
DEVELOPMENT Synbat - The Wrath of Grapes - Rifting - 25th Hour - I Married a Witch - The Hunt for Skinwalker
PRE-PRODUCTION Ditch - Over the River
PRODUCTION The Best Evidence
POST PRODUCTION Falling
UPCOMING RELEASES States of Grace
CREDITS Poltergeist 1&2 - Stephen King's Sleepwalkers - Marked for Death - Cool World - Immortals (Series) - Great Balls of Fire - Who Killed Atlanta's Children - Visitors from the Unknown

Mark Victor .Producer/Writer
Mark Skelly .Producer
Sarah Johnson .Director, Development

VIEW ASKEW PRODUCTIONS, INC.
PO Box 93339
Los Angeles, CA 90093
PHONE .323-969-9423
FAX .323-969-9008
EMAIL .gailmstanley@aol.com
TYPES Features
HAS DEAL WITH The Weinstein Company
CREDITS Jay and Silent Bob Strike Back - Dogma - Clerks 1&2 - Mallrats - Chasing Amy - Jersey Girl

Kevin Smith .President
Scott Mosier .VP
Gail Stanley .Assistant to Kevin Smith/Director, Development

VILLAGE ROADSHOW PICTURES
3400 Riverside Dr., Ste. 900
Burbank, CA 91505
PHONE .818-260-6000
FAX .818-260-6001
WEB SITE .www.villageroadshowpictures.com
TYPES Animation - Features
HAS DEAL WITH Warner Bros. Pictures
PROVIDES DEAL TO This is that corporation
DEVELOPMENT Get Smart - Shantaram - Major Movie Star - Other People's Wishes - The Dirty Dozen (Remake) - Market Forces
PRE-PRODUCTION Ocean's Thirteen - I Am Legend
PRODUCTION The Brave One - License To Wed - Happy Feet - Music & Lyrics
POST PRODUCTION Unaccompanied Minors - The Reaping - The Visiting - Lucky You
CREDITS Charlie and the Chocolate Factory - The Matrix 1-3 - Ocean's Eleven - Ocean's Twelve - Mystic River - Training Day - Three Kings - Constantine - Analyze This - The Lake House - Two Weeks Notice - Miss Congeniality - The Dukes of Hazzard - Zoolander - Cats & Dogs - Deep Blue Sea - Swordfish - Don't Say a Word - Space Cowboys
SUBMISSION POLICY No unsolicited submissions

Bruce Berman .Chairman/CEO
Steve Krone .President/COO
Dana Goldberg .President, Production
Reid Sullivan .Executive VP/CFO
Jeffrey Lampert .Executive VP, Worldwide Feature Production
Melissa Anna .Sr. VP, Distribution & Media
Kevin Berg .VP, Legal & Financial Affairs
Anna Dergan .VP, Administration & Operations
Jordanna Fraiberg .VP, Production
Joel Goldstein .VP, Business & Legal Affairs
Joseph Hanratty .VP, Controller
Kellie Maltagliati .VP, Marketing & Publicity
Jonny Romano .Director, Physical & Post-Production
Linda Cuevas .Manager, Marketing & Distribution
Fred Klein .Creative Executive
Suzy Figueroa .Executive Assistant to B. Berman
Remi Guyton .Executive Assistant to D. Goldberg
Amy Van Haun .Executive Assistant to R. Sullivan, K. Berg & J. Goldstein

DIMITRI VILLARD PRODUCTIONS
8721 Santa Monica Blvd., Ste. 100
Los Angeles, CA 90069-4507
PHONE .310-229-4545
FAX .310-362-8898
EMAIL .dvillard@gmail.com
TYPES Features - Made-for-TV/Cable Movies
DEVELOPMENT Headhunter - Where's Harry?
CREDITS Say Nothing - Flight of the Navigator - Once Bitten - In Love & War

Dimitri Villard .President
Susan Danforth .Assistant

VISIONBOX MEDIA GROUP
3272 Motor Ave., Ste. G
Los Angeles, CA 90034
PHONE .310-204-4686
FAX .310-204-4603
EMAIL .info@visionboxmedia.com
WEB SITE .www.visionboxmedia.com
TYPES Documentaries - Features - TV Series
DEVELOPMENT Morningstar - Immaculate Conception - The Last Date Movie - Cousin Ginny
COMPLETED UNRELEASED Believe In Me - The L.A. Riot Spectacular
CREDITS Falling Like This - Teddy Bears' Picnic - Charlotte Sometimes - The Invisibles - The Cooler - Love Object - Tortilla Soup - Never Die Alone
SUBMISSION POLICY Solicited projects only

John Manulis .CEO
Chris Miller .President, Post Production
Bill Newcomb .Director, Administration & Post Production
Randy Weiss .Director, Development & Production

VIVIANO FELDMAN ENTERTAINMENT
8383 Wilshire Blvd., Ste. 202
Beverly Hills, CA 90211
PHONE .323-866-0700
FAX .323-866-0704
EMAIL .viviano_feldman_entertainment@yahoo.com
TYPES Animation - Direct-to-Video/DVD - Features - Miniseries - Reality TV - Specials - Theatre - TV Series
DEVELOPMENT Jack and Jill (Sony) - American Crawl - Finders Keepers - Freedom House (Warner Bros.)
CREDITS Three to Tango - Family Sins - Caught in the Act - Nightmare Man - Alibi - Strange Love - Pitfall - Magic Hour - Letters from Joe - Mom's Got a Date with a Vampire - Strange Hearts
COMMENTS Affiliated with PGA

Bettina Sofia Viviano .President/Producer/Manager
Richard Feldman .President/Producer/Manager
Sarah Dale .Creative Executive

JON VOIGHT ENTERTAINMENT
10203 Santa Monica Blvd.
Los Angeles, CA 90067
PHONE .310-843-0223
FAX .310-553-9895
EMAIL .develop@crystal-sky.com
TYPES Features - Made-for-TV/Cable Movies
CREDITS Film: The Karate Dog - Baby Geniuses; TV: The Princess & the Barrio Boy - The Fixer

Jon Voight .Actor/Producer
Dorothy Koster .Manager

VON ZERNECK-SERTNER FILMS

13425 Ventura Blvd., Ste. 301
Sherman Oaks, CA 91423
PHONE .818-789-2766
FAX .818-789-2768
EMAIL .kellygarrett@vzsfilms.com
TYPES Features - Made-for-TV/Cable Movies - TV Series
HAS DEAL WITH Sony Pictures Television
PRODUCTION Category 7: The End of the World - For One Night - Haunting Sarah
COMPLETED UNRELEASED Vinegar Hill
CREDITS Scott Turow's Reversible Errors - Category 6: Day of Destruction - Wes Craven Presents Don't Look Down - The Mystery of Natalie Wood - Ambulance Girl - We Were the Mulvaneys

Robert Sertner .Partner
Frank von Zerneck .Partner
Danielle von Zerneck Fearnley .Producer
Stacy Mandelberg .Sr. VP, Development
Randy Sutter .Sr. VP, Production
Peter Sadowski .VP, Production
Laurence Ducceschi .Director, Production
Kelly Garrett .Director, Development
Nancy Mouton .Executive Assistant

VOX3 FILMS

180 Varick St., Ste. 1002
New York, NY 10014
PHONE .212-741-0406
FAX .212-741-0424
EMAIL .contact@vox3films.com
WEB SITE .www.vox3films.com
TYPES Direct-to-Video/DVD - Features - Made-for-TV/Cable Movies
DEVELOPMENT Stained Glass - Man and Boy - Under the Frog - Skin and Teeth - Sightings
PRE-PRODUCTION Crawling at Night - The Last Word
PRODUCTION Never Forever - Broken English
POST PRODUCTION Feel
UPCOMING RELEASES Fur
CREDITS America Brown - Game 6
COMMENTS Accepts scripts from agents only

Andrew Fierberg .Founder/Producer
Christina Weiss Lurie .Founder/Producer
Steven Shainberg .Founder/Director/Producer
Kelly McCormick .VP, Development
Mamta Trivedi .Director, Production

VOY PICTURES

9220 W. Sunset Blvd., Ste. 309
West Hollywood, CA 90069
PHONE .310-550-1019/212-204-8331
FAX .310-388-0775/212-202-5240
EMAIl .contact@voygroup.com
WEB SITE .www.voypictures.com
SECOND WEB SITE .www.voygroup.com
TYPES Direct-to-Video/DVD - Documentaries - Features - Reality TV - TV Series
DEVELOPMENT Public Emily
CREDITS Favela Rising
SUBMISSION POLICY See Web site
COMMENTS English-language Latino films and television

Fernando Espuelas .CEO
Brian Field .COO
Lourdes Diaz .President
Ted Perkins .Head, Distribution
Dino Hainline .Creative Executive
Jonathan Martofel .Development Assistant

VULCAN PRODUCTIONS

505 Fifth Ave. South, Ste. 900
Seattle, WA 98104
PHONE .206-342-2277
WEB SITE .www.vulcanproductions.com
TYPES Documentaries - Features
POST PRODUCTION Where God Left His Shoes
CREDITS Features: Hard Candy - Bickford Schmeckler's Cool Ideas - Far From Heaven - Coastlines - The Safety of Objects - The Luzhin Defense - Titus - Men With Guns; Documentaries: Rx for Survival: Heroes - Rx for Survival: A Global Health Challenge - No Direction Home: Bob Dylan - National Geographic's Strange Days on Planet Earth - Lightning in a Bottle - Black Sky: Winning the X Prize - Black Sky: The Race for Space - Martin Scorsese Presents The Blues - Evolution - Cracking the Code of Life - Me & Isaac Newton - Inspirations

Paul Allen .Chairman & Founder
Jody Patton .President & CEO
Richard Hutton .VP, Media Development
Michael Caldwell .Director, Motion Picture Productions
Bonnie Benjamin-Phariss .Director, Documentary Productions
Pamela Rosenstein .Manager, Documentary Productions
Jennifer Senkler .Assistant Manager, Documentary Productions
Jason Hunke .Sr. Director, Marketing & Publicity
Michael Nank .Manager, Marketing & Publicity

RAYMOND WAGNER PRODUCTIONS, INC.

10377 Rochester Ave.
Los Angeles, CA 90024
PHONE .310-278-1970
FAX .310-274-2662
TYPES Features - Made-for-TV/Cable Movies - TV Series
DEVELOPMENT Demolished Man (Paramount) - The Stars My Destination (Universal) - The Alibi Club - The Ghosts - Men Are Dogs - Harry's Lot
CREDITS Turner & Hooch - Run - Snow Day - Maniac Magee

Raymond Wagner .President/Producer
Christine McBride .Director, Development

WALDEN FILMS

953 Fourth St., Ste. 305
Santa Monica, CA 90403
PHONE .202-912-6524
EMAIL .waldencine@aol.com
TYPES Features - TV Series
DEVELOPMENT Poe - Expedition - Liecatcher
CREDITS A&E Biography - The Napoleon Murder Mystery - White House: 200th Anniversary - Crime & Punishment

Noah Morowitz .Executive Producer/Director

WALDEN MEDIA

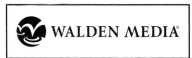

1888 Century Park East, 14th Fl.
Los Angeles, CA 90067

PHONE .310-887-1000/617-451-5420
FAX .310-887-1001
WEB SITE .www.walden.com

TYPES	Features
PROVIDES DEAL TO	Bristol Bay Productions - Gran Via Productions
DEVELOPMENT	The Chronicles of Narnia: Prince Caspian - Tortoise and Hippo - Manhunt - Rebels - Treasure Island - Kid Mayor - The Giver - Biblionauts - Carlisle School - Nim's Island - The City of Ember - The Dark Is Rising Sequence - City of the Beasts - Heat - Tom Quixote - Untitled Edgar Allen Poe Project - Untitled Sherlock Holmes Project - The Westing Game
PRE-PRODUCTION	Journey to the Center of the Earth (3-D)
PRODUCTION	Waterhorse - Mr. Magorium's Wonder Emporium
POST PRODUCTION	Bridge to Terabithia - Amazing Grace
UPCOMING RELEASES	Charlotte's Web
CREDITS	How to Eat Fried Worms - Hoot - The Chronicles of Narnia: The Lion, the Witch and the Wardrobe - I Am David - Because of Winn-Dixie - Around the World in 80 Days - Holes - Ghosts of the Abyss - Pulse: a STOMP Odyssey
COMMENTS	Parent company: Anschutz Film Group; Production deal with Penguin Young Readers Group; East Coast office: 294 Washington St., 7th Fl., Boston, MA 02108

Cary Granat .CEO
David Weil .CEO, Anschutz Film Group
Micheal Flaherty .Co-Founder/President (Boston)
Jess Wittenberg .COO
Francesca Lindley .CFO
Frances X. Flaherty .Executive VP, General Counsel
Alex Schwartz .Executive VP, Production
Chris DeMoulin .Executive VP, Marketing
Gordon Tichell .Sr. VP, Finance/Controller
Jim Meenaghan .Sr. VP, Business & Legal Affairs
Jackie Levine .Sr. VP, Production
Doug Jones .Sr. VP, Physical Production
Frank Smith .Sr. VP, Business & Legal Affairs
Randy Testa .VP, Education & Professional Development (Boston)
Karin Le Maire Crounse .VP, Project Development (Boston)
Lindsay Fellows .VP, Music
Jay Galston .VP, Finance & Strategic Planning
Debbie Kovacs .VP, Publishing (Boston)
Mylan Stepanovich .VP, Physical Production
Jonas Thaler .VP, Post Production
Brian Crounse .Director, Research & Large Format Projects (Boston)
Tommy Finkelstein .Director, Business & Legal Affairs
David Kaufmann .Director, Development
Evan Turner .Director, Development
Jared Mass .Creative Executive
Bonnie Solomon .Creative Executive

WALKER/FITZGIBBON TV/FILMS

233 N. Wetherly Dr.
Beverly Hills, CA 90211

PHONE .866-884-3501/310-205-3500
FAX .310-205-3502
EMAIL .walkerfitz@aol.com
WEB SITE .www.walkerfitzgibbon.com

TYPES	Documentaries - Features - Made-for-TV/Cable Movies - Music Videos - Specials - TV Series
DEVELOPMENT	Centac - Centac 26 - INK: Crime Beat
CREDITS	Tributo a Nuestros Heroes (NBC Telemundo/Universal) - Gloria Estefan: Live & Rewrapped (Estefan Television Productions) - Intimate Portrait: Gloria Estefan (Lifetime TV); Documentaries: Shakira - Andy Garcia/Cachao (Sony Music/VH1/MTV Latin America)
COMMENTS	East Coast office: 3183 NE 166 St., North Miami Beach, FL 33160

Mo Fitzgibbon .Producer/Director
Robert W. Walker .Executive Producer/Director
Fernando Viquez .Co-Producer
Victoria Rose .Development & Business Affairs (NY)
Nora Castillo .Production Manager

WALTZING CLOUDS, INC.

12242 Nelson Rd.
Moorpark, CA 93021

PHONE .805-553-9094

TYPES	Documentaries - Features - Made-for-TV/Cable Movies - Miniseries - Theatre - TV Series
DEVELOPMENT	The Investigation - Dual - The Searchers - Voss
PRE-PRODUCTION	Ernest Hemingway's The Old Man and the Sea
CREDITS	Dead Ahead - The Ticket - The Hunted - Overlord

Stuart Cooper .President/Writer/Director
Kelly Korzon .VP, Development & Production

WARDENCLYFFE ENTERTAINMENT

8899 Beverly Blvd., Ste. 603
Los Angeles, CA 90048

PHONE .310-273-9664
FAX .310-273-9658

TYPES	Features
DEVELOPMENT	The Alchemist - Mockingbird - U.S.S. Pueblo
UPCOMING RELEASES	American Gothic
CREDITS	Dave Barry's Complete Guide to Guys - Kart Racer - Blizzard - Iron Will - Survivors - Wooly Boys - With You or Without You - Virginia's Run
SUBMISSION POLICY	No unsolicited material

Robert Schwartz .Producer/President
Brandon Kienzle .Director, Development

WARNER BROS. ANIMATION

15303 Ventura Blvd., Bldg. E
Sherman Oaks, CA 91403
PHONE .818-977-8700
WEB SITE www.warnerbros.com
TYPES Animation - Features - Direct-to-Video/DVD - Syndication - TV Series

Sander D. Schwartz .President, Warner Bros. Animation
Andy Lewis .Executive VP/General Manager
Howard Schwartz .Sr. VP, Domestic Production
Kim Christianson .VP, Creative Affairs
Toshiyuki Hiruma .VP, International Production
Timothy R. Iverson .VP, Post Production
Peter Steckelman .VP, Business & Legal Affairs

WARNER BROS. DIGITAL DISTRIBUTION

4000 Warner Blvd.
Burbank, CA 91522-0001
PHONE .818-954-6000
WEB SITE www.warnerbros.com
TYPES Internet Content - Mobile Content

Simon Kenny .President

WARNER BROS. ENTERTAINMENT INC.

4000 Warner Blvd.
Burbank, CA 91522-0001
PHONE .818-954-6000
WEB SITE www.warnerbros.com
TYPES Animation - Direct-to-Video/DVD - Documentaries - Features - TV Series

Barry M. Meyer .Chairman/CEO
Alan F. Horn .President/COO
Gary Credle .Executive VP, Administration & Studio Operations
Susan N. Fleishman .Executive VP, Corporate Communications
Richard J. Fox .Executive VP, International
Diane Nelson .Executive VP, Global Brand Management
Edward A. Romano .Executive VP/CFO
Bruce Rosenblum .President, Warner Bros. Television Group
John A. Schulman .Executive VP/General Counsel
Kevin Tsujihara .President, Warner Bros. Home Entertainment Group
Josh Berger .Executive VP, Managing Director, Warner Bros. Entertainment UK
Bill Ireton .President/Representative Director, Warner Entertainment Japan
Iris Knobloch .Président-Directeur Général, Warner Bros. France S.A.
Darcy Antonellis .Executive VP, Distribution Technology Operations
Leigh Chapman .Sr. VP/Chief Employment Counsel
Michael Goodnight .Sr. VP/Assistant Corporate Controller
James L. Halsey .Sr. VP/CIO
Reginald Harpur .Sr. VP/Controller
Dean Marks .Sr. VP, Intellectual Property, Corporate Business Development & Strategy
Gaetano Mastropasqua .Sr. VP/Corporate Global Promotions & Partner Relations
Gary Meisel .Sr. VP, Corporate Business Development & Strategy
Steven Mertz .Sr. VP/General Counsel, Europe
Jim Noonan .Sr. VP, Worldwide Strategic Promotions & Communications, Warner Bros. Home Entertainment Group
Zazi Pope .Sr. VP/Deputy General Counsel
Sheldon Presser .Sr. VP/Deputy General Counsel
Lisa Rawlins .Sr. VP, Studio & Production Affairs
Andrea Marozas .Sr. VP, Corporate Communications, Theatrical
Scott Rowe .Sr. VP, Corporate Communications
Laura Valan .Sr. VP, TV Financial Management
Kiko Washington .Sr. VP, Worldwide Human Resources
Clarissa Weirick .Sr. VP/General Counsel, Corporate Business Development & Strategy

(Continued)

WARNER BROS. ENTERTAINMENT INC. (Continued)

Jeremy Williams .Sr. VP/Deputy General Counsel
Marc Brandon .VP, Antipiracy Internet Operations
Amber Fredman .VP, Brand Management
Vicky Goldberg .VP, Recruitment & Employee Development
Irika Slavin .VP, Brand Management
List St. Amand .VP, Brand Management
Sandy Yi .VP, Brand Management
Alison Cressey .Group Marketing Director, Warner Bros. Entertainment UK
Patrick Strafford .Group Commercial Marketing Director, Warner Bros. Entertainment UK

WARNER BROS. ONLINE

505 N. Brand Blvd., 4th Fl.
Glendale, CA 91203
PHONE .818-977-7900
FAX .818-977-3135
WEB SITE www.warnerbros.com
TYPES Internet Content - Mobile Content

Justin Herz .VP, Client Services
Darryl LaRue .VP, Sales & Business Development
Michael Lewis .VP, Business & Legal Affairs/General Counsel
Staci Miller .VP, Operations & Brand Strategy
Brian Moreno .VP, Strategic Marketing
Brian Ober .VP, Finance & Administration
Khalid Oreif .VP, Technology & Engineering
Billy Wright .VP, Worldwide Wireless

WARNER BROS. PICTURES

4000 Warner Blvd.
Burbank, CA 91522-0001
PHONE .818-954-6000
WEB SITE www.warnerbros.com
TYPES Features

Jeff Robinov .President, Production
Steven Papazian .President, Physical Production
Doug Frank .President, Music Operations
Steve Spira .President, Worldwide Business Affairs
Patti Connolly .Executive VP, Business Affairs
Lynn Harris .Executive VP, Production
Kevin McCormick .Executive VP, Theatrical Production
Marc Solomon .Executive VP, Post Production & Visual Effects
Courtenay Valenti .Executive VP, Production
Keith Zajic .Executive VP, Business Affairs, Music
Musette Buckley .Sr. VP, Production Resources
Daniel B. Butler .Sr. VP, Business & Legal Affairs, Music
Chris De Faria .Sr. VP, Physical Production & Visual Effects
Bill Draper .Sr. VP, Physical Production
Jessica Goodman .Sr. VP, Production
Lora Kennedy .Sr. VP, Feature Casting
Dan Lin .Sr. VP, Production
Lisa Margolis .Sr. VP, Business & Legal Affairs, Music
Mark Scoon .Sr. VP, Physical Production
Greg Silverman .Sr. VP, Production
Frank J. Urioste .Sr. VP, Creative
Kristy Carlson .VP, Casting
Suzi Civita .VP, Music
Ellen Schwartz .VP, Music Development
Virginia Tweedy .VP, Business Affairs Administration
Teresa Wayne .VP, Story & Creative Administration
Gary LeMel .Advisor, Warner Bros. Pictures Music/CEO, Warner Sunset Soundtracks

WARNER BROS. TELEVISION PRODUCTION

4000 Warner Blvd.
Burbank, CA 91522-0001
PHONE .818-954-6000
WEB SITE .www.warnerbros.com
TYPES TV Series

Peter Roth .President
Leonard Goldstein .Executive VP, Creative Affairs
Brett Paul .Executive VP, Business Affairs, Operations & Finance
Judith Zaylor .Executive VP, Production
Mary V. Buck .Sr. VP, Casting
Adam Glick .Sr. VP, Business Affairs
Melinda Hage .Sr. VP, Current Programming
Hank Lachmund .Sr. VP, Labor Relations
Gregg Maday .Sr. VP, Movies & Miniseries
Sharon Magnuson .Sr. VP, Publicity
Marianne Cracchiolo Mago .Sr. VP, Comedy Development
Geriann McIntosh .Sr. VP, Administration
Marjorie Neufeld .Sr. VP/General Counsel, Legal Affairs
Susan Rovner .Sr. VP, Drama Development
David Sacks .Sr. VP, Current Programming
Bronwyn Savasta .Sr. VP, Music
Tony Sepulveda .Sr. VP, Casting
Christina Smith .Sr. VP, Financial Administration
Jody Zucker .Sr. VP/Deputy General Counsel, Legal Affairs
Wendy Baldikoski .VP, Comedy Development
Clancy Collins .VP, Current Programming
Gay M. Di Fusco .VP, Music Clearance & Licensing
Nannette Diacovo .VP, Legal Affairs
Jay Gendron .VP, Business Affairs
Mindy Hahn-Seiffert .VP, Research
Vicky Herman .VP, Production
Henry Johnson .VP, Production
Heather Kadin .VP, Drama Development
Rachel Kaplan .VP, Drama Development
Lisa Lang .VP, Comedy Development
Lisa Lewis .VP, Production
Dan Limerick .VP, Business Affairs
Jennifer Littlehales .VP, WBTV Production
Mara Lopez .VP, Post Production
Sue Palladino .VP, Business Affairs
Ellen Rauch .VP, Production
Margaret Simon .VP, Casting (NY)
Rick Smith .VP, Estimating
John Stuckmeyer .VP, Production
Adrienne Turner .VP, Current Programming
Sam Wolfson .VP, Labor Relations
Barbara Zuckerman .VP, Legal Affairs
Jeanne Cotton .Director, Current Programming
Stephanie Groves .Director, Current Programming
Lisa Roos .Director, Drama Development
Odetta Watkins .Director, Current Programming
Rebecca Franko .Manager, Current Programming

WARNER BROS. THEATRE VENTURES

4000 Warner Blvd.
Burbank, CA 91522-0001
PHONE .818-954-6000
WEB SITE .www.warnerbros.com

Gregg Maday .Executive VP
Raymond Wu .VP, Business & Legal Affairs

*WARNER HORIZON TELEVISION

c/o Warner Bros.
4000 Warner Blvd.
Burbank, CA 91522-0001
PHONE .818-954-6000
WEB SITE .www.warnerbros.com
TYPES Reality TV - TV Series

Peter Roth .President, Warner Bros. Television
David Auerbach .Sr. VP, Alternative Programming
Alan Saxe .Sr. VP, Business Affairs
Shelley Zimmerman .Sr. VP, Scripted Programming

WARNER INDEPENDENT PICTURES

4000 Warner Blvd.
Burbank, CA 91522-0001
PHONE .818-954-6000
WEB SITE .www.warnerindependent.com
TYPES Features
PROVIDES DEAL TO Bonne Pioche - Cherry Road Films, LLC

Polly Cohen .President
Steven Friedlander .Executive VP, Domestic Distribution
Laura Kim .Executive VP, Marketing & Publicity
Paul Federbush .Sr. VP, Co-Production & Acquisitions
Despina Beazoglou .VP, Business & Legal Affairs
Tracey Bing .VP, Production & Acquisitions
Lauren Craniotes .VP, Production
David Magedman .VP, Distribution
Erin O'Neil .VP, Creative Advertising

WARREN MILLER ENTERTAINMENT

2540 Frontier Ave., Bldg. 104
Boulder, CO 80301
PHONE .303-442-3430
FAX .303-998-7208
WEB SITE .www.warrenmiller.com
TYPES Direct-to-Video/DVD - Documentaries - Features - Made-for-TV/Cable Movies - TV Series
PRODUCTION Epic Conditions (The Weather Channel) - Destination Wild (Fox Sports)
POST PRODUCTION Warren Miller's Off the Grid
CREDITS Ultimate Playground (OLN) - 2005 U.S. Freeskiing Open (NBC) - Dalton Highway (OLN) - World's Best: Top Ten Ski Resorts (Travel Channel) - Warren Miller's Higher Ground - Superior Beings (ESPN) - Global Adventures (OLN) - Inside: Avalanches (Discovery) - Toyota: There & Back (OLN) - Warren Miller's Thrills & Spills - Wild Survival with Corbin Bernsen - Amstel Light Iceland Open (OLN) - Guy's Guide to Colorado (Spike TV)

Jamie Pentz .Executive Producer
Doug Powell .General Manager
Chris Keig .Head, Production
Jeff Moore .Director, Development
Ginger Sheehy .Manager, Development

WARRIOR POETS

407 Broome St., Ste. 7B
New York, NY 10013
PHONE .212-219-7617
FAX .212-219-2920
TYPES Documentaries - Features - Reality TV - TV Series
HAS DEAL WITH Sony Pictures Television
DEVELOPMENT The Republican War on Science
PRODUCTION Public Nuisance
POST PRODUCTION Class Act
CREDITS 30 Days (F/X) - Super Size Me - I Bet You Will (MTV)

Morgan Spurlock .Producer
Dana Palmer .Office Manager
Jeremy Chilnick .Assistant to Producer

WASS-STEIN
500 S. Buena Vista St., Animation 2B-4
Burbank, CA 91521
PHONE . . . . See Below
FAX 818-563-9889
TYPES TV Series
HAS DEAL WITH Touchstone Television
CREDITS Less Than Perfect

Nina Wass . . . . Partner (818-560-1950)
Gene Stein . . . . Partner (818-560-1985)
Catherine Dunn . . . . Assistant to Nina Wass
Kevin Lappin . . . . Assistant to Gene Stein

***WATER CHANNEL**
2602 Grand Ave.
Everett, WA 98201
PHONE 425-259-0575
FAX 425-259-2077
EMAIL . . . . inquiries@waterchannel.com
WEB SITE . . . . www.waterchannel.com
TYPES Specials - TV Series
COMMENTS Network focused on the water recreation and sports lifestyle; Programming and production office: 400 N. 34th St., #216, Seattle, WA 98103, phone: 206-547-2730, fax: 206-547-2744

Jack King . . . . Chairman of the Board
Art Lindgren . . . . President/CEO
Robert Shipstad . . . . CCO
Jay Cascio . . . . Executive VP, Production & Creative Services
George Sullivan . . . . Executive VP, Sales & Marketing
Howard Fried . . . . Director, Programming & Operations
John Schoonover . . . . Director, Creative Services
Blair Christie . . . . Executive Producer
Greg Obata . . . . Sr. Director, Corporate Operations
Tom Picard . . . . Corporate Strategy

WATERMARK
5555 Melrose Ave., Swanson Bldg., 3rd Fl.
Los Angeles, CA 90038
PHONE 323-956-5000
TYPES Features - TV Series
HAS DEAL WITH Paramount Pictures
DEVELOPMENT Bob the Musical - Henry's List of Wrongs - The Spiderwick Chronicles - Looking for Alaska - The Boys (CBS Pilot) - Blindsided - The Dice Man - Closed for Christmas

Jessica Tuchinsky . . . . Partner
Mark Waters . . . . Partner
Veronica Brooks . . . . VP
Chris Goodwin . . . . Assistant
Kate Sullivan . . . . Assistant

WATERSHED FILMS
833 Moraga Dr., Ste. 1
Los Angeles, CA 90049
PHONE 310-472-8750
EMAIL . . . . watershedfilms@earthlink.net
TYPES Documentaries - Features - Reality TV - TV Series
CREDITS Plato's Run - The Dinosaur Hunter - Tall Tales - One in Eight - VH1 50 Greatest Album Covers
COMMENTS Deal with Tijuana Entertainment

James Brooke . . . . Producer
Neil DeGroot . . . . Producer
Wally Parks . . . . Producer

WATSON POND PRODUCTIONS
c/o Twentieth Century Fox
10201 W. Pico Blvd., Bldg. 41, Ste. 100
Los Angeles, CA 90035
PHONE 310-369-5701
FAX 310-969-0287
TYPES Reality TV - TV Series
HAS DEAL WITH Twentieth Century Fox Television

Brad Johnson . . . . President
Katy McCaffrey . . . . VP
Jon Radler . . . . Assistant

WE: WOMEN'S ENTERTAINMENT
200 Jericho Quadrangle
Jericho, NY 11753
PHONE 516-803-3000
WEB SITE . . . . www.we.tv
TYPES Documentaries - Reality TV - Specials - TV Series
PRE-PRODUCTION Doggie Daycare - Mrs. America 2006 - Women on Death Row 2
PRODUCTION She House 2006 - America's Cutest Puppies - Bride vs. Bride - Platinum Weddings - Cheerleader U. - Women at War: Coming Home
POST PRODUCTION Dirty Dancing - Designer to the Stars: Kari Whitman - Hair Trauma - Unwrapping Macy's - USA Today/WE Weight-Loss Challenge
UPCOMING RELEASES Vietnam Nurses with Dana Delaney
CREDITS Swimsuit Secrets Revealed - Cinematherapy - She House - 3 Men and a Chick Flick - Full Frontal Fashion: Under the Tents - Bridezillas - Tammy Faye: Death Defying - Women on Death Row - John Edward: Cross Country - Skating's Next Star - Two Funny: Cotter & Louise - Secret Lives of Women - Other Side of the Cell - Mrs. America - Mrs. World - Daddy's Spoiled Little Girl - Ghost Moms - Mom's Dream Day - Dad's Dream Day - Style Me with Rachel Hunter - Supersize Surgery

Kim Martin . . . . General Manager
Steve Cheskin . . . . Sr. VP Programming
Elizabeth Doree . . . . VP, Scheduling
Gena McCarthy . . . . VP, Development & Production
Kathleen Farrell . . . . Executive Producer, Programming
Roseanne Lopopolo . . . . Executive Producer, Programming
Annabelle McDonald . . . . Executive Producer, Programming
Gary Pipa . . . . Director, Scheduling
Theresa Patiri . . . . Director, Production Operations

JIM WEDAA PRODUCTIONS

6399 Wilshire Blvd., Ste 1011
Los Angeles, CA 90048
PHONE .323-852-6966
FAX .323-852-6969
EMAIL .jim@jimwedaaproductions.com
WEB SITE .www.jimwedaaproductions.com

TYPES	Features - Made-for-TV/Cable Movies - TV Series
DEVELOPMENT	The Blue Wall - Public Displays of Affection (PDA) - Whispers in Bedlam - The Demonologists - Saint Ex - Terrington Prep
CREDITS	Mission to Mars - Big Trouble - Black Dog - Red Team - Nine Lives

Jim Wedaa .President
Kristen Clayville .Assistant to Jim Wedaa

WEED ROAD PICTURES

4000 Warner Blvd., Bldg. 81, Ste. 115
Burbank, CA 91522
PHONE .818-954-3771/818-954-3464
FAX .818-954-3061

TYPES	Features
HAS DEAL WITH	Warner Bros. Pictures
DEVELOPMENT	Doom Patrol - Indianapolis - Woodrow Wilson Dime - Eddie Dickens & the Awful End - The Ha Ha - When the Wind Blows - The Extraordinary Adventures of Alfred Kropp - Heart Shaped Box
PRE-PRODUCTION	Tonight He Comes - I Am Legend
CREDITS	Mr. & Mrs. Smith - Constantine - Starsky & Hutch - Lost in Space - Deep Blue Sea

Akiva Goldsman .Producer
Kerry Foster .President, Production
Matt Smith .Creative Executive
Dan Rosenfelt .Story Editor
Max Boyer .1st Assistant to Akiva Goldsman
Trent Olsen .2nd Assistant to Akiva Goldsman
Jeremy Bailey .Assistant to Matt Smith

WEEKEND FILMS/MAIN STREET FILM COMPANY

2802 Main St., Ste. 1
Santa Monica, CA 90405
PHONE .310-399-9577
FAX .310-399-9515

TYPES	Features
DEVELOPMENT	Walk of Fame - Silver Strike - Slowman - Where You Are - Earthquake Weather - My Life in Orange
PRE-PRODUCTION	Drive Away Dykes
CREDITS	Because of Winn-Dixie - The First $20 Million - Bedazzled - Multiplicity - Groundhog Day - The League of Extraordinary Gentlemen - Gas Food Lodging - Mi Vida Loca - Carnivale - Grace of My Heart - Sugar Town
SUBMISSION POLICY	No query letters or unsolicited materials

Trevor Albert .Producer
Dan Hassid .Producer
Kym Bye .Development Executive
Troy Benjamin .Assistant

THE WEINSTEIN COMPANY

345 Hudson St., 13th Fl.
New York, NY 10014
PHONE .646-862-3400
FAX .917-368-7000
WEB SITE .www.weinsteinco.com
SECOND WEB SITE .www.twcpublicity.com

TYPES	Features
PROVIDES DEAL TO	Cube Vision - Mirage Enterprises - Outerbanks Entertainment - Trancas International Films - View Askew Productions, Inc.
DEVELOPMENT	Escape from Planet Earth - Kung Fu High School - Panic - Teenage Mutant Ninja Turtles 4 - The Impossible Adventures of Phineas Roone - The Equalizer - Hood vs. Evil - Knight Rider
PRODUCTION	Fan Boys - The Nanny Diaries
UPCOMING RELEASES	Factory Girl - Breaking & Entering - Killshot - Grind House - Igor - Stormbreaker - Bobby - Miss Potter - Guilty Pleasures - Arthur & The Invisibles; TV: Project Catwalk
CREDITS	Film: Wordplay - Derailed - Transamerica - Mrs. Henderson Presents - Hoodwinked - The Matador - Wolf Creek - The Libertine - Doogal - Lucky Number Slevin - Clerks II - The Protector; TV: Project Runway - Project Greenlight
COMMENTS	Second East Coast office: 375 Greenwich St., 3rd Fl., New York, NY 10013; phone: 212-941-3800; fax: 212-941-3949; West Coast address: 5700 Wilshire Blvd., Ste. 600, Los Angeles, CA 90036; phone: 323-207-3200; fax: 323-954-0997; Distribution deal with Genius Products Inc., Motion Picture Distribution LP (Canada) and Roadshow Films

Bob Weinstein .Co-Chairman (NY)
Harvey Weinstein .Co-Chairman (NY)
Glen Basner .President, International (NY)
Michael Cole .Co-President, Production (LA)
Steve Bunnell .Chairman, Domestic Distribution (NY)
Larry Madden .Executive VP, Finance/CFO (NY)
Peter Hurwitz .General Counsel (NY)
Timothy A. Clawson .Executive VP, Physical & Post Production (NY)
Gary Faber .Executive VP, Marketing (NY)
Maeva Gatineau .Executive VP/Co-Head, Acquisitions (UK)
Michelle Krumm .Executive VP/Co-Head, Acquisitions (LA)
Charles Layton .Executive VP, Office of the Co-Chairman (NY)
Barry Littman .Executive VP, Business & Legal Affairs (LA)
Irwin Reiter .Executive VP, Accounting & Financial Reporting (NY)
Eric Roth .Executive VP, Business & Legal Affairs (LA)
Colin Vaines .Executive VP, European Production & Development (UK)
Liz Biber .Sr. VP, Publicity (LA)
Kelly Carmichael .Sr. VP, Production & Casting (NY)
Liz Berger Dagan .Sr. VP, Publicity (NY)
Carla Gardini .Sr. VP, Production (LA)
Matthew Garner .Sr. VP, Post Production (UK)
Andrew Kim .Sr. VP, Finance & Business Development (NY)
Matthew Landon .Sr. VP, Post Production (NY)
Matthew Stein .Sr. VP, Production, Dimension Films (NY)
Dani Weinstein .Sr. VP, Publicity (NY)
Jonathan Fuhrman .VP, Business & Legal Affairs (NY)
Lisa Giannokopulos .VP, Regional Publicity (NY)
Rachel Levy .VP, Motion Picture Music (LA)
Bey Logan .VP, Acquisitions & Co-Production (Asia)
Diana Peters .VP, Publicity (NY)

(Continued)

THE WEINSTEIN COMPANY (Continued)

Eric Robinson . . . . . VP, Production & Development (NY)
Sarah Levinson Rothman . . . . . VP, Corporate Communications (NY)
Michael Rothstein . . . . . VP, International Sales (NY)
Barbara Schneeweiss . . . . . VP, TV & Film Production & Development (LA)
Sara Finmann Serlen . . . . . VP, Publicity (NY)
Paula Woods . . . . . VP, International Publicity (UK)
Stephen Bruno . . . . . Director, Marketing (NY)
Brendan Deneen . . . . . Director, Production & Development (NY)
Ben Famiglietti . . . . . Director, Production & Development (NY)
Emily Feingold . . . . . Director, Corporate Communications (NY)
Ethan Noble . . . . . Director, Marketing (NY)
Elena Zilberman . . . . . Director, Publicity (NY)
Julie Cloutier . . . . . Manager, Corporate Communications & Publicity (NY)
Pantea Ghaderi . . . . . Manager, Publicity (LA)
Teni Khachaturian . . . . . Manager, Publicity (LA)

WEINSTOCK PRODUCTIONS

140 S. Irving Blvd.
Los Angeles, CA 90004
PHONE 323-465-1976
TYPES Features
UPCOMING RELEASES Fracture
CREDITS Sleepover - Joe Gould's Secret - Where the Money Is

Charles Weinstock . . . . . Producer

JERRY WEINTRAUB PRODUCTIONS

c/o Warner Bros.
4000 Warner Blvd., Bungalow 1
Burbank, CA 91522-0001
PHONE 818-954-2500
FAX 818-954-1399
TYPES Features
HAS DEAL WITH Warner Bros. Pictures
DEVELOPMENT The Wild Bunch - Rodeo Gal
PRODUCTION Ocean's Thirteen
POST PRODUCTION Nancy Drew
CREDITS Ocean's Twelve - Ocean's Eleven - Vegas Vacation - The Specialist - Diner - Nashville - Soldier - Avengers - Karate Kid 1-4
SUBMISSION POLICY No unsolicited material accepted

Jerry Weintraub . . . . . Producer
Rob Guralnick . . . . . President
Susan Ekins . . . . . VP, Physical Production
Leigh Boniello . . . . . Development Executive
Kimberly Pinkstaff . . . . . Executive Assistant to Jerry Weintraub

WEINTRAUB/KUHN PRODUCTIONS

1450 Second St.
Santa Monica, CA 90401
PHONE 310-458-3300
FAX 310-458-3302
TYPES Direct-to-Video/DVD - Documentaries - Features - Made-for-TV/Cable Movies - TV Series
DEVELOPMENT They Only Come Out at Midnight - Angels on Horseback
PRE-PRODUCTION Vampire on the Orient Express - Monkey Love
COMPLETED UNRELEASED Patton's Ghost Corps (Documentary)
CREDITS High Road to China - The New Adventures of Robin Hood - Enter the Dragon - The Devil's Arithmetic - Perilous - Amazons and Gladiators - Endangered Species - Dream Warrior - Curse of the Dragon - La Femme Musketeer

Fred Weintraub . . . . . Producer
Tom Kuhn . . . . . Producer
Jackie Weintraub . . . . . VP, Development
Maxwell Meltzer . . . . . Business Affairs

WELLER/GROSSMAN PRODUCTIONS

5200 Lankershim Blvd., Ste. 500
North Hollywood, CA 91601
PHONE 818-755-4800
FAX 818-755-4820
WEB SITE . . . . . www.wellergrossman.com
TYPES Documentaries - Reality TV - TV Series
HAS DEAL WITH Discovery Health Channel - Food Network - The History Channel - Home & Garden Television (HGTV)
PRODUCTION Word of Mouth (Food Network) - The TurnAround (CNN) - Freemasons - National Geographic
CREDITS Your Reality Checked (Fine Living) - Beyond the Da Vinci Code (Documentary) - That's Clever! - Bar-B-Que with Bobby Flay - Strictly Dr. Drew - Tasty Travels with Rachael Ray (Food Network) - Look What I Did! (HGTV) - Hangar 18 (History Channel) - John Lithgow's Paloozaville

Gary H. Grossman . . . . . Executive Producer
Robb Weller . . . . . Executive Producer
Steve Lange . . . . . Executive Producer
Noel Poole . . . . . CFO
Debbie Supnik . . . . . Development

JOHN WELLS PRODUCTIONS

c/o Warner Bros. Studios
4000 Warner Blvd., Bldg. 1
Burbank, CA 91522-0001
PHONE 818-954-1687
FAX 818-954-3657
TYPES Features - TV Series
HAS DEAL WITH Warner Bros. Television Production
PROVIDES DEAL TO Harms Way Productions - Killer Films, Inc.
DEVELOPMENT Wartime Lies
CREDITS Duma - Nearing Grace - Smith - The Good Thief - White Oleander - ER - The West Wing - Third Watch - China Beach - Presidio Med - The Big Time - Citizen Baines - Trinity - Doom

John Wells . . . . . Writer/Producer (818-954-1687)
Andrew Stearn . . . . . President, TV (818-954-7568)
Ned Haspel . . . . . Executive VP, Finance & Business Affairs (818-954-5115)
Laura Holstein . . . . . Executive VP, Features (818-954-5341)
John Levey . . . . . Sr. VP, Casting (818-954-4080)
Chris Selak . . . . . Sr. VP, TV (818-954-3629)
Joy Ann Daffern . . . . . VP, Human Resources & Administration (818-954-5276)
Reeva Mandelbaum . . . . . VP, Research (818-954-4135)
Lisa Morales . . . . . VP, Features (818-954-3542)
Shelagh M. O'Brien . . . . . Director, Production (818-954-5441)
Dan Hadl . . . . . Director, Finance & Business Affairs (818-954-3609)
Matt Skiena . . . . . Story Editor, Features (818-954-5341)
Jinny Joung . . . . . Executive Assistant to John Wells (818-954-1687)
Dennis Defrehn . . . . . Assistant to Andrew Stearn (818-954-7568)
Jared Geoffroy . . . . . Finance & Business Affairs Coordinator (818-954-5440)
Jesse Spencer . . . . . Assistant to Chris Selak (818-954-3629)
Jonathan Stopek . . . . . Assistant to Lisa Morales (818-954-3542)
Melanie Burgess . . . . . Assistant to John Levey (818-954-4080)

CLIFFORD WERBER PRODUCTIONS

1630 Stewart St., Ste. 120
Santa Monica, CA 90404
PHONE .310-309-8467
FAX .310-828-4132
TYPES Direct-to-Video/DVD - Features - Made-for-TV/Cable Movies
DEVELOPMENT Sydney White and the Seven Dorks - Degree of Difficulty - Stealing Cars - Minding the Marys
POST PRODUCTION One Part Sugar
CREDITS Family Tree - A Cinderella Story

Clifford Werber .Producer
Daniel Manus .Creative Executive

WERNER-GOLD-MILLER

4024 Radford Ave., Bungalow 20
Studio City, CA 91604
PHONE .818-655-5301
FAX .818-655-8340
TYPES TV Series
CREDITS 20 Good Years - Happy Hour

Tom Werner .Producer
Eric Gold .Producer/Manager
Jimmy Miller .Producer/Manager
Mike Clements .President
Russ Buchholz .Creative Executive

SIMON WEST PRODUCTIONS

5555 Melrose Ave., Dressing Room Bldg., Rm. 109
Hollywood, CA 90038
PHONE .323-956-8994
FAX .323-862-2205
TYPES Commercials - Features - TV Series
HAS DEAL WITH CBS Paramount Network Television
CREDITS When a Stranger Calls - Black Hawk Down - Con Air - The General's Daughter - Lara Croft: Tomb Raider - Keen Eddie (Paramount/Fox) - Harry Green and Eugene (Paramount/ABC) - Close to Home (Warner Bros. TV/CBS)

Simon West .Director/Producer
Jib Polhemus .President, Production
Grant Brostrom .Assistant
Kevin Hurley .Assistant

WESTERN SANDBLAST

3780 Wilshire Blvd., 7th Fl.
Los Angeles, CA 90010
PHONE .213-637-8633
FAX .213-637-0110
WEB SITE .www.sandblast.com
TYPES Features - Made-for-TV/Cable Movies - TV Series

Dan Pyne .No Title
John Mankiewicz .No Title
Susan Ruskin .No Title
Erich Anderson .No Title
Aaron Lipstadt .No Title
Eyde Belasco .No Title
Max Flynn .No Title

WHEELHOUSE ENTERTAINMENT

15464 Ventura Blvd.
Sherman Oaks, CA 91403-3002
PHONE .818-461-3599
FAX .818-907-0819
WEB SITE .www.wheelhouseentertainment.com
TYPES Documentaries - Features - TV Series
CREDITS Braveheart - The Man in the Iron Mask - Pearl Harbor - We Were Soldiers
SUBMISSION POLICY No submissions

Randall Wallace .Director/Writer/Producer
Danielle Lemmon .VP/Producer
Stephen Zapotoczny .VP/Producer
Derek Owen .Manager, Creative Services & Technology
Jill Rytie .Manager, Production & Development
Kevin Gugle .Assistant to Randall Wallace

WHITE SNEAKERS, INC.

14061 Roblar Rd.
Sherman Oaks, CA 91423
PHONE .818-905-1183
FAX .818-905-0705
EMAIL .whitesneakersinc@adelphia.net
TYPES Animation - Direct-to-Video/DVD - Documentaries - Features - Made-for-TV/Cable Movies - Reality TV - Specials - TV Series
DEVELOPMENT Let Us Prey - Blithering Bunnies (Animated Feature) - Bad Blood - Zen and the Brain (Documentary Series/Special) - Seven Mysteries of Life (Documentary Series) - Louis & Bark (Animated Feature); TV: Late Night Nutz - Julianne - The William Saroyan Short Story Playhouse
PRE-PRODUCTION The William Saroyan Experience (Live Attraction/Exhibition)
CREDITS Annual Prism Awards (FX Network) - Animals of the NFL (National Geographic Special) - William Saroyan's The Parsley Garden - National Geographic's GeoKids (Video Series) - Jim Hensen's Muppet Babies

Hank Saroyan .Producer/Writer/Director/CEO
Jennie Trias .Development/Acquistion

WHITELIGHT ENTERTAINMENT

5200 Lankershim Blvd., Ste. 350
North Hollywood, CA 91601
PHONE .818-655-9747
FAX .818-763-8121

TYPES	Features - TV Series
DEVELOPMENT	Harold Arlen's Over the Rainbow - Lupin 3 - Homestretch - On My Honor
PRE-PRODUCTION	The Best Christmas Pageant Ever - Brimstone
PRODUCTION	Crossing Paths
CREDITS	Minority Report - Lost World: Jurassic Park - Schindler's List - Jurassic Park - Hook

Gerald R. Molen .Chairman/CEO/Partner
Chet Thomas .President, Production & Development/Partner
David Ranes .Partner
Chris Taylor .Assistant

WHITEWATER FILMS

2232 S. Cotner Ave.
Los Angeles, CA 90064
PHONE .310-575-5800
FAX .310-575-5802
EMAIL .info@whitewaterfilms.com
WEB SITE .www.whitewaterfilms.com

TYPES	Features - TV Series
DEVELOPMENT	Talent Pool - Pushing Forty - Bulldogs - Burnt Bridge Road - The Strangers - Levittown - The Living End - Zombie, Esq. - Greta
POST PRODUCTION	Kabluey
CREDITS	Nearing Grace - Mean Creek - Halloween: Resurrection - Bad Boys - American Dreamer - Life Goes On
SUBMISSION POLICY	No unsolicited material

Rick Rosenthal .President
Jeff Balis .Producer
Rhoades Rader .Producer
Ryan Peterson .Director, Development
Doug Sutherland .Production Executive

WHOOP INC./ONE HO PRODUCTIONS/ LIL' WHOOP PRODUCTIONS

375 Greenwich St.
New York, NY 10013
PHONE .212-941-2074

TYPES	Animation - Features - Made-for-TV/Cable Movies - Reality TV - Specials - Theatre - TV Series
DEVELOPMENT	Shop/Shop - Ask Whoopi - Harlem - Concierge - Destined to Witness - Sketch Off - At Her Majesty's Request
CREDITS	Just for Kicks - Whoopi's Littleburg - Hollywood Squares - Strong Medicine - Ruby's Bucket of Blood - Call Me Claus - What Makes a Family - Whoopi (NBC)

Whoopi Goldberg .Executive Producer
Tom Leonardis .President/Executive Producer/Director, Development
Shannon McCandless .Assistant

WHYADUCK PRODUCTIONS, INC.

4804 Laurel Canyon Blvd., PMB 502
North Hollywood, CA 91607
PHONE .818-980-5355
EMAIL .duckprods@aol.com
WEB SITE .www.duckprods.com

TYPES	Documentaries - Features - TV Series
DEVELOPMENT	The Sirens of Titan
PRODUCTION	Dick Gregory: The Color of Funny - Kurt Vonnegut: American Made
CREDITS	Lenny Bruce: Swear to Tell the Truth - Mother Night - W.C. Fields Straight Up - Curb Your Enthusiasm - Mort Sahl: The Loyal Opposition - The Marx Brothers in a Nutshell
SUBMISSION POLICY	No unsolicited submissions
COMMENTS	ABC Pilot deal

Robert B. Weide .President/Producer

WIDEAWAKE, INC.

8752 Rangely Ave.
Los Angeles, CA 90048
PHONE .310-652-9200

TYPES	Features - Reality TV - TV Series
DEVELOPMENT	Destiny - Big Brothers - The Holiday Club - Soulmates
CREDITS	The Girl Next Door

Luke Greenfield .Writer/Director/Producer
Matthew Seigel .Producer
Nik Frank-Lehrer .Assistant

WIGRAM PRODUCTIONS

4000 Warner Blvd., Bldg. 81, Rm. 215
PHONE .818-954-2412
FAX .818-954-6538

TYPES	Features
HAS DEAL WITH	Warner Bros. Pictures
PRODUCTION	Harry Potter and the Order of the Phoenix

Lionel Wigram .Producer
Peter Eskelsen .Creative Executive

DAN WIGUTOW PRODUCTIONS

534 La Guardia Pl., Ste. 3
New York, NY 10012
PHONE .212-477-1328
FAX .212-254-6902

TYPES	Features - Made-for-TV/Cable Movies - Miniseries - TV Series
DEVELOPMENT	Arson Project - Revenge of the Middle Aged Woman: Sequel - Devil's Cargo
CREDITS	Murder on Pleasant Drive (Made-for-TV Movie) - Revenge of the Middle-Aged Woman - In a Child's Name (Miniseries) - Brave New World - Hunt for the Unicorn Killer (Miniseries) - Peter Benchley's The Beast (Miniseries) - Raising Waylon

Dan Wigutow .Executive Producer
Laura Brownson .Producer
Tara DeJulio .Story Editor

WILD AT HEART FILMS, LLC
10100 Santa Monica Blvd., Ste. 1300
Los Angeles, CA 90067
PHONE .310-205-0550
FAX .310-855-0177
TYPES Animation - Features - Internet Content - Made-for-TV/Cable Movies - Reality TV - TV Series
DEVELOPMENT Personal Foul (Showtime) - Ooh LA LA - The New York Christmas Movie (Sony/Revolution) - Heart of the Atom - A Not So Royal Wedding - War Paint
PRE-PRODUCTION The 12 (Sci Fi) - Fractured - NAAC (Spike TV) - 35th of May
PRODUCTION We Choose Freedom
CREDITS Jackpot - Northfork - In and Out

James Egan .CEO/Producer/Writer
Marlise Karlin .Producer
Boris Geiger .Business Affairs
Demetrius Moore .Assistant to the Producers

WILD BRAIN, INC.
660 Alabama St.
San Francisco, CA 94110
PHONE .415-553-8000
FAX .415-553-8009
EMAIL .info@wildbrain.com
WEB SITE .www.wildbrain.com
TYPES Animation - Commercials - Internet Content - TV Series

Charles Rivkin .President & CEO
Andrea Mansour .Executive Producer, Commercials
Randey Arnold-Kraft .Director, Human Resources

WILDRICE PRODUCTIONS
12439 Magnolia Blvd., Ste. 173
North Hollywood, CA 91607
PHONE .818-487-2765
FAX .818-753-9830
EMAIL .joelrice@wildriceproductions.com
TYPES Features - Made-for-TV/Cable Movies - Miniseries - Reality TV - TV Series
DEVELOPMENT Reviving Ophelia - Breast Cancer Husand - The Inn Crowd
PRODUCTION Shredderman
COMPLETED UNRELEASED This Time Around (Pilot)
CREDITS Recipe For a Perfect Christmas - Searching for David's Heart - Love Rules! - I Want to Marry Ryan Banks - Picking Up & Dropping Off - Code 1114 - One Kill - About Sarah - Half a Dozen Babies - Sleeping with the Devil - Breaking Through

Joel S. Rice .Executive Producer
Richard Joel .Reality Executive Producer
Tom Novac .Reality Executive Producer
Jeremy Diller .Development Assistant

WILDWELL FILMS
1516 Rosalia Rd., Loft 7
Los Angeles, CA 90027
PHONE .323-662-4050
WEB SITE .www.m4our.com/wake
TYPES Documentaries - Features
DEVELOPMENT Sleepwalking - Venus - The Dead Girls - The Lucky Day - Dark Corner
PRE-PRODUCTION Magic Hour
CREDITS Spirit of '76 - Bram Stoker's Dracula - Traveling Light - Wake
SUBMISSION POLICY Agent submission or legal representative only
COMMENTS Fiercely independent

Susan Landau Finch .Producer/Writer
Henry LeRoy Finch .Director/Writer

WILDWOOD ENTERPRISES, INC.
335 N. Maple Dr., Ste. 354
Beverly Hills, CA 90210
PHONE .310-246-7707
TYPES Features
CREDITS Quiz Show - A River Runs Through It - Ordinary People - The Horse Whisperer - The Legend of Bagger Vance - The Slums of Beverly Hills - The Motorcycle Diaries
SUBMISSION POLICY No unsolicited material

Robert Redford .Owner
Connie Wethington .Development
Bill Holderman .Development

ELLYN WILLIAMS PRODUCTIONS
1100 Alta Loma Road
Los Angeles, CA 90069
PHONE .310-659-2889
FAX .310-289-9472
TYPES Made-for-TV/Cable Movies - TV Series
DEVELOPMENT Lost & Found (MOW) - I Think I Love You (MOW) - A Passion For More (Series) - Night Over Water - An Empty Plate - The Road Taken - Garden of Evil (MOW) - Tripping the Prom Queen (Series)
PRE-PRODUCTION The Party Never Stops
CREDITS Fantasia: Life Is Not a Fairy Tale - A Mother's Testimony - The Third Twin - Boot Camp - The Stalking of Laurie Show - Hunger Point

Ellyn Williams .Executive Producer
Laura Lizer .Business Manager

WILMARK ENTERTAINMENT, INC.
1752 Reed St.
Redondo Beach, CA 90278
PHONE .310-529-4836
EMAIL .willbaronet@yahoo.com
TYPES Documentaries - Features - Made-for-TV/Cable Movies - TV Series
DEVELOPMENT Rookies - 10 Things Your Man Isn't Talking to You About
PRODUCTION Battle (Feature)
CREDITS Any Day Now - Beauty - Vendetta - Intimate Portraits - Trapped (USA, MOW) - CSI: Miami - Medical Investigation (NBC)

Mark Israel .President
Wili Baronet .VP

BRAD WILSON PRODUCTIONS, INC.
4120 Burbank Blvd.
Burbank, CA 91505
PHONE .818-845-8811
FAX .818-845-8868
EMAIL .brad@bradwilson.biz
WEB SITE .www.bradwilson.biz

TYPES	Direct-to-Video/DVD - Features - Made-for-TV/Cable Movies - TV Series
DEVELOPMENT	Believers Among Us Vol. 2 - Town Policy - King: A Dream Denied
POST PRODUCTION	The Fallen
CREDITS	A Family Thing - Left Luggage - Don't Let Go - The Ghost Club - One of Them - Undercover Kids - Believers Among Us

Brad Wilson .Producer
Laura Roberts .Head, Development

WILSON/WOODS PRODUCTIONS
10641 La Grange Ave., Ste. 304
Los Angeles, CA 90025
PHONE .310-470-6924

TYPES	Features - Made-for-TV/Cable Movies
DEVELOPMENT	Krystal Turns 18 - Silver Wings
CREDITS	The Elf Who Saved Christmas (USA) - The Elf and the Magic Key (USA) - The Miracle of the Cards (PAX)

Lee Wilson .Producer
Robert Woods .Producer

WIND DANCER PRODUCTION GROUP
200 W. 57th St., Ste. 601
New York, NY 10019-3211
PHONE .212-765-4772/626-356-4618
FAX .212-765-4775/626-356-4619

TYPES	Features - TV Series
DEVELOPMENT	DILLIGAF
PRE-PRODUCTION	Daughter of the Queen of Sheba - Harv the Barbarian
UPCOMING RELEASES	Walker
CREDITS	What Women Want - Where the Heart Is - Firelight - Home Improvement - Thunder Alley - Soul Man - Costello
COMMENTS	West Coast office: 745 S. Marengo Ave., Ste. 204, Pasadena, CA 91106

Matt Williams .Principal
David McFadzean .Principal
Carmen Finestra .Principal
Dete Meserve .Executive VP

THE WINER COMPANY
4636 Van Nuys Blvd.
Van Nuys, CA 91403
PHONE .310-395-0058
FAX .310-395-8850
EMAIL .hwinerco@aol.com

TYPES	Features - Made-for-TV/Cable Movies
DEVELOPMENT	In Hiding - Addict - Custom of the Country - Ground Zero - Conversations with a Fat Girl - Mermaid Dreams
PRE-PRODUCTION	The Price
CREDITS	Dive from Clausen's Pier - Lucky 7 - Damaged Care - Jeremiah - Riot - House Arrest - Space Camp - Infidelity

Harry Winer .President

WINGNUT FILMS LTD.
PO Box 15-208
Miramar Wellington 6003, New Zealand
PHONE .64-4-388-9939
FAX .64-4-388-9449

TYPES	Features
DEVELOPMENT	Halo - The Lovely Bones
CREDITS	King Kong - The Lord of the Rings - The Frighteners - Heavenly Creatures - Meet the Feebles - Braindead - Bad Taste
SUBMISSION POLICY	No unsolicited submissions accepted

Peter Jackson .Director/Producer

WINKLER FILMS
211 S. Beverly Dr., Ste. 200
Beverly Hills, CA 90212
PHONE .310-858-5780

TYPES	Features - Miniseries
HAS DEAL WITH	Sony Pictures Entertainment
DEVELOPMENT	A Perfect Divorce - A Cop Between - Chariots of the Gods (Sci Fi Miniseries)
PRE-PRODUCTION	Home of the Brave
CREDITS	The Net 2.0 - Rocky - Goodfellas - Raging Bull - The Right Stuff - The Net - At First Sight - Life as a House - The Shipping News - Enough - De-Lovely

Irwin Winkler .CEO
Rob Cowan .President
Selina Gomeau .Assistant to Irwin Winkler
Julie Milstead .Assistant to Rob Cowan

WINSOME PRODUCTIONS
1505 Fourth St., Ste. 216
Santa Monica, CA 90401
PHONE .310-656-3300
FAX .310-656-3301
EMAIL .info@winsomeprods.com

TYPES	Documentaries - Features - Made-for-TV/Cable Movies - Reality TV
DEVELOPMENT	The Canine Chronicles - Born to Die
COMPLETED UNRELEASED	Lucky 13
CREDITS	Keeping Up with the Steins - It's Always Something: The Gilda Radner Story - Common Ground - The Mary Tyler Moore Reunion Special - Who Makes You Laugh? - Class Clowns - Love with a Twist - Night Creatures

A.D. Oppenheim .Producer/Writer
Daniel L. Oppenheim .Producer/VP, Production
Joy Pollack .VP, Development
Matt Wolpert .Development Associate

STAN WINSTON PRODUCTIONS

7032 Valjean Ave.
Van Nuys, CA 91406
PHONE 818-782-0870
WEB SITE ....www.stanwinstonproductions.com
TYPES Features - Made-for-TV/Cable Movies - TV Series
DEVELOPMENT Desolate - Certifiable - The Suffering - Courtney Crumrin - Me & My Monster
PRE-PRODUCTION The Deaths of Ian
POST PRODUCTION Skinwalkers
CREDITS The Day the World Ended - Hellraiser: Deader - Earth vs. the Spider - How to Make a Monster - She Creature - Teenage Caveman - Wrong Turn
SUBMISSION POLICY No submissions accepted, other than those via an agent signatory to the WGA who has received permission to send material; All other submissions will be returned unread

Stan Winston ....President/Director/Producer (818-782-0870)
Brian J. Gilbert ....Producer
Ryan Murphy ....Story Editor

RALPH WINTER PRODUCTIONS, INC.

c/o Twentieth Century Fox Film Corporation
10201 W. Pico Blvd., Bldg. 6, Ste. 101
Los Angeles, CA 90035
PHONE 310-369-4723/310-369-8860
FAX 310-969-0727/310-369-3262
TYPES Direct-to-Video/DVD - Features - Made-for-TV/Cable Movies - TV Series
HAS DEAL WITH Twentieth Century Fox
DEVELOPMENT Breaking the Box - The Purpose Driven Life - One-Third - Fantastic Four (Sequel)
CREDITS X-Men 1-3 - The Visitation - The Fantastic Four - Planet of the Apes - Inspector Gadget - Left Behind: The Movie - Mighty Joe Young - Hackers - Star Trek 4-6 - Shoot or Be Shot - Hangman's Curse - Blizzard

Ralph Winter ....Producer
Susana Zepeda ....VP, Development & Production
Allison Calleri ....Production & Development
Melinda Nishioka ....Development

WITT-THOMAS-HARRIS PRODUCTIONS

11901 Santa Monica Blvd., Ste. 596
West Los Angeles, CA 90025
PHONE 310-472-6004/818-762-7500
FAX 310-476-5015/818-762-7540
EMAIL ....pwittproductions@aol.com
TYPES Features - TV Series
CREDITS Film: Insomnia - Three Kings - Final Analysis - Dead Poets Society; TV: Soap - Benson - Empty Nest - John Larroquette Show - The Golden Girls - Blossom
COMMENTS Second office: 11240 Magnolia Blvd., Ste. 201, North Hollywood, CA 91601

Paul Junger Witt ....Partner
Tony Thomas ....Partner (818-762-7500)
Susan Harris ....Partner
Ellen Benjamin ....Assistant to Mssrs. Witt and Harris
Marlene Fuentes ....Assistant to Mr. Thomas

WOLF FILMS, INC.

100 Universal City Plaza, Bldg. 2252
Universal City, CA 91608-1085
PHONE 818-777-6969/212-627-0088
FAX 818-866-1446/212-627-0957
TYPES Features - TV Series
HAS DEAL WITH NBC Universal Television Studio
DEVELOPMENT Bury My Heart at Wounded Knee
CREDITS Law & Order - Law & Order: Special Victims Unit - Law & Order: Criminal Intent - Conviction

Dick Wolf ....Executive Producer, Creator, Law & Order/Law & Order: SVU/ Law & Order: Criminal Intent
Arthur Forney ....Co-Executive Producer, Law & Order/Law & Order: SVU/ Law & Order: Criminal Intent
Peter Jankowski ....Executive Producer, Law & Order/Law & Order: SVU/ Law & Order: Criminal Intent
Nena Rodrigue ....Head, Development
Tony Ganz ....Features
Neal Baer ....Executive Producer, Law & Order: SVU
Walon Green ....Executive Producer, Law & Order
Ted Kotcheff ....Executive Producer, Law & Order: SVU
Warren Leight ....Executive Producer, Law & Order: Criminal Intent
Nicholas Wootton ....Executive Producer, Law & Order
Fred Berner ....Executive Producer, Law & Order: Criminal Intent
Matthew Penn ....Executive Producer, Law & Order
Rick Eid ....Executive Producer, Law & Order

FRED WOLF FILMS

4222 W. Burbank Blvd.
Burbank, CA 91505
PHONE 818-846-0611
FAX 818-846-0979
EMAIL ....administration@fredwolffilms.com
WEB SITE ....www.fredwolffilms.com
TYPES Animation - Direct-to-Video/DVD - Features - TV Series
DEVELOPMENT Zoe and Moe - Brittany the Cyber-Chick - Judge Courtney
CREDITS The Fantastic Voyages of Sinbad - Teenage Mutant Ninja Turtles - Zorro

Fred Wolf ....President
Cheryl Wadsworth ....Director, Administration
Liz Wolf ....Production Supervisor

WOLFMILL ENTERTAINMENT

9027 Larke Ellen Circle
Los Angeles, CA 90035-4222
PHONE 310-559-1622
FAX 310-559-1623
EMAIL ....craig@wolfmill.com
WEB SITE ....www.wolfmill.com
TYPES Animation - Features - TV Series
DEVELOPMENT Ponytailers - Astounding Space Thrills
PRE-PRODUCTION Cabo
CREDITS Pocket Dragon Adventures - T.H.U.N.D.E.R. Agents
COMMENTS Deals with Sceneries International and Pictor Media

Craig Miller ....Partner
Marv Wolfman ....Partner
Richard Rosen ....Business Affairs

THE WOLPER ORGANIZATION

4000 Warner Blvd., Bldg. 14, Ste. 200
Burbank, CA 91522-0001

PHONE .818-954-1421/818-954-3505
FAX .818-954-1593/818-954-2319

TYPES: Features - Made-for-TV/Cable Movies - Miniseries - Reality TV - TV Series
HAS DEAL WITH: Warner Bros. Pictures
DEVELOPMENT: Love and Terror - T-Rex - The Last Woman - The Swarm - 40 Days - Momo - Hell Bound - On the Brinks - Stephen King's It - Behind the Enterprise - Used - Ringling Bros. and Barnum & Bailey Circus: Celebrity Version - Citizen Jane - The Witching Hour - Wolfen - Sybil
PRE-PRODUCTION: The Year Without Santa Claus (NBC)
PRODUCTION: Earth Angel (Lifetime) - War on Drugs (Showtime)
POST PRODUCTION: Sybil - God or the Girl (or Holy Joe) (A&E) - Penn & Teller: Off the Deep End (NBC)
CREDITS: L.A. Confidential - Murder in the 1st - Surviving Picasso - Thornbirds - Roots - Mists of Avalon - Queen - Penn & Teller: Bullshit - Helter Skelter - Stephen King's Salem's Lot - North and South - Snow Wonder - Instant Beauty Pageant (E! Entertainment Television)
SUBMISSION POLICY: No unsolicited material
COMMENTS: Development office: 4000 Warner Blvd., Bldg. 14, Ste. 202, Burbank, CA 91522-0001

Mark M. Wolper .President/Executive Producer
Kevin Nicklaus .VP, Development
Kathleen Doise .Executive Assistant
Sam Alexander .Development Assistant

WONDERFILMS

1416 N. La Brea Ave.
Los Angeles, CA 90028

PHONE .323-802-1656

TYPES: Features - Made-for-TV/Cable Movies
DEVELOPMENT: It's Just a Game - Sabrina Dhawan Project - Dick Contino's Blues - SanTosh Sivan Project
POST PRODUCTION: Kerala
COMPLETED UNRELEASED: Beautiful Ohio
CREDITS: Bigger Than the Sky - Water - Cherish - The Terrorist - Asoka - Sixteen Years of Alcohol
SUBMISSION POLICY: No unsolicited submission
COMMENTS: Formerly Accomplice Films

Mark Burton .Producer
Marina Davis .Assistant

WONDERLAND SOUND AND VISION

8739 Sunset Blvd.
West Hollywood, CA 90069

PHONE .310-659-4451
FAX .310-659-4482

TYPES: Features - TV Series
HAS DEAL WITH: Columbia Pictures - Warner Bros. Television Production
DEVELOPMENT: Revenge of the Nerds (Remake)
PRODUCTION: We Are Marshall (Warner Bros. Pictures)
CREDITS: Films: Stay Alive - Charlie's Angels: Full Throttle; TV: Supernatural (The WB) - The O.C. (Fox) - The Mountain - Fastlane

McG .No Title
Peter Johnson .No Title
Jeanne Allgood .No Title
David Manpearl .No Title
Anna Mastro .No Title
Kris Warren .No Title
Andy Shapiro .No Title
Jeff Bruckner .No Title
Jeff Grosvenor .No Title
Megan Zaitz .No Title
Erica Arbelaez .No Title
Sandra Mucke .No Title

THE WOOFENILL WORKS, INC.

516 E. 81st St., Ste. 3
New York, NY 10028-2530

PHONE .212-734-2578
FAX .212-734-3186
EMAIL .prymeva@earthlink.net

TYPES: Direct-to-Video/DVD - Features - Made-for-TV/Cable Movies - Miniseries - TV Series
DEVELOPMENT: Genesis - Thunderwulf
PRE-PRODUCTION: This Side of Heaven
CREDITS: Murder Between Friends - Exit - All American Murder - Double Crossed: The Barry Seales Story - Catch Me Killer - Man Outside - The Brewster Project
SUBMISSION POLICY: Send query with synopsis by email

Joseph K. Landsman .Chairman/CEO
Jan A. Koster .President/Creative Director
Ronald Tanet .Executive Producer/Corporate Counsel
Robert L. Cohen .VP, Production/Supervising Producer
Robert J. Nichols .VP/Corporate Counsel
Jonathan Stathakis .Production/Distribution Consultant
Kathy Winthrop .Creative Executive

WORKING TITLE FILMS
9720 Wilshire Blvd., 4th Fl.
Beverly Hills, CA 90212
PHONE .310-777-3100/44-207-307-3000
FAX .310-777-5243
WEB SITE www.workingtitlefilms.com
TYPES Features
HAS DEAL WITH Universal Pictures
DEVELOPMENT The Troubleshooter - Definitely, Maybe
CREDITS United 93 - Bean - Dead Man Walking - Fargo - Four Weddings and a Funeral - Notting Hill - Elizabeth - Bridget Jones's Diary - About a Boy - O Brother Where Art Thou? - The Big Lebowski - Billy Elliot - High Fidelity - Love Actually - Thirteen - Wimbledon - Shaun of the Dead - The Interpreter - Pride & Prejudice - Nanny McPhee
SUBMISSION POLICY No unsolicited submissions
COMMENTS UK office: Oxford House, 76 Oxford St., London W1D 1BS, United Kingdom

Tim Bevan .Co-Chairman
Eric Fellner .Co-Chairman
Liza Chasin .President, Production (US)
Debra Hayward .Executive Producer
Natascha Wharton .Head, Film/WT2
Michelle Wright .Head, Physical Production
Angela Morrison .COO
Nick Angel .Music Supervisor
Chris Clark .Sr. VP, Development (US)
Amelia Granger .Literary Acquisitions Executive (UK)
Dan McRae .Development Executive (UK)
Evan Hayes .Creative Executive (US)

WORKSHOP PICTURES, INC.
4645 Van Nuys Blvd., Ste. 202
Sherman Oaks, CA 91403
PHONE .818-788-2183
EMAIL .info@workshoppictures.com
WEB SITE www.workshoppictures.com
TYPES Commercials - Features - Made-for-TV/Cable Movies - Music Videos
DEVELOPMENT Baja - Big Kill
PRE-PRODUCTION The Seat at the Table
CREDITS The Metro Chase

Dennis LaValle .Chairman/CEO
Chris W. Fallin .President/COO
James D. Benson .VP/CFO
Scott Martin .Director, Development

WORLD FILM SERVICES, INC.
630 Fifth Ave., Ste. 1505
New York, NY 10111
PHONE .212-632-3456
FAX .212-632-3457
TYPES Features - TV Series
CREDITS A Passage to India - The Dresser - Beautiful Thing

John Heyman .CEO
Pamela Osowski .VP
Mark Montgomery .Development
Roy Krost .Canada

WORLD INTERNATIONAL NETWORK
811 N. Catalina Ave., Ste. 2304
Redondo Beach, CA 90277
PHONE .310-937-9967
FAX .310-372-8540
TYPES Features - Made-for-TV/Cable Movies
CREDITS The Perfect Nanny - The Perfect Wife - Yesterday's Children - Blind Obsession - Rain - A Mother's Testimony - She's No Angel - Living with Fear - Seduced by a Thief - Redemption of the Ghost - Cloverbend - Perilous - Spirit

Larry Gershman .Chairman/CEO
Martha Mikita .Executive VP/CFO
Zana Thompson .Controller

WORLD OF WONDER PRODUCTIONS
6650 Hollywood Blvd., Ste. 400
Hollywood, CA 90028
PHONE .323-603-6300
FAX .323-603-6301
EMAIL .wow@worldofwonder.net
WEB SITE www.worldofwonder.net
TYPES Documentaries - Features - TV Series
CREDITS Showbiz Moms and Dads - Party Monster - Shock Video: Too Hot for the Box - Gay Hollywood - Women on Top: Hollywood Power - Monica in Black and White - Brilliant but Cancelled - The Eyes of Tammy Faye - Inside Deep Throat - Showdogs Moms & Dads - Gay Republicans - The Hidden Fuhrer - Sports Kids Moms and Dads - Movies That Shook the World - Transgeneration - Party Party - Power Lesbians - Camp Michael Jackson - Vivid Valley - Andy Warhol: The Complete Picture - Secret Rulers of the World

Fenton Bailey .Executive Producer/Co-Director
Randy Barbato .Executive Producer/Co-Director
David Schiff .Head, Development
Thomas Wolf .Head, Technology
Jordan Ruden .Production Manager
Fred Paccone .COO
Craig Browner .Production Supervisor

WORLDWIDE BIGGIES
1515 Broadway, 38th Fl.
New York, NY 10036
PHONE 212-846-7521
FAX 212-846-1873
WEB SITE .....www.worldwidebiggies.com
TYPES Features - Internet Content - TV Series
HAS DEAL WITH Nickelodeon/MTVN Kids & Family Group
DEVELOPMENT War Dance (Shine Global)
COMMENTS Includes Biggies Broadband and Shine Global (Nonprofit documentary division); Additional deals with Cranium, Inc. and Virgin USA

Albie Hecht .....CEO
Kari Kim .....Production & Development
Susan MacLaury .....Executive Director, Shine Global

WORLDWIDE PANTS, INC.
1697 Broadway
New York, NY 10019
PHONE 212-975-5300/323-575-5600
FAX 212-975-4780
WEB SITE .....www.cbs.com
TYPES Animation - Features - TV Series
PRODUCTION Let's Rob
CREDITS Strangers with Candy: The Movie - The Late Late Show - Everybody Loves Raymond - The Late Show with David Letterman - Ed
SUBMISSION POLICY No unsolicited submissions; Pitches in writing to New York office only
COMMENTS The Late Late Show office: 7800 Beverly Blvd., Ste. 244, Los Angeles, CA 90036

Rob Burnett .....President/CEO
David Letterman .....Comptroller
Valerie Schaer .....Executive VP

WPT ENTERPRISES, INC.
5700 Wilshire Blvd., Ste. 350
Los Angeles, CA 90036
PHONE 323-330-9900
FAX 323-330-9901
WEB SITE .....www.worldpokertour.com
TYPES Direct-to-Video/DVD - Internet Content - Mobile Content - TV Series
PRODUCTION Professional Poker Tour
CREDITS World Poker Tour
SUBMISSION POLICY No unsolicited submissions

Steven Lipscomb .....President/CEO
Peter Hughes .....COO
Todd Steele .....CFO
Robyn Moder .....Executive VP, WPT Studios
Adam Pliska .....General Counsel
Natalie Zweben .....Director, Marketing

NORTON WRIGHT PRODUCTIONS
13331 Moorpark St., Ste. 308
Sherman Oaks, CA 91423
PHONE 818-990-3058
TYPES Features - Made-for-TV/Cable Movies - TV Series
DEVELOPMENT All at Sea - A Stolen Mind
CREDITS Night of the Wolf - Murderous Intent - Angel Flight Down - Rescue of Flight 232 - Sadie & Son - Haunted by Her Past
SUBMISSION POLICY Script submissions via agent only

Norton Wright .....Executive Producer/Writer
Susan Watson .....Director, Development

WWE FILMS
345 N. Maple Dr., Ste. 201
Beverly Hills, CA 90210
PHONE 310-285-5300
FAX 310-285-9914
WEB SITE .....www.wwe.com
TYPES Direct-to-Video/DVD - Features - TV Series

Joel Simon .....President (310-285-5301)
Jed Blaugrund .....VP (310-285-5303)
Richard Lowell .....Creative Executive (310-285-5302)

X FILME CREATIVE POOL GMBH
Kurfuerstenstrasse 57
Berlin 10785, Germany
PHONE 49-30-230-833-11
FAX 49-30-230-833-22
EMAIL .....info@x-filme.de
WEB SITE .....www.x-filme.net
TYPES Features
DEVELOPMENT Veronika - Dschingis
PRE-PRODUCTION Goodbye Bafana
PRODUCTION Prince Edouard, Max Minsky and Me - The Three Robbers
POST PRODUCTION Lovelive - Das Herz Ist ein Dunkler Wald - Mein Fueher: The Truly Truest Truth About Adolf Hitler
UPCOMING RELEASES A Friend of Mine
CREDITS Silent Night - Life is All You Get - Wintersleepers - Run Lola Run - The Giraffe - Gigantic - Paul is Dead - The Princess & the Warrior - Never Mind the Wall - Heidi M. - Heaven - Herz - I'm the Father - Goodbye, Lenin! - True - Learning to Lie - Love in Thoughts - Soundless - Agnes & His Brothers - En Garde - Go for Zucker! - Underexposure - Küss Mich, Hexe! - Summer in Berlin - Imagine Me & You - Love Me Do - The Red Cockatoo - Digging for Belladonna

Tom Tykwer .....Founder/Managing Partner/Director
Stefan Arndt .....Founder/Managing Partner/Producer
Wolfgang Becker .....Founder/Managing Partner/Director
Dani Levy .....Founder/Managing Partner/Director
Manuela Stehr .....Co-Manager/Producer

XINGU FILMS LTD.
12 Cleveland Row, St. James's
London SW1A 1DH, United Kingdom
PHONE 44-20-7451-0600
FAX 44-20-7451-0601
EMAIL .....anita@xingufilms.com
TYPES Documentaries - Features
DEVELOPMENT A Dog Called Grk - Fifth Business - The Provider - South of the Border, West of the Sun
UPCOMING RELEASES Alpha Male - A Guide to Recognizing Your Saints
COMPLETED UNRELEASED Cheeky
CREDITS The Grotesque - Boys from Brazil - Moving the Mountain - The Sweatbox - A Kind of Childhood
SUBMISSION POLICY Email submissions to alex@xingufilms.com

Trudie Styler .....Chairman/Producer/Director
Anita Sumner .....CEO/Co-Producer
Travis Swords .....Producer
Dorothee Inderfurth .....Associate Producer
Alex Francis .....Head, Development

YAHOO! MEDIA GROUP/YAHOO! STUDIOS
2450 Broadway
Santa Monica, CA 90404
PHONE 310-907-2700
FAX 310-907-2701
WEB SITE .....www.yahoo.com
TYPES Internet Content - Mobile Content
CREDITS Kevin Sites in the Hot Zone

Terry Semel .....CEO
Lloyd Braun .....Head, Original Content
David Katz .....Head, Yahoo! Studios
Vince Broady .....Head, Games, Entertainment & Youth Properties
Karin Timpone .....Head, Marketing
Cammie Dunaway .....Chief Marketing Officer
Scott Moore .....Head, News, Finance, Technology & Health

YARI FILM GROUP (YFG)
10850 Wilshire Blvd., 6th Fl.
Los Angeles, CA 90024
PHONE 310-234-8970
FAX 310-234-8975
TYPES Features
HAS DEAL WITH Universal Pictures
PROVIDES DEAL TO Brooklyn Media
DEVELOPMENT The Entity - Chasing Dinner - Kickin' It Old Skool - Resurrecting the Champ - Crazy Dog
PRE-PRODUCTION Man on a Ledge - Stain
PRODUCTION Painted Veil - Hoax
POST PRODUCTION Illusionist - First Snow
UPCOMING RELEASES Winter Passing - Haven - Find Me Guilty
COMPLETED UNRELEASED Matador - Dave Chappelle Project - Even Money
CREDITS Prime - Thumbsucker - Crash - Hostage - A Love Song for Bobby Long

Bob Yari .....Partner
Bill Immerman .....Sr. Executive VP/CAO, Yari Film Group
Neil Sacker .....COO/General Counsel
David Glasser .....Managing Partner, Syndicate Films
Brad Jenkel .....Executive VP, Production
Erin Eggers .....Creative Executive
Ian Watermeier .....Creative Executive
Shelly Strong .....VP, Production & Finance
Dan Stutz .....VP, Business & Legal Affairs
Isabel White .....VP, Publicity
Andrea Hanson .....Assistant to Bob Yari
Gabriel Polsky .....Assistant to Neil Sacker
Katie Johnson .....Assistant to Isabel White

MARK YELLEN PRODUCTIONS
183 S. Orange Dr.
Los Angeles, CA 90036
PHONE 323-935-5525
FAX 323-935-5755
EMAIL .....mypfilms@earthlink.net
TYPES Commercials - Direct-to-Video/DVD - Features - Made-for-TV/Cable Movies - Music Videos
DEVELOPMENT Wolftrap - Between a Rock and a Hard Place - The Yards Between Us - Alter Arrangement - Rev - Shadow Creek - Doo Lister's Blues - Days Like This
PRE-PRODUCTION Crash Bandits
CREDITS Montana - Shiloh - Where the Rivers Flow North - Shiloh Season - Fist of the North Star - Blast - The Big Squeeze - One Good Turn - Puerto Vallarta Squeeze

Mark Yellen .....Producer
Brook Philips .....Director, Development
Liz Reed .....Assistant

***YELLOW CAB PICTURES**
6500 Wilshire Blvd., Ste. 2240
Los Angeles, CA 90048
PHONE 323-655-1010
EMAIL .....info@yellowcabpictures.com
WEB SITE .....www.yellowcabpictures.com
TYPES Features - Reality TV - TV Series
DEVELOPMENT TV: Dirty Old Men - The Strip - Crossed Palms - Art Theft Unit - FUNdamentals; Features: Grasp - Ex-Boyfriend Project
PRE-PRODUCTION Parallel

Harley Bauer .....Producer
Robert Flutie .....Producer

YORKTOWN PRODUCTIONS, LTD.
18 Gloucester Ln., 4th Fl.
Toronto, ON M4Y 1L5, Canada
PHONE 416-923-2787
FAX 416-923-8580
TYPES Features
CREDITS The Statement - Moonstruck - The Hurricane - A Soldier's Story - In the Heat of the Night - Thomas Crown Affair (1968) - Fiddler on the Roof - Jesus Christ Superstar - Only You
SUBMISSION POLICY No unsolicited material accepted

Norman Jewison .....Director/Producer
Michael Jewison .....Producer
Kim Briggs .....Assistant to Norman Jewison
Winnie Wong .....Office Manager

MIKE YOUNG PRODUCTIONS LLC
A Moonscoop Company
20335 Ventura Blvd., Ste. 225
Woodland Hills, CA 91364
PHONE .818-999-0062
FAX .818-999-0172
EMAIL .info@mikeyoungproductions.com
WEB SITE .www.mikeyoungproductions.com
SECOND WEB SITE .www.taffyentertainment.com
TYPES Animation - Commercials - Direct-to-Video/DVD - TV Series
DEVELOPMENT El Corazon - Bad Egg - Hero 108
PRE-PRODUCTION Cosmic Quantum Ray
PRODUCTION Growing Up Creepie - I Got a Rocket - Dive Olly Dive
POST PRODUCTION Bratz
CREDITS He-Man and the Master of the Universe (Cartoon Network) - Clifford's Puppy Days (PBS) - Pet Alien (Cartoon Network) - Jakers! The Adventures of Piggley Winks (PBS) - Toddworld (TLC)

Mike Young .Co-CEO
Bill Schultz .Co-CEO
Liz Young .President
Josh Fisher .VP, Creative Affairs
Cary Silver .VP, Production
Rita Street .VP, Development

THE SAUL ZAENTZ COMPANY
2600 Tenth St.
Berkeley, CA 94710
PHONE .510-549-1528
TYPES Features
CREDITS One Flew Over the Cuckoo's Nest - Amadeus - The English Patient

Saul Zaentz .Producer

ZALOOM FILM
16055 Ventura Blvd., Ste. 535
Encinco, CA 91436
PHONE .818-905-1180
TYPES Animation - Features - Made-for-TV/Cable Movies - TV Series
CREDITS Encino Man - Hearts of Darkness - H-E-Double Hockey Sticks - The Cape (Series) - The Sports Pages - The Whole Shebang - Wonderful World of Disney Telefilm Series - PAX Network Family Film Series
SUBMISSION POLICY No unsolicited submissions

George Zaloom .Writer/Producer
David Hanson .Writer/Producer
Bruno Fortuna .VP, Development (Film)
Robin Goodfellow .VP, Development (TV)

THE ZANUCK COMPANY
9465 Wilshire Blvd., Ste. 930
Beverly Hills, CA 90212
PHONE .310-274-0261
FAX .310-273-9217
EMAIL .zanuckco@aol.com
TYPES Features - TV Series
HAS DEAL WITH DreamWorks SKG
CREDITS Charlie and the Chocolate Factory - Big Fish - Road to Perdition - Planet of the Apes - Deep Impact - The Verdict - Cocoon - The Sting - Driving Miss Daisy - Jaws - Rush - True Crime - Rules of Engagement - Academy Awards® 2000 - Reign of Fire
SUBMISSION POLICY No unsolicited submissions

Richard D. Zanuck .Producer (310-274-0261)
Lili Fini Zanuck .Producer/Director (310-274-0209)
Harrison Zanuck .Producer (310-274-5929)

ZEMECKIS/NEMEROFF FILMS
264 S. La Cienega Blvd., Ste. 238
Beverly Hills, CA 90211
PHONE .310-552-3333
FAX .310-552-3334
TYPES Features
DEVELOPMENT 14 Minutes and 59 Seconds
PRE-PRODUCTION Thicker
CREDITS Enfants Terribles
SUBMISSION POLICY No unsolicited submissions

Leslie Zemeckis .Actress/Producer
Terry Nemeroff .Writer/Director/Producer

ZENTROPA
Filmbyen 22
Hvidovre 2650, Denmark
PHONE .45-3-678-0055/45-3-686-8788
FAX .45-3-678-0077/45-3-686-8789
EMAIL .receptionen@filmbyen.com
WEB SITE .www.zentropa.dk
TYPES Features - TV Series
CREDITS Hvordan vi slipper af med de andre - Chacun, dans sa nuit - Råzone - Red Road - Princess - Liv - Dolph & Wulff med venner - De Skrev historie: Dolph - Efter brylluppet - Drømmen

Lars von Trier .Producer/Director
Peter Aalbaek Jensen .Managing Director
Meta Louise Foldager .Producer

ZEPHYR FILMS LTD.
33 Percy St.
London W1T 2DF, UK
PHONE .44-207-255-3555
FAX .44-207-255-3777
EMAIL .info@zephyrfilms.co.uk
WEB SITE .www.zephyrfilms.co.uk
TYPES Features
DEVELOPMENT White Rose - Last Station - Peter and Catherine
POST PRODUCTION Angels & Virgins - The Last Legion - Young Hannibal - Penelope
CREDITS Wah-Wah - The Upside of Anger - Asylum

Chris Curling .Producer
Phil Robertson .Producer
Luke Carey .Producer's Assistant
Polly West .Producer's Assistant

ZERO PICTURES

171 Pier Ave., Ste. 317
Santa Monica, CA 90405
PHONE 310-450-9040
EMAIL . . . . .participate@zeropictures.com
WEB SITE . . . . .www.zeropictures.com
TYPES Documentaries - Features - TV Series
CREDITS Charlotte Sometimes - Phoenix Point - Surrender - Lucinda's Spell - Hero, Lover, Fool - The Wooden Gun - Dogstar - Lou Lou - Self Storage - Mic and the Claw - The Invisibles - Welcome Says the Angel - Prometheus Bound - Is That All There Is? - Falling Like This

Michael Kastenbaum . . . . .Filmmaker
Marc Ambrose . . . . .Filmmaker
Louise Fenton . . . . .Filmmaker
Garrison Williams . . . . .Web Designer

ZIEGER PRODUCTIONS

331 Maple Dr., 3rd Fl.
Beverly Hills, CA 90210
PHONE 310-276-6177
FAX 310-276-9477
WEB SITE . . . . .www.ziegerproductions.com
TYPES Features - Reality TV - TV Series
DEVELOPMENT Sex, Drugs and Mozart - The Bureau - Knight & Day
PRE-PRODUCTION Under Arrest
CREDITS The Skulls 2
COMMENTS In partnership with Massimo Cristaldi for their 250+ titles in the Italian Film Library

Michele Zieger . . . . .Producer
Krasimir Karamfilov . . . . .Creative Executive

ZINGY INC.

500 Fashion Ave.
New York, NY 10018
PHONE 212-477-8601
EMAIL . . . . .pr@zingy.com
WEB SITE . . . . .www.zingy.com
TYPES Internet Content - Mobile Content
COMMENTS Partnerships with Nickelodeon & Viacom Consumer Products, and Bernie Mac; Original mobisodes, new series, and short-form entertainment created under Zingy Originals, and represented by International Creative Management, Inc. (ICM)

Debra Bluman . . . . .VP, Marketing & Sales
Scott Debson . . . . .VP, Licensing & Publishing
Chris Bellitti .Director, Corporate Communications

ZINKLER FILMS

9000 Sunset Blvd., Ste. 1101
West Hollywood, CA 90069
PHONE 310-288-0482
FAX 310-288-0470
WEB SITE . . . . .www.zinklerfilms.com
SECOND WEB SITE .www.guptapublishing.com
TYPES Direct-to-Video/DVD - Documentaries - Features - Internet Content - Reality TV - Specials
DEVELOPMENT Beady - All American Game (Quality Urban Theatrical) - Sight for Sore Eyes - Oy and Honey - Pit Fighting Championship Series - Web site Stations
PRE-PRODUCTION Significant Other
PRODUCTION Untitled Feature
POST PRODUCTION Messiah
CREDITS One More Round - 911 Hollywood Emergency - Wisegirls - Heartland - Forever 21 - Boys Klub
SUBMISSION POLICY Email synopsis and package info to submissions@zinklerfilms.com or visit company Web site; Unrepresented singers or unpublished songwriters may send demos for house soundtracks (no Web site inquiries)
COMMENTS Screenplays with packaged attachments only for co-productions (see Web site); Indie festival productions up to $500,000, major motion pictures up to $15 million; Music/talent and urban concept screenplays welcome if clean; Mailing address: PO Box 629, Beverly Hills, CA 90213

Jessica Russell . . . . .Producer/President
Arrika Russell . . . . .Producer/Writer
Dennis Holahan . . . . .Attorney
Michael Holtz . . . . .Attorney
Kate Miller . . . . .Assistant Producer/Head, Development
Richard Ginsberg . . . . .Music Attorney
Jing Zhang . . . . .Assistant to Ms. Russell

LAURA ZISKIN PRODUCTIONS

10202 W. Washington Blvd., Astaire Bldg., Ste. 1310
Culver City, CA 90232
PHONE 310-244-7373
FAX 310-244-0073
TYPES Features - Made-for-TV/Cable Movies - TV Series
HAS DEAL WITH Columbia Pictures
DEVELOPMENT 79th Annual Academy Awards - Deus Ex - Katharine Graham Project - Me & My Monster - How I Paid For College - How To Be Good - Morgan's Summit - The Spellman Files - Untitled Jason McElwain Feature
PRODUCTION Spider-Man 3
CREDITS Spider-Man 2 - Dinner with Friends - 74th Annual Academy Awards - Pretty Woman - To Die For - As Good as It Gets - Fail Safe - Spider-Man - Hero - What About Bob?

Laura Ziskin . . . . .Producer
Renee Witt . . . . .Sr. VP, Creative Affairs (NY)
Pam Oas Williams . . . . .Sr. VP, TV & Features
Jake Bauman . . . . .Story Editor (NY)
Sasha Mervyn . . . . .Story Editor (LA)
Ryan Behnke . . . . .Assistant to Laura Ziskin

RON ZISKIN PRODUCTIONS, INC.

4428 Arcola Ave.
Toluca Lake, CA 91602
PHONE . . . 310-963-7600
EMAIL . . . ron.ziskin@verizon.net
TYPES Features - Made-for-TV/Cable Movies - Miniseries - Reality TV - Syndication - TV Series
CREDITS American Gladiators - Unwed Father - Sandblast - Stealing Sinatra - The Courage to Love - Winning Women - SoapCenter - Futuresport - Born American - The Goodbye Girl - Comfort and Joy

Ron Ziskin . . . President
Maddie Miyoshi . . . VP, Development

FREDERICK ZOLLO PRODUCTIONS, INC.

257 W. 52nd St., 2nd Fl.
New York, NY 10019
PHONE . . . 212-957-1300
FAX . . . 212-957-1315
TYPES Documentaries - Features - Made-for-TV/Cable Movies - Theatre - TV Series
CREDITS The Paper - Quiz Show - In the Gloaming - Mississippi Burning - Hurlyburly - Ghosts of Mississippi - Lansky - Naked in New York; Theatre: The Goat (New York) - Chitty Chitty Bang Bang (London)

Frederick Zollo . . . Producer
Vince Maggio . . . Producer
Eric Chaney . . . Development

ZUCKER PRODUCTIONS

1250 Sixth St., Ste. 201
Santa Monica, CA 90401
PHONE . . . 310-656-9202
FAX . . . 310-656-9220
TYPES Features
DEVELOPMENT You Are Here - Untitled Warner Bros. Project - Yakuza Girl
PRE-PRODUCTION Friends with Benefits
CREDITS Rat Race - Unconditional Love - My Best Friend's Wedding - My Life - Ghost - Ruthless People - Airplane! - First Knight

Jerry Zucker . . . No Title
Janet Zucker . . . No Title
Jason Benesh . . . No Title
Sean Gesell . . . No Title
Jenny Wood . . . No Title

ZUCKER/NETTER PRODUCTIONS

1411 Fifth St., Ste. 402
Santa Monica, CA 90401
PHONE . . . 310-394-1644
FAX . . . 310-899-6722
TYPES Features
HAS DEAL WITH Twentieth Century Fox - Fox 2000
DEVELOPMENT 8 Track - Life of Pi - Rule No. 3 - Chasing the Whale - Into the Light
POST PRODUCTION Scary Movie 4 - Untitled Onion Sketch Movie
UPCOMING RELEASES Flicka
CREDITS Fever Pitch - My Boss's Daughter - Dude, Where's My Car? - Phone Booth - Scary Movie 3
SUBMISSION POLICY Through agency only

Gil Netter . . . Chairman/Producer
David Zucker . . . Producer/Director/Writer
Tom Carstens . . . Creative Executive

ZUCKERMAN ENTERTAINMENT

c/o Donald Zuckerman
343 N. Orange Dr.
Los Angeles, CA 90036
PHONE . . . 323-692-0131
FAX . . . 323-692-0126
EMAIL . . . donaldzucker@earthlink.net
TYPES Direct-to-Video/DVD - Documentaries - Features - Made-for-TV/Cable Movies
POST PRODUCTION Broken Bridges - Suffering Man's Charity
UPCOMING RELEASES Secret of the Code (Documentary) - Dishdogz
CREDITS Greenstreet Hooligans - Mayor of Sunset Strip - The Man from Elysian Fields - Thick as Thieves - Big Brass Ring - Beat - Say Nothing - Dogtown - The Low Life - The Adventures of Tom Sawyer

Donald Zuckerman . . . Producer
Katy Cooper . . . Assistant

SECTION D

TV SHOWS AND STAFF

***20 GOOD YEARS (NBC/30 mins.)**
c/o Werner-Gold-Miller
4024 Radford Ave., 4th Fl., Bldg. 3
Studio City, CA 91604
PHONE .818-655-7050
PRODUCTION COMPANIES Warner Bros. Television Production - Werner-Gold-Miller

Mike Clements .Executive Producer
Eric Gold .Executive Producer
Marsh McCall .Executive Producer/Showrunner
Jimmy Miller .Executive Producer
Tom Werner .Executive Producer
Kirk Rudell .Co-Executive Producer
Mike Teverbaugh .Co-Executive Producer
Eric Zicklin .Co-Executive Producer
Patricia Breen .Co-Producer
Robert H. Cohen .Consulting Producer
Michael Leeson .Consulting Producer/Creator
Samantha McIntyre .Staff Writer
Sung Suh .Staff Writer
Hugh Webber .Staff Writer

24 (Fox/60 mins.)
21050 Lassen St.
Chatsworth, CA 91311
PHONE .818-717-5400
FAX .818-717-5450
WEB SITE .www.fox.com/24
PRODUCTION COMPANIES Imagine Television - Twentieth Century Fox Television

Joel Surnow .Executive Producer/Creator
Bob Cochran .Executive Producer/Creator
Brian Grazer .Executive Producer
Howard Gordon .Executive Producer/Showrunner
Evan Katz .Executive Producer/Showrunner
Jon Cassar .Executive Producer/Director
Keifer Sutherland .Executive Producer
Manny Coto .Co-Executive Producer
David Fury .Co-Executive Producer
Stephen Kronish .Co-Executive Producer
Michael Loceff .Co-Executive Producer
Paul Gadd .Producer
Michael Klick .Producer/UPM
Brad Turner .Producer/Director
Debi Manwiller .Casting Director

***3 LBS. (CBS/60 mins.)**
34-12 36th St., Ste. 131
Astoria, NY 11106
PHONE .718-706-5000
FAX .718-706-5050
PRODUCTION COMPANY CBS Paramount Network Television

Peter Ocko .Executive Producer/Showrunner/Creator
Scott Kaufer .Executive Producer
Matt McGuiness .Supervising Producer
Davey Holmes .Co-Producer
Jessica Boll .Staff Writer
Pat McCorkle .Casting Director
Kelly Gillespie .Casting Associate

30 DAYS (FX/60 mins.)
c/o Warrior Poets
407 Broome St., Ste. 7B
New York, NY 10013
PHONE .212-219-7617
FAX .212-219-2920
WEB SITE .www.fxnetworks.com/shows/originals/30days/main.html
PRODUCTION COMPANIES Actual Reality Pictures - Reveille, LLC - Warrior Poets

Morgan Spurlock .Executive Producer/Creator
R.J. Cutler .Executive Producer
Ben Silverman .Executive Producer
Mark Koops .Executive Producer
H.T. Owens .Executive Producer

***30 ROCK (NBC/30 mins.)**
c/o Silvercup Studios
42-22 22nd St.
Long Island City, NY 11101
PHONE .718-906-2000
PRODUCTION COMPANIES Broadway Video Entertainment - NBC Universal Television Studio

Lorne Michaels .Executive Producer
Tina Fey .Executive Producer/Creator
JoAnn Alfano .Executive Producer
Marci Klein .Executive Producer
David Miner .Executive Producer
Robert Carlock .Co-Executive Producer
John Riggi .Co-Executive Producer
Jack Burditt .Co-Executive Producer
David Finkel .Co-Executive Producer
Brett Baer .Co-Executive Producer
Matt Hubbard .Co-Producer
Jerry Kupfer .Line Producer
Jennifer McNamara .Casting Director
Adam Bernstein .Supervising Producer
Kay Cannon .Staff Writer
Daisy Gardner .Staff Writer

7TH HEAVEN (The CW/60 mins.)
c/o North Shore Productions
4301 Exposition Blvd.
Santa Monica, CA 90404
PHONE .310-998-5700
WEB SITE .www.cwtv.com/cw-7heaven.html
PRODUCTION COMPANY CBS Paramount Network Television

Brenda Hampton .Executive Producer/Creator
Chris Olsen .Co-Executive Producer
Jeff Olsen .Co-Executive Producer
Elaine Arata .Consulting Producer
Jeff Rogers .Supervising Producer
Vicki Huff .Producer
Lindsley Parsons III .UPM/Line Producer
Shawn Kostanian .Associate Producer
Pam Cotton .Coordinating Producer

ACCORDING TO JIM (ABC/30 mins.)

c/o CBS Studio City Center
4024 Radford Ave., Bldg. 4
Studio City, CA 91604
PHONE .818-655-5094
FAX .818-655-8668
WEB SITE abc.go.com/primetime/accordingtojim/index.html
PRODUCTION COMPANY Touchstone Television

Warren Bell .Executive Producer/Showrunner
Suzanne Bukinik .Executive Producer
Jonathan Stark .Executive Producer/Creator
Marc Gurvitz .Executive Producer
John D. Beck .Co-Executive Producer
Ron Hart .Co-Executive Producer
Hayes Jackson .Co-Executive Producer
Bob Heath .Co-Executive Producer/UPM
John Peaslee .Consulting Producer
Judd Pillot .Consulting Producer
Christi Ayo .Co-Producer
Harry Hannigan .Co-Producer
Sylvia Green .Executive Story Editor
Chris Nowak .Story Editor
Allison Bosch .Casting Director

ALL OF US (The CW/30 mins.)

100 Universal City Plaza, Bldg. 3213
Universal City, CA 91608
PHONE .818-954-7300
FAX .818-655-0165
WEB SITE .www.cwtv.com/cw-allofus.html
PRODUCTION COMPANIES Overbrook Entertainment - Warner Bros. Television Production
COMMENTS Writers' office: 4024 Radford Ave., Admin. Bldg., Ste. 290, Studio City, CA 91604

Jada Pinkett Smith .Executive Producer/Creator
Will Smith .Executive Producer/Creator
James Lassiter .Executive Producer
Jeff Strauss .Executive Producer/Showrunner
Arthur Harris .Executive Producer
Betsy Borns .Consulting Producer/Creator
Stacy A. Littlejohn .Consulting Producer
Lori Lakin-Hutcherson .Consulting Producer
Royale Watkins .Creative Consultant
Leo Clarke .Line Producer
Jared Bush .Co-Producer
Ray Lancon .Executive Story Editor
Terence Paul Winter .Executive Story Editor
Jewel Wormley .Executive Story Editor
Chad Drew .Staff Writer
Monica Swann .Casting Director

THE AMAZING RACE (CBS/60 mins.)

c/o World Race Productions, Inc.
7800 Beverly Blvd.
Los Angeles, CA 90036
PHONE .310-577-9381
FAX .310-577-9473
WEB SITE .www.cbs.com/primetime/amazing_race
PRODUCTION COMPANIES Jerry Bruckheimer Television - Touchstone Television

Jerry Bruckheimer .Executive Producer
Bertram van Munster .Executive Producer/Co-Creator
Jonathan Littman .Executive Producer
Screech Washington .Executive Producer
Elise Doganieri .Executive Producer/Co-Creator
Amy Chacon .Co-Executive Producer
Evan Weinstein .Co-Executive Producer

AMERICAN DAD (Fox/30 mins.)

5700 Wilshire Blvd., Ste. 475
Los Angeles, CA 90036
PHONE .323-857-8900/323-857-8800
FAX .323-857-8945/323-857-8938
WEB SITE .www.fox.com/americandad
PRODUCTION COMPANY Twentieth Century Fox Television
COMMENTS Writers' office: 5700 Wilshire Blvd., Ste. 325, Los Angeles, CA 90036

Seth MacFarlane .Executive Producer/Creator
Mike Barker .Executive Producer/Creator
Matt Weitzman .Executive Producer/Creator
Kenny Schwartz .Executive Producer
Rick Wiener .Executive Producer
David Zuckerman .Executive Producer
Jim Bernstein .Co-Executive Producer
David Hemingson .Co-Executive Producer
Michael Shipley .Co-Executive Producer
Dan Vebber .Co-Executive Producer
Jonathon Fener .Supervising Producer
Ron Hughart .Supervising Director
Anthony Lioi .Supervising Director
Brian Boyle .Supervising Producer
Nahnatchka Khan .Supervising Producer
Kara Vallow .Producer
Diana Ritchey .Animation Producer
Mark Douglas .Associate Producer
Steve Hely .Executive Story Editor
Chris McKenna .Executive Story Editor
Matt McKenna .Executive Story Editor
Laura McCreary .Story Editor
Eric Durbin .Staff Writer
Rick Williams .Staff Writer
Linda Lamontagne .Casting Director

AMERICAN IDOL (Fox/60 mins.)

7800 Beverly Blvd., Ste. 251
Los Angeles, CA 90036
PHONE .323-575-8000
WEB SITE .www.idolonfox.com
PRODUCTION COMPANIES 19 Entertainment, Inc. - FremantleMedia North America

Simon Fuller .Executive Producer/Creator
Cecile Frot-Coutaz .Executive Producer
Nigel Lythgoe .Executive Producer
Ken Warrick .Executive Producer
Charles Boyd .Supervising Producer
James Breen .Sr. Producer
Simon Lythgoe .Producer
Megan Michaels .Producer
Patrick Lynn .Coordinating Producer
Wylleen May .Executive in Charge of Production
Eric Lapoint .Head, Accounting
Mike Hofferth .Production Manager

AMERICA'S FUNNIEST VIDEOS (ABC/60 mins.)
12233 W. Olympic Blvd., Ste. 170
Los Angeles, CA 90064
PHONE .310-442-5600
FAX .310-442-5604
WEB SITE .www.afv.tv
SECOND WEB SITE .www.vdbp.com
PRODUCTION COMPANY Vin Di Bona Productions

Vin Di Bona .Executive Producer
Todd Thicke .Co-Executive Producer/Writer
Michele Nasraway .Co-Executive Producer
J. Elvis Weinstein .Consulting Producer/Writer
Trace Beaulieu .Writer
Michael Palleschi .Writer
Gina Di Bona .Production Consultant
Gerald Jaskulski .Line Producer
Tomika Dalmer-Ciaccio .Line Producer
Tom Bergeron .Producer
Richard Connor .Coordinating Producer
Joe Bellon .Coordinating Producer
Greg Bellon .Coordinating Producer

AMERICA'S NEXT TOP MODEL (The CW/60 mins.)
c/o Bankable Productions
6310 San Vicente Blvd., Ste. 505
Los Angeles, CA 90048
PHONE .323-934-4308
FAX .323-934-4387
WEB SITE .www.cwtv.com/cw-antm2.html
PRODUCTION COMPANIES 10x10 Entertainment - Bankable Productions

Tyra Banks .Executive Producer/Creator
Anthony Dominici .Executive Producer
Ken Mok .Executive Producer

THE APPRENTICE (NBC/60 mins.)
c/o Mark Burnett Productions
640 N. Sepulveda Blvd.
Los Angeles, CA 90049
PHONE .310-903-5400
PRODUCTION COMPANY Mark Burnett Productions

Donald Trump .Executive Producer
Mark Burnett .Executive Producer
Jay Bienstock .Executive Producer
Jamie Canniffe .Co-Executive Producer
Page Feldman .Co-Executive Producer
Conrad Riggs .Co-Executive Producer

AVERAGE JOE (NBC/60 mins.)
c/o Krasnow Productions
2700 Colorado Ave., Ste. 450
Santa Monica, CA 90404
PHONE .310-255-4824
FAX .310-255-4804
WEB SITE .www.nbc.com/nbc/Average_Joe
PRODUCTION COMPANIES FremantleMedia North America - Krasnow Productions - NBC Universal Television Studio

Andrew Glassman .Executive Producer
Stuart Krasnow .Executive Producer
Jason Raff .Supervising Producer

THE BACHELOR (ABC/60 mins.)
3500 W. Olive St., Ste. 600
Burbank, CA 91505
PHONE .818-972-0077
FAX .818-972-0986
WEB SITE .abc.go.com/primetime/bachelor/index.html
PRODUCTION COMPANIES Next Entertainment - Warner Horizon Television

Mike Fleiss .Executive Producer
Lisa Levenson .Executive Producer
David Bohnert .Co-Executive Producer
Martin Hilton .Co-Executive Producer
Monica Stock .Supervising Producer
Robyn Kass .Talent Executive

BATTLESTAR GALACTICA (Sci Fi/60 mins.)
c/o GFP Productions
3500 Cornett Rd., Bldg. C North
Vancouver, BC V5M 2H5, Canada
PHONE .604-453-6650/818-777-1934
FAX .604-453-6651/818-866-4193
WEB SITE .www.scifi.com/battlestar
PRODUCTION COMPANIES NBC Universal Television Studio - Sky Networks

David Eick .Executive Producer
Ronald D. Moore .Executive Producer
Mark Verheiden .Co-Executive Producer
Michael Angeli .Co-Executive Producer
Harvey Frand .Supervising Producer
Michael Taylor .Supervising Producer
Bradley Thompson .Producer
David Weddle .Producer
Paul Leonard .Co-Producer
Ron French .Line Producer
Chris Randolph .Production Manager
Anne Cofell Saunders .Story Editor
Carol Kritzer .Casting Director
Robert Ulrich .Casting Director

***BIG DAY (ABC/30 mins.)**
10202 W. Washington Blvd.
Culver City, CA 90232
PHONE .310-244-3290
PRODUCTION COMPANIES Allenford Productions Inc. - Sony Pictures Television

Matthew Carlson .Executive Producer/Showrunner
Josh Goldsmith .Executive Producer/Creator
Cathy Yuspa .Executive Producer/Creator
Justin Adler .Co-Executive Producer
Bob Nickman .Co-Executive Producer
Jason Fisher .Producer
Maggie Bondur .Consulting Producer
Bill Daly .Consulting Producer
Dan Kopelman .Consulting Producer
Jessica Goldstein .Executive Story Editor
Chrissy Pietrosh .Executive Story Editor
Dylann Brander .Casting Director
Megan Branman .Casting Director

BIG LOVE (HBO/60 mins.)
c/o Triple Love Productions
27420 Avenue Scott
Santa Clarita, CA 91355
PHONE 661-362-6800
FAX 661-362-6844
WEB SITE .....www.hbo.com/events/biglove/
PRODUCTION COMPANIES HBO Entertainment - Playtone Productions

Tom Hanks .....Executive Producer
Gary Goetzman .....Executive Producer
Mark V. Olsen .....Executive Producer/Creator
Will Scheffer .....Executive Producer/Creator
David Knoller .....Executive Producer
Mimi Friedman .....Supervising Producer
Jeanette Collins .....Supervising Producer
Bernadette Caulfield .....Producer
Doug Jung .....Producer
Peter Friedlander .....Co-Producer
Steve Turner .....Co-Producer
Lance Black .....Executive Story Editor
Eileen Myers .....Executive Story Editor
Doug Stockstill .....Staff Writer
Jennifer Svidler .....Staff Writer

THE BIGGEST LOSER (NBC/60 mins.)
c/o 3 Ball Productions
1600 Rosecrans Ave., Bldg. 7, 2nd Fl.
Manhattan Beach, CA 90266
PHONE 310-727-3337
FAX 310-727-3339
WEB SITE .....www.nbc.com/The_Biggest_Loser
PRODUCTION COMPANIES 25/7 Productions - 3 Ball Productions - NBC Universal Television Studio - Reveille, LLC

Dave Broome .....Executive Producer
John Foy .....Executive Producer
Todd Nelson .....Executive Producer
JD Roth .....Executive Producer
Ben Silverman .....Executive Producer
Elayne Cilic .....Supervising Producer
Mark Koops .....Co-Executive Producer
Howard Owens .....Co-Executive Producer
Troy Searer .....Co-Executive Producer
Eric Westmore .....Line Producer
Allison Kaz .....Casting Director

THE BLACK DONNELLYS (NBC/60 mins.)
203 Meserole Ave., 2nd Fl.
New York, NY 11222
PHONE .....718-389-2803/310-315-9002 (Writer's office)
FAX 718-383-6878
PRODUCTION COMPANIES Blackfriars Bridge - NBC Universal Television Studio

Paul Haggis .....Executive Producer/Showrunner/Creator
Bobby Moresco .....Executive Producer/Showrunner
Mark R. Harris .....Co-Executive Producer
Sean Whitesell .....Co-Executive Producer
Jeff F. King .....Supervising Producer
Rafael Alvarez .....Producer
Laurence Becsey .....Producer
Kim Clements .....Producer
Dana Maksimovich .....Co-Producer
Mick Betancourt .....Staff Writer
Laurie Huntsler .....Staff Writer
Gary Lennon .....Staff Writer
Alexa Fogel .....Casting Director

THE BOLD AND THE BEAUTIFUL (CBS/30 mins.)
7800 Beverly Blvd., Ste. 3371
Los Angeles, CA 90036
PHONE 323-575-4138
FAX 323-655-8760

Lee Phillip Bell .....Co-Creator
Bradley Bell .....Executive Producer/Head Writer
Rhonda Friedman .....Supervising Producer
Ron Weaver .....Sr. Producer
Cynthia J. Popp .....Producer
Adam Dusevoir .....Associate Producer
Michael Minnis .....Associate Head Writer
Jerry Birn .....Story Consultant
Betsy Snyder .....Story Consultant
Rex Best .....Writer
John Chambers .....Writer
Fred Johnson .....Writer
Tracy Ann Kelly .....Writer
Patrick Mulcahey .....Writer
Christy Elaine Dooley .....Casting Director

BONES (Fox/60 mins.)
c/o Twentieth Century Fox Television
10201 W. Pico Blvd., Bldg. 99, Ste. 430
Los Angeles, CA 90035
PHONE 310-369-1800/310-369-4086
FAX 310-969-0094
WEB SITE .....www.fox.com/bones
PRODUCTION COMPANIES Josephson Entertainment - Twentieth Century Fox Television
COMMENTS Writers' office: 10201 W. Pico Blvd., Bldg. 80, Ste. 3, Los Angeles, CA 90035

Barry Josephson .....Executive Producer
Kathy Reichs .....Executive Producer
Hart Hanson .....Executive Producer/Creator/Showrunner
Stephen Nathan .....Executive Producer
Steve Beers .....Co-Executive Producer
Gary Glasberg .....Co-Executive Producer
Tony Wharmby .....Co-Executive Producer
Scott Williams .....Co-Executive Producer
Janet Tamaro .....Supervising Producer
Jan DeWitt .....Producer/UPM
Christopher Ambrose .....Co-Producer
Elizabeth Benjamin .....Co-Producer
Noah Hawley .....Executive Story Editor
Karine Rosenthal .....Staff Writer
Rick Millikan .....Casting Director

BOSTON LEGAL (ABC/60 mins.)
c/o David E. Kelley Productions
1600 Rosecrans Ave., Bldg. 4-B
Manhattan Beach, CA 90266
PHONE . . . 310-727-2200
WEB SITE . . . abc.go.com/primetime/bostonlegal/index.html
PRODUCTION COMPANIES David E. Kelley Productions - Twentieth Century Fox Television

David E. Kelley . . . Executive Producer/Creator
Bill D'Elia . . . Executive Producer
Janet Leahy . . . Executive Producer
Mike Listo . . . Co-Executive Producer
Steve Robin . . . Supervising Producer
Janet Knutsen . . . Producer/UPM
Bob Breech . . . Consulting Producer
Lawrence Broch . . . Consulting Producer
Phoef Sutton . . . Consulting Producer
Susan Dickes . . . Consulting Producer
Andrew Kreisberg . . . Producer
Michael Reisz . . . Co-Producer
Craig Turk . . . Co-Producer
Anne Uemura . . . Associate Producer
Sandy Golden . . . Staff Writer
Karen Wyscarver . . . Staff Writer
Ken Miller . . . Casting Director
Nikki Valko . . . Casting Director
Rick Silverman . . . Production Executive

***THE CLASS (CBS/30 mins.)**
c/o Warner Bros. Television
4000 Warner Blvd.
Burbank, CA 91522
PHONE . . . 818-954-4365
FAX . . . 818-954-3024
PRODUCTION COMPANY Warner Bros. Television Production

David Crane . . . Executive Producer/Showrunner/Creator
Jeffrey Klarik . . . Executive Producer/Showrunner/Creator
Mike Sikowitz . . . Co-Executive Producer
Brian Buckner . . . Consulting Producer
Jonathan Green . . . Co-Producer
Amanda Lasher . . . Co-Producer
Gabe Miller . . . Co-Producer
Steve Molaro . . . Co-Producer
Corey Nickerson . . . Co-Producer
Ed Roe . . . Co-Producer
Lisa Helfrich-Jackson . . . Line Producer
Sue Murphy . . . Executive Story Editor
Gavin Steckler . . . Staff Writer
Bruce Newberg . . . Casting Director

CLOSE TO HOME (CBS/60 mins.)
c/o Sony Pictures Studios
10202 W. Washington Blvd., Myrna Loy Bldg., 2nd Fl.
Culver City, CA 90232
PHONE . . . 310-244-7242
FAX . . . 310-244-1970
WEB SITE . . . www.cbs.com/primetime/close_to_home
PRODUCTION COMPANIES Jerry Bruckheimer Television - Warner Bros. Television Production

Jerry Bruckheimer . . . Executive Producer
Jim Leonard . . . Creator
Jonathan Littman . . . Executive Producer
Eric Overmyer . . . Executive Producer/Showrunner
Bill Fordes . . . Co-Executive Producer
Jill Danton . . . Producer
Kevin Dowling . . . Producer
Elwood Reid . . . Producer
Antoinette Stella . . . Producer
Tom Smuts . . . Co-Producer
Lindsay Sturman . . . Co-Producer
Leo Geter . . . Executive Story Editor
Alison McDonald . . . Staff Writer
Nikki Toscano . . . Staff Writer
Carrie Audino . . . Casting Director
Laura Schiff . . . Casting Director
Sari Knight . . . Casting Associate

THE CLOSER (TNT/60 mins.)
c/o Raleigh Studios
5300 Melrose Ave., #225E
Los Angeles, CA 90038
PHONE . . . 323-871-4410
FAX . . . 323-871-4411
WEB SITE . . . alt.tnt.tv/tntoriginals/closer
PRODUCTION COMPANIES The Shephard/Robin Company - Warner Bros. Television Production

James Duff . . . Executive Producer/Creator
Michael Robin . . . Executive Producer
Greer Shephard . . . Executive Producer
Wendy West . . . Co-Executive Producer
Adam Belanoff . . . Supervising Producer
Andrew Sacks . . . Producer
Michael Weiss . . . Producer
Hunt Baldwin . . . Co-Producer
John Coveny . . . Co-Producer
Gil Garcetti . . . Consulting Producer
Steven Kane . . . Story Editor
Bruce Newberg . . . Casting Director

THE COLBERT REPORT (Comedy Central/30 mins.)
513 W. 54th St.
New York, NY 10019
PHONE . . . 212-649-6200
FAX . . . 212-649-6288
WEB SITE . . . www.colbertnation.com
PRODUCTION COMPANIES Busboy Productions - Spartina Productions

Stephen Colbert . . . Executive Producer
Ben Karlin . . . Executive Producer
Jon Stewart . . . Executive Producer
Richard Korson . . . Executive in Charge for Busboy Productions
Lou Wallach . . . Executive in Charge for Comedy Central
Richard Dahm . . . Supervising Producer
Allison Silverman . . . Supervising Producer
Glenn Eichler . . . Consulting Producer
Tom Purcell . . . Consulting Producer
Meredith Bennett . . . Line Producer
John Bedolis . . . Coordinating Producer
Kim Gamble . . . Segment Producer
Matt Lappin . . . Segment Producer
Mike Brumm . . . Writer
Eric Drysdale . . . Writer
Rob Dubbin . . . Writer
Peter Gwinn . . . Writer
Jay Katsir . . . Writer
Laura Krafft . . . Writer
Frank Lesser . . . Writer
Emily Lazar . . . Talent Booker

COLD CASE (CBS/60 mins.)
4000 Warner Blvd., Bldg. 185
Burbank, CA 91522
PHONE . . . 818-954-3399
FAX . . . 818-954-2832
WEB SITE . . . www.cbs.com/primetime/cold_case
PRODUCTION COMPANIES Jerry Bruckheimer Television - CBS Paramount Network Television - Warner Bros. Television Production

Meredith Stiehm . . . Executive Producer/Creator/Showrunner
Jerry Bruckheimer . . . Executive Producer
Jonathan Littman . . . Executive Producer
Veena Sud . . . Executive Producer/Showrunner
Tyler Bensinger . . . Co-Executive Producer
Samantha Corbin-Miller . . . Co-Executive Producer
Jennifer Johnson . . . Supervising Producer
Greg Plagman . . . Supervising Producer
David Barrett . . . Consulting Producer
Merri Howard . . . Producer
Liz Garcia . . . Co-Producer
Eric Shelton . . . Story Editor
Gavin Harris . . . Staff Writer
Tom Pettit . . . Staff Writer

COPS (Fox/30 mins.)
c/o Langley Productions
1111 Broadway
Santa Monica, CA 90401
PHONE .310-449-5300
FAX .310-449-5330
WEB SITE www.cops.com
PRODUCTION COMPANIES Langley Productions - Twentieth Century Fox Television

John Langley .Executive Producer/Creator
Doug Waterman .Supervising Producer
Jimmy Langley .Producer
Bryan Collins .Coordinating Producer

CRIMINAL MINDS (CBS/60 mins.)
8660 Hayden Pl.
Culver City, CA 90232
PHONE .310-840-7474
FAX .310-840-7475
WEB SITE .www.cbs.com/primetime/criminal_minds
PRODUCTION COMPANIES CBS Paramount Network Television - Touchstone Television

Edward Allen Bernero .Executive Producer/Showrunner
Mark Gordon .Executive Producer
Deb Spera .Executive Producer
Jeff Davis .Co-Executive Producer/Creator
Simon Mirren .Co-Executive Producer
Aaron Zelman .Co-Executive Producer
Chris Mundy .Co-Executive Producer
Charles Carroll .Producer
Debra J. Fisher .Producer
Erica Messer .Producer
Frank Conway .Co-Producer/UPM
Gigi Coello-Bannon .Co-Producer
Andrew Wilder .Executive Story Editor
Ed Napier .Story Editor
Amanda Bernero .Researcher
Rick Dunkle .Script Coordinator
Oanh Ly .Writers' Assistant
Jess Prosser .Writers' Assistant
April Webster .Casting Director
Scott David .Casting Associate
Gina Garcia .Casting Associate
Rosalie Escobar .Assistant to Edward Allen Bernero

CROSSING JORDAN (NBC/60 mins.)
100 Universal City Plaza, Bldg. 5225, 2nd Fl.
Universal City, CA 91608
PHONE .818-733-5588
FAX .818-733-3710
WEB SITE .www.nbc.com/Crossing_Jordan
PRODUCTION COMPANIES NBC Universal Television Studio - Tailwind Productions

Tim Kring .Executive Producer/Creator
Dennis Hammer .Executive Producer
Jon Cowan .Executive Producer/Showrunner
Kathy McCormick .Executive Producer/Showrunner
Robert Rovner .Executive Producer/Showrunner
Allan Arkush .Executive Producer/Director
Rob Fresco .Co-Executive Producer
Melissa Byer .Supervising Producer
Treena Hancock .Supervising Producer
Skip Beaudine .Producer/UPM
Natalie Hart .Casting Director
Jason La Padura .Casting Director

CSI: CRIME SCENE INVESTIGATION (CBS/60 mins.)
100 Universal City Plaza, Bldg. 2128, Ste. B
Universal City, CA 91608
PHONE .818-777-4274
FAX .818-733-4274
WEB SITE .www.cbs.com/primetime/csi
PRODUCTION COMPANIES Alliance Atlantis - Jerry Bruckheimer Television - CBS Paramount Network Television

Jerry Bruckheimer .Executive Producer
Carol Mendelsohn .Executive Producer/Co-Showrunner
Ann Donahue .Executive Producer
Naren Shankar .Executive Producer/Co-Showrunner
Anthony Zuiker .Executive Producer/Creator
Jonathan Littman .Executive Producer
Cynthia Chvatal .Executive Producer
William Petersen .Executive Producer
Kenneth Fink .Co-Executive Producer
Louis Milito .Co-Executive Producer
Sarah Goldfinger .Supervising Producer
Richard Lewis .Supervising Producer/Director
Steven Felder .Producer
Phil Conserva .Co-Producer
Carol Kritzer .Casting Director
Andy Henry .Casting Associate

CSI: MIAMI (CBS/60 mins.)
1600 Rosecrans Ave., Bldg. 4A, 2nd Fl.
Manhattan Beach, CA 90266
PHONE .310-727-5959
FAX .310-727-5960
WEB SITE .www.cbs.com/primetime/csi_miami
PRODUCTION COMPANIES Alliance Atlantis - Jerry Bruckheimer Television - CBS Paramount Network Television

Jerry Bruckheimer .Executive Producer
Jonathan Littman .Executive Producer
Ann Donahue .Executive Producer/Showrunner/Creator
Carol Mendelsohn .Executive Producer/Creator
Anthony Zuiker .Executive Producer/Creator
Elizabeth Devine .Co-Executive Producer
Sunil Nayar .Co-Executive Producer
Gina Lamar .Supervising Producer
Barry O'Brien .Supervising Producer
Sam Hill .Producer
Ildy Modrovich .Producer
Don Tardino .Producer
Marco Black .UPM
Marc Dube .Co-Producer
Scott Lautanen .Co-Producer
Corey Miller .Co-Producer
Melissa Black .Associate Producer
Doreen Blauschild .Associate Producer
Eric Mirich .Associate Producer
John Haynes .Executive Story Editor
Brian Davidson .Story Editor
Kristal Houghton .Story Editor
Nan Dutton .Casting Director

CSI: NY (CBS/60 mins.)

c/o CBS Studio City Center
4024 Radford Ave., Bldg. 2
Studio City, CA 91604
PHONE 818-655-5511
FAX 818-655-8247
WEB SITE ....www.cbs.com/primetime/csi_ny
PRODUCTION COMPANIES Alliance Atlantis - Jerry Bruckheimer Television - CBS Paramount Network Television
COMMENTS Writers' office: 4024 Radford Ave., Bldg. 8, Studio City, CA 91604

Jerry Bruckheimer ....Executive Producer
Anthony Zuiker ....Executive Producer/Showrunner/Creator
Ann Donahue ....Executive Producer/Creator
Carol Mendelsohn ....Executive Producer/Creator
Jonathan Littman ....Executive Producer
Pam Veasey ....Executive Producer/Showrunner
Peter Lenkov ....Executive Producer
Wendy Battles ....Co-Executive Producer
Tim Lea ....Supervising Producer
Ken Solarz ....Consulting Producer
Zachary Reiter ....Executive Story Editor
Samantha Humphrey ....Story Editor
Gary Sinise ....Producer
Rob Bailey ....Producer
Vikki Williams ....Producer
Geoff Hemwall ....Co-Producer
Todd Coe ....Line Producer
Barbara Fiorentino ....Casting Director
Rebecca Mangieri ....Casting Director

THE DAILY SHOW WITH JON STEWART (Comedy Central/30 mins.)

604 W. 52nd St.
New York, NY 10019
PHONE 212-468-1700
FAX 212-468-1890
WEB SITE ....www.comedycentral.com/shows/the_daily_show/index.jhtml
PRODUCTION COMPANY Hello Doggie, Inc.

Jon Stewart ....Executive Producer
Ben Karlin ....Executive Producer
Kahane Corn ....Co-Executive Producer
DJ Javerbaum ....Head Writer/Supervising Producer
Rachel Axler ....Writer
Kevin Bleger ....Writer
Rich Blomquist ....Writer
Steve Bodow ....Writer
Tim Carvell ....Writer
JR Havlan ....Writer
Scott Jacobson ....Writer
Rob Kutner ....Writer
Sam Means ....Writer
Jason Reich ....Writer
Jason Ross ....Writer
Hilary Kun ....Talent Booker

DANCING WITH THE STARS (ABC/60 mins.)

4144 Lankershim Blvd., #200
North Hollywood, CA 91602
PHONE 818-299-9660
WEB SITE ....abc.go.com/primetime/dancing/index.html
PRODUCTION COMPANY BBC Worldwide Americas

Conrad Green ....Executive Producer
Richard Hopkins ....Executive Producer
Izzie Pick ....Supervising Producer
Linda Giambrone ....Producer

*DAY BREAK (ABC/60 mins.)

4585 Electronics Pl., 2nd Fl.
Los Angeles, CA 90039
PHONE 818-553-2929
FAX 818-553-2930
PRODUCTION COMPANIES Gross Entertainment - Touchstone Television

Jeffrey Bell ....Executive Producer/Showrunner
Rob Bowman ....Executive Producer
Matthew Gross ....Executive Producer
Richard Heus ....Co-Executive Producer
Steve Maeda ....Co-Executive Producer
Paul Zbyszewski ....Co-Executive Producer/Creator
David Graziano ....Supervising Producer
Henry Alonso Myers ....Supervising Producer
Taye Diggs ....Producer
Abe Hoch ....Producer
Charles Murray ....Co-Producer
John Hlavin ....Staff Writer
Jenny Lynn ....Staff Writer
Angela Russo ....Staff Writer
David Booth ....Writers' Assistant
Robert Ulrich ....Casting Director

DAYS OF OUR LIVES (NBC/60 mins.)

3000 W. Alameda Ave.
Burbank, CA 91523
PHONE 818-840-4089
FAX 818-840-4968

Ken Corday ....Executive Producer
Steve Wyman ....Co-Executive Producer
James E. Reilly ....Consulting Producer/Head Writer
Roy Steinberg ....Supervising Producer
Janet Spellman-Rider ....Sr. Coordinating Producer
Tom Walker ....Sr. Coordinating Producer
Peter Brash ....Writer
Rick Draughon ....Writer
Jeanne Marie Ford ....Writer
Sofia Landon Geier ....Writer
Victor Gialanella ....Writer
Renee Godelia ....Writer
Susan Kirshenbaum ....Writer
Bruce Neckels ....Writer
Jodie Scholz ....Writer
Michael Slade ....Writer
Fran Bascom ....Casting Director
Linda Poindexter ....Casting Director

THE DEAD ZONE (USA/60 mins.)

3330 Bridgeway St.
Vancouver, BC V5K 5E9, Canada
PHONE 604-296-2000
FAX 604-296-2020
WEB SITE ....www.usanetwork.com/series/thedeadzone
PRODUCTION COMPANIES Lionsgate - Piller/Segan
COMMENTS Writers' office: 7025 Santa Monica Blvd., Los Angeles, CA 90038

Lloyd Segan ....Executive Producer (323-817-1113/604-296-2018)
Tommy Thompson ....Executive Producer/Showrunner (323-817-1100)
Shawn Piller ....Co-Executive Producer/Creator (604-296-2009/323-817-1101)
Christina Lynch ....Supervising Producer
Loren Segan ....Supervising Producer
Michael Taylor ....Supervising Producer
Robert Petrovicz ....Producer (604-296-2008)
Kira Domaschuk ....Co-Producer (604-296-2006)
Anthony Michael Hall ....Co-Producer
Amber Woodward ....Associate Producer
James Morris ....Staff Writer
Shin Shimosawa ....Staff Writer
Adam Targum ....Staff Writer
Sue Brouse ....Casting Director (Vancouver) (604-990-9543)
Shawn Dawson ....Casting Director (LA) (818-623-1818)

DESPERATE HOUSEWIVES (ABC/60 mins.)

c/o Touchstone Television
3800 W. Alameda Ave.
Burbank, CA 91505
PHONE . . . . 818-733-3773/310-369-1296 (Casting)
FAX 818-733-3775
WEB SITE . . . . abc.go.com/primetime/desperate/index.html
PRODUCTION COMPANY Touchstone Television
COMMENTS Writers' office: 100 Universal City Plaza, Bldg. 2128, Universal City, CA 91608

Marc Cherry . . . . Executive Producer/Creator
George W. Perkins . . . . Executive Producer
Bob Daily . . . . Co-Executive Producer
David Grossman . . . . Co-Executive Producer
Joe Keenan . . . . Co-Executive Producer
Kevin Murphy . . . . Co-Executive Producer
Joey Murphy . . . . Co-Executive Producer
John Pardee . . . . Co-Executive Producer
Larry Shaw . . . . Co-Executive Producer
Susan Jaffe . . . . Supervising Producer
Alex Cunningham . . . . Producer
Stephanie Hagen . . . . Producer
Charlie Skouras . . . . Producer
Sabrina Wind . . . . Producer
Kevin Etten . . . . Co-Producer
Jeff Greenstein . . . . Consulting Producer
Charles Pratt . . . . Consulting Producer
Jenna Bans . . . . Executive Story Editor
Josh Senter . . . . Executive Story Editor
Dahvi Waller . . . . Staff Writer
Scott Genkinger . . . . Casting Director
Junie Lowry-Johnson . . . . Casting Director

*DIRT (FX/60 mins.)

c/o Coquette Productions
8105 W. 3rd St.
West Hollywood, CA 90048
PHONE 323-801-1000
FAX 323-801-1001
PRODUCTION COMPANIES Coquette Productions - Touchstone Television

David Arquette . . . . Executive Producer
Matthew Carnahan . . . . Executive Producer/Creator
Courteney Cox-Arquette . . . . Executive Producer
Joel Fields . . . . Co-Executive Producer/Showrunner
Chris Long . . . . Co-Executive Producer
Thea Mann . . . . Producer
Sascha Schneider . . . . Line Producer
Barbara Fiorentino . . . . Casting Director

DRAWN TOGETHER (Comedy Central/30 mins.)

c/o Comedy Central
2049 Century Park East, Ste. 4000
Los Angeles, CA 90067
PHONE 310-407-4700
FAX 310-407-4796
WEB SITE . . . www.comedycentral.com/shows/drawn_together/index.jhtml
COMMENTS Animated

Matt Silverstein . . . . Executive Producer/Creator
Dave Jeser . . . . Executive Producer/Creator
Adam Hamburger . . . . Consulting Producer
David Hamburger . . . . Consulting Producer
Joshua Krist . . . . Consulting Producer

THE ELLEN DEGENERES SHOW (Syndicated/60 mins.)

3000 W. Alameda Ave., Ste. 2700
Burbank, CA 91523
PHONE 818-260-5600
FAX 818-260-5601
WEB SITE . . . . www.ellendegeneres.com
SECOND WEB SITE . . . . www.ellentv.com
PRODUCTION COMPANIES NBC Entertainment - Telepictures Productions - Warner Bros. Television Production

Mary Connelly . . . . Executive Producer
Ellen DeGeneres . . . . Executive Producer
Ed Glavin . . . . Executive Producer
Andy Lassner . . . . Executive Producer
Derek Westervelt . . . . Coordinating Producer
Jason Gabel . . . . Sr. Producer
Jonathan Norman . . . . Sr. Producer
Melissa Geiger Schrift . . . . Sr. Producer
Vikki Ernst . . . . Producer
Karen Kilgariff . . . . Head Writer
Karen Anderson . . . . Writer
Alison Balian . . . . Writer
Liz Feldman . . . . Writer
Kevin Leman . . . . Writer
Margaret Smith . . . . Writer
Christopher Miele . . . . . Product Placement Producer/Audience Giveaways
Melissa Little . . . . Publicist
Danny Ceballos . . . . Writer
Lori Blackman . . . . Sr. Talent Executive
Corey Palent . . . . Talent Executive

ENTOURAGE (HBO/30 mins.)

6330 San Vicente Blvd., 5th Fl.
Los Angeles, CA 90048
PHONE 323-330-6060
FAX 323-934-8680
WEB SITE . . . . www.hbo.com/entourage
PRODUCTION COMPANY HBO Entertainment

Doug Ellin . . . . Executive Producer
Steve Levinson . . . . Executive Producer
Mark Wahlberg . . . . Executive Producer
Marc Abrams . . . . Co-Executive Producer
Mike Benson . . . . Co-Executive Producer
Julian Farino . . . . Co-Executive Producer
Rob Weiss . . . . Co-Executive Producer
Denis Biggs . . . . Supervising Producer
Brian Burns . . . . Producer
Wayne Carmona . . . . Producer/UPM
Lori Jo Nemhauser . . . . Producer
Sheila Jaffe . . . . Casting Director
Georgianne Walken . . . . Casting Director
Vanessa Rodriguez . . . . Casting Associate

ER (NBC/60 mins.)
c/o Warner Bros. Television
4000 Warner Blvd., Bldg. 133, Rm. 204
Burbank, CA 91522
PHONE .818-954-3830
FAX .818-954-3847
WEB SITE .www.nbc.com/ER
PRODUCTION COMPANIES Amblin Entertainment - Constant C. Productions - Warner Bros. Television Production

John Wells .Executive Producer
Michael Crichton .Executive Producer/Creator
Christopher Chulack .Executive Producer
R. Scott Gemmill .Executive Producer/Showrunner
David Zabel .Executive Producer
Richard Thorpe .Produced By
Joe Sachs .Co-Executive Producer
Janine Sherman Barrois .Co-Executive Producer
Lydia Woodward .Consulting Producer
Tommy Burns .Producer/UPM
Wendy Spence Rosato .Producer
Virgil Williams .Producer
Lisa Zwerling .Producer
Karen Maser .Staff Writer
John Levey .Casting Director

EVERYBODY HATES CHRIS (The CW/30 mins.)
c/o Paramount Studios
5555 Melrose Ave., Bldg. 213, Ste. 320
Hollywood, CA 90038
PHONE .323-956-1500
FAX .323-862-1588
WEB SITE .www.cwtv.com/cw-ehc.html
PRODUCTION COMPANIES 3 Arts Entertainment, Inc. - CBS Paramount Network Television - Chris Rock Entertainment, Inc.

Chris Rock .Executive Producer/Co-Creator
Ali LeRoi .Executive Producer/Showrunner/Co-Creator
Michael Rotenberg .Executive Producer
Dave Becky .Executive Producer
Don Reo .Professional Writer
Rodney Barnes .Co-Executive Producer
Andrew Orenstein .Co-Executive Producer
Alyson Fouse .Supervising Producer
Jim Michaels .Producer
Chuck Sklar .Producer
Devon Shepard .Consulting Producer
Frank Sebastiano .Consulting Producer
Kali Londono .Producer Trainee
Aeysha Carr .Script Coordinator
Adrienne Carter .Story Editor
Kim Coleman .Casting Director
Vickie Thomas .Casting Director

EXTREME MAKEOVER: HOME EDITION (ABC/60 mins.)
c/o Endemol USA, Inc.
9255 Sunset Blvd., Ste. 1100
Los Angeles, CA 90069
PHONE .323-785-2262
FAX .323-785-2426
WEB SITE .abc.go.com/primetime/xtremehome/index.html
PRODUCTION COMPANIES Endemol USA, Inc. - Lock and Key Productions

Craig Armstrong .Executive Producer
Denise Cramsey .Executive Producer/Showrunner
Luis Barreto .Co-Executive Producer
Janelle Fiorito .Co-Executive Producer
Star Price .Co-Executive Producer
Mark Rains .Producer

FAMILY GUY (Fox/30 mins.)
5700 Wilshire Blvd., Ste. 325
Los Angeles, CA 90035
PHONE .323-857-8800
FAX .323-857-8835
WEB SITE .www.familyguy.com
PRODUCTION COMPANY Twentieth Century Fox Television
COMMENTS Animated

Seth MacFarlane .Executive Producer/Creator/Showrunner
David Goodman .Executive Producer/Showrunner
Chris Sheridan .Executive Producer
Mark Hentemann .Co-Executive Producer
Danny Smith .Co-Executive Producer
Shannon Smith .Animation Producer
Alex Borstein .Producer
Steve Callaghan .Producer
Mike Henry .Producer
Alec Sulkin .Producer
Kara Vallow .Producer
Wellesley Wild .Producer
Kirker Butler .Co-Producer
Kim Fertman .Associate Producer
Tom Devanney .Consultant
Cherry Chevapravatdumrong .Story Editor
Patrick Meighan .Story Editor
John Viener .Story Editor
Linda Lamontagne .Casting Director

***FRIDAY NIGHT LIGHTS (NBC/60 mins.)**
5010 Burleson Rd.
Austin, TX 78744
PHONE .512-707-6900
FAX .512-707-8820
PRODUCTION COMPANIES Film 44 - Imagine Television - NBC Universal Television Studio

Peter Berg .Executive Producer/Creator
Brian Grazer .Executive Producer
Jason Katims .Executive Producer/Showrunner
David Nevins .Executive Producer
Sarah Aubrey .Co-Executive Producer
John Cameron .Co-Executive Producer
Jeffrey Reiner .Co-Executive Producer
Jeff Henry .Co-Producer
Mike Lewis .Co-Producer
Nan Bernstein .Line Producer
David Boyd .Director, Photography
Cary White .Production Designer
Linda Lowy .Casting Director

***THE GAME (The CW/30 mins.)**
c/o Grammnet Productions
5555 Melrose Ave., Wilder Bldg., Ste. 114
Los Angeles, CA 90038
PHONE .323-956-5547
FAX .323-862-2284
WEB SITE .www.cwtv.com/cw thegame.html
PRODUCTION COMPANIES CBS Paramount Network Television - Grammnet Productions

Mara Brock Akil .Executive Producer/Showrunner/Creator
Dan Dugan .Executive Producer
Kelsey Grammer .Executive Producer
Steve Stark .Executive Producer
Tim Edwards .Co-Executive Producer
Anne Flett-Giordano .Co-Executive Producer
Chuck Ranberg .Co-Executive Producer
Kenny Smith .Co-Executive Producer
Erica Montolfo .Producer
Kenya Barris .Consulting Producer
Sara V. Finney-Johnson .Consulting Producer
Julie Bean .Staff Writer
Suzanne Goddard-Smythe .Casting Director

THE GEORGE LOPEZ SHOW (ABC/30 mins.)
c/o Warner Bros. Television
4000 Warner Blvd., Bldg. 19, Rm. 229
Burbank, CA 91522
PHONE 818-954-3332
FAX 818-954-3371
WEB SITE . . . . abc.go.com/primetime/georgelopez/en/index.html
PRODUCTION COMPANIES Fortis Films - Mohawk Productions - Warner Bros. Television Production

Robert Borden . . . . Executive Producer/Creator/Showrunner
Sandra Bullock . . . . Executive Producer
Dave Caplan . . . . Executive Producer
Bruce Helford . . . . Executive Producer/Creator
Paul Kaplan . . . . Executive Producer
George Lopez . . . . Executive Producer/Creator
Deborah Oppenheimer . . . . Executive Producer
Mark Torgove . . . . Executive Producer
Jim Hope . . . . Co-Executive Producer
Rick Nyholm . . . . Co-Executive Producer
Luisa Leschin . . . . Supervising Producer
John Morey . . . . Supervising Producer
Frank Pace . . . . Producer
Allen Zipper . . . . Creative Consultant
Michael Loftus . . . . Story Editor
Kathy Fischer . . . . Staff Writer
Stacey Levy . . . . Casting Director
Andrew Wohlwend . . . . ABC/Disney Fellow

GHOST WHISPERER (CBS/60 mins.)
100 Universal City Plaza, Bldg. 5225, Rm. 106
Univeral City, CA 91608
PHONE 818-733-3080
FAX 818-733-3482
WEB SITE . . . . www.cbs.com/primetime/ghost_whisperer
PRODUCTION COMPANIES Paramount Pictures - Sander/Moses Productions, Inc. - Touchstone Television

John Gray . . . . Executive Producer/Creator/Showrunner
Kim Moses . . . . Executive Producer
Ian Sander . . . . Executive Producer
James Van Praagh . . . . Co-Executive Producer
Jed Seidel . . . . Co-Executive Producer
Jim Kouf . . . . Co-Executive Producer
Elle Johnson . . . . Supervising Producer
Jeannine Renshaw . . . . Supervising Producer
Jennifer Love Hewitt . . . . Producer
Catherine Butterfield . . . . Producer
David Fallon . . . . Producer
Barbara Black . . . . Producer/UPM
Mary Courtney . . . . Producer/Supervisor
Breen Frazier . . . . Co-Producer
Juanita Diana Feeney . . . . Co-Producer
Donna Rosenstein . . . . Casting Director
Liz Lang . . . . Associate Casting Director

GILMORE GIRLS (The CW/60 mins.)
4000 Warner Blvd., Bldg. 193, Rm. 201
Burbank, CA 91522
PHONE 818-954-3115
WEB SITE . . . . www.cwtv.com/cw-gilmoregirls.html
PRODUCTION COMPANY Warner Bros. Television Production

David Rosenthal . . . . Executive Producer
Rebecca Rand Kirshner . . . . Co-Executive Producer
Gina Fattore . . . . Co-Executive Producer
Gayle Abrams . . . . Co-Executive Producer
Rina Mimoun . . . . Consulting Producer
David Babcock . . . . Consulting Producer
Patricia Fass Palmer . . . . Producer
Helen Pai . . . . Producer
Mara Casey . . . . Casting Director
Jami Rudofsky . . . . Casting Director

GIRLFRIENDS (The CW/30 mins.)
c/o CBS Radford Studios
4024 Radford Ave., Bungalow 3
Studio City, CA 91604
PHONE 818-655-5590
FAX 818-655-8317
WEB SITE . . . . www.cwtv.com/cw-girlfriends.html
PRODUCTION COMPANIES CBS Paramount Network Television - Grammnet Productions

Kelsey Grammer . . . . Executive Producer
Mara Brock Akil . . . . Executive Producer/Creator
Regina Hicks . . . . Executive Producer
Mark Alton Brown . . . . Consulting Producer
Dee LaDuke . . . . Consulting Producer
Dan Dugan . . . . Producer/UPM
Karin Gist . . . . Producer
Mary Fukuto . . . . Co-Producer
Michele Marburger . . . . Story Editor
Kevin Marburger . . . . Story Editor
Prentice Penny . . . . Staff Writer
Vincent Brown . . . . Staff Writer
Susie Johnson . . . . Production Coordinator

GREY'S ANATOMY (ABC/60 mins.)
c/o Prospect Studios
4151 Prospect Ave., Los Feliz Tower, 4th Fl.
Los Angeles, CA 90027
PHONE 323-671-4650
FAX 323-671-4365
WEB SITE . . . . abc.go.com/primetime/greysanatomy/index.html
PRODUCTION COMPANY Touchstone Television

Shonda Rhimes . . . . Executive Producer/Creator/Showrunner
Betsy Beers . . . . Executive Producer
Mark Gordon . . . . Executive Producer
Krista Vernoff . . . . Executive Producer
Peter Horton . . . . Co-Executive Producer
Mark Wilding . . . . Co-Executive Producer
Debora Cahn . . . . Supervising Producer
Tony Phelan . . . . Supervising Producer
Joan Rater . . . . Supervising Producer
Gabrielle Stanton . . . . Supervising Producer
Harry Werksman . . . . Supervising Producer
Allan Heinberg . . . . Consulting Producer
Kip Koenig . . . . Consulting Producer
Rob Corn . . . . Producer
Zoanne Clack . . . . Executive Story Editor/Consultant
Stacy McKee . . . . Story Editor
Carolina Paiz . . . . Staff Writer
Linda Lowy . . . . Casting Director
John Brace . . . . Casting Director

***HAPPY HOUR (Fox/30 mins.)**
4024 Rafdord Ave.
Studio City, CA 91604
PHONE 818-655-6484
PRODUCTION COMPANIES Warner Bros. Television Production - Werner-Gold-Miller

Jackie Filgo . . . . Executive Producer/Showrunner
Jeff Filgo . . . . Executive Producer/Showrunner
Tom Werner . . . . Executive Producer
Eric Gold . . . . Executive Producer
Jimmy Miller . . . . Executive Producer
Rob Deshotel . . . . Co-Executive Producer
Casey Johnson . . . . Supervising Producer
David Windsor . . . . Supervising Producer
Sally Bradford . . . . Consulting Producer
Marc Solakian . . . . Line Producer
Mark Brazill . . . . Consultant
Jim Reynolds . . . . Story Editor
Shawn Simmonds . . . . Staff Writer
Julie Ashton . . . . Casting Director

HELL'S KITCHEN (Fox/60 mins.)
c/o Granada America
15303 Ventura Blvd., Bldg. C, Ste. 800
Sherman Oaks, CA 91403
PHONE . . . 818-455-4600
FAX . . . 818-455-4700
WEB SITE . . . www.fox.com/hellskitchen
PRODUCTION COMPANY Upper Ground Enterprises, Inc.

Paul Jackson . . . Executive Producer
Layla Sabih . . . Executive Producer
Arthur Smith . . . Executive Producer
Kent Weed . . . Executive Producer
Andy Scheer . . . Co-Executive Producer
Sandi Johnson . . . Supervising Producer
Faye Stapleton . . . Supervising Producer
Trice Barto . . . Producer
Nancy Gunn . . . Producer
Yun Lingner . . . Producer
Peter Tartaglia . . . Producer

***HELP ME HELP YOU (ABC/30 mins.)**
5555 Melrose Ave., Wilder Bldg., 2nd Fl.
Los Angeles, CA 90038
PHONE . . . 323-956-2800
FAX . . . 323-862-2808
PRODUCTION COMPANY Regency Television

Jenni Konner . . . Executive Producer/Creator
Alex Reid . . . Executive Producer/Showrunner
Ali Rushfield . . . Executive Producer/Creator
Rodney Rothman . . . Co-Executive Producer
Linda Wallem . . . Co-Executive Producer
Ron Weiner . . . Supervising Producer
Joel Madison . . . Consulting Producer
Jim Simons . . . UPM
Janis Carr . . . Associate Producer
Daley Haggar . . . Staff Writer
Chester Tam . . . Staff Writer
Colin Daniel . . . Casting Director
Brett Greenstein . . . Casting Director

***HEROES (NBC/60 mins.)**
c/o Sunset Gower Studios
1438 N. Gower St.
Hollywood, CA 90028
PHONE . . . 323-468-7900
FAX . . . 323-468-7901
PRODUCTION COMPANY NBC Universal Television Studio

Dennis Hammer . . . Executive Producer
Tim Kring . . . Executive Producer/Showrunner/Creator
Jesse Alexander . . . Co-Executive Producer
Natalie Chaidez . . . Co-Executive Producer
Michael C. Green . . . Co-Executive Producer
Jeph Loeb . . . Co-Executive Producer
Adam Armus . . . Supervising Producer
Kay Foster . . . Supervising Producer
Greg Beeman . . . Producer
Aron Eli Coleite . . . Co-Producer
Bryan Fuller . . . Consulting Producer
Skip Baudine . . . Line Producer
Natalie Hart . . . Casting Director
Jason La Padura . . . Casting Director
Joe Pokaski . . . Staff Writer

***HIDDEN PALMS (The CW/60 mins.)**
c/o Sunset Gower Studios
1438 N Gower St., Box 23, Bldg. 70, Ste 200
Hollywood, CA 90028
PHONE . . . 310-581-7367
FAX . . . 310-858-6947
PRODUCTION COMPANIES Lionsgate - Outerbanks Entertainment

Kevin Williamson . . . Executive Producer/Creator
Scott Winant . . . Co-Executive Producer
Dan Arkin . . . Supervising Producer
Steve Blackman . . . Producer
Barbie Kligman . . . Producer
John Kousakas . . . Line Producer
Paula Yoo . . . Story Editor
Brian Holdman . . . Staff Writer
Lesli Gelles . . . Casting Director
Greg Orson . . . Casting Director

HOUSE (Fox/60 mins.)
10201 W. Pico Blvd., Bldg. 89, Rm. 230
Los Angeles, CA 90035
PHONE . . . 310-369-3100
FAX . . . 310-969-1100
WEB SITE . . . www.fox.com/house
PRODUCTION COMPANIES Bad Hat Harry Productions - Heel & Toe Films - NBC Universal Television Studio - Shore Z Productions

Paul Attanasio . . . Executive Producer
Katie Jacobs . . . Executive Producer
David Shore . . . Executive Producer/Creator
Bryan Singer . . . Executive Producer
Daniel Sackheim . . . Executive Producer
Thomas L. Moran . . . Co-Executive Producer
Doris Egan . . . Co-Executive Producer
Russel Friend . . . Co-Executive Producer
Garrett Lerner . . . Co-Executive Producer
Leonard Dick . . . Supervising Producer
Peter Blake . . . Consulting Producer
Lawrence Kaplow . . . Producer
Liz Friedman . . . Co-Producer
Steven Heth . . . Co-Producer
Marcy Kaplan . . . Co-Producer
David Foster . . . Executive Story Editor
David Hoselton . . . Executive Story Editor
Sara Hess . . . Story Editor
Pam Davis . . . Staff Writer
Gerrit Van der Meer . . . Producer/UPM
Dustin Paddock . . . Script Coordinator
Stephanie Laffin . . . Casting Director
Amy Lippens . . . Casting Director

HOW I MET YOUR MOTHER (CBS/30 mins.)

c/o Twentieth Century Fox Television
10201 W. Pico Blvd., Trailer 795
Los Angeles, CA 90035
PHONE . . . . . 310-369-3355/310-369-3220 (Writers' office)
FAX 310-969-0361
WEB SITE . . . . . www.cbs.com/primetime/how_i_met_your_mother
PRODUCTION COMPANY Twentieth Century Fox Television

Carter Bays . . . . . Executive Producer/Creator/Showrunner
Pamela Fryman . . . . . Executive Producer/Director
Greg Malins . . . . . Executive Producer/Showrunner
Craig Thomas . . . . . Executive Producer/Creator/Showrunner
Stephen Lloyd . . . . . Co-Executive Producer
Kristin Newman . . . . . Co-Executive Producer
Suzy Greenberg . . . . . UPM/Producer
Chris Harris . . . . . Producer
Jamie Rhonheimer . . . . . Producer
Rob Greenberg . . . . . Consulting Producer
Rob Fox . . . . . Associate Producer
Stew Halpern . . . . . Post Associate Producer
Missy Alexander . . . . . Production Coordinator
Brenda Hsueh . . . . . Executive Story Editor
Kourtney Kang . . . . . Executive Story Editor
Gloria Calderon Kellet . . . . . Story Editor
Maria Ferrari . . . . . Staff Writer

IN CASE OF EMERGENCY (ABC/30 mins.)

c/o LA Center Studios
1201 West 5th St., Ste. M270
Los Angeles, CA 90017
PHONE 213-534-3112
PRODUCTION COMPANIES Bushwacker Productions - Touchstone Television

Emile Levisetti . . . . . Executive Producer
Howard J. Morris . . . . . Executive Producer/Showrunner/Creator
Jon Kinnally . . . . . Co-Executive Producer
Bob Kushell . . . . . Co-Executive Producer
Tracy Poust . . . . . Co-Executive Producer
David Feeney . . . . . Consulting Producer
Jack Kenny . . . . . Consulting Producer
Roz Moore . . . . . Consulting Producer
Mychelle Deschamps . . . . . Line Producer
Jenny Lee . . . . . Staff Writer
Eric Siegel . . . . . Staff Writer
Eric Wasserman . . . . . Staff Writer
Dava Waite . . . . . Casting Director

*JERICHO (CBS/60 mins.)

c/o Calvert Studios
15001 Calvert St.
Van Nuys, CA 91411
PHONE 818-778-2330
FAX 818-373-4121
PRODUCTION COMPANIES CBS Paramount Network Television - Junction Entertainment

Carol Barbee . . . . . Executive Producer/Showrunner
Stephen Chbosky . . . . . Executive Producer/Creator
Jon Turteltaub . . . . . Executive Producer
Dan O'Shannon . . . . . Co-Executive Producer
Jack Clements . . . . . Supervising Producer
Mike Ostrowski . . . . . Supervising Producer
Dan Shotz . . . . . Producer
Nancy Won . . . . . Producer
Karim Zreik . . . . . Producer
Ellie Herman . . . . . Consulting Producer

JIMMY KIMMEL LIVE (ABC/60 mins.)

6834 Hollywood Blvd., Ste. 600
Hollywood, CA 90028
PHONE 323-860-5900
WEB SITE . . . . . www.jimmykimmellive.net
PRODUCTION COMPANIES 12:05 am Productions - Touchstone Television

Jimmy Kimmel . . . . . Executive Producer
Doug DeLuca . . . . . Co-Executive Producer
Jason Schrift . . . . . Co-Executive Producer
Jill Leiderman . . . . . Executive Producer
Erin Irwin . . . . . Supervising Producer
Chris Fraticelli . . . . . Producer
Seth Weldner . . . . . Comedy Producer
Craig Powell . . . . . Comedy Co-Producer
Patrick Friend . . . . . Field Producer
Caroline Krabach . . . . . Field Producer
Jeff Sammon . . . . . Field Producer
Jennifer Sharron . . . . . Field Producer
Ken Crosby . . . . . Segment Producer
Adam Spiegelman . . . . . Segment Producer
Rich Brown . . . . . Human Interest Producer
David Craig . . . . . Line Producer
J Graigory . . . . . Production Coordinator
Steve O'Donnell . . . . . Head Writer
Tony Barbieri . . . . . Writer
Jonathan Bines . . . . . Writer
Will Burke . . . . . Writer
Gary Greenberg . . . . . Writer
Sal Iacono . . . . . Writer
Bill Kelley . . . . . Writer
Jacob Lentz . . . . . Writer
Paul Raff . . . . . Writer
Richard Rosner . . . . . Writer
David Weinstein . . . . . Writer
Amber Bickham . . . . . Casting
Michael Greggs . . . . . Casting

*JUSTICE (Fox/60 mins.)

1201 W. 5th St., Ste. F-190
Los Angeles, CA 90017
PHONE 213-534-3443
FAX 213-534-3412
PRODUCTION COMPANIES Jerry Bruckheimer Television - Warner Bros. Television Production

Jerry Bruckheimer . . . . . Executive Producer
Jonathan Littman . . . . . Executive Producer
Jonathan Shapiro . . . . . Executive Producer/Showrunner
David McNally . . . . . Executive Producer/Director
Tim Marx . . . . . Producer
KristieAnne Reed . . . . . Consulting Producer
Greg Ferguson . . . . . UPM

KIDNAPPED (NBC/60 mins.)
34-02 Starr Ave., 1st Fl.
New York, NY 11101
PHONE .718-906-3100
FAX .718-906-3131
PRODUCTION COMPANIES 25C Productions - Sony Pictures Television

Carl Beverly .Executive Producer
Michael Dinner .Executive Producer
David Greenwalt .Executive Producer/Showrunner
Jason Smilovic .Executive Producer/Creator
Sarah Timberman .Executive Producer
Jan Oxenberg .Co-Executive Producer
Ken Topolsky .Co-Executive Producer
Byron Balasco .Consulting Producer
David J. Burke .Consulting Producer
Jeff King .Consulting Producer
Tyler Mitchell .Consulting Producer
Duppy Demetrius .Executive Story Editor
Sam Catlin .Story Editor
Hilly Hicks .Staff Writer
Bonnie Finnegan .Casting Director
Mark Scott .Casting Director

THE KING OF QUEENS (CBS/30 mins.)
c/o Sony Pictures Entertainment
10202 W. Washington Blvd., David Lean Bldg., Ste. 410
Culver City, CA 90232
PHONE .310-244-3343
FAX .310-244-0443
WEB SITE .www.cbs.com/primetime/king_of_queens
PRODUCTION COMPANIES CBS Paramount Network Television - Sony Pictures Television

David Bickel .Executive Producer
Chris Downey .Executive Producer
Kevin James .Executive Producer
Rock Reuben .Executive Producer
Rob Schiller .Executive Producer/Director
Tony Sheehan .Executive Producer/Showrunner
Jeff Sussman .Executive Producer
Ilana Wernick .Executive Producer
Liz Astrof .Co-Executive Producer
Michael J. Weithorn .Creator/Creative Consultant
Nick Bakay .Consulting Producer
Jim Kukucka .Producer/UPM
Owen Ellickson .Co-Producer
Mike Soccio .Co-Producer
Dennis Regan .Executive Story Editor
Cami Patton .Casting Director

KING OF THE HILL (Fox/30 mins.)
15821 Ventura Blvd., Ste. 280
Encino, CA 91436
PHONE .818-501-5079
FAX .818-501-5761
WEB SITE .www.fox.com/kingofthehill
PRODUCTION COMPANIES 3 Arts Entertainment, Inc. - Twentieth Century Fox Television
COMMENTS Animated

Greg Daniels .Executive Producer/Creator
Mike Judge .Executive Producer/Creator
John Altschuler .Executive Producer/Showrunner
David Krinsky .Executive Producer/Showrunner
Jim Dauterive .Executive Producer
Howard Klein .Executive Producer
Michael Rotenberg .Executive Producer
Garland Testa .Executive Producer
Joe Boucher .Supervising Producer
Greg Cohen .Supervising Producer
Tony Gama-Lobo .Supervising Producer
Rebecca May .Supervising Producer
Christy Stratton .Supervising Producer
Paul Corrigan .Consulting Producer
Dan McGrath .Consulting Producer
Dave Schiff .Consulting Producer
Brad Walsh .Consulting Producer
Mark McJimsey .Producer
Erin Ehrlich .Co-Producer
Judah Mille .Co-Producer
Murray Miller .Co-Producer
Michael Branch .Associate Producer
Robert Parigi .Associate Producer
Tim Croston .Executive Story Editor
Chip Hall .Executive Story Editor
Blake McCorkmick .Executive Story Editor
Sanjay Shay .Staff Writer
Scott Muller .Casting Associate

***THE KNIGHTS OF PROSPERITY (ABC/30 mins.)**
c/o Silvercup Studios
42-22 22nd St., Ste. 320
Long Island City, NY 11101
PHONE .718-906-2333
FAX .718-906-2339
PRODUCTION COMPANIES Touchstone Television - Worldwide Pants, Inc.

Jon D. Beckerman .Executive Producer/Creator
Rob Burnett .Executive Producer/Creator
David Letterman .Executive Producer
Eric Horsted .Co-Executive Producer
Merrill Karpf .Co-Executive Producer
Steve Tompkins .Co-Executive Producer
Donal Logue .Producer
Karey Dornetto .Staff Writer
Dylan Morgan .Staff Writer
Josh Siegal .Staff Writer
Alaine Alldaffer .Casting Director

THE L WORD (Showtime/60 mins.)

8275 Manitoba St.
Vancouver, BC V5X 4L8, Canada
PHONE .604-419-1300
FAX .604-419-1301
WEB SITE www.sho.com/site/lword/home.do
PRODUCTION COMPANY Anonymous Content

Ilene Chaiken .Executive Producer/Creator/Showrunner
Larry Kennar .Executive Producer
Rose Lam .Executive Producer
Ellie Herman .Co-Executive Producer
Elizabeth Hunter .Co-Executive Producer
David Stenn .Co-Executive Producer
Rose Troche .Co-Executive Producer
Kathy Greenberg .Producer/Creator
A.M. Homes .Producer
Elizabeth Ziff .Producer
Susan Miller .Consulting Producer
Mark Zakarin .Consulting Producer
Kim Speer .Line Producer
Cherien Dabis .Staff Writer
Ariel Schrag .Staff Writer
Beth Klein .Casting Director (LA)
Coreen Mayrs .Casting Director (Vancouver)

LAS VEGAS (NBC/60 mins.)

9336 W. Washington Blvd., Bldg. F
Culver City, CA 90232
PHONE .310-202-4488/310-202-4490 (Writers' office)
FAX .310-202-4489/310-202-4491 (Writers' office)
WEB SITE www.nbc.com/Las_Vegas
PRODUCTION COMPANIES DreamWorks Television - NBC Universal Television Studio

Gary Scott Thompson .Executive Producer/Creator
Gardner Stern .Executive Producer
Justin Falvey .Executive Producer
Darryl Frank .Executive Producer
Kim Newton .Executive Producer
Matt Pyken .Executive Producer
David Solomon .Co-Executive Producer/Director
Rob Cullen .Consulting Producer
Mark Cullen .Consulting Producer
Matt Miller .Supervising Producer
Scott Steindorff .Creative Consultant
Stephen Sassen .Producer
Jill Cargerman .Co-Producer
Julie Herlocker .Co-Producer
Lorie Zerweck .Co-Producer/UPM
Kevin Garnett .Staff Writer
Joanna Philbin .Staff Writer
Cami Patton .Casting Director

LAST CALL WITH CARSON DALY (NBC/30 mins.)

c/o NBC Studios
3000 W. Alameda Ave., Bungalow 1600
Burbank, CA 91523
PHONE .818-260-5070
FAX .818-260-5080
WEB SITE www.nbc.com/Last_Call_with_Carson_Daly
PRODUCTION COMPANIES Carson Daly Productions - NBC Universal Television Studio
COMMENTS Friday show is 60 minutes

Carson Daly .Producer/Host
David Friedman .Executive Producer
Guy Oseary .Executive Producer
Steve Paley .Director
Nicolle Yaron .Producer
Chris Conte .Line Producer
Richard Eagan .Segment Producer
Kip Madsen .Segment Producer
Drew Ogier .Segment Producer
Dave King .Head Writer
Alan Yang .Writer
Mike Hammeke .Production Manager
Jamie Granet .Talent Executive
Diana Miller .Talent Producer
Michelle Stuart .Talent Producer

LAST COMIC STANDING (NBC/60 mins.)

c/o Peter Engel Productions
330 Bob Hope Dr., Ste. C-113
Burbank, CA 91523
PHONE .323-993-7324
PRODUCTION COMPANIES Peter Engel Productions - Magical Elves - NBC Universal Television Studio

Dan Cutforth .Executive Producer
Peter Engel .Executive Producer
Barry Katz .Executive Producer
Jane Lipsitz .Executive Producer
Rob Fox .Co-Executive Producer
Leslie Radakovich .Supervising Producer
Kerry Holmwood .Producer
Brittany Levin-Lovett .Producer
Javier Winnik .Producer

THE LATE LATE SHOW WITH CRAIG FERGUSON (CBS/60 mins.)

c/o CBS Television City
7800 Beverly Blvd., Ste. 244
Los Angeles, CA 90036
PHONE .323-575-5600
FAX .323-575-5656
WEB SITE www.cbs.com/latenight/latelate
PRODUCTION COMPANY Worldwide Pants, Inc.

Peter Lassally .Executive Producer
Gary Considine .Co-Executive Producer
Brian McAloon .Director
Cathy Hoeven .Supervising Producer
Alisa Gichon .Talent Executive
David Nickoll .Head Writer
Ted Mulkerin .Writer
Joe O'Brien .Writer
Ned Rice .Writer
Joe Strazzullo .Writer
Michael Naidus .Sr. Segment Producer
Tom Keaney .Segment Producer
Jamie Browder .Talent Coordinator
David Podemski .Writers' Assistant

LATE NIGHT WITH CONAN O'BRIEN (NBC/60 mins.)

c/o NBC Studios
Rockefeller Center, Studio 6-A
New York, NY 10112
PHONE 212-664-3737
FAX 212-664-4622
WEB SITE . . www.nbc.com/Late_Night_with_Conan_O'Brien/index.shtml
PRODUCTION COMPANY Broadway Video Entertainment

Lorne Michaels . . . . Executive Producer
Jeff Ross . . . . Executive Producer
Mike Sweeney . . . . Head Writer
Daniel Ferguson . . . . Supervising Producer
Frank Smiley . . . . Supervising Producer
Allan Kartun . . . . Director
Tracy King . . . . Producer
Conan O'Brien . . . . Producer
Jim Pitt . . . . Talent Executive
Debbie Wunder . . . . Music Coordinator
Paula Davis . . . . Talent Booker
Cecelia Pleva . . . . Casting Director

THE LATE SHOW WITH DAVID LETTERMAN (CBS/60 mins.)

c/o Worldwide Pants, Inc.
1697 Broadway
New York, NY 10019
PHONE 212-975-5300
FAX 212-975-4734
WEB SITE . . . . www.cbs.com/latenight/lateshow
PRODUCTION COMPANY Worldwide Pants, Inc.

Jude Brennan . . . . Executive Producer
Rob Burnett . . . . Executive Producer
Barbara Gaines . . . . Executive Producer
Peter Lassally . . . . Executive Producer
David Letterman . . . . Executive Producer
Maria Pope . . . . Executive Producer
Eric Stangel . . . . Head Writer
Justin Stangel . . . . Head Writer
Jon D. Beckerman . . . . Supervising Producer
Jerry Foley . . . . Supervising Producer/Director
Matt Roberts . . . . Supervising Producer
Sheila Rogers . . . . Producer
Nancy Agostini . . . . Associate Producer

LAW & ORDER (NBC/60 mins.)

100 Universal City Plaza, Bldg. 2252
Universal City, CA 91608
PHONE 818-777-6969
FAX 818-866-1226/212-627-0957
WEB SITE . . . . www.nbc.com/Law_&_Order
PRODUCTION COMPANIES NBC Universal Television Studio - Wolf Films, Inc.
COMMENTS East Coast office: Pier 62, Hudson River at W. 23rd St., New York, NY 10011

Dick Wolf . . . . Executive Producer/Creator
Walon Green . . . . Executive Producer
Nicholas Wootton . . . . Executive Producer/Showrunner
Matthew Penn . . . . Executive Producer
Peter Jankowski . . . . Executive Producer
Richard Sweren . . . . Co-Executive Producer
Arthur Forney . . . . Co-Executive Producer
Chris Levinson . . . . Co-Executive Producer
Robert Nathan . . . . Co-Executive Producer
Luke Reiter . . . . Co-Executive Producer
David Wilcox . . . . Co-Executive Producer
Peter Giuliano . . . . Produced By
Gary Karr . . . . Supervising Producer
David Slack . . . . Executive Story Editor
Sonny Postiglione . . . . Staff Writer
John Roche . . . . Writers' Assistant
Lynn Kressel . . . . Casting Director
Suzanne Ryan . . . . Casting Director

LAW & ORDER: CRIMINAL INTENT (NBC/60 mins.)

Chelsea Piers, Pier 62, Ste. 305
New York, NY 10011
PHONE 212-336-6350
FAX 212-336-6363
WEB SITE . . . . www.nbc.com/Law_&_Order:_Criminal_Intent
PRODUCTION COMPANIES NBC Universal Television Studio - Wolf Films, Inc.
COMMENTS East Coast office: Pier 62, Hudson River at W. 23rd St., New York, NY 10011

Dick Wolf . . . . Executive Producer
Peter Jankowksi . . . . Executive Producer
Warren Leight . . . . Executive Producer/Showrunner
Norberto Barba . . . . Co-Executive Producer
Gerry Conway . . . . Co-Executive Producer
Arthur Forney . . . . Co-Executive Producer
Michael Kewley . . . . Supervising Producer
Stephanie Sengupta . . . . Supervising Producer
Charlie Rubin . . . . Supervising Producer
John L. Roman . . . . Producer
Diana Son . . . . Producer
Mary Rae Thewlis . . . . Producer
Michael Smith . . . . Co-Producer
Gina Gionfriddo . . . . Story Editor
Lynn Kressel . . . . Casting Director

LAW & ORDER: SPECIAL VICTIMS UNIT (NBC/60 mins.)

100 Universal City Plaza, Bldg. 2252, Rm. 201
Universal City, CA 91608
PHONE 818-777-6969/201-662-7170
FAX 201-662-7175
WEB SITE . . . . www.nbc.com/Law_&_Order:_Special_Victims_Unit
PRODUCTION COMPANIES NBC Universal Television Studio - Wolf Films, Inc.
COMMENTS East Coast office: 5801 West Side Ave., North Bergen, NJ 07047

Dick Wolf . . . . Executive Producer
Ted Kotcheff . . . . Executive Producer
Neal Baer . . . . Executive Producer/Showrunner
Peter Jankowksi . . . . Executive Producer
Patrick Harbinson . . . . Co-Executive Producer
Arthur Forney . . . . Co-Executive Producer
David DeClerque . . . . Produced By
Dawn DeNoon . . . . Co-Executive Producer
Jonathan Greene . . . . Co-Executive Producer
Amanda Green . . . . Co-Executive Producer
Randy Roberts . . . . Supervising Producer
Peter Leto . . . . Producer
Gail Barringer . . . . Producer
Sheyna Smith . . . . Co-Producer
Judith McCreary . . . . Consulting Producer
Paul Grellong . . . . Story Editor
Allison Intrieri . . . . Staff Writer

LOST (ABC/60 mins.)
500 S. Buena Vista, Bldg. 23
Burbank, CA 91521
PHONE 818-560-7223/808-733-2100
WEB SITE ....abc.go.com/primetime/lost/index.html
PRODUCTION COMPANIES Bad Robot Productions - Touchstone Television
COMMENTS Hawaii office: 680 Iwilei Rd., Ste. 495, Honolulu, HI 96817

J.J. Abrams ....Executive Producer/Co-Creator
Damon Lindelof ....Executive Producer/Co-Creator
Bryan Burk ....Executive Producer
Carlton Cuse ....Executive Producer
Jeff Pinkner ....Co-Executive Producer
Monica Breen ....Supervising Producer
Drew Goddard ....Supervising Producer
Adam Horowitz ....Supervising Producer
Edward Kitsis ....Supervising Producer
Allison Schapker ....Supervising Producer
Liz Sarnoff ....Producer
Christina Kim ....Staff Writer
Gregg Nations ....Script Coordinator
April Webster ....Casting Director
Noreen O'Toole ....Assistant to Damon Lindelof

LUCKY LOUIE (HBO/30 mins.)
c/o HBO Original Programming
2500 Broadway, Ste. 400
Santa Monica, CA 90404
PHONE 323-860-8128
FAX 323-860-8126
PRODUCTION COMPANIES Dreams Eno Productions - HBO Media Ventures

Dave Becky ....Executive Producer
Louis C.K. ....Executive Producer
Vic Kaplan ....Executive Producer
Mike Royce ....Executive Producer/Showrunner
Kit Boss ....Co-Executive Producer
Leo Clarke ....Producer
Andrew Weyman ....Producer
Tracy Katsky ....Consulting Producer
Mary Fitzgerald ....Staff Writer
Juel Bestrop ....Casting Director
Jeanne Mark McCarthy ....Casting Director

MAD TV (Fox/60 mins.)
c/o Hollywood Center Studios
1040 N. Las Palmas, Bldg. 2
Hollywood, CA 90038
PHONE 323-860-8999
FAX 323-860-8997
EMAIL ....info@madtv.com
WEB SITE ....www.madtv.com
PRODUCTION COMPANY Girl Group Company

Dick Blasucci ....Executive Producer
Quincy Jones ....Executive Producer
David Salzman ....Executive Producer
Bryan Adams ....Co-Executive Producer
Steven Cragg ....Co-Executive Producer
John Crane ....Co-Executive Producer
Lauren Dombrowski ....Co-Executive Producer
Steven Haft ....Co-Executive Producer
Michael Hitchcock ....Co-Executive Producer
Jennifer Joyce ....Supervising Producer
Bruce Leddy ....Supervising Producer/Director
Bruce McCoy ....Supervising Producer
Scott Sites ....Producer
Nicole Garcia ....Casting Director

MARTHA (Syndicated/60 mins.)
226 W. 26th St., 3rd Fl.
New York, NY 10001
PHONE 917-438-5700
FAX 917-438-5703
WEB SITE ....www.marthastewart.com/martha
PRODUCTION COMPANY MSLO Productions, Inc.

Martha Stewart ....Executive Producer
Mark Burnett ....Executive Producer
Rob Dauber ....Co-Executive Producer
Conrad Riggs ....Co-Executive Producer
Laurie Rich ....Executive in Charge of Production
Bob McKinnon ....Director
Jeffry Culbreth ....Supervising Producer
Christina Deyo ....Supervising Producer
Meredith Paige ....Supervising Producer
Deb Savo ....Supervising Producer
Lisa Wagner ....Supervising Producer
Shara Kabakow ....Line Producer
Greta Anthony ....Producer
George Davilas ....Producer
Barbara Fight ....Producer
Stephanie Fitzhugh ....Producer
Ann MacMullan ....Producer
Ashley Sparks ....Producer
Simone Swink ....Producer
Lenore Welby ....Producer
Suzanne Bass ....Coordinating Producer
Jana Petrosini ....Web Producer
James Avenell ....Talent Booker
Anduin Havens ....Art Director
Diane Trafford ....Audience Coordinator
Angie Ketterman ....TV Chef
Wes Martin ....TV Chef

MASTERS OF HORROR (Showtime/60 mins.)
8651 Eastlake Dr.
Burnaby, BC V5A 4T7
PHONE 604-444-1100
FAX 604-444-1116
WEB SITE ....www.sho.com/site/mastersofhorror/home.do
PRODUCTION COMPANIES IDT Entertainment - Industry Entertainment Partners

Keith Addis ....Executive Producer
Morris Berger ....Executive Producer
Steve Brown ....Executive Producer
Andrew Deane ....Executive Producer
Mick Garris ....Executive Producer
John W. Hyde ....Executive Producer
Lisa Richardson ....Producer
Tom Rowe ....Producer
Adam Goldworm ....Co-Producer/Production Executive
Ben Browning ....Co-Producer/Production Executive
Stacey Jade Smart ....Executive in Charge of Production
Lindsey Kroeger ....Casting Director
David Rapaport ....Casting Director

MEDIUM (NBC/60 mins.)
1600 Rosecrans Ave., Bldg. 2A, 3rd Fl.
Manhattan Beach, CA 90266
PHONE .310-727-2121
FAX .310-727-2122
WEB SITE .www.nbc.com/Medium
PRODUCTION COMPANIES CBS Paramount Network Television - Grammnet Productions

Glenn Gordon Caron .Executive Producer
Kelsey Grammer .Executive Producer
Steve Stark .Executive Producer
Rene Echevarria .Executive Producer
Ronald L. Schwary .Executive Producer
Robert Doherty .Supervising Producer
Moira Kirland .Supervising Producer
Debbie Cass .Producer/UPM
Diane Adema-John .Executive Story Editor
Rob Pearlstein .Executive Story Editor
Melinda Hsu .Story Editor
Judy Race .Production Coordinator
Irene Cagen .Casting Director
Meg Liberman .Casting Director

MONK (USA/60 mins.)
846 N. Cahuenga Blvd.
Los Angeles, CA 90038
PHONE .323-993-5304
FAX .323-993-5395
WEB SITE .www.usanetwork.com/series/monk
PRODUCTION COMPANY NBC Universal Television Studio

David Hoberman .Executive Producer
Andy Breckman .Executive Producer
Tony Shalhoub .Executive Producer
Randy Zisk .Executive Producer/Director
Fern Field .Co-Executive Producer
Tom Scharpling .Co-Executive Producer
Jonathan Collier .Consulting Producer
Anthony Santa Croce .Producer/UPM
Sheridan Thayer .Co-Producer
Scott Collins .Co-Producer
Daniel Dratch .Producer
Joe Toplyn .Producer
Hy Conrad .Co-Producer
Amy Britt .Casting Director
Anya Colloff .Casting Director

***MY BOYS (TBS/30 mins.)**
c/o Paramount Pictures Lot
5555 Melrose Ave., Bldg. 213
Los Angeles, CA 90038
PHONE .323-956-2700
FAX .323-862-2270
PRODUCTION COMPANIES Pariah - Remote Broadcasting - Sony Pictures Television

Gavin Polone .Executive Producer
Jamie Tarses .Executive Producer
Betsy Thomas .Executive Producer
Cindy Caponera .Supervising Producer
Ken Ornstein .Producer/UPM
Rick Singer .Producer
Eric Gilliland .Consulting Producer
Rob Ulin .Creative Consultant
RJ Visciglia .Associate Producer
Courtney Lilly .Executive Story Editor
Brendan Smith .Staff Writer
Tracy Lilienfield .Casting Director
Laura Adler .Casting Assistant

MY NAME IS EARL (NBC/30 mins.)
c/o City Studios
7700 Balboa Blvd.
Van Nuys, CA 91406-2219
PHONE .818-780-3362
WEB SITE .www.nbc.com/My_Name_Is_Earl
PRODUCTION COMPANY Twentieth Century Fox Television

Greg Garcia .Creator/Executive Producer
Mark Buckland .Executive Producer
Bobby Bowman .Executive Producer
Barbie Adler .Co-Executive Producer
Victor Fresco .Consulting Producer
Brad Copeland .Consulting Producer
Tim Stack .Consulting Producer
J.B. Cook .Supervising Producer
Erika Kaestle .Supervising Producer
Patrick McCarthy .Supervising Producer
Mike Pennie .Supervising Producer
Danielle Sanchez-Witzel .Producer
Kat Likkel .Producer
John Hoberg .Producer
Mike Mariano .Producer
Kim Hamberg .Associate Producer
Matt Simon .Associate Producer
Hilary Winston .Executive Story Editor
Vali Chandrasekaran .Story Editor

NAKED TRUCKER & T-BONES (Comedy Central/30 mins.)
c/o Hollywood Center Studios
1040 N. Las Palmas
Los Angeles, CA 90038
PHONE .323-860-8290
WEB SITE . . . .www.comedycentral.com/shows/naked_trucker/index.jhtml
PRODUCTION COMPANY Parallel Entertainment, Inc.

Dave Gruber Allen .Executive Producer
Donick Cary .Executive Producer
Norm Hiscock .Executive Producer
David Koechner .Executive Producer
J.P. Williams .Executive Producer

NANNY 911 (Fox/60 mins.)
c/o Granada America
15303 Ventura Blvd., Ste. 800
Sherman Oaks, CA 91403
PHONE .818-455-4600
FAX .818-455-4700
WEB SITE .www.fox.com/nanny911
PRODUCTION COMPANY Granada America

Paul Jackson .Executive Producer
Bruce Toms .Executive Producer
Gerry McKean .Co-Executive Producer
Michael Shevloff .Co-Executive Producer

NCIS (CBS/60 mins.)
c/o Sunset Gower Studios
1438 N. Gower St., Box 25
Hollywood, CA 90028
PHONE 323-468-4500
FAX 323-468-4599
WEB SITE . . . . www.cbs.com/primetime/ncis
PRODUCTION COMPANIES Belisarius Productions - CBS Paramount Network Television

Donald P. Bellisario . . . . Executive Producer/Creator
Chas. Floyd Johnson . . . . Co-Executive Producer
Mark Horowitz . . . . Co-Executive Producer
John C. Kelley . . . . Co-Executive Producer
Julie Watson . . . . Supervising Producer
David Bellisario . . . . Producer
Avery Drewe . . . . Producer
Mark Schilz . . . . Producer
Josh Rexon . . . . Co-Producer
Richie Owens . . . . Associate Producer
Shane Brennan . . . . Consulting Producer
Robert Palm . . . . Consulting Producer
Nell Scovell . . . . Consulting Producer
Steven Kriozere . . . . Co-Producer
Steven Binder . . . . Executive Story Editor
David North . . . . Story Editor
Susan Bluestein . . . . Casting Director
Camille St. Cyr . . . . Casting Director

THE NEW ADVENTURES OF OLD CHRISTINE (CBS/30 mins.)
4000 Warner Blvd., Bldg. 136, Ste. 119
Burbank, CA 91522-0001
PHONE 818-954-5032
FAX 818-954-6277
WEB SITE . . . . www.cbs.com/primetime/old_christine
PRODUCTION COMPANY Warner Bros. Television Production

Kari Lizer . . . . Executive Producer/Creator/Showrunner
Andy Ackerman . . . . Executive Producer/Director
Jen Crittenden . . . . Co-Executive Producer
Jeff Astrof . . . . Co-Executive Producer
Adam Barr . . . . Co-Executive Producer
Jonathan Goldstein . . . . Supervising Producer
Katie Palmer . . . . Executive Story Editor
Danielle Evenson . . . . Staff Writer
Lisa Helfrich Jackson . . . . Line Producer
Katherine Eckert . . . . Casting Director

***THE NINE (ABC/60 mins.)**
c/o Warner Bros. Television Production
4000 Warner Blvd.
Burbank, CA 91522
PHONE 213-534-3500
FAX 213-534-3501
PRODUCTION COMPANY Warner Bros. Television Production

Alex Graves . . . . Executive Producer
Hank Steinberg . . . . Executive Producer/Creator
Tom Garrigus . . . . Co-Executive Producer
K.J. Steinberg . . . . Co-Executive Producer/Creator
Tom Szentgyorgyi . . . . Co-Executive Producer
Joy Gregory . . . . Producer
Perry Husman . . . . Producer
Ted Humphrey . . . . Co-Producer
Nicole Mirante . . . . Co-Producer
John G. Smith . . . . UPM
Gayliann Harvey . . . . Production Coordinator
Jason Wilborn . . . . Staff Writer
Onalee Hunter . . . . Writers' Assistant
Carrie Audino . . . . Casting Director
Laura Schiff . . . . Casting Director

NIP/TUCK (FX/60 mins.)
5555 Melrose Ave., Modular Bldg., 1st Fl.
Los Angeles, CA 90038
PHONE 323-956-2400
WEB SITE . . . . www.fxnetworks.com/shows/originals/niptuck/main.html
PRODUCTION COMPANIES The Shephard/Robin Company - Warner Bros. Television Production

Ryan Murphy . . . . Executive Producer/Creator
Michael Robin . . . . Executive Producer
Greer Shephard . . . . Executive Producer
Lyn Greene . . . . Supervising Producer
Richard Levine . . . . Supervising Producer
Sean Jablonski . . . . Producer
Jennifer Salt . . . . Co-Producer
Michael Weiss . . . . Co-Producer
Pat McKee . . . . Line Producer
Hank Chilton . . . . Story Editor
Brad Falchuk . . . . Staff Writer

***NOTES FROM THE UNDERBELLY (ABC/30 mins.)**
c/o The Tannenbaum Company
4000 Warner Blvd., Bldg. 146, Rm. 206
Burbank, CA 91522
PHONE 818-977-1640
FAX 818-977-7484
PRODUCTION COMPANIES Tannenbaum Company - Warner Bros. Television Production

Barry Sonnenfeld . . . . Executive Producer
Eric Tannenbaum . . . . Executive Producer
Kim Tannenbaum . . . . Executive Producer
Stacy Traub . . . . Executive Producer/Showrunner/Creator
Gary Murphy . . . . Co-Executive Producer
Steve Joe . . . . Supervising Producer
Greg Schaffer . . . . Supervising Producer
Lesley Lake Webster . . . . Producer
Jana Hunter . . . . Consulting Producer
Mitch Hunter . . . . Consulting Producer
John Quaintance . . . . Co-Producer
Shira Zeltzer Goldman . . . . Staff Writer
Brett Benner . . . . Casting Director
Debby Romano . . . . Casting Director

NUMB3RS (CBS/60 mins.)
c/o LA Center Studios
1201 W. 5th St., M180
Los Angeles, CA 90017
PHONE 213-534-3852
FAX 213-534-3856
WEB SITE www.cbs.com/primetime/numb3rs
PRODUCTION COMPANIES CBS Paramount Network Television - Scott Free Productions

Ridley Scott . . . . Executive Producer
Tony Scott . . . . Executive Producer
Barry Schindel . . . . Executive Producer/Showrunner
Nick Falacci . . . . Executive Producer/Creator
Cheryl Heuton . . . . Executive Producer/Creator
David Zucker . . . . Executive Producer
Lewis Abel . . . . Co-Executive Producer
Andrew Dettman . . . . Co-Executive Producer
Don McGill . . . . Co-Executive Producer
Robert Port . . . . Consulting Producer
Julie Hebert . . . . Consulting Producer
Ken Sanzel . . . . Consultant
Michael Attanasio . . . . Producer/UPM
John Behring . . . . Producer/Director
Christine Larson-Nitzche . . . . Producer/UPM
Sean Crouch . . . . Staff Writer
J. David Harden . . . . Staff Writer
Mark Saks . . . . Casting Director

THE O.C. (Fox/60 mins.)
c/o Raleigh Studios
1600 Rosecrans Ave., Bldg. 6-A, 2nd Fl.
Manhattan Beach, CA 90266
PHONE .310-727-2838
FAX .310-727-2839
WEB SITE .www.fox.com/oc
PRODUCTION COMPANIES Warner Bros. Television Production - Wonderland Sound and Vision

Robert DeLaurentis .Executive Producer/Showrunner
McG .Executive Producer
Stephanie Savage .Executive Producer
Josh Schwartz .Executive Producer/Creator
John Stephens .Co-Executive Producer
Ian Toynton .Co-Executive Producer
J.J. Philbin .Producer
Lisa Cochran-Neilan .Co-Producer
Ben Kunde .Co-Producer
David Calloway .Line Producer
Leila Gerstein .Executive Story Editor
Mark Fish .Staff Writer
Alexandra Patsavas .Music Supervisor

THE OFFICE (NBC/30 mins.)
c/o NBC Universal Television Studio
100 Universal City Plaza
Universal City, CA 91608
PHONE .818-786-6666
WEB SITE .www.nbc.com/The_Office
PRODUCTION COMPANIES NBC Universal Television Studio - Reveille, LLC

Greg Daniels .Executive Producer/Showrunner/Creator
Ricky Gervais .Executive Producer/Creator
Howard Klein .Executive Producer
Stephen Merchant .Executive Producer/Creator
Ben Silverman .Executive Producer
Jennifer Celotta .Co-Executive Producer
Paul Lieberstein .Co-Executive Producer
Kent Zbornak .Co-Executive Producer
B.J. Novak .Supervising Producer
Mike Schur .Supervising Producer
Brent Forrester .Consulting Producer
Larry Wilmore .Consulting Producer
Mindy Kaling .Executive Story Editor
Lee Eisenberg .Story Editor
Justin Spitzer .Story Editor
Gene Stupinsky .Story Editor
Caroline Williams .Staff Writer
Allison Jones .Casting Director

ONE LIFE TO LIVE (ABC/60 mins.)
56 W. 66th St.
New York, NY 10023
PHONE .212-456-7777
WEB SITE .abc.go.com/daytime/onelifetolive/index.html
PRODUCTION COMPANY ABC Daytime

Frank Valentini .Executive Producer
Suzanne Flynn .Producer
John Tumino .Producer
Shelley Honigbaum .Coordinating Producer
Dena Higley .Head Writer
Jackie Van Belle .Assistant Producer
Shelly Altman .Breakdown Writer
Ron Carlivati .Breakdown Writer
Victor Glalanella .Breakdown Writer
Janet Iacobuzoio .Breakdown Writer
Leslie Nipkow .Script Editor
Mark Christopher .Script Writer
Carolyn Culliton .Script Writer
Michelle Poteet Lisanti .Script Writer
Fran Myers .Script Writer
Ginger Redmon .Script Writer
Chirs Van Etten .Continuity Supervisor
Julie Madison .Casting Director

ONE TREE HILL (The CW/60 mins.)
1223 N. 23rd St.
Wilmington, NC 28405
PHONE .910-343-3770/818-977-1883
FAX .910-343-3777/818-977-1460
WEB SITE .www.cwtv.com/cw-onetreehill.html
PRODUCTION COMPANIES Tollin/Robbins Productions - Warner Bros. Television Production
COMMENTS Writers' office: 411 N. Hollywood Way, Bldg. 248R, Burbank, CA 91505

Joe Davola .Executive Producer
Brian Robbins .Executive Producer
Mark Schwahn .Executive Producer/Creator/Showrunner
Mike Tollin .Executive Producer
Greg Prange .Co-Executive Producer
Bill Brown .Consulting Producer
David Hartley .Producer/UPM
Adele Lim .Co-Producer
Dawn Urbont .Co-Producer
Terrence Coli .Executive Story Editor
Mike Herro .Story Editor
John A. Norris .Story Editor
David Strauss .Story Editor
Michelle Furtney-Goodman .Staff Writer
Brett Benner .Casting Director (Los Angeles)
Lisa Mae Fincannon .Casting Director (Wilmington)
Craig Fincannon .Casting Director (Wilmington)
Debby Romano .Casting Director (Los Angeles)

PASSIONS (NBC/60 mins.)
4024 Radford Ave.
Studio City, CA 91604
PHONE .818-655-5454
FAX .818-655-8375
WEB SITE .www.nbc.com/passions
PRODUCTION COMPANIES NBC Universal Television Studio - Outpost Farms, Inc.

James E. Reilly .Creator/Head Writer/Consulting Producer
Lisa de Cazotte .Executive Producer
Richard Schilling .Supervising Producer
Mary-Kelly Weir .Producer
Timothy Stevens .Associate Producer
Jeanne Haney .Sr. Coordinating Producer
Denise Mark .Coordinating Producer
Clem Egan .Writer
N. Gail Lawrence .Writer
Marlene Clark Poulter .Writer
Pete T. Rich .Writer
Peggy Schibi .Writer
Maralyn Thoma .Writer
Darrell Ray Thomas Jr. .Writer
Nancy Williams Watt .Writer
Petros Tagoryan .Publicity Coordinator
Jackie Briskey .Casting Director (Principals)
Dana Olsen .Casting Director (Under Fives/Extras)

PRISON BREAK (Fox/60 mins.)
999 Metro Media Pl.
Dallas, IL 75247
PHONE .214-951-9200
FAX .214-905-1079
WEB SITE .www.fox.com/prisonbreak
PRODUCTION COMPANIES Adelstein Productions - Original Film
COMMENTS Writers' office: 12233 W. Olympic Blvd., #210, Los Angeles, CA 90064

Marty Adelstein .Executive Producer
Neal Moritz .Executive Producer
Dawn Parouse .Executive Producer
Mike Pavone .Executive Producer
Brett Ratner .Executive Producer
Paul Scheuring .Executive Producer/Creator/Showrunner
Matt Olmstead .Co-Executive Producer
Zack Estrin .Co-Executive Producer
Kevin Hooks .Co-Executive Producer
Nick Santora .Co-Executive Producer
Karyn Usher .Consulting Producer
Garry Brown .Producer
Agatha Warren .Associate Producer
Monica Macer .Staff Writer
Scott Genkinger .Casting Director
Junie Lowry-Johnson .Casting Director

PROJECT RUNWAY (Bravo/60 mins.)
915 Broadway, 20th Fl.
New York, NY 10010
PHONE .212-627-0001
FAX .212-627-1110
WEB SITE .www.projectrunway.com
PRODUCTION COMPANIES Full Picture - Magical Elves - The Weinstein Company

Jane Cha .Executive Producer
Desiree Gruber .Executive Producer

PSYCH (USA/60 mins.)
c/o Tagline Pictures
9250 Wilshire Blvd., Ground Fl.
Beverly Hills, CA 90212
PHONE .310-595-1500
FAX .310-595-1505
PRODUCTION COMPANIES NBC Universal Television Studio - Tagline Pictures

Steve Franks .Executive Producer/Creator
Chris Henze .Executive Producer
Kelly Kulchak .Executive Producer
Liz Marx .Casting Director

QUEER EYE (Bravo/60 mins.)
100 Avenue of the Americas
New York, NY 10013
PHONE .212-581-8200
FAX .212-581-8201
WEB SITE .www.bravotv.com/Queer_Eye_for_the_Straight_Guy
PRODUCTION COMPANY Scout Productions

David Collins .Executive Producer/Creator
Michael Williams .Executive Producer
David Metzler .Executive Producer
Linda Lea .Executive Producer
Joel K. Savitt .Executive in Charge of Production
Lynn Sadofsky .Co-Executive Producer
Donna MacLetchie .Producer
Sheila Cabano .Production Executive
Gigi Caucey .Production Manager

***RAINES (NBC/60 mins.)**
c/o Raleigh Studios
5300 Melrose Ave.
Los Angeles, CA 90038
PHONE .323-960-4725

Preston Fischer .Executive Producer
Peter Noah .Executive Producer
Graham Yost .Executive Producer/Showrunner/Creator
Jennifer Cecil .Co-Executive Producer
Fred Golan .Co-Executive Producer
Josh Singer .Supervising Producer
Felix Alcala .Producer
Bruce Rasmussen .Consulting Producer
Taylor Elmore .Story Editor
Dave Andron .Staff Writer
Wendy Calhoun .Staff Writer
Moira Walley-Beckett .Staff Writer
Meg Liberman .Casting Director

REAL TIME WITH BILL MAHER (HBO/60 mins.)
7800 Beverly Blvd.
Los Angeles, CA 90036
PHONE .323-575-7700
EMAIL .tickets@realtimehbo.com
WEB SITE .www.hbo.com/billmaher
PRODUCTION COMPANY HBO Entertainment

Brad Grey .Executive Producer
Marc Gurvitz .Executive Producer
Scott Carter .Executive Producer
Bill Maher .Executive Producer
Sheila Griffiths .Executive Producer
Dean Johnson .Co-Executive Producer
Billy Martin .Co-Executive Producer

REBA (The CW/30 mins.)
10201 W. Pico Blvd., Bldg. 38, Rm. 125
Los Angeles, CA 90035
PHONE .310-369-7322
FAX .310-969-3323
WEB SITE .thewb.warnerbros.com/web/show.jsp?id=RB
PRODUCTION COMPANIES Acme Productions - Twentieth Century Fox Television

Kevin Abbott .Executive Producer/Showrunner
Don Beck .Executive Producer
Matt Berry .Executive Producer
Pat Bullard .Executive Producer
Chris Case .Executive Producer
Michael Hanel .Executive Producer
Reba McEntire .Executive Producer
Mindy Schultheis .Executive Producer
Jason Shubb .Producer
Stevie Ray Fromstein .Consultant
Steve Stajich .Consultant
Chris Atwood .Staff Writer
Greg Orson .Casting Director

RENO 911! (Comedy Central/30 mins.)
c/o Hilarious Productions
9465 Wilshire Blvd., Ste. 950
Beverly Hills, CA 90212
PHONE 323-785-2902
FAX 323-785-2147
WEB SITE . . . .www.comedycentral.com/shows/reno_911/index.jhtml
COMMENTS Production office: Hollywood Production Center, 1149 N. Gower St., #271, Los Angeles, CA 90038

Thomas Lennon . . . .Executive Producer
Robert Ben Garant . . . .Executive Producer
Kerri Kenney-Silver . . . .Executive Producer
John Landgraf . . . .Executive Producer
Danny DeVito . . . .Executive Producer
Michael Shamberg . . . .Executive Producer
Stacey Sher . . . .Executive Producer
Peter Principato . . . .Co-Executive Producer
Paul Young . . . .Co-Executive Producer
Michael Patrick Jann . . . .Director/Consulting Producer
Penny Adams . . . .Producer

RESCUE ME (FX/60 mins.)
c/o Canterbury Productions
176 Grand St., 4th Fl.
New York, NY 10013
PHONE 212-941-7204
FAX 212-965-8630
WEB SITE . . . .www.fxnetworks.com/shows/originals/rescueme/main.html
PRODUCTION COMPANIES Apostle - DreamWorks Television - Sony Pictures Television

Denis Leary . . . .Executive Producer
Peter Tolan . . . .Executive Producer
Jim Serpico . . . .Executive Producer
Kerry Orent . . . .Producer
Tom Sellitti . . . .Producer
Leslie Tolan . . . .Producer
Evan Reilly . . . .Co-Producer
Julie Tucker . . . .Casting Director

***RULES OF ENGAGEMENT (CBS/30 mins.)**
c/o Sony Pictures Television
10202 W. Washington Blvd.
Culver City, CA 90232
PHONE 310-244-4000
PRODUCTION COMPANY Sony Pictures Television

Andy Ackerman . . . .Executive Producer
Jack Giarraputo . . . .Executive Producer
Tom Hertz . . . .Executive Producer/Showrunner/Creator
Doug Robinson . . . .Executive Producer
Adam Sandler . . . .Executive Producer
Jon Sherman . . . .Co-Executive Producer
Vanessa McCarthy . . . .Producer
Barbara Stoll . . . .Line Producer
Stephen A. Holland . . . .Executive Story Editor
Michael Haukom . . . .Story Editor
Leslie Litt . . . .Casting Director
Suzanne Goddard-Smythe . . . .Casting Director

***RUNAWAY (The CW/60 mins.)**
c/o Darren Star Productions
10202 W. Washington Blvd., Fred Astaire Bldg., Ste. 2210
Culver City, CA 90232
PHONE 416-631-7776
FAX 416-631-7862
WEB SITE . . . .www.cwtv.com/cw-runaway.html
PRODUCTION COMPANIES Sony Pictures Television - Darren Star Productions

Darren Star . . . .Executive Producer
Ed Zuckerman . . . .Executive Producer/Showrunner
Dana Baratta . . . .Co-Executive Producer
Susie Fitzgerald . . . .Co-Executive Producer
Chad Hodge . . . .Co-Executive Producer/Creator
John E. Pogue . . . .Producer
Lynn Raynor . . . .Producer
Luke Schelhaas . . . .Producer
Meredith Philpott . . . .Staff Writer
Hannah Shakespeare . . . .Staff Writer
Lesli Gelles . . . .Casting Director
Greg Orson . . . .Casting Director

THE SARAH SILVERMAN PROGRAMME (Comedy Central/30 mins.)
c/o Comedy Central
2049 Century Park East, Ste. 4000
Los Angeles, CA 90067
PHONE 310-407-4700
FAX 310-407-4796
PRODUCTION COMPANY Comedy Central

Heidi Herzon . . . .Executive Producer
Rob Schrab . . . .Executive Producer
Sarah Silverman . . . .Executive Producer
Dan Sterling . . . .Executive Producer
Erin O'Malley . . . .Producer

SATURDAY NIGHT LIVE (NBC/90 mins.)
30 Rockefeller Plaza, 17th Fl.
New York, NY 10112
PHONE 212-664-4511
FAX 212-664-2485
WEB SITE . . . .www.nbc.com/Saturday_Night_Live
PRODUCTION COMPANY Broadway Video

Lorne Michaels . . . .Executive Producer
Dennis McNicholas . . . .Head Writer
Seth Meyers . . . .Head Writer
Andrew Steele . . . .Head Writer
Ken Aymong . . . .Supervising Producer
Michael Bosze . . . .Producer
Steve Higgins . . . .Producer
Marci Klein . . . .Producer
Michael Shoemaker . . . .Producer
James Signorelli . . . .Producer
Ayala Cohen . . . .Co-Producer
Hillary Selesnick Hunn . . . .Co-Producer

***SAVED (TNT/60 mins.)**
3500 Cornett Rd.
Vancouver, BC V5M 2H5, Canada
PHONE 604-453-4820
FAX 604-453-4821
PRODUCTION COMPANIES Brightlight Pictures, Inc. - fox 21 - Imagine Television - Sarabande Productions

David Manson .....Executive Producer/Creator/Showrunner
David Nevins .....Executive Producer
Joe Dougherty .....Co-Executive Producer
Sandy Kroopf .....Supervising Producer
Matthew Carlisle .....Producer
John Mankiewicz .....Producer
Barry Pullman .....Producer
Shawn Williamson .....Producer
Kira Arne .....Co-Producer
Ann Hamilton .....Consulting Producer
Libby Goldstein .....Casting Director
Junie Lowry Johnson .....Casting Director

SCRUBS (NBC/30 mins.)
12629 Riverside Dr., 3rd Fl.
Valley Village, CA 91607
PHONE 818-623-1880, x104
FAX 818-623-2552
WEB SITE .....www.nbc.com/Scrubs
PRODUCTION COMPANIES Doozer - Touchstone Television

Bill Lawrence .....Executive Producer/Creator/Showrunner
Tim Hobert .....Executive Producer
Tad Quill .....Executive Producer
Neil Goldman .....Co-Executive Producer
Garrett Donovan .....Co-Executive Producer
Bill Callahan .....Co-Executive Producer
Janae Bakken .....Producer
Angela Nissel .....Producer
Mike Schwartz .....Producer
Deb Fordham .....Producer
Mark Stegemann .....Producer
Aseem Batra .....Executive Story Editor
Kevin Biegel .....Executive Story Editor
Dave Tennant .....Staff Writer
Andrew Schwarzman .....Staff Writer
Clarence Livingston .....Staff Writer
Randall Winston .....Line Producer
Liz Newman .....Line Producer
Brett Benner .....Casting Director
Debby Romano .....Casting Director

***SHARK (CBS/60 mins.)**
c/o Twentieth Century Fox Television
10201 W. Pico. Bldg. 226
Los Angeles, CA 90035
PHONE 310-369-7475
FAX 310-969-2600
PRODUCTION COMPANIES Imagine Television - Twentieth Century Fox Television

Ian Biederman .....Executive Producer/Creator
Brian Grazer .....Executive Producer
Red Holcomb .....Executive Producer
David Nevins .....Executive Producer
Ed Redlich .....Executive Producer/Showrunner
Keith Eisner .....Co-Executive Producer
Bill Chais .....Producer
Rod Holcomb .....Producer
Michael Oates Palmer .....Producer
Mimi Schmir .....Consulting Producer
Bob Del Valle .....Line Producer
Yolanda Lawrence .....Story Editor
Devon Greggory .....Staff Writer
Rick Millikan .....Casting Director

THE SHIELD (FX/60 mins.)
c/o Prospect Studios
4151 Prospect Ave., Silverlake Bldg., 2nd Fl.
Los Angeles, CA 90027
PHONE 323-671-4161
FAX 323-671-5511
WEB SITE .....www.fxnetworks.com/shows/originals/the_shield/main.html
PRODUCTION COMPANIES Fox Television Studios - Sony Pictures Television

Shawn Ryan .....Executive Producer/Creator
Glen Mazzara .....Executive Producer
Charles H. Eglee .....Executive Producer
Scott Rosenbaum .....Co-Executive Producer
Kurt Sutter .....Co-Executive Producer
Adam E. Fierro .....Supervising Producer
Michael Chiklis .....Producer
Kevin Cremin .....Producer
Liz Craft .....Producer
Sarah Fain .....Producer
Wendy Weidman .....Casting
Barbara Florentino .....Casting
Rebecca Mangieri .....Casting

THE SHOWBIZ SHOW WITH DAVID SPADE (Comedy Central/30 mins.)
c/o Central Productions
5800 Sunset Blvd., Bldg. 11, Ste. 202
Los Angeles, CA 90028
PHONE 323-762-7000
WEB SITE .....www.comedycentral.com/shows/showbiz_show/index.jhtml
PRODUCTION COMPANIES Brillstein-Grey Entertainment - Central Productions - Pariah

David Spade .....Executive Producer
Eddie Feldman .....Executive Producer
Hugh Fink .....Executive Producer
Gavin Polone .....Executive Producer
Peter Traugott .....Executive Producer

THE SIMPSONS (Fox/30 mins.)
10201 W. Pico Blvd., Bldg. 203
Los Angeles, CA 90035
PHONE .310-369-3959
FAX .310-369-3852
WEB SITE www.thesimpsons.com
PRODUCTION COMPANIES Film Roman, Inc. - Gracie Films - Twentieth Century Fox Television
COMMENTS Animated

James L. Brooks .Executive Producer
Matt Groening .Executive Producer
Al Jean .Executive Producer/Showrunner
Tim Long .Executive Producer
Ian Maxtone-Graham .Executive Producer
Carolyn Omine .Executive Producer
Matt Selman .Executive Producer
Stewart Burns .Co-Executive Producer
Joel Cohen .Co-Executive Producer
Kevin Curran .Co-Executive Producer
John Frink .Co-Executive Producer
Dana Gould .Co-Executive Producer
Don Payne .Co-Executive Producer
Michael Price .Co-Executive Producer
Dan Greaney .Producer
Ron Hauge .Producer
David Mirkin .Producer
Richard Raynis .Producer
Mike Reiss .Producer
Richard Sakai .Producer
Denise Sirkot .Producer
Matt Warburton .Producer
Bonnie Pietila .Producer/Casting Consultant
Jeff Westbrook .Co-Producer
Dominique Braud .Co-Producer, Post Production
Richard Chung .Animation Co-Producer
Larina Adamson .Supervising Producer
Marc Wilmore .Supervising Producer
Felicia Nalivansky .Associate Producer
Danny Chun .Story Editor

***THE SINGLES TABLE (NBC/30 mins.)**
5555 Melrose Ave., Cooper Bldg., Rm. 105
Los Angeles, CA 90038
PHONE .323-956-4200
FAX .323-862-2373
PRODUCTION COMPANY Twentieth Century Fox Television

Bill Martin .Executive Producer/Showrunner/Creator
Mike Schiff .Executive Producer/Showrunner/Creator
Mark Hudis .Co-Executive Producer
Chris Kelly .Co-Executive Producer
Christine Zander .Co-Executive Producer
Abraham Higginbotham .Supervising Producer
Lew Schneider .Consulting Producer
Shawn Wilt .Line Producer
Mary Fitzgerald .Staff Writer
Jonathan Howard .Staff Writer
Alexis Frank Koczara .Casting Director
Christine Smith Shevchenko .Casting Director

***SIX DEGREES (ABC/60 mins.)**
53-16 35th St., 4th Fl.
Long Island City, NY 11101
PHONE .718-906-3300
FAX .718-906-3333
PRODUCTION COMPANIES Bad Robot Productions - Touchstone Television

J.J. Abrams .Executive Producer
Bryan Burk .Executive Producer
Carol Flint .Executive Producer/Showrunner
Raven Metzner .Executive Producer/Creator
Stuart Zicherman .Executive Producer/Creator
Julie Rottenberg .Supervising Producer
Brad Winters .Supervising Producer
Laura Wolner .Supervising Producer
Elisa Zuritsky .Supervising Producer
Jace Alexander .Producer
Peter Elkoff .Producer
Jane Raab .Producer
Dave Dworetzky .Co-Producer
Peter Parnell .Consulting Producer
Margo Meyers .Line Producer
Pang Ni Landrum .Story Editor
Neil Goldberg .Staff Writer
Gayle Keller .Casting Director
Noel Eisenberg .Assistant to Carol Flint
Jessica Kantor .Assistant to Stuart Zicherman & Raven Metzner
Kevin Kuffa .Casting Assistant

SLEEPER CELL (Showtime/60 mins.)
c/o Showtime Productions
10880 Wilshire Blvd., Ste. 1600
Los Angeles, CA 90024
PHONE .818-672-8060
FAX .818-672-8870
PRODUCTION COMPANY Showtime Networks Inc.

Ethan Reiff .Executive Producer
Cyrus Voris .Executive Producer
Ann Kindberg .Producer
Angel Dean Lopez .Staff Writer
Kamran Pasha .Staff Writer
Alexander Woo .Staff Writer

SMALLVILLE (The CW/60 mins.)
4000 Warner Blvd., Bldg. 160, Ste. 200
Burbank, CA 91522
PHONE .818-977-4050
FAX .818-977-2404
WEB SITE www.cwtv.com/cw-smallville.html
PRODUCTION COMPANIES Smallville Studios, Inc. - Tollin/Robbins Productions - Warner Bros. Television Production

Alfred Gough .Executive Producer/Showrunner/Co-Creator
Miles Millar .Executive Producer/Showrunner/Co-Creator
Ken Horton .Executive Producer
Brian Robbins .Executive Producer
Mike Tollin .Executive Producer
Joe Davola .Executive Producer
Steven S. DeKnight .Co-Executive Producer
John Litvack .Co-Executive Producer
James Marshall .Co-Executive Producer
Brian Peterson .Co-Executive Producer
Todd Slavkin .Co-Executive Producer
Kelly Souders .Co-Executive Producer
Darren Swimmer .Co-Executive Producer
Rob Maier .Producer
Jae Marchant .Producer
Tim Scanlan .Producer
David Willson .Producer
Holly Harold .Executive Story Editor
Turi Meyer .Executive Story Editor
Al Septien .Executive Story Editor
Tracy Bellomo .Staff Writer
Caroline Dries .Staff Writer
Deedee Bradley .Casting Director (US)
Coreen Mayrs .Casting Director (Canada)

SO YOU THINK YOU CAN DANCE (Fox/60 mins.)
c/o 19 Entertainment
9440 Santa Monica Blvd., Ste. 705
Beverly Hills, CA 90210
PHONE .310-777-1940
FAX .310-777-1949
WEB SITE www.fox.com/dance
PRODUCTION COMPANIES 19 Entertainment, Inc. - dick clark productions, inc.

Simon Fuller .Executive Producer
Nigel Lythgoe .Executive Producer
Allen Shapiro .Executive Producer

SOUTH PARK (Comedy Central/30 mins.)
c/o Comedy Central
2049 Century Park East, Ste. 4000
Los Angeles, CA 90067
PHONE .310-407-4700
FAX .310-407-4796
WEB SITE www.southparkstudios.com
PRODUCTION COMPANY Comedy Central
COMMENTS Animated

Trey Parker .Executive Producer/Creator
Matt Stone .Executive Producer/Creator
Anne Garefino .Executive Producer
Frank Agnone .Supervising Producer
Jennifer Howell .Supervising Producer
Pam Brady .Consulting Producer
Vernon Chatman .Consulting Producer
Kyle McCulloch .Consulting Producer
Theresa Mulligan .Consulting Producer

***STANDOFF (Fox/60 mins.)**
c/o Twentieth Century Fox Television
10201 W. Pico Blvd., Bldg. 1/100
PHONE .310-369-5500
FAX .310-969-0701
PRODUCTION COMPANY Twentieth Century Fox Television

Craig Silverstein .Executive Producer/Showrunner
Glen Mazzara .Executive Producer/Showrunner
Tim Story .Executive Producer
Juan Carlos Coto .Co-Executive Producer
Linda Gase .Co-Executive Producer
Jonathan Glassner .Co-Executive Producer
David Levinson .Consulting Producer
Marc David Alpert .Producer
Stacy Rukeyser .Executive Story Editor
Adam Targum .Story Editor
Joy Kecken .Staff Writer
Angela Terry .Casting Director
Barbara Stordahl .Casting Director

STARGATE: ATLANTIS (Sci Fi/60 mins.)
2400 Boundary Rd.
Burnaby, BC V5M 3Z3, Canada
PHONE .604-292-8560
FAX .604-292-8550
WEB SITE www.scifi.com/atlantis
PRODUCTION COMPANY Pegasus Productions III, Inc.

Robert Cooper .Executive Producer
Joseph Mallozzi .Executive Producer
Paul Mullie .Executive Producer
N. John Smith .Executive Producer
Brad Wright .Executive Producer
Carl Binder .Co-Executive Producer
Martin Wood .Supervising Producer
Martin Gero .Co-Producer
Stuart Aikeng .Casting Director
Sean Cossey .Casting Director

STARGATE: SG-1 (Sci Fi/60 mins.)
2400 Boundary Rd.
Burnaby, BC V5M 3Z3, Canada
PHONE .604-292-8500
FAX .604-292-8550
WEB SITE www.scifi.com/stargate
PRODUCTION COMPANY Kawoosh! Productions X, Inc.

Robert Cooper .Executive Producer
Joseph Mallozzi .Executive Producer
Paul Mullie .Executive Producer
N. John Smith .Executive Producer
Brad Wright .Executive Producer
Carl Binder .Co-Executive Producer
John G. Lenic .Producer
Andy Mikita .Producer
Martin Gero .Co-Producer
Stuart Aikins .Casting Director (Canada)
Sean Cossey .Casting Director (Canada)

STUDIO 60 ON THE SUNSET STRIP (NBC/60 mins.)
4000 Warner Blvd., Bldg. 131
Burbank, CA 91522
PHONE .818-954-1515
FAX .818-954-5677/818-954-1008
PRODUCTION COMPANIES Shoe Money Productions - Warner Bros. Television Production
COMMENTS Writers' office: 4000 Warner Blvd., Bldg. 139, Rm. 107, Burbank, CA 91522

Thomas Schlamme .Executive Producer
Aaron Sorkin .Executive Producer/Creator
Eli Attie .Co-Executive Producer
Timothy Busfield .Producer
Dylan Massin .Line Producer
Julie DeJoie .Associate Producer
Mindy Kanaskae .Associate Producer
Lauren Lohman .Associate Producer
Dana Calvo .Story Editor
Mark McKinney .Story Editor
Christina Booth .Staff Writer
Jessica Brickman .Staff Writer
David Handleman .Staff Writer
Cinque Henderson .Staff Writer
Melissa Myers .Staff Writer
Amy Turner .Staff Writer
Meg Lieberman .Casting Director

SUPERNANNY (ABC/60 mins.)
3800 Barham Blvd., Ste. 210
Los Angeles, CA 90068
PHONE .323-904-4680
FAX .323-904-4681
WEB SITE abc.go.com/primetime/supernanny/index.html

Nick Powell .Executive Producer/Creator
Nick Emmerson .Executive Producer
Craig Armstrong .Executive Producer
Kirsty Robson .Executive in Charge

SUPERNATURAL (The CW/60 mins.)
8085 Glenwood Dr.
Vancouver, BC V3N 5C8, Canada
PHONE .604-529-1466
FAX .604-529-1444
WEB SITE .www.cwtv.com/cw-supernatural.html
PRODUCTION COMPANIES Warner Bros. Television Production - Wonderland Sound and Vision
COMMENTS Writers' office: 3400 Riverside Dr., 7th Fl., Burbank, CA 91505

Eric Kripke .Executive Producer/Showrunner/Creator
McG .Executive Producer
John Shiban .Executive Producer
Robert Singer .Executive Producer
Kim Manners .Co-Executive Producer
Phil Sgriccia .Supervising Producer
Peter Johnson .Producer
Cyrus Yavneh .Producer
Brigitta Lauren .Executive Assistant to Robert Singer
Emily McLaughlin .Executive Assistant to Eric Kripke
Heike Brandstatter .Casting Director (Canada)
Coreen Mayrs .Casting Director (Canada)
Robert Ulrich .Casting Director (US)

SURVIVOR (CBS/60 mins.)
c/o Mark Burnett Productions
640 N. Sepulveda Blvd.
Los Angeles, CA 90049
PHONE .310-903-5400
WEB SITE .www.cbs.com/primetime/survivor
PRODUCTION COMPANY Mark Burnett Productions

Mark Burnett .Executive Producer
Charlie Parsons .Executive Producer
Tom Shelly .Executive Producer
Doug McCallie .Co-Executive Producer
Conrad Riggs .Co-Executive Producer
Kevin Green .Co-Executive Producer
Scott Putman .Line Producer
John Kirhoffer .Producer
Daniel Munday .Producer
Jesse Jensen .Producer
Jeff Probst .Producer/Host

***'TIL DEATH (Fox/30 mins.)**
c/o Sony Pictures Television
10202 W. Washington Blvd.
Culver City, CA 90232
PHONE .310-244-3434
FAX .310-244-1183
PRODUCTION COMPANIES Montrose Productions - Sony Pictures Television

Josh Goldsmith .Executive Producer/Creator/Showrunner
Cathy Yuspa .Executive Producer/Creator/Showrunner
Patti Carr .Co-Executive Producer
Al Higgins .Co-Executive Producer
Lara Runnels .Co-Executive Producer
Alex Barnow .Producer
Annette Davis .Producer/UPM
Marc Firek .Producer
Nick Bakay .Consulting Producer
DJ Nash .Executive Story Editor
Vijal Patel .Staff Writer
Tammara Billik .Casting Director

THE TONIGHT SHOW WITH JAY LENO (NBC/60 mins.)
c/o Big Dog Productions
3000 W. Alameda Ave., Rm. 2190
Burbank, CA 91523
PHONE .818-840-2222
PRODUCTION COMPANY NBC Entertainment

Gary Considine .Executive Producer
Debbie Vickers .Executive Producer
Ellen Brown .Director
Larry Goitia .Supervising Producer
Patti M. Grant .Supervising Producer
Michael Alexander .Producer
Tracie Fiss .Producer
Walter Lewis .Associate Producer

TRADING SPOUSES: MEET YOUR NEW MOMMY (Fox/60 mins.)
c/o Rocket Science Laboratories
8441 Santa Monica Blvd.
West Hollywood, CA 90069
PHONE .323-802-0500
FAX .323-802-0599
WEB SITE .www.fox.com/tradingspouses
PRODUCTION COMPANY Rocket Science Laboratories

Chris Cowan .Executive Producer
Jean-Michel Michenaud .Executive Producer

***TRAVELER (ABC/60 mins.)**
1201 W. 5th St., Ste. F-360
Los Angeles, CA 90017
PHONE .323-956-8411
PRODUCTION COMPANIES The Jinks/Cohen Company - Warner Bros. Television Production

Bruce Cohen .Executive Producer
Charlie Craig .Executive Producer/Showrunner
David Digilio .Creator
Dan Jinks .Executive Producer
Norman Morrill .Co-Executive Producer
Vanessa Reisen .Co-Producer
Eli Talbert .Consulting Producer
John Stark .Line Producer
Michael Alaimo .Executive Story Editor
Henry Robles .Executive Story Editor
Katie Wech .Staff Writer
Ed Fowler .Writers' Assistant
Jim Martin .Writers' Assistant/Assistant to Charlie Craig & David DiGilio
Ken Miller .Casting Director
Nikki Valko .Casting Director
Julie Whitesell .Script Production Assistant

TWO AND A HALF MEN (CBS/30 mins.)
c/o Warner Bros.
4000 Warner Blvd., Bldg. 160
Burbank, CA 91522
PHONE . . . 818-977-1777
FAX . . . 818-977-3737
PRODUCTION COMPANIES Chuck Lorre Productions - Tannenbaum Company - Warner Bros. Television Production

Chuck Lorre . . . Executive Producer/Showrunner/Creator
Kim Tannenbaum . . . Executive Producer
Eric Tannenbaum . . . Executive Producer
Lee Aronsohn . . . Executive Producer
Mark Burg . . . Executive Producer
Oren Koules . . . Executive Producer
Pamela Fryman . . . Executive Producer
Don Foster . . . Co-Executive Producer
Susan Beavers . . . Co-Executive Producer
Eddie Gorodetsky . . . Co-Executive Producer
Mark Roberts . . . Co-Executive Producer
Michael Collier . . . Producer
Jim Patterson . . . Producer
Joe Bella . . . Co-Producer
Eric Lapidus . . . Consulting Producer/Creator
Mike Collier . . . Line Producer
Adam Waring . . . Story Editor
Mark Sweet . . . Staff Writer
Ken Miller . . . Casting Director
Nikki Valco . . . Casting Director

THE TYRA BANKS SHOW (Syndicated/60 mins.)
7800 Beverly Blvd., #202
Los Angeles, CA 90036
PHONE . . . 323-575-8200
FAX . . . 323-575-8250
WEB SITE . . . www.tyrashow.com
PRODUCTION COMPANIES Bankable Productions - Handprint Entertainment - Telepictures Productions

Tyra Banks . . . Executive Producer
Benny Medina . . . Executive Producer
Alex Duda . . . Executive Producer
John Redmann . . . Executive Producer
Rachel Miskowiec . . . Co-Executive Producer
Bruce Catania . . . Executive in Charge of Production
Carolyn London . . . Creative Consultant
Evolyn Brooks . . . Supervising Producer
Lisa Momberger . . . Executive Assistant to Tyra Banks
Stephanie Kun . . . Executive Assistant to Kevin Applegate & John Redmann

***UGLY BETTY (ABC/60 mins.)**
c/o Reveille, LLC
100 Universal Plaza, Bungalow 5180/5170
Universal City, CA 91608
PHONE . . . 718-906-2223
PRODUCTION COMPANIES Reveille, LLC - Touchstone Television

Salma Hayek . . . Executive Producer
Silvio Horta . . . Executive Producer/Creator
James Parriott . . . Executive Producer/Showrunner
Ben Silverman . . . Executive Producer
Jose Tamez . . . Executive Producer
Teri Weinberg . . . Executive Producer
Sheila R. Lawrence . . . Co-Executive Producer
James Hayman . . . Producer
Cameron Litvack . . . Co-Producer
Marco Pennette . . . Consulting Producer
Don Todd . . . Consulting Producer
Mark Baker . . . Line Producer
Dailyn Rodriguez . . . Story Editor
Veronica Becker . . . Staff Writer
Sarah Kucserka . . . Staff Writer
Myra Jo Martino . . . Staff Writer
Libby Goldstein . . . Casting Director
Junie Lowry-Johnson . . . Casting Director

THE UNIT (CBS/60 mins.)
c/o Twentieth Century Fox Television
10201 W. Pico Blvd., Bldg. 88
Los Angeles, CA 90035
PHONE . . . 661-294-2005
FAX . . . 661-294-2019
WEB SITE . . . www.cbs.com/primetime/the_unit
PRODUCTION COMPANY Twentieth Century Fox Television

David Mamet . . . Executive Producer/Creator
Shawn Ryan . . . Executive Producer/Creator/Showrunner
Todd Kessler . . . Co-Executive Producer
Vahan Moosekian . . . Co-Executive Producer
Daniel Voll . . . Co-Executive Producer
Eric Haney . . . Supervising Producer
Lynn Mamet . . . Supervising Producer
Sharon Lee Watson . . . Producer
Patti Wolfe . . . Consulting Producer
Emily Halpern . . . Staff Writer
Randy Huggins . . . Staff Writer

***VANISHED (Fox/60 mins.)**
c/o Paramount Pictures
5555 Melrose Ave.
Hollywood, CA 90038
PHONE . . . 310-369-1000
PRODUCTION COMPANY Twentieth Century Fox Television

Paul Redford . . . Executive Producer/Showrunner
Mimi Leder . . . Executive Producer/Director
Carla Kettner . . . Co-Executive Producer
Chris Black . . . Co-Executive Producer
Dan Dworkin . . . Supervising Producer
Jay Beattie . . . Supervising Producer
Ed Milkovich . . . Producer
Michael Cedar . . . Co-Producer/UPM
J.R. Orci . . . Co-Producer
Kelly Wheeler . . . Production Associate Producer
Melinda Hsu . . . Executive Story Editor
Matt Lau . . . Staff Writer
Cami Patton . . . Casting Director

VERONICA MARS (The CW/60 mins.)
4705 Ruffin Rd., Stages Bldg. 4&5
San Diego, CA 92123
PHONE . . . 858-715-6405/818-752-5471
FAX . . . 858-627-9370/818-754-8848
WEB SITE . . . www.cwtv.com/cw-veronica.html
PRODUCTION COMPANIES Silver Pictures - Warner Bros. Television Production
COMMENTS Writers' office: 10844 Burbank Blvd., North Hollywood, CA 91601

Diane Ruggiero . . . Executive Producer
Stu Segall . . . Executive Producer
Joel Silver . . . Executive Producer
Rob Thomas . . . Executive Producer/Showrunner/Creator
Jennifer Gwartz . . . Co-Executive Producer
Danielle Stokdyk . . . Co-Executive Producer
Howard Grigsby . . . Producer
Dan Etheridge . . . Producer
Paul Kurta . . . Line Producer
John Enbom . . . Executive Story Editor
Phil Klemmer . . . Executive Story Editor
Jonathan Moskin . . . Story Editor
David Mulei . . . Story Editor
Deedee Bradley . . . Casting Director (LA)
D. Candis Paule . . . Casting Director (San Diego)

THE WAR AT HOME (Fox/30 mins.)
c/o Acme Productions
4000 Warner Blvd., Bldg. 19, Rm. 140
Burbank, CA 91522
PHONE .818-954-7115
FAX .818-954-7210
WEB SITE www.fox.com/warathome
PRODUCTION COMPANIES Acme Productions - Warner Bros. Television Production

Michael Hanel .Executive Producer
Mindy Schultheis .Executive Producer
Rob Lotterstein .Executive Producer/Creator/Showrunner
Stephen Engel .Co-Executive Producer
Claudia Lonow .Co-Executive Producer
Andy Cadiff .Producer
Darin Henry .Producer
Michael Davidoff .Consulting Producer
Jennifer Glickman .Consulting Producer
Bill Kunstler .Consulting Producer
Al Lowenstein .Line Producer
David Holden .Staff Writer
Ryan Shankel .Staff Writer
Susan Vash .Casting Director
Adam Blutt .Assistant to Mindy Schultheis & Michael Hanel

***WATERFRONT (CBS/60 mins.)**
c/o Warner Bros. Television
4000 Warner Blvd.
Burbank, CA 91522
PHONE .401-333-9844
FAX .401-333-9845
PRODUCTION COMPANY Warner Bros. Television Production

Jack Orman .Executive Producer/Showrunner/Creator
Joe Pantoliano .Executive Producer
Michael Berns .Co-Executive Producer
Ed Bianchi .Co-Executive Producer
Nick Thiel .Co-Executive Producer
Yahlin Chang .Supervising Producer
Jill Abbinanti .Staff Writer
Jeremy Carver .Staff Writer
Janet Lin .Staff Writer
Carrie Audino .Casting Director
Laura Schiff .Casting Director

WHAT ABOUT BRIAN (ABC/60 mins.)
c/o Bad Robot Productions
500 S. Buena Vista St., Production Bldg., Rm. 361
Burbank, CA 91521
PHONE .818-560-4355
FAX .818-560-7189
PRODUCTION COMPANIES Bad Robot Productions - Touchstone Television

J.J. Abrams .Executive Producer
Bryan Burk .Executive Producer
Jonathan Pontell .Executive Producer/Director
Josh Reims .Executive Producer/Showrunner
Dana Stevens .Executive Producer/Creator
Mark Perry .Consulting Producer
Kate Angelo .Supervising Producer
Liz Tigelaar .Producer
Bob Williams .Producer
Mike Foley .Co-Producer
Stephen Hootstein .Co-Producer
Ross Cantor .Staff Writer
Nancy Jack .Staff Writer

WIFE SWAP (ABC/60 mins.)
c/o RDF Media
440 Ninth Ave., 11th Fl.
New York, NY 10001
PHONE .212-404-1463
FAX .212-404-1423
WEB SITE .abc.go.com/primetime/wifeswap/index.html
PRODUCTION COMPANY RDF Media

Michael Davies .Executive Producer
Stephen Lambert .Creator
Wendy Roth .Executive Producer
Cristin Cricco .Co-Executive Producer
Mike Gamson .Co-Executive Producer
Stephanie Schwam .Co-Executive Producer
Lisa Pitt .Casting Director
Michael Raptis .Casting Director

THE WIRE (HBO/60 mins.)
1801 S. Clinton St.
Baltimore, MD 21224
PHONE .410-537-6550
FAX .410-537-6588
WEB SITE www.hbo.com/thewire
PRODUCTION COMPANY HBO Entertainment

David Simon .Executive Producer/Creator
Nina K. Noble .Executive Producer
Joe Chappelle .Co-Executive Producer
Eric Overmyer .Consulting Producer
Ed Burns .Producer
Karen Thorson .Producer
William F. Zorzi .Story Editor
Kia Corthron .Writer
Dennis Lehane .Writer
George Pelecanos .Writer
Richard Price .Writer
Chris Collins .Staff Writer
Alexa L. Fogel CSA .Casting Director
Pat Moran CSA .Casting Director (Baltimore)

WITHOUT A TRACE (CBS/60 mins.)
c/o Warner Bros. Television
4000 Warner Blvd., Bldg. 36, Rm. 123
Burbank, CA 91522
PHONE .818-954-1707
FAX .818-954-6165
WEB SITE www.cbs.com/primetime/without_a_trace
PRODUCTION COMPANY Warner Bros. Television Production

Jerry Bruckheimer .Executive Producer
Jonathan Littman .Executive Producer
Jan Nash .Executive Producer/Showrunner
Hank Steinberg .Executive Producer/Creator
Greg Walker .Executive Producer/Showrunner
David Amann .Executive Producer
Jonathan Kaplan .Co-Executive Producer
David Goodman .Supervising Producer
Jose Molina .Supervising Producer
Gwendolyn Parker .Producer
Scott White .Producer
Byron Balasco .Co-Producer
Diego Gutierrez .Co-Producer
Nancy Van Doornewaard .Co-Producer
David Mongan .Story Editor
Amanda Segel Marks .Story Editor
Alicia Kirk .Staff Writer
Gary Zuckerbrod .Casting Director

WORKSHEET

DATE	PROJECT	CONTACT	NOTES

SECTION E

INDEX BY TYPE

Animation

19 Entertainment, Inc.
40 Acres & A Mule Filmworks, Inc.
777 Entertainment Group, Ltd.
Aardman Animations
Adult Swim
Agamemnon Films, Inc.
Alliance Atlantis
American Blackguard, Inc.
Anonymous Creators Productions
Appleseed Entertainment, LLC
Ardustry Entertainment
Artists, Inc.
Atomic Cartoons, Inc.
Automatic Pictures, Inc.
Avalanche! Entertainment
Bang Zoom! Entertainment
Harve Bennett Productions
BET Networks
Big Pix Inc.
Bleiberg Entertainment
BloodWorks, LLC
BLT Productions Ltd.
Blue Sky Studios
Blue Tulip Productions
Blueprint Entertainment
Braga Productions
Broadway Video
Buena Vista Motion Pictures Group
Tim Burton Productions
C2 Pictures
Caldera/De Fanti Entertainment
Cartoon Network
CastleBright Studios
Cataland Films
Chanticleer Films
Charlotte Street Films
Chartoff Productions
Chiodo Bros. Productions, Inc.
CinéGroupe
CineMagic Entertainment
Circle of Confusion Productions
City Entertainment
Clarity Pictures, LLC
The Collective
Comedy Central
Comic Book Movies, LLC/Branded Entertainment/Batfilm Productions
Concrete Pictures
Cookie Jar Entertainment
CrazyDreams Entertainment
Creanspeak Productions LLC
Creative Capers Entertainment
Crystal Spring Productions, Inc.
Cube Vision
Curious Pictures
Dark Horse Entertainment
DFZ Productions
Disney ABC Cable Networks Group
Walt Disney Television Animation
Disney-ABC Television Group
DisneyToon Studios
The Donners' Company
Bonny Dore Productions
Double Edge Entertainment
DreamWorks Animation SKG
DreamWorks SKG
E Entertainment, LLC
EARS XXI
Echelon Entertainment World Distribution & Prod.
Ralph Edwards Productions
Elkins Entertainment
Emmett/Furla Films
Empire Pictures Incorporated
Endgame Entertainment
Ensemble Entertainment

Animation (Continued)

Enteraktion Studios
Epic Level Entertainment, Ltd.
Euphoria Entertainment
EuropaCorp Films
Evergreen Films, LLC
Evolving Pictures Entertainment
Eye on the Ball Films, Inc.
Film Roman, Inc.
Films By Jove
Firm Films
Flame Ventures LLC
Foothill Entertainment, Inc.
Foremost Films
Forest Park Pictures
Frederator Studios
Gerber Pictures
Ghost Robot
Frederic Golchan Productions
Goldcrest Films International, Inc.
John Goldwyn Productions
Gorilla Pictures
Gotham Entertainment Group
The Gotham Group, Inc.
Gracie Films
Grammnet Productions
Greasy Entertainment
Guardian Entertainment, Ltd.
Hand Picked Films
The Hatchery
Hazy Mills Productions
Hella Good Moving Pictures
The Jim Henson Company
here! Networks
Highway 9 Films
HIT Entertainment
Hyperion Studio
Ideal Entertainment, Inc.
IDT Entertainment
ImageMovers
Imagi Services (USA)
Imagination Productions, Inc.
IMAX Corporation
ISBE Productions
Janicek-Marino Creative
JibJab Media Inc.
Kadokawa Pictures USA
Kanpai Pictures
David Kirschner Productions
Klasky Csupo, Inc.
Konwiser Brothers
Robert Kosberg Productions
Laika Entertainment
Larco Productions, Inc.
Larger Than Life Productions
The Late Bloomer Company, Ltd.
Latitude Television LLC
Arnold Leibovit Entertainment
Lett/Reese International Productions
Lighthouse Productions
Lion Rock Productions
Lionsgate
Liquid Theory
Lonetree Entertainment
Lucasfilm Ltd.
The Tom Lynch Company
Madison Road Entertainment
Magic Light Pictures
Mandoki Productions, Inc.
Marvel Studios, Inc.
Bill Melendez Productions
MGA Entertainment/MGA Entertainment Films
Mike's Movies/Michael Peyser Productions
Mindfire Entertainment
The Mirisch Corporation
Mission Entertainment

Animation (Continued)

Mobile Streams
MobiTV
Mode of 8
Moving Pictures, DPI
MTV Networks
MTV Networks Latin America (MTVNLA)
Murphy Boyz Productions
Muse Entertainment Enterprises
The N
Nala Films
National Geographic Kids' Prog. & Prod.
National Lampoon
Nelvana Communications, Inc.
New Generation Films, Inc.
Nickelodeon Movies
Nickelodeon/MTVN Kids & Family Group
Noggin
O Entertainment
Sam Okun Productions, Inc.
Lin Oliver Productions
The Orphanage
George Paige Associates, Inc.
Paraskevas Studios
Parkchester Pictures
P.A.T. Productions
Peculiar Films
Phase Two Productions
Piranha Pictures, Inc.
Pixar Animation Studios
Planet Grande Pictures
Platinum Studios, LLC
Playtime Productions
Playtone Productions
Plotpoint, Inc.
Poor Boys Productions
Popular Arts Entertainment, Inc.
PorchLight Entertainment
POW! Entertainment
Precis Productions, Inc.
Protozoa Pictures
Proud Mary Entertainment
Radar Pictures
Rafelson Media
Red Wagon Entertainment
REGAN
Relevant Entertainment Group
Renegade Animation, Inc.
Rhino Films
Rice & Beans Productions
RichCrest Animation Studios
River Road Entertainment
RKO Pictures, LLC
Phil Roman Entertainment
Rough Draft Studios
Ruby-Spears Productions
Edward Saxon Productions (ESP)
Scarab Productions
Scholastic Entertainment
Schwartz & Company, Inc.
Sci Fi Channel
Seaside Productions
SekretAgent Productions
Sesame Workshop
Jon Shestack Productions
Silver Lion Films
Silver Nitrate Pictures
Silvers/Koster Productions, Inc.
The Gene Simmons Company
Sitting Ducks Productions
Smart Entertainment
Sony Pictures Animation
Sony Pictures Imageworks
Sparky Pictures
Spike TV
Spirit Horse Productions

Animation (Continued)

Jane Startz Productions, Inc.
The Howard Stern Production Company
Stone and Company Entertainment
Sunrise Entertainment
Sunswept Entertainment
SUperFInger Entertainment
Sweeney Entertainment
Symbolic Action
Synchronicity Productions
Martin Tahse Productions
Tempest Entertainment
Nancy Tenenbaum Films
Teocalli Entertainment
Threshold Entertainment
TLC Entertainment
TMC Entertainment
TOKYOPOP Inc.
Triage Entertainment
Trigger Street Independent
Turner Entertainment Group
Twentieth Century Fox Animation
Two Oceans Entertainment Group
Underground Films
Universal Pictures
Urban Entertainment
Vanguard Films/Vanguard Animation
Village Roadshow Pictures
Viviano Feldman Entertainment
Warner Bros. Animation
Warner Bros. Entertainment Inc.
White Sneakers, Inc.
Whoop Inc./One Ho Prod./Lil' Whoop Prod.
Wild At Heart Films, LLC
Wild Brain, Inc.
Fred Wolf Films
Wolfmill Entertainment
Worldwide Pants, Inc.
Mike Young Productions LLC
Zaloom Film

Commercials

@radical.media
3 Ring Circus Films
The 7th Floor
9.14 Pictures
900 Films
A Band Apart
Aardman Animations
Alturas Films
American Blackguard, Inc.
Anonymous Creators Productions
Artists, Inc.
Atomic Cartoons, Inc.
Bay Films
Belladonna Productions
Blue Tulip Productions
Boxx Communications, LLC
Braverman Productions, Inc.
Tim Burton Productions
Cafe Productions
Carson Signature Films, Inc.
CatchLight Films
Catfish Productions
Chameleon Entertainment
City Lights Media Group
Clarity Pictures, LLC
Concrete Pictures
CrazyDreams Entertainment
Curious Pictures
Digital Domain, Inc.
Digital Ranch Productions
EARS XXI
Emotional Pictures Corporation
Evergreen Films, LLC
Fallout

Commercials (Continued)

Film Roman, Inc.
Five Sisters Productions
Frazier | Chipman Entertainment
Ghost Robot
Ginty Films International
Go Go Luckey Productions
Gordonstreet Pictures
Grisham Films USA
Guardian Entertainment, Ltd.
The Jim Henson Company
Josselyne Herman & Assoc./Moving Image Films
Hollywood East Entertainment, Inc.
Homerun Entertainment, Inc.
Hypnotic
International Television Group (ITG) - Epix Films
Janicek-Marino Creative
Klasky Csupo, Inc.
Konwiser Brothers
L.I.F.T. Productions
Laika Entertainment
Lightstone Entertainment, Inc.
Liquid Theory
Live Animals
Londine Productions
Luminair Entertainment
M3 Television
Mandoki Productions, Inc.
ManifestoVision
The Matthau Company, Inc.
Bill Melendez Productions
Merchant-Ivory
MGA Entertainment/MGA Entertainment Films
Mission Entertainment
MobiTV
Monster Productions
MRB Productions, Inc.
Norsemen Television Productions, LLC
North By Northwest Entertainment
Nova Pictures
Open Road Films
The Orphanage
The Over the Hill Gang
Piranha Pictures, Inc.
Pollywog Entertainment, Inc
Rafelson Media
Red Door Films/David Poulshock Productions, Inc.
Tim Reid Productions, Inc.
Renegade Animation, Inc.
Rubicon
Runaway Productions
Senza Pictures
Silvers/Koster Productions, Inc.
Slipnot! Productions/SPG
Spirit Horse Productions
Star Entertainment Group, Inc.
Stick Figure Productions
Super Delicious Productions
Symbolic Entertainment
Threshold Entertainment
Treasure Entertainment
TriCoast Studios
Tri-Elite Entertainment, Ltd.
VanDerKloot Film & Television
Vanguard Productions
Joseph S. Vecchio Entertainment
Versus
Simon West Productions
Wild Brain, Inc.
Workshop Pictures, Inc.
Mark Yellen Productions
Mike Young Productions LLC

Direct-to-Video/DVD

100% Entertainment
19 Entertainment, Inc.
3Wolves Productions
57-T Productions, Inc.
6 Pictures
777 Entertainment Group, Ltd.
7ponies productions
8790 Pictures, Inc.
900 Films
A Band Apart
A&E Network
AEI-Atchity Entertainment International, Inc.
Agua Films
Alchemy Entertainment
Altitude Entertainment
American Blackguard, Inc.
Anonymous Creators Productions
Mark Archer Entertainment
Ardustry Entertainment
Arjay Entertainment
Arlington Entertainment, Inc.
Artists, Inc.
The Asylum
Atomic Cartoons, Inc.
Avalon Television, Inc.
Bad Boy Films
Bang Zoom! Entertainment
BET Networks
Big Pix Inc.
Black Folk Entertainment
BloodWorks, LLC
Blue Rider Pictures
Bogner Entertainment, Inc.
Bob Booker Productions
Boxx Communications, LLC
Braga Productions
Brainstorm Media
Brave New Films
Braverman Productions, Inc.
John Brister Films
Brookwell McNamara Entertainment, Inc.
Bunim/Murray Productions, Inc.
C2 Pictures
Camelot Entertainment Group, Inc.
Capital Arts Entertainment
Carson Signature Films, Inc.
CatchLight Films
Chiodo Bros. Productions, Inc.
CinéGroupe
Cinema Libre Studio
CineMagic Entertainment
Cinetic
Cineville LLC
City Lights Media Group
The Collective
Comic Book Movies, LLC/Branded Entertainment/Batfilm Productions
Concorde-New Horizons
Concrete Pictures
Cookie Jar Entertainment
Robert Cort Productions
Court TV Networks
Creanspeak Productions LLC
Creative Capers Entertainment
Crystal Spring Productions, Inc.
CSM Communications
Curious Pictures
Dakota North Entertainment/Dakota Films
Dark Horse Entertainment
Destiny Pictures
Digital Ranch Productions
Dimension Films
DisneyToon Studios
Bonny Dore Productions
Dream Entertainment, Inc.

Direct-to-Video/DVD (Continued)

E Entertainment, LLC
EARS XXI
East of Doheny/Lexington Road Productions
Echelon Entertainment World Distribution & Prod.
Echo Lake Productions
Abra Edelman Productions
Ralph Edwards Productions
Elkins Entertainment
Ensemble Entertainment
Enteraktion Studios
Entertainment Studios, Inc.
Epic Level Entertainment, Ltd.
Epigram Entertainment
Epiphany Pictures, Inc.
The Robert Evans Company
Evolution
Evolving Pictures Entertainment
Eye in the Sky Entertainment
Farrell/Minoff Productions
Fierce Entertainment, LLC
Film Roman, Inc.
FilmEngine
Filmstreet, Inc.
Flame Ventures LLC
Flying A Studios, Inc.
Focus Features/Rogue Pictures
Foothill Entertainment, Inc.
Bonnie Forbes Productions
The Foxboro Company, Inc.
FremantleMedia North America
Chuck Fries Productions, Inc.
Gallant Entertainment
Generate
Gerber Pictures
Ginty Films International
Go Go Luckey Productions
Gordonstreet Pictures
Gotham Entertainment Group
The Gotham Group, Inc.
Graymark Productions Inc.
Robert Greenwald Productions
Greenwood Avenue Entertainment
Greystone Television and Films
Ken Gross Management
Gross-Weston Productions
Guardian Entertainment, Ltd.
G-Unit Television & Films
Haft Entertainment
Half Shell Entertainment
Hand Picked Films
The Harris Company
The Hatchery
The Jim Henson Company
here! Networks
Josselyne Herman & Assoc./Moving Image Films
Bryan Hickox Pictures, Inc.
Highway 9 Films
HII Entertainment
Hyperion Studio
IFM Film Associates, Inc.
Imagi Services (USA)
IMG Media
Ironworks Production
Janicek-Marino Creative
Kinetic Filmworks
Klasky Csupo, Inc.
Konwiser Brothers
Fred Kuehnert Productions
The Kushner-Locke Company
L.I.F.T. Productions
Latham Entertainment
Leisure Time Enterprises
Malcolm Leo Productions
Lighthouse Productions
Linkletter/Kritzer

Direct-to-Video/DVD (Continued)

Lionsgate
Peter Locke Productions
Londine Productions
Lonetree Entertainment
Longbow Productions
Longfellow Pictures
Lynn Loring Productions
Lucky Crow Films
Luminair Entertainment
The Tom Lynch Company
M3 Television
Madison Road Entertainment
Guy Magar Films
Michael Mailer Films
Mainline Releasing
Managed Passion Films
The Marshak/Zachary Company
Martin Chase Productions
Marvel Studios, Inc.
Maverick Films
Bill Melendez Productions
MGA Entertainment/MGA Entertainment Films
Michael Meltzer Productions
Mindfire Entertainment
mod3productions
Monster Productions
Morningstar Entertainment
Motion Picture Corporation of America
Moving Pictures, DPI
MPH Entertainment, Inc.
MRB Productions, Inc.
Murphy Boyz Productions
Namesake Entertainment
Nasser Entertainment Group
National Lampoon
Nelvana Communications, Inc.
New Concorde
New Generation Films, Inc.
New Wave Entertainment
New Wave Entertainment
Nickelodeon Movies
Nickelodeon/MTVN Kids & Family Group
Noble House Entertainment, Inc.
North By Northwest Entertainment
Northstar Entertainment
Numenorean Films
O Entertainment
O.N.C. Entertainment Inc.
Old School Pictures, LLC
Lin Oliver Productions
Open Road Films
Original Film
George Paige Associates, Inc.
Parallel Entertainment, Inc.
Paraskevas Studios
Patchett Kaufman Entertainment
Paulist Productions
PAYASO Entertainment
Peculiar Films
Phoenix Pictures
Piranha Pictures, Inc.
Pollywog Entertainment, Inc
Popular Arts Entertainment, Inc.
PorchLight Entertainment
POW! Entertainment
Primetime Pictures
Proud Mary Entertainment
Pterodactyl Productions Inc.
Q Media Partners
Rafelson Media
Raffaella Productions, Inc.
Red Door Films/David Poulshock Productions, Inc.
Red Hen Productions
Red Wagon Entertainment
REGAN

Direct-to-Video/DVD (Continued)

Tim Reid Productions, Inc.
Relevant Entertainment Group
Renaissance Pictures
RHI Entertainment
Rive Gauche Entertainment
RKO Pictures, LLC
Phil Roman Entertainment
Roserock Films
Runaway Productions
Rupert Productions, Inc.
S Pictures, Inc.
Schwartz & Company, Inc.
Seraphim Films
Serendipity Productions, Inc.
Seven Arts Pictures
Seven Summits Pictures & Management
Shoreline Entertainment, Inc.
Shutt-Jones Productions
Signature Pictures
Silver Nitrate Pictures
Silverline Entertainment, Inc.
Silvers/Koster Productions, Inc.
The Gene Simmons Company
Sirocco Media
Sitting Ducks Productions
Sixth Way Productions
Slipnot! Productions/SPG
Smart Entertainment
SMG Productions
Sparky Pictures
Spirit Horse Productions
Spyglass Entertainment Group
Jane Startz Productions, Inc.
Steamroller Productions, Inc.
Stoneworks Television
Mike Sullivan Productions, Inc.
Symbolic Action
The Syndicate
TAE Productions/Medeacom Productions
Tapestry Films, Inc.
Taurus Entertainment Company
Teocalli Entertainment
Threshold Entertainment
TLC Entertainment
TOKYOPOP Inc.
Tomorrow Film Corporation
Treasure Entertainment
TriCoast Studios
Tri-Elite Entertainment, Ltd.
Troma Entertainment, Inc.
Tudor Management Group
Twilight Pictures, Inc.
Two Sticks Productions
Underground Films
Urban Entertainment
VanDerKloot Film & Television
Vanguard Productions
Vantage Enterprises, Inc.
Joseph S. Vecchio Entertainment
Mark Victor Productions
Viviano Feldman Entertainment
Vox3 Films
VOY Pictures
Warner Bros. Animation
Warner Bros. Entertainment Inc.
Warren Miller Entertainment
Weintraub/Kuhn Productions
Clifford Werber Productions
White Sneakers, Inc.
Brad Wilson Productions, Inc.
Ralph Winter Productions, Inc.
Fred Wolf Films
The Woofenill Works, Inc.
WPT Enterprises, Inc.
WWE Films

Direct-to-Video/DVD (Continued)

Mark Yellen Productions
Mike Young Productions LLC
Zinkler Films
Zuckerman Entertainment

Documentaries

@radical.media
44 Blue Productions, Inc.
4th Row Films
777 Entertainment Group, Ltd.
7ponies productions
9.14 Pictures
900 Films
A Band Apart
A&E Network
Aberration Films
Acappella Pictures
Actual Reality Pictures
Actuality Productions
Adirondack Pictures
AEI-Atchity Entertainment International, Inc.
Agamemnon Films, Inc.
Ahimsa Films
Alameda Films
Alliance Atlantis
Altitude Entertainment
Alturas Films
AMC
American Blackguard, Inc.
American Zoetrope
Angelika
Animal Planet
Animus Films
Anonymous Creators Productions
Appleseed Entertainment, LLC
Loreen Arbus Productions, Inc.
Archer Entertainment
Mark Archer Entertainment
Arden Entertainment
Article 19 Films
The Artists' Colony
Asylum Entertainment
Avalanche! Entertainment
Baldwin Entertainment Group, Ltd.
Bang Zoom! Entertainment
Barwood Films
Bates Entertainment
Suzanne Bauman Productions
June Beallor Productions
Dave Bell Associates
Belladonna Productions
BET Networks
Big Pix Inc.
BloodWorks, LLC
Blossom Films
Blue Rider Pictures
Bona Fide Productions
Boneyard Entertainment
Boxx Communications, LLC
David Brady Productions
Braga Productions
Brainstorm Media
Braverman Productions, Inc.
Bravo
Broadway Video
Bunim/Murray Productions, Inc.
Burrud Productions
Cafe Productions
Cairo/Simpson Entertainment, Inc.
Camden Pictures
Carson Signature Films, Inc.
Cataland Films
Catapult Films
CatchLight Films
Catfish Productions

Documentaries (Continued)

Chanticleer Films
Chiodo Bros. Productions, Inc.
Cinema 21 Group
Cinema Libre Studio
CineMagic Entertainment
CineSon Productions Inc.
Cinetic
Cineville LLC
City Entertainment
City Lights Media Group
Clarity Pictures, LLC
Class 5 Films
Comic Book Movies, LLC/Branded Entertainment/Batfilm Productions
Con Artists Productions
Concrete Pictures
Court TV Networks
Creanspeak Productions LLC
Crystal Spring Productions, Inc.
CSM Communications
Dalaklis-McKeown Entertainment, Inc.
di Bonaventura Pictures, Inc.
Digital Ranch Productions
Discovery Channel
Discovery Health Channel
Discovery Networks, U.S.
Bonny Dore Productions
E! Networks
EARS XXI
Earthworks Films
East of Doheny/Lexington Road Productions
Echelon Entertainment World Distribution & Prod.
Rona Edwards Productions/ES Entertainment
El Norte Productions
Electric Entertainment
Elkins Entertainment
Emerging Pictures
Emotional Pictures Corporation
Endgame Entertainment
Ensemble Entertainment
Enteraktion Studios
Entertainment Studios, Inc.
Epic Level Entertainment, Ltd.
Epiphany Pictures, Inc.
ESPN Original Entertainment (EOE)
Euphoria Entertainment
Evergreen Films, LLC
Evolution
Exile Entertainment
Exxcell Entertainment, Inc./Exxcell Films
Eye in the Sky Entertainment
Face Productions/Jennilind Productions
Farrell/Minoff Productions
Fierce Entertainment, LLC
Film Garden Entertainment, Inc.
Firm Films
Firm Television
Five Mile River Films, Ltd.
Florentine Films
Foothill Entertainment, Inc.
Bonnie Forbes Productions
Fort Hill Productions
Fortress Entertainment
Four Boys Films
Frazier | Chipman Entertainment
Budd Friedman Digital
Funny Boy Films
G4 TV
Galán Entertainment
Gallant Entertainment
Generate
Gerber Pictures
Ghost Robot
Go Go Luckey Productions
Dan Gordon Productions

Documentaries (Continued)

Gordonstreet Pictures
Gorilla Pictures
GreeneStreet Films
Robert Greenwald Productions
Greenwood Avenue Entertainment
The Greif Company
Greystone Television and Films
Grinning Dog Pictures
Grisham Films USA
Allison Grodner Productions, Inc.
Grosso Jacobson Communications Corp.
The Group Entertainment
GSN
G-Unit Television & Films
Haft Entertainment
Half Shell Entertainment
Peter Hankwitz Production & Management
Harbor Lights Productions
Harding & Associates
The Harris Company
HBO Documentaries & Family
Paul Heller Productions
here! Networks
Josselyne Herman & Assoc./Moving Image Films
Bryan Hickox Pictures, Inc.
Highway 9 Films
The History Channel
Hollywood East Entertainment, Inc.
Homerun Entertainment, Inc.
Hope Enterprises, Inc.
I.E. Productions, Inc.
The Idea Factory
Imaginarium Entertainment Group
IMAX Corporation
IMG Media
The Independent Film Channel (IFC)
Indigo Films
Interloper Films
Ironworks Production
Ishtar Films
j.k. livin productions
Janicek-Marino Creative
Jaret Entertainment
JCS Entertainment II
JTN Productions
Jupiter Entertainment
Jurist Productions
K2 Pictures, Inc.
Kahn Power Pictures
Kanpai Pictures
Kareem Productions
KCET
kdd Productions, LLC
KLS Communications, Inc.
Konwiser Brothers
Krainin Productions, Inc.
L.I.F.T. Productions
Lancaster Gate Entertainment
Langley Productions
LaSalleHolland
Last Straw Productions
The Late Bloomer Company, Ltd.
Latin Hollywood Films
Latitude Television LLC
Launa Newman Productions (LNP)
Andrew Lauren Productions
LeFrak Productions
Malcolm Leo Productions
Linkletter/Kritzer
Lion Television U.S.
Lionsgate
Live Animals
LivePlanet
LMNO Productions
Lonetree Entertainment

Documentaries (Continued)

Longbow Productions
L'Orange
Lucky Crow Films
Luminair Entertainment
The Tom Lynch Company
MacGillivray Freeman Films
Mainline Releasing
Mandalay Sports Action Entertainment & Mandalay Integrated Media Entertainment
Niki Marvin Productions, Inc.
Timothy Marx Productions, Inc.
Merchant-Ivory
Mike's Movies/Michael Peyser Productions
Miramax Films
Mission Entertainment
mod3productions
Mode of 8
Morningstar Entertainment
Motion Picture Production, Inc.
Moving Pictures, DPI
Moxie Firecracker Films
MPH Entertainment, Inc.
Mr. Mudd
MSNBC
MTV Networks Latin America (MTVNLA)
Murphy Boyz Productions
Muse Entertainment Enterprises
Muse Productions, Inc.
MWG Productions
Myriad Pictures
Nasser Entertainment Group
National Geographic Feature Films
NBC News
Neo Art & Logic
Next Wednesday
Norsemen Television Productions, LLC
North By Northwest Entertainment
NorthSouth Productions
O.N.C. Entertainment Inc.
Sam Okun Productions, Inc.
Old Dime Box Productions, Inc.
Olmos Productions, Inc.
One Step Productions
Open Road Films
Orchard Films
George Paige Associates, Inc.
Palomar Pictures
Paradigm Studio
Parkway Productions
Participant Productions
Paulist Productions
Daniel L. Paulson Productions
PBS
Peace Arch Entertainment Group Inc.
Periscope Entertainment, LLC
Perry Films
The Todd Phillips Company
Pie Town Productions
Pilgrim Films & Television, Inc.
Pink Sneakers Productions
Plan B Entertainment
Planet Grande Pictures
Playboy Entertainment Group, Inc.
Playtone Productions
Plum Pictures
Poetry & Pictures Inc.
Pollywog Entertainment, Inc
Paul Pompian Productions, Inc.
Popular Arts Entertainment, Inc.
Port Magee Pictures, Inc.
Pretty Matches Productions
Prometheus Entertainment
Prospect Pictures
QVF Inc.
Rafelson Media

Documentaries (Continued)

Rainstorm Entertainment, Inc.
Peggy Rajski Productions
Reason Pictures
Red Om Films, Inc.
REGAN
Tim Reid Productions, Inc.
Reveille, LLC
Rhino Films
Rive Gauche Entertainment
River Road Entertainment
Riverrock Entertainment Group
RKO Pictures, LLC
Rocket Science Laboratories
Rope The Moon Productions
Zvi Howard Rosenman Productions
Gay Rosenthal Productions
Rupert Productions, Inc.
S Pictures, Inc.
Alan Sacks Productions, Inc.
Sacred Dogs Entertainment, LLC
Saturn Films
Edward Saxon Productions (ESP)
Schwartz & Company, Inc.
Sci Fi Channel
Scott Free Productions
Scout Productions
SenArt Films
Seven Summits Pictures & Management
Shoot the Moon Productions
Shoreline Entertainment, Inc.
Showtime Networks Inc.
Sierra Club Productions
Sinovoi Entertainment
Sixth Way Productions
Slipnot! Productions/SPG
Snapdragon Films, Inc.
Solaris
Solo Entertainment Group
Sony BMG Feature Films
Spike TV
Spirit Horse Productions
Spitfire Pictures
Steamroller Productions, Inc.
Scott Sternberg Productions
The Stevens Company
Stick Figure Productions
Stone and Company Entertainment
Stoneworks Television
Storm Entertainment
Mel Stuart Productions, Inc.
StudioCanal (US)
Sundance Channel
Suntaur/Elsboy Entertainment
SUperFlnger Entertainment
Sweeney Entertainment
Synchronicity Productions
TAE Productions/Medeacom Productions
Taillight TV
Taylor Made Films
Grazka Taylor Productions
Teocalli Entertainment
This is that corporation
Thunderbird Pictures
Timeline Films
TLC
TMC Entertainment
Tollin/Robbins Productions
Tommy Boy Films
Trancas International Films
Travel Channel
Treasure Entertainment
Trezza Entertainment
Triage Entertainment
TriCoast Studios
Trigger Street Independent

Documentaries (Continued)

Trillion Entertainment, Inc.
Trillium Productions, Inc.
Turner Entertainment Group
Twilight Pictures, Inc.
Two Oceans Entertainment Group
Underground Films
Valhalla Motion Pictures
VanDerKloot Film & Television
Vanguard Productions
Vantage Enterprises, Inc.
Joseph S. Vecchio Entertainment
Versus
VH1
Visionbox Media Group
VOY Pictures
Vulcan Productions
Walker/Fitzgibbon TV/Films
Waltzing Clouds, Inc.
Warner Bros. Entertainment Inc.
Warren Miller Entertainment
Warrior Poets
Watershed Films
WE: Women's Entertainment
Weintraub/Kuhn Productions
Weller/Grossman Productions
Wheelhouse Entertainment
White Sneakers, Inc.
Whyaduck Productions, Inc.
Wildwell Films
WilMark Entertainment, Inc.
Winsome Productions
World of Wonder Productions
Xingu Films Ltd.
Zero Pictures
Zinkler Films
Frederick Zollo Productions, Inc.
Zuckerman Entertainment

Features

@radical.media
100% Entertainment
1492 Pictures
19 Entertainment, Inc.
21 Laps Entertainment
2929 Productions
3 Arts Entertainment, Inc.
3 Ring Circus Films
360 Pictures/FGM Entertainment
3n1 Entertainment
3Wolves Productions
40 Acres & A Mule Filmworks, Inc.
44 Blue Productions, Inc.
4th Row Films
57-T Productions, Inc.
6 Pictures
777 Entertainment Group, Ltd.
7ponies productions
The 7th Floor
8790 Pictures, Inc.
9.14 Pictures
900 Films
A Band Apart
A Wink and a Nod Productions
Aardman Animations
Abandon Pictures, Inc.
Aberration Films
Acappella Pictures
Act III Productions
Actual Reality Pictures
Ad Hominem Enterprises
Orly Adelson Productions
Adelstein Productions
Adirondack Pictures
AEI-Atchity Entertainment International, Inc.
Agamemnon Films, Inc.

Features (Continued)

Agua Films
Ahimsa Films
Alameda Films
Alchemy Entertainment
Alcon Entertainment, LLC
A-Line Pictures
Alliance Atlantis
Altitude Entertainment
Alturas Films
AM Productions & Management
Ambush Entertainment
American Blackguard, Inc.
American Work
American Zoetrope
Amicus Entertainment Limited
And Then Productions
Andell Entertainment
Craig Anderson Productions
Angelika
Angry Films, Inc.
Animus Films
Anonymous Creators Productions
Antidote International Films, Inc.
Apartment 3B Productions
Apatow Productions
Apostle
Appian Way
Apple & Honey Film Corp.
Appleseed Entertainment, LLC
Archer Entertainment
Mark Archer Entertainment
Ardustry Entertainment
Armada Pictures
Armagh Films, Inc.
Arramis Films
Ars Nova
Article 19 Films
The Artists' Colony
Artists Production Group (APG)
Artists, Inc.
Ascendant Pictures
Asgaard Entertainment
Asls Productions
Asylum Entertainment
The Asylum
Atlas Entertainment
Atman Entertainment
Atmosphere Entertainment MM, LLC
Automatic Pictures, Inc.
The AV Club
Avalanche! Entertainment
Avenue Pictures
aWounded Knee
The Axelrod/Edwards Company
Baby Cow Productions Ltd.
Back Lot Pictures
Bad Boy Films
Bad Hat Harry Productions
The Badham Company
Barnet Bain Films
John Baldecchi Productions
Baldwin Entertainment Group, Ltd.
Ballyhoo, Inc.
Bang Zoom! Entertainment
Bankable Productions
Banyan Tree Films
Alan Barnette Productions
Barnholtz Entertainment
Barnstorm Films
Barwood Films
Bates Entertainment
Battle Plan Productions
The Bauer Company
Bauer Martinez Entertainment
Carol Baum Productions

Features (Continued)

Suzanne Bauman Productions
Bay Films
Bayonne Entertainment
Bazmark, Inq.
BBC Films
BBC Worldwide Americas
Beacon
June Beallor Productions
The Bedford Falls Company
Beech Hill Films
Dave Bell Associates
Belladonna Productions
Lawrence Bender Productions
Benderspink
Harve Bennett Productions
Berlanti Productions
Rick Berman Productions
BET Networks
Big Beach
Big Light Productions
Big Pix Inc.
Bigel Entertainment
Black & White Productions
Black Folk Entertainment
Black Sheep Entertainment
Blackfriars Bridge
Bleiberg Entertainment
BloodWorks, LLC
Blossom Films
Blue Bay Productions
Blue Print
Blue Rider Pictures
Blue Sky Studios
Blue Star Pictures
Blue Tulip Productions
Bluebird House
Blueline Productions
Blueprint Films
Blumhouse Productions
Bobker/Kruger Films
Bodega Bay Productions, Inc.
Bogner Entertainment, Inc.
Boku Films
Bold Films
Bona Fide Productions
Boneyard Entertainment
Bonne Pioche
Boxx Communications, LLC
Boz Productions
David Brady Productions
Braga Productions
Brainstorm Media
Brancato/Salke Productions
Brandman Productions
Braun Entertainment Group, Inc.
David Braun Productions
Brave New Films
Braverman Productions, Inc.
Bravo
Paulette Breen Productions
The Bregman Entertainment Group
Bregman Productions
The Bremer Goff Company
Bridge Films, LLC
Brightlight Pictures, Inc.
Brillstein-Grey Entertainment
John Brister Films
Bristol Bay Productions
British Lion
Broad Strokes Entertainment
Broadway Video
Broadway Video Entertainment
Broken Lizard Industries
Broken Road Productions
Brooklyn Films

Features (Continued)

Brooklyn Media
Brooksfilms Limited
Brookwell McNamara Entertainment, Inc.
Bonnie Bruckheimer Productions
Jerry Bruckheimer Films & Television
The Bubble Factory
Buckaroo Entertainment
Buena Vista Motion Pictures Group
Bull's Eye Entertainment
Bungalow 78 Productions
Bunim/Murray Productions, Inc.
Burleigh Filmworks
Burnside Entertainment, Inc.
Burnt Orange Productions
Burrud Productions
Tim Burton Productions
Busboy Productions
Butchers Run Films
Byrum Power & Light
C2 Pictures
Cafe Productions
Cairo/Simpson Entertainment, Inc.
Caldera/De Fanti Entertainment
Callahan Filmworks
John Calley Productions
Camden Pictures
Camelot Entertainment Group, Inc.
Camelot Pictures
Colleen Camp Productions
Canary Films
Cannell Studios
Reuben Cannon Productions
Capital Arts Entertainment
Anne Carlucci Productions
Carrie Productions, Inc.
Carsey-Werner Films
Carson Signature Films, Inc.
The Thomas Carter Company
Cartoon Network
Castle Rock Entertainment
CastleBright Studios
Cataland Films
Catapult Films
CatchLight Films
Cates/Doty Productions
Catfish Productions
Cattleya
Cecchi Gori Pictures
Centropolis Entertainment
CFP Productions
Stokely Chaffin Productions
Chanticleer Films
Charlotte Street Films
Chartoff Productions
Cherry Road Films, LLC
Cheyenne Enterprises
Chicagofilms
Chick Flicks
China Film Group
Chiodo Bros. Productions, Inc.
Chotzen/Jenner Productions
Chris/Rose Productions
ChubbCo Film Co.
Cider Mill Productions
Cine Mosaic
CineCity Pictures
CinéGroupe
Cinema 21 Group
Cinema Libre Studio
Cinema Seven Productions
CineMagic Entertainment
CineSon Productions Inc.
Cinetic
Cineville LLC
Circle of Confusion Productions

Features (Continued)

City Entertainment
City Lights Media Group
Civilian Pictures
CJ Entertainment America
Clarity Pictures, LLC
Class 5 Films
Clear Pictures Entertainment Inc.
Patricia Clifford Productions
Cobblestone Films
Code Entertainment
Colebrook Road, Inc.
The Collective
The Colleton Company
Colomby Films
Colossal Entertainment
Columbia Pictures
Comic Book Movies, LLC/Branded Entertainment/Batfilm Productions
Completion Films
Concept Entertainment
Concorde-New Horizons
Concrete Entertainment
Concrete Pictures
Constantin Film Development, Inc./Constantin TV
ContentFilm
Contrafilm
Conundrum Entertainment
Cooper's Town Productions
Coquette Productions
The Core
Cornice Entertainment
Robert Cort Productions
Cosgrove-Meurer Productions
Cindy Cowan Entertainment, Inc.
Craftsman Films
Crane Wexelblatt Entertainment
Crave Films
Craven/Maddalena Films
CrazyDreams Entertainment
Creanspeak Productions LLC
Creative Capers Entertainment
Creative Coalition
Creative Impulse Entertainment
Creature Entertainment
Crossroads Films
Crystal Lake Entertainment, Inc.
Crystal Sky Pictures, LLC
Crystal Spring Productions, Inc.
Cube Vision
Curb Entertainment
Curious Pictures
Current Entertainment
C/W Productions
Cyan Pictures
Cypress Films, Inc.
Dakota North Entertainment/Dakota Films
The Sean Daniel Company
Lee Daniels Entertainment
Danjaq, LLC
Dark Horse Entertainment
Dark Trick Films
Darkwoods Productions
Alan David Management
Davis Entertainment Company
Daybreak Productions
DC Comics
Dino De Laurentiis Company
De Line Pictures
Michael De Luca Productions
de Passe Entertainment
Deacon Entertainment
Deep River Productions
Deja View Productions Ltd.
Departure Studios
Destiny Pictures

Features (Continued)

Detour
Deutsch/Open City Films
DFZ Productions
di Bonaventura Pictures, Inc.
Di Novi Pictures
Louis DiGiaimo & Associates, Ltd.
Digital Domain, Inc.
Dimension Films
The Walt Disney Company
DisneyToon Studios
DNA Films
Dominant Pictures
Donaldson/Sanders Entertainment
The Donners' Company
Bonny Dore Productions
Chris Dorr Productions
Double Edge Entertainment
Double Feature Films
Double Nickel Entertainment
Jean Doumanian Productions
Jeff Dowd & Associates
Dream Entertainment, Inc.
DreamWorks Animation SKG
DreamWorks SKG
Dreyfuss/James Productions
Driven Entertainment
Duly Noted
E Entertainment, LLC
Ealing Studios
EARS XXI
Earthworks Films
East of Doheny/Lexington Road Productions
The Ebersole-Hughes Company
Echelon Entertainment World Distribution & Prod.
Echo Lake Productions
Abra Edelman Productions
The Edelstein Company
Eden Rock Media, Inc.
EDKO Films Ltd.
Edmonds Entertainment
Rona Edwards Productions/ES Entertainment
Eighth Square Entertainment
El Dorado Pictures
El Norte Productions
Electric Entertainment
Element Films
Elevation Filmworks
Elixir Films
Elkins Entertainment
Embassy Row LLC
Ember Entertainment Group
Emerald City Productions, Inc.
Emerging Pictures
Emmett/Furla Films
Empire Pictures Incorporated
Endgame Entertainment
Energy Entertainment
Ensemble Entertainment
Enteraktion Studios
entitled entertainment
EntPro, Inc.
Epic Level Entertainment, Ltd.
Epidemic Pictures & Management
Epigram Entertainment
Epiphany Pictures, Inc.
Stefanie Epstein Productions
Escape Artists II
Esparza-Katz Productions
Esperanto Films
Eternity Pictures, Inc.
Euphoria Entertainment
EuropaCorp Films
The Robert Evans Company
Everyman Pictures
Evolution Entertainment

Features (Continued)

Evolving Pictures Entertainment
Exile Entertainment
Exxcell Entertainment, Inc./Exxcell Films
Eye in the Sky Entertainment
Eye on the Ball Films, Inc.
Face Productions/Jennilind Productions
Fade In Films
Fair Dinkum Productions
Fallout
Farrell Paura Productions, LLC
Farrell/Minoff Productions
The Phil Fehrle Company
The Feldman Company
Edward S. Feldman Company
Zachary Feuer Films
Adam Fields Productions
Fierce Entertainment, LLC
Fifty Cannon Entertainment, LLC
Filbert Steps Productions
Film & Music Entertainment, Ltd. (F&ME)
Film 44
Film Bridge International
Film Crash
The Film Department
Film Farm
Film Roman, Inc.
FilmColony
FilmEngine
FilmFour
Films By Jove
Filmsmith
Filmstreet, Inc.
Wendy Finerman Productions
Firebrand Productions
Firm Films
First Look Pictures
Fisher Productions
Five Sisters Productions
Flame Ventures LLC
Flashpoint Entertainment
Flavor Unit Entertainment
Flower Films, Inc.
Flying A Studios, Inc.
Focus Features/Rogue Pictures
Foothill Entertainment, Inc.
Bonnie Forbes Productions
Foremost Films
Forensic Films, Inc.
Foresight Unlimited
Forest Park Pictures
Fort Hill Productions
Fortis Films
Fortress Entertainment
Forward Entertainment
Forward Pass, Inc.
David Foster Productions
Foundation Entertainment
Four Boys Films
Fox Atomic
The Foxboro Company, Inc.
FR Productions
Frazier | Chipman Entertainment
Jack Freedman Productions
Joel Freeman Productions, Inc.
Frelaine
Fresh Paint
Fresh Produce Films
Fried Films
Daniel Fried Productions
Chuck Fries Productions, Inc.
Front Street Pictures, Inc.
Fuller Films, Inc.
Funny Boy Films
Furst Films
Furthur Films

Features (Continued)

Fuse Entertainment
Gallant Entertainment
Gambit Pictures
Garlin Pictures, Inc.
Generate
Generation Entertainment
Genrebend Productions, Inc.
Gerber Pictures
Ghost House Pictures
Ghost Robot
Gigantic Pictures
Gillen & Price
Roger Gimbel Productions, Inc.
Ginty Films International
Giraffe Productions
Gittes, Inc.
Glatzer Productions
Go Girl Media
Go Go Luckey Productions
The Goatsingers
Goepp Circle Productions
Goff-Kellam Productions
Frederic Golchan Productions
Gold Circle Films
Goldcrest Films International, Inc.
Goldenring Productions
The Goldstein Company
John Goldwyn Productions
Good Kop Films
The Goodman Company
The Mark Gordon Company
Dan Gordon Productions
Gordonstreet Pictures
Gorilla Pictures
Gotham Entertainment Group
The Gotham Group, Inc.
Gracie Films
Grade A Entertainment
Michael Grais Productions
Grammnet Productions
Gran Via Productions
Grand Productions, Inc.
Gray Angel Productions
Graymark Productions Inc.
Greasy Entertainment
Sarah Green Film Corp.
GreeneStreet Films
Robert Greenwald Productions
The Greif Company
Greystone Television and Films
Merv Griffin Entertainment
Nick Grillo Productions
Grisham Films USA
Dan Grodnik Productions
Gross Entertainment
Ken Gross Management
Beth Grossbard Productions
Grossbart Kent Productions
Grosso Jacobson Communications Corp.
Gross-Weston Productions
Groundswell Production
The Group Entertainment
Gryphon Films
Guardian Entertainment, Ltd.
G-Unit Television & Films
Gunn Films
Guy Walks Into a Bar
H. Beale Company
H2F Entertainment
H2O Motion Pictures
Haft Entertainment
Half Shell Entertainment
Hand Picked Films
Handprint Entertainment
Peter Hankwitz Production & Management

Features (Continued)

Harbor Lights Productions
Harding & Associates
Harding-Kurtz Entertainment
Harms Way Productions
Harpo Films, Inc.
The Harris Company
Hart Sharp Entertainment, Inc.
The Hatchery
Hazy Mills Productions
HBO Films
HDNet Films
The Hecht Company
Heel & Toe Films
Hella Good Moving Pictures
Paul Heller Productions
Rosilyn Heller Productions
Hell's Kitchen Ltd.
Henderson Productions, Inc.
The Jim Henson Company
here! Networks
Josselyne Herman & Assoc./Moving Image Films
Heyday Films
Bryan Hickox Pictures, Inc.
High Horse Films
Highway 9 Films
S. Hirsch Company, Inc./Seemore Films
HIT Entertainment
Hock Films, Inc.
Gary Hoffman Productions
Jason Hoffs Productions
Hollywood Gang Productions, LLC
Hopscotch Pictures
HorsePower Entertainment
Humble Journey Films
Peter Hyams Productions, Inc.
Hyde Park Entertainment
Hyperion Studio
Hypnotic
I.E. Productions, Inc.
Icon Productions, LLC
The Idea Factory
Ideal Entertainment, Inc.
Identity Films
IDT Entertainment
IFM Film Associates, Inc.
ImageMovers
Imageries Entertainment
Imagi Services (USA)
Imaginarium Entertainment Group
Imagination Productions, Inc.
Imagine Entertainment
IMAX Corporation
Impact Pictures
In Cahoots
Incognito Entertainment
The Independent Film Channel (IFC)
InDigEnt
Industry Entertainment Partners
Infinitum Nihil
Infinity Features Entertainment
Infinity Media, Inc.
Infront Productions
Initial Entertainment Group
Integrated Films & Management
Intermedia Film Equities USA, Inc.
International Arts Entertainment
International Television Group (ITG) - Epix Films
Interscope/Shady/Aftermath Films
Intrepid Pictures
Intuition Productions
InVenture Entertainment
Invitation Entertainment
Iridium Entertainment
Irish DreamTime
Ironworks Production

Features (Continued)

ISBE Productions
Ithaka
Ixtlan
j.k. livin productions
J2 Pictures/J2TV
Jack Angel Productions Inc.
Tom Jacobson Productions
Jaffilms, LLC
Janicek-Marino Creative
January Films
Janus Films, LLC
Jaret Entertainment
Melinda Jason Company
JBE Productions
Jeff Wald Entertainment
Jersey Films
The Jinks/Cohen Company
Joada Productions, Inc.
Joel Films
John Fogel Entertainment Group
Johnenelly Productions
Bridget Johnson Films
Don Johnson Productions
Tony Jonas Productions
Josephson Entertainment
JPH Productions
JT Entertainment
Judge-Belshaw Entertainment, Inc.
Junction Entertainment
Junction Films
Jurist Productions
Just Singer Entertainment
Kadokawa Pictures USA
Kahn Power Pictures
Kanpai Pictures
Kaplan/Perrone Entertainment, LLC
Kareem Productions
Marty Katz Productions
Jon Katzman Productions
The Kaufman Company
kdd Productions, LLC
Keckins Projects, Ltd.
Keller Entertainment Group
David E. Kelley Productions
The Kennedy/Marshall Company
Kenneth Johnson Productions
Kenwright USA/Bill Kenwright Ltd.
Diana Kerew Productions
The Kerner Entertainment Company
Ketcham Films
Key Creatives, LLC
KeyLight Entertainment Group
Keystone Entertainment, Inc.
Killer Films, Inc.
Sidney Kimmel Entertainment
Kinetic Filmworks
Kinetic Pictures
Kintop Pictures
David Kirschner Productions
Sam Kitt/Future Films
Klasky Csupo, Inc.
KLS Communications, Inc.
The Konigsberg-Smith Company
Konwiser Brothers
Kopelson Entertainment
Robert Kosberg Productions
Krainin Productions, Inc.
The Jonathan Krane Group
Krasnoff Foster Productions
Sid & Marty Krofft Pictures Corporation
Fred Kuehnert Productions
Kurtzman/Orci
The Kushner-Locke Company
L.I.F.T. Productions
The Ladd Company

Features (Continued)

David Ladd Films
Laika Entertainment
Lakeshore Entertainment Group LLC
Lancaster Gate Entertainment
David Lancaster Productions
Lance Entertainment, Inc.
The Landsburg Company
Landscape Entertainment
Liz Selzer Lang Productions
Langley Productions
Larco Productions, Inc.
Larger Than Life Productions
Larkin-Goldstein Production
LaSalleHolland
Rick Lashbrook Films
Last Straw Productions
The Late Bloomer Company, Ltd.
Latham Entertainment
Latin Hollywood Films
Latitude Television LLC
Laugh Factory Entertainment
Launchpad Productions
Andrew Lauren Productions
Robert Lawrence Productions
LeFrak Productions
Legendary Pictures
Arnold Leibovit Entertainment
The Jerry Leider Company
Leisure Time Enterprises
Lemon Sky Productions, Inc.
Malcolm Leo Productions
Letnom Productions
Level 1 Entertainment
Zane W. Levitt Productions/Zeta Entertainment
Licht Entertainment Corporation
Liddell Entertainment
Barbara Lieberman Productions
The Hal Lieberman Company
Light Renegade Entertainment, Inc.
Lighthouse Entertainment
Lighthouse Productions
Lightstone Entertainment, Inc.
Lightstorm Entertainment
Linkletter/Kritzer
Lion Eyes Entertainment
Lion Rock Productions
Lionsgate
George Litto Productions, Inc.
LivePlanet
LJ Film
Lloyd Entertainment
Mike Lobell Productions
Peter Locke Productions
Londine Productions
Lone Star Film Group
Lonetree Entertainment
Longbow Productions
Longfellow Pictures
L'Orange
Lynn Loring Productions
Lotus Pictures
Love Spell Entertainment
Lucasfilm Ltd.
Lucid Pictures
Lucky Crow Films
Luminair Entertainment
Luminous Entertainment
Luna Ray Films
Lunaria Films
Dan Lupovitz Productions
A.C. Lyles Productions, Inc.
The Tom Lynch Company
Macari/Edelstein Films
Macedon Media, Inc.
Macgowan Films

Features (Continued)

Mad Chance
Madhouse Entertainment
Madison Road Entertainment
Guy Magar Films
Magic Light Pictures
Magnet Management
Magnetic Film
Michael Mailer Films
Main Line Pictures
Mainline Releasing
MakeMagic Productions
Maloof Productions
Malpaso Productions
Managed Passion Films
Management 360
Mandalay Pictures
Mandalay Sports Action Entertainment & Mandalay Integrated Media Entertainment
Mandate Pictures
Mandeville Films
Mandoki Productions, Inc.
Mandy Films
Mango Tree Pictures
The Manhattan Project, Ltd.
The Manheim Company
Manifest Film Company
ManifestoVision
James Manos Productions, Inc.
Maple Shade Films
Laurence Mark Productions
The Marshak/Zachary Company
Martin Chase Productions
Marvel Studios, Inc.
Niki Marvin Productions, Inc.
MarVista Entertainment
Timothy Marx Productions, Inc.
Mase/Kaplan Productions, Inc.
Matador Pictures
The Matthau Company, Inc.
Maverick Films
Maya Pictures
Mayhem Pictures
The Mayhem Project
MBST Entertainment, Inc.
Media 8 Entertainment
Media Financial International, LLC
Media Four
Media Talent Group
Medusa Film
Melee Entertainment
Bill Melendez Productions
Barry Mendel Productions
MERCER Film Group Inc.
Merchant-Ivory
Metro-Goldwyn-Mayer Studios, Inc. (MGM)
Patricia K. Meyer Productions
MGA Entertainment/MGA Entertainment Films
Michael Meltzer Productions
Terence Michael Productions, Inc.
Midnight Sun Pictures
Mike's Movies/Michael Peyser Productions
Millennium Films
Mindfire Entertainment
Mirage Enterprises
Miramax Films
Miranda Entertainment
The Mirisch Corporation
Misher Films
Renée Missel Productions
Mission Entertainment
MM Productions
MobiTV
Mobius International
mod3productions
Mode of 8

Features (Continued)

Mojo Films
Monster Productions
Montage Entertainment
The Montecito Picture Company
Moonstone Entertainment
Moore/Cramer Productions
Morgan Creek Productions
John Morrissey Productions
Jeff Morton Productions
Mosaic Media Group
Moshag Productions, Inc.
Motion Picture Corporation of America
Motion Picture Invest
Motor City Films
Moving Pictures, DPI
Mozark Productions
MPH Entertainment, Inc.
Mr. Mudd
MRB Productions, Inc.
MTV Films
Murphy Boyz Productions
Muse Entertainment Enterprises
Muse Productions, Inc.
Mutual Film Company
MWG Productions
Myriad Pictures
Nala Films
Namesake Entertainment
Nanas Entertainment
Nash Entertainment
National Geographic Feature Films
National Lampoon
NBC Universal Corporate
Neal Street Productions Ltd.
Neighbors Entertainment
Nelvana Communications, Inc.
Neo Art & Logic
Mace Neufeld Productions
NEU-MAN-FILMS, Inc.
New Amsterdam Entertainment, Inc.
New City Pictures, Inc.
New Concorde
New Crime Productions
New Deal Productions
New England Productions, Inc.
New Generation Films, Inc.
New Line Cinema
New Redemption Pictures
New Wave Entertainment
New Wave Management
Vincent Newman Entertainment
Peter Newman Productions, Inc.
Newmarket Capital Group
Next Wednesday
Nickelodeon Movies
Nickelodeon/MTVN Kids & Family Group
Nightstar Productions, Inc.
Nine Yards Entertainment
Nitelite Entertainment
Noble House Entertainment, Inc.
Norsemen Television Productions, LLC
North By Northwest Entertainment
Northstar Entertainment
Nova Pictures
Nuance Productions
Numenorean Films
Nuyorican
O Entertainment
O.N.C. Entertainment Inc.
Lynda Obst Productions
Ocean Pictures
Odd Lot Entertainment
Offspring Entertainment
Sam Okun Productions, Inc.
Old Dime Box Productions, Inc.

Features (Continued)

Old School Pictures, LLC
Lin Oliver Productions
Olmos Productions, Inc.
Omnibus
On Stilts Productions
Once A Frog Productions
Once Upon A Time Films, Ltd.
One Step Productions
One Voice Entertainment, Inc.
Open Road Films
Original Film
The Orphanage
Out of the Blue . . . Entertainment
Outerbanks Entertainment
Outlaw Productions
The Over the Hill Gang
Overbrook Entertainment
Oxygen Media
OZLA Pictures, Inc.
Pacifica International Film & TV Corporation
George Paige Associates, Inc.
Palomar Pictures
Panamax Films
Pandemonium
Pantheon Entertainment Corp.
Paradigm Studio
Paradox Productions, Inc.
Parallel Entertainment, Inc.
Paramount Pictures
Paramount Pictures Production Division
Paramount Vantage/Paramount Classics
Paraskevas Studios
Pariah
Park Ex Pictures
Parkchester Pictures
Parkway Productions
Participant Productions
Partizan
P.A.T. Productions
Patchett Kaufman Entertainment
Pathfinder Pictures, LLC
Patriot Pictures, LLC
Paulist Productions
Daniel L. Paulson Productions
PAYASO Entertainment
Peace Arch Entertainment Group Inc.
Pearl Pictures
Peculiar Films
Peirce Pictures
Penn Station Entertainment
Zak Penn's Company
Periscope Entertainment, LLC
Permut Presentations
Persistent Entertainment
Peters Entertainment
Daniel Petrie Jr. & Company
D. Petrie Productions, Inc.
Stephen Pevner, Inc.
Pfeffer Film
The Todd Phillips Company
Phoenix Pictures
Picturehouse
Pierce Williams Entertainment
Pilgrim Films & Television, Inc.
Piller/Segan
Pink Slip Pictures
Piranha Pictures, Inc.
The Pitt Group
Pixar Animation Studios
Plan B Entertainment
Platform Entertainment
Platinum Dunes
Platinum Studios, LLC
Marc Platt Productions
Playtime Productions

Features (Continued)

Playtone Productions
Plotpoint, Inc.
Plum Pictures
PLUS Entertainment, Inc.
Poetry & Pictures Inc.
Point Road, Inc.
Martin Poll Films, Ltd.
Pollywog Entertainment, Inc
The Polson Company
Paul Pompian Productions, Inc.
Poor Boys Productions
PorchLight Entertainment
Port Magee Pictures, Inc.
Potboiler Productions
P.O.V. Company
POW! Entertainment
Power Up
Practical Pictures
Edward R. Pressman Film Corporation
Pretty Dangerous Films
Pretty Matches Productions
Pretty Pictures
Primary Productions
Primetime Pictures
Principal Entertainment
Principato-Young Entertainment
Production Logistics, Inc.
Production Partners, Inc.
Prospect Pictures
Protozoa Pictures
Proud Mary Entertainment
Pterodactyl Productions Inc.
QED International
Quinta Communications USA
QVF Inc.
Qwerty Films
Radar Pictures
Radiant Productions
The Radmin Company
Rafelson Media
Raffaella Productions, Inc.
Rainbow Film Company/Rainbow Releasing
Rainforest Films
Rainstorm Entertainment, Inc.
Peggy Rajski Productions
Random House Films
Randwell Productions
Rat Entertainment/Rat TV
Raygun Productions
Reason Pictures
Recorded Picture Company
Red Bird Productions
Red Door Films/David Poulshock Productions, Inc.
Red Hen Productions
Red Hour Films
Red Om Films, Inc.
Red Strokes Entertainment
Red Wagon Entertainment
Marian Rees Associates
REGAN
Regency Enterprises
Regent
Tim Reid Productions, Inc.
Reiner/Greisman
Relativity Media LLC
Relevant Entertainment Group
Renaissance Pictures
Renfield Productions
Reveille, LLC
Revelations Entertainment
Revolution Studios
Reynolds Entertainment
Rhino Films
Rice & Beans Productions
Rive Gauche Entertainment

Features (Continued)

River One Films
River Road Entertainment
Riverrock Entertainment Group
RKO Pictures, LLC
Roberts/David Films, Inc.
Amy Robinson Productions
Rocket Entertainment
Rocket Science Laboratories
Rocklin Entertainment
Stan Rogow Productions
Phil Roman Entertainment
ROOM 101, Inc.
Room 9 Entertainment
Rope The Moon Productions
Alex Rose Productions, Inc.
Zvi Howard Rosenman Productions
Rosenzweig Films
Roserock Films
Roth/Arnold Productions
Rough Diamond Productions
Rough Draft Studios
Roundtable Entertainment
Ruby-Spears Productions
The Ruddy Morgan Organization, Inc./
Albert S. Ruddy Productions
Scott Rudin Productions
Runaway Productions
Rupert Productions, Inc.
S Pictures, Inc.
Sachs Judah Productions
Alan Sacks Productions, Inc.
Sacred Dogs Entertainment, LLC
Saltire Entertainment
Salty Features
Samoset, Inc./Sacret, Inc.
Samuel Goldwyn Films
Samuelson Productions Limited
Sandcastle 5 Productions
Sander/Moses Productions, Inc.
Sanford/Pillsbury Productions
Saphier Productions
Sarabande Productions
Arthur Sarkissian Productions
Saturn Films
Edward Saxon Productions (ESP)
Scarab Productions
Paul Schiff Productions
Scholastic Entertainment
Joel Schumacher Productions
Faye Schwab Productions/MMA, Inc.
Schwartz & Company, Inc.
Steven Schwartz Productions, Inc.
Sci Fi Channel
Scott Free Productions
Scout Productions
Screen Gems
SE8 Group
Seaside Productions
Seed Productions
Segue Productions, Inc.
SekretAgent Productions
Dylan Sellers Productions
SenArt Films
Senator Entertainment, Inc.
Senza Pictures
Seraphim Films
Serenade Films
Serendipity Point Films
Serendipity Productions, Inc.
Seven Arts Pictures
Seven Summits Pictures & Management
ShadowCatcher Entertainment
Shady Acres Entertainment
Jon Shestack Productions
Shoe Money Productions

Features (Continued)

Shoot the Moon Productions
Shoreline Entertainment, Inc.
Showtime Independent Films
Shukovsky English Entertainment
The Shuman Company
Shutt-Jones Productions
Sierra Club Productions
Signature Pictures
Silly Robin Productions
Silver Dream Productions
Silver Lion Films
Silver Nitrate Pictures
Silver Pictures
Casey Silver Productions
Silverline Entertainment, Inc.
Silvers/Koster Productions, Inc.
The Gene Simmons Company
Simmons/Lathan
The Robert Simonds Company
Simsie Films/Media Savant Pictures
Single Cell Pictures
Sinovoi Entertainment
Sirocco Media
Sitting Ducks Productions
Sixth Way Productions
Skylark Entertainment, Inc.
Skyline Pictures, LLC
Slipnot! Productions/SPG
Smart Entertainment
SMG Productions
Gary Smith Company
Smoke House
Snapdragon Films, Inc.
Sneak Preview Entertainment, Inc.
Snowfall Films/Windchill Films
Sobini Films
Solaris
Solo Entertainment Group
Solo One Productions
The Sommers Company
Sony BMG Feature Films
Sony Online Entertainment
Sony Pictures Animation
Sony Pictures Digital
Sony Pictures Entertainment
Sony Pictures Imageworks
South Productions, LLC
South Side Films
Southern Cross the Dog
Southern Skies, Inc.
Southpaw Entertainment
Sparky Pictures
Spice Factory
Spirit Horse Productions
Spitfire Pictures
Spring Creek Productions, Inc.
Spyglass Entertainment Group
St. Amos Productions
Stampede Entertainment
Star Entertainment Group, Inc.
Starbucks Entertainment
Darren Star Productions
Starry Night Entertainment
Jane Startz Productions, Inc.
State Street Pictures
Station 3
Steamroller Productions, Inc.
The Howard Stern Production Company
The Stevens Company
Joel Stevens Entertainment
Stick Figure Productions
Stone Village Pictures, LLC
Stone vs. Stone
Storm Entertainment
Story and Film, Inc.

Features (Continued)

Storyline Entertainment
Strike Entertainment
Mel Stuart Productions, Inc.
StudioCanal (US)
Studios International
Sub Rosa Productions, Inc.
Mike Sullivan Productions, Inc.
Summerland Entertainment
Summers Entertainment
Summit Entertainment
Sunlight Productions
Sunrise Entertainment
Sunset Canyon Productions
Sunswept Entertainment
Suntaur/Elsboy Entertainment
Superb Entertainment
SUperFInger Entertainment
Ronald Suppa Productions, Inc.
Sweeney Entertainment
Symbolic Entertainment
Symphony Pictures, Inc.
Synchronicity Productions
The Syndicate
TAE Productions/Medeacom Productions
Tag Entertainment, Inc.
Tagline Pictures
Martin Tahse Productions
Tailfish Productions
Talisman Pacific
Tannenbaum Company
Tapestry Films, Inc.
Taryn Productions
Taurus Entertainment Company
Taylor Made Films
Grazka Taylor Productions
Michael Taylor Productions
Team Todd
Teitelbaum Artists Group
Tempest Entertainment
Tempesta Films
Temple Hill Productions
Nancy Tenenbaum Films
Teocalli Entertainment
Terra Firma Films
This is that corporation
Larry Thompson Organization
Thousand Words
Three Strange Angels, Inc.
Threshold Entertainment
Thunder Road Pictures
Thunderbird Pictures
Tiara Blu Films
Tidewater Entertainment, Inc.
Tig Productions, Inc.
The Steve Tisch Company
TLC Entertainment
TOKYOPOP Inc.
Tollin/Robbins Productions
Tommy Boy Films
Tomorrow Film Corporation
Tooley Productions
Tornell Productions
Totem Productions
Tower of Babble Entertainment
Trancas International Films
Traveler's Rest Films
Treasure Entertainment
Tree Line Film
Trezza Entertainment
Tribeca Productions
TriCoast Studios
Tricor Entertainment
Tri-Elite Entertainment, Ltd.
Trigger Street Independent
Trillion Entertainment, Inc.

Features (Continued)

Trillium Productions, Inc.
Trilogy Entertainment Group
TriStar Pictures
Troma Entertainment, Inc.
Trunity, a Mediar Company, a Division of True Mediar, a Unity Corpbopoly
T-Squared Productions
Tudor Management Group
Tule River Films
The Turman Inc. Picture Company
TurtleBack Productions, Inc.
Norman Twain Productions
Twentieth Century Fox
Twentieth Century Fox - Fox 2000
Twentieth Century Fox - Searchlight Pictures
Twentieth Century Fox Animation
Twilight Pictures, Inc.
Two Oceans Entertainment Group
Two Sticks Productions
Type A Films
Ufland Productions
Underground Films
Union Entertainment
Union Square Entertainment
Universal Operations Group
Universal Pictures
Universal Studios
Unpainted Pictures
Untitled Entertainment
Urban Entertainment
Renée Valente Productions
Valhalla Motion Pictures
VanDerKloot Film & Television
Vanguard Films/Vanguard Animation
Vanguard Productions
Vantage Enterprises, Inc.
The Vault, Inc.
Joseph S. Vecchio Entertainment
Verdon-Cedric Productions
Versus
Vertigo Entertainment
Viacom Entertainment Group
Mark Victor Productions
View Askew Productions, Inc.
Village Roadshow Pictures
Dimitri Villard Productions
Visionbox Media Group
Viviano Feldman Entertainment
Jon Voight Entertainment
von Zerneck-Sertner Films
Vox3 Films
VOY Pictures
Vulcan Productions
Raymond Wagner Productions, Inc.
Walden Films
Walden Media
Walker/Fitzgibbon TV/Films
Waltzing Clouds, Inc.
Wardenclyffe Entertainment
Warner Bros. Animation
Warner Bros. Entertainment Inc.
Warner Bros. Pictures
Warner Independent Pictures
Warren Miller Entertainment
Warrior Poets
Watermark
Watershed Films
Jim Wedaa Productions
Weed Road Pictures
Weekend Films/Main Street Film Company
The Weinstein Company
Weinstock Productions
Jerry Weintraub Productions
Weintraub/Kuhn Productions
John Wells Productions

Features (Continued)

Clifford Werber Productions
Simon West Productions
Western Sandblast
Wheelhouse Entertainment
White Sneakers, Inc.
WhiteLight Entertainment
Whitewater Films
Whoop Inc./One Ho Prod./Lil' Whoop Prod.
Whyaduck Productions, Inc.
WideAwake, Inc.
Wigram Productions
Dan Wigutow Productions
Wild At Heart Films, LLC
WildRice Productions
Wildwell Films
Wildwood Enterprises, Inc.
WilMark Entertainment, Inc.
Brad Wilson Productions, Inc.
Wilson/Woods Productions
Wind Dancer Production Group
The Winer Company
WingNut Films Ltd.
Winkler Films
Winsome Productions
Stan Winston Productions
Ralph Winter Productions, Inc.
Witt-Thomas-Harris Productions
Wolf Films, Inc.
Fred Wolf Films
Wolfmill Entertainment
The Wolper Organization
WonderFilms
Wonderland Sound and Vision
The Woofenill Works, Inc.
Working Title Films
Workshop Pictures, Inc.
World Film Services, Inc.
World International Network
World of Wonder Productions
Worldwide Biggies
Worldwide Pants, Inc.
Norton Wright Productions
WWE Films
X Filme Creative Pool GmbH
Xingu Films Ltd.
Yari Film Group (YFG)
Mark Yellen Productions
Yellow Cab Pictures
Yorktown Productions, Ltd.
The Saul Zaentz Company
Zaloom Film
The Zanuck Company
Zemeckis/Nemeroff Films
Zentropa
Zephyr Films Ltd.
Zero Pictures
Zieger Productions
Zinkler Films
Laura Ziskin Productions
Ron Ziskin Productions, Inc.
Frederick Zollo Productions, Inc.
Zucker Productions
Zucker/Netter Productions
Zuckerman Entertainment

Internet Content

4th Row Films
A Band Apart
ABC Family
Actuality Productions
Alchemy Entertainment
Alturas Films
American Blackguard, Inc.
Amp'd Mobile
Anonymous Creators Productions

Internet Content (Continued)

AOL Media Networks
Arjay Entertainment
Avalanche! Entertainment
Barnholtz Entertainment
Bigel Entertainment
Broad Strokes Entertainment
Mark Burnett Productions
Cartoon Network
CinéGroupe
CineMagic Entertainment
Circle of Confusion Productions
City Entertainment
The Collective
Comedy Central
Cookie Jar Entertainment
Creative Capers Entertainment
CSM Communications
Disney Online
DIY Network
Donaldson/Sanders Entertainment
Bonny Dore Productions
EARS XXI
Electric Entertainment
Film Roman, Inc.
Flame Ventures LLC
Fox Atomic
Fox Mobile Entertainment
Fox Reality
FremantleMedia North America
Budd Friedman Digital
G4 TV
Generate
Google Inc.
The Gotham Group, Inc.
GSN
G-Unit Television & Films
Half Shell Entertainment
HBO Media Ventures
The Jim Henson Company
here! Networks
The History Channel
Homerun Entertainment, Inc.
IAC/InterActiveCorp
Imagination Productions, Inc.
Janicek-Marino Creative
JibJab Media Inc.
Klasky Csupo, Inc.
Robert Kosberg Productions
Latitude Television LLC
Linkletter/Kritzer
Londine Productions
L'Orange
M3 Television
Mandalay Sports Action Entertainment & Mandalay Integrated Media Entertainment
Merchant-Ivory
Mindfire Entertainment
Mode of 8
Mondo Media
The Mottola Company
MSN Originals
MTV Networks
MTV Networks Latin America (MTVNLA)
Murphy Boyz Productions
National Lampoon
New Wave Entertainment
Nitelite Entertainment
NorthSouth Productions
Oxygen Media
Paramount Digital Media Group
Pariah
Parkway Productions
P.A.T. Productions
Popular Arts Entertainment, Inc.
Precis Productions, Inc.

Internet Content (Continued)

Proteus
Q Media Partners
REGAN
Rice & Beans Productions
Rive Gauche Entertainment
Rocket Entertainment
Rupert Productions, Inc.
Sander/Moses Productions, Inc.
Sci Fi Channel
Screen Door Entertainment
Senza Pictures
SiTV
SlingShot Media
Smart Entertainment
SOAPnet
SUperFInger Entertainment
Symbolic Action
Treasure Entertainment
Triage Entertainment
Troma Entertainment, Inc.
TV Guide Channel
Joseph S. Vecchio Entertainment
Veoh Networks, Inc.
Versus
Warner Bros. Digital Distribution
Warner Bros. Online
Wild At Heart Films, LLC
Wild Brain, Inc.
Worldwide Biggies
WPT Enterprises, Inc.
Yahoo! Media Group/Yahoo! Studios
Zingy Inc.
Zinkler Films

Made-for-TV/Cable Movies

100% Entertainment
3 Ring Circus Films
4th Row Films
57-T Productions, Inc.
6 Pictures
A Wink and a Nod Productions
A&E Network
ABC Entertainment Television Group
ABC Family
Orly Adelson Productions
AEI-Atchity Entertainment International, Inc.
Agamemnon Films, Inc.
Agua Films
Alexander/Enright & Associates
Alliance Atlantis
Altitude Entertainment
AM Productions & Management
Ambush Entertainment
American Blackguard, Inc.
Amicus Entertainment Limited
Craig Anderson Productions
Angelika
Apple & Honey Film Corp.
Appleseed Entertainment, LLC
Archer Entertainment
Arlington Entertainment, Inc.
The Artists' Colony
Asls Productions
Atman Entertainment
Atmosphere Entertainment MM, LLC
Automatic Pictures, Inc.
Avenue Pictures
The Axelrod/Edwards Company
The Badham Company
Barnet Bain Films
John Baldecchi Productions
Bankable Productions
Alan Barnette Productions
Barnholtz Entertainment
Barnstorm Films

Made-for-TV/Cable Movies (Continued)

Barracuda Productions
Barwood Films
Bates Entertainment
The Bauer Company
Carol Baum Productions
Bayonne Entertainment
BBC Worldwide Americas
June Beallor Productions
Dave Bell Associates
Harve Bennett Productions
BET Networks
Big Pix Inc.
BLT Productions Ltd.
Blue Rider Pictures
Blue Star Pictures
Blue Tulip Productions
Bluebird House
Blueline Productions
Blueprint Entertainment
Bogner Entertainment, Inc.
Boneyard Entertainment
Boxx Communications, LLC
David Brady Productions
Braga Productions
Brainstorm Media
Brandman Productions
Braun Entertainment Group, Inc.
David Braun Productions
Brave New Films
Bravo
Paulette Breen Productions
The Bregman Entertainment Group
The Bremer Goff Company
Brightlight Pictures, Inc.
John Brister Films
British Lion
Broad Strokes Entertainment
Brooklyn Films
Brookwell McNamara Entertainment, Inc.
Bonnie Bruckheimer Productions
Bunim/Murray Productions, Inc.
Burleigh Filmworks
Bushwacker Productions
C2 Pictures
Cafe Productions
Cairo/Simpson Entertainment, Inc.
Caldera/De Fanti Entertainment
Camelot Entertainment Group, Inc.
Camelot Pictures
Reuben Cannon Productions
Maj Canton Productions
Capital Arts Entertainment
Anne Carlucci Productions
Carson Signature Films, Inc.
The Thomas Carter Company
Catapult Films
Catfish Productions
CBS Entertainment
CBS Paramount Network Television
Chanticleer Films
Charlotte Street Films
Chartoff Productions
Chic Productions
Chick Flicks
Chiodo Bros. Productions, Inc.
Chotzen/Jenner Productions
Chris/Rose Productions
ChubbCo Film Co.
CinéGroupe
CineMagic Entertainment
City Entertainment
City Lights Media Group
Clarity Pictures, LLC
dick clark productions, inc.
Clear Pictures Entertainment Inc.

Made-for-TV/Cable Movies (Continued)

Patricia Clifford Productions
CMT: Country Music Television
Cobblestone Films
The Collective
The Colleton Company
Colomby Films
Colossal Entertainment
Completion Films
Con Artists Productions
Concept Entertainment
Robert Cort Productions
Corymore Entertainment
Cosgrove-Meurer Productions
Court TV Networks
Crane Wexelblatt Entertainment
Craven/Maddalena Films
CrazyDreams Entertainment
Creanspeak Productions LLC
Creative Impulse Entertainment
CRPI Entertainment
Crystal Spring Productions, Inc.
CSM Communications
Curious Pictures
Cypress Point Productions
Dakota North Entertainment/Dakota Films
The Sean Daniel Company
Davis Entertainment Company
de Passe Entertainment
Deja View Productions Ltd.
Destiny Pictures
Louis DiGiaimo & Associates, Ltd.
Disney ABC Cable Networks Group
Donaldson/Sanders Entertainment
Bonny Dore Productions
Chris Dorr Productions
Double Nickel Entertainment
Jean Doumanian Productions
Dreyfuss/James Productions
Duly Noted
E Entertainment, LLC
The Ebersole-Hughes Company
Echo Lake Productions
Abra Edelman Productions
The Edelstein Company
Rona Edwards Productions/ES Entertainment
Eighth Square Entertainment
El Dorado Pictures
Electric Entertainment
Elkins Entertainment
Emerging Pictures
Empire Pictures Incorporated
Endgame Entertainment
Ensemble Entertainment
EntPro, Inc.
Epic Level Entertainment, Ltd.
Epigram Entertainment
Epiphany Pictures, Inc.
Stefanie Epstein Productions
Esparza-Katz Productions
Euphoria Entertainment
Evolution
Exxcell Entertainment, Inc./Exxcell Films
Face Productions/Jennilind Productions
Farrell/Minoff Productions
The Phil Fehrle Company
The Feldman Company
Zachary Feuer Films
Fierce Entertainment, LLC
Film Bridge International
Film Roman, Inc.
FilmColony
Filmstreet, Inc.
Wendy Finerman Productions
Firebrand Productions
Firm Television

Made-for-TV/Cable Movies (Continued)

Preston Stephen Fischer Company
Fisher Productions
Five Mile River Films, Ltd.
Flame Ventures LLC
Flying A Studios, Inc.
Foothill Entertainment, Inc.
Bonnie Forbes Productions
Fortress Entertainment
Four Boys Films
Fox Television Studios
The Foxboro Company, Inc.
Frazier | Chipman Entertainment
Jack Freedman Productions
Joel Freeman Productions, Inc.
Fresh Produce Films
Daniel Fried Productions
Chuck Fries Productions, Inc.
Front Street Pictures, Inc.
Furst Films
FX
Galán Entertainment
Gallant Entertainment
Garlin Pictures, Inc.
Generate
Genrebend Productions, Inc.
Gerber Pictures
Leeza Gibbons Enterprises (LGE)
Roger Gimbel Productions, Inc.
Ginty Films International
Go Girl Media
Go Go Luckey Productions
Goldcrest Films International, Inc.
Goldenring Productions
John Goldwyn Productions
Good Game
The Mark Gordon Company
Gordonstreet Pictures
Gotham Entertainment Group
The Gotham Group, Inc.
Grade A Entertainment
Michael Grais Productions
Granada America
Grand Productions, Inc.
GRB Entertainment
Robert Greenwald Productions
Greenwood Avenue Entertainment
The Greif Company
Merv Griffin Entertainment
Nick Grillo Productions
Grisham Films USA
Dan Grodnik Productions
Ken Gross Management
Beth Grossbard Productions
Grosso Jacobson Communications Corp.
Gross-Weston Productions
Guardian Entertainment, Ltd.
H. Beale Company
Haft Entertainment
Hallmark Hall of Fame Productions, Inc.
Hand Picked Films
Harbor Lights Productions
Harding-Kurtz Entertainment
Harpo Films, Inc.
The Harris Company
Hart Sharp Entertainment, Inc.
The Hatchery
Hazy Mills Productions
HBO Films
The Hecht Company
Paul Heller Productions
Rosilyn Heller Productions
The Jim Henson Company
here! Networks
Josselyne Herman & Assoc./Moving Image Films
Bryan Hickox Pictures, Inc.

Made-for-TV/Cable Movies (Continued)

HIT Entertainment
Gary Hoffman Productions
Hopscotch Pictures
Humble Journey Films
Hyperion Studio
I.E. Productions, Inc.
The Idea Factory
IFM Film Associates, Inc.
Imageries Entertainment
Imagination Productions, Inc.
The Independent Film Channel (IFC)
Integrated Films & Management
Intuition Productions
ISBE Productions
Ishtar Films
Ithaka
Jack Angel Productions Inc.
Jackhole Industries
Jaffe/Braunstein Films, LLC
Melinda Jason Company
JBE Productions
JCS Entertainment II
Joada Productions, Inc.
Johnenelly Productions
Bridget Johnson Films
JPH Productions
JTN Productions
Jurist Productions
Just Singer Entertainment
Kahn Power Pictures
Jon Katzman Productions
The Kaufman Company
KCET
kdd Productions, LLC
Keckins Projects, Ltd.
Keep Clear
Keller Entertainment Group
Kenneth Johnson Productions
Diana Kerew Productions
Ketcham Films
Kinetic Pictures
David Kirschner Productions
Sam Kitt/Future Films
KLS Communications, Inc.
The Konigsberg-Smith Company
Konwiser Brothers
Kopelson Entertainment
Robert Kosberg Productions
Krainin Productions, Inc.
L.I.F.T. Productions
Lancaster Gate Entertainment
Lance Entertainment, Inc.
Landscape Entertainment
Liz Selzer Lang Productions
Larkin-Goldstein Production
Last Straw Productions
The Late Bloomer Company, Ltd.
Latitude Television LLC
Laugh Factory Entertainment
LeFrak Productions
The Jerry Leider Company
Leisure Time Enterprises
The Levinson/Fontana Company
Licht Entertainment Corporation
Barbara Lieberman Productions
Lifetime Television (Los Angeles)
Lifetime Television (New York)
Lighthouse Entertainment
Linkletter/Kritzer
Lion Television U.S.
Lionsgate
LivePlanet
Peter Locke Productions
Londine Productions
Lonetree Entertainment

Made-for-TV/Cable Movies (Continued)

Longbow Productions
Lynn Loring Productions
Lotus Pictures
Lucky Crow Films
Luna Ray Films
Lunaria Films
Dan Lupovitz Productions
The Tom Lynch Company
Macedon Media, Inc.
Guy Magar Films
Michael Mailer Films
Mainline Releasing
Managed Passion Films
Mandalay Pictures
Mandalay Sports Action Entertainment & Mandalay Integrated Media Entertainment
Mandy Films
Mango Tree Pictures
The Manhattan Project, Ltd.
The Manheim Company
Manifest Film Company
James Manos Productions, Inc.
The Marshak/Zachary Company
Martin Chase Productions
Niki Marvin Productions, Inc.
MarVista Entertainment
Timothy Marx Productions, Inc.
Mase/Kaplan Productions, Inc.
The Matthau Company, Inc.
Maverick Films
Maya Pictures
Media Four
MERCER Film Group Inc.
Merchant-Ivory
Metro-Goldwyn-Mayer Studios, Inc. (MGM)
Patricia K. Meyer Productions
Michael Meltzer Productions
Terence Michael Productions, Inc.
Mindfire Entertainment
The Mirisch Corporation
Moore/Cramer Productions
John Morrissey Productions
Jeff Morton Productions
Motion Picture Corporation of America
Motion Picture Production, Inc.
Moving Pictures, DPI
MPH Entertainment, Inc.
MTV Networks
Murphy Boyz Productions
Muse Entertainment Enterprises
MWG Productions
Myriad Pictures
Namesake Entertainment
Nanas Entertainment
Nash Entertainment
Nasser Entertainment Group
National Geographic Feature Films
National Lampoon
NBC Entertainment
NBC Universal Television Studio
Neighbors Entertainment
Mace Neufeld Productions
NEU-MAN-FILMS, Inc.
New Amsterdam Entertainment, Inc.
New City Pictures, Inc.
New Concorde
New England Productions, Inc.
New Line Cinema
New Line Television
New Redemption Pictures
New Wave Entertainment
Nightstar Productions, Inc.
Nine Yards Entertainment
Nitelite Entertainment
Noble House Entertainment, Inc.

Made-for-TV/Cable Movies (Continued)

Norsemen Television Productions, LLC
North By Northwest Entertainment
Nova Pictures
Nuance Productions
Numenorean Films
O Entertainment
O.N.C. Entertainment Inc.
Lynda Obst Productions
Sam Okun Productions, Inc.
Old Dime Box Productions, Inc.
Old School Pictures, LLC
Lin Oliver Productions
Olmos Productions, Inc.
Omnibus
On Stilts Productions
Once A Frog Productions
Once Upon A Time Films, Ltd.
One Step Productions
The Orphanage
The Over the Hill Gang
Oxygen Media
George Paige Associates, Inc.
Pantheon Entertainment Corp.
Park Ex Pictures
Patchett Kaufman Entertainment
Paulist Productions
Daniel L. Paulson Productions
PAYASO Entertainment
Peace Arch Entertainment Group Inc.
Persistent Entertainment
Daniel Petrie Jr. & Company
D. Petrie Productions, Inc.
Phoenix Pictures
Piller/Segan
Piranha Pictures, Inc.
The Pitt Group
Plan B Entertainment
Marc Platt Productions
PLUS Entertainment, Inc.
Martin Poll Films, Ltd.
The Polson Company
Paul Pompian Productions, Inc.
Poor Boys Productions
PorchLight Entertainment
Port Magee Pictures, Inc.
P.O.V. Company
POW! Entertainment
Pretty Matches Productions
Primetime Pictures
Program Partners
Prometheus Entertainment
Proud Mary Entertainment
Q Media Partners
QVF Inc.
Radiant Productions
Rafelson Media
Raffaella Productions, Inc.
Randwell Productions
Red Hen Productions
Red Om Films, Inc.
Marian Rees Associates
REGAN
Regent
Revelations Entertainment
Reynolds Entertainment
RHI Entertainment
Rice & Beans Productions
Rive Gauche Entertainment
River One Films
RKO Pictures, LLC
Rocket Science Laboratories
Stan Rogow Productions
Rope The Moon Productions
Rosemont Productions International, Ltd.
Zvi Howard Rosenman Productions

Made-for-TV/Cable Movies (Continued)

Rosenzweig Films
S Pictures, Inc.
Alan Sacks Productions, Inc.
Sacred Dogs Entertainment, LLC
Samoset, Inc./Sacret, Inc.
Sander/Moses Productions, Inc.
Sanford/Pillsbury Productions
Sanitsky Company
Sarabande Productions
Edward Saxon Productions (ESP)
Faye Schwab Productions/MMA, Inc.
Schwartz & Company, Inc.
Sci Fi Channel
Scott Free Productions
Serendipity Productions, Inc.
Seven Summits Pictures & Management
ShadowCatcher Entertainment
Shore View Entertainment
Shoreline Entertainment, Inc.
Showtime Networks Inc.
Silver Lion Films
Silverline Entertainment, Inc.
Silvers/Koster Productions, Inc.
Simsie Films/Media Savant Pictures
Sinovoi Entertainment
Sitting Ducks Productions
Skylark Entertainment, Inc.
Skyline Pictures, LLC
Slipnot! Productions/SPG
Smart Entertainment
SMG Productions
Gary Smith Company
Snapdragon Films, Inc.
Sneak Preview Entertainment, Inc.
Snowfall Films/Windchill Films
Solo One Productions
Sony Pictures Television
South Side Films
Southern Skies, Inc.
Southpaw Entertainment
Spike TV
Spirit Horse Productions
Spring Creek Productions, Inc.
St. Amos Productions
Station 3
Joel Stevens Entertainment
Stoneworks Television
Storyline Entertainment
Studios International
Sub Rosa Productions, Inc.
Mike Sullivan Productions, Inc.
Summerland Entertainment
Sunrise Entertainment
Suntaur/Elsboy Entertainment
Sweeney Entertainment
Symphony Pictures, Inc.
Synchronicity Productions
Tag Entertainment, Inc.
Tagline Pictures
Martin Tahse Productions
Taurus Entertainment Company
Grazka Taylor Productions
Michael Taylor Productions
Team Todd
Teocalli Entertainment
This is that corporation
Larry Thompson Organization
Tiara Blu Films
Touchstone Television
Trancas International Films
Treasure Entertainment
Trezza Entertainment
Tribeca Productions
TriCoast Studios
Tri-Elite Entertainment, Ltd.

Made-for-TV/Cable Movies (Continued)

Trillium Productions, Inc.
Tudor Management Group
The Turman Inc. Picture Company
Turner Entertainment Group
Turner Network Television (TNT)
TurtleBack Productions, Inc.
Norman Twain Productions
Twilight Pictures, Inc.
Two Oceans Entertainment Group
Two Sticks Productions
Ufland Productions
Underground Films
Unpainted Pictures
USA Network
Renée Valente Productions
Valhalla Motion Pictures
Vanguard Productions
Vantage Enterprises, Inc.
Joseph S. Vecchio Entertainment
VH1
Mark Victor Productions
Dimitri Villard Productions
Jon Voight Entertainment
von Zerneck-Sertner Films
Vox3 Films
Raymond Wagner Productions, Inc.
Walker/Fitzgibbon TV/Films
Waltzing Clouds, Inc.
Warren Miller Entertainment
Jim Wedaa Productions
Weintraub/Kuhn Productions
Clifford Werber Productions
Western Sandblast
White Sneakers, Inc.
Whoop Inc./One Ho Prod./Lil' Whoop Prod.
Dan Wigutow Productions
Wild At Heart Films, LLC
WildRice Productions
Ellyn Williams Productions
WilMark Entertainment, Inc.
Brad Wilson Productions, Inc.
Wilson/Woods Productions
The Winer Company
Winsome Productions
Stan Winston Productions
Ralph Winter Productions, Inc.
The Wolper Organization
WonderFilms
The Woofenill Works, Inc.
Workshop Pictures, Inc.
World International Network
Norton Wright Productions
Mark Yellen Productions
Zaloom Film
Laura Ziskin Productions
Ron Ziskin Productions, Inc.
Frederick Zollo Productions, Inc.
Zuckerman Entertainment

Miniseries

51 Minds Entertainment
9.14 Pictures
A Band Apart
ABC Family
AEI-Atchity Entertainment International, Inc.
AMC
Arlington Entertainment, Inc.
Armagh Films, Inc.
Bad Hat Harry Productions
Alan Barnette Productions
The Bauer Company
Bayonne Entertainment
BBC Worldwide Americas
Harve Bennett Productions
BLT Productions Ltd.

Miniseries (Continued)

Blue Tulip Productions
Blueprint Entertainment
Paulette Breen Productions
The Bregman Entertainment Group
Brooklyn Films
Butchers Run Films
C2 Pictures
Cairo/Simpson Entertainment, Inc.
Caldera/De Fanti Entertainment
John Calley Productions
Catfish Productions
CBS Paramount Network Television
Chic Productions
CinéGroupe
Cinema 21 Group
CineMagic Entertainment
Class 5 Films
Con Artists Productions
CSM Communications
Cypress Point Productions
de Passe Entertainment
Discovery Networks, U.S.
Donaldson/Sanders Entertainment
Bonny Dore Productions
EARS XXI
Echelon Entertainment World Distribution & Prod.
Echo Lake Productions
The Edelstein Company
Eden Rock Media, Inc.
David Eick Productions
El Dorado Pictures
Electric Entertainment
Empire Pictures Incorporated
Ensemble Entertainment
Euphoria Entertainment
Exxcell Entertainment, Inc./Exxcell Films
Face Productions/Jennilind Productions
Fierce Entertainment, LLC
Film Roman, Inc.
Firm Television
Preston Stephen Fischer Company
Fisher Productions
Foresight Unlimited
David Foster Productions
Generate
Roger Gimbel Productions, Inc.
Go Go Luckey Productions
Goldenring Productions
The Gotham Group, Inc.
Granada America
Ken Gross Management
Beth Grossbard Productions
Grosso Jacobson Communications Corp.
Gross-Weston Productions
The Harris Company
The Hatchery
Hazy Mills Productions
HBO Films
The Jim Henson Company
Humble Journey Films
Imagine Television
Intuition Productions
Invitation Entertainment
ISBE Productions
Johnenelly Productions
Tony Jonas Productions
JTN Productions
Just Singer Entertainment
Kahn Power Pictures
KCET
Keep Clear
Diana Kerew Productions
David Kirschner Productions
KLS Communications, Inc.
The Konigsberg-Smith Company

Miniseries (Continued)

Kopelson Entertainment
Krainin Productions, Inc.
L.I.F.T. Productions
David Ladd Films
Liz Selzer Lang Productions
Larkin-Goldstein Production
The Late Bloomer Company, Ltd.
Leisure Time Enterprises
Barbara Lieberman Productions
Linkletter/Kritzer
Live Animals
Longbow Productions
Lynn Loring Productions
Maverick Films
Maya Pictures
Merchant-Ivory
Mindfire Entertainment
Morningstar Entertainment
Motion Picture Corporation of America
Muse Entertainment Enterprises
MWG Productions
Myriad Pictures
Nash Entertainment
Nasser Entertainment Group
NBC Universal Television Studio
Mace Neufeld Productions
Nitelite Entertainment
O.N.C. Entertainment Inc.
Sam Okun Productions, Inc.
The Orphanage
The Over the Hill Gang
Patchett Kaufman Entertainment
Pearl Pictures
Marc Platt Productions
Playtone Productions
Pretty Matches Productions
Proud Mary Entertainment
Raffaella Productions, Inc.
REGAN
Relevant Entertainment Group
RHI Entertainment
Rive Gauche Entertainment
S Pictures, Inc.
Sander/Moses Productions, Inc.
Sarabande Productions
Schwartz & Company, Inc.
Sci Fi Channel
Showtime Networks Inc.
Silver Dream Productions
Smart Entertainment
SMG Productions
Studios International
Summers Entertainment
Suntaur/Elsboy Entertainment
TMC Entertainment
Tribeca Productions
Tri-Elite Entertainment, Ltd.
Ufland Productions
Underground Films
Joseph S. Vecchio Entertainment
Viviano Feldman Entertainment
Waltzing Clouds, Inc.
Dan Wigutow Productions
WildRice Productions
Winkler Films
The Wolper Organization
The Woofenill Works, Inc.
Ron Ziskin Productions, Inc.

Mobile Content

@radical.media
100% Entertainment
9 Squared
Abandon Pictures, Inc.
Actuality Productions

Mobile Content (Continued)

Air2web, Inc.
Airborne Entertainment
Alchemy Entertainment
Alturas Films
Amp'd Mobile
Anonymous Creators Productions
AOL Media Networks
Arjay Entertainment
Avalanche! Entertainment
Bleiberg Entertainment
Buena Vista Television
Mark Burnett Productions
Cartoon Network
Chameleon Entertainment
The Cielo Group, Inc.
CinéGroupe
Cinema-Electric Inc.
CineMagic Entertainment
Comedy Central
Comedy Time
Creative Capers Entertainment
CSM Communications
Disney Online
Donaldson/Sanders Entertainment
Bonny Dore Productions
Chris Dorr Productions
EARS XXI
Enpocket
Film Roman, Inc.
Flame Ventures LLC
Fox Atomic
Fox Mobile Entertainment
Fox Reality
FremantleMedia North America
Generate
Google Inc.
GoTV Networks
Groove Mobile
GSN
Guardian Entertainment, Ltd.
The Gurin Company
HBO Media Ventures
The Jim Henson Company
here! Networks
The History Channel
IAC/InterActiveCorp
The Idea Factory
Janicek-Marino Creative
JibJab Media Inc.
Kareem Productions
Klasky Csupo, Inc.
Latitude Television LLC
Linkletter/Kritzer
LivePlanet
Londine Productions
L'Orange
Mandalay Sports Action Entertainment & Mandalay Integrated Media Entertainment
Mindfire Entertainment
Mobile Streams
MobiTV
Mondo Media
The Mottola Company
MSpot
MTV Networks
MTV Networks Latin America (MTVNLA)
Murphy Boyz Productions
National Lampoon
New Wave Entertainment
O.N.C. Entertainment Inc.
The Over the Hill Gang
Paramount Digital Media Group
Pariah
P.A.T. Productions
Piranha Pictures, Inc.

Mobile Content (Continued)

Platinum Studios, LLC
Popular Arts Entertainment, Inc.
POW! Entertainment
Proteus
Q Media Partners
REGAN
Rive Gauche Entertainment
Rocket Entertainment
Sci Fi Channel
Senza Pictures
Simsie Films/Media Savant Pictures
SiTV
SkyZone Entertainment
Sling Media
Smart Entertainment
SOAPnet
Sub Rosa Productions, Inc.
SUperFInger Entertainment
Symbolic Action
Symbolic Entertainment
Taurus Entertainment Company
Treasure Entertainment
Triage Entertainment
Troma Entertainment, Inc.
TV Guide Channel
Joseph S. Vecchio Entertainment
Veoh Networks, Inc.
Warner Bros. Digital Distribution
Warner Bros. Online
WPT Enterprises, Inc.
Yahoo! Media Group/Yahoo! Studios
Zingy Inc.

Music Videos

@radical.media
19 Entertainment, Inc.
777 Entertainment Group, Ltd.
The 7th Floor
9.14 Pictures
A Band Apart
Alchemy Entertainment
Alturas Films
American Blackguard, Inc.
Anonymous Creators Productions
Artists, Inc.
Belladonna Productions
Boxx Communications, LLC
The Bregman Entertainment Group
Tim Burton Productions
Cafe Productions
CatchLight Films
Chameleon Entertainment
City Lights Media Group
CJ Entertainment America
CMT: Country Music Television
Concrete Pictures
Crossroads Films
CSM Communications
Cube Vision
Curious Pictures
Digital Domain, Inc.
Bonny Dore Productions
Driven Entertainment
Eye in the Sky Entertainment
Eye on the Ball Films, Inc.
Fallout
Film Roman, Inc.
Frazier | Chipman Entertainment
Ghost Robot
Ginty Films International
Go Go Luckey Productions
The Group Entertainment
Guardian Entertainment, Ltd.
G-Unit Television & Films
The Jim Henson Company

Music Videos (Continued)

Josselyne Herman & Assoc./Moving Image Films
Hollywood East Entertainment, Inc.
House of Rock Productions, Inc.
Interloper Films
International Television Group (ITG) - Epix Films
K2 Pictures, Inc.
L.I.F.T. Productions
Laika Entertainment
LaSalleHolland
Lightstone Entertainment, Inc.
Liquid Theory
Live Animals
Londine Productions
M3 Television
The Matthau Company, Inc.
Merchant-Ivory
Mission Entertainment
MobiTV
Monster Productions
MRB Productions, Inc.
Open Road Films
The Orphanage
The Over the Hill Gang
Partizan
Piranha Pictures, Inc.
Pollywog Entertainment, Inc
Rafelson Media
Rupert Productions, Inc.
Sacred Dogs Entertainment, LLC
Senza Pictures
Silvers/Koster Productions, Inc.
Sixth Way Productions
Slipnot! Productions/SPG
Spirit Horse Productions
Stick Figure Productions
Sub Rosa Productions, Inc.
Symbolic Entertainment
Taillight TV
Trancas International Films
Treasure Entertainment
Tri-Elite Entertainment, Ltd.
Troma Entertainment, Inc.
Vanguard Productions
Walker/Fitzgibbon TV/Films
Workshop Pictures, Inc.
Mark Yellen Productions

Reality TV

19 Entertainment, Inc.
3 Ball Productions
3 Ring Circus Films
40 Acres & A Mule Filmworks, Inc.
44 Blue Productions, Inc.
4th Row Films
51 Minds Entertainment
777 Entertainment Group, Ltd.
7ponies productions
9.14 Pictures
900 Films
A Band Apart
ABC Daytime
ABC Entertainment Television Group
ABC Family
Actual Reality Pictures
Actuality Productions
Orly Adelson Productions
AEI-Atchity Entertainment International, Inc.
Agua Films
Altitude Entertainment
Anonymous Creators Productions
Loreen Arbus Productions, Inc.
Ardustry Entertainment
Arjay Entertainment
Asylum Entertainment
Atmosphere Entertainment MM, LLC

Reality TV (Continued)

Avalanche! Entertainment
Avalon Television, Inc.
The Axelrod/Edwards Company
Bad Boy Films
Bankable Productions
Banyan Productions
Bayonne Entertainment
June Beallor Productions
BET Networks
Bigel Entertainment
Stu Billett Productions
BloodWorks, LLC
Blue Rider Pictures
Blue Tulip Productions
Blueprint Entertainment
Boneyard Entertainment
Bob Booker Productions
Boxx Communications, LLC
Boz Productions
Braverman Productions, Inc.
Bravo
The Bremer Goff Company
Jerry Bruckheimer Films & Television
Bunim/Murray Productions, Inc.
Mark Burnett Productions
Bushwacker Productions
Cairo/Simpson Entertainment, Inc.
Maj Canton Productions
Carson Signature Films, Inc.
CBS Entertainment
Chameleon Entertainment
Chic Productions
CineMagic Entertainment
City Entertainment
The Collective
Comedy Central
Concrete Pictures
The Core
Court TV Networks
Creanspeak Productions LLC
Creative Differences
Crystal Spring Productions, Inc.
CSM Communications
Cube Vision
The CW
Cypress Point Productions
Dakota North Entertainment/Dakota Films
Dalaklis-McKeown Entertainment, Inc.
Alan David Management
Vin Di Bona Productions
Digital Ranch Productions
Discovery Networks, U.S.
Donaldson/Sanders Entertainment
Bonny Dore Productions
Double Nickel Entertainment
E! Networks
EARS XXI
Earthview Inc.
Edmonds Entertainment
Ralph Edwards Productions
Rona Edwards Productions/ES Entertainment
Embassy Row LLC
Emmett/Furla Films
Endemol USA Latino
Endemol USA, Inc.
Peter Engel Productions
Epic Level Entertainment, Ltd.
Epidemic Pictures & Management
ESPN Original Entertainment (EOE)
Euphoria Entertainment
Everyman Pictures
Evolution
Evolving Pictures Entertainment
Eyeworks Touchdown
Fierce Entertainment, LLC

Reality TV (Continued)

Film Garden Entertainment, Inc.
Filmstreet, Inc.
Firm Films
Firm Television
Flame Ventures LLC
Food Network
Bonnie Forbes Productions
Forest Park Pictures
Fortress Entertainment
Fox Cable Networks
Fox Reality
The Foxboro Company, Inc.
Franzke Entertainment Inc.
Frazier | Chipman Entertainment
Fremantle Productions Latin America
FremantleMedia North America
Budd Friedman Digital
Full Picture
Fuse Entertainment
FX
Galán Entertainment
Garlin Pictures, Inc.
Generate
Leeza Gibbons Enterprises (LGE)
Giraffe Productions
Go Girl Media
Go Go Luckey Productions
The Goodman Company
Gotham Entertainment Group
Granada America
GRB Entertainment
Robert Greenwald Productions
The Greif Company
Greystone Television and Films
Merv Griffin Entertainment
Grinning Dog Pictures
Allison Grodner Productions, Inc.
Gross Entertainment
Grosso Jacobson Communications Corp.
Guardian Entertainment, Ltd.
The Gurin Company
Haft Entertainment
Harbor Lights Productions
Harding & Associates
Harding-Kurtz Entertainment
Hazy Mills Productions
The Jim Henson Company
here! Networks
Josselyne Herman & Assoc./Moving Image Films
Bryan Hickox Pictures, Inc.
Highway 9 Films
S. Hirsch Company, Inc./Seemore Films
Hollywood East Entertainment, Inc.
Homerun Entertainment, Inc.
HorsePower Entertainment
House of Rock Productions, Inc.
Humble Journey Films
The Idea Factory
Imagine Television
Incognito Entertainment
Indigo Films
ION Media Networks, Inc.
ISBE Productions
Ithaka
J2 Pictures/J2TV
Jackhole Industries
Janicek-Marino Creative
Jay & Tony Show Productions
JBE Productions
JCS Entertainment II
Jeff Wald Entertainment
Johnenelly Productions
JT Entertainment
JTN Productions
Junction Films

Reality TV (Continued)

Jupiter Entertainment
Kandor Entertainment
Kanpai Pictures
KCET
Keep Clear
KLS Communications, Inc.
Konwiser Brothers
Robert Kosberg Productions
Krasnow Productions
L.I.F.T. Productions
Liz Selzer Lang Productions
Langley Productions
Larkin-Goldstein Production
Last Straw Productions
Latitude Television LLC
Launa Newman Productions (LNP)
Leisure Time Enterprises
Letnom Productions
Lifetime Television (Los Angeles)
Lifetime Television (New York)
Linkletter/Kritzer
Lion Television U.S.
Liquid Theory
Live Animals
LivePlanet
LMNO Productions
Longbow Productions
Lucky Crow Films
The Tom Lynch Company
Madhouse Entertainment
Madison Road Entertainment
Magnetic Film
Maloof Productions
Mandalay Sports Action Entertainment & Mandalay Integrated Media Entertainment
Mango Tree Pictures
The Marshak/Zachary Company
The Matthau Company, Inc.
Maverick Films
Terence Michael Productions, Inc.
Mindfire Entertainment
Mobile Streams
mod3productions
Mode of 8
Moore/Cramer Productions
Morningstar Entertainment
Motion Picture Production, Inc.
The Mottola Company
Moving Pictures, DPI
MPH Entertainment, Inc.
MTV Networks
MTV Networks Latin America (MTVNLA)
Murphy Boyz Productions
MWG Productions
Nash Entertainment
Nasser Entertainment Group
National Lampoon
NBC Entertainment
NBC Universal Television Studio
NEU-MAN-FILMS, Inc.
New Line Television
New Redemption Pictures
New Screen Concepts, Inc.
New Wave Management
Next Entertainment
Nightstar Productions, Inc.
Nitelite Entertainment
Noble House Entertainment, Inc.
Norsemen Television Productions, LLC
NorthSouth Productions
Nova Pictures
Nuyorican
Sam Okun Productions, Inc.
Omnibus
Orchard Films

Reality TV (Continued)

Original Productions
The Over the Hill Gang
Oxygen Media
Pariah
P.A.T. Productions
Patchett Kaufman Entertainment
Daniel L. Paulson Productions
PBS
Pearl Pictures
Daniel Petrie Jr. & Company
Pie Town Productions
Pierce Williams Entertainment
Pilgrim Films & Television, Inc.
Pink Sneakers Productions
Planet Grande Pictures
Playboy Entertainment Group, Inc.
Playtone Productions
PLUS Entertainment, Inc.
Pollywog Entertainment, Inc
Paul Pompian Productions, Inc.
Popular Arts Entertainment, Inc.
Port Magee Pictures, Inc.
POW! Entertainment
Precis Productions, Inc.
Program Partners
Prometheus Entertainment
Proud Mary Entertainment
Q Media Partners
Rafelson Media
RDF Media
Red Om Films, Inc.
REGAN
Relevant Entertainment Group
Renegade 83
Reveille, LLC
Rive Gauche Entertainment
Rocket Science Laboratories
Gay Rosenthal Productions
Heidi Rotbart Management
Rubicon
Rupert Productions, Inc.
S Pictures, Inc.
Sacred Dogs Entertainment, LLC
Sander/Moses Productions, Inc.
Schwartz & Company, Inc.
Sci Fi Channel
Scout Productions
Screen Door Entertainment
Senza Pictures
Shoreline Entertainment, Inc.
Silver Pictures
Silvers/Koster Productions, Inc.
The Gene Simmons Company
Simsie Films/Media Savant Pictures
Sirocco Media
SiTV
Slipnot! Productions/SPG
SMG Productions
A. Smith & Co. Productions
SOAPnet
Sony Pictures Television
Spike TV
Spirit Horse Productions
Station 3
Scott Sternberg Productions
Stick Figure Productions
Stone and Company Entertainment
Stoneworks Television
style.
Sub Rosa Productions, Inc.
Mike Sullivan Productions, Inc.
Super Delicious Productions
SUperFInger Entertainment
Ronald Suppa Productions, Inc.
The Syndicate

Reality TV (Continued)

Taillight TV
Tannenbaum Company
Larry Thompson Organization
Tiara Blu Films
TMC Entertainment
Tooley Productions
Trancas International Films
Triage Entertainment
Tribeca Productions
Tribune Entertainment Company
Tri-Elite Entertainment, Ltd.
Trigger Street Independent
Turner Entertainment Group
Twentieth Television
Twilight Pictures, Inc.
USA Network
Vanguard Productions
Joseph S. Vecchio Entertainment
Versus
VH1
Mark Victor Productions
Viviano Feldman Entertainment
VOY Pictures
Warner Horizon Television
Warrior Poets
Watershed Films
Watson Pond Productions
WE: Women's Entertainment
Weller/Grossman Productions
White Sneakers, Inc.
Whoop Inc./One Ho Prod./Lil' Whoop Prod.
WideAwake, Inc.
Wild At Heart Films, LLC
WildRice Productions
Winsome Productions
The Wolper Organization
Yellow Cab Pictures
Zieger Productions
Zinkler Films
Ron Ziskin Productions, Inc.

Specials

51 Minds Entertainment
9.14 Pictures
A Wink and a Nod Productions
ABC Family
Actuality Productions
Ambassador Entertainment Inc.
American Blackguard, Inc.
AOL Media Networks
Loreen Arbus Productions, Inc.
Arden Entertainment
Arjay Entertainment
Asylum Entertainment
BET Networks
Boneyard Entertainment
The Bregman Entertainment Group
Carson Signature Films, Inc.
Cates/Doty Productions
CBS Paramount Network Television
dick clark productions, inc.
Cossette Productions
Court TV Networks
CSM Communications
Curious Pictures
Dalaklis-McKeown Entertainment, Inc.
de Passe Entertainment
Discovery Networks, U.S.
Donaldson/Sanders Entertainment
Bonny Dore Productions
E! Networks
EARS XXI
Emotional Pictures Corporation
Entertainment Studios, Inc.
Film Garden Entertainment, Inc.

Specials (Continued)

Film Roman, Inc.
Fox Broadcasting Company
FremantleMedia North America
G4 TV
Generate
Leeza Gibbons Enterprises (LGE)
Roger Gimbel Productions, Inc.
Go Go Luckey Productions
GRB Entertainment
Merv Griffin Entertainment
Grosso Jacobson Communications Corp.
GSN
The Gurin Company
Haft Entertainment
Hand Picked Films
Harding & Associates
HBO Entertainment
The Jim Henson Company
here! Networks
Josselyne Herman & Assoc./Moving Image Films
The History Channel
HIT Entertainment
Hollywood East Entertainment, Inc.
House of Rock Productions, Inc.
The Idea Factory
Imagination Productions, Inc.
Imagine Television
Janicek-Marino Creative
JTN Productions
Jupiter Entertainment
K2 Pictures, Inc.
Kandor Entertainment
Kanpai Pictures
Keep Clear
Robert Kosberg Productions
Krainin Productions, Inc.
The Landsburg Company
Leisure Time Enterprises
Linkletter/Kritzer
Liquid Theory
Live Animals
Longbow Productions
The Tom Lynch Company
Madison Road Entertainment
Mandalay Sports Action Entertainment & Mandalay Integrated Media Entertainment
Scott Mauro Entertainment, Inc.
Media Four
Mindfire Entertainment
mod3productions
Morningstar Entertainment
MRB Productions, Inc.
MSNBC
MTV Networks Latin America (MTVNLA)
Murphy Boyz Productions
Nasser Entertainment Group
National Lampoon
NBC Universal Television Studio
Nitelite Entertainment
Northstar Entertainment
Nuyorican
O.N.C. Entertainment Inc.
Original Productions
Oxygen Media
George Paige Associates, Inc.
Parallel Entertainment, Inc.
Pariah
Patchett Kaufman Entertainment
Perry Films
Planet Grande Pictures
Playboy Entertainment Group, Inc.
Popular Arts Entertainment, Inc.
Precis Productions, Inc.
REGAN
Rive Gauche Entertainment
Gay Rosenthal Productions
S Pictures, Inc.
Alan Sacks Productions, Inc.
Sacred Dogs Entertainment, LLC
Sander/Moses Productions, Inc.
George Schlatter Productions
Schwartz & Company, Inc.
Screen Door Entertainment
Showtime Networks Inc.
SiTV
Smart Entertainment
A. Smith & Co. Productions
Gary Smith Company
SOAPnet
Andrew Solt Productions
Spike TV
Scott Sternberg Productions
The Stevens Company
Stoneworks Television
SUperFInger Entertainment
Taillight TV
TBS
Telemundo Network
Tenth Planet Productions
Teocalli Entertainment
TMC Entertainment
Triage Entertainment
Tri-Elite Entertainment, Ltd.
TV Guide Channel
TV One, LLC
Joseph S. Vecchio Entertainment
Versus
Viviano Feldman Entertainment
Walker/Fitzgibbon TV/Films
Water Channel
WE: Women's Entertainment
White Sneakers, Inc.
Whoop Inc./One Ho Prod./Lil' Whoop Prod.
Zinkler Films

Theatre

@radical.media
Ars Nova
Baldwin Entertainment Group, Ltd.
Carol Baum Productions
BET Networks
Blossom Films
The Bregman Entertainment Group
Brooksfilms Limited
Cossette Productions
Bonny Dore Productions
Jean Doumanian Productions
East of Doheny/Lexington Road Productions
Eighth Square Entertainment
Elkins Entertainment
Endgame Entertainment
entitled entertainment
EntPro, Inc.
Fisher Productions
Foundation Entertainment
Four Boys Films
The Foxboro Company, Inc.
Chuck Fries Productions, Inc.
Fuller Films, Inc.
Hart Sharp Entertainment, Inc.
Henderson Productions, Inc.
The Jim Henson Company
Infront Productions
Ithaka
Joel Films
Kareem Productions
Kenwright USA/Bill Kenwright Ltd.
Konwiser Brothers
Larco Productions, Inc.
Macedon Media, Inc.
Mainline Releasing
The Manhattan Project, Ltd.
Laurence Mark Productions
MBST Entertainment, Inc.
Merchant-Ivory
Miller/Boyett Productions
Mr. Mudd
National Lampoon
Neal Street Productions Ltd.
Nitelite Entertainment
Lin Oliver Productions
On Stilts Productions
Stephen Pevner, Inc.
Marc Platt Productions
Playtone Productions
PLUS Entertainment, Inc.
Pollywog Entertainment, Inc
Prospect Pictures
Rafelson Media
Red Bird Productions
REGAN
Relevant Entertainment Group
Alan Sacks Productions, Inc.
Seed Productions
ShadowCatcher Entertainment
Silver Nitrate Pictures
Suntaur/Elsboy Entertainment
Synchronicity Productions
Takes On Productions
Taurus Entertainment Company
Arielle Tepper Productions
Tribeca Productions
Norman Twain Productions
Underground Films
Untitled Entertainment
Upright Citizens Brigade
Viviano Feldman Entertainment
Waltzing Clouds, Inc.
Whoop Inc./One Ho Prod./Lil' Whoop Prod.
Frederick Zollo Productions, Inc.

TV Series

@radical.media
19 Entertainment, Inc.
21 Laps Entertainment
25C Productions
3 Arts Entertainment, Inc.
3n1 Entertainment
40 Acres & A Mule Filmworks, Inc.
44 Blue Productions, Inc.
4th Row Films
51 Minds Entertainment
57-T Productions, Inc.
777 Entertainment Group, Ltd.
7ponies productions
The 7th Floor
9.14 Pictures
900 Films
A Band Apart
A&E Network
Aardman Animations
ABC Daytime
ABC Entertainment Television Group
ABC Family
ABC Sports
Aberration Films
Acappella Pictures
Acme Productions
Act III Productions
Actual Reality Pictures
Actuality Productions
Orly Adelson Productions
Adelstein Productions
Adult Swim
AEI-Atchity Entertainment International, Inc.

TV Series (Continued)

Agua Films
Alchemy Entertainment
Alcon Entertainment, LLC
Alexander/Enright & Associates
Alliance Atlantis
Altitude Entertainment
AM Productions & Management
Ambassador Entertainment Inc.
Ambush Entertainment
AMC
American Blackguard, Inc.
And Then Productions
Craig Anderson Productions
Angelika
Angry Films, Inc.
Animal Planet
Animus Films
Anonymous Creators Productions
Apartment 3B Productions
Apatow Productions
Apostle
Appleseed Entertainment, LLC
Loreen Arbus Productions, Inc.
Archer Entertainment
Arden Entertainment
Ardustry Entertainment
Arlington Entertainment, Inc.
Ars Nova
The Artists' Colony
Artists Production Group (APG)
Asylum Entertainment
Atman Entertainment
Atmosphere Entertainment MM, LLC
Atomic Cartoons, Inc.
Automatic Pictures, Inc.
Avalanche! Entertainment
Avalon Television, Inc.
Avenue Pictures
The Axelrod/Edwards Company
Baby Cow Productions Ltd.
Bad Boy Films
Bad Hat Harry Productions
Bad Robot Productions
The Badham Company
Baldwin Entertainment Group, Ltd.
Ballyhoo, Inc.
Bang Zoom! Entertainment
Bankable Productions
Banyan Productions
Alan Barnette Productions
Barnstorm Films
Barracuda Productions
Barwood Films
Bates Entertainment
Battle Plan Productions
The Bauer Company
Carol Baum Productions
Suzanne Bauman Productions
Bayonne Entertainment
BBC Films
BBC Worldwide Americas
June Beallor Productions
The Bedford Falls Company
Beech Hill Films
Belisarius Productions
Dave Bell Associates
Bell-Phillip TV Productions, Inc.
Lawrence Bender Productions
Benderspink
Harve Bennett Productions
Berlanti Productions
Rick Berman Productions
BET Networks
Big Cattle Productions
Big Light Productions

TV Series (Continued)

Big Pix Inc.
Bigel Entertainment
Stu Billett Productions
Black Folk Entertainment
Black Sheep Entertainment
Blackfriars Bridge
BLT Productions Ltd.
Blue Rider Pictures
Blue Star Pictures
Blue Tulip Productions
Bluebird House
Blueline Productions
Blueprint Entertainment
Blumhouse Productions
Steven Bochco Productions
Bodega Bay Productions, Inc.
Bogner Entertainment, Inc.
Boku Films
Boneyard Entertainment
Bob Booker Productions
Boxx Communications, LLC
Boz Productions
David Brady Productions
Braga Productions
Brainstorm Media
Brancato/Salke Productions
Brandman Productions
Braun Entertainment Group, Inc.
David Braun Productions
Brave New Films
Bravo
Paulette Breen Productions
The Bregman Entertainment Group
The Bremer Goff Company
Brightlight Pictures, Inc.
Brillstein-Grey Entertainment
John Brister Films
Broad Strokes Entertainment
Broadway Video
Broadway Video Entertainment
Broken Road Productions
Brooklyn Films
Brookwell McNamara Entertainment, Inc.
Jerry Bruckheimer Films & Television
Buena Vista Television
Bull's Eye Entertainment
Bungalow 78 Productions
Bunim/Murray Productions, Inc.
Burleigh Filmworks
Mark Burnett Productions
Burnside Entertainment, Inc.
Burrud Productions
Al Burton Productions
Busboy Productions
Bushwacker Productions
Byrum Power & Light
C2 Pictures
Cairo/Simpson Entertainment, Inc.
Caldera/De Fanti Entertainment
Callahan Filmworks
Camelot Entertainment Group, Inc.
Camelot Pictures
Colleen Camp Productions
Reuben Cannon Productions
Maj Canton Productions
Capital Arts Entertainment
Anne Carlucci Productions
Carrie Productions, Inc.
Carson Daly Productions
Carson Signature Films, Inc.
The Thomas Carter Company
Cartoon Network
Cataland Films
Cates/Doty Productions
Catfish Productions

TV Series (Continued)

CBS Corporation
CBS Entertainment
CBS Paramount International Television
CBS Paramount Network Television
CBS Paramount Worldwide Television Distribution
CBS Sports
Stokely Chaffin Productions
Chanticleer Films
Charles Bros.
Charles Floyd Johnson Productions
Charlotte Street Films
Cheyenne Enterprises
Chic Productions
Chicagofilms
Chiodo Bros. Productions, Inc.
Chotzen/Jenner Productions
Chris/Rose Productions
CinéGroupe
Cinema 21 Group
CineMagic Entertainment
Cinetic
Circle of Confusion Productions
City Entertainment
Clarity Pictures, LLC
dick clark productions, inc.
Class IV Productions
Clear Pictures Entertainment Inc.
Patricia Clifford Productions
CMT: Country Music Television
CNBC
Cobblestone Films
Code Entertainment
The Collective
The Colleton Company
Colomby Films
Colossal Entertainment
Comedy Arts Studios
Comedy Central
Comic Book Movies, LLC/Branded Entertainment/Batfilm Productions
Con Artists Productions
Concept Entertainment
Concorde-New Horizons
Concrete Entertainment
Concrete Pictures
Contrafilm
Cookie Jar Entertainment
Coquette Productions
The Core
Cornice Entertainment
Corymore Entertainment
Cosgrove-Meurer Productions
Cossette Productions
Court TV Networks
Cindy Cowan Entertainment, Inc.
Craftsman Films
Crane Wexelblatt Entertainment
Craven/Maddalena Films
Creanspeak Productions LLC
Creative Capers Entertainment
Creative Coalition
Creative Differences
Creative Impulse Entertainment
Crossroads Films
CRPI Entertainment
Crystal Lake Entertainment, Inc.
Crystal Spring Productions, Inc.
CSM Communications
Cube Vision
Curious Pictures
The CW
Dakota North Entertainment/Dakota Films
Dalaklis-McKeown Entertainment, Inc.
The Sean Daniel Company
Dark Horse Entertainment

TV Series (Continued)

Darkwoods Productions
Alan David Management
Davis Entertainment Company
Daybreak Productions
Dino De Laurentiis Company
de Passe Entertainment
Destiny Pictures
DFZ Productions
Vin Di Bona Productions
di Bonaventura Pictures, Inc.
Di Novi Pictures
Louis DiGiaimo & Associates, Ltd.
Digital Ranch Productions
Discovery Channel
Discovery Health Channel
Discovery Networks, U.S.
Disney ABC Cable Networks Group
Walt Disney Television Animation
Disney-ABC Television Group
DIY Network
Dominant Pictures
Donaldson/Sanders Entertainment
The Donners' Company
Doozer
Bonny Dore Productions
Double Nickel Entertainment
Jean Doumanian Productions
DreamWorks SKG
Dreyfuss/James Productions
Driven Entertainment
E! Networks
EARS XXI
Earthworks Films
East of Doheny/Lexington Road Productions
The Ebersole-Hughes Company
Echelon Entertainment World Distribution & Prod.
Echo Lake Productions
Abra Edelman Productions
The Edelstein Company
Edmonds Entertainment
Ralph Edwards Productions
Rona Edwards Productions/ES Entertainment
David Eick Productions
Eighth Square Entertainment
El Dorado Pictures
El Norte Productions
Electric Entertainment
Elkins Entertainment
Embassy Row LLC
Ember Entertainment Group
Emotional Pictures Corporation
Empire Pictures Incorporated
Endemol USA Latino
Endemol USA, Inc.
Endgame Entertainment
Peter Engel Productions
Ensemble Entertainment
Enteraktion Studios
Epic Level Entertainment, Ltd.
Epidemic Pictures & Management
Epigram Entertainment
Epiphany Pictures, Inc.
Epitome Pictures, Inc.
Stefanie Epstein Productions
Escape Artists II
Esparza-Katz Productions
ESPN Original Entertainment (EOE)
Euphoria Entertainment
The Robert Evans Company
Evergreen Films, LLC
Everyman Pictures
Evolution
Evolution Entertainment
Evolving Pictures Entertainment
Exxcell Entertainment, Inc./Exxcell Films

TV Series (Continued)

Face Productions/Jennilind Productions
Fair Dinkum Productions
Fallout
Farrell Paura Productions, LLC
Farrell/Minoff Productions
The Feldman Company
Zachary Feuer Films
Fierce Entertainment, LLC
Fifty Cannon Entertainment, LLC
Film 44
Film Crash
Film Farm
Film Garden Entertainment, Inc.
Film Roman, Inc.
FilmEngine
Films By Jove
Filmstreet, Inc.
Fine Living
Firebrand Productions
Firm Films
Firm Television
Preston Stephen Fischer Company
Fisher Productions
Five Mile River Films, Ltd.
Five Sisters Productions
Flame Ventures LLC
Flashpoint Entertainment
Flying A Studios, Inc.
Food Network
Foothill Entertainment, Inc.
Bonnie Forbes Productions
Forest Park Pictures
Fort Hill Productions
Fortis Films
Fortress Entertainment
Forward Entertainment
Forward Pass, Inc.
Foundation Entertainment
Four Boys Films
fox 21
Fox Broadcasting Company
Fox Cable Networks
Fox News Channel
Fox Reality
Fox Sports Network
Fox Television Studios
Franzke Entertainment Inc.
Frazier | Chipman Entertainment
Frederator Studios
Jack Freedman Productions
Joel Freeman Productions, Inc.
Fremantle Productions Latin America
FremantleMedia North America
Fresh Paint
Fresh Produce Films
Daniel Fried Productions
Budd Friedman Digital
Chuck Fries Productions, Inc.
Front Street Pictures, Inc.
Full Picture
Fuller Films, Inc.
Funny Boy Films
Furst Films
Fuse Entertainment
FX
G4 TV
Galán Entertainment
Gallant Entertainment
Garlin Pictures, Inc.
Generate
Generation Entertainment
Genrebend Productions, Inc.
Gerber Pictures
Gillen & Price
Ginty Films International

TV Series (Continued)

Giraffe Productions
Glatzer Productions
Go Girl Media
Go Go Luckey Productions
Go Time Entertainment
Goepp Circle Productions
Goldenring Productions
Good Game
The Goodman Company
The Mark Gordon Company
Dan Gordon Productions
Gordonstreet Pictures
Gotham Entertainment Group
The Gotham Group, Inc.
Gracie Films
Grade A Entertainment
Michael Grais Productions
Grammnet Productions
Gran Via Productions
Granada America
Grand Productions, Inc.
GRB Entertainment
Greasy Entertainment
Robert Greenwald Productions
Greenwood Avenue Entertainment
The Greif Company
Greystone Television and Films
Merv Griffin Entertainment
Nick Grillo Productions
Grinning Dog Pictures
Grisham Films USA
Dan Grodnik Productions
Gross Entertainment
Ken Gross Management
Beth Grossbard Productions
Grossbart Kent Productions
Grosso Jacobson Communications Corp.
Gross-Weston Productions
The Group Entertainment
GSN
Guardian Entertainment, Ltd.
Gunn Films
The Gurin Company
Guy Walks Into a Bar
H. Beale Company
H2F Entertainment
Haft Entertainment
Half Shell Entertainment
Hand Picked Films
Handprint Entertainment
Peter Hankwitz Production & Management
Harbor Lights Productions
Harding & Associates
Harding-Kurtz Entertainment
Dean Hargrove Productions
Harms Way Productions
Harpo Films, Inc.
The Harris Company
The Hatchery
Hazy Mills Productions
HBO Entertainment
HDNet
The Hecht Company
Heel & Toe Films
Hella Good Moving Pictures
The Jim Henson Company
here! Networks
Josselyne Herman & Assoc./Moving Image Films
Heyday Films
Bryan Hickox Pictures, Inc.
High Horse Films
Highway 9 Films
S. Hirsch Company, Inc./Seemore Films
The History Channel
HIT Entertainment

TV Series (Continued)

Hock Films, Inc.
Gary Hoffman Productions
Hollywood East Entertainment, Inc.
Home & Garden Television (HGTV)
Homerun Entertainment, Inc.
Hope Enterprises, Inc.
Hopscotch Pictures
HorsePower Entertainment
House of Rock Productions, Inc.
Humble Journey Films
Peter Hyams Productions, Inc.
Hyperion Studio
Hypnotic
I.E. Productions, Inc.
Icon Productions, LLC
The Idea Factory
Ideal Entertainment, Inc.
IDT Entertainment
IFM Film Associates, Inc.
Imageries Entertainment
Imagi Services (USA)
Imaginarium Entertainment Group
Imagination Productions, Inc.
Imagine Television
IMG Media
In Cahoots
Incognito Entertainment
The Independent Film Channel (IFC)
Indigo Films
Industry Entertainment Partners
Infinity Features Entertainment
Infront Productions
Integrated Films & Management
International Arts Entertainment
International Television Group (ITG) - Epix Films
Intuition Productions
InVenture Entertainment
Invitation Entertainment
ION Media Networks, Inc.
Ironworks Production
Is Or Isn't Entertainment
ISBE Productions
Ithaka
j.k. livin productions
J2 Pictures/J2TV
Jack Angel Productions Inc.
Jackhole Industries
Tom Jacobson Productions
Jaffe/Braunstein Films, LLC
Janicek-Marino Creative
January Films
Jaret Entertainment
Melinda Jason Company
Jay & Tony Show Productions
JBE Productions
JCS Entertainment II
Jeff Wald Entertainment
The Jinks/Cohen Company
Johnenelly Productions
Don Johnson Productions
Tony Jonas Productions
Josephson Entertainment
JPH Productions
JT Entertainment
JTN Productions
Judge-Belshaw Entertainment, Inc.
Junction Entertainment
Junction Films
Jupiter Entertainment
Jurist Productions
Just Singer Entertainment
K2 Pictures, Inc.
Kadokawa Pictures USA
Kandor Entertainment
Kanpai Pictures

TV Series (Continued)

Kaplan/Perrone Entertainment, LLC
Jon Katzman Productions
The Kaufman Company
KCET
kdd Productions, LLC
Keckins Projects, Ltd.
Keep Clear
Keller Entertainment Group
David E. Kelley Productions
Kenneth Johnson Productions
Diana Kerew Productions
The Kerner Entertainment Company
Ketcham Films
Key Creatives, LLC
Kinetic Pictures
King World Productions, Inc.
David Kirschner Productions
Klasky Csupo, Inc.
KLS Communications, Inc.
KoMut Entertainment
Konwiser Brothers
Kopelson Entertainment
Robert Kosberg Productions
Krasnoff Foster Productions
Krasnow Productions
Sid & Marty Krofft Pictures Corporation
Kurtzman/Orci
The Kushner-Locke Company
L.I.F.T. Productions
David Ladd Films
The Landsburg Company
Landscape Entertainment
Liz Selzer Lang Productions
Langley Productions
Larco Productions, Inc.
Larkin-Goldstein Production
LaSalleHolland
Last Straw Productions
The Late Bloomer Company, Ltd.
Latham Entertainment
Latin Hollywood Films
Latitude Television LLC
Laugh Factory Entertainment
Launa Newman Productions (LNP)
LeFrak Productions
Arnold Leibovit Entertainment
The Jerry Leider Company
Leisure Time Enterprises
Lemon Sky Productions, Inc.
Malcolm Leo Productions
Letnom Productions
Lett/Reese International Productions
The Levinson/Fontana Company
Licht Entertainment Corporation
Liddell Entertainment
Barbara Lieberman Productions
Lifetime Television (Los Angeles)
Lifetime Television (New York)
Lighthouse Entertainment
Lighthouse Productions
Lightstone Entertainment, Inc.
Linkletter/Kritzer
Lion Eyes Entertainment
Lion Rock Productions
Lion Television U.S.
Lionsgate
James Lipton Productions
Liquid Theory
The Littlefield Company
Live Animals
LivePlanet
Lloyd Entertainment
LMNO Productions
Peter Locke Productions
Logo

TV Series (Continued)

Londine Productions
Lonetree Entertainment
Lynn Loring Productions
Love Spell Entertainment
Lucasfilm Ltd.
Luminair Entertainment
Lunaria Films
Dan Lupovitz Productions
A.C. Lyles Productions, Inc.
The Tom Lynch Company
M3 Television
Macedon Media, Inc.
Macgowan Films
Madhouse Entertainment
Guy Magar Films
Michael Mailer Films
Maloof Productions
Management 360
Mandalay Pictures
Mandalay Sports Action Entertainment & Mandalay Integrated Media Entertainment
Mandeville Films
Mandy Films
Mango Tree Pictures
The Manheim Company
Manifest Film Company
ManifestoVision
James Manos Productions, Inc.
Laurence Mark Productions
The Marshak/Zachary Company
Martha Stewart Living Omnimedia, Inc.
Martin Chase Productions
Martin/Stein Productions
Marvel Studios, Inc.
Niki Marvin Productions, Inc.
MarVista Entertainment
Timothy Marx Productions, Inc.
Mase/Kaplan Productions, Inc.
The Matthau Company, Inc.
Maverick Films
Mayhem Pictures
MBST Entertainment, Inc.
Media Four
Media Talent Group
Bill Melendez Productions
MERCER Film Group Inc.
Merchant-Ivory
Patricia K. Meyer Productions
MGA Entertainment/MGA Entertainment Films
Michael Meltzer Productions
Midnight Sun Pictures
Miller/Boyett Productions
Mindfire Entertainment
Miranda Entertainment
The Mirisch Corporation
Misher Films
MobiTV
mod3productions
Mode of 8
Mojo Films
Monster Productions
Montage Entertainment
Moore/Cramer Productions
Morningstar Entertainment
Jeff Morton Productions
Mosaic Media Group
Moshag Productions, Inc.
Motion Picture Production, Inc.
Motor City Films
The Mottola Company
Moving Pictures, DPI
Mozark Productions
MPH Entertainment, Inc.
Mr. Mudd
MRB Productions, Inc.

TV Series (Continued)

MSNBC
MTV Networks
MTV Networks Latin America (MTVNLA)
Murphy Boyz Productions
Muse Entertainment Enterprises
Mutual Film Company
MWG Productions
My Network TV
Myriad Pictures
The N
Namesake Entertainment
Nanas Entertainment
Nash Entertainment
Nasser Entertainment Group
National Geographic Feature Films
National Geographic Kids' Prog. & Prod.
National Lampoon
NBC Entertainment
NBC Sports
NBC Universal Cable Entertainment
NBC Universal Corporate
NBC Universal Television Studio
Neighbors Entertainment
Nelvana Communications, Inc.
Neo Art & Logic
Mace Neufeld Productions
NEU-MAN-FILMS, Inc.
New Amsterdam Entertainment, Inc.
New Concorde
New England Productions, Inc.
New Generation Films, Inc.
New Line Cinema
New Line Television
New Redemption Pictures
New Wave Entertainment
New Wave Management
Vincent Newman Entertainment
Peter Newman Productions, Inc.
Next Entertainment
Next Wednesday
Nickelodeon/MTVN Kids & Family Group
Nightstar Productions, Inc.
Nine Yards Entertainment
Nitelite Entertainment
Noggin
Norsemen Television Productions, LLC
NorthSouth Productions
Northstar Entertainment
Nova Pictures
Nuance Productions
Numenorean Films
Nuyorican
O Entertainment
O.N.C. Entertainment Inc.
Lynda Obst Productions
Offspring Entertainment
Sam Okun Productions, Inc.
Old Dime Box Productions, Inc.
Old School Pictures, LLC
Lin Oliver Productions
Olmos Productions, Inc.
Omnibus
Once A Frog Productions
Once Upon A Time Films, Ltd.
One Voice Entertainment, Inc.
Open Road Films
Orchard Films
Original Productions
The Orphanage
Outerbanks Entertainment
Outlaw Productions
The Over the Hill Gang
Overbrook Entertainment
Oxygen Media
OZLA Pictures, Inc.

TV Series (Continued)

George Paige Associates, Inc.
Palomar Pictures
Paradigm Studio
Paradox Productions, Inc.
Paraskevas Studios
Pariah
Park Ex Pictures
Parkchester Pictures
Parkway Productions
P.A.T. Productions
Patriot Pictures, LLC
Paulist Productions
Daniel L. Paulson Productions
PAYASO Entertainment
PBS
Peace Arch Entertainment Group Inc.
Pearl Pictures
Peculiar Films
Periscope Entertainment, LLC
Permut Presentations
Perry Films
Persistent Entertainment
Daniel Petrie Jr. & Company
D. Petrie Productions, Inc.
Phase Two Productions
Phoenix Pictures
Pie Town Productions
Pilgrim Films & Television, Inc.
Piller/Segan
Pink Slip Pictures
Pink Sneakers Productions
The Pitt Group
Planet Grande Pictures
Platinum Studios, LLC
Marc Platt Productions
Playboy Entertainment Group, Inc.
Playtime Productions
Playtone Productions
Plotpoint, Inc.
Plum Pictures
Martin Poll Films, Ltd.
Pollywog Entertainment, Inc
The Polson Company
Paul Pompian Productions, Inc.
Poor Boys Productions
Popular Arts Entertainment, Inc.
PorchLight Entertainment
Port Magee Pictures, Inc.
P.O.V. Company
POW! Entertainment
Power Up
Practical Pictures
Precis Productions, Inc.
Edward R. Pressman Film Corporation
Pretty Matches Productions
Pretty Pictures
Principato-Young Entertainment
Production Partners, Inc.
Program Partners
Prometheus Entertainment
Prospect Pictures
Protozoa Pictures
Proud Mary Entertainment
Pterodactyl Productions Inc.
Q Media Partners
QVF Inc.
Radar Pictures
The Radmin Company
Rafelson Media
Raffaella Productions, Inc.
Rat Entertainment/Rat TV
RDF Media
Red Bird Productions
Red Board Productions
Red Dog Entertainment

TV Series (Continued)

Red Door Films/David Poulshock Productions, Inc.
Red Om Films, Inc.
Red Strokes Entertainment
Red Wagon Entertainment
REGAN
Regency Television
Regent
Tim Reid Productions, Inc.
Relevant Entertainment Group
Renaissance Pictures
Renegade 83
Renegade Animation, Inc.
Renfield Productions
Reveille, LLC
Revelations Entertainment
Rice & Beans Productions
Rive Gauche Entertainment
Riverrock Entertainment Group
Rocket Entertainment
Rocket Science Laboratories
Rocklin Entertainment
Stan Rogow Productions
Al Roker Productions
Phil Roman Entertainment
Alex Rose Productions, Inc.
Rosemont Productions International, Ltd.
Zvi Howard Rosenman Productions
Gay Rosenthal Productions
Rosenzweig Films
Heidi Rotbart Management
Joe Roth Television
Rough Draft Studios
Roundtable Entertainment
Rubicon
Ruby-Spears Productions
The Ruddy Morgan Organization, Inc./
Albert S. Ruddy Productions
S Pictures, Inc.
Sachs Judah Productions
Alan Sacks Productions, Inc.
Sacred Dogs Entertainment, LLC
Samoset, Inc./Sacret, Inc.
Sander/Moses Productions, Inc.
Sanitsky Company
Saphier Productions
Sarabande Productions
Arthur Sarkissian Productions
Saturn Films
Edward Saxon Productions (ESP)
Scarab Productions
Paul Schiff Productions
George Schlatter Productions
Scholastic Entertainment
Faye Schwab Productions/MMA, Inc.
Schwartz & Company, Inc.
Steven Schwartz Productions, Inc.
Sci Fi Channel
Scott Free Productions
Scout Productions
Screen Door Entertainment
Ryan Seacrest Productions
Seed Productions
SekretAgent Productions
Dylan Sellers Productions
Senza Pictures
Seraphim Films
Serendipity Point Films
Sesame Workshop
Seven Summits Pictures & Management
Shady Acres Entertainment
The Shephard/Robin Company
Jon Shestack Productions
Shoe Money Productions
Shoot the Moon Productions
Shore View Entertainment

TV Series (Continued)

Shoreline Entertainment, Inc.
Showtime Networks Inc.
Shukovsky English Entertainment
The Shuman Company
Shutt-Jones Productions
Sierra Club Productions
Silly Robin Productions
Silver Lion Films
Silver Pictures
Casey Silver Productions
The Fred Silverman Company
Silvers/Koster Productions, Inc.
The Gene Simmons Company
Single Cell Pictures
Sinovoi Entertainment
Sirocco Media
Sitting Ducks Productions
SiTV
Sixth Way Productions
Sky Networks
Skylark Entertainment, Inc.
Sleuth
Slipnot! Productions/SPG
Smart Entertainment
SMG Productions
A. Smith & Co. Productions
Smoke House
Snapdragon Films, Inc.
Sneak Preview Entertainment, Inc.
SOAPnet
Solaris
Solo Entertainment Group
Solo One Productions
Andrew Solt Productions
The Sommers Company
Sony Pictures Entertainment
Sony Pictures Imageworks
Sony Pictures Television
Sony Pictures Television International
South Productions, LLC
South Side Films
Southern Skies, Inc.
Southpaw Entertainment
Spacedog
Spike TV
Spirit Horse Productions
Spyglass Entertainment Group
St. Amos Productions
Stampede Entertainment
Darren Star Productions
Starry Night Entertainment
Jane Startz Productions, Inc.
State Street Pictures
Station 3
Steamroller Productions, Inc.
The Howard Stern Production Company
Scott Sternberg Productions
Joel Stevens Entertainment
Stick Figure Productions
Stone and Company Entertainment
Stone Village Pictures, LLC
Stone vs. Stone
Stoneworks Television
Story and Film, Inc.
Storyline Entertainment
Mel Stuart Productions, Inc.
Studios International
style.
Sub Rosa Productions, Inc.
Mike Sullivan Productions, Inc.
Summerland Entertainment
Sundance Channel
Sunlight Productions
Suntaur/Elsboy Entertainment

TV Series (Continued)

Super Delicious Productions
Superb Entertainment
SUperFInger Entertainment
Sweeney Entertainment
Symphony Pictures, Inc.
Synchronicity Productions
TAE Productions/Medeacom Productions
Tagline Pictures
Tailfish Productions
Taillight TV
Takes On Productions
Talisman Pacific
Tannenbaum Company
Taryn Productions
Taurus Entertainment Company
Taylor Made Films
Michael Taylor Productions
TBS
Teitelbaum Artists Group
Telemundo Network
Telepictures Productions
Teocalli Entertainment
Larry Thompson Organization
Threshold Entertainment
Thunder Road Pictures
Thunderbird Pictures
Tiara Blu Films
Tidewater Entertainment, Inc.
TLC
TLC Entertainment
TMC Entertainment
TOKYOPOP Inc.
Tollin/Robbins Productions
Tommy Boy Films
Tooley Productions
Touchstone Television
Tower of Babble Entertainment
Trancas International Films
Travel Channel
Traveler's Rest Films
Tree Line Film
Triage Entertainment
Tribeca Productions
Tribune Entertainment Company
TriCoast Studios
Tricor Entertainment
Tri-Elite Entertainment, Ltd.
Trigger Street Independent
Trillium Productions, Inc.
Trilogy Entertainment Group
T-Squared Productions
Tudor Management Group
Turner Entertainment Group
Turner Network Television (TNT)
TurtleBack Productions, Inc.
TV Guide Channel
TV One, LLC
TV Repair
Norman Twain Productions
Twentieth Century Fox Television
Twentieth Television
Twilight Pictures, Inc.
Two Oceans Entertainment Group
Underground Films
Untitled Entertainment
Upright Citizens Brigade
Urban Entertainment
USA Network
Renée Valente Productions
Valhalla Motion Pictures
VanDerKloot Film & Television
Vanguard Productions
Vantage Enterprises, Inc.
Joseph S. Vecchio Entertainment

TV Series (Continued)

Versus
Vertigo Entertainment
VH1
Viacom Entertainment Group
Mark Victor Productions
Visionbox Media Group
Viviano Feldman Entertainment
von Zerneck-Sertner Films
VOY Pictures
Raymond Wagner Productions, Inc.
Walden Films
Walker/Fitzgibbon TV/Films
Waltzing Clouds, Inc.
Warner Bros. Animation
Warner Bros. Entertainment Inc.
Warner Bros. Television Production
Warner Horizon Television
Warren Miller Entertainment
Warrior Poets
Wass-Stein
Water Channel
Watermark
Watershed Films
Watson Pond Productions
WE: Women's Entertainment
Jim Wedaa Productions
Weintraub/Kuhn Productions
Weller/Grossman Productions
John Wells Productions
Werner-Gold-Miller
Simon West Productions
Western Sandblast
Wheelhouse Entertainment
White Sneakers, Inc.
WhiteLight Entertainment
Whitewater Films
Whoop Inc./One Ho Prod./Lil' Whoop Prod.
Whyaduck Productions, Inc.
WideAwake, Inc.
Dan Wigutow Productions
Wild At Heart Films, LLC
Wild Brain, Inc.
WildRice Productions
Ellyn Williams Productions
WilMark Entertainment, Inc.
Brad Wilson Productions, Inc.
Wind Dancer Production Group
Stan Winston Productions
Ralph Winter Productions, Inc.
Witt-Thomas-Harris Productions
Wolf Films, Inc.
Fred Wolf Films
Wolfmill Entertainment
The Wolper Organization
Wonderland Sound and Vision
The Woofenill Works, Inc.
World Film Services, Inc.
World of Wonder Productions
Worldwide Biggies
Worldwide Pants, Inc.
WPT Enterprises, Inc.
Norton Wright Productions
WWE Films
Yellow Cab Pictures
Mike Young Productions LLC
Zaloom Film
The Zanuck Company
Zentropa
Zero Pictures
Zieger Productions
Laura Ziskin Productions
Ron Ziskin Productions, Inc.
Frederick Zollo Productions, Inc.

SECTION F

INDEX BY NAME

Aagaard, Ken .CBS Sports, p. 88
Aaron, Paul .Suntaur/Elsboy Entertainment, p. 305
Aaronson, Ellen .Johnenelly Productions, p. 182
Aaronson, Stephanie .PBS, p. 251
Abarbanell, Rachel .Lynda Obst Productions, p. 241
Abaro, Alison .The Mayhem Project, p. 213
Abate, Ciro .Fox Broadcasting Company, p. 139
Abbinanti, Jill .Waterfront, p. 379
Abbott, Kevin .Reba, p. 372
Abdul-Jabbar, Kareem .Kareem Productions, p. 185
Abdy, Pamela .Paramount Pictures Production Division, p. 248
Abel, Dawn .CBS Paramount Worldwide Television Dist., p. 88
Abel, Lewis .Numb3rs, p. 370
Abernethy, Jack .My Network TV, p. 228
Abernethy, Peet R. .Stephen Pevner, Inc., p. 253
Aboulache, Perla .Olmos Productions, Inc., p. 242
Abraham, David .Discovery Networks, U.S., p. 111
Abraham, David .TLC, p. 314
Abraham, Harriet .ABC Daytime, p. 44
Abraham, Jake .InDigEnt, p. 173
Abraham, James .Daybreak Productions, p. 108
Abraham, Marc .Strike Entertainment, p. 303
Abraham, Nancy .HBO Documentaries & Family, p. 162
Abraham, Peggy Jo .E! Networks, p. 117
Abrahams, Lauren .Michael De Luca Productions, p. 108
Abramo, Joe .Sobini Films, p. 293
Abrams, Dan .MSNBC, p. 225
Abrams, Gayle .Gilmore Girls, p. 362
Abrams, Gerald W. .Cypress Point Productions, p. 106
Abrams, J.J. .What About Brian, p. 379
Abrams, J.J. .Six Degrees, p. 375
Abrams, J.J. .Lost, p. 368
Abrams, J.J. .Bad Robot Productions, p. 60
Abrams, Marc .Entourage, p. 360
Abrams, Peter .Tapestry Films, Inc., p. 308
Abramson, Brad .VH1, p. 330
Abramson, Lawrence .Incognito Entertainment, p. 173
Abramson, Stephen D. .New Line Cinema, p. 234
Abrego, Cris .51 Minds Entertainment, p. 42
Abreo, Jasa .Tig Productions, Inc., p. 313
Abril, Jason .Brooklyn Films, p. 77
Acker, Rachel .The Collective, p. 96
Ackerman, Andy .The New Adventures of Old Christine, p. 370
Ackerman, Andy .Rules of Engagement, p. 373
Ackerman, Aric .@radical.media, p. 38
Ackerman, Corey .Southpaw Entertainment, p. 297
Ackerman, Jim .VH1, p. 330
Ackerman, Rickey .Arnold Shapiro Productions, p. 285
Acland, Norma .Carsey-Werner Films, p. 84
Adair, Todd .Fox Broadcasting Company, p. 139
Adamovich, Dennis .Cartoon Network, p. 84
Adams, Bryan .Mad TV, p. 368
Adams, Joel .Krainin Productions, Inc., p. 190
Adams, Penny .RENO 911!, p. 373
Adams, Steven .Luna Ray Films, p. 204
Adamson, Laird .HDNet Films, p. 163
Adamson, Larina .The Simpsons, p. 375
Adderton, Peter .Amp'd Mobile, p. 51
Addis, Keith .Masters of Horror, p. 368
Addis, Keith .Industry Entertainment Partners, p. 174
Adelman, Barry .dick clark productions, inc., p. 94
Adelson, Orly .Orly Adelson Productions, p. 46
Adelstein, Marty .Prison Break, p. 372
Adelstein, Marty .Adelstein Productions, p. 47
Adema-John, Diane .Medium, p. 369
Adilman, Glenn .Sony Pictures Television, p. 296
Adler, Barbie .My Name Is Earl, p. 369
Adler, Ben .Cobblestone Films, p. 96
Adler, Jacqui .Cobblestone Films, p. 96
Adler, Justin .Big Day, p. 355
Adler, Kasey .Intrepid Pictures, p. 176
Adler, Kate .CBS Paramount Network Television, p. 87
Adler, Laura .My Boys, p. 369
Adler, Paul .TV Guide Channel, p. 321
Adler-Galloway, Connie .Murphy Boyz Productions, p. 227
Adrian, Michael .HDNet, p. 163
Affleck, Ben .LivePlanet, p. 201
Afineevsky, Evgeny .New Generation Films, Inc., p. 234
Aftergood, Braden .Film 44, p. 131
Agala, Jeffery .Atomic Cartoons, Inc., p. 58
Agin, Jonas .The Tom Lynch Company, p. 205
Agnone, Frank .South Park, p. 376
Agostini, Nancy .The Late Show with David Letterman, p. 367
Aguilar, Michael .Penn Station Entertainment, p. 252
Aguirre, Robb .Robert Lawrence Productions, p. 195
Ahn, Henry .NBC Universal Cable Entertainment, p. 231
Ahr, Meredith .NBC Entertainment, p. 230
Ahrendt, Chad .Laurence Mark Productions, p. 210
Aidem, Larry .Sundance Channel, p. 304
Aiello, Patrick .Hyde Park Entertainment, p. 169
Aikeng, Stuart .Stargate: Atlantis, p. 376
Aikins, Stuart .Stargate: SG-1, p. 376
Ailes, Roger .My Network TV, p. 228
Ailes, Roger .Fox News Channel, p. 139
Aissa, Rod .MTV Networks, p. 226
Ajir, Kasra .Station 3, p. 300
Akens, Susan .CBS Paramount International Television, p. 87
Akil, Mara Brock .The Game, p. 361
Akil, Mara Brock .Girlfriends, p. 362
Akkad, Malek .Trancas International Films, p. 316
Alaimo, Michael .Traveler, p. 377
Albani, Steve .Comedy Central, p. 98
Albano, Frank .E! Networks, p. 117
Albelda, Randy .Dan Lupovitz Productions, p. 204
Albert, Trevor .Weekend Films/Main Street Film Company, p. 337
Albolote, Edward .Bay Films, p. 63
Albrecht, Chris .HBO Entertainment, p. 162
Albright, Gary .Cartoon Network, p. 84
Albright, Molly .Picturehouse, p. 254
Alcala, Felix .Raines, p. 372
Alcantar, Gerald .Fox Broadcasting Company, p. 139
Aldrich, Matt .Suntaur/Elsboy Entertainment, p. 305
Aldridge, Leslie Ann .National Geographic Giant Screen Films & Special Projects, p. 229
Alegret, Orlando .Ensemble Entertainment, p. 124
Alesevich, Matt .The Foxboro Company, Inc., p. 140
Alessandri, Fernando .Once Upon A Time Films, Ltd., p. 243
Alessandri, Rick .ESPN Original Entertainment (EOE), p. 127
Alessi, Tony .Intermedia Film Equities USA, Inc., p. 175
Alex, Michael .MTV Networks, p. 226
Alexander, Andy .Burnt Orange Productions, p. 80
Alexander, Chris .Twentieth Century Fox Television, p. 323
Alexander, Chris .Alcon Entertainment, LLC, p. 49
Alexander, Craig .New Line Cinema, p. 234
Alexander, Erin .JT Entertainment, p. 182
Alexander, Jace .Six Degrees, p. 375
Alexander, Jesse .Heroes, p. 363
Alexander, Les .Alexander/Enright & Associates, p. 49
Alexander, Linda .MTV Networks Latin America (MTVNLA), p. 226
Alexander, Marc .St. Amos Productions, p. 299
Alexander, Michael .The Tonight Show with Jay Leno, p. 377
Alexander, Missy .How I Met Your Mother, p. 364
Alexander, Sam .The Wolper Organization, p. 344
Alexander, Stacy .VH1, p. 330
Alexandria, Petra .Laurence Mark Productions, p. 210
Alexanian, Alexis .Elixir Films, p. 121
Alexanian, David .Elixir Films, p. 121
Alfandary, Jack .Fremantle Productions Latin America, p. 142
Alfano, JoAnn .30 Rock, p. 353
Alfano, JoAnn .Broadway Video Entertainment, p. 76
Alfieri, Richard .EntPro, Inc., p. 125
Alfieri, Tom .NBC Entertainment, p. 230
Alfrey, Dennis .here! Networks, p. 165
Alison, Rosie .Heyday Films, p. 166
Alkin, Luke .BBC Films, p. 64
Allain, Alicia .The Robert Evans Company, p. 127
Allain, Stephanie .Southern Cross the Dog, p. 297
Alldaffer, Alaine .The Knights of Prosperity, p. 365
Allegra, Gerette .Sony Pictures Television, p. 296
Allen, Byron .Entertainment Studios, Inc., p. 125

Allen, Dave Gruber . . . . .Naked Trucker & T-Bones, p. 369
Allen, Debbie . . . . .Red Bird Productions, p. 267
Allen, Gayle . . . . .Current TV, LLC, p. 105
Allen, Kenton . . . . .BBC Films, p. 64
Allen, Paul . . . . .Vulcan Productions, p. 332
Allensworth, David . . . . .VH1, p. 330
Allen-Turner, Richard . . . . .Avalon Television, Inc., p. 58
Allgood, Jeanne . . . . .Wonderland Sound and Vision, p. 344
Allicon, George . . . . .H2F Entertainment, p. 158
Allison, Brooke . . . . .Summerland Entertainment, p. 304
Allman, Betsy . . . . .Pie Town Productions, p. 254
Alloul, Marc . . . . .Airborne Entertainment, p. 48
Allyn, Heather . . . . .SMG Productions, p. 292
Almog, Tal . . . . .Regency Enterprises, p. 268
Aloe, Mary L. .Proud Mary Entertainment, p. 263
Alovera, Shirley . . . . .Pacifica International Film & TV Corp,, p. 246
Alpert, David . . . . .Circle of Confusion Productions, p. 93
Alpert, Marc David . . . . .Standoff, p. 376
Alpert, Sasha . . . . .Bunim/Murray Productions, Inc., p. 79
Alsop, C. Scott . . . . .Exxcell Entertainment, Inc./Exxcell Films, p. 129
Alterman, Kent . . . . .New Line Cinema, p. 234
Altman, Mark A. . . . . .Mindfire Entertainment, p. 217
Altman, Robert . . . . .Sandcastle 5 Productions, p. 279
Altman, Shelly . . . . .One Life to Live, p. 371
Altmann, Phil . . . . .Strike Entertainment, p. 303
Altobell, Jennifer . . . . .HBO Films, p. 162
Altounian, Brian . . . . .Platinum Studios, LLC, p. 257
Altschuler, John . . . . .King of the Hill, p. 365
Alvarez, Matt . . . . .Cube Vision, p. 104
Alvarez, Rafael . . . . .The Black Donnellys, p. 356
Alvarez-Garmon, Felix . . . . .IMG Media, p. 172
Alvelda, Dr. Phillip . . . . .MobiTV, p. 219
Alves, Carina . . . . .Plum Pictures, p. 258
Amann, David . . . . .Without a Trace, p. 379
Amato, Len . . . . .Spring Creek Productions, Inc., p. 298
Amaya, Rey . . . . .Sander/Moses Productions, Inc., p. 279
Ambado, Ethan . . . . .Goldenring Productions, p. 149
Ambrose, Christopher . . . . .Bones, p. 356
Ambrose, Marc . . . . .Zero Pictures, p. 349
Ambrosio, Anthony . . . . .CBS Corporation, p. 86
Ames, Lindsey . . . . .The Robert Simonds Company, p. 290
Amin, Alexa . . . . .Regency Enterprises, p. 268
Amin, Mark . . . . .Lionsgate, p. 200
Amin, Mark . . . . .Sobini Films, p. 293
Amirshahi, Bobby . . . . .Spike TV, p. 298
Amirshahi, Bobby . . . . .Comedy Central, p. 98
Ammar, Tarak Ben . . . . .Quinta Communications USA, p. 264
Ampel, Gordon . . . . .Focus Features/Rogue Pictures, p. 136
Amritraj, Ashok . . . . .Hyde Park Entertainment, p. 169
Amsden, Liz .Sub Rosa Productions, Inc., p. 303
Anderle, Darryl . . . . .Funny Boy Films, p. 143
Andersen, Jon .Sub Rosa Productions, Inc., p. 303
Anderson, Ashley . . . . .The Matthau Company, Inc., p. 212
Anderson, Craig . . . . .CrazyDreams Entertainment, p. 102
Anderson, Craig . . . . .Craig Anderson Productions, p. 52
Anderson, David . . . . .TV Guide Channel, p. 321
Anderson, Erich . . . . .Western Sandblast, p. 339
Anderson, James . . . . .Cartoon Network, p. 84
Anderson, Jeff . . . . .Allison Grodner Productions, Inc., p. 155
Anderson, Karen . . . . .The Ellen DeGeneres Show, p. 360
Anderson, Kimberly . . . . .L.I.F.T. Productions, p. 191
Anderson, Paul W.S. . . . . .Impact Pictures, p. 173
Anderson, Scott W. . . . . .Once Upon A Time Films, Ltd., p. 243
Anderson, Steve . . . . .ABC Sports, p. 45
Anderson, Steve . . . . .ESPN Original Entertainment (EOE), p. 127
Anderson, Susan . . . . .Focus Features/Rogue Pictures, p. 136
Andre, Fabian . . . . .Bunim/Murray Productions, Inc., p. 79
Andrews, Dave . . . . .GSN, p. 157
Andrews, John . . . . .Klasky Csupo, Inc., p. 189
Andrews, Patrice . . . . .Granada America, p. 152
Andrialis, Courtney . . . . .Deutsch/Open City Films, p. 109
Andrialis, Courtney . . . . .HDNet Films, p. 163
Andron, Dave . . . . .Raines, p. 372
Andrus, Mike . . . . .Antidote International Films, Inc., p. 53
Ang, Hui Keng . . . . .Sony Pictures Television International, p. 296
Angel, Dan . . . . .The Hatchery, p. 161
Angel, Nick . . . . .Working Title Films, p. 345
Angeli, Michael . . . . .Battlestar Galactica, p. 355
Angelo, Kate . . . . .What About Brian, p. 379
Anglewicz, Nicholas . . . . .Endgame Entertainment, p. 124
Anisi, Tannaz . . . . .Mainline Releasing, p. 207
Ankeles, Alex . . . . .Mosaic Media Group, p. 222
Anna, Melissa .Village Roadshow Pictures, p. 331
Annison, Jeff . . . . .MobiTV, p. 219
Ann-Margret . . . . .AM Productions & Management, p. 50
Ansell, Julie . . . . .Gracie Films, p. 151
Antholis, Kary . . . . .HBO Films, p. 162
Anthony, Greta . . . . .MARTHA, p. 368
Antonellis, Darcy . . . . .Warner Bros. Entertainment Inc., p. 334
Antonini, Lydia . . . . .JibJab Media Inc., p. 181
Anufrieeva, Svetlana . . . . .New Generation Films, Inc., p. 234
Anunciation, Derrick . . . .Echelon Entertainment World Dist. & Prod., p. 119
Apatow, Judd . . . . .Apatow Productions, p. 53
Apelian, Lauri . . . . .Matador Pictures, p. 212
Apfelbaum, Jillian . . . . .Ars Nova, p. 55
Apostolou, Theano . . . . .AMC, p. 50
Appel, Steve . . . . .ION Media Networks, Inc., p. 177
Appling, Susan . . . . .Kenneth Johnson Productions, p. 186
Arad, Ari . . . . .Marvel Studios, Inc., p. 211
Arad, Avi . . . . .Marvel Studios, Inc., p. 211
Arad, Ittay . . . . .360 Pictures/FGM Entertainment, p. 41
Arai, Taka . . . . .Pathfinder Pictures, LLC, p. 250
Arata, Elaine . . . . .7th Heaven, p. 353
Arau, Sergio . . . . .Eye on the Ball Films, Inc., p. 129
Arbelaez, Erica . . . . .Wonderland Sound and Vision, p. 344
Arbiter, Devin . . . . .O.N.C. Entertainment Inc., p. 240
Arbus, Loreen . . . . .Loreen Arbus Productions, Inc., p. 54
Archer, Mark . . . . .Mark Archer Entertainment, p. 54
Arcuri, Vincent J. . . . . .Leeza Gibbons Enterprises (LGE), p. 146
Arden, Dan . . . . .Arden Entertainment, p. 54
Aresco, Michael L. . . . . .CBS Sports, p. 88
Argott, Don . . . . .9.14 Pictures, p. 43
Arias, Francisco . . . . .CBS Paramount Network Television, p. 87
Aries, Lee Tsu . . . . .Nickelodeon/MTVN Kids & Family Group, p. 237
Arizmendi, Yareli . . . . .Eye on the Ball Films, Inc., p. 129
Arkin, Dan . . . . .Hidden Palms, p. 363
Arkush, Allan . . . . .Crossing Jordan, p. 358
Arkuss, Jeff . . . . .Fox Atomic, p. 138
Arleta, Derek . . . . .New Line Cinema, p. 234
Armbrust, Aynsley . . . . .Untitled Entertainment, p. 327
Armbrust, Tobin . . . . .Spitfire Pictures, p. 298
Armor, Kim . . . . .Versus, p. 329
Armstrong, Annie . . . . .Tribeca Productions, p. 318
Armstrong, Craig . . . . .Extreme Makeover: Home Edition, p. 361
Armstrong, Craig . . . . .Supernanny, p. 376
Armstrong, Dwight . . . . .Untitled Entertainment, p. 327
Armstrong, Laura . . . . .Endemol USA, Inc., p. 123
Armstrong, Michael D. . . . . .BET Networks, p. 66
Armstrong, Scot . . . . .American Work, p. 51
Armus, Adam . . . . .Heroes, p. 363
Arndt, Stefan . . . . .X Filme Creative Pool GmbH, p. 346
Arne, Kira . . . . .Saved, p. 374
Arnett, Sharon . . . . .Vin Di Bona Productions, p. 110
Arnold, Michael J. . . . . .Imagi Services (USA), p. 171
Arnold, Sandy . . . . .Bill Melendez Productions, p. 215
Arnold, Susan . . . . .Roth/Arnold Productions, p. 275
Arnold-Kraft, Randey . . . . .Wild Brain, Inc., p. 341
Arnspiger, Paula . . . . .Spitfire Pictures, p. 298
Arocho, Lourdes . . . . .New Line Television, p. 235
Aromando, Phil . . . . .Hock Films, Inc., p. 167
Aronoff, Marisa . . . . .Fox Reality, p. 140
Aronofsky, Darren . . . . .Protozoa Pictures, p. 263
Aronsohn, Lee . . . . .Two and a Half Men, p. 378
Aronson, Pete . . . . .Generate, p. 145
Aronson, Scott . . . . .Melee Entertainment, p. 214
Arquette, David . . . . .Dirt, p. 360
Arquette, David . . . . .Coquette Productions, p. 101
Arson, Brenda . . . . .Gorilla Pictures, p. 150
Arundale, Jennifer .MERCER Film Group Inc., p. 215
Arundale, Scott . . . . .MERCER Film Group Inc., p. 215

Asbell, Kevin .... Treasure Entertainment, p. 317
Asbell, Steve .... Twentieth Century Fox, p. 322
Ascheim, Tom .... Noggin, p. 239
Ascheim, Tom .... The N, p. 228
Ascheim, Tom .... Nickelodeon/MTVN Kids & Family Group, p. 237
Ascoli, M. Alessandra .... Screen Door Entertainment, p. 283
Ashamana, Greg .... Dalaklis-McKeown Entertainment, Inc., p. 106
Ashburn, Athena .... Sirocco Media, p. 290
Ashburn, Matthew .... Sirocco Media, p. 290
Asher, Bob .... Dalaklis-McKeown Entertainment, Inc., p. 106
Ashley, Heather .... mistRE films, p. 218
Ashman, Eric .... Proteus, p. 263
Ashton, Julie .... Happy Hour, p. 362
Ashurst, James .... Travel Channel, p. 316
Ashworth, Cynthia .... Oxygen Media, p. 245
Askanas, Paula .... Sony Pictures Television, p. 296
Askin, Shebnem .... 2929 Productions, p. 40
Asner, Matthew .... mod3productions, p. 219
Aspinwall, Maria K. .... Tudor Management Group, p. 320
Astrof, Jeff .... The New Adventures of Old Christine, p. 370
Astrof, Liz .... The King of Queens, p. 365
Ataei, Soheila .... G4 TV, p. 144
Atchity, Ken .... AEI-Atchity Entertainment Intl., Inc., p. 47
Athas, Nick .... Olmos Productions, Inc., p. 242
Atkins, Sean .... A. Smith & Co. Productions, p. 292
Atkinson, Kathy .... Fox Broadcasting Company, p. 139
Attanasio, Michael .... Numb3rs, p. 370
Attanasio, Paul .... House, p. 363
Attanasio, Paul .... Heel & Toe Films, p. 163
Attie, Eli .... Studio 60 on the Sunset Strip, p. 376
Atwater, Martha .... Scholastic Entertainment, p. 281
Atwell, Robert P. .... Camelot Entertainment Group, Inc., p. 82
Atwood, Chris .... Reba, p. 372
Aubrey, Sarah .... Friday Night Lights, p. 361
Aubrey, Sarah .... Film 44, p. 131
Aubry, Jonathan .... here! Networks, p. 165
Audino, Carrie .... The Nine, p. 370
Audino, Carrie .... Waterfront, p. 379
Audino, Carrie .... Close to Home, p. 357
Auerbach, David .... Warner Horizon Television, p. 335
Auerbach, Gary .... Go Go Luckey Productions, p. 147
Auerbach, Jeffrey .... Charlotte Street Films, p. 89
Auerbach, Julie .... Go Go Luckey Productions, p. 147
Auerbach, Michael .... King World Productions, Inc., p. 188
Aug, Boyd .... Joada Productions, Inc., p. 181
Augsberger, Jana .... Eden Rock Media, Inc., p. 120
Augsberger, Thomas .... Eden Rock Media, Inc., p. 120
Auritt, Polly .... Film 44, p. 131
Auspitz, Sara .... Endemol USA, Inc., p. 123
Austin, Ian .... Lonetree Entertainment, p. 202
Austin, Jeanne .... 1492 Pictures, p. 38
Austin, Mark .... Intermedia Film Equities USA, Inc., p. 175
Austin, Steve .... Tag Entertainment, Inc., p. 307
Austin-Bruns, Emily V. .... New Amsterdam Entertainment, Inc., p. 233
Avallone, Susan .... Unpainted Pictures, p. 327
Avenell, James .... MARTHA, p. 368
Averill, Howard .... NBC Entertainment, p. 230
Avery, Kelley .... Paramount Pictures, p. 248
Avila, Ernie .... Original Productions, p. 244
Aviv, Oren .... Buena Vista Motion Pictures Group, p. 78
Avner, Andrew .... Heel & Toe Films, p. 163
Avnet, Jon .... Brooklyn Films, p. 77
Avruskin, Milt .... David Brady Productions, p. 72
Axelrod, Jonathan .... The Axelrod/Edwards Company, p. 59
Axler, Rachel .... The Daily Show With Jon Stewart, p. 359
Axume, Elias .... Myriad Pictures, p. 228
Ayer, David .... Crave Films, p. 102
Ayers, Julie .... New Wave Management, p. 236
Aymong, Ken .... Saturday Night Live, p. 373
Ayo, Christi .... According to Jim, p. 354
Azpiazu, Stefanie .... This is that corporation, p. 312
Azusa, Dominique .... Chotzen/Jenner Productions, p. 90
Azzolino, Mike .... Jerry Bruckheimer Films & Television, p. 78
Babatunde-Bey, Jana .... Overbrook Entertainment, p. 245
Babcock, David .... Gilmore Girls, p. 362
Babcock, Hayley .... Fox Television Studios, p. 140
Babcock, Jim .... Cartoon Network, p. 84
Babiszewski, Jason .... Code Entertainment, p. 96
Baca, Ian .... Joel Stevens Entertainment, p. 301
Bachmaier, Joerg .... Endemol USA, Inc., p. 123
Badagliacca, Mark .... Paramount Pictures, p. 248
Badell-Slaughter, Cindy .... CBS Entertainment, p. 86
Bader, Jeffrey .... ABC Entertainment Television Group, p. 45
Badham, John .... The Badham Company, p. 60
Badlam, Robb .... Filbert Steps Productions, p. 131
Badstibner, Jim .... Offspring Entertainment, p. 241
Baek, Jenny .... Armada Pictures, p. 55
Baer, Amy .... Columbia Pictures, p. 97
Baer, Brett .... 30 Rock, p. 353
Baer, Donald .... Discovery Networks, U.S., p. 111
Baer, Neal .... Law & Order: Special Victims Unit, p. 367
Baer, Neal .... Wolf Films, Inc., p. 343
Baer, Willi E. .... Eternity Pictures, Inc., p. 127
Baez, Carlos .... A&E Network, p. 44
Bagley, Sarah .... Arielle Tepper Productions, p. 312
Bailey, Dick .... Tribune Entertainment Company, p. 318
Bailey, Fenton .... World of Wonder Productions, p. 345
Bailey, Jeremy .... Weed Road Pictures, p. 337
Bailey, Kerry .... Craig Anderson Productions, p. 52
Bailey, Miranda .... Ambush Entertainment, p. 50
Bailey, Rob .... CSI: NY, p. 359
Bailey, Sean .... LivePlanet, p. 201
Bain, Allen .... The 7th Floor, p. 43
Bain, Barnet .... Barnet Bain Films, p. 60
Baird, Tracey .... Dakota North Entertainment/Dakota Films, p. 106
Bajaria, Bela .... CBS Entertainment, p. 86
Bakay, Nick .... The King of Queens, p. 365
Bakay, Nick .... 'Til Death, p. 377
Baker, Bridget .... NBC Universal Cable Entertainment, p. 231
Baker, Mark .... Ugly Betty, p. 378
Baker, Martin .... IMG Media, p. 172
Baker, Matthew .... Recorded Picture Company, p. 266
Baker, Mike .... Enpocket, p. 124
Baker, Neil .... E! Networks, p. 117
Baker, Patrick .... Misher Films, p. 218
Baker, Paxton .... BET Networks, p. 66
Baker, Simon .... Sony Pictures Entertainment, p. 295
Baker, Susan M. .... June Beallor Productions, p. 64
Baker, Tiffany .... Misher Films, p. 218
Baker-Riker, Margery .... CBS News, p. 87
Bakish, Bob .... MTV Networks, p. 226
Bakken, Janae .... Scrubs, p. 374
Bakshi, Mark .... Paramount Pictures Production Division, p. 248
Balaban, Bob .... Chicagofilms, p. 90
Balaker, Courtney .... Neo Art & Logic, p. 232
Balasco, Byron .... Without a Trace, p. 379
Balasco, Byron .... Kidnapped, p. 365
Baldasare, John .... Industry Entertainment Partners, p. 174
Baldecchi, John .... John Baldecchi Productions, p. 60
Baldikoski, Wendy .... Warner Bros. Television Production, p. 335
Baldwin, Alec .... El Dorado Pictures, p. 120
Baldwin, Erin .... Laika Entertainment, p. 191
Baldwin, Howard .... Baldwin Entertainment Group, Ltd., p. 60
Baldwin, Hunt .... The Closer, p. 357
Baldwin, Karen .... Baldwin Entertainment Group, Ltd., p. 60
Baldwin, Nathaniel .... Baldwin Entertainment Group, Ltd., p. 60
Balian, Alison .... The Ellen DeGeneres Show, p. 360
Balian, Gina .... HBO Entertainment, p. 162
Balis, Jeff .... Whitewater Films, p. 340
Ball, Chelsey .... Josselyne Herman & Assoc./Moving Image Films, p. 166
Ball, Chris .... Newmarket Capital Group, p. 236
Ball, Jennifer .... A&E Network, p. 44
Ballas-Traynor, Lucia .... MTV Networks, p. 226
Ballering, Richard .... Touchstone Television, p. 316
Ballivian, Nicole .... Cinema Libre Studio, p. 92
Balsam, Mark .... Peace Arch Entertainment Group Inc., p. 251
Banal, Shannon .... Bleiberg Entertainment, p. 68
Bancroft, Libby .... Mutual Film Company, p. 227
Bandman, Jake .... Shoot the Moon Productions, p. 286
Bangert, Charles .... New Screen Concepts, Inc., p. 235

Bank, Brenda .MRB Productions, Inc., p. 224
Bankoff, Jim .AOL Media Networks, p. 53
Banks, Brian .CBS Paramount Network Television, p. 87
Banks, Susan .TV One, LLC, p. 322
Banks, Tyra .America's Next Top Model, p. 355
Banks, Tyra .The Tyra Banks Show, p. 378
Banks, Tyra .Bankable Productions, p. 61
Bankston, Matt .Hazy Mills Productions, p. 161
Bannister, Thomas .Angelika, p. 52
Bans, Jenna .Desperate Housewives, p. 360
Bantle, Scott .G4 TV, p. 144
Barab, Martin J. .Bauer Martinez Entertainment, p. 63
Barak, Deborah .CBS Paramount Network Television, p. 87
Barak, Deborah .CBS Entertainment, p. 86
Baratta, Dana .Runaway, p. 373
Barba, Norberto .Law & Order: Criminal Intent, p. 367
Barbato, Randy .World of Wonder Productions, p. 345
Barbee, Carol .Jericho, p. 364
Barbee, Matt .Untitled Entertainment, p. 327
Barber, Anna .SMG Productions, p. 292
Barber, Gary .Spyglass Entertainment Group, p. 299
Barber, Karen .A Band Apart, p. 43
Barber, Karen .Lawrence Bender Productions, p. 65
Barber, Shawn .Mobile Streams, p. 219
Barbera, Michele .Lonetree Entertainment, p. 202
Barbieri, Tony .Jimmy Kimmel Live, p. 364
Barcellos, Christian .Bravo, p. 74
Barcinas, Tamra .Endemol USA, Inc., p. 123
Barclay, Mark .Strike Entertainment, p. 303
Bardasano, Carole .Fremantle Productions Latin America, p. 142
Barden, Lee .Comedy Central, p. 98
Bardwil, Steve .Buena Vista Motion Pictures Group, p. 78
Barg, Meredith .Darren Star Productions, p. 300
Barger, Tony .Joel Schumacher Productions, p. 281
Bario, Holly .Universal Pictures, p. 326
Barish, Leora .Fuller Films, Inc., p. 143
Barker, Clive .Seraphim Films, p. 284
Barker, Doug .ION Media Networks, Inc., p. 177
Barker, Mike .American Dad, p. 354
Barlassina, Chiara .Merchant-Ivory, p. 215
Barlow, Edward .Spitfire Pictures, p. 298
Barlow, Nate .Automatic Pictures, Inc., p. 58
Barnathan, Michael .1492 Pictures, p. 38
Barneburg, Aimee .East of Doheny/Lexington Road Prod., p. 118
Barnes, Dean .Fox Television Studios, p. 140
Barnes, Jonas .Original Film, p. 244
Barnes, Paul .Florentine Films, p. 135
Barnes, Rodney .Everybody Hates Chris, p. 361
Barnett, Kevin .Conundrum Entertainment, p. 100
Barnett, Peter J. .Nova Pictures, p. 240
Barnett, Steve .Atmosphere Entertainment MM, LLC, p. 58
Barnette, Alan .Alan Barnette Productions, p. 61
Barnhill, Matthew .BET Networks, p. 66
Barnholtz, Barry .Barnholtz Entertainment, p. 62
Barnholtz, Kate .Barnholtz Entertainment, p. 62
Barnow, Alex .'Til Death, p. 377
Barnum, Rob .Cyan Pictures, p. 105
Baron, Caroline .A-Line Pictures, p. 49
Baron, Fred .Twentieth Century Fox, p. 322
Baron, Nina .Picturehouse, p. 254
Baron, Pam .Twentieth Century Fox Television, p. 323
Baron, Peter .MTV Networks, p. 226
Baron, Seth .Peter Hankwitz Production & Mgmt., p. 160
Barone, Randall .ABC Daytime, p. 44
Baronet, Wili .WilMark Entertainment, Inc., p. 341
Barquet, Arturo .Universal Pictures, p. 326
Barr, Adam .The New Adventures of Old Christine, p. 370
Barr, Tally .Dakota North Entertainment/Dakota Films, p. 106
Barrau, Claire .Bonne Pioche, p. 71
Barrero, Nestor .Universal Studios, p. 326
Barret, Jean-Christophe .Bonne Pioche, p. 71
Barreto, Luis .Extreme Makeover: Home Edition, p. 361
Barrett, David .Cold Case, p. 357
Barrett, Jason .Alchemy Entertainment, p. 48
Barrie, Lynn .Twentieth Century Fox Television, p. 323
Barrie, Michael .Imagination Productions, Inc., p. 171
Barringer, Gail .Law & Order: Special Victims Unit, p. 367
Barrington, Dave .My Network TV, p. 228
Barris, Kenya .The Game, p. 361
Barris, Robin .Imagine Entertainment, p. 172
Barron, Robert .Twentieth Century Fox Television, p. 323
Barros, Alvaro .MTV Networks Latin America (MTVNLA), p. 226
Barroso, Emilio Diez .Nala Films, p. 228
Barrosse, Paul .Gay Rosenthal Productions, p. 275
Barry, Jonathan .Nuyorican, p. 240
Barry, Josh .ABC Entertainment Television Group, p. 45
Barry, Sumithra .NBC Entertainment, p. 230
Barrymore, Drew .Flower Films, Inc., p. 135
Bartee, Jeff .MobiTV, p. 219
Barth, Aimée .Forest Park Pictures, p. 137
Bartis, David .Hypnotic, p. 170
Bartlett, Helen .Barnstorm Films, p. 62
Bartlett, Lee .Fox Broadcasting Company, p. 139
Barto, Trice .Hell's Kitchen, p. 363
Bartok, Mike .Viacom Entertainment Group, p. 330
Barton, Al .Columbia Pictures, p. 97
Barton, Kimberly .Penn Station Entertainment, p. 252
Bartoo, Todd .PorchLight Entertainment, p. 259
Bartosh, Wendy .Twentieth Century Fox Television, p. 323
Baruch, Jonathan .Relevant Entertainment Group, p. 270
Baruh, Brad .M3 Television, p. 205
Barzee, Anastasia .East of Doheny/Lexington Road Prod., p. 118
Bascom, Fran .Days of Our Lives, p. 359
Baseman, Neal .Twentieth Century Fox Television, p. 323
Bashoff, Jaclyn .Gray Angel Productions, p. 152
Basile, Mary Beth .Mojo Films, p. 220
Baskerville, Bob .DIY Network, p. 113
Baskin, Alex .Evolution, p. 128
Baskin, Ellen .Epigram Entertainment, p. 125
Basner, Glen .The Weinstein Company, p. 337
Bass, Matt .HBO Films, p. 162
Bass, Suzanne .MARTHA, p. 368
Bassman, Sabrina .Schwartz & Company, Inc., p. 281
Bastian, Rene .Belladonna Productions, p. 65
Basulto, David .Clarity Pictures, LLC, p. 94
Basulto, Loren .Clarity Pictures, LLC, p. 94
Basunia, Taj .Spice Factory, p. 298
Bateman, Laine .Storyline Entertainment, p. 302
Bates, Edward J. .Bates Entertainment, p. 62
Bates, Rheanna .Everyman Pictures, p. 128
Bates, Rochelle .Bates Entertainment, p. 62
Batra, Aseem .Scrubs, p. 374
Batter, John .DreamWorks Animation SKG, p. 116
Batti-McClure, Tahira .Sci Fi Channel, p. 282
Battista, Rich .TV Guide Channel, p. 321
Battles, Wendy .CSI: NY, p. 359
Battsek, Daniel .Miramax Films, p. 217
Baucom, Pam .Florentine Films, p. 135
Baudine, Skip .Heroes, p. 363
Bauer, Harley .Yellow Cab Pictures, p. 347
Bauer, Martin R. .The Bauer Company, p. 63
Baughan, Bristol .Reason Pictures, p. 266
Baugin, Judith .ContentFilm, p. 100
Baum, Carol .Carol Baum Productions, p. 63
Baum, David .Latin Hollywood Films, p. 194
Baum, Michael .Handprint Entertainment, p. 160
Baum, Shiva .Alex Rose Productions, Inc., p. 274
Bauman, Beau .Tower of Babble Entertainment, p. 316
Bauman, Jake .Laura Ziskin Productions, p. 349
Bauman, Suzanne .Suzanne Bauman Productions, p. 63
Baumann, William T. .PorchLight Entertainment, p. 259
Baumgard, Caroline .Endemol USA, Inc., p. 123
Baxter, Peter .SMG Productions, p. 292
Baxter, Stuart .Sony Pictures Television International, p. 296
Bay, Michael .Platinum Dunes, p. 257
Bay, Michael .Digital Domain, Inc., p. 110
Bay, Michael .Bay Films, p. 63
Bayer, Hally .Cookie Jar Entertainment, p. 100
Baynes, Andrea .Alexander/Enright & Associates, p. 49
Bayoud, Alexis .Outerbanks Entertainment, p. 245

Bays, Carter . . . . . How I Met Your Mother, p. 364
Bazalgette, Peter . . . . . Endemol USA, Inc., p. 123
Beallor, June . . . . . June Beallor Productions, p. 64
Bean, Henry . . . . . Fuller Films, Inc., p. 143
Bean, Julie . . . . . The Game, p. 361
Beanes, David . . . . . Universal Operations Group, p. 326
Bear, Emily . . . . . Miramax Films, p. 217
Beattie, Alex . . . . . In Cahoots, p. 173
Beattie, Jay . . . . . Vanished, p. 378
Beatty, Kim . . . . . North By Northwest Entertainment, p. 239
Beatty, Thomas . . . . . Lakeshore Entertainment Group LLC, p. 192
Beaty, Naomi . . . . . Maverick Films, p. 213
Beaubaire, David . . . . . DreamWorks SKG, p. 116
Beauchamp, Todd . . . . . TriCoast Studios, p. 318
Beaudine, Skip . . . . . Crossing Jordan, p. 358
Beaulieu, Trace . . . . . America's Funniest Videos, p. 355
Beavers, Susan . . . . . Two and a Half Men, p. 378
Beazoglou, Despina . . . . . Warner Independent Pictures, p. 335
Beccar Varela, Jeronimo . . . . . Frederic Golchan Productions, p. 148
Beck, Carrie . . . . . MTV Films, p. 225
Beck, Don . . . . . Reba, p. 372
Beck, Gordon . . . . . USA Network, p. 327
Beck, J. . . . . . First Look Pictures, p. 134
Beck, John D. . . . . . According to Jim, p. 354
Beck, Q . . . . . Nickelodeon Movies, p. 237
Becker, Holly . . . . . Sidney Kimmel Entertainment, p. 187
Becker, Kimberly . . . . . Managed Passion Films, p. 208
Becker, Veronica . . . . . Ugly Betty, p. 378
Becker, Wolfgang . . . . . X Filme Creative Pool GmbH, p. 346
Beckerman, Jon D. . . . . . The Knights of Prosperity, p. 365
Beckerman, Jon D. . . . . . The Late Show with David Letterman, p. 367
Beckett, Lee . . . . . Media Financial International, LLC, p. 214
Beckman, Deanna . . . . . Untitled Entertainment, p. 327
Beckman, Preston . . . . . Fox Broadcasting Company, p. 139
Becky, Dave . . . . . Everybody Hates Chris, p. 361
Becky, Dave . . . . . Lucky Louie, p. 368
Becky, Dave . . . . . 3 Arts Entertainment, Inc., p. 40
Becsey, Laurence . . . . . The Black Donnellys, p. 356
Becsey, Laurence . . . . . Blackfriars Bridge, p. 68
Bedard, Michael . . . . . Sitting Ducks Productions, p. 290
Beddor, Frank . . . . . Automatic Pictures, Inc., p. 58
Bedolis, John . . . . . The Colbert Report, p. 357
Bedusa, Susan . . . . . 4th Row Films, p. 42
Beeber, Jay . . . . . Black Sheep Entertainment, p. 68
Beece, Debby . . . . . Oxygen Media, p. 245
Beeks, Steve . . . . . Lionsgate, p. 200
Beeman, Greg . . . . . Heroes, p. 363
Beeman, Ryan . . . . . Intrepid Pictures, p. 176
Beers, Betsy . . . . . Grey's Anatomy, p. 362
Beers, Libby . . . . . Lifetime Television (Los Angeles), p. 198
Beers, Steve . . . . . Bones, p. 356
Beers, Thom . . . . . Original Productions, p. 244
Beers, Tim . . . . . Original Productions, p. 244
Begg, Isabel . . . . . BBC Films, p. 64
Beggs, Kevin . . . . . Lionsgate, p. 200
Begnaud, Troy . . . . . Evolution Entertainment, p. 128
Behl, Aaron . . . . . Broken Lizard Industries, p. 76
Behnke, Ryan . . . . . Laura Ziskin Productions, p. 349
Behr, Karinne . . . . . Bauer Martinez Entertainment, p. 63
Behring, John . . . . . Numb3rs, p. 370
Behrman, Jason "Bear" . . . . . Highway 9 Films, p. 166
Behrman, Mellany . . . . . Highway 9 Films, p. 166
Beier, Erica . . . . . New Line Cinema, p. 234
Beil, Mani . . . . . Nickelodeon Movies, p. 237
Beiter, Debbie . . . . . Comedy Central, p. 98
Belanoff, Adam . . . . . The Closer, p. 357
Belasco, Eyde . . . . . Western Sandblast, p. 339
Belcastro, Dana M. . . . . . New Line Cinema, p. 234
Belgrad, Doug . . . . . Columbia Pictures, p. 97
Belinkoff, Kevin . . . . . GSN, p. 157
Belker, Thanda . . . . . Sony Pictures Television International, p. 296
Belkin, Jeffrey . . . . . Foremost Films, p. 137
Belkin, Jeffrey . . . . . Double Nickel Entertainment, p. 115
Bell, Ali . . . . . Heyday Films, p. 166
Bell, Art . . . . . Court TV Networks, p. 102
Bell, Bradley . . . . . The Bold and the Beautiful, p. 356
Bell, Bradley . . . . . Bell-Phillip TV Productions, Inc., p. 65
Bell, Brian . . . . . Canary Films, p. 83
Bell, David L. . . . . . Dave Bell Associates, p. 65
Bell, Jeffrey . . . . . Day Break, p. 359
Bell, Jill Hudson . . . . . Fox Broadcasting Company, p. 139
Bell, Jim . . . . . NBC News, p. 230
Bell, Lee Phillip . . . . . The Bold and the Beautiful, p. 356
Bell, Lee Phillip . . . . . Bell-Phillip TV Productions, Inc., p. 65
Bell, Ross Grayson . . . . . Atman Entertainment, p. 57
Bell, Torrey . . . . . Bravo, p. 74
Bell, Warren . . . . . According to Jim, p. 354
Bella, Joe . . . . . Two and a Half Men, p. 378
Bellflower, Nellie . . . . . KeyLight Entertainment Group, p. 187
Bellisario, David . . . . . NCIS, p. 370
Bellisario, David . . . . . Belisarius Productions, p. 65
Bellisario, Donald P. . . . . . NCIS, p. 370
Bellisario, Donald P. . . . . . Belisarius Productions, p. 65
Bellitti, Chris . . . . . Zingy Inc., p. 349
Bello, Morella . . . . . Touchstone Television, p. 316
Bellomo, Lisa . . . . . Pretty Pictures, p. 261
Bellomo, Tracy . . . . . Smallville, p. 375
Bellon, Greg . . . . . America's Funniest Videos, p. 355
Bellon, Joe . . . . . America's Funniest Videos, p. 355
Bellville, Hercules . . . . . Recorded Picture Company, p. 266
Belshaw, George . . . . . Judge-Belshaw Entertainment, Inc., p. 183
Belson, Kristine . . . . . DreamWorks Animation SKG, p. 116
Belt, Mimi . . . . . Telemundo Network, p. 310
Beltzner, Jeff . . . . . Evolving Pictures Entertainment, p. 128
Benattar, Rick . . . . . Thunder Road Pictures, p. 313
Benavente, David M. . . . . . Telepictures Productions, p. 311
Bendele, George . . . . . Funny Boy Films, p. 143
Bender, Chris . . . . . Benderspink, p. 66
Bender, Lawrence . . . . . A Band Apart, p. 43
Bender, Lawrence . . . . . Lawrence Bender Productions, p. 65
Bender, Myles . . . . . Focus Features/Rogue Pictures, p. 136
Bender, Quinn . . . . . New City Pictures, Inc., p. 233
Bender, Ted . . . . . Principato-Young Entertainment, p. 262
Benedek, Melinda . . . . . Showtime Networks Inc., p. 287
Benesh, Jason . . . . . Zucker Productions, p. 350
Benjamin, Elizabeth . . . . . Bones, p. 356
Benjamin, Ellen . . . . . Witt-Thomas-Harris Productions, p. 343
Benjamin, Linda . . . . . Intermedia Film Equities USA, Inc., p. 175
Benjamin, Stuart . . . . . Baldwin Entertainment Group, Ltd., p. 60
Benjamin, Troy . . . . . Weekend Films/Main Street Film Company, p. 337
Benjamin-Phariss, Bonnie . . . . . Vulcan Productions, p. 332
Benn, Grace . . . . . Sony Pictures Television, p. 296
Benner, Brett . . . . . One Tree Hill, p. 371
Benner, Brett . . . . . Scrubs, p. 374
Benner, Brett . . . . . Notes From the Underbelly, p. 370
Bennett, Douglas . . . . . National Lampoon, p. 230
Bennett, Harve . . . . . Harve Bennett Productions, p. 66
Bennett, Jana . . . . . BBC Worldwide Americas, p. 64
Bennett, Jay . . . . . Original Productions, p. 244
Bennett, Jennifer . . . . . Alliance Atlantis, p. 49
Bennett, Kent . . . . . Licht Entertainment Corporation, p. 197
Bennett, Meredith . . . . . The Colbert Report, p. 357
Bennett, Michael . . . . . MRB Productions, Inc., p. 224
Bennett, Rob . . . . . MSN Originals, p. 224
Bennett, Sylvia . . . . . PBS, p. 251
Bennett, Tye . . . . . Paulette Breen Productions, p. 74
Benoit, Melva . . . . . Fox Broadcasting Company, p. 139
Bensinger, Tyler . . . . . Cold Case, p. 357
Benson, Alison . . . . . Pretty Matches Productions, p. 261
Benson, James D. . . . . . Workshop Pictures, Inc., p. 345
Benson, Julie . . . . . Contrafilm, p. 100
Benson, Michael . . . . . Altitude Entertainment, p. 49
Benson, Mike . . . . . Entourage, p. 360
Benson, Peter . . . . . Guardian Entertainment, Ltd., p. 157
Benson, Scott . . . . . Guardian Entertainment, Ltd., p. 157
Benson, Stuart . . . . . Sundance Channel, p. 304
Bentley, Robert . . . . . TV Guide Channel, p. 321
Bentley, Trevor . . . . . Atomic Cartoons, Inc., p. 58
Benun, Robert . . . . . Lakeshore Entertainment Group LLC, p. 192
Benz, Gary R. . . . . . GRB Entertainment, p. 153

Beougher, Francine . . . . .Sony Pictures Television, p. 296
Berenson, Matt . . . . .Carsey-Werner Films, p. 84
Berfield, Justin . . . . .J2 Pictures/J2TV, p. 178
Berg, Jon . . . . .Guy Walks Into a Bar, p. 158
Berg, Kevin . . . . .CBS Paramount Network Television, p. 87
Berg, Kevin . . . . .Village Roadshow Pictures, p. 331
Berg, Meredith . . . . .Platinum Studios, LLC, p. 257
Berg, Peter . . . . .Friday Night Lights, p. 361
Berg, Peter . . . . .Film 44, p. 131
Berg, Rick . . . . .Code Entertainment, p. 96
Berger, Albert . . . . .Bona Fide Productions, p. 71
Berger, Josh . . . . .Warner Bros. Entertainment Inc., p. 334
Berger, Karen . . . . .DC Comics, p. 108
Berger, Lisa . . . . .E! Networks, p. 117
Berger, Morris . . . . .Masters of Horror, p. 368
Berger, Morris . . . . .IDT Entertainment, p. 171
Bergeron, Tom .America's Funniest Videos, p. 355
Bergman, Alan . . . . .Buena Vista Motion Pictures Group, p. 78
Bergman, Debra Grieco .Columbia Pictures, p. 97
Bergman, Ram . . . . .Gordonstreet Pictures, p. 150
Bergman, Royce . . . . .Storyline Entertainment, p. 302
Bergmann, Peter .The Over the Hill Gang, p. 245
Bergstein, David . . . . .Mobius International, p. 219
Berk, Jason . . . . .Union Square Entertainment, p. 325
Berk, Jeff . . . . .Norsemen Television Productions, LLC, p. 239
Berk, Michele . . . . .Lotus Pictures, p. 203
Berk, Stefanie . . . . .Playtone Productions, p. 258
Berke, Beth . . . . .Sony Pictures Entertainment, p. 295
Berlanti, Greg . . . . .Berlanti Productions, p. 66
Berlin, Carey . . . . .DNA Films, p. 114
Berlin, Mieke ter Poorten . . . . .Tudor Management Group, p. 320
Berliner, Marc . . . . .Bad Hat Harry Productions, p. 59
Berman, Amy . . . . .HBO Films, p. 162
Berman, Andy . . . . .Misher Films, p. 218
Berman, Bruce . . . . .Village Roadshow Pictures, p. 331
Berman, Burt . . . . .Paramount Pictures Production Division, p. 248
Berman, Gail . . . . .Paramount Pictures, p. 248
Berman, Jennifer . . . . .De Line Pictures, p. 108
Berman, Joel . . . . .CBS Paramount Worldwide Television Dist., p. 88
Berman, Melissa . . . . .Berlanti Productions, p. 66
Berman, Richard C. . . . . .Lancaster Gate Entertainment, p. 192
Berman, Rick . . . . .Rick Berman Productions, p. 66
Bermann, Georges . . . . .Partizan, p. 250
Bermudez-Key, Klaudia . . . . . .Sony Pictures Television International, p. 296
Bernal, Aida . . . . .Nuyorican, p. 240
Bernard, Claire Rose . . . . .CastleBright Studios, p. 85
Bernard, Joe . . . . .Telemundo Network, p. 310
Bernard, Nicole .Fox Broadcasting Company, p. 139
Bernardi, David . . . . .Imagine Entertainment, p. 172
Bernath, David . . . . .Comedy Central, p. 98
Berner, Fred . . . . .Wolf Films, Inc., p. 343
Bernero, Amanda . . . . .Criminal Minds, p. 358
Bernero, Edward Allen . . . . .Criminal Minds, p. 358
Berney, Bob . . . . .Picturehouse, p. 254
Bernheim, Nicolas . . . . .Seven Summits Pictures & Management, p. 285
Berning, Melvin . . . . .A&E Network, p. 44
Berns, Ashley . . . . .Circle of Confusion Productions, p. 93
Berns, Michael . . . . .Waterfront, p. 379
Bernstein, Adam . . . . .30 Rock, p. 353
Bernstein, Andrew . . . . .Paul Schiff Productions, p. 280
Bernstein, Armyan . . . . .Beacon, p. 64
Bernstein, Jim . . . . .American Dad, p. 354
Bernstein, Lewis . . . . .Sesame Workshop, p. 285
Bernstein, Melissa . . . . .Gran Via Productions, p. 152
Bernstein, Michael . . . . .Actual Reality Pictures, p. 46
Bernstein, Nan . . . . .Friday Night Lights, p. 361
Bernstein, Nancy . . . . .DreamWorks Animation SKG, p. 116
Bernstein, Nick . . . . .NBC Entertainment, p. 230
Bernstein, Scott . . . . .Universal Pictures, p. 326
Bernstein-Baker, Lori . . . . .Twentieth Television, p. 324
Berro, Benson . . . . .Endemol USA, Inc., p. 123
Berry, John . . . . .Latin Hollywood Films, p. 194
Berry, Jonathan . . . . .DreamWorks SKG, p. 116
Berry, Matt . . . . .Reba, p. 372
Bersch, Steven . . . . .Twentieth Century Fox, p. 322
Berson, David . . . . .Tribune Entertainment Company, p. 318
Bert, Victoria . . . . .Al Roker Productions, p. 274
Bertelle, Ralph . . . . .Paramount Vantage/Paramount Classics, p. 248
Berthiaume, Dave . . . . .Flying A Studios, Inc., p. 135
Bertner, Brad . . . . .3 Arts Entertainment, Inc., p. 40
Berwick, Frances . . . . .Bravo, p. 74
Besman, Michael . . . . .Ballyhoo, Inc., p. 60
Besnoy, Dana . . . . .Pie Town Productions, p. 254
Bess, Ivan . . . . .Sarah Green Film Corp., p. 153
Bess, Janet . . . . .Concrete Pictures, p. 99
Besser, Matt . . . . .Upright Citizens Brigade, p. 327
Besson, Luc . . . . .EuropaCorp Films, p. 127
Best, Rex . . . . .The Bold and the Beautiful, p. 356
Bestall, Rikki Lea .Krasnoff Foster Productions, p. 190
Bestrop, Juel . . . . .Lucky Louie, p. 368
Betancourt, Mick . . . . .The Black Donnellys, p. 356
Bettag, Tom . . . . .Discovery Channel, p. 111
Bettag, Tom . . . . .Discovery Networks, U.S., p. 111
Bevan, Michael . . . . .GSN, p. 157
Bevan, Tim . . . . .Working Title Films, p. 345
Beverly, Carl . . . . .Kidnapped, p. 365
Beverly, Carl . . . . .25C Productions, p. 40
Beverly, Sharon .Rive Gauche Entertainment, p. 272
Beyda, Katherine . . . . .New Line Cinema, p. 234
Bhai, Amyn . . . . .Proud Mary Entertainment, p. 263
Bialow, Adam . . . . .Lionsgate, p. 200
Bianchi, Ed . . . . .Waterfront, p. 379
Bianco, Jim . . . . .Dalaklis-McKeown Entertainment, Inc., p. 106
Bibby, Roslyn . . . . .FX, p. 144
Biber, Liz . . . . .The Weinstein Company, p. 337
Biber, Liz . . . . .Dimension Films, p. 111
Bickel, David . . . . .The King of Queens, p. 365
Bickham, Amber . . . . .Jimmy Kimmel Live, p. 364
Biddix, Joe . . . . .Untitled Entertainment, p. 327
Biddle, Adrienne . . . . .Focus Features/Rogue Pictures, p. 136
Bieber, Jayne . . . . .New Line Cinema, p. 234
Bieber, Jayne . . . . .New Line Television, p. 235
Biederman, Ian . . . . .Shark, p. 374
Biegel, Kevin . . . . .Scrubs, p. 374
Bienstock, Jay . . . . .The Apprentice, p. 355
Bienstock, Marc . . . . .Mainline Releasing, p. 207
Biewend, Janis . . . . .New Screen Concepts, Inc., p. 235
Bigel, Daniel . . . . .Bigel Entertainment, p. 67
Biggar, Maggie . . . . .Fortis Films, p. 137
Biggs, Denis . . . . .Entourage, p. 360
Bilanjian, Sossi . . . . .DisneyToon Studios, p. 113
Bilger, Arthur H. . . . . .Veoh Networks, Inc., p. 329
Bill, Tony . . . . .Barnstorm Films, p. 62
Billeci, Bob . . . . .Sony Pictures Television International, p. 296
Billett, Stu . . . . .Stu Billett Productions, p. 67
Billik, Tammara . . . .'Til Death, p. 377
Billik, Tara . . . . .Craven/Maddalena Films, p. 102
Billingsly, Matt . . . . .Harms Way Productions, p. 160
Bilsky, Bethany . . . . .Mad Chance, p. 206
Binder, Carl . . . . .Stargate: SG-1, p. 376
Binder, Carl . . . . .Stargate: Atlantis, p. 376
Binder, Jack . . . . .Sunlight Productions, p. 305
Binder, Mike . . . . .Sunlight Productions, p. 305
Binder, Steven . . . . .NCIS, p. 370
Binder, Steven . . . . .Belisarius Productions, p. 65
Bines, Jonathan . . . . .Jimmy Kimmel Live, p. 364
Bing, Tracey . . . . .Warner Independent Pictures, p. 335
Binkow, Gary . . . . .The Collective, p. 96
Biondo, John . . . . .Mandate Pictures, p. 209
Birchfield-Eick, Jenny . . . . .JBE Productions, p. 180
Bird, Andy . . . . .The Walt Disney Company, p. 112
Birkhahn, Jonathan . . . . .King World Productions, Inc., p. 188
Birman Ripstein, Daniel . . . . .Alameda Films, p. 48
Birmingham, Robert . . . . .Fred Kuehnert Productions, p. 190
Birn, Jerry . . . . .The Bold and the Beautiful, p. 356
Birnbaum, Michael . . . . .Empire Pictures Incorporated, p. 123
Birnbaum, Roger . . . . .Spyglass Entertainment Group, p. 299
Biscotti, Gina . . . . .Barwood Films, p. 62
Bissell, Robin . . . . .Larger Than Life Productions, p. 193
Bittler, David . . . . .Logo, p. 202

Blachman, Rochel . . . . .Phoenix Pictures, p. 254
Black, Alison . . . . .H2F Entertainment, p. 158
Black, Barbara . . . . .Ghost Whisperer, p. 362
Black, Chris . . . . .Vanished, p. 378
Black, Eric . . . . .Pie Town Productions, p. 254
Black, Jack . . . . .Black & White Productions, p. 67
Black, Lance . . . . .Big Love, p. 356
Black, Marco . . . . .CSI: Miami, p. 358
Black, Marnie . . . . .MTV Networks, p. 226
Black, Melissa . . . . .CSI: Miami, p. 358
Black, Mike . . . . .Taryn Productions, p. 308
Black, Todd . . . . .Escape Artists II, p. 126
Blacker, Peter . . . . .Telemundo Network, p. 310
Blackman, David . . . . .Laurence Mark Productions, p. 210
Blackman, Lori . . . . .The Ellen DeGeneres Show, p. 360
Blackman, Steve . . . . .Hidden Palms, p. 363
Blackwell, Deborah . . . . .Disney ABC Cable Networks Group, p. 112
Blackwell, Deborah . . . . .SOAPnet, p. 293
Blackwood, Carolyn . . . . .New Line Cinema, p. 234
Blahd, Doug . . . . .Namesake Entertainment, p. 228
Blain, Adam . . . . .JT Entertainment, p. 182
Blair, Seth . . . . .Norsemen Television Productions, LLC, p. 239
Blake, Jeff . . . . .Sony Pictures Entertainment, p. 295
Blake, Juliet . . . . .Scholastic Entertainment, p. 281
Blake, Meredith . . . . .Participant Productions, p. 249
Blake, Peter . . . . .House, p. 363
Blanchard, Kara . . . . .This is that corporation, p. 312
Blanco, Rick . . . . .Cartoon Network, p. 84
Blaney, Jane . . . . .USA Network, p. 327
Blank, Matthew C. . . . . .Showtime Networks Inc., p. 287
Blas, John . . . . .Buena Vista Motion Pictures Group, p. 78
Blasband, Katherine . . . . .Tapestry Films, Inc., p. 308
Blasucci, Dick . . . . .Mad TV, p. 368
Blatt, Greg . . . . .IAC/InterActiveCorp, p. 170
Blaugrund, Jed . . . . .WWE Films, p. 346
Blauschild, Doreen . . . . .CSI: Miami, p. 358
Blaylock, William . . . . .Seven Summits Pictures & Management, p. 285
Bleck, Jack . . . . .DreamWorks SKG, p. 116
Bleger, Kevin . . . . .The Daily Show With Jon Stewart, p. 359
Bleiberg, Ehud . . . . .Bleiberg Entertainment, p. 68
Bliss, Howard . . . . .Union Entertainment, p. 325
Bliss, Tom . . . . .Strike Entertainment, p. 303
Bloch, Cheryl . . . . .Face Productions/Jennilind Productions, p. 129
Bloch, David . . . . .Focus Features/Rogue Pictures, p. 136
Block, Bill . . . . .QED International, p. 264
Block, Ira . . . . .Jurist Productions, p. 183
Block, Nicole W. . . . . .Screen Door Entertainment, p. 283
Block, Peter . . . . .Lionsgate, p. 200
Blodgett, Sean . . . . .Star Entertainment Group, Inc., p. 299
Blohm, Jennifer . . . . .DisneyToon Studios, p. 113
Blomquist, Alan .Parallel Entertainment, Inc., p. 247
Blomquist, Rich . . . . .The Daily Show With Jon Stewart, p. 359
Bloodgood, Brian . . . . .Comedy Central, p. 98
Bloodworth-Thomason, Linda . . . . .Mozark Productions, p. 223
Bloom, Barbara . . . . .CBS Entertainment, p. 86
Bloom, Dianne . . . . .Angry Films, Inc., p. 52
Bloom, Kevin . . . . .Stone and Company Entertainment, p. 301
Bloomfield, David . . . . .Escape Artists II, p. 126
Bloomfield, Jodea . . . . .Crystal Sky Pictures, LLC, p. 104
Bloys, Casey . . . . .HBO Entertainment, p. 162
Blue, Steven . . . . .E! Networks, p. 117
Bluestein, Susan . . . . .NCIS, p. 370
Bluestone, Mark . . . . .Sony Pictures Television International, p. 296
Bluhm, David . . . . .GoTV Networks, p. 151
Blum, Jason . . . . .Blumhouse Productions, p. 70
Blum, Jennifer . . . . .1492 Pictures, p. 38
Blum, T. Alex . . . . .Colebrook Road, Inc., p. 96
Bluman, Debra . . . . .Zingy Inc., p. 349
Blumberg, Daniel . . . . .Film Crash, p. 132
Blumberg, Stuart . . . . .Class 5 Films, p. 95
Blume, Bonnie . . . . .The Mirisch Corporation, p. 218
Blume, Eric . . . . .Comedy Central, p. 98
Blumenfeld, Steven . . . . .Current TV, LLC, p. 105
Blumenfield, Jay . . . . .Jay & Tony Show Productions, p. 180
Blumenthal, Jason . . . . .Escape Artists II, p. 126
Blumenthal, Josh . . . . .Media Financial International, LLC, p. 214
Blunck, Joachim . . . . .Bunim/Murray Productions, Inc., p. 79
Blutt, Adam . . . . .The War at Home, p. 379
Blutt, Adam . . . . .Acme Productions, p. 46
Boardman, Tom . . . . .Benderspink, p. 66
Bobker, Daniel . . . . .Bobker/Kruger Films, p. 70
Bocaccio, Gerard . . . . .Silver Pictures, p. 289
Bochco, Dayna Kalins . . . . .Steven Bochco Productions, p. 70
Bochco, Steven . . . . .Steven Bochco Productions, p. 70
Bocsi, Steve . . . . .Odd Lot Entertainment, p. 241
Boden, Bob . . . . .Fox Reality, p. 140
Bodenheimer, George . . . . .The Walt Disney Company, p. 112
Bodenheimer, George . . . . .ABC Sports, p. 45
Bodenheimer, George . . . . .ESPN Original Entertainment (EOE), p. 127
Bodow, Steve . . . . .The Daily Show With Jon Stewart, p. 359
Boehm, Ted . . . . .Tapestry Films, Inc., p. 308
Boehm, Tyler . . . . .Sobini Films, p. 293
Bogach, Lewis . . . . .CMT: Country Music Television, p. 95
Bogner, Jonathan .Bogner Entertainment, Inc., p. 71
Bogosian, Dave .Entertainment Studios, Inc., p. 125
Bohn, Andy . . . . .Morgan Creek Productions, p. 221
Bohn, Tim . . . . .Cypress Films, Inc., p. 106
Bohnert, David . . . . .The Bachelor, p. 355
Boland, John . . . . .PBS, p. 251
Bolkus, Ed . . . . .New Line Television, p. 235
Boll, Jessica . . . . .3 lbs., p. 353
Bolt, Jeremy . . . . .Impact Pictures, p. 173
Bolt, Karen . . . . .Carrie Productions, Inc., p. 83
Bolter, Howard . . . . .E! Networks, p. 117
Boltho, Alexei . . . . .BBC Films, p. 64
Bombassei, James . . . . .Viacom Entertainment Group, p. 330
Bondesen, Mikkel . . . . .Fuse Entertainment, p. 144
Bondur, Maggie . . . . .Big Day, p. 355
Bonfiglio, Mike . . . .@radical.media, p. 38
Boniello, Leigh .Jerry Weintraub Productions, p. 338
Bonifer, Janet . . . . .Carsey-Werner Films, p. 84
Bonnett, Adam . . . . .Disney ABC Cable Networks Group, p. 112
Bonney, Denise . . . . .Brightlight Pictures, Inc., p. 75
Booke, Alexandra . . . . .Klasky Csupo, Inc., p. 189
Booker, Barry . . . . .Silver Nitrate Pictures, p. 288
Booker, Bob . . . . .Bob Booker Productions, p. 71
Booker, Laura . . . . .Bob Booker Productions, p. 71
Boone, Cooper . . . . .100% Entertainment, p. 38
Boorstein, Joan . . . . .Showtime Networks Inc., p. 287
Boortz, Jeff . . . . .Concrete Pictures, p. 99
Booth, Christina .Studio 60 on the Sunset Strip, p. 376
Booth, David . . . . .Day Break, p. 359
Borba, Janet Graham . . . . .HBO Films, p. 162
Borde, Emmanuelle . . . . .Sony Pictures Digital, p. 295
Borden, Robert . . . . .The George Lopez Show, p. 362
Border, W.K. . . . . .Neo Art & Logic, p. 232
Boreland, Val . . . . .Comedy Central, p. 98
Borgeson, Linda . . . . .Miramax Films, p. 217
Borja, Eric . . . . .Groundswell Production, p. 156
Borkent, Jules . . . . .Nickelodeon/MTVN Kids & Family Group, p. 237
Borlaug, Natalie . . . . .The Todd Phillips Company, p. 254
Born, Jennie . . . . .Buena Vista Television, p. 79
Borns, Betsy . . . . .All of Us, p. 354
Bornstein, Garner . . . . .Airborne Entertainment, p. 48
Borodi, Leslie . . . . .New Generation Films, Inc., p. 234
Boros, Stuart . . . . .Dino De Laurentiis Company, p. 108
Borstein, Alex . . . . .Family Guy, p. 361
Borsten, Joan . . . . .Films By Jove, p. 133
Borza, Michael . . . . .Turner Network Television (TNT), p. 321
Bosch, Allison . . . . .According to Jim, p. 354
Bosch, Anja . . . . .PorchLight Entertainment, p. 259
Boss, Kit . . . . .Lucky Louie, p. 368
Bost, Walter Michael . . . . .Sparky Pictures, p. 297
Bostick, Michael . . . . .Shady Acres Entertainment, p. 285
Bosze, Michael . . . . .Saturday Night Live, p. 373
Botstein, Sarah . . . . .Florentine Films, p. 135
Botta, Pasquale . . . . .Cinema Seven Productions, p. 92
Bottinelli, Connie . . . . .Grinning Dog Pictures, p. 154
Bottino, Lou . . . . .Rick Berman Productions, p. 66
Botwick, Terry . . . . .Vanguard Films/Vanguard Animation, p. 328

Boucher, Joe ....King of the Hill, p. 365
Boudart, Noella ....Reason Pictures, p. 266
Boughn, Lacy ....Escape Artists II, p. 126
Boughn, Lacy ....The Steve Tisch Company, p. 314
Boulet-Gercourt, Jill ....Martha Stewart Living Omnimedia, Inc., p. 211
Bounds, Ian ....Symbolic Entertainment, p. 306
Bourbeau, Crystal ....GreeneStreet Films, p. 153
Bourgoujian, Lisa ....LMNO Productions, p. 201
Bourke, Alison ....The Independent Film Channel (IFC), p. 173
Bourne, Andrew ....The Littlefield Company, p. 200
Boutrous, Victor ....Jaffe/Braunstein Films, LLC, p. 179
Bouttier, Brett ....Telepictures Productions, p. 311
Bouttier, Sheila ....Telepictures Productions, p. 311
Bove, Christof ....USA Network, p. 327
Bover, Lynne ....kdd Productions, LLC, p. 185
Bowden, C.J. ....SlingShot Media, p. 291
Bowden, Tim ....SekretAgent Productions, p. 283
Bowen, Marty ....Temple Hill Productions, p. 311
Bowen, Sarah ....Imagine Entertainment, p. 172
Bower, Bruce ....Twentieth Television, p. 324
Bowers, Dave ....Banyan Productions, p. 61
Bowland, Jeff ....Coquette Productions, p. 101
Bowles, Adriene ....Focus Features/Rogue Pictures, p. 136
Bowles, Bryan ....Sony Pictures Television, p. 296
Bowles, Jill ....Bungalow 78 Productions, p. 79
Bowles, Luke Parker ....Hart Sharp Entertainment, Inc., p. 161
Bowman, Bobby ....My Name Is Earl, p. 369
Bowman, Brooke ....ABC Family, p. 45
Bowman, Quinton ....BET Networks, p. 66
Bowman, Rob ....Day Break, p. 359
Boyd, Aaron ....Centropolis Entertainment, p. 88
Boyd, Andrew ....Mandate Pictures, p. 209
Boyd, Charles ....American Idol, p. 354
Boyd, David ....Friday Night Lights, p. 361
Boyd, Mellany ....TriCoast Studios, p. 318
Boyer, Ben ....Sky Networks, p. 291
Boyer, Max ....Weed Road Pictures, p. 337
Boyett, Robert L. ....Miller/Boyett Productions, p. 217
Boykin, Deena ....Cartoon Network, p. 84
Boyle, Brian ....American Dad, p. 354
Boyle, David ....Radar Pictures, p. 264
Boyle, Kevin ....Valhalla Motion Pictures, p. 328
Boyle, Sean ....Lifetime Television (Los Angeles), p. 198
Boyter, Cale ....New Line Cinema, p. 234
Bozonelis, Lia ....Picturehouse, p. 254
Bozotti, Filippo ....Article 19 Films, p. 56
Brace, Cindy ....Ginty Films International, p. 146
Brace, John ....Grey's Anatomy, p. 362
Bracken, Michael ....The Gotham Group, Inc., p. 151
Bradford, Sally ....Happy Hour, p. 362
Bradley, Ashley ....Trillion Entertainment, Inc., p. 319
Bradley, Deedee ....Smallville, p. 375
Bradley, Deedee ....Veronica Mars, p. 378
Bradley, Jeanie ....Sony Pictures Television, p. 296
Bradley, Jim ....Merv Griffin Entertainment, p. 154
Bradley, Rick ....Leeza Gibbons Enterprises (LGE), p. 146
Bradley, Suzanne ....Piller/Segan, p. 255
Bradstreet, Kyle ....The Levinson/Fontana Company, p. 197
Brady, David ....David Brady Productions, p. 72
Brady, Matt R. ....MRB Productions, Inc., p. 224
Brady, Pam ....South Park, p. 376
Braga, Brannon ....Braga Productions, p. 72
Bragg, Brendan ....Integrated Films & Management, p. 175
Bragg, Chip ....Tollin/Robbins Productions, p. 315
Braine, Gordon (Tim) ....Popular Arts Entertainment, Inc., p. 259
Bramberg, Greta ....Shady Acres Entertainment, p. 285
Brambilla, Elizabeth ....Picturehouse, p. 254
Bramhall, Adrienne ....Sierra Club Productions, p. 287
Bramhall, Sam ....Twentieth Century Fox Television, p. 323
Bramnick, Flory ....Sony Pictures Television, p. 296
Brancato, Chris ....Brancato/Salke Productions, p. 73
Branch, Michael ....King of the Hill, p. 365
Branch, Rita ....3Wolves Productions, p. 41
Brandenstein, A.J. ....DreamWorks SKG, p. 116
Brander, Dylann ....Big Day, p. 355
Brandes, David ....Apple & Honey Film Corp., p. 53
Brandis, Bernardine ....Buena Vista Motion Pictures Group, p. 78
Brandl, Darren ....S. Hirsch Company, Inc./Seemore Films, p. 167
Brandler, Zach ....Evolution Entertainment, p. 128
Brandman, Michael ....Brandman Productions, p. 73
Brandman, Miles ....Brandman Productions, p. 73
Brandon, Marc ....Warner Bros. Entertainment Inc., p. 334
Brandstatter, Heike ....Supernatural, p. 377
Brandstein, Jonathan ....MBST Entertainment, Inc., p. 213
Branman, Megan ....Big Day, p. 355
Branton, Michael ....GRB Entertainment, p. 153
Brar, Rene ....Stone and Company Entertainment, p. 301
Brash, Peter ....Days of Our Lives, p. 359
Bratches, Sean ....ABC Sports, p. 45
Bratman, Josh ....Michael De Luca Productions, p. 108
Braud, Dominique ....The Simpsons, p. 375
Brauer, Jeffrey ....Universal Pictures, p. 326
Braun, Cece ....CBS Paramount International Television, p. 87
Braun, David ....David Braun Productions, p. 73
Braun, Lloyd ....Yahoo! Media Group/Yahoo! Studios, p. 347
Braun, Neil ....IDT Entertainment, p. 171
Braun, Zev ....Braun Entertainment Group, Inc., p. 73
Braune, Judy ....PBS, p. 251
Braunstein, Howard ....Jaffe/Braunstein Films, LLC, p. 179
Bravakis, John ....Triage Entertainment, p. 317
Braverman, Alan N. ....The Walt Disney Company, p. 112
Braverman, Alan N. ....ABC Entertainment Television Group, p. 45
Braverman, Alex ....Braverman Productions, Inc., p. 73
Braverman, Chuck ....Braverman Productions, Inc., p. 73
Braverman, Marilyn ....Braverman Productions, Inc., p. 73
Brazill, Mark ....Happy Hour, p. 362
Brazzell, Anka ....Red Strokes Entertainment, p. 267
Break, Steven ....Bauer Martinez Entertainment, p. 63
Breakman, Gil ....G4 TV, p. 144
Breay, Lara ....Red Hour Films, p. 267
Brecher, Emily ....Granada America, p. 152
Breckman, Andy ....Monk, p. 369
Breech, Bob ....Boston Legal, p. 357
Breech, Bob ....David E. Kelley Productions, p. 186
Breen, James ....American Idol, p. 354
Breen, Monica ....Lost, p. 368
Breen, Patricia ....20 Good Years, p. 353
Breen, Paulette ....Paulette Breen Productions, p. 74
Bregman, Anthony ....This is that corporation, p. 312
Bregman, Buddy ....The Bregman Entertainment Group, p. 74
Bregman, Martin ....Bregman Productions, p. 75
Bregman, Michael ....Bregman Productions, p. 75
Breil, Ilan ....Mosaic Media Group, p. 222
Bremer, Michael ....The Bremer Goff Company, p. 75
Brener, Marc ....Infront Productions, p. 175
Brener, Richard ....New Line Cinema, p. 234
Brennan, Bill ....Sci Fi Channel, p. 282
Brennan, Jude ....The Late Show with David Letterman, p. 367
Brennan, Patrick ....Team Todd, p. 310
Brennan, Shane ....NCIS, p. 370
Brennan, Tracie ....Al Roker Productions, p. 274
Brennan, Wendy ....The Bubble Factory, p. 78
Brenner, Chris ....Creature Entertainment, p. 103
Brenner, Robbie ....Davis Entertainment Company, p. 107
Brescia, Christopher ....Miramax Films, p. 217
Bresnan, Jennifer ....The CW, p. 105
Bress, Danny ....Identity Films, p. 170
Brewer, Craig ....Southern Cross the Dog, p. 297
Brewer, Georg ....DC Comics, p. 108
Brewer, Ginny ....Jon Shestack Productions, p. 286
Brewer, Sandra ....Buena Vista Television, p. 79
Brezner, Larry ....MBST Entertainment, Inc., p. 213
Brian, Laurie ....Indigo Films, p. 174
Brickhouse, LouAnne ....Buena Vista Motion Pictures Group, p. 78
Brickman, Jessica ....Studio 60 on the Sunset Strip, p. 376
Bricknell, Tim ....Mirage Enterprises, p. 217
Bridges, Jeff ....Asls Productions, p. 57
Bridgett, Sharla Sumpter ....Tollin/Robbins Productions, p. 315
Briede, Amy ....Graymark Productions Inc., p. 153
Brien, Jeb ....The Mottola Company, p. 223

Briganti, Irena . . . . .Fox News Channel, p. 139
Briggs, Kim . . . . .Yorktown Productions, Ltd., p. 347
Briggs, Scott . . . . .Alcon Entertainment, LLC, p. 49
Brillstein, Bernie . . . . .Brillstein-Grey Entertainment, p. 75
Brinkman, Tamara . . . . .Boxx Communications, LLC, p. 72
Briskey, Jackie . . . . .Passions, p. 371
Briskman, Louis . . . . .CBS Corporation, p. 86
Brister, John H. . . . . .John Brister Films, p. 75
Brito, Brandon . . . . .Nickelodeon Movies, p. 237
Britt, Amy . . . . .Monk, p. 369
Broadbent, Graham . . . . .Blue Print, p. 69
Broady, Vince . . . . .Yahoo! Media Group/Yahoo! Studios, p. 347
Broccoli, Barbara . . . . .Danjaq, LLC, p. 107
Broch, Lawrence . . . . .Boston Legal, p. 357
Brock, Sarah . . . . .CMT: Country Music Television, p. 95
Brockman, Kevin . . . . .Disney-ABC Television Group, p. 113
Brockman, Kevin . . . . .ABC Entertainment Television Group, p. 45
Brockway, Jody . . . . .Granada America, p. 152
Broder, Esq., Merav . . . . .Two Sticks Productions, p. 325
Brodlie, Matt . . . . .Paramount Vantage/Paramount Classics, p. 248
Brodsky, Leigh Anne . . . . .Nickelodeon/MTVN Kids & Family Group, p. 237
Brody, Jeb . . . . .Big Beach, p. 67
Broido, Joe . . . . .PorchLight Entertainment, p. 259
Brokaw, Cary . . . . .Avenue Pictures, p. 59
Bromley, Scott . . . . .Cyan Pictures, p. 105
Bromstad, Angela . . . . .NBC Universal Television Studio, p. 231
Bronson, John . . . . .Madison Road Entertainment, p. 206
Brooke, James . . . . .Watershed Films, p. 336
Brooker, Richard . . . . .Boxx Communications, LLC, p. 72
Brookins, Charlie Jordan . . . . .MTV Films, p. 225
Brooks, Abbie . . . . .Playtime Productions, p. 257
Brooks, Brooke . . . . .Davis Entertainment Company, p. 107
Brooks, David . . . . .Focus Features/Rogue Pictures, p. 136
Brooks, Elaine . . . . .style., p. 303
Brooks, Elizabeth . . . . .GoTV Networks, p. 151
Brooks, Evolyn . . . . .The Tyra Banks Show, p. 378
Brooks, Fleming .Casey Silver Productions, p. 289
Brooks, Garth . . . . .Red Strokes Entertainment, p. 267
Brooks, James L. . . . . .The Simpsons, p. 375
Brooks, James L. . . . . .Gracie Films, p. 151
Brooks, Jennifer . . . . .Lakeshore Entertainment Group LLC, p. 192
Brooks, Mel . . . . .Brooksfilms Limited, p. 77
Brooks, Michael . . . . .Rafelson Media, p. 265
Brooks, Paul . . . . .Gold Circle Films, p. 148
Brooks, Rebecca . . . . .Gambit Pictures, p. 144
Brooks, Stanley M. . . . . .Once Upon A Time Films, Ltd., p. 243
Brooks, Tim .Lifetime Television (New York), p. 198
Brooks, Veronica . . . . .Watermark, p. 336
Brookwell, David . . . . .Brookwell McNamara Entertainment, Inc., p. 77
Brookwell, Rick . . . . .Greystone Television and Films, p. 154
Broome, Dave . . . . .The Biggest Loser, p. 356
Brosnan, Pierce . . . . .Irish DreamTime, p. 177
Brostrom, Grant . . . . .Simon West Productions, p. 339
Brotman, P. Arden . . . . .Sacred Dogs Entertainment, LLC, p. 278
Broucek, Paul B. . . . . .New Line Cinema, p. 234
Broughton, Emma . . . . .BBC Films, p. 64
Brouse, Sue . . . . .The Dead Zone, p. 359
Broussard, Stephen . . . . .Marvel Studios, Inc., p. 211
Browder, Jamie . . . . .The Late Late Show with Craig Ferguson, p. 366
Brown, Ben . . . . .Safran Company, p. 278
Brown, Bill . . . . .One Tree Hill, p. 371
Brown, Christopher . . . . .Urban Entertainment, p. 327
Brown, Cynthia . . . . .CBS Entertainment, p. 86
Brown, Dave . . . . .Benderspink, p. 66
Brown, David .The Manhattan Project, Ltd., p. 210
Brown, Effie . . . . .Duly Noted, p. 117
Brown, Ellen . . . . .The Tonight Show with Jay Leno, p. 377
Brown, Eryn .Industry Entertainment Partners, p. 174
Brown, Garry . . . . .Prison Break, p. 372
Brown, Janet . . . . .Cinetic, p. 93
Brown, Jayme . . . . .Loreen Arbus Productions, Inc., p. 54
Brown, Joe . . . . .Bravo, p. 74
Brown, Jon . . . . .Ensemble Entertainment, p. 124
Brown, Katherine . . . . .Intrepid Pictures, p. 176
Brown, Keith . . . . .Spike TV, p. 298
Brown, Kevin .Lawrence Bender Productions, p. 65
Brown, Kristin . . . . .TLC, p. 314
Brown, Mark Alan . . . . .Renfield Productions, p. 270
Brown, Mark Alton . . . . .Girlfriends, p. 362
Brown, Michael H. . . . . .Regency Enterprises, p. 268
Brown, Nicole . . . . .Marc Platt Productions, p. 257
Brown, Rich . . . . .Jimmy Kimmel Live, p. 364
Brown, Sam . . . . .New Line Cinema, p. 234
Brown, Seth . . . . .S Pictures, Inc., p. 277
Brown, Stephen . . . . .Twentieth Television, p. 324
Brown, Steve . . . . .Masters of Horror, p. 368
Brown, Tawnya . . . . .Next Entertainment, p. 236
Brown, Vincent . . . . .Girlfriends, p. 362
Browne, Don . . . . .Telemundo Network, p. 310
Browner, Craig . . . . .World of Wonder Productions, p. 345
Brownfield, David . . . . .CBS Entertainment, p. 86
Browning, Ben . . . . .Masters of Horror, p. 368
Browning, Ben . . . . .Industry Entertainment Partners, p. 174
Browning, Mary . . . . .Strike Entertainment, p. 303
Browning, Michelle . . . . .Lonetree Entertainment, p. 202
Brownson, Laura .Dan Wigutow Productions, p. 340
Brownstein, Lee . . . . .Kandor Entertainment, p. 184
Brubaker, James D. . . . . .Universal Pictures, p. 326
Bruce, Donald . . . . .Bold Films, p. 71
Bruce, Pamela K. . . . . .Once A Frog Productions, p. 242
Bruckheimer, Bonnie . . . . .Bonnie Bruckheimer Productions, p. 77
Bruckheimer, Jerry . . . . .Cold Case, p. 357
Bruckheimer, Jerry . . . . .The Amazing Race, p. 354
Bruckheimer, Jerry . . . . .CSI: Miami, p. 358
Bruckheimer, Jerry . . . . .Justice, p. 364
Bruckheimer, Jerry . . . . .Close to Home, p. 357
Bruckheimer, Jerry . . . . .Without a Trace, p. 379
Bruckheimer, Jerry . . . . .CSI: NY, p. 359
Bruckheimer, Jerry . . . . .CSI: Crime Scene Investigation, p. 358
Bruckheimer, Jerry . . . . .Jerry Bruckheimer Films & Television, p. 78
Bruckner, Jeff . . . . .Wonderland Sound and Vision, p. 344
Brucks, Bryan . . . . .The Syndicate, p. 307
Brumm, Mike . . . . .The Colbert Report, p. 357
Brune, Ray . . . . .Merv Griffin Entertainment, p. 154
Bruning, Richard . . . . .DC Comics, p. 108
Brunner, Alex . . . . .Spitfire Pictures, p. 298
Bruno, Stephen . . . . .The Weinstein Company, p. 337
Bruns, Emerson . . . . .Glatzer Productions, p. 147
Brunswick, Marc . . . . .Gunn Films, p. 158
Brunt, Daniel . . . . .Room 9 Entertainment, p. 274
Brustrom, Jeff . . . . .Disney ABC Cable Networks Group, p. 112
Brutocao, Matt . . . . .Fried Films, p. 142
Bryant, Blake . . . . .Buena Vista Television, p. 79
Bryant, Samantha . . . . .Tribeca Productions, p. 318
Bryer, Liana . . . . .Barnholtz Entertainment, p. 62
Bryman, Gary . . . . .Rocket Entertainment, p. 273
Bryson, Louise Henry . . . . .Lifetime Television (Los Angeles), p. 198
Bucatinsky, Dan . . . . .Is Or Isn't Entertainment, p. 177
Buccieri, Paul . . . . .Twentieth Television, p. 324
Buchholz, Russ . . . . .Werner-Gold-Miller, p. 339
Buchwald, Don . . . . .The Howard Stern Production Company, p. 301
Buchwald-Paletz, Jennifer . . . . .The Thomas Carter Company, p. 84
Buck, Mary V. . . . . .Warner Bros. Television Production, p. 335
Buckingham, Simon . . . . .Mobile Streams, p. 219
Buckland, Mark . . . . .My Name Is Earl, p. 369
Buckley, Christine . . . . .Lakeshore Entertainment Group LLC, p. 192
Buckley, Kristen . . . . .Nickelodeon/MTVN Kids & Family Group, p. 237
Buckley, Musette . . . . .Warner Bros. Pictures, p. 334
Buckner, Brian . . . . .The Class, p. 357
Buclow, David . . . . .Brookwell McNamara Entertainment, Inc., p. 77
Budnick, Scott . . . . .The Todd Phillips Company, p. 254
Budow, Aileen . . . . .Comedy Central, p. 98
Buechler, John . . . . .Imageries Entertainment, p. 171
Buenting, Bob . . . . .TV One, LLC, p. 322
Bufalini, Veronica . . . . .Picturehouse, p. 254
Bugg, Emily . . . . .Evolution Entertainment, p. 128
Buhaj, Marc . . . . .Cartoon Network, p. 84
Buitenveld, Jeff . . . . .C/W Productions, p. 105
Bukinik, Suzanne . . . . .According to Jim, p. 354
Bulhack, David . . . . .IMG Media, p. 172

Bull, Tom . . . . .Production Partners, Inc., p. 262
Bullard, Jeff . . . . .The Matthau Company, Inc., p. 212
Bullard, Pat . . . . .Reba, p. 372
Bullock, Paul . . . . .Blueprint Entertainment, p. 70
Bullock, Sandra . . . . .The George Lopez Show, p. 362
Bullock, Sandra . . . . .Fortis Films, p. 137
Bullough, Miles . . . . .Aardman Animations, p. 44
Bulnes, Melissa . . . . .David Braun Productions, p. 73
Bunch, Stacey . . . . .Nuance Productions, p. 240
Bundy, Patsy . . . . .King World Productions, Inc., p. 188
Bunker, Mihoko . . . . .OZLA Pictures, Inc., p. 246
Bunnell, Mike . . . . .Current TV, LLC, p. 105
Bunnell, Steve . . . . .The Weinstein Company, p. 337
Bunting, Clark . . . . .Discovery Networks, U.S., p. 111
Buquicchio, Frank A. . . . . .New Line Television, p. 235
Buraglio, Elizabeth . . . . .Original Film, p. 244
Burditt, Jack . . . . .30 Rock, p. 353
Bures, Angela . . . . .The Collective, p. 96
Burford, Anne . . . . .Charles Floyd Johnson Productions, p. 89
Burg, Mark . . . . .Two and a Half Men, p. 378
Burg, Mark . . . . .Evolution Entertainment, p. 128
Burgess, Brandon . . . . .ION Media Networks, Inc., p. 177
Burgess, Melanie . . . . .John Wells Productions, p. 338
Burgos, Max . . . . .The Collective, p. 96
Burk, Bryan . . . . .Bad Robot Productions, p. 60
Burk, Bryan . . . . .What About Brian, p. 379
Burk, Bryan . . . . .Six Degrees, p. 375
Burk, Bryan . . . . .Lost, p. 368
Burke, David J. . . . . .Kidnapped, p. 365
Burke, James . . . . .entitled entertainment, p. 125
Burke, Jim . . . . .Ad Hominem Enterprises, p. 46
Burke, Will . . . . .Jimmy Kimmel Live, p. 364
Burleigh, Stephen . . . . .Burleigh Filmworks, p. 80
Burnett, Angelina . . . . .Dominant Pictures, p. 114
Burnett, Mark . . . . .The Apprentice, p. 355
Burnett, Mark . . . . .Survivor, p. 377
Burnett, Mark . . . . .MARTHA, p. 368
Burnett, Mark . . . . .Mark Burnett Productions, p. 80
Burnett, Rob . . . . .The Knights of Prosperity, p. 365
Burnett, Rob . . . . .The Late Show with David Letterman, p. 367
Burnett, Rob . . . . .Worldwide Pants, Inc., p. 346
Burnley, Jay . . . . .Palomar Pictures, p. 246
Burns, Brian . . . . .Entourage, p. 360
Burns, Ed . . . . .The Wire, p. 379
Burns, Joanne . . . . .Twentieth Television, p. 324
Burns, Ken . . . . .Florentine Films, p. 135
Burns, Kevin J. . . . . .Prometheus Entertainment, p. 263
Burns, Michael . . . . .Lionsgate, p. 200
Burns, Steve . . . . .Discovery Networks, U.S., p. 111
Burns, Stewart . . . . .The Simpsons, p. 375
Burns, Tommy . . . . .ER, p. 361
Burr, Kristin . . . . .Buena Vista Motion Pictures Group, p. 78
Burrell, Mark . . . . .Half Shell Entertainment, p. 159
Burroughs, Ryan . . . . .Suzanne Bauman Productions, p. 63
Burrows, James . . . . .Charles Bros., p. 89
Burrows, John . . . . .Paul Pompian Productions, Inc., p. 259
Burrud, John . . . . .Burrud Productions, p. 80
Burrus, Richard . . . . .Sony Pictures Television, p. 296
Burry, Allen . . . . .Furthur Films, p. 144
Burton, Al . . . . .Al Burton Productions, p. 80
Burton, Charity . . . . .Five Sisters Productions, p. 135
Burton, Gabrielle C. . . . . .Five Sisters Productions, p. 135
Burton, Gabrielle B. . . . . .Five Sisters Productions, p. 135
Burton, Jennifer . . . . .Five Sisters Productions, p. 135
Burton, Maria . . . . .Five Sisters Productions, p. 135
Burton, Mark . . . . .WonderFilms, p. 344
Burton, Roger . . . . .Five Sisters Productions, p. 135
Burton, Tim . . . . .Tim Burton Productions, p. 81
Burton, Ursula . . . . .Five Sisters Productions, p. 135
Busby, Kathy . . . . .New Line Cinema, p. 234
Busfield, Timothy . . . . .Studio 60 on the Sunset Strip, p. 376
Bush, Jared . . . . .All of Us, p. 354
Butan, Marc . . . . .2929 Productions, p. 40
Butazzoni, Fernando . . . . .Joel Films, p. 181
Buting, Yang . . . . .China Film Group, p. 90
Butler, Alex . . . . .Agamemnon Films, Inc., p. 47
Butler, Daniel B. . . . . .Warner Bros. Pictures, p. 334
Butler, David . . . . .HDNet, p. 163
Butler, Joshua . . . . .Kinetic Pictures, p. 188
Butler, Kirker . . . . .Family Guy, p. 361
Butler-Sloss, William . . . . .Fifty Cannon Entertainment, LLC, p. 131
Butterfield, Catherine . . . . .Ghost Whisperer, p. 362
Butters, Melvin . . . . .Barnholtz Entertainment, p. 62
Buttlar, Kim . . . . .Spyglass Entertainment Group, p. 299
Butts, Daphne . . . . .Bankable Productions, p. 61
Bye, Kym . . . . .Weekend Films/Main Street Film Company, p. 337
Byer, Melissa . . . . .Crossing Jordan, p. 358
Bymel, Suzan . . . . .Management 360, p. 208
Bynder, David . . . . .PorchLight Entertainment, p. 259
Byrens, Sharon . . . . .Turner Network Television (TNT), p. 321
Byrens, Sharon . . . . .TBS, p. 309
Byrne, Myra . . . . .Triage Entertainment, p. 317
Byrne, Peter . . . . .HIT Entertainment, p. 167
Byrum, John . . . . .Byrum Power & Light, p. 81
C.K., Louis . . . . .Lucky Louie, p. 368
Caamaño-Loquet, Darlene . . . . .Nala Films, p. 228
Caaro-Evans, Nigel . . . . .FremantleMedia North America, p. 142
Cabano, Sheila . . . . .Queer Eye, p. 372
Cacheula, Mike . . . . .Laika Entertainment, p. 191
Cadiff, Andy . . . . .The War at Home, p. 379
Cadrez, Glenn . . . . .BloodWorks, LLC, p. 68
Cage, Nicolas . . . . .Saturn Films, p. 280
Cagen, Irene . . . . .Medium, p. 369
Cagle, Jeff . . . . .Air2web, Inc., p. 48
Cahn, Debora . . . . .Grey's Anatomy, p. 362
Caire, John . . . . .Reynolds Entertainment, p. 271
Cairns, Thomas . . . . .NBC Entertainment, p. 230
Cairo, Judy . . . . .Cairo/Simpson Entertainment, Inc., p. 81
Calabrese, Peter . . . . .Q Media Partners, p. 264
Calandra, Steve . . . . .Buena Vista Television, p. 79
Calastro, Edna . . . . .New Screen Concepts, Inc., p. 235
Caldera-De Fanti, Carolyn . . . . .Caldera/De Fanti Entertainment, p. 82
Calderone, Tom . . . . .VH1, p. 330
Caldon, Patrick . . . . .DC Comics, p. 108
Caldwell, Michael . . . . .Vulcan Productions, p. 332
Caleb, Ruth . . . . .BBC Films, p. 64
Calfo, Francie . . . . .ABC Entertainment Television Group, p. 45
Calhoun, Cory . . . . .Flame Ventures LLC, p. 135
Calhoun, Wendy . . . . .Raines, p. 372
Califano, Gary . . . . .MRB Productions, Inc., p. 224
Call, C. Brad . . . . .Digital Domain, Inc., p. 110
Callaghan, Mike . . . . .Motion Picture Corporation of America, p. 222
Callaghan, Steve . . . . .Family Guy, p. 361
Callahan, Bill . . . . .Scrubs, p. 374
Callahan, Patrice . . . . .Twentieth Television, p. 324
Callender, Colin . . . . .HBO Films, p. 162
Calleri, Allison . . . . .Ralph Winter Productions, Inc., p. 343
Calley, John . . . . .John Calley Productions, p. 82
Callif, Dustin . . . . .Spacedog, p. 297
Calloway, Blake . . . . .Sci Fi Channel, p. 282
Calloway, David . . . . .The O.C., p. 371
Calpeter, Lynn . . . . .NBC Universal Corporate, p. 231
Calvo, Dana . . . . .Studio 60 on the Sunset Strip, p. 376
Camacho, Blanca . . . . .Edward R. Pressman Film Corporation, p. 261
Camagna, Andy . . . . .The Sommers Company, p. 294
Cameron, James . . . . .Lightstorm Entertainment, p. 199
Cameron, John . . . . .Friday Night Lights, p. 361
Cameron, John . . . . .Film 44, p. 131
Cameron, Kisha Imani . . . . .Completion Films, p. 99
Camon, Alessandro . . . . .Edward R. Pressman Film Corporation, p. 261
Camp, Colleen . . . . .Colleen Camp Productions, p. 82
Campbell, Billy . . . . .Discovery Networks, U.S., p. 111
Campbell, Bruce . . . . .NBC Universal Corporate, p. 231
Campbell, Cherri . . . . .Serendipity Point Films, p. 284
Campbell, John . . . . .Jerry Bruckheimer Films & Television, p. 78
Campbell, Joyce . . . . .KCET, p. 185
Campbell, Paul . . . . .IDT Entertainment, p. 171
Campbell, Teresa . . . . .Intl. Television Group (ITG) - Epix Films, p. 176
Campo, Darren . . . . .Court TV Networks, p. 102
Cannan, Megan . . . . .Jaffilms, LLC, p. 179

Cannell, Stephen J. . . . . .Cannell Studios, p. 83
Canniffe, Jamie . . . . .The Apprentice, p. 355
Cannold, Debra . . . . .Patchett Kaufman Entertainment, p. 250
Cannon, Julie . . . . .Rope The Moon Productions, p. 274
Cannon, Kay . . . . .30 Rock, p. 353
Cannon, Reuben . . . . .Reuben Cannon Productions, p. 83
Cannon, Vivian . . . . .Original Film, p. 244
Canter, Kassie . . . . .Oxygen Media, p. 245
Canter, Rob . . . . .Dalaklis-McKeown Entertainment, Inc., p. 106
Canterna, Paul . . . . .Seven Summits Pictures & Management, p. 285
Cantillon, Elizabeth . . . . .Columbia Pictures, p. 97
Canton, Maj . . . . .Maj Canton Productions, p. 83
Canton, Mark . . . . .Atmosphere Entertainment MM, LLC, p. 58
Cantor, Ross . . . . .What About Brian, p. 379
Cantor, Steven . . . . .Stick Figure Productions, p. 301
Capanna, Henry . . . . .The Syndicate, p. 307
Caplan, Dave . . . . .The George Lopez Show, p. 362
Caplan, David . . . . .Hollywood Gang Productions, LLC, p. 168
Caplan, David . . . . .Cecchi Gori Pictures, p. 88
Caplin, Lee . . . . .Cineville LLC, p. 93
Caponera, Cindy . . . . .My Boys, p. 369
Caprielian, Stephanie . . . . .Universal Studios, p. 326
Caprio, Nicholas .Gay Rosenthal Productions, p. 275
Capus, Steve . . . . .NBC News, p. 230
Caraet, Rose . . . . .de Passe Entertainment, p. 108
Caramalis, Chris M. . . . . .DC Comics, p. 108
Carbone, V.J. . . . . .Focus Features/Rogue Pictures, p. 136
Carbonetti, Angela . . . . .Untitled Entertainment, p. 327
Cardinal, Eric . . . . .The CW, p. 105
Carey, Anne . . . . .This is that corporation, p. 312
Carey, Jack . . . . .TV Guide Channel, p. 321
Carey, Luke . . . . .Zephyr Films Ltd., p. 348
Carey, Tony . . . . .Fox Cable Networks, p. 139
Cargerman, Jill . . . . .Las Vegas, p. 366
Carliner, Rob . . . . .Butchers Run Films, p. 81
Carlisle, Matthew . . . . .Saved, p. 374
Carlivati, Ron . . . . .One Life to Live, p. 371
Carlock, Robert . . . . .30 Rock, p. 353
Carlson, Kristy . . . . .Warner Bros. Pictures, p. 334
Carlson, Matthew . . . . .Big Day, p. 355
Carlton, Peter . . . . .FilmFour, p. 133
Carlucci, Anne . . . . .Anne Carlucci Productions, p. 83
Carmichael, Jamie . . . . .ContentFilm, p. 100
Carmichael, Kelly . . . . .The Weinstein Company, p. 337
Carmichael, Seth . . . . .Goldcrest Films International, Inc., p. 149
Carmona, Wayne . . . . .Entourage, p. 360
Carnahan, Matthew . . . . .Dirt, p. 360
Carner, Charles Robert . . . . .South Side Films, p. 297
Carney, Amy . . . . .Sony Pictures Television, p. 296
Carolin, Reid . . . . .Peirce Pictures, p. 252
Carolla, Adam . . . . .Jackhole Industries, p. 178
Carollo, Gina . . . . .Cineville LLC, p. 93
Caron, Glenn Gordon . . . . .Medium, p. 369
Carr, Aeysha . . . . .Everybody Hates Chris, p. 361
Carr, Eric . . . . .Focus Features/Rogue Pictures, p. 136
Carr, Gary . . . . .NorthSouth Productions, p. 239
Carr, Janis . . . . .Help Me Help You, p. 363
Carr, Louis . . . . .BET Networks, p. 66
Carr, Patti . . . .'Til Death, p. 377
Carrabba, Joe . . . . .The Bubble Factory, p. 78
Carrasquillo, Millie . . . . .Telemundo Network, p. 310
Carrelli, Bari . . . . .Actuality Productions, p. 46
Carrie, Stephanie . . . . .57-T Productions, Inc., p. 42
Carrillo, Laura . . . . .New Line Cinema, p. 234
Carroll, Charles . . . . .Criminal Minds, p. 358
Carroll, Ed . . . . .The Independent Film Channel (IFC), p. 173
Carroll, Ed . . . . .AMC, p. 50
Carroll, Greg . . . . .IMG Media, p. 172
Carroll, Ryan . . . . .Buckaroo Entertainment, p. 78
Carroll, Willard . . . . .Hyperion Studio, p. 169
Carruthers, Julie . . . . .ABC Daytime, p. 44
Carsey, Marcy . . . . .Oxygen Media, p. 245
Carsey, Marcy . . . . .Carsey-Werner Films, p. 84
Carson, Beaux . . . . .Carson Signature Films, Inc., p. 84
Carson, Bryon . . . . .Urban Entertainment, p. 327
Carson, Chris . . . . .King World Productions, Inc., p. 188
Carson, Joey .Bunim/Murray Productions, Inc., p. 79
Carstens, Tom . . . . .Zucker/Netter Productions, p. 350
Carstenson, Toni Pace . . . . .Suzanne Bauman Productions, p. 63
Carter, Adrienne . . . . .Everybody Hates Chris, p. 361
Carter, Doug . . . . .Buena Vista Motion Pictures Group, p. 78
Carter, Karl . . . . .Current TV, LLC, p. 105
Carter, Scott . . . . .Real Time with Bill Maher, p. 372
Carter, Susie Singer . . . . .Go Girl Media, p. 147
Carter, Thomas . . . . .Station 3, p. 300
Carter, Thomas . . . . .The Thomas Carter Company, p. 84
Cartier, Mark . . . . .Poor Boys Productions, p. 259
Carty, Jill . . . . .MakeMagic Productions, p. 207
Carty, Ryan . . . . .Clarity Pictures, LLC, p. 94
Caruso, Ruth . . . . .Carson Daly Productions, p. 84
Carvell, Tim . . . . .The Daily Show With Jon Stewart, p. 359
Carver, Benedict . . . . .Crystal Sky Pictures, LLC, p. 104
Carver, Jeremy . . . . .Waterfront, p. 379
Cary, Allen . . . . .Mojo Films, p. 220
Cary, Donick . . . . .Naked Trucker & T-Bones, p. 369
Casady, Guymon . . . . .Management 360, p. 208
Casagrande, Jill . . . . .Disney ABC Cable Networks Group, p. 112
Casalese, Mauro . . . . .Atomic Cartoons, Inc., p. 58
Casares, Lillian . . . . .Latin Hollywood Films, p. 194
Casazza, Brian . . . . .9 Squared, p. 43
Cascio, Jay . . . . .Water Channel, p. 336
Case, Chris . . . . .Reba, p. 372
Caserta, Jennifer . . . . .The Independent Film Channel (IFC), p. 173
Casey, Brian . . . . .Once A Frog Productions, p. 242
Casey, Dan . . . . .Laika Entertainment, p. 191
Casey, Mara . . . . .Gilmore Girls, p. 362
Casey, Michael . . . . .Starbucks Entertainment, p. 299
Cass, Debbie . . . . .Medium, p. 369
Cassar, Jon . . . . .24, p. 353
Cassel, Sam . . . . .Scott Rudin Productions, p. 277
Cassell, Karen . . . . .Turner Network Television (TNT), p. 321
Cassels, Sean . . . . .LeFrak Productions, p. 195
Cassidy, Carolyn . . . . .NBC Entertainment, p. 230
Cassidy, Jason . . . . .Miramax Films, p. 217
Cassidy, Nicole . . . . .Parkway Productions, p. 249
Castaldo, Amie . . . . .Senza Pictures, p. 284
Castaldo, Mark . . . . .Destiny Pictures, p. 109
Castallo, Chris . . . . .NBC Entertainment, p. 230
Castaner, Berta . . . . .Telemundo Network, p. 310
Casterline, Dale . . . . .King World Productions, Inc., p. 188
Castillo, Brian . . . . .Blue Rider Pictures, p. 69
Castillo, Nora . . . . .Walker/Fitzgibbon TV/Films, p. 333
Caston, Joe . . . . .Crave Films, p. 102
Castro, Andrea . . . . .Benderspink, p. 66
Castro, Richard . . . . .Cinema Libre Studio, p. 92
Catania, Bruce . . . . .The Tyra Banks Show, p. 378
Cates, Gilbert . . . . .Cates/Doty Productions, p. 85
Cates, Michelle . . . . .Gran Via Productions, p. 152
Cates, Valerie . . . . .Random House Films, p. 266
Catlin, Sam . . . . .Kidnapped, p. 365
Catmull, Dr. Edwin E. . . . . .Pixar Animation Studios, p. 256
Catmull, Ed . . . . .The Walt Disney Company, p. 112
Catmull, Ed . . . . .Buena Vista Motion Pictures Group, p. 78
Catterjee, Shashwata . . . . .The Hal Lieberman Company, p. 197
Caucey, Gigi . . . . .Queer Eye, p. 372
Caulfield, Bernadette . . . . .Big Love, p. 356
Cauthen, Kelley . . . . .Mainline Releasing, p. 207
Cavalier, Liz . . . . .Automatic Pictures, Inc., p. 58
Cavallo, Bob . . . . .The Walt Disney Company, p. 112
Cavallo, Lucy . . . . .CBS Entertainment, p. 86
Cavanaugh, Francis . . . . .CBS Entertainment, p. 86
Cavanaugh, Mary Jeanne . . . . .Oxygen Media, p. 245
Cawley, Michael . . . . .The Goatsingers, p. 148
Ceballos, Danny . . . . .The Ellen DeGeneres Show, p. 360
Ceballos, Jennifer . . . . .The Sommers Company, p. 294
Ceccarelli, Chris . . . . .Madison Road Entertainment, p. 206
Cecil, Jennifer . . . . .Raines, p. 372
Cedar, Michael . . . . .Vanished, p. 378
Cegielski, Craig . . . . .Lionsgate, p. 200
Celani, Renato . . . . .Samuelson Productions Limited, p. 279

Celeboglu, Eren . . . . .Doozer, p. 114
Celestino, Lyndsy . . . . .Nancy Tenenbaum Films, p. 311
Celotta, Jennifer . . . . .The Office, p. 371
Cervini, Rich . . . . .King World Productions, Inc., p. 188
Cesa, Bob . . . . .Twentieth Television, p. 324
Cesa, Bob . . . . .My Network TV, p. 228
Ceslik, Carolyn . . . . .CBS Entertainment, p. 86
Cetiner, Leman . . . . .Silverline Entertainment, Inc., p. 289
Cha, Jane . . . . .Project Runway, p. 372
Cha, Jane . . . . .Full Picture, p. 143
Chacamaty, Carol . . . . .Brooklyn Films, p. 77
Chacon, Amy . . . . .The Amazing Race, p. 354
Chacona, Marica . . . . .Showtime Networks Inc., p. 287
Chader, Lisa . . . . .CMT: Country Music Television, p. 95
Chaffin, Stokely . . . . .Stokely Chaffin Productions, p. 88
Chaidez, Natalie . . . . .Heroes, p. 363
Chaiken, Ilene . . . . .The L Word, p. 366
Chaikin, Judy . . . . .One Step Productions, p. 243
Chaiklin, Rebecca . . . . .Article 19 Films, p. 56
Chaires, Becky . . . . .Sony Pictures Digital, p. 295
Chais, Bill . . . . .Shark, p. 374
Chak, Yelena . . . . .Jerry Bruckheimer Films & Television, p. 78
Chamberlain, Barry . . . . .CBS Paramount International Television, p. 87
Chambers, Brian . . . . .Twentieth Century Fox Television, p. 323
Chambers, Ernest . . . . .Merv Griffin Entertainment, p. 154
Chambers, Essie . . . . .The N, p. 228
Chambers, Jennifer . . . . .Maverick Films, p. 213
Chambers, John . . . . .The Bold and the Beautiful, p. 356
Chamoy, Mike . . . . .Zak Penn's Company, p. 252
Champion, Gill . . . . .POW! Entertainment, p. 260
Chan, Larry . . . . .Foresight Unlimited, p. 137
Chandler, Fred . . . . .Twentieth Century Fox, p. 322
Chandler, Joe . . . . .NBC Universal Television Studio, p. 231
Chandrasekaran, Vali . . . . .My Name Is Earl, p. 369
Chandrasekhar, Jay . . . . .Broken Lizard Industries, p. 76
Chaney, Eric . . . . .Frederick Zollo Productions, Inc., p. 350
Chang, Anita S. . . . . .Rat Entertainment/Rat TV, p. 266
Chang, Kevin . . . . .Misher Films, p. 218
Chang, Sandra . . . . .Industry Entertainment Partners, p. 174
Chang, Terence . . . . .Lion Rock Productions, p. 199
Chang, Yahlin . . . . .Waterfront, p. 379
Chang, Yee Yeo . . . . .Killer Films, Inc., p. 187
Changnon, Pola . . . . .Cartoon Network, p. 84
Chanley, Sandy . . . . .Production Partners, Inc., p. 262
Channer, Richard . . . . .JT Entertainment, p. 182
Channing-Williams, Simon . . . . .Potboiler Productions, p. 260
Chapman, Leigh . . . . .Warner Bros. Entertainment Inc., p. 334
Chapman, Melanie . . . . .The Bubble Factory, p. 78
Chappelle, Joe . . . . .The Wire, p. 379
Charalambous, Chris . . . . .Irish DreamTime, p. 177
Charbanic, Diane . . . . .New Line Cinema, p. 234
Charles, Glen . . . . .Charles Bros., p. 89
Charles, Les . . . . .Charles Bros., p. 89
Charpentier, Mark . . . . .Conundrum Entertainment, p. 100
Chartoff, Ira . . . . .Endemol USA, Inc., p. 123
Chartoff, Robert . . . . .Chartoff Productions, p. 89
Chase, Debra Martin . . . . .Martin Chase Productions, p. 211
Chasey, Skip . . . . .Imagine Television, p. 172
Chasin, Liza . . . . .Working Title Films, p. 345
Chasin, Seth . . . . .Playboy Entertainment Group, Inc., p. 257
Chasman, Steven . . . . .Current Entertainment, p. 105
Chatman, Vernon . . . . .South Park, p. 376
Chatterjee, Rahul . . . . .Lighthouse Entertainment, p. 198
Chatton, Charlotte . . . . .Departure Studios, p. 109
Chau, Micheline . . . . .Lucasfilm Ltd., p. 203
Chavez, Albert . . . . .SiTV, p. 290
Chavez, Arturo . . . . .Lionsgate, p. 200
Chavez, Christina . . . . .Mondo Media, p. 220
Chavez Jr., Elio . . . . .Imagine Television, p. 172
Chbosky, Stephen . . . . .Jericho, p. 364
Cheddy, Geoff . . . . .Brillstein-Grey Entertainment, p. 75
Cheeks, George . . . . .MTV Networks, p. 226
Chen, Christopher C. . . . . .Endgame Entertainment, p. 124
Chen, Jiande . . . . .Sony Pictures Television International, p. 296
Chen, Sibyl . . . . .Mandate Pictures, p. 209
Cheng, Albert . . . . .Disney-ABC Television Group, p. 113
Cheng, John . . . . .Rat Entertainment/Rat TV, p. 266
Chenzira-Pinnock, Haj . . . . .Red Wagon Entertainment, p. 268
Cheong, Amy . . . . .Jeff Wald Entertainment, p. 180
Cherkas, Vicki . . . . .GreeneStreet Films, p. 153
Chern, Bianca . . . . .Imagine Television, p. 172
Chernin, Peter . . . . .Fox Broadcasting Company, p. 139
Cherniss, Matt . . . . .FX, p. 144
Chernov, Jeffrey . . . . .Spyglass Entertainment Group, p. 299
Cherry, Judd . . . . .21 Laps Entertainment, p. 38
Cherry, Marc . . . . .Desperate Housewives, p. 360
Cheskin, Steve . . . . .WE: Women's Entertainment, p. 336
Chestnut, Colette . . . . .MTV Networks, p. 226
Cheung, Vince . . . . .Rice & Beans Productions, p. 272
Chevapravatdumrong, Cherry . . . . .Family Guy, p. 361
Chew, Sukee . . . . .Hopscotch Pictures, p. 169
Chianese, Joseph . . . . .Sony Pictures Entertainment, p. 295
Chiarabaglio, Janet . . . . .Mike Lobell Productions, p. 201
Chiaramonte, Deborah . . . . .DreamWorks SKG, p. 116
Chiarelli, Pete . . . . .Kurtzman/Orci, p. 191
Chiavelli, Matthew . . . . .Sci Fi Channel, p. 282
Chicorel, Steve . . . . .Chic Productions, p. 90
Chicorel, Steve . . . . .Shoreline Entertainment, Inc., p. 286
Chiklis, Michael . . . . .The Shield, p. 374
Childers, Kesila . . . . .The Core, p. 101
Chilek, Melanie . . . . .Sony Pictures Television, p. 296
Chilnick, Jeremy . . . . .Warrior Poets, p. 335
Chilton, Hank . . . . .Nip/Tuck, p. 370
Chimenz, Marco . . . . .Cattleya, p. 86
Chin, Diana . . . . .Silver Dream Productions, p. 288
Chin, Elaine . . . . .HBO Films, p. 162
Chin, Victor . . . . .TOKYOPOP Inc., p. 315
Chiocchi, Frank . . . . .Universal Pictures, p. 326
Chiodi, Joel . . . . .GSN, p. 157
Chiodo, Charles . . . . .Chiodo Bros. Productions, Inc., p. 90
Chiodo, Edward . . . . .Chiodo Bros. Productions, Inc., p. 90
Chiodo, Stephen . . . . .Chiodo Bros. Productions, Inc., p. 90
Chipman, Garett . . . . .Frazier | Chipman Entertainment, p. 141
Chisarick, Jodi . . . . .Twentieth Television, p. 324
Chiu, Linda Sophie . . . . .Myriad Pictures, p. 228
Chiurco, Jennifer . . . . .Haft Entertainment, p. 159
Choi, Diana . . . . .Playtone Productions, p. 258
Choi, William . . . . .Management 360, p. 208
Chotzen, Yvonne . . . . .Chotzen/Jenner Productions, p. 90
Chouinard, Sandra . . . . .Fred Kuehnert Productions, p. 190
Chow, Calvin . . . . .Platinum Studios, LLC, p. 257
Chramosta, Paul . . . . .Zane W. Levitt Prod./Zeta Ent., p. 197
Christensen, Hayden . . . . .Forest Park Pictures, p. 137
Christensen, Maren . . . . .Universal Studios, p. 326
Christensen, Tove . . . . .Forest Park Pictures, p. 137
Christenson, Eric . . . . .Initial Entertainment Group, p. 175
Christiansen, Dorthea . . . . .Creative Impulse Entertainment, p. 103
Christiansen, Robert W. . . . . .Chris/Rose Productions, p. 90
Christianson, Kim . . . . .Warner Bros. Animation, p. 334
Christianson, Vicki . . . . .Icon Productions, LLC, p. 170
Christie, Blair . . . . .Water Channel, p. 336
Christie, Julie . . . . .Eyeworks Touchdown, p. 129
Christie, Tom . . . . .Showtime Networks Inc., p. 287
Christodoro, Jonathan . . . . .First Look Pictures, p. 134
Christopher, Amy . . . . .Fox Broadcasting Company, p. 139
Christopher, Mark . . . . .One Life to Live, p. 371
Chu, Andrea . . . . .The Sean Daniel Company, p. 106
Chu, Sean . . . . .Sony Pictures Television International, p. 296
Chua, Damon . . . . .Impact Pictures, p. 173
Chubb, Caldecot . . . . .ChubbCo Film Co., p. 91
Chugerman, Randi . . . . .Touchstone Television, p. 316
Chukudebelu, Chika . . . . .Humble Journey Films, p. 169
Chulack, Christopher . . . . .ER, p. 361
Chun, Danny . . . . .The Simpsons, p. 375
Chun, Matt . . . . .here! Networks, p. 165
Chung, Edwin . . . . .NBC Entertainment, p. 230
Chung, Richard . . . . .The Simpsons, p. 375
Church, Adam . . . . .Mobius International, p. 219
Church, Bartow . . . . .Apostle, p. 53
Church, Karen . . . . .CBS Entertainment, p. 86

Chvatal, Cynthia .CSI: Crime Scene Investigation, p. 358
Chvatal, Cynthia .High Horse Films, p. 166
Ciardi, Mark .Mayhem Pictures, p. 213
Ciccone, Dawn .PBS, p. 251
Cilic, Elayne .The Biggest Loser, p. 356
Cingoli, Marco .Sony Pictures Television International, p. 296
Circosta, Chris .Telepictures Productions, p. 311
Cirigliano, Jim .Arden Entertainment, p. 54
Cisneroz, Lisa Marie .Bang Zoom! Entertainment, p. 61
Citrano, Laura .entitled entertainment, p. 125
Civiello, Laura .G4 TV, p. 144
Civita, Suzi .Warner Bros. Pictures, p. 334
Civrais, Nathalie .Sony Pictures Television International, p. 296
Clack, Zoanne .Grey's Anatomy, p. 362
Clafin, Richard .Martha Stewart Living Omnimedia, Inc., p. 211
Claggett, Rita .Exxcell Entertainment, Inc./Exxcell Films, p. 129
Clark, Chad .Alcon Entertainment, LLC, p. 49
Clark, Chris .Working Title Films, p. 345
Clark, Dick .dick clark productions, inc., p. 94
Clark, Dylan .Universal Pictures, p. 326
Clark, Greg .Untitled Entertainment, p. 327
Clark, Jason .Fox Broadcasting Company, p. 139
Clark, Larry .Legendary Pictures, p. 195
Clark, Peter J. .Port Magee Pictures, Inc., p. 260
Clark, Shannon .Mr. Mudd, p. 224
Clark, Sherryl .Kopelson Entertainment, p. 189
Clarke, Allison .Bravo, p. 74
Clarke, Krystyna .CSM Communications, p. 104
Clarke, Leah .DNA Films, p. 114
Clarke, Leo .Lucky Louie, p. 368
Clarke, Leo .All of Us, p. 354
Clary, Susan .NEU-MAN-FILMS, Inc., p. 232
Clavell, Ana .Taurus Entertainment Company, p. 309
Clawson, David .Michael Taylor Productions, p. 309
Clawson, Timothy A. .The Weinstein Company, p. 337
Claybourne, Doug .Poetry & Pictures Inc., p. 258
Clayton, Greg .Spirit Horse Productions, p. 298
Clayton, Martin .CMT: Country Music Television, p. 95
Clayville, Kristen .Jim Wedaa Productions, p. 337
Cleary, Sean .CBS Paramount International Television, p. 87
Clem, Mitch .The Marshak/Zachary Company, p. 211
Clemente, Rosa .Joel Films, p. 181
Clements, Becky .Brillstein-Grey Entertainment, p. 75
Clements, Jack .Jericho, p. 364
Clements, Kim .The Black Donnellys, p. 356
Clements, Mike .20 Good Years, p. 353
Clements, Mike .Werner-Gold-Miller, p. 339
Clemmer, Ronnie D. .Longbow Productions, p. 203
Clendenin, Thomas .CNBC, p. 96
Clifford, Jeffrey .The Montecito Picture Company, p. 220
Clifford, Patricia .Patricia Clifford Productions, p. 95
Clifton, Lisa .TBS, p. 309
Clifton, Lisa .Turner Network Television (TNT), p. 321
Clifton, Sidney .Film Roman, Inc., p. 132
Cline, Kelly .Fox Cable Networks, p. 139
Cline, Kelly .FX, p. 144
Clodfelter, Jason .Sony Pictures Television, p. 296
Clooney, George .Smoke House, p. 292
Close, Glenn .Trillium Productions, Inc., p. 319
Close, Megan .Kopelson Entertainment, p. 189
Cloutier, Julie .The Weinstein Company, p. 337
Cobette, Candice .Southern Cross the Dog, p. 297
Cochran, Bob .24, p. 353
Cochran, Connie .Landscape Entertainment, p. 193
Cochran, Patrick .IFM Film Associates, Inc., p. 171
Cochran, Yolanda .Alcon Entertainment, LLC, p. 49
Cochran-Neilan, Lisa .The O.C., p. 371
Cockrell, John .D. Petrie Productions, Inc., p. 253
Cockrill, Ellen .Universal Pictures, p. 326
Codikow, Stacy .Power Up, p. 260
Coe, Todd .CSI: NY, p. 359
Coelen, Chris .RDF Media, p. 266
Coello-Bannon, Gigi .Criminal Minds, p. 358
Coffey, Grace .Twentieth Century Fox Television, p. 323
Coffey, Moira .King World Productions, Inc., p. 188
Cogan, Rene .Newmarket Capital Group, p. 236
Cogar, Billy .here! Networks, p. 165
Coggins, Chris .Escape Artists II, p. 126
Cohan, Matthew .Bay Films, p. 63
Cohen, Adam .Super Delicious Productions, p. 305
Cohen, Adam .Martin Poll Films, Ltd., p. 259
Cohen, Alexis .Atlas Entertainment, p. 57
Cohen, Amanda .Original Film, p. 244
Cohen, Andrew .Bravo, p. 74
Cohen, Andrew .Apatow Productions, p. 53
Cohen, Andrew .NBC Universal Cable Entertainment, p. 231
Cohen, Andy .Grade A Entertainment, p. 151
Cohen, Ayala .Saturday Night Live, p. 373
Cohen, Barney .Pterodactyl Productions Inc., p. 263
Cohen, Betty .Lifetime Television (New York), p. 198
Cohen, Bob .Twentieth Century Fox, p. 322
Cohen, Bruce .Traveler, p. 377
Cohen, Bruce .The Jinks/Cohen Company, p. 181
Cohen, Charles .Metro-Goldwyn-Mayer Studios, Inc. (MGM), p. 215
Cohen, Dan .Buena Vista Television, p. 79
Cohen, David .ABC Entertainment Television Group, p. 45
Cohen, Ellen .Sony Pictures Television, p. 296
Cohen, Greg .King of the Hill, p. 365
Cohen, Ivan .Pterodactyl Productions Inc., p. 263
Cohen, Jaclyn Rann .Nickelodeon/MTVN Kids & Family Group, p. 237
Cohen, Jed .Buena Vista Television, p. 79
Cohen, Joel .The Simpsons, p. 375
Cohen, John .Twentieth Century Fox Animation, p. 323
Cohen, Jon .Davis Entertainment Company, p. 107
Cohen, Larry .Larco Productions, Inc., p. 193
Cohen, Lawrence .Merv Griffin Entertainment, p. 154
Cohen, Lee .CineMagic Entertainment, p. 92
Cohen, Lindsay .Tannenbaum Company, p. 308
Cohen, Marty .Paramount Pictures Production Division, p. 248
Cohen, Michael .City Lights Media Group, p. 94
Cohen, Neil A. .A&E Network, p. 44
Cohen, Philip .Universal Pictures, p. 326
Cohen, Polly .Warner Independent Pictures, p. 335
Cohen, Robert H. .20 Good Years, p. 353
Cohen, Robert L. .The Woofenill Works, Inc., p. 344
Cohen, Seth .Comedy Central, p. 98
Cohen, Shari .Blueprint Entertainment, p. 70
Cohen, Stacy .Roserock Films, p. 275
Cohen, Todd .Reveille, LLC, p. 270
Cohen-Cutler, Olivia .ABC Entertainment Television Group, p. 45
Cohen-Dickler, Susan .Banyan Productions, p. 61
Cohn, David .MTV Networks, p. 226
Cohn, Elie .Langley Productions, p. 193
Cohn, Laina .Evolution Entertainment, p. 128
Cohn, Marjorie .Nickelodeon/MTVN Kids & Family Group, p. 237
Coifman, Vanessa .Senator Entertainment, Inc., p. 284
Colagiovanni, Elizabeth .Alcon Entertainment, LLC, p. 49
Colbert, Ritch .Program Partners, p. 262
Colbert, Stephen .The Colbert Report, p. 357
Cole, Alex .Nine Yards Entertainment, p. 238
Cole, Bob .King World Productions, Inc., p. 188
Cole, Chad .Evolution Entertainment, p. 128
Cole, Michael .The Weinstein Company, p. 337
Cole, Suzanne .Universal Pictures, p. 326
Coleite, Aron Eli .Heroes, p. 363
Coleman, Beth .Spike TV, p. 298
Coleman, Eric .Nickelodeon/MTVN Kids & Family Group, p. 237
Coleman, Kim .Everybody Hates Chris, p. 361
Coleman, Lewis .DreamWorks Animation SKG, p. 116
Coleman, Rob .Lucasfilm Ltd., p. 203
Coleman, Ryan .The Sean Daniel Company, p. 106
Coleman, Ryan F. .The Bedford Falls Company, p. 65
Coleman, Scott .Mandate Pictures, p. 209
Coleman-Smith, Salaam .style., p. 303
Coleman-Smith, Salaam .E! Networks, p. 117
Coletta, Joanna .Bill Melendez Productions, p. 215
Colfer, Evan .Myriad Pictures, p. 228
Coli, Terrence .One Tree Hill, p. 371
Colichman, Paul .Regent, p. 269
Colichman, Paul .here! Networks, p. 165

Colleton, Sara . . . . The Colleton Company, p. 97
Collette, Scott . . . . Foresight Unlimited, p. 137
Collier, Jonathan . . . . Monk, p. 369
Collier, Michael . . . . Two and a Half Men, p. 378
Collier, Mike . . . . Two and a Half Men, p. 378
Colligan, Megan . . . . Paramount Vantage/Paramount Classics, p. 248
Collins, Bryan . . . . Cops, p. 358
Collins, Chris . . . . The Wire, p. 379
Collins, Clancy . . . . Warner Bros. Television Production, p. 335
Collins, David . . . . Queer Eye, p. 372
Collins, David . . . . Scout Productions, p. 282
Collins, David J. . . . . Sunset Canyon Productions, p. 305
Collins, Gregory . . . . Burnt Orange Productions, p. 80
Collins, Jeanette . . . . Big Love, p. 356
Collins, Meghann . . . . Tollin/Robbins Productions, p. 315
Collins, Peter . . . . Benderspink, p. 66
Collins, Scott . . . . Monk, p. 369
Collins, Timothy . . . . Focus Features/Rogue Pictures, p. 136
Colloff, Anya . . . . Monk, p. 369
Colombie, Nicole . . . . Duly Noted, p. 117
Colomby, Harry . . . . Colomby Films, p. 97
Colonna, JoAnne . . . . Brillstein-Grey Entertainment, p. 75
Colpaert, Carl . . . . Cineville LLC, p. 93
Coluccio, Branon . . . . New Wave Entertainment, p. 235
Columbus, Chris . . . . 1492 Pictures, p. 38
Colwell, Traci . . . . Twentieth Century Fox Television, p. 323
Combs, Sean . . . . Bad Boy Films, p. 59
Combs, Troy . . . . Gay Rosenthal Productions, p. 275
Comerford, John . . . . Paradigm Studio, p. 247
Common, Elizabeth . . . . Old Dime Box Productions, Inc., p. 242
Compare, Brian . . . . Court TV Networks, p. 102
Compere, Sha-Kim . . . . Flavor Unit Entertainment, p. 135
Comstock, Beth . . . . NBC Universal Corporate, p. 231
Comstock, Tiffany . . . . HDNet, p. 163
Conaty, Erica . . . . NBC Universal Cable Entertainment, p. 231
Conboy, Liberty . . . . Tudor Management Group, p. 320
Condolora, Paul . . . . Cartoon Network, p. 84
Congelose, Angela . . . . Furthur Films, p. 144
Conlon, Clare Anne . . . . New Line Cinema, p. 234
Connelly, Cindy . . . . Tribune Entertainment Company, p. 318
Connelly, Mary . . . . The Ellen DeGeneres Show, p. 360
Connolly, Patti . . . . Warner Bros. Pictures, p. 334
Connor, Darby . . . . Carson Signature Films, Inc., p. 84
Connor, Michael J. . . . . Universal Operations Group, p. 326
Connor, Richard . . . . America's Funniest Videos, p. 355
Conrad, Hy . . . . Monk, p. 369
Conroy, Kevin . . . . AOL Media Networks, p. 53
Conserva, Phil . . . . CSI: Crime Scene Investigation, p. 358
Considine, Gary . . . . The Tonight Show with Jay Leno, p. 377
Considine, Gary . . . . The Late Late Show with Craig Ferguson, p. 366
Constantine, Jason . . . . Lionsgate, p. 200
Constantino, Victor . . . . Mayhem Pictures, p. 213
Conte, Chris . . . . Last Call with Carson Daly, p. 366
Converse, Michael . . . . The Hal Lieberman Company, p. 197
Conway, Dyan Austin . . . . Marian Rees Associates, p. 268
Conway, Frank . . . . Criminal Minds, p. 358
Conway, Gerry . . . . Law & Order: Criminal Intent, p. 367
Coogan, Steve . . . . Baby Cow Productions Ltd., p. 59
Cook, Bob . . . . Twentieth Television, p. 324
Cook, Bob . . . . My Network TV, p. 228
Cook, Chris . . . . Madhouse Entertainment, p. 206
Cook, Dane . . . . SUperFInger Entertainment, p. 306
Cook, Greg . . . . Automatic Pictures, Inc., p. 58
Cook, J.B. . . . . My Name Is Earl, p. 369
Cook, Julie . . . . CastleBright Studios, p. 85
Cook, Marshall . . . . Pollywog Entertainment, Inc, p. 259
Cook, Richard . . . . The Walt Disney Company, p. 112
Cook, Richard . . . . Buena Vista Motion Pictures Group, p. 78
Cook, Winship . . . . Edward S. Feldman Company, p. 130
Cooke, Stuart . . . . Recorded Picture Company, p. 266
Cookler, Weston . . . . Misher Films, p. 218
Cooley, Ben . . . . Black & White Productions, p. 67
Cooper, Bob . . . . Landscape Entertainment, p. 193
Cooper, BP . . . . Symbolic Entertainment, p. 306
Cooper, David . . . . The Vault, Inc., p. 329
Cooper, Jessica . . . . The Matthau Company, Inc., p. 212
Cooper, Katy . . . . Zuckerman Entertainment, p. 350
Cooper, Kimberly . . . . Twentieth Century Fox, p. 322
Cooper, Matt . . . . The Vault, Inc., p. 329
Cooper, Robert . . . . Stargate: SG-1, p. 376
Cooper, Robert . . . . Stargate: Atlantis, p. 376
Cooper, Stuart . . . . Waltzing Clouds, Inc., p. 333
Coote, Gregory . . . . Latitude Television LLC, p. 195
Copeland, Brad . . . . My Name Is Earl, p. 369
Copeland, Conor . . . . Red Wagon Entertainment, p. 268
Copeland, John . . . . Evergreen Films, LLC, p. 128
Copeland, Tiffani . . . . Grammnet Productions, p. 152
Copen, Erin . . . . Asylum Entertainment, p. 57
Coplan, Amanda . . . . The Film Department, p. 132
Copland, Liesl . . . . Cinetic, p. 93
Coppola, Adrienne-Stout . . . . EARS XXI, p. 118
Coppola, Christopher . . . . EARS XXI, p. 118
Corbin-Miller, Samantha . . . . Cold Case, p. 357
Corcoran, Ed . . . . Blue Sky Studios, p. 69
Corcoran, Karen . . . . Silvers/Koster Productions, Inc., p. 289
Corday, Evan . . . . Evolution Entertainment, p. 128
Corday, Ken . . . . Days of Our Lives, p. 359
Corigliano, Mary . . . . Court TV Networks, p. 102
Corley, Al . . . . Code Entertainment, p. 96
Corman, Catherine . . . . New Concorde, p. 233
Corman, Cis . . . . Barwood Films, p. 62
Corman, Julie . . . . New Concorde, p. 233
Corman, Roger . . . . Concorde-New Horizons, p. 99
Corman, Roger . . . . New Concorde, p. 233
Corn, Kahane . . . . The Daily Show With Jon Stewart, p. 359
Corn, Rob . . . . Grey's Anatomy, p. 362
Cornfeld, Stuart . . . . Red Hour Films, p. 267
Cornish, Kevin . . . . RKO Pictures, LLC, p. 273
Corpas, Aisha . . . . New Line Television, p. 235
Corrado, Ed . . . . H2F Entertainment, p. 158
Corral, Pete . . . . Columbia Pictures, p. 97
Corrao, Lauren . . . . Comedy Central, p. 98
Correa, Robert . . . . CBS Sports, p. 88
Corren, Andy . . . . Generate, p. 145
Corrente, Michael . . . . Iridium Entertainment, p. 177
Corrigan, Paul . . . . King of the Hill, p. 365
Corrington, Joyce . . . . Bunim/Murray Productions, Inc., p. 79
Cort, Robert . . . . Robert Cort Productions, p. 101
Cortés, Lisa . . . . Lee Daniels Entertainment, p. 106
Corthron, Kia . . . . The Wire, p. 379
Corvo, David . . . . NBC News, p. 230
Corzo, Robert S. . . . . Regency Enterprises, p. 268
Cosgrove, Ben . . . . Paramount Pictures Production Division, p. 248
Cosgrove, John . . . . Cosgrove-Meurer Productions, p. 101
Coskan, Zeynep . . . . Everyman Pictures, p. 128
Cossette, John . . . . Cossette Productions, p. 101
Cossey, Sean . . . . Stargate: SG-1, p. 376
Cossey, Sean . . . . Stargate: Atlantis, p. 376
Costa, Mark . . . . New Line Television, p. 235
Costa, Mike . . . . Outerbanks Entertainment, p. 245
Costigan, Michael . . . . Scott Free Productions, p. 282
Costner, Kevin . . . . Tig Productions, Inc., p. 313
Coston, Suzanne . . . . de Passe Entertainment, p. 108
Cotner, Ben . . . . Paramount Vantage/Paramount Classics, p. 248
Coto, Juan Carlos . . . . Standoff, p. 376
Coto, Manny . . . . 24, p. 353
Cotten, Joshua . . . . Mandalay Sports Action Entertainment & Mandalay Integrated Media Entertainment, p. 208
Cotter, Alysia . . . . Legendary Pictures, p. 195
Cotter, Colin . . . . Initial Entertainment Group, p. 175
Cotton, Jeanne . . . . Warner Bros. Television Production, p. 335
Cotton, Nancy . . . . Con Artists Productions, p. 99
Cotton, Pam . . . . 7th Heaven, p. 353
Cotton, Rick . . . . NBC Universal Corporate, p. 231
Cottone, Lucia . . . . Lifetime Television (Los Angeles), p. 198
Cottone, Phil . . . . Cataland Films, p. 85
Cottrill, Geoff . . . . Starbucks Entertainment, p. 299
Couch, John . . . . Ralph Edwards Productions, p. 120
Coughlin, Janine . . . . Alliance Atlantis, p. 49
Coulter, Ronni . . . . Columbia Pictures, p. 97

Courtemanche, Jill . . . . . Sobini Films, p. 293
Courtney, Christopher . . . . . New City Pictures, Inc., p. 233
Courtney, Mary . . . . . Ghost Whisperer, p. 362
Coveny, John . . . . . The Closer, p. 357
Cowan, Chris . . . . . Trading Spouses: Meet Your New Mommy, p. 377
Cowan, Chris . . . . . Rocket Science Laboratories, p. 273
Cowan, Cindy . . . . . Cindy Cowan Entertainment, Inc., p. 102
Cowan, Denys . . . . . BET Networks, p. 66
Cowan, Jon . . . . . Crossing Jordan, p. 358
Cowan, Michael Lionello . . . . . Spice Factory, p. 298
Cowan, Rich . . . . . North By Northwest Entertainment, p. 239
Cowan, Rob . . . . . Winkler Films, p. 342
Cowin, Kimberly . . . . . Pink Sneakers Productions, p. 255
Cox, Joel . . . . . Malpaso Productions, p. 208
Cox, Penney Finkelman . . . . . Sony Pictures Animation, p. 295
Cox-Arquette, Courteney . . . . . Dirt, p. 360
Cox-Arquette, Courteney . . . . . Coquette Productions, p. 101
Cox-Hagen, Nigel . . . . . VH1, p. 330
Coyle, Chris . . . . . Mobile Streams, p. 219
Cozzi, Giovanni . . . . . Emerging Pictures, p. 122
Cozzini, Allison . . . . . IMG Media, p. 172
Crabbe, Peter . . . . . Evergreen Films, LLC, p. 128
Craft, Liz . . . . . The Shield, p. 374
Cragg, Steven . . . . . Mad TV, p. 368
Craig, Charlie . . . . . Traveler, p. 377
Craig, David . . . . . Jimmy Kimmel Live, p. 364
Craig, Douglas . . . . . Discovery Networks, U.S., p. 111
Craig, Michele . . . . . Hazy Mills Productions, p. 161
Cramer, Grant . . . . . Moore/Cramer Productions, p. 221
Cramer, Peter . . . . . Universal Pictures, p. 326
Cramsey, Denise . . . . . Extreme Makeover: Home Edition, p. 361
Crane, A.D. . . . . . Sub Rosa Productions, Inc., p. 303
Crane, Amanda . . . . . Film Garden Entertainment, Inc., p. 132
Crane, David . . . . . The Class, p. 357
Crane, John . . . . . Mad TV, p. 368
Crane, Peter . . . . . Crane Wexelblatt Entertainment, p. 102
Craniotes, Lauren . . . . . Warner Independent Pictures, p. 335
Crase, Vanessa . . . . . Station 3, p. 300
Craven, Wes . . . . . Craven/Maddalena Films, p. 102
Crawford, Steve . . . . . Nine Yards Entertainment, p. 238
Crean, Kelly . . . . . Creanspeak Productions LLC, p. 103
Credle, Gary . . . . . Warner Bros. Entertainment Inc., p. 334
Cremin, Kevin . . . . . The Shield, p. 374
Crenna, Maria . . . . . CBS Paramount Network Television, p. 87
Cressey, Alison . . . . . Warner Bros. Entertainment Inc., p. 334
Crevello, Drew . . . . . Mandate Pictures, p. 209
Cricco, Cristin . . . . . Wife Swap, p. 379
Crichton, Michael . . . . . ER, p. 361
Crill, R. Michael . . . . . Comedy Time, p. 98
Crisman, Ryan . . . . . Red Door Films/David Poulshock Prod., Inc., p. 267
Cristall, Erin . . . . . New Line Television, p. 235
Crittenden, Jen . . . . . The New Adventures of Old Christine, p. 370
Croce, Anthony Santa . . . . . Monk, p. 369
Crocker, Jeff . . . . . Sixth Way Productions, p. 291
Crofford, Keith . . . . . Adult Swim, p. 47
Crofford, Keith . . . . . Cartoon Network, p. 84
Crompton, Dorothy . . . . . Rive Gauche Entertainment, p. 272
Crompton, Sarah . . . . . Impact Pictures, p. 173
Cronin, Daria . . . . . Cartoon Network, p. 84
Cronin, Mark . . . . . 51 Minds Entertainment, p. 42
Cronin, Rich . . . . . GSN, p. 157
Crosby, Ken . . . . . Jimmy Kimmel Live, p. 364
Cross, Chris . . . . . Sub Rosa Productions, Inc., p. 303
Cross, Courtney . . . . . TriCoast Studios, p. 318
Cross, Suzanne . . . . . Sub Rosa Productions, Inc., p. 303
Croston, Tim . . . . . King of the Hill, p. 365
Crouch, Sean . . . . . Numb3rs, p. 370
Crounse, Brian . . . . . Walden Media, p. 333
Crounse, Karin Le Maire . . . . . Walden Media, p. 333
Crye, John . . . . . Newmarket Capital Group, p. 236
Crystal, Billy . . . . . Face Productions/Jennilind Productions, p. 129
Csupo, Gabor . . . . . Klasky Csupo, Inc., p. 189
Cuarón, Alfonso . . . . . Esperanto Films, p. 126
Cuarón, Carlos . . . . . Esperanto Films, p. 126
Cuban, Mark . . . . . HDNet, p. 163
Cuban, Mark . . . . . 2929 Productions, p. 40
Cubillas, Al . . . . . Laika Entertainment, p. 191
Cucci, John . . . . . Spike TV, p. 298
Cucci, John . . . . . Comedy Central, p. 98
Cuenca, Al . . . . . Alcon Entertainment, LLC, p. 49
Cuevas, Linda . . . . . Village Roadshow Pictures, p. 331
Culbreth, Jeffry . . . . . MARTHA, p. 368
Culea, Melinda . . . . . Blueline Productions, p. 69
Cullen, Elizabeth . . . . . Oxygen Media, p. 245
Cullen, Mark . . . . . Las Vegas, p. 366
Cullen, Rob . . . . . Las Vegas, p. 366
Culliton, Carolyn . . . . . One Life to Live, p. 371
Culp, Anna . . . . . Imagine Entertainment, p. 172
Culpepper, Clinton . . . . . Screen Gems, p. 283
Cummings, Patti . . . . . Ensemble Entertainment, p. 124
Cummings, Seth . . . . . Amp'd Mobile, p. 51
Cummins, Emily . . . . . Red Wagon Entertainment, p. 268
Cunningham, Alex . . . . . Desperate Housewives, p. 360
Cunningham, Donna . . . . . Sony Pictures Television International, p. 296
Cunningham, John . . . . . DC Comics, p. 108
Cunningham, Lyna . . . . . Level 1 Entertainment, p. 197
Cunningham, Sean S. . . . . . Crystal Lake Entertainment, Inc., p. 103
Cunningham, Teresa . . . . . DC Comics, p. 108
Curb, Carole . . . . . Curb Entertainment, p. 104
Curling, Chris . . . . . Zephyr Films Ltd., p. 348
Curmi, Patricia . . . . . QVF Inc., p. 264
Curran, Kevin . . . . . The Simpsons, p. 375
Curren, Lois . . . . . MTV Networks, p. 226
Currey, Gail . . . . . Lucasfilm Ltd., p. 203
Curry, Anne E. . . . . . Old Dime Box Productions, Inc., p. 242
Curry, Kevin . . . . . Seaside Productions, p. 283
Curry, Sheena . . . . . G-Unit Television & Films, p. 157
Curtis, Debra . . . . . Sony Pictures Television, p. 296
Curtis, Grant . . . . . Ghost House Pictures, p. 145
Curtis, Grant . . . . . Renaissance Pictures, p. 270
Cusack, Brendan . . . . . Boxx Communications, LLC, p. 72
Cusack, Chris . . . . . Stoneworks Television, p. 302
Cusack, John . . . . . New Crime Productions, p. 233
Cuse, Carlton . . . . . Lost, p. 368
Cusick, Richard . . . . . TV Guide Channel, p. 321
Custodio, Primo . . . . . Universal Studios, p. 326
Cutforth, Dan . . . . . Last Comic Standing, p. 366
Cutler, Devin . . . . . Media 8 Entertainment, p. 214
Cutler, R.J. . . . . . 30 Days, p. 353
Cutler, R.J. . . . . . Actual Reality Pictures, p. 46
Cutler, Viruna . . . . . Thunder Road Pictures, p. 313
Cutler-Rubenstein, Devorah . . . . . Noble House Entertainment, Inc., p. 238
Cybriwsky, Mary . . . . . Atlas Entertainment, p. 57
Cygielman, Jamie . . . . . HIT Entertainment, p. 167
Czarkowski, Joseph . . . . . Discovery Networks, U.S., p. 111
Czernin, Peter . . . . . Blue Print, p. 69
Da Matta, Flavia . . . . . Fremantle Productions Latin America, p. 142
Dabis, Cherien . . . . . The L Word, p. 366
Daccord, Julie . . . . . Miramax Films, p. 217
Daeenejad, Saeed . . . . . Intermedia Film Equities USA, Inc., p. 175
Daffern, Joy Ann . . . . . John Wells Productions, p. 338
Dagan, Liz Berger . . . . . The Weinstein Company, p. 337
Dagnino, Thomas . . . . . Alcon Entertainment, LLC, p. 49
Dagres, Todd . . . . . Veoh Networks, Inc., p. 329
Dahlia, B . . . . . Paradigm Studio, p. 247
Dahm, Richard . . . . . The Colbert Report, p. 357
Daily, Bob . . . . . Desperate Housewives, p. 360
Dain, Patrick . . . . . Red Hour Films, p. 267
Dalaklis, Charles . . . . . Dalaklis-McKeown Entertainment, Inc., p. 106
Dale, Sarah . . . . . Viviano Feldman Entertainment, p. 331
D'Alessio, David . . . . . Andrew Lauren Productions, p. 195
Daley, Joe . . . . . Seraphim Films, p. 284
Dalmer-Ciaccio, Tomika . . . . . America's Funniest Videos, p. 355
Daltas, Alex . . . . . Trilogy Entertainment Group, p. 319
Dalton, Robb . . . . . IMG Media, p. 172
Dalvi, Salil . . . . . NBC Universal Corporate, p. 231
Daly, Ann . . . . . DreamWorks Animation SKG, p. 116
Daly, Ann . . . . . DreamWorks SKG, p. 116
Daly, Bill . . . . . Big Day, p. 355
Daly, Carson . . . . . Last Call with Carson Daly, p. 366

Daly, Carson . . . . .Carson Daly Productions, p. 84
Daly, Patrick . . . . .Jean Doumanian Productions, p. 115
Dam, Allen . . . . .Anonymous Creators Productions, p. 52
Damaschke, Bill . . . . .DreamWorks Animation SKG, p. 116
Damato, Vince . . . . .Landscape Entertainment, p. 193
Damiano, John . . . . .NBC Universal Corporate, p. 231
D'Amico, Kirk . . . . .Myriad Pictures, p. 228
Damon, Mark . . . . .Foresight Unlimited, p. 137
Damon, Matt . . . . .LivePlanet, p. 201
Damsker, Corey . . . . .Hollywood East Entertainment, Inc., p. 168
Dana, Jennifer . . . . .Andrew Lauren Productions, p. 195
Danaher-Dorr, Karen . . . . .kdd Productions, LLC, p. 185
Danella, Guy . . . . .Gold Circle Films, p. 148
Daneshvari, Gitty . . . . .Contrafilm, p. 100
Danforth, Susan . . . . .Dimitri Villard Productions, p. 331
Dang, Binh . . . . .Steamroller Productions, Inc., p. 300
Dangel, Julie . . . . .Element Films, p. 121
D'Angelo, Carr . . . . .Unpainted Pictures, p. 327
D'Angelo, Joe . . . . .Hyde Park Entertainment, p. 169
D'Angelo, Nick . . . . .Twentieth Century Fox - Fox 2000, p. 323
Daniel, Colin . . . . .Help Me Help You, p. 363
Daniel, Gregg L. . . . . .Rainstorm Entertainment, Inc., p. 265
Daniel, Sean . . . . .The Sean Daniel Company, p. 106
Daniel, Tiffany . . . . .Heyday Films, p. 166
Danielak, Yarek . . . . .Armada Pictures, p. 55
Daniels, Alan . . . . .Sony Pictures Television, p. 296
Daniels, Greg . . . . .King of the Hill, p. 365
Daniels, Greg . . . . .The Office, p. 371
Daniels, Lee . . . . .Lee Daniels Entertainment, p. 106
Daniels, Nancy . . . . .CBS Entertainment, p. 86
Daniels, Susanne . . . . .Lifetime Television (Los Angeles), p. 198
Daniels, Tricia . . . . .TV Guide Channel, p. 321
Dann, Marlene . . . . .Court TV Networks, p. 102
Dannenberg, Randy . . . . .Media 8 Entertainment, p. 214
Danska, Jennifer . . . . .E! Networks, p. 117
Dante, Joe . . . . .Renfield Productions, p. 270
Danto, Joan . . . . .here! Networks, p. 165
Danton, Jill . . . . .Close to Home, p. 357
Darabont, Frank . . . . .Darkwoods Productions, p. 107
Darby, Alleta . . . . .MPH Entertainment, Inc., p. 224
Darby, Geoffrey . . . . .Oxygen Media, p. 245
Darden, Shelly . . . . .Mr. Mudd, p. 224
Dargan, Janet Tsai . . . . .Sony Pictures Television International, p. 296
Darian, Craig . . . . .Tricor Entertainment, p. 318
D'Arinzo, Debbie . . . . .Court TV Networks, p. 102
Darmody, Julie . . . . .Mosaic Media Group, p. 222
Darmour, Valerie . . . . .Moxie Firecracker Films, p. 223
Darnell, Mike . . . . .Fox Broadcasting Company, p. 139
Daro, Elizabeth . . . . .Sitting Ducks Productions, p. 290
Darondeau, Yves . . . . .Bonne Pioche, p. 71
Daruty, Michael . . . . .Universal Operations Group, p. 326
Dauber, Rob . . . . .MARTHA, p. 368
Dauber, Rob . . . . .Martha Stewart Living Omnimedia, Inc., p. 211
Dauchy, Derek . . . . .Davis Entertainment Company, p. 107
Dauterive, Jim . . . . .King of the Hill, p. 365
Davatzes, Nickolas . . . . .A&E Network, p. 44
Davey, Bruce . . . . .Icon Productions, LLC, p. 170
Davey, Chris . . . . .Media Talent Group, p. 214
Davey, Jim . . . . .Nickelodeon/MTVN Kids & Family Group, p. 237
David, Alan . . . . .Alan David Management, p. 107
David, Kerry . . . . .Lucky Crow Films, p. 204
David, Lorena . . . . .Roberts/David Films, Inc., p. 273
David, Pierre . . . . .Lance Entertainment, Inc., p. 192
David, Scott . . . . .Criminal Minds, p. 358
David, Stephen . . . . .The Idea Factory, p. 170
David Williams, Denise . . . . .MakeMagic Productions, p. 207
Davidoff, Michael . . . . .The War at Home, p. 379
Davids, Daniel . . . . .The History Channel, p. 167
Davids, Daniel . . . . .A&E Network, p. 44
Davids, Hollace . . . . .Universal Pictures, p. 326
Davidson, Boaz . . . . .Millennium Films, p. 217
Davidson, Brian . . . . .CSI: Miami, p. 358
Davidson, Chris . . . . .CBS Entertainment, p. 86
Davidson, Jennifer . . . . .Sony Pictures Television, p. 296
Davidson, Jennifer . . . . .Pie Town Productions, p. 254
Davidson, Jon . . . . .New Line Cinema, p. 234
Davidson, Tom . . . . .Sony Pictures Television International, p. 296
Davies, Michael . . . . .Wife Swap, p. 379
Davies, Michael . . . . .Embassy Row LLC, p. 122
Davies, Rob . . . . .Atomic Cartoons, Inc., p. 58
Davies, Scott . . . . .Atomic Cartoons, Inc., p. 58
Davila, Christine . . . . .Team Todd, p. 310
Davilas, George . . . . .MARTHA, p. 368
Davine, Howard . . . . .Touchstone Television, p. 316
Davis, Annette . . . .'Til Death, p. 377
Davis, Ayo . . . . .Touchstone Television, p. 316
Davis, Brad . . . . .Disney Online, p. 112
Davis, Carin . . . . .Film Roman, Inc., p. 132
Davis, Christina . . . . .CBS Entertainment, p. 86
Davis, Dorothy . . . . .The Kerner Entertainment Company, p. 187
Davis, Jeff . . . . .Criminal Minds, p. 358
Davis, Jerry . . . . .IDT Entertainment, p. 171
Davis, Jodi . . . . .Nickelodeon/MTVN Kids & Family Group, p. 237
Davis, John A. . . . . .Davis Entertainment Company, p. 107
Davis, Jonathan .Fox Broadcasting Company, p. 139
Davis, Laura . . . . .Roundtable Entertainment, p. 276
Davis, Marina . . . . .WonderFilms, p. 344
Davis, Michelle . . . . .Norsemen Television Productions, LLC, p. 239
Davis, Pam . . . . .House, p. 363
Davis, Paula .Late Night with Conan O'Brien, p. 367
Davis, Roger . . . . .Lonetree Entertainment, p. 202
Davis, Sid . . . . .Platinum Studios, LLC, p. 257
Davis, Stephanie . . . . .3 Arts Entertainment, Inc., p. 40
Davis, Todd . . . . .Harpo Films, Inc., p. 161
Davis, Wade . . . . .Viacom Entertainment Group, p. 330
Davison, Doug . . . . .Vertigo Entertainment, p. 330
Davison, Michael . . . . .Saturn Films, p. 280
Davola, Joe . . . . .Smallville, p. 375
Davola, Joe . . . . .One Tree Hill, p. 371
Davola, Joe . . . . .Tollin/Robbins Productions, p. 315
Davy, Ildi Toth . . . . .Curb Entertainment, p. 104
Dawkins, Deborah . . . . .Jupiter Entertainment, p. 183
Dawkins, Keith . . . . .Nickelodeon/MTVN Kids & Family Group, p. 237
Daws, Sally . . . . .FX, p. 144
Dawson, Rachel . . . .@radical.media, p. 38
Dawson, Shawn . . . . .The Dead Zone, p. 359
Day, Kathy . . . . .Mace Neufeld Productions, p. 232
Day, Lisa . . . . .Participant Productions, p. 249
De Bont, Jan . . . . .Blue Tulip Productions, p. 69
de Cazotte, Lisa . . . . .Passions, p. 371
de Crinis, Jackie . . . . .USA Network, p. 327
De Fanti, Jean-Luc . . . . .Caldera/De Fanti Entertainment, p. 82
De Faria, Chris . . . . .Warner Bros. Pictures, p. 334
De Fusco, Nicole . . . . .Oxygen Media, p. 245
De Guttadauro, Lorenzo . . . . .USA Network, p. 327
De Joie, Julie . . . . .Shoe Money Productions, p. 286
de la Fuente, Lauren . . . . .G4 TV, p. 144
De Laurentiis, Dino . . . . .Dino De Laurentiis Company, p. 108
De Laurentiis, Martha . . . . .Dino De Laurentiis Company, p. 108
De Laurentiis, Raffaella . . . . .Raffaella Productions, Inc., p. 265
De Leon, Lorraine . . . . .Relevant Entertainment Group, p. 270
de Lespinois, Pierre . . . . .Evergreen Films, LLC, p. 128
De Line, Donald . . . . .De Line Pictures, p. 108
De Luca, Michael . . . . .Michael De Luca Productions, p. 108
De Maio, Lorenzo . . . . .Dino De Laurentiis Company, p. 108
De Marco, Joseph . . . . .Twentieth Century Fox - Searchlight Pictures, p. 323
De Napoli, Thomas . . . . .Cine Mosaic, p. 91
De Niro, Robert . . . . .Tribeca Productions, p. 318
De Nobile, Dennis . . . . .LivePlanet, p. 201
De Pace, Mark . . . . .Ghost Robot, p. 146
de Passe, Suzanne . . . . .de Passe Entertainment, p. 108
de Puthod, Marie . . . . .The Bregman Entertainment Group, p. 74
De Souza, Paul . . . . .Fuller Films, Inc., p. 143
Dean, Lillian . . . . .Fortis Films, p. 137
Deane, Andrew . . . . .Masters of Horror, p. 368
Deane, Andrew . . . . .Industry Entertainment Partners, p. 174
Deas, Alex . . . . .Davis Entertainment Company, p. 107
DeBasc, Dafna . . . . .Untitled Entertainment, p. 327
DeBaun, Susan . . . . .CNBC, p. 96
Debbs, James . . . . .Antidote International Films, Inc., p. 53

Debeenie, Christina .Nasser Entertainment Group, p. 229
DeBenedettis, Paul .MTV Networks, p. 226
DeBevoise, Charlie .NorthSouth Productions, p. 239
DeBevoise, Marc .IDT Entertainment, p. 171
Debiec, Chris .Nova Pictures, p. 240
DeBitetto, Robert .A&E Network, p. 44
Debson, Scott .Zingy Inc., p. 349
DeCamargo, Simone .Neo Art & Logic, p. 232
Decker, David .Telepictures Productions, p. 311
Decker, Jennifer .Stone and Company Entertainment, p. 301
DeClerque, David .Law & Order: Special Victims Unit, p. 367
DeCordoba, Louise .Paramount Vantage/Paramount Classics, p. 248
DeCrane, David .Lance Entertainment, Inc., p. 192
DeFrancis, Amber .Benderspink, p. 66
Defrehn, Dennis .John Wells Productions, p. 338
DeGeneres, Ellen .The Ellen DeGeneres Show, p. 360
Degraff, Cary .The Collective, p. 96
DeGroot, Neil .Watershed Films, p. 336
Deiboldt, Kevin .The Levinson/Fontana Company, p. 197
Deighton, Joshua .Sidney Kimmel Entertainment, p. 187
DeJesus, Dani .Craig Anderson Productions, p. 52
DeJoie, Julie .Studio 60 on the Sunset Strip, p. 376
DeJulio, James .Half Shell Entertainment, p. 159
DeJulio, Tara .Dan Wigutow Productions, p. 340
DeKnight, Steven S. .Smallville, p. 375
Del Deo, Adam .Endgame Entertainment, p. 124
Del Prete, Deborah .Odd Lot Entertainment, p. 241
Del Sol, Elizabeth .Scarab Productions, p. 280
Del Valle, Bob .Shark, p. 374
Delaney, Audrey .Media 8 Entertainment, p. 214
Delaney, John .Scott Rudin Productions, p. 277
Delaney, Lynn .Jaffe/Braunstein Films, LLC, p. 179
Delaney, Tim .Showtime Networks Inc., p. 287
DeLang, J.R. .Twentieth Century Fox, p. 322
DeLaurentis, Francesca .Radar Pictures, p. 264
DeLaurentis, Robert .The O.C., p. 371
Delavigne, Anne .ABC Entertainment Television Group, p. 45
Delbridge, Eddie .TV Guide Channel, p. 321
D'Elia, Bill .Boston Legal, p. 357
D'Elia, Robin Seidner .New Line Television, p. 235
Dellaverson, John .Lionsgate, p. 200
DeLuca, Doug .Jimmy Kimmel Live, p. 364
DeLuca, Doug .Jackhole Industries, p. 178
DeLuca, Len .ESPN Original Entertainment (EOE), p. 127
DeMarco, Raymond .The Group Entertainment, p. 156
Demarco, Robyn .MTV Networks, p. 226
DeMasters, Gina .Firebrand Productions, p. 134
Demato, Richard .Fuse Entertainment, p. 144
Demberg, Lisa .Fox Television Studios, p. 140
Dembrowski, Christi .Infinitum Nihil, p. 174
Demetrius, Duppy .Kidnapped, p. 365
Demey, Frederic .Cineville LLC, p. 93
Demko, Tom .The Bauer Company, p. 63
DeMontreux, Debbie .The Independent Film Channel (IFC), p. 173
DeMoulin, Chris .Walden Media, p. 333
DeMoulin, Chris .Bristol Bay Productions, p. 76
Demyanenko, Alex .VH1, p. 330
Deneen, Brendan .The Weinstein Company, p. 337
Denise, Debbie .Sony Pictures Imageworks, p. 295
Denny-Gardner, Lucy .King World Productions, Inc., p. 188
DeNoon, Dawn .Law & Order: Special Victims Unit, p. 367
Densham, Nevin .Trilogy Entertainment Group, p. 319
Densham, Pen .Trilogy Entertainment Group, p. 319
Denton, Stephanie .Lionsgate, p. 200
Depoe, Suzanne .Ginty Films International, p. 146
DePollo, Daryl .Ken Gross Management, p. 155
Depp, Johnny .Infinitum Nihil, p. 174
Derenzo, Ray .MobiTV, p. 219
Dergan, Anna .Village Roadshow Pictures, p. 331
DeRosa, Christina .CastleBright Studios, p. 85
DeRose, Frank .Lifetime Television (New York), p. 198
Desai, Naren .Brillstein-Grey Entertainment, p. 75
Desai, Shaleen .fox 21, p. 138
DeSanto, F.J. .Comic Book Movies, LLC/Branded Entertainment/ Batfilm Productions, p. 99
DeSanto, Gunilla .Sci Fi Channel, p. 282
Deschamps, Mychelle .In Case of Emergency, p. 364
Deshotel, Rob .Happy Hour, p. 362
Desiderio, C.S.P., Father Frank .Paulist Productions, p. 250
Desmond, Steve .The Pitt Group, p. 256
Dettman, Andrew .Numb3rs, p. 370
Detwiler, Kristen .Michael De Luca Productions, p. 108
Deutch, Jim .Actuality Productions, p. 46
Deutchman, Ira .Emerging Pictures, p. 122
Deutchman, Jack .New Line Cinema, p. 234
Deutscher, Andrew .Sony Pictures Television, p. 296
Devan, Bruce .O Entertainment, p. 240
Devanney, Tom .Family Guy, p. 361
Devereux, Elizabeth .1492 Pictures, p. 38
Devi-McConnell, Anita .TV Guide Channel, p. 321
Devine, Elizabeth .CSI: Miami, p. 358
Devine, Zanne .Beacon, p. 64
DeVito, Danny .RENO 911!, p. 373
DeVito, Danny .Jersey Films, p. 180
Devlin, Dean .Electric Entertainment, p. 121
Devlin, Tom .Entertainment Studios, Inc., p. 125
Dewey, Sandra .Turner Network Television (TNT), p. 321
Dewey, Sandra .TBS, p. 309
DeWitt, Jan .Bones, p. 356
Dexter, Alison .Nickelodeon/MTVN Kids & Family Group, p. 237
Dexter, John .here! Networks, p. 165
Deyarmin, James .Cinema Seven Productions, p. 92
Deyo, Christina .MARTHA, p. 368
Di Bona, Cara .Vin Di Bona Productions, p. 110
Di Bona, Gina .America's Funniest Videos, p. 355
Di Bona, Vin .America's Funniest Videos, p. 355
Di Bona, Vin .Vin Di Bona Productions, p. 110
di Bonaventura, Lorenzo .di Bonaventura Pictures, Inc., p. 110
Di Franco, Paul .Capital Arts Entertainment, p. 83
Di Fusco, Gay M. .Warner Bros. Television Production, p. 335
Di Loreto, Dante .Kenwright USA/Bill Kenwright Ltd., p. 186
Di Novi, Denise .Di Novi Pictures, p. 110
Di Pasquale, Mara .Peace Arch Entertainment Group Inc., p. 251
Di Prisco, Mary Ellen .SOAPnet, p. 293
Di Trani, Mimi .Untitled Entertainment, p. 327
Diacovo, Nannette .Warner Bros. Television Production, p. 335
Diamant, Illana .Signature Pictures, p. 288
Diamant, Moshe .Signature Pictures, p. 288
Diamond, Daniel .Seven Arts Pictures, p. 285
Diamond, Daniel .Crystal Sky Pictures, LLC, p. 104
Diamond, Peter .NBC Sports, p. 231
Diaz, Armando .TAE Productions/Medeacom Productions, p. 307
Diaz, Jocelyn .ABC Entertainment Television Group, p. 45
Diaz, Leyani .Agua Films, p. 48
Diaz, Lourdes .Agua Films, p. 48
Diaz, Lourdes .VOY Pictures, p. 332
Diaz, Nina .MTV Networks, p. 226
Diaz, Philippe .Cinema Libre Studio, p. 92
Diaz, Roger .TAE Productions/Medeacom Productions, p. 307
Dibari Jr., Anthony .MTV Networks, p. 226
Dibble, Laurel .High Horse Films, p. 166
DiBlasi, Anthony .Seraphim Films, p. 284
DiCunio, Jerry .NBC Universal Television Studio, p. 231
DiCaprio, Leonardo .Appian Way, p. 53
Dice, Ken .Discovery Networks, U.S., p. 111
Dick, Andy .Pollywog Entertainment, Inc, p. 259
Dick, Leonard .House, p. 363
Dickerman, Samuel .Columbia Pictures, p. 97
Dickes, Susan .Boston Legal, p. 357
Dickler, Jan .Banyan Productions, p. 61
Dickler, Liz .Touchstone Television, p. 316
Dickman, Donna .Focus Features/Rogue Pictures, p. 136
Dickstein, Joe .Mainline Releasing, p. 207
DiDio, Daniel .DC Comics, p. 108
Diener, Todd .Brillstein-Grey Entertainment, p. 75
Dietrich, Beth .The History Channel, p. 167
Diggs, Taye .Day Break, p. 359
DiGiaimo, Lou .Louis DiGiaimo & Associates, Ltd., p. 110
DiGiaimo Jr., Lou .Louis DiGiaimo & Associates, Ltd., p. 110
Digilio, David .Traveler, p. 377

Diller, Barry . . . . .IAC/InterActiveCorp, p. 170
Diller, Jeremy . . . . .WildRice Productions, p. 341
Dillon, Matt . . . . .Banyan Tree Films, p. 61
DiMartino, Regina . . . . .Fox Television Studios, p. 140
Dimbort, Danny . . . . .Millennium Films, p. 217
DiNallo, Barbara . . . . .StudioCanal (US), p. 303
Diner, Jerry . . . . .Monster Productions, p. 220
Dinga, Nat . . . . .Sunlight Productions, p. 305
Dingley, Michael . . . . .Home & Garden Television (HGTV), p. 168
Dinielli, Keith . . . . .John Baldecchi Productions, p. 60
Dinner, Michael . . . . .Kidnapped, p. 365
Dinsmoor, Miles . . . . .Concrete Pictures, p. 99
Dinsmore, Jayson . . . . .NBC Entertainment, p. 230
Dion, Garrick . . . . .Bold Films, p. 71
Dion, Garrick . . . . .David Lancaster Productions, p. 192
Dionne, Max . . . . .Contrafilm, p. 100
DiRaffaele, Michelle . . . . .Mandalay Pictures, p. 208
Dirksen, Jennah . . . . .Scott Free Productions, p. 282
DiSalvo, Joe . . . . .King World Productions, Inc., p. 188
DiSanto, Tony . . . . .MTV Networks, p. 226
Disco, Michael . . . . .New Line Cinema, p. 234
Disharoon, Scott . . . . .entitled entertainment, p. 125
Ditrinco, Linda . . . . .Focus Features/Rogue Pictures, p. 136
Dix, A.J. . . . . .FilmEngine, p. 133
Dix, Greg F. . . . . .AEI-Atchity Entertainment Intl., Inc., p. 47
Dix, Michele Megan . . . . .VH1, p. 330
Dizol, Crystal . . . . .CastleBright Studios, p. 85
Dobbins, E. Brian . . . . .Principato-Young Entertainment, p. 262
Dobie, Doug . . . . .Amp'd Mobile, p. 51
Doble, Paul . . . . .The Mayhem Project, p. 213
Dobson, Connie . . . . .Roger Gimbel Productions, Inc., p. 146
Dodd, Ted . . . . .Twentieth Century Fox, p. 322
Doden, Jeff . . . . .Pink Sneakers Productions, p. 255
Dodson, Neal . . . . .Dylan Sellers Productions, p. 284
Doel, Frances . . . . .New Concorde, p. 233
Dogan, Damla . . . . .VH1, p. 330
Doganieri, Elise . . . . .The Amazing Race, p. 354
Doganieri, Elise . . . . .Earthview Inc., p. 118
Doggett, Leryn . . . . .O Entertainment, p. 240
Doherty, Neal . . . . .The Konigsberg-Smith Company, p. 189
Doherty, Robert . . . . .Medium, p. 369
Doise, Kathleen . . . . .The Wolper Organization, p. 344
Dolan, Michael . . . . .Viacom Entertainment Group, p. 330
Dolcemaschio, Steve . . . . .E! Networks, p. 117
Dolgen, Lauren . . . . .MTV Networks, p. 226
Domaschuk, Kira . . . . .The Dead Zone, p. 359
Dombrowski, Lauren . . . . .Mad TV, p. 368
Dominello, Jim . . . . .Persistent Entertainment, p. 253
Domingo, Annie . . . . .Myriad Pictures, p. 228
Dominici, Anthony . . . . .America's Next Top Model, p. 355
Don, Laurie . . . . .The Jim Henson Company, p. 165
Donahue, Ann . . . . .CSI: NY, p. 359
Donahue, Ann . . . . .CSI: Crime Scene Investigation, p. 358
Donahue, Ann . . . . .CSI: Miami, p. 358
Donahue, Nikki . . . . .Sub Rosa Productions, Inc., p. 303
Donald, James L. . . . . .Starbucks Entertainment, p. 299
Donaldson, Peter . . . . .Donaldson/Sanders Entertainment, p. 114
Donatelli, Christian . . . . .Benderspink, p. 66
Donen, Josh . . . . .Buckaroo Entertainment, p. 78
Donen, Nikki . . . . .Oxygen Media, p. 245
Donlon, Jim . . . . .Focus Features/Rogue Pictures, p. 136
Donnars, Dave . . . . .Orchard Films, p. 243
Donnelly, David . . . . .The Artists' Colony, p. 56
Donner, Lauren Shuler . . . . .The Donners' Company, p. 114
Donner, Richard . . . . .The Donners' Company, p. 114
Donnermeyer, Nicholas . . . . .Bleiberg Entertainment, p. 68
D'Onofrio, Mark . . . . .Goff-Kellam Productions, p. 148
Donovan, Garrett . . . . .Scrubs, p. 374
Donovan, Kemper . . . . .Circle of Confusion Productions, p. 93
Donovan, Lauren . . . . .CNBC, p. 96
Dooley, Christy Elaine . . . . .The Bold and the Beautiful, p. 356
Dopher, Ken . . . . .Sony Online Entertainment, p. 294
Doqui, Pamela Palmer . . . . .Type A Films, p. 325
Doran, Lindsay . . . . .Three Strange Angels, Inc., p. 313
Dore, Bonny . . . . .Bonny Dore Productions, p. 114
Doree, Elizabeth . . . . .WE: Women's Entertainment, p. 336
Dorfman, Brian . . . . .NBC Entertainment, p. 230
Dorfman, Rick . . . . .Relevant Entertainment Group, p. 270
Dorgan, James V. . . . . .Telepictures Productions, p. 311
Dormun, Alphonso . . . . .VanDerKloot Film & Television, p. 328
Dornbusch, Ryan . . . . .Revelations Entertainment, p. 271
Dornetto, Karey . . . . .The Knights of Prosperity, p. 365
Dorr, Christopher . . . . .Chris Dorr Productions, p. 114
Dorrell, Torrie . . . . .Sony Online Entertainment, p. 294
Doshi, Sunil . . . . .Proteus, p. 263
Doty, Dennis . . . . .Cates/Doty Productions, p. 85
Doty, Lance . . . . .aWounded Knee, p. 59
Dougherty, Jen . . . . .Salty Features, p. 278
Dougherty, Jennifer . . . . .Nash Entertainment, p. 229
Dougherty, Joe . . . . .Saved, p. 374
Douglas, Esther . . . . .Fifty Cannon Entertainment, LLC, p. 131
Douglas, Jay . . . . .CastleBright Studios, p. 85
Douglas, Mark . . . . .American Dad, p. 354
Douglas, Michael . . . . .Furthur Films, p. 144
Doumanian, Jean . . . . .Jean Doumanian Productions, p. 115
Douridas, Chris . . . . .Hella Good Moving Pictures, p. 164
Dowd, Jeff . . . . .Jeff Dowd & Associates, p. 115
Dowling, Kevin . . . . .Close to Home, p. 357
Downey, Chris . . . . .The King of Queens, p. 365
Downey, Greg . . . . .NBC Entertainment, p. 230
Downey, Mike . . . . .Film & Music Entertainment, Ltd. (F&ME), p. 131
Doyle, Amy . . . . .MTV Networks, p. 226
Doyle, Bobby L. . . . . .New Line Cinema, p. 234
Doyle, David . . . . .Discovery Networks, U.S., p. 111
Doyle, David . . . . .Animal Planet, p. 52
Doyle, Ken . . . . .Twentieth Television, p. 324
Drachkovitch, Rasha . . . . .44 Blue Productions, Inc., p. 41
Drachkovitch, Stephanie . . . . .44 Blue Productions, Inc., p. 41
Draizin, Doug . . . . .Epigram Entertainment, p. 125
Drake, Jed . . . . .ESPN Original Entertainment (EOE), p. 127
Drake, Joe . . . . .Mandate Pictures, p. 209
Drake, Scott . . . . .CNBC, p. 96
Drake-Earl, Joanna . . . . .Current TV, LLC, p. 105
Draper, Bill . . . . .Warner Bros. Pictures, p. 334
Dratch, Daniel . . . . .Monk, p. 369
Draughon, Rick . . . . .Days of Our Lives, p. 359
Dray, Julia . . . . .Broken Lizard Industries, p. 76
Dresp, Jeanne . . . . .Red Dog Entertainment, p. 267
Drew, Chad . . . . .All of Us, p. 354
Drewe, Avery . . . . .NCIS, p. 370
Drewe, Avery . . . . .Belisarius Productions, p. 65
Dreyfuss, Christie . . . . .Nelvana Communications, Inc., p. 232
Dreyfuss, Richard . . . . .Dreyfuss/James Productions, p. 117
Dries, Caroline . . . . .Smallville, p. 375
Driessen, Christine . . . . .ABC Sports, p. 45
Driessen, Christine . . . . .ESPN Original Entertainment (EOE), p. 127
Dripps, Bazyl . . . . .VanDerKloot Film & Television, p. 328
Drobnyk, Christian . . . . .Discovery Networks, U.S., p. 111
Drobnyk, Christian . . . . .TLC, p. 314
Drumm, Tom . . . . .Safran Company, p. 278
Drummond, Diane . . . . .Jerry Bruckheimer Films & Television, p. 78
Dryfoos, Glenn . . . . .Telemundo Network, p. 310
Dryke, Sean . . . . .O.N.C. Entertainment Inc., p. 240
Drysdale, Eric . . . . .The Colbert Report, p. 357
Duan, Lewei . . . . .Echelon Entertainment World Dist. & Prod., p. 119
Duarte, Chris . . . . .MakeMagic Productions, p. 207
Dubbin, Rob . . . . .The Colbert Report, p. 357
Dube, Marc . . . . .CSI: Miami, p. 358
Dubelko, Bob . . . . .Carsey-Werner Films, p. 84
Dubelko, Michael . . . . .Cannell Studios, p. 83
Dubin, Michael . . . . .here! Networks, p. 165
Dubinet, Ann . . . . .Myriad Pictures, p. 228
Dubnicek, Jack . . . . .The Donners' Company, p. 114
Dubois, Dana . . . . .NBC Universal Television Studio, p. 231
Dubuc, Nancy . . . . .A&E Network, p. 44
Ducard, Malik . . . . .Lionsgate, p. 200
Ducceschi, Laurence . . . . .von Zerneck-Sertner Films, p. 332
Duchan, Peter . . . . .Chicagofilms, p. 90
Duchovny, David . . . . .And Then Productions, p. 51
Ducocq, Alexandra . . . . .Seed Productions, p. 283

Ducsay, Robert ... The Sommers Company, p. 294
Duda, Alex ... The Tyra Banks Show, p. 378
Duda, Matthew ... Showtime Independent Films, p. 287
Duda, Matthew ... Showtime Networks Inc., p. 287
Dudelson, James G. ... Taurus Entertainment Company, p. 309
Dudelson, Robert F. ... Taurus Entertainment Company, p. 309
Dudelson, Scott ... Taurus Entertainment Company, p. 309
Dudelson, Stanley E. ... Taurus Entertainment Company, p. 309
Dudevoir, Leon ... New Line Cinema, p. 234
Duff, James ... The Closer, p. 357
Duffell, Julie ... O.N.C. Entertainment Inc., p. 240
Duffy, Jeanette ... Superb Entertainment, p. 305
Dufour, Marie-Christine ... CinéGroupe, p. 91
Dufresne, Dani ... Melee Entertainment, p. 214
Dufresne, Rachel ... Shoreline Entertainment, Inc., p. 286
Dugan, Dan ... The Game, p. 361
Dugan, Dan ... Girlfriends, p. 362
Dugan, Randy ... Bunim/Murray Productions, Inc., p. 79
Dugdale, Rick ... Daniel Petrie Jr. & Company, p. 253
Duka, Daniel ... Mandate Pictures, p. 209
Duke, Alan ... G4 TV, p. 144
Dulany, Kelleigh ... Comedy Central, p. 98
Dummer, Vicki ... ABC Entertainment Television Group, p. 45
Dummler, Scott ... Luminair Entertainment, p. 204
Dumont, Carrie ... Cookie Jar Entertainment, p. 100
Dumont, Richard ... Twentieth Television, p. 324
Dumontet, Gilbert ... Screen Gems, p. 283
Dumouchel, Ellen ... Conundrum Entertainment, p. 100
Dunaway, Cammie ... Yahoo! Media Group/Yahoo! Studios, p. 347
Dunbar, Dave ... Paramount Vantage/Paramount Classics, p. 248
Duncan, Dayton ... Florentine Films, p. 135
Duncan, Scott ... Trillion Entertainment, Inc., p. 319
Duncan, Tai ... Paul Schiff Productions, p. 280
Duncombe, Charles ... Rocket Science Laboratories, p. 273
Dungey, Channing ... Touchstone Television, p. 316
Dungey, Channing ... ABC Entertainment Television Group, p. 45
Dunkelgrun, Laura ... New Wave Management, p. 236
Dunkle, Rick ... Criminal Minds, p. 358
Dunlap, Lindsay ... Ember Entertainment Group, p. 122
Dunleavy, Catherine ... USA Network, p. 327
Dunlevy, Nicholas ... Twentieth Century Fox - Searchlight Pictures, p. 323
Dunn, Catherine ... Wass-Stein, p. 336
Dunn, James ... Twentieth Century Fox Television, p. 323
Dunn, Shari ... Arden Entertainment, p. 54
Dunnam, Charlotte ... Tenth Planet Productions, p. 311
Dunning, Dr. Ted ... Veoh Networks, Inc., p. 329
Dunn-Leonard, Barbara ... Ralph Edwards Productions, p. 120
Dunphy, Dennis ... Telemundo Network, p. 310
Duran, Venecia ... Vanguard Films/Vanguard Animation, p. 328
Durbin, Eric ... American Dad, p. 354
Durel, Mark ... Harpo Films, Inc., p. 161
Durkin, Ginny ... Shady Acres Entertainment, p. 285
Durrani, Nusrat ... MTV Networks, p. 226
Durso, Ed ... ABC Sports, p. 45
Durso, Ed ... ESPN Original Entertainment (EOE), p. 127
Dusedau, Neal ... Barry Mendel Productions, p. 215
Dusevoir, Adam ... The Bold and the Beautiful, p. 356
Dusevoir, Adam ... Bell-Phillip TV Productions, Inc., p. 65
Dussault, Mike ... Tannenbaum Company, p. 308
Dust, Brittany ... Scott Sternberg Productions, p. 301
Dutton, Nan ... CSI: Miami, p. 358
Duvall, Robert ... Butchers Run Films, p. 81
Duzinski, Amy ... Parkchester Pictures, p. 249
Dvornik, Mark ... CBS Paramount Worldwide Television Dist., p. 88
Dworetzky, Dave ... Six Degrees, p. 375
Dworkin, Dan ... Vanished, p. 378
Dwyer, Cathy ... Greenwood Avenue Entertainment, p. 154
Dwyer, Maria ... here! Networks, p. 165
Dyer, Julia ... Act III Productions, p. 46
Dyer, Scott ... Nelvana Communications, Inc., p. 232
Dynner, Susan ... Aberration Films, p. 46
Dyson, Eliza ... John Goldwyn Productions, p. 149
D'Zurilla, Mike ... Twentieth Century Fox Television, p. 323
Eagan, Jason ... Ars Nova, p. 55
Eagan, Richard ... Last Call with Carson Daly, p. 366
Earley, Joe ... Fox Broadcasting Company, p. 139
Easley, Mehrak ... Original Film, p. 244
East, Guy ... Spitfire Pictures, p. 298
Easterly, Andrew ... TriCoast Studios, p. 318
Eastwood, Clint ... Malpaso Productions, p. 208
Eastwood, Joseph ... EntPro, Inc., p. 125
Eaton, Bob ... ESPN Original Entertainment (EOE), p. 127
Eaton, Diane ... Norsemen Television Productions, LLC, p. 239
Ebbs, Donna ... Disney ABC Cable Networks Group, p. 112
Ebel, Kathy ... Good Game, p. 149
Eberhart, Joli ... Bay Films, p. 63
Ebersol, Dick ... NBC Sports, p. 231
Ebersole, P. David ... The Ebersole-Hughes Company, p. 119
Eberts, Christopher ... Ascendant Pictures, p. 56
Eberts, Martha ... Sony Pictures Television International, p. 296
Ecclesine, Steve ... Brookwell McNamara Entertainment, Inc., p. 77
Echevarria, Rene ... Medium, p. 369
Eck, John ... NBC Universal Corporate, p. 231
Eckerling, Liz ... American Zoetrope, p. 51
Eckert, Katherine ... The New Adventures of Old Christine, p. 370
Eckert, Kristine ... Entertainment Studios, Inc., p. 125
Eddings, Ryle ... Periscope Entertainment, LLC, p. 252
Edelbaum, Jana ... Janus Films, LLC, p. 179
Edelist, Susan ... fox 21, p. 138
Edelman, Abra ... Abra Edelman Productions, p. 119
Edelstein, Michael ... The Edelstein Company, p. 119
Edelstein, Neal ... Macari/Edelstein Films, p. 205
Edgar, Angie ... Alchemy Entertainment, p. 48
Edgar, Rob ... Union Entertainment, p. 325
Edmonds, Kenneth "Babyface" ... Edmonds Entertainment, p. 120
Edmonds, Tracey E. ... Edmonds Entertainment, p. 120
Edrich, Kathy ... Fox Broadcasting Company, p. 139
Edwards, Brian ... DreamWorks SKG, p. 116
Edwards, Chris ... HDNet Films, p. 163
Edwards, Gary ... Ralph Edwards Productions, p. 120
Edwards, Karyn ... Brightlight Pictures, Inc., p. 75
Edwards, Kelly ... The Axelrod/Edwards Company, p. 59
Edwards, Rona ... Rona Edwards Productions/ES Entertainment, p. 120
Edwards, Tim ... The Game, p. 361
Egan, Clem ... Passions, p. 371
Egan, Doris ... House, p. 363
Egan, Eddie ... Universal Pictures, p. 326
Egan, Gail ... Potboiler Productions, p. 260
Egan, James ... Wild At Heart Films, LLC, p. 341
Egber, Lauren ... Principal Entertainment, p. 262
Eggebeen, Rachel ... Paramount Vantage/Paramount Classics, p. 248
Egger, Toni ... Discovery Networks, U.S., p. 111
Egger, Toni ... Discovery Health Channel, p. 111
Eggers, Erin ... Yari Film Group (YFG), p. 347
Eglee, Charles H. ... The Shield, p. 374
Eguia, Vicky ... Picturehouse, p. 254
Ehimika, Jessica ... H2F Entertainment, p. 158
Ehrhard, John ... Pink Sneakers Productions, p. 255
Ehrlich, Erin ... King of the Hill, p. 365
Ehrlich, Martin ... Versus, p. 329
Ehrlich, Phyllis ... Cartoon Network, p. 84
Ehrman, Jesse ... Dylan Sellers Productions, p. 284
Eichinger, Bernd ... Constantin Film Dev., Inc./Constantin TV, p. 100
Eichler, David ... New Line Cinema, p. 234
Eichler, Glenn ... The Colbert Report, p. 357
Eick, David ... Battlestar Galactica, p. 355
Eick, David ... David Eick Productions, p. 120
Eid, Rick ... Wolf Films, Inc., p. 343
Eigen, Sam ... Shoreline Entertainment, Inc., p. 286
Eigendorff, Richard ... MTV Networks, p. 226
Einbinder, Bette ... Universal Pictures, p. 326
Einhorn, Stephen L. ... New Line Cinema, p. 234
Einziger, Scott ... Next Entertainment, p. 236
Eisen, Andrea ... Artists, Inc., p. 56
Eisen, Marshall ... MTV Networks, p. 226
Eisen, Pamela ... Capital Arts Entertainment, p. 83
Eisenberg, Lee ... The Office, p. 371
Eisenberg, Noel ... Six Degrees, p. 375
Eisenman, Julia ... Endgame Entertainment, p. 124
Eisner, Keith ... Shark, p. 374

Eisner, Les . . . . Twentieth Television, p. 324
Eisner, Michael . . . . Veoh Networks, Inc., p. 329
Ekins, Susan . . . . Jerry Weintraub Productions, p. 338
Elbin, Debbie . . . . Sony Pictures Television International, p. 296
Elder, Daniel . . . . Luminair Entertainment, p. 204
Elder, Elizabeth . . . . Luminair Entertainment, p. 204
Elder, George . . . . Luminair Entertainment, p. 204
Eldridge, Tony . . . . Lonetree Entertainment, p. 202
Elgarresta, Emilce . . . . Telemundo Network, p. 310
Elias, Dani . . . . Brightlight Pictures, Inc., p. 75
Elias, Georges . . . . Platinum Studios, LLC, p. 257
Elias, Mikail . . . . 3Wolves Productions, p. 41
Elice, Jeremy . . . . AMC, p. 50
Eliot, Jeanette . . . . NBC Entertainment, p. 230
Elkins, Hillard . . . . Elkins Entertainment, p. 122
Elkoff, Peter . . . . Six Degrees, p. 375
Ellenberg, Michael . . . . Scott Rudin Productions, p. 277
Ellickson, Owen . . . . The King of Queens, p. 365
Ellin, Doug . . . . Entourage, p. 360
Elliot, John . . . . Mosaic Media Group, p. 222
Elliott, Karen . . . . Universal Studios, p. 326
Elliott, Kjose . . . . Lakeshore Entertainment Group LLC, p. 192
Elliott, Mike . . . . Capital Arts Entertainment, p. 83
Ellis, Michael . . . . Camelot Entertainment Group, Inc., p. 82
Ellis, Riley Kathryn . . . . Twentieth Century Fox, p. 322
Ellis, Riley Kathryn . . . . Twentieth Century Fox - Fox 2000, p. 323
Ellis, Roger R. . . . . mistRE films, p. 218
Ellis, Suzann . . . . Beacon, p. 64
Ellison, Adam . . . . Lemon Sky Productions, Inc., p. 196
Ellner, Erik . . . . New Line Cinema, p. 234
Ellsworth, Thomas . . . . GoTV Networks, p. 151
Ellzey, Lisa . . . . Twentieth Century Fox, p. 322
Elmer, Lauren . . . . Elevation Filmworks, p. 121
Elmo, Tina . . . . Scout Productions, p. 282
Elmore, Taylor . . . . Raines, p. 372
Elwood, Kelly . . . . Cookie Jar Entertainment, p. 100
Emery, Brent . . . . Maverick Films, p. 213
Emma, Tom . . . . MarVista Entertainment, p. 212
Emmerich, Roland . . . . Centropolis Entertainment, p. 88
Emmerich, Toby . . . . New Line Cinema, p. 234
Emmerich, Ute . . . . Centropolis Entertainment, p. 88
Emmerson, Nick . . . . Supernanny, p. 376
Emmerson, Steve . . . . Fierce Entertainment, LLC, p. 131
Emmett, Randall . . . . Emmett/Furla Films, p. 123
Emmick, Len . . . . Air2web, Inc., p. 48
Emmitt, Palmer . . . . Farrell Paura Productions, LLC, p. 130
Emrey, Thomas . . . . Universal Pictures, p. 326
Enbom, John . . . . Veronica Mars, p. 378
Endara II, Robert G. . . . . Larry Thompson Organization, p. 312
Ender, Chris . . . . CBS Corporation, p. 86
Ender, Chris . . . . CBS Entertainment, p. 86
Endicott, Evan . . . . Ad Hominem Enterprises, p. 46
Endore-Kaiser, Guy . . . . Paramount Vantage/Paramount Classics, p. 248
Eng, Carol . . . . MTV Networks, p. 226
Engel, Charles . . . . NBC Universal Television Studio, p. 231
Engel, David . . . . Circle of Confusion Productions, p. 93
Engel, Peter . . . . Last Comic Standing, p. 366
Engel, Peter . . . . Peter Engel Productions, p. 124
Engel, Stephen . . . . The War at Home, p. 379
Engel, Tim . . . . Buena Vista Motion Pictures Group, p. 78
Engelen, Jeffrey . . . . PorchLight Entertainment, p. 259
Engelson, Trevor . . . . Underground Films, p. 325
England, Chrissie . . . . Industrial Light & Magic (ILM), p. 174
England, Susan . . . . Goldcrest Films International, Inc., p. 149
Engle, Ryan . . . . Kopelson Entertainment, p. 189
Englehart, Rozanne . . . . Sony Pictures Television International, p. 296
Engleman, Jim . . . . Buena Vista Television, p. 79
Engler, Craig . . . . Sci Fi Channel, p. 282
English, Diane . . . . Shukovsky English Entertainment, p. 287
Engstrom, Jewell . . . . Disney ABC Cable Networks Group, p. 112
Ennis, Susan . . . . HBO Entertainment, p. 162
Ennis, Tom . . . . 19 Entertainment, Inc., p. 38
Enright, Don . . . . Alexander/Enright & Associates, p. 49
Enslin, Erin . . . . Baldwin Entertainment Group, Ltd., p. 60
Epstein, Andrew . . . . Apatow Productions, p. 53
Epstein, Brad . . . . Buena Vista Motion Pictures Group, p. 78
Epstein, Ruth . . . . Front Street Pictures, Inc., p. 143
Epstein, Stefanie . . . . Stefanie Epstein Productions, p. 126
Erhardt, Ed . . . . ABC Sports, p. 45
Erhardt, Ed . . . . ESPN Original Entertainment (EOE), p. 127
Erlicht, Jamie . . . . Sony Pictures Television, p. 296
Erlinger, Michael . . . . ABC Entertainment Television Group, p. 45
Ernst, Vikki . . . . The Ellen DeGeneres Show, p. 360
Ernster-Rivera, Dawn . . . . DisneyToon Studios, p. 113
Erwich, Craig . . . . Fox Broadcasting Company, p. 139
Eschenasy, Avy . . . . Focus Features/Rogue Pictures, p. 136
Escobar, Ramón . . . . Telemundo Network, p. 310
Escobar, Rosalie . . . . Criminal Minds, p. 358
Escott, Mike . . . . Principal Entertainment, p. 262
Esenwein, Wolfgang . . . . Motion Picture Invest, p. 222
Eskelsen, Peter . . . . Wigram Productions, p. 340
Eskenas, Jon . . . . Orly Adelson Productions, p. 46
Esmailzadeh, Kourosh . . . . Storm Entertainment, p. 302
Esparza, Moctesuma . . . . Maya Pictures, p. 213
Esparza, Moctesuma . . . . Esparza-Katz Productions, p. 126
Esparza, Tonantzin . . . . Maya Pictures, p. 213
Espiedra, Natasha . . . . Frelaine, p. 142
Espinosa, Mike . . . . Entertainment Studios, Inc., p. 125
Espuelas, Fernando . . . . VOY Pictures, p. 332
Esquibel, Irma . . . . Evolution Entertainment, p. 128
Essick, Amanda . . . . GreeneStreet Films, p. 153
Estenson, Kenneth C. . . . . Disney-ABC Television Group, p. 113
Estey-McLoughlin, Hilary . . . . Telepictures Productions, p. 311
Estrem, Jeanette . . . . MWG Productions, p. 228
Estrin, Leah . . . . Imagine Entertainment, p. 172
Estrin, Zack . . . . Prison Break, p. 372
Etheridge, Dan . . . . Veronica Mars, p. 378
Etkind, Marc . . . . The History Channel, p. 167
Etten, Kevin . . . . Desperate Housewives, p. 360
Etting, Brian R. . . . . Garlin Pictures, Inc., p. 145
Etting, Josh . . . . Garlin Pictures, Inc., p. 145
Eugster, Carlo . . . . Out of the Blue . . . Entertainment, p. 244
Evanoff, Lorraine . . . . Element Films, p. 121
Evans Jr., Charles . . . . Acappella Pictures, p. 46
Evans, Derek . . . . Spyglass Entertainment Group, p. 299
Evans, Jane . . . . Focus Features/Rogue Pictures, p. 136
Evans, Kattie . . . . National Geographic Feature Films, p. 229
Evans, Leigh . . . . Red Wagon Entertainment, p. 268
Evans, Marc . . . . Paramount Pictures Production Division, p. 248
Evans, Marc . . . . Intrepid Pictures, p. 176
Evans, Nancy . . . . Trillium Productions, Inc., p. 319
Evans, Robert . . . . The Robert Evans Company, p. 127
Evans, Tim . . . . Morningstar Entertainment, p. 221
Evashevski, Kassie . . . . Plan B Entertainment, p. 256
Evashevski, Kassie . . . . Brillstein-Grey Entertainment, p. 75
Evenson, Danielle . . . . The New Adventures of Old Christine, p. 370
Everitt, Darren . . . . Greasy Entertainment, p. 153
Evershed, John . . . . Mondo Media, p. 220
Everson, Carolyn . . . . MTV Networks, p. 226
Ewalt, Darrell . . . . HDNet, p. 163
Ewart, Bill . . . . Montage Entertainment, p. 220
Ewers, Erik . . . . Florentine Films, p. 135
Ewing, Michael . . . . Callahan Filmworks, p. 82
Exarhos, Tina . . . . MTV Networks, p. 226
Eyal, Irad . . . . City Lights Media Group, p. 94
Ezhuthachan, Aditya . . . . Palomar Pictures, p. 246
Ezrin, Sarah . . . . Misher Films, p. 218
Ezso, Kathy . . . . Cannell Studios, p. 83
Faber, Gary . . . . The Weinstein Company, p. 337
Fagan, Robert . . . . L'Orange, p. 203
Fagin, Josh . . . . Solaris, p. 293
Fahart, Carol . . . . Twentieth Century Fox Television, p. 323
Faigen, Alexa . . . . Initial Entertainment Group, p. 175
Faigenblum, David . . . . Concept Entertainment, p. 99
Faillace, Maria . . . . Twentieth Century Fox - Fox 2000, p. 323
Fain, Jana . . . . Big Light Productions, p. 67
Fain, Sarah . . . . The Shield, p. 374
Fairall, Sandy . . . . Latin Hollywood Films, p. 194
Faires, Jay . . . . Lionsgate, p. 200
Fairfield, David . . . . Malcolm Leo Productions, p. 196

Faitro, Jennifer ....Dalaklis-McKeown Entertainment, Inc., p. 106
Falacci, Nick ....Numb3rs, p. 370
Falbo, Michael ....Blumhouse Productions, p. 70
Falcetti, Charlie ....Sony Pictures Entertainment, p. 295
Falchuk, Brad ....Nip/Tuck, p. 370
Falco, Randel A. ....NBC Universal Cable Entertainment, p. 231
Falco, Tracy ....Andell Entertainment, p. 51
Fallin, Chris W. ....Workshop Pictures, Inc., p. 345
Fallon, David ....Ghost Whisperer, p. 362
Falvey, Justin ....Las Vegas, p. 366
Falvey, Justin ....DreamWorks SKG, p. 116
Falvey, Samie Kim ....ABC Entertainment Television Group, p. 45
Famiglietti, Ben ....The Weinstein Company, p. 337
Fan, Gloria ....Mosaic Media Group, p. 222
Fan, Gloria ....Atlas Entertainment, p. 57
Fantasia, Steve ....Kahn Power Pictures, p. 184
Farah, Mike ....Southern Cross the Dog, p. 297
Farella, Vivi ....Sinovoi Entertainment, p. 290
Farino, Julian ....Entourage, p. 360
Farkas, Salina ....TriCoast Studios, p. 318
Farrell, Candace ....Merv Griffin Entertainment, p. 154
Farrell, Jennifer ....Sub Rosa Productions, Inc., p. 303
Farrell, Joseph ....Farrell Paura Productions, LLC, p. 130
Farrell, Juliana ....Groundswell Production, p. 156
Farrell, Kathleen ....WE: Women's Entertainment, p. 336
Farrell, Mike ....Farrell/Minoff Productions, p. 130
Farrell, Rebecca ....J2 Pictures/J2TV, p. 178
Farrell, Tom ....Banyan Productions, p. 61
Farrelly, Bobby ....Conundrum Entertainment, p. 100
Farrelly, Peter ....Conundrum Entertainment, p. 100
Farris, Susie ....New Line Cinema, p. 234
Fastook, Steve ....CNBC, p. 96
Fattore, Gina ....Gilmore Girls, p. 362
Faulkner, Judy ....Laurence Mark Productions, p. 210
Faust, Helen ....Buena Vista Television, p. 79
Favale, Vincent P. ....CBS Entertainment, p. 86
Fay, William ....Legendary Pictures, p. 195
Fazio, Debra ....Spike TV, p. 298
Fazlagic Sr., Jesenko ....VanDerKloot Film & Television, p. 328
Fear, Maureen Poon ....Di Novi Pictures, p. 110
Fearnley, Danielle von Zerneck ....von Zerneck-Sertner Films, p. 332
Febrizio, Nick ....A&E Network, p. 44
Feder, Steven ....Black Sheep Entertainment, p. 68
Federbush, Paul ....Warner Independent Pictures, p. 335
Fee, Edward ....di Bonaventura Pictures, Inc., p. 110
Feeney, David ....In Case of Emergency, p. 364
Feeney, Juanita Diana ....Ghost Whisperer, p. 362
Feeney, Michael ....A&E Network, p. 44
Fehrle, Marieke ....The Phil Fehrle Company, p. 130
Fehrle, Phil ....The Phil Fehrle Company, p. 130
Feig, Ellen ....Epigram Entertainment, p. 125
Feig, Erik ....Summit Entertainment, p. 304
Feige, Kevin ....Marvel Studios, Inc., p. 211
Feigen, Ben ....Nine Yards Entertainment, p. 238
Feiken, Jennifer ....Google Inc., p. 149
Fein, Marc ....Versus, p. 329
Feingold, Ben ....Columbia Pictures, p. 97
Feingold, Carly ....Craven/Maddalena Films, p. 102
Feingold, Emily ....The Weinstein Company, p. 337
Feinman, Mitch ....Fox Mobile Entertainment, p. 139
Feinstein, Rorri ....Samuel Goldwyn Films, p. 279
Feist, John ....CSM Communications, p. 104
Feld, John C. ....CMT: Country Music Television, p. 95
Feld, Rob ....ManifestoVision, p. 210
Felder, Steven ....CSI: Crime Scene Investigation, p. 358
Feldman, Beth ....CBS Corporation, p. 86
Feldman, Beth ....CBS Entertainment, p. 86
Feldman, Bob ....DreamWorks Animation SKG, p. 116
Feldman, Ed ....Edward S. Feldman Company, p. 130
Feldman, Eddie ....The Showbiz Show with David Spade, p. 374
Feldman, Eric ....here! Networks, p. 165
Feldman, J.J. ....Pearl Pictures, p. 252
Feldman, Jackie ....Reynolds Entertainment, p. 271
Feldman, Josh ....Cartoon Network, p. 84
Feldman, Leslee ....DreamWorks SKG, p. 116
Feldman, Liz ....The Ellen DeGeneres Show, p. 360
Feldman, Page ....The Apprentice, p. 355
Feldman, Richard ....Viviano Feldman Entertainment, p. 331
Feldman, Steven ....The Cielo Group, Inc., p. 91
Feldman, Todd ....The Feldman Company, p. 130
Feller, Michael ....Fox Sports Network, p. 140
Fellner, Eric ....Working Title Films, p. 345
Fellows, Lindsay ....Bristol Bay Productions, p. 76
Fellows, Lindsay ....Walden Media, p. 333
Felsher, Andy ....FremantleMedia North America, p. 142
Felsot, Jesse ....Treasure Entertainment, p. 317
Feltheimer, Jon ....Lionsgate, p. 200
Felts, Jason ....J2 Pictures/J2TV, p. 178
Fenady, Andrew ....Universal Pictures, p. 326
Fener, Jonathon ....American Dad, p. 354
Fenster, Chet ....Kinetic Pictures, p. 188
Fenton, Chris ....H2F Entertainment, p. 158
Fenton, Louise ....Zero Pictures, p. 349
Ferguson, Craig ....Terra Firma Films, p. 312
Ferguson, Daniel ....Late Night with Conan O'Brien, p. 367
Ferguson, Greg ....Justice, p. 364
Ferguson, Holly ....Arielle Tepper Productions, p. 312
Ferguson, Karen ....DisneyToon Studios, p. 113
Ferhrle, Jim ....The Phil Fehrle Company, p. 130
Ferleger, Daniel ....Paramount Pictures, p. 248
Fermin, Marisa ....Twentieth Television, p. 324
Ferneau, Laurie ....Firm Television, p. 134
Ferrari, Alex R. ....MTV Networks, p. 226
Ferrari, Maria ....How I Met Your Mother, p. 364
Ferraro, Nikki ....Showtime Networks Inc., p. 287
Ferrell, Lisa ....JCS Entertainment II, p. 180
Ferrell, Rodney ....Twentieth Century Fox - Fox 2000, p. 323
Ferrie, Jared ....Evolution Entertainment, p. 128
Ferro, Jon ....Lionsgate, p. 200
Ferrone, Matt ....Love Spell Entertainment, p. 203
Ferry, Anita ....j.k. livin productions, p. 178
Fertman, Kim ....Family Guy, p. 361
Ferwerda, Elliot ....QED International, p. 264
Feuer, Zachary ....Zachary Feuer Films, p. 130
Fey, Tina ....30 Rock, p. 353
Fiacchino, Tommaso ....Cherry Road Films, LLC, p. 89
Ficarra, John J. ....DC Comics, p. 108
Fichandler, Mark ....Court TV Networks, p. 102
Ficken, Amy ....Intuition Productions, p. 176
Fidlow, Bennett J. ....Vanguard Productions, p. 329
Fidz, Rene ....Guardian Entertainment, Ltd., p. 157
Fiedler, Andy ....The Tom Lynch Company, p. 205
Field, Brian ....VOY Pictures, p. 332
Field, Fern ....Monk, p. 369
Field, Gwen ....Creanspeak Productions LLC, p. 103
Field, Gwen ....Simsie Films/Media Savant Pictures, p. 290
Field, Peter ....Pie Town Productions, p. 254
Field, Ted W. ....Radar Pictures, p. 264
Fields, Adam ....Adam Fields Productions, p. 130
Fields, Ira ....Court TV Networks, p. 102
Fields, Joel ....Dirt, p. 360
Fields, Julie ....G4 TV, p. 144
Fields, Simon ....Nuyorican, p. 240
Fierberg, Andrew ....Vox3 Films, p. 332
Fierman, Stephanie ....DC Comics, p. 108
Fierro, Adam E. ....The Shield, p. 374
Fierson, Jeff ....Original Film, p. 244
Fight, Barbara ....MARTHA, p. 368
Figueroa, Suzy ....Village Roadshow Pictures, p. 331
Filgo, Jackie ....Happy Hour, p. 362
Filgo, Jeff ....Happy Hour, p. 362
Filippelli, Rachel ....NBC Entertainment, p. 230
Filoni, Dave ....Lucasfilm Ltd., p. 203
Fincannon, Craig ....One Tree Hill, p. 371
Fincannon, Lisa Mae ....One Tree Hill, p. 371
Finch, Henry LeRoy ....Wildwell Films, p. 341
Finch, Kathleen ....DIY Network, p. 113
Finch, Susan Landau ....Wildwell Films, p. 341
Fine, Delia ....A&E Network, p. 44
Fine, Jared ....PLUS Entertainment, Inc., p. 258

Fine, Joshua . . . . Marvel Studios, Inc., p. 211
Fine, Kristin . . . . The Collective, p. 96
Finerman, Wendy . . . . Wendy Finerman Productions, p. 134
Finestra, Carmen . . . . Wind Dancer Production Group, p. 342
Fineza, Rich . . . . GSN, p. 157
Fink, Hugh . . . . The Showbiz Show with David Spade, p. 374
Fink, Jonny . . . . Tollin/Robbins Productions, p. 315
Fink, Kenneth . . . . CSI: Crime Scene Investigation, p. 358
Finkel, David . . . . 30 Rock, p. 353
Finkelstein, Mindy . . . . Foremost Films, p. 137
Finkelstein, Rick . . . . Universal Studios, p. 326
Finkelstein, Rick . . . . Universal Pictures, p. 326
Finkelstein, Tommy . . . . Bristol Bay Productions, p. 76
Finkelstein, Tommy . . . . Walden Media, p. 333
Finley, Lynn . . . . Disney ABC Cable Networks Group, p. 112
Finn, Catherin . . . . Mode of 8, p. 219
Finn, Pat . . . . Rubicon, p. 276
Finn, Sarah . . . . Sony Pictures Television, p. 296
Finnegan, Bonnie . . . . Kidnapped, p. 365
Finnell, Michael . . . . Renfield Productions, p. 270
Finnerty, James . . . . The Levinson/Fontana Company, p. 197
Finney-Johnson, Sara V. . . . . The Game, p. 361
Fiore Jr., Anthony R. . . . . Spirit Horse Productions, p. 298
Fiorentino, Barbara . . . . Dirt, p. 360
Fiorentino, Barbara . . . . CSI: NY, p. 359
Fiorito, Janelle . . . . Extreme Makeover: Home Edition, p. 361
Firek, Marc . . . . 'Til Death, p. 377
Firestone, Karen . . . . Pink Slip Pictures, p. 255
Fisch, David . . . . SlingShot Media, p. 291
Fisch, Stephanie . . . . Endemol USA Latino, p. 123
Fischer, A.B. . . . . The Shuman Company, p. 287
Fischer, Allen . . . . Principato-Young Entertainment, p. 262
Fischer, Brad . . . . Phoenix Pictures, p. 254
Fischer, Jonathan . . . . Intrepid Pictures, p. 176
Fischer, Kathy . . . . The George Lopez Show, p. 362
Fischer, Preston . . . . Raines, p. 372
Fischer, Preston . . . . Preston Stephen Fischer Company, p. 134
Fish, Mark . . . . The O.C., p. 371
Fish, Steve . . . . Twentieth Television, p. 324
Fisher, Bob . . . . Comedy Time, p. 98
Fisher, Danny . . . . City Lights Media Group, p. 94
Fisher, Debra J. . . . . Criminal Minds, p. 358
Fisher, Jack . . . . City Lights Media Group, p. 94
Fisher, Jason . . . . Big Day, p. 355
Fisher, Josh . . . . Mike Young Productions LLC, p. 348
Fisher, Lucy . . . . Red Wagon Entertainment, p. 268
Fisher, Ricka . . . . Fisher Productions, p. 134
Fisher, Steven . . . . Logo, p. 202
Fishman, Bill . . . . Fallout, p. 129
Fishman, Jim . . . . Fallout, p. 129
Fiss, Tracie . . . . The Tonight Show with Jay Leno, p. 377
Fitz, Lindsay . . . . NBC Sports, p. 231
Fitzgerald, Brehan . . . . Twentieth Century Fox, p. 322
Fitzgerald, Brendan . . . . Sony Pictures Television International, p. 296
Fitzgerald, John . . . . CMT: Country Music Television, p. 95
Fitzgerald, Julie . . . . Trilogy Entertainment Group, p. 319
Fitzgerald, Kevin . . . . NBC Entertainment, p. 230
Fitzgerald, Mary . . . . The Singles Table, p. 375
Fitzgerald, Mary . . . . Lucky Louie, p. 368
Fitzgerald, Susie . . . . Runaway, p. 373
Fitzgerald, Susie . . . . Darren Star Productions, p. 300
Fitzgibbon, Mo . . . . Walker/Fitzgibbon TV/Films, p. 333
Fitzhugh, Stephanie . . . . MARTHA, p. 368
Fitzmaurice, Ellen . . . . Lonetree Entertainment, p. 202
Fitzmorris, Brian . . . . Scott Mauro Entertainment, Inc., p. 212
Fitzpatrick, Eileen . . . . A&E Network, p. 44
Fitzpatrick, Terry . . . . Sesame Workshop, p. 285
Fladell, Matthew . . . . Barnholtz Entertainment, p. 62
Flaherty, Frances X. . . . . Walden Media, p. 333
Flaherty, Micheal . . . . Walden Media, p. 333
Flaherty, Neal . . . . Benderspink, p. 66
Flam, Bryan . . . . Trilogy Entertainment Group, p. 319
Flannery, Will . . . . Fox Cable Networks, p. 139
Flavin, John . . . . Boku Films, p. 71
Fleary, Kim . . . . The CW, p. 105
Fleder, Gary . . . . Mojo Films, p. 220
Fleischer, Robert . . . . Mobile Streams, p. 219
Fleischman, Tracy . . . . Robert Greenwald Productions, p. 153
Fleishman, Susan N. . . . . Warner Bros. Entertainment Inc., p. 334
Fleiss, Mike . . . . The Bachelor, p. 355
Fleiss, Mike . . . . Next Entertainment, p. 236
Fleming, David . . . . Mosaic Media Group, p. 222
Fleming, Drew . . . . Concrete Pictures, p. 99
Fleming, Eric . . . . Launa Newman Productions (LNP), p. 195
Flett-Giordano, Anne . . . . The Game, p. 361
Fleury, Laura . . . . A&E Network, p. 44
Flick, Felicia . . . . Brooksfilms Limited, p. 77
Flint, Carol . . . . Six Degrees, p. 375
Flischel, Karen . . . . here! Networks, p. 165
Flock, John . . . . Peace Arch Entertainment Group Inc., p. 251
Florentino, Barbara . . . . The Shield, p. 374
Flores, Craig J. . . . . Cecchi Gori Pictures, p. 88
Flores, Craig J. . . . . Hollywood Gang Productions, LLC, p. 168
Florio, Maria . . . . Earthworks Films, p. 118
Floro, Kathryn . . . . Blue Star Pictures, p. 69
Floyd, Chris . . . . Universal Pictures, p. 326
Flutie, Robert . . . . Yellow Cab Pictures, p. 347
Flynn, Beau . . . . Contrafilm, p. 100
Flynn, Kathy . . . . MTV Networks, p. 226
Flynn, Max . . . . Western Sandblast, p. 339
Flynn, Steve . . . . Focus Features/Rogue Pictures, p. 136
Flynn, Suzanne . . . . One Life to Live, p. 371
Flynn, Tara . . . . Brancato/Salke Productions, p. 73
Fogel, Alexa . . . . The Black Donnellys, p. 356
Fogel, Alexa L. . . . . Beech Hill Films, p. 65
Fogel, John . . . . John Fogel Entertainment Group, p. 182
Fogel CSA, Alexa L. . . . . The Wire, p. 379
Fogelson, Adam . . . . Universal Pictures, p. 326
Fogelson, Susie . . . . Food Network, p. 136
Foldager, Meta Louise . . . . Zentropa, p. 348
Foldes, Lawrence D. . . . . Star Entertainment Group, Inc., p. 299
Foldy, Peter . . . . Filmstreet, Inc., p. 133
Foley, Jack . . . . Focus Features/Rogue Pictures, p. 136
Foley, Jerry . . . . The Late Show with David Letterman, p. 367
Foley, Mike . . . . What About Brian, p. 379
Foliart, Cheryl . . . . Touchstone Television, p. 316
Folks, Carolyn . . . . Entertainment Studios, Inc., p. 125
Folta, Carl . . . . CBS Corporation, p. 86
Fong, Ramsey . . . . Killer Films, Inc., p. 187
Fong, Wenda . . . . Fox Broadcasting Company, p. 139
Fong, Zana . . . . Eternity Pictures, Inc., p. 127
Fontana, Tom . . . . The Levinson/Fontana Company, p. 197
Foonberg, Annie . . . . Alchemy Entertainment, p. 48
Forbes, Bonnie . . . . Bonnie Forbes Productions, p. 137
Forbes, Brett . . . . Fortress Entertainment, p. 137
Forbis, Wil . . . . Gryphon Films, p. 157
Forcey, Daniel . . . . Platinum Studios, LLC, p. 257
Ford, Elisabeth . . . . Arielle Tepper Productions, p. 312
Ford, Jack . . . . Sony Pictures Television International, p. 296
Ford, Jeanne Marie . . . . Days of Our Lives, p. 359
Ford, Kelly . . . . Burleigh Filmworks, p. 80
Fordes, Bill . . . . Close to Home, p. 357
Fordham, Deb . . . . Scrubs, p. 374
Forgey, Allison . . . . Macedon Media, Inc., p. 205
Forkner, Ben . . . . Management 360, p. 208
Form, Andrew . . . . Platinum Dunes, p. 257
Forman, Jason . . . . Infinitum Nihil, p. 174
Forman, Michael C. . . . . Big Cattle Productions, p. 67
Forney, Arthur . . . . Law & Order: Special Victims Unit, p. 367
Forney, Arthur . . . . Law & Order: Criminal Intent, p. 367
Forney, Arthur . . . . Law & Order, p. 367
Forney, Arthur . . . . Wolf Films, Inc., p. 343
Forrest, Kristen . . . . Taillight TV, p. 308
Forrest, Tom . . . . Taillight TV, p. 308
Forrester, Brent . . . . The Office, p. 371
Forstmann, Ted . . . . IMG Media, p. 172
Fort, Annie . . . . ABC Family, p. 45
Forte, Deborah . . . . Scholastic Entertainment, p. 281
Forte, Kate . . . . Harpo Films, Inc., p. 161
Fortis, Gil . . . . Mobius International, p. 219

Fortuna, Bruno . . . . Zaloom Film, p. 348
Foster, David . . . . House, p. 363
Foster, David . . . . David Foster Productions, p. 138
Foster, Don . . . . Two and a Half Men, p. 378
Foster, Gary . . . . Krasnoff Foster Productions, p. 190
Foster, Greg . . . . IMAX Corporation, p. 172
Foster, Jeff . . . . Vin Di Bona Productions, p. 110
Foster, Kay . . . . Heroes, p. 363
Foster, Kerry . . . . Weed Road Pictures, p. 337
Foster, Missy . . . . 21 Laps Entertainment, p. 38
Foster, Nick . . . . IDT Entertainment, p. 171
Foster, Yolanda . . . . NBC Universal Corporate, p. 231
Fournier, Teri . . . . New Line Cinema, p. 234
Fouse, Alyson . . . . Everybody Hates Chris, p. 361
Fouthorap, Robert . . . . CNBC, p. 96
Fowler, Ed . . . . Traveler, p. 377
Fowler, Elizabeth . . . . Clear Pictures Entertainment Inc., p. 95
Fowler, Melody . . . . Harpo Films, Inc., p. 161
Fox, Brad . . . . E! Networks, p. 117
Fox, Heather . . . . Adelstein Productions, p. 47
Fox, Judy . . . . Michael Grais Productions, p. 151
Fox, Karen . . . . Fox Broadcasting Company, p. 139
Fox, Kimberly . . . . QED International, p. 264
Fox, Richard J. . . . . Warner Bros. Entertainment Inc., p. 334
Fox, Rob . . . . How I Met Your Mother, p. 364
Fox, Rob . . . . Last Comic Standing, p. 366
Fox, Tony . . . . Comedy Central, p. 98
Foy, John . . . . The Biggest Loser, p. 356
Fragner, Lisa . . . . Twentieth Century Fox Animation, p. 323
Fragner, Lisa . . . . Blue Sky Studios, p. 69
Fraiberg, Jordanna . . . . Village Roadshow Pictures, p. 331
Fraiche, Gaylyn . . . . Martin Chase Productions, p. 211
Fraikorn, Beth . . . . Artists, Inc., p. 56
Frakes, Jonathan . . . . Goepp Circle Productions, p. 148
Francis, Alex . . . . Xingu Films Ltd., p. 347
Francis, Eddie . . . . Curb Entertainment, p. 104
Francis, Jane . . . . fox 21, p. 138
Francis, Kara . . . . Regency Enterprises, p. 268
Francis, Kevin . . . . Arlington Entertainment, Inc., p. 55
Francisco, Juan . . . . Darkwoods Productions, p. 107
Frand, Harvey . . . . Battlestar Galactica, p. 355
Franek, Clemens . . . . Conundrum Entertainment, p. 100
Frank, Barry . . . . IMG Media, p. 172
Frank, Darryl . . . . Las Vegas, p. 366
Frank, Darryl . . . . DreamWorks SKG, p. 116
Frank, David M. . . . . Indigo Films, p. 174
Frank, Doug . . . . Warner Bros. Pictures, p. 334
Frank, Geanne . . . . Revelations Entertainment, p. 271
Frank, Kaylin . . . . Buena Vista Motion Pictures Group, p. 78
Frank, Kristin . . . . Logo, p. 202
Frank, Paul . . . . Firm Television, p. 134
Frank, Scott JT . . . . Epiphany Pictures, Inc., p. 126
Frank, Ted . . . . NBC Entertainment, p. 230
Frankel, Jennie . . . . Magnet Management, p. 207
Frankel, Joseph . . . . Stefanie Epstein Productions, p. 126
Frankel, Matthew . . . . AMC, p. 50
Frankel, Matthew . . . . The Independent Film Channel (IFC), p. 173
Frankie, Richard . . . . Sony Pictures Television, p. 296
Frank-Lehrer, Nik . . . . WideAwake, Inc., p. 340
Franklin, Michelle . . . . MakeMagic Productions, p. 207
Franklin, Paul . . . . Twentieth Television, p. 324
Franko, Rebecca . . . . Warner Bros. Television Production, p. 335
Franks, Martin . . . . CBS Corporation, p. 86
Franks, Steve . . . . Psych, p. 372
Franz, Julia . . . . Touchstone Television, p. 316
Franzke, David . . . . Franzke Entertainment Inc., p. 141
Fraser, Andy . . . . Morgan Creek Productions, p. 221
Fraser, Dianne . . . . Industry Entertainment Partners, p. 174
Fraticelli, Chris . . . . Jimmy Kimmel Live, p. 364
Frattini, Salli . . . . MTV Networks, p. 226
Fratto, Adam . . . . Piller/Segan, p. 255
Frazee, John . . . . CBS News, p. 87
Frazier . . . . Atmosphere Entertainment MM, LLC, p. 58
Frazier, Breen . . . . Ghost Whisperer, p. 362
Frazier, Carrie . . . . HBO Films, p. 162
Frazier, Kelly . . . . Frazier | Chipman Entertainment, p. 141
Frederick, Barbra . . . . The Core, p. 101
Frederick, Doug . . . . Sony Pictures Television, p. 296
Frederick, Michael . . . . Stone and Company Entertainment, p. 301
Frederickson, Gray . . . . Graymark Productions Inc., p. 153
Fredman, Amber . . . . Warner Bros. Entertainment Inc., p. 334
Freed, Jamie . . . . Nine Yards Entertainment, p. 238
Freedman, Dan . . . . Mandate Pictures, p. 209
Freedman, Jack . . . . Jack Freedman Productions, p. 141
Freedman, Jeffrey . . . . Paramount Vantage/Paramount Classics, p. 248
Freedman, Mimi . . . . The Greif Company, p. 154
Freedman, Steve . . . . Intermedia Film Equities USA, Inc., p. 175
Freeling, Isa . . . . Ironworks Production, p. 177
Freeman, Joel . . . . Joel Freeman Productions, Inc., p. 141
Freeman, Morgan . . . . Revelations Entertainment, p. 271
Freeman, Scott . . . . Bunim/Murray Productions, Inc., p. 79
Freer, Randy . . . . Fox Cable Networks, p. 139
Freer, Randy . . . . Fox Sports Network, p. 140
Freet, Chad . . . . Regency Enterprises, p. 268
Freid, Jocelyn . . . . CBS Paramount Network Television, p. 87
Freilich, Victor . . . . New Generation Films, Inc., p. 234
Freimark, Daryl . . . . New Line Cinema, p. 234
Freis, Esq., Jon H. . . . . Creanspeak Productions LLC, p. 103
Fremes, John . . . . Element Films, p. 121
French, Gary . . . . Touchstone Television, p. 316
French, Jamie . . . . NBC Entertainment, p. 230
French, Kathleen . . . . Evolution, p. 128
French, Ron . . . . Battlestar Galactica, p. 355
Frenkel, Nick . . . . 3 Arts Entertainment, Inc., p. 40
Fresco, Rob . . . . Crossing Jordan, p. 358
Fresco, Victor . . . . My Name Is Earl, p. 369
Freston, Tom . . . . Viacom Entertainment Group, p. 330
Frey, Derek . . . . Tim Burton Productions, p. 81
Frey, Jeff . . . . Interloper Films, p. 175
Frieberg, Mickey . . . . Morningstar Entertainment, p. 221
Fried, Andrew . . . . @radical.media, p. 38
Fried, Daniel . . . . Daniel Fried Productions, p. 143
Fried, Howard . . . . Water Channel, p. 336
Fried, Mitch . . . . Comedy Central, p. 98
Fried, Rob . . . . Fried Films, p. 142
Friedberg, Adam . . . . Guy Walks Into a Bar, p. 158
Friedenson, Shyama . . . . Lionsgate, p. 200
Friedgen, Christina . . . . Sony Pictures Television, p. 296
Friedlander, Peter . . . . Big Love, p. 356
Friedlander, Peter . . . . Playtone Productions, p. 258
Friedlander, Steven . . . . Warner Independent Pictures, p. 335
Friedman, Amy . . . . Nickelodeon/MTVN Kids & Family Group, p. 237
Friedman, Budd . . . . Budd Friedman Digital, p. 143
Friedman, Darin . . . . Management 360, p. 208
Friedman, David . . . . Last Call with Carson Daly, p. 366
Friedman, Dawn . . . . Vin Di Bona Productions, p. 110
Friedman, Liz . . . . House, p. 363
Friedman, Louis G. . . . . Production Logistics, Inc., p. 262
Friedman, Marcie . . . . Odd Lot Entertainment, p. 241
Friedman, Mickey . . . . Rupert Productions, Inc., p. 277
Friedman, Mimi . . . . Big Love, p. 356
Friedman, Paul . . . . CBS News, p. 87
Friedman, Rhonda . . . . The Bold and the Beautiful, p. 356
Friedman, Rhonda . . . . Bell-Phillip TV Productions, Inc., p. 65
Friedman, Robert . . . . Spike TV, p. 298
Friedman, Russell . . . . Sci Fi Channel, p. 282
Friedman, Saul . . . . Bunim/Murray Productions, Inc., p. 79
Friedman, Stephen . . . . MTV Networks, p. 226
Friedman, Steve . . . . ION Media Networks, Inc., p. 177
Friedman, Steve . . . . CBS News, p. 87
Friedman, Zoe . . . . Comedy Central, p. 98
Friedrich, Garth . . . . Davis Entertainment Company, p. 107
Friend, John . . . . Cartoon Network, p. 84
Friend, Patrick . . . . Jimmy Kimmel Live, p. 364
Friend, Russel . . . . House, p. 363
Friendly, David T. . . . . Deep River Productions, p. 109
Fries, Ava . . . . Chuck Fries Productions, Inc., p. 143
Fries, Charles W. . . . . Chuck Fries Productions, Inc., p. 143
Frink, John . . . . The Simpsons, p. 375
Frith, Sara . . . . New Line Cinema, p. 234

Frodsham, Lisa . . . . .TV Guide Channel, p. 321
Fromstein, Stevie Ray . . . . .Reba, p. 372
Frons, Brian . . . . .Disney-ABC Television Group, p. 113
Frons, Brian . . . . .ABC Daytime, p. 44
Frost, Jeff . . . . .Touchstone Television, p. 316
Frot-Coutaz, Cecile . . . . .American Idol, p. 354
Frot-Coutaz, Cecile . . . . .FremantleMedia North America, p. 142
Froude, Christian . . . . .L.I.F.T. Productions, p. 191
Frumkes, Edward .Mutual Film Company, p. 227
Fry Hengst, Cori . . . . .Giraffe Productions, p. 147
Frydman, Marc . . . . .Battle Plan Productions, p. 63
Fryman, Pamela .How I Met Your Mother, p. 364
Fryman, Pamela . . . . .Two and a Half Men, p. 378
Fu, Taoyun . . . . .Chic Productions, p. 90
Fuchs, Scott .Broad Strokes Entertainment, p. 76
Fuentes, Marlene . . . . .Witt-Thomas-Harris Productions, p. 343
Fugard, Berenice . . . . .Paramount Vantage/Paramount Classics, p. 248
Fuhrman, Jonathan . . . . .The Weinstein Company, p. 337
Fujita, Mark . . . . .Bang Zoom! Entertainment, p. 61
Fukuda, Atsushi . . . . .Sony Pictures Television International, p. 296
Fukunaga, John . . . . .Sony Pictures Television International, p. 296
Fukuto, Jay . . . . .MGA Ent./MGA Ent. Films, p. 216
Fukuto, Mary . . . . .Girlfriends, p. 362
Fulle, Jenny . . . . .Sony Pictures Imageworks, p. 295
Fuller, Brad . . . . .Platinum Dunes, p. 257
Fuller, Bryan . . . . .Heroes, p. 363
Fuller, Simon . . . . .American Idol, p. 354
Fuller, Simon . . . . .So You Think You Can Dance, p. 376
Fuller, Simon . . . . .19 Entertainment, Inc., p. 38
Fuller, Taylor . . . . .Tribune Entertainment Company, p. 318
Fung, Stacy . . . . .Regency Television, p. 269
Funk, Judd . . . . .New Line Cinema, p. 234
Furer, Ken . . . . .Bona Fide Productions, p. 71
Furie, Lori . . . . .Columbia Pictures, p. 97
Furla, George . . . . .Emmett/Furla Films, p. 123
Furness, Deborra-lee . . . . .Seed Productions, p. 283
Furnish, David . . . . .Rocket Pictures Limited, p. 273
Furr, Tom . . . . .Playboy Entertainment Group, Inc., p. 257
Furst, Bryan . . . . .Furst Films, p. 143
Furst, Sean . . . . .Furst Films, p. 143
Furtney-Goodman, Michelle . . . . .One Tree Hill, p. 371
Furuichi, Natsu . . . . .Hart Sharp Entertainment, Inc., p. 161
Fury, David . . . . .24, p. 353
Fyvolent, Robert . . . . .Newmarket Capital Group, p. 236
Gabel, Jason .The Ellen DeGeneres Show, p. 360
Gabler, Elizabeth . . . . .Twentieth Century Fox - Fox 2000, p. 323
Gabriel, Larry . . . . .Platform Entertainment, p. 256
Gad, Joseph . . . . .3Wolves Productions, p. 41
Gadarian, David . . . . .Parkchester Pictures, p. 249
Gadarian, Kathryne . . . . .FremantleMedia North America, p. 142
Gadd, Paul . . . . .24, p. 353
Gaelen, Nancy . . . . .Alturas Films, p. 50
Gaffney, Peter . . . . .The History Channel, p. 167
Gagliano, Ted . . . . .Twentieth Century Fox, p. 322
Gaines, Barbara . . . . .The Late Show with David Letterman, p. 367
Gaines, Jeremy . . . . .MSNBC, p. 225
Gaither, Julie . . . . .Moxie Firecracker Films, p. 223
Gal, Peter . . . . .Nickelodeon/MTVN Kids & Family Group, p. 237
Galán, Nely . . . . .Galán Entertainment, p. 144
Galano, Camela . . . . .New Line Cinema, p. 234
Gale, David . . . . .MTV Networks, p. 226
Gale, David . . . . .MTV Films, p. 225
Galkin, Matthew . . . . .Stick Figure Productions, p. 301
Gallant, Michael O. . . . . .Gallant Entertainment, p. 144
Gallen, Joel . . . . .Tenth Planet Productions, p. 311
Gallers, Lainie . . . . .Turner Network Television (TNT), p. 321
Galloway, Steve . . . . .TOKYOPOP Inc., p. 315
Galper, Giselle . . . . .American Zoetrope, p. 51
Galston, Jay . . . . .Walden Media, p. 333
Galston, Jay . . . . .Bristol Bay Productions, p. 76
Gama-Lobo, Tony . . . . .King of the Hill, p. 365
Gamarra, Eddie . . . . .The Gotham Group, Inc., p. 151
Gambino, David . . . . .Silver Pictures, p. 289
Gamble, Kim . . . . .The Colbert Report, p. 357
Gamson, Mike . . . . .Wife Swap, p. 379
Ganczewski, Damian . . . . .Once Upon A Time Films, Ltd., p. 243
Gandin, Rachel . . . . .Sidney Kimmel Entertainment, p. 187
Ganeless, Michele . . . . .Comedy Central, p. 98
Gangi, Barbara . . . . .Paulist Productions, p. 250
Ganis, Sid . . . . .Out of the Blue . . . Entertainment, p. 244
Ganz, Tony . . . . .Wolf Films, Inc., p. 343
Garant, Robert Ben . . . . .RENO 911!, p. 373
Garbus, Liz . . . . .Moxie Firecracker Films, p. 223
Garcetti, Gil . . . . .The Closer, p. 357
Garcia, Alex . . . . .Bad Hat Harry Productions, p. 59
Garcia, Andy . . . . .CineSon Productions Inc., p. 92
Garcia, Gina . . . . .Criminal Minds, p. 358
Garcia, Greg . . . . .My Name Is Earl, p. 369
Garcia, Ivette . . . . .Tollin/Robbins Productions, p. 315
Garcia, Kenneth . . . . .Reason Pictures, p. 266
Garcia, Liz . . . . .Cold Case, p. 357
Garcia, Mario . . . . .The Bauer Company, p. 63
Garcia, Mike . . . . .HBO Entertainment, p. 162
Garcia, Natalie . . . . .Sony Pictures Television International, p. 296
Garcia, Nicole . . . . .Mad TV, p. 368
Garcia, Richard . . . . .ION Media Networks, Inc., p. 177
Garcia, Sadath . . . . .Lynda Obst Productions, p. 241
Gard, Jo . . . . .Twentieth Century Fox Television, p. 323
Gardini, Carla . . . . .The Weinstein Company, p. 337
Gardini, Gina . . . . .Cattleya, p. 86
Gardner, Cindy . . . . .NBC Universal Corporate, p. 231
Gardner, Cindy . . . . .Universal Studios, p. 326
Gardner, Daisy . . . . .30 Rock, p. 353
Gardner, David . . . . .Principato-Young Entertainment, p. 262
Gardner, Dede . . . . .Plan B Entertainment, p. 256
Gardner, Erika . . . . .The Gurin Company, p. 158
Gardner, Lindsay . . . . .Fox Cable Networks, p. 139
Gardner, Lynn . . . . .A&E Network, p. 44
Garduño, Anna . . . . .Darkwoods Productions, p. 107
Garefino, Anne . . . . .South Park, p. 376
Garefino, Anne . . . . .Trunity, a Mediar Company, a Division of True Mediar, a Unity Corpbopoly, p. 320
Garel-Jones, Ivan . . . . .Granada America, p. 152
Garfield, Harry . . . . .Universal Pictures, p. 326
Garfinkel, Gary . . . . .Showtime Networks Inc., p. 287
Garfinkle, David . . . . .Renegade 83, p. 270
Garner, Joseph . . . . .The Todd Phillips Company, p. 254
Garner, Matthew . . . . .The Weinstein Company, p. 337
Garner, Scott . . . . .Disney ABC Cable Networks Group, p. 112
Garner, Todd . . . . .Broken Road Productions, p. 77
Garnett, Kevin . . . . .Las Vegas, p. 366
Garrett, David . . . . .Summit Entertainment, p. 304
Garrett, Geoff . . . . .Crystal Lake Entertainment, Inc., p. 103
Garrett, Kelly . . . . .von Zerneck-Sertner Films, p. 332
Garrett, Steve . . . . .Paramount Vantage/Paramount Classics, p. 248
Garrigus, Tom . . . . .The Nine, p. 370
Garris, Mick . . . . .Masters of Horror, p. 368
Garrison, Amanda . . . . .Participant Productions, p. 249
Garrow, Gillian . . . . .Arlington Entertainment, Inc., p. 55
Garson, Leslie . . . . .Leeza Gibbons Enterprises (LGE), p. 146
Gartner, Alex . . . . .Atlas Entertainment, p. 57
Garvey, Lisa . . . . .Sidney Kimmel Entertainment, p. 187
Garvey, Michael . . . . .VH1, p. 330
Garvin, Philip . . . . .HDNet, p. 163
Gary, Danielle . . . . .The Core, p. 101
Gase, Linda . . . . .Standoff, p. 376
Gaspin, Jeff . . . . .NBC Entertainment, p. 230
Gaspin, Jeff . . . . .Sleuth, p. 291
Gaspin, Jeff . . . . .NBC Universal Cable Entertainment, p. 231
Gast, Tannya . . . . .Twentieth Television, p. 324
Gaston, Jim . . . . .Touchstone Television, p. 316
Gateley, Liz . . . . .MTV Networks, p. 226
Gatens, Kary McHoul . . . . .Fox Broadcasting Company, p. 139
Gates, Stephen . . . . .Evolution Entertainment, p. 128
Gatineau, Maeva . . . . .The Weinstein Company, p. 337
Gatins, George . . . . .Mosaic Media Group, p. 222
Gatsby, Jill . . . . .Larco Productions, Inc., p. 193
Gatta, Joe . . . . .Millennium Films, p. 217
Gatti, Rosa . . . . .ESPN Original Entertainment (EOE), p. 127
Gaulding, Shannon . . . . .Columbia Pictures, p. 97

Gaulke, Ann . . . Telemundo Network, p. 310
Gauthier, Zig . . . GSN, p. 157
Gauvin, Jean . . . Cookie Jar Entertainment, p. 100
Gavin, Dolores . . . The History Channel, p. 167
Gaylord, Chuck . . . Universal Pictures, p. 326
Gaylord, Michael D. . . . Nickelodeon/MTVN Kids & Family Group, p. 237
Gaynor, Eric . . . Sony Pictures Digital, p. 295
Gazeley, Jaye . . . Front Street Pictures, Inc., p. 143
Gazica, Michele . . . Buena Vista Motion Pictures Group, p. 78
Gazull, Jordi . . . Columbia Pictures, p. 97
Gazzolo, Pierluigi . . . MTV Networks Latin America (MTVNLA), p. 226
Geary, Robert . . . Columbia Pictures, p. 97
Geddie, Bill . . . ABC Daytime, p. 44
Geer, Shawn . . . Pollywog Entertainment, Inc, p. 259
Geffen, David . . . DreamWorks SKG, p. 116
Geier, Sofia Landon . . . Days of Our Lives, p. 359
Geiger, Boris . . . Wild At Heart Films, LLC, p. 341
Geiger, Sara . . . Stone Village Pictures, LLC, p. 302
Geist, Libby . . . Shoot the Moon Productions, p. 286
Gelb, Audrey . . . Touchstone Television, p. 316
Gelber, Danielle . . . Showtime Networks Inc., p. 287
Geletko, Judy . . . Avenue Pictures, p. 59
Gelfan, Greg . . . Twentieth Century Fox, p. 322
Gelfand, Dan . . . here! Networks, p. 165
Gelfand, Lindsay . . . American Work, p. 51
Gelinas, Stefanie . . . FremantleMedia North America, p. 142
Geller, Aaron . . . Avenue Pictures, p. 59
Geller, Glenn . . . CBS Paramount Network Television, p. 87
Geller, Mark . . . Paramount Vantage/Paramount Classics, p. 248
Geller, Nancy . . . HBO Entertainment, p. 162
Gelles, Lesli . . . Runaway, p. 373
Gelles, Lesli . . . Hidden Palms, p. 363
Gemmill, R. Scott . . . ER, p. 361
Genard, Susan . . . Camden Pictures, p. 82
Gendron, Jay . . . Warner Bros. Television Production, p. 335
Genelius, Sandra . . . CBS News, p. 87
Genest, Frederic . . . Partizan, p. 250
Genier, Joe . . . Capital Arts Entertainment, p. 83
Genkinger, Scott . . . Desperate Housewives, p. 360
Genkinger, Scott . . . Prison Break, p. 372
Genot, Beau J. . . . Glatzer Productions, p. 147
Genson, Melissa . . . New Line Television, p. 235
Gentilli, Veronica . . . Touchstone Television, p. 316
Geoffray, Jeff . . . Blue Rider Pictures, p. 69
Geoffroy, Jared . . . John Wells Productions, p. 338
Georgaris, Dean . . . Penn Station Entertainment, p. 252
George, Chris . . . Artists Production Group (APG), p. 56
George, Gene L. . . . Regent, p. 269
George, Mike . . . TriCoast Studios, p. 318
Geraci, Ron . . . Nickelodeon/MTVN Kids & Family Group, p. 237
Gerber, Bill . . . Gerber Pictures, p. 145
Gerber, Chuck . . . ABC Sports, p. 45
Gerber, Chuck . . . ESPN Original Entertainment (EOE), p. 127
Gerber, Jennifer . . . Andell Entertainment, p. 51
Gerbson, Steve . . . Harding-Kurtz Entertainment, p. 160
Germani, Lisa . . . TV Guide Channel, p. 321
Gero, Martin . . . Stargate: Atlantis, p. 376
Gero, Martin . . . Stargate: SG-1, p. 376
Gerse, Steven W. . . . Buena Vista Motion Pictures Group, p. 78
Gersh, Bruce . . . ABC Entertainment Television Group, p. 45
Gersh, Lisa . . . Oxygen Media, p. 245
Gershman, Larry . . . World International Network, p. 345
Gerson, David . . . Focus Features/Rogue Pictures, p. 136
Gerson, Rochelle . . . Carsey-Werner Films, p. 84
Gerstein, Leila . . . The O.C., p. 371
Gervais, Ricky . . . The Office, p. 371
Gesell, Sean . . . Zucker Productions, p. 350
Geter, Leo . . . Close to Home, p. 357
Gethers, Peter . . . Random House Films, p. 266
Getman, Arlene . . . Twentieth Century Fox Television, p. 323
Gettleson, Harvey . . . East of Doheny/Lexington Road Prod., p. 118
Getto, Paul . . . Focus Features/Rogue Pictures, p. 136
Geyer, Tracy . . . Rocket Science Laboratories, p. 273
Ghaderi, Pantea . . . The Weinstein Company, p. 337
Ghio, Janet . . . Vin Di Bona Productions, p. 110
Giaime, Janine . . . Anonymous Creators Productions, p. 52
Gialanella, Victor . . . Days of Our Lives, p. 359
Giambrone, Linda . . . Dancing with the Stars, p. 359
Giannetti, Andrea . . . Columbia Pictures, p. 97
Giannini, Aron . . . The Collective, p. 96
Giannokopulos, Lisa . . . The Weinstein Company, p. 337
Gianopulos, James . . . Twentieth Century Fox, p. 322
Giarraputo, Jack . . . Rules of Engagement, p. 373
Gibb, James . . . Tailfish Productions, p. 307
Gibbons, Leeza . . . Leeza Gibbons Enterprises (LGE), p. 146
Gibbons, Stephanie . . . FX, p. 144
Gibgot, Jennifer . . . Offspring Entertainment, p. 241
Gibson, Jake . . . Pie Town Productions, p. 254
Gichon, Alisa . . . The Late Late Show with Craig Ferguson, p. 366
Gieseke, Jessica . . . Darkwoods Productions, p. 107
Gigliotti, Donna . . . Tempesta Films, p. 311
Gilardi Jr., Jack . . . Evolving Pictures Entertainment, p. 128
Gilbert, Brian J. . . . Stan Winston Productions, p. 343
Gilbert, Gary . . . Camelot Pictures, p. 82
Gilbert, Katie . . . Indigo Films, p. 174
Gilbert, Larry . . . Con Artists Productions, p. 99
Gilbert, Paul . . . Sony Pictures Television International, p. 296
Gilbert, Suzie . . . Ixtlan, p. 178
Gil-Besson, Rene . . . Signature Pictures, p. 288
Gildea, John . . . Cookie Jar Entertainment, p. 100
Giles, Tanya . . . Nickelodeon/MTVN Kids & Family Group, p. 237
Gill, Alison . . . DC Comics, p. 108
Gill, Codessa . . . Endemol USA, Inc., p. 123
Gill, Mark . . . The Film Department, p. 132
Gillen, Anne Marie . . . Gillen & Price, p. 146
Gillen, Paddy . . . Atomic Cartoons, Inc., p. 58
Gillespie, Alexandra . . . Fox Broadcasting Company, p. 139
Gillespie, Kelly . . . 3 lbs., p. 353
Gillespie, Mike . . . Telemundo Network, p. 310
Gilliland, Carrye . . . Everyman Pictures, p. 128
Gilliland, Eric . . . My Boys, p. 369
Gillmer, Bruce . . . VH1, p. 330
Gillogly, Carrie . . . Gerber Pictures, p. 145
Gilmore, Charissa . . . Touchstone Television, p. 316
Gilroy, Henry . . . Lucasfilm Ltd., p. 203
Gilula, Stephen . . . Twentieth Century Fox - Searchlight Pictures, p. 323
Gimbel, Roger . . . Roger Gimbel Productions, Inc., p. 146
Ginnane, Antony I. . . . IFM Film Associates, Inc., p. 171
Ginsberg, Caryn . . . PBS, p. 251
Ginsberg, Richard . . . Zinkler Films, p. 349
Ginsberg, Yitzhak . . . Dream Entertainment, Inc., p. 116
Ginsburg, Glenn . . . Comedy Central, p. 98
Ginter, Gabrielle . . . Charlotte Street Films, p. 89
Ginty, Robert . . . Ginty Films International, p. 146
Gionfriddo, Gina . . . Law & Order: Criminal Intent, p. 367
Giordano, Kristan . . . TV Guide Channel, p. 321
Giovanni, Marita . . . Ishtar Films, p. 178
Giraldo, John . . . New Line Cinema, p. 234
Girard, Judy . . . Home & Garden Television (HGTV), p. 168
Girolamo, Gina . . . NBC Universal Television Studio, p. 231
Gist, Karin . . . Girlfriends, p. 362
Gitelson, Rick . . . Plotpoint, Inc., p. 258
Gitlin, Mimi Polk . . . Lion Eyes Entertainment, p. 199
Gitlin, Richard . . . Lion Eyes Entertainment, p. 199
Gittes, Harry . . . Gittes, Inc., p. 147
Giuliano, Peter . . . Law & Order, p. 367
Given, Andy . . . Columbia Pictures, p. 97
Gladstein, Richard N. . . . FilmColony, p. 133
Gladstone, James . . . Lionsgate, p. 200
Gladstone, Katie . . . HDNet, p. 163
Gladstone, Noel . . . MTV Networks Latin America (MTVNLA), p. 226
Glaize, Finley . . . Brooklyn Media, p. 77
Glalanella, Victor . . . One Life to Live, p. 371
Glankler, Rick . . . HIT Entertainment, p. 167
Glantz, Jillian . . . David Foster Productions, p. 138
Glasberg, Gary . . . Bones, p. 356
Glascoe, Jon . . . Cypress Films, Inc., p. 106
Glaser, Jeffrey . . . Twentieth Century Fox Television, p. 323
Glasgow, Ra'uf . . . Reynolds Entertainment, p. 271
Glass, Elisabeth . . . HDNet, p. 163

Glasser, David . . . . . Yari Film Group (YFG), p. 347
Glassey, Rich . . . . . GreeneStreet Films, p. 153
Glassman, Andrew . . . . . Average Joe, p. 355
Glassman, Jennifer . . . . . ISBE Productions, p. 177
Glassman, Michael . . . . . Outlaw Productions, p. 245
Glassman, Rick . . . . . Twentieth Century Fox Television, p. 323
Glassner, Jonathan . . . . . Standoff, p. 376
Glatter, Emily . . . . . New Line Cinema, p. 234
Glatzer, Peter . . . . . Glatzer Productions, p. 147
Glavin, Ed . . . . . The Ellen DeGeneres Show, p. 360
Glazer, Alan . . . . . Mosaic Media Group, p. 222
Glazer, Alan . . . . . Atlas Entertainment, p. 57
Gleeson, Mark . . . . . Sony Pictures Television International, p. 296
Glenn-Chesloff, Leslie . . . . . Lifetime Television (New York), p. 198
Glick, Adam . . . . . Warner Bros. Television Production, p. 335
Glickman, Jennifer . . . . . The War at Home, p. 379
Glickman, Jonathan . . . . . Spyglass Entertainment Group, p. 299
Globe, Anne . . . . . DreamWorks Animation SKG, p. 116
Glotzbach, Liz . . . . . Twentieth Century Fox - Searchlight Pictures, p. 323
Glotzer, Liz . . . . . Castle Rock Entertainment, p. 85
Glover, Danny . . . . . Carrie Productions, Inc., p. 83
Gnan, Anita . . . . . Brandman Productions, p. 73
Goddard, Drew . . . . . Lost, p. 368
Goddard, Melissa . . . . . Concept Entertainment, p. 99
Goddard-Smythe, Suzanne . . . . . The Game, p. 361
Goddard-Smythe, Suzanne . . . . . Rules of Engagement, p. 373
Godelia, Renee . . . . . Days of Our Lives, p. 359
Godfrey, Christopher . . . . . Everyman Pictures, p. 128
Godfrey, Rachel . . . . . Heyday Films, p. 166
Godfrey, Wayne . . . . . Goldcrest Films International, Inc., p. 149
Godfrey, Wyck . . . . . Temple Hill Productions, p. 311
Godwin, Wayne . . . . . PBS, p. 251
Goerg, Markus . . . . . Prospect Pictures, p. 263
Goetz, Jared . . . . . Buena Vista Television, p. 79
Goetzman, Gary . . . . . Big Love, p. 356
Goetzman, Gary . . . . . Playtone Productions, p. 258
Goff, Gina G. . . . . . Goff-Kellam Productions, p. 148
Goff, Paul . . . . . The Bremer Goff Company, p. 75
Goger, Chris . . . . . Enteraktion Studios, p. 124
Gogolak, Charlie . . . . . Benderspink, p. 66
Goicouria, Luis . . . . . MTV Networks Latin America (MTVNLA), p. 226
Going, Geoffrey . . . . . Gallant Entertainment, p. 144
Goit, Whitney . . . . . A&E Network, p. 44
Goitia, Larry . . . . . The Tonight Show with Jay Leno, p. 377
Golan, Fred . . . . . Raines, p. 372
Golchan, Frederic . . . . . Frederic Golchan Productions, p. 148
Gold, Bob . . . . . Taryn Productions, p. 308
Gold, Danny . . . . . mod3productions, p. 219
Gold, Eric . . . . . Happy Hour, p. 362
Gold, Eric . . . . . 20 Good Years, p. 353
Gold, Eric . . . . . Mosaic Media Group, p. 222
Gold, Eric . . . . . Werner-Gold-Miller, p. 339
Gold, Josh . . . . . The Todd Phillips Company, p. 254
Gold, Robin . . . . . Janus Films, LLC, p. 179
Gold, Steve . . . . . Tri-Elite Entertainment, Ltd., p. 319
Gold, Ted . . . . . Fox Broadcasting Company, p. 139
Goldberg, Amanda . . . . . Mandy Films, p. 209
Goldberg, Dan . . . . . The Montecito Picture Company, p. 220
Goldberg, Dan . . . . . FremantleMedia North America, p. 142
Goldberg, Dana . . . . . Village Roadshow Pictures, p. 331
Goldberg, Daniel . . . . . The Todd Phillips Company, p. 254
Goldberg, Darren . . . . . The 7th Floor, p. 43
Goldberg, David . . . . . Endemol USA, Inc., p. 123
Goldberg, Eliot . . . . . Ryan Seacrest Productions, p. 283
Goldberg, Gail . . . . . Buena Vista Motion Pictures Group, p. 78
Goldberg, Joel . . . . . CBS Entertainment, p. 86
Goldberg, Judy . . . . . Impact Pictures, p. 173
Goldberg, Keith . . . . . New Line Cinema, p. 234
Goldberg, Kira . . . . . DreamWorks SKG, p. 116
Goldberg, Leonard . . . . . Mandy Films, p. 209
Goldberg, Mandy . . . . . Esperanto Films, p. 126
Goldberg, Neil . . . . . Six Degrees, p. 375
Goldberg, Rich . . . . . Mainline Releasing, p. 207
Goldberg, T.S. . . . . . Ember Entertainment Group, p. 122
Goldberg, Vicky . . . . . Warner Bros. Entertainment Inc., p. 334
Goldberg, Whoopi . . . Whoop Inc./One Ho Prod./Lil' Whoop Prod., p. 340
Goldberger, Gary . . . . . Craig Anderson Productions, p. 52
Golden, Kit . . . . . The Manhattan Project, Ltd., p. 210
Golden, Nathan . . . . . George Schlatter Productions, p. 280
Golden, Peter . . . . . CBS Entertainment, p. 86
Golden, Sandy . . . . . Boston Legal, p. 357
Goldenberg, Josh . . . . . Generate, p. 145
Goldenring, Jane . . . . . Goldenring Productions, p. 149
Goldenson, Max . . . . . MWG Productions, p. 228
Goldfine, Phillip . . . . . Steamroller Productions, Inc., p. 300
Goldfinger, Sarah . . . . . CSI: Crime Scene Investigation, p. 358
Goldhirsh, Ben . . . . . Reason Pictures, p. 266
Goldin, Gregg . . . . . MTV Films, p. 225
Golding, Jono . . . . . Phase Two Productions, p. 253
Goldman, Brian . . . . . here! Networks, p. 165
Goldman, Danny . . . . . Sony Pictures Television International, p. 296
Goldman, David . . . . . Touchstone Television, p. 316
Goldman, David . . . . . Comedy Time, p. 98
Goldman, Greg . . . . . RDF Media, p. 266
Goldman, Kevin . . . . . CNBC, p. 96
Goldman, Larry . . . . . LMNO Productions, p. 201
Goldman, Mark . . . . . Current TV, LLC, p. 105
Goldman, Michael . . . . . The Collective, p. 96
Goldman, Michael . . . . . Comedy Time, p. 98
Goldman, Nancy . . . . . Letnom Productions, p. 196
Goldman, Neil . . . . . Scrubs, p. 374
Goldman, Nicole . . . . . The Jim Henson Company, p. 165
Goldman, Shira Zeltzer . . . . . Notes From the Underbelly, p. 370
Goldman, Tami . . . . . Jerry Bruckheimer Films & Television, p. 78
Goldschein, Gil . . . . . Bunim/Murray Productions, Inc., p. 79
Goldsman, Akiva . . . . . Weed Road Pictures, p. 337
Goldsmith, Brian . . . . . Mandate Pictures, p. 209
Goldsmith, Josh . . . . . Big Day, p. 355
Goldsmith, Josh . . . . . 'Til Death, p. 377
Goldsmith-Vein, Ellen . . . . . The Gotham Group, Inc., p. 151
Goldstein Esq., Charles Terry . . . . . Sub Rosa Productions, Inc., p. 303
Goldstein, David . . . . . Universal Operations Group, p. 326
Goldstein, Gary W. . . . . . The Goldstein Company, p. 149
Goldstein, Jessica . . . . . Big Day, p. 355
Goldstein, Joel . . . . . Village Roadshow Pictures, p. 331
Goldstein, Jonathan . . . . . The New Adventures of Old Christine, p. 370
Goldstein, Laurie . . . . . Nightstar Productions, Inc., p. 238
Goldstein, Leonard . . . . . Warner Bros. Television Production, p. 335
Goldstein, Libby . . . . . Saved, p. 374
Goldstein, Libby . . . . . Ugly Betty, p. 378
Goldstein, Michael R. . . . . . Larkin-Goldstein Production, p. 194
Goldstein, Sarah . . . . . E! Networks, p. 117
Goldstein, Wayne . . . . . Sony Pictures Television, p. 296
Goldstone, Alex . . . . . Fuse Entertainment, p. 144
Goldstone, John . . . . . Fort Hill Productions, p. 137
Goldworm, Adam . . . . . Masters of Horror, p. 368
Goldworm, Adam . . . . . Industry Entertainment Partners, p. 174
Goldwyn, Danny . . . . . Playtime Productions, p. 257
Goldwyn, John . . . . . John Goldwyn Productions, p. 149
Goldwyn, Peter . . . . . Samuel Goldwyn Films, p. 279
Goldwyn Jr., Samuel . . . . . Samuel Goldwyn Films, p. 279
Golenberg, Jeff . . . . . The Collective, p. 96
Golightly, Norm . . . . . Saturn Films, p. 280
Golin, Craig . . . . . Film Garden Entertainment, Inc., p. 132
Golingay, Harold . . . . . Echelon Entertainment World Dist. & Prod., p. 119
Gollust, Allison . . . . . NBC News, p. 230
Golod, Ksana . . . . . Tailfish Productions, p. 307
Gomeau, Selina . . . . . Winkler Films, p. 342
Gomez, Mike . . . . . Tommy Boy Films, p. 315
Gonda, Kelly . . . . . East of Doheny/Lexington Road Prod., p. 118
Gonda, Lou . . . . . East of Doheny/Lexington Road Prod., p. 118
Gonnella, Trish . . . . . Michael Mailer Films, p. 207
Gonsalves, Lee . . . . . Tribune Entertainment Company, p. 318
Gonzales, Carlos . . . . . Fremantle Productions Latin America, p. 142
Gonzales, Phil . . . . . CBS Entertainment, p. 86
Gonzales, Robert . . . . . Disney Online, p. 112
Gonzalez, Dale . . . . . Air2web, Inc., p. 48
Gonzalez, Francisco . . . . . Motion Picture Corporation of America, p. 222
Gonzalez, Nikki . . . . . CNBC, p. 96
Gonzalez, Robert . . . . . Adam Fields Productions, p. 130

Gonzalez, Rosa .Planet Grande Pictures, p. 256
Gonzalez, Tomas .Fremantle Productions Latin America, p. 142
Gonzalez-Turner, Genevieve .Mandeville Films, p. 209
Goode, Marianne .Lifetime Television (Los Angeles), p. 198
Gooder, Mark .Icon Productions, LLC, p. 170
Goodfellow, Robin .Zaloom Film, p. 348
Goodman, Adam .DreamWorks SKG, p. 116
Goodman, David .HBO Entertainment, p. 162
Goodman, David .Without a Trace, p. 379
Goodman, David .Family Guy, p. 361
Goodman, Dean .ION Media Networks, Inc., p. 177
Goodman, Gary .Lionsgate, p. 200
Goodman, Ilyssa .The Goodman Company, p. 149
Goodman, Jessica .Warner Bros. Pictures, p. 334
Goodman, Joe .Namesake Entertainment, p. 228
Goodman, Jonas .Front Street Pictures, Inc., p. 143
Goodman, Jordan .The Gurin Company, p. 158
Goodman, Leah .The Polson Company, p. 259
Goodman, Randi .New Line Television, p. 235
Goodnight, Michael .Warner Bros. Entertainment Inc., p. 334
Goodwin, Chris .Watermark, p. 336
Goore, Phil .New Line Cinema, p. 234
Gorai, Tom .ShadowCatcher Entertainment, p. 285
Gordon, Adam .Comedy Arts Studios, p. 98
Gordon, Charles .Daybreak Productions, p. 108
Gordon, Dan .Dan Gordon Productions, p. 150
Gordon, Donovan .BET Networks, p. 66
Gordon, Howard .24, p. 353
Gordon, John .BET Networks, p. 66
Gordon, Lauren .Di Novi Pictures, p. 110
Gordon, Marc .Firm Films, p. 134
Gordon, Mark .Criminal Minds, p. 358
Gordon, Mark .Grey's Anatomy, p. 362
Gordon, Mark .The Mark Gordon Company, p. 150
Gordon, Stuart .Red Hen Productions, p. 267
Gordon, Susan .CBS Corporation, p. 86
Gore, Al .Current TV, LLC, p. 105
Gore, Craig .Jon Katzman Productions, p. 185
Gorfain, Louis .New Screen Concepts, Inc., p. 235
Gorham, Keith .Universal Studios, p. 326
Gorman, Sean .The Hatchery, p. 161
Gorodetsky, Eddie .Two and a Half Men, p. 378
Gorodetzky, Karen .Capital Arts Entertainment, p. 83
Gorski, Roberta "Ro" .Crave Films, p. 102
Goss, Alan .Battle Plan Productions, p. 63
Goss, Beth .Universal Pictures, p. 326
Gottlieb, Bill J. .Gorilla Pictures, p. 150
Gottlieb, Meyer .Samuel Goldwyn Films, p. 279
Gottwald, Mark .Mindfire Entertainment, p. 217
Gough, Alfred .Smallville, p. 375
Goularte, Jill .Revelations Entertainment, p. 271
Goulbourne, Raymond .BET Networks, p. 66
Gould, Andrew .Tempest Entertainment, p. 311
Gould, Cheryl .NBC News, p. 230
Gould, Dana .The Simpsons, p. 375
Goumas, Liz .Face Productions/Jennilind Productions, p. 129
Governale, Frank .CBS News, p. 87
Governale, Joshua .Fox Broadcasting Company, p. 139
Gozukizil, Esrin .ABC Entertainment Television Group, p. 45
Graboff, Marc .NBC Entertainment, p. 230
Grace, Florence .TriStar Pictures, p. 319
Grace, Francey .Ambush Entertainment, p. 50
Grace, Jasmine .CastleBright Studios, p. 85
Grace, Tara .The Kennedy/Marshall Company, p. 186
Grad, Nick .FX, p. 144
Graddick, Herndon .Current TV, LLC, p. 105
Graden, Brian .VH1, p. 330
Graden, Brian .MTV Networks, p. 226
Graden, Brian .CMT: Country Music Television, p. 95
Graden, Brian .Logo, p. 202
Grady, Austin .Charles Floyd Johnson Productions, p. 89
Graff, Aaron .Sarabande Productions, p. 280
Graham, Erica .Everyman Pictures, p. 128
Graham, Kristen Guertin .Fox Broadcasting Company, p. 139
Graham, Lauren .Good Game, p. 149
Graham, Matt .Robert Greenwald Productions, p. 153
Graigory, J .Jimmy Kimmel Live, p. 364
Grais, Michael .Michael Grais Productions, p. 151
Gralnick, Jeff .NBC News, p. 230
Gramm, Colton .Brillstein-Grey Entertainment, p. 75
Grammer, Kelsey .Girlfriends, p. 362
Grammer, Kelsey .Medium, p. 369
Grammer, Kelsey .The Game, p. 361
Grammer, Kelsey .Grammnet Productions, p. 152
Granat, Cary .Walden Media, p. 333
Granat, Cary .Bristol Bay Productions, p. 76
Grande, Mark .The Howard Stern Production Company, p. 301
Granet, Jamie .Last Call with Carson Daly, p. 366
Granger, Amelia .Working Title Films, p. 345
Granger, Don .C/W Productions, p. 105
Grant, Christopher .Reveille, LLC, p. 270
Grant, Michael .Moonstone Entertainment, p. 220
Grant, Patti M. .The Tonight Show with Jay Leno, p. 377
Grantowitz, Steve .Marvel Studios, Inc., p. 211
Grarut, Gene .Epiphany Pictures, Inc., p. 126
Grasso, Maria .Lifetime Television (Los Angeles), p. 198
Grave, Elizabeth .Groundswell Production, p. 156
Graves, Alex .The Nine, p. 370
Gray, Elektra .The Independent Film Channel (IFC), p. 173
Gray, Gordon .Mayhem Pictures, p. 213
Gray, John .Ghost Whisperer, p. 362
Gray, Steven .PBS, p. 251
Gray, Thomas K. .Imagi Services (USA), p. 171
Gray, Toni .Film Garden Entertainment, Inc., p. 132
Grayson, Alissa .Universal Pictures, p. 326
Grayson, Kevin .Paramount Vantage/Paramount Classics, p. 248
Grazer, Brian .Shark, p. 374
Grazer, Brian .Friday Night Lights, p. 361
Grazer, Brian .24, p. 353
Grazer, Brian .Imagine Television, p. 172
Grazer, Brian .Imagine Entertainment, p. 172
Graziano, David .Day Break, p. 359
Greaney, Dan .The Simpsons, p. 375
Greco, Paul .PBS, p. 251
Green, Amanda .Law & Order: Special Victims Unit, p. 367
Green, Blair .Focus Features/Rogue Pictures, p. 136
Green, Chris .Sacred Dogs Entertainment, LLC, p. 278
Green, Conrad .Dancing with the Stars, p. 359
Green, Dave .HDNet, p. 163
Green, Jonathan .The Class, p. 357
Green, Josh .Emerging Pictures, p. 122
Green, Kevin .Survivor, p. 377
Green, Michael C. .Heroes, p. 363
Green, Michael .The Collective, p. 96
Green, Sarah .Sarah Green Film Corp., p. 153
Green, Stanley H. .Burrud Productions, p. 80
Green, Sylvia .According to Jim, p. 354
Green, Todd .The Independent Film Channel (IFC), p. 173
Green, Todd .AMC, p. 50
Green, Tracy .Lion Television U.S., p. 199
Green, Trey .Noble House Entertainment, Inc., p. 238
Green, Walon .Law & Order, p. 367
Green, Walon .Wolf Films, Inc., p. 343
Green, Whitney .Buena Vista Motion Pictures Group, p. 78
Greenberg, Gary .Jimmy Kimmel Live, p. 364
Greenberg, George .Fox Sports Network, p. 140
Greenberg, Jamie .Sesame Workshop, p. 285
Greenberg, Josh .MTV Networks Latin America (MTVNLA), p. 226
Greenberg, Kathy .The L Word, p. 366
Greenberg, Marc .Mainline Releasing, p. 207
Greenberg, Paul .TV Guide Channel, p. 321
Greenberg, Randy .Platinum Studios, LLC, p. 257
Greenberg, Rob .How I Met Your Mother, p. 364
Greenberg, Sarah .Lionsgate, p. 200
Greenberg, Scott .Film Roman, Inc., p. 132
Greenberg, Suzy .How I Met Your Mother, p. 364
Greenblatt, Lisa .Platinum Dunes, p. 257
Greenblatt, Robert .Showtime Independent Films, p. 287
Greenblatt, Robert .Showtime Networks Inc., p. 287
Greenblatt, William R. .Symphony Pictures, Inc., p. 306

Greenburg, Michael . . . . Big Pix Inc., p. 67
Greene, Danielle . . . . ABC Entertainment Television Group, p. 45
Greene, Jonathan . . . . Law & Order: Special Victims Unit, p. 367
Greene, Lyn . . . . Nip/Tuck, p. 370
Greene, Mary Putnam . . . . Brillstein-Grey Entertainment, p. 75
Greene, Robert . . . . 4th Row Films, p. 42
Greener, Adam . . . . 3 Ball Productions, p. 40
Greenfield, Luke . . . . WideAwake, Inc., p. 340
Greenfield, Matthew . . . Twentieth Century Fox - Searchlight Pictures, p. 323
Greenspan, Alan . . . . International Arts Entertainment, p. 176
Greenspan, Alison . . . . Di Novi Pictures, p. 110
Greenspun, Danny . . . . Stone Village Pictures, LLC, p. 302
Greenspun, Robin . . . . Stone Village Pictures, LLC, p. 302
Greenstein, Brett . . . . Help Me Help You, p. 363
Greenstein, Jane . . . . NBC Entertainment, p. 230
Greenstein, Jeff . . . . Desperate Housewives, p. 360
Greenwald, Robert . . . . Robert Greenwald Productions, p. 153
Greenwalt, David . . . . Kidnapped, p. 365
Greer, Elissa . . . . New Line Cinema, p. 234
Greggory, Devon . . . . Shark, p. 374
Greggs, Michael . . . . Jimmy Kimmel Live, p. 364
Gregory, Joy . . . . The Nine, p. 370
Gregory, Shannon . . . . Davis Entertainment Company, p. 107
Greif, B. Billie . . . . I.E. Productions, Inc., p. 170
Greif, Leslie . . . . The Greif Company, p. 154
Greiner, Jim . . . . A&E Network, p. 44
Greisman, Alan . . . . Reiner/Greisman, p. 269
Grellong, Paul . . . . Law & Order: Special Victims Unit, p. 367
Greves, Kurt . . . . AMC, p. 50
Grey, Brad . . . . Paramount Pictures, p. 248
Grey, Brad . . . . Real Time with Bill Maher, p. 372
Grey, Lawrence . . . . Fox Atomic, p. 138
Gribbon, Barry . . . . Homerun Entertainment, Inc., p. 168
Gribbon, Jennifer . . . . Homerun Entertainment, Inc., p. 168
Grieder, Steve . . . . Nickelodeon/MTVN Kids & Family Group, p. 237
Griffin, Adam . . . . The Collective, p. 96
Griffin, John . . . . Spike TV, p. 298
Griffin, Merv . . . . Merv Griffin Entertainment, p. 154
Griffin, Peggy . . . . Cates/Doty Productions, p. 85
Griffin, Phil . . . . NBC News, p. 230
Griffin, Rachel . . . . MGA Ent./MGA Ent. Films, p. 216
Griffin, Tony . . . . Merv Griffin Entertainment, p. 154
Griffis, Noelle . . . . Big Beach, p. 67
Griffith, JoAnne Adams . . . . MTV Networks, p. 226
Griffith, Sarah . . . . Pink Sneakers Productions, p. 255
Griffiths, Jim . . . . Playboy Entertainment Group, Inc., p. 257
Griffiths, Sheila . . . . Real Time with Bill Maher, p. 372
Grifka, Allan . . . . The Collective, p. 96
Grigg, Ronnie . . . . Peters Entertainment, p. 253
Grigsby, Howard . . . . Veronica Mars, p. 378
Grill, Steve . . . . The Artists' Colony, p. 56
Grillo, Nick . . . . Nick Grillo Productions, p. 154
Grimshaw, Paul . . . . The Orphanage, p. 244
Grimston, Jane . . . . Brightlight Pictures, Inc., p. 75
Grindle, Summer . . . . El Dorado Pictures, p. 120
Grindlinger, Meredith . . . . Mandate Pictures, p. 209
Grindon, Michael . . . . Sony Pictures Television International, p. 296
Grisanti, Jennifer . . . . CBS Paramount Network Television, p. 87
Grodanz, Melanie . . . . Grammnet Productions, p. 152
Grodner, Allison . . . . Allison Grodner Productions, Inc., p. 155
Grodnik, Daniel L. . . . . Dan Grodnik Productions, p. 155
Groening, Matt . . . . The Simpsons, p. 375
Grogin, Scott . . . . Fox Broadcasting Company, p. 139
Gronenthal, Harold . . . . AMC, p. 50
Gronenthal, Harold . . . . The Independent Film Channel (IFC), p. 173
Gronfein, Jim . . . . Twentieth Television, p. 324
Groom, Mickey . . . . John Fogel Entertainment Group, p. 182
Gross, Kenneth H. . . . . Ken Gross Management, p. 155
Gross, Lesly . . . . Mutual Film Company, p. 227
Gross, Marcy . . . . Gross-Weston Productions, p. 156
Gross, Matthew . . . . Day Break, p. 359
Gross, Matthew . . . . Gross Entertainment, p. 155
Grossbard, Beth . . . . Beth Grossbard Productions, p. 155
Grossbard, Beth . . . . Craig Anderson Productions, p. 52
Grossbart, Jack . . . . Grossbart Kent Productions, p. 156
Grossman, Brad . . . . Imagine Entertainment, p. 172
Grossman, David . . . . Desperate Housewives, p. 360
Grossman, Gary H. . . . . Weller/Grossman Productions, p. 338
Grossman, Jed . . . . Lionsgate, p. 200
Grossmann, Aurelia . . . . Partizan, p. 250
Grosso, Nikki Allyn . . . . Jersey Films, p. 180
Grosso, Sonny . . . . Grosso Jacobson Comm. Corp., p. 156
Grosvenor, Ed . . . . Sub Rosa Productions, Inc., p. 303
Grosvenor, Jeff . . . . Wonderland Sound and Vision, p. 344
Groubert, Mark . . . . Black Sheep Entertainment, p. 68
Groves, Phil . . . . IMAX Corporation, p. 172
Groves, Stephanie . . . . Warner Bros. Television Production, p. 335
Gruber, Desiree . . . . Project Runway, p. 372
Gruber, Desiree . . . . Full Picture, p. 143
Grudman, Nora . . . . Bravo, p. 74
Grund, Christine . . . . Renegade 83, p. 270
Grundahl, Marcus . . . . Antidote International Films, Inc., p. 53
Grunfeld, Jacqui . . . . Touchstone Television, p. 316
Gruosso, Gerard . . . . A&E Network, p. 44
Grushow, Sandy . . . . Phase Two Productions, p. 253
Gryphon, Robert . . . . Gryphon Films, p. 157
Guber, Peter . . . . Mandalay Pictures, p. 208
Gubert, George . . . . Buena Vista Television, p. 79
Guerin, Jean . . . . USA Network, p. 327
Guerin, Terry . . . . Tapestry Films, Inc., p. 308
Guerrero, Luis . . . . Esparza-Katz Productions, p. 126
Guerrero, Luis . . . . Maya Pictures, p. 213
Guevara, Janie Sakura . . . . Blackfriars Bridge, p. 68
Gugle, Kevin . . . . Wheelhouse Entertainment, p. 339
Gugliotta, Greg . . . . Nitelite Entertainment, p. 238
Guido, Tony . . . . RHI Entertainment, p. 271
Guidone, Kimberly . . . . East of Doheny/Lexington Road Prod., p. 118
Guillen, Roger . . . . Sci Fi Channel, p. 282
Gulko, Harlan . . . . Focus Features/Rogue Pictures, p. 136
Gulliver, William . . . . MM Productions, p. 218
Guma, Jesse . . . . Lightstone Entertainment, Inc., p. 199
Gummersall, Joshua . . . . The Bedford Falls Company, p. 65
Gumpert, Andrew . . . . Columbia Pictures, p. 97
Gunby, Tami . . . . Alexander/Enright & Associates, p. 49
Gundlach, Joan . . . . A&E Network, p. 44
Gunn, Andrew . . . . Gunn Films, p. 158
Gunn, Jon . . . . Lucky Crow Films, p. 204
Gunn, Nancy . . . . Hell's Kitchen, p. 363
Gunther, Sara . . . . Penn Station Entertainment, p. 252
Gupta, Nav . . . . CastleBright Studios, p. 85
Guralnick, Rob . . . . Jerry Weintraub Productions, p. 338
Gur-Arieh, Civan . . . . Interloper Films, p. 175
Gurin, Phil . . . . The Gurin Company, p. 158
Gurney, Robin . . . . Imagine Television, p. 172
Gurvitz, Marc . . . . Real Time with Bill Maher, p. 372
Gurvitz, Marc . . . . According to Jim, p. 354
Gurvitz, Marc . . . . Brillstein-Grey Entertainment, p. 75
Gustawes, Gus . . . . j.k. livin productions, p. 178
Gustawes, Mark . . . . j.k. livin productions, p. 178
Guth, Paulina . . . . Enteraktion Studios, p. 124
Guthrie, Jeffrey . . . . HBO Films, p. 162
Guthrie, Sheila . . . . CBS Paramount Network Television, p. 87
Gutierrez, Diego . . . . Without a Trace, p. 379
Guyton, Remi . . . . Village Roadshow Pictures, p. 331
Gwartz, Jennifer . . . . Veronica Mars, p. 378
Gwen, Jill . . . . Twentieth Century Fox - Searchlight Pictures, p. 323
Gwinn, Peter . . . . The Colbert Report, p. 357
Gyngell, David . . . . Granada America, p. 152
Ha, Schuyler . . . . Initial Entertainment Group, p. 175
Haas, Andrew . . . . De Line Pictures, p. 108
Haas, Bryan . . . . Michael De Luca Productions, p. 108
Haber, Ben . . . . Broken Road Productions, p. 77
Hache, Emily . . . . DisneyToon Studios, p. 113
Hacken, Carla . . . . Twentieth Century Fox - Fox 2000, p. 323
Hackett, Michael . . . . Gambit Pictures, p. 144
Hackett, Stephen . . . . King World Productions, Inc., p. 188
Hackner, Lisa . . . . Telepictures Productions, p. 311
Hadl, Dan . . . . John Wells Productions, p. 338
Haeussermann, Nicole . . . . Ascendant Pictures, p. 56
Haffner, Craig . . . . Greystone Television and Films, p. 154

Haft, Jeremy . . . . .MRB Productions, Inc., p. 224
Haft, Steven . . . . .Mad TV, p. 368
Haft, Steven . . . . .Haft Entertainment, p. 159
Hagar, David W. . . . . .Greenwood Avenue Entertainment, p. 154
Hage, Melinda . . . . .Warner Bros. Television Production, p. 335
Hagee, Erin . . . . .Southern Cross the Dog, p. 297
Hagen, Erica . . . . .John Calley Productions, p. 82
Hagen, Stephanie .Desperate Housewives, p. 360
Hagerty, Erin . . . . .Thousand Words, p. 313
Haggar, Daley . . . . .Help Me Help You, p. 363
Haggis, Paul . . . . .The Black Donnellys, p. 356
Haggis, Paul . . . . .Blackfriars Bridge, p. 68
Hagopian, Kip . . . . .Segue Productions, Inc., p. 283
Hague, Bill . . . . .King World Productions, Inc., p. 188
Hahn, Cynthia . . . . .Beacon, p. 64
Hahn, Nina . . . . .Nickelodeon/MTVN Kids & Family Group, p. 237
Hahn-Seiffert, Mindy . . . . .Warner Bros. Television Production, p. 335
Haight, Martha . . . . .Cheyenne Enterprises, p. 89
Hail, David . . . . .The Tom Lynch Company, p. 205
Haiman, Evan . . . . .HDNet, p. 163
Haimes, Marc . . . . .DreamWorks SKG, p. 116
Haimes, Ted . . . . .FremantleMedia North America, p. 142
Haimovitz, Jules .dick clark productions, inc., p. 94
Hainey, Evan . . . . .Untitled Entertainment, p. 327
Hainline, Dino . . . . .VOY Pictures, p. 332
Hair, Ross . . . . .Sony Pictures Television International, p. 296
Hake, Ward . . . . .Twentieth Century Fox Television, p. 323
Halby, Karen L. . . . . .Sony Pictures Entertainment, p. 295
Haldar, Neil . . . . .SkyZone Entertainment, p. 291
Hale, Bryan . . . . .Evolution, p. 128
Hale, Susan . . . . .TOKYOPOP Inc., p. 315
Hale, Susan . . . . .Upright Citizens Brigade, p. 327
Halfon, Lianne . . . . .Mr. Mudd, p. 224
Haljun, Tory . . . . .Playtone Productions, p. 258
Hall, Anthony Michael . . . . .The Dead Zone, p. 359
Hall, Billie E. . . . . .Lett/Reese International Productions, p. 196
Hall, Chip . . . . .King of the Hill, p. 365
Hall, Gary . . . . .Twentieth Century Fox Television, p. 323
Hall, Gina . . . . .Tollin/Robbins Productions, p. 315
Hall, Lori . . . . .CSM Communications, p. 104
Hall, Meredith . . . . .Nancy Tenenbaum Films, p. 311
Hall, Nancy Mosher .Alan Barnette Productions, p. 61
Hall, Philip . . . . .Sunswept Entertainment, p. 305
Hall, Philip . . . . .Media 8 Entertainment, p. 214
Hall, Sharon . . . . .Sony Pictures Television, p. 296
Hall, Stewart . . . . .Media 8 Entertainment, p. 214
Hall, Vondie Curtis . . . . .Motor City Films, p. 223
Halleen, Tom . . . . .AMC, p. 50
Hallett, Dean . . . . .Twentieth Century Fox, p. 322
Halliday, Lisa . . . . .Harpo Films, Inc., p. 161
Hallin, Paula . . . . .Shoe Money Productions, p. 286
Hallman, Drew . . . . .Pie Town Productions, p. 254
Halmi Sr., Robert . . . . .RHI Entertainment, p. 271
Halmi Jr., Robert . . . . .RHI Entertainment, p. 271
Halper, Tara . . . . .New Line Television, p. 235
Halperin, Dan . . . . .Epiphany Pictures, Inc., p. 126
Halperin, Missy .Fox Broadcasting Company, p. 139
Halpern, Emily . . . . .The Unit, p. 378
Halpern, James . . . . .David Eick Productions, p. 120
Halpern, Noreen . . . . .Blueprint Entertainment, p. 70
Halpern, Stew . . . . .How I Met Your Mother, p. 364
Hals, Matthew . . . . .Permut Presentations, p. 252
Halsey, James L. . . . . .Warner Bros. Entertainment Inc., p. 334
Halvorson, Robert J. . . . . .Proud Mary Entertainment, p. 263
Hamada, Walter . . . . .H2F Entertainment, p. 158
Hamann, Justin . . . . .Cheyenne Enterprises, p. 89
Hamberg, Kim . . . . .My Name Is Earl, p. 369
Hamburger, Adam . . . . .Drawn Together, p. 360
Hamburger, David . . . . .Drawn Together, p. 360
Hamburger, Kevin . . . . .Telepictures Productions, p. 311
Hamilton, Ann . . . . .Saved, p. 374
Hamilton, Art . . . . .Colossal Entertainment, p. 97
Hamilton, Chad . . . . .Paramount Vantage/Paramount Classics, p. 248
Hamilton, Lisa . . . . .DreamWorks SKG, p. 116
Hamilton, Marcy Levitas . . . . .TriCoast Studios, p. 318
Hamilton, Strath . . . . .TriCoast Studios, p. 318
Hamilton-Shaw, Steve . . . . .Rocket Pictures Limited, p. 273
Hamlin, David . . . . .East of Doheny/Lexington Road Prod., p. 118
Hamm, Bill . . . . .Ghost House Pictures, p. 145
Hamm, Bill . . . . .Renaissance Pictures, p. 270
Hammack, Lourri . . . . .Laika Entertainment, p. 191
Hammeke, Mike . . . . .Last Call with Carson Daly, p. 366
Hammer, Bonnie . . . . .Sci Fi Channel, p. 282
Hammer, Bonnie . . . . .USA Network, p. 327
Hammer, Bonnie . . . . .NBC Universal Cable Entertainment, p. 231
Hammer, Dennis . . . . .Crossing Jordan, p. 358
Hammer, Dennis . . . . .Heroes, p. 363
Hammer, Stuart . . . . .Revelations Entertainment, p. 271
Hamori, Andras . . . . .H2O Motion Pictures, p. 159
Hampton, Brenda . . . . .7th Heaven, p. 353
Hamrick, Shari . . . . .Spirit Horse Productions, p. 298
Han, Howard . . . . .Trilogy Entertainment Group, p. 319
Han, Jane . . . . .Sony BMG Feature Films, p. 294
Hancock, Treena . . . . .Crossing Jordan, p. 358
Handel, Ari . . . . .Protozoa Pictures, p. 263
Handleman, David . . . . .Studio 60 on the Sunset Strip, p. 376
Handy, Dagan . . . . .Shady Acres Entertainment, p. 285
Hanel, Michael . . . . .The War at Home, p. 379
Hanel, Michael . . . . .Reba, p. 372
Hanel, Michael . . . . .Acme Productions, p. 46
Haney, Eric . . . . .The Unit, p. 378
Haney, Jana . . . . .Marvel Studios, Inc., p. 211
Haney, Jeanne . . . . .Passions, p. 371
Hanks, Nicholas . . . . .Sidney Kimmel Entertainment, p. 187
Hanks, Poppy . . . . .State Street Pictures, p. 300
Hanks, Tom . . . . .Big Love, p. 356
Hanks, Tom . . . . .Playtone Productions, p. 258
Hankwitz, Peter . . . . .Peter Hankwitz Production & Mgmt., p. 160
Hanley, Chris . . . . .Muse Productions, Inc., p. 227
Hanley, Roberta . . . . .Muse Productions, Inc., p. 227
Hanna, Matt . . . . .VH1, p. 330
Hannaway, Dorian . . . . .CBS Entertainment, p. 86
Hannibal, Ellie . . . . .Rick Berman Productions, p. 66
Hannigan, Harry . . . . .According to Jim, p. 354
Hanratty, Joseph . . . . .Village Roadshow Pictures, p. 331
Hansen, Ash . . . . .Braverman Productions, Inc., p. 73
Hansen, Douglas E. . . . . .Endgame Entertainment, p. 124
Hansen, Gale . . . . .Relativity Media LLC, p. 269
Hansen, Libby . . . . .USA Network, p. 327
Hansen, Molly . . . . .Digital Domain, Inc., p. 110
Hansen, Sam . . . . .The Jinks/Cohen Company, p. 181
Hanson, Andrea . . . . .Yari Film Group (YFG), p. 347
Hanson, David . . . . .Zaloom Film, p. 348
Hanson, Eric . . . . .Letnom Productions, p. 196
Hanson, Hart . . . . .Bones, p. 356
Hanson, Michelle . . . . .Entertainment Studios, Inc., p. 125
Hanson, Paul . . . . .QED International, p. 264
Hanson, Randall C. . . . . .King World Productions, Inc., p. 188
Harbert, Ted . . . . .E! Networks, p. 117
Harbert, Ted . . . . .style., p. 303
Harbin, Kim . . . . .Buena Vista Television, p. 79
Harbinson, Patrick . . . . .Law & Order: Special Victims Unit, p. 367
Hardart, Paul . . . . .Adirondack Pictures, p. 47
Hardart, Tom . . . . .Adirondack Pictures, p. 47
Harden, J. David . . . . .Numb3rs, p. 370
Harding, Dave . . . . .Harding & Associates, p. 160
Harding, Dave . . . . .Harding-Kurtz Entertainment, p. 160
Hardy, Jim . . . . .Hope Enterprises, Inc., p. 169
Hardy, Kerry Schmidt . . . . .Sony Pictures Television, p. 296
Hardy, Rob . . . . .Rainforest Films, p. 265
Hargett-Aupetit, Hester .Raffaella Productions, Inc., p. 265
Hargreaves-Heald, Rachel . . . . .Heyday Films, p. 166
Hargrove, Dean . . . . .Dean Hargrove Productions, p. 160
Hargrove, Jason . . . . . .Twentieth Century Fox - Searchlight Pictures, p. 323
Haring, Matt . . . . .900 Films, p. 43
Harlan, Brad . . . . .North By Northwest Entertainment, p. 239
Harlin, Renny . . . . .Midnight Sun Pictures, p. 216
Harlow II, Bryce N. . . . . .CBS Corporation, p. 86
Harman, Damon . . . . .Chameleon Entertainment, p. 89
Harmelin, Sara . . . . .Silver Pictures, p. 289

Harms, Kristin . . . . Harms Way Productions, p. 160
Harold, Holly . . . . Smallville, p. 375
Harper, Kent . . . . Hella Good Moving Pictures, p. 164
Harper, Robert . . . . Twentieth Century Fox, p. 322
Harpur, Reginald . . . . Warner Bros. Entertainment Inc., p. 334
Harrington, Eamon . . . . Planet Grande Pictures, p. 256
Harrington, Eric . . . . Ronald Suppa Productions, Inc., p. 306
Harris, Alissa . . . . Twentieth Century Fox Television, p. 323
Harris, Ann . . . . Sony Pictures Television International, p. 296
Harris, Ariana . . . . Lawrence Bender Productions, p. 65
Harris, Arthur . . . . All of Us, p. 354
Harris, Arthur . . . . CBS Sports, p. 88
Harris, Bill . . . . A&E Network, p. 44
Harris, Brad . . . . InVenture Entertainment, p. 176
Harris, Carolyn . . . . Raygun Productions, p. 266
Harris, Chris . . . . How I Met Your Mother, p. 364
Harris, Dan . . . . The Harris Company, p. 161
Harris, Gavin . . . . Cold Case, p. 357
Harris, Greg . . . . CBS Entertainment, p. 86
Harris, Jonathan . . . . Twentieth Century Fox Television, p. 323
Harris, Lynn . . . . Warner Bros. Pictures, p. 334
Harris, Mark R. . . . . The Black Donnellys, p. 356
Harris, Mark R. . . . . The Harris Company, p. 161
Harris, Petersen . . . . CFP Productions, p. 88
Harris, Pippa . . . . Neal Street Productions Ltd., p. 232
Harris, Stephanie . . . . Buena Vista Motion Pictures Group, p. 78
Harris, Susan . . . . Witt-Thomas-Harris Productions, p. 343
Harrison, Dan . . . . Sleuth, p. 291
Harrison, Donna . . . . Tribune Entertainment Company, p. 318
Harrison, Dustin . . . . Gorilla Pictures, p. 150
Harrison, Hal . . . . CBS Paramount Network Television, p. 87
Harrison, Joan . . . . Discovery Networks, U.S., p. 111
Harrison, Joan . . . . TLC, p. 314
Harrison, Matthew . . . . Film Crash, p. 132
Hart, Ali . . . . Relevant Entertainment Group, p. 270
Hart, Brad . . . . CBS Paramount Worldwide Television Dist., p. 88
Hart, Jason . . . . Krainin Productions, Inc., p. 190
Hart, Natalie . . . . Crossing Jordan, p. 358
Hart, Natalie . . . . Heroes, p. 363
Hart, Ron . . . . According to Jim, p. 354
Hart, Ron . . . . Sam Okun Productions, Inc., p. 242
Hart, Veronica . . . . HIT Entertainment, p. 167
Hartford, Scott . . . . Prometheus Entertainment, p. 263
Hartley, Alli . . . . Tomorrow Film Corporation, p. 315
Hartley, David . . . . One Tree Hill, p. 371
Hartley, Sam . . . . Asylum Entertainment, p. 57
Hartley, Ted . . . . RKO Pictures, LLC, p. 273
Hartman, Andrea . . . . NBC Entertainment, p. 230
Hartman, Hope . . . . ABC Entertainment Television Group, p. 45
Hartman, Rome . . . . CBS News, p. 87
Hartmann, Rogers . . . . Code Entertainment, p. 96
Hartrey, Amanda . . . . Ambush Entertainment, p. 50
Hart-Smith, Heather . . . . Twentieth Television, p. 324
Hartwell, Jane . . . . DreamWorks Animation SKG, p. 116
Hartwick, Amy . . . . ABC Entertainment Television Group, p. 45
Hartwick, Joe . . . . Twentieth Century Fox, p. 322
Harvey, Brian . . . . ABC Entertainment Television Group, p. 45
Harvey, Brian . . . . Touchstone Television, p. 316
Harvey, Caroline . . . . Mirage Enterprises, p. 217
Harvey, Gavin . . . . Versus, p. 329
Harvey, Gayliann . . . . The Nine, p. 370
Harwood, Robyn . . . . Phase Two Productions, p. 253
Hashimoto, Stacy . . . . Triage Entertainment, p. 317
Haskett, Erin . . . . Infinity Features Entertainment, p. 174
Haskins, Rick . . . . The CW, p. 105
Haskovec, Alison . . . . Intermedia Film Equities USA, Inc., p. 175
Haspel, Ned . . . . John Wells Productions, p. 338
Hassan, Mazen . . . . 21 Laps Entertainment, p. 38
Hassel, Molly . . . . Catfish Productions, p. 86
Hassell, Tom . . . . Picturehouse, p. 254
Hassid, Dan . . . . Weekend Films/Main Street Film Company, p. 337
Hassig, John . . . . Jaffe/Braunstein Films, LLC, p. 179
Hatamiya, Kim . . . . Sony Pictures Television International, p. 296
Hatanaka, Gregory . . . . Pathfinder Pictures, LLC, p. 250
Hatch, Abram . . . . Darren Star Productions, p. 300
Hatcher, Jan . . . . GSN, p. 157
Hatcher, Teri . . . . ISBE Productions, p. 177
Hauge, Ron . . . . The Simpsons, p. 375
Haukom, Michael . . . . Rules of Engagement, p. 373
Hauptman, Andrew . . . . Andell Entertainment, p. 51
Hauptman, Dustin . . . . Rubicon, p. 276
Hauptman, Ellen Bronfman . . . . Andell Entertainment, p. 51
Hause, Rob . . . . G4 TV, p. 144
Havens, Anduin . . . . MARTHA, p. 368
Havlan, JR . . . . The Daily Show With Jon Stewart, p. 359
Hawk, Tony . . . . 900 Films, p. 43
Hawkins, Kim . . . . Indigo Films, p. 174
Hawley, Heather . . . . Krasnoff Foster Productions, p. 190
Hawley, Jane . . . . BBC Films, p. 64
Hawley, Noah . . . . Bones, p. 356
Hawley, Richard . . . . Merchant-Ivory, p. 215
Hayashigawa, Nathan . . . . Andrew Lauren Productions, p. 195
Hayden, Laurette . . . . USA Network, p. 327
Hayden, Marianne . . . . Carson Daly Productions, p. 84
Hayek, Salma . . . . Ugly Betty, p. 378
Hayes, Alex . . . . Fifty Cannon Entertainment, LLC, p. 131
Hayes, Evan . . . . Working Title Films, p. 345
Hayes, Jocelyn . . . . Killer Films, Inc., p. 187
Hayes, John . . . . Cube Vision, p. 104
Hayes, Sean . . . . Hazy Mills Productions, p. 161
Hayman, James . . . . Ugly Betty, p. 378
Haynes, Brian . . . . Crystal Spring Productions, Inc., p. 104
Haynes, John . . . . CSI: Miami, p. 358
Hayward, Bob . . . . Summit Entertainment, p. 304
Hayward, Chuck . . . . State Street Pictures, p. 300
Hayward, Debra . . . . Working Title Films, p. 345
Hazen, Samantha . . . . Current Entertainment, p. 105
Heacock, Jessica . . . . Spike TV, p. 298
Healey, Janet . . . . IDT Entertainment, p. 171
Healy, Kimberly . . . . PorchLight Entertainment, p. 259
Healy, Michael . . . . Disney ABC Cable Networks Group, p. 112
Heard, Michael . . . . Twentieth Century Fox, p. 322
Heaston, Jodi . . . . Ascendant Pictures, p. 56
Heath, Bob . . . . According to Jim, p. 354
Heath, Robyn . . . . 2929 Productions, p. 40
Heaton, Patricia . . . . Four Boys Films, p. 138
Hebenstreit, Cory . . . . Benderspink, p. 66
Hebenstreit, David . . . . Cube Vision, p. 104
Heberer, Sandy . . . . PBS, p. 251
Hebert, Julie . . . . Numb3rs, p. 370
Hecht, Albie . . . . Worldwide Biggies, p. 346
Hecht, Duffy . . . . The Hecht Company, p. 163
Hecht-Ward, Liz . . . . Main Line Pictures, p. 207
Heckman, Carrie . . . . Civilian Pictures, p. 94
Heder, Dan . . . . Greasy Entertainment, p. 153
Heder, Doug . . . . Greasy Entertainment, p. 153
Heder, Jon . . . . Greasy Entertainment, p. 153
Hedges, James . . . . ABC Entertainment Television Group, p. 45
Hedrick, Rebecca . . . . Blue Bay Productions, p. 68
Heed, Mary . . . . A&E Network, p. 44
Heffernan, Kevin . . . . Broken Lizard Industries, p. 76
Heffner, Daniel Jason . . . . Serendipity Productions, Inc., p. 284
Hegarty, Bridget . . . . CBS Paramount Network Television, p. 87
Hegedus-Lum, Dorka . . . . 2929 Productions, p. 40
Hegeman, John . . . . Fox Atomic, p. 138
Hegyes, Stephen . . . . Brightlight Pictures, Inc., p. 75
Heidelberger, Mark . . . . Treasure Entertainment, p. 317
Heidenreich, Eric . . . . Cinetic, p. 93
Heinberg, Allan . . . . Grey's Anatomy, p. 362
Heineman, Alex . . . . Focus Features/Rogue Pictures, p. 136
Helberg, Dan . . . . Stone and Company Entertainment, p. 301
Helfand, Michael . . . . Screen Gems, p. 283
Helfant, Michael . . . . Marvel Studios, Inc., p. 211
Helford, Bruce . . . . The George Lopez Show, p. 362
Helfrich Jackson, Lisa . . . . The New Adventures of Old Christine, p. 370
Helfrich-Jackson, Lisa . . . . The Class, p. 357
Heller, Art . . . . Andrew Lauren Productions, p. 195
Heller, Davida . . . . Radar Pictures, p. 264
Heller, Lisa . . . . HBO Documentaries & Family, p. 162
Heller, Paul . . . . Paul Heller Productions, p. 164

Heller, Rick . . . . .Interscope/Shady/Aftermath Films, p. 176
Heller, Rosilyn . . . . .Rosilyn Heller Productions, p. 164
Helm, C. J. . . . . .A Wink and a Nod Productions, p. 43
Hely, Steve . . . . .American Dad, p. 354
Hemenez, Linnea . . . . .GSN, p. 157
Hemingson, David . . . . .American Dad, p. 354
Hemwall, Geoff . . . . .CSI: NY, p. 359
Hendee, Lynn . . . . .Chartoff Productions, p. 89
Henderson, Amy . . . . .Brainstorm Media, p. 72
Henderson, Cinque . . . . .Studio 60 on the Sunset Strip, p. 376
Henderson, Joe . . . . .The Jim Henson Company, p. 165
Henderson, Katie . . . . .Nine Yards Entertainment, p. 238
Henderson, Mark . . . . .Norsemen Television Productions, LLC, p. 239
Henderson Moore, Nina . . . . .BET Networks, p. 66
Hendler, David . . . . .Sony Pictures Entertainment, p. 295
Hendricks, Adam . . . . .The Jinks/Cohen Company, p. 181
Hendricks, Bruce . . . . .Buena Vista Motion Pictures Group, p. 78
Hendricks, John S. . . . . .Discovery Networks, U.S., p. 111
Hendrickson, Elek .Temple Hill Productions, p. 311
Hendrickson, Mike .Twentieth Century Fox, p. 322
Hendrixson, Jason . . . . .H2F Entertainment, p. 158
Henkel, Christoph . . . . .Cineville LLC, p. 93
Henne, Brette . . . . .VH1, p. 330
Hennelly, Denis Henry . . . . .Open Road Films, p. 243
Henney, James . . . . .The Syndicate, p. 307
Henning, Stefanie . . . . .Fox Television Studios, p. 140
Henri, Maddie . . . . .Home & Garden Television (HGTV), p. 168
Henrion, Amandine . . . . .Bonne Pioche, p. 71
Henry, Andy . . . . .CSI: Crime Scene Investigation, p. 358
Henry, Darin . . . . .The War at Home, p. 379
Henry, Fleur . . . . .Sub Rosa Productions, Inc., p. 303
Henry, Jeff . . . . .Friday Night Lights, p. 361
Henry, Mike . . . . .Family Guy, p. 361
Henry, Roger . . . . .Discovery Networks, U.S., p. 111
Hensleigh, Eleo . . . . .ABC Entertainment Television Group, p. 45
Hensleigh, Eleo . . . . .Disney-ABC Television Group, p. 113
Hensleigh, Eleo . . . . .Disney ABC Cable Networks Group, p. 112
Henson, Brian . . . . .The Jim Henson Company, p. 165
Henson, Lisa . . . . .The Jim Henson Company, p. 165
Hentemann, Mark . . . . .Family Guy, p. 361
Henze, Chris . . . . .Psych, p. 372
Henze, Chris . . . . .Tagline Pictures, p. 307
Heppe, Ryan . . . . .David Foster Productions, p. 138
Herbst, Scott . . . . .Lakeshore Entertainment Group LLC, p. 192
Herbst-Brady, Elizabeth . . . . .Twentieth Television, p. 324
Heredia, Stephanie . . . . . .TAE Productions/Medeacom Productions, p. 307
Herlihy, Shannon . . . . .Endemol USA, Inc., p. 123
Herlocker, Julie . . . . .Las Vegas, p. 366
Herman, Elaine . . . .Josselyne Herman & Assoc./Moving Image Films, p. 166
Herman, Ellie . . . . .The L Word, p. 366
Herman, Ellie . . . . .Jericho, p. 364
Herman, Harvey . . .Josselyne Herman & Assoc./Moving Image Films, p. 166
Herman, Vicky . . . . .Warner Bros. Television Production, p. 335
Hermann, Randy . . . . .Mandalay Pictures, p. 208
Herman-Saccio, Josselyne . . . . .Josselyne Herman & Assoc./ Moving Image Films, p. 166
Hernandez, Amanda . . . . .City Entertainment, p. 93
Hernandez, Maria E. . . . . .dick clark productions, inc., p. 94
Herr, Claudia . . . . .Random House Films, p. 266
Herrera, Henry . . . . .Joel Films, p. 181
Herrington, Suzanne . . . . .Ocean Pictures, p. 241
Herro, Mike . . . . .One Tree Hill, p. 371
Hersh, Ed . . . . .Court TV Networks, p. 102
Hershey, Thomas . . . . .Sony Pictures Imageworks, p. 295
Hershman, Kim . . . . .Touchstone Television, p. 316
Herskovic, Patricia .Jack Freedman Productions, p. 141
Herskovitz, Marshall . . . . .The Bedford Falls Company, p. 65
Hertz, Judah . . . . .Invitation Entertainment, p. 177
Hertz, Tom . . . . .Rules of Engagement, p. 373
Herz, Adam . . . . .Terra Firma Films, p. 312
Herz, Justin . . . . .Warner Bros. Online, p. 334
Herz, Michael . . . . .Troma Entertainment, Inc., p. 320
Herzfeld, John . . . . .New Redemption Pictures, p. 235
Herzig, Amy . . . . .CBS Entertainment, p. 86
Herzog, Doug . . . . .Comedy Central, p. 98
Herzog, Doug . . . . .Spike TV, p. 298
Herzon, Heidi . . . . .The Sarah Silverman Programme, p. 373
Heslov, Grant . . . . .Smoke House, p. 292
Hess, Sara . . . . .House, p. 363
Hester, Jean . . . . .Touchstone Television, p. 316
Heston, Fraser C. . . . . .Agamemnon Films, Inc., p. 47
Heth, Steven . . . . .House, p. 363
Hetzel, Eric . . . . .Robert Cort Productions, p. 101
Heus, Richard . . . . .Day Break, p. 359
Heuser, H. Michael . . . . .Storm Entertainment, p. 302
Heuton, Cheryl . . . . .Numb3rs, p. 370
Hewitt, Jennifer Love . . . . .Ghost Whisperer, p. 362
Hewitt, Jennifer Love . . . . .Love Spell Entertainment, p. 203
Heyman, David . . . . .Heyday Films, p. 166
Heyman, Helena . . . . .Industry Entertainment Partners, p. 174
Heyman, John . . . . .World Film Services, Inc., p. 345
Heyman, Mark . . . . .Protozoa Pictures, p. 263
Heymann, Tom . . . . .A&E Network, p. 44
Hickman, Mark . . . . .NorthSouth Productions, p. 239
Hickox, S. Bryan . . . . .Bryan Hickox Pictures, Inc., p. 166
Hicks, Andi . . . . .Timeline Films, p. 314
Hicks, Heather . . . . .KoMut Entertainment, p. 189
Hicks, Hilly . . . . .Kidnapped, p. 365
Hicks, John . . . . .Arramis Films, p. 55
Hicks, Nate . . . . .Comic Book Movies, LLC/Branded Entertainment/ Batfilm Productions, p. 99
Hicks, Regina . . . . .Girlfriends, p. 362
Hicks, Russell . . . . .Nickelodeon/MTVN Kids & Family Group, p. 237
Hidalgo, Jorge . . . . .Telemundo Network, p. 310
Higginbotham, Abraham . . . . .The Singles Table, p. 375
Higgins, Al . . . .'Til Death, p. 377
Higgins, Angelique . . . . .Irish DreamTime, p. 177
Higgins, Bob . . . . .Cartoon Network, p. 84
Higgins, David W. . . . . .Launchpad Productions, p. 195
Higgins, J. Paul . . . . .JPH Productions, p. 182
Higgins, Lisa . . . . .Endemol USA, Inc., p. 123
Higgins, Maria . . . . .dick clark productions, inc., p. 94
Higgins, Steve . . . . .Saturday Night Live, p. 373
High, Joel . . . . .Lionsgate, p. 200
Higley, Dena . . . . .One Life to Live, p. 371
Hildebrand, Erin . . . . .Picturehouse, p. 254
Hildebrand, Frank . . . . .River Road Entertainment, p. 272
Hildebrand, Jodi . . . . .Sidney Kimmel Entertainment, p. 187
Hill, Eddie . . . . .Nickelodeon/MTVN Kids & Family Group, p. 237
Hill, Gregg . . . . .AMC, p. 50
Hill, Gregg . . . . .The Independent Film Channel (IFC), p. 173
Hill, Michael . . . . .Paramount Pictures Production Division, p. 248
Hill, Michael . . . . .HBO Entertainment, p. 162
Hill, Sam . . . . .CSI: Miami, p. 358
Hill, Stephen . . . . .BET Networks, p. 66
Hillebrand, Steve . . . . .Hollywood East Entertainment, Inc., p. 168
Hilliard, Michael . . . .@radical.media, p. 38
Hillman, David . . . . .Lifetime Television (Los Angeles), p. 198
Hillman, Elizabeth . . . . .Discovery Channel, p. 111
Hilman, Tom . . . . .Playtime Productions, p. 257
Hilton, Jennifer . . . . .Liddell Entertainment, p. 197
Hilton, Martin . . . . .The Bachelor, p. 355
Hilton, Ronald . . . . .Enteraktion Studios, p. 124
Hinajosa, Jude . . . . .Proud Mary Entertainment, p. 263
Hinton, Solomon . . . . .The Collective, p. 96
Hippisley Coxe, Nick . . . . .Catfish Productions, p. 86
Hirsch, Gary . . . . .Screen Gems, p. 283
Hirsch, Marc . . . . .CBS Paramount Worldwide Television Dist., p. 88
Hirsch, Saryl . . . . .Samuelson Productions Limited, p. 279
Hirsch, Steven R. . . . . .King World Productions, Inc., p. 188
Hirsch, Steven . . . . .S. Hirsch Company, Inc./Seemore Films, p. 167
Hirschegger, Andrea . . . . .The Montecito Picture Company, p. 220
Hirschfeld, Marc . . . . .NBC Entertainment, p. 230
Hirschorn, Michael . . . . .VH1, p. 330
Hirsh, Michael . . . . .Cookie Jar Entertainment, p. 100
Hiruma, Toshiyuki . . . . .Warner Bros. Animation, p. 334
Hiscock, Norm . . . . .Naked Trucker & T-Bones, p. 369
Hitchcock, James . . . . .CMT: Country Music Television, p. 95
Hitchcock, Michael . . . . .Mad TV, p. 368
Hitzig, Rupert . . . . .Rupert Productions, Inc., p. 277

Hlavin, John . . . . . Day Break, p. 359
Hoberg, John . . . . . My Name Is Earl, p. 369
Hoberman, David . . . . . Monk, p. 369
Hoberman, David . . . . . Mandeville Films, p. 209
Hobert, Tim . . . . . Scrubs, p. 374
Hoch, Abe . . . . . Day Break, p. 359
Hochman, Jessica . . . . . Grammnet Productions, p. 152
Hochmuth, Steve . . . . . Apostle, p. 53
Hock, Jonathan . . . . . Hock Films, Inc., p. 167
Hodge, Chad . . . . . Runaway, p. 373
Hodges, John . . . . . John Goldwyn Productions, p. 149
Hoerr, Mark . . . . . HBO Films, p. 162
Hoeven, Cathy . . . . . The Late Late Show with Craig Ferguson, p. 366
Hoffberg, Jonathan . . . . . Treasure Entertainment, p. 317
Hofferth, Mike . . . . . American Idol, p. 354
Hoffman, Alison . . . . . AMC, p. 50
Hoffman, Beth . . . . . Twentieth Century Fox Television, p. 323
Hoffman, Derek . . . . . The Donners' Company, p. 114
Hoffman, Gary . . . . . Gary Hoffman Productions, p. 167
Hoffman, Janette Jensen "JJ" . . . . . Eighth Square Entertainment, p. 120
Hoffman, John . . . . . HBO Documentaries & Family, p. 162
Hoffman, Kate . . . . . Seven Arts Pictures, p. 285
Hoffman, Laura . . . . . PorchLight Entertainment, p. 259
Hoffman, Mark . . . . . CNBC, p. 96
Hoffman, Paul . . . . . Twentieth Century Fox, p. 322
Hoffman, Peter M. . . . . . Seven Arts Pictures, p. 285
Hoffman, Philip Seymour . . . . . Cooper's Town Productions, p. 100
Hoffman, Susan . . . . . Seven Arts Pictures, p. 285
Hoffmeister, Jennifer . . . . . Strike Entertainment, p. 303
Hoffs, Jason . . . . . Jason Hoffs Productions, p. 168
Hogan, Michael . . . . . Hart Sharp Entertainment, Inc., p. 161
Hohauser, Ron . . . . . Marvel Studios, Inc., p. 211
Holahan, Dennis . . . . . Zinkler Films, p. 349
Holcman, Brad . . . . . fox 21, p. 138
Holcomb, Red . . . . . Shark, p. 374
Holcomb, Rod . . . . . Shark, p. 374
Holden, Ben . . . . . Spitfire Pictures, p. 298
Holden, David . . . . . The War at Home, p. 379
Holden, Susan . . . . . Curious Pictures, p. 104
Holden-Garland, Beth . . . . . Untitled Entertainment, p. 327
Holderman, Bill . . . . . Wildwood Enterprises, Inc., p. 341
Holdman, Brian . . . . . Hidden Palms, p. 363
Holdren, Ken . . . . . The Montecito Picture Company, p. 220
Holdridge, John . . . . . King World Productions, Inc., p. 188
Holdsworth, Carol . . . . . MarVista Entertainment, p. 212
Holland, Gill . . . . . The Group Entertainment, p. 156
Holland, Jeff . . . . . Hopscotch Pictures, p. 169
Holland, Stephen A. . . . . . Rules of Engagement, p. 373
Hollander, Russell . . . . . Buckaroo Entertainment, p. 78
Hollander, Susan . . . . . Belisarius Productions, p. 65
Holleschau, Randy . . . . . CrazyDreams Entertainment, p. 102
Hollinger, Mark . . . . . Discovery Networks, U.S., p. 111
Hollis, James . . . . . Myriad Pictures, p. 228
Holm, Karen . . . . . Disney ABC Cable Networks Group, p. 112
Holmberg, Erik . . . . . New Line Cinema, p. 234
Holmes, Davey . . . . . 3 lbs., p. 353
Holmes, Elizabeth . . . . . New Wave Management, p. 236
Holmes, Jill . . . . . VH1, p. 330
Holmgren, Steve . . . . . HDNet Films, p. 163
Holmwood, Kerry . . . . . Last Comic Standing, p. 366
Holst, Lynn . . . . . RHI Entertainment, p. 271
Holstein, Laura . . . . . John Wells Productions, p. 338
Holtz, Michael . . . . . Zinkler Films, p. 349
Holtz, Nathan . . . . . Imaginarium Entertainment Group, p. 171
Holtzman, Scott . . . . . Buena Vista Motion Pictures Group, p. 78
Holzgraf, Sarah . . . . . Sixth Way Productions, p. 291
Holzman, Miriam . . . . . Fox Mobile Entertainment, p. 139
Homan, Eric . . . . . Frederator Studios, p. 141
Homes, A.M. . . . . . The L Word, p. 366
Homewood, Alison . . . . . HIT Entertainment, p. 167
Hommel, Carolyn . . . . . Bravo, p. 74
Hong, Bradley . . . . . CineMagic Entertainment, p. 92
Hong, Herman . . . . . Longbow Productions, p. 203
Honigbaum, Shelley . . . . . One Life to Live, p. 371
Honore, James . . . . . Columbia Pictures, p. 97
Hood, Lucy . . . . . Fox Mobile Entertainment, p. 139
Hooker, Scott . . . . . MSNBC, p. 225
Hooks, Kevin . . . . . Prison Break, p. 372
Hookstratten, Jon . . . . . Fox Broadcasting Company, p. 139
Hool, Conrad . . . . . Silver Lion Films, p. 288
Hool, Lance . . . . . Silver Lion Films, p. 288
Hooper, Meghan . . . . . Just Singer Entertainment, p. 184
Hootstein, Stephen . . . . . What About Brian, p. 379
Hoover, Julie . . . . . Disney-ABC Television Group, p. 113
Hoover, Tina . . . . . Endemol USA, Inc., p. 123
Hope, Jim . . . . . The George Lopez Show, p. 362
Hope, Linda . . . . . Hope Enterprises, Inc., p. 169
Hope, Ted . . . . . This is that corporation, p. 312
Hopkins, Alicia . . . . . Tapestry Films, Inc., p. 308
Hopkins, Anderson . . . . . Shady Acres Entertainment, p. 285
Hopkins, Anne . . . . . Marian Rees Associates, p. 268
Hopkins, Brian . . . . . NorthSouth Productions, p. 239
Hopkins, Dale . . . . . G4 TV, p. 144
Hopkins, Joel . . . . . Touchstone Television, p. 316
Hopkins, Mike . . . . . Fox Cable Networks, p. 139
Hopkins, Richard . . . . . Dancing with the Stars, p. 359
Hopper, Laura . . . . . Deep River Productions, p. 109
Hopper, Nate . . . . . Sony Pictures Animation, p. 295
Hoppes, Shawna . . . . . Centropolis Entertainment, p. 88
Hopwood, David . . . . . Atmosphere Entertainment MM, LLC, p. 58
Hora, Steve . . . . . Edward R. Pressman Film Corporation, p. 261
Horasawa, Mie . . . . . CBS Paramount International Television, p. 87
Horberg, William . . . . . Sidney Kimmel Entertainment, p. 187
Horenstein, Chelsea . . . . . Peter Newman Productions, Inc., p. 236
Hori, Karen . . . . . Langley Productions, p. 193
Hori, Takeo . . . . . Antidote International Films, Inc., p. 53
Horn, Alan F. . . . . . Warner Bros. Entertainment Inc., p. 334
Hornstock, Joel . . . . . Twentieth Century Fox Television, p. 323
Horovitz, Rachael . . . . . Longfellow Pictures, p. 203
Horowitz, Adam . . . . . Lost, p. 368
Horowitz, Erin . . . . . ABC Entertainment Television Group, p. 45
Horowitz, James M. . . . . . Universal Pictures, p. 326
Horowitz, Jennifer . . . . . Miramax Films, p. 217
Horowitz, John . . . . . Cinetic, p. 93
Horowitz, Jordan . . . . . Camelot Pictures, p. 82
Horowitz, Mark . . . . . NCIS, p. 370
Horowitz, Mark . . . . . Belisarius Productions, p. 65
Horsted, Eric . . . . . The Knights of Prosperity, p. 365
Horta, Silvio . . . . . Ugly Betty, p. 378
Horton, Chris . . . . . Cinetic, p. 93
Horton, Ken . . . . . Smallville, p. 375
Horton, Peter . . . . . Grey's Anatomy, p. 362
Horwitz, Ed . . . . . LMNO Productions, p. 201
Horwitz, Leah . . . . . VH1, p. 330
Hoselton, David . . . . . House, p. 363
Hoster, Terra . . . . . Generate, p. 145
Hotz, Mark . . . . . NBC Universal Cable Entertainment, p. 231
Houghton, Kristal . . . . . CSI: Miami, p. 358
Houlehan, Maggie . . . . . Parallel Entertainment, Inc., p. 247
House, Andy . . . . . Sony Pictures Television, p. 296
Houser, Catherine . . . . . MTV Networks, p. 226
Houser, Jeff . . . . . Rive Gauche Entertainment, p. 272
Houshour, Brad . . . . . Rafelson Media, p. 265
Howard, Andrew . . . . . Incognito Entertainment, p. 173
Howard, Ashley . . . . . National Geographic Giant Screen Films & Special Projects, p. 229
Howard, Jonathan . . . . . The Singles Table, p. 375
Howard, Josh . . . . . CNBC, p. 96
Howard, Kelsey . . . . . Primetime Pictures, p. 262
Howard, Merri . . . . . Cold Case, p. 357
Howard, Ron . . . . . Imagine Television, p. 172
Howard, Ron . . . . . Imagine Entertainment, p. 172
Howard, Shari . . . . . Nickelodeon/MTVN Kids & Family Group, p. 237
Howard, Thordis . . . . . Bravo, p. 74
Howarter, Laurie . . . . . Fox Television Studios, p. 140
Howe, Dave . . . . . Sci Fi Channel, p. 282
Howe, Dave . . . . . NBC Universal Cable Entertainment, p. 231
Howe, Travis . . . . . Sony Pictures Television, p. 296
Howe, Worth . . . . . Scott Mauro Entertainment, Inc., p. 212
Howell, Jennifer . . . . . South Park, p. 376

Howell, Jennifer . . . . .Trunity, a Mediar Company, a Division of True Mediar, a Unity Corpbopoly, p. 320
Howell, Jeremy . . . . .Troma Entertainment, Inc., p. 320
Howell, Jerri . . . . .E! Networks, p. 117
Howells, Ted . . . . .Beacon, p. 64
Howie, Nina . . . . .TBS, p. 309
Howsam, Erik . . . . .di Bonaventura Pictures, Inc., p. 110
Howsam, Gary . . . . .Peace Arch Entertainment Group Inc., p. 251
Hoyer, Donn . . . . .George Schlatter Productions, p. 280
Hrycun, Kristine . . . . .Castle Rock Entertainment, p. 85
Hsia, Lisa . . . . .Bravo, p. 74
Hsiung, Susette . . . . .Disney ABC Cable Networks Group, p. 112
Hsu, Melinda . . . . .Medium, p. 369
Hsu, Melinda . . . . .Vanished, p. 378
Hsueh, Brenda . . . . .How I Met Your Mother, p. 364
Hubbard, Linsey . . . . .The Fred Silverman Company, p. 289
Hubbard, Matt . . . . .30 Rock, p. 353
Huber, Barbara . . . . .Radiant Productions, p. 265
Huber, Bob . . . . .Fox Broadcasting Company, p. 139
Huck, Lori . . . . .New Line Television, p. 235
Hudis, Mark . . . . .The Singles Table, p. 375
Hudlin, Reginald . . . . .BET Networks, p. 66
Hudson, David . . . . .Turner Network Television (TNT), p. 321
Hudson, David . . . . .TBS, p. 309
Hudson, Laura . . . . .3n1 Entertainment, p. 41
Hudson, Laura . . . . .Driven Entertainment, p. 117
Huff, Vicki . . . . .7th Heaven, p. 353
Hufnail, Mark . . . . .MPH Entertainment, Inc., p. 224
Huggins, Erica . . . . .Imagine Entertainment, p. 172
Huggins, Randy . . . . .The Unit, p. 378
Hughart, Ron . . . . .American Dad, p. 354
Hughes, Gina Degnan . . . . .AMC, p. 50
Hughes, Jonathan . . . . .Trilogy Entertainment Group, p. 319
Hughes, Kassie . . . . .mistRE films, p. 218
Hughes, Palmerston . . . . .Filmstreet, Inc., p. 133
Hughes, Peter . . . . .WPT Enterprises, Inc., p. 346
Hughes, Sarah L. . . . . .Touchstone Television, p. 316
Hughes, Sarah . . . . .ABC Entertainment Television Group, p. 45
Hughes, Stephanie . . . . .Alchemy Entertainment, p. 48
Hughes, Todd . . . . .The Ebersole-Hughes Company, p. 119
Hugo, Carly . . . . .The Group Entertainment, p. 156
Huie, Stefanie . . . . .Icon Productions, LLC, p. 170
Hull, Richard . . . . .Avalanche! Entertainment, p. 58
Hult, Mary Ann . . . . .Picturehouse, p. 254
Humperdinck, Engelbert . . . . .AM Productions & Management, p. 50
Humphrey, Bridget . . . . .Cider Mill Productions, p. 91
Humphrey, Samantha . . . . .CSI: NY, p. 359
Humphrey, Ted . . . . .The Nine, p. 370
Hundal, Raj . . . . .Single Cell Pictures, p. 290
Hunke, Jason . . . . .Vulcan Productions, p. 332
Hunn, Hillary Selesnick . . . . .Saturday Night Live, p. 373
Hunt, Brian . . . . .NBC Universal Cable Entertainment, p. 231
Hunt, David . . . . .Four Boys Films, p. 138
Hunte, Karen Robinson . . . . .KCET, p. 185
Hunter, Andrew . . . . .MTV Networks, p. 226
Hunter, Elizabeth . . . . .The L Word, p. 366
Hunter, Jamila . . . . .Twentieth Century Fox Television, p. 323
Hunter, Jana . . . . .Notes From the Underbelly, p. 370
Hunter, Mitch . . . . .Notes From the Underbelly, p. 370
Hunter, Onalee . . . . .The Nine, p. 370
Hunter, Pat . . . . .PBS, p. 251
Hunter, Robert C. . . . . .Exxcell Entertainment, Inc./Exxcell Films, p. 129
Huntsberry, Frederick . . . . .Paramount Pictures, p. 248
Huntsler, Laurie . . . . .The Black Donnellys, p. 356
Huntsman, James . . . . .Asgaard Entertainment, p. 57
Hurd, Gale Anne . . . . .Valhalla Motion Pictures, p. 328
Hurley, Kevin . . . . .Simon West Productions, p. 339
Hurwitz, Marietta . . . . .Bravo, p. 74
Hurwitz, Peter . . . . .The Weinstein Company, p. 337
Husain, Rebecca . . . . .Mandoki Productions, Inc., p. 209
Husman, Perry . . . . .The Nine, p. 370
Hussain, Asger . . . . .Lee Daniels Entertainment, p. 106
Hussey, Margaret . . . . .Pie Town Productions, p. 254
Huston, Anjelica . . . . .Gray Angel Productions, p. 152
Hutcherson, Jarvee . . . . .Tri-Elite Entertainment, Ltd., p. 319
Hutchinson, David . . . . .Program Partners, p. 262
Hutchison, Julie . . . . .Universal Pictures, p. 326
Huth, Denise . . . . .Darkwoods Productions, p. 107
Hutton, Patti . . . . .Universal Studios, p. 326
Hutton, Richard . . . . .Vulcan Productions, p. 332
Huwiler, Macie . . . . .A&E Network, p. 44
Hyams, Peter .Peter Hyams Productions, Inc., p. 169
Hyatt, Joel . . . . .Current TV, LLC, p. 105
Hyde, Bo . . . . .Cherry Road Films, LLC, p. 89
Hyde, John W. . . . . .Masters of Horror, p. 368
Hyde, John W. . . . . .Film Roman, Inc., p. 132
Hyman, Scott .Sneak Preview Entertainment, Inc., p. 293
Iaccarino, Jessica . . . . .Hollywood East Entertainment, Inc., p. 168
Iacobuzoio, Janet . . . . .One Life to Live, p. 371
Iacono, Peter . . . . .Columbia Pictures, p. 97
Iacono, Sal . . . . .Jimmy Kimmel Live, p. 364
Ianniello, Joseph . . . . .CBS Corporation, p. 86
Ibañez, Adriana . . . . .Telemundo Network, p. 310
Ice Cube . . . . .Cube Vision, p. 104
Ichise, Take . . . . .OZLA Pictures, Inc., p. 246
Igbokwe, Pearlena . . . . .Showtime Networks Inc., p. 287
Ige, Eileen . . . . .Twentieth Century Fox Television, p. 323
Iger, Robert . . . . .The Walt Disney Company, p. 112
Iger, Robert . . . . .Pixar Animation Studios, p. 256
Ignjatovic, Jesse . . . . .MTV Networks, p. 226
Ignon, Alex . . . . .King World Productions, Inc., p. 188
Ikeda, Megumi . . . . .NBC Universal Cable Entertainment, p. 231
Ikeman, Jesse . . . . .Blueprint Entertainment, p. 70
Ilagan, Mandel . . . . .Fox Reality, p. 140
Illovitch, Barry . . . . .Entertainment Studios, Inc., p. 125
Imhoff, David . . . . .New Line Cinema, p. 234
Imhoff, David . . . . .New Line Television, p. 235
Imm, Tima . . . . .VH1, p. 330
Immergut, Scott . . . . .Symbolic Action, p. 306
Immerman, Bill . . . . .Yari Film Group (YFG), p. 347
Immucci, Erica . . . . .National Geographic Giant Screen Films & Special Projects, p. 229
Impastato, J.P. . . . . .Serenade Films, p. 284
Imperato, Thomas . . . . .Twentieth Century Fox, p. 322
Imperato, Thomas . . . . .Regency Enterprises, p. 268
Inderfurth, Dorothee . . . . .Xingu Films Ltd., p. 347
Infantolino, Joseph . . . . .Beech Hill Films, p. 65
Inga, Joe . . . . .Crystal Sky Pictures, LLC, p. 104
Inglee, Lawrence . . . . .The Mark Gordon Company, p. 150
Ingold, Jeff . . . . .NBC Entertainment, p. 230
Inouye, Richard . . . . .Tribune Entertainment Company, p. 318
Inserra, Lovisa . . . . .Cypress Films, Inc., p. 106
Insogna, Julie . . . . .Oxygen Media, p. 245
Interian, Arturo . . . . .Lifetime Television (Los Angeles), p. 198
Intrieri, Allison . . . . .Law & Order: Special Victims Unit, p. 367
Introcaso-Davis, Amy . . . . .Bravo, p. 74
Ioannou, Sofia . . . . .MTV Networks Latin America (MTVNLA), p. 226
Iovine, Jimmy .Interscope/Shady/Aftermath Films, p. 176
Ipson, Jason Todd . . . . .Asgaard Entertainment, p. 57
Ipson Burke, Jaime . . . . .Asgaard Entertainment, p. 57
Ireland, Sam . . . . .Untitled Entertainment, p. 327
Ireton, Bill . . . . .Warner Bros. Entertainment Inc., p. 334
Irvin, Karen . . . . .Code Entertainment, p. 96
Irvine, Tracy . . . . .Steamroller Productions, Inc., p. 300
Irwin, Erin . . . . .Jimmy Kimmel Live, p. 364
Irwin, Gary E. . . . . .9.14 Pictures, p. 43
Isaac, Margaret French . . . . . .Vanguard Films/Vanguard Animation, p. 328
Isaacs, Stanley . . . . .100% Entertainment, p. 38
Isaacson, Barry . . . . .Farrell Paura Productions, LLC, p. 130
Isaacson, Donna . . . . .Twentieth Century Fox, p. 322
Isaacson, Sara . . . . .Lifetime Television (Los Angeles), p. 198
Isenhour, Stacey . . . . .Cartoon Network, p. 84
Ishak, Sabrina Bonet . . . . .Fox Broadcasting Company, p. 139
Ishiyama, Shingo . . . . .Sony Pictures Television International, p. 296
Iso, Christine . . . . .Pacifica International Film & TV Corp,, p. 246
Israel, Amy . . . . .Paramount Vantage/Paramount Classics, p. 248
Israel, Jesse . . . . .Alcon Entertainment, LLC, p. 49
Israel, Mark . . . . .WilMark Entertainment, Inc., p. 341
Ivers, Jeff . . . . .Participant Productions, p. 249
Iverson, Timothy R. . . . . .Warner Bros. Animation, p. 334

Ivey, Laura . . . . .Odd Lot Entertainment, p. 241
Ivory, James . . . . .Merchant-Ivory, p. 215
Iwanyk, Basil . . . . .Thunder Road Pictures, p. 313
Iwata, Mary Ellen . . . . .Home & Garden Television (HGTV), p. 168
Izaac, Raymond . . . . .Gordonstreet Pictures, p. 150
Jabali, Renata . . . . .Fremantle Productions Latin America, p. 142
Jablin, David . . . . .Imagination Productions, Inc., p. 171
Jablonski, Sean . . . . .Nip/Tuck, p. 370
Jack, Brent . . . . .Mandate Pictures, p. 209
Jack, Nancy . . . . .What About Brian, p. 379
Jackman, Hugh . . . . .Seed Productions, p. 283
Jackovich, Karen G. . . . . .Sub Rosa Productions, Inc., p. 303
Jacks, Jim . . . . .Frelaine, p. 142
Jackson, Ariana . . . . .Andrew Lauren Productions, p. 195
Jackson, Brandi . . . . .Red Wagon Entertainment, p. 268
Jackson, Carly Rose . . . . .Epiphany Pictures, Inc., p. 126
Jackson, Curtis "50 Cent" . . . . .G-Unit Television & Films, p. 157
Jackson, Cynthia . . . . .PBS, p. 251
Jackson, Dallas . . . . .Davis Entertainment Company, p. 107
Jackson, Genise . . . . .Comedy Central, p. 98
Jackson, George . . . . .Camelot Entertainment Group, Inc., p. 82
Jackson, Hayes . . . . .According to Jim, p. 354
Jackson, Jennifer . . . . .Studios International, p. 303
Jackson, Marlon . . . . .Sci Fi Channel, p. 282
Jackson, Matt . . . . .Paramount Pictures Production Division, p. 248
Jackson, Michael . . . . .IAC/InterActiveCorp, p. 170
Jackson, Patti . . . . .Universal Pictures, p. 326
Jackson, Paul . . . . .Hell's Kitchen, p. 363
Jackson, Paul . . . . .Nanny 911, p. 369
Jackson, Paul . . . . .Farrell Paura Productions, LLC, p. 130
Jackson, Peter . . . . .WingNut Films Ltd., p. 342
Jackson, Peter E. . . . . .Evolving Pictures Entertainment, p. 128
Jackson, Read . . . . .Fox Sports Network, p. 140
Jackson, Sarah . . . . .Seven Summits Pictures & Management, p. 285
Jackson, Scott . . . . .Vin Di Bona Productions, p. 110
Jacobs, Doug . . . . .Court TV Networks, p. 102
Jacobs, Garrett . . . . .Krasnow Productions, p. 190
Jacobs, Holly . . . . .Fox Television Studios, p. 140
Jacobs, John . . . . .Smart Entertainment, p. 292
Jacobs, Josh . . . . .Electric Entertainment, p. 121
Jacobs, Katie . . . . .House, p. 363
Jacobs, Katie . . . . .Heel & Toe Films, p. 163
Jacobs, Mara . . . . .New Wave Entertainment, p. 235
Jacobs, Michael . . . . .MarVista Entertainment, p. 212
Jacobs, Rick . . . . .Lifetime Television (Los Angeles), p. 198
Jacobs, Shannon . . . . .CBS Corporation, p. 86
Jacobson, Danny . . . . .Infront Productions, p. 175
Jacobson, Janet . . . . .RHI Entertainment, p. 271
Jacobson, Joanne . . . . .Logo, p. 202
Jacobson, Lawrence S. . . . . .Grosso Jacobson Comm. Corp., p. 156
Jacobson, Marie . . . . .Sony Pictures Television International, p. 296
Jacobson, Scott . . . . .The Daily Show With Jon Stewart, p. 359
Jacobson, Tom .Tom Jacobson Productions, p. 179
Jacquemotte, Justin . . . . .Lawrence Bender Productions, p. 65
Jafari, Maher . . . . .The Edelstein Company, p. 119
Jaffa, Michael .Madison Road Entertainment, p. 206
Jaffe, Alix . . . . .CBS Entertainment, p. 86
Jaffe, Bob . . . . .Jaffilms, LLC, p. 179
Jaffe, Michael . . . . .Jaffe/Braunstein Films, LLC, p. 179
Jaffe, Sheila . . . . .Entourage, p. 360
Jaffe, Stanley R. . . . . .Jaffilms, LLC, p. 179
Jaffe, Susan . . . . .Desperate Housewives, p. 360
Jaffe, Toby . . . . .Original Film, p. 244
Jaffe, Wendy . . . . .Lionsgate, p. 200
Jaffin, Lindsey . . . . .Heel & Toe Films, p. 163
Jaglin, Mike . . . . .Comedy Time, p. 98
Jaglom, Henry . . . . .Rainbow Film Co./Rainbow Releasing, p. 265
Jalon, Hedi . . . . .Kopelson Entertainment, p. 189
Jam, Kia . . . . .Ascendant Pictures, p. 56
James, Caroline .Steven Bochco Productions, p. 70
James, Freddy . . . . .DIY Network, p. 113
James, Gavin . . . . .Intermedia Film Equities USA, Inc., p. 175
James, Jay . . . . .E! Networks, p. 117
James, Judith . . . . .Dreyfuss/James Productions, p. 117
James, Kevin . . . . .The King of Queens, p. 365
Jameson, Andrew . . . . .Maloof Productions, p. 208
Jameson, Jerry . . . . .Twentieth Television, p. 324
Jamieson, JJ . . . . .Last Straw Productions, p. 194
Jamieson, Tana Nugent . . . . .A&E Network, p. 44
Janicek, Jim . . . . .Janicek-Marino Creative, p. 179
Janis-Mashayekhi, Susan . . . . .Pink Sneakers Productions, p. 255
Jankowksi, Peter . . . . .Law & Order: Special Victims Unit, p. 367
Jankowksi, Peter . . . . .Law & Order: Criminal Intent, p. 367
Jankowski, Peter . . . . .Law & Order, p. 367
Jankowski, Peter . . . . .Wolf Films, Inc., p. 343
Jann, Michael Patrick . . . . .RENO 911!, p. 373
Jansen, Marc . . . . .The Gurin Company, p. 158
Jaquet, Brian . . . . .Sling Media, p. 291
Jarach, Lucas .Solo Entertainment Group, p. 294
Jarchow, Stephen P. . . . . .Regent, p. 269
Jarchow, Stephen P. . . . . .here! Networks, p. 165
Jaret, Adam . . . . .Jaret Entertainment, p. 180
Jaret, Seth . . . . .Jaret Entertainment, p. 180
Jarrett, Rikki . . . . .Muse Productions, Inc., p. 227
Jarzynski, Kevin . . . . .Kopelson Entertainment, p. 189
Jashni, John . . . . .Legendary Pictures, p. 195
Jaskulski, Gerald . . . . .America's Funniest Videos, p. 355
Jason, Jack . . . . .Solo One Productions, p. 294
Jason, Melinda . . . . .Melinda Jason Company, p. 180
Javerbaum, DJ . . . . .The Daily Show With Jon Stewart, p. 359
Jay, Chris Ann . . . . .Epiphany Pictures, Inc., p. 126
Jay, Lidia . . . . .Gorilla Pictures, p. 150
Jaysen, Peter . . . . .Moving Pictures, DPI, p. 223
Jean, Al . . . . .The Simpsons, p. 375
Jebb, Andrew . . . . .Nash Entertainment, p. 229
Jeffers, Lorelei . . . . .Touchstone Television, p. 316
Jeffers, Susannah . . . . .Twentieth Century Fox Television, p. 323
Jeffries, Janet . . . . .A Band Apart, p. 43
Jeffries, Janet . . . . .Lawrence Bender Productions, p. 65
Jelline, Moe . . . . .Tannenbaum Company, p. 308
Jenkel, Brad . . . . .Yari Film Group (YFG), p. 347
Jenkins, Chris . . . . .Universal Operations Group, p. 326
Jenkins, Jeff . . . . .Bunim/Murray Productions, Inc., p. 79
Jenkins, Jennifer . . . . .Lifetime Television (Los Angeles), p. 198
Jenkins, Jim . . . . .Lionsgate, p. 200
Jenkins, Stacey . . . . .VH1, p. 330
Jenkinson, Michael . . . . .Urban Entertainment, p. 327
Jenner, William . . . . .Chotzen/Jenner Productions, p. 90
Jennings, Michele L. . . . . .Hyperion Studio, p. 169
Jensen, Elsa . . . . .Darren Star Productions, p. 300
Jensen, Jesse . . . . .Survivor, p. 377
Jensen, Peter Aalbaek . . . . .Zentropa, p. 348
Jensen, Steven . . . . .Keep Clear, p. 186
Jerome, Al . . . . .KCET, p. 185
Jerou, Gaby . . . . .Southpaw Entertainment, p. 297
Jeser, Dave . . . . .Drawn Together, p. 360
Jeurgens, Kate . . . . .Disney ABC Cable Networks Group, p. 112
Jevons, Dan . . . . .Union Entertainment, p. 325
Jewison, Michael . . . . .Yorktown Productions, Ltd., p. 347
Jewison, Norman . . . . .Yorktown Productions, Ltd., p. 347
Jha, Manish . . . . .ESPN Original Entertainment (EOE), p. 127
Jin, Zhongqiang . . . . .China Film Group, p. 90
Jinks, Dan . . . . .Traveler, p. 377
Jinks, Dan . . . . .The Jinks/Cohen Company, p. 181
Jitner, Barbara Martinez . . . . .El Norte Productions, p. 121
Joblove, George . . . . .Sony Pictures Imageworks, p. 295
Jobs, Steven P. . . . . .Pixar Animation Studios, p. 256
Joe, Michael . . . . .Universal Pictures, p. 326
Joe, Steve . . . . .Notes From the Underbelly, p. 370
Joel, Richard . . . . .WildRice Productions, p. 341
Joffe, Adam . . . . .Sony Online Entertainment, p. 294
Joffe, Tatyana . . . . .QED International, p. 264
Johansmeier, Elissa . . . . .Fox Broadcasting Company, p. 139
John, Elton . . . . .Rocket Pictures Limited, p. 273
Johns, Paul A. . . . . .VanDerKloot Film & Television, p. 328
Johnsen, George . . . . .Threshold Entertainment, p. 313
Johnsen, Julie . . . . .Mandy Films, p. 209
Johnson, Ann . . . . .Twentieth Century Fox Television, p. 323
Johnson, Bob L. . . . . .Luna Ray Films, p. 204
Johnson, Brad . . . . .Watson Pond Productions, p. 336

Johnson, Bret .Universal Pictures, p. 326
Johnson, Bridget .Bridget Johnson Films, p. 182
Johnson, Broderick .Alcon Entertainment, LLC, p. 49
Johnson, Brooke Bailey .Food Network, p. 136
Johnson, Brown .Nickelodeon/MTVN Kids & Family Group, p. 237
Johnson, Bruce D. .PorchLight Entertainment, p. 259
Johnson, Bryce .Artists Production Group (APG), p. 56
Johnson, Casey .Happy Hour, p. 362
Johnson, Chas. Floyd .NCIS, p. 370
Johnson, Chas. Floyd .Charles Floyd Johnson Productions, p. 89
Johnson, Chas. Floyd .Belisarius Productions, p. 65
Johnson, Christina .The Mark Gordon Company, p. 150
Johnson, David .FremantleMedia North America, p. 142
Johnson, Dean .Real Time with Bill Maher, p. 372
Johnson, Dmitri M. .The Gotham Group, Inc., p. 151
Johnson, Don .Don Johnson Productions, p. 182
Johnson, Doug .Management 360, p. 208
Johnson, Elle .Ghost Whisperer, p. 362
Johnson, Eric M. .Asylum Entertainment, p. 57
Johnson, Fred .The Bold and the Beautiful, p. 356
Johnson, Henry .Warner Bros. Television Production, p. 335
Johnson, Jan .Laika Entertainment, p. 191
Johnson, Jeff .CrazyDreams Entertainment, p. 102
Johnson, Jennifer .Cold Case, p. 357
Johnson, Junie Lowry .Saved, p. 374
Johnson, Katie .Yari Film Group (YFG), p. 347
Johnson, Keith .Grosso Jacobson Comm. Corp., p. 156
Johnson, Kenneth .Kenneth Johnson Productions, p. 186
Johnson, Lance .Escape Artists II, p. 126
Johnson, Marcia .East of Doheny/Lexington Road Prod., p. 118
Johnson, Mark .Gran Via Productions, p. 152
Johnson, Mark S. .Twentieth Century Fox Television, p. 323
Johnson, Mike .Out of the Blue . . . Entertainment, p. 244
Johnson, Peter .Supernatural, p. 377
Johnson, Peter .Wonderland Sound and Vision, p. 344
Johnson, Richard R. .DC Comics, p. 108
Johnson, Robert L. .BET Networks, p. 66
Johnson, Robert W. .Buena Vista Motion Pictures Group, p. 78
Johnson, Ryan R. .Pretty Dangerous Films, p. 261
Johnson, Sandi .Hell's Kitchen, p. 363
Johnson, Sarah .Mark Victor Productions, p. 330
Johnson, Sheila K. .E! Networks, p. 117
Johnson, Sue .ABC Daytime, p. 44
Johnson, Susie .Girlfriends, p. 362
Johnson, Teresa .Universal Pictures, p. 326
Johnston, Gaby .FremantleMedia North America, p. 142
Johnston, Jesse .Thousand Words, p. 313
Johnston, Stephen R. .Goldcrest Films International, Inc., p. 149
Jolly, Susanna .And Then Productions, p. 51
Jonas, Robin .Tig Productions, Inc., p. 313
Jonas, Tony .Tony Jonas Productions, p. 182
Jones, Allison .The Office, p. 371
Jones, Amorette .IDT Entertainment, p. 171
Jones, Brandon .Landscape Entertainment, p. 193
Jones, Cameron .Fifty Cannon Entertainment, LLC, p. 131
Jones, Cosmo .Spacedog, p. 297
Jones, Dennis E. .Deja View Productions Ltd., p. 109
Jones, Doug .Walden Media, p. 333
Jones, Doug .Bristol Bay Productions, p. 76
Jones, Gary .Kinetic Filmworks, p. 188
Jones, Janine .SMG Productions, p. 292
Jones, Jina .Platinum Studios, LLC, p. 257
Jones, Joanna .Gold Circle Films, p. 148
Jones, Kathy .Shady Acres Entertainment, p. 285
Jones, Kathy .Shutt-Jones Productions, p. 287
Jones, Kenna .National Geographic Feature Films, p. 229
Jones, Khaki .Cartoon Network, p. 84
Jones, Kristin .Miramax Films, p. 217
Jones, Larry .Nickelodeon/MTVN Kids & Family Group, p. 237
Jones, Leandra .Arjay Entertainment, p. 55
Jones, Loretha .MTV Films, p. 225
Jones, Lynsey .Tom Jacobson Productions, p. 179
Jones, Monique .Sidney Kimmel Entertainment, p. 187
Jones, Pam .Reiner/Greisman, p. 269
Jones, Quincy .Mad TV, p. 368
Jones, Richard .CBS Corporation, p. 86
Jones, Ryan .State Street Pictures, p. 300
Jones, Sherwood .Tapestry Films, Inc., p. 308
Jones, Tina .Atlas Entertainment, p. 57
Jordan, Ashley .Tollin/Robbins Productions, p. 315
Jose, Kimberly .Jean Doumanian Productions, p. 115
Josefsberg, Lisa .Catapult Films, p. 85
Joseph, Rosalie .ABC Entertainment Television Group, p. 45
Josephson, Barry .Bones, p. 356
Josephson, Barry .Josephson Entertainment, p. 182
Josey, Bill .TOKYOPOP Inc., p. 315
Joskow, Suzanne .The Harris Company, p. 161
Jossen, Barry .Touchstone Television, p. 316
Josten, Walter .Blue Rider Pictures, p. 69
Joubert, Marc .LivePlanet, p. 201
Joung, Jinny .John Wells Productions, p. 338
Jovovich, Milla .Creature Entertainment, p. 103
Joyce, Jennifer .Mad TV, p. 368
Joyce, Sheena M. .9.14 Pictures, p. 43
Judah, Jeff .Sachs Judah Productions, p. 277
Judge, Jonathan .Judge-Belshaw Entertainment, Inc., p. 183
Judge, Mike .King of the Hill, p. 365
Juergens, Kate .ABC Family, p. 45
Jullian, Kara .Comedy Time, p. 98
Jun, Richard .CJ Entertainment America, p. 94
Jung, Doug .Big Love, p. 356
Juni, Susannah .New Line Cinema, p. 234
Jurgensen, Andy .Sidney Kimmel Entertainment, p. 187
Juris, Marc .Court TV Networks, p. 102
Jussim, Jared .Sony Pictures Entertainment, p. 295
Justice, Hardy .Tribeca Productions, p. 318
Justus, Matthew .Moxie Firecracker Films, p. 223
Juvonen, Nancy .Flower Films, Inc., p. 135
Kaam, Caroline .New Line Television, p. 235
Kabakow, Shara .MARTHA, p. 368
Kacandes, Georgia .Paramount Vantage/Paramount Classics, p. 248
Kadera, Mary .PBS, p. 251
Kadin, Heather .Warner Bros. Television Production, p. 335
Kadin, Jonathan .Columbia Pictures, p. 97
Kadison, Zak .Gold Circle Films, p. 148
Kadlec, Meredith .here! Networks, p. 165
Kaestle, Erika .My Name Is Earl, p. 369
Kagan, Russell .Proteus, p. 263
Kahane, Nathan .Mandate Pictures, p. 209
Kahane, Rob .The Collective, p. 96
Kahl, Kelly .CBS Entertainment, p. 86
Kahler, Clay .Grosso Jacobson Comm. Corp., p. 156
Kahn, Harvey .Front Street Pictures, Inc., p. 143
Kahn, Jenette .Double Nickel Entertainment, p. 115
Kahn, Jeremy .Kahn Power Pictures, p. 184
Kahn, Susan .Brainstorm Media, p. 72
Kahrs, Kenneth L. .Universal Studios, p. 326
Kalafatic, Helen .Laika Entertainment, p. 191
Kalagian, Terry .Cartoon Network, p. 84
Kalfus, Bryan .Offspring Entertainment, p. 241
Kaling, Mindy .The Office, p. 371
Kalle, Superna .Sony Pictures Television International, p. 296
Kalmacoff, Toni .di Bonaventura Pictures, Inc., p. 110
Kalos, Lauren .PBS, p. 251
Kalouria, Sheraton .Martha Stewart Living Omnimedia, Inc., p. 211
Kamen, Jon .@radical.media, p. 38
Kamin, Dianne .Nine Yards Entertainment, p. 238
Kamins, Ken .Key Creatives, LLC, p. 187
Kanaan, Greg .Red Dog Entertainment, p. 267
Kanalz III, Hank .DC Comics, p. 108
Kanaskae, Mindy .Studio 60 on the Sunset Strip, p. 376
Kane, Darren .Stone and Company Entertainment, p. 301
Kane, Linda Calabrese .Banyan Productions, p. 61
Kane, Steven .The Closer, p. 357
Kane-Ritsch, Julie .The Gotham Group, Inc., p. 151
Kang, Kourtney .How I Met Your Mother, p. 364
Kang, Peter .Twentieth Century Fox, p. 322
Kanner, Cynthia Davis .HBO Films, p. 162
Kanter, Nancy .Disney ABC Cable Networks Group, p. 112
Kantor, Jessica .Six Degrees, p. 375

Kanyuck, Scott . . . . . New Line Cinema, p. 234
Kapfer, Darius . . . . . S. Hirsch Company, Inc./Seemore Films, p. 167
Kaplan, Aaron . . . . . Kaplan/Perrone Entertainment, LLC, p. 184
Kaplan, Andy . . . . . Sony Pictures Television International, p. 296
Kaplan, Ashley . . . . . Current TV, LLC, p. 105
Kaplan, Avram Butch . . . . . Mase/Kaplan Productions, Inc., p. 212
Kaplan, Brad . . . . . Evolution Entertainment, p. 128
Kaplan, Christian . . . . . Twentieth Century Fox, p. 322
Kaplan, Dena . . . . . GSN, p. 157
Kaplan, Howard . . . . . Morgan Creek Productions, p. 221
Kaplan, Jill . . . . . Principal Entertainment, p. 262
Kaplan, Jonathan . . . . . Without a Trace, p. 379
Kaplan, Marcy . . . . . House, p. 363
Kaplan, Marjorie . . . . . Discovery Networks, U.S., p. 111
Kaplan, Neil . . . . . Trilogy Entertainment Group, p. 319
Kaplan, Paul . . . . . The George Lopez Show, p. 362
Kaplan, Paula . . . . . Nickelodeon/MTVN Kids & Family Group, p. 237
Kaplan, Rachel . . . . . Warner Bros. Television Production, p. 335
Kaplan, Steven G. . . . . . Rainstorm Entertainment, Inc., p. 265
Kaplan, Vic . . . . . Lucky Louie, p. 368
Kaplow, Lawrence . . . . . House, p. 363
Kapp, Lauren . . . . . NBC News, p. 230
Kappock, Kevin . . . . . LMNO Productions, p. 201
Kaprall, Mandy . . . . . Twentieth Century Fox Television, p. 323
Karamfilov, Krasimir . . . . . Zieger Productions, p. 349
Karas, Jay . . . . . Kanpai Pictures, p. 184
Karasick, Adam . . . . . Tree Line Film, p. 317
Karlin, Ben . . . . . The Colbert Report, p. 357
Karlin, Ben . . . . . The Daily Show With Jon Stewart, p. 359
Karlin, Ben . . . . . Busboy Productions, p. 81
Karlin, Marlise . . . . . Wild At Heart Films, LLC, p. 341
Karnes, David . . . . . CBS Paramount Network Television, p. 87
Karp, Scott . . . . . The Syndicate, p. 307
Karpen, Andrew . . . . . Focus Features/Rogue Pictures, p. 136
Karpf, Merrill . . . . . The Knights of Prosperity, p. 365
Karr, Gary . . . . . Law & Order, p. 367
Karsch, Andrew . . . . . Longfellow Pictures, p. 203
Karsh, Michael . . . . . National Geographic Kids' Prog. & Prod., p. 229
Kartun, Allan . . . . . Late Night with Conan O'Brien, p. 367
Karz, Mike . . . . . Generate, p. 145
Karzen, Rachel . . . . . E! Networks, p. 117
Kasanoff, Larry . . . . . Threshold Entertainment, p. 313
Kasdan, Jessica . . . . . Playtime Productions, p. 257
Kasdan, Sheldon . . . . . Universal Studios, p. 326
Kasha, Kevin . . . . . New Line Cinema, p. 234
Kasper, Pam . . . . . Ocean Pictures, p. 241
Kass, Robyn . . . . . The Bachelor, p. 355
Kassan, Adam . . . . . Paramount Vantage/Paramount Classics, p. 248
Kassar, Mario . . . . . C2 Pictures, p. 81
Kassen, Adam . . . . . Trigger Street Independent, p. 319
Kassen, Mark . . . . . Trigger Street Independent, p. 319
Kassov, Andrew . . . . . Platform Entertainment, p. 256
Kastenbaum, Michael . . . . . Zero Pictures, p. 349
Kastin, Alena . . . . . East of Doheny/Lexington Road Prod., p. 118
Kastner, Dillon . . . . . Cinema Seven Productions, p. 92
Kastner, Elliott . . . . . Cinema Seven Productions, p. 92
Kates, Gian Pablo . . . . . Telemundo Network, p. 310
Katims, Jason . . . . . Friday Night Lights, p. 361
Katsir, Jay . . . . . The Colbert Report, p. 357
Katsky, Tracy . . . . . Lucky Louie, p. 368
Katsumoto, Ken . . . . . Lionsgate, p. 200
Katz, Barry . . . . . Last Comic Standing, p. 366
Katz, Barry . . . . . New Wave Management, p. 236
Katz, Campbell . . . . . Marty Katz Productions, p. 185
Katz, Claudia . . . . . Rough Draft Studios, p. 276
Katz, David . . . . . Yahoo! Media Group/Yahoo! Studios, p. 347
Katz, Evan . . . . . 24, p. 353
Katz, Jeff . . . . . New Line Cinema, p. 234
Katz, Jon . . . . . Edward R. Pressman Film Corporation, p. 261
Katz, Jonathan . . . . . Turner Entertainment Group, p. 320
Katz, Lisa . . . . . Twentieth Century Fox Television, p. 323
Katz, Marty . . . . . Marty Katz Productions, p. 185
Katz, Robert F. . . . . . K2 Pictures, Inc., p. 184
Katz, Robert . . . . . Esparza-Katz Productions, p. 126
Katz, Robert . . . . . Amicus Entertainment Limited, p. 51
Katz, Stacy . . . . . CineCity Pictures, p. 91
Katzenberg, Jeffrey . . . . . DreamWorks Animation SKG, p. 116
Katzenberg, Jeffrey . . . . . DreamWorks SKG, p. 116
Katzman, Jon . . . . . Jon Katzman Productions, p. 185
Kaufer, Scott . . . . . 3 lbs., p. 353
Kauffman, Ken . . . . . MGA Ent./MGA Ent. Films, p. 216
Kaufman, Amy . . . . . Primary Productions, p. 261
Kaufman, Katherine . . . . . PorchLight Entertainment, p. 259
Kaufman, Kenneth . . . . . Patchett Kaufman Entertainment, p. 250
Kaufman, Lloyd . . . . . Troma Entertainment, Inc., p. 320
Kaufman, Mark S. . . . . . New Line Cinema, p. 234
Kaufman, Pam . . . . . Nickelodeon/MTVN Kids & Family Group, p. 237
Kaufman, Paul A. . . . . . The Kaufman Company, p. 185
Kaufman, Romy . . . . . Universal Pictures, p. 326
Kaufman, Victor . . . . . IAC/InterActiveCorp, p. 170
Kaufmann, David . . . . . Walden Media, p. 333
Kavanagh-Payne, Jo . . . . . Foothill Entertainment, Inc., p. 136
Kavanaugh, Ryan . . . . . Relativity Media LLC, p. 269
Kaviar, Brent . . . . . New Line Cinema, p. 234
Kawalec, J.C. . . . . . Twentieth Television, p. 324
Kawas, Lance K.R. . . . . . New Generation Films, Inc., p. 234
Kay, Douglas . . . . . Mondo Media, p. 220
Kay, Kevin . . . . . Spike TV, p. 298
Kaye, Josh . . . . . Cinema-Electric Inc., p. 92
Kaye, Martin L. . . . . . CBS Sports, p. 88
Kaz, Allison . . . . . The Biggest Loser, p. 356
Kazanjian, Howard . . . . . Tricor Entertainment, p. 318
Keach, James . . . . . Catfish Productions, p. 86
Keaney, Tom . . . . . The Late Late Show with Craig Ferguson, p. 366
Kearns, Deette . . . . . Focus Features/Rogue Pictures, p. 136
Keating, Shannon . . . . . Twentieth Television, p. 324
Keats, Laura . . . . . Go Girl Media, p. 147
Kecken, Joy . . . . . Standoff, p. 376
Kedas, Jeannie . . . . . MTV Networks, p. 226
Keegan, Jim . . . . . Lionsgate, p. 200
Keenan, Joe . . . . . Desperate Housewives, p. 360
Keeter, Tom . . . . . Sony Pictures Television International, p. 296
Keig, Chris . . . . . Warren Miller Entertainment, p. 335
Keitel, Harvey . . . . . The Goatsingers, p. 148
Keith, Richard . . . . . Catfish Productions, p. 86
Kellam, Laura A. . . . . . Goff-Kellam Productions, p. 148
Keller, Corinna . . . . . MTV Networks Latin America (MTVNLA), p. 226
Keller, David . . . . . Keller Entertainment Group, p. 186
Keller, Gayle . . . . . Six Degrees, p. 375
Keller, J.A. . . . . . Ember Entertainment Group, p. 122
Keller, Jaret . . . . . New Line Television, p. 235
Keller, Max . . . . . Keller Entertainment Group, p. 186
Keller, Micheline . . . . . Keller Entertainment Group, p. 186
Keller, Steve . . . . . Nickelodeon/MTVN Kids & Family Group, p. 237
Kellet, Gloria Calderon . . . . . How I Met Your Mother, p. 364
Kelley, Bill . . . . . Jimmy Kimmel Live, p. 364
Kelley, David E. . . . . . Boston Legal, p. 357
Kelley, David E. . . . . . David E. Kelley Productions, p. 186
Kelley, John C. . . . . . NCIS, p. 370
Kelley, John . . . . . USA Network, p. 327
Kelley, John C. . . . . . Belisarius Productions, p. 65
Kelley, Kirk . . . . . Laika Entertainment, p. 191
Kellison, Daniel . . . . . Jackhole Industries, p. 178
Kellman, Samson . . . . . Epiphany Pictures, Inc., p. 126
Kellner, Melissa . . . . . Sony Pictures Television, p. 296
Kelloway, Krista . . . . . Brightlight Pictures, Inc., p. 75
Kelly, Ann . . . . . TAE Productions/Medeacom Productions, p. 307
Kelly, Audrey . . . . . Fade In Films, p. 129
Kelly, Brendan . . . . . New Line Television, p. 235
Kelly, Chris . . . . . The Singles Table, p. 375
Kelly, Jen . . . . . Double Nickel Entertainment, p. 115
Kelly, Justin . . . . . Seven Arts Pictures, p. 285
Kelly, Kristen . . . . . VH1, p. 330
Kelly, Michael . . . . . POW! Entertainment, p. 260
Kelly, Patrick . . . . . Turner Network Television (TNT), p. 321
Kelly, Patrick . . . . . TBS, p. 309
Kelly, Tracy Ann . . . . . The Bold and the Beautiful, p. 356
Kelly-Brown, Kathy . . . . . NBC Universal Corporate, p. 231
Kelso, Meegan . . . . . MBST Entertainment, Inc., p. 213
Kelty, Ellen . . . . . Norman Twain Productions, p. 322

Kemezis, Nikki ... TV Guide Channel, p. 321
Kemp, Barry ... Bungalow 78 Productions, p. 79
Kenchelian, Mark ... Walt Disney Television Animation, p. 113
Kendig, Patricia ... Columbia Pictures, p. 97
Kendrick, Katherine ... DreamWorks Animation SKG, p. 116
Kenealy, Heather ... CastleBright Studios, p. 85
Kennar, Larry ... The L Word, p. 366
Kennar, Larry ... Code Entertainment, p. 96
Kennedy, Donald ... Columbia Pictures, p. 97
Kennedy, Ilene ... Court TV Networks, p. 102
Kennedy, John ... Epiphany Pictures, Inc., p. 126
Kennedy, Kathleen ... The Kennedy/Marshall Company, p. 186
Kennedy, Lora ... Warner Bros. Pictures, p. 334
Kennedy, Maria ... Discovery Networks, U.S., p. 111
Kennedy, Rory ... Moxie Firecracker Films, p. 223
Kennedy, Steve A. ... Daniel L. Paulson Productions, p. 251
Kenney, Brendan ... American Zoetrope, p. 51
Kenney, Gordon ... Tri-Elite Entertainment, Ltd., p. 319
Kenney-Silver, Kerri ... RENO 911!, p. 373
Kenny, Jack ... In Case of Emergency, p. 364
Kenny, Simon ... Warner Bros. Digital Distribution, p. 334
Kenshole, Fiona ... Laika Entertainment, p. 191
Kent, Alainee ... Recorded Picture Company, p. 266
Kent, Billy ... The AV Club, p. 58
Kent, Linda L. ... Grossbart Kent Productions, p. 156
Kent, Philip ... Turner Entertainment Group, p. 320
Kent, Steven ... Sony Pictures Television International, p. 296
Kenwright, Bill ... Kenwright USA/Bill Kenwright Ltd., p. 186
Kenyon, Heather ... Cartoon Network, p. 84
Kephart, Taylor ... Lynda Obst Productions, p. 241
Kerchner, Rob ... Capital Arts Entertainment, p. 83
Kerew, Diana ... Diana Kerew Productions, p. 186
Kerger, Paula ... PBS, p. 251
Kerkeniakova, Teodora ... River Road Entertainment, p. 272
Kerner, Jordan ... The Kerner Entertainment Company, p. 187
Kernis, Lee ... Brillstein-Grey Entertainment, p. 75
Kerr, Alex ... Shady Acres Entertainment, p. 285
Kerrigan, Sheila ... Ascendant Pictures, p. 56
Kershaw, Jamie ... DreamWorks SKG, p. 116
Kertes, Kevin ... New Line Cinema, p. 234
Keshishian, Aleen ... Brillstein-Grey Entertainment, p. 75
Kessel, Robert ... Hart Sharp Entertainment, Inc., p. 161
Kesselman, Josh ... Principal Entertainment, p. 262
Kessler, Carolyn ... Concrete Entertainment, p. 99
Kessler, Gary ... Euphoria Entertainment, p. 127
Kessler, Todd ... The Unit, p. 378
Kessll, Brad ... Gold Circle Films, p. 148
Ketabi, Afshin ... Casey Silver Productions, p. 289
Ketai, Ben ... Ghost House Pictures, p. 145
Ketai, Ben ... Renaissance Pictures, p. 270
Ketcham, Jerry ... Buena Vista Motion Pictures Group, p. 78
Ketcham, John ... Ketcham Films, p. 187
Ketterman, Angie ... MARTHA, p. 368
Kettner, Carla ... Vanished, p. 378
Ketvertis, George ... SMG Productions, p. 292
Kewley, Michael ... Law & Order: Criminal Intent, p. 367
Khachaturian, Teni ... The Weinstein Company, p. 337
Khan, Nulmulchka ... American Dad, p. 354
Khanna, Jai ... Brillstein-Grey Entertainment, p. 75
Kidd, Mark ... Graymark Productions Inc., p. 153
Kidman, Nicole ... Blossom Films, p. 68
Kienzle, Brandon ... Wardenclyffe Entertainment, p. 333
Kiernan, Peter ... Management 360, p. 208
Kikumoto, Jan ... Capital Arts Entertainment, p. 83
Kiley, Mike ... TOKYOPOP Inc., p. 315
Kilgariff, Karen ... The Ellen DeGeneres Show, p. 360
Killilea, Kim ... Nickelodeon/MTVN Kids & Family Group, p. 237
Killion, Brandon ... Original Productions, p. 244
Killion, Justin ... Kaplan/Perrone Entertainment, LLC, p. 184
Kim, Andrew ... The Weinstein Company, p. 337
Kim, Anna ... Four Boys Films, p. 138
Kim, Chris ... @radical.media, p. 38
Kim, Christina ... Lost, p. 368
Kim, Clara ... Untitled Entertainment, p. 327
Kim, Elizabeth ... Lionsgate, p. 200
Kim, Helen Lee ... Mandate Pictures, p. 209
Kim, Jae ... The Mark Gordon Company, p. 150
Kim, Ji-Yeon ... LJ Film, p. 201
Kim, Joseph ... Paulist Productions, p. 250
Kim, Kari ... Worldwide Biggies, p. 346
Kim, Laura ... Warner Independent Pictures, p. 335
Kim, Peggy ... The History Channel, p. 167
Kim, So-Hee ... LJ Film, p. 201
Kim, Ted ... CJ Entertainment America, p. 94
Kimball, Charlie ... Pretty Pictures, p. 261
Kimball, Scott ... 6 Pictures, p. 42
Kimmel, Jimmy ... Jimmy Kimmel Live, p. 364
Kimmel, Jimmy ... Jackhole Industries, p. 178
Kimmel, Sidney ... Sidney Kimmel Entertainment, p. 187
Kimmett, Deborah ... David Brady Productions, p. 72
Kinberg, Mali ... Mandate Pictures, p. 209
Kindberg, Ann ... Sleeper Cell, p. 375
Kinder, Jeff ... VanDerKloot Film & Television, p. 328
King, Alex ... Keller Entertainment Group, p. 186
King, Crystal ... Picturehouse, p. 254
King, Curt ... NBC Universal Television Studio, p. 231
King, Dave ... Last Call with Carson Daly, p. 366
King, Ed ... Rocket Pictures Limited, p. 273
King, Graham ... Initial Entertainment Group, p. 175
King, Jack ... Water Channel, p. 336
King, Jeff ... Kidnapped, p. 365
King, Jeff F. ... The Black Donnellys, p. 356
King, Jonathan ... Focus Features/Rogue Pictures, p. 136
King, Marc Thomas ... HBO Films, p. 162
King, Nicole ... Management 360, p. 208
King, Rob ... Braverman Productions, Inc., p. 73
King, Robin ... King World Productions, Inc., p. 188
King, Roger ... King World Productions, Inc., p. 188
King, Tracy ... Late Night with Conan O'Brien, p. 367
Kinnally, Jon ... In Case of Emergency, p. 364
Kinney-Sterns, Endyia ... BET Networks, p. 66
Kirby, Lynne ... Sundance Channel, p. 304
Kirch, Susan ... DisneyToon Studios, p. 113
Kirchen, Bill ... The Montecito Picture Company, p. 220
Kirhoffer, John ... Survivor, p. 377
Kirk, Alicia ... Without a Trace, p. 379
Kirk, Michael ... Renaissance Pictures, p. 270
Kirk, Michael ... Ghost House Pictures, p. 145
Kirk, Robert ... Digital Ranch Productions, p. 110
Kirkwood, Gene ... Interscope/Shady/Aftermath Films, p. 176
Kirland, Moira ... Medium, p. 369
Kirman, Roger ... Touchstone Television, p. 316
Kirsch, Rebecca ... Electric Entertainment, p. 121
Kirschenbaum, Jeffrey ... Universal Pictures, p. 326
Kirschner, David ... David Kirschner Productions, p. 188
Kirsh, Debbie ... Comedy Central, p. 98
Kirshbaum, Jeff ... Cafe Productions, p. 81
Kirshen, Ames ... Marvel Studios, Inc., p. 211
Kirshenbaum, Susan ... Days of Our Lives, p. 359
Kirshner, Rebecca Rand ... Gilmore Girls, p. 362
Kirtman, Nate ... NBC Entertainment, p. 230
Kirven, Cindy ... Endgame Entertainment, p. 124
Kisilevsky, Lauren ... Type A Films, p. 325
Kitchens, Craig ... Camelot Entertainment Group, Inc., p. 82
Kitsis, Edward ... Lost, p. 368
Kitt, Sam ... Sam Kitt/Future Films, p. 188
Kittle, T. L. ... Renfield Productions, p. 270
Kivowitz, Courtney ... Benderspink, p. 66
Kiwitt, Sidney ... Lotus Pictures, p. 203
Klainberg, Lesli ... Orchard Films, p. 243
Klaits, Elyse ... The Kennedy/Marshall Company, p. 186
Klamert, Ron ... TOKYOPOP Inc., p. 315
Klarik, Jeffrey ... The Class, p. 357
Klarman, Jason ... Bravo, p. 74
Klarman, Jason ... NBC Universal Cable Entertainment, p. 231
Klasky, Arlene ... Klasky Csupo, Inc., p. 189
Klawitter, Michael ... Bregman Productions, p. 75
Kleberg, Fredrick A. ... Exxcell Entertainment, Inc./Exxcell Films, p. 129
Klehm, Kit ... 6 Pictures, p. 42
Kleiman, Alana ... Twentieth Century Fox Television, p. 323

Klein, Alan .The Independent Film Channel (IFC), p. 173
Klein, Amanda .Pariah, p. 249
Klein, Beth .The L Word, p. 366
Klein, Beth .Showtime Networks Inc., p. 287
Klein, Fred .Village Roadshow Pictures, p. 331
Klein, Gene .Hypnotic, p. 170
Klein, Howard .King of the Hill, p. 365
Klein, Howard .The Office, p. 371
Klein, Howard .3 Arts Entertainment, Inc., p. 40
Klein, Jennifer .Apartment 3B Productions, p. 53
Klein, JJ .21 Laps Entertainment, p. 38
Klein, Joanna .Regency Television, p. 269
Klein, Lizzy .Good Kop Films, p. 149
Klein, Marci .Saturday Night Live, p. 373
Klein, Marci .30 Rock, p. 353
Klein, Michael .Discovery Networks, U.S., p. 111
Klein, Michael .The Axelrod/Edwards Company, p. 59
Klein, Ray .Norsemen Television Productions, LLC, p. 239
Klein, Sharon .Twentieth Century Fox Television, p. 323
Kleinbart, Philip .Robert Greenwald Productions, p. 153
Kleinberg, Joe .Odd Lot Entertainment, p. 241
Kleiner, Jeremy .Plan B Entertainment, p. 256
Kleinerman, Brad .DisneyToon Studios, p. 113
Kleinman, Joe .Star Entertainment Group, Inc., p. 299
Klemann, Gwen .P.A.T. Productions, p. 250
Klemmer, Phil .Veronica Mars, p. 378
Klewans, Margo .SekretAgent Productions, p. 283
Klibansky, Andrei .Red Wagon Entertainment, p. 268
Klibansky, Natasha .The Ladd Company, p. 191
Klick, Michael .24, p. 353
Kligman, Barbie .Hidden Palms, p. 363
Kline, Gerry .Platinum Studios, LLC, p. 257
Kline, Robert D. .TAE Productions/Medeacom Productions, p. 307
Kline, Wayne .Farrell Paura Productions, LLC, p. 130
Klingenstein, Alan .Filbert Steps Productions, p. 131
Klinsport, Brian .Incognito Entertainment, p. 173
Kliot, Jason .Deutsch/Open City Films, p. 109
Kliot, Jason .HDNet Films, p. 163
Klores, Dan .Shoot the Moon Productions, p. 286
Klubien, Jorgen .Laika Entertainment, p. 191
Kluft, Stephanie .Sidney Kimmel Entertainment, p. 187
Knell, Gary E. .Sesame Workshop, p. 285
Knight, Eric .And Then Productions, p. 51
Knight, Sari .Close to Home, p. 357
Knizek, Craig .Nuance Productions, p. 240
Knobloch, Iris .Warner Bros. Entertainment Inc., p. 334
Knoller, David .Big Love, p. 356
Knox, Travis .Storyline Entertainment, p. 302
Knutsen, Janet .Boston Legal, p. 357
Koa, Jonathan .NBC Universal Television Studio, p. 231
Kobayashi, Junko .POW! Entertainment, p. 260
Kobayashi, Yuka .POW! Entertainment, p. 260
Koch, Chris .Reason Pictures, p. 266
Koch, Jonathan .Asylum Entertainment, p. 57
Koch-Stone, Alexandra .Paramount Pictures Production Division, p. 248
Kocsis, Tom .Conundrum Entertainment, p. 100
Koczara, Alexis Frank .The Singles Table, p. 375
Koechner, David .Naked Trucker & T-Bones, p. 369
Koenen, Kimberly .Craftsman Films, p. 102
Koenig, Kip .Grey's Anatomy, p. 362
Koenigsberg, Neil .Asls Productions, p. 57
Koffler, Pamela .Killer Films, Inc., p. 187
Koga, Dave .Comedy Central, p. 98
Koh, Charlotte .Twentieth Century Fox - Searchlight Pictures, p. 323
Kohan, David .KoMut Entertainment, p. 189
Kohl, Pam .3 Arts Entertainment, Inc., p. 40
Kohn, Michael .GSN, p. 157
Kohn, Sharon Lester .Rainbow Film Co./Rainbow Releasing, p. 265
Kohorn, Larry .Columbia Pictures, p. 97
Kois, Dan .Scott Rudin Productions, p. 277
Kolar, Susan .Sesame Workshop, p. 285
Kolb, Ken .Twentieth Television, p. 324
Kolb, Leslie .Tom Jacobson Productions, p. 179
Kolbrenner, Adam .Madhouse Entertainment, p. 206
Kolde, Kevin .Frederator Studios, p. 141
Kolker, Samantha .di Bonaventura Pictures, Inc., p. 110
Koll, David .Platinum Studios, LLC, p. 257
Koll, P.J. .The Artists' Colony, p. 56
Kollappallil, Patricia .Animal Planet, p. 52
Kolodner, Eva .Salty Features, p. 278
Koltai-Levine, Marian .Picturehouse, p. 254
Komarnicki, Todd .Guy Walks Into a Bar, p. 158
Komesar, Lloyd .Buena Vista Television, p. 79
Komodikis, Maria .A&E Network, p. 44
Kong, Bill .EDKO Films Ltd., p. 120
Konialian, Elise .Untitled Entertainment, p. 327
Konigsberg, Frank .The Konigsberg-Smith Company, p. 189
Konner, Jenni .Help Me Help You, p. 363
Konop, Kelli .Mandate Pictures, p. 209
Konrad, Cathy .Tree Line Film, p. 317
Konwiser, Kern .Konwiser Brothers, p. 189
Konwiser, Kip .Konwiser Brothers, p. 189
Konzelman, Chuck .Numenorean Films, p. 240
Koondel, Scott .CBS Paramount Worldwide Television Dist., p. 88
Koonin, Steve .Turner Network Television (TNT), p. 321
Koonin, Steve .TBS, p. 309
Koops, Mark .30 Days, p. 353
Koops, Mark .The Biggest Loser, p. 356
Koops, Mark .Reveille, LLC, p. 270
Koornick, Jason .Eye in the Sky Entertainment, p. 129
Kopelevich, Roman .Bleiberg Entertainment, p. 68
Kopelman, Dan .Big Day, p. 355
Kopeloff, Eric .Gotham Entertainment Group, p. 150
Kopelson, Anne .Kopelson Entertainment, p. 189
Kopelson, Arnold .Kopelson Entertainment, p. 189
Kopelson, Evan .Kopelson Entertainment, p. 189
Kopf, Megan .MSNBC, p. 225
Kopf, Megan .NBC News, p. 230
Koplin, Sarah .Centropolis Entertainment, p. 88
Koplovitz, Elysa .Good Kop Films, p. 149
Koppel, Ted .Discovery Channel, p. 111
Koppel, Ted .Discovery Networks, U.S., p. 111
Korda, Cathy .ABC Entertainment Television Group, p. 45
Kordestani, Ronak .The Gotham Group, Inc., p. 151
Korerat, Barrett .Circle of Confusion Productions, p. 93
Korn, Barbra .Untitled Entertainment, p. 327
Kornblau, Craig .Universal Pictures, p. 326
Korson, Richard .The Colbert Report, p. 357
Korson, Richard .Busboy Productions, p. 81
Korzon, Kelly .Waltzing Clouds, Inc., p. 333
Kosberg, Robert .Nash Entertainment, p. 229
Kosberg, Robert .Robert Kosberg Productions, p. 190
Kosinski, Geyer .Media Talent Group, p. 214
Kosner, John .ESPN Original Entertainment (EOE), p. 127
Kosove, Andrew A. .Alcon Entertainment, LLC, p. 49
Kosse, David .Universal Pictures, p. 326
Kostanian, Shawn .7th Heaven, p. 353
Koster, Dorothy .Jon Voight Entertainment, p. 331
Koster, Dorothy .Crystal Sky Pictures, LLC, p. 104
Koster, Iren .Silvers/Koster Productions, Inc., p. 289
Koster, Jan A. .The Woofenill Works, Inc., p. 344
Kostura, Annmarie .NBC Entertainment, p. 230
Kotcheff, Ted .Law & Order: Special Victims Unit, p. 367
Kotcheff, Ted .Wolf Films, Inc., p. 343
Koth, David .Untitled Entertainment, p. 327
Kouf, Jim .Ghost Whisperer, p. 362
Koules, Oren .Two and a Half Men, p. 378
Koules, Oren .Evolution Entertainment, p. 128
Kounelias, Christina .New Line Cinema, p. 234
Kousakas, John .Hidden Palms, p. 363
Kousakis, Anastasia .SenArt Films, p. 284
Kovacevich, Igor .Tule River Films, p. 320
Kovacs, Debbie .Walden Media, p. 333
Koyatch, Louis .Silvers/Koster Productions, Inc., p. 289
Krabach, Caroline .Jimmy Kimmel Live, p. 364
Kraemer, Joanne .Bryan Hickox Pictures, Inc., p. 166
Krafft, Laura .The Colbert Report, p. 357
Kraft, Robert .Twentieth Century Fox, p. 322
Krainin, Julian .Krainin Productions, Inc., p. 190
Krakower, Susan .CNBC, p. 96

Krakowsky, Shinaan .Greystone Television and Films, p. 154
Kraman, Kyla .Marvel Studios, Inc., p. 211
Kramer, Andrew .Dimension Films, p. 111
Kramer, James .Sony Pictures Television International, p. 296
Kramer, Jeremy .DreamWorks SKG, p. 116
Kramer, Jon .Rive Gauche Entertainment, p. 272
Kramer, Larry .CBS Entertainment, p. 86
Kramer, Lee .Bull's Eye Entertainment, p. 79
Kramer, Max .H2F Entertainment, p. 158
Krane, Jonathan D. .The Jonathan Krane Group, p. 190
Krane, Joshua .G4 TV, p. 144
Krantz, Tony .Flame Ventures LLC, p. 135
Kranzler, Eric .Management 360, p. 208
Krask, Sylvia J. .Buena Vista Motion Pictures Group, p. 78
Krasno, John .Stick Figure Productions, p. 301
Krasnoff, Russ .Krasnoff Foster Productions, p. 190
Krasnow, Stuart .Average Joe, p. 355
Krasnow, Stuart .Krasnow Productions, p. 190
Krasnow, Stuart .FremantleMedia North America, p. 142
Krastins, Gints .Sneak Preview Entertainment, Inc., p. 293
Kraus, James .Carsey-Werner Films, p. 84
Krause, Mitchell .MM Productions, p. 218
Krause, Robin .Sub Rosa Productions, Inc., p. 303
Krauss, Andrea .here! Networks, p. 165
Krauss, Christina Avis .Grosso Jacobson Comm. Corp., p. 156
Krauss, Jonathan .Columbia Pictures, p. 97
Kravas, Khristina .Groundswell Production, p. 156
Kravetz, Andy .John Fogel Entertainment Group, p. 182
Kravitz, Bill .Rough Diamond Productions, p. 276
Kravitz, Miriam .Alan David Management, p. 107
Kregness, Lisa .Constantin Film Dev., Inc./Constantin TV, p. 100
Kreisberg, Andrew .Boston Legal, p. 357
Kreisberg, Stacy .Fox Television Studios, p. 140
Kreischer, Kottie .The Collective, p. 96
Krentzin, Thomas .New Concorde, p. 233
Kressel, Lynn .Law & Order: Criminal Intent, p. 367
Kressel, Lynn .Law & Order, p. 367
Kretzmer, Maggie .Two Sticks Productions, p. 325
Krevoy, Brad .Motion Picture Corporation of America, p. 222
Krikorian, Blake .Sling Media, p. 291
Krikorian, Jason .Sling Media, p. 291
Krim, Rick .VH1, p. 330
Kring, Tim .Heroes, p. 363
Kring, Tim .Crossing Jordan, p. 358
Krinsky, David .King of the Hill, p. 365
Kriozere, Steven .NCIS, p. 370
Kripke, Eric .Supernatural, p. 377
Kripner, Stephen .Taurus Entertainment Company, p. 309
Krislovich, Danica .Madison Road Entertainment, p. 206
Krist, Joshua .Drawn Together, p. 360
Kristol, Mark .Sidney Kimmel Entertainment, p. 187
Kritzer, Carol .CSI: Crime Scene Investigation, p. 358
Kritzer, Carol .Battlestar Galactica, p. 355
Kritzer, Eddie .Linkletter/Kritzer, p. 199
Krochmal, Jenny .Prometheus Entertainment, p. 263
Kroeger, Lindsey .Masters of Horror, p. 368
Krofft, Marty .Sid & Marty Krofft Pictures Corporation, p. 190
Krofft, Sid .Sid & Marty Krofft Pictures Corporation, p. 190
Kroll, Jon .New Line Cinema, p. 234
Kroll, Jon .New Line Television, p. 235
Kromwell, Chloe .Hella Good Moving Pictures, p. 164
Krone, Steve .Village Roadshow Pictures, p. 331
Kronish, Stephen .24, p. 353
Kroopf, Sandy .Saved, p. 374
Kroopf, Scott .Intermedia Film Equities USA, Inc., p. 175
Kroopnick, Steve .Triage Entertainment, p. 317
Krost, Roy .World Film Services, Inc., p. 345
Krueger, Clayton .FX, p. 144
Kruger, Ehren .Bobker/Kruger Films, p. 70
Krumm, Michelle .The Weinstein Company, p. 337
Krupat, Michael .City Lights Media Group, p. 94
Krupp, Philip M. .Braun Entertainment Group, Inc., p. 73
Krushel, Kenneth .Proteus, p. 263
Kubena, Kent .2929 Productions, p. 40
Kubitz, Andy .CBS Entertainment, p. 86
Kubsch, Chris .Lucasfilm Ltd., p. 203
Kucenski, Tony .Rupert Productions, Inc., p. 277
Kuciak, Michael .AEI-Atchity Entertainment Intl., Inc., p. 47
Kucserka, Sarah .Ugly Betty, p. 378
Kudrow, Lisa .Is Or Isn't Entertainment, p. 177
Kuehnert, Fred T. .Fred Kuehnert Productions, p. 190
Kuffa, Kevin .Six Degrees, p. 375
Kughn, Richard .Longbow Productions, p. 203
Kuhl, Chris .Marc Platt Productions, p. 257
Kuhlman, Reenie .Discovery Health Channel, p. 111
Kuhn, Adam .Silver Pictures, p. 289
Kuhn, Michael .Qwerty Films, p. 264
Kuhn, Tom .Weintraub/Kuhn Productions, p. 338
Kujawski, Peter .Focus Features/Rogue Pictures, p. 136
Kukoff, David .JTN Productions, p. 183
Kukucka, Jim .The King of Queens, p. 365
Kulchak, Kelly .Psych, p. 372
Kulchak, Kelly .Tagline Pictures, p. 307
Kulikowski, Chris .Element Films, p. 121
Kulzer, Robert .Constantin Film Dev., Inc./Constantin TV, p. 100
Kun, Hilary .The Daily Show With Jon Stewart, p. 359
Kun, Stephanie .The Tyra Banks Show, p. 378
Kunath, Pam .Columbia Pictures, p. 97
Kunath, Pam .Screen Gems, p. 283
Kunde, Ben .The O.C., p. 371
Kung, Steven .Edward Saxon Productions (ESP), p. 280
Kunis, Marc .TMC Entertainment, p. 314
Kunisada, Megumi .Bang Zoom! Entertainment, p. 61
Kunstler, Bill .The War at Home, p. 379
Kuperberg, Frederick .Disney ABC Cable Networks Group, p. 112
Kupetz, Dan .CBS Paramount Network Television, p. 87
Kupfer, Jerry .30 Rock, p. 353
Kurian, Anil .Intrepid Pictures, p. 176
Kurian, Asha .Pfeffer Film, p. 253
Kurland, Kim Fitzgerald .Fox Broadcasting Company, p. 139
Kuroda, Andee .Kanpai Pictures, p. 184
Kurrasch, Anne .Showtime Networks Inc., p. 287
Kurta, Paul .Veronica Mars, p. 378
Kurtz, Gary .Harding-Kurtz Entertainment, p. 160
Kurtzman, Alex .Kurtzman/Orci, p. 191
Kurtzman, Howard .Twentieth Century Fox Television, p. 323
Kurzweil, Jordan .AOL Media Networks, p. 53
Kushell, Bob .In Case of Emergency, p. 364
Kushman, Elizabeth .Kadokawa Pictures USA, p. 184
Kushner, Donald .Junction Films, p. 183
Kutkauskaite, Marcele .Laurence Mark Productions, p. 210
Kutner, Rob .The Daily Show With Jon Stewart, p. 359
Kutney, Sara .Odd Lot Entertainment, p. 241
Kuzon, Tiffany .Evolution Entertainment, p. 128
Kwak, Rick .ContentFilm, p. 100
Kwapis, Ken .In Cahoots, p. 173
Kwolek, Jean .Handprint Entertainment, p. 160
Kyber, Casey .Twentieth Century Fox Television, p. 323
Kyle, Brenda .Touchstone Television, p. 316
Kyle, Craig .Marvel Studios, Inc., p. 211
Kyle, Liisa .Sparky Pictures, p. 297
La Maina, Francis .dick clark productions, inc., p. 94
La Padura, Jason .Crossing Jordan, p. 358
La Padura, Jason .Heroes, p. 363
La Salle, Eriq .Humble Journey Films, p. 169
Labbe, Rico .MRB Productions, Inc., p. 224
LaBelle, Betty .Touchstone Television, p. 316
LaBelle, Rob .Infinity Features Entertainment, p. 174
Labunka, Iya .Buena Vista Motion Pictures Group, p. 78
Lacey, Lorene .Twilight Pictures, Inc., p. 324
Lacey, Scarlett .Robert Cort Productions, p. 101
Lacey, Theophilus .Program Partners, p. 262
Lachaud, Dorothée .Bonne Pioche, p. 71
Lacheim, Ken .Morningstar Entertainment, p. 221
Lachmund, Hank .Warner Bros. Television Production, p. 335
Lachniet, Todd .Norsemen Television Productions, LLC, p. 239
Lacy, Phillip .American Blackguard, Inc., p. 50
Lacy, Robert .Intermedia Film Equities USA, Inc., p. 175
Ladd Jr., Alan .The Ladd Company, p. 191
Ladd, David .David Ladd Films, p. 191

Ladd, Diane . . . . .Exxcell Entertainment, Inc./Exxcell Films, p. 129
LaDuke, Dee . . . . .Girlfriends, p. 362
Lafazia, Alex .Tollin/Robbins Productions, p. 315
Laffin, Stephanie . . . . .House, p. 363
LaFortune, Victoria . . . . .Touchstone Television, p. 316
Lai, Anne . . . . .Scott Free Productions, p. 282
Lai, Jeffrey R. . . . . .Disney ABC Cable Networks Group, p. 112
Laiblin, Kristel . . . . .Strike Entertainment, p. 303
Laikin, Daniel S. . . . . .National Lampoon, p. 230
Laikind, Daniel . . . . .Stick Figure Productions, p. 301
Laing, Stephanie Cone . . . . .Takes On Productions, p. 308
Lajeski, Glen . . . . .Buena Vista Motion Pictures Group, p. 78
Lakin-Hutcherson, Lori . . . . .All of Us, p. 354
Lam, Aaron . . . . .Buckaroo Entertainment, p. 78
Lam, Rose . . . . .The L Word, p. 366
Lamal, Andre . . . . .Lakeshore Entertainment Group LLC, p. 192
Lamar, Gina . . . . .CSI: Miami, p. 358
Lamba, Sanjeev . . . . .Dimension Films, p. 111
Lambert, Bob . . . . .Buena Vista Motion Pictures Group, p. 78
Lambert, John . . . . .Regent, p. 269
Lambert, Stephen . . . . .RDF Media, p. 266
Lambert, Stephen . . . . .Wife Swap, p. 379
Lamberth, Josie .Jeff Wald Entertainment, p. 180
Lambeth, Welch . . . . .L.I.F.T. Productions, p. 191
Lammi, Edward . . . . .Sony Pictures Television, p. 296
LaMont, Alfredo . . . . .Relevant Entertainment Group, p. 270
Lamontagne, Linda . . . . .Family Guy, p. 361
Lamontagne, Linda . . . . .American Dad, p. 354
LaMonte, Lou . . . . .Intl. Television Group (ITG) - Epix Films, p. 176
Lampert, Jeffrey . . . . .Village Roadshow Pictures, p. 331
Lampitoc, Emerlynn . . . . .Edmonds Entertainment, p. 120
Lampley, Bree Walker . . . . .Crystal Spring Productions, Inc., p. 104
Lampley, Jim . . . . .Crystal Spring Productions, Inc., p. 104
Lamprecht, Ron . . . . .NBC Universal Cable Entertainment, p. 231
Lan, Tian . . . . .Paramount Pictures Production Division, p. 248
Lancaster, Barbara . . . . .Turner Network Television (TNT), p. 321
Lancaster, Barbara . . . . .TBS, p. 309
Lancaster, David . . . . .Bold Films, p. 71
Lancaster, David . . . . .David Lancaster Productions, p. 192
Lancaster, Laura . . . . .NBC Universal Television Studio, p. 231
Lance, Peter . . . . .Cinema 21 Group, p. 91
Lancellotti, Stephen . . . . .Jean Doumanian Productions, p. 115
Lancon, Ray . . . . .All of Us, p. 354
Land, Stephen . . . . .Jupiter Entertainment, p. 183
Landau, Dan . . . . .Crossroads Films, p. 103
Landau, Jon . . . . .Lightstorm Entertainment, p. 199
Landau, Tania . . . . .Original Film, p. 244
Landau, Yair . . . . .Sony Pictures Digital, p. 295
Landau, Yair . . . . .Sony Pictures Entertainment, p. 295
Landels, Ryan . . . . .The Sommers Company, p. 294
Landes, Raymond J. . . . . .New Line Cinema, p. 234
Landgraf, John . . . . .Fox Cable Networks, p. 139
Landgraf, John . . . . .RENO 911!, p. 373
Landgraf, John . . . . .FX, p. 144
Landin, Marlen . . . . .SiTV, p. 290
Landin, Vicky . . . . .Pie Town Productions, p. 254
Landon, Matthew . . . . .The Weinstein Company, p. 337
Landrum, Pang Ni . . . . .Six Degrees, p. 375
Landsberg, Kathy . . . . .Pariah, p. 249
Landsburg, Alan . . . . .The Landsburg Company, p. 193
Landsman, Joseph K. . . . . .The Woofenill Works, Inc., p. 344
Landy, Kevin . . . . .USA Network, p. 327
Lane, Jeff . . . . .Pfeffer Film, p. 253
Lane, Matt . . . . .Union Square Entertainment, p. 325
Lane, Rebecca . . . . .Endemol USA, Inc., p. 123
Lane, Ryan .Intermedia Film Equities USA, Inc., p. 175
Lang, Lisa . . . . .Warner Bros. Television Production, p. 335
Lang, Liz . . . . .Ghost Whisperer, p. 362
Lang, Liz Selzer . . . . .Liz Selzer Lang Productions, p. 193
Lang, Michael . . . . .Fox Cable Networks, p. 139
Lang, Rocky . . . . .Harbor Lights Productions, p. 160
Lang, Victoria . . . . .PLUS Entertainment, Inc., p. 258
Langan, Christine . . . . .BBC Films, p. 64
Langdon, Reuben . . . . .Artists, Inc., p. 56
Lange, Cassidy . . . . . . .Twentieth Century Fox - Searchlight Pictures, p. 323
Lange, Dan . . . . .Picturehouse, p. 254
Lange, John . . . . .Picturehouse, p. 254
Lange, Steve . . . . .Weller/Grossman Productions, p. 338
Langer, Jeremy . . . . .Fox Sports Network, p. 140
Langer, Pat . . . . .Lifetime Television (New York), p. 198
Langford, David . . . . .The Radmin Company, p. 265
Langley, Donna . . . . .Universal Pictures, p. 326
Langley, Jimmy . . . . .Cops, p. 358
Langley, John . . . . .Cops, p. 358
Langley, John . . . . .Langley Productions, p. 193
Langley, Morgan . . . . .Langley Productions, p. 193
Langlois, Jim . . . . .Neighbors Entertainment, p. 232
Lanham, Nancy . . . . .Vincent Newman Entertainment, p. 236
Lansbury, Angela . . . . .Corymore Entertainment, p. 101
Lansdell, Marcus . . . . .City Lights Media Group, p. 94
Lansdowne, Rob .VanDerKloot Film & Television, p. 328
Lantos, Robert . . . . .Serendipity Point Films, p. 284
LaPaglia, Anthony . . . . .Last Straw Productions, p. 194
Lapides, Howard . . . . .The Core, p. 101
Lapidus, Eric . . . . .Two and a Half Men, p. 378
LaPietra, Aldo . . . . .Alturas Films, p. 50
LaPlaca, Chris . . . . .ESPN Original Entertainment (EOE), p. 127
LaPlume, Chandra . . . . .Taillight TV, p. 308
Lapoint, Eric . . . . .American Idol, p. 354
Lappin, Arthur . . . . .Hell's Kitchen Ltd., p. 164
Lappin, Kevin . . . . .Wass-Stein, p. 336
Lappin, Matt . . . . .The Colbert Report, p. 357
Large, Gailor . . . . .Jason Hoffs Productions, p. 168
Larian, Isaac . . . . .MGA Ent./MGA Ent. Films, p. 216
Larkham, Tavis . . . . .The Greif Company, p. 154
Larkin, Michael G. . . . . .Larkin-Goldstein Production, p. 194
Larkowski, Amy . . . . .Sony Pictures Television International, p. 296
Larner, Drew . . . . .Bauer Martinez Entertainment, p. 63
LaRose, Scott . . . . .Monster Productions, p. 220
Larouche, Pierre . . . . .Park Ex Pictures, p. 249
Larson, Graham . . . . .Identity Films, p. 170
Larson, James . . . . .Arjay Entertainment, p. 55
Larsonneur, Florence . . . . .Recorded Picture Company, p. 266
Larson-Nitzche, Christine . . . . .Numb3rs, p. 370
LaRue, Darryl . . . . .Warner Bros. Online, p. 334
LaSalle, Lillian . . . . .LaSalleHolland, p. 194
Laserson, Lillian . . . . .DC Comics, p. 108
Lashbrook, Rick . . . . .Rick Lashbrook Films, p. 194
Lasher, Amanda . . . . .The Class, p. 357
Lasher, Estelle . . . . .Principal Entertainment, p. 262
Lassally, Peter . . . . .The Late Late Show with Craig Ferguson, p. 366
Lassally, Peter . . . . .The Late Show with David Letterman, p. 367
Lassally, Tom . . . . .3 Arts Entertainment, Inc., p. 40
Lasseter, John . . . . .The Walt Disney Company, p. 112
Lasseter, John . . . . .Pixar Animation Studios, p. 256
Lasseter, John . . . . .Buena Vista Motion Pictures Group, p. 78
Lassiter, James . . . . .All of Us, p. 354
Lassiter, James . . . . .Overbrook Entertainment, p. 245
Lassner, Andy . . . . .The Ellen DeGeneres Show, p. 360
LaStaiti, Scott . . . . .Stone Village Pictures, LLC, p. 302
Latcham, Jeremy . . . . .Marvel Studios, Inc., p. 211
Latham, Jill . . . . .Kopelson Entertainment, p. 189
Latham, Taylor . . . . .Gerber Pictures, p. 145
Latham, Walter . . . . .Latham Entertainment, p. 194
Lathan, Stan . . . . .Simmons/Lathan, p. 289
Latt, David J. . . . . .TV Repair, p. 322
Latt, David Michael . . . . .The Asylum, p. 57
Lattaker-Johnson, Robyn . . . . .BET Networks, p. 66
Lattman, Ally . . . . .Lionsgate, p. 200
Lau, Matt . . . . .Vanished, p. 378
Lauder, Karen . . . . .Abandon Pictures, Inc., p. 44
Lauderdale, Katherine . . . . .PBS, p. 251
Lauren, Andrew . . . . .Andrew Lauren Productions, p. 195
Lauren, Brigitta . . . . .Supernatural, p. 377
Laurenson, Jamie . . . . .BBC Films, p. 64
Lautanen, Scott . . . . .CSI: Miami, p. 358
LaVaccare, MJ . . . . .Fox Broadcasting Company, p. 139
Lavagnino, Tom . . . . .Genrebend Productions, Inc., p. 145
LaValle, Dennis . . . . .Workshop Pictures, Inc., p. 345
Laverty, Karen . . . . .SMG Productions, p. 292

LaVigne, James . . . . Furthur Films, p. 144
Lavin, David . . . . CBS Paramount Network Television, p. 87
Law, Susan . . . . Sony Pictures Television, p. 296
Lawenda, David . . . . Spike TV, p. 298
Lawler, Colleen . . . . Symbolic Action, p. 306
Lawler, Mary . . . . TBS, p. 309
Lawler, Mary . . . . Turner Network Television (TNT), p. 321
Lawn, Kevin . . . . New Crime Productions, p. 233
Lawrence, Bill . . . . Scrubs, p. 374
Lawrence, Bill . . . . Doozer, p. 114
Lawrence, Jon . . . . Endemol USA, Inc., p. 123
Lawrence, N. Gail . . . . Passions, p. 371
Lawrence, Robert . . . . Robert Lawrence Productions, p. 195
Lawrence, Sheila R. . . . . Ugly Betty, p. 378
Lawrence, Yolanda . . . . Shark, p. 374
Lawson, Kelli Richardson . . . . BET Networks, p. 66
Lawson, Ken . . . . Twentieth Television, p. 324
Lawson, Peter . . . . Miramax Films, p. 217
Lawton, Rosalind . . . . Miramax Films, p. 217
Laybourne, Geraldine . . . . Oxygen Media, p. 245
Layne, Barry . . . . National Lampoon, p. 230
Layne, Cooper . . . . HorsePower Entertainment, p. 169
Layton, Charles . . . . The Weinstein Company, p. 337
Lazar, Andrew . . . . Mad Chance, p. 206
Lazar, Emily . . . . The Colbert Report, p. 357
Lazarus, Herb . . . . Carsey-Werner Films, p. 84
Lazarus, Mark . . . . Turner Network Television (TNT), p. 321
Lazarus, Mark . . . . TBS, p. 309
Lazarus, Mark . . . . Turner Entertainment Group, p. 320
Lazin, Lauren . . . . MTV Networks, p. 226
Lazzo, Mike . . . . Adult Swim, p. 47
Lea, Judy . . . . Gorilla Pictures, p. 150
Lea, Linda . . . . Queer Eye, p. 372
Lea, Tim . . . . CSI: NY, p. 359
Leahy, Janet . . . . Boston Legal, p. 357
Leahy, Mike . . . . Neo Art & Logic, p. 232
Leamon, Koren . . . . Taillight TV, p. 308
Leaney, Angela . . . . Nickelodeon/MTVN Kids & Family Group, p. 237
Leanza, Chris . . . . 25C Productions, p. 40
Lear, Andrew . . . . The Core, p. 101
Lear, Norman . . . . Act III Productions, p. 46
Leary, Denis . . . . Rescue Me, p. 373
Leary, Denis . . . . Apostle, p. 53
Leavell, Chris . . . . Indigo Films, p. 174
Leavy, David . . . . Discovery Networks, U.S., p. 111
Lebda, Doug . . . . IAC/InterActiveCorp, p. 170
Leblanc, Edith . . . . L.I.F.T. Productions, p. 191
LeBlanc, Matt . . . . Fort Hill Productions, p. 137
Leblang, Steve . . . . FX, p. 144
LeBoff, Jared . . . . Marc Platt Productions, p. 257
LeClair, Ben . . . . Black & White Productions, p. 67
Leclere, Tiffany . . . . Media 8 Entertainment, p. 214
Leddy, Bruce . . . . Mad TV, p. 368
Leder, Geraldine . . . . Twentieth Century Fox Television, p. 323
Leder, Mimi . . . . Vanished, p. 378
Lederman, Jodi . . . . Amp'd Mobile, p. 51
Lederman, Nina . . . . Joe Roth Television, p. 275
Lee, Alan . . . . Double Edge Entertainment, p. 115
Lee, Christopher Dehau . . . . Melee Entertainment, p. 214
Lee, Damon . . . . Deacon Entertainment, p. 109
Lee, David . . . . New Screen Concepts, Inc., p. 235
Lee, Debra L. . . . . BET Networks, p. 66
Lee, Douglas . . . . Metro-Goldwyn-Mayer Studios, Inc. (MGM), p. 215
Lee, Eileen . . . . Harpo Films, Inc., p. 161
Lee, Erica . . . . Thunder Road Pictures, p. 313
Lee, Ike . . . . JT Entertainment, p. 182
Lee, Jeff . . . . Proteus, p. 263
Lee, Jenny . . . . In Case of Emergency, p. 364
Lee, Jim . . . . DC Comics, p. 108
Lee, Jimmy . . . . Buena Vista Television, p. 79
Lee, Keli . . . . Touchstone Television, p. 316
Lee, Keli . . . . ABC Entertainment Television Group, p. 45
Lee, Kevin . . . . Anonymous Creators Productions, p. 52
Lee, Kevin . . . . Bunim/Murray Productions, Inc., p. 79
Lee, Linda . . . . George Litto Productions, Inc., p. 201
Lee, Marta . . . . George Schlatter Productions, p. 280
Lee, Mary . . . . Mandate Pictures, p. 209
Lee, Michelle . . . . The Mark Gordon Company, p. 150
Lee, Pat Tourk . . . . Moffitt-Lee Productions, p. 219
Lee, Paul . . . . ABC Family, p. 45
Lee, Paul . . . . Disney ABC Cable Networks Group, p. 112
Lee, Rob . . . . Bayonne Entertainment, p. 63
Lee, Rob . . . . Lonetree Entertainment, p. 202
Lee, Rolly . . . . Saturn Films, p. 280
Lee, Roy . . . . Vertigo Entertainment, p. 330
Lee, Sammy . . . . Media 8 Entertainment, p. 214
Lee, Seung-jae . . . . LJ Film, p. 201
Lee, Spike . . . . 40 Acres & A Mule Filmworks, Inc., p. 41
Lee, Stan . . . . POW! Entertainment, p. 260
Lee, Steven . . . . Anonymous Creators Productions, p. 52
Leepson, David . . . . Fox Sports Network, p. 140
Leeson, Michael . . . . 20 Good Years, p. 353
Lefevre, Mina . . . . ABC Family, p. 45
Lefkowitz, Bruce . . . . FX, p. 144
Lefler, Bradley . . . . Management 360, p. 208
LeFrak, Francine . . . . LeFrak Productions, p. 195
LeGoy, Keith . . . . Sony Pictures Television International, p. 296
Legrand, Brian . . . . Andrew Solt Productions, p. 294
Lehane, Dennis . . . . The Wire, p. 379
Lehman, Nicholas . . . . MTV Networks, p. 226
Lehrer, Eli . . . . Bravo, p. 74
Lehrer, Harvey . . . . JTN Productions, p. 183
Leib, Mitchell . . . . Buena Vista Motion Pictures Group, p. 78
Leibold, Katy . . . . @radical.media, p. 38
Leibovit, Arnold . . . . Arnold Leibovit Entertainment, p. 196
Leibowitz, Richard . . . . Union Entertainment, p. 325
Leider, Jerry . . . . The Jerry Leider Company, p. 196
Leiderman, Jill . . . . Jimmy Kimmel Live, p. 364
Leifer, Stephanie . . . . Touchstone Television, p. 316
Leigh-Bell, Patrick . . . . Jupiter Entertainment, p. 183
Leight, Warren . . . . Law & Order: Criminal Intent, p. 367
Leight, Warren . . . . Wolf Films, Inc., p. 343
Leingang, Lisa . . . . CBS Entertainment, p. 86
Leipzig, Adam . . . . National Geographic Feature Films, p. 229
Leissner, Janet . . . . CBS News, p. 87
Leitch, Kathy . . . . Flying A Studios, Inc., p. 135
Leiviska, Nancy . . . . Cube Vision, p. 104
Leman, Kevin . . . . The Ellen DeGeneres Show, p. 360
Lemchen, Bob . . . . Fox Television Studios, p. 140
Lemcoff, Veronica . . . . Twentieth Century Fox - Searchlight Pictures, p. 323
LeMel, Gary . . . . Warner Bros. Pictures, p. 334
Lemire, Michel . . . . CinéGroupe, p. 91
Lemme, Steve . . . . Broken Lizard Industries, p. 76
Lemmon, Danielle . . . . Wheelhouse Entertainment, p. 339
Lemons, Jayme . . . . Coquette Productions, p. 101
Lemus, Adriana . . . . Twentieth Century Fox Television, p. 323
Lena, Hank . . . . HDNet, p. 163
Lenard, Brian . . . . RDF Media, p. 266
Lenard, Warren . . . . New Line Cinema, p. 234
Lenic, John G. . . . . Stargate: SG-1, p. 376
Lenig, Christine . . . . Cosgrove-Meurer Productions, p. 101
Lenkov, Peter . . . . CSI: NY, p. 359
Lennon, Gary . . . . The Black Donnellys, p. 356
Lennon, Thomas . . . . RENO 911!, p. 373
Lentz, Frank . . . . Current TV, LLC, p. 105
Lentz, Jacob . . . . Jimmy Kimmel Live, p. 364
Leo, Jerry . . . . Bravo, p. 74
Leo, Malcolm . . . . Malcolm Leo Productions, p. 196
Leon, Ed . . . . SiTV, p. 290
Leonarczyk, Gregory . . . . Periscope Entertainment, LLC, p. 252
Leonard, Franklin . . . . Appian Way, p. 53
Leonard, Jeff . . . . Two Sticks Productions, p. 325
Leonard, Jim . . . . Close to Home, p. 357
Leonard, Marc . . . . Logo, p. 202
Leonard, Maxine . . . . Myriad Pictures, p. 228
Leonard, Paul . . . . Battlestar Galactica, p. 355
Leonard, Samantha . . . . Pie Town Productions, p. 254
Leonardis, Tom . . . . Whoop Inc./One Ho Prod./Lil' Whoop Prod., p. 340
Leonelli, Nadia . . . . ManifestoVision, p. 210
Leoni, Téa . . . . And Then Productions, p. 51

Leonsis, Ted . . . AOL Media Networks, p. 53
Lerner, Avi . . . Millennium Films, p. 217
Lerner, Garrett . . . House, p. 363
Lerner, Jeffrey . . . Sony Pictures Television International, p. 296
LeRoi, Ali . . . Everybody Hates Chris, p. 361
Leschin, Luisa . . . The George Lopez Show, p. 362
Lesher, John . . . Paramount Pictures, p. 248
Lesher, John . . . Paramount Vantage/Paramount Classics, p. 248
Lesinski, Tom . . . Paramount Digital Media Group, p. 248
Lesinski, Tom . . . Paramount Pictures, p. 248
Leslie, Chad . . . Shoreline Entertainment, Inc., p. 286
Leslie, Jack . . . The Donners' Company, p. 114
Leslie, Kris . . . DreamWorks Animation SKG, p. 116
Lessans, Greg . . . Terra Firma Films, p. 312
Lesser, Frank . . . The Colbert Report, p. 357
Lesser, Norman . . . Buena Vista Television, p. 79
Letarte, Michelle . . . Renegade 83, p. 270
Lethcoe, Jason . . . Scarab Productions, p. 280
Leto, Peter . . . Law & Order: Special Victims Unit, p. 367
Lett III, Frank T. . . . Lett/Reese International Productions, p. 196
Lett, Franklin . . . Lett/Reese International Productions, p. 196
Letta, Giampaolo . . . Medusa Film, p. 214
Letterman, David . . . The Late Show with David Letterman, p. 367
Letterman, David . . . The Knights of Prosperity, p. 365
Letterman, David . . . Worldwide Pants, Inc., p. 346
Leutwyler, Matthew . . . Ambush Entertainment, p. 50
Levenson, Lisa . . . The Bachelor, p. 355
Levenson, Lisa . . . Next Entertainment, p. 236
Levenstein, Mark . . . HBO Films, p. 162
Leventman, Leslie . . . MTV Networks, p. 226
Levett, Jen . . . Original Film, p. 244
Levey, Alan . . . Buena Vista Motion Pictures Group, p. 78
Levey, John . . . ER, p. 361
Levey, John . . . John Wells Productions, p. 338
Levey, Lynne . . . Comedy Central, p. 98
Levi, Jo . . . Cosgrove-Meurer Productions, p. 101
Levi, Judah . . . 3Wolves Productions, p. 41
Levin, Adam . . . Cinema-Electric Inc., p. 92
Levin, Barbara . . . NBC News, p. 230
Levin, Berna . . . Tollin/Robbins Productions, p. 315
Levin, Carl . . . Prospect Pictures, p. 263
Levin, Daniel . . . Platform Entertainment, p. 256
Levin, Drew . . . TMC Entertainment, p. 314
Levin, Gail . . . Paramount Pictures Production Division, p. 248
Levin, Jody A. . . . New Line Cinema, p. 234
Levin, Jordan . . . Generate, p. 145
Levin, Sam . . . The Matthau Company, Inc., p. 212
Levin, Samantha . . . Keckins Projects, Ltd., p. 185
Levin, Stacey . . . Twentieth Century Fox Television, p. 323
Levin, Steve . . . SiTV, p. 290
Levin, Susan . . . Silver Pictures, p. 289
Levin, Sydney . . . New Line Television, p. 235
Levin, Wayne . . . Lionsgate, p. 200
Levine, Bruce . . . mod3productions, p. 219
Levine, Dan . . . Paramount Pictures Production Division, p. 248
Levine, David . . . Fuse Entertainment, p. 144
Levine, Ellen . . . Vantage Enterprises, Inc., p. 329
Levine, Gary . . . Showtime Networks Inc., p. 287
Levine, Jackie . . . Bristol Bay Productions, p. 76
Levine, Jackie . . . Walden Media, p. 333
Levine, Jeff . . . Gold Circle Films, p. 148
Levine, Jeffrey . . . Spring Creek Productions, Inc., p. 298
Levine, Jennifer . . . Untitled Entertainment, p. 327
Levine, Richard . . . Nip/Tuck, p. 370
Levine, Stephanie . . . Regency Television, p. 269
Levine, Tyler . . . January Films, p. 179
Levin-Lovett, Brittany . . . Last Comic Standing, p. 366
Levinsohn, Gary . . . Mutual Film Company, p. 227
Levinson, Barry . . . The Levinson/Fontana Company, p. 197
Levinson, Chris . . . Law & Order, p. 367
Levinson, David . . . Standoff, p. 376
Levinson, Jena . . . The Late Bloomer Company, Ltd., p. 194
Levinson, Lee . . . The Late Bloomer Company, Ltd., p. 194
Levinson, Sarah . . . Playtime Productions, p. 257
Levinson, Steve . . . Entourage, p. 360
Levisetti, Emile . . . In Case of Emergency, p. 364
Levisetti, Emile . . . Bushwacker Productions, p. 81
Levison, Susan . . . Fox Broadcasting Company, p. 139
Levitas, Andrew J. . . . SekretAgent Productions, p. 283
Levitt, Zane W. . . . Zane W. Levitt Prod./Zeta Ent., p. 197
Levitz, Paul . . . DC Comics, p. 108
Levy, Aurelie . . . New Crime Productions, p. 233
Levy, Dani . . . X Filme Creative Pool GmbH, p. 346
Levy, David Guy . . . Periscope Entertainment, LLC, p. 252
Levy, Debbie . . . The Hal Lieberman Company, p. 197
Levy, Don . . . Sony Pictures Digital, p. 295
Levy, Doug . . . Fox Sports Network, p. 140
Levy, Howard . . . Buena Vista Television, p. 79
Levy, Jennifer . . . VH1, p. 330
Levy, Joey . . . Marc Platt Productions, p. 257
Levy, John . . . Columbia Pictures, p. 97
Levy, Josh . . . Josephson Entertainment, p. 182
Levy, Justin . . . Film 44, p. 131
Levy, Lawrence . . . Catapult Films, p. 85
Levy, Nikki . . . Gold Circle Films, p. 148
Levy, Rachel . . . Dimension Films, p. 111
Levy, Rachel . . . The Weinstein Company, p. 337
Levy, Rob . . . Untitled Entertainment, p. 327
Levy, Robert L. . . . Tapestry Films, Inc., p. 308
Levy, Sarah Kirshbaum . . . Nickelodeon/MTVN Kids & Family Group, p. 237
Levy, Sharon . . . Spike TV, p. 298
Levy, Shawn . . . 21 Laps Entertainment, p. 38
Levy, Stacey . . . The George Lopez Show, p. 362
Levy, Stuart J. . . . TOKYOPOP Inc., p. 315
Levy, Zoë . . . Bluebird House, p. 69
Levy-Hinte, Jeffrey . . . Antidote International Films, Inc., p. 53
Lewand, Beth . . . Comedy Central, p. 98
Lewellen, Michael . . . BET Networks, p. 66
Lewis, Andy . . . Warner Bros. Animation, p. 334
Lewis, Ann . . . E! Networks, p. 117
Lewis, Claudia . . . Twentieth Century Fox - Searchlight Pictures, p. 323
Lewis, Damon . . . Krasnow Productions, p. 190
Lewis, Jenny . . . Daniel L. Paulson Productions, p. 251
Lewis, Laura . . . Twentieth Century Fox, p. 322
Lewis, Lisa . . . Warner Bros. Television Production, p. 335
Lewis, Lisa . . . VanDerKloot Film & Television, p. 328
Lewis, Michael . . . Warner Bros. Online, p. 334
Lewis, Mike . . . Friday Night Lights, p. 361
Lewis, Potter . . . Generation Entertainment, p. 145
Lewis, Richard . . . CSI: Crime Scene Investigation, p. 358
Lewis, Richard . . . Sidney Kimmel Entertainment, p. 187
Lewis, Richard Barton . . . Southpaw Entertainment, p. 297
Lewis, Ryan . . . Fuse Entertainment, p. 144
Lewis, Stephanie . . . Thousand Words, p. 313
Lewis, Walter . . . The Tonight Show with Jay Leno, p. 377
Li, Jimmy . . . Media 8 Entertainment, p. 214
Liakhoff, Laurence . . . Bonne Pioche, p. 71
Libby, Dru . . . Bravo, p. 74
Liber, Reuben . . . Motion Picture Corporation of America, p. 222
Liber, Rodney . . . Blue Bay Productions, p. 68
Liberatore, Lindsey . . . The Mark Gordon Company, p. 150
Liberman, Meg . . . Medium, p. 369
Liberman, Meg . . . Raines, p. 372
Licata, Richard . . . Showtime Networks Inc., p. 287
Licht, Andrew . . . Licht Entertainment Corporation, p. 197
Lichtenstein, Demian . . . Lightstone Entertainment, Inc., p. 199
Lichtenstein, Jim . . . Pie Town Productions, p. 254
Liddell, Mickey . . . Liddell Entertainment, p. 197
Liddell, Susy . . . BBC Films, p. 64
Liddi, Nicolina . . . QED International, p. 264
Lieb, Eric . . . Fox Atomic, p. 138
Lieberman, Arthur . . . POW! Entertainment, p. 260
Lieberman, Barbara . . . Barbara Lieberman Productions, p. 197
Lieberman, Cynthia . . . Sony Pictures Television, p. 296
Lieberman, Hal . . . The Hal Lieberman Company, p. 197
Lieberman, Linda . . . IMG Media, p. 172
Lieberman, Meg . . . Studio 60 on the Sunset Strip, p. 376
Lieberman, Todd . . . Mandeville Films, p. 209
Lieberstein, Paul . . . The Office, p. 371
Lieblein, Sharon Chazin . . . Nickelodeon/MTVN Kids & Family Group, p. 237

Liebling, Deborah . . . . . Twentieth Century Fox, p. 322
Liebman, Brett A. . . . . . Playtime Productions, p. 257
Liebman, Jonathan . . . . . Brillstein-Grey Entertainment, p. 75
Lierle, Susan . . . . . E! Networks, p. 117
Liggins, Alfred . . . . . TV One, LLC, p. 322
Lightsey, Eddie . . . . . American Blackguard, Inc., p. 50
Liguori, Peter . . . . . Fox Broadcasting Company, p. 139
Lihani, Robert . . . . . Digital Ranch Productions, p. 110
Likkel, Kat . . . . . My Name Is Earl, p. 369
Lilico, Mark . . . . . Humble Journey Films, p. 169
Lilienfield, Tracy . . . . . My Boys, p. 369
Lillie, Lauren . . . . . Deutsch/Open City Films, p. 109
Lillie, Lauren . . . . . HDNet Films, p. 163
Lillis, Julia . . . . . Patriot Pictures, LLC, p. 250
Lilly, Courtney . . . . . My Boys, p. 369
Lim, Adele . . . . . One Tree Hill, p. 371
Lima, Alison . . . . . DreamWorks SKG, p. 116
Liman, Doug . . . . . Hypnotic, p. 170
Limerick, Dan . . . . . Warner Bros. Television Production, p. 335
Lin, Andrew . . . . . Paramount Vantage/Paramount Classics, p. 248
Lin, Dan . . . . . Warner Bros. Pictures, p. 334
Lin, Janet . . . . . Waterfront, p. 379
Lindahl, Carl . . . . . The History Channel, p. 167
Linde, David . . . . . Universal Pictures, p. 326
Lindelof, Damon . . . . . Lost, p. 368
Linden, Jay . . . . . NBC Universal Corporate, p. 231
Lindgren, Art . . . . . Water Channel, p. 336
Lindley, Francesca . . . . . Bristol Bay Productions, p. 76
Lindley, Francesca . . . . . Walden Media, p. 333
Lindman, Sarah . . . . . Noggin, p. 239
Lindsay, Mark . . . . . Sidney Kimmel Entertainment, p. 187
Lindsey, Erin . . . . . Twentieth Century Fox - Fox 2000, p. 323
Lineberry, Veronika . . . . . King World Productions, Inc., p. 188
Ling, Laura . . . . . Current TV, LLC, p. 105
Lingner, Yun . . . . . Hell's Kitchen, p. 363
Linklater, Richard . . . . . Detour, p. 109
Linkletter, Art . . . . . Linkletter/Kritzer, p. 199
Linn, Chris . . . . . MTV Networks, p. 226
Linn, Jason . . . . . New Line Cinema, p. 234
Linsky, Sam . . . . . Turner Network Television (TNT), p. 321
Linville, Geoffrey . . . . . Serenade Films, p. 284
Linz, Felipe . . . . . Deep River Productions, p. 109
Lioi, Anthony . . . . . American Dad, p. 354
Lioud, Christophe . . . . . Bonne Pioche, p. 71
Lippens, Amy . . . . . House, p. 363
Lipscomb, Steven . . . . . WPT Enterprises, Inc., p. 346
Lipsitz, Jane . . . . . Last Comic Standing, p. 366
Lipstadt, Aaron . . . . . Western Sandblast, p. 339
Lipstone, Howard . . . . . The Landsburg Company, p. 193
Lipton, James . . . . . James Lipton Productions, p. 200
Lisanti, Michelle Poteet . . . . . One Life to Live, p. 371
Lisberger, Peggy . . . . . PorchLight Entertainment, p. 259
Lischak, Bill . . . . . First Look Pictures, p. 134
Lisio, Mary . . . . . Actual Reality Pictures, p. 46
Liska, Kathy . . . . . The Donners' Company, p. 114
Liss, Ira . . . . . Industry Entertainment Partners, p. 174
Lister, Gary . . . . . New Wave Entertainment, p. 235
Listo, Mike . . . . . Boston Legal, p. 357
Litinsky, Irene . . . . . Muse Entertainment Enterprises, p. 227
Litt, Leslie . . . . . Rules of Engagement, p. 373
Litt, Stefan . . . . . Columbia Pictures, p. 97
Littin, Matt . . . . . Cinetic, p. 93
Little, Melissa . . . . . The Ellen DeGeneres Show, p. 360
Little, Quentin . . . . . HDNet Films, p. 163
Littlefield, Davien . . . . . Cooper's Town Productions, p. 100
Littlefield, Warren . . . . . The Littlefield Company, p. 200
Littlehales, Jennifer . . . . . Warner Bros. Television Production, p. 335
Littlejohn, Stacy A. . . . . . All of Us, p. 354
Littman, Barry . . . . . The Weinstein Company, p. 337
Littman, Jill . . . . . Handprint Entertainment, p. 160
Littman, Jonathan . . . . . CSI: NY, p. 359
Littman, Jonathan . . . . . Close to Home, p. 357
Littman, Jonathan . . . . . Without a Trace, p. 379
Littman, Jonathan . . . . . CSI: Crime Scene Investigation, p. 358
Littman, Jonathan . . . . . Justice, p. 364
Littman, Jonathan . . . . . Cold Case, p. 357
Littman, Jonathan . . . . . CSI: Miami, p. 358
Littman, Jonathan . . . . . The Amazing Race, p. 354
Littman, Jonathan . . . . . Jerry Bruckheimer Films & Television, p. 78
Littmann, Paul . . . . . Sony Pictures Television International, p. 296
Litto, Andria . . . . . George Litto Productions, Inc., p. 201
Litto, George . . . . . George Litto Productions, Inc., p. 201
Litvack, Cameron . . . . . Ugly Betty, p. 378
Litvack, John . . . . . Smallville, p. 375
Litvak, Michael . . . . . Bold Films, p. 71
Liu, Marilyn . . . . . Brightlight Pictures, Inc., p. 75
Liuag, Robert . . . . . G4 TV, p. 144
Livingston, Clarence . . . . . Scrubs, p. 374
Lizer, Kari . . . . . The New Adventures of Old Christine, p. 370
Lizer, Laura . . . . . Ellyn Williams Productions, p. 341
Llano, Jenny . . . . . Fremantle Productions Latin America, p. 142
Lloyd, Lauren . . . . . Lloyd Entertainment, p. 201
Lloyd, Samantha . . . . . Red Hour Films, p. 267
Lloyd, Stephen . . . . . How I Met Your Mother, p. 364
Lo, Andria . . . . . Mondo Media, p. 220
Lo, April . . . . . Elevation Filmworks, p. 121
Lo, Ken . . . . . Sony Pictures Television International, p. 296
Lobell, Mike . . . . . Mike Lobell Productions, p. 201
LoCascio, Fran . . . . . Evergreen Films, LLC, p. 128
LoCascio, Steve . . . . . King World Productions, Inc., p. 188
Loceff, Michael . . . . . 24, p. 353
Locke, Peter . . . . . Peter Locke Productions, p. 202
Locker, Ken . . . . . Cookie Jar Entertainment, p. 100
Lodin, Laura . . . . . National Geographic Feature Films, p. 229
Loeb, Jeph . . . . . Heroes, p. 363
Loesch, Margaret . . . . . The Hatchery, p. 161
Lofaro, Phil . . . . . Buena Vista Motion Pictures Group, p. 78
Loftus, Michael . . . . . The George Lopez Show, p. 362
Logan, Bey . . . . . The Weinstein Company, p. 337
Logan, Sandi . . . . . Touchstone Television, p. 316
Loggia, Audrey . . . . . Merv Griffin Entertainment, p. 154
Logue, Donal . . . . . The Knights of Prosperity, p. 365
Logue, Gerry . . . . . Lifetime Television (New York), p. 198
Logue, Sara . . . . . here! Networks, p. 165
Loh, Grace . . . . . New Crime Productions, p. 233
Lohman, Lauren . . . . . Studio 60 on the Sunset Strip, p. 376
Lohr, Noel . . . . . Intermedia Film Equities USA, Inc., p. 175
Lollar, Kimberly . . . . . Parallel Entertainment, Inc., p. 247
Lombard, Ken . . . . . Starbucks Entertainment, p. 299
Lombardo, Michael . . . . . HBO Entertainment, p. 162
Lomis, Eileen . . . . . Columbia Pictures, p. 97
Loncar, Marilyn . . . . . CBS Paramount Network Television, p. 87
London, Carolyn . . . . . The Tyra Banks Show, p. 378
London, Carolyn . . . . . Bankable Productions, p. 61
London, Michael . . . . . Groundswell Production, p. 156
Londono, Kali . . . . . Everybody Hates Chris, p. 361
Long, Bruce . . . . . National Lampoon, p. 230
Long, Chris . . . . . Dirt, p. 360
Long, Tim . . . . . The Simpsons, p. 375
Longardi, Francesca . . . . . Cattleya, p. 86
Longarzo, Jerry . . . . . Fox Television Studios, p. 140
Longbottom, Hannah . . . . . Film & Music Entertainment, Ltd. (F&ME), p. 131
Longi, Steven A. . . . . . Permut Presentations, p. 252
Longmuir, Virginia . . . . . Lakeshore Entertainment Group LLC, p. 192
Lonow, Claudia . . . . . The War at Home, p. 379
Lookofsky, Jacqueline . . . . . Samoset, Inc./Sacret, Inc., p. 278
Loos, Rob . . . . . TLC Entertainment, p. 314
Loparco, Elissa . . . . . Regency Enterprises, p. 268
Loparo, Michelle . . . . . Sub Rosa Productions, Inc., p. 303
Lopez, Angel Dean . . . . . Sleeper Cell, p. 375
Lopez, Anthony . . . . . Latin Hollywood Films, p. 194
Lopez, Carlos . . . . . Mutual Film Company, p. 227
Lopez, Diana . . . . . Furthur Films, p. 144
Lopez, George . . . . . The George Lopez Show, p. 362
Lopez, Jennifer . . . . . Nuyorican, p. 240
Lopez, JJ . . . . . MarVista Entertainment, p. 212
Lopez, Judi . . . . . AMC, p. 50
Lopez, Judi . . . . . The Independent Film Channel (IFC), p. 173
Lopez, Mara . . . . . Warner Bros. Television Production, p. 335
Lopez, Suzanne . . . . . FremantleMedia North America, p. 142

Lopez, Tery . . . . Maya Pictures, p. 213
Lopopolo, Roseanne . . . . WE: Women's Entertainment, p. 336
Lops, Peter . . . . My Network TV, p. 228
Lorber, Marc B. . . . . Barracuda Productions, p. 62
Lord, Peter . . . . Aardman Animations, p. 44
Lorenz, Carsten . . . . Miranda Entertainment, p. 218
Lorenz, Robert . . . . Malpaso Productions, p. 208
Loring, Lynn . . . . Lynn Loring Productions, p. 203
Lorraine, Lynda . . . . Teocalli Entertainment, p. 312
Lorre, Chuck . . . . Two and a Half Men, p. 378
Losnegard, Chris . . . . Prospect Pictures, p. 263
Lotterstein, Rob . . . . The War at Home, p. 379
Loud, Delilah . . . . King World Productions, Inc., p. 188
Loughery, Don . . . . Sony Pictures Television, p. 296
Louie, Nina . . . . Sony Pictures Television, p. 296
Louis, Lindy . . . . Pfeffer Film, p. 253
Louzil, Eric . . . . Echelon Entertainment World Dist. & Prod., p. 119
Love, Sandi . . . . Elkins Entertainment, p. 122
Loveall, Chris . . . . The Edelstein Company, p. 119
Lovick, Josanne B. . . . . BLT Productions Ltd., p. 68
Lowell, Richard . . . . WWE Films, p. 346
Lowenstein, Al . . . . The War at Home, p. 379
Lowery, Bob . . . . Concrete Pictures, p. 99
Lowery, William . . . . Underground Films, p. 325
Lowitt, Paula . . . . DC Comics, p. 108
Lowry, Brenda . . . . Bravo, p. 74
Lowry, Hunt . . . . Roserock Films, p. 275
Lowry-Johnson, Junie . . . . Desperate Housewives, p. 360
Lowry-Johnson, Junie . . . . Prison Break, p. 372
Lowry-Johnson, Junie . . . . Ugly Betty, p. 378
Lowy, Linda . . . . Friday Night Lights, p. 361
Lowy, Linda . . . . Grey's Anatomy, p. 362
Loy, Eric . . . . Identity Films, p. 170
Lozano, John . . . . South Side Films, p. 297
Lozitsky, Hayley . . . . E! Networks, p. 117
Lubaroff, Terri Feldman . . . . Humble Journey Films, p. 169
Luber, Matt . . . . Nine Yards Entertainment, p. 238
Lubetkin, Dan . . . . Avalon Television, Inc., p. 58
Lucas, George . . . . Lucasfilm Ltd., p. 203
Lucas, Jeff . . . . Comedy Central, p. 98
Lucas, Jennifer . . . . Entertainment Studios, Inc., p. 125
Lucas, Joe . . . . CBS Paramount International Television, p. 87
Lucchesi, Gary . . . . Lakeshore Entertainment Group LLC, p. 192
Luce, Dave . . . . FremantleMedia North America, p. 142
Luchs, Stacey M. . . . . David E. Kelley Productions, p. 186
Lucioni, Danella . . . . CastleBright Studios, p. 85
Luckenbill, Wendy . . . . NBC Entertainment, p. 230
Luczak, Renata . . . . Comedy Central, p. 98
Ludlow, Graham . . . . Colossal Entertainment, p. 97
Ludwin, Rick . . . . NBC Entertainment, p. 230
Luegenbiehl, Kelly . . . . ABC Entertainment Television Group, p. 45
Luff, Brad . . . . The Mayhem Project, p. 213
Lugger, Shannon . . . . Ghost House Pictures, p. 145
Lugger, Shannon . . . . Renaissance Pictures, p. 270
Luhrmann, Amanda . . . . Bazmark, Inq., p. 63
Luhrmann, Baz . . . . Bazmark, Inq., p. 63
Lui, Brenna . . . . AEI-Atchity Entertainment Intl., Inc., p. 47
Luisi, Michael . . . . Miramax Films, p. 217
Lukasiewicz, Mark . . . . NBC News, p. 230
Luker, Kyle . . . . The Group Entertainment, p. 156
Lulla, Azina . . . . Tomorrow Film Corporation, p. 315
Lundberg, Daniela Taplin . . . . Plum Pictures, p. 258
Lundberg, Kyle . . . . Altitude Entertainment, p. 49
Lundberg, Robert . . . . Latitude Television LLC, p. 195
Luong, Huy . . . . Once Upon A Time Films, Ltd., p. 243
Lupovitz, Dan . . . . Dan Lupovitz Productions, p. 204
Luria, James . . . . AOL Media Networks, p. 53
Lurie, Christina Weiss . . . . Vox3 Films, p. 332
Lurie, Rod . . . . Battle Plan Productions, p. 63
Lusitana, Donna E. . . . . Greystone Television and Films, p. 154
Lust, Jason . . . . The Jim Henson Company, p. 165
Lustgarten, Jessica . . . . Elevation Filmworks, p. 121
Lux, David . . . . Twentieth Century Fox, p. 322
Ly, Oanh . . . . Criminal Minds, p. 358
Lyle, David . . . . Fox Cable Networks, p. 139
Lyle, David . . . . Fox Reality, p. 140
Lyles, A.C. . . . . A.C. Lyles Productions, Inc., p. 205
Lynas, Jeff . . . . Blueprint Entertainment, p. 70
Lynch, Bonita . . . . Bravo, p. 74
Lynch, Cheryl Buysse . . . . Fox Television Studios, p. 140
Lynch, Christina . . . . The Dead Zone, p. 359
Lynch, Joan . . . . ESPN Original Entertainment (EOE), p. 127
Lynch, Thomas W. . . . . The Tom Lynch Company, p. 205
Lyne, Susan . . . . Martha Stewart Living Omnimedia, Inc., p. 211
Lynn, Jenny . . . . Day Break, p. 359
Lynn, Patrick . . . . American Idol, p. 354
Lynn, Richard W. . . . . USA Network, p. 327
Lynne, Michael . . . . New Line Cinema, p. 234
Lynton, Michael . . . . Sony Pictures Entertainment, p. 295
Lyons, Ann . . . . IFM Film Associates, Inc., p. 171
Lyons, Anthony J. . . . . IFM Film Associates, Inc., p. 171
Lyons, Charlie . . . . Beacon, p. 64
Lyons, John . . . . Focus Features/Rogue Pictures, p. 136
Lyons, Sidney H. . . . . CBS Entertainment, p. 86
Lyons, Suzanne . . . . Snowfall Films/Windchill Films, p. 293
Lyster, Russ . . . . Louis DiGiaimo & Associates, Ltd., p. 110
Lythgoe, Nigel . . . . American Idol, p. 354
Lythgoe, Nigel . . . . So You Think You Can Dance, p. 376
Lythgoe, Simon . . . . American Idol, p. 354
Lytton, Chris . . . . Morgan Creek Productions, p. 221
Ma, Ivana . . . . Generate, p. 145
Maatta, John . . . . The CW, p. 105
Macaluso, Yvette . . . . Digital Domain, Inc., p. 110
Macari, Mike . . . . Macari/Edelstein Films, p. 205
Macaulay, Caroline . . . . Lion Rock Productions, p. 199
Macaulay, Scott . . . . Forensic Films, Inc., p. 137
Macdonald, Andrew . . . . DNA Films, p. 114
MacDonald, Chad . . . . Program Partners, p. 262
MacDonald, Dean . . . . Mondo Media, p. 220
MacDonald, Duncan . . . . Fox Atomic, p. 138
MacDonald, Steve . . . . Twentieth Television, p. 324
Mace, Dave . . . . Logo, p. 202
Macedo, Iona . . . . Columbia Pictures, p. 97
Macer, Monica . . . . Prison Break, p. 372
MacFarlane, Seth . . . . American Dad, p. 354
MacFarlane, Seth . . . . Family Guy, p. 361
MacGillivray, Greg . . . . MacGillivray Freeman Films, p. 205
Macgowan, Marian . . . . Macgowan Films, p. 206
Macias, Lori . . . . SlingShot Media, p. 291
Macias, Stephen . . . . here! Networks, p. 165
Mack, David . . . . Departure Studios, p. 109
Mack, Josh . . . . Stone Village Pictures, LLC, p. 302
Mackall, Kevin . . . . MTV Networks, p. 226
Mackay, David . . . . Brave New Films, p. 73
Mackiewicz, Liz . . . . Media 8 Entertainment, p. 214
MacKinney, Ted . . . . Mosaic Media Group, p. 222
MacKinney, Ted . . . . Atlas Entertainment, p. 57
MacLaury, Susan . . . . Worldwide Biggies, p. 346
MacLetchie, Donna . . . . Queer Eye, p. 372
MacMullan, Ann . . . . MARTHA, p. 368
MacNair, Swanna . . . . Misher Films, p. 218
MacPherson, Margo . . . . Brightlight Pictures, Inc., p. 75
MacPherson, Scoot . . . . Court TV Networks, p. 102
Macri, Dean . . . . The Cielo Group, Inc., p. 91
Macy, Steve . . . . Shoreline Entertainment, Inc., p. 286
Macy, Trevor . . . . Intrepid Pictures, p. 176
Madariaga, Elizabeth . . . . Blueprint Entertainment, p. 70
Maday, Charles . . . . The History Channel, p. 167
Maday, Gregg . . . . Warner Bros. Television Production, p. 335
Maday, Gregg . . . . Warner Bros. Theatre Ventures, p. 335
Maddalena, Marianne . . . . Craven/Maddalena Films, p. 102
Madden, David . . . . Fox Television Studios, p. 140
Madden, Larry . . . . The Weinstein Company, p. 337
Madden, Molly . . . . 3 Arts Entertainment, Inc., p. 40
Madden, Ollie . . . . Intermedia Film Equities USA, Inc., p. 175
Madden, Robert V. . . . . King World Productions, Inc., p. 188
Maddoch, Jason . . . . Emmett/Furla Films, p. 123
Maddock, Brent . . . . Stampede Entertainment, p. 299
Maddox, Anthony . . . . Bad Boy Films, p. 59
Maddox, Steve . . . . Sony Pictures Television, p. 296

Madhavan, A.K. .RichCrest Animation Studios, p. 272
Madigan, Alyson .Frelaine, p. 142
Madison, Joel .Help Me Help You, p. 363
Madison, Julie .One Life to Live, p. 371
Madison, Meg .Revelations Entertainment, p. 271
Madison, Paula .NBC Universal Corporate, p. 231
Madonna .Maverick Films, p. 213
Mador, Jennifer .VanDerKloot Film & Television, p. 328
Madsen, Kip .Last Call with Carson Daly, p. 366
Madson, Ken .Parallel Entertainment, Inc., p. 247
Maeda, Steve .Day Break, p. 359
Mafoutsis, John .MTV Networks Latin America (MTVNLA), p. 226
Magar, Guy .Guy Magar Films, p. 206
Magedman, David .Warner Independent Pictures, p. 335
Maggini, Tia .Red Wagon Entertainment, p. 268
Maggio, Vince .Frederick Zollo Productions, Inc., p. 350
Maggioni, Alex .E! Networks, p. 117
Magnuson, Sharan .Warner Bros. Television Production, p. 335
Mago, Marianne Cracchiolo .Warner Bros. Television Production, p. 335
Magpiong, Bret .Andell Entertainment, p. 51
Maguire, Kiran .Nine Yards Entertainment, p. 238
Maguire, Patrick .ABC Entertainment Television Group, p. 45
Maguire, Patrick .Touchstone Television, p. 316
Mahan, Mike .dick clark productions, inc., p. 94
Maher, Bill .Real Time with Bill Maher, p. 372
Maier, Rob .Smallville, p. 375
Mailer, Michael .Michael Mailer Films, p. 207
Maio, Juliana .Lighthouse Productions, p. 198
Majerus, Greg .Moonstone Entertainment, p. 220
Makarewicz, Andrew .CinéGroupe, p. 91
Makhlout, David .IFM Film Associates, Inc., p. 171
Makkos, Suzanna .Fox Broadcasting Company, p. 139
Makler, Todd .The Over the Hill Gang, p. 245
Maksimovich, Dana .The Black Donnellys, p. 356
Malacrida, Dave .MGA Ent./MGA Ent. Films, p. 216
Maleki, Salvy .O Entertainment, p. 240
Maleski, Michael .Proteus, p. 263
Malhotra, Ravi .Patriot Pictures, LLC, p. 250
Malik, Sanjoy .Air2web, Inc., p. 48
Malina, Maggie .VH1, p. 330
Malins, Greg .How I Met Your Mother, p. 364
Malkovich, John .Mr. Mudd, p. 224
Mallhi, Sonny .Vertigo Entertainment, p. 330
Mallman, Stephan .Recorded Picture Company, p. 266
Malloy, Angela .3 Ball Productions, p. 40
Mallozzi, Joseph .Stargate: SG-1, p. 376
Mallozzi, Joseph .Stargate: Atlantis, p. 376
Malone, Stanley .PorchLight Entertainment, p. 259
Maloney, Eric .Primetime Pictures, p. 262
Maloof, Adrienne .Maloof Productions, p. 208
Maloof, Gavin .Maloof Productions, p. 208
Maloof, George .Maloof Productions, p. 208
Maloof, Joe .Maloof Productions, p. 208
Maloof, Phil .Maloof Productions, p. 208
Maltagliati, Kellie .Village Roadshow Pictures, p. 331
Maltin, Samantha .Nickelodeon/MTVN Kids & Family Group, p. 237
Malykont, Ethan .Union Entertainment, p. 325
Mamet, David .The Unit, p. 378
Mamet, Lynn .The Unit, p. 378
Manasse, Patrick .Spitfire Pictures, p. 298
Manchester, Amy .Asylum Entertainment, p. 57
Mancini, Tessa .Norman Twain Productions, p. 322
Mancino, Jennifer .The Mark Gordon Company, p. 150
Mancuso, Renee .Lakeshore Entertainment Group LLC, p. 192
Mancuso Jr., Frank .360 Pictures/FGM Entertainment, p. 41
Mandala, Steven .Telemundo Network, p. 310
Mandel, Hillary .IMG Media, p. 172
Mandel, Laura Danford .Telepictures Productions, p. 311
Mandel, Mark .ABC Sports, p. 45
Mandelbaum, Reeva .John Wells Productions, p. 338
Mandelberg, Stacy .von Zerneck-Sertner Films, p. 332
Mandoki, Luis .Mandoki Productions, Inc., p. 209
Manela, Mariana .A. Smith & Co. Productions, p. 292
Manetti, Carolyn .Maple Shade Films, p. 210
Mangan IV, Thomas J. .River One Films, p. 272
Mangano, Stephanie .Touchstone Television, p. 316
Mangano, Stephanie .Buena Vista Motion Pictures Group, p. 78
Mangieri, Rebecca .CSI: NY, p. 359
Mangieri, Rebecca .The Shield, p. 374
Mangold, James .Tree Line Film, p. 317
Manham, Nadav .LaSalleHolland, p. 194
Manheim, Michael .The Manheim Company, p. 210
Maniaci, Sal .Nickelodeon/MTVN Kids & Family Group, p. 237
Manis, Brian D. .Davis Entertainment Company, p. 107
Mankiewicz, John .Saved, p. 374
Mankiewicz, John .Western Sandblast, p. 339
Mankoff, Doug .Echo Lake Productions, p. 119
Mann, Gary .Comedy Central, p. 98
Mann, Michael .Forward Pass, Inc., p. 138
Mann, Patricia .The Littlefield Company, p. 200
Mann, Shalom .Sony Pictures Digital, p. 295
Mann, Thea .Dirt, p. 360
Mann, Thea .Coquette Productions, p. 101
Mann, Travis .Crystal Sky Pictures, LLC, p. 104
Manne, Karen .Touchstone Television, p. 316
Manners, Kim .Supernatural, p. 377
Manning, Michelle .MM Productions, p. 218
Manor, Arnon .CatchLight Films, p. 85
Manos Jr., James .James Manos Productions, Inc., p. 210
Manpearl, David .Wonderland Sound and Vision, p. 344
Mansell, Richard .Recorded Picture Company, p. 266
Mansfield, Pancho .Spike TV, p. 298
Manson, Arla Sorkin .Sarabande Productions, p. 280
Manson, David .Saved, p. 374
Manson, David .Sarabande Productions, p. 280
Mansour, Andrea .Wild Brain, Inc., p. 341
Manulis, John .Visionbox Media Group, p. 331
Manulis, John .Foundation Entertainment, p. 138
Manus, Daniel .Clifford Werber Productions, p. 339
Manville, Reed .CBS Paramount Worldwide Television Dist., p. 88
Manwiller, Debi .24, p. 353
Manze, Vince .NBC Entertainment, p. 230
Maquiling, David .Angelika, p. 52
Marano, Gabriel .Fox Television Studios, p. 140
Marburger, Kevin .Girlfriends, p. 362
Marburger, Michele .Girlfriends, p. 362
Marcantonio, AJ .Shoe Money Productions, p. 286
Marcello, Vanessa .Artists Production Group (APG), p. 56
Marchant, Byron .BET Networks, p. 66
Marchant, Joe .Smallville, p. 375
Marchick, Jenny .Mandeville Films, p. 209
Marco, Daisy .Cannell Studios, p. 83
Marcus, Andrew .Relativity Media LLC, p. 269
Marcus, Irwin .Touchstone Television, p. 316
Marcus, Matthew .Triage Entertainment, p. 317
Marcus, Michael E. .Cornice Entertainment, p. 101
Margara, Penny .Periscope Entertainment, LLC, p. 252
Margol, Bill .Discovery Networks, U.S., p. 111
Margol, Bill .Travel Channel, p. 316
Margolin, Judy .Parkchester Pictures, p. 249
Margolis, Brad .The Edelstein Company, p. 119
Margolis, Bruce .Twentieth Century Fox Television, p. 323
Margolis, Lisa .Warner Bros. Pictures, p. 334
Margulies, Alan .AM Productions & Management, p. 50
Mariani, E. Nicholas .Mike's Movies/Michael Peyser Prod., p. 216
Mariano, Joy .Arnold Shapiro Productions, p. 285
Mariano, Mike .My Name Is Earl, p. 369
Marin, Alexander .Sony Pictures Television International, p. 296
Marincic, Richard .Platinum Studios, LLC, p. 257
Marinelli, Janice .Buena Vista Television, p. 79
Marino, Joe .Stick Figure Productions, p. 301
Marino, Len .Janicek-Marino Creative, p. 179
Marinoff, Deborah .Abandon Pictures, Inc., p. 44
Mark, Denise .Passions, p. 371
Mark, Laurence .Laurence Mark Productions, p. 210
Markel, Katrina .Braverman Productions, Inc., p. 73
Markle, Peter .Blueline Productions, p. 69
Markley, Ed .Southern Skies, Inc., p. 297
Markley, Jodi .ESPN Original Entertainment (EOE), p. 127
Markline, Mark .Universal Pictures, p. 326

Marko, David . . . . CBS Entertainment, p. 86
Markowitz, Michelle . . . . Magnet Management, p. 207
Marks, Brad . . . . Media Talent Group, p. 214
Marks, Dean . . . . Warner Bros. Entertainment Inc., p. 334
Marks, Mike . . . . Brillstein-Grey Entertainment, p. 75
Marks, Molly . . . . Barracuda Productions, p. 62
Marks, Rebecca . . . . NBC Entertainment, p. 230
Marks, Stephen . . . . Evolution Entertainment, p. 128
Marlon, Christopher . . . . Code Entertainment, p. 96
Marmur, Ori . . . . Original Film, p. 244
Marozas, Andrea . . . . Warner Bros. Entertainment Inc., p. 334
Marsak, Lindsay . . . . here! Networks, p. 165
Marsh, Gary K. . . . . Disney ABC Cable Networks Group, p. 112
Marsh, Tony . . . . Jay & Tony Show Productions, p. 180
Marshak, Darryl . . . . The Marshak/Zachary Company, p. 211
Marshal, Paul . . . . O Entertainment, p. 240
Marshall, Adam . . . . Energy Entertainment, p. 124
Marshall, Alex . . . . Spice Factory, p. 298
Marshall, Bonnie K. . . . . David Brady Productions, p. 72
Marshall, Frank . . . . The Kennedy/Marshall Company, p. 186
Marshall, Garry . . . . Henderson Productions, Inc., p. 164
Marshall, James . . . . Smallville, p. 375
Marshall, Michael E. . . . . Marvel Studios, Inc., p. 211
Marshall, Penny . . . . Parkway Productions, p. 249
Marshall, Sam . . . . Burnt Orange Productions, p. 80
Marshall, Tresha . . . . Sony Pictures Television, p. 296
Marshall-Daniels, Meryl . . . . Two Oceans Entertainment Group, p. 324
Marter, Annie . . . . GreeneStreet Films, p. 153
Martin, Bill . . . . The Singles Table, p. 375
Martin, Billy . . . . Real Time with Bill Maher, p. 372
Martin, Catherine . . . . Bazmark, Inq., p. 63
Martin, Damon . . . . Departure Studios, p. 109
Martin, David . . . . Avalon Television, Inc., p. 58
Martin, Erin E. . . . . Lunaria Films, p. 204
Martin, Gary . . . . Columbia Pictures, p. 97
Martin, Jeremy . . . . Dark Trick Films, p. 107
Martin, Jim . . . . Traveler, p. 377
Martin, Jonathon Komack . . . . Dark Trick Films, p. 107
Martin, Kim . . . . WE: Women's Entertainment, p. 336
Martin, Nic . . . . Ealing Studios, p. 118
Martin, Nikki . . . . G-Unit Television & Films, p. 157
Martin, Ross . . . . MTV Networks, p. 226
Martin, Sam . . . . HBO Films, p. 162
Martin, Scott . . . . Workshop Pictures, Inc., p. 345
Martin, Steve . . . . Martin/Stein Productions, p. 211
Martin, Wes . . . . MARTHA, p. 368
Martin, Wrye . . . . Civilian Pictures, p. 94
Martin, Wrye . . . . L'Orange, p. 203
Martinelli, Carlo . . . . Bona Fide Productions, p. 71
Martinez, Dan . . . . Universal Pictures, p. 326
Martinez, Naomi . . . . Fox Television Studios, p. 140
Martinez, Philippe . . . . Bauer Martinez Entertainment, p. 63
Martino, Myra Jo . . . . Ugly Betty, p. 378
Martino, Virginia . . . . New Line Cinema, p. 234
Martinsen, Dan . . . . Nickelodeon/MTVN Kids & Family Group, p. 237
Martofel, Jonathan . . . . VOY Pictures, p. 332
Marvin, Niki . . . . Niki Marvin Productions, Inc., p. 211
Marx, Eric . . . . Sony Pictures Television, p. 296
Marx, Hilary . . . . Broadway Video Entertainment, p. 76
Marx, Liz . . . . Psych, p. 372
Marx, Tim . . . . Justice, p. 364
Marx, Timothy . . . . Timothy Marx Productions, Inc., p. 212
Mas, Juan . . . . North By Northwest Entertainment, p. 239
Masada, Jamie . . . . Laugh Factory Entertainment, p. 195
Maschwitz, Stuart . . . . The Orphanage, p. 244
Mascolo, Mark . . . . Shukovsky English Entertainment, p. 287
Maser, Karen . . . . ER, p. 361
Mashariki, Zola . . . . Twentieth Century Fox - Searchlight Pictures, p. 323
Masi, James . . . . Sobini Films, p. 293
Mason, Brendan . . . . Beech Hill Films, p. 65
Mason, Gabriel . . . . Vertigo Entertainment, p. 330
Mason, Linda . . . . CBS News, p. 87
Mason, Lynn . . . . Zane W. Levitt Prod./Zeta Ent., p. 197
Masquelier, Michel . . . . IMG Media, p. 172
Mass, Jared . . . . Walden Media, p. 333
Massey, Dave . . . . Bobker/Kruger Films, p. 70
Massey, Joanna . . . . CBS Corporation, p. 86
Massey, Joanna . . . . CBS Entertainment, p. 86
Massie, Bob . . . . IMG Media, p. 172
Massin, Dylan . . . . Studio 60 on the Sunset Strip, p. 376
Mastro, Anna . . . . Wonderland Sound and Vision, p. 344
Mastropasqua, Gaetano . . . . Warner Bros. Entertainment Inc., p. 334
Matalas, Terry . . . . Braga Productions, p. 72
Matalon, David . . . . Regency Enterprises, p. 268
Mate, Lowell . . . . Flame Ventures LLC, p. 135
Mater, Rick . . . . The CW, p. 105
Mathenge, Nimo . . . . Once Upon A Time Films, Ltd., p. 243
Mathews, Martin . . . . Keckins Projects, Ltd., p. 185
Mathison, Lori . . . . Film Bridge International, p. 132
Matlin, Marlee . . . . Solo One Productions, p. 294
Matson, Chris . . . . HDNet Films, p. 163
Matsuhsima, Arata . . . . Sony Pictures Television International, p. 296
Mattera, Larry . . . . Amp'd Mobile, p. 51
Matthau, Charles . . . . The Matthau Company, Inc., p. 212
Matthew, Marcia . . . . Dream Entertainment, Inc., p. 116
Matthews, Andrew . . . . New Line Cinema, p. 234
Matthews, Gina . . . . Roundtable Entertainment, p. 276
Mattis, David . . . . Circle of Confusion Productions, p. 93
Mattis, Lawrence . . . . Circle of Confusion Productions, p. 93
Matukewicz, Joe . . . . Paramount Vantage/Paramount Classics, p. 248
Matz, Zachary . . . . Filmsmith, p. 133
Mauceri, Mark . . . . Playboy Entertainment Group, Inc., p. 257
Maul, Chris . . . . Grammnet Productions, p. 152
Maurer, Joshua D. . . . . City Entertainment, p. 93
Mauro, Scott . . . . Scott Mauro Entertainment, Inc., p. 212
Mavinkurve, Nik . . . . Marc Platt Productions, p. 257
Maxtone-Graham, Ian . . . . The Simpsons, p. 375
Maxwell, Chris . . . . Twentieth Century Fox - Searchlight Pictures, p. 323
May, Corey . . . . SekretAgent Productions, p. 283
May, Rebecca . . . . King of the Hill, p. 365
May, Robert . . . . SenArt Films, p. 284
May, Wylleen . . . . American Idol, p. 354
Mayberry, Del . . . . Fox Broadcasting Company, p. 139
Maybruck, Nadine . . . . Arthur Sarkissian Productions, p. 280
Maydew, Sam . . . . The Collective, p. 96
Mayer, Vivian . . . . Universal Pictures, p. 326
Mayfield, Debra . . . . Charles Floyd Johnson Productions, p. 89
Mayfield, Debra . . . . Belisarius Productions, p. 65
Maynard, Ghen . . . . CBS Entertainment, p. 86
Mayo, Jennifer . . . . ABC Entertainment Television Group, p. 45
Mayo, John . . . . New Line Television, p. 235
Mayrs, Coreen . . . . Supernatural, p. 377
Mayrs, Coreen . . . . Smallville, p. 375
Mayrs, Coreen . . . . The L Word, p. 366
Mayzurk, Jeff . . . . E! Networks, p. 117
Mazalian, Josh . . . . Double Edge Entertainment, p. 115
Mazer, Nicole . . . . Nickelodeon/MTVN Kids & Family Group, p. 237
Mazur, Mare . . . . KCET, p. 185
Mazur, Paula . . . . Film Farm, p. 132
Mazza, Tom . . . . Madison Road Entertainment, p. 206
Mazzara, Glen . . . . The Shield, p. 374
Mazzara, Glen . . . . Standoff, p. 376
Mazzocone, Carl . . . . Main Line Pictures, p. 207
Mazzocone, Carl . . . . Evolution Entertainment, p. 128
Mazzola, Kara . . . . FR Productions, p. 141
Mazzu, Joanne . . . . Sony Pictures Television, p. 296
McAboy, Scott . . . . fox 21, p. 138
McAlevey, Peter . . . . Thunderbird Pictures, p. 313
McAloon, Brian . . . . The Late Late Show with Craig Ferguson, p. 366
McBride, Christine . . . . Raymond Wagner Productions, Inc., p. 332
McBride, Scot . . . . MTV Networks Latin America (MTVNLA), p. 226
McCabe, Claire . . . . VH1, p. 330
McCaffrey, Dan . . . . Sony Pictures Television International, p. 296
McCaffrey, Katy . . . . Watson Pond Productions, p. 336
McCall, Andrea . . . . DreamWorks SKG, p. 116
McCall, Joan . . . . Joada Productions, Inc., p. 181
McCall, Lael . . . . Blueprint Entertainment, p. 70
McCall, Marsh . . . . 20 Good Years, p. 353
McCallie, Doug . . . . Survivor, p. 377
McCandless, Shannon . . . . Whoop Inc./One Ho Prod./Lil' Whoop Prod., p. 340

McCann, David . . . . .Buena Vista Motion Pictures Group, p. 78
McCanny, Jane . . . . .KeyLight Entertainment Group, p. 187
McCarley, Mike . . . . .NBC Sports, p. 231
McCarthy, Bill . . . . .Carsey-Werner Films, p. 84
McCarthy, David . . . . .CRPI Entertainment, p. 103
McCarthy, Dottie . . . . .The Stevens Company, p. 301
McCarthy, Gena . . . . .WE: Women's Entertainment, p. 336
McCarthy, Jeanne Mark . . . . .Lucky Louie, p. 368
McCarthy, Lillah . . . . .Turner Network Television (TNT), p. 321
McCarthy, Lillah . . . . .TBS, p. 309
McCarthy, Patrick . . . . .My Name Is Earl, p. 369
McCarthy, Vanessa . . . . .Rules of Engagement, p. 373
McCartney, Bret D. . . . . .Trancas International Films, p. 316
McCauley, Darryl . . . . .SUperFInger Entertainment, p. 306
McClard, Lauren . . . . .Ahimsa Films, p. 48
McClellan, Cyndi . . . . .E! Networks, p. 117
McClellan, Kevin . . . . .E! Networks, p. 117
McClelland, Megan . . . . .Frederic Golchan Productions, p. 148
McClintock, Dana . . . . .CBS Corporation, p. 86
McClintock, Jim . . . . .ABC Entertainment Television Group, p. 45
McCloskey, Shane . . . . .Element Films, p. 121
McCluggage, Kerry . . . . .Craftsman Films, p. 102
McClure, Holly .Namesake Entertainment, p. 228
McConaghey, Richard . . . . .Davis Entertainment Company, p. 107
McConaughey, Matthew . . . . .j.k. livin productions, p. 178
McConnell, Fran . . . . .Sony Pictures Television International, p. 296
McCorkindale, Laura . . . . .Bluebird House, p. 69
McCorkle, Pat . . . . .3 lbs., p. 353
McCorkmick, Blake . . . . .King of the Hill, p. 365
McCormack, Eric . . . . .Big Cattle Productions, p. 67
McCormick, Colleen . . . . .Lifetime Television (Los Angeles), p. 198
McCormick, Gary . . . . .Fine Living, p. 133
McCormick, Gary . . . . .DIY Network, p. 113
McCormick, Kathy . . . . .Crossing Jordan, p. 358
McCormick, Kelly . . . . .Vox3 Films, p. 332
McCormick, Kevin . . . . .Warner Bros. Pictures, p. 334
McCoy, Bruce . . . . .Mad TV, p. 368
McCoy, Wendy . . . . .Versus, p. 329
McCracken, Craig . . . . .Cartoon Network, p. 84
McCray, Brigitte . . . . .Oxygen Media, p. 245
McCreary, Judith . . . . .Law & Order: Special Victims Unit, p. 367
McCreary, Laura . . . . .American Dad, p. 354
McCreary, Lori . . . . .Revelations Entertainment, p. 271
McCrory, Shelley . . . . .NBC Universal Television Studio, p. 231
McCullagh, Nathaniel . . . . .Barbara Lieberman Productions, p. 197
McCulloch, Kyle . . . . .South Park, p. 376
McCumber, Chris . . . . .USA Network, p. 327
McCurry, Pilar . . . . .Columbia Pictures, p. 97
McDermott, Anne . . . . .Sneak Preview Entertainment, Inc., p. 293
McDonald, Alison . . . . .Close to Home, p. 357
McDonald, Annabelle . . . . .WE: Women's Entertainment, p. 336
McDonald, Michael . . . . .Touchstone Television, p. 316
McDonald, Michael . . . . .ABC Entertainment Television Group, p. 45
McDonnell, Ed . . . . .Maple Shade Films, p. 210
McDonough, Candice . . . . .New Line Cinema, p. 234
McDonough, Linda . . . . .Odd Lot Entertainment, p. 241
McElroy, Jill . . . . .Benderspink, p. 66
McElwaine, Guy .Morgan Creek Productions, p. 221
McEntegart, Rob . . . . .Mandate Pictures, p. 209
McEntire, Reba . . . . .Reba, p. 372
McFadden, Grant . . . . .Bold Films, p. 71
McFadden, Johnathon . . . . .Baldwin Entertainment Group, Ltd., p. 60
McFadden-Roan, Colin . . . . .fox 21, p. 138
McFadzean, David . . . . .Wind Dancer Production Group, p. 342
McFern, Dennis . . . . .Airborne Entertainment, p. 48
McG . . . . .The O.C., p. 371
McG . . . . .Supernatural, p. 377
McG . . . . .Wonderland Sound and Vision, p. 344
McGahey, Michael . . . . .Klasky Csupo, Inc., p. 189
McGhee, George .BBC Worldwide Americas, p. 64
McGill, Don . . . . .Numb3rs, p. 370
McGill, Rebecca . . . . .Flame Ventures LLC, p. 135
McGinnis, J.R. . . . . .Sony Pictures Television, p. 296
McGinty, Caitlin . . . . .Bushwacker Productions, p. 81
McGoldrick, Bill . . . . .Spike TV, p. 298
McGoun, Martyn . . . . .Mobile Streams, p. 219
McGowan, Betsy . . . . .The CW, p. 105
McGowan, Darin .Renegade Animation, Inc., p. 270
McGowan, Gretchen . . . . .HDNet Films, p. 163
McGrath, Benson . . . . .Anonymous Creators Productions, p. 52
McGrath, Dan . . . . .King of the Hill, p. 365
McGrath, Judith . . . . .MTV Networks, p. 226
McGrath, Judith . . . . .VH1, p. 330
McGrath, Tracy . . . . .Dimension Films, p. 111
McGuiness, Matt . . . . .3 lbs., p. 353
McGuinness, Carolyn . . . . .Harpo Films, Inc., p. 161
McGuire, David . . . . .Telepictures Productions, p. 311
McGuire, J.A. . . . . .Ember Entertainment Group, p. 122
McGuire, Paul . . . . .The CW, p. 105
McGuirk, Terence . . . . .Turner Entertainment Group, p. 320
McGurk, Chris . . . . .IDT Entertainment, p. 171
McHale, Judith A. . . . . .Discovery Networks, U.S., p. 111
McHugh, Jonathan . . . . .BloodWorks, LLC, p. 68
McHugh, Peter . . . . .The Gotham Group, Inc., p. 151
McIlhargey, Navid . . . . .Silver Pictures, p. 289
McInnes, Campbell . . . . .New Line Cinema, p. 234
McIntosh, Geriann . . . . .Warner Bros. Television Production, p. 335
McIntyre, Samantha . . . . .20 Good Years, p. 353
McJimsey, Mark . . . . .King of the Hill, p. 365
McKairnes, Jim . . . . .Discovery Networks, U.S., p. 111
McKean, Gerry . . . . .Nanny 911, p. 369
McKeaney, Brian . . . . .Patchett Kaufman Entertainment, p. 250
McKee, Pat . . . . .Nip/Tuck, p. 370
McKee, Stacy . . . . .Grey's Anatomy, p. 362
McKenna, Chris . . . . .American Dad, p. 354
McKenna, James . . . . .CBS News, p. 87
McKenna, Matt . . . . .American Dad, p. 354
McKeown, Allan . . . . .Takes On Productions, p. 308
McKeown, Theresa . . . . .Dalaklis-McKeown Entertainment, Inc., p. 106
McKillop, David . . . . .Discovery Networks, U.S., p. 111
McKinney, Mark . . . . .Studio 60 on the Sunset Strip, p. 376
McKinnon, Bob . . . . .MARTHA, p. 368
McKinnon, Don . . . . .Starbucks Entertainment, p. 299
McKinnon, Laverne . . . . .CBS Entertainment, p. 86
McKnight, Jane . . . . .Media Four, p. 214
McKnight, John . . . . .Exxcell Entertainment, Inc./Exxcell Films, p. 129
McLaren, Jenny . . . . .Mirage Enterprises, p. 217
McLaughlin, Christian . . . . .Beacon, p. 64
McLaughlin, Emily . . . . .Supernatural, p. 377
McLaughlin, Josh . . . . .The Mark Gordon Company, p. 150
McLaughlin, Melinda . . . . .A&E Network, p. 44
McLaughlin, Stacey . . . . .Principal Entertainment, p. 262
McLean, Bill . . . . .E! Networks, p. 117
McLean, Chrissie . . . . .C/W Productions, p. 105
McLean, Colin . . . . .TV Guide Channel, p. 321
McLeod, David . . . . .Buena Vista Television, p. 79
McLeroy, Val . . . . .Epigram Entertainment, p. 125
McLoughlin, Linda . . . . .Fremantle Productions Latin America, p. 142
McMahon, John . . . . .Sony Pictures Television International, p. 296
McManus, Marsha .Principal Entertainment, p. 262
McManus, Sean . . . . .CBS News, p. 87
McManus, Sean . . . . .CBS Sports, p. 88
McMaster, Emily . . . . .Big Beach, p. 67
McMillan, Katie . . . . .Element Films, p. 121
McMillian, Beatrice . . . . .Andrew Solt Productions, p. 294
McMinn, Robert . . . . .Lakeshore Entertainment Group LLC, p. 192
McNally, David . . . . .Justice, p. 364
McNamara, James M. . . . . .Panamax Films, p. 246
McNamara, Jennifer . . . . .30 Rock, p. 353
McNamara, Jennifer . . . . .NBC Entertainment, p. 230
McNamara, Julie . . . . .CBS Paramount Network Television, p. 87
McNamara, Sean . . . . .Brookwell McNamara Entertainment, Inc., p. 77
McNaughton, Amee . . . . .Twentieth Century Fox - Fox 2000, p. 323
McNeely, Milinda . . . . .ABC Entertainment Television Group, p. 45
McNeely, Milinda . . . . .Touchstone Television, p. 316
McNeil, Craig . . . . .Granada America, p. 152
McNichol, Megan . . . . .Mayhem Pictures, p. 213
McNicholas, Dennis . . . . .Saturday Night Live, p. 373
McNulty, Tom . . . . .21 Laps Entertainment, p. 38
McPartland, Tip . . . . .TMC Entertainment, p. 314

McPartlin, Peter . . . . .Miramax Films, p. 217
McPherson, Stephen . . . . .ABC Entertainment Television Group, p. 45
McQuilken, Kim . . . . .Cartoon Network, p. 84
McRae, Dan . . . . .Working Title Films, p. 345
McRitchie, Greig . . . . .Universal Pictures, p. 326
McRoberts, Anna . . . . .Keystone Entertainment, Inc., p. 187
McShane, Chris . . . . .Busboy Productions, p. 81
McTeague, Patti . . . . .Disney-ABC Television Group, p. 113
McTeague, Patti . . . . .Disney ABC Cable Networks Group, p. 112
Mead, Shannon . . . . .Burrud Productions, p. 80
Meade, Kim . . . . .Mandeville Films, p. 209
Meadows, Mike . . . . .New Wave Entertainment, p. 235
Meagher, Kevin . . . . .Popular Arts Entertainment, Inc., p. 259
Means, Sam . . . . .The Daily Show With Jon Stewart, p. 359
Mechanic, Bill . . . . .Pandemonium, p. 246
Mechanic, Carol .Showtime Networks Inc., p. 287
Medanich, Roger . . . . .Chiodo Bros. Productions, Inc., p. 90
Medavoy, Mike . . . . .Phoenix Pictures, p. 254
Medina, Benny . . . . .The Tyra Banks Show, p. 378
Medina, Benny .Handprint Entertainment, p. 160
Medjuck, Joe . . . . .The Montecito Picture Company, p. 220
Mednick, Scott . . . . .Legendary Pictures, p. 195
Medwid, Lisa . . . . .John Calley Productions, p. 82
Meehan, Glenn .44 Blue Productions, Inc., p. 41
Meehan, Timothy . . . . .Mojo Films, p. 220
Meenaghan, Jim . . . . .Walden Media, p. 333
Meenaghan, Jim . . . . .Bristol Bay Productions, p. 76
Mefford, Karl . . . . .The Montecito Picture Company, p. 220
Mehl, Chris . . . . .Mandalay Sports Action Entertainment & Mandalay Integrated Media Entertainment, p. 208
Mehlman, Alexandra . . . . .Imageries Entertainment, p. 171
Mehlman, Gary . . . . .Imageries Entertainment, p. 171
Mehr, Adam . . . . .Gold Circle Films, p. 148
Mehta, Salil . . . . .ABC Sports, p. 45
Mehta, Salil . . . . .ESPN Original Entertainment (EOE), p. 127
Meidel, Greg . . . . .CBS Paramount Worldwide Television Dist., p. 88
Meier, Rhiannon . . . . .Blue Star Pictures, p. 69
Meier, Seth William . . . . .Burnside Entertainment, Inc., p. 80
Meighan, Patrick . . . . .Family Guy, p. 361
Meil, Jason . . . . .Current TV, LLC, p. 105
Meir, Donna Friedman . . . .National Geographic Kids' Prog. & Prod., p. 229
Meisel, Gary . . . . .Warner Bros. Entertainment Inc., p. 334
Meisinger, Robyn . . . . .Madhouse Entertainment, p. 206
Meisler, Kevin . . . . .Orly Adelson Productions, p. 46
Meissner, Christine . . . . .Moonstone Entertainment, p. 220
Meister, Eddie . . . . .Buena Vista Television, p. 79
Mejia, Edward .Moshag Productions, Inc., p. 222
Mekles, David . . . . .Q Media Partners, p. 264
Melamede, Yael . . . . .Salty Features, p. 278
Melbye, Lisa . . . . .MGA Ent./MGA Ent. Films, p. 216
Meledandri, Christopher . . . . . . .Twentieth Century Fox Animation, p. 323
Melendez, Bill .Bill Melendez Productions, p. 215
Melendez, Christian "Kiki" . . . . .Latin Hollywood Films, p. 194
Melendez, Miguel . . . . .Overbrook Entertainment, p. 245
Mellen, Chase . . . . .Silver Lion Films, p. 288
Mellish, Craig . . . . .Florentine Films, p. 135
Mellner, Shirley . . . . .Martin Poll Films, Ltd., p. 259
Melnick, Jeff .Eighth Square Entertainment, p. 120
Melnick, Steven . . . . .Twentieth Century Fox Television, p. 323
Melnik, Robert . . . . .Lionsgate, p. 200
Meltzer, Howard . . . . .TurtleBack Productions, Inc., p. 321
Meltzer, Maxwell . . . . .Weintraub/Kuhn Productions, p. 338
Meltzer, Michael L. . . . . .Michael Meltzer Productions, p. 216
Melville, Sarah . . . . .PBS, p. 251
Memel, Jana Sue . . . . .Chanticleer Films, p. 89
Memel, Mindi . . . . .Chanticleer Films, p. 89
Menchel, Michael . . . . .Relevant Entertainment Group, p. 270
Mendel, Barry . . . . .Barry Mendel Productions, p. 215
Mendelsohn, Brad . . . . .Industry Entertainment Partners, p. 174
Mendelsohn, Carol . . . . .CSI: Crime Scene Investigation, p. 358
Mendelsohn, Carol . . . . .CSI: NY, p. 359
Mendelsohn, Carol . . . . .CSI: Miami, p. 358
Mendelsohn, Kelly . . . . .Revelations Entertainment, p. 271
Mendelsohn, Michael .Patriot Pictures, LLC, p. 250
Mendes, Sam .Neal Street Productions Ltd., p. 232
Mendez, Robert . . . . .Disney-ABC Television Group, p. 113
Mendoza, Azalia . . . . .Silver Lion Films, p. 288
Mendoza, Edy . . . . .CBS Entertainment, p. 86
Meneses, Isabel N. . . . . .Joel Films, p. 181
Menna, Christine . . . . .New Line Television, p. 235
Mensing Jr., Richard J. .CBS Entertainment, p. 86
Mercado, Robert . . . . .Cineville LLC, p. 93
Mercer, Tracy . . . . .Revelations Entertainment, p. 271
Mercer, Willie . . . . .Tagline Pictures, p. 307
Merchant, Stephen . . . . .The Office, p. 371
Mercier, Kevin .Screen Door Entertainment, p. 283
Mercurio, Jim . . . . .Montage Entertainment, p. 220
Merilees, Rob . . . . .Infinity Features Entertainment, p. 174
Meringoff, William .Joada Productions, Inc., p. 181
Merlino, Jennifer . . . . .Untitled Entertainment, p. 327
Merlob, Michael . . . . .Sunrise Entertainment, p. 305
Meron, Neil . . . . .Storyline Entertainment, p. 302
Merrell, Aaron .Sidney Kimmel Entertainment, p. 187
Merrick, Rodney . . . . .Malcolm Leo Productions, p. 196
Merrifield, Gary . . . . .Comedy Central, p. 98
Merrill, Dina . . . . .RKO Pictures, LLC, p. 273
Mertz, Steven . . . . .Warner Bros. Entertainment Inc., p. 334
Mervyn, Sasha . . . . .Laura Ziskin Productions, p. 349
Meserve, Dete . . . . .Wind Dancer Production Group, p. 342
Messer, Arnold . . . . .Phoenix Pictures, p. 254
Messer, Erica . . . . .Criminal Minds, p. 358
Messer, Fran . . . . .Nanas Entertainment, p. 229
Messick, Jill . . . . .Broadway Video Entertainment, p. 76
Messier, Linda . . . . .Traveler's Rest Films, p. 317
Messina, Gabriella . . . . .Home & Garden Television (HGTV), p. 168
Messina, Michael . . . . .New Amsterdam Entertainment, Inc., p. 233
Metcalf, Kim . . . . .Jerry Bruckheimer Films & Television, p. 78
Metcalf, Mitch . . . . .NBC Entertainment, p. 230
Metrose, Ian . . . . .CBS Entertainment, p. 86
Metrose, Lauri . . . . .CBS Paramount Network Television, p. 87
Metwalli, Mona . . . . .dick clark productions, inc., p. 94
Metz, Marsha . . . . .Constantin Film Dev., Inc./Constantin TV, p. 100
Metz, Meredith .Walt Disney Television Animation, p. 113
Metz, Meredith . . . . .Disney ABC Cable Networks Group, p. 112
Metz III, Tom W. . . . . .Lion Rock Productions, p. 199
Metzger, Bridget . . . . .VanDerKloot Film & Television, p. 328
Metzler, David . . . . .Queer Eye, p. 372
Metzler, David . . . . .Scout Productions, p. 282
Metzner, Raven . . . . .Six Degrees, p. 375
Meurer, Terry . . . . .Cosgrove-Meurer Productions, p. 101
Meyer, Barry M. . . . . .Warner Bros. Entertainment Inc., p. 334
Meyer, Kris . . . . .Conundrum Entertainment, p. 100
Meyer, Nick . . . . .Lionsgate, p. 200
Meyer, Patricia K. . . . . .Patricia K. Meyer Productions, p. 216
Meyer, Ron . . . . .NBC Universal Corporate, p. 231
Meyer, Ron . . . . .Universal Studios, p. 326
Meyer, Sophie . . . . .Ealing Studios, p. 118
Meyer, Turi . . . . .Smallville, p. 375
Meyerink, Victoria Paige . . . . .Star Entertainment Group, Inc., p. 299
Meyers, Andy . . . . .M3 Television, p. 205
Meyers, Bryan . . . . .Magnetic Film, p. 207
Meyers, Howard . . . . .Focus Features/Rogue Pictures, p. 136
Meyers, Margo . . . . .Six Degrees, p. 375
Meyers, Seth . . . . .Saturday Night Live, p. 373
Meyerson, Aaron . . . . .Oxygen Media, p. 245
Micallef, Amanda . . . . .Rope The Moon Productions, p. 274
Micallef, Eddie . . . . .Burnside Entertainment, Inc., p. 80
Michael, Terence . . . . .Terence Michael Productions, Inc., p. 216
Michaels, David .Hella Good Moving Pictures, p. 164
Michaels, Jim . . . . .Everybody Hates Chris, p. 361
Michaels, Joe . . . . .MSN Originals, p. 224
Michaels, Joel . . . . .C2 Pictures, p. 81
Michaels, Lorne . . . . .30 Rock, p. 353
Michaels, Lorne . . . . .Late Night with Conan O'Brien, p. 367
Michaels, Lorne . . . . .Saturday Night Live, p. 373
Michaels, Lorne . . . . .Broadway Video, p. 76
Michaels, Lorne . . . . .Broadway Video Entertainment, p. 76
Michaels, Megan . . . . .American Idol, p. 354
Michaels, Steve . . . . .Asylum Entertainment, p. 57
Michalchyshyn, Laura . . . . .Sundance Channel, p. 304

Michas, Ryan . . . . .Stone Village Pictures, LLC, p. 302
Michelle, Brianne . . . . .Summerland Entertainment, p. 304
Michels, Peter . . . . .Forest Park Pictures, p. 137
Michels, Scott . . . . .CBS Paramount International Television, p. 87
Michenaud, Jean-Michel . . .Trading Spouses: Meet Your New Mommy, p. 377
Michenaud, Jean-Michel . . . . .Rocket Science Laboratories, p. 273
Michiel, Aaron . . . . .Relativity Media LLC, p. 269
Mickelson, Robert . . . . .Film Farm, p. 132
Middelton, Sarisa .Carrie Productions, Inc., p. 83
Middleton, James . . . . .C2 Pictures, p. 81
Middleton, Polly . . . . .Paul Pompian Productions, Inc., p. 259
Midgen, Toby . . . . .Lakeshore Entertainment Group LLC, p. 192
Miele, Christopher . . . . .The Ellen DeGeneres Show, p. 360
Migliore, Bill . . . . .Class 5 Films, p. 95
Mihailovich, Vera .Forward Entertainment, p. 138
Mika, Andre . . . . .AOL Media Networks, p. 53
Mikita, Andy . . . . .Stargate: SG-1, p. 376
Mikita, Martha . . . . .World International Network, p. 345
Milam, Julian . . . . .The Bedford Falls Company, p. 65
Milam, Matthew . . . . .Mandate Pictures, p. 209
Milano, Lin . . . . .Broad Strokes Entertainment, p. 76
Milch, David . . . . .Red Board Productions, p. 267
Milchan, Arnon . . . . .Regency Enterprises, p. 268
Milchan-Lambert, Alexandra . . . . .Regency Enterprises, p. 268
Miles, Joanna . . . . .Brandman Productions, p. 73
Milich, Matt . . . . .Armada Pictures, p. 55
Milio, Jim . . . . .MPH Entertainment, Inc., p. 224
Milito, Louis . . . . .CSI: Crime Scene Investigation, p. 358
Milkovich, Ed . . . . .Vanished, p. 378
Millar, Miles . . . . .Smallville, p. 375
Millard, Bryan . . . . .Circle of Confusion Productions, p. 93
Mille, Judah . . . . .King of the Hill, p. 365
Miller, Andrew . . . . .Mirage Enterprises, p. 217
Miller, Angela . . . . .Revelations Entertainment, p. 271
Miller, Brian . . . . .Cartoon Network, p. 84
Miller, Carmen M. . . . . .Eternity Pictures, Inc., p. 127
Miller, Chelsea . . . . .Shoreline Entertainment, Inc., p. 286
Miller, Chris . . . . .Visionbox Media Group, p. 331
Miller, Chris . . . . .Flower Films, Inc., p. 135
Miller, Christina . . . . .Cartoon Network, p. 84
Miller, Corey . . . . .CSI: Miami, p. 358
Miller, Craig . . . . .Wolfmill Entertainment, p. 343
Miller, Darren . . . . .C/W Productions, p. 105
Miller, Diana . . . . .Last Call with Carson Daly, p. 366
Miller, Diane .Tomorrow Film Corporation, p. 315
Miller, Gabe . . . . .The Class, p. 357
Miller, Herman . . . . .Euphoria Entertainment, p. 127
Miller, Jeff . . . . .Kinetic Filmworks, p. 188
Miller, Jeffrey . . . . .Buena Vista Motion Pictures Group, p. 78
Miller, Jessica . . . . .Chic Productions, p. 90
Miller, Jim . . . . .Mandate Pictures, p. 209
Miller, Jimmy . . . . .20 Good Years, p. 353
Miller, Jimmy . . . . .Happy Hour, p. 362
Miller, Jimmy . . . . .Mosaic Media Group, p. 222
Miller, Jimmy . . . . .Werner-Gold-Miller, p. 339
Miller, John . . . . .NBC Entertainment, p. 230
Miller, Jonathan . . . . .AOL Media Networks, p. 53
Miller, Jonathan D. . . . . .NBC Sports, p. 231
Miller, Kate . . . . .Zinkler Films, p. 349
Miller, Ken . . . . .Boston Legal, p. 357
Miller, Ken . . . . .Traveler, p. 377
Miller, Ken . . . . .Two and a Half Men, p. 378
Miller, Kenny . . . . .Noggin, p. 239
Miller, Kenny . . . . .The N, p. 228
Miller, Kimberly . . . . .Radiant Productions, p. 265
Miller, Laura K. . . . . .Intermedia Film Equities USA, Inc., p. 175
Miller, Lori . . . . .The Vault, Inc., p. 329
Miller, Mark . . . . .Industrial Light & Magic (ILM), p. 174
Miller, Matt . . . . .Las Vegas, p. 366
Miller, Michelle . . . . .1492 Pictures, p. 38
Miller, Murray . . . . .King of the Hill, p. 365
Miller, Nancy Jacobs . . . . .Film Garden Entertainment, Inc., p. 132
Miller, Nathan . . . . .Johnenelly Productions, p. 182
Miller, Nick . . . . .Atlas Entertainment, p. 57
Miller, Nick . . . . .Code Entertainment, p. 96
Miller, Nicki . . . . .Steven Schwartz Productions, Inc., p. 281
Miller, Olaf . . . . .Atomic Cartoons, Inc., p. 58
Miller, Paul . . . . .Crossroads Films, p. 103
Miller, Perkins . . . . .NBC Sports, p. 231
Miller, Richard . . . . .Guardian Entertainment, Ltd., p. 157
Miller, Seth A. . . . . .Moshag Productions, Inc., p. 222
Miller, Staci . . . . .Warner Bros. Online, p. 334
Miller, Steve . . . . .New Line Cinema, p. 234
Miller, Susan . . . . .The L Word, p. 366
Miller, Thomas L. .Miller/Boyett Productions, p. 217
Miller, Todd . . . . .Sony Pictures Television International, p. 296
Miller, Troy . . . . .Dakota North Entertainment/Dakota Films, p. 106
Miller, Vicky . . . . .Turner Entertainment Group, p. 320
Miller, Zach . . . . .Reason Pictures, p. 266
Millero, Ralph . . . . .Mirage Enterprises, p. 217
Millerton, Heather . . . . .Fade In Films, p. 129
Millikan, Rick . . . . .Shark, p. 374
Millikan, Rick . . . . .Bones, p. 356
Millikin, Brian . . . . .Piller/Segan, p. 255
Milliner, Todd . . . . .Hazy Mills Productions, p. 161
Mills, Alan W. . . . . .The Marshak/Zachary Company, p. 211
Mills, Chris . . . . .Magnet Management, p. 207
Mills, Christian . . . . .Hyperion Studio, p. 169
Mills, Rob . . . . .ABC Entertainment Television Group, p. 45
Mills, Scott . . . . .BET Networks, p. 66
Milne, Ian . . . . .The Syndicate, p. 307
Milne, Jeff . . . . .Pathfinder Pictures, LLC, p. 250
Milo, Nancy . . . . .Touchstone Television, p. 316
Miloro, Andrea . . . . .Sony Pictures Animation, p. 295
Milstead, Julie . . . . .Winkler Films, p. 342
Milstein, Andrew . . . . .Buena Vista Motion Pictures Group, p. 78
Milstein, Edward L. . . . . .Level 1 Entertainment, p. 197
Milton, Meredith . . . . .Summit Entertainment, p. 304
Mimoun, Rina . . . . .Gilmore Girls, p. 362
Min, Eric . . . . .Seven Arts Pictures, p. 285
Mincheff, Roger . . . . .Spacedog, p. 297
Miner, David . . . . .30 Rock, p. 353
Miner, David . . . . .3 Arts Entertainment, Inc., p. 40
Miner, Mark . . . . .Paramount Pictures Production Division, p. 248
Minerd, Dean . . . . .Evolution, p. 128
Ming, Melvin . . . . .Sesame Workshop, p. 285
Minghella, Anthony . . . . .Mirage Enterprises, p. 217
Minnis, Michael . . . . .The Bold and the Beautiful, p. 356
Minoff, Marvin . . . . .Farrell/Minoff Productions, p. 130
Minoli, Lorenzo .Five Mile River Films, Ltd., p. 134
Minor, Zac . . . . .A Band Apart, p. 43
Minor, Zac . . . . .Lawrence Bender Productions, p. 65
Minson, Whitney . . . . .Launa Newman Productions (LNP), p. 195
Minster, Mary Ann . . . . .Comedy Central, p. 98
Mintz, Alan . . . . .Starbucks Entertainment, p. 299
Mirabello, Doug . . . . .Rick Berman Productions, p. 66
Miranda, Jada . . . . .HBO Entertainment, p. 162
Mirante, Nicole . . . . .The Nine, p. 370
Mirch, Jason . . . . .Evolution Entertainment, p. 128
Mircheff, Alex . . . . .Original Film, p. 244
Mirich, Eric . . . . .CSI: Miami, p. 358
Mirisch, Walter . . . . .The Mirisch Corporation, p. 218
Mirkin, David . . . . .The Simpsons, p. 375
Mirren, Simon . . . . .Criminal Minds, p. 358
Mischler, Michael . . . . . . .CBS Paramount Worldwide Television Dist., p. 88
Misenhimer, Tim . . . . .Neighbors Entertainment, p. 232
Misher, Danielle . . . . .TriStar Pictures, p. 319
Misher, Kevin . . . . .Misher Films, p. 218
Miskowiec, Rachel . . . . .The Tyra Banks Show, p. 378
Mislove, Michael . . . . .KeyLight Entertainment Group, p. 187
Missel, Renée . . . . .Renée Missel Productions, p. 218
Mitas, Robert . . . . .Furthur Films, p. 144
Mitchell, Collin . . . . .Untitled Entertainment, p. 327
Mitchell, Dan . . . . .Reason Pictures, p. 266
Mitchell, Deborah .Entertainment Studios, Inc., p. 125
Mitchell, Elvis . . . . .Columbia Pictures, p. 97
Mitchell, Eric . . . . .Baldwin Entertainment Group, Ltd., p. 60
Mitchell, Mark . . . . .Arjay Entertainment, p. 55
Mitchell, Tyler . . . . .Kidnapped, p. 365
Mitcheltree, Leigh . . . . .The Bubble Factory, p. 78

Mittweg, Rolf . . . . . New Line Cinema, p. 234
Miyaki, Bruce . . . . . Vanguard Productions, p. 329
Miyares, Beth . . . . . Fox Broadcasting Company, p. 139
Miyoshi, Maddie . . . . . Ron Ziskin Productions, Inc., p. 350
Mizel, Matthew . . . . . Offspring Entertainment, p. 241
Moder, Robyn . . . . . WPT Enterprises, Inc., p. 346
Modrovich, Ildy . . . . . CSI: Miami, p. 358
Moehring, Jay . . . . . Dalaklis-McKeown Entertainment, Inc., p. 106
Moffitt, John . . . . . Moffitt-Lee Productions, p. 219
Moffly, George . . . . . Piranha Pictures, Inc., p. 256
Mogollon, Diana R. . . . . . Galán Entertainment, p. 144
Mohamad, Michael . . . . . The History Channel, p. 167
Mohr, Jay . . . . . Giraffe Productions, p. 147
Mok, Ken . . . . . America's Next Top Model, p. 355
Molaro, Steve . . . . . The Class, p. 357
Molasky, Andrew . . . . . Stone Village Pictures, LLC, p. 302
Moldo, Julie G. . . . . . Amicus Entertainment Limited, p. 51
Molen, Gerald R. . . . . . WhiteLight Entertainment, p. 340
Molen, Laura . . . . . Spike TV, p. 298
Molen, Steven . . . . . DreamWorks SKG, p. 116
Molina, David . . . . . Creative Capers Entertainment, p. 103
Molina, Jose . . . . . Without a Trace, p. 379
Molina, Vibiana . . . . . Twentieth Century Fox Television, p. 323
Molinier, Catherine . . . . . CBS Paramount International Television, p. 87
Moloshok, Jim . . . . . HBO Media Ventures, p. 162
Momberger, Lisa . . . . . The Tyra Banks Show, p. 378
Momberger, Lisa . . . . . Bankable Productions, p. 61
Monaco, Karen . . . . . Keckins Projects, Ltd., p. 185
Monaghan, Kevin . . . . . NBC Sports, p. 231
Moneo, Teresa . . . . . Focus Features/Rogue Pictures, p. 136
Mongan, David . . . . . Without a Trace, p. 379
Monger, Cori . . . . . Generate, p. 145
Mongiardo, John . . . . . here! Networks, p. 165
Monier-Williams, Jennifer . . . . . Sesame Workshop, p. 285
Monreal, Leslie . . . . . ION Media Networks, Inc., p. 177
Monroe, Magnus . . . . . Tree Line Film, p. 317
Monson, Tim . . . . . Platinum Studios, LLC, p. 257
Montana, Sammy . . . . . Trancas International Films, p. 316
Montanio, Ben . . . . . Rice & Beans Productions, p. 272
Monteleone, Antonietta . . . . . National Geographic Giant Screen Films & Special Projects, p. 229
Montepare, Jon . . . . . Fresh Produce Films, p. 142
Montford, Susan . . . . . Angry Films, Inc., p. 52
Montgomery, Heather . . . . . QED International, p. 264
Montgomery, Mark . . . . . World Film Services, Inc., p. 345
Monther, Jill . . . . . Foothill Entertainment, Inc., p. 136
Montillot, Franck . . . . . Partizan, p. 250
Montolfo, Erica . . . . . The Game, p. 361
Montoya, Scott . . . . . PAYASO Entertainment, p. 251
Moomey, Kristie . . . . . TBS, p. 309
Moomey, Kristie . . . . . Turner Network Television (TNT), p. 321
Moon, Matthew . . . . . Echelon Entertainment World Dist. & Prod., p. 119
Moon, Mike . . . . . Walt Disney Television Animation, p. 113
Mooney, Andrew . . . . . The Walt Disney Company, p. 112
Moonves, Leslie . . . . . CBS Corporation, p. 86
Moonves, Leslie . . . . . CBS Entertainment, p. 86
Moore, Bryan . . . . . Fortis Films, p. 137
Moore, David . . . . . Tule River Films, p. 320
Moore, Demetrius . . . . . Wild At Heart Films, LLC, p. 341
Moore, Jane Lawton . . . . . Robert Kosberg Productions, p. 190
Moore, Jeff . . . . . Warren Miller Entertainment, p. 335
Moore, John . . . . . Point Road, Inc., p. 258
Moore, Matt . . . . . The Jinks/Cohen Company, p. 181
Moore, Mindy . . . . . Fox Television Studios, p. 140
Moore, Nate . . . . . Participant Productions, p. 249
Moore, Rich . . . . . Rough Draft Studios, p. 276
Moore, Rob . . . . . Paramount Pictures, p. 248
Moore, Ronald D. . . . . . Battlestar Galactica, p. 355
Moore, Roz . . . . . In Case of Emergency, p. 364
Moore, Scott . . . . . Yahoo! Media Group/Yahoo! Studios, p. 347
Moore, Sherilyn . . . . . Sub Rosa Productions, Inc., p. 303
Moore, Stephen . . . . . Aardman Animations, p. 44
Moore, Terry . . . . . Moore/Cramer Productions, p. 221
Moore, W. Jay . . . . . Maloof Productions, p. 208
Moore, Wendy . . . . . Dan Grodnik Productions, p. 155
Moosekian, Vahan . . . . . The Unit, p. 378
Morales, Deborah . . . . . Kareem Productions, p. 185
Morales, Ibra . . . . . Telemundo Network, p. 310
Morales, Lisa . . . . . John Wells Productions, p. 338
Moran, Katrina . . . . . Granada America, p. 152
Moran, Linda . . . . . Belladonna Productions, p. 65
Moran, Megan . . . . . Red Wagon Entertainment, p. 268
Moran CSA, Pat . . . . . The Wire, p. 379
Moran, Patrick . . . . . Twentieth Century Fox Television, p. 323
Moran, Sean . . . . . MTV Networks, p. 226
Moran, Thomas L. . . . . . House, p. 363
Moran, Tom . . . . . Totem Productions, p. 316
Moran, Tom . . . . . Scott Free Productions, p. 282
Morayniss, John . . . . . Blueprint Entertainment, p. 70
Moreau, Melanie . . . . . CMT: Country Music Television, p. 95
Morehouse, Clark . . . . . Tribune Entertainment Company, p. 318
Moreland, Rob . . . . . Vanguard Films/Vanguard Animation, p. 328
Morell, Jared . . . . . Endgame Entertainment, p. 124
Morelli, Cecilia . . . . . Primary Productions, p. 261
Morelli, Vanessa . . . . . Twentieth Century Fox - Searchlight Pictures, p. 323
Moreno, Brian . . . . . Warner Bros. Online, p. 334
Moreno, Frank . . . . . New Concorde, p. 233
Moresco, Bobby . . . . . The Black Donnellys, p. 356
Moresco, J.B. . . . . . Don Johnson Productions, p. 182
Moretti, Luz . . . . . Moonstone Entertainment, p. 220
Morewitz, Brian . . . . . ABC Entertainment Television Group, p. 45
Morey, John . . . . . The George Lopez Show, p. 362
Morgan, Andre . . . . . The Ruddy Morgan Organization, Inc./ Albert S. Ruddy Productions, p. 276
Morgan, Dylan . . . . . The Knights of Prosperity, p. 365
Morgan, Jana . . . . . Rubicon, p. 276
Morgan, Kendall . . . . . Cherry Road Films, LLC, p. 89
Morgan, Lana . . . . . The Matthau Company, Inc., p. 212
Morgan, Mark . . . . . Maverick Films, p. 213
Morgan, Peter . . . . . O.N.C. Entertainment Inc., p. 240
Moritz, Neal . . . . . Prison Break, p. 372
Moritz, Neal . . . . . Original Film, p. 244
Morley, Mike . . . . . The Group Entertainment, p. 156
Morong, Donna . . . . . Buena Vista Motion Pictures Group, p. 78
Morono, Aimee . . . . . Rosenzweig Films, p. 275
Morowitz, Noah . . . . . Walden Films, p. 332
Morri, Kirk . . . . . Neo Art & Logic, p. 232
Morrill, Norman . . . . . Traveler, p. 377
Morrill, Sharon . . . . . DisneyToon Studios, p. 113
Morris, Bernie . . . . . Magnetic Film, p. 207
Morris, Dolores . . . . . HBO Documentaries & Family, p. 162
Morris, Howard J. . . . . . In Case of Emergency, p. 364
Morris, James . . . . . The Dead Zone, p. 359
Morris, Jill . . . . . Focus Features/Rogue Pictures, p. 136
Morris, John . . . . . IMG Media, p. 172
Morris, Parker . . . . . Arthur Sarkissian Productions, p. 280
Morris, Seth . . . . . Upright Citizens Brigade, p. 327
Morrisey, Audrey . . . . . Live Animals, p. 201
Morrison, Angela . . . . . Working Title Films, p. 345
Morrison, Brett . . . . . Gryphon Films, p. 157
Morrison, Briegh . . . . . Solaris, p. 293
Morrison, Gloria . . . . . Echelon Entertainment World Dist. & Prod., p. 119
Morrison, Kevin . . . . . BET Networks, p. 66
Morrison, Lori . . . . . Heidi Rotbart Management, p. 275
Morrison, Robyn . . . . . International Arts Entertainment, p. 176
Morrison, Vanessa . . . . . Twentieth Century Fox, p. 322
Morrissey, John . . . . . Sony Pictures Television, p. 296
Morrissey, John . . . . . John Morrissey Productions, p. 221
Morse, Annie . . . . . Spitfire Pictures, p. 298
Morse, Elizabeth . . . . . Q Media Partners, p. 264
Mortensen, Zachary . . . . . Ghost Robot, p. 146
Mortimer, Meg . . . . . Principal Entertainment, p. 262
Morton, Jeff . . . . . Jeff Morton Productions, p. 222
Morton, Kristen . . . . . Capital Arts Entertainment, p. 83
Morton, Nick . . . . . Baldwin Entertainment Group, Ltd., p. 60
Mosawi, Anthony . . . . . The Mayhem Project, p. 213
Moser, Diane . . . . . The Bubble Factory, p. 78
Moser, John . . . . . Showtime Networks Inc., p. 287
Moses, Ben . . . . . Appleseed Entertainment, LLC, p. 54
Moses, Kim . . . . . Ghost Whisperer, p. 362

Moses, Kim .Sander/Moses Productions, Inc., p. 279
Moses, Lynne .Appleseed Entertainment, LLC, p. 54
Moses, Michael .Universal Pictures, p. 326
Mosier, Scott .View Askew Productions, Inc., p. 331
Moskin, Jonathan .Veronica Mars, p. 378
Mosko, Steve .Sony Pictures Television, p. 296
Moskow, Jacqueline R. .New Line Cinema, p. 234
Moskowitz, Jeffrey M. .Gary Smith Company, p. 292
Mosquera, Lumumba .Dimension Films, p. 111
Moss, Adam .Columbia Pictures, p. 97
Mostow, Fera .Touchstone Television, p. 316
Moszkowicz, Martin .Constantin Film Dev., Inc./Constantin TV, p. 100
Mott, Bob .New Line Cinema, p. 234
Mottola, Tommy .The Mottola Company, p. 223
Moulton, Kelly .The Colleton Company, p. 97
Mountain, Erik .John Brister Films, p. 75
Mouscardy, Thomas .Comedy Central, p. 98
Moussa, Isis .CBS Paramount International Television, p. 87
Mouton, Nancy .von Zerneck-Sertner Films, p. 332
Mower, Mark .Moshag Productions, Inc., p. 222
Moy, Karen .Columbia Pictures, p. 97
Moy, Stephanie .Nine Yards Entertainment, p. 238
Moyer, Jennifer .The Sean Daniel Company, p. 106
Mu, Tiejun .China Film Group, p. 90
Mucha, Zenia .The Walt Disney Company, p. 112
Mucke, Sandra .Wonderland Sound and Vision, p. 344
Mudd, Victoria .Earthworks Films, p. 118
Mueller, Matthew .Echelon Entertainment World Dist. & Prod., p. 119
Mueller, Roni .CBS Entertainment, p. 86
Mueller, Roni .CBS Paramount Network Television, p. 87
Muhl, Phillip E. .Buena Vista Motion Pictures Group, p. 78
Mulcahey, Patrick .The Bold and the Beautiful, p. 356
Mulderrig, Steve .Tribune Entertainment Company, p. 318
Mulei, David .Veronica Mars, p. 378
Mulein, Jeni .Original Film, p. 244
Mulholland, Jim .Imagination Productions, Inc., p. 171
Mulingbayan, Cheryl .Firm Television, p. 134
Mulkerin, Ted .The Late Late Show with Craig Ferguson, p. 366
Mullen, Patrick .David Ladd Films, p. 191
Muller, Scott .King of the Hill, p. 365
Mullie, Paul .Stargate: Atlantis, p. 376
Mullie, Paul .Stargate: SG-1, p. 376
Mulligan, Billy .Jane Startz Productions, Inc., p. 300
Mulligan, Theresa .South Park, p. 376
Mullin, Jennifer .FremantleMedia North America, p. 142
Mulvey, Logan .Symbolic Entertainment, p. 306
Mumford, David .Sony Pictures Television, p. 296
Munch, Axel .Silverline Entertainment, Inc., p. 289
Munday, Daniel .Survivor, p. 377
Mundy, Chris .Criminal Minds, p. 358
Munekata, Ken .Columbia Pictures, p. 97
Muniz, Ish .Intl. Television Group (ITG) - Epix Films, p. 176
Munro, Nanette .Peter Locke Productions, p. 202
Murch, Rachel .East of Doheny/Lexington Road Prod., p. 118
Murchison, John .HBO Films, p. 162
Murdoch, K. Rupert .Fox Broadcasting Company, p. 139
Murdoch, Susan .QVF Inc., p. 264
Murphey, Michael S. .Bodega Bay Productions, Inc., p. 70
Murphy, Bill .Murphy Boyz Productions, p. 227
Murphy, Billy .Touchstone Television, p. 316
Murphy, Diane .Miller/Boyett Productions, p. 217
Murphy, Don .Angry Films, Inc., p. 52
Murphy, Doug .Nelvana Communications, Inc., p. 232
Murphy, Gary .Notes From the Underbelly, p. 370
Murphy, Joey .Desperate Housewives, p. 360
Murphy, John .Civilian Pictures, p. 94
Murphy, Kevin .Desperate Housewives, p. 360
Murphy Jr., Ray .Murphy Boyz Productions, p. 227
Murphy, Rowena .Zane W. Levitt Prod./Zeta Ent., p. 197
Murphy, Ryan .Nip/Tuck, p. 370
Murphy, Ryan .Stan Winston Productions, p. 343
Murphy, Sara .Cooper's Town Productions, p. 100
Murphy, Sue .The Class, p. 357
Murphy, Tony .Goldcrest Films International, Inc., p. 149
Murphy-Gibb, Dwina .Sacred Dogs Entertainment, LLC, p. 278
Murray, Charles .Day Break, p. 359
Murray, Jarrod .Adelstein Productions, p. 47
Murray, Jonathan .Bunim/Murray Productions, Inc., p. 79
Murray, Patrick .Studios International, p. 303
Murray, Patrick .Myriad Pictures, p. 228
Murray, Rachel .Type A Films, p. 325
Murray, Ray .Banyan Productions, p. 61
Musselman, Jennifer .Nickelodeon/MTVN Kids & Family Group, p. 237
Musselman, Mark .Serendipity Point Films, p. 284
Musso, Anna .Ad Hominem Enterprises, p. 46
Musso, Eugene .Code Entertainment, p. 96
Mutchnick, Max .KoMut Entertainment, p. 189
Mutrux, Gail .Pretty Pictures, p. 261
Myers, Bill .Home & Garden Television (HGTV), p. 168
Myers, Dan .HDNet, p. 163
Myers, Eileen .Big Love, p. 356
Myers, Fran .One Life to Live, p. 371
Myers, Henry Alonso .Day Break, p. 359
Myers, Jeff .New Wave Entertainment, p. 235
Myers, Kimberly .Maya Pictures, p. 213
Myers, Melissa .Studio 60 on the Sunset Strip, p. 376
Myers, Sergio .7ponies productions, p. 42
Myles, Nick .Persistent Entertainment, p. 253
Myman, Adam .ABC Entertainment Television Group, p. 45
Myron, Ben .Leisure Time Enterprises, p. 196
Myron, Cynthia .Epiphany Pictures, Inc., p. 126
Nabatoff, Diane .Tiara Blu Films, p. 313
Nachmanoff, Elena .NBC News, p. 230
Nadler, Lindsay .Miramax Films, p. 217
Nadler, Maud .HBO Films, p. 162
Nagel, Stacey .ION Media Networks, Inc., p. 177
Nagenda, Tendo .Plan B Entertainment, p. 256
Nagler, Harvey .CBS News, p. 87
Naidus, Michael .The Late Late Show with Craig Ferguson, p. 366
Naito, Ramsey .Cartoon Network, p. 84
Najarian, John .E! Networks, p. 117
Nalivansky, Felicia .The Simpsons, p. 375
Nalle, Ned .Playboy Entertainment Group, Inc., p. 257
Nanas, Herb .Nanas Entertainment, p. 229
Nandan, Ravi .American Work, p. 51
Nank, Michael .Vulcan Productions, p. 332
Napier, Ed .Criminal Minds, p. 358
Napier, Laura .Poetry & Pictures Inc., p. 258
Napleton, Brian .Belisarius Productions, p. 65
Napoliello, Ira .Jason Hoffs Productions, p. 168
Narez, Alfredo .Air2web, Inc., p. 48
Nash, Bruce .Nash Entertainment, p. 229
Nash, DJ .'Til Death, p. 377
Nash, Jan .Without a Trace, p. 379
Nash, Marney Hochman .Fox Television Studios, p. 140
Nash, Michael .Landscape Entertainment, p. 193
Nash, Robyn .Nash Entertainment, p. 229
Nasrabadi, Amir .DisneyToon Studios, p. 113
Nasraway, Michele .America's Funniest Videos, p. 355
Nasser, Jack .Nasser Entertainment Group, p. 229
Nasser, Joe .Nasser Entertainment Group, p. 229
Nath, Bernadette .Epiphany Pictures, Inc., p. 126
Nathan, Deborah .QVF Inc., p. 264
Nathan, Robert .Law & Order, p. 367
Nathan, Robert .Cinetic, p. 93
Nathan, Stephen .Bones, p. 356
Nathanson, Laura .ABC Family, p. 45
Nathanson, Laura .Disney ABC Cable Networks Group, p. 112
Nathanson, Michael G. .O.N.C. Entertainment Inc., p. 240
Nations, Gregg .Lost, p. 368
Naumann, Kim .Planet Grande Pictures, p. 256
Nava, Gregory .El Norte Productions, p. 121
Navarrete, Allan .Discovery Networks, U.S., p. 111
Navarro, Irene .900 Films, p. 43
Navarro, Kenn .Mondo Media, p. 220
Nayar, Deepak .Kintop Pictures, p. 188
Nayar, Sunil .CSI: Miami, p. 358
Nayfeld, Mikhail .Mandate Pictures, p. 209
Naylor, Peter .NBC Universal Corporate, p. 231
Nazarian, Sam .Element Films, p. 121

Neal, David . . . NBC Sports, p. 231
Neal, Greg . . . Food Network, p. 136
Nealon, Liz . . . Sesame Workshop, p. 285
Nealy, Todd . . . Primetime Pictures, p. 262
Neber, Cece . . . The Donners' Company, p. 114
Necessary, Gary . . . George Schlatter Productions, p. 280
Neckels, Bruce . . . Days of Our Lives, p. 359
Nedick, Mitch . . . The CW, p. 105
Nedivi, Ben . . . Millennium Films, p. 217
Nee, John . . . DC Comics, p. 108
Needham, John . . . Sony Online Entertainment, p. 294
Neely, Francie . . . Timeline Films, p. 314
Neely, Hugh Munro . . . Timeline Films, p. 314
Neely, Matt . . . Spirit Horse Productions, p. 298
Neesan, Paul . . . The Kerner Entertainment Company, p. 187
Neifing, Stephanie . . . Sander/Moses Productions, Inc., p. 279
Neil, Doug . . . Universal Pictures, p. 326
Neimand, Gabrielle . . . Strike Entertainment, p. 303
Neinstein, Paul . . . Paramount Pictures, p. 248
Neisser, Winifred White . . . Sony Pictures Television, p. 296
NeJame, George . . . Tribune Entertainment Company, p. 318
Nelson, Anne R. . . . CBS Entertainment, p. 86
Nelson, Diane . . . Warner Bros. Entertainment Inc., p. 334
Nelson, Erik . . . Lionsgate, p. 200
Nelson, Erik . . . Creative Differences, p. 103
Nelson, Julie . . . The Gotham Group, Inc., p. 151
Nelson, Julie . . . Indigo Films, p. 174
Nelson, Kate . . . SOAPnet, p. 293
Nelson, Kathy . . . Universal Pictures, p. 326
Nelson, Paul . . . Mosaic Media Group, p. 222
Nelson, Phyllis . . . Touchstone Television, p. 316
Nelson, Todd . . . The Biggest Loser, p. 356
Nelson, Todd . . . 3 Ball Productions, p. 40
Nemeroff, Terry . . . Zemeckis/Nemeroff Films, p. 348
Nemes, Scott . . . Adelstein Productions, p. 47
Nemeth, Stephen . . . Rhino Films, p. 272
Nemhauser, Lori Jo . . . Entourage, p. 360
Nesvig, Jon . . . Fox Broadcasting Company, p. 139
Nett, Eleanor . . . Endgame Entertainment, p. 124
Netter, Gil . . . Zucker/Netter Productions, p. 350
Neufeld, Mace . . . Mace Neufeld Productions, p. 232
Neufeld, Marjorie . . . Warner Bros. Television Production, p. 335
Neuhaus, Eric . . . Court TV Networks, p. 102
Neuhauser, Alice . . . The Kushner-Locke Company, p. 191
Neuman, David . . . Current TV, LLC, p. 105
Neuman, Jeffrey R. . . . NEU-MAN-FILMS, Inc., p. 232
Neutz, Bobby . . . Namesake Entertainment, p. 228
Neutz, Kelly . . . Namesake Entertainment, p. 228
Nevins, David . . . Friday Night Lights, p. 361
Nevins, David . . . Saved, p. 374
Nevins, David . . . Shark, p. 374
Nevins, David . . . Imagine Television, p. 172
Nevins, Sheila . . . HBO Documentaries & Family, p. 162
Newberg, Bruce . . . The Closer, p. 357
Newberg, Bruce . . . The Class, p. 357
Newberger, Patty . . . Comedy Central, p. 98
Newby, Kelly . . . Jeff Wald Entertainment, p. 180
Newcomb, Bill . . . Visionbox Media Group, p. 331
Newell, Erin . . . Level 1 Entertainment, p. 197
Newell, Mike . . . Fifty Cannon Entertainment, LLC, p. 131
Newling, Caro . . . Neal Street Productions Ltd., p. 232
Newman, Ari . . . Media Financial International, LLC, p. 214
Newman, Eric . . . Strike Entertainment, p. 303
Newman, Gary . . . Twentieth Century Fox Television, p. 323
Newman, George . . . Trancas International Films, p. 316
Newman, Jason . . . Untitled Entertainment, p. 327
Newman, Joshua . . . Cyan Pictures, p. 105
Newman, Kristin . . . How I Met Your Mother, p. 364
Newman, Liz . . . Scrubs, p. 374
Newman, Michael . . . Room 9 Entertainment, p. 274
Newman, Nancy . . . MTV Networks, p. 226
Newman, Peter . . . Peter Newman Productions, Inc., p. 236
Newman, Salli . . . Firebrand Productions, p. 134
Newman, Vincent . . . Vincent Newman Entertainment, p. 236
Newman-Minson, Launa . . . Launa Newman Productions (LNP), p. 195
Newmann, Michael . . . Tommy Boy Films, p. 315
Newmyer, Deb . . . Outlaw Productions, p. 245
Newport, Bob . . . Alcon Entertainment, LLC, p. 49
Newson, Michael . . . Twentieth Television, p. 324
Newton, Briana . . . Harpo Films, Inc., p. 161
Newton, Kim . . . Las Vegas, p. 366
Nezami, Susan . . . New Line Cinema, p. 234
Nguyen, Dantram . . . The Donners' Company, p. 114
Ngyman, Maggie . . . Tri-Elite Entertainment, Ltd., p. 319
Nicholls, Alexis . . . The Collective, p. 96
Nichols, Nicole . . . Disney-ABC Television Group, p. 113
Nichols, Nicole . . . Disney ABC Cable Networks Group, p. 112
Nichols, Robert J. . . . The Woofenill Works, Inc., p. 344
Nichols, Sara . . . Emotional Pictures Corporation, p. 123
Nicholson, Ellen . . . 2929 Productions, p. 40
Nicholson-Salke, Jennifer . . . Twentieth Century Fox Television, p. 323
Nickell, Hunter . . . Fox Cable Networks, p. 139
Nickels, Kurt . . . Trunity, a Mediar Company, a Division of True Mediar, a Unity Corpbopoly, p. 320
Nickerson, Corey . . . The Class, p. 357
Nickerson, Dede . . . Paramount Pictures Production Division, p. 248
Nickerson, Julia . . . Big Cattle Productions, p. 67
Nickerson, Robyn . . . Class 5 Films, p. 95
Nicklaus, Kevin . . . The Wolper Organization, p. 344
Nickman, Bob . . . Big Day, p. 355
Nickoll, David . . . The Late Late Show with Craig Ferguson, p. 366
Nicolaides, Scott . . . Sidney Kimmel Entertainment, p. 187
Nicolella, Nicholas . . . Gross Entertainment, p. 155
Nicolini-Glazer, Christiane . . . Rive Gauche Entertainment, p. 272
Niederhoffer, Galt . . . Plum Pictures, p. 258
Nielsen, Anne . . . Universal Studios, p. 326
Niemeyer, Scott . . . Gold Circle Films, p. 148
Nies, Gabe . . . Twentieth Century Fox Television, p. 323
Nieto, Marina . . . NBC Entertainment, p. 230
Nieves, Jennifer . . . 360 Pictures/FGM Entertainment, p. 41
Nieves, Nestor . . . New Line Cinema, p. 234
Nikol, Tom . . . Sony Pictures Television, p. 296
Nikolic, Iliana . . . Elevation Filmworks, p. 121
Nipkow, Leslie . . . One Life to Live, p. 371
Nishimoto, Tiffany . . . El Dorado Pictures, p. 120
Nishioka, Melinda . . . Ralph Winter Productions, Inc., p. 343
Nissel, Angela . . . Scrubs, p. 374
Nittoli, Andrea . . . Laugh Factory Entertainment, p. 195
Nixon, Jon . . . Chameleon Entertainment, p. 89
Nixon, Sasha . . . Partizan, p. 250
Noah, Peter . . . Raines, p. 372
Noble, Ethan . . . The Weinstein Company, p. 337
Noble, Nina K. . . . The Wire, p. 379
Nocero, Gina . . . A&E Network, p. 44
Noe, Scott . . . Boxx Communications, LLC, p. 72
Nogawski, John . . . CBS Paramount Worldwide Television Dist., p. 88
Nolan, Niamh . . . Hell's Kitchen Ltd., p. 164
Nolfi, George . . . Gambit Pictures, p. 144
Noll, David . . . City Lights Media Group, p. 94
Nollman, Alyssa . . . Five Mile River Films, Ltd., p. 134
Nonaka, J. David . . . Lionsgate, p. 200
Noon, Bryan . . . Touchstone Television, p. 316
Noonan, Jim . . . Warner Bros. Entertainment Inc., p. 334
Nordby, Erik . . . Q Media Partners, p. 264
Nordlander, Charles . . . Food Network, p. 136
Nordling, Lee . . . Platinum Studios, LLC, p. 257
Normal, Henry . . . Baby Cow Productions Ltd., p. 59
Norman, Christina . . . MTV Networks, p. 226
Norman, Jonathan . . . The Ellen DeGeneres Show, p. 360
Norman, Mark . . . Cartoon Network, p. 84
Norman, Suzanne . . . CMT: Country Music Television, p. 95
Norris, Carly . . . Vertigo Entertainment, p. 330
Norris, John A. . . . One Tree Hill, p. 371
North, David . . . NCIS, p. 370
North, David . . . Belisarius Productions, p. 65
Northrup, Curt . . . Granada America, p. 152
Norton, Deborah . . . Sony Pictures Television, p. 296
Norton, Edward . . . Class 5 Films, p. 95
Norton, Jim . . . Class 5 Films, p. 95
Norton, Troy . . . The Gurin Company, p. 158

Norwood, Nicole .....Touchstone Television, p. 316
Noss, Terry .....RichCrest Animation Studios, p. 272
Nossokoff, Brian .....Broken Lizard Industries, p. 76
Notary, Terry .....Scarab Productions, p. 280
Nourse, Scott .....Sony Pictures Digital, p. 295
Novac, Tom .....WildRice Productions, p. 341
Novak, B.J. .....The Office, p. 371
Novak, Jennifer .....Parallel Entertainment, Inc., p. 247
Noveck, Gregory .....DC Comics, p. 108
Novick, Lynn .....Florentine Films, p. 135
Novick, Mason .....Benderspink, p. 66
Novoa, Joel .....Joel Films, p. 181
Novoa, Joseph .....Joel Films, p. 181
Nowak, Chris .....According to Jim, p. 354
Nowlin, Kendall .....Lance Entertainment, Inc., p. 192
Nowocinski, Erin .....Imagine Television, p. 172
Nowotny, Robert A. .....Teocalli Entertainment, p. 312
Nozik, Michael .....Serenade Films, p. 284
Nugent, Barry .....E! Networks, p. 117
Nugent, Ginny .....HBO Films, p. 162
Nugent, Nelle .....The Foxboro Company, Inc., p. 140
Nulman, Andy .....Airborne Entertainment, p. 48
Nunan, Tom .....Bull's Eye Entertainment, p. 79
Nunes, Vasco .....Interloper Films, p. 175
Nunez, Alec .....Furthur Films, p. 144
Nunez, Diana .....Elkins Entertainment, p. 122
Nuñez Jr., Armando .....CBS Paramount International Television, p. 87
Nuñez, Armando .....CBS Paramount Worldwide Television Dist., p. 88
Nunnari, Gianni .....Cecchi Gori Pictures, p. 88
Nunnari, Gianni .....Hollywood Gang Productions, LLC, p. 168
Nusbaum, Karen .....Nash Entertainment, p. 229
Nussbaum, Karl .....Film Crash, p. 132
Nutter, David .....Genrebend Productions, Inc., p. 145
Nuzzi, Dominick .....ABC Daytime, p. 44
Nyberg, Tracey .....Overbrook Entertainment, p. 245
Nyholm, Rick .....The George Lopez Show, p. 362
Nystedt, Colleen .....New City Pictures, Inc., p. 233
Oakes, Jon .....Original Film, p. 244
Oakes, Steve .....Curious Pictures, p. 104
Oakley, Nick .....Granada America, p. 152
O'Bannon, Rockne S. .....Creative Impulse Entertainment, p. 103
Obata, Greg .....Water Channel, p. 336
Ober, Brian .....Warner Bros. Online, p. 334
O'Brien, Barry .....CSI: Miami, p. 358
O'Brien, Conan .....Late Night with Conan O'Brien, p. 367
O'Brien, Deborah .....ABC Entertainment Television Group, p. 45
O'Brien, Deborah .....Touchstone Television, p. 316
O'Brien, Joe .....The Late Late Show with Craig Ferguson, p. 366
O'Brien, Nora .....Sci Fi Channel, p. 282
O'Brien, Shelagh M. .....John Wells Productions, p. 338
Obst, Lynda .....Lynda Obst Productions, p. 241
Obst, Oliver .....Tom Jacobson Productions, p. 179
Ockman, Aaron .....Neo Art & Logic, p. 232
Ocko, Peter .....3 lbs., p. 353
O'Con, Pauline .....Fox Broadcasting Company, p. 139
O'Connell, Brian .....MRB Productions, Inc., p. 224
O'Connell, David .....Bravo, p. 74
O'Connell, Dr. Libby .....A&E Network, p. 44
O'Connell, Jennifer .....NBC Entertainment, p. 230
O'Connell, Katie .....NBC Entertainment, p. 230
O'Connor, Ann .....Universal Studios, p. 326
O'Connor, Dennis .....Picturehouse, p. 254
O'Connor, Dennis .....HBO Films, p. 162
O'Connor, Gavin .....Solaris, p. 293
O'Connor, Gregory .....Solaris, p. 293
O'Connor, Mark .....Twentieth Century Fox, p. 322
O'Connor, Pat .....HDNet, p. 163
O'Connor, Rachel .....Columbia Pictures, p. 97
O'Connor, Shannon .....CBS Entertainment, p. 86
Odell, Benjamin .....Panamax Films, p. 246
Oden, Kathryn .....Laurence Mark Productions, p. 210
Oden, Murray .....Norsemen Television Productions, LLC, p. 239
O'Donnell, Stacey .....Bunim/Murray Productions, Inc., p. 79
O'Donnell, Steve .....Jimmy Kimmel Live, p. 364
Oedekerk, Steve .....O Entertainment, p. 240
Offsay, Jerry .....Parkchester Pictures, p. 249
Offutt, Amber .....Participant Productions, p. 249
Ogawa, Carl .....Berlanti Productions, p. 66
Ogier, Drew .....Last Call with Carson Daly, p. 366
Oglesby, Marsha .....Brooklyn Films, p. 77
Oh, James .....Fox Broadcasting Company, p. 139
Oh, Jun .....Beacon, p. 64
Oh, William .....Comedy Central, p. 98
O'Hair, Tim .....Armagh Films, Inc., p. 55
O'Hara, Robin .....Forensic Films, Inc., p. 137
O'Hara, Ryan .....TV Guide Channel, p. 321
Ohman, Danny .....SiTV, p. 290
Ohoven, Michael .....Infinity Media, Inc., p. 174
Oillataguerre, Peter .....Universal Pictures, p. 326
Okada, Erin .....Alcon Entertainment, LLC, p. 49
Okada, Mami .....Bang Zoom! Entertainment, p. 61
Okamoto, Bryan .....Endgame Entertainment, p. 124
O'Karma, Hank .....New Screen Concepts, Inc., p. 235
O'Keefe, Dana .....Cinetic, p. 93
O'Keefe, Sean .....Union Entertainment, p. 325
O'Keefe, Terence M. .....Vanguard Productions, p. 329
Okun, Sam .....Sam Okun Productions, Inc., p. 242
Olde, Jeff .....VH1, p. 330
Oldfield, Barney .....Angelika, p. 52
Oldman, Gary .....SE8 Group, p. 283
Oldre, Chris .....Buena Vista Television, p. 79
Olin, Jason .....A Band Apart, p. 43
Olin, Jason .....Lawrence Bender Productions, p. 65
Olin, Lisa J. .....Jack Angel Productions Inc., p. 178
Olin, Zack .....ABC Entertainment Television Group, p. 45
Olivas, Xochitl L. .....Grammnet Productions, p. 152
Oliver, Lin .....Lin Oliver Productions, p. 242
Oliver, Whitney .....Daniel L. Paulson Productions, p. 251
Olmos, Bodie James .....Olmos Productions, Inc., p. 242
Olmos, Edward James .....Olmos Productions, Inc., p. 242
Olmstead, Jane .....Camelot Entertainment Group, Inc., p. 82
Olmstead, Matt .....Prison Break, p. 372
Olschan, Rachel .....Electric Entertainment, p. 121
Olsen, Chris .....7th Heaven, p. 353
Olsen, Dana .....Passions, p. 371
Olsen, Erik .....Silver Pictures, p. 289
Olsen, Jeff .....7th Heaven, p. 353
Olsen, Kim .....Code Entertainment, p. 96
Olsen, Mark V. .....Big Love, p. 356
Olsen, Mark .....Trigger Street Independent, p. 319
Olsen, Peter .....A&E Network, p. 44
Olsen, Trent .....Weed Road Pictures, p. 337
Olshansky, Rick .....NBC Universal Television Studio, p. 231
Olson, Edward .....Latitude Television LLC, p. 195
Olson, Kirk .....Sony Pictures Television, p. 296
Olson, Paige .....Buena Vista Motion Pictures Group, p. 78
Olson, Robyn .....Gay Rosenthal Productions, p. 275
Oltman, David .....Guardian Entertainment, Ltd., p. 157
Olynyk, Signe .....Twilight Pictures, Inc., p. 324
O'Malley, Deidre .....Mondo Media, p. 220
O'Malley, Erin .....The Sarah Silverman Programme, p. 373
Oman, Chad .....Jerry Bruckheimer Films & Television, p. 78
Omine, Carolyn .....The Simpsons, p. 375
O'Neil, Erin .....Warner Independent Pictures, p. 335
O'Neil, Robert .....Universal Operations Group, p. 326
O'Neill, Eileen .....Discovery Health Channel, p. 111
O'Neill, Eileen .....Discovery Networks, U.S., p. 111
O'Neill, Eileen .....Twentieth Television, p. 324
O'Neill, Evelyn .....Management 360, p. 208
O'Neill, Matt .....Dan Gordon Productions, p. 150
O'Neill, Steven .....NBC Universal Television Studio, p. 231
Ong, Brad .....Nickelodeon Movies, p. 237
Ong, Laureen .....Fox Cable Networks, p. 139
Ontiveros, Lupe .....Latin Hollywood Films, p. 194
Opatut, Eileen .....Logo, p. 202
Openden, Lori .....The CW, p. 105
Oppenheim, A.D. .....Winsome Productions, p. 342
Oppenheim, Daniel L. .....Winsome Productions, p. 342
Oppenheimer, Deborah .....The George Lopez Show, p. 362
Oppenheimer, Joe .....BBC Films, p. 64

Optican, Tony . . . . Sci Fi Channel, p. 282
Orci, J.R. . . . . Vanished, p. 378
Orci, Roberto . . . . Kurtzman/Orci, p. 191
Ordesky, Mark . . . . New Line Cinema, p. 234
Oreif, Khalid . . . . Warner Bros. Online, p. 334
O'Reilly, Colin . . . . Smart Entertainment, p. 292
O'Reilly, Karri . . . . David Lancaster Productions, p. 192
Oren, Leslie . . . . Fox Television Studios, p. 140
Orengo, Angel . . . . Sony Pictures Television International, p. 296
Orenstein, Andrew . . . . Everybody Hates Chris, p. 361
Orenstein, Fern . . . . CBS Entertainment, p. 86
Orent, Kerry . . . . Rescue Me, p. 373
O'Riain, Adrienne . . . . Apostle, p. 53
Orlando, John . . . . Circle of Confusion Productions, p. 93
Orloski, Brynne . . . . Vanguard Films/Vanguard Animation, p. 328
Orman, Jack . . . . Waterfront, p. 379
Ornekian, Dikran . . . . The Sommers Company, p. 294
Ornstein, Ken . . . . My Boys, p. 369
Ornston, David E. . . . . Two Sticks Productions, p. 325
Orr Jr., Steven . . . . Buena Vista Television, p. 79
Orrell-Jones, Duncan . . . . Buena Vista Motion Pictures Group, p. 78
Orson, Greg . . . . Hidden Palms, p. 363
Orson, Greg . . . . Reba, p. 372
Orson, Greg . . . . Runaway, p. 373
Ortega, Jennifer . . . . CMT: Country Music Television, p. 95
Ortega-Cowan, Roman . . . . Relevant Entertainment Group, p. 270
Ortenberg, Tom . . . . Lionsgate, p. 200
Ortez, Johnny . . . . Funny Boy Films, p. 143
Ortiguero, Julius . . . . Cinema Seven Productions, p. 92
Ortiz, Sandra . . . . Twentieth Century Fox Television, p. 323
Ortiz, Stuart . . . . Red Hen Productions, p. 267
Ortiz, Tito . . . . The Mark Gordon Company, p. 150
Osako, Rick . . . . CatchLight Films, p. 85
Osborne, Barrie M. . . . . Emerald City Productions, Inc., p. 122
Osborne, India . . . . Seaside Productions, p. 283
Osborne, Nick . . . . Underground Films, p. 325
Oseary, Guy . . . . Last Call with Carson Daly, p. 366
Oseary, Guy . . . . Maverick Films, p. 213
Oseary, Guy . . . . Untitled Entertainment, p. 327
O'Shannon, Dan . . . . Jericho, p. 364
O'Shea, Brian . . . . Odd Lot Entertainment, p. 241
O'Shea, Michael . . . . Double Nickel Entertainment, p. 115
Osher, Bob . . . . Columbia Pictures, p. 97
Osorio, Paulette . . . . Focus Features/Rogue Pictures, p. 136
Osowski, Pamela . . . . World Film Services, Inc., p. 345
Osteen, Talia . . . . Blueprint Films, p. 70
Ostroff, Dawn . . . . The CW, p. 105
Ostroff, Donna . . . . Mirage Enterprises, p. 217
Ostrowski, Mike . . . . Jericho, p. 364
Oswaks, Robert . . . . Sony Pictures Television, p. 296
Oswald, George . . . . Fox Broadcasting Company, p. 139
O'Toole, Noreen . . . . Lost, p. 368
Ottinger, Chris . . . . Fox Television Studios, p. 140
Ouweleen, Michael . . . . Cartoon Network, p. 84
Overbeeke, H. David . . . . NBC Universal Corporate, p. 231
Overmyer, Eric . . . . The Wire, p. 379
Overmyer, Eric . . . . Close to Home, p. 357
Ow, Ricky . . . . Sony Pictures Television International, p. 296
Owen, Derek . . . . Wheelhouse Entertainment, p. 339
Owens, H.T. . . . . 30 Days, p. 353
Owens, Howard . . . . The Biggest Loser, p. 356
Owens, Howard . . . . Reveille, LLC, p. 270
Owens, Richie . . . . NCIS, p. 370
Oxenberg, Dina . . . . Emmett/Furla Films, p. 123
Oxenberg, Jan . . . . Kidnapped, p. 365
Oyco, Ivan . . . . Spyglass Entertainment Group, p. 299
Oyola, Gerardo . . . . Telemundo Network, p. 310
Ozn, Robert . . . . One Voice Entertainment, Inc., p. 243
Paarte, Heta . . . . Focus Features/Rogue Pictures, p. 136
Pacacha, Claire . . . . This is that corporation, p. 312
Paccone, Fred . . . . World of Wonder Productions, p. 345
Pace, Bill . . . . Longbow Productions, p. 203
Pace, Frank . . . . The George Lopez Show, p. 362
Pachasa, Arlene . . . . Sam Okun Productions, Inc., p. 242
Pacheco, Stephanie . . . . CBS Paramount International Television, p. 87
Pachler, Christoph . . . . Sony Pictures Television International, p. 296
Packard, Chris . . . . Fox Mobile Entertainment, p. 139
Packer, Jim . . . . Metro-Goldwyn-Mayer Studios, Inc. (MGM), p. 215
Packer, William . . . . Rainforest Films, p. 265
Packman, Scott . . . . Metro-Goldwyn-Mayer Studios, Inc. (MGM), p. 215
Paddison, Gordon . . . . New Line Cinema, p. 234
Paddock, Dustin . . . . House, p. 363
Padgham, Karin . . . . Recorded Picture Company, p. 266
Padnos, Jamie . . . . Showtime Networks Inc., p. 287
Padwa, Sabrina . . . . @radical.media, p. 38
Pagano, Chuck . . . . ABC Sports, p. 45
Pagano, Chuck . . . . ESPN Original Entertainment (EOE), p. 127
Page, Albert . . . . Mandeville Films, p. 209
Page, Allison . . . . Food Network, p. 136
Page, Kathy . . . . Paulette Breen Productions, p. 74
Paglino, Joe . . . . Discovery Networks, U.S., p. 111
Pahl, Jane . . . . Janicek-Marino Creative, p. 179
Pai, Helen . . . . Gilmore Girls, p. 362
Paige, George . . . . George Paige Associates, Inc., p. 246
Paige, Meredith . . . . MARTHA, p. 368
Paine, Nicholas . . . . EARS XXI, p. 118
Paisner, Bruce L. . . . . Actuality Productions, p. 46
Paitchel, Debbie . . . . Court TV Networks, p. 102
Paiz, Carolina . . . . Grey's Anatomy, p. 362
Palacio, Ricardo . . . . Nala Films, p. 228
Palaski, Courtenay . . . . Cartoon Network, p. 84
Palef, Bonnie . . . . Snapdragon Films, Inc., p. 293
Palen, Tim . . . . Lionsgate, p. 200
Palent, Corey . . . . The Ellen DeGeneres Show, p. 360
Palermo, John . . . . Seed Productions, p. 283
Paley, Jon . . . . Curious Pictures, p. 104
Paley, Steve . . . . Last Call with Carson Daly, p. 366
Palik, Betty . . . . Muse Entertainment Enterprises, p. 227
Palladino, Anthony . . . . Arlington Entertainment, Inc., p. 55
Palladino, Sue . . . . Warner Bros. Television Production, p. 335
Palleschi, Michael . . . . America's Funniest Videos, p. 355
Pallotta, Tommy . . . . Ghost Robot, p. 146
Palluth, Ed . . . . The Independent Film Channel (IFC), p. 173
Palluth, Ed . . . . AMC, p. 50
Palm, Erica . . . . Red Hour Films, p. 267
Palm, Robert . . . . NCIS, p. 370
Palmer, Amanda Morgan . . . . Shady Acres Entertainment, p. 285
Palmer, Amy . . . . Davis Entertainment Company, p. 107
Palmer, Dana . . . . Warrior Poets, p. 335
Palmer, Glendon . . . . Humble Journey Films, p. 169
Palmer, Joe . . . . Atlas Entertainment, p. 57
Palmer, Katie . . . . The New Adventures of Old Christine, p. 370
Palmer, Linda . . . . Runaway Productions, p. 277
Palmer, Michael . . . . Krasnoff Foster Productions, p. 190
Palmer, Michael Oates . . . . Shark, p. 374
Palmer, Patricia Fass . . . . Gilmore Girls, p. 362
Palmerton, John . . . . Turner Network Television (TNT), p. 321
Palmerton, John . . . . TBS, p. 309
Palotay, Marc . . . . Universal Studios, p. 326
Panay, Andrew . . . . Tapestry Films, Inc., p. 308
Pandit, Ani . . . . Cinetic, p. 93
Panitch, Sanford . . . . Regency Enterprises, p. 268
Pantaleo, Jeff . . . . Partizan, p. 250
Pantazis, Stacey . . . . Anne Carlucci Productions, p. 83
Pantoliano, Joe . . . . Waterfront, p. 379
Pao, Alice . . . . Misher Films, p. 218
Paolantonio, Bill . . . . LMNO Productions, p. 201
Papandrea, Bruna . . . . Groundswell Production, p. 156
Papanek, John . . . . ESPN Original Entertainment (EOE), p. 127
Papazian, Steven . . . . Warner Bros. Pictures, p. 334
Papero, Pat . . . . Segue Productions, Inc., p. 283
Pappas, George . . . . Cinema Seven Productions, p. 92
Paquette, Eric . . . . Screen Gems, p. 283
Paraskevas, Betty . . . . Paraskevas Studios, p. 249
Paraskevas, Michael . . . . Paraskevas Studios, p. 249
Paratore, Jim . . . . Telepictures Productions, p. 311
Parcero, Charmaine . . . . Acappella Pictures, p. 46
Pardee, John . . . . Desperate Housewives, p. 360
Parducci, Anne . . . . Lionsgate, p. 200
Parigi, Robert . . . . King of the Hill, p. 365

Paris, Margaret . . . . .Sony Pictures Television, p. 296
Paris, Russ . . . . .Columbia Pictures, p. 97
Parish, Scott . . . . .Alcon Entertainment, LLC, p. 49
Parisot, Pierre . . . . .Atlas Entertainment, p. 57
Park, Joy . . . . .CineMagic Entertainment, p. 92
Park, Nick . . . . .Aardman Animations, p. 44
Park, Richard . . . . .SkyZone Entertainment, p. 291
Parker, Carole . . . . .Jaffe/Braunstein Films, LLC, p. 179
Parker, Darby . . . . .Rick Lashbrook Films, p. 194
Parker, Gary . . . . .Grinning Dog Pictures, p. 154
Parker, Gwendolyn . . . . .Without a Trace, p. 379
Parker, Hutch . . . . .Twentieth Century Fox, p. 322
Parker, Jessica . . . . .Samuelson Productions Limited, p. 279
Parker, John . . . . .TOKYOPOP Inc., p. 315
Parker, John .Lemon Sky Productions, Inc., p. 196
Parker, Lita . . . . .New Line Cinema, p. 234
Parker, Matt . . . . .The Group Entertainment, p. 156
Parker, Pamela . . . . .Sony Pictures Television International, p. 296
Parker, Sarah Jessica . . . . .Pretty Matches Productions, p. 261
Parker, Trey . . . . .South Park, p. 376
Parker, Trey . . . . .Trunity, a Mediar Company, a Division of True Mediar, a Unity Corpbopoly, p. 320
Parkis, Steve . . . . .Disney Online, p. 112
Parks, Wally . . . . .Watershed Films, p. 336
Parnell, Brad . . . . .6 Pictures, p. 42
Parnell, Peter . . . . .Six Degrees, p. 375
Parouse, Dawn . . . . .Prison Break, p. 372
Parr, Chris . . . . .CMT: Country Music Television, p. 95
Parr, Stuart . . . . .Interscope/Shady/Aftermath Films, p. 176
Parr, Victoria . . . . .Samuelson Productions Limited, p. 279
Parriott, James . . . . .Ugly Betty, p. 378
Parseghian, Gene . . . . .Untitled Entertainment, p. 327
Parsons, Charlie . . . . .Survivor, p. 377
Parsons III, Lindsley . . . . .7th Heaven, p. 353
Part, Ron .Twentieth Century Fox Television, p. 323
Pascal, Amy . . . . .Columbia Pictures, p. 97
Pascal, Amy . . . . .Sony Pictures Entertainment, p. 295
Paschal, Brian . . . . .The Hal Lieberman Company, p. 197
Paseornek, Michael . . . . .Lionsgate, p. 200
Pasha, Kamran . . . . .Sleeper Cell, p. 375
Pasquin, John . . . . .Paradox Productions, Inc., p. 247
Passman, David .The Bedford Falls Company, p. 65
Patchett, Tom . . . . .Patchett Kaufman Entertainment, p. 250
Patel, Mina . . . . .CBS Paramount International Television, p. 87
Patel, Palak . . . . .Spring Creek Productions, Inc., p. 298
Patel, Rachna . . . . .Smoke House, p. 292
Patel, Vijal . . . .'Til Death, p. 377
Patent, Leslie . . . . .Comedy Arts Studios, p. 98
Patiri, Theresa .WE: Women's Entertainment, p. 336
Patmore-Gibbs, Suzanne . . . . . .ABC Entertainment Television Group, p. 45
Patrick, Joe . . . . .Metro-Goldwyn-Mayer Studios, Inc. (MGM), p. 215
Patrone-Werdiger, Jesse . . . . .Amy Robinson Productions, p. 273
Patsavas, Alexandra . . . . .The O.C., p. 371
Patterson, Casey . . . . .Spike TV, p. 298
Patterson, Jim . . . . .Two and a Half Men, p. 378
Patterson, Michael . . . . .Buena Vista Television, p. 79
Patterson, Ryan . . . . .Maco Noufeld Productions, p. 232
Pattison, Nikki . . . . .Next Entertainment, p. 236
Patton, Cami . . . . .The King of Queens, p. 365
Patton, Cami . . . . .Vanished, p. 378
Patton, Cami . . . . .Las Vegas, p. 366
Patton, Jody . . . . .Vulcan Productions, p. 332
Patzelt, Kevin . . . . .Bang Zoom! Entertainment, p. 61
Paul, Brett . . . . .Warner Bros. Television Production, p. 335
Paul, DJ . . . . .Sixth Way Productions, p. 291
Paul, Hank . . . . .Crystal Sky Pictures, LLC, p. 104
Paul, Samuel J. . . . . .Sundance Channel, p. 304
Paul, Steven . . . . .Crystal Sky Pictures, LLC, p. 104
Paule, D. Candis . . . . .Veronica Mars, p. 378
Paulson, Daniel L. . . . . .Daniel L. Paulson Productions, p. 251
Paulson, Eric . . . . .Playtone Productions, p. 258
Paura, Catherine . . . . .Farrell Paura Productions, LLC, p. 130
Pavone, Mike . . . . .Prison Break, p. 372
Pavoni, David . . . . .Motion Picture Production, Inc., p. 223
Payne, Alexander . . . . .Ad Hominem Enterprises, p. 46
Payne, Don . . . . .The Simpsons, p. 375
Payne, Gregory B. . . . . .Foothill Entertainment, Inc., p. 136
Payne, Judd . . . . .Persistent Entertainment, p. 253
Payne, Travis . . . . .Cinema 21 Group, p. 91
Peabody, Wyatt . . . . .Rafelson Media, p. 265
Peace, Kristin . . . . .TV Guide Channel, p. 321
Peak, Kearie . . . . .Electric Entertainment, p. 121
Pear, Winston . . . . .Rat Entertainment/Rat TV, p. 266
Pearl, Debra . . . . .Catfish Productions, p. 86
Pearl, Gary . . . . .Pearl Pictures, p. 252
Pearl, Michael . . . . .ABC Sports, p. 45
Pearlman, Steve . . . . .Class IV Productions, p. 95
Pearlstein, Rob . . . . .Medium, p. 369
Pearse, Annette . . . . .Arlington Entertainment, Inc., p. 55
Pearson, Mark . . . . .Twentieth Century Fox Television, p. 323
Pearson, Reece . . . . .Flame Ventures LLC, p. 135
Pease, Martha .Lifetime Television (New York), p. 198
Peaslee, John . . . . .According to Jim, p. 354
Peck, Adam . . . . .Synchronicity Productions, p. 306
Peck, Alison . . . . .C/W Productions, p. 105
Pedde, Giovanni . . . . .CBS Paramount International Television, p. 87
Pederson, Bob . . . . .Comedy Central, p. 98
Pedowitz, Mark . . . . .Touchstone Television, p. 316
Pedregal, Carl . . . . .Lionsgate, p. 200
Peele, Bart . . . . .Bunim/Murray Productions, Inc., p. 79
Peerce, Larry . . . . .Synchronicity Productions, p. 306
Peirce, Kimberly . . . . .Peirce Pictures, p. 252
Pelecanos, George . . . . .The Wire, p. 379
Pellereau, Adrian . . . . .Sneak Preview Entertainment, Inc., p. 293
Pellet, Gail . . . . .Trezza Entertainment, p. 317
Pellicano, Elke . . . . .Nancy Tenenbaum Films, p. 311
Pelman, Yoram .Tomorrow Film Corporation, p. 315
Pelphrey, Jennifer . . . . .Cartoon Network, p. 84
Peltier, Melissa Jo .MPH Entertainment, Inc., p. 224
Pelzer, Jeremy . . . . .Ealing Studios, p. 118
Pena, Kelly . . . . .Disney ABC Cable Networks Group, p. 112
Pence, Carol . . . . .Namesake Entertainment, p. 228
Pendleton, Sitarah . . . . .TV One, LLC, p. 322
Penha, Lisa . . . . .The Independent Film Channel (IFC), p. 173
Penn, David . . . . .Slipnot! Productions/SPG, p. 292
Penn, Matthew . . . . .Law & Order, p. 367
Penn, Matthew . . . . .Wolf Films, Inc., p. 343
Penn, Zak . . . . .Zak Penn's Company, p. 252
Pennette, Marco . . . . .Ugly Betty, p. 378
Pennie, Mike . . . . .My Name Is Earl, p. 369
Penny, Prentice . . . . .Girlfriends, p. 362
Penotti, John . . . . .GreeneStreet Films, p. 153
Pentz, Jamie . . . . .Warren Miller Entertainment, p. 335
Penvari, Jannie . . . . .Lucid Pictures, p. 204
Peoples, Theresa . . . . .Cannell Studios, p. 83
Pepper, Nicholas . . . . .ABC Entertainment Television Group, p. 45
Pereat, Jean Pierre . . . . .Evolving Pictures Entertainment, p. 128
Perello, Richard . . . . .Broken Lizard Industries, p. 76
Perello, Richard . . . . .Cataland Films, p. 85
Perer, Langley . . . . .Benderspink, p. 66
Perez, Arturo . . . . .Fremantle Productions Latin America, p. 142
Perez, Dinah . . . . .Light Renegade Entertainment, Inc., p. 198
Perez, Leo . . . . .SiTV, p. 290
Perez, Raul . . . . .Columbia Pictures, p. 97
Perez, Roman . . . . .M3 Television, p. 205
Perez-Brown, Cynthia . . . . .The Ruddy Morgan Organization, Inc./ Albert S. Ruddy Productions, p. 276
Pergola, Chris . . . . .Comedy Central, p. 98
Perini, Jennifer . . . . .Everyman Pictures, p. 128
Perkins, George W. . . . . .Desperate Housewives, p. 360
Perkins, George W. . . . . .New England Productions, Inc., p. 233
Perkins, Nancy . . . . .NBC Universal Television Studio, p. 231
Perkins, Ted . . . . .VOY Pictures, p. 332
Permut, David . . . . .Permut Presentations, p. 252
Pernworth, Julie . . . . .CBS Entertainment, p. 86
Perrette, Jean-Briac . . . . .NBC Universal Cable Entertainment, p. 231
Perrier, Delphine . . . . .Mandate Pictures, p. 209
Perrone, Sean . . . . .Kaplan/Perrone Entertainment, LLC, p. 184
Perry, Craig . . . . .Practical Pictures, p. 261
Perry, Dana Heinz . . . . .Perry Films, p. 253

Perry, Hart . . . Perry Films, p. 253
Perry, Kiana . . . Liquid Theory, p. 200
Perry, Mark . . . What About Brian, p. 379
Perryman, Jacquie . . . Twentieth Century Fox Television, p. 323
Persinger, Marshall . . . Fresh Produce Films, p. 142
Pertan, Ersin . . . Michael De Luca Productions, p. 108
Pesmen, Paula DuPré . . . 1492 Pictures, p. 38
Pessin, Marilyn . . . Act III Productions, p. 46
Petal, Malcolm . . . L.I.F.T. Productions, p. 191
Peter-Contesse, Nathalie . . . Hollywood Gang Productions, LLC, p. 168
Peter-Contesse, Nathalie . . . Cecchi Gori Pictures, p. 88
Peters, Anita . . . Laika Entertainment, p. 191
Peters, Christine . . . CFP Productions, p. 88
Peters, David . . . Montage Entertainment, p. 220
Peters, Diana . . . The Weinstein Company, p. 337
Peters, Jon . . . Peters Entertainment, p. 253
Peters, Michael . . . Paul Heller Productions, p. 164
Peters, Rachel . . . Archer Entertainment, p. 54
Peters, Rori . . . SiTV, p. 290
Petersen, Jori . . . SOAPnet, p. 293
Petersen, William . . . CSI: Crime Scene Investigation, p. 358
Petersen, William . . . High Horse Films, p. 166
Petersen, Wolfgang . . . Radiant Productions, p. 265
Peterson, Bonnie . . . MPH Entertainment, Inc., p. 224
Peterson, Brian . . . Smallville, p. 375
Peterson, Chris . . . Stone Village Pictures, LLC, p. 302
Peterson, Clark . . . Story and Film, Inc., p. 302
Peterson, Jason . . . Symbolic Entertainment, p. 306
Peterson, Jay . . . K2 Pictures, Inc., p. 184
Peterson, Nathan . . . Cyan Pictures, p. 105
Peterson, Ryan . . . Whitewater Films, p. 340
Petitti, Tony . . . CBS Sports, p. 88
Petraglia, Lisa . . . Touchstone Television, p. 316
Petretti, James . . . Sony Pictures Television, p. 296
Petrie Jr., Dan . . . Daniel Petrie Jr. & Company, p. 253
Petrie, Dorothea G. . . . D. Petrie Productions, Inc., p. 253
Petrie, June . . . D. Petrie Productions, Inc., p. 253
Petrocelli, Patrick . . . Trigger Street Independent, p. 319
Petrosini, Jana . . . MARTHA, p. 368
Petrosova, Natalya . . . Odd Lot Entertainment, p. 241
Petrovicz, Robert . . . The Dead Zone, p. 359
Petruniak, Jennifer . . . Alcon Entertainment, LLC, p. 49
Petry, Jerry . . . NBC Entertainment, p. 230
Petta, Daman . . . JibJab Media Inc., p. 181
Pett-Dante, Cynthia . . . Brillstein-Grey Entertainment, p. 75
Pettigrew, Jacques . . . CinéGroupe, p. 91
Pettit, Tom . . . Cold Case, p. 357
Pett-Joseph, Andrea . . . Brillstein-Grey Entertainment, p. 75
Petty, Meredith . . . Archer Entertainment, p. 54
Pettyjohn, Scarlett . . . Element Films, p. 121
Petulla, Mark . . . Lifetime Television (Los Angeles), p. 198
Petzel, Christopher . . . Fierce Entertainment, LLC, p. 131
Pevner, Stephen . . . Stephen Pevner, Inc., p. 253
Pew, Michele . . . Concrete Pictures, p. 99
Peyser, Michael . . . Mike's Movies/Michael Peyser Prod., p. 216
Pfautch, Jennifer . . . Deacon Entertainment, p. 109
Pfeffer, Rachel . . . Pfeffer Film, p. 253
Pfeiffer, Carolyn . . . Burnt Orange Productions, p. 80
Pfeiffer, Darin . . . Colleen Camp Productions, p. 82
Pfeiffer, Jeremy . . . Boxx Communications, LLC, p. 72
Pflieger, Kim . . . Pie Town Productions, p. 254
Pham, Annie . . . Spacedog, p. 297
Phegan, Tanya . . . DNA Films, p. 114
Phelan, Shauna . . . Furst Films, p. 143
Phelan, Tony . . . Grey's Anatomy, p. 362
Phelps, Jill Farren . . . ABC Daytime, p. 44
Philbin, J.J. . . . The O.C., p. 371
Philbin, Joanna . . . Las Vegas, p. 366
Philion, Brittany . . . Lion Rock Productions, p. 199
Philips, Brian . . . CMT: Country Music Television, p. 95
Philips, Brook . . . Mark Yellen Productions, p. 347
Philips, Dan . . . Laika Entertainment, p. 191
Philips, Todd . . . Krainin Productions, Inc., p. 190
Phillips, Alissa . . . Michael De Luca Productions, p. 108
Phillips, Amy . . . Versus, p. 329
Phillips, Bill . . . Turner Network Television (TNT), p. 321
Phillips, Bill . . . TBS, p. 309
Phillips, Byron . . . BET Networks, p. 66
Phillips, Guy . . . BBC Worldwide Americas, p. 64
Phillips, Louis . . . Phoenix Pictures, p. 254
Phillips, Marci . . . ABC Entertainment Television Group, p. 45
Phillips, Michael . . . Lighthouse Productions, p. 198
Phillips, Nicholas . . . Screen Gems, p. 283
Phillips, Stephanie . . . Mandate Pictures, p. 209
Phillips, Todd . . . The Todd Phillips Company, p. 254
Phillips Jr., William . . . Universal Studios, p. 326
Philpott, Meredith . . . Runaway, p. 373
Phoenix, Joy . . . A&E Network, p. 44
Phung, Quan . . . Twentieth Century Fox Television, p. 323
Pianigiani, Linda . . . di Bonaventura Pictures, Inc., p. 110
Picard, Lynn . . . Lifetime Television (New York), p. 198
Picard, Tom . . . Water Channel, p. 336
Piccoli, Pier Paolo . . . PLUS Entertainment, Inc., p. 258
Pichirallo, Joe . . . Overbrook Entertainment, p. 245
Pick, Izzie . . . Dancing with the Stars, p. 359
Pickering, Pamela . . . Dino De Laurentiis Company, p. 108
Pickrum, Michael . . . BET Networks, p. 66
Picollec, Laurence . . . Bonne Pioche, p. 71
Piechota, Pauline . . . Adirondack Pictures, p. 47
Pielak, Nolan . . . Dream Entertainment, Inc., p. 116
Piepenkotter, Julie . . . Disney ABC Cable Networks Group, p. 112
Pierce, Gerald . . . Universal Pictures, p. 326
Pierce, Michael . . . Pierce Williams Entertainment, p. 255
Pierce, Tricia . . . Symphony Pictures, Inc., p. 306
Pierson, Joseph . . . Cypress Films, Inc., p. 106
Pierson, Priscilla . . . Turner Network Television (TNT), p. 321
Pierson, Priscilla . . . TBS, p. 309
Pierson, Travis . . . CBS Entertainment, p. 86
Pietila, Bonnie . . . The Simpsons, p. 375
Pietrosh, Chrissy . . . Big Day, p. 355
Piette, Jason . . . Spice Factory, p. 298
Piggott, Zorana . . . Film & Music Entertainment, Ltd. (F&ME), p. 131
Pilat, Andrea . . . Pie Town Productions, p. 254
Pilcher, Lydia Dean . . . Cine Mosaic, p. 91
Piligian, Craig M. . . . Pilgrim Films & Television, Inc., p. 255
Piller, Shawn . . . The Dead Zone, p. 359
Piller, Shawn . . . Piller/Segan, p. 255
Pillot, Judd . . . According to Jim, p. 354
Pillsbury, Sarah . . . Sanford/Pillsbury Productions, p. 279
Pincus, Ira . . . Blueprint Entertainment, p. 70
Pincus, Josh . . . Cyan Pictures, p. 105
Pine, Steve . . . Nasser Entertainment Group, p. 229
Pini, Robert . . . New Line Cinema, p. 234
Pink, Jeremy . . . CNBC, p. 96
Pinkner, Jeff . . . Lost, p. 368
Pinkney, Rose Catherine . . . TV One, LLC, p. 322
Pinkstaff, Kimberly . . . Jerry Weintraub Productions, p. 338
Pinkwater, Jeremy . . . Luminair Entertainment, p. 204
Pinnolis, Toni . . . British Lion, p. 76
Pino, Diego Del . . . Moore/Cramer Productions, p. 221
Pintauro, Frank . . . Showtime Networks Inc., p. 287
Pinter, Hannah . . . Peter Engel Productions, p. 124
Pinto, Lynette . . . NBC Universal Cable Entertainment, p. 231
Pinvidic, Brant . . . GRB Entertainment, p. 153
Pipa, Gary . . . WE: Women's Entertainment, p. 336
Piper, Todd . . . Comedy Time, p. 98
Pipski, Daniel . . . LivePlanet, p. 201
Pirie, Iain . . . 19 Entertainment, Inc., p. 38
Pirnia, Tara . . . Maverick Films, p. 213
Piro, Whitney . . . The Pitt Group, p. 256
Pistor, Julia . . . Nickelodeon Movies, p. 237
Pitt, Adina . . . Nickelodeon/MTVN Kids & Family Group, p. 237
Pitt, Jim . . . Late Night with Conan O'Brien, p. 367
Pitt, Lisa . . . Wife Swap, p. 379
Pitt, Lou . . . The Pitt Group, p. 256
Pivcevic, Anne . . . BBC Films, p. 64
Place, Jess I. . . . Braun Entertainment Group, Inc., p. 73
Plager, Joey . . . Lifetime Television (Los Angeles), p. 198
Plagman, Greg . . . Cold Case, p. 357
Planco, Johnnie . . . Untitled Entertainment, p. 327

Plante, Ron . . . Lifetime Television (New York), p. 198
Platt, Jeremy . . . Double Nickel Entertainment, p. 115
Platt, Jodie . . . Touchstone Television, p. 316
Platt, Marc . . . Marc Platt Productions, p. 257
Platt, Warren . . . Mobile Streams, p. 219
Plaza, Jacqueline . . . Echelon Entertainment World Dist. & Prod., p. 119
Plec, Julie . . . Benderspink, p. 66
Pless, Judith . . . Showtime Networks Inc., p. 287
Plestis, Craig . . . NBC Entertainment, p. 230
Pleva, Cecelia . . . Late Night with Conan O'Brien, p. 367
Pliska, Adam . . . WPT Enterprises, Inc., p. 346
Plotkin, Andrew . . . Class IV Productions, p. 95
Plum, Steve . . . Twentieth Century Fox, p. 322
Plumer, Cliff . . . Lucasfilm Ltd., p. 203
Plunkett, Kevin . . . ABC Entertainment Television Group, p. 45
Plutte, Steve . . . Homerun Entertainment, Inc., p. 168
Poage, Sarah . . . 44 Blue Productions, Inc., p. 41
Pobjoy, Bruce A. . . . Summerland Entertainment, p. 304
Podemski, David . . . The Late Late Show with Craig Ferguson, p. 366
Poehler, Amy . . . Upright Citizens Brigade, p. 327
Pogue, John E. . . . Runaway, p. 373
Poindexter, Linda . . . Days of Our Lives, p. 359
Poitier, Sidney . . . Verdon-Cedric Productions, p. 329
Pokaski, Joe . . . Heroes, p. 363
Poku, Dee . . . Paramount Vantage/Paramount Classics, p. 248
Polakoff, David . . . Granada America, p. 152
Polaner, Melissa . . . Nickelodeon/MTVN Kids & Family Group, p. 237
Polhemus, Jib . . . Simon West Productions, p. 339
Polidoro, Jay . . . Gerber Pictures, p. 145
Polis, Michael R. . . . The Jim Henson Company, p. 165
Poll, Martin . . . Martin Poll Films, Ltd., p. 259
Pollack, Jeff . . . Handprint Entertainment, p. 160
Pollack, Joy . . . Winsome Productions, p. 342
Pollack, Noah . . . VH1, p. 330
Pollack, Ross . . . Sony Pictures Television International, p. 296
Pollack, Sara . . . Big Beach, p. 67
Pollack, Susanna . . . BBC Worldwide Americas, p. 64
Pollack, Sydney . . . Mirage Enterprises, p. 217
Pollison, David . . . Ghost House Pictures, p. 145
Pollison, David . . . Renaissance Pictures, p. 270
Pollock, James B. . . . Ralph Edwards Productions, p. 120
Pollock, Tom . . . The Montecito Picture Company, p. 220
Pollok, Stuart . . . Saltire Entertainment, p. 278
Polone, Gavin . . . My Boys, p. 369
Polone, Gavin . . . The Showbiz Show with David Spade, p. 374
Polone, Gavin . . . Pariah, p. 249
Polousky, Jayne . . . Broken Road Productions, p. 77
Polsky, Gabriel . . . Yari Film Group (YFG), p. 347
Polson, Beth . . . The Polson Company, p. 259
Poltermann, Barry . . . Civilian Pictures, p. 94
Poltrack, David . . . CBS Corporation, p. 86
Polvino, Marisa . . . Iridium Entertainment, p. 177
Polydoros, Mike . . . Lionsgate, p. 200
Pompian, Paul . . . Paul Pompian Productions, Inc., p. 259
Pongracic, Lisa . . . HBO Entertainment, p. 162
Ponomarev, Dmitri . . . TV Guide Channel, p. 321
Ponte, Jessica . . . National Geographic Feature Films, p. 229
Pontell, Jonathan . . . What About Brian, p. 379
Poole, Noel . . . Weller/Grossman Productions, p. 338
Poon, Troy Craig . . . MTV Films, p. 225
Pope, Braxton . . . Ithaka, p. 178
Pope, Brian . . . dick clark productions, inc., p. 94
Pope, David . . . Danjaq, LLC, p. 107
Pope, Deanna . . . Sid & Marty Krofft Pictures Corporation, p. 190
Pope, Jennifer . . . AEI-Atchity Entertainment Intl., Inc., p. 47
Pope, Katherine . . . NBC Entertainment, p. 230
Pope, Maria . . . The Late Show with David Letterman, p. 367
Pope, Martin . . . Magic Light Pictures, p. 207
Pope, Zazi . . . Warner Bros. Entertainment Inc., p. 334
Popp, Cynthia J. . . . The Bold and the Beautiful, p. 356
Popp, Cynthia J. . . . Bell-Phillip TV Productions, Inc., p. 65
Port, George . . . MarVista Entertainment, p. 212
Port, Robert . . . Numb3rs, p. 370
Portello, Beth . . . Cinema Libre Studio, p. 92
Porter, Elizabeth . . . Comedy Central, p. 98
Porter, Vince . . . Showtime Networks Inc., p. 287
Portner, Matt . . . GreeneStreet Films, p. 153
Portolese, James . . . Signature Pictures, p. 288
Posner, Carli . . . Patriot Pictures, LLC, p. 250
Poster, Meryl . . . Superb Entertainment, p. 305
Postiglione, Sonny . . . Law & Order, p. 367
Postlewaite, Ashley Q. . . . Renegade Animation, Inc., p. 270
Poticha, Eric . . . The Jim Henson Company, p. 165
Potkins, Michael . . . Infinity Features Entertainment, p. 174
Pottash, Bruce . . . CBS Paramount Worldwide Television Dist., p. 88
Potter, Scott . . . New Wave Entertainment, p. 235
Potts, Amanda . . . Benderspink, p. 66
Pouiphanvongxay, Oubansack . . . Evolution Entertainment, p. 128
Poul, Alan . . . Boku Films, p. 71
Poulshock, David . . . Red Door Films/David Poulshock Prod., Inc., p. 267
Poulter, Marlene Clark . . . Passions, p. 371
Poust, Tracy . . . In Case of Emergency, p. 364
Poverelli, Samantha . . . Turner Network Television (TNT), p. 321
Poverelli, Samantha . . . TBS, p. 309
Powell, Alison . . . Scott Sternberg Productions, p. 301
Powell, Craig . . . Jimmy Kimmel Live, p. 364
Powell, Dan . . . Comedy Central, p. 98
Powell, Doug . . . Warren Miller Entertainment, p. 335
Powell, James . . . VanDerKloot Film & Television, p. 328
Powell, Nick . . . Supernanny, p. 376
Powell, Norman S. . . . Vantage Enterprises, Inc., p. 329
Powell, Shirley . . . Turner Entertainment Group, p. 320
Power, Derek . . . Kahn Power Pictures, p. 184
Power, Ilene Kahn . . . Kahn Power Pictures, p. 184
Powers, Davis . . . Current TV, LLC, p. 105
Powers, Peggy . . . Broadway Video Entertainment, p. 76
Praagh, James Van . . . Ghost Whisperer, p. 362
Prager, Marlin . . . Legendary Pictures, p. 195
Prange, Greg . . . One Tree Hill, p. 371
Prasad, Krishna . . . RichCrest Animation Studios, p. 272
Pratico, Natalie . . . Sony Pictures Television International, p. 296
Pratt, Ben . . . Maloof Productions, p. 208
Pratt, Charles . . . Desperate Housewives, p. 360
Press, Terry . . . DreamWorks Animation SKG, p. 116
Presser, Renee . . . Lifetime Television (New York), p. 198
Presser, Sheldon . . . Warner Bros. Entertainment Inc., p. 334
Pressman, Edward R. . . . Edward R. Pressman Film Corporation, p. 261
Prevett, Michael . . . Relevant Entertainment Group, p. 270
Price, Jody . . . Gillen & Price, p. 146
Price, Marc . . . Budd Friedman Digital, p. 143
Price, Michael . . . The Simpsons, p. 375
Price, Paula . . . Epigram Entertainment, p. 125
Price, Richard . . . The Wire, p. 379
Price, Star . . . Extreme Makeover: Home Edition, p. 361
Priess, Don . . . Go Girl Media, p. 147
Primorac, Rafael . . . Arramis Films, p. 55
Primuth, David . . . GSN, p. 157
Prince, Jonathan . . . Once A Frog Productions, p. 242
Principato, Peter . . . RENO 911!, p. 373
Principato, Peter . . . Principato-Young Entertainment, p. 262
Prindle, Jared . . . 900 Films, p. 43
Priou, Emmanuel . . . Bonne Pioche, p. 71
Pritzker, Gigi . . . Odd Lot Entertainment, p. 241
Probst, Jeff . . . Survivor, p. 377
Procop, Amy . . . Original Productions, p. 244
Profera, Toni . . . The Core, p. 101
Proietto, Marci . . . Twentieth Century Fox Television, p. 323
Prokop, Paul . . . New Line Cinema, p. 234
Proner, Pierre . . . Merchant-Ivory, p. 215
Prosper, Derick . . . G-Unit Television & Films, p. 157
Prosser, Jess . . . Criminal Minds, p. 358
Protho, Nichelle . . . Urban Entertainment, p. 327
Protzel, Marc . . . Peter Hyams Productions, Inc., p. 169
Proud, Geoffrey . . . Jupiter Entertainment, p. 183
Prupas, Jesse . . . Muse Entertainment Enterprises, p. 227
Prupas, Michael . . . Muse Entertainment Enterprises, p. 227
Pryor, Jeff . . . Metro-Goldwyn-Mayer Studios, Inc. (MGM), p. 215
Puckhaber, George . . . Original Productions, p. 244
Pugliese, Charles . . . Killer Films, Inc., p. 187
Pullman, Barry . . . Saved, p. 374

Pullman, Maresa .Scott Free Productions, p. 282
Pura, Sarah .Untitled Entertainment, p. 327
Purcell, Tom .The Colbert Report, p. 357
Puri, Steven .Red Wagon Entertainment, p. 268
Purohit, Vinayak .RichCrest Animation Studios, p. 272
Pusateri, Nicole .@radical.media, p. 38
Putman, Fred .Dave Bell Associates, p. 65
Putman, Scott .Survivor, p. 377
Putnam, Aaron .Motion Picture Production, Inc., p. 223
Putnam, Keri .Miramax Films, p. 217
Putney, Troy .The Bedford Falls Company, p. 65
Putt, James .Initial Entertainment Group, p. 175
Pyken, Matt .Las Vegas, p. 366
Pyne, Ben .ABC Family, p. 45
Pyne, Ben .ABC Sports, p. 45
Pyne, Ben .ESPN Original Entertainment (EOE), p. 127
Pyne, Dan .Western Sandblast, p. 339
Quaintance, John .Notes From the Underbelly, p. 370
Queen, James .Scott Rudin Productions, p. 277
Queen Latifah .Flavor Unit Entertainment, p. 135
Quenqua, Nicole .Focus Features/Rogue Pictures, p. 136
Quested, John .Goldcrest Films International, Inc., p. 149
Quested, Nick .Goldcrest Films International, Inc., p. 149
Quijano, Eric .Playtone Productions, p. 258
Quill, Tad .Scrubs, p. 374
Quimby, Amy .Home & Garden Television (HGTV), p. 168
Quin-Harkin, Anne .Stone Village Pictures, LLC, p. 302
Quinn, Keith .LivePlanet, p. 201
Quinn, Mary .Brightlight Pictures, Inc., p. 75
Quiroz, Eva .Relativity Media LLC, p. 269
Quoss, Victoria .Versus, p. 329
Raab, Jane .Six Degrees, p. 375
Raab, Tracey .Twentieth Century Fox Television, p. 323
Rabbin, Sandra .Black Folk Entertainment, p. 67
Rabinowitz, Tal .Sony Pictures Television, p. 296
Rabins, Sandra .Sony Pictures Animation, p. 295
Race, Judy .Medium, p. 369
Radakovich, Leslie .Last Comic Standing, p. 366
Radcliffe, Mark .1492 Pictures, p. 38
Rader, Rhoades .Whitewater Films, p. 340
Radford, Mary .The Kennedy/Marshall Company, p. 186
Radford, Renate .NBC Entertainment, p. 230
Radice, Frank .NBC Entertainment, p. 230
Radler, Jon .Watson Pond Productions, p. 336
Radmin, Linne .The Radmin Company, p. 265
Radovanov, Danica .Josephson Entertainment, p. 182
Rae, Jolene .Ronald Suppa Productions, Inc., p. 306
Rafalowski, Mark .Rive Gauche Entertainment, p. 272
Rafelson, Peter .Rafelson Media, p. 265
Raff, Jason .Average Joe, p. 355
Raff, Paul .Jimmy Kimmel Live, p. 364
Raffanello, Nicole .CMT: Country Music Television, p. 95
Ragsdale, Kevin .Pretty Dangerous Films, p. 261
Raimi, Sam .Renaissance Pictures, p. 270
Raimi, Sam .Ghost House Pictures, p. 145
Raimi, Sam .Buckaroo Entertainment, p. 78
Raimo, Michelle .Nickelodeon Movies, p. 237
Rains, Mark .Extreme Makeover: Home Edition, p. 361
Rains, Mark .GRB Entertainment, p. 153
Rajkowski, Rebecca .In Cahoots, p. 173
Rajski, Peggy .Peggy Rajski Productions, p. 265
Raleigh, Chris .GSN, p. 157
Ramanna, Seema .RichCrest Animation Studios, p. 272
Rambert, Omarr .Overbrook Entertainment, p. 245
Ramet, Valeska .Stone Village Pictures, LLC, p. 302
Ramey, Sarah .Edward R. Pressman Film Corporation, p. 261
Ramirez, Diane .Echelon Entertainment World Dist. & Prod., p. 119
Ramis, Harold .Ocean Pictures, p. 241
Ramnath, Monika .Mandate Pictures, p. 209
Ramras, Golan .Kadokawa Pictures USA, p. 184
Ranberg, Chuck .The Game, p. 361
Randall, Gary A. .Grand Productions, Inc., p. 152
Randall, Rebecca .Caldera/De Fanti Entertainment, p. 82
Randolph, Chris .Battlestar Galactica, p. 355
Randolph, Jennifer .Court TV Networks, p. 102
Randolph, Marjorie .Buena Vista Motion Pictures Group, p. 78
Randt, Clark .Paramount Pictures Production Division, p. 248
Ranes, David .WhiteLight Entertainment, p. 340
Rankin, Jenny .Clear Pictures Entertainment Inc., p. 95
Rann-Cohen, Jaclyn .Nickelodeon/MTVN Kids & Family Group, p. 237
Ranta, Chris .Odd Lot Entertainment, p. 241
Rapaport, David .Masters of Horror, p. 368
Raphaelson, Josh .Program Partners, p. 262
Rapp, Amy .NorthSouth Productions, p. 239
Rappaport, Daniel .Management 360, p. 208
Rappaport, Ryan .Twentieth Century Fox Television, p. 323
Rappaport, Seth .Edmonds Entertainment, p. 120
Raptis, Michael .Wife Swap, p. 379
Rashid, Khadijah .Cinema Libre Studio, p. 92
Rasmussen, Bruce .Raines, p. 372
Rasser, Kim .Robert Cort Productions, p. 101
Rast, Alan .Fox Broadcasting Company, p. 139
Rasulo, James .The Walt Disney Company, p. 112
Rater, Joan .Grey's Anatomy, p. 362
Rath, Dave .Generate, p. 145
Rathauser, Michael .Lionsgate, p. 200
Ratner, Aaron .Mindfire Entertainment, p. 217
Ratner, Brett .Prison Break, p. 372
Ratner, Brett .Rat Entertainment/Rat TV, p. 266
Ratthe, Mathieu .Melee Entertainment, p. 214
Rattray, Celine .Plum Pictures, p. 258
Raubicheck, Marie .Comedy Central, p. 98
Rauch, Ellen .Warner Bros. Television Production, p. 335
Rauch, Michael .Showtime Networks Inc., p. 287
Raudonis, Mark .Bunim/Murray Productions, Inc., p. 79
Raufi, Caroline .Hyde Park Entertainment, p. 169
Raven, Abbe .The History Channel, p. 167
Raven, Abbe .A&E Network, p. 44
Ravetch, Joshua .New Line Cinema, p. 234
Rawlings, Marshall .Alturas Films, p. 50
Rawlins, Lisa .Warner Bros. Entertainment Inc., p. 334
Rawlinson, Peter .Battle Plan Productions, p. 63
Ray, Aaron .The Collective, p. 96
Rayne, Allison .The Film Department, p. 132
Raynis, Richard .The Simpsons, p. 375
Raynor, Lynn .Runaway, p. 373
Raynor, Lynn .P.O.V. Company, p. 260
Rea, Jodie .Twentieth Television, p. 324
Reading, Austin .Liquid Theory, p. 200
Reading, Julie Kellman .Liquid Theory, p. 200
Ready, David .di Bonaventura Pictures, Inc., p. 110
Reaney, Paul .FremantleMedia North America, p. 142
Reardon, Danielle .Kadokawa Pictures USA, p. 184
Reardon, John .Tribune Entertainment Company, p. 318
Rebo, Barry .Emerging Pictures, p. 122
Redford, Paul .Vanished, p. 378
Redford, Robert .Wildwood Enterprises, Inc., p. 341
Redick, Shaun .The Collective, p. 96
Redier-Linsk, Donna .Fox Broadcasting Company, p. 139
Redlich, Ed .Shark, p. 374
Redmann, John .The Tyra Banks Show, p. 378
Redmon, Ginger .One Life to Live, p. 371
Redstone, Sumner .CBS Corporation, p. 86
Reed, David .Stokely Chaffin Productions, p. 88
Reed, Drew .Twentieth Century Fox - Fox 2000, p. 323
Reed, Jason T. .Buena Vista Motion Pictures Group, p. 78
Reed, KristieAnne .Justice, p. 364
Reed, KristieAnne .Jerry Bruckheimer Films & Television, p. 78
Reed, Liz .Mark Yellen Productions, p. 347
Reed, Nikki .Bungalow 78 Productions, p. 79
Reed, Patty .Roserock Films, p. 275
Reed, Sylvia .Telemundo Network, p. 310
Reeder, Zac .MarVista Entertainment, p. 212
Reekie, Blair .Peace Arch Entertainment Group Inc., p. 251
Rees, Marian .Marian Rees Associates, p. 268
Reese-Lett, Della .Lett/Reese International Productions, p. 196
Reeves, Gary .Ardustry Entertainment, p. 54
Regal, Kelly .Turner Entertainment Group, p. 320
Regan, Dennis .The King of Queens, p. 365
Regan, Jennifer .Mandate Pictures, p. 209

Regan, Judith .REGAN, p. 268
Regen, Michael .Melee Entertainment, p. 214
Regina, Chris .Sci Fi Channel, p. 282
Register, Sam .Cartoon Network, p. 84
Reich, Allon .DNA Films, p. 114
Reich, Jason .The Daily Show With Jon Stewart, p. 359
Reichman, Donna Pearlmutter .HBO Films, p. 162
Reichman, Justin .Bravo, p. 74
Reichs, Kathy .Bones, p. 356
Reid, Alex .Help Me Help You, p. 363
Reid, Daphne .Tim Reid Productions, Inc., p. 269
Reid, Douglas .Last Straw Productions, p. 194
Reid, Elwood .Close to Home, p. 357
Reid, Eric .Lakeshore Entertainment Group LLC, p. 192
Reid, Kendrick .Comedy Central, p. 98
Reid, Marc .Lakeshore Entertainment Group LLC, p. 192
Reid, Melissa .Jerry Bruckheimer Films & Television, p. 78
Reid, Tim .Tim Reid Productions, Inc., p. 269
Reiff, Ethan .Sleeper Cell, p. 375
Reigg, Brandon .ABC Entertainment Television Group, p. 45
Reihel, Michelle .Valhalla Motion Pictures, p. 328
Reilly, Ann .The Feldman Company, p. 130
Reilly, Evan .Rescue Me, p. 373
Reilly, James E. .Days of Our Lives, p. 359
Reilly, James E. .Passions, p. 371
Reilly, Kevin .NBC Entertainment, p. 230
Reimink, Greg .Rubicon, p. 276
Reimond, Nick .Emmett/Furla Films, p. 123
Reims, Josh .What About Brian, p. 379
Reiner, Jeffrey .Friday Night Lights, p. 361
Reiner, Rob .Reiner/Greisman, p. 269
Reiner, Rob .Castle Rock Entertainment, p. 85
Reinhardt-Locke, Robin .MTV Networks, p. 226
Reinhart, Mark .here! Networks, p. 165
Reinish, Jennie .The Montecito Picture Company, p. 220
Reis, Matthew .Benderspink, p. 66
Reis, Tiffany .Asylum Entertainment, p. 57
Reisen, Vanessa .Traveler, p. 377
Reiser, Paul .Nuance Productions, p. 240
Reiss, Geoff .ESPN Original Entertainment (EOE), p. 127
Reiss, John .NBC News, p. 230
Reiss, Mike .The Simpsons, p. 375
Reisz, Michael .Boston Legal, p. 357
Reiter, Gabe .Robert Cort Productions, p. 101
Reiter, Irwin .The Weinstein Company, p. 337
Reiter, Luke .Law & Order, p. 367
Reiter, Zachary .CSI: NY, p. 359
Reitman, Ivan .The Montecito Picture Company, p. 220
Rejtig, Mark .Disney ABC Cable Networks Group, p. 112
Relles, Stefani .Fox Broadcasting Company, p. 139
Renfroe, Jay .Renegade 83, p. 270
Renshaw, Jeannine .Ghost Whisperer, p. 362
Renzetti, Rob .Cartoon Network, p. 84
Reo, Don .Everybody Hates Chris, p. 361
Repola, Art .Buena Vista Motion Pictures Group, p. 78
Resetar, Edward .Untitled Entertainment, p. 327
Resnick, Jason .Focus Features/Rogue Pictures, p. 136
Resnick, Jodie .Disney Online, p. 112
Resnick, Mark .Twentieth Century Fox, p. 322
Resteghini, Marc .Twentieth Century Fox, p. 322
Reuben, Rock .The King of Queens, p. 365
Revitte, Joe .Banyan Tree Films, p. 61
Rexon, Josh .NCIS, p. 370
Reyes-Smith, Vanessa .Nickelodeon/MTVN Kids & Family Group, p. 237
Reynard, Mel .Recorded Picture Company, p. 266
Reynolds, Carol .CRPI Entertainment, p. 103
Reynolds, Eric .New Line Cinema, p. 234
Reynolds, Fred .CBS Corporation, p. 86
Reynolds, Jim .Happy Hour, p. 362
Reynolds, Kelley Feldsott .Reynolds Entertainment, p. 271
Reynolds, Matthew .Casey Silver Productions, p. 289
Reynolds, Patrick F. .Reynolds Entertainment, p. 271
Reynolds, Ryan .Dark Trick Films, p. 107
Reynolds, Tom .BET Networks, p. 66
Reznack-Byrum, Karin .Byrum Power & Light, p. 81
Rhee, Tammie .Orchard Films, p. 243
Rhimes, Shonda .Grey's Anatomy, p. 362
Rhodes, Katie .Untitled Entertainment, p. 327
Rhodes, Mark .Marvel Studios, Inc., p. 211
Rhodes, Matthew .Persistent Entertainment, p. 253
Rhonheimer, Jamie .How I Met Your Mother, p. 364
Rhulen, Anthony .FilmEngine, p. 133
Rhys, Timothy .Camden Pictures, p. 82
Rhyu, Cindy .LJ Film, p. 201
Ribble, Alana .The Ruddy Morgan Organization, Inc./ Albert S. Ruddy Productions, p. 276
Ricci, Stephen .Crystal Spring Productions, Inc., p. 104
Rice, Cindi .Epic Level Entertainment, Ltd., p. 125
Rice, Dennis .Buena Vista Motion Pictures Group, p. 78
Rice, Joel S. .WildRice Productions, p. 341
Rice, Ned .The Late Late Show with Craig Ferguson, p. 366
Rice, Peter .Twentieth Century Fox - Searchlight Pictures, p. 323
Rice, Peter .Fox Atomic, p. 138
Rice, Richard .Concrete Pictures, p. 99
Rich, Laurie .MARTHA, p. 368
Rich, Marvin .Paulette Breen Productions, p. 74
Rich, Pete T. .Passions, p. 371
Rich, Stephanie .2929 Productions, p. 40
Richard, Alfredo .Telemundo Network, p. 310
Richards, Celia .Macgowan Films, p. 206
Richards, Mike .dick clark productions, inc., p. 94
Richards, Steve .Silver Pictures, p. 289
Richardson, Julie .Imaginarium Entertainment Group, p. 171
Richardson, Lisa .Masters of Horror, p. 368
Richardson, Lynne .Mandate Pictures, p. 209
Richardson, Mike .Dark Horse Entertainment, p. 107
Richbourg, Eli .Joel Schumacher Productions, p. 281
Riche, Alan .Sunrise Entertainment, p. 305
Riche, Peter .Sunrise Entertainment, p. 305
Riches, Shane .Poor Boys Productions, p. 259
Riches, Victor .Poor Boys Productions, p. 259
Richman, Adam .Double Nickel Entertainment, p. 115
Richmond, Bruce .HBO Entertainment, p. 162
Ricopero, Luiza .Myriad Pictures, p. 228
Ricord, Raymond .ABC Entertainment Television Group, p. 45
Riddle, Andy .National Geographic Kids' Prog. & Prod., p. 229
Ridenhour, Chris .Evolution Entertainment, p. 128
Rider, Marti .Sony Pictures Television, p. 296
Rieber, John .G4 TV, p. 144
Riesenberg, Pete .Chuck Fries Productions, Inc., p. 143
Rifkin, Arnold .Cheyenne Enterprises, p. 89
Rigal, Rene .State Street Pictures, p. 300
Riggi, John .30 Rock, p. 353
Riggs, Conrad .Survivor, p. 377
Riggs, Conrad .MARTHA, p. 368
Riggs, Conrad .The Apprentice, p. 355
Riggs, Conrad .Mark Burnett Productions, p. 80
Riklin, Matt .Bridge Films, LLC, p. 75
Riley, Dan .Port Magee Pictures, Inc., p. 260
Riley, M. .Mosaic Media Group, p. 222
Riley, Margaret .Brillstein-Grey Entertainment, p. 75
Riley, Sean .FX, p. 144
Riley, Sharon G. .Pie Town Productions, p. 254
Rimawi, David .The Asylum, p. 57
Rindel, Gaby .Joel Films, p. 181
Rindel, Santiago .Joel Films, p. 181
Riney, Shelly .Mandalay Pictures, p. 208
Ringe, Benjamin .Banyan Productions, p. 61
Rinzel, Alison .CBS Entertainment, p. 86
Riordan, Bob .Twentieth Television, p. 324
Ripstein, Alfredo .Alameda Films, p. 48
Risafi, Peter .Comedy Central, p. 98
Risher, Sara .Chick Flicks, p. 90
Rister, Laura .Untitled Entertainment, p. 327
Ritchey, Diana .American Dad, p. 354
Ritchie, Lauren A. .New Line Cinema, p. 234
Ritt, Martina .Riverrock Entertainment Group, p. 273
Rivas, Renee .Keckins Projects, Ltd., p. 185
Rivera, Patricia .Mandate Pictures, p. 209
Rivers, Melissa .Keep Clear, p. 186

Rivin, Ruth . . . . LMNO Productions, p. 201
Rivkin, Charles . . . . Wild Brain, Inc., p. 341
Rizor, Joel . . . . Screen Door Entertainment, p. 283
Rizzotti, Patrick . . . . Fortress Entertainment, p. 137
Roach, Jay . . . . Everyman Pictures, p. 128
Roach, Jessica . . . . Beth Grossbard Productions, p. 155
Roach, Julie . . . . Initial Entertainment Group, p. 175
Roach, Michael . . . . Fox Broadcasting Company, p. 139
Roban, Michael . . . . Stone Village Pictures, LLC, p. 302
Robb, Edie . . . . Station 3, p. 300
Robb, R.D. . . . . Station 3, p. 300
Robbins, Brian . . . . Smallville, p. 375
Robbins, Brian . . . . One Tree Hill, p. 371
Robbins, Brian . . . . Tollin/Robbins Productions, p. 315
Robbins, Joan . . . . Entertainment Studios, Inc., p. 125
Robbins, Kate . . . . Snowfall Films/Windchill Films, p. 293
Roberts, Ann Lewis . . . . Buena Vista Television, p. 79
Roberts, Ben . . . . Humble Journey Films, p. 169
Roberts, Beth . . . . NBC Entertainment, p. 230
Roberts, Cam . . . . Colomby Films, p. 97
Roberts, Chris . . . . Ascendant Pictures, p. 56
Roberts, Dick . . . . Sony Pictures Television, p. 296
Roberts, Ed . . . . Joada Productions, Inc., p. 181
Roberts, Gary D. . . . . Twentieth Century Fox, p. 322
Roberts, Ian . . . . Upright Citizens Brigade, p. 327
Roberts, J.B. . . . . Tagline Pictures, p. 307
Roberts, Jack . . . . Comic Book Movies, LLC/Branded Entertainment/ Batfilm Productions, p. 99
Roberts, John P. . . . . GSN, p. 157
Roberts, Julia . . . . Red Om Films, Inc., p. 267
Roberts, Laura . . . . Brad Wilson Productions, Inc., p. 342
Roberts, Mark . . . . Two and a Half Men, p. 378
Roberts, Mark . . . . Roberts/David Films, Inc., p. 273
Roberts, Matt . . . . The Late Show with David Letterman, p. 367
Roberts, Michael . . . . The CW, p. 105
Roberts, Nancy . . . . Stampede Entertainment, p. 299
Roberts, Randy . . . . Law & Order: Special Victims Unit, p. 367
Roberts, Vincent H. . . . . Disney ABC Cable Networks Group, p. 112
Robertson, Amy Salko . . . . The AV Club, p. 58
Robertson, John . . . . Silly Robin Productions, p. 288
Robertson, Matt . . . . Nuyorican, p. 240
Robertson, Phil . . . . Zephyr Films Ltd., p. 348
Robin, Michael . . . . The Closer, p. 357
Robin, Michael . . . . Nip/Tuck, p. 370
Robin, Michael . . . . The Shephard/Robin Company, p. 286
Robin, Steve . . . . Boston Legal, p. 357
Robinov, Jeff . . . . Warner Bros. Pictures, p. 334
Robins, Sean . . . . Broken Road Productions, p. 77
Robinson, Amy . . . . Amy Robinson Productions, p. 273
Robinson, Brian . . . . ESPN Original Entertainment (EOE), p. 127
Robinson, Brian . . . . Morgan Creek Productions, p. 221
Robinson, Butch . . . . Humble Journey Films, p. 169
Robinson, Cindy . . . . Jupiter Entertainment, p. 183
Robinson, David . . . . Lee Daniels Entertainment, p. 106
Robinson, David C. . . . . Morgan Creek Productions, p. 221
Robinson, Doug . . . . Rules of Engagement, p. 373
Robinson, Elizabeth . . . . Principal Entertainment, p. 262
Robinson, Eric . . . . The Weinstein Company, p. 337
Robinson, James G. . . . . Morgan Creek Productions, p. 221
Robinson, John . . . . Blueprint Entertainment, p. 70
Robinson, Marcello . . . . 777 Entertainment Group, Ltd., p. 42
Robinson, Mary . . . . Proud Mary Entertainment, p. 263
Robinson, Randy . . . . Randwell Productions, p. 266
Robinson, Rebecca . . . . Black & White Productions, p. 67
Robinson, Regan . . . . Spacedog, p. 297
Robinson, Trisha . . . . Brainstorm Media, p. 72
Robles, Henry . . . . Traveler, p. 377
Robson, Kirsty . . . . Supernanny, p. 376
Roby, Sara . . . . DreamWorks SKG, p. 116
Rocco, Nikki . . . . Universal Pictures, p. 326
Rocco, Vicki . . . . Hyde Park Entertainment, p. 169
Roche, John . . . . Law & Order, p. 367
Rochkind, Glen . . . . CNBC, p. 96
Rock, Bobby . . . . American Zoetrope, p. 51
Rock, Chris . . . . Everybody Hates Chris, p. 361
Rocklin, Nicole . . . . Rocklin Entertainment, p. 274
Rockwell, David . . . . New City Pictures, Inc., p. 233
Rockwell, Simon . . . . RDF Media, p. 266
Rocourt II, Guy . . . . Letnom Productions, p. 196
Roddy, Jessica . . . . 2929 Productions, p. 40
Rodgers, Greg . . . . Mutual Film Company, p. 227
Rodgers, Johnathan . . . . TV One, LLC, p. 322
Rodman, Anne . . . . Phoenix Pictures, p. 254
Rodman, Cheryl . . . . Spyglass Entertainment Group, p. 299
Rodman, Patrick . . . . Bang Zoom! Entertainment, p. 61
Rodman, Rene . . . . PorchLight Entertainment, p. 259
Rodrigue, Nena . . . . Wolf Films, Inc., p. 343
Rodriguez, Dailyn . . . . Ugly Betty, p. 378
Rodriguez, Lydia . . . . Keckins Projects, Ltd., p. 185
Rodriguez, Matthew . . . . Twentieth Television, p. 324
Rodriguez, Rick . . . . Sony Pictures Television International, p. 296
Rodriguez, Rosalind . . . . Endemol USA Latino, p. 123
Rodriguez, Vanessa . . . . Entourage, p. 360
Rodriguez, Yolanda . . . . Michael Taylor Productions, p. 309
Rodríguez, Tatiana . . . . MTV Networks Latin America (MTVNLA), p. 226
Roe, Ed . . . . The Class, p. 357
Roe Reyes, Jennifer . . . . Letnom Productions, p. 196
Roeding, Cyriac . . . . CBS Entertainment, p. 86
Roedy, Bill . . . . MTV Networks, p. 226
Roenfeldt, Gretel . . . . Boxx Communications, LLC, p. 72
Roepke, Gene . . . . 21 Laps Entertainment, p. 38
Roewe, Jay . . . . HBO Films, p. 162
Rogawski, Julia . . . . Cinetic, p. 93
Rogers, Carl . . . . Alcon Entertainment, LLC, p. 49
Rogers, Jeff . . . . 7th Heaven, p. 353
Rogers, Jennifer . . . . The Mayhem Project, p. 213
Rogers, Sheila . . . . The Late Show with David Letterman, p. 367
Rogge, Eric . . . . Film Farm, p. 132
Rogier, Timothy . . . . The Jinks/Cohen Company, p. 181
Rogow, Stan . . . . Stan Rogow Productions, p. 274
Rohan, Hanh . . . . JibJab Media Inc., p. 181
Rohr, Kathleen Burns . . . . Pilgrim Films & Television, Inc., p. 255
Rohrlich, Joe . . . . Vincent Newman Entertainment, p. 236
Rohrs Jr., John . . . . Sony Pictures Television, p. 296
Roker, Al . . . . Al Roker Productions, p. 274
Roker, Vicki . . . . Lakeshore Entertainment Group LLC, p. 192
Rollins Westin, Sherrie . . . . Sesame Workshop, p. 285
Rollman, Eric . . . . Marvel Studios, Inc., p. 211
Rolontz, Lee . . . . VH1, p. 330
Roman, Danny . . . . Scott Rudin Productions, p. 277
Roman, John L. . . . . Law & Order: Criminal Intent, p. 367
Roman, Phil . . . . Phil Roman Entertainment, p. 274
Romano, Anthony . . . . Hand Picked Films, p. 159
Romano, Debby . . . . Scrubs, p. 374
Romano, Debby . . . . Notes From the Underbelly, p. 370
Romano, Debby . . . . One Tree Hill, p. 371
Romano, Edward A. . . . . Warner Bros. Entertainment Inc., p. 334
Romano, Jonny . . . . Village Roadshow Pictures, p. 331
Romano, Marianne . . . . Nickelodeon/MTVN Kids & Family Group, p. 237
Romano, Nicole . . . . Protozoa Pictures, p. 263
Romero, Dolly . . . . SiTV, p. 290
Romero, Thamar . . . . Nickelodeon/MTVN Kids & Family Group, p. 237
Romilly, Sara D. . . . . New Line Cinema, p. 234
Rona, Andrew . . . . Focus Features/Rogue Pictures, p. 136
Rone, David . . . . Fox Cable Networks, p. 139
Rone, David . . . . Fox Sports Network, p. 140
Ronquillo, Kristine . . . . AM Productions & Management, p. 50
Ronson, Steve . . . . A&E Network, p. 44
Ronzoni, Cindy . . . . GSN, p. 157
Rood, John . . . . ABC Family, p. 45
Rood, John . . . . Disney ABC Cable Networks Group, p. 112
Roodman, Joel . . . . Gotham Entertainment Group, p. 150
Roongcharoen, Ellen . . . . Echelon Entertainment World Dist. & Prod., p. 119
Roos, Fred . . . . FR Productions, p. 141
Roos, Lisa . . . . Warner Bros. Television Production, p. 335
Root, Antony . . . . Sony Pictures Television International, p. 296
Root, Jane . . . . Discovery Networks, U.S., p. 111
Root, Jane . . . . Discovery Channel, p. 111
Rosales, Frank . . . . Discovery Networks, U.S., p. 111
Rosato, Wendy Spence . . . . ER, p. 361

Roscoe, Patrick ....Playtone Productions, p. 258
Rose, Alexandra ....Alex Rose Productions, Inc., p. 274
Rose, Jacobus ....Skylark Entertainment, Inc., p. 291
Rose, Michael ....Magic Light Pictures, p. 207
Rose, Sara ....Picturehouse, p. 254
Rose, Tyler ....Fuse Entertainment, p. 144
Rose, Victoria ....Walker/Fitzgibbon TV/Films, p. 333
Rosello, Mark ....Norsemen Television Productions, LLC, p. 239
Rosemont, David A. ......Rosemont Productions International, Ltd., p. 275
Rosemont, Norman ......Rosemont Productions International, Ltd., p. 275
Rosen, Eric ....Roth/Arnold Productions, p. 275
Rosen, Josh ....Indigo Films, p. 174
Rosen, Ken ....Phoenix Pictures, p. 254
Rosen, Lance ....Paradigm Studio, p. 247
Rosen, Marc ....Heyday Films, p. 166
Rosen, Matt ....Chris Dorr Productions, p. 114
Rosen, Noah ....Circle of Confusion Productions, p. 93
Rosen, Richard ....Wolfmill Entertainment, p. 343
Rosen, Rick ....Cinema Libre Studio, p. 92
Rosen Esq., Robert C. ....Star Entertainment Group, Inc., p. 299
Rosen, Susie ....Magnetic Film, p. 207
Rosenbaum, Scott ....The Shield, p. 374
Rosenberg, Billy ....Lynda Obst Productions, p. 241
Rosenberg, Daniel ....InVenture Entertainment, p. 176
Rosenberg, Joe ....Radar Pictures, p. 264
Rosenberg, Julia ....January Films, p. 179
Rosenberg, Kevin ....John Baldecchi Productions, p. 60
Rosenberg, Michael ....Imagine Entertainment, p. 172
Rosenberg, Michael ....Maverick Films, p. 213
Rosenberg, Paul ....Interscope/Shady/Aftermath Films, p. 176
Rosenberg, Rick ....Chris/Rose Productions, p. 90
Rosenberg, Scott Mitchell ....Platinum Studios, LLC, p. 257
Rosenberg, Tom ....Lakeshore Entertainment Group LLC, p. 192
Rosenblatt, Bart ....Code Entertainment, p. 96
Rosenblum, Bruce ....Warner Bros. Entertainment Inc., p. 334
Rosenblum, John Frank ....Epic Level Entertainment, Ltd., p. 125
Rosenblum, John Frank ....Lighthouse Productions, p. 198
Rosenblum, Kim ....Nickelodeon/MTVN Kids & Family Group, p. 237
Rosenblum, Paul ....Quinta Communications USA, p. 264
Rosenfeld, Madelon ....Jurist Productions, p. 183
Rosenfelt, Adam ....Element Films, p. 121
Rosenfelt, Dan ....Weed Road Pictures, p. 337
Rosenfelt, Karen ....Sunswept Entertainment, p. 305
Rosenfelt, Scott .........................I.E. Productions, Inc., p. 170
Rosenman, Zvi Howard ....Zvi Howard Rosenman Productions, p. 275
Rosenstein, Donna ....Ghost Whisperer, p. 362
Rosenstein, Nina ....HBO Entertainment, p. 162
Rosenstein, Pamela ....Vulcan Productions, p. 332
Rosenthal, Dave ....Principato-Young Entertainment, p. 262
Rosenthal, David ....Gilmore Girls, p. 362
Rosenthal, Gay ....Gay Rosenthal Productions, p. 275
Rosenthal, Jane ....Tribeca Productions, p. 318
Rosenthal, Jim ....New Line Cinema, p. 234
Rosenthal, Jim ....New Line Television, p. 235
Rosenthal, Karine ....Bones, p. 356
Rosenthal, Lee E. ....Paramount Pictures Production Division, p. 248
Rosenthal, Rick ....Whitewater Films, p. 340
Rosenthal, Risa ....A&E Network, p. 44
Rosenzweig, Alison ....Rosenzweig Films, p. 275
Rosenzweig, Josh ....here! Networks, p. 165
Roses, Joanna ....Nickelodeon/MTVN Kids & Family Group, p. 237
Rosette, Nancy ....VanDerKloot Film & Television, p. 328
Roskin, Marc ....Electric Entertainment, p. 121
Rosner, Richard ....Jimmy Kimmel Live, p. 364
Ross, Damon ....Nickelodeon Movies, p. 237
Ross, Douglas ....Evolution, p. 128
Ross, Gary ....Larger Than Life Productions, p. 193
Ross, Glenn ....Universal Pictures, p. 326
Ross, Jason ....The Daily Show With Jon Stewart, p. 359
Ross, Jeff ....Late Night with Conan O'Brien, p. 367
Ross, Jeremy ....TOKYOPOP Inc., p. 315
Ross, Jeremy ....Vanguard Films/Vanguard Animation, p. 328
Ross, Marcia ....Buena Vista Motion Pictures Group, p. 78
Ross, Marcy ....Fox Broadcasting Company, p. 139
Ross, Rich ....Disney ABC Cable Networks Group, p. 112
Ross, Tess ....FilmFour, p. 133
Rossellini, Victoria ....Twentieth Century Fox, p. 322
Rossi, Amanda ....The Asylum, p. 57
Rosta, Tim ....MTV Networks, p. 226
Rostami, Sara ....Creanspeak Productions LLC, p. 103
Rotbart, Heidi ....Heidi Rotbart Management, p. 275
Rotenberg, Lesli ....PBS, p. 251
Rotenberg, Michael ....Everybody Hates Chris, p. 361
Rotenberg, Michael ....King of the Hill, p. 365
Rotenberg, Michael ....3 Arts Entertainment, Inc., p. 40
Roth, Donna Arkoff ....Roth/Arnold Productions, p. 275
Roth, Doug ....Sony Pictures Television, p. 296
Roth, Elisa ....NBC Universal Television Studio, p. 231
Roth, Eric ....The Weinstein Company, p. 337
Roth, Heather ....ABC Entertainment Television Group, p. 45
Roth, JD ....The Biggest Loser, p. 356
Roth, JD ....3 Ball Productions, p. 40
Roth, Jeffrey ....Focus Features/Rogue Pictures, p. 136
Roth, Jodi ....CBS Entertainment, p. 86
Roth, Kim ....Imagine Entertainment, p. 172
Roth, Michael J. ....Sneak Preview Entertainment, Inc., p. 293
Roth, Peter ....Warner Bros. Television Production, p. 335
Roth, Peter ....Warner Horizon Television, p. 335
Roth, Scott ....Twentieth Television, p. 324
Roth, Stephanie ....Sony Pictures Entertainment, p. 295
Roth, Wendy ....RDF Media, p. 266
Roth, Wendy ....Wife Swap, p. 379
Rothbart, Corrie ....Bauer Martinez Entertainment, p. 63
Rothbart, Daniel ....Nickelodeon Movies, p. 237
Rothbart, Jonathan ....The Orphanage, p. 244
Rothberg, Russell ....Fox Broadcasting Company, p. 139
Rothenberg, Steve ....Lionsgate, p. 200
Rothman, Aaron ....Comedy Central, p. 98
Rothman, Alison ....Twentieth Century Fox Television, p. 323
Rothman, Rachel ....Maverick Films, p. 213
Rothman, Rodney ....Help Me Help You, p. 363
Rothman, Sarah Levinson ....The Weinstein Company, p. 337
Rothman, Tom ....Twentieth Century Fox, p. 322
Rothstein, Josh ....Double Feature Films, p. 115
Rothstein, Lauren ....Industry Entertainment Partners, p. 174
Rothstein, Michael ....The Weinstein Company, p. 337
Rothstein, Richard ....NBC Universal Television Studio, p. 231
Rothwell, Tim ....Marvel Studios, Inc., p. 211
Rotmensz, Nathan ....Chameleon Entertainment, p. 89
Rott, Betsy ....E! Networks, p. 117
Rottenberg, Julie ....Six Degrees, p. 375
Rottinghaus, Aaron ....Bold Films, p. 71
Rou, Alison ....ABC Entertainment Television Group, p. 45
Roumel, Katie ....Killer Films, Inc., p. 187
Rousso, Mark ....New Wave Management, p. 236
Roven, Charles ....Mosaic Media Group, p. 222
Roven, Charles ....Atlas Entertainment, p. 57
Rovner, Robert ....Crossing Jordan, p. 358
Rovner, Susan ....Warner Bros. Television Production, p. 335
Rowe, Scott ....Warner Bros. Entertainment Inc., p. 334
Rowe, Tom ....Masters of Horror, p. 368
Rowland, Jen ....Super Delicious Productions, p. 305
Rowland, Jon ....The Harris Company, p. 161
Rowles, Johnny ....Starry Night Entertainment, p. 300
Roybal, Mark ....Scott Rudin Productions, p. 277
Royce, Mike ....Lucky Louie, p. 368
Royce, Yemaya ....Steven Bochco Productions, p. 70
Rozenfeld, Kim ....ABC Entertainment Television Group, p. 45
Rubbert, Neil ....Boxx Communications, LLC, p. 72
Rubenfeld, Paul ....Imaginarium Entertainment Group, p. 171
Rubenstein, Ira ....Sony Pictures Digital, p. 295
Rubin, Charlie ....Law & Order: Criminal Intent, p. 367
Rubin, Cheryl ....DC Comics, p. 108
Rubin Esq., Gerald ....The Jerry Leider Company, p. 196
Rubin, Michael ....MSNBC, p. 225
Rubin, Scott ....National Lampoon, p. 230
Rubino, Joanne ....The Greif Company, p. 154
Rubino-Bradway, Caitlen ....LeFrak Productions, p. 195
Rubinstein, Richard P. ....New Amsterdam Entertainment, Inc., p. 233
Rubio, Raquel ....Pandemonium, p. 246

Ruby, Joseph . . . . .Ruby-Spears Productions, p. 276
Ruchim, Arik . . . . .C/W Productions, p. 105
Rudd, Larry . . . . .Taryn Productions, p. 308
Rudd, Rebekah . . . . .Spyglass Entertainment Group, p. 299
Ruddy, Al . . . . .The Ruddy Morgan Organization, Inc./ Albert S. Ruddy Productions, p. 276
Rudell, Kirk . . . . .20 Good Years, p. 353
Ruden, Jordan . . . . .World of Wonder Productions, p. 345
Ruderman, Melissa . . . . .Handprint Entertainment, p. 160
Rudin, Scott . . . . .Scott Rudin Productions, p. 277
Rudman, Melissa . . . . .Fox Reality, p. 140
Rudofsky, Jami . . . . .Gilmore Girls, p. 362
Ruggeri, Tyler . . . . .Exile Entertainment, p. 128
Ruggiero, Diane . . . . .Veronica Mars, p. 378
Rugolo, Gina . . . . .Relevant Entertainment Group, p. 270
Ruiz, Jonathan . . . . .Regency Enterprises, p. 268
Rukeyser, Stacy . . . . .Standoff, p. 376
Runnels, Lara . . . .'Til Death, p. 377
Runyan, Jenni . . . . .Comedy Central, p. 98
Ruocco, Kindra . . . . .Cinema Libre Studio, p. 92
Rupert-Shibata, Christy . . . . .CNBC, p. 96
Ruppenthal, John . . . . .PBS, p. 251
Rush, Colleen Fahey . . . . .VH1, p. 330
Rush, Colleen Fahey . . . . .MTV Networks, p. 226
Rushfield, Ali . . . . .Help Me Help You, p. 363
Rushnell, Hilary . . . . .Lion Television U.S., p. 199
Ruskin, Morris . . . . .Shoreline Entertainment, Inc., p. 286
Ruskin, Susan . . . . .Western Sandblast, p. 339
Russell, Arrika . . . . .Zinkler Films, p. 349
Russell, Dan . . . . .Discovery Networks, U.S., p. 111
Russell, Dan . . . . .Animal Planet, p. 52
Russell, Dylan . . . . .Stone Village Pictures, LLC, p. 302
Russell, Jessica . . . . .Zinkler Films, p. 349
Russell, Kerry . . . . .ChubbCo Film Co., p. 91
Russell, Patrick . . . . .Sony BMG Feature Films, p. 294
Russell, Shannon . . . . .Epiphany Pictures, Inc., p. 126
Russo, Alana . . . . .NBC Sports, p. 231
Russo, Angela . . . . .Day Break, p. 359
Russo, Sylvester . . . . .King World Productions, Inc., p. 188
Ruta, Nick .Baldwin Entertainment Group, Ltd., p. 60
Rutten, Stephanie . . . . .Lonetree Entertainment, p. 202
Ruttenberg, Brett . . . . .The Collective, p. 96
Ruzicka, Tom . . . . .Universal Pictures, p. 326
Ryan, Ann . . . . .Gary Hoffman Productions, p. 167
Ryan, Chris . . . . .K2 Pictures, Inc., p. 184
Ryan, Chris . . . . .Disney ABC Cable Networks Group, p. 112
Ryan, Christine . . . . .Con Artists Productions, p. 99
Ryan, Christopher T. . . . . .CBS Entertainment, p. 86
Ryan, Laurissa .CMT: Country Music Television, p. 95
Ryan, Luke . . . . .New Line Cinema, p. 234
Ryan, Shannon .Fox Broadcasting Company, p. 139
Ryan, Shawn . . . . .The Unit, p. 378
Ryan, Shawn . . . . .The Shield, p. 374
Ryan, Suzanne . . . . .Law & Order, p. 367
Ryan, Trevor . . . . .Di Novi Pictures, p. 110
Ryder, Aaron . . . . .Newmarket Capital Group, p. 236
Ryder, Aaron . . . . .Raygun Productions, p. 266
Rydzewski, Ellen . . . . .Current TV, LLC, p. 105
Rytie, Jill . . . . .Wheelhouse Entertainment, p. 339
Saade, John . . . . .ABC Entertainment Television Group, p. 45
Saari, Per . . . . .Blossom Films, p. 68
Saavedra, Craig M. . . . . .Starry Night Entertainment, p. 300
Saban, Lena . . . . .Grosso Jacobson Comm. Corp., p. 156
Sabih, Layla . . . . .Hell's Kitchen, p. 363
Sabin, Edward . . . . .Fox Television Studios, p. 140
Sablosky, Scott . . . . .Grossbart Kent Productions, p. 156
Sacca, Chris . . . . .Google Inc., p. 149
Saccani, Damien . . . . .Cider Mill Productions, p. 91
Sacchi, John . . . . .Lionsgate, p. 200
Saccio, Michael . . .Josselyne Herman & Assoc./Moving Image Films, p. 166
Sachs, Benjamin . . . . .The Todd Phillips Company, p. 254
Sachs, Gabe . . . . .Sachs Judah Productions, p. 277
Sachs, Jason . . . . .Beacon, p. 64
Sachs, Joe . . . . .ER, p. 361
Sachs, Patty . . . . .Belisarius Productions, p. 65
Sack, Reuben . . . . .The Matthau Company, Inc., p. 212
Sacker, Neil . . . . .Yari Film Group (YFG), p. 347
Sackheim, Daniel . . . . .House, p. 363
Sacks, Alan . . . . .Alan Sacks Productions, Inc., p. 277
Sacks, Andrew . . . . .The Closer, p. 357
Sacks, David . . . . .Warner Bros. Television Production, p. 335
Sacks, David . . . . .Room 9 Entertainment, p. 274
Sadeghi, Marc . . . . .The Orphanage, p. 244
Sadofsky, Lynn . . . . .Queer Eye, p. 372
Sadowski, Peter .von Zerneck-Sertner Films, p. 332
Saduski, Kirk . . . . .Playtone Productions, p. 258
Saetre, Linda . . . . .Bonne Pioche, p. 71
Safady, Rita . . . . .Flame Ventures LLC, p. 135
Safarian, Golareh . . . . .Q Media Partners, p. 264
Safavi, Mandy . . . . .Out of the Blue . . . Entertainment, p. 244
Saffer, Wendy . . . . .Serendipity Point Films, p. 284
Safford, Tony . . . . .Twentieth Century Fox, p. 322
Safinick, Ron . . . . .Sobini Films, p. 293
Safran, Peter . . . . .Safran Company, p. 278
Saftler, Chuck . . . . .FX, p. 144
Sagastume, Gustavo . . . . .PBS, p. 251
Sahagen, Peter D. . . . . .Ardustry Entertainment, p. 54
Saigh, Rita . . . . .Nasser Entertainment Group, p. 229
Sajak, Pat . . . . .P.A.T. Productions, p. 250
Sakai, Richard . . . . .The Simpsons, p. 375
Sakai, Richard . . . . .Gracie Films, p. 151
Sakamoto, Kaeko .Bang Zoom! Entertainment, p. 61
Saks, Mark . . . . .Numb3rs, p. 370
Sakurada, Jennifer . . . . .Myriad Pictures, p. 228
Sakurai, Yuko . . . . .OZLA Pictures, Inc., p. 246
Salamoff, Paul . . . . .Bold Films, p. 71
Salamoff, Paul J. .David Lancaster Productions, p. 192
Salamone, Lisa . . . . .Walt Disney Television Animation, p. 113
Salamone, Lisa . . . . .Disney ABC Cable Networks Group, p. 112
Saleem, Haroon . . . . .Overbrook Entertainment, p. 245
Saleh, Angelika . . . . .Angelika, p. 52
Salemi, Joseph . . . . .Lotus Pictures, p. 203
Sales, Brett . . . . .Loreen Arbus Productions, Inc., p. 54
Salim, Anna . . . . .Blueprint Entertainment, p. 70
Salimi, Firoze . . . . .The Artists' Colony, p. 56
Salke, Alan . . . . .Sidney Kimmel Entertainment, p. 187
Salke, Albert J. . . . . .Brancato/Salke Productions, p. 73
Salley, John . . . . .Black Folk Entertainment, p. 67
Salomon, Shirley . . . . .BET Networks, p. 66
Saloomey, Rick . . . . .TV Guide Channel, p. 321
Salt, Jennifer . . . . .Nip/Tuck, p. 370
Salter, Robbie . . . . .Jerry Bruckheimer Films & Television, p. 78
Salvaterra, Chris . . . . .Participant Productions, p. 249
Salvatore, Richard . . . . .Two Sticks Productions, p. 325
Salvatore, Rob . . . . .Half Shell Entertainment, p. 159
Salvino, Frank . . . . .New Line Cinema, p. 234
Salzberg, David G. . . . . .Mandalay Sports Action Entertainment & Mandalay Integrated Media Entertainment, p. 208
Salzman, David . . . . .Mad TV, p. 368
Samet, Jessica . . . . .Lifetime Television (Los Angeles), p. 198
Sami, Elisabeth . . . . .CNBC, p. 96
Sammon, Jeff . . . . .Jimmy Kimmel Live, p. 364
Samples, Jim . . . . .Adult Swim, p. 47
Samples, Jim . . . . .Cartoon Network, p. 84
Sams, Louise . . . . .Turner Entertainment Group, p. 320
Samuels, Kathy . . . . .CBS Paramount Worldwide Television Dist., p. 88
Samuels, Ron . . . . .Invitation Entertainment, p. 177
Samuelson, Couper . . . . .2929 Productions, p. 40
Samuelson, Marc .Samuelson Productions Limited, p. 279
Samuelson, Peter . . . . .Samuelson Productions Limited, p. 279
San Pedro, Joyce . . . . .Out of the Blue . . . Entertainment, p. 244
Sanchez, Aaron H. . . . . .Old Dime Box Productions, Inc., p. 242
Sanchez, Deanna . . . . .2929 Productions, p. 40
Sanchez, Padra . . . . .Pink Sneakers Productions, p. 255
Sanchez, Susan . . . . .Camelot Entertainment Group, Inc., p. 82
Sanchez, Tony . . . . .Universal Operations Group, p. 326
Sanchez-Witzel, Danielle . . . . .My Name Is Earl, p. 369
Sandberg, Ryan . . . . .TLC Entertainment, p. 314
Sandell, Mary . . . . .Laika Entertainment, p. 191
Sander, Ian . . . . .Ghost Whisperer, p. 362

Sander, Ian .Sander/Moses Productions, Inc., p. 279
Sanderlin, Ann Marie .Gunn Films, p. 158
Sanders, Bill .Sony Pictures Digital, p. 295
Sanders, Elisa .Taillight TV, p. 308
Sanders, Jay .Donaldson/Sanders Entertainment, p. 114
Sanders, Randall .Paulette Breen Productions, p. 74
Sanders, Vernon .NBC Universal Television Studio, p. 231
Sanderson, Jay .JTN Productions, p. 183
Sanderson, Lisa .Red Strokes Entertainment, p. 267
Sanderson, Madeleine .Partizan, p. 250
Sandler, Aaron .Alan Barnette Productions, p. 61
Sandler, Adam .Rules of Engagement, p. 373
Sandler, Andrew .CastleBright Studios, p. 85
Sandler, Luke .Outlaw Productions, p. 245
Sandler, Tara .Pie Town Productions, p. 254
Sandor, Julie .Ambush Entertainment, p. 50
Sandoval, Adrianne .Forward Entertainment, p. 138
Sandoval, Jerry .Cube Vision, p. 104
Sands, Jill Greenberg .Noggin, p. 239
Sands, Jill Greenberg .The N, p. 228
Sands, Jill Greenberg .Nickelodeon/MTVN Kids & Family Group, p. 237
Sands, Ned .Nickelodeon/MTVN Kids & Family Group, p. 237
Sands, Rick .Metro-Goldwyn-Mayer Studios, Inc. (MGM), p. 215
Sandstede, Monica .Landscape Entertainment, p. 193
Sandston, Pat .Jerry Bruckheimer Films & Television, p. 78
Sandvoss, Peter .Hyperion Studio, p. 169
Sandvoss, Steve .Hyperion Studio, p. 169
Sandzimier, Bruce .Touchstone Television, p. 316
Sanford, Midge .Sanford/Pillsbury Productions, p. 279
Sanford, Zac .Suntaur/Elsboy Entertainment, p. 305
Sanitsky, Larry .Sanitsky Company, p. 279
Sanjenis, Elizabeth .Telemundo Network, p. 310
Sanping, Han .China Film Group, p. 90
Sansoy, Sabri .GSN, p. 157
Santa Cruz, Will .Barnholtz Entertainment, p. 62
Santana, Macos .Telemundo Network, p. 310
Santor, Louis .Regency Enterprises, p. 268
Santora, Nick .Prison Break, p. 372
Santoro, Caryn .The Bubble Factory, p. 78
Sanz-Agero, Jenna .Media 8 Entertainment, p. 214
Sanzel, Ken .Numb3rs, p. 370
Sapan, Joshua .AMC, p. 50
Sapan, Joshua .The Independent Film Channel (IFC), p. 173
Saperstein, Marc J. .NBC Universal Corporate, p. 231
Saperstein, Richard .Dimension Films, p. 111
Saphier, Peter .Saphier Productions, p. 280
Sapot, Alex .Grand Productions, Inc., p. 152
Saraf, Peter .Big Beach, p. 67
Sardar, Gian .Blackfriars Bridge, p. 68
Sardo, Sal .Buena Vista Television, p. 79
Sarjeant, Debbie .L.I.F.T. Productions, p. 191
Sarkar, Sam .Infinitum Nihil, p. 174
Sarkes, Tim .Brillstein-Grey Entertainment, p. 75
Sarkissian, Arthur .Arthur Sarkissian Productions, p. 280
Sarnoff, Bret .Carsey-Werner Films, p. 84
Sarnoff, Liz .Lost, p. 368
Sarnoff, Tim .Sony Pictures Imageworks, p. 295
Saroyan, Hank .White Sneakers, Inc., p. 339
Sassen, Stephen .Las Vegas, p. 366
Satin, Scott .Nash Entertainment, p. 229
Sato, Ron .Sony Pictures Television International, p. 296
Saucy, Allison .Clarity Pictures, LLC, p. 94
Sauer, Steve .Media Four, p. 214
Saunders, Anne Cofell .Battlestar Galactica, p. 355
Saunders, Scott .Film Crash, p. 132
Savage, Niki .Sachs Judah Productions, p. 277
Savage, Stephanie .The O.C., p. 371
Savasta, Bronwyn .Warner Bros. Television Production, p. 335
Savia, Emile .Grisham Films USA, p. 155
Saviano, John .Old School Pictures, LLC, p. 242
Savin, Adina .Disney ABC Cable Networks Group, p. 112
Savitch, Annette .The Todd Phillips Company, p. 254
Savitt, Brandi .Senza Pictures, p. 284
Savitt, Joel K. .Queer Eye, p. 372
Savitt, Joel K. .Scout Productions, p. 282
Savo, Deb .MARTHA, p. 368
Saxe, Alan .Warner Horizon Television, p. 335
Saxon, Ed .Edward Saxon Productions (ESP), p. 280
Saypoff, Todd .Bravo, p. 74
Sayre, Liz .Twentieth Century Fox - Searchlight Pictures, p. 323
Scali, Lois .Pixar Animation Studios, p. 256
Scalise, Nikki .Twentieth Century Fox - Searchlight Pictures, p. 323
Scanlan, Kristy .Threshold Entertainment, p. 313
Scanlan, Paul .MobiTV, p. 219
Scanlan, Tim .Smallville, p. 375
Scarano, Amanda .Irish DreamTime, p. 177
Scavella, Donna .E! Networks, p. 117
Scavetta, Joseph .FremantleMedia North America, p. 142
Schaberg, Marc .Element Films, p. 121
Schacher, Marc .Tribune Entertainment Company, p. 318
Schaefer, Fred .PorchLight Entertainment, p. 259
Schaeffer, James .Main Line Pictures, p. 207
Schaeffer, Paul .Mandalay Pictures, p. 208
Schaer, Valerie .Worldwide Pants, Inc., p. 346
Schaffer, Anne-Elisa .East of Doheny/Lexington Road Prod., p. 118
Schaffer, Greg .Notes From the Underbelly, p. 370
Schamus, James .Focus Features/Rogue Pictures, p. 136
Schankowitz, Peter J. .Vin Di Bona Productions, p. 110
Schanzer, Kenneth .NBC Sports, p. 231
Schapiro, Larry .Nine Yards Entertainment, p. 238
Schapker, Allison .Lost, p. 368
Scharbo, Grant .Roundtable Entertainment, p. 276
Scharf, Dan .The Jim Henson Company, p. 165
Scharpling, Tom .Monk, p. 369
Schaum, Rounsevelle .Camelot Entertainment Group, Inc., p. 82
Schechter, Morgan .Prospect Pictures, p. 263
Scheer, Andy .Hell's Kitchen, p. 363
Scheffer, Will .Big Love, p. 356
Scheidlinger, Rob .Omnibus, p. 242
Scheiner, Laura .Noble House Entertainment, Inc., p. 238
Scheinman, Andrew .Castle Rock Entertainment, p. 85
Schelhaas, Luke .Runaway, p. 373
Schembri, Chris .Discovery Networks, U.S., p. 111
Schenck, Jeff .Regent, p. 269
Schenck, Kirk .RDF Media, p. 266
Schenk, Nick .Go Time Entertainment, p. 148
Schenz, Gregory R. .Beacon, p. 64
Scherma, Frank .@radical.media, p. 38
Scheuring, Paul .Prison Break, p. 372
Schibi, Peggy .Passions, p. 371
Schiessel, Peter .Participant Productions, p. 249
Schiff, Dave .King of the Hill, p. 365
Schiff, David .World of Wonder Productions, p. 345
Schiff, Gunther .George Schlatter Productions, p. 280
Schiff, Laura .Waterfront, p. 379
Schiff, Laura .The Nine, p. 370
Schiff, Laura .Close to Home, p. 357
Schiff, Mike .The Singles Table, p. 375
Schiff, Paul .Paul Schiff Productions, p. 280
Schiff-Abrams, Zach .Michael De Luca Productions, p. 108
Schiller, Abbie .ABC Daytime, p. 44
Schiller, Lawrence .KLS Communications, Inc., p. 189
Schiller, Rob .The King of Queens, p. 365
Schilling, Richard .Passions, p. 371
Schillinger, Erica .Untitled Entertainment, p. 327
Schilz, Mark .NCIS, p. 370
Schimik, Erika .Lionsgate, p. 200
Schimmel, John .Ascendant Pictures, p. 56
Schimpf, Barbara .Arnold Leibovit Entertainment, p. 196
Schindel, Barry .Numb3rs, p. 370
Schindler, Deborah .Columbia Pictures, p. 97
Schirmann, Abigail .Mandate Pictures, p. 209
Schlamme, Thomas .Studio 60 on the Sunset Strip, p. 376
Schlamme, Thomas .Shoe Money Productions, p. 286
Schlatter, George .George Schlatter Productions, p. 280
Schlatter, Maria S. .George Schlatter Productions, p. 280
Schlichter, Brian K. .Lancaster Gate Entertainment, p. 192
Schlichting, Johannes .Constantin Film Dev., Inc./Constantin TV, p. 100
Schlossman, Michael .Red Dog Entertainment, p. 267
Schmidbauer, Kerstin .Constantin Film Dev., Inc./Constantin TV, p. 100

Schmidt, Aaron . . . . .Creanspeak Productions LLC, p. 103
Schmidt, Anne . . . . .Sidney Kimmel Entertainment, p. 187
Schmidt, Glenn D. . . . . .Mobile Streams, p. 219
Schmidt, John . . . . .ContentFilm, p. 100
Schmidt, Kyle . . . . .The Kennedy/Marshall Company, p. 186
Schmir, Mimi . . . . .Shark, p. 374
Schmitz, Jerome . . . . .Sony Pictures Digital, p. 295
Schneeweiss, Barbara . . . . .The Weinstein Company, p. 337
Schneider, David Coplan . . . . .Lightstone Entertainment, Inc., p. 199
Schneider, Don . . . . .E Entertainment, LLC, p. 118
Schneider, Elia . . . . .Joel Films, p. 181
Schneider, Ibi . . . . .Joel Films, p. 181
Schneider, Jay . . . . .TV One, LLC, p. 322
Schneider, John . . . . .Johnenelly Productions, p. 182
Schneider, Lew . . . . .The Singles Table, p. 375
Schneider, Mike . . . . .The Kennedy/Marshall Company, p. 186
Schneider, Rafael . . . . .Joel Films, p. 181
Schneider, Rick . . . . .Scarab Productions, p. 280
Schneider, Rob . . . . .Sweeney Entertainment, p. 306
Schneider, Sascha . . . . .Dirt, p. 360
Schneider, Stacy . . . . .Pie Town Productions, p. 254
Schneider, Steven . . . . .ROOM 101, Inc., p. 274
Schoentag, Andy . . . . .Walt Disney Television Animation, p. 113
Scholer, Amanda . . . . .Universal Pictures, p. 326
Scholnick, Mark . . . . .Bravo, p. 74
Scholz, Jodie . . . . .Days of Our Lives, p. 359
Schoneboom, Sallie . . . . .Sci Fi Channel, p. 282
Schoonover, John . . . . .Water Channel, p. 336
Schornak, Brian . . . . .Laurence Mark Productions, p. 210
Schorr, Robin . . . . .River Road Entertainment, p. 272
Schotz, Eric . . . . .LMNO Productions, p. 201
Schrab, Rob . . . . .The Sarah Silverman Programme, p. 373
Schrag, Ariel . . . . .The L Word, p. 366
Schreiber, Michael . . . . .Tapestry Films, Inc., p. 308
Schreiberg, Stu . . . . .Triage Entertainment, p. 317
Schreier, Eric . . . . .FX, p. 144
Schrift, Jason . . . . .Jimmy Kimmel Live, p. 364
Schrift, Melissa Geiger . . . . .The Ellen DeGeneres Show, p. 360
Schriver, Kate . . . . .Lakeshore Entertainment Group LLC, p. 192
Schroeder, Adam . . . . .Regency Enterprises, p. 268
Schroeder-Telleson, Dawn . . . .Sony Pictures Television International, p. 296
Schube, Peter . . . . .The Jim Henson Company, p. 165
Schubert, Neil . . . . .Lifetime Television (Los Angeles), p. 198
Schuermann, Martin . . . . .Intermedia Film Equities USA, Inc., p. 175
Schulman, Cathy . . . . .Bull's Eye Entertainment, p. 79
Schulman, Irv . . . . .Buena Vista Television, p. 79
Schulman, John A. . . . . .Warner Bros. Entertainment Inc., p. 334
Schulman, Mark .3 Arts Entertainment, Inc., p. 40
Schultheis, Mindy . . . . .The War at Home, p. 379
Schultheis, Mindy . . . . .Reba, p. 372
Schultheis, Mindy . . . . .Acme Productions, p. 46
Schultz, Bill . . . . .Mike Young Productions LLC, p. 348
Schultz, Bob . . . . .Twilight Pictures, Inc., p. 324
Schultz, Howard D. . . . . .Starbucks Entertainment, p. 299
Schultz, T.C. . . . . .Sony Pictures Television International, p. 296
Schultze, Bradford .Precis Productions, Inc., p. 261
Schulze, Rob . . . . .Paramount Vantage/Paramount Classics, p. 248
Schumacher, Joel . . . . .Joel Schumacher Productions, p. 281
Schumacher, Thomas . . . . .Buena Vista Motion Pictures Group, p. 78
Schumaecker, Kate . . . . .Superb Entertainment, p. 305
Schuman, Stacey . . . . .Eyeworks Touchdown, p. 129
Schupack, Linda . . . . .AMC, p. 50
Schur, Mike . . . . .The Office, p. 371
Schur, Seth . . . . .Saturn Films, p. 280
Schuster, Jack . . . . .Mandate Pictures, p. 209
Schuurmans, Niels . . . . .Spike TV, p. 298
Schuyler, Linda . . . . .Epitome Pictures, Inc., p. 126
Schwab, Faye . . . . .Faye Schwab Productions/MMA, Inc., p. 281
Schwab, Ken . . . . .Turner Network Television (TNT), p. 321
Schwab, Ken . . . . .TBS, p. 309
Schwahn, Mark . . . . .One Tree Hill, p. 371
Schwake, Paul . . . . .Level 1 Entertainment, p. 197
Schwam, Stephanie . . . . .Wife Swap, p. 379
Schwartz, Alex . . . . .Walden Media, p. 333
Schwartz, Ellen . . . . .Warner Bros. Pictures, p. 334
Schwartz, Gil . . . . .CBS Corporation, p. 86
Schwartz, Howard . . . . .Warner Bros. Animation, p. 334
Schwartz, Jill . . . . .FremantleMedia North America, p. 142
Schwartz, Josh . . . . .The O.C., p. 371
Schwartz, Kenny . . . . .American Dad, p. 354
Schwartz, Leslie . . . . .MSNBC, p. 225
Schwartz, Mike . . . . .Scrubs, p. 374
Schwartz, Rick . . . . .Blueprint Films, p. 70
Schwartz, Robert . . . . .Picturehouse, p. 254
Schwartz, Robert . . . . .SMG Productions, p. 292
Schwartz, Robert . . . . .Wardenclyffe Entertainment, p. 333
Schwartz, Robin . . . . .Regency Television, p. 269
Schwartz, Ron . . . . .Lionsgate, p. 200
Schwartz, Russell . . . . .HBO Entertainment, p. 162
Schwartz, Russell . . . . .New Line Cinema, p. 234
Schwartz, Sander D. . . . . .Warner Bros. Animation, p. 334
Schwartz, Steven . . . . .Steven Schwartz Productions, Inc., p. 281
Schwartz, Stuart . . . . .Cosgrove-Meurer Productions, p. 101
Schwartz, William A. . . . . .Schwartz & Company, Inc., p. 281
Schwary, Ronald L. . . . . .Medium, p. 369
Schwarz, Anne . . . . .Fox Broadcasting Company, p. 139
Schwarz, David . . . . .Spike TV, p. 298
Schwarzman, Andrew . . . . .Scrubs, p. 374
Schweickert, Joyce . . . . .Luminous Entertainment, p. 204
Schweitzer, Amanda . . . . .Seed Productions, p. 283
Schweitzer, Jenny . . . . .Canary Films, p. 83
Schwimmer, Michael . . . . .SiTV, p. 290
Scolaro, Jesse . . . . .The 7th Floor, p. 43
Scoon, Mark . . . . .Warner Bros. Pictures, p. 334
Scott, Brandon . . . . .Klasky Csupo, Inc., p. 189
Scott, Jessica . . . . .Filbert Steps Productions, p. 131
Scott, Mark . . . . .Kidnapped, p. 365
Scott, Ridley . . . . .Numb3rs, p. 370
Scott, Ridley . . . . .Scott Free Productions, p. 282
Scott, Seann William . . . . .Identity Films, p. 170
Scott, Steve . . . . .Universal Pictures, p. 326
Scott, Tim . . . . .Go Time Entertainment, p. 148
Scott, Tony . . . . .Numb3rs, p. 370
Scott, Tony . . . . .Totem Productions, p. 316
Scott, Tony . . . . .Scott Free Productions, p. 282
Scott-Hansen, Claudia . . . . .HIT Entertainment, p. 167
Scovell, Nell . . . . .NCIS, p. 370
Scurlock, Aliana . . . . .Martin Poll Films, Ltd., p. 259
Seabourne, Yolanda . . . . .Vin Di Bona Productions, p. 110
Seabury, Bryan . . . . .Gran Via Productions, p. 152
Seabury, Bryan . . . . .CBS Paramount Network Television, p. 87
Seacrest, Ryan . . . . .Ryan Seacrest Productions, p. 283
Seagal, Steven . . . . .Steamroller Productions, Inc., p. 300
Sealy, Dr. Pete . . . . .Veoh Networks, Inc., p. 329
Searer, Troy . . . . .The Biggest Loser, p. 356
Sears, Jeff . . . . .DIY Network, p. 113
Sears, Mike . . . . .Norsemen Television Productions, LLC, p. 239
Sears, Steven . . . . .Artists, Inc., p. 56
Sebastiano, Frank . . . . .Everybody Hates Chris, p. 361
Sedeak, Nabil . . . . .Bauer Martinez Entertainment, p. 63
Seeger, Allyson . . . . .The Mark Gordon Company, p. 150
Seekman, Dan . . . . .L.I.F.T. Productions, p. 191
Segal, Brigitte . . . . .Quinta Communications USA, p. 264
Segal, Peter . . . . .Callahan Filmworks, p. 82
Segal, Philip . . . . .Original Productions, p. 244
Segall, Stu . . . . .Veronica Mars, p. 378
Segan, Lloyd . . . . .The Dead Zone, p. 359
Segan, Lloyd . . . . .Piller/Segan, p. 255
Segan, Loren . . . . .The Dead Zone, p. 359
Segel Marks, Amanda . . . . .Without a Trace, p. 379
Seibert, Fred . . . . .Frederator Studios, p. 141
Seidan, Stephanie . . . . .Faye Schwab Productions/MMA, Inc., p. 281
Seidel, Bruce . . . . .Food Network, p. 136
Seidel, Jed . . . . .Ghost Whisperer, p. 362
Seidelman, Arthur Allan . . . . .EntPro, Inc., p. 125
Seigel, Matthew . . . . .WideAwake, Inc., p. 340
Selak, Chris . . . . .John Wells Productions, p. 338
Seldin, Colleen . . . . .Miramax Films, p. 217
Selick, Henry . . . . .Laika Entertainment, p. 191
Selig, Keri . . . . .Intuition Productions, p. 176

Selig, Roni .Buena Vista Television, p. 79
Sellers, Dylan .Dylan Sellers Productions, p. 284
Sellitti, Tom .Rescue Me, p. 373
Sellitti, Tom .Apostle, p. 53
Selman, Matt .The Simpsons, p. 375
Seltzer, David .Management 360, p. 208
Semel, Terry .Yahoo! Media Group/Yahoo! Studios, p. 347
Semiao, Ron .ESPN Original Entertainment (EOE), p. 127
Semon, Sam .CBS Entertainment, p. 86
Senders, Roger .CBS Entertainment, p. 86
Sengupta, Momita .MTV Films, p. 225
Sengupta, Stephanie .Law & Order: Criminal Intent, p. 367
Senkler, Jennifer .Vulcan Productions, p. 332
Senter, Josh .Desperate Housewives, p. 360
Seppala, Eric .Farrell Paura Productions, LLC, p. 130
Septien, Al .Smallville, p. 375
Sepulveda, Christopher .Simsie Films/Media Savant Pictures, p. 290
Sepulveda, Tony .Warner Bros. Television Production, p. 335
Serafini, Adriano .Latin Hollywood Films, p. 194
Serlen, Sara Finmann .The Weinstein Company, p. 337
Serpico, Jim .Rescue Me, p. 373
Serpico, Jim .Apostle, p. 53
Serrano, Kimi .Sony Pictures Television, p. 296
Sertner, Robert .von Zerneck-Sertner Films, p. 332
Serwatka, David .Bravo, p. 74
Seto, Adrian .E! Networks, p. 117
Setos, Andrew .Fox Broadcasting Company, p. 139
Severson, Aaron .Platinum Studios, LLC, p. 257
Severson, Jak .Madison Road Entertainment, p. 206
Sevilla, Enid N. .Paulist Productions, p. 250
Seward, Amanda .Film Bridge International, p. 132
Sexton, Adam .Groove Mobile, p. 155
Sexton, Adrian .Lionsgate, p. 200
Sexton, Courtney .Participant Productions, p. 249
Seymour, Jane .Catfish Productions, p. 86
Sgriccia, Phil .Supernatural, p. 377
Sha Money XL .G-Unit Television & Films, p. 157
Shader, Josh .Terra Firma Films, p. 312
Shadyac, Tom .Shady Acres Entertainment, p. 285
Shafer, Martin .Castle Rock Entertainment, p. 85
Shah, Ash .Silver Nitrate Pictures, p. 288
Shah, Bhupen .Sling Media, p. 291
Shah, Sundip .Silver Nitrate Pictures, p. 288
Shahar, Martine .TBS, p. 309
Shahar, Martine .Turner Network Television (TNT), p. 321
Shaheen, Nick .David Kirschner Productions, p. 188
Shainberg, Steven .Vox3 Films, p. 332
Shakespeare, Hannah .Runaway, p. 373
Shakespeare, Sue .Creative Capers Entertainment, p. 103
Shakespeare, Terry .Creative Capers Entertainment, p. 103
Shalek, Caren .PorchLight Entertainment, p. 259
Shalhoub, Tony .Monk, p. 369
Shalit, Nevin .New Line Television, p. 235
Shall, David .FremantleMedia North America, p. 142
Shamberg, Carla Santos .Double Feature Films, p. 115
Shamberg, Michael .RENO 911!, p. 373
Shamberg, Michael .Double Feature Films, p. 115
Shamir, Pami .Granada America, p. 152
Shane, Michel .Hand Picked Films, p. 159
Shane, Rachel .Red Wagon Entertainment, p. 268
Shani, Libby .Sunswept Entertainment, p. 305
Shankar, Naren .CSI: Crime Scene Investigation, p. 358
Shankel, Ryan .The War at Home, p. 379
Shankman, Adam .Offspring Entertainment, p. 241
Shanks, Russell .Sony Online Entertainment, p. 294
Shankwiler, Dave .Lionsgate, p. 200
Shannon, Cathy .@radical.media, p. 38
Shannon, Steve .TV Guide Channel, p. 321
Shanti, Alys .Robert Greenwald Productions, p. 153
Shapiro, Alexandra .USA Network, p. 327
Shapiro, Allen .Mosaic Media Group, p. 222
Shapiro, Allen .So You Think You Can Dance, p. 376
Shapiro, Allen .Atlas Entertainment, p. 57
Shapiro, Andra .Nickelodeon/MTVN Kids & Family Group, p. 237
Shapiro, Andy .Wonderland Sound and Vision, p. 344
Shapiro, Arnold .Arnold Shapiro Productions, p. 285
Shapiro, Barry .Hollywood East Entertainment, Inc., p. 168
Shapiro, Dmitry .Veoh Networks, Inc., p. 329
Shapiro, Ellen .Heel & Toe Films, p. 163
Shapiro, Evan .The Independent Film Channel (IFC), p. 173
Shapiro, Jenny .Traveler's Rest Films, p. 317
Shapiro, Jon .Ideal Entertainment, Inc., p. 170
Shapiro, Jonathan .Justice, p. 364
Shapiro, Julie A. .New Line Cinema, p. 234
Shapiro, Julie A. .New Line Television, p. 235
Shapiro, Lucy .Groundswell Production, p. 156
Shapiro, Peter .Ideal Entertainment, Inc., p. 170
Shapiro, Stephanie .Krasnoff Foster Productions, p. 190
Shapiro-Mathes, Angela .Fox Television Studios, p. 140
Shardo, JC .JCS Entertainment II, p. 180
Sharenow, Robert .A&E Network, p. 44
Shareshian, Steven .Playtone Productions, p. 258
Sharkey, Debra .South Side Films, p. 297
Sharkey, Lisa .Al Roker Productions, p. 274
Sharma, Tanya .Sub Rosa Productions, Inc., p. 303
Sharon, Jo .Nash Entertainment, p. 229
Sharp, Jeffrey .Hart Sharp Entertainment, Inc., p. 161
Sharp, Jim .Twentieth Century Fox Television, p. 323
Sharp, Jim .Comedy Central, p. 98
Sharpless, Dana .Twentieth Century Fox Television, p. 323
Sharron, Jennifer .Jimmy Kimmel Live, p. 364
Shattuck, Lianne Siegel .Twentieth Century Fox Television, p. 323
Shaw, Anthony .Corymore Entertainment, p. 101
Shaw, Larry .Desperate Housewives, p. 360
Shay, Andrea .Regency Television, p. 269
Shay, Heather .CastleBright Studios, p. 85
Shay, Sanjay .King of the Hill, p. 365
Shaye, Robert K. .New Line Cinema, p. 234
Shea, John .MTV Networks, p. 226
Shea, Martin .CBS Corporation, p. 86
Shearmur, Allison .Paramount Pictures Production Division, p. 248
Sheehan, Bob .CBS Paramount Worldwide Television Dist., p. 88
Sheehan, Jordan .Scott Free Productions, p. 282
Sheehan, Tony .The King of Queens, p. 365
Sheehan, Veronica .Turner Entertainment Group, p. 320
Sheehy, Ginger .Warren Miller Entertainment, p. 335
Sheets, Tom .Fox Broadcasting Company, p. 139
Sheinberg, Bill .The Bubble Factory, p. 78
Sheinberg, Jon .The Bubble Factory, p. 78
Sheinberg, Sid .The Bubble Factory, p. 78
Shelburne, Dana .Twentieth Century Fox Television, p. 323
Sheldon, David .Joada Productions, Inc., p. 181
Sheldon, Valarie .Digital Ranch Productions, p. 110
Shelly, Tom .Survivor, p. 377
Shelton, Colette .Lifetime Television (Los Angeles), p. 198
Shelton, Eric .Cold Case, p. 357
Shemtov, Eyal .SiTV, p. 290
Sheng, Bob .Double Edge Entertainment, p. 115
Shenkler, Craig .Steven Bochco Productions, p. 70
Shepard, Alexandra .Playboy Entertainment Group, Inc., p. 257
Shepard, Devon .Everybody Hates Chris, p. 361
Shepard, Sarah .Appian Way, p. 53
Shephard, Greer .The Closer, p. 357
Shephard, Greer .Nip/Tuck, p. 370
Shephard, Greer .The Shephard/Robin Company, p. 286
Shepherd, Andrew .Noble House Entertainment, Inc., p. 238
Shepherd, Richard .The Turman Inc. Picture Company, p. 320
Sher, Stacey .RENO 911!, p. 373
Sher, Stacey .Double Feature Films, p. 115
Sherak, William .Blue Star Pictures, p. 69
Sheridan, Chris .Family Guy, p. 361
Sheridan, Jim .Hell's Kitchen Ltd., p. 164
Sherlock, Dan .Disney Online, p. 112
Sherman, Danny .Principal Entertainment, p. 262
Sherman, Eric .VH1, p. 330
Sherman, Eric P. .Bang Zoom! Entertainment, p. 61
Sherman, Heidi .Regency Enterprises, p. 268
Sherman, Jon .Rules of Engagement, p. 373
Sherman, Lisa .Logo, p. 202
Sherman, Steven .Talisman Pacific, p. 308

Sherman, Thom . . . . The CW, p. 105
Sherman, Zack . . . . Flame Ventures LLC, p. 135
Sherman Barrois, Janine . . . . ER, p. 361
Sherrill, Rick . . . . Sony Pictures Television, p. 296
Sherwood, Jenni . . . . HBO Films, p. 162
Sherwood, Karen Kehela . . . . Imagine Entertainment, p. 172
Shestack, Jon . . . . Jon Shestack Productions, p. 286
Sheth, Jay . . . . Air2web, Inc., p. 48
Shevchenko, Christine Smith . . . . The Singles Table, p. 375
Shevick, Jerry . . . . Actuality Productions, p. 46
Shevloff, Michael . . . . Nanny 911, p. 369
Shiban, John . . . . Supernatural, p. 377
Shields, Cory . . . . NBC Universal Corporate, p. 231
Shields, Joanna . . . . Google Inc., p. 149
Shields, Margaret . . . . Stampede Entertainment, p. 299
Shields, Mark . . . . South Side Films, p. 297
Shik, Marjorie . . . . Cheyenne Enterprises, p. 89
Shikiar, David . . . . Screen Door Entertainment, p. 283
Shimer, Julie . . . . Playtone Productions, p. 258
Shimosawa, Shin . . . . The Dead Zone, p. 359
Shin, Mira . . . . Scott Rudin Productions, p. 277
Shine, Bill . . . . Fox News Channel, p. 139
Shintani, Roberta . . . . Dino De Laurentiis Company, p. 108
Shin-Wannemacher, Nani . . . . A&E Network, p. 44
Shiozaki, Andrew . . . . Anonymous Creators Productions, p. 52
Shipley, Michael . . . . American Dad, p. 354
Shipstad, Robert . . . . Water Channel, p. 336
Shmuger, Marc . . . . Universal Pictures, p. 326
Shoemaker, Michael . . . . Saturday Night Live, p. 373
Shojai, David . . . . Seven Summits Pictures & Management, p. 285
Shore, David . . . . House, p. 363
Shore, Jeff . . . . E! Networks, p. 117
Shore, Jonathan . . . . Brightlight Pictures, Inc., p. 75
Shore, Richard . . . . First Look Pictures, p. 134
Short, Doug . . . . Buena Vista Motion Pictures Group, p. 78
Short, Trevor . . . . Millennium Films, p. 217
Shotz, Dan . . . . Jericho, p. 364
Shotz, Dan . . . . Junction Entertainment, p. 183
Shotz, Todd . . . . Cheyenne Enterprises, p. 89
Shreves, Catherine . . . . L.I.F.T. Productions, p. 191
Shubb, Jason . . . . Reba, p. 372
Shukovsky, Joel . . . . Shukovsky English Entertainment, p. 287
Shulman, Jessica . . . . Bobker/Kruger Films, p. 70
Shulman, Marcia . . . . Fox Broadcasting Company, p. 139
Shulman, Michael . . . . Starry Night Entertainment, p. 300
Shuman, Jason . . . . Blue Star Pictures, p. 69
Shuman, Lawrence . . . . The Shuman Company, p. 287
Shur, Laura . . . . Al Roker Productions, p. 274
Shuter, Rich . . . . DreamWorks SKG, p. 116
Shutt, Buffy . . . . Shady Acres Entertainment, p. 285
Shutt, Buffy . . . . Shutt-Jones Productions, p. 287
Shuttleworth, Lucy . . . . Spice Factory, p. 298
Shwarzstein, Meyer . . . . Brainstorm Media, p. 72
Shwer, Robyn . . . . Fresh Paint, p. 142
Sicherman, Steve . . . . Twentieth Century Fox Television, p. 323
Siddons, Bill . . . . The Core, p. 101
Sideropoulos, John . . . . 3 Ring Circus Films, p. 40
Siderow, Norman . . . . Creative Coalition, p. 103
Sidlow, Carol . . . . Face Productions/Jennilind Productions, p. 129
Siebens, Jennifer . . . . CBS News, p. 87
Siebert, Steven . . . . Lighthouse Entertainment, p. 198
Siega, Marcos . . . . Prospect Pictures, p. 263
Siegal, Josh . . . . The Knights of Prosperity, p. 365
Siegel, Adam . . . . Marc Platt Productions, p. 257
Siegel, Eric . . . . In Case of Emergency, p. 364
Siegel, Joshua . . . . Fresh Paint, p. 142
Siegel, Lloyd . . . . NBC News, p. 230
Siegel, Noel . . . . Fox Reality, p. 140
Siegel, Rebecca . . . . Sky Networks, p. 291
Siegel, Ross . . . . Guy Walks Into a Bar, p. 158
Siegrist, Tom . . . . Twentieth Century Fox, p. 322
Sienega, Corey . . . . David Kirschner Productions, p. 188
Sieras, Charisma . . . . Allison Grodner Productions, Inc., p. 155
Sievernich, Chris . . . . Armada Pictures, p. 55
Sighvatsson, Joni . . . . Palomar Pictures, p. 246
Signorelli, James . . . . Saturday Night Live, p. 373
Signorotti, Ron . . . . New Line Cinema, p. 234
Sikorska, Magdalena . . . . Lighthouse Productions, p. 198
Sikowitz, Mike . . . . The Class, p. 357
Silberman, Dan . . . . A&E Network, p. 44
Silberwasser, Luis . . . . Discovery Networks, U.S., p. 111
Silfen, Lori . . . . New Line Cinema, p. 234
Silk, Jon . . . . Benderspink, p. 66
Silla, Virginie . . . . EuropaCorp Films, p. 127
Sillars, Laura . . . . Home & Garden Television (HGTV), p. 168
Silveira, Ron . . . . Universal Operations Group, p. 326
Silver, Cary . . . . Mike Young Productions LLC, p. 348
Silver, Casey . . . . Casey Silver Productions, p. 289
Silver, Darryl M. . . . . The Idea Factory, p. 170
Silver, Gary . . . . CBS Entertainment, p. 86
Silver, Joel . . . . Veronica Mars, p. 378
Silver, Joel . . . . Silver Pictures, p. 289
Silver, Josh . . . . Sneak Preview Entertainment, Inc., p. 293
Silverberg, Maryn . . . . Contrafilm, p. 100
Silverberg, Sabrina . . . . MTV Networks, p. 226
Silverman, Allison . . . . The Colbert Report, p. 357
Silverman, Ben . . . . The Office, p. 371
Silverman, Ben . . . . Ugly Betty, p. 378
Silverman, Ben . . . . The Biggest Loser, p. 356
Silverman, Ben . . . . 30 Days, p. 353
Silverman, Benjamin . . . . Reveille, LLC, p. 270
Silverman, Fred . . . . The Fred Silverman Company, p. 289
Silverman, Geoff . . . . Principal Entertainment, p. 262
Silverman, Greg . . . . Warner Bros. Pictures, p. 334
Silverman, Lloyd A. . . . . The Artists' Colony, p. 56
Silverman, Mark . . . . A&E Network, p. 44
Silverman, Mark . . . . Disney ABC Cable Networks Group, p. 112
Silverman, Rich . . . . John Baldecchi Productions, p. 60
Silverman, Rick . . . . Boston Legal, p. 357
Silverman, Rick . . . . David E. Kelley Productions, p. 186
Silverman, Sarah . . . . The Sarah Silverman Programme, p. 373
Silverman, Tom . . . . Tommy Boy Films, p. 315
Silvers, Tracey . . . . Silvers/Koster Productions, Inc., p. 289
Silverstein, Craig . . . . Standoff, p. 376
Silverstein, Matt . . . . Drawn Together, p. 360
Silverstone, Aileen . . . . Florentine Films, p. 135
Silverstone, Alicia . . . . Concrete Entertainment, p. 99
Silverthorn, Linda . . . . Seven Arts Pictures, p. 285
Simicich, Ed . . . . Court TV Networks, p. 102
Simiens, Germaine . . . . New Concorde, p. 233
Simkin, Michael . . . . Offspring Entertainment, p. 241
Simmer, David . . . . Leisure Time Enterprises, p. 196
Simmonds, Shawn . . . . Happy Hour, p. 362
Simmons, Dottie . . . . HBO Films, p. 162
Simmons, Gene . . . . The Gene Simmons Company, p. 289
Simmons, Russell . . . . Simmons/Lathan, p. 289
Simon, Annie . . . . Playtime Productions, p. 257
Simon, Chandra . . . . Orchard Films, p. 243
Simon, Chuck . . . . Stoneworks Television, p. 302
Simon, Chuck . . . . S Pictures, Inc., p. 277
Simon, David . . . . The Wire, p. 379
Simon, Hali . . . . Peter Hankwitz Production & Mgmt., p. 160
Simon, Joel . . . . WWE Films, p. 346
Simon, Margaret . . . . Warner Bros. Television Production, p. 335
Simon, Matt . . . . My Name Is Earl, p. 369
Simon, Perry . . . . Shore View Entertainment, p. 286
Simon, Stephanie . . . . Untitled Entertainment, p. 327
Simonds, Robert . . . . The Robert Simonds Company, p. 290
Simonelli, John . . . . Graymark Productions Inc., p. 153
Simonian, Andrew . . . . The Gurin Company, p. 158
Simons, Jim . . . . Help Me Help You, p. 363
Simons, Scott . . . . Slipnot! Productions/SPG, p. 292
Simpson, Aaron . . . . JibJab Media Inc., p. 181
Simpson, Bradford . . . . Appian Way, p. 53
Simpson, Jennifer . . . . Type A Films, p. 325
Simpson, Joe . . . . JT Entertainment, p. 182
Simpson, Michael . . . . Cairo/Simpson Entertainment, Inc., p. 81
Sims, Jen . . . . Gay Rosenthal Productions, p. 275
Sims, Kelley . . . . Revelations Entertainment, p. 271
Sinclair, Nigel . . . . Spitfire Pictures, p. 298

Singer, Andrew .... .Broadway Video Entertainment, p. 76
Singer, Andy .... .Home & Garden Television (HGTV), p. 168
Singer, Bryan .... .House, p. 363
Singer, Bryan .... .Bad Hat Harry Productions, p. 59
Singer, Charlie .... .MTV Networks Latin America (MTVNLA), p. 226
Singer, Joey .... .Go Girl Media, p. 147
Singer, Josh .... .Raines, p. 372
Singer, Maurice .... .Apostle, p. 53
Singer, Rick .... .My Boys, p. 369
Singer, Robert .... .Supernatural, p. 377
Singer, Sheri .... .Just Singer Entertainment, p. 184
Singerman, Ira .... .Sobini Films, p. 293
Singerman, Matt .... .TV Guide Channel, p. 321
Singh, Arielle .... .Intrepid Pictures, p. 176
Singh, Jaspreet .... .Proteus, p. 263
Singh, Vinay .... .This is that corporation, p. 312
Singleton, Joan .... .8790 Pictures, Inc., p. 43
Singleton, John .... .New Deal Productions, p. 233
Singleton, Ralph .... .8790 Pictures, Inc., p. 43
Sinise, Gary .... .CSI: NY, p. 359
Sinkus, Christi .... .Trancas International Films, p. 316
Sinovoi, Lana .... .Sinovoi Entertainment, p. 290
Sinovoi, Maxwell .... .Sinovoi Entertainment, p. 290
Sinton, Frank .... .Asylum Entertainment, p. 57
Sirkot, Denise .... .The Simpsons, p. 375
Sirkot, Denise .... .Gracie Films, p. 151
Sirulnick, David .... .MTV Networks, p. 226
Siruni, Aram .... .Colleen Camp Productions, p. 82
Sisk, Bradford .... .Bankable Productions, p. 61
Siskin, Alex .... .Out of the Blue . . . Entertainment, p. 244
Sites, Scott .... .Mad TV, p. 368
Skalski, Mary Jane .... .Next Wednesday, p. 236
Skeeters, Kim .... .Escape Artists II, p. 126
Skeeters, Kim .... .The Steve Tisch Company, p. 314
Skelly, Mark .... .Mark Victor Productions, p. 330
Skerbelis, Monika .... .Rona Edwards Productions/ES Entertainment, p. 120
Skiena, Matt .... .John Wells Productions, p. 338
Skinner, David .... .ShadowCatcher Entertainment, p. 285
Skinner, Geoff .... .Nash Entertainment, p. 229
Skipper, John .... .ABC Sports, p. 45
Skipper, John .... .ESPN Original Entertainment (EOE), p. 127
Sklar, Chuck .... .Everybody Hates Chris, p. 361
Skolarus, Ed .... .Fox Reality, p. 140
Skoll, Jeff .... .Participant Productions, p. 249
Skolnik, Michael .... .Article 19 Films, p. 56
Skorlich, Jennifer .... .NBC Universal Cable Entertainment, p. 231
Skouras, Charlie .... .Desperate Housewives, p. 360
Skowronski, Lauren .... .NBC News, p. 230
Skwarek, Diane .... .The Landsburg Company, p. 193
Slack, David .... .Law & Order, p. 367
Slade, Becka .... .New Screen Concepts, Inc., p. 235
Slade, Michael .... .Days of Our Lives, p. 359
Slater, Todd .... .Baldwin Entertainment Group, Ltd., p. 60
Slava, Kris .... .Bravo, p. 74
Slava, Kris .... .NBC Universal Cable Entertainment, p. 231
Slavick, Aaron .... .Once Upon A Time Films, Ltd., p. 243
Slavin, Iriku .... .Warner Bros. Entertainment Inc., p. 334
Slavkin, Todd .... .Smallville, p. 375
Slay, Ray .... .NBC Entertainment, p. 230
Slesinski, Frank .... .Rat Entertainment/Rat TV, p. 266
Sloan, Donna .... .Lionsgate, p. 200
Sloan, Harry E. .... .Metro-Goldwyn-Mayer Studios, Inc. (MGM), p. 215
Sloan, Lea .... .PBS, p. 251
Sloan, Michael .... .Star Entertainment Group, Inc., p. 299
Sloss, John .... .InDigEnt, p. 173
Sloss, John .... .Cinetic, p. 93
Slump, Megan .... .Graymark Productions Inc., p. 153
Slutzky, Elliot .... .Miramax Films, p. 217
Small, Alison .... .Liddell Entertainment, p. 197
Small, Kahli .... .Focus Features/Rogue Pictures, p. 136
Smart, Stacey Jade .... .Masters of Horror, p. 368
Smedley, John .... .Sony Online Entertainment, p. 294
Smee, Bill .... .Discovery Networks, U.S., p. 111
Smerling, Max .... .Lakeshore Entertainment Group LLC, p. 192
Smiley, Frank .... .Late Night with Conan O'Brien, p. 367
Smiley, Stu .... .Comedy Arts Studios, p. 98
Smilovic, Jason .... .Kidnapped, p. 365
Smith, Anne .... .TBS, p. 309
Smith, Anne .... .Turner Network Television (TNT), p. 321
Smith, Arthur .... .Hell's Kitchen, p. 363
Smith, Arthur .... .A. Smith & Co. Productions, p. 292
Smith, Blake .... .Scott Free Productions, p. 282
Smith, Bradford .... .CFP Productions, p. 88
Smith, Brendan .... .My Boys, p. 369
Smith, Bruce .... .Hyperion Studio, p. 169
Smith, Carol .... .Numenorean Films, p. 240
Smith, Christie .... .Management 360, p. 208
Smith, Christina .... .Warner Bros. Television Production, p. 335
Smith, Craig .... .Sony Pictures Television, p. 296
Smith, Dan .... .Playboy Entertainment Group, Inc., p. 257
Smith, Danny .... .Family Guy, p. 361
Smith, Drew .... .The Konigsberg-Smith Company, p. 189
Smith, Emily .... .Disney Online, p. 112
Smith, Eric .... .Sony Pictures Television, p. 296
Smith, Eric .... .Norsemen Television Productions, LLC, p. 239
Smith, Erik .... .Seven Arts Pictures, p. 285
Smith, Frank .... .Bristol Bay Productions, p. 76
Smith, Frank .... .Walden Media, p. 333
Smith, Gary .... .Gary Smith Company, p. 292
Smith, Gwenn .... .TBS, p. 309
Smith, Gwenn .... .Turner Network Television (TNT), p. 321
Smith, Jada Pinkett .... .All of Us, p. 354
Smith, Jake .... .IMG Media, p. 172
Smith, Jennifer .... .Rive Gauche Entertainment, p. 272
Smith, Jerry .... .Enteraktion Studios, p. 124
Smith, John G. .... .The Nine, p. 370
Smith, Jonah .... .Thousand Words, p. 313
Smith, Jonna .... .New Line Cinema, p. 234
Smith, Karen .... .dick clark productions, inc., p. 94
Smith, Kenny .... .The Game, p. 361
Smith, Kevin .... .View Askew Productions, Inc., p. 331
Smith, Linda .... .Michael Meltzer Productions, p. 216
Smith, Lucas .... .Endgame Entertainment, p. 124
Smith, Madelon .... .David Ladd Films, p. 191
Smith, Margaret .... .The Ellen DeGeneres Show, p. 360
Smith, Matt .... .Weed Road Pictures, p. 337
Smith, Matt .... .SekretAgent Productions, p. 283
Smith, Matthew .... .Myriad Pictures, p. 228
Smith, Maureen .... .Discovery Networks, U.S., p. 111
Smith, Maureen .... .Animal Planet, p. 52
Smith, Melissa .... .Emmett/Furla Films, p. 123
Smith, Michael .... .Law & Order: Criminal Intent, p. 367
Smith, Michael .... .Food Network, p. 136
Smith, Michael .... .Principal Entertainment, p. 262
Smith, N. John .... .Stargate: SG-1, p. 376
Smith, N. John .... .Stargate: Atlantis, p. 376
Smith, Nova .... .Lee Daniels Entertainment, p. 106
Smith, Pam .... .Twentieth Century Fox Television, p. 323
Smith, Paul .... .Columbia Pictures, p. 97
Smith, Paula .... .Clear Pictures Entertainment Inc., p. 95
Smith, Peter .... .Universal Pictures, p. 326
Smith, Rachel .... .The Independent Film Channel (IFC), p. 173
Smith, Rick .... .Warner Bros. Television Production, p. 335
Smith, Robert .... .Endemol USA, Inc., p. 123
Smith, Roger .... .AM Productions & Management, p. 50
Smith, Roger Guenveur .... .Luna Ray Films, p. 204
Smith, Russ .... .Mr. Mudd, p. 224
Smith, Sarah .... .Tapestry Films, Inc., p. 308
Smith, Sarita .... .Discovery Networks, U.S., p. 111
Smith, Shannon .... .Family Guy, p. 361
Smith, Sheyna .... .Law & Order: Special Victims Unit, p. 367
Smith, Syd .... .Universal Pictures, p. 326
Smith, Will .... .All of Us, p. 354
Smith, Will .... .Overbrook Entertainment, p. 245
Smith, Zack .... .Gary Smith Company, p. 292
Smithberg, Madeleine .... .Current TV, LLC, p. 105
Smith-Kite, Miura .... .Playtone Productions, p. 258
Smolsky, Charles .... .Sony Pictures Television, p. 296
Smuts, Tom .... .Close to Home, p. 357
Smyer, Danielle Christine .... .TriCoast Studios, p. 318

Snedeker, Brian . . . . DisneyToon Studios, p. 113
Snegaroff, Gary . . . . E! Networks, p. 117
Snell, Peter R. E. . . . . British Lion, p. 76
Snider, Stacey . . . . DreamWorks SKG, p. 116
Snyder, Betsy . . . . The Bold and the Beautiful, p. 356
Snyder, Fonda . . . . Cookie Jar Entertainment, p. 100
Snyder, Meghan . . . . Red Wagon Entertainment, p. 268
Snyder, Robert . . . . Keckins Projects, Ltd., p. 185
Snyder, Robyn . . . . Anne Carlucci Productions, p. 83
Soaper, Pamela . . . . CBS Entertainment, p. 86
Sobel, Sarah . . . . Dimension Films, p. 111
Sobhani, Bob . . . . Magnet Management, p. 207
Sobolewski, Chris . . . . David Foster Productions, p. 138
Soby Jr., Peter . . . . 6 Pictures, p. 42
Soccio, Mike . . . . The King of Queens, p. 365
Sodha, Jitesh . . . . Mobile Streams, p. 219
Soisson, Joel . . . . Neo Art & Logic, p. 232
Solakian, Marc . . . . Happy Hour, p. 362
Solarz, Ken . . . . CSI: NY, p. 359
Solberg, John . . . . FX, p. 144
Solis, Vicente . . . . MTV Networks Latin America (MTVNLA), p. 226
Solomon, Bonnie . . . . Walden Media, p. 333
Solomon, Bonnie . . . . Bristol Bay Productions, p. 76
Solomon, Cary . . . . Numenorean Films, p. 240
Solomon, Christian Halsey . . . . Solo Entertainment Group, p. 294
Solomon, David . . . . Las Vegas, p. 366
Solomon, Lee . . . . Solo Entertainment Group, p. 294
Solomon, Marc . . . . Warner Bros. Pictures, p. 334
Solomon, Mitch . . . . Magnet Management, p. 207
Solomon, Richard . . . . The Bedford Falls Company, p. 65
Soloway, Arnold . . . . The Over the Hill Gang, p. 245
Solt, Andrew . . . . Andrew Solt Productions, p. 294
Somers, Mary . . . . Bravo, p. 74
Sommers, Stephen . . . . The Sommers Company, p. 294
Son, Diana . . . . Law & Order: Criminal Intent, p. 367
Sondervan, Sofia . . . . Sony BMG Feature Films, p. 294
Song, Jean . . . . Summit Entertainment, p. 304
Sonnenberg, Mark . . . . Discovery Networks, U.S., p. 111
Sonnenfeld, Barry . . . . Notes From the Underbelly, p. 370
Sorcher, Robert . . . . AMC, p. 50
Soref, Dror . . . . Skyline Pictures, LLC, p. 291
Sorensen, Ridd . . . . Atomic Cartoons, Inc., p. 58
Sorenson, Carsten . . . . The Orphanage, p. 244
Sorenson, Tara . . . . National Geographic Kids' Prog. & Prod., p. 229
Sorkin, Aaron . . . . Studio 60 on the Sunset Strip, p. 376
Sorrenti, Anne Marie . . . . Blueprint Entertainment, p. 70
Sorrentino, Scott . . . . Platform Entertainment, p. 256
Sortito, Karen . . . . Spyglass Entertainment Group, p. 299
Soter, Paul . . . . Broken Lizard Industries, p. 76
Soth, Norith . . . . Pathfinder Pictures, LLC, p. 250
Souders, Kelly . . . . Smallville, p. 375
Soulsby, Dan . . . . DisneyToon Studios, p. 113
Soultan, Alfred . . . . New Generation Films, Inc., p. 234
Sourian, Mark . . . . DreamWorks SKG, p. 116
Sousa, Guy . . . . FX, p. 144
South, Frank . . . . South Productions, LLC, p. 297
South, Margaret . . . . South Productions, LLC, p. 297
Spade, David . . . . The Showbiz Show with David Spade, p. 374
Spadone, Paul . . . . Mike Sullivan Productions, Inc., p. 304
Spain, Brian . . . . Mandalay Pictures, p. 208
Spak, Joanna . . . . Walt Disney Television Animation, p. 113
Sparks, Ashley . . . . MARTHA, p. 368
Spatt, Michael . . . . New Line Cinema, p. 234
Spaulding, Andrew D. . . . . Echo Lake Productions, p. 119
Spears, Kenneth . . . . Ruby-Spears Productions, p. 276
Spector, Ben . . . . Dominant Pictures, p. 114
Spector, John . . . . Sony Pictures Television, p. 296
Speed, Chuck . . . . Mindfire Entertainment, p. 217
Speed, Scott . . . . Hollywood East Entertainment, Inc., p. 168
Speed, Tracy . . . . Lifetime Television (Los Angeles), p. 198
Speer, Kim . . . . The L Word, p. 366
Speiser, Rachel . . . . Twentieth Century Fox Television, p. 323
Spellman-Rider, Janet . . . . Days of Our Lives, p. 359
Spencer, Jesse . . . . John Wells Productions, p. 338
Spencer, Tim . . . . Focus Features/Rogue Pictures, p. 136
Spera, Deb . . . . Criminal Minds, p. 358
Spera, Deborah . . . . The Mark Gordon Company, p. 150
Sperber, Stephanie . . . . Universal Pictures, p. 326
Spevak, Albert . . . . Ambassador Entertainment Inc., p. 50
Spiegel, Andrea . . . . Twilight Pictures, Inc., p. 324
Spiegelman, Adam . . . . Jimmy Kimmel Live, p. 364
Spiegelman, David . . . . New Line Cinema, p. 234
Spiegelman, David . . . . New Line Television, p. 235
Spiegelman, David . . . . Junction Entertainment, p. 183
Spielberg, Steven . . . . DreamWorks SKG, p. 116
Spies, James . . . . Battle Plan Productions, p. 63
Spina, Dario . . . . Spike TV, p. 298
Spindel, Abigail . . . . Longfellow Pictures, p. 203
Spink, Brian . . . . Benderspink, p. 66
Spink, J.C. . . . . Benderspink, p. 66
Spinks, Lynwood . . . . Relativity Media LLC, p. 269
Spira, Steve . . . . Warner Bros. Pictures, p. 334
Spiridellis, Evan . . . . JibJab Media Inc., p. 181
Spiridellis, Gregg . . . . JibJab Media Inc., p. 181
Spiroff, Tom . . . . Macedon Media, Inc., p. 205
Spitale, Emily . . . . Logo, p. 202
Spitalnik, Joel . . . . A-Line Pictures, p. 49
Spitz, David . . . . Lionsgate, p. 200
Spitzer, Justin . . . . The Office, p. 371
Spivak, Jason . . . . Sony Pictures Digital, p. 295
Spotnitz, Frank . . . . Big Light Productions, p. 67
Sprecher, Samantha . . . . Face Productions/Jennilind Productions, p. 129
Sprecher, Sue . . . . MarVista Entertainment, p. 212
Spring, Greg . . . . Pie Town Productions, p. 254
Spring, James . . . . Ealing Studios, p. 118
Spring, Sara . . . . Paramount Pictures Production Division, p. 248
Springborn, Beatrice . . . . Raygun Productions, p. 266
Springer, Justin . . . . LivePlanet, p. 201
Springer, Linda . . . . Paramount Pictures Production Division, p. 248
Sprouse, Michael . . . . Playboy Entertainment Group, Inc., p. 257
Sproxton, David . . . . Aardman Animations, p. 44
Spurling, Hugh . . . . Bauer Martinez Entertainment, p. 63
Spurlock, Morgan . . . . 30 Days, p. 353
Spurlock, Morgan . . . . Warrior Poets, p. 335
Squyres, Phil . . . . Sony Pictures Television, p. 296
St. Amand, List . . . . Warner Bros. Entertainment Inc., p. 334
St. Clair, Beau . . . . Irish DreamTime, p. 177
St. Cyr, Camille . . . . NCIS, p. 370
St. Ivanyi, Andra . . . . Pacifica International Film & TV Corp,, p. 246
St. Pierre, Danny . . . . Lionsgate, p. 200
St. Vincent, Alyssa . . . . Piranha Pictures, Inc., p. 256
Stabilini, Giovanni . . . . Cattleya, p. 86
Stack, Thomas . . . . Columbia Pictures, p. 97
Stack, Tim . . . . My Name Is Earl, p. 369
Staeger, Nadine . . . . Mango Tree Pictures, p. 210
Staeger, Will . . . . Mango Tree Pictures, p. 210
Stafford, Clay . . . . American Blackguard, Inc., p. 50
Staggs, Sandra . . . . Seven Arts Pictures, p. 285
Staggs, Thomas O. . . . . The Walt Disney Company, p. 112
Stahlberg, Michael . . . . Slipnot! Productions/SPG, p. 292
Stajich, Steve . . . . Reba, p. 372
Stallings, Kitty . . . . Dave Bell Associates, p. 65
Stam, Erin . . . . Spyglass Entertainment Group, p. 299
Stambouli, Romina . . . . Joel Films, p. 181
Stamen, Jessica . . . . Echo Lake Productions, p. 119
Stamos, John . . . . St. Amos Productions, p. 299
Stamos, Nick . . . . Mindfire Entertainment, p. 217
Stamp, Philip . . . . Lucasfilm Ltd., p. 203
Stanford, Halle . . . . The Jim Henson Company, p. 165
Stangel, Eric . . . . The Late Show with David Letterman, p. 367
Stangel, Justin . . . . The Late Show with David Letterman, p. 367
Stangel, Suzzanne . . . . George Schlatter Productions, p. 280
Stanghetti, Nikki . . . . Midnight Sun Pictures, p. 216
Stanhope, Hiroko . . . . OZLA Pictures, Inc., p. 246
Stankevich, E. Michael . . . . Mr. Mudd, p. 224
Stanley, Cheryl . . . . ABC Entertainment Television Group, p. 45
Stanley, Christopher . . . . Blue Tulip Productions, p. 69
Stanley, Gail . . . . View Askew Productions, Inc., p. 331
Stanton, Gabrielle . . . . Grey's Anatomy, p. 362
Stapf, David . . . . CBS Paramount Network Television, p. 87

Staples, Will . . . . . Union Entertainment, p. 325
Stapleton, Faye . . . . . Hell's Kitchen, p. 363
Star, Darren . . . . . Runaway, p. 373
Star, Darren . . . . . Darren Star Productions, p. 300
Stark, Benjamin . . . . . Pretty Matches Productions, p. 261
Stark, John . . . . . Traveler, p. 377
Stark, Jonathan . . . . . According to Jim, p. 354
Stark, Michael . . . . . Bryan Hickox Pictures, Inc., p. 166
Stark, Steve . . . . . Medium, p. 369
Stark, Steve . . . . . The Game, p. 361
Stark, Steve . . . . . Grammnet Productions, p. 152
Starke, David . . . . . Twentieth Century Fox, p. 322
Starkenburg, Michael . . . . . TV Guide Channel, p. 321
Starkey, Ken . . . . . King World Productions, Inc., p. 188
Starler, Alisa . . . . . C/W Productions, p. 105
Starllworth, Monikka . . . . . Motor City Films, p. 223
Starobin, David . . . . . Piranha Pictures, Inc., p. 256
Starr, Shane . . . . . Samuel Goldwyn Films, p. 279
Startz, Jane . . . . . Jane Startz Productions, Inc., p. 300
Stathakis, Jonathan . . . . . The Woofenill Works, Inc., p. 344
Stay, Rebecca . . . . . Is Or Isn't Entertainment, p. 177
Stearn, Andrew . . . . . John Wells Productions, p. 338
Stebor, Ben . . . . . The Radmin Company, p. 265
Steckelman, Peter . . . . . Warner Bros. Animation, p. 334
Steckler, Gavin . . . . . The Class, p. 357
Steckler, Jeremy . . . . . Twentieth Century Fox - Searchlight Pictures, p. 323
Steel, Justin . . . . . Ithaka, p. 178
Steele, Andrew . . . . . Saturday Night Live, p. 373
Steele, Todd . . . . . WPT Enterprises, Inc., p. 346
Steen, Jeremiah . . . . . Jerry Bruckheimer Films & Television, p. 78
Steenveld, Charles . . . . . Reveille, LLC, p. 270
Steers, Chad . . . . . The Gotham Group, Inc., p. 151
Stefanidis, Christopher . . . . . Buena Vista Television, p. 79
Stegemann, Mark . . . . . Scrubs, p. 374
Stehr, Manuela . . . . . X Filme Creative Pool GmbH, p. 346
Stein, Bruce . . . . . The Hatchery, p. 161
Stein, Gene . . . . . Wass-Stein, p. 336
Stein, Jeremy . . . . . Generation Entertainment, p. 145
Stein, Jeremy . . . . . Jon Shestack Productions, p. 286
Stein, Joan . . . . . Martin/Stein Productions, p. 211
Stein, Lauren . . . . . NBC Universal Television Studio, p. 231
Stein, Mark . . . . . Level 1 Entertainment, p. 197
Stein, Matthew . . . . . Dimension Films, p. 111
Stein, Matthew . . . . . The Weinstein Company, p. 337
Stein, Robert . . . . . Comedy Central, p. 98
Stein, Scott . . . . . Harpo Films, Inc., p. 161
Steinberg, Bruce . . . . . HIT Entertainment, p. 167
Steinberg, David . . . . . Stokely Chaffin Productions, p. 88
Steinberg, David . . . . . MBST Entertainment, Inc., p. 213
Steinberg, Dawn . . . . . Sony Pictures Television, p. 296
Steinberg, Eric . . . . . CBS Entertainment, p. 86
Steinberg, Erica . . . . . Universal Pictures, p. 326
Steinberg, Hank . . . . . Without a Trace, p. 379
Steinberg, Hank . . . . . The Nine, p. 370
Steinberg, Jeremy . . . . . Fox News Channel, p. 139
Steinberg, K.J. . . . . . The Nine, p. 370
Steinberg, Roy . . . . . Days of Our Lives, p. 359
Steindorff, Scott . . . . . Las Vegas, p. 366
Steindorff, Scott . . . . . Stone Village Pictures, LLC, p. 302
Steiner, Ezekiel . . . . . Brillstein-Grey Entertainment, p. 75
Steingart, Jon . . . . . Ars Nova, p. 55
Steinhauser, Sharon . . . . . Radar Pictures, p. 264
Steinke, Paul . . . . . Buena Vista Motion Pictures Group, p. 78
Steinman, Adam . . . . . Lion Television U.S., p. 199
Steisel, Susanna . . . . . Florentine Films, p. 135
Stella, Antoinette . . . . . Close to Home, p. 357
Stellato, Lou . . . . . MTV Networks, p. 226
Stellman, Michael . . . . . Snapdragon Films, Inc., p. 293
Stelzer, Peter . . . . . On Stilts Productions, p. 242
Stenftenagel, Amy . . . . . Gunn Films, p. 158
Stenn, David . . . . . The L Word, p. 366
Stenson, Mike . . . . . Jerry Bruckheimer Films & Television, p. 78
Stepanek, Sheila . . . . . Partizan, p. 250
Stepanovich, Mylan . . . . . Walden Media, p. 333
Stepanovich, Mylan . . . . . Bristol Bay Productions, p. 76
Stephan, Natasha . . . . . Nickelodeon Movies, p. 237
Stephen, Elizabeth Guber . . . . . Mandalay Pictures, p. 208
Stephens, Cordelia . . . . . Belladonna Productions, p. 65
Stephens, John . . . . . The O.C., p. 371
Stephens, Loren . . . . . One Step Productions, p. 243
Stephenson, Gary . . . . . The Tom Lynch Company, p. 205
Sterling, Christy . . . . . Imagine Entertainment, p. 172
Sterling, Dan . . . . . The Sarah Silverman Programme, p. 373
Sterman, Jason . . . . . Totem Productions, p. 316
Stern, Gardner . . . . . Las Vegas, p. 366
Stern, Howard . . . . . The Howard Stern Production Company, p. 301
Stern, Jackie . . . . . The Core, p. 101
Stern, James D. . . . . . Endgame Entertainment, p. 124
Stern, Jay . . . . . Rat Entertainment/Rat TV, p. 266
Stern, Julie . . . . . Lifetime Television (Los Angeles), p. 198
Stern, Mark . . . . . Sci Fi Channel, p. 282
Stern, Mark . . . . . NBC Universal Cable Entertainment, p. 231
Stern, Sandra . . . . . Lionsgate, p. 200
Stern, Sandy . . . . . Single Cell Pictures, p. 290
Sternberg, David . . . . . Fox Cable Networks, p. 139
Sternberg, Marc . . . . . The Shuman Company, p. 287
Sternberg, Phil . . . . . Super Delicious Productions, p. 305
Sternberg, Scott . . . . . Scott Sternberg Productions, p. 301
Sternfeld, Alan . . . . . Q Media Partners, p. 264
Sternschein, Evan . . . . . Discovery Networks, U.S., p. 111
Stevens, Andy . . . . . Moving Pictures, DPI, p. 223
Stevens, Dana . . . . . What About Brian, p. 379
Stevens, Fisher . . . . . GreeneStreet Films, p. 153
Stevens Jr., George . . . . . The Stevens Company, p. 301
Stevens, Greg . . . . . Stampede Entertainment, p. 299
Stevens, Jaime . . . . . Universal Pictures, p. 326
Stevens, Joel . . . . . Joel Stevens Entertainment, p. 301
Stevens, Michael . . . . . The Stevens Company, p. 301
Stevens, Scott . . . . . Burnside Entertainment, Inc., p. 80
Stevens, Tim . . . . . New Line Cinema, p. 234
Stevens, Timothy . . . . . Passions, p. 371
Stevenson, Bo . . . . . Playtone Productions, p. 258
Stevenson, Justine . . . . . Evolution Entertainment, p. 128
Stevenson, Marc . . . . . Front Street Pictures, Inc., p. 143
Stevenson, Natalie . . . . . Last Straw Productions, p. 194
Stevenson, Timothy I. . . . . . The Gotham Group, Inc., p. 151
Stewart, Anita . . . . . Sesame Workshop, p. 285
Stewart, Greg . . . . . Evolution, p. 128
Stewart, Jill . . . . . Station 3, p. 300
Stewart, Jon . . . . . The Daily Show With Jon Stewart, p. 359
Stewart, Jon . . . . . The Colbert Report, p. 357
Stewart, Jon . . . . . Busboy Productions, p. 81
Stewart, Martha . . . . . MARTHA, p. 368
Stewart, Martha . . . . . Martha Stewart Living Omnimedia, Inc., p. 211
Stewart, Sari . . . . . The Orphanage, p. 244
Stewart, Scott . . . . . The Orphanage, p. 244
Stewart, Terry . . . . . New Line Cinema, p. 234
Stewart, Trevor . . . . . Madhouse Entertainment, p. 206
Stiehm, Meredith . . . . . Cold Case, p. 357
Stier, Geoff . . . . . Paramount Vantage/Paramount Classics, p. 248
Still, Lance . . . . . New Line Cinema, p. 234
Stiller, Ben . . . . . Red Hour Films, p. 267
Stillman, Lori . . . . . Pacifica International Film & TV Corp,, p. 246
Stine, Beth . . . . . Relevant Entertainment Group, p. 270
Stipe, Michael . . . . . Single Cell Pictures, p. 290
Stirdivant, Bethany . . . . . Fuse Entertainment, p. 144
Stirling, Mike . . . . . FilmEngine, p. 133
Stirling, Rich . . . . . FilmEngine, p. 133
Stock, Monica . . . . . The Bachelor, p. 355
Stockhammer, Cynthia . . . . . Endemol USA, Inc., p. 123
Stockstill, Doris . . . . . Dean Hargrove Productions, p. 160
Stockstill, Doug . . . . . Big Love, p. 356
Stockton, Lance . . . . . Zak Penn's Company, p. 252
Stodel, Guy . . . . . New Line Cinema, p. 234
Stoff, Erwin . . . . . 3 Arts Entertainment, Inc., p. 40
Stohn, Stephen . . . . . Epitome Pictures, Inc., p. 126
Stokdyk, Danielle . . . . . Veronica Mars, p. 378
Stolhanske, Erik . . . . . Broken Lizard Industries, p. 76
Stolhanske, Lainie . . . . . Management 360, p. 208
Stoll, Barbara . . . . . Rules of Engagement, p. 373

Stoller, Bryan Michael . . . . .Northstar Entertainment, p. 239
Stolper, Stella . . . . .VH1, p. 330
Stone, Adam . . . . .Mandalay Pictures, p. 208
Stone, Alexandra . . . . .Recorded Picture Company, p. 266
Stone, Bill . . . . .Amp'd Mobile, p. 51
Stone, Brian . . . . .The Orphanage, p. 244
Stone, Bridget . . . . .Renée Missel Productions, p. 218
Stone, Cindy . . . . .Taurus Entertainment Company, p. 309
Stone, Dave . . . . .Bunim/Murray Productions, Inc., p. 79
Stone, David .Rocket Science Laboratories, p. 273
Stone, Erik . . . . .Davis Entertainment Company, p. 107
Stone, Matt . . . . .South Park, p. 376
Stone, Matt . . . . .Trunity, a Mediar Company, a Division of True Mediar, a Unity Corpbopoly, p. 320
Stone, Nancy Rae . . . . .Beacon, p. 64
Stone, Oliver . . . . .Ixtlan, p. 178
Stone, Robert . . . . .Stone vs. Stone, p. 302
Stone, Scott A. . . . . .Stone and Company Entertainment, p. 301
Stone, Webster . . . . .Stone vs. Stone, p. 302
Stopek, Jonathan .John Wells Productions, p. 338
Stordahl, Barbara . . . . .Standoff, p. 376
Storey, Erik . . . . .Sci Fi Channel, p. 282
Stork, Carl . . . . .Digital Domain, Inc., p. 110
Storm, Glenda . . . . .Shady Acres Entertainment, p. 285
Storm, Shelley . . . . .Asylum Entertainment, p. 57
Story, Tim . . . . .Standoff, p. 376
Stossel, Kristi . . . . .The Gurin Company, p. 158
Stotsky, Adam . . . . .Sci Fi Channel, p. 282
Stott, Jennifer . . . . .Picturehouse, p. 254
Stoudt, Charlotte . . . . .Sarabande Productions, p. 280
Strache, Ray . . . . .Twentieth Century Fox, p. 322
Strafford, Patrick . . . . .Warner Bros. Entertainment Inc., p. 334
Strain, Sherri . . . . .The Asylum, p. 57
Straka, Angie . . . . .CBS Corporation, p. 86
Strange, Michael . . . . .Keystone Entertainment, Inc., p. 187
Stratton, Christy . . . . .King of the Hill, p. 365
Strauss, Carolyn . . . . .HBO Entertainment, p. 162
Strauss, David . . . . .One Tree Hill, p. 371
Strauss, Jeff . . . . .All of Us, p. 354
Strauss, Melissa . . . . .KoMut Entertainment, p. 189
Strauss, Peter . . . . .Mandalay Pictures, p. 208
Strauss, Ricky . . . . .Participant Productions, p. 249
Strauss, Scott . . . . .Screen Gems, p. 283
Strazzullo, Joe . . . . .The Late Late Show with Craig Ferguson, p. 366
Street, Rita .Mike Young Productions LLC, p. 348
Streisand, Barbra . . . . .Barwood Films, p. 62
Stresemann, Gretchen . . . .Paramount Vantage/Paramount Classics, p. 248
Striegel, Stephanie . . . . .Bigel Entertainment, p. 67
Stringer, David Sean . . . . .Spirit Horse Productions, p. 298
Stringfellow, Stu . . . . .Entertainment Studios, Inc., p. 125
Stroh, Ernst "Etchie" . . . . .Moonstone Entertainment, p. 220
Stroh, Shahar . . . . .Moonstone Entertainment, p. 220
Stroh, Yael . . . . .Moonstone Entertainment, p. 220
Stroman, Gwenn . . . . .Flower Films, Inc., p. 135
Strong, Shelly . . . . .Yari Film Group (YFG), p. 347
Struber, Larry . . . . .Precis Productions, Inc., p. 261
Stryker, Andrew .Tollin/Robbins Productions, p. 315
Stuart, Mel . . . . .Mel Stuart Productions, Inc., p. 303
Stuart, Michelle . . . . .Last Call with Carson Daly, p. 366
Stubbs, Will . . . . .Davis Entertainment Company, p. 107
Stuckmeyer, John . . . . .Warner Bros. Television Production, p. 335
Stuecken, Matthew . . . . .The Sommers Company, p. 294
Stulwich, Kim . . . . .Mindfire Entertainment, p. 217
Stuparich De La Barra, Tamara . . . . .Foresight Unlimited, p. 137
Stupinsky, Gene . . . . .The Office, p. 371
Sturman, Lindsay . . . . .Close to Home, p. 357
Stutler, Jay . . . . .Walt Disney Television Animation, p. 113
Stutman, Gary . . . . .Morgan Creek Productions, p. 221
Stutz, Dan . . . . .Yari Film Group (YFG), p. 347
Styler, Trudie . . . . .Xingu Films Ltd., p. 347
Suarez, Elizabeth . . . . .PBS, p. 251
Subramanyam, Radha . . .Nickelodeon/MTVN Kids & Family Group, p. 237
Suchan, Casey . . . . .Open Road Films, p. 243
Sucherman, Greg . . . . .Universal Pictures, p. 326
Sud, Veena . . . . .Cold Case, p. 357
Sugerman, Andrew . . . . .Pantheon Entertainment Corp., p. 247
Sugerman, Chad . . . . . . .Comic Book Movies, LLC/Branded Entertainment/ Batfilm Productions, p. 99
Suh, Sung . . . . .20 Good Years, p. 353
Suh, Ted . . . . .9 Squared, p. 43
Sulatycky, Annemarie . . . . .Alliance Atlantis, p. 49
Sulkin, Alec . . . . .Family Guy, p. 361
Sullivan, Dan . . . . .C/W Productions, p. 105
Sullivan, Dennis . . . . .Hallmark Hall of Fame Productions, Inc., p. 159
Sullivan, George . . . . .Water Channel, p. 336
Sullivan, Jack . . . . .Broadway Video, p. 76
Sullivan, Jack . . . . .Broadway Video Entertainment, p. 76
Sullivan, Kate . . . . .Watermark, p. 336
Sullivan, Kelly . . . . .Touchstone Television, p. 316
Sullivan, Larry . . . . .Regency Television, p. 269
Sullivan, Mike . . . . .Mike Sullivan Productions, Inc., p. 304
Sullivan, Reid . . . . .Village Roadshow Pictures, p. 331
Sullivan, Susan . . . . .MSNBC, p. 225
Sullivan, Tim . . . . .Court TV Networks, p. 102
Summers, Cathleen . . . . .Summers Entertainment, p. 304
Summers, Matt . . . . .Saturn Films, p. 280
Sumner, Anita . . . . .Xingu Films Ltd., p. 347
Sumpter, Shelly . . . . .Nickelodeon/MTVN Kids & Family Group, p. 237
Suncic, Mailys Ann-Charlotte . . . . .Trillion Entertainment, Inc., p. 319
Sundae . . . . .Fallout, p. 129
Sundell, Alexandra . . . . .Regency Enterprises, p. 268
Sunderland, James . . . . .FremantleMedia North America, p. 142
Sunderland, Lawren . . . . .Rope The Moon Productions, p. 274
Sundwall, Fredrik . . . . .ManifestoVision, p. 210
Supnik, Debbie .Weller/Grossman Productions, p. 338
Suppa, Ronald . . . . .Ronald Suppa Productions, Inc., p. 306
Suratt, Dan .Lifetime Television (New York), p. 198
Surnow, Joel . . . . .24, p. 353
Suro, Maira . . . . .Renegade 83, p. 270
Suser, Andrew . . . . .LMNO Productions, p. 201
Suskind, Beth . . . . .Pie Town Productions, p. 254
Sussman, Danny . . . . .Brillstein-Grey Entertainment, p. 75
Sussman, David . . . . .MTV Networks, p. 226
Sussman, Jack . . . . .CBS Entertainment, p. 86
Sussman, Jeff . . . . .The King of Queens, p. 365
Sutherland, Doug . . . . .Whitewater Films, p. 340
Sutherland, Keifer . . . . .24, p. 353
Sutter, Kurt . . . . .The Shield, p. 374
Sutter, Randy . . . . .von Zerneck-Sertner Films, p. 332
Sutton, Phoef . . . . .Boston Legal, p. 357
Svidler, Jennifer . . . . .Big Love, p. 356
Swain, Brett . . . . .DisneyToon Studios, p. 113
Swallow, John . . . . .Universal Pictures, p. 326
Swallow, Karen . . . . .1492 Pictures, p. 38
Swaney, Joseph . . . . .Cartoon Network, p. 84
Swann, Kim . . . . .Q Media Partners, p. 264
Swann, Monica . . . . .All of Us, p. 354
Swanson, Bruce . . . . .CBS Paramount International Television, p. 87
Swanson, Kelly Coogan . . . . .RHI Entertainment, p. 271
Swanson, Neely . . . . .David E. Kelley Productions, p. 186
Swartz, Rob . . . . .Sci Fi Channel, p. 282
Swedlin, Rosalie . . . . .Industry Entertainment Partners, p. 174
Sweeney, Anne . . . . .The Walt Disney Company, p. 112
Sweeney, Anne . . . . .ABC Entertainment Television Group, p. 45
Sweeney, Anne . . . . .Disney-ABC Television Group, p. 113
Sweeney, Anne . . . . .Disney ABC Cable Networks Group, p. 112
Sweeney, David . . . . .Sweeney Entertainment, p. 306
Sweeney, Mike .Late Night with Conan O'Brien, p. 367
Sweet, Brian . . . . .Shoreline Entertainment, Inc., p. 286
Sweet, Mark . . . . .Two and a Half Men, p. 378
Sweigart, Linda . . . . .O Entertainment, p. 240
Sweren, Richard . . . . .Law & Order, p. 367
Swett, Hilary . . . . .Boz Productions, p. 72
Swezey, Stuart . . . . .Original Productions, p. 244
Swimmer, Darren . . . . .Smallville, p. 375
Swink, Simone . . . . .MARTHA, p. 368
Swofford, Steve . . . . .DisneyToon Studios, p. 113
Swords, Travis . . . . .Xingu Films Ltd., p. 347
Sykes, Melissa . . . . .Home & Garden Television (HGTV), p. 168
Symons, Genevieve . . . . .Altitude Entertainment, p. 49

Symons, Kel . . . . .Mace Neufeld Productions, p. 232
Sypniewski, David . . . . .Amp'd Mobile, p. 51
Syvan, Lemore . . . . .Elevation Filmworks, p. 121
Szelest, Jenelle . . . . .Brainstorm Media, p. 72
Szentgyorgyi, Tom . . . . .The Nine, p. 370
Szew, Fernando .MarVista Entertainment, p. 212
Szew, Joseph . . . . .MarVista Entertainment, p. 212
Szimonisz, Greg . . . . .Dreyfuss/James Productions, p. 117
Szymanski, Stanley . . . . .Sony Pictures Imageworks, p. 295
Tackaberry, Tony . . . . .Lion Television U.S., p. 199
Taddeo, Kim . . . . .Murphy Boyz Productions, p. 227
Tafuri, Joe . . . . .Sony Pictures Television, p. 296
Tagoryan, Petros . . . . .Passions, p. 371
Tague, Stephen . . . . .CBS Paramount International Television, p. 87
Tahse, Martin . . . . .Martin Tahse Productions, p. 307
Taitz, Daniel . . . . .Oxygen Media, p. 245
Taja, Darryl . . . . .Epidemic Pictures & Management, p. 125
Takahashi, Anne . . . . .Senza Pictures, p. 284
Takano, Kent . . . . .Fine Living, p. 133
Takiyama, Masao . . . . .Columbia Pictures, p. 97
Talbert, Eli . . . . .Traveler, p. 377
Talbott, James . . . . .Flying A Studios, Inc., p. 135
Talley, Geoff . . . . .Bayonne Entertainment, p. 63
Tam, Chester . . . . .Help Me Help You, p. 363
Tamaro, Janet . . . . .Bones, p. 356
Tamez, Jose . . . . .Ugly Betty, p. 378
Tan, Jun . . . . .Ambush Entertainment, p. 50
Tandler, Sharla . . . . .Two Sticks Productions, p. 325
Tanet, Ronald . . . . .The Woofenill Works, Inc., p. 344
Tanguay, Dale . . . . .TriCoast Studios, p. 318
Tann, Steve . . . . .Touchstone Television, p. 316
Tann, Zach . . . . .Magnet Management, p. 207
Tannenbaum, Eric . . . . .Two and a Half Men, p. 378
Tannenbaum, Eric . . . . .Notes From the Underbelly, p. 370
Tannenbaum, Eric . . . . .Tannenbaum Company, p. 308
Tannenbaum, Kim . . . . .Notes From the Underbelly, p. 370
Tannenbaum, Kim . . . . .Two and a Half Men, p. 378
Tannenbaum, Kim . . . . .Tannenbaum Company, p. 308
Tannyan, Aida . . . . .Serendipity Point Films, p. 284
Tanter, Miles .Alexander/Enright & Associates, p. 49
Tantillo, Megan . . . . .Lifetime Television (Los Angeles), p. 198
Tanz, Larry . . . . .LivePlanet, p. 201
Tao, Steve .FremantleMedia North America, p. 142
Tapert, Robert . . . . .Renaissance Pictures, p. 270
Tapert, Robert . . . . .Ghost House Pictures, p. 145
Taplin, Jeff . . . . .Infinitum Nihil, p. 174
Tapper, Cara . . . . .Super Delicious Productions, p. 305
Tappon, Drew . . . . .MTV Networks, p. 226
Tarantino, Quentin . . . . .A Band Apart, p. 43
Tardino, Don . . . . .CSI: Miami, p. 358
Targum, Adam . . . . .Standoff, p. 376
Targum, Adam . . . . .The Dead Zone, p. 359
Tarmey, Kerri . . . . .A&E Network, p. 44
Tarpinian, Gary .Morningstar Entertainment, p. 221
Tarses, Jamie . . . . .My Boys, p. 369
Tarses, Jamie . . . . .Pariah, p. 249
Tartaglia, Peter . . . . .Hell's Kitchen, p. 363
Tartikoff, Jenny . . . . .NBC News, p. 230
Tartikoff, Lilly . . . . .H. Beale Company, p. 158
Tassler, Nina . . . . .CBS Entertainment, p. 86
Tat, Randy . . . . .CFP Productions, p. 88
Tate, Sandy . . . . .Flavor Unit Entertainment, p. 135
Tatevosian, Karen . . . . .Sony Pictures Television, p. 296
Taube, Larry . . . . .Principal Entertainment, p. 262
Tauber, Jim . . . . .Sidney Kimmel Entertainment, p. 187
Taubman, Lawrence . . . . .CineCity Pictures, p. 91
Taufen, Regina . . . . .21 Laps Entertainment, p. 38
Tavel, Connie . . . . .Forward Entertainment, p. 138
Taweel, George . . . . .TLC Entertainment, p. 314
Taxter, Maureen . . . . .Nickelodeon/MTVN Kids & Family Group, p. 237
Taylor, Blake . . . . .TriCoast Studios, p. 318
Taylor, Brigham . . . . .Buena Vista Motion Pictures Group, p. 78
Taylor, Camille . . . . .Crossroads Films, p. 103
Taylor, Chris . . . . .WhiteLight Entertainment, p. 340
Taylor, Geoffrey . . . . .Taylor Made Films, p. 309
Taylor, Grazka . . . . .Grazka Taylor Productions, p. 309
Taylor, Gregg . . . . .The Kennedy/Marshall Company, p. 186
Taylor, Jamie . . . . .Twentieth Century Fox - Searchlight Pictures, p. 323
Taylor, Jason . . . . .MobiTV, p. 219
Taylor, Jason . . . . .Bad Hat Harry Productions, p. 59
Taylor, Jim . . . . .Ad Hominem Enterprises, p. 46
Taylor, Josh . . . . .Principal Entertainment, p. 262
Taylor, Lesley . . . . .Cookie Jar Entertainment, p. 100
Taylor, Mark . . . . .TBS, p. 309
Taylor, Mark . . . . .Turner Network Television (TNT), p. 321
Taylor, Mark . . . . .Nickelodeon/MTVN Kids & Family Group, p. 237
Taylor, Michael . . . . .Battlestar Galactica, p. 355
Taylor, Michael . . . . .The Dead Zone, p. 359
Taylor, Michael . . . . .Peace Arch Entertainment Group Inc., p. 251
Taylor, Michael . . . . .Michael Taylor Productions, p. 309
Taylor, Minna . . . . .Fox Broadcasting Company, p. 139
Taylor, Quinn . . . . .ABC Entertainment Television Group, p. 45
Taylor, Sam . . . . .Film & Music Entertainment, Ltd. (F&ME), p. 131
Taylor, Sheila Hanahan . . . . .Practical Pictures, p. 261
Taylor, Tom . . . . .T-Squared Productions, p. 320
Taylor, Toper . . . . .Cookie Jar Entertainment, p. 100
Taylor, Warren . . . . .Bill Melendez Productions, p. 215
Teach, Andy . . . . .Sony Pictures Television, p. 296
Teaton, Kenneth . . . . .The Foxboro Company, Inc., p. 140
Teitel, Robert . . . . .State Street Pictures, p. 300
Teitelbaum, Mark . . . . .Teitelbaum Artists Group, p. 310
Teitelman, Mark . . . . .MRB Productions, Inc., p. 224
Telegdy, Paul . . . . .BBC Worldwide Americas, p. 64
Tellem, Nancy . . . . .CBS Paramount Network Television, p. 87
Tellem, Nancy . . . . .CBS Entertainment, p. 86
Templeton, Deborah . . . . .Barnholtz Entertainment, p. 62
Templeton, Gary . . . . .P.A.T. Productions, p. 250
Templeton, Scott . . . . .Pie Town Productions, p. 254
Tenenbaum, Andrew D. . . . . .MBST Entertainment, Inc., p. 213
Tenenbaum, Nancy .Nancy Tenenbaum Films, p. 311
Tenenbaum, Stephen . . . . .MBST Entertainment, Inc., p. 213
Tennant, Dave . . . . .Scrubs, p. 374
Tennenbaum, Andrew R. . . . . .Flashpoint Entertainment, p. 135
Tepper, Arielle . . . . .Arielle Tepper Productions, p. 312
Tepper, Stanley . . . . .Emmett/Furla Films, p. 123
Teran, Victor .Sidney Kimmel Entertainment, p. 187
Terry, Angela . . . . .Standoff, p. 376
Terry, Laura . . . . .David Foster Productions, p. 138
Terry-Goldsby, Allyson . . . . . . .Sony Pictures Television International, p. 296
Tertzakian, Anoosh . . . . .MarVista Entertainment, p. 212
Testa, Garland . . . . .King of the Hill, p. 365
Testa, Randy . . . . .Walden Media, p. 333
Teverbaugh, Mike . . . . .20 Good Years, p. 353
Textor, John . . . . .Digital Domain, Inc., p. 110
Thal, Jeffrey . . . . .Ensemble Entertainment, p. 124
Thaler, Jonas . . . . .Walden Media, p. 333
Thaler, Jonas . . . . .Bristol Bay Productions, p. 76
Thayer, Sheridan . . . . .Monk, p. 369
Thayer, Tom . . . . .Traveler's Rest Films, p. 317
Theeranuntawat, Paninee . . . . .Morningstar Entertainment, p. 221
Thelen, George . . . . .Q Media Partners, p. 264
Thewlis, Mary Rae . . . . .Law & Order: Criminal Intent, p. 367
Thicke, Todd . . . . .America's Funniest Videos, p. 355
Thiel, Nick . . . . .Waterfront, p. 379
Thoday, Jon . . . . .Avalon Television, Inc., p. 58
Thoma, Maralyn . . . . .Passions, p. 371
Thomas, Allison .Larger Than Life Productions, p. 193
Thomas, Bernard . . . . .Arlington Entertainment, Inc., p. 55
Thomas, Betsy . . . . .My Boys, p. 369
Thomas, Betty . . . . .Dominant Pictures, p. 114
Thomas, Bradley . . . . .Conundrum Entertainment, p. 100
Thomas, Chet . . . . .WhiteLight Entertainment, p. 340
Thomas, Craig . . . . .How I Met Your Mother, p. 364
Thomas, Danielle . . . . .Untitled Entertainment, p. 327
Thomas Jr., Darrell Ray . . . . .Passions, p. 371
Thomas, Dawn . . . . .Overbrook Entertainment, p. 245
Thomas, Deborah . . . . .NBC Universal Corporate, p. 231
Thomas, Gwynne . . . . .Buena Vista Television, p. 79
Thomas, Heather . . . . .Agamemnon Films, Inc., p. 47
Thomas, Jeremy . . . . .Recorded Picture Company, p. 266

Thomas, Marlena . . . . . Spyglass Entertainment Group, p. 299
Thomas, Nigel . . . . . Matador Pictures, p. 212
Thomas, Rob . . . . . Veronica Mars, p. 378
Thomas, Stina . . . . . Pie Town Productions, p. 254
Thomas, Tippi . . . . . Lance Entertainment, Inc., p. 192
Thomas, Tony . . . . . Witt-Thomas-Harris Productions, p. 343
Thomas, Vickie . . . . . Everybody Hates Chris, p. 361
Thomases, Amy . . . . . Universal Pictures, p. 326
Thomason, Harry . . . . . Mozark Productions, p. 223
Thomason, Jamie . . . . . DisneyToon Studios, p. 113
Thompson, Alison . . . . . Focus Features/Rogue Pictures, p. 136
Thompson, Barnaby . . . . . Ealing Studios, p. 118
Thompson, Bill . . . . . Picturehouse, p. 254
Thompson, Bob . . . . . Fox Cable Networks, p. 139
Thompson, Bob . . . . . Fox Sports Network, p. 140
Thompson, Bradley . . . . . Battlestar Galactica, p. 355
Thompson, Byron . . . . . Light Renegade Entertainment, Inc., p. 198
Thompson, David . . . . . BBC Films, p. 64
Thompson, Eric . . . . . Maverick Films, p. 213
Thompson, Gary Scott . . . . . Las Vegas, p. 366
Thompson, Jeanne . . . . . Sunrise Entertainment, p. 305
Thompson, Kelly . . . . . Larry Thompson Organization, p. 312
Thompson, Larry . . . . . Larry Thompson Organization, p. 312
Thompson, Mark . . . . . BBC Worldwide Americas, p. 64
Thompson, Shannon . . . . . Harpo Films, Inc., p. 161
Thompson, Tommy . . . . . The Dead Zone, p. 359
Thompson, William . . . . . Fuse Entertainment, p. 144
Thompson, Zana . . . . . World International Network, p. 345
Thoms, Donald . . . . . Discovery Networks, U.S., p. 111
Thomson, Julie . . . . . Valhalla Motion Pictures, p. 328
Thomson, Richard . . . . . Guardian Entertainment, Ltd., p. 157
Thorman, Dan . . . . . Madison Road Entertainment, p. 206
Thorn, Michael . . . . . Adelstein Productions, p. 47
Thornton, Michael . . . . . Buena Vista Television, p. 79
Thorpe, Richard . . . . . ER, p. 361
Thorson, Karen . . . . . The Wire, p. 379
Thrasher, Chris . . . . . Power Up, p. 260
Thrasher, Lisa . . . . . Power Up, p. 260
Threinen, Derek . . . . . National Geographic Giant Screen Films & Special Projects, p. 229
Thwaites, David . . . . . Phoenix Pictures, p. 254
Tiballi, Nancy . . . . . Latin Hollywood Films, p. 194
Tibbels, Kirkland . . . . . Funny Boy Films, p. 143
Tibbets, Daniel . . . . . GoTV Networks, p. 151
Tichell, Gordon . . . . . Bristol Bay Productions, p. 76
Tichell, Gordon . . . . . Walden Media, p. 333
Tichy, Bree . . . . . The Jinks/Cohen Company, p. 181
Tidwell, Johnnie . . . . . TAE Productions/Medeacom Productions, p. 307
Tierney, Kevin . . . . . Park Ex Pictures, p. 249
Tiesiera, Tiffany . . . . . Marty Katz Productions, p. 185
Tigelaar, Liz . . . . . What About Brian, p. 379
Tiles, Neal . . . . . G4 TV, p. 144
Tilkin, Lori . . . . . Lion Rock Productions, p. 199
Tillan, Jose . . . . . MTV Networks Latin America (MTVNLA), p. 226
Tilley, Dylan . . . . . Morningstar Entertainment, p. 221
Tillinghast, Charlie . . . . . MSNBC, p. 225
Tillman Jr., George . . . . . State Street Pictures, p. 300
Timberman, Sarah . . . . . Kidnapped, p. 365
Timberman, Sarah . . . . . 25C Productions, p. 40
Timmons, Lauren . . . . . SenArt Films, p. 284
Timon, Halla . . . . . Fort Hill Productions, p. 137
Timoner, Ondi . . . . . Interloper Films, p. 175
Timpone, Karin . . . . . Yahoo! Media Group/Yahoo! Studios, p. 347
Tindal, Calvin . . . . . Buena Vista Motion Pictures Group, p. 78
Tingle, Terri . . . . . Turner Entertainment Group, p. 320
Tinker, John . . . . . 3n1 Entertainment, p. 41
Tipton, Chris . . . . . Davis Entertainment Company, p. 107
Tirola, Douglas . . . . . 4th Row Films, p. 42
Tisch, Steve . . . . . Escape Artists II, p. 126
Tisch, Steve . . . . . The Steve Tisch Company, p. 314
Tischler-Blue, Victory . . . . . Sacred Dogs Entertainment, LLC, p. 278
To, Tony . . . . . Studios International, p. 303
Toback, Stephen . . . . . DisneyToon Studios, p. 113
Tober, Jeff . . . . . Motion Picture Production, Inc., p. 223
Tocantins, Nicole . . . . . Is Or Isn't Entertainment, p. 177
Todd, Don . . . . . Ugly Betty, p. 378
Todd, Jennifer . . . . . Team Todd, p. 310
Todd, Norman . . . . . Infinitum Nihil, p. 174
Todd, Suzanne . . . . . Team Todd, p. 310
Todman Jr., Bill . . . . . Level 1 Entertainment, p. 197
Todoroff, Tom . . . . . 57-T Productions, Inc., p. 42
Toffler, Van . . . . . VH1, p. 330
Toffler, Van . . . . . MTV Networks, p. 226
Toffler, Van . . . . . CMT: Country Music Television, p. 95
Tolan, Leslie . . . . . Rescue Me, p. 373
Tolan, Peter . . . . . Rescue Me, p. 373
Toledo-Arencibia, Biana . . . . . Telemundo Network, p. 310
Tollin, Mike . . . . . One Tree Hill, p. 371
Tollin, Mike . . . . . Smallville, p. 375
Tollin, Mike . . . . . Tollin/Robbins Productions, p. 315
Tolmach, Matt . . . . . Columbia Pictures, p. 97
Tomassi Lindman, Sarah . . . . . The N, p. 228
Tomita, Sandra . . . . . The Goldstein Company, p. 149
Tomko, Carole . . . . . Discovery Networks, U.S., p. 111
Tompkins, Steve . . . . . The Knights of Prosperity, p. 365
Toms, Bob . . . . . ABC Sports, p. 45
Toms, Bruce . . . . . Nanny 911, p. 369
Tong, Stanley . . . . . Double Edge Entertainment, p. 115
Tongue, Chris . . . . . Dark Horse Entertainment, p. 107
Tooley, Tucker . . . . . Media Talent Group, p. 214
Tooley, Tucker . . . . . Tooley Productions, p. 315
Toplyn, Joe . . . . . Monk, p. 369
Topolsky, Ken . . . . . Kidnapped, p. 365
Toporovich, Jaime . . . . . Mandy Films, p. 209
Topping, Jenno . . . . . Fresh Paint, p. 142
Torgove, Mark . . . . . The George Lopez Show, p. 362
Tornell, Lisa . . . . . Tornell Productions, p. 315
Torres, Carlos . . . . . Buena Vista Television, p. 79
Torres, Jesus . . . . . Sony Pictures Television International, p. 296
Torres, Oscar . . . . . Bobker/Kruger Films, p. 70
Torres, Vanessa . . . . . Broad Strokes Entertainment, p. 76
Torresblanco, Frida . . . . . Esperanto Films, p. 126
Toscano, Nikki . . . . . Close to Home, p. 357
Tovar, Juan . . . . . Esperanto Films, p. 126
Tow, Andrew . . . . . here! Networks, p. 165
Tower, Carlos . . . . . The Mark Gordon Company, p. 150
Tower, Jon . . . . . L.I.F.T. Productions, p. 191
Towey, Gael . . . . . Martha Stewart Living Omnimedia, Inc., p. 211
Toynton, Ian . . . . . The O.C., p. 371
Tozzi, Riccardo . . . . . Cattleya, p. 86
Tracey, Amanda . . . . . Twentieth Century Fox Television, p. 323
Tracy, Brett . . . . . Lynn Loring Productions, p. 203
Trafford, Diane . . . . . MARTHA, p. 368
Trahan, Terry . . . . . Parkway Productions, p. 249
Tran, Bic . . . . . Lakeshore Entertainment Group LLC, p. 192
Trapani, Andy . . . . . Integrated Films & Management, p. 175
Traub, Stacy . . . . . Notes From the Underbelly, p. 370
Traugott, Peter . . . . . The Showbiz Show with David Spade, p. 374
Traugott, Peter . . . . . Brillstein-Grey Entertainment, p. 75
Tredinnick, Ryan . . . . . GSN, p. 157
Treglia, Tammy . . . . . Vin Di Bona Productions, p. 110
Treisman, Jonathan . . . . . Buena Vista Motion Pictures Group, p. 78
Trejo, Martin . . . . . Mandalay Sports Action Entertainment & Mandalay Integrated Media Entertainment, p. 208
Treloar, Atlanta . . . . . Cindy Cowan Entertainment, Inc., p. 102
Tremayne, Charles . . . . . Granada America, p. 152
Trench, Tracey . . . . . East of Doheny/Lexington Road Prod., p. 118
Trepanier, Jeanne . . . . . Terence Michael Productions, Inc., p. 216
Treston, Arik . . . . . Cinema Libre Studio, p. 92
Trezza, Alan . . . . . Scott Free Productions, p. 282
Trezza, James Francis . . . . . Trezza Entertainment, p. 317
Trias, Jennie . . . . . White Sneakers, Inc., p. 339
Trier, Lars von . . . . . Zentropa, p. 348
Trilling, Wendi . . . . . CBS Entertainment, p. 86
Trimmer, Carrie . . . . . A&E Network, p. 44
Trivedi, Mamta . . . . . Vox3 Films, p. 332
Troche, Rose . . . . . The L Word, p. 366
Trojan, Janice . . . . . Universal Pictures, p. 326
Trojan, Jeffrey . . . . . DC Comics, p. 108
Tropea, Silvana . . . . . Class 5 Films, p. 95

Trotiner, Glen .Burnside Entertainment, Inc., p. 80
Trott, Jesse . . . . .L'Orange, p. 203
Trotta, Heidi . . . . .Buena Vista Motion Pictures Group, p. 78
Troutwine, Chad . . . . .Departure Studios, p. 109
Troy, Cassandra .Teitelbaum Artists Group, p. 310
Truesdell, Ember . . . . .Flower Films, Inc., p. 135
Truesdell, Keith . . . . .Production Partners, Inc., p. 262
Truitt, Lisa . . . . .National Geographic Giant Screen Films & Special Projects, p. 229
Truman, Brian .Landscape Entertainment, p. 193
Trump, Donald . . . . .The Apprentice, p. 355
Trump, Michelle . . . . .James Manos Productions, Inc., p. 210
Trunkey, Christopher . . . . .Phoenix Pictures, p. 254
Tse, Simon . . . . .CineMagic Entertainment, p. 92
Tseckares, Steve . . . . .E! Networks, p. 117
Tseng, Amelie . . . . .Bravo, p. 74
Tsui, Daren . . . . .MSpot, p. 225
Tsujihara, Kevin . . . . .Warner Bros. Entertainment Inc., p. 334
Tucci, Richard D. . . . . .Parkway Productions, p. 249
Tuchinsky, Jessica . . . . .Watermark, p. 336
Tuchman, Bruce . . . . . .Metro-Goldwyn-Mayer Studios, Inc. (MGM), p. 215
Tucker, Brandie . . . . .Endemol USA, Inc., p. 123
Tucker, Julie . . . . .Rescue Me, p. 373
Tuckerman, David . . . . .New Line Cinema, p. 234
Tuckerman, Jonathan . . . . .Benderspink, p. 66
Tuckfield, Tristen . . . . .The Ebersole-Hughes Company, p. 119
Tudor, Marty . . . . .Tudor Management Group, p. 320
Tuffin, Christopher . . . . .BloodWorks, LLC, p. 68
Tugend, Jennie Lew . . . . .Kadokawa Pictures USA, p. 184
Tukan, Zambak . . . . .Alcon Entertainment, LLC, p. 49
Tull, Thomas . . . . .Legendary Pictures, p. 195
Tumino, John . . . . .One Life to Live, p. 371
Tumminia, James . . . . .George Paige Associates, Inc., p. 246
Tumulty, Elizabeth . . . . .The CW, p. 105
Tunnicliffe, Andy . . . . .Guy Walks Into a Bar, p. 158
Tureaud, Christian . . . . .Mandalay Sports Action Entertainment & Mandalay Integrated Media Entertainment, p. 208
Turen, Kevin . . . . .First Look Pictures, p. 134
Turgis, Amelie . . . . .Recorded Picture Company, p. 266
Turk, Craig . . . . .Boston Legal, p. 357
Turman, Lawrence . . . . .The Turman Inc. Picture Company, p. 320
Turner, Adrienne . . . . .Warner Bros. Television Production, p. 335
Turner, Amy . . . . .Studio 60 on the Sunset Strip, p. 376
Turner, Angela . . . . .Sony Pictures Television, p. 296
Turner, Barbara . . . . .Trezza Entertainment, p. 317
Turner, Bob . . . . .IDT Entertainment, p. 171
Turner, Brad . . . . .24, p. 353
Turner, Bryan . . . . .Melee Entertainment, p. 214
Turner, Clem . . . . .Guardian Entertainment, Ltd., p. 157
Turner, Evan . . . . .Walden Media, p. 333
Turner, Hans . . . . .Mobius International, p. 219
Turner, Jennifer . . . . .NBC Universal Television Studio, p. 231
Turner, Keith . . . . .NBC Universal Corporate, p. 231
Turner, Kelli . . . . .New Line Cinema, p. 234
Turner, Steve . . . . .Big Love, p. 356
Turner-Moody, Mae . . . . .Sony Pictures Imageworks, p. 295
Turrisi, Kim . . . . .Lin Oliver Productions, p. 242
Turteltaub, Jon . . . . .Jericho, p. 364
Turteltaub, Jon . . . . .Junction Entertainment, p. 183
Turtletaub, Marc . . . . .Big Beach, p. 67
Turtletaub, Marc . . . . .Deep River Productions, p. 109
Tuschman, Bob . . . . .Food Network, p. 136
Tuzon, Rita . . . . .Fox Cable Networks, p. 139
Twain, Dena . . . . .Temple Hill Productions, p. 311
Twain, Norman . . . . .Norman Twain Productions, p. 322
Twardosz, Sebastian . . . . .Craftsman Films, p. 102
Tweedy, Virginia . . . . .Warner Bros. Pictures, p. 334
Twilley, Robert . . . . .Jupiter Entertainment, p. 183
Tykwer, Tom . . . . .X Filme Creative Pool GmbH, p. 346
Tyler, Bridget . . . . .Red Wagon Entertainment, p. 268
Tyler, Marianne . . . . .Harve Bennett Productions, p. 66
Tyler, Miri . . . . .Joe Roth Television, p. 275
Tyrer, William . . . . .Newmarket Capital Group, p. 236
Tyus-Adair, Kathryn . . . . .Trillion Entertainment, Inc., p. 319
Uemura, Anne . . . . .Boston Legal, p. 357
Ufland, Harry J. . . . . .Ufland Productions, p. 325
Ufland, Mary Jane . . . . .Ufland Productions, p. 325
Uhls, Jim . . . . .Peculiar Films, p. 252
Uhls, Yalda Tehranian . . . . .Peculiar Films, p. 252
Ulbrich, Ed . . . . .Digital Domain, Inc., p. 110
Ulin, Rob . . . . .My Boys, p. 369
Ullman, Shawn . . . . .Laugh Factory Entertainment, p. 195
Ulrich, Robert . . . . .Day Break, p. 359
Ulrich, Robert . . . . .Battlestar Galactica, p. 355
Ulrich, Robert . . . . .Supernatural, p. 377
Ulrich, Robyn . . . . .DIY Network, p. 113
Ulrich, Robyn . . . . .Fine Living, p. 133
Underhill, Erin . . . . .NBC Entertainment, p. 230
Underwood, Tracy . . . . .Blumhouse Productions, p. 70
Ungar, Gary . . . . .Exile Entertainment, p. 128
Unger, Bill . . . . .Tidewater Entertainment, Inc., p. 313
Unger, George . . . . .Neighbors Entertainment, p. 232
Unterman, Zac . . . . .Smart Entertainment, p. 292
Upson, Erin . . . . .Scott Free Productions, p. 282
Upton, Mike . . . . .2929 Productions, p. 40
Urann, Michael . . . . .Odd Lot Entertainment, p. 241
Urban, Anna . . . . .Apostle, p. 53
Urbanski, Douglas . . . . .SE8 Group, p. 283
Urbina, Yvette . . . . .Fox Broadcasting Company, p. 139
Urbont, Ariana . . . . .MTV Networks, p. 226
Urbont, Dawn . . . . .One Tree Hill, p. 371
Urdang, Kellie . . . . .Jerry Bruckheimer Films & Television, p. 78
Urdang, Leslie . . . . .Serenade Films, p. 284
Uribe, Julie . . . . .FremantleMedia North America, p. 142
Urioste, Frank J. . . . . .Warner Bros. Pictures, p. 334
Urofsky, Matthew . . . . .Electric Entertainment, p. 121
Usher, Karyn . . . . .Prison Break, p. 372
Ushiroku, Masaki . . . . .Sony Pictures Television International, p. 296
Uslan, David . . . . .Comic Book Movies, LLC/Branded Entertainment/ Batfilm Productions, p. 99
Uslan, Michael . . . . .Comic Book Movies, LLC/Branded Entertainment/ Batfilm Productions, p. 99
Ussery, Terdema . . . . .HDNet, p. 163
Utley, Nancy . . . . .Twentieth Century Fox - Searchlight Pictures, p. 323
Uyeda, Robert . . . . .Mutual Film Company, p. 227
Uzielli, Al . . . . .Leisure Time Enterprises, p. 196
Vachon, Christine . . . . .Killer Films, Inc., p. 187
Vadas, Kristen Connolly . . . . .Oxygen Media, p. 245
Vahradian, Mark . . . . .di Bonaventura Pictures, Inc., p. 110
Vaines, Colin . . . . .The Weinstein Company, p. 337
Vaisman, Edward . . . . .Avenue Pictures, p. 59
Vait, Annette . . . . .Luminous Entertainment, p. 204
Vajna, Andrew . . . . .C2 Pictures, p. 81
Valan, Laura .Warner Bros. Entertainment Inc., p. 334
Valaskakis, Ion . . . . .Airborne Entertainment, p. 48
Valco, Nikki . . . . .Two and a Half Men, p. 378
Valenta, Nick . . . . .Adelstein Productions, p. 47
Valente, Renée . . . . .Renée Valente Productions, p. 328
Valenti, Courtenay . . . . .Warner Bros. Pictures, p. 334
Valenti, Matt . . . . .Atman Entertainment, p. 57
Valentine, Dean . . . . .Symbolic Action, p. 306
Valentine, Jared . . . . .Infinity Features Entertainment, p. 174
Valentini, Frank . . . . .One Life to Live, p. 371
Valentini, Frank . . . . .ABC Daytime, p. 44
Valenzuela, Lisa . . . . . . .Dakota North Entertainment/Dakota Films, p. 106
Valhouli, Alex . . . . .Mandate Pictures, p. 209
Valine, Julie . . . . .The Robert Simonds Company, p. 290
Valko, Nikki . . . . .Traveler, p. 377
Valko, Nikki . . . . .Boston Legal, p. 357
Valleau, Dave . . . . .Infinity Features Entertainment, p. 174
Valleau, Pete . . . . .Infinity Features Entertainment, p. 174
Vallow, Kara . . . . .American Dad, p. 354
Vallow, Kara . . . . .Family Guy, p. 361
Valverde, Rawley . . . . .Current TV, LLC, p. 105
Van Amburg, Zackary . . . . .Sony Pictures Television, p. 296
Van Arragon, Brad . . . . .Brightlight Pictures, Inc., p. 75
Van Arsdale, Taylor . . . . .Tailfish Productions, p. 307
Van Belle, Jackie . . . . .One Life to Live, p. 371
Van Citters, Darrell . . . . .Renegade Animation, Inc., p. 270
Van der Meer, Gerrit . . . . .House, p. 363

Van Doornewaard, Nancy .Without a Trace, p. 379
Van Etten, Chirs . . . . .One Life to Live, p. 371
Van Fleet, Alex . . . . .Hyde Park Entertainment, p. 169
Van Haun, Amy . . . . .Village Roadshow Pictures, p. 331
Van Hoff, Stephanie .Fox Television Studios, p. 140
Van Hook, Kevin . . . . .Film Roman, Inc., p. 132
Van Hoy, Carrie .The Gotham Group, Inc., p. 151
Van Kempen, Michelle . . . . .Film Garden Entertainment, Inc., p. 132
Van Lowe, Ehrich . . . . .Frazier | Chipman Entertainment, p. 141
van Munster, Bertram . . . . .The Amazing Race, p. 354
van Munster, Bertram . . . . .Earthview Inc., p. 118
van Riet, Hans . . . . .House of Rock Productions, Inc., p. 169
Van Syckle, Richard . . . . .CMT: Country Music Television, p. 95
Van Til, Desi . . . . .Roth/Arnold Productions, p. 275
Vanderbeke, Larry . . . . .Twentieth Television, p. 324
VanDerKloot, William . . . . .VanDerKloot Film & Television, p. 328
Vandervelde, John . . . . .Cookie Jar Entertainment, p. 100
VanderWier, Terry . . . . .Bryan Hickox Pictures, Inc., p. 166
Vann, Michael . . . . .Arjay Entertainment, p. 55
Vanzo, Gregg . . . . .Rough Draft Studios, p. 276
Vanzo, Scott . . . . .Rough Draft Studios, p. 276
Vargas, Stephanie . . . . .Trezza Entertainment, p. 317
Varo, Sandy . . . . .CBS Entertainment, p. 86
Varvi, John . . . . .FX, p. 144
Vash, Susan . . . . .The War at Home, p. 379
Vasquez, Lalo .Shady Acres Entertainment, p. 285
Vasquez, Lalo . . . . .Shutt-Jones Productions, p. 287
Vassos, Costa . . . . .Front Street Pictures, Inc., p. 143
Vaughan, Craig . . . . .Fox Mobile Entertainment, p. 139
Vaughan, Doug . . . . .NBC News, p. 230
Veal, Branson . . . . .MRB Productions, Inc., p. 224
Veasey, Pam . . . . .CSI: NY, p. 359
Vebber, Dan . . . . .American Dad, p. 354
Vecchio, Joseph S. . . . . .Joseph S. Vecchio Entertainment, p. 329
Vecchione, Andy . . . . .here! Networks, p. 165
Veenstra, Joel . . . . .Alcon Entertainment, LLC, p. 49
Vega, Rose Marie . . . . .Alliance Atlantis, p. 49
Veisel, Cathy . . . . .Fox Television Studios, p. 140
Veley, Jason . . . . .State Street Pictures, p. 300
Velez, Alberto . . . . .Sony Pictures Imageworks, p. 295
Velez, Max . . . . .Roberts/David Films, Inc., p. 273
Vella, Vivienne . . . . .Telepictures Productions, p. 311
Velvet, Tina . . . . .HorsePower Entertainment, p. 169
Veneziano, Ariel . . . . .GreeneStreet Films, p. 153
Ventani, Pietro . . . . .Sony Pictures Television International, p. 296
Ventimiglia, Gary . . . . .Valhalla Motion Pictures, p. 328
Vento-Hall, Joan . . . . .Chameleon Entertainment, p. 89
Vercelli, Donald . . . . .Sony Online Entertainment, p. 294
Verderame, Andy . . . . .Court TV Networks, p. 102
Verdi, David . . . . .NBC News, p. 230
Verdin, Julia . . . . .Rough Diamond Productions, p. 276
Verheiden, Mark . . . . .Battlestar Galactica, p. 355
Verkin, Billy . . . . .Fred Kuehnert Productions, p. 190
Vermilion, Kevin . . . . .Power Up, p. 260
Verna, Tracy . . . . .FremantleMedia North America, p. 142
Vernetti, Joanna . . . . .Super Delicious Productions, p. 305
Verno, Helen . . . . .Sony Pictures Television, p. 296
Vernoff, Krista . . . . .Grey's Anatomy, p. 362
Vernon, Lori Imbler . . . . .Chartoff Productions, p. 89
Vernon, Ryan . . . . .The Pitt Group, p. 256
Veverka, Peter . . . . .Point Road, Inc., p. 258
Viane, Chuck . . . . .Buena Vista Motion Pictures Group, p. 78
Vicente, Joana . . . . .Deutsch/Open City Films, p. 109
Vicente, Joana . . . . .HDNet Films, p. 163
Vickers, Debbie . . . . .The Tonight Show with Jay Leno, p. 377
Victor, Daniel . . . . .Sesame Workshop, p. 285
Victor, Daniel J. . . . . .Boneyard Entertainment, p. 71
Victor, Diana . . . . .This is that corporation, p. 312
Victor, Mark . . . . .Mark Victor Productions, p. 330
Victor, Richard M. . . . . .Boneyard Entertainment, p. 71
Vidov, Oleg . . . . .Films By Jove, p. 133
Vidov, Sergei . . . . .Films By Jove, p. 133
Vidra, Guy . . . . .Proteus, p. 263
Viener, John . . . . .Family Guy, p. 361
Vignola, Charles . . . . .Jerry Bruckheimer Films & Television, p. 78
Vila, Scott . . . . .A&E Network, p. 44
Vilar, Christine . . . . .Mondo Media, p. 220
Villacorta, John . . . . .Touchstone Television, p. 316
Villadolid, Paul . . . . .CMT: Country Music Television, p. 95
Villalpando, Armando . . . . .TV Guide Channel, p. 321
Villard, Dimitri . . . . .Dimitri Villard Productions, p. 331
Villarreal, William . . . . .Sony Pictures Imageworks, p. 295
Villas, Lee . . . . .King World Productions, Inc., p. 188
Villegas, Michael . . . . .Touchstone Television, p. 316
Vina, Adrian . . . . .New Redemption Pictures, p. 235
Vince, Lyn . . . . .Infinity Features Entertainment, p. 174
Vince, Robert . . . . .Keystone Entertainment, Inc., p. 187
Vince, William . . . . .Infinity Features Entertainment, p. 174
Vincent, Cheri . . . . .Twentieth Television, p. 324
Vinciquerra, Anthony . . . . .Fox Cable Networks, p. 139
Vinciquerra, Tony . . . . .Fox Broadcasting Company, p. 139
Vines, Greg . . . . .Andrew Solt Productions, p. 294
Vinnitski, Alexander H. . . . . .New Generation Films, Inc., p. 234
Vinson, Tripp . . . . .Contrafilm, p. 100
Viola, David . . . . .Filbert Steps Productions, p. 131
Viola, Mary . . . . .Thunder Road Pictures, p. 313
Viquez, Fernando .Walker/Fitzgibbon TV/Films, p. 333
Virvez, Dionicio . . . . .Tri-Elite Entertainment, Ltd., p. 319
Viscidi, Marcus .Lemon Sky Productions, Inc., p. 196
Visciglia, RJ . . . . .My Boys, p. 369
Vishnevsky, Ian . . . . .Treasure Entertainment, p. 317
Vitale, Ruth . . . . .First Look Pictures, p. 134
Vitale, Thomas . . . . .Sci Fi Channel, p. 282
Vitale, Thomas . . . . .NBC Universal Cable Entertainment, p. 231
Vitallo-Hook, Lisbeth . . . . .Andell Entertainment, p. 51
Vito, Sabrina . . . . .Tagline Pictures, p. 307
Viviano, Bettina Sofia . . . . .Viviano Feldman Entertainment, p. 331
Vlassopulos, Jon . . . . .Endemol USA, Inc., p. 123
Vodde, Michael . . . . .Martin Tahse Productions, p. 307
Vogel, Jordanna . . . . .Mission Entertainment, p. 218
Vogel, M. Scott . . . . .Mission Entertainment, p. 218
Vogtner, Alina . . . . .MTV Networks Latin America (MTVNLA), p. 226
Voight, Jon . . . . .Jon Voight Entertainment, p. 331
Volk-Weiss, Brian . . . . .New Wave Management, p. 236
Voll, Daniel . . . . .The Unit, p. 378
Vollack, Lia . . . . .Columbia Pictures, p. 97
Volturno, Jeanette . . . . .CatchLight Films, p. 85
von der Leyen, Robin . . . . .Constantin Film Dev., Inc./Constantin TV, p. 100
von Gal, Peter . . . . .RHI Entertainment, p. 271
von Zerneck, Frank . . . . .von Zerneck-Sertner Films, p. 332
Vonk, Jake . . . . .Twentieth Century Fox Television, p. 323
Voorhees, Tucker . . . . .3 Arts Entertainment, Inc., p. 40
Voris, Cyrus . . . . .Sleeper Cell, p. 375
Voye, Tay . . . . .North By Northwest Entertainment, p. 239
Vradenburg, Alissa . . . . .Untitled Entertainment, p. 327
Vye, Heather . . . . .Initial Entertainment Group, p. 175
Wacek, Eddie . . . . .Dino De Laurentiis Company, p. 108
Wachel, Sarah . . . . .Cineville LLC, p. 93
Wachs, Hannah . . . . .Trunity, a Mediar Company, a Division of True Mediar, a Unity Corpbopoly, p. 320
Wachsberger, Patrick . . . . .Summit Entertainment, p. 304
Wachtel, Jeff . . . . .USA Network, p. 327
Wachtell, Jennifer . . . . .Initial Entertainment Group, p. 175
Wachter, Catherine . . . . .The Goldstein Company, p. 149
Waddington, Alastair . . . . .IMG Media, p. 172
Wade, Celeste . . . . .Driven Entertainment, p. 117
Wade, Celeste . . . . .3n1 Entertainment, p. 41
Wade, Chris . . . . .Imagine Entertainment, p. 172
Wade, LeslieAnne . . . . .CBS Sports, p. 88
Wade, Todd . . . . .Runaway Productions, p. 277
Wadlow, Jeff . . . . .Tower of Babble Entertainment, p. 316
Wadsworth, Cheryl . . . . .Fred Wolf Films, p. 343
Wadsworth, Steve . . . . .The Walt Disney Company, p. 112
Waehner, Kevin . . . . .Gold Circle Films, p. 148
Wager, Jamie . . . . .Alcon Entertainment, LLC, p. 49
Wagner, Jake . . . . .Energy Entertainment, p. 124
Wagner, Lauren . . . . .Tollin/Robbins Productions, p. 315
Wagner, Lisa . . . . .MARTHA, p. 368
Wagner, Meredith . . . . .Lifetime Television (New York), p. 198
Wagner, Natalie . . . . .Foothill Entertainment, Inc., p. 136

Wagner, Paula ....C/W Productions, p. 105
Wagner, Raymond ....Raymond Wagner Productions, Inc., p. 332
Wagner, Todd ....2929 Productions, p. 40
Wahl, Dale ....Laika Entertainment, p. 191
Wahlberg, Mark ....Entourage, p. 360
Wain, Margot ....CBS Entertainment, p. 86
Waite, Dava ....In Case of Emergency, p. 364
Waite, Jeanne McHale ....Banyan Productions, p. 61
Waits-Smith, Kalia ....Kanpai Pictures, p. 184
Walby, Christine ....Blumhouse Productions, p. 70
Wald, Jeff ....Jeff Wald Entertainment, p. 180
Wald, Michael ....Sony Pictures Television International, p. 296
Walden, Dana ....Twentieth Century Fox Television, p. 323
Waldron, Michael ....Cypress Point Productions, p. 106
Waldron-Harding, Roslyn ....Article 19 Films, p. 56
Walens, Rachel ....Radiant Productions, p. 265
Walk, Cymbre ....The Group Entertainment, p. 156
Walken, Georgianne ....Entourage, p. 360
Walker III, Alexander ....New Generation Films, Inc., p. 234
Walker Jr., Alexander ....New Generation Films, Inc., p. 234
Walker, Brian ....NBC Sports, p. 231
Walker, Darrell ....BET Networks, p. 66
Walker, Galen ....Imagi Services (USA), p. 171
Walker, Greg ....Without a Trace, p. 379
Walker, Lakesha ....Berlanti Productions, p. 66
Walker, Malvena ....Lakeshore Entertainment Group LLC, p. 192
Walker, Mark ....Boxx Communications, LLC, p. 72
Walker, Matt ....DisneyToon Studios, p. 113
Walker, Rick ....The Asylum, p. 57
Walker, Robert W. ....Walker/Fitzgibbon TV/Films, p. 333
Walker, Scott ....Boxx Communications, LLC, p. 72
Walker, Tom ....Days of Our Lives, p. 359
Walkley, David ....E! Networks, p. 117
Wall, Barbara ....Lionsgate, p. 200
Wall, Mary ....Artists, Inc., p. 56
Wall, Rosemary ....Indigo Films, p. 174
Wallace, Alex ....NBC News, p. 230
Wallace, Randall ....Wheelhouse Entertainment, p. 339
Wallach, Allison ....Lifetime Television (New York), p. 198
Wallach, David ....Jupiter Entertainment, p. 183
Wallach, Lou ....The Colbert Report, p. 357
Wallach, Lou ....Comedy Central, p. 98
Wallau, Alex ....ABC Entertainment Television Group, p. 45
Wallem, Linda ....Help Me Help You, p. 363
Waller, Dahvi ....Desperate Housewives, p. 360
Walley-Beckett, Moira ....Raines, p. 372
Walls, Charlotte ....Matador Pictures, p. 212
Walmsley, Patrick ....Lion Eyes Entertainment, p. 199
Walsh, Abigail ....Goldcrest Films International, Inc., p. 149
Walsh, Adriana ....Enteraktion Studios, p. 124
Walsh, Brad ....King of the Hill, p. 365
Walsh, John ....ESPN Original Entertainment (EOE), p. 127
Walsh, Jonna ....Gay Rosenthal Productions, p. 275
Walsh, Kevin ....Twentieth Television, p. 324
Walsh, Matt ....Upright Citizens Brigade, p. 327
Walsh, Mike ....Twentieth Century Fox Television, p. 323
Walsh, Tom ....Enteraktion Studios, p. 124
Walter, Greg ....3 Arts Entertainment, Inc., p. 40
Walters, Gary Michael ....Bold Films, p. 71
Walthers, Kal ....Buena Vista Motion Pictures Group, p. 78
Walton, Ed ....De Line Pictures, p. 108
Walton III, M. Dal ....Emmett/Furla Films, p. 123
Walz, Jon Alon ....Motion Picture Production, Inc., p. 223
Wanamaker, Keirsten ....Nickelodeon/MTVN Kids & Family Group, p. 237
Wandell, Morgan ....Touchstone Television, p. 316
Wander, Ellen S. ....Film Bridge International, p. 132
Wang, Andrew ....Storyline Entertainment, p. 302
Wang, Edward C. ....Gittes, Inc., p. 147
Wang, Jason ....Tannenbaum Company, p. 308
Wang, Mike ....MRB Productions, Inc., p. 224
Wang, Sherry ....Cinema-Electric Inc., p. 92
Wang, Shirley ....Vanguard Productions, p. 329
Wanke, Christina ....Randwell Productions, p. 266
Warburton, Matt ....The Simpsons, p. 375
Ward, Charlie ....Red Hour Films, p. 267
Ward, Geoffrey C. ....Florentine Films, p. 135
Ward, Jennifer ....Echelon Entertainment World Dist. & Prod., p. 119
Ward, Jim ....Lucasfilm Ltd., p. 203
Ward, Laurel ....Ocean Pictures, p. 241
Ward, Paul ....Nickelodeon/MTVN Kids & Family Group, p. 237
Ward, Ron ....Merv Griffin Entertainment, p. 154
Ware, Charlyn ....Lionsgate, p. 200
Waring, Adam ....Two and a Half Men, p. 378
Warner, Paula ....Touchstone Television, p. 316
Warner, Tom ....Sony Pictures Television, p. 296
Warren, Agatha ....Prison Break, p. 372
Warren, Andy ....NBC Universal Television Studio, p. 231
Warren, Danny ....Grammnet Productions, p. 152
Warren, Kris ....Wonderland Sound and Vision, p. 344
Warren, Suzanne ....Pandemonium, p. 246
Warrick, Ken ....American Idol, p. 354
Warshauer, Matt ....Good Game, p. 149
Warun, Kenneth ....ABC Entertainment Television Group, p. 45
Warwick, Ken ....FremantleMedia North America, p. 142
Washington, Kiko ....Warner Bros. Entertainment Inc., p. 334
Washington, Screech ....The Amazing Race, p. 354
Wass, Nina ....Wass-Stein, p. 336
Wasserman, Eric ....In Case of Emergency, p. 364
Wassermann, Pax ....Stick Figure Productions, p. 301
Waterman, Doug ....Cops, p. 358
Waterman, Doug ....Langley Productions, p. 193
Waterman, Shana C. ....25C Productions, p. 40
Watermeier, Ian ....Yari Film Group (YFG), p. 347
Waters, Mark ....Watermark, p. 336
Watkin, John ....Planet Grande Pictures, p. 256
Watkins, Odetta ....Warner Bros. Television Production, p. 335
Watkins, Royale ....All of Us, p. 354
Watkins, Teresa ....RDF Media, p. 266
Watson, Bill L. ....EARS XXI, p. 118
Watson, Eric ....Protozoa Pictures, p. 263
Watson, John ....Trilogy Entertainment Group, p. 319
Watson, Julie ....NCIS, p. 370
Watson, Julie ....Belisarius Productions, p. 65
Watson, Luke ....MRB Productions, Inc., p. 224
Watson, Peter ....Recorded Picture Company, p. 266
Watson, Sharon Lee ....The Unit, p. 378
Watson, Susan ....Norton Wright Productions, p. 346
Watson, Tom ....Logo, p. 202
Watt, Nancy Williams ....Passions, p. 371
Watters, James ....Universal Operations Group, p. 326
Watts, Adrienne ....VanDerKloot Film & Television, p. 328
Watts, Emma ....Twentieth Century Fox, p. 322
Watts, Jeff ....Boxx Communications, LLC, p. 72
Waugh, James ....Suntaur/Elsboy Entertainment, p. 305
Wax, Jonathan ....Fox Broadcasting Company, p. 139
Wayne, Bob ....DC Comics, p. 108
Wayne, Christina ....AMC, p. 50
Wayne, Michael ....Sony Pictures Digital, p. 295
Wayne, Teresa ....Warner Bros. Pictures, p. 334
Weakley, Craig ....Twentieth Television, p. 324
Weatherford, Jim ....Cookie Jar Entertainment, p. 100
Weatherholtz, Jenny ....Broken Lizard Industries, p. 76
Weathersby, Cassius Vernon ....Londine Productions, p. 202
Weathersby, Joshua ....Londine Productions, p. 202
Weathersby, Nadine ....Londine Productions, p. 202
Weaver, Brooklyn ....Energy Entertainment, p. 124
Weaver, Matthew ....Prospect Pictures, p. 263
Weaver, Ron ....The Bold and the Beautiful, p. 356
Weaver, Ron ....Bell-Phillip TV Productions, Inc., p. 65
Webb, Bill ....Buena Vista Television, p. 79
Webb, Laurie ....Mirage Enterprises, p. 217
Webb, Leighton ....Fox Mobile Entertainment, p. 139
Webb, Lewin ....Peace Arch Entertainment Group Inc., p. 251
Webber, Hugh ....20 Good Years, p. 353
Weber, Jonathan ....Key Creatives, LLC, p. 187
Weber, Marco ....Senator Entertainment, Inc., p. 284
Weber, Michael ....Discovery Networks, U.S., p. 111
Weber, Mike ....Radar Pictures, p. 264
Webster, Aisla ....Brightlight Pictures, Inc., p. 75
Webster, Angela ....Pink Sneakers Productions, p. 255

Webster, April . . . . . Criminal Minds, p. 358
Webster, April . . . . . Lost, p. 368
Webster, Lesley Lake . . . . . Notes From the Underbelly, p. 370
Wech, Katie . . . . . Traveler, p. 377
Wechsler, Ron . . . . . ESPN Original Entertainment (EOE), p. 127
Wedaa, Jim . . . . . Jim Wedaa Productions, p. 337
Weddle, David . . . . . Battlestar Galactica, p. 355
Wedge, Chris . . . . . Blue Sky Studios, p. 69
Wee, James . . . . . SkyZone Entertainment, p. 291
Weed, Kent . . . . . Hell's Kitchen, p. 363
Weed, Kent . . . . . A. Smith & Co. Productions, p. 292
Wegner, Kolie . . . . . L.I.F.T. Productions, p. 191
Wegner, Steven P. . . . . . Alcon Entertainment, LLC, p. 49
Wegner, Esq., William E. . . . . . Tricor Entertainment, p. 318
Wehrenberg, Erin Gough . . . . . NBC Entertainment, p. 230
Weiant, Ted . . . . . Dave Bell Associates, p. 65
Weibel, Irene . . . . . Nelvana Communications, Inc., p. 232
Weide, Robert B. . . . . . Whyaduck Productions, Inc., p. 340
Weidenfeld, Nick . . . . . Adult Swim, p. 47
Weidman, Wendy . . . . . The Shield, p. 374
Weil, David . . . . . Bristol Bay Productions, p. 76
Weil, David . . . . . Walden Media, p. 333
Weil, Leah . . . . . Sony Pictures Entertainment, p. 295
Weinberg, Dan . . . . . ESPN Original Entertainment (EOE), p. 127
Weinberg, Jason . . . . . Untitled Entertainment, p. 327
Weinberg, Larry . . . . . E Entertainment, LLC, p. 118
Weinberg, Matthew . . . . . Guy Walks Into a Bar, p. 158
Weinberg, Teri . . . . . Ugly Betty, p. 378
Weinberg, Teri . . . . . Reveille, LLC, p. 270
Weinberger, Alex . . . . . Touchstone Television, p. 316
Weiner, Andrew . . . . . Ithaka, p. 178
Weiner, Jake . . . . . Benderspink, p. 66
Weiner, Ron . . . . . Help Me Help You, p. 363
Weiner, William S. . . . . . Regency Enterprises, p. 268
Weingarten, Caryn . . . . . Mosaic Media Group, p. 222
Weinger, Todd . . . . . Lion Rock Productions, p. 199
Weingroff, Jennifer . . . . . CBS Paramount International Television, p. 87
Weinlein, Thad . . . . . Artists, Inc., p. 56
Weinstein, Adam . . . . . ION Media Networks, Inc., p. 177
Weinstein, Bob . . . . . Dimension Films, p. 111
Weinstein, Bob . . . . . The Weinstein Company, p. 337
Weinstein, Dani . . . . . The Weinstein Company, p. 337
Weinstein, David . . . . . Jimmy Kimmel Live, p. 364
Weinstein, Erika . . . . . Darren Star Productions, p. 300
Weinstein, Evan . . . . . The Amazing Race, p. 354
Weinstein, Harvey . . . . . The Weinstein Company, p. 337
Weinstein, J. Elvis . . . . . America's Funniest Videos, p. 355
Weinstein, Paula . . . . . Spring Creek Productions, Inc., p. 298
Weinstock, Charles . . . . . Weinstock Productions, p. 338
Weinstock, Josh . . . . . Generate, p. 145
Weinstock, Marc . . . . . Screen Gems, p. 283
Weinstock, Nicholas . . . . . Twentieth Century Fox Television, p. 323
Weintraub, Anthony . . . . . A-Line Pictures, p. 49
Weintraub, Fred . . . . . Weintraub/Kuhn Productions, p. 338
Weintraub, Jackie . . . . . Weintraub/Kuhn Productions, p. 338
Weintraub, Jerry . . . . . Jerry Weintraub Productions, p. 338
Weir, Mary-Kelly . . . . . Passions, p. 371
Weirick, Clarissa . . . . . Warner Bros. Entertainment Inc., p. 334
Weisel, Sol . . . . . Playboy Entertainment Group, Inc., p. 257
Weiser, John . . . . . Sony Pictures Television, p. 296
Weisfeld, Zak . . . . . Jupiter Entertainment, p. 183
Weisinger, Daniel . . . . . Junction Films, p. 183
Weisman, Michael . . . . . NBC Entertainment, p. 230
Weiss, Amy . . . . . Brillstein-Grey Entertainment, p. 75
Weiss, Barry . . . . . Sony Pictures Imageworks, p. 295
Weiss, Ben . . . . . Fortress Entertainment, p. 137
Weiss, Bruce . . . . . Ironworks Production, p. 177
Weiss, Evan . . . . . Handprint Entertainment, p. 160
Weiss, Jason . . . . . MTV Films, p. 225
Weiss, Jeff . . . . . Sony Pictures Television, p. 296
Weiss, Juliana . . . . . MPH Entertainment, Inc., p. 224
Weiss, Michael . . . . . Nip/Tuck, p. 370
Weiss, Michael . . . . . The Closer, p. 357
Weiss, Michele . . . . . New Line Cinema, p. 234
Weiss, Randy . . . . . Visionbox Media Group, p. 331
Weiss, Randy . . . . . Foundation Entertainment, p. 138
Weiss, Rob . . . . . Entourage, p. 360
Weiss, Staci . . . . . 19 Entertainment, Inc., p. 38
Weissberg, Andrew . . . . . The History Channel, p. 167
Weisse, Noemie . . . . . Sony Pictures Television International, p. 296
Weissenborn, Jamie . . . . . Sony Pictures Television International, p. 296
Weissman, Lauren C. . . . . . Kadokawa Pictures USA, p. 184
Weissman, Stuart . . . . . Scott Mauro Entertainment, Inc., p. 212
Weithorn, Michael J. . . . . . The King of Queens, p. 365
Weitz, Brett . . . . . fox 21, p. 138
Weitz, Jory . . . . . Hella Good Moving Pictures, p. 164
Weitzman, Matt . . . . . American Dad, p. 354
Welby, Lenore . . . . . MARTHA, p. 368
Welch, Jennifer . . . . . Sidney Kimmel Entertainment, p. 187
Welch, Sam . . . . . aWounded Knee, p. 59
Welch, Shane . . . . . Foothill Entertainment, Inc., p. 136
Weldele, Phillip . . . . . Al Burton Productions, p. 80
Weldner, Seth . . . . . Jimmy Kimmel Live, p. 364
Welker, Kara . . . . . Generate, p. 145
Weller, Robb . . . . . Weller/Grossman Productions, p. 338
Wells, Clark . . . . . Di Novi Pictures, p. 110
Wells, Jason . . . . . Sony Pictures Television International, p. 296
Wells, John . . . . . ER, p. 361
Wells, John . . . . . John Wells Productions, p. 338
Wendschuh, Dooma . . . . . SekretAgent Productions, p. 283
Wendt, Laura . . . . . Nickelodeon/MTVN Kids & Family Group, p. 237
Wenokur, Bob . . . . . Lionsgate, p. 200
Wensel, Brian . . . . . Paramount Pictures Production Division, p. 248
Wentworth, John A. . . . . . CBS Paramount Network Television, p. 87
Wentworth, John A. . . . . . King World Productions, Inc., p. 188
Wentworth, John A. . . . . . CBS Paramount Worldwide Television Dist., p. 88
Werbe, Susan . . . . . The History Channel, p. 167
Werber, Clifford . . . . . Clifford Werber Productions, p. 339
Werksman, Harry . . . . . Grey's Anatomy, p. 362
Werner, Tom . . . . . 20 Good Years, p. 353
Werner, Tom . . . . . Happy Hour, p. 362
Werner, Tom . . . . . Oxygen Media, p. 245
Werner, Tom . . . . . Carsey-Werner Films, p. 84
Werner, Tom . . . . . Werner-Gold-Miller, p. 339
Wernick, Ilana . . . . . The King of Queens, p. 365
Wernick, Sandy . . . . . Brillstein-Grey Entertainment, p. 75
Wertz, Sharla . . . . . Jupiter Entertainment, p. 183
Wesley, James . . . . . Lifetime Television (New York), p. 198
West, Denmark . . . . . MTV Networks, p. 226
West, Joella . . . . . Comedy Central, p. 98
West, Palmer . . . . . Thousand Words, p. 313
West, Polly . . . . . Zephyr Films Ltd., p. 348
West, Ron . . . . . Tagline Pictures, p. 307
West, Simon . . . . . Simon West Productions, p. 339
West, Wendy . . . . . The Closer, p. 357
Westbrook, Jeff . . . . . The Simpsons, p. 375
Westergaard, Troy . . . . . Orly Adelson Productions, p. 46
Westerman, Erin . . . . . Gunn Films, p. 158
Westervelt, Derek . . . . . The Ellen DeGeneres Show, p. 360
Westheimer, Erica . . . . . Lone Star Film Group, p. 202
Westheimer, Fred . . . . . Lone Star Film Group, p. 202
Westman, Kit . . . . . Sub Rosa Productions, Inc., p. 303
Westmore, Eric . . . . . The Biggest Loser, p. 356
Weston, Ann . . . . . Gross-Weston Productions, p. 156
Weston, Brad . . . . . Paramount Pictures Production Division, p. 248
Westphal, John . . . . . Sony Pictures Television, p. 296
Wethington, Connie . . . . . Wildwood Enterprises, Inc., p. 341
Wexelblatt, Linda Curran . . . . . Crane Wexelblatt Entertainment, p. 102
Wexler, Joshua . . . . . Threshold Entertainment, p. 313
Wexler, Scott . . . . . 3 Arts Entertainment, Inc., p. 40
Weyermann, Diane . . . . . Participant Productions, p. 249
Weyman, Andrew . . . . . Lucky Louie, p. 368
Wharmby, Tony . . . . . Bones, p. 356
Wharton, Natascha . . . . . Working Title Films, p. 345
Whedon, Zack . . . . . Red Board Productions, p. 267
Wheeler, Garrett . . . . . Platform Entertainment, p. 256
Wheeler, Jay . . . . . Program Partners, p. 262
Wheeler, Kelly . . . . . Vanished, p. 378
Wheeler, Michael . . . . . David Brady Productions, p. 72
Wheelock, Martha . . . . . Ishtar Films, p. 178

Whelan, Colin . . . . Dalaklis-McKeown Entertainment, Inc., p. 106
Whelley, Eileen . . . . NBC Universal Corporate, p. 231
Whifler, Graeme . . . . Cafe Productions, p. 81
Whitaker, Jim . . . . Imagine Entertainment, p. 172
Whitcomb, Brad . . . . Departure Studios, p. 109
White, Aurelia . . . . Actuality Productions, p. 46
White, Ayu . . . . CineMagic Entertainment, p. 92
White, Belinda . . . . Silver Lion Films, p. 288
White, Ben . . . . MTV Networks, p. 226
White, Beth . . . . HBO Entertainment, p. 162
White, Bonnie . . . . Exxcell Entertainment, Inc./Exxcell Films, p. 129
White, Cary . . . . Friday Night Lights, p. 361
White, Harry . . . . ContentFilm, p. 100
White, Isabel . . . . Yari Film Group (YFG), p. 347
White, J.P. . . . . Hyperion Studio, p. 169
White, Mike . . . . Black & White Productions, p. 67
White, Roberta . . . . Pie Town Productions, p. 254
White, Scott . . . . Without a Trace, p. 379
White, Stiles . . . . Hyperion Studio, p. 169
Whitehead, Glenn . . . . HBO Films, p. 162
Whitesell, Julie . . . . Traveler, p. 377
Whitesell, Sean . . . . The Black Donnellys, p. 356
Whitham, Jeremy . . . . BBC Worldwide Americas, p. 64
Whitney, Steve . . . . Relevant Entertainment Group, p. 270
Whittaker, Susan . . . . Two Oceans Entertainment Group, p. 324
Wholey, Karin . . . . HBO Films, p. 162
Wick, Douglas . . . . Red Wagon Entertainment, p. 268
Wickstrom, Kate . . . . ShadowCatcher Entertainment, p. 285
Widmaier, William Louis . . . . Platinum Studios, LLC, p. 257
Widman, Jarrett . . . . Sub Rosa Productions, Inc., p. 303
Wiener, Aaron . . . . Entertainment Studios, Inc., p. 125
Wiener, Jenny . . . . Ars Nova, p. 55
Wiener, Rick . . . . American Dad, p. 354
Wieshofer, Marni . . . . Lionsgate, p. 200
Wigan, Gareth . . . . Columbia Pictures, p. 97
Wiggins, David . . . . Neighbors Entertainment, p. 232
Wight, Nancie . . . . Airborne Entertainment, p. 48
Wigram, Lionel . . . . Wigram Productions, p. 340
Wigutow, Dan . . . . Dan Wigutow Productions, p. 340
Wilber, Tricia . . . . ABC Family, p. 45
Wilber, Tricia . . . . Disney ABC Cable Networks Group, p. 112
Wilborn, Jason . . . . The Nine, p. 370
Wilburn, Clinton . . . . Turner Network Television (TNT), p. 321
Wilburn, Clinton . . . . TBS, p. 309
Wilcox, David . . . . Law & Order, p. 367
Wild, Wellesley . . . . Family Guy, p. 361
Wilde, Sarah Jane . . . . Code Entertainment, p. 96
Wilder, Andrew . . . . Criminal Minds, p. 358
Wildhack, John . . . . ESPN Original Entertainment (EOE), p. 127
Wilding, Mark . . . . Grey's Anatomy, p. 362
Wildzumas, Cristina . . . . Hypnotic, p. 170
Wilensky, Adam . . . . Fox Mobile Entertainment, p. 139
Wiley, Martin . . . . TriCoast Studios, p. 318
Wilhem, Christopher . . . . Tooley Productions, p. 315
Wilhite, Tom . . . . Hyperion Studio, p. 169
Wilhm, Colin . . . . Principal Entertainment, p. 262
Wilkes, Justin . . . . @radical.media, p. 30
Wilkes, Peter . . . . Lionsgate, p. 200
Wilkinson, Rob . . . . Focus Features/Rogue Pictures, p. 136
Will, John . . . . Joel Stevens Entertainment, p. 301
Willaman, Karen . . . . Double Feature Films, p. 115
Williams, Aaron . . . . Twentieth Century Fox, p. 322
Williams, Barry . . . . Macedon Media, Inc., p. 205
Williams, Beth . . . . East of Doheny/Lexington Road Prod., p. 118
Williams, Bob . . . . What About Brian, p. 379
Williams, Bob . . . . Arjay Entertainment, p. 55
Williams, Carlos . . . . Touchstone Television, p. 316
Williams, Caroline . . . . The Office, p. 371
Williams, Ellyn . . . . Ellyn Williams Productions, p. 341
Williams, Garrison . . . . Zero Pictures, p. 349
Williams, J.P. . . . . Naked Trucker & T-Bones, p. 369
Williams, J.P. . . . . Parallel Entertainment, Inc., p. 247
Williams, Jeremy . . . . Warner Bros. Entertainment Inc., p. 334
Williams, Jessica . . . . Parallel Entertainment, Inc., p. 247
Williams, John H. . . . . Vanguard Films/Vanguard Animation, p. 328
Williams, Kim . . . . Reuben Cannon Productions, p. 83
Williams, Linda . . . . Tommy Boy Films, p. 315
Williams, Lindsay . . . . The Gotham Group, Inc., p. 151
Williams, Maria . . . . Film 44, p. 131
Williams, Mark C. . . . . Pierce Williams Entertainment, p. 255
Williams, Marsha E. . . . . . Nickelodeon/MTVN Kids & Family Group, p. 237
Williams, Matt . . . . Wind Dancer Production Group, p. 342
Williams, Michael . . . . Queer Eye, p. 372
Williams, Michael . . . . Scout Productions, p. 282
Williams, Montel . . . . Letnom Productions, p. 196
Williams, Pam Oas . . . . Laura Ziskin Productions, p. 349
Williams, Phillip . . . . DIY Network, p. 113
Williams, R.J. . . . . Arjay Entertainment, p. 55
Williams, Rick . . . . American Dad, p. 354
Williams, Scott . . . . Bones, p. 356
Williams, Scott . . . . NBC Entertainment, p. 230
Williams, Sharon . . . . Disney-ABC Television Group, p. 113
Williams, Sharon . . . . ABC Entertainment Television Group, p. 45
Williams, Tim . . . . GreeneStreet Films, p. 153
Williams, Tom . . . . Gran Via Productions, p. 152
Williams, Vikki . . . . CSI: NY, p. 359
Williams, Virgil . . . . ER, p. 361
Williams, Virginia . . . . HDNet Films, p. 163
Williamson, Glenn . . . . Back Lot Pictures, p. 59
Williamson, Kevin . . . . Hidden Palms, p. 363
Williamson, Kevin . . . . Outerbanks Entertainment, p. 245
Williamson, Melissa . . . . Blueprint Entertainment, p. 70
Williamson, Norby . . . . ABC Sports, p. 45
Williamson, Norby . . . . ESPN Original Entertainment (EOE), p. 127
Williamson, Shawn . . . . Saved, p. 374
Williamson, Shawn . . . . Brightlight Pictures, Inc., p. 75
Williger, David S. . . . . P.A.T. Productions, p. 250
Willis, Marlea . . . . A&E Network, p. 44
Willman, Brent . . . . GSN, p. 157
Willner, Jeff . . . . TriCoast Studios, p. 318
Wills, Monnie . . . . Tom Jacobson Productions, p. 179
Wills, Patricio . . . . Telemundo Network, p. 310
Willson, David . . . . Smallville, p. 375
Wilmore, Larry . . . . The Office, p. 371
Wilmore, Marc . . . . The Simpsons, p. 375
Wilson, Andrew . . . . Evolution Entertainment, p. 128
Wilson, Brad . . . . Brad Wilson Productions, Inc., p. 342
Wilson, Brian . . . . David Foster Productions, p. 138
Wilson, Don . . . . Gorilla Pictures, p. 150
Wilson, Ed . . . . Fox Broadcasting Company, p. 139
Wilson, Eric . . . . GoTV Networks, p. 151
Wilson, Jason . . . . Shady Acres Entertainment, p. 285
Wilson, John F. . . . . PBS, p. 251
Wilson, Julie . . . . Twentieth Century Fox Television, p. 323
Wilson, Karina . . . . Concept Entertainment, p. 99
Wilson, Keri . . . . Mirage Enterprises, p. 217
Wilson, Lee . . . . Wilson/Woods Productions, p. 342
Wilson, Lisa . . . . Hyde Park Entertainment, p. 169
Wilson, Meg . . . . IMAX Corporation, p. 172
Wilson, Michael . . . . Danjaq, LLC, p. 107
Wilson, Mitsy . . . . Fox Broadcasting Company, p. 139
Wilson, Molly . . . . HBO Films, p. 162
Wilson, Rob . . . . Ixtlan, p. 178
Wilson, S.S. . . . . Stampede Entertainment, p. 299
Wilson, Skye . . . . Super Delicious Productions, p. 305
Wilson, Veronica . . . . David E. Kelley Productions, p. 186
Wilt, Shawn . . . . The Singles Table, p. 375
Wiltgen, Jessica . . . . Lloyd Entertainment, p. 201
Wimer, Michael . . . . Centropolis Entertainment, p. 88
Winant, Scott . . . . Hidden Palms, p. 363
Wind, Sabrina . . . . Desperate Housewives, p. 360
Winder, Catherine . . . . Lucasfilm Ltd., p. 203
Windsor, David . . . . Happy Hour, p. 362
Wineblatt, Martha . . . . Krainin Productions, Inc., p. 190
Winer, Harry . . . . The Winer Company, p. 342
Winfrey, Oprah . . . . Oxygen Media, p. 245
Winfrey, Oprah . . . . Harpo Films, Inc., p. 161
Winick, Gary . . . . InDigEnt, p. 173
Winikoff, Cami . . . . Sobini Films, p. 293
Winkler, Henry . . . . Fair Dinkum Productions, p. 129

Winkler, Irwin . . . . . . Winkler Films, p. 342
Winkler, Kirstin . . . . . . Centropolis Entertainment, p. 88
Winkler, Richard . . . . . . Curious Pictures, p. 104
Winks, Wendy . . . . . . A Wink and a Nod Productions, p. 43
Winn, Kate . . . . . . A&E Network, p. 44
Winn, Pam . . . . . . HBO Films, p. 162
Winn, Patrick . . . . . . Camelot Entertainment Group, Inc., p. 82
Winnik, Javier . . . . . . Last Comic Standing, p. 366
Winograde, Jana . . . . . . ABC Entertainment Television Group, p. 45
Winshell, Allison . . . . . . PBS, p. 251
Winston, China . . . . . . Joada Productions, Inc., p. 181
Winston, Hilary . . . . . . My Name Is Earl, p. 369
Winston, Randall . . . . . . Scrubs, p. 374
Winston, Stan . . . . . . Stan Winston Productions, p. 343
Winter, Michael . . . . . . Versus, p. 329
Winter, Ralph . . . . . . Ralph Winter Productions, Inc., p. 343
Winter, Terence Paul . . . . . . All of Us, p. 354
Winters, Brad . . . . . . Six Degrees, p. 375
Winterstern, Henry . . . . . . First Look Pictures, p. 134
Winterton, Brian . . . . . . Dark Trick Films, p. 107
Winthrop, Kathy . . . . . . The Woofenill Works, Inc., p. 344
Winvick, Chris . . . . . . Integrated Films & Management, p. 175
Wise, Elizabeth . . . . . . Lifetime Television (Los Angeles), p. 198
Wise, Malissa . . . . . . Platinum Studios, LLC, p. 257
Wise, Robert . . . . . . Creative Differences, p. 103
Wiseman, John . . . . . . Paramount Pictures Production Division, p. 248
Wiseman, John . . . . . . Paramount Vantage/Paramount Classics, p. 248
Wiseman, Marci . . . . . . fox 21, p. 138
Wishart, Karen . . . . . . TV One, LLC, p. 322
Witherspoon, Reese . . . . . . Type A Films, p. 325
Witlin, Alixandre . . . . . . City Entertainment, p. 93
Witoshkin, Christina . . . . . . Blue Sky Studios, p. 69
Witsken, Mark . . . . . . Brave New Films, p. 73
Witt, Paul Junger . . . . . . Witt-Thomas-Harris Productions, p. 343
Witt, Renee . . . . . . Laura Ziskin Productions, p. 349
Wittenberg, Jess . . . . . . Walden Media, p. 333
Wittenberg, Jess . . . . . . Bristol Bay Productions, p. 76
Wohl, Lauren . . . . . . New Line Television, p. 235
Wohlwend, Andrew . . . . . . The George Lopez Show, p. 362
Woinsky, Orin . . . . . . Landscape Entertainment, p. 193
Wolarsky, Nina . . . . . . Smoke House, p. 292
Wolarsky, Nina . . . . . . Hart Sharp Entertainment, Inc., p. 161
Wolf, Dick . . . . . . Law & Order: Special Victims Unit, p. 367
Wolf, Dick . . . . . . Law & Order: Criminal Intent, p. 367
Wolf, Dick . . . . . . Law & Order, p. 367
Wolf, Dick . . . . . . Wolf Films, Inc., p. 343
Wolf, Fred . . . . . . Fred Wolf Films, p. 343
Wolf, Jeff . . . . . . Sony Pictures Television, p. 296
Wolf, Liz . . . . . . Fred Wolf Films, p. 343
Wolf, Mary Ann . . . . . . NBC Entertainment, p. 230
Wolf, Michael J. . . . . . . MTV Networks, p. 226
Wolf, Mike . . . . . . Film Roman, Inc., p. 132
Wolf, Penny . . . . . . Peace Arch Entertainment Group Inc., p. 251
Wolf, Thomas . . . . . . World of Wonder Productions, p. 345
Wolfe, Dan . . . . . . Universal Pictures, p. 326
Wolfe, Elizabeth . . . . . . DisneyToon Studios, p. 113
Wolfe, Jordan . . . . . . Shady Acres Entertainment, p. 285
Wolfe, Katrina . . . . . . Dimension Films, p. 111
Wolfe, Melissa . . . . . . Frederator Studios, p. 141
Wolfe, Patti . . . . . . The Unit, p. 378
Wolfe, Steven J. . . . . . . Sneak Preview Entertainment, Inc., p. 293
Wolff, Bill . . . . . . MSNBC, p. 225
Wolff, Russell . . . . . . ABC Sports, p. 45
Wolff, Russell . . . . . . ESPN Original Entertainment (EOE), p. 127
Wolfman, Marv . . . . . . Wolfmill Entertainment, p. 343
Wolfson, Michael . . . . . . AOL Media Networks, p. 53
Wolfson, Sam . . . . . . Warner Bros. Television Production, p. 335
Wolf-Weiss, Abby . . . . . . Smoke House, p. 292
Wolloff, Marc . . . . . . Popular Arts Entertainment, Inc., p. 259
Wolner, Laura . . . . . . Six Degrees, p. 375
Wolper, Mark M. . . . . . . The Wolper Organization, p. 344
Wolpert, Matt . . . . . . Winsome Productions, p. 342
Wolthoff, David . . . . . . The Shuman Company, p. 287
Wolz, Silke . . . . . . Dream Entertainment, Inc., p. 116
Wombwell, Andy . . . . . . Rhino Films, p. 272
Won, Nancy . . . . . . Jericho, p. 364
Wong, Andrea . . . . . . ABC Entertainment Television Group, p. 45
Wong, Chi-Li . . . . . . AEI-Atchity Entertainment Intl., Inc., p. 47
Wong, Max . . . . . . Pink Slip Pictures, p. 255
Wong, Winnie . . . . . . Yorktown Productions, Ltd., p. 347
Woo, Alexander . . . . . . Sleeper Cell, p. 375
Woo, Angeles . . . . . . Lion Rock Productions, p. 199
Woo, John . . . . . . Lion Rock Productions, p. 199
Woo, Kim . . . . . . Lion Rock Productions, p. 199
Wood, Doris . . . . . . The Manhattan Project, Ltd., p. 210
Wood, Gwen . . . . . . PBS, p. 251
Wood, Jenny . . . . . . Zucker Productions, p. 350
Wood, Martin . . . . . . Stargate: Atlantis, p. 376
Wood, Michael . . . . . . BBC Films, p. 64
Wood, Michael S. . . . . . . Rocket Science Laboratories, p. 273
Wood, Terry . . . . . . CBS Paramount Worldwide Television Dist., p. 88
Wood, Terry . . . . . . King World Productions, Inc., p. 188
Woodbeck-Natkin, Victoria . . . . . . Lonetree Entertainment, p. 202
Woodford, Brent . . . . . . The Walt Disney Company, p. 112
Woodlief, Eryl . . . . . . Odd Lot Entertainment, p. 241
Woodrow, Danielle . . . . . . VH1, p. 330
Woods, Clark . . . . . . Metro-Goldwyn-Mayer Studios, Inc. (MGM), p. 215
Woods, Paula . . . . . . The Weinstein Company, p. 337
Woods, Robert . . . . . . Wilson/Woods Productions, p. 342
Woodward, Amber . . . . . . The Dead Zone, p. 359
Woodward, Anne . . . . . . Station 3, p. 300
Woodward, Lydia . . . . . . ER, p. 361
Woodward, Scott . . . . . . TV Guide Channel, p. 321
Woolf, Jennifer . . . . . . Keckins Projects, Ltd., p. 185
Wooster, Mark . . . . . . Universal Studios, p. 326
Wootton, Nicholas . . . . . . Law & Order, p. 367
Wootton, Nicholas . . . . . . Wolf Films, Inc., p. 343
Wormley, Jewel . . . . . . All of Us, p. 354
Wright, Adam . . . . . . PorchLight Entertainment, p. 259
Wright, Billy . . . . . . Warner Bros. Online, p. 334
Wright, Bob . . . . . . NBC Universal Corporate, p. 231
Wright, Brad . . . . . . Stargate: SG-1, p. 376
Wright, Brad . . . . . . Stargate: Atlantis, p. 376
Wright, Brian . . . . . . Lifetime Television (Los Angeles), p. 198
Wright, Crystal . . . . . . Universal Studios, p. 326
Wright, Daniel . . . . . . Guardian Entertainment, Ltd., p. 157
Wright, Daniel . . . . . . CrazyDreams Entertainment, p. 102
Wright, Heather . . . . . . Aardman Animations, p. 44
Wright, Jane . . . . . . BBC Films, p. 64
Wright, Jennifer . . . . . . Samuel Goldwyn Films, p. 279
Wright, Michael . . . . . . TBS, p. 309
Wright, Michael . . . . . . Turner Network Television (TNT), p. 321
Wright, Michelle . . . . . . Working Title Films, p. 345
Wright, Miklos . . . . . . Lightstone Entertainment, Inc., p. 199
Wright, Norton . . . . . . Norton Wright Productions, p. 346
Wright, Pandit . . . . . . Discovery Networks, U.S., p. 111
Wright, Richard . . . . . . Lakeshore Entertainment Group LLC, p. 192
Wu, Grace . . . . . . NBC Entertainment, p. 230
Wu, Raymond . . . . . . Warner Bros. Theatre Ventures, p. 335
Wulbrun, Karyn . . . . . . E! Networks, p. 117
Wunder, Debbie . . . . . . Late Night with Conan O'Brien, p. 367
Wurtzel, Alan . . . . . . NBC Universal Corporate, p. 231
Wyatt, Patricia . . . . . . HIT Entertainment, p. 167
Wyman, Brad . . . . . . Junction Films, p. 183
Wyman, Mark . . . . . . Columbia Pictures, p. 97
Wyman, Steve . . . . . . Days of Our Lives, p. 359
Wymer, Darin . . . . . . Tony Jonas Productions, p. 182
Wymore, Patrick . . . . . . Junction Entertainment, p. 183
Wynn, Jordan . . . . . . The Mark Gordon Company, p. 150
Wyscarver, Karen . . . . . . Boston Legal, p. 357
Xydis, Bobby . . . . . . Leeza Gibbons Enterprises (LGE), p. 146
Yaloff, Mark . . . . . . QED International, p. 264
Yaloff, Mark . . . . . . Key Creatives, LLC, p. 187
Yamada, Kaido . . . . . . Pathfinder Pictures, LLC, p. 250
Yamaki, Jennie . . . . . . Mandate Pictures, p. 209
Yan, Luo . . . . . . Silver Dream Productions, p. 288
Yang, Alan . . . . . . Last Call with Carson Daly, p. 366
Yang, Janet . . . . . . Manifest Film Company, p. 210
Yang, Nina . . . . . . Double Edge Entertainment, p. 115
Yang, Steve . . . . . . Double Edge Entertainment, p. 115

Yani, Andrew .Merv Griffin Entertainment, p. 154
Yannich, Richard .CBS Paramount International Television, p. 87
Yanover, Paul .Disney Online, p. 112
Yap, Robert .Silverline Entertainment, Inc., p. 289
Yapp, Jeffrey .MTV Networks, p. 226
Yari, Bob .Yari Film Group (YFG), p. 347
Yaron, Nicolle .Last Call with Carson Daly, p. 366
Yasui, Todd .Fox Broadcasting Company, p. 139
Yasutake, Kenji .Revelations Entertainment, p. 271
Yates, Chris .Sony Online Entertainment, p. 294
Yates, Tony .RDF Media, p. 266
Yates, Yvette .PAYASO Entertainment, p. 251
Yavneh, Cyrus .Supernatural, p. 377
Yeallourides, Constantine .Sam Okun Productions, Inc., p. 242
Yee, Joan .CBS Entertainment, p. 86
Yeldham, Rebecca .Ahimsa Films, p. 48
Yellen, Linda .Keckins Projects, Ltd., p. 185
Yellen, Mark .Mark Yellen Productions, p. 347
Yellen, Martin .Keckins Projects, Ltd., p. 185
Yen, Peggy .Tenth Planet Productions, p. 311
Yeomans, Liz .Underground Films, p. 325
Yerxa, Ron .Bona Fide Productions, p. 71
Yeung, Irene .Vertigo Entertainment, p. 330
Yi, Sandy .Warner Bros. Entertainment Inc., p. 334
Yim, Yoonah .Echelon Entertainment World Dist. & Prod., p. 119
Yoo, Andrew .Treasure Entertainment, p. 317
Yoo, Paula .Hidden Palms, p. 363
York, Sherri .SOAPnet, p. 293
Yorn, Julie .Firm Films, p. 134
Yoshikawa, Max .New Concorde, p. 233
Yost, Graham .Raines, p. 372
Young, Alex .Twentieth Century Fox, p. 322
Young, Alex .Josephson Entertainment, p. 182
Young, Brian .Untitled Entertainment, p. 327
Young, Chris .Hyperion Studio, p. 169
Young, Craig .Mike Sullivan Productions, Inc., p. 304
Young, Eugene .FremantleMedia North America, p. 142
Young, Inman .Sixth Way Productions, p. 291
Young, J.R. .Renaissance Pictures, p. 270
Young, J.R. .Ghost House Pictures, p. 145
Young, Janelle .The Littlefield Company, p. 200
Young, Jason .Twentieth Century Fox, p. 322
Young, Jim .Animus Films, p. 52
Young, John Sacret .Samoset, Inc./Sacret, Inc., p. 278
Young, Lenny .Tempest Entertainment, p. 311
Young, Liz .Mike Young Productions LLC, p. 348
Young, Mal .19 Entertainment, Inc., p. 38
Young, Mark .PorchLight Entertainment, p. 259
Young, Mike .Mike Young Productions LLC, p. 348
Young, Paul .RENO 911!, p. 373
Young, Paul .Principato-Young Entertainment, p. 262
Young, Saskia .Lynda Obst Productions, p. 241
Young, Scott .Norsemen Television Productions, LLC, p. 239
Young, Suzanne .HBO Films, p. 162
Young, T.L. .Pathfinder Pictures, LLC, p. 250
Young, Tanya .Noggin, p. 239
Young, Tanya .The N, p. 228
Youngblood, Chad .Fine Living, p. 133
Youngblood, Steve .Nickelodeon/MTVN Kids & Family Group, p. 237
Younge, Patrick .Discovery Networks, U.S., p. 111
Younge, Patrick .Travel Channel, p. 316
Yousem, Jordan .The Core, p. 101
Yu, Jain .Nickelodeon Movies, p. 237
Yu, Kannie .Lifetime Television (Los Angeles), p. 198
Yun, Hai-young .CJ Entertainment America, p. 94
Yuspa, Cathy .Big Day, p. 355
Yuspa, Cathy .'Til Death, p. 377
Yuspa, Margaret .Comedy Central, p. 98
Zabel, David .ER, p. 361
Zaccaria, David .Telepictures Productions, p. 311
Zachary, Susan .The Marshak/Zachary Company, p. 211
Zadak, Joel .Principato-Young Entertainment, p. 262
Zadan, Craig .Storyline Entertainment, p. 302
Zadikoff, Adam .Room 9 Entertainment, p. 274
Zaentz, Saul .The Saul Zaentz Company, p. 348
Zagin, David .A&E Network, p. 44
Zahavi, Natan .Tapestry Films, Inc., p. 308
Zaitz, Megan .Wonderland Sound and Vision, p. 344
Zajic, Keith .Warner Bros. Pictures, p. 334
Zakai, Amotz .Echo Lake Productions, p. 119
Zakarin, Mark .The L Word, p. 366
Zakrzewski, Rita .Columbia Pictures, p. 97
Zalaznick, Lauren .Bravo, p. 74
Zalaznick, Lauren .NBC Universal Cable Entertainment, p. 231
Zales, Teresa .Neo Art & Logic, p. 232
Zaloom, George .Zaloom Film, p. 348
Zambri, Lisa .Contrafilm, p. 100
Zamudio, Roger .3Wolves Productions, p. 41
Zandazma, Pooneh .Apartment 3B Productions, p. 53
Zander, Christine .The Singles Table, p. 375
Zane, Edwin .Motion Picture Production, Inc., p. 223
Zanitsch, Noel .Lance Entertainment, Inc., p. 192
Zanuck, Dean .DFZ Productions, p. 109
Zanuck, Harrison .The Zanuck Company, p. 348
Zanuck, Lili Fini .The Zanuck Company, p. 348
Zanuck, Richard D. .The Zanuck Company, p. 348
Zapotoczny, Stephen .Wheelhouse Entertainment, p. 339
Zappala, Tom .ABC Family, p. 45
Zappala, Tom .Disney ABC Cable Networks Group, p. 112
Zappy, Leah .Brooksfilms Limited, p. 77
Zarghami, Cyma .Nickelodeon/MTVN Kids & Family Group, p. 237
Zaslav, David M. .Sleuth, p. 291
Zaslav, David M. .CNBC, p. 96
Zaslav, David M. .NBC Universal Cable Entertainment, p. 231
Zaslaw, Diana .Indigo Films, p. 174
Zasuly, Peter .Harding-Kurtz Entertainment, p. 160
Zaylor, Judith .Warner Bros. Television Production, p. 335
Zbornak, Kent .The Office, p. 371
Zbyszewski, Paul .Day Break, p. 359
Zebrowski-Heller, Kathy .Paul Heller Productions, p. 164
Zehr, John .ESPN Original Entertainment (EOE), p. 127
Zehren, Anne .Current TV, LLC, p. 105
Zeidel, Andrew .Airborne Entertainment, p. 48
Zektser, Igor .New Generation Films, Inc., p. 234
Zel, Antoinette .Telemundo Network, p. 310
Zelin, Jason .Brooklyn Media, p. 77
Zelman, Aaron .Criminal Minds, p. 358
Zelniker, Richard .Lucid Pictures, p. 204
Zelniker, Tram Nguyen .Lucid Pictures, p. 204
Zelon, David .Mandalay Pictures, p. 208
Zeman, Joshua .Ghost Robot, p. 146
Zemeckis, Leslie .Zemeckis/Nemeroff Films, p. 348
Zenga, Bo .Boz Productions, p. 72
Zenkel, Gary .NBC Sports, p. 231
Zepeda, Susana .Ralph Winter Productions, Inc., p. 343
Zermeno, Michael .Nickelodeon Movies, p. 237
Zerweck, Lorie .Las Vegas, p. 366
Zetumer, Josh .Elixir Films, p. 121
Zhang, Jing .Zinkler Films, p. 349
Ziannis, Bessy .Airborne Entertainment, p. 48
Zicherman, Stuart .Six Degrees, p. 375
Zicklin, Eric .20 Good Years, p. 353
Zicko, Heather .Guy Walks Into a Bar, p. 158
Zieger, Michele .Zieger Productions, p. 349
Zieger, Michele .Maverick Films, p. 213
Ziegert, Britta .Pantheon Entertainment Corp., p. 247
Ziegler, Tim .Starbucks Entertainment, p. 299
Zierhut, Monica .Buena Vista Motion Pictures Group, p. 78
Ziev, Stephanie .Oxygen Media, p. 245
Ziff, Elizabeth .The L Word, p. 366
Ziff, Emily .Cooper's Town Productions, p. 100
Zigler, Vivi .NBC Entertainment, p. 230
Zilber, Christina .Trillion Entertainment, Inc., p. 319
Zilber, Laurent .Trillion Entertainment, Inc., p. 319
Zilberman, Elena .The Weinstein Company, p. 337
Zim, Jake .Fox Atomic, p. 138
Zimet, Vic .New Screen Concepts, Inc., p. 235
Zimmer, Karen S. .New Line Cinema, p. 234
Zimmerly, Deborah .Go Girl Media, p. 147
Zimmerman, Ed .Sony Pictures Television, p. 296

Zimmerman, Rachel .Sunlight Productions, p. 305
Zimmerman, Scott . . . . .Evolution Entertainment, p. 128
Zimmerman, Shelley . . . . .Warner Horizon Television, p. 335
Zimmerman, Stewart . . . . .Sony Pictures Television, p. 296
Zinberg, Margo . . . . .Nickelodeon/MTVN Kids & Family Group, p. 237
Zinkin, Benjamin . . . . .New Line Cinema, p. 234
Zinner, Peter . . . . .David Braun Productions, p. 73
Zipper, Allen . . . . .The George Lopez Show, p. 362
Zipperman, Barbara . . . . .Sony Pictures Animation, p. 295
Zisk, Randy . . . . .Monk, p. 369
Ziskin, Laura . . . . .Laura Ziskin Productions, p. 349
Ziskin, Ron . . . . .Ron Ziskin Productions, Inc., p. 350
Zivic, Jennifer . . . . .HIT Entertainment, p. 167
Zizzi, Suzanne . . . . .Lion Rock Productions, p. 199
Zlotnick, Lorey . . . . .Fox Reality, p. 140
Zlotnik, Carmi . . . . .HBO Media Ventures, p. 162
Zloto, Danielle . . . . .Bay Films, p. 63
Zoda, Sam . . . . .Granada America, p. 152
Zoll, Shara . . . . .Sci Fi Channel, p. 282
Zoller, Glenn . . . . .Gigantic Pictures, p. 146
Zollo, Frederick . . . . .Frederick Zollo Productions, Inc., p. 350
Zomek, Shauna . . . . .Mandeville Films, p. 209
Zoradi, Mark . . . . .Buena Vista Motion Pictures Group, p. 78
Zorzi, William F. . . . . .The Wire, p. 379
Zoshak, Becky . . . . .The Radmin Company, p. 265
Zotnowski, Robert . . . . .CBS Entertainment, p. 86
Zoumas, Michael . . . . .Epic Level Entertainment, Ltd., p. 125
Zreik, Karim . . . . .Jericho, p. 364
Zreik, Karim . . . . .Junction Entertainment, p. 183
Zrimc, Claire . . . . .SOAPnet, p. 293
Zubick, Kim .The Robert Simonds Company, p. 290
Zucker, David . . . . .Numb3rs, p. 370
Zucker, David . . . . .Scott Free Productions, p. 282
Zucker, David . . . . .Zucker/Netter Productions, p. 350
Zucker, Holly Schiffer . . . . .HBO Films, p. 162
Zucker, Janet . . . . .Zucker Productions, p. 350
Zucker, Jeff . . . . .NBC Universal Television Studio, p. 231
Zucker, Jeff . . . . .NBC Entertainment, p. 230
Zucker, Jeff . . . . .NBC News, p. 230
Zucker, Jerry . . . . .Zucker Productions, p. 350
Zucker, Jody . . . . .Warner Bros. Television Production, p. 335
Zuckerbrod, Gary . . . . .Without a Trace, p. 379
Zuckerman, Barbara . . . . .Warner Bros. Television Production, p. 335
Zuckerman, David . . . . .American Dad, p. 354
Zuckerman, Donald . . . . .Zuckerman Entertainment, p. 350
Zuckerman, Ed . . . . .Runaway, p. 373
Zuckerman, Jodi . . . . .Participant Productions, p. 249
Zuckerman, Maria . . . . .HBO Films, p. 162
Zuiker, Anthony . . . . .CSI: Miami, p. 358
Zuiker, Anthony . . . . .CSI: NY, p. 359
Zuiker, Anthony . . . . .CSI: Crime Scene Investigation, p. 358
Zulfer, Catherine . . . . .Playboy Entertainment Group, Inc., p. 257
Zupan, Lisa .Wendy Finerman Productions, p. 134
Zurier, Ben . . . . .VH1, p. 330
Zuritsky, Elisa . . . . .Six Degrees, p. 375
Zwagil, Stuart . . . . .44 Blue Productions, Inc., p. 41
Zwarg, David .Brillstein-Grey Entertainment, p. 75
Zweben, Natalie . . . . .WPT Enterprises, Inc., p. 346
Zweibel, Alan . . . . .Silly Robin Productions, p. 288
Zwerling, Lisa . . . . .ER, p. 361
Zwick, Edward .The Bedford Falls Company, p. 65
Zwieg, Cody . . . . .Craven/Maddalena Films, p. 102